Nivaldo J. Tro

Introductory Chemistry

Fourth Custom Edition for Pasadena City College

Taken from:
Introductory Chemistry, Fifth Edition
by Nivaldo J. Tro

Cover Art: Courtesy of Pearson Learning Solutions.

Taken from:

Introductory Chemistry, Fifth Edition
by Nivaldo J. Tro
Copyright © 2015, 2011, 2009, 2006, 2003 by Pearson Education, Inc.
Upper Saddle River, New Jersey 07458

Pearson Learning Solutions, 501 Boylston Street, Suite 900, Boston, MA 02116
A Pearson Education Company
www.pearsoned.com

Printed in the United States of America

1 2 3 4 5 6 7 8 9 10 V0CR 18 17 16 15 14

000200010271911049

LA

ISBN 10: 1-269-92427-3
ISBN 13: 978-1-269-92427-6

About the Author

Nivaldo Tro, is a Professor of Chemistry at Westmont College in Santa Barbara, California, where he has been a faculty member since 1990. He received his Ph.D. in chemistry from Stanford University for work on developing and using optical techniques to study the adsorption and desorption of molecules to and from surfaces in ultra high vacuum. He then went on to the University of California at Berkeley, where he did post doctoral research on ultrafast reaction dynamics in solution. Since coming to Westmont, Professor Tro has been awarded grants from the American Chemical Society Petroleum Research Fund, from Research Corporation, and from the National Science Foundation to study the dynamics of various processes occurring in thin adlayer films adsorbed on dielectric surfaces. He has been honored as Westmont's outstanding teacher of the year three times and has also received the college's outstanding researcher of the year award. Professor Tro lives in Santa Barbara with his wife, Ann, and their four children, Michael, Ali, Kyle, and Kaden. In his leisure time, Professor Tro enjoys mountain biking, surfing, reading to his children, and being outdoors with his family.

Brief Contents

Contents

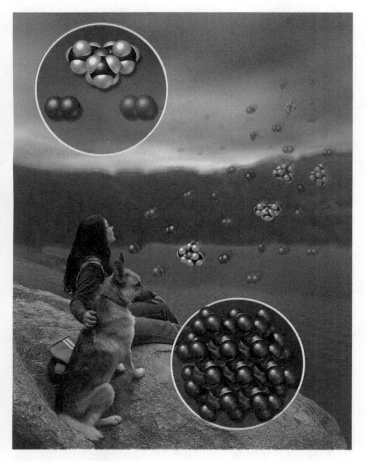

4 Atoms and Elements
94

3 Matter and Energy
56

5 Molecules and Compounds
128

8 Quantities in Chemical Reactions 248

9 Electrons in Atoms and the Periodic Table 284

10 Chemical Bonding   324

11 Gases   358

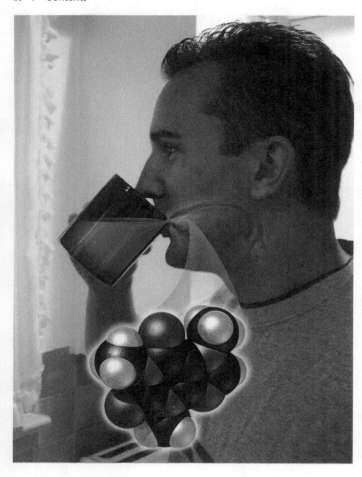

13 Solutions   446

12 Liquids, Solids, and Intermolecular Forces   410

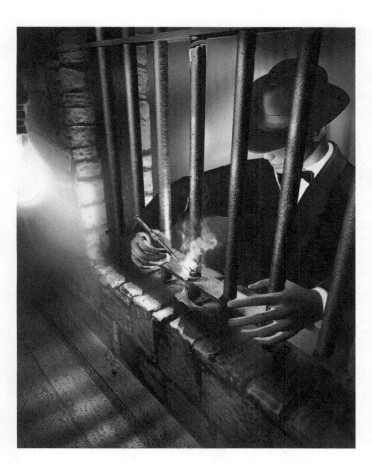

14 Acids and Bases   486

Problem-Solving Procedures

To the Student

This book is for *you*, and every text feature is meant to help you learn. I have two main goals for you in this course: to see chemistry as you never have before and to develop the problem-solving skills you need to succeed in chemistry.

I want you to experience chemistry in a new way. I have written each chapter to show you that chemistry is not just something that happens in a laboratory; chemistry surrounds you at every moment. I have worked with several outstanding artists to develop photographs and art that will help you visualize the molecular world. From the opening example to the closing chapter, you will *see* chemistry. My hope is that when you finish this course, you will think differently about your world because you understand the molecular interactions that underlie everything around you.

My second goal is for you to develop problem-solving skills. No one succeeds in chemistry—or in life, really—without the ability to solve problems. I can't give you a formula for problem solving, but I can give you strategies that will help you develop the *chemical intuition* you need to understand chemical reasoning.

Look for several recurring structures throughout this book designed to help you master problem solving. The most important ones are (1) a four-step process (Sort, Strategize, Solve, and Check) designed to help you learn how to solve problems; (2) the solution map, a visual aid that helps you navigate your way through problems; (3) the two-column Examples, in which the left column explains in clear and simple language the purpose of each step of the solution shown in the right column; and (4) the three-column Examples, which describe a problem-solving procedure while demonstrating how it is applied to two different Examples. In addition, you will find a For More Practice feature at the end of each worked Example that directs you to the end-of-chapter problems that provide more opportunity to practice the skill(s) covered in the Example. In this edition, I have added a new tool for you at the end of each chapter: a Self-Assessment Quiz. These quizzes are designed to help you test yourself on the core concepts and skills of each chapter. You can also use them as you prepare for exams. Before an exam, take the quiz associated with each chapter that the exam will cover. The questions you miss on the quiz will reveal the areas you need to spend the most time studying.

Lastly, I hope this book leaves you with the knowledge that chemistry is *not* reserved only for those with some superhuman intelligence level. With the right amount of effort and some clear guidance, anyone can master chemistry, including you.

Sincerely,

Nivaldo J. Tro
tro@westmont.edu

To the Instructor

I thank all of you who have used any of the first four editions of *Introductory Chemistry*—you have made this book the most widely selling book in its market, and for that I am extremely grateful. The preparation of the fifth edition has enabled me to continue to refine the book to meet its fundamental purpose: teaching chemical skills in the context of relevance.

Introductory Chemistry is designed for a one-semester, college-level, introductory or preparatory chemistry course. Students taking this course need to develop problem-solving skills—but they also must see *why* these skills are important to them and to their world. *Introductory Chemistry* extends chemistry from the laboratory to the student's world. It motivates students to learn chemistry by demonstrating the role it plays in their daily lives.

This is a visual book. Wherever possible, I have used images to help communicate the subject. In developing chemical principles, for example, I worked with several artists to develop multipart images that show the connection between everyday processes visible to the eye and the molecular interactions responsible for those processes. This art has been further refined and improved in the fifth edition, making the visual impact sharper and more targeted to student learning. For example, you will note a hierarchical system of labeling in many of the images: The white-boxed labels are the most important, the tan-tint boxes are the second most important, and unboxed labels are the third most important. This allows me to treat related labels and annotations within an image in the same way, so that the relationships between them are immediately evident. My intent is to create an art program that teaches and that presents complex information clearly and concisely. Many of the illustrations showing molecular depictions of a real-world object or process have three parts: macroscopic (what we can see with our eyes); molecular and atomic (space-filling models that depict what the molecules and atoms are doing); and symbolic (how chemists represent the molecular and atomic world). The goal is for the student to begin to see the connections between the macroscopic world, the molecular world, and the representation of the molecular world with symbols and formulas.

I have also refined the problem-solving pedagogy to include four steps: Sort, Strategize, Solve, and Check. The *solution map*, which has been part of this book since the first edition, is now part of the *Strategize* step. This four-step procedure is meant to guide students as they learn chemical problem solving. Extensive flowcharts are also incorporated throughout the book, allowing students to visualize the organization of chemical ideas and concepts. The color scheme used in both the solution maps and the flowcharts is designed to have pedagogical value. More specifically, the solution maps utilize the colors of the visible spectrum—always in the same order, from violet to red.

Throughout the worked Examples in this book, I use a *two- or three-column* layout in which students learn a general procedure for solving problems of a particular type as they see this procedure applied to one or two worked Examples. In this format, the *explanation* of how to solve a problem is placed directly beside the actual steps in the *solution* of the problem. Many of you have said that you use a similar technique in lecture and office hours. Since students have specifically asked for connections between Examples and end-of-chapter problems, I include a For More Practice feature at the end of each worked Example that lists the review examples and end-of-chapter problems that provide additional opportunities to practice the skill(s) covered in the Example.

A successful new feature in the second edition was the Conceptual Checkpoints, a series of short questions that students can use to test their mastery of key concepts as they read through a chapter. Emphasizing understanding rather than calculation, they are designed to be easy to answer if the student has grasped the essential concept but difficult if he or she has not. Your positive remarks on this new feature prompted me to continue adding more of these to the fifth edition, including questions that highlight visualization of the molecular world.

This edition has allowed me to add four new global features to the book: Learning Outcomes (LOs), Group Questions, Self-Assessment Quizzes, and Interactive Worked Examples. You will find the learning outcomes underneath most section heads—many of the LOs are repeated in the end of chapter material with an associated worked example. You will find the Group Questions following the chapter exercises. You can assign these as homework if you would like, but you can also use them as in class activities to encourage active learning and peer-to-peer engagement. The Self-Assessment Quizzes are at the very beginning of the chapter review material. These quizzes are designed so that students can test themselves on the core concepts and skills of each chapter. I encourage my students to use these quizzes as they prepare for exams. For example, if my exam covers Chapters 5–8, I assign the quizzes for those chapters for credit (you can do this in MasteringChemistry®). Students then get a sort of pretest on the core material that will be on the exam. The Interactive Worked Examples are a new digital asset that we created for this edition. These examples are available in MasteringChemistry® and at the following website: www.pearsonhighered.com/irc. Each Interactive Worked Example walks the student through a key example from the book (the examples that have been made interactive are marked with a play icon in the book). At a key point in the Interactive Worked Example, the video pauses and the student is asked a question. These questions are designed to encourage students to be active in the learning process. Once the student answers the question, the video resumes to the end. A follow-up question can then be assigned for credit in MasteringChemistry®.

My goal in this new edition is to continue to help you make learning a more active (rather than passive) process for your students. The new Group Questions can help make your classroom more active. The new Conceptual Checkpoints, along with the new Self-Assessment Quizzes, make reading the book a more active process. The addition of the Interactive Worked Examples makes the media experience active as well. Research consistently shows that students learn better when they are actively engaged in the process. I hope the tools that I have provided here continue to aid you in teaching your students more effectively. Please feel free to e-mail me with any questions or comments you might have. I look forward to hearing from you as you use this book in your course.

Sincerely,

Nivaldo J. Tro
tro@westmont.edu

Preface

New to This Edition

NEW! Key Learning Outcomes have been added to each chapter section. Learning outcomes correlate to the Chemical Skills and Examples in the end-of-chapter material and to MasteringChemistry®. Each section (after the introductory sections) has at least one learning outcome that summarizes the key learning objective of the material to help students focus their learning and assess their progress.

NEW! Self-Assessment Quizzes. Each chapter contains a 10-15 question multiple choice self-assessment quiz. These quizzes are designed to help students review the chapter material and prepare for exams.

NEW! 3–4 Questions for Group Work have been added to the end-of-chapter problems in each chapter to facilitate guided-inquiry learning both inside and outside the classroom.

NEW! 20 Interactive Worked Examples. Interactive Worked Examples are digital versions of the text's worked examples that make Tro's unique problem-solving strategies interactive, bringing his award-winning teaching directly to all students using his text. In these digital versions, students are instructed how to break down problems using Tro's proven Sort, Strategize, Solve, and Check technique. The Interactive Worked Examples can be accessed by scanning the QR code on the back cover allowing students to quickly access an office-hour type experience.

These problems are incorporated into MasteringChemistry® as assignable tutorial activities and are also available for download and distribution via the Instructor Resource Center (IRC) for instructional and classroom use.

More than 20 New Conceptual Checkpoints are in the fifth edition and are designed to make reading the book an active process. The checkpoints encourage students to stop and think about the ideas just presented before moving on and also provide a tool for self-assessment.

Interest Box Questions are now numbered in the Everyday Chemistry, Chemistry in the Environment, Chemistry in the Media, and Chemistry and Health boxes so that they can easily be assigned.

Cross-references to the Math Appendix, now indicated by a +/− icon in the fifth edition, are more visible and allow students to locate additional resources more easily.

Additional Features

- **A student-friendly, step-by-step, problem-solving approach is presented throughout** the book (fully introduced and explained in Chapter 2): Tro's unique two-and three-column examples help guide students through problems step-by-step using Sort, Strategize, Solve, and Check. "Relationships Used" are also included in most worked examples.

- **In all chapters, figure labels follow a consistent hierarchy.** Three types of labels appear in the art. The most important information is in white shadow boxes; the second most important is in tinted boxes (with no border); and the third level of labels is unboxed.
- **All figures and figure captions have been carefully examined, and images and labels have been replaced or revised when needed** to improve the teaching focus of the art program.
- **Every end-of-chapter question has been carefully reviewed** by the author and editor and accordingly revised and/or replaced when necessary.

Some significant improvements have been made to key content areas as well. These include:

- To reflect recent changes made by IUPAC that introduce more uncertainty in atomic masses, the periodic tables on the inside front cover of the book and all subsequent periodic tables in the text containing atomic masses now include the modified following atomic masses: Li 6.94; S 32.06; Ge 72.63; Se 78.97; and Mo 95.95.
- In Chapter 1, *The Chemical World,* key wording about chemicals as well as the definition of chemistry have been changed to more strongly reflect particles and properties connection.
- In Section 2.3, *Significant Figures: Writing Numbers to Reflect Precision,* clarification has been added about trailing zeros in the significant digits discussion in Section 2.3.
- In Section 3.8, *Energy,* a new schematic has been added to the photo of the dam to better illustrate the concept of potential energy, and there is a new figure, Figure 3.15, *Potential Energy of Raised Weight.*
- Several new subheadings have been added to Chapter 5 to help students better navigate the material; Table 5.3, *Some Common Polyatomic Ions,* has been moved to an earlier place in Chapter 5; and fourth edition Example 5.7, *Writing Formulas for Ionic Compounds,* has been replaced with fifth edition Example 5.7, *Writing Formulas for Ionic Compounds Containing Polyatomic Ions.*
- In Chapter 6, Chemistry in the Environment box *Chlorine in Chlorofluorocarbons* has been revised and updated. Figure 6.3, *The Ozone Shield,* has been updated and revised to include a molecular perspective and be a better teaching tool and Figure 6.4, *Growth of the Ozone Hole,* has been updated with 2010 data.
- The transition between balancing chemical equations to investigating types of reactions at the beginning of Section 7.5, *Aqueous Solutions and Solubility: Compounds Dissolved in Water,* has been sharpened to help students relate Section 7.5 to the previous section.
- Figure 7.7, *Solubility Rules Flowchart,* has been edited so that Ca^{2+}, Sr^{2+}, and Ba^{2+} are in periodic table order throughout for easier memorization.
- The phrase "global warming" has been replaced with "climate change" throughout Chapter 8, *Quantities in Chemical Reactions,* and Figure 8.2, *Climate Change,* has been updated to include global temperature data for 2011 and 2012.
- In Section 9.1, *Blimps, Balloons, and Models of the Atom,* more emphasis has been placed on the relationship between atomic structure and properties in the discussion of helium and hydrogen.
- In Section 9.4, *The Bohr Model: Atoms with Orbits,* new introductory material has been added to emphasize the relationship between light emission and electron motion.

- Orbital representations in figures throughout Chapter 9 have been modified to be more accurate.
- Throughout Chapter 10, *Chemical Bonding*, the term *Lewis theory* has been replaced with *Lewis model*.
- In Chapter 11, *Gases*, an update about how newer jets pressurize their cabins has been added to the Everyday Chemistry box, *Airplane Cabin Pressurization*, and Table 11.5, *Changes in Pollutant Levels for Major U.S. Cities, 1980–2010*, has been updated to include the most recent available data.
- Content has been revised and material has been added to improve clarity in the subsection entitled *Surface Tension* in Section 12.3, *Intermolecular Forces in Action: Surface Tension and Viscosity*. Also, the caption for Figure 12.5, *Origin of Surface Tension*, has been revised and the phase inset figures in Figure 12.16, *Heating Curve during Melting*, have been corrected to show the phases more accurately.
- The new title for Section 12.6, *Types of Intermolecular Forces: Dispersion, Dipole–Dipole, Hydrogen Bonding, and Ion–Dipole*, reflects new content and new material about ion–dipole forces, including new Figure 12.25, *Ion–Dipole Forces*. Also, ion–dipole forces have been added to Table 12.5, *Types of Intermolecular Forces*, and the art in the table now depicts space-filling models of the molecules.
- Content in Section 13.3, *Solutions of Solids Dissolved in Water: How to Make Rock Candy*, links the discussion of solvent–solute interactions to the discussion of intermolecular forces in Chapter 12.
- Figure 14.19, *How Buffers Resist pH Change*, has been changed to be more useful and easier for students to understand.
- Section 14.11, *Acid Rain: An Environmental Problem Related to Fossil Fuel Combustion*, has been cut.
- New, brief introductory statements have been added to Section 15.6, *Calculating and Using Equilibrium Constants*, and in Section 15.10, *The Effect of a Temperature Change on Equilibrium*, numbers that indicate sequence have been added to the three unnumbered equations that indicate how equilibrium changes when heat is added or removed from exothermic and endothermic reactions.
- The title of Figure 16.12, *Used Voltaic Cell*, has been corrected, and the art has been slightly modified.
- Figure 16.18, *Schematic Diagram of a Fuel-Cell Breathalyzer*, in the box Everyday Chemistry: *The Fuel-Cell Breathalyzer* has also been modified for accuracy.
- Clarification has been added in Section 18.10, *Aromatic Hydrocarbons*, in the discussion of the carbon–carbon bonds in benzene.

The design and features of this text have been conceived to work together as an integrated whole with a single purpose: to help students understand chemical principles and to master problem-solving skills in a context of relevance. Students must be able not only to grasp chemical concepts and solve chemical problems, but also to understand how those concepts and problem-solving skills are relevant to their other courses, their eventual career paths, and their daily lives.

Teaching Principles

The development of basic chemical principles—such as those of atomic structure, chemical bonding, chemical reactions, and the gas laws—is one of the main goals of this text. Students must acquire a firm grasp of these principles in order to succeed in the general chemistry sequence or the chemistry courses that support the allied health curriculum. To that end, the book integrates qualitative and quantitative material and proceeds from concrete concepts to more abstract ones.

Organization of the Text

The main divergence in topic ordering among instructors teaching introductory and preparatory chemistry courses is the placement of electronic structure and chemical bonding. Should these topics come early, at the point where models for the atom are being discussed? Or should they come later, after the student has been exposed to chemical compounds and chemical reactions? Early placement gives students a theoretical framework within which they can understand compounds and reactions. However, it also presents students with abstract models before they understand why they are necessary. I have chosen a later placement for the following reasons:

1. **A later placement provides greater flexibility.** An instructor who wants to cover atomic theory and bonding earlier can simply cover Chapters 9 and 10 after Chapter 4. However, if atomic theory and bonding were placed earlier, it would be more difficult for the instructor to skip these chapters and come back to them later.

2. **A later placement allows earlier coverage of topics that students can more easily visualize.** Coverage of abstract topics too early in a course can lose some students. Chemical compounds and chemical reactions are more tangible than atomic orbitals, and their relevance is easier to demonstrate to the beginning student.

3. **A later placement gives students a reason to learn an abstract theory.** Once students learn about compounds and reactions, they are more easily motivated to learn a theory that explains compounds and reactions in terms of underlying causes.

4. **A later placement follows the scientific method.** In science, we normally make observations, form laws, and then build models or theories that explain our observations and laws. A later placement follows this ordering.

Nonetheless, I know that every course is unique and that each instructor chooses to cover topics in his or her own way. Consequently, I have written each chapter for maximum flexibility in topic ordering. In addition, the book is offered in two formats. The full version, *Introductory Chemistry*, contains 19 chapters, including organic chemistry and biochemistry. The shorter version, *Introductory Chemistry Essentials*, contains 17 chapters and omits these topics.

Print and Media Resources

For the Instructor

MasteringChemistry®
MasteringChemistry® is the first adaptive-learning online homework and tutorial system. Instructors can create online assignments for their students by choosing from a wide range of items, including end-of-chapter problems and research-enhanced tutorials. Assignments are automatically graded with up-to-date diagnostic information, helping instructors pinpoint where students struggle either individually or for the class as a whole. These questions can be used asynchro-

nously outside of class as well. For the fifth edition, 20 new Interactive Worked Examples have been added to the Study Area. Icons appear next to examples indicating that a digital version is available.

NEW! Learning Catalytics™

Learning Catalytics™ is a "bring your own device" student engagement, assessment, and classroom intelligence system. With Learning Catalytics™ you can:

- Assess students in real time, using open-ended tasks to probe student understanding.
- Understand immediately where students are and adjust your lecture accordingly.
- Improve your students' critical-thinking skills.
- Access rich analytics to understand student performance.
- Add your own questions to make Learning Catalytics™ fits your course exactly.
- Manage student interactions with intelligent grouping and timing.

Learning Catalytics™ is a technology that has grown out of twenty years of cutting edge research, innovation, and implementation of interactive teaching and peer instruction. Learning Catalytics™ is included with the purchase of Mastering with eText. Students purchasing Mastering without eText will be able to upgrade their Mastering accounts to include access to Learning Catalytics™. Michael Everest of Westmont College has written a set of questions in Learning Catalytics™ that correlates directly to the topics and concepts in *Introductory Chemistry*, 5e and encourages group-based inquiry learning.

NEW! Adaptive Follow-up Assignments in MasteringChemistry®

Instructors now have the ability to assign adaptive follow-up assignments to students. Content delivered to students as part of adaptive learning will be automatically personalized for each individual based on strengths and weaknesses identified by his or her performance on Mastering parent assignments.

NEW! Dynamic Study Modules, designed to enable students to study effectively on their own, as well as help students quickly access and learn the nomenclature they need to be more successful in chemistry. These modules can be accessed on smartphones, tablets, and computers and results can be tracked in the MasteringChemistry® Gradebook. How it works:

1. Students receive an initial set of questions and benefit from the metacognition involved with asking them to indicate how confident they are with their answer.
2. After answering each set of questions, students review their answers.
3. Each question has explanation material that reinforces the correct answer response and addresses the misconceptions found in the wrong answer choices.
4. Once students review the explanations, they are presented with a new set of questions. Students cycle through this dynamic process of test-learn-retest until they achieve mastery of the material.

Instructor's Manual with Complete Solutions (0-321-94906-4) by Mark Ott of Jackson Community College, and Matthew Johll of Illinois Valley Community College. This manual features lecture outlines with presentation suggestions, teaching tips, suggested in-class demonstrations, and topics for classroom discussion. It also contains full solutions to all the end-of-chapter problems from the text.

TestGen Testbank (0-321-94933-1) by Michael Hauser of St. Louis Community College. This download-only test bank includes more than 2000 questions and is available on the Instructor's Resource Center.

Instructor's Resource Materials (0-321-94932-3) This resource provides an integrated collection of resources to help instructors make efficient and effective use of their time and is available for download from the Instructor's Resource Center. The package features the following:

- All the art from the text, including figures and tables in JPG and PDF formats; movies; animations; Interactive Molecules; and the Instructor's Resource Manual files.
- Four PowerPoint™ presentations: (1) a lecture outline presentation for each chapter, (2) all the art from the text, (3) the worked Examples from the text, and (4) clicker questions.
- TestGen, a computerized version of the Test Item File that allows instructors to create and tailor exams to fit their needs.

Instructor's Guide for Student's Guided Activity Workbook (0-321-96118-8) by Michael Everest of Westmont College. This manual features assessible outcomes, facilitation tips, and demonstration suggestions to help integrate guided-inquiry learning in the classroom and is available for download on the Instructor's Resource Center.

For the Student

Pearson eText offers students the power to create notes, highlight text in different colors, create bookmarks, zoom, and view single or multiple pages. Access to the Pearson eText for *Introductory Chemistry*, Fifth Edition, is available for purchase either as a standalone item (ISBN 0-321-93363-X) or within MasteringChemistry® (ISBN 0-321-93434-2).

Study Guide (0-321-94905-6) by Donna Friedman of St. Louis Community College—Florissant Valley. Each chapter of the Study Guide contains an overview, key learning outcomes, a chapter review, as well as practice problems for each major concept in the text. Each chapter is followed by two or three self-tests with answers so students can check their work.

Student's Selected Solution Manual (0-321-94907-2) by Matthew Johll of Illinois Valley Community College. The manual provides solutions to those problems that have a short answer in the text's Answers section (problems numbered in blue in the text).

NEW! Student's Guided Activity Workbook (0-321-94908-0) by Michael Everest of Westmont College. This set of guided-inquiry activities enables students to construct chemical knowledge and related skills on their own. Each activity begins by presenting some information (as a table, figure, graph, text, etc.). Students, working in groups of 3–4, answer questions designed to draw their attention to the important concepts and trends exemplified in the information. Through their active participation in the learning process, students learn not only chemistry, but also a wide range of additional skills such as information processing, problem solving, deductive reasoning, and teamwork. There are approximately three complete worksheets to accompany each chapter in *Introductory Chemistry*, and each worksheet should take students from 50–60 minutes to complete. The activities can be used in place of, or as a supplement to, a lecture-based pedagogy. This supplement is available through Pearson Custom Library www.pearsoncustomlibrary.com.

Acknowledgments

This book has been a group effort, and there are many people whose help has meant a great deal to me. First and foremost, I would like to thank my editors, Adam Jaworski and Chris Hess. I appreciate your commitment to and energy for this project. You are both incredibly bright and insightful editors, and I am lucky to get to work with you. As always, I am grateful to Paul Corey, the president of the Science Division at Pearson, for his unwavering support.

I am also in a continual state of awe and gratitude to Erin Mulligan, my development editor and friend. Thanks, Erin, for all your outstanding help and advice. Thanks also to my project editor, Coleen Morrison. Coleen, your guidance and attention to details kept this project running smoothly from start to finish. I am so grateful. I would also like to thank Jonathan Cottrell, my marketing manager, whose creativity in describing and promoting the book is without equal. Thanks also to the MasteringChemistry® team who continue to provide and promote the best online homework system on the planet.

I also appreciate the expertise and professionalism of my copy editor, Betty Pessagno, as well as the skill and diligence of Francesca Monaco and her colleagues at codeMantra. I am a picky author, and they always accommodated my seemingly endless requests. Thank you, Francesca. Thanks as well to my project manager, Beth Sweeten, managing editor Gina Cheselka, and the rest of the Pearson team—they are part of a first-class operation. This text has benefited immeasurably from their talents and hard work. I owe a special debt of gratitude to Quade Paul, who continues to make my ideas come alive in his chapter-opener and cover art.

I am grateful for the support of my colleagues Allan Nishimura, David Marten, Stephen Contakes, Kristi Lazar, Carrie Hill, Michael Everest, and Heidi Henes-Vanbergen, who have supported me in my department while I worked on this book. I am also grateful to Katherine Han, who helped me with the Self-Assessment Quizzes. I owe a special debt of gratitude to Michael Tro. He has been helping me with manuscript preparation, proofreading, organizing art manuscripts, and tracking changes in end-of-chapter material for the past three years. Michael has been reliable, accurate, and invaluable. Thanks Mikee!

I am grateful to those who have given so much to me personally while writing this book. First on that list is my wife, Ann. Her patience and love for me are beyond description. I also thank my children, Michael, Ali, Kyle, and Kaden, whose smiling faces and love of life always inspire me. I come from a large Cuban family, whose closeness and support most people would envy. Thanks to my parents, Nivaldo and Sara; my siblings, Sarita, Mary, and Jorge; my siblings-in-law, Jeff, Nachy, Karen, and John; my nephews and nieces, Germain, Danny, Lisette, Sara, and Kenny. These are the people with whom I celebrate life.

Lastly, I am indebted to the many reviewers, listed next, whose ideas are scattered throughout this book. They have corrected me, inspired me, and sharpened my thinking on how best to teach this subject we call chemistry. I deeply appreciate their commitment to this project.

Reviewers of the 5th Edition

Alyse Dilts
Harrisburg Area Community College

Claire Cohen
University of Toledo

Craig McClure
University of Alabama — Birmingham

Ebru Buyuktanir
Stark State College

Edward Lee
Texas Tech University

James Zubricky
University of Toledo

Janice Webster
Ivy Tech Community College —Terre Haute

Jennifer Firestine
Lindenwood University

Kathy Flynn
College of the Canyons

Michael Hauser
St. Louis Community College — Meramec

Michael Rodgers
Southeast Missouri State University

Robert Culp
California State University — Fresno

Rosa Davila
College of Southern Idaho

Sara Harvey
Los Angeles Pierce College

Scott Bunge
Kent State University

Sylvia Esjornson
Southwestern Oklahoma State University

Virginia Miller
Montgomery College

5th Edition Accuracy Reviewers

Alyse Dilts
Harrisburg Area Community College

Connie Lee
Montgomery County Community College

Kent McCorkle
Fresno City College

Lance Lund
Anoka-Ramsey Community College

Stevenson Flemer Jr.
University of Vermont

Reviewers of the 4th Edition

Brian G. Dixon
Massachusetts Maritime Academy

Bruce E. Hodson
Baylor University

Carmela Byrnes
MiraCosta College

Carmela Magliocchi Brynes
MiraCosta College

Chuck Laland
Black Hawk College

Clarissa Sorenson-Unruh
Central New Mexico Community College

David Vanderlinden
Des Moines Area Community College

Donald R. Jones
Lincoln Land Community College

Donna Friedman
St. Louis Community College—Florissant Valley

Farkhondeh Khalili
Massachusetts Bay Community College

Geoff Mitchell
Washington International School

Guy Dadson
Fullerton College

Jack F. McKenna
St. Cloud State University

Jason Serin
Glendale Community College

Jeannine Eddleton
Virginia Tech

Jeffrey Allison
Austin Community College

Jerod Gross
Roanoke Benson High School

Jie Song
Univeristy of Michigan—Flint

John Petty
University of South Alabama

Joseph Bergman
Illinois Central College

Kelly Beefus
Anoka-Ramsey Community College

Lara Baxley
California Polytechnic State University

Laurie Leblanc
Cuyamaca College

Luther D. Giddings
Salt Lake Community College

Marcus Giotto
Quinsigamond Community College

Margaret Kiminsky
Monroe Community College

Maria Cecilia D. de Mesa
Baylor University

Martha R. Kellner
Westminster College

Maru Grant
Ohlone College

Meg Osterby
Western Technical College

Melodie Graber
Oakton Community College

Michael A. Hauser
St. Louis Community College

Mikhail V. Barybin
The University of Kansas

Nancy Lee
MiraCosta College

Rebecca Krystyniak
Saint Cloud State

Richard Lavallee
Santa Monica College

Ron Erickson
University of Iowa

Simon Bott
University of Houston

Steven Socol
McHenry Community College

Tamara E. Hanna
Texas Tech University

Tammy S. Gummersheimer
Schenectady County Community College

Timothy Dudley
Villanova University

Vicki MacMurdo
Anoka-Ramsey Community College

Vidyullata C. Waghulde
St. Louis Community—Meramec

Virginia Miller
Montgomery College

Youngju Sohn
Florida Institute of Technology

Reviewers of the 3rd Edition

Anthony P. Toste
Missouri State University

Benjamin Arrowood
Ohio University

Carol A. Martinez
Central New Mexico Community College

Carrie Woodcock
Eastern Michigan University

Donna G. Friedman
St. Louis Community College

Erick Fuoco
Daley College

Joe Bergman
Illinois Central College

John Thurston
University of Iowa

Kathleen Thrush Shaginaw
Particular Solutions, Inc.

Kresimir Rupnik
Louisiana State University

Kurt Allen Teets
Okaloosa-Walton College

Laurie Leblanc
Grossmont College

Martha R. Joseph
Westminster College

Mary Sohn
Florida Tech

Melodie A. Graber
Oakton Community College

Michael A. Hauser
St Louis Community College, Meramec Campus

Pong (David) Shieh
Wharton College

Sharlene J. Dzugan
University of Cumberlands

Thomas Dzugan
University of Cumberlands

Timothy Dudley
Villanova University

Timothy Kreider
University of Medicine & Dentistry of New Jersey

Reviewers of the 2nd Edition

Blake Key
Northwestern Michigan College

Bryan E. Breyfogle
Southwest Missouri State University

Carl A. Hoeger
University of California—San Diego

Carol A. Martinez
Albuquerque Technical Vocational Institute

Charles Michael McCallum
University of the Pacific

Colin Bateman
Brevard Community College

Crystal Gambino
Manatee Community College

David S. Ballantine, Jr.
Northern Illinois University

Deborah G. Simon
Santa Fe Community College

Donald R. Jones
Lincoln Land Community College

Donna G. Friedman
St. Louis Community College—Florissant Valley

Donna K. Howell
Angelo State University

Eric L. Trump
Emporia State University

Frank Carey
Wharton County Junior College

James G. Tarter
College of Southern Idaho

Kirk Kawagoe
Fresno City College

Laurie LeBlanc
Cuyamaca College

Lynne Zeman
Kirkwood Community College

Mary Sohn
Florida Institute of Technology

Mary Urban
College of Lake County

Michael Hauser
St. Louis Community College—Meramec

Michele Berkey
San Juan College

Michelle Driessen
University of Minnesota—Minneapolis

Morris Bramlett
University of Arkansas—Monticello

Newton P. Hillard, Jr.
Eastern New Mexico University

Nichole Jackson
Odessa College

Peter-John Stanskas
San Bernardino Valley College

Rebecca A. Krystyniak
St. Cloud State University

Richard Watt
University of New Mexico

Robbey C. Culp
Fresno City College

Robin McCann
Shippensburg University

Ronald C. Marks
Warner Southern College

Roy Kennedy
Massachusetts Bay Community College

Ruth M. Topich
Virginia Commonwealth University

Steve Gunther
Albuquerque Technical Vocational Institute

Steven R. Boone
Central Missouri State University

T. G. Jackson
University of South Alabama

Theodore Sakano
Rockland Community College

Victor Ryzhov
Northern Illinois University

Reviewers of the 1st Edition

Bill Nickels
Schoolcraft College

Bob Perkins
Kwantlen University College

Bryan E. Breyfogle
Southwest Missouri State University

C. Michael McCallum
University of the Pacific

Calvin D. Tormanen
Central Michigan University

Carl J. Carrano
Southwest Texas State University

Caryn Prudenté
University of Southern Maine

Christine V. Bilicki
Pasadena City College

Connie M. Roberts
Henderson State University

Danny R. Bedgood
Arizona State University

Donald C. Davis
College of Lake County

Donna G. Friedman
St. Louis Community College at Florissant Valley

Dwayne Gergens
San Diego Mesa College

Eric L. Trump
Emporia State University

George Goth
Skyline College

Jan Gryko
Jacksonville State University

Jeffery A. Schneider
SUNY—Oswego

Kathy Mitchell
St. Petersburg Junior College

Kim D. Summerhays
University of San Francisco

Laura Andersson
Big Bend Community College

Leslie Wo-Mei Fung
Loyola University of Chicago

Lori Allen
University of Wisconsin—Parkside

Mark Porter
Texas Tech University

Rill Ann Reuter
Winona State University

Ronald H. Takata
Honolulu Community College

Roy Kennedy
Massachusetts Bay Community College

Warren Bosch
Elgin Community College

A Consistent Problem-Solving Strategy

Drawing from Professor Tro's experience in the classroom with his own students, *Introductory Chemistry*, **Fifth Edition** brings chemistry out of the laboratory and into the world—helping you learn chemistry by showing you how it manifests in your daily lives. Clear, specific examples are woven throughout to tell the story of chemistry. The **Fifth Edition** is also available with MasteringChemistry®, the premier online homework and assessment tool.

A CONSISTENT STRATEGY FOR SOLVING PROBLEMS helps you develop the skills you need to succeed in your chemistry course. Tro's unique two- and three-column examples help guide students through problems step-by-step using *Sort, Strategize, Solve, and Check.*

Two-Column Examples
All but the simplest examples are presented in a unique two-column format.

- The left column explains the purpose of each step, while the right column shows how the step is executed.

- This format will help you think about the reason for each step in the solution and fit the steps together.

Solution Maps
Many of the examples use a unique visual approach in the *Strategize Step*, where you'll be shown how to draw a solution map for a problem.

Three-Column Examples
Procedures for solving certain problems are presented in a unique three-column format.

- The first column outlines the problem-solving procedure and explains the reasoning that underlies each step.

- The second and third columns show two similar but slightly different examples to solve this class of problem.

- Seeing the method applied to solve two related problems helps you understand the general procedure in a way that no single example could convey.

Skillbuilder Exercises
Every worked example is followed by at least one similar (but unworked) Skillbuilder exercise.

For More Practice
These follow every worked example, linking you to in-chapter examples and end-of-chapter problems that give you a chance to practice the skills explained in each worked example.

NEW! INTERACTIVE WORKED EXAMPLES

Interactive Worked Examples are digital versions of the text's worked examples that make Tro's unique problem-solving strategies interactive, bringing his award-winning teaching directly to all students using his text. In these digital versions, students are instructed how to break down problems using Tro's proven *Sort, Strategize, Solve, and Check* technique. The Interactive Worked Examples can be accessed by scanning the QR code on the back cover allowing students to quickly access an office-hour type experience.

These problems are incorporated into MasteringChem stry® as assignable tutorial activities and are also available for download and distribution via the Instructor Resource Center (IRC) for instructional and classroom use.

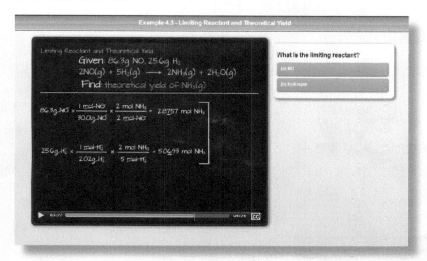

CONCEPTUAL UNDERSTANDING completes the picture. In every chemistry course you take, success requires more than problem-solving skills. Real understanding of concepts will help you see why these skills are important to you and to your world.

Conceptual Checkpoints

Conceptual questions enhance understanding of chemical principles, encourage you to stop and think about the ideas just presented, and provide a tool to assess your own progress. Answers and explanations are given at the end of each chapter. More than 20 new **Conceptual Checkpoints** have been added—many with a focus on visualization and drawing.

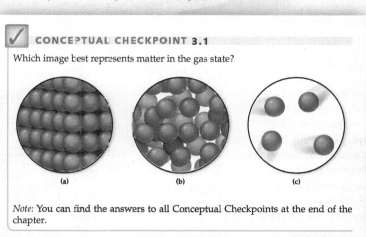

Visualizing Chemistry
Creates Deeper Understanding

BY CONNECTING the macroscopic and microscopic worlds, visualizing concepts brings chemistry to life and creates a deeper understanding that will serve you throughout the course.

Chapter Openers
Dr. Tro opens each chapter with a specific example of a concept to grab your attention, stepping back to make a more general and relatable analogy, and then going back into specifics. This style reflects Dr. Tro's teaching methodology, effectively used in his own classroom.

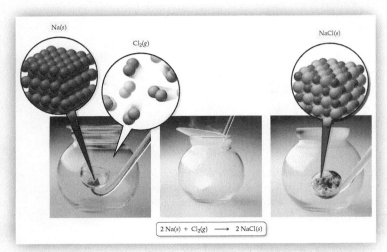

MACROSCOPIC TO MICROSCOPIC ART

The goal is for you to connect what you see and experience with the molecules responsible and with the way chemists represent those molecules.

Many illustrations have three parts:

- a macroscopic image (what you can see with your eyes)
- a microscopic image (what the molecules are doing)
- a symbolic representation (how chemists represent the process with symbols and equations)

INTEREST BOXES

Four different types of interest boxes apply chemistry to everyday events and topics. The questions within these boxes have been numbered so they may be assigned.

- **Chemistry in the Environment** boxes discuss environmental issues that are closely tied to chemistry, such as the reactions involved in ozone depletion.
- **Everyday Chemistry** boxes demonstrate the importance of chemistry in everyday situations, such as bleaching your hair.
- **Chemistry in the Media** boxes discuss chemical topics that have been in the news recently, such as the controversy over oxygenated fuels.
- **Chemistry and Health** boxes focus on personal health and fitness topics, as well as biomedical topics.

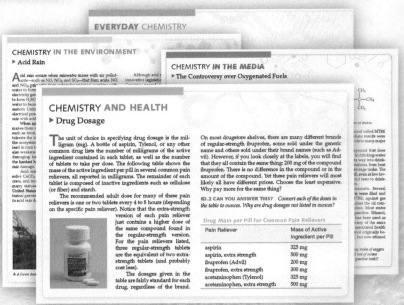

Enhanced End-of-Chapter Material

CHAPTER REVIEW

Consistent review material at the end of each chapter helps reinforce what you've learned.

Chemical Principles

The left column summarizes the key principles that you should take away from the chapter, and the right column tells why each topic is important for you to understand.

Chemical Principles	Relevance
Uncertainty: Scientists report measured quantities so that the number of digits reflects the certainty in the measurement. Write measured quantities so that every digit is certain except the last, which is estimated.	**Uncertainty:** Measurement is a hallmark of science, and you must communicate the precision of a measurement with the measurement so that others know how reliable the measurement is. When you write or manipulate measured quantities, you must show and retain the precision with which the original measurement was made.
Units: Measured quantities usually have units associated with them. The SI unit for length is the meter; for mass, the kilogram; **and for time, the second. Prefix multipliers such as** *kilo-* or *milli-* are often used in combination with these basic units. The SI units of volume are units of length raised to the third power; liters or milliliters are often used as well.	**Units:** The units in a measured quantity communicate what the quantity actually is. Without an agreed-on system of units, scientists could not communicate their measurements. Units are also important in calculations, and the tracking of units throughout a calculation is essential.
Density: The density of a substance is its mass divided by its volume, $d = m/V$, and is usually reported in units of grams per cubic centimeter or grams per milliliter. Density is a fundamental property of all substances and generally differs from one substance to another.	**Density:** The density of substances is an important consideration in choosing materials for manufacturing and production. Airplanes, for example, are made of low-density materials, while bridges are made of higher-density materials. Density is important as a conversion factor between mass and volume and vice versa.

NEW! Chemical Skills with Key Learning Outcomes

The left column describes the key skills you should know after reading the chapter, which often correlate to a *Key Learning Outcome* that has been added at the section level. The right column contains a worked example illustrating that skill.

Chemical Skills	Examples
LO: Express very large and very small numbers using scientific notation (Section 2.2). To express a number in scientific notation: • Move the decimal point to obtain a number between 1 and 10. • Write the decimal part multiplied by 10 raised to the number of places you moved the decimal point. • The exponent is positive if you moved the decimal point to the left and negative if you moved the decimal point to the right.	**EXAMPLE 2.18 SCIENTIFIC NOTATION** Express the number 45,000,000 in scientific notation. $$45,000,000$$ $$4.5 \times 10^7$$

CHAPTER IN REVIEW

Self-Assessment Quiz

Q1. How many atoms are there in 5.8 mol helium?
- (a) 23.2 atoms
- (b) 9.6×10^{-24} atoms
- (c) 5.8×10^{23} atoms
- (d) 3.5×10^{24} atoms

Q2. A sample of pure silver has a mass of 155 g. How many moles of silver are in the sample?
- (a) 1.44 mol
- (b) 1.67×10^4 mol
- (c) 0.696 mol
- (d) 155 mol

NEW! Chapter Self-Assessment Quiz

The end of each chapter consists of 10–15 multiple-choice questions that are similar to those on other standardized exams and will also be assignable and randomized in MasteringChemistry®.

NEW! *Group-Based* Questions

have been added to the end-of-chapter problems in each chapter, facilitating guided-inquiry learning both inside and outside the classroom. A new *Guided Activity Workbook* (available in the Pearson Custom Library (www.pearsoncustomlibrary.com)) has also been created to use alongside Tro's textbook. A set of interactive *Critical Thinking Questions* that is tailored toward guided learning is also available for instructors at the Instructor Resource Center (www.pearsonhighered.com/irc).

QUESTIONS FOR GROUP WORK

Discuss these questions with the group and record your consensus answer.

121. Complete the following table.

Particle	Mass (amu)	Charge	In the nucleus? (yes/no)	# in ³²S atom	# in ⁷⁹Br⁻ ion
Proton					
Neutron					
Electron					

122. Make a sketch of an oxygen atom. Include the correct number of protons, electrons, and neutrons for the most abundant isotope. Use the following symbols: proton = •, neutron = o, electron = •.

123. The table at right includes data similar to that used by Mendeleev when he made the periodic table. Write on a small card the symbol, atomic mass, and a stable compound formed by each element. Arrange your cards in order of increasing atomic mass. Do you observe any repeating patterns? Describe any patterns you observe. (*Hint:* There is one missing element somewhere in the pattern.)

Element	Atomic Mass	Stable Compound	Element	Atomic Mass	Stable Compound
Be	9	$BeCl_2$	O	16	H_2O
S	32	H_2S	Ga	69.7	GaH_3
F	19	F_2	As	75	AsF_3
Ca	40	$CaCl_2$	C	12	CH_4
Li	7	LiCl	K	39	KCl
Si	28	SiH_4	Mg	24.3	$MgCl_2$
Cl	35.4	Cl_2	Se	79	H_2Se
B	10.8	BH_3	Al	27	AlH_3
Ge	72.6	GeH_4	Br	80	Br_2
N	14	NF_3	Na	23	NaCl

124. Arrange the cards from Question 123 so that mass increases from left to right and elements with similar properties are above and below each other. Copy the periodic table you have invented onto a piece of paper. There is one element missing. Predict its mass and a stable compound it might form.

Additional End-of-Chapter Features
- Key Terms
- Review Questions
- Problems by Topic
- Cumulative Problems
- Conceptual Problems
- Highlight Problems

MasteringChemistry® for Students

www.masteringchemistry.com

MASTERINGCHEMISTRY® TUTORIALS guide you through the most challenging topics while helping to make connections between related chemical concepts. Immediate feedback and tutorial assistance help you understand and master concepts and skills in chemistry—allowing you to retain more knowledge and perform better in this course and beyond.

MasteringChemistry® is the only system to provide instantaneous feedback specific to the most common wrong answers. You can submit an answer and receive immediate, error-specific feedback. Simpler subproblems—hints—are provided upon request.

NEW! Pause and Predict Video Quizzes ask you to predict the outcome of experiments and demonstrations as you watch the videos; a set of multiple choice questions challenges you to apply the concepts from the video to related scenarios. These videos are also available in web and mobile-friendly formats through the Study Area of MasteringChemistry and in the Pearson eText.

Math Remediation links found in selected tutorials launch algorithmically generated math exercises that give you unlimited opportunity for practice and mastery of math skills. Math Remediation exercises provide additional practice and free up class and office-hour time to focus on the chemistry. Exercises include guided solutions, sample problems, and learning aids for extra help and offer helpful feedback when you enter incorrect answers.

NEW! Simulations, assignable in MasteringChemistry, include those developed by the PhET Chemistry Group, and the leading authors in simulation development covering some of the most difficult chemistry concepts.

MasteringChemistry® for Instructors
www.masteringchemistry.com

The Mastering platform was developed by scientists for science students and instructors. Mastering has been refined from data-driven insights derived from over a decade of real-world use by faculty and students.

NEW! Learning Catalytics™ is a "bring your own device" student engagement, assessment, and classroom intelligence system. With Learning Catalytics™ you can:

- Assess students in real time, using open-ended tasks to probe student understanding.
- Understand immediately where students are and adjust your lecture accordingly.
- Improve your students' critical-thinking skills.
- Access rich analytics to understand student performance.
- Add your own questions to make Learning Catalytics™ fit your course exactly.
- Manage student interactions with intelligent grouping and timing.

Learning Catalytics™ is included with the purchase of Mastering with eText. Students purchasing Mastering without eText will be able to upgrade their Mastering accounts to include access to Learning Catalytics™.

NEW! Adaptive Follow-Up Assignments
Instructors now have the ability to assign adaptive follow-up assignments to students. Content delivered to students as part of adaptive learning will be automatically personalized for each individual based on strengths and weaknesses identified by his or her performance on Mastering parent assignments.

NEW! Dynamic Study Modules, designed to enable students to study effectively on their own as well as help students quickly access and learn the nomenclature they need to be more successful in chemistry. These modules can be accessed on smartphones, tablets, and computers and results can be tracked in the MasteringChemistry® Gradebook. How it works:

1. Students receive an initial set of questions and benefit from the metacognition involved with asking them to indicate how confident they are with their answer.
2. After answering each set of questions, students review their answers.
3. Each question has explanation material that reinforces the correct answer response and addresses the misconceptions found in the wrong answer choices.
4. Once students review the explanations, they are presented with a new set of questions. Students cycle through this dynamic process of test-learn-retest until they achieve mastery of the material.

NEW! Learning Outcomes
Let Mastering do the work in tracking student performance against your learning outcomes:

- Add your own or use the publisher provided learning outcomes.
- View class performance against the specified learning outcomes.
- Export results to a spreadsheet that you can further customize and share with your chair, dean, administrator, or accreditation board.

Soda pop is a mixture of carbon dioxide and water and a few other substances that contribute flavor and color. When soda pop is poured into a glass, some of the carbon dioxide molecules come out of the mixture, producing the familiar fizz.

The Chemical World

"*Imagination is more important than knowledge.*"—Albert Einstein (1879–1955)

CHAPTER OUTLINE

1.1 Soda Pop Fizz

Carbon dioxide molecule

Oxygen atom | Carbon atom | Oxygen atom

Water molecule

Hydrogen atom | Oxygen atom | Hydrogen atom

Open a can of soda pop and you hear the familiar "chchchch" of pressure release. Take a sip and you feel the carbon dioxide bubbles on your tongue. If you shake the can before you open it, you are sprayed with the bubbly liquid. A can of soda pop, like most familiar items in our daily lives, is a chemical mixture containing mostly sugar, water, and carbon dioxide. The unique combination of these substances gives soda pop its properties. Have you ever wondered why soda pop tastes sweet? To understand why, you need to understand sugar and solutions of sugar with water. We will learn about solutions in Chapter 13. Have you ever wondered why soda fizzes when you open it? To understand the reason, you need to understand gases and their ability to dissolve in liquids and how that ability varies with changing pressure. We will learn about gases in Chapter 11. And if you want to know why drinking too much soda pop makes you gain weight, you need to understand energy and the production of energy by chemical reactions. We will discuss energy in Chapter 3 and chemical reactions in Chapter 7. You don't need to venture any farther than your own home and your own everyday experiences to encounter chemical questions. Chemicals compose virtually everything in our world: the soda; this book; your pencil; indeed, even your own body.

Chemists are particularly interested in the connections between the properties of substances and the structure of the particles that compose them. For example, why does soda pop fizz? Like all common substances, soda pop is ultimately composed of tiny particles called *atoms*. Atoms are so small that a single drop of soda contains about one billion trillion of them. In soda, as in many substances, these atoms are bound together to form several different types of *molecules*. The molecules important to fizzing are carbon dioxide and water. Carbon dioxide molecules consist of three atoms—one carbon and two oxygen atoms—held together in a straight line by chemical bonds. Water molecules also consist of three atoms—one oxygen and two hydrogen atoms—bonded together, but rather than being straight like carbon dioxide, the water molecule is bent.

▶ Virtually everything around you is composed of chemicals.

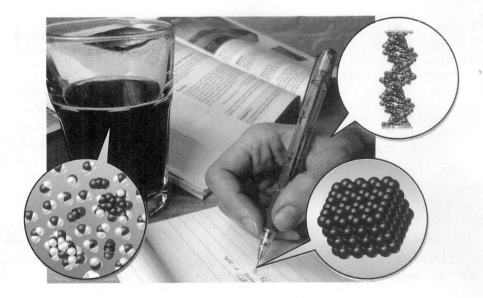

We will explore the nature of atoms, molecules, and chemical bonds more fully in later chapters. For now, think of atoms and molecules as tiny particles that compose all common matter, and chemical bonds as the attachments that hold atoms together.

The details of how atoms bond together to form a molecule—straight, bent, or some other shape—as well as the type of atoms in the molecule, determine *everything* about the substance that the molecule composes. The characteristics of water molecules make water a liquid at room temperature. The characteristics of carbon dioxide molecules make carbon dioxide a gas at room temperature. The characteristics of sugar molecules allow them to interact with our taste buds to produce the sensation of sweetness.

The makers of soda pop use *pressure* (the result of collisions between gaseous molecules and the surfaces around them) to force gaseous carbon dioxide molecules to mix with liquid water molecules. As long as the can of soda is sealed, the carbon dioxide molecules remain mixed with the water molecules, held there by pressure. When the can is opened, the pressure is released and carbon dioxide molecules escape out of the soda mixture (▼ Figure 1.1). As they do, they create bubbles—the familiar fizz of soda pop.

▲ **FIGURE 1.1 Where the fizz comes from** Bubbles in soda pop are pockets of carbon dioxide gas molecules escaping out of the liquid water.

1.2   Chemicals Compose Ordinary Things

LO: Recognize that chemicals make
up virtually everything we come
into contact with in our world.
*(Note: Most of the sections in
the chapters in this book link to
a Learning Objective (LO), which
is listed at the beginning of the
section).*

Is soda pop composed of chemicals? Yes. In fact, nothing that we can hold or touch is *not* made of chemicals. When most people think of chemicals, however, they may envision a can of paint thinner in their garage, or recall a headline about a river polluted by industrial waste. But chemicals compose ordinary things, too. Chemicals compose the air we breathe and the water we drink. They compose toothpaste, Tylenol®, and toilet paper. Chemicals make up virtually everything we come into contact with. Chemistry explains the properties and behavior of chemicals, in the broadest sense, by helping us understand the molecules that compose them.

▲ People often have a very narrow view of chemicals, thinking of them only as dangerous poisons or pollutants.

▲ Chemists are interested in knowing why ordinary things, such as water, are the way they are. When a chemist sees a pitcher of water, she thinks of the molecules that compose the liquid and how those molecules determine its properties.

As you experience the world around you, molecules are interacting to create your experience. Imagine watching a sunset. Molecules are involved in every step. Molecules in air interact with light from the sun, scattering away the blue and green light and leaving the red and orange light to create the color you see. Molecules in your eyes absorb that light and as a result are altered in a way that sends a signal to your brain. Molecules in your brain then interpret the signal to produce images and emotions. This whole process—mediated by molecules—creates the evocative experience of seeing a sunset.

Chemists are interested in why ordinary substances are the way they are. Why is water a liquid? Why is salt a solid? Why does soda fizz? Why is a sunset red? Throughout this book, you will learn the answers to these questions and many others. *You will learn the connections between the behavior of matter and the structure of the particles that compose it.*

1.3   All Things Are Made of Atoms and Molecules

LO: Recognize that all things are made
of atoms and molecules.

Nobel laureate Richard Feynman, in a lecture to first-year physics students at the California Institute of Technology, said that the most important idea in all human knowledge is that *all things are made of atoms*. Since atoms are usually bound together to form molecules, however, a chemist might add the concept of *molecules* to Feynman's bold assertion. This simple idea—that all things are made of atoms and molecules—explains much about our world and our experience of it. Atoms and molecules determine how matter behaves—if they were different, matter would be different. The nature of water molecules, for example, determines how water behaves. The nature of sugar molecules determines how sugar behaves, and the molecules that compose humans determine much about how our bodies behave.

◀ Richard Feynman (1918–1988), Nobel Prize–winning physicist and popular professor at California Institute of Technology.

There is a direct connection between the world of atoms and molecules and the world we experience every day. Chemists explore this connection. They seek to understand it. A good, simple definition of **chemistry** is *the science that tries to understand how matter behaves by studying how atoms and molecules behave.*

1.4   The Scientific Method: How Chemists Think

LO: Identify and understand the key characteristics of the scientific method: observation, the formulation of hypotheses, the testing of hypotheses by experiment, and the formulation of laws and theories.

Chemists use the **scientific method**—a way of learning that emphasizes observation and experimentation—to understand the world. The scientific method stands in contrast to ancient Greek philosophies that emphasized *reason* as the way to understand the world. Although the scientific method is not a rigid procedure that automatically leads to a definitive answer, it does have key characteristics that distinguish it from other ways of acquiring knowledge. These key characteristics include observation, the formulation of hypotheses, the testing of hypotheses by experiment, and the formulation of laws and theories.

The first step in acquiring scientific knowledge (▼ Figure 1.2) is often the **observation** or measurement of some aspect of nature. Some observations are simple, requiring nothing more than the naked eye. Other observations rely on the use of sensitive instrumentation. Occasionally, an important observation happens entirely by chance. Alexander Fleming (1881–1955), for example, discovered penicillin when he observed a bacteria-free circle around a certain mold that had accidentally grown on a culture plate. Regardless of how these observations occur, they usually involve the measurement or description of some aspect of the physical world. For example, Antoine Lavoisier (1743–1794), a French chemist who studied *combustion*, burned substances in closed containers. He carefully measured the mass of each container and its contents before and after burning the substance inside, noting that there was no change in the mass during combustion. Lavoisier made an *observation* about the physical world.

Combustion means burning. The mass of an object is a measure of the quantity of matter within it.

Observations often lead scientists to formulate a **hypothesis**, a tentative interpretation or explanation of the observations. Lavoisier explained his observations on combustion by hypothesizing that combustion involved the combination of a substance with a component of air. A good hypothesis is *falsifiable*, which means that further testing has the potential to prove it wrong. Hypotheses are tested by **experiments**, highly controlled observations designed to validate or invalidate hypotheses. The results of an experiment may confirm a hypothesis or show the hypothesis to be mistaken in some way. In the latter case, the hypothesis may have to be modified, or even discarded and replaced by an alternative hypothesis. Either way, the new or revised hypothesis must also be tested through further experimentation.

Sometimes a number of similar observations lead to the development of a **scientific law**, a brief statement that summarizes past observations and predicts future ones. For example, based on his observations of combustion, Lavoisier developed the **law of conservation of mass**, which states, "In a chemical reaction

▲ **FIGURE 1.2   The scientific method**

▶ (Right) Painting of the French chemist Antoine Lavoisier and his wife, Marie, who helped him in his work by illustrating his experiments, recording results, and translating scientific articles from English. [*Source:* Jacques Louis David (French, 1748–1825). "Antoine-Laurent Lavoisier (1743–1794) and His Wife (Marie-Anne-Pierrette Paulze, 1758–1836)," 1788, oil on canvas, H. 102-1/4 in. W. 76-5/8 in. (259.7 × 194.6 cm). The Metropolitan Museum of Art, Purchase, Mr. and Mrs. Charles Wrightsman Gift, in honor of Everett Fahy, 1977. (1977.10) Image copyright © The Metropolitan Museum of Art.] (Far right) John Dalton, the English chemist who formulated the atomic theory.

matter is neither created nor destroyed." This statement grew out of Lavoisier's observations, and it predicted the outcome of similar experiments on *any* chemical reaction. Laws are also subject to experiments, which can prove them wrong or validate them.

| Scientific theories are also called *models*.

One or more well-established hypotheses may form the basis for a scientific **theory**. Theories provide a broader and deeper explanation for observations and laws. They are models of the way nature is, and they often predict behavior that extends well beyond the observations and laws on which they are founded. A good example of a theory is the **atomic theory** of John Dalton (1766–1844). Dalton explained the law of conservation of mass, as well as other laws and observations, by proposing that all matter was composed of small, indestructible particles called atoms. Dalton's theory was a model of the physical world—it went beyond the laws and observations of the time to explain these laws and observations.

Theories are also tested and validated by experiments. Notice that the scientific method begins with observation, and then laws, hypotheses, and theories are developed based on those observations. Experiments, which are carefully controlled observations, determine the validity of laws, hypotheses, or theories. If a law, hypothesis, or theory is inconsistent with the findings of an experiment, it must be revised and new experiments must be conducted to test the revisions. Over time, scientists eliminate poor theories, and good theories—those consistent with experiments—remain Established theories with strong experimental support are the most powerful pieces of scientific knowledge. People unfamiliar with science sometimes say, "That is just a theory," as if theories were mere speculations. However, well-tested theories are as close to truth as we get in science. For example, the idea that all matter is made of atoms is "just a theory," but it is a theory with 200 years of experimental evidence to support it, including the recent imaging of atoms themselves (◀ Figure 1.3). Established theories should not be taken lightly—they are the pinnacle of scientific understanding.

▲ **FIGURE 1.3 Are atoms real?** The atomic theory has 200 years of experimental evidence to support it, including recent images, such as this one, of atoms themselves. This image shows the Kanji (a system of Japanese writing using Chinese characters) for "atom" written with individual iron atoms on top of a copper surface.

✓ **CONCEPTUAL CHECKPOINT 1.1**

Which statement most resembles a scientific theory?

(a) When the pressure on a sample of oxygen gas is increased 10%, the volume of the gas decreases by 10%.

(b) The volume of a gas is inversely proportional to its pressure.

(c) A gas is composed of small particles in constant motion.

(d) A gas sample has a mass of 15.8 g and a volume of 10.5 L.

Note: The answers to all Conceptual Checkpoints appear at the end of the chapter.

EVERYDAY CHEMISTRY

▶ Combustion and the Scientific Method

Early chemical theories attempted to explain common phenomena such as combustion. Why did things burn? What was happening to a substance when it burned? Could something that was burned be unburned? Early chemists burned different substances and made observations to try to answer these questions. They observed that substances stop burning when placed in a closed container. They found that many metals burn to form a white powder that they called a *calx* (now we know that these white powders are oxides of the metal) and that the metal could be recovered from the calx, or unburned, by combining the calx with charcoal and heating it.

Chemists in the first part of the eighteenth century formed a theory about combustion to explain these observations. In this theory, combustion involved a fundamental substance that they called *phlogiston*. This substance was present in anything that burned and was released during combustion. Flammable objects were flammable because they contained phlogiston. When things burned in a closed container, they didn't burn for very long because the space within the container became saturated with phlogiston. When things burned in the open, they continued to burn until all of the phlogiston within them was gone. This theory also explained how metals that had burned could be unburned. Charcoal was a phlogiston-rich material—they knew this because it burned so well—and when it was combined with a calx, which was a metal that had been emptied of its phlogiston, it transferred some of its phlogiston into the calx, converting the calx back into the unburned form of the metal. The phlogiston theory was consistent with all of the observations of the time and was widely accepted as valid.

Like any theory, the phlogiston theory was tested continually by experiment. One set of experiments, conducted in the mid–eighteenth century by Louis-Bernard Guyton de Morveau (1737–1816), consisted of weighing metals before and after burning them. In every case the metals *gained* weight when they were burned. This observation is inconsistent with the phlogiston theory, which predicted that metals should *lose* weight because phlogiston was supposed to be lost during combustion. Clearly, the phlogiston theory needed modification.

The first modification was that phlogiston was a very light substance so that it actually "buoyed up" the materials that contained it. Thus when phlogiston was released, the material became heavier. Such a modification seemed to fit the observations but also seemed far-fetched. Antoine Lavoisier developed a more likely explanation by devising a completely new theory of combustion. Lavoisier proposed that, when a substance burned, it actually took something *out* of the air, and when it unburned, it released something back into the air. Lavoisier said that burning objects *fixed* (attached or bonded) the air and that the *fixed* air was released during unburning. In a confirming experiment (▼ Figure 1.4), Lavoisier roasted a mixture of calx and charcoal with the aid of sunlight focused by a giant burning lens, and found that a huge volume of "fixed air" was released in the process. The scientific method worked. The phlogiston theory was proven wrong, and a new theory of combustion took its place—a theory that, with a few refinements, is still valid today.

B1.1 CAN YOU ANSWER THIS?   *What is the difference between a law and a theory? How does the example of the phlogiston theory demonstrate this difference?*

▲ **FIGURE 1.4 Focusing on combustion** The great burning lens belonging to the Academy of Sciences. Lavoisier used a similar lens in 1777 to show that a mixture of *calx* (metal oxide) and charcoal released a large volume of *fixed air* when heated.

1.5   A Beginning Chemist: How to Succeed

You are a beginning chemist. This may be your first chemistry course, but it may not be your last. To succeed as a beginning chemist, keep the following ideas in mind. First, chemistry requires curiosity and imagination. If you are content knowing that the sky is blue, but don't care *why* it is blue, then you may have to rediscover your curiosity. I say "rediscover" because even children—or better, *especially* children—have this kind of curiosity. To succeed as a chemist, you must have the curiosity and imagination of a child—*you must want to know the why of things.*

Second, chemistry requires calculation. Throughout this course, you will be asked to calculate answers and quantify information. *Quantification* involves measurement as part of observation—it is one of the most important tools in science. Quantification allows you to go beyond merely saying that this object is hot and that one is cold or that this one is large and that one is small. It allows you to specify the difference precisely. For example, two samples of water may feel equally hot to your hand, but when you measure their temperatures, you may find that one is 40 °C and the other is 44 °C. Even small differences can be important in a calculation or experiment, so assigning numbers to observations and manipulating those numbers become very important in chemistry.

Lastly, chemistry requires commitment. To succeed in this course, you must commit to learning chemistry. Roald Hoffman, winner of the 1981 Nobel Prize for chemistry, said,

> I like the idea that human beings can do anything they want to. They need to be trained sometimes. They need a teacher to awaken the intelligence within them. But to be a chemist requires no special talent, I'm glad to say. Anyone can do it, with hard work.

Professor Hoffman is right. The key to success in this course is hard work—that requires commitment. You must do your work regularly and carefully. If you do, you will succeed, and you will be rewarded by seeing a whole new world—the world of molecules and atoms. This world exists beneath the surface of nearly everything you encounter. I welcome you to this world and consider it a privilege, together with your professor, to be your guide.

▲ To succeed as a scientist, you must have the curiosity of a child.

CHAPTER IN REVIEW

Self-Assessment Quiz

Q1. Where can you find chemicals?

(a) In a hardware store

(b) In a chemical stockroom

(c) All around you and even inside of you

(d) All of the above

Q2. Which statement best defines chemistry?

(a) The science that studies solvents, drugs, and insecticides

(b) The science that studies the connections between the properties of matter and the particles that compose that matter

(c) The science that studies air and water pollution

(d) The science that seeks to understand processes that occur only in chemical laboratories

Q3. According to the scientific method, what is a law?

(a) A short statement that summarizes a large number of observations

(b) A fact that can never be refuted

(c) A model that gives insight into how nature is

(d) An initial guess with explanatory power

Q4. Which statement is an example of an observation?

(a) In a chemical reaction, matter is conserved.

(b) All matter is made of atoms.

(c) When a given sample of gasoline is burned in a closed container, the mass of the container and its contents does not change.

(d) Atoms bond to one another by sharing electrons.

Q5. Which characteristic is necessary for success in understanding chemistry?

(a) Curiosity

(b) Calculation

(c) Commitment

(d) All of the above

Answers 1:d, 2:b, 3:a, 4:c, 5:d

Chemical Principles

Matter and Molecules: Chemists are interested in all matter, even ordinary matter such as water or air. You don't need to go to a chemical storeroom to find chemicals because they are all around you. Chemistry is the science that studies the connections between the properties of matter and the particles that compose that matter.

Relevance

Matter and Molecules: Chemists want to understand matter for several reasons. First, chemists are simply curious—they want to know why. Why are some substances reactive and others not? Why are some substances gases, some liquids, and others solids? Chemists are also practical; they want to understand matter so that they can control it and produce substances that are useful to society and to humankind.

The Scientific Method: Chemists employ the scientific method, which makes use of observations, hypotheses, laws, theories, and experiments. Observations involve measuring or observing some aspect of nature. Hypotheses are tentative interpretations of the observations. Laws summarize the results of a large number of observations, and theories are models that explain and give the underlying causes for observations and laws. Hypotheses, laws, and theories must be tested and validated by experiment. If they are not confirmed, they are revised and tested through further experimentation.

The Scientific Method: The scientific method is a way to understand the world. Since the inception of the scientific method, knowledge about the natural world has grown rapidly. The application of the scientific method has produced technologies that have raised living standards throughout the world with advances such as increased food production, rapid transportation, unparalleled access to information, and longer life spans.

Success as a Beginning Chemist: To succeed as a beginning chemist, you must be curious and imaginative, be willing to do calculations, and be committed to learning the material.

Success as a Beginning Chemist: Understanding chemistry will give you a deeper appreciation for the world in which you live, and if you choose science as a career, it will be a foundation upon which you will continue to build.

KEY TERMS

atomic theory **[1.4]**
chemistry **[1.3]**
experiment **[1.4]**

hypothesis **[1.4]**
law of conservation
    of mass **[1.4]**

observation **[1.4]**
scientific law **[1.4]**
scientific method **[1.4]**

theory **[1.4]**

EXERCISES

QUESTIONS

Answers to all questions numbered in blue appear in the Answers section at the back of the book.

1. Why does soda fizz?
2. What are chemicals? Give some examples.
3. What do chemists try to do? How do they understand the natural world?
4. What is meant by the statement, "Matter does what molecules do"? Give an example.
5. Define *chemistry*.
6. How is chemistry connected to everyday life? How is chemistry relevant outside the chemistry laboratory?
7. Explain the scientific method.

8. Cite an example from this chapter of the scientific method at work.
9. What is the difference between a law and a theory?
10. What is the difference between a hypothesis and a theory?
11. What is wrong with the statement, "It is just a theory"?
12. What is the law of conservation of mass, and who discovered it?
13. What is the atomic theory, and who formulated it?
14. What are three things you need to do to succeed in this course?

PROBLEMS

Note: The exercises in the Problems section are paired, and the answers to the odd-numbered exercises (numbered in blue) appear in the Answers section at the back of the book.

15. Examine the opening figure of this chapter. Use the information in Section 1.1 to identify the two molecules sitting next to the cola glass and identify each of the atoms within each molecule.

16. Examine Figure 1.1 and, from a molecular point of view, explain why soda pop fizzes. What molecules are inside the bubbles in a glass of soda pop?

17. Classify each statement as an observation, a law, or a theory.
    (a) When a metal is burned in a closed container, the sum of the masses of the container and its contents does not change.
    (b) Matter is made of atoms.
    (c) Matter is conserved in chemical reactions.
    (d) When wood is burned in a closed container, its mass does not change.

18. Classify each statement as an observation, a law, or a theory.
    (a) The star closest to Earth is moving away from Earth at high speed.
    (b) A body in motion stays in motion unless acted upon by a force.
    (c) The universe began as a cosmic explosion called the Big Bang.
    (d) A stone dropped from an altitude of 450 m falls to the ground in 9.6 s.

19. A student prepares several samples of the same gas and measures their mass and volume. The results are tabulated as follows. Formulate a tentative law from the measurements.

Mass of Gas (in g)	Volume of Gas (in L)
22.5	1.60
35.8	2.55
70.2	5.00
98.5	7.01

20. A student measures the volume of a gas sample at several different temperatures. The results are tabulated as follows. Formulate a tentative law from the measurements.

Temperature of Gas (in K)	Volume of Gas (in L)
298	4.55
315	4.81
325	4.96
335	5.11

21. A chemist in an imaginary universe does an experiment that attempts to correlate the size of an atom with its chemical reactivity. The results are tabulated as follows.

Size of Atom	Chemical Reactivity
small	low
medium	intermediate
large	high

(a) Formulate a law from this data.

(b) Formulate a theory to explain the law.

22. A chemist decomposes several samples of water into hydrogen and oxygen and measures the mass of the hydrogen and the oxygen obtained. The results are tabulated as follows.

Sample Number	Grams of Hydrogen	Grams of Oxygen
1	1.5	12
2	2	16
3	2.5	20

(a) Summarize these observations in a short statement.

Next, the chemist decomposes several samples of carbon dioxide into carbon and oxygen. The results are tabulated as follows:

Sample Number	Grams of Carbon	Grams of Oxygen
1	0.5	1.3
2	1.0	2.7
3	1.5	4.0

(b) Summarize these observations in a short statement.

(c) Formulate a law from the observations in (a) and (b).

(d) Formulate a theory that might explain your law in (c).

QUESTIONS FOR GROUP WORK

Discuss these questions with the group and record your consensus answer.

23. The manufacturer of a particular brand of toothpaste claims that the brand contains "no chemicals." Using a few grammatically correct English sentences, describe what you think the company means by that statement. Would a scientist consider the manufacturer's statement to be correct? Why or why not?

24. Make a list (including up to ten items) of all the atoms or molecules group members can name off the top of their heads. Get at least one contribution from each group member.

25. In your own words, provide a brief definition for each of the following: observation, law, hypothesis, and theory.

26. How curious are you? How good are your quantitative skills? How hard are you willing to work to succeed in chemistry? Answer these questions individually on a scale of 1 (=not at all) to 5 (=very), then share your answers with your group. Report the group average for each question.

▶Answers to Conceptual Checkpoints

1.1 (c) Answers a and d are observations. Answer b is a scientific law. Answer c is the only answer that proposes a *model* for what a gas is like.

Global Temperature
(meteorological stations)

△ The graph in this image displays average global temperatures (relative to the mean) over the past 100 years.

Measurement and Problem Solving

2

"The important thing in science is not so much to obtain new facts as to discover new ways of thinking about them."—Sir William Lawrence Bragg (1890–1971)

CHAPTER OUTLINE

2.1 Measuring Global Temperatures

Global warming has become a household term. Average global temperatures affect agriculture, weather, and ocean levels. The media report that global temperatures are increasing. These reports are based on the work of scientists who—after analyzing records from thousands of temperature-measuring stations around the world—concluded that average global temperatures have risen by 0.6 °C in the last century.

> A unit is a standard, agreed-on quantity by which other quantities are measured.

Notice how the scientists reported their results. What if they had reported a temperature increase of simply 0.6 without any *units*? The result would be unclear. Units are extremely important in reporting and working with scientific measurements, and they must always be included. Suppose that the scientists had included additional zeros in their results—for example, 0.60 °C or 0.600 °C—or that they had reported the number their computer displayed after averaging many measurements, something like 0.58759824 °C. Would these convey the same information? Not really. Scientists adhere to a standard way of reporting measured quantities in which the number of reported digits reflects the precision in the measurement—more digits, more precision; fewer digits, less precision. Numbers are usually written so that the uncertainty is indicated by the last reported digit. For example, by reporting a temperature increase of 0.6 °C, the scientists mean 0.6 ± 0.1 °C (± means plus or minus). The temperature rise could be as much as 0.7 °C or as little as 0.5 °C, but it is not 1.0 °C. The degree of certainty in this particular measurement is critical, influencing political decisions that directly affect people's lives.

2.2 Scientific Notation: Writing Large and Small Numbers

> LO: Express very large and very small numbers using scientific notation.

Science constantly pushes the boundaries of the very large and the very small. We can, for example, now measure time periods as short as 0.000000000000001 second and distances as great as 14,000,000,000 light-years. Because the many zeros in these numbers are cumbersome to write, we use **scientific notation** to write them more compactly. In scientific notation, 0.000000000000001 is 1×10^{-15}, and

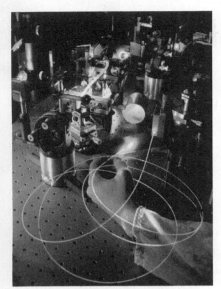

▲ Lasers such as this one can measure time periods as short as 1×10^{-15} s.

14,000,000,000 is 1.4×10^{10}. A number written in scientific notation consists of a **decimal part**, a number that is usually between 1 and 10, and an **exponential part**, 10 raised to an **exponent**, n.

$$1.2 \times 10^{-10} \longleftarrow \text{exponent } (n)$$

decimal part   exponential part

A positive exponent (n) means 1 multiplied by 10 n times.

$$10^0 = 1$$

$$10^1 = 1 \times 10 = 10$$

$$10^2 = 1 \times 10 \times 10 = 100$$

$$10^3 = 1 \times 10 \times 10 \times 10 = 1000$$

A negative exponent ($-n$) means 1 divided by 10 n times.

$$10^{-1} = \frac{1}{10} = 0.1$$

$$10^{-2} = \frac{1}{10 \times 10} = 0.01$$

$$10^{-3} = \frac{1}{10 \times 10 \times 10} = 0.001$$

To convert a number to scientific notation, we move the decimal point (either to the left or to the right, as needed) to obtain a number between 1 and 10 and then multiply that number (the decimal part) by 10 raised to the power that reflects the movement of the decimal point. For example, to write 5983 in scientific notation, we move the decimal point to the left three places to get 5.983 (a number between 1 and 10) and then multiply the decimal part by 1000 to compensate for moving the decimal point.

$$5983 = 5.983 \times 1000$$

1000 is 10^3

$$= 5.983 \times 10^3$$

We can do this in one step by counting how many places we move the decimal point to obtain a number between 1 and 10 and then writing the decimal part multiplied by 10 raised to the number of places we moved the decimal point.

$$5983 = 5.983 \times 10^3$$
3 2 1

If the decimal point is moved to the left, as in the previous example, the exponent is positive. If the decimal is moved to the right, the exponent is negative.

The Mathematics Review Appendix (p. MR-2) includes a review of mathematical operations for numbers written in scientific notation.

$$0.00034 = 3.4 \times 10^{-4}$$
$$\underset{1\,2\,3\,4}{\smile}$$

To express a number in scientific notation:

1. Move the decimal point to obtain a number between 1 and 10.
2. Write the result from Step 1 multiplied by 10 raised to the number of places you moved the decimal point.
   - The exponent is positive if you moved the decimal point to the left.
   - The exponent is negative if you moved the decimal point to the right.

Remember, large numbers have positive exponents and small numbers have negative exponents

---

EXAMPLE 2.1   SCIENTIFIC NOTATION

The 2013 U.S. population was estimated to be 315,000,000 people. Express this number in scientific notation.

To obtain a number between 1 and 10, move the decimal point to the left eight decimal places; the exponent is 8. Because you move the decimal point to the left, the sign of the exponent is positive.

SOLUTION

$315{,}000{,}000$ people $= 3.15 \times 10^8$ people

▶ **SKILLBUILDER 2.1 | Scientific Notation**

The total U.S national debt in 2013 was approximately $16,342,000,000,000. Express this number in scientific notation.

Note: The answers to all Skillbuilders appear at the end of the chapter.

▶ **FOR MORE PRACTICE**   Example 2.18; Problems 31, 32

EXAMPLE 2.2   SCIENTIFIC NOTATION

The radius of a carbon atom is approximately 0.000000000070 m. Express this number in scientific notation.

To obtain a number between 1 and 10, move the decimal point to the right 11 decimal places; therefore, the exponent is 11. Because you moved the decimal point to the right, the sign of the exponent is negative.

SOLUTION

0.000000000070 m $= 7.0 \times 10^{-11}$ m

▶ **SKILLBUILDER 2.2 | Scientific Notation**

Express the number 0.000038 in scientific notation.

▶ **FOR MORE PRACTICE**   Problems 33, 34.

 CONCEPTUAL CHECKPOINT 2.1

The radius of a dust speck is 4.5×10^{-3} mm. What is the correct value of this number in decimal notation (i.e., express the number without using scientific notation)?

(a) 4500 mm

(b) 0.045 mm

(c) 0.0045 mm

(d) 0.00045 mm

Note: The answers to all Conceptual Checkpoints appear at the end of the chapter.

2.3   Significant Figures: Writing Numbers to Reflect Precision

LO: Report measured quantities to the right number of digits.

LO: Determine which digits in a number are significant.

▲ Because pennies come in whole numbers, seven pennies means 7.00000. . . pennies. This is an exact number and therefore never limits significant figures in calculations.

▲ Our knowledge of the amount of gold in a 10-g gold bar depends on how precisely it was measured.

If we tell someone we have seven pennies, our meaning is clear. Pennies come in whole numbers, and seven pennies means seven whole pennies—it is unlikely that we would have 7.4 pennies. However, if we tell someone that we have a 10-g gold bar, the meaning is *unclear*. Our knowledge of the actual amount of gold in the bar depends on how precisely it was measured, which in turn depends on the scale or balance used to make the measurement. As we just learned, measured quantities are written to reflect the uncertainty in the measurement. If the gold measurement is rough, we could describe the bar as containing "10 g of gold." If a more precise balance is used, we can write the gold content as "10.0 g." We could report an even more precise measurement as "10.00 g."

We report scientific numbers so that every digit is certain except the last, which we estimate. For example, if a reported measurement is:

$$\underset{\underset{\text{certain}}{\uparrow\ \ \uparrow}}{\underline{45.87}2}\ \ \underset{\textit{estimated}}{}$$

We know that the first four digits are certain; the last digit is estimated.

Suppose that we weigh an object on a balance with marks at every 1 g, and the pointer is between the 1-g mark and the 2-g mark (▼ Figure 2.1) but much closer to the 1-g mark. To record the measurement, we mentally divide the space between the 1- and 2-g marks into 10 equal spaces and estimate the position of the pointer. In this case, the pointer indicates about 1.2 g. We write the measurement as 1.2 g, indicating that we are sure of the "1" but have estimated the ".2."

If we measure an object using a balance with marks every tenth of a gram, we need to write the result with more digits. For example, suppose that on this more precise balance the pointer is between the 1.2-g mark and the 1.3-g mark (▼ Figure 2.2). We again divide the space between the two marks into 10 equal spaces and estimate the third digit. In the case of the nut shown in Figure 2.2, we report 1.26 g. Digital balances usually have readouts that report the mass to the correct number of digits.

1.2 g

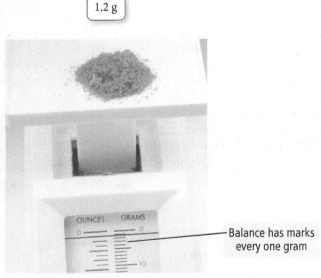

▲ **FIGURE 2.1   Estimating tenths of a gram**   This balance has markings every 1 g, so we estimate to the tenths place. To estimate between markings, we mentally divide the space into 10 equal spaces and estimate the last digit. This reading is 1.2 g.

— Balance has marks every one gram

1.26 g

— Balance has marks every tenth of a gram

▲ **FIGURE 2.2   Estimating hundredths of a gram**   Because this scale has markings every 0.1 g, we estimate to the hundredths place. The correct reading is 1.26 g.

EXAMPLE 2.3 REPORTING THE RIGHT NUMBER OF DIGITS

The bathroom scale in ▼ Figure 2.3 has markings at every 1 lb. Report the reading to the correct number of digits.

▲ FIGURE 2.3 **Reading a bathroom scale**

SOLUTION

Because the pointer is between the 147- and 148-lb markings, you mentally divide the space between the markings into 10 equal spaces and estimate the next digit. In this case, you should report the result as:

147.7 lb

What if you estimated a little differently and wrote 147.6 lb? In general, one unit of difference in the last digit is acceptable because the last digit is estimated and different people might estimate it slightly differently. However, if you wrote 147.2 lb, you would clearly be wrong.

▶SKILLBUILDER 2.3 | **Reporting the Right Number of Digits**

You use a thermometer to measure the temperature of a backyard hot tub, and you obtain the reading shown in ▼ Figure 2.4. Record the temperature reading to the correct number of digits.

◀ FIGURE 2.4 **Reading a thermometer**

▶**FOR MORE PRACTICE** Example 2.19; Problems 41, 42.

Counting Significant Figures

The non–place-holding digits in a measurement are **significant figures** (or **significant digits**). As we have seen, these significant figures represent the precision of a measured quantity—the greater the number of significant figures, the greater the precision of the measurement. We can determine the number of significant figures in a written number fairly easily; however, if the number contains zeros, we must distinguish between the zeros that are significant and those that simply mark the decimal place. In the number 0.002, for example, the leading zeros mark the decimal place; they *do not* add to the precision of the measurement. In the number 0.00200, however, the trailing zeros *do* add to the precision of the measurement.

To determine the number of significant figures in a number, we follow these rules:

1. All nonzero digits are significant.

1.05   0.0110

2. Interior zeros (zeros between two numbers) are significant.

4.0208   50.1

3. Trailing zeros (zeros to the right of a nonzero number) that fall after a decimal point are significant.

5.10   3.00

4. Trailing zeros that fall before a decimal point are significant.

$$\underline{50}.00 \qquad 17\underline{00}.24$$

When a number is expressed in scientific notation, all trailing zeros are significant.

5. Leading zeros (zeros to the left of the first nonzero number) are not significant. They only serve to locate the decimal point.

For example, the number 0.0005 has only one significant digit.

6. Trailing zeros at the end of a number, but before an *implied* decimal point, are ambiguous and should be avoided by using scientific notation.

For example, it is unclear if the number 350 has two or three significant figures. We can avoid confusion by writing the number as 3.5×10^2 to indicate two significant figures or as 3.50×10^2 to indicate three.

Exact Numbers

Some books put a decimal point after one or more trailing zeros if the zeros are to be considered significant. We avoid that practice in this book, but you should be aware of it.

Exact numbers have an unlimited number of significant figures. Exact numbers originate from three sources:

- Exact counting of discrete objects. For example, 3 atoms means 3.00000 . . . atoms.

- *Defined quantities*, such as the number of centimeters in 1 m. Because 100 cm is defined as 1 m,

$$100\ cm = 1\ m \text{ means } 100.00000 \ldots cm = 1.0000000 \ldots m$$

Note that some conversion factors (see Section 2.6) are defined quantities while others are not.

- Integral numbers that are part of an equation. For example, in the equation,
$radius = \dfrac{diameter}{2}$, the number 2 is exact and therefore has an unlimited number of significant figures.

EXAMPLE 2.4 **DETERMINING THE NUMBER OF SIGNIFICANT FIGURES IN A NUMBER**

How many significant figures are in each number?

(a) 0.0035
(b) 1.080
(c) 2371
(d) 2.97×10^5
(e) 1 dozen = 12
(f) 100.00
(g) 100,000

	SOLUTION
The 3 and the 5 are significant (rule 1). The leading zeros only mark the decimal place and are not significant (rule 5).	(a) 0.0035 two significant figures
The interior zero is significant (rule 2), and the trailing zero is significant (rule 3). The 1 and the 8 are also significant (rule 1).	(b) 1.080 four significant figures
All digits are significant (rule 1).	(c) 2371 four significant figures
All digits in the decimal part are significant (rule 1).	(d) 2.97×10^5 three significant figures
Defined numbers are exact and therefore have an unlimited number of significant figures.	(e) 1 dozen = 12 unlimited significant figures

The 1 is significant (rule 1), and the trailing zeros before the decimal point are significant (rule 4). The trailing zeros after the decimal point are also significant (rule 3).	**(f)** 100.00 five significant figures
This number is ambiguous. Write as 1×10^5 to indicate one significant figure or as 1.00000×10^5 to indicate six significant figures.	**(g)** 100,000 ambiguous

▶**SKILLBUILDER 2.4 | Determining the Number of Significant Figures in a Number**

How many significant figures are in each number?

(a) 58.31
(b) 0.00250
(c) 2.7×10^3
(d) 1 cm = 0.01 m
(e) 0.500
(f) 2100

▶**FOR MORE PRACTICE**   Example 2.20; Problems 43, 44, 45, 46, 47, 48.

CHEMISTRY **IN THE MEDIA**

▶ **The COBE Satellite and Very Precise Measurements That Illuminate Our Cosmic Past**

Since the earliest times, humans have wondered about the origins of our planet. Scientists have probed this question and developed theories for how the universe and the Earth began. The most accepted theory today about the origin of the universe is the Big Bang theory. According to the Big Bang theory, the universe began in a tremendous expansion about 13.7 billion years ago and has been expanding ever since. A measurable prediction of this theory is the presence of a remnant "background radiation" from the expansion of the universe. That remnant radiation is characteristic of the current temperature of the universe. When the Big Bang occurred, the temperature of the universe was very hot and the associated radiation very bright. Today, 13.7 billion years later, the temperature of the universe is very cold and the background radiation very faint.

In the early 1960s, Robert H. Dicke, P. J. E. Peebles, and their colleagues at Princeton University began to build a device to measure this background radiation and by doing so take a direct look into the cosmological past and provide evidence for the Big Bang theory. At about the same time, quite by accident, Arno Penzias and Robert Wilson of Bell Telephone Laboratories measured excess radio noise on one of their communications satellites. As it turned out, this noise was the background radiation that the Princeton scientists were looking for. The two groups published papers together in 1965 reporting their findings along with the corresponding current temperature of the universe, about 3 degrees above absolute zero, or 3 K. We will define temperature measurement scales in Chapter 3. For now, know that 3 K is an extremely low temperature (454 degrees below zero on the Fahrenheit scale).

In 1989, NASA's Goddard Space Flight Center developed the Cosmic Background Explorer (COBE) satellite to measure the background radiation more precisely. The COBE satellite determined that the background radiation corresponded to a universe with a temperature of 2.735 K. (Notice the difference in significant figures from the previous measurement.) It went on to measure tiny fluctuations in the background radiation that amount to temperature differences of 1 part in 100,000. These fluctuations, though small, are an important prediction of the Big Bang theory. Scientists announced that the COBE satellite had produced the strongest evidence yet for the Big Bang theory of the creation of the universe. This is the way that science works. Measurement, and precision in measurement, are important to understanding the world—so important that we dedicate most of this chapter to the concept of measurement.

B2.1 CAN YOU ANSWER THIS?   *How many significant figures are there in each of the preceding temperature measurements (3 K, 2.735 K)?*

◀ The COBE satellite, launched in 1989 to measure background radiation. Background radiation is a remnant of the Big Bang—the expansion that is believed to have formed the universe.

CONCEPTUAL CHECKPOINT 2.2

The Curiosity Rover on the surface of Mars recently measured a daily low temperature of −65.19 °C. What is implied range of the actual temperature?

(a) between −65.190 °C and −65.199 °C

(b) between −65.18 °C and −65.20 °C

(c) between −65.1 °C and −65.2 °C

(d) exactly −65.19 °C

2.4   Significant Figures in Calculations

LO: Round numbers to the correct number of significant figures.

LO: Determine the correct number of significant figures in the results of multiplication and division calculations.

LO: Determine the correct number of significant figures in the results of addition and subtraction calculations.

LO: Determine the correct number of significant figures in the results of calculations involving both addition/subtraction and multiplication/division.

When we use measured quantities in calculations, the results of the calculation must reflect the precision of the measured quantities. We should not lose or gain precision during mathematical operations.

Multiplication and Division

In multiplication or division, the result carries the same number of significant figures as the factor with the fewest significant figures.

For example:

$$\underset{\text{(3 sig. figures)}}{5.02} \times \underset{\text{(5 sig. figures)}}{89.665} \times \underset{\text{(2 sig. figures)}}{0.10} = 45.0118 = \underset{\text{(2 sig. figures)}}{45}$$

We round the intermediate result (in blue) to two significant figures to reflect the least precisely known factor (0.10), which has two significant figures.

In division, we follow the same rule.

$$\underset{\text{(4 sig. figures)}}{5.892} \div \underset{\text{(3 sig. figures)}}{6.10} = 0.96590 = \underset{\text{(3 sig. figures)}}{0.966}$$

We round the intermediate result (in blue) to three significant figures to reflect the least precisely known factor (6.10), which has three significant figures.

Rounding

When we round to the correct number of significant figures:

we round down if the last (or leftmost) digit dropped is 4 or less;
we round up if the last (or leftmost) digit dropped is 5 or more.

For example, when we round each of these numbers to two significant figures:

2.33 rounds to 2.3
2.37 rounds to 2.4
2.34 rounds to 2.3
2.35 rounds to 2.4

We consider only the *last (or leftmost) digit being dropped* when we decide in which direction to round—we ignore all digits to the right of it. For example, to round 2.349 to two significant figures, only the 4 in the hundredths place (2.3**4**9) determines which direction to round—the 9 is irrelevant.

2.349 rounds to 2.3

For calculations involving multiple steps, we round only the final answer—we do not round the intermediate results. This prevents small rounding errors from affecting the final answer.

EXAMPLE 2.5 **SIGNIFICANT FIGURES IN MULTIPLICATION AND DIVISION**

Perform each calculation to the correct number of significant figures.

(a) $1.01 \times 0.12 \times 53.51 \div 96$
(b) $56.55 \times 0.920 \div 34.2585$

Round the intermediate result (in blue) to two significant figures to reflect the two significant figures in the least precisely known quantities (0.12 and 96).	**SOLUTION** **(a)** $1.01 \times 0.12 \times 53.51 \div 96 = 0.067556 = 0.068$
Round the intermediate result (in blue) to three significant figures to reflect the three significant figures in the least precisely known quantity (0.920).	**(b)** $56.55 \times 0.920 \div 34.2585 = 1.51863 = 1.52$

▶**SKILLBUILDER 2.5** | **Significant Figures in Multiplication and Division**

Perform each calculation to the correct number of significant figures.

(a) $1.10 \times 0.512 \times 1.301 \times 0.005 \div 3.4$
(b) $4.562 \times 3.99870 \div 89.5$

▶**FOR MORE PRACTICE** Examples 2.21, 2.22; Problems 57, 58, 59, 60.

Addition and Subtraction

In addition or subtraction, the result has the same number of decimal places as the quantity with the fewest decimal places.

For example:

$$
\begin{array}{r}
5.74 \\
0.823 \\
+\,2.651 \\
\hline
9.214 = 9.21
\end{array}
$$

It is sometimes helpful to draw a vertical line directly to the right of the number with the fewest decimal places. The line shows the number of decimal places that should be in the answer.

We round the intermediate answer (in blue) to two decimal places because the quantity with the fewest decimal places (5.74) has two decimal places.

For subtraction, we follow the same rule. For example:

$$
\begin{array}{r}
4.8 \\
-\,3.965 \\
\hline
0.835 = 0.8
\end{array}
$$

We round the intermediate answer (in blue) to one decimal place because the quantity with the fewest decimal places (4.8) has one decimal place. Remember: *For multiplication and division, the quantity with the fewest **significant figures** determines the number of significant figures in the answer. For addition and subtraction, the quantity with the fewest **decimal places** determines the number of decimal places in the answer.* In multiplication and division we focus on significant figures, but in addition and subtraction we focus on decimal places. When a problem involves addition and subtraction, the answer may have a different number of significant figures than the initial quantities. For example:

$$28.02 - 27.99 = 0.03$$

Initial quantities each have four significant figures

Answer has only one significant figure

The answer has only one significant figure, even though the initial quantities each had four significant figures.

EXAMPLE 2.6   SIGNIFICANT FIGURES IN ADDITION AND SUBTRACTION

Perform the calculations to the correct number of significant figures.

(a)   0.987
     +125.1
     −1.22

(b)   0.765
     −3.449
     −5.98

Round the intermediate answer (in blue) to one decimal place to reflect the quantity with the fewest decimal places (125.1). Notice that 125.1 is not the quantity with the fewest significant figures—it has four while the other quantities only have three—but because it has the fewest decimal places, it determines the number of decimal places in the answer.	**SOLUTION**
	
	(a) 0.987
	     +125.1
	     −1.22
	     124.867 = 124.9

Round the intermediate answer (in blue) to two decimal places to reflect the quantity with the fewest decimal places (5.98).	(b) 0.765
	     −3.449
	     −5.98
	     −8.664 = −8.66

▶**SKILLBUILDER 2.6 | Significant Figures in Addition and Subtraction**

Perform the calculations to the correct number of significant figures.

(a)   2.18
     +5.621
     +1.5870
     −1.8

b)   7.876
     −0.56
     +123.792

▶**FOR MORE PRACTICE**   Example 2.23; Problems 61, 62, 63, 64.

Calculations Involving Both Multiplication/Division and Addition/Subtraction

In calculations involving both multiplication/division and addition/subtraction, we do the steps in parentheses first; determine the correct number of significant figures in the intermediate answer; then complete the remaining steps.

For example:

$$3.489 \times (5.67 - 2.3)$$

We complete the subtraction step first.

$$5.67 - 2.3 = 3.37$$

We use the subtraction rule to determine that the intermediate answer (3.37) has only one significant decimal place. To avoid small errors, we do not round at this point; instead, we underline the least significant figure as a reminder.

$$= 3.489 \times 3.3\underline{7}$$

We then complete the multiplication step.

$$3.489 \times 3.3\underline{7} = 11.758 = 12$$

The multiplication rule indicates that the intermediate answer (11.758) rounds to two significant figures (12) because it is limited by the two significant figures in 3.3$\underline{7}$.

| **EXAMPLE 2.7** | **SIGNIFICANT FIGURES IN CALCULATIONS INVOLVING BOTH MULTIPLICATION/ DIVISION AND ADDITION/SUBTRACTION** |

Perform the calculations to the correct number of significant figures.

(a) $6.78 \times 5.903 \times (5.489 - 5.01)$
(b) $19.667 - (5.4 \times 0.916)$

Do the step in parentheses first. Use the subtraction rule to mark 0.479 to two decimal places because 5.01, the number in the parentheses with the least number of decimal places, has two.	**SOLUTION** **(a)** $6.78 \times 5.903 \times (5.489 - 5.01)$ $= 6.78 \times 5.903 \times (0.479)$ $= 6.78 \times 5.903 \times 0.47\underline{9}$
Then perform the multiplication and round the answer to two significant figures because the number with the least number of significant figures has two.	$6.78 \times 5.903 \times 0.47\underline{9} = 19.1707$ $= 19$
Do the step in parentheses first. The number with the least number of significant figures within the parentheses (5.4) has two, so mark the answer to two significant figures.	**(b)** $19.667 - (5.4 \times 0.916)$ $= 19.667 - (4.9\underline{4}64)$ $= 19.667 - 4.9\underline{4}64$
Then perform the subtraction and round the answer to one decimal place because the number with the least number of decimal places has one.	$19.667 - 4.9\underline{4}64 = 14.7206$ $= 14.7$

▶**SKILLBUILDER 2.7** | **Significant Figures in Calculations Involving Both Multiplication/Division and Addition/Subtraction**

Perform each calculation to the correct number of significant figures.
(a) $3.897 \times (782.3 - 451.88)$
(b) $(4.58 \div 1.239) - 0.578$

▶**FOR MORE PRACTICE** Example 2.24; Problems 65, 66, 67, 68.

 CONCEPTUAL CHECKPOINT 2.3

Which calculation would have its result reported to the *greater* number of significant figures?
(a) $3 + (15/12)$
(b) $(3 + 15)/12$

2.5 The Basic Units of Measurement

LO: Recognize and work with the SI base units of measurement, prefix multipliers, and derived units.

By themselves, numbers have little meaning. Read this sentence: When my son was 7 he walked 3, and when he was 4 he could throw his baseball 8 and tell us that his school was 5 away. The sentence is confusing. We don't know what the numbers mean because the **units** are missing. The meaning becomes clear, however, when we add the missing units to the numbers: When my son was 7 *months old* he walked 3 *steps*, and when he was 4 *years old* he could throw his baseball 8 *feet* and tell us that his school was 5 *minutes* away. Units make all the difference. In chemistry, units are critical. Never write a number by itself; always use its associated units—otherwise your work will be as confusing as the initial sentence.

The two most common unit systems are the **English system**, used in the United States, and the **metric system**, used in most of the rest of the world. The English system uses units such as inches, yards, and pounds, while the metric system uses centimeters, meters, and kilograms. The most convenient system for science measurements is based on the metric system and is called the **International System** of units or **SI units**. SI units are a set of standard units agreed on by scientists throughout the world.

The abbreviation *SI* comes from the French *le Système International*.

▲ Science uses instruments to make measurements. Every instrument is calibrated in a particular unit without which the measurements would be meaningless.

TABLE 2.1 Important SI Base Units

Quantity	Unit	Symbol
length	meter	m
mass	kilogram	kg
time	second	s
temperature*	kelvin	K

*Temperature units are discussed in Chapter 3.

The Base Units

Table 2.1 lists the common SI base units. They include the **meter (m)** as the base unit of length; the **kilogram (kg)** as the base unit of mass; and the **second (s)** as the base unit of time. Each of these base units is precisely defined. The meter is defined as the distance light travels in a certain period of time: 1/299,792,458 s (▼ Figure 2.5).

◀ **FIGURE 2.5 The base unit of length** The definition of a meter, established by international agreement in 1983, is the distance that light travels in vacuum in 1/299,792,458 s. Question: Why is such a precise standard necessary?

▲ **FIGURE 2.6   The base unit of mass**   A duplicate of the international standard kilogram, called kilogram 20, is kept at the National Institute of Standards and Technology near Washington, D.C.

▲ **FIGURE 2.7   The base unit of time**   The second is defined, using an atomic clock, as the duration of 9,192,631,770 periods of the radiation emitted from a certain transition in a cesium-133 atom.

Because the mass of the block of metal used to define a kilogram has changed slightly over the years, scientists are currently working on alternate ways to define the kilogram.

A nickel (5 cents) has a mass of about 5 g.

(The speed of light is 3.0×10^8 m/s.) The kilogram is defined as the mass of a block of metal kept at the International Bureau of Weights and Measures at Sèvres, France (▲ Figure 2.6). The second is defined using an atomic standard (▲ Figure 2.7).

Most people are familiar with the SI base unit of time, the second. However, if you live in the United States, you may be less familiar with the meter and the kilogram. The meter is slightly longer than a yard (a yard is 36 in. while a meter is 39.37 in.). A 100-yd football field measures only 91.4 m.

The kilogram is a measure of mass, which is different from weight. The **mass** of an object is a measure of the quantity of matter within it, while the weight of an object is a measure of the gravitational pull on that matter. Consequently, weight depends on gravity while mass does not. If you were to weigh yourself on Mars, for example, the lower gravity would pull you toward the scale less than Earth's gravity would, resulting in a lower weight. A 150-lb person on Earth weighs only 57 lb on Mars. However, the person's mass, the quantity of matter in his or her body, remains the same. A kilogram of mass is the equivalent of 2.205 lb of weight on Earth, so if we express mass in kilograms, a 150-lb person on Earth has a mass of approximately 68 kg. A second common unit of mass is the gram (g), defined as follows:

$$1000 \text{ g} = 10^3 \text{ g} = 1 \text{ kg}$$

Prefix Multipliers

The SI system employs **prefix multipliers** (Table 2.2) with the base units. These multipliers change the value of the unit by powers of 10. For example, the kilometer (km) features the prefix *kilo-*, meaning 1000 or 10^3. Therefore:

$$1 \text{ km} = 1000 \text{ m} = 10^3 \text{ m}$$

Similarly, the millisecond (ms) has the prefix *milli-*, meaning 0.001 or 10^{-3}.

$$1 \text{ ms} = 0.001 \text{ s} = 10^{-3} \text{ s}$$

The prefix multipliers allow us to express a wide range of measurements in units that are similar in size to the quantity we are measuring. We choose the prefix multiplier that is most convenient for a particular measurement. For example, to measure the diameter of a quarter, we use centimeters because a quarter has

▲ The diameter of a quarter is about 2.43 cm.
Question: Why would we *not* use meters to measure a quarter?

TABLE 2.2 SI Prefix Multipliers

Prefix	Symbol	Meaning	Multiplier	
tera-	T	trillion	1,000,000,000,000	(10^{12})
giga-	G	billion	1,000,000,000	(10^{9})
mega-	M	million	1,000,000	(10^{6})
kilo-	k	thousand	1,000	(10^{3})
hecto-	h	hundred	100	10^{2}
deca-	da	ten	10	10^{1}
deci-	d	tenth	0.1	(10^{-1})
centi-	c	hundredth	0.01	(10^{-2})
milli-	m	thousandth	0.001	(10^{-3})
micro-	μ	millionth	0.000001	(10^{-6})
nano-	n	billionth	0.000000001	(10^{-9})
pico-	p	trillionth	0.000000000001	(10^{-12})
femto-	f	quadrillionth	0.000000000000001	(10^{-15})

a diameter of about 2.43 cm. A centimeter is a common metric unit and is about equivalent to the width of a pinky finger (2.54 cm = 1 in.). The millimeter could also work to express the diameter of the quarter; the same quarter measures 24.3 mm. The kilometer, however, would not work as well because, in that unit, the quarter's diameter is 0.0000243 km. We pick a unit similar in size to (or smaller than) the quantity we are measuring. Consider expressing the length of a short chemical bond, about 1.2×10^{-10} m. Which prefix multiplier should we use? The most convenient one is probably the picometer (pico = 10^{-12}). Chemical bonds measure about 120 pm.

TABLE 2.3 Some Common Units and Their Equivalents

Length

1 kilometer (km) = 0.6214 mile (mi)	
1 meter (m) = 39.37 inches (in.)	
= 1.094 yards (yd)	
1 foot (ft) = 30.48 centimeters (cm)	
1 inch (in.) = 2.54 centimeters (cm)	
(exact)	

Mass

1 kilogram (kg) = 2.205 pounds (lb)	
1 pound (lb) = 453.59 grams (g)	
1 ounce (oz) = 28.35 grams (g)	

Volume

1 liter (L) = 1000 milliliters (mL)	
= 1000 cubic centimeters (cm³)	
1 liter (L) = 1.057 quarts (qt)	
1 U.S gallon (gal) = 3.785 liters (L)	

✓ **CONCEPTUAL CHECKPOINT 2.4**

Which is the most convenient unit to use to express the dimensions of a polio virus, which is about 2.8×10^{-8} m in diameter?

(a) Mm

(b) mm

(c) μm

(d) nm

Derived Units

A derived unit is formed from other units. For example, many units of **volume**, a measure of space, are derived units. Any unit of length, when cubed (raised to the third power), becomes a unit of volume. Therefore, cubic meters (m^3), cubic centimeters (cm^3), and cubic millimeters (mm^3) are all units of volume. A three-bedroom house has a volume of about 630 m^3, a can of soda pop has a volume of about 350 cm^3, and a rice grain has a volume of about 3 mm^3. We also use the **liter (L)** and milliliter (mL) to express volume (although these are not derived units). A gallon is equal to 3.785 L. A milliliter is equivalent to 1 cm^3. Table 2.3 lists some common units and their equivalents.

2.6 Problem Solving and Unit Conversion

LO: Convert between units.

Problem solving is one of the most important skills you will acquire in this course. Not only will this skill help you succeed in chemistry, but it will help you to learn how to think critically, which is important in every area of knowledge. When my daughter was a freshman in high school, she came to me for help on an algebra problem. The problem went something like this:

> The Mathematics Review Appendix (p. MR-1) includes a review of how to solve algebraic problems for a variable.

> Sam and Sara live 11 miles apart. Sam leaves his house traveling at 6 miles per hour toward Sara's house. Sara leaves her house traveling at 3 miles per hour toward Sam's house. How much time elapses until Sam and Sara meet?

Solving the problem requires setting up the equation $11 - 6t = 3t$. Although my daughter could solve this equation for t quite easily, getting to the equation from the problem statement was another matter—that process requires *critical thinking*, and that was the skill she needed to learn to successfully solve the problem. You can't succeed in chemistry—or in life, really—without developing critical thinking skills. Learning how to solve chemical problems helps you develop these kinds of skills.

Although no simple formula applies to every problem, you can learn problem-solving strategies and begin to develop some chemical intuition. You can think of many of the problems in this book as *unit conversion problems*, where you are given one or more quantities and asked to convert them into different units. Other problems require the use of *specific equations* to get to the information you are trying to find. In the sections that follow, you will find strategies to help you solve both of these types of problems. Of course, many problems contain both conversions and equations, requiring the combination of these strategies, and some problems may require an altogether different approach, but the basic tools you learn here can be applied to those problems as well.

Converting Between Units

> Using units as a guide to solving problems is called dimensional analysis.

Units are critical in calculations. Knowing how to work with and manipulate units in calculations is a crucial part of problem solving. In calculations, units help determine correctness. You should always include units in calculations, and you can think of many calculations as converting from one unit to another. You can multiply, divide, and cancel units like any other algebraic quantity.

Remember:

1. Always write every number with its associated unit. Never ignore units; they are critical.
2. Always include units in your calculations, dividing them and multiplying them as if they were algebraic quantities. Do not let units magically appear or disappear in calculations. Units must flow logically from beginning to end.

Consider converting 17.6 in. to centimeters. You know from Table 2.3 that 1 in. = 2.54 cm. To determine how many centimeters are in 17.6 in., perform the conversion:

$$17.6 \text{ in.} \times \frac{2.54 \text{ cm}}{1 \text{ in.}} = 44.7 \text{ cm}$$

The unit *in.* cancels and you are left with *cm* as your final unit. The quantity $\frac{2.54 \text{ cm}}{1 \text{ in.}}$ is a **conversion factor** between *in.* and *cm*—it is a quotient with *cm* on top and *in.* on bottom.

For most conversion problems, you are given a quantity in some units and asked to convert the quantity to another unit. These calculations take the form:

$$\text{information given} \times \text{conversion factor(s)} = \text{information sought}$$

$$\cancel{\text{given unit}} \times \frac{\text{desired unit}}{\cancel{\text{given unit}}} = \text{desired unit}$$

You can construct conversion factors from any two quantities known to be equivalent. In this example, 2.54 cm = 1 in., so construct the conversion factor by dividing both sides of the equality by 1 in. and canceling the units.

$$2.54 \text{ cm} = 1 \text{ in.}$$

$$\frac{2.54 \text{ cm}}{1 \text{ in.}} = \frac{1 \cancel{\text{in.}}}{1 \cancel{\text{in.}}}$$

$$\frac{2.54 \text{ cm}}{1 \text{ in.}} = 1$$

The quantity $\dfrac{2.54 \text{ cm}}{1 \text{ in.}}$ is equal to 1 and you can use it to convert between inches and centimeters.

What if you want to perform the conversion the other way, from centimeters to inches? If you try to use the same conversion factor, the units do not cancel correctly.

$$44.7 \text{ cm} \times \frac{2.54 \text{ cm}}{1 \text{ in.}} = \frac{114 \text{ cm}^2}{\text{in.}}$$

The units in the answer, as well as the value of the answer, are incorrect. The unit $\text{cm}^2/\text{in.}$ is not correct, and, based on your knowledge that centimeters are smaller than inches, you know that 44.7 cm cannot be equivalent to 114 in. In solving problems, always check if the final units are correct, and consider whether or not the magnitude of the answer makes sense. In this case, the mistake was in how the conversion factor was used. You must invert it.

$$44.7 \cancel{\text{ cm}} \times \frac{1 \text{ in.}}{2.54 \cancel{\text{ cm}}} = 17.6 \text{ in.}$$

You can invert conversion factors because they are equal to 1 and the inverse of 1 is 1.

$$\frac{1}{1} = 1$$

Therefore,

$$\frac{2.54 \text{ cm}}{1 \text{ in.}} = 1 = \frac{1 \text{ in.}}{2.54 \text{ cm}}$$

You can diagram conversions using a **solution map**. A solution map is a visual outline that shows the strategic route required to solve a problem. For unit conversion, the solution map focuses on units and how to convert from one unit to another. The solution map for converting from inches to centimeters is:

in. ⟶ cm

$$\frac{2.54 \text{ cm}}{1 \text{ in.}}$$

The solution map for converting from centimeters to inches is:

$$\frac{1 \text{ in.}}{2.54 \text{ cm}}$$

Each arrow in a solution map for a unit conversion has an associated conversion factor, with the units of the previous step in the denominator and the units of the following step in the numerator. For one-step problems such as these, the solution map is only moderately helpful, but for multistep problems, it becomes a powerful way to develop a problem-solving strategy. In the section that follows, you will learn how to incorporate solution maps into an overall problem-solving strategy.

 CONCEPTUAL CHECKPOINT 2.5

Which conversion factor should you use to convert 4 ft to inches (12 in. = 1 ft)?

(a) $\dfrac{12 \text{ in.}}{1 \text{ ft}}$ (b) $\dfrac{1 \text{ ft}}{12 \text{ in.}}$ (c) $\dfrac{1 \text{ in.}}{12 \text{ ft}}$ (d) $\dfrac{12 \text{ ft}}{1 \text{ in.}}$

General Problem-Solving Strategy

In this book, we use a standard problem-solving procedure that you can adapt to many of the problems encountered in chemistry and beyond. Solving any problem essentially requires that you assess the information given in the problem and devise a way to get to the requested information. In other words, you need to:

- Identify the starting point (the *given* information).
- Identify the end point (what you must *find*).
- Devise a way to get from the starting point to the end point using what is given as well as what you already know or can look up. You can use a *solution map* to diagram the steps required to get from the starting point to the end point.

In graphic form, this progression looks like this:

Given $\longrightarrow$ Solution Map $\longrightarrow$ Find

Beginning students often have trouble knowing how to start solving a chemistry problem. Although no problem-solving procedure is applicable to all problems, the following four-step procedure can be helpful in working through many of the numerical problems you will encounter in this book.

1. **Sort**. Begin by sorting the information in the problem. *Given* information is the basic data provided by the problem—often one or more numbers with their associated units. The given information is the starting point for the problem. *Find* indicates what the problem is asking you to find (the end point of the problem).

2. **Strategize**. This is usually the hardest part of solving a problem. In this process, you must create a solution map—the series of steps that will get you from the given information to the information you are trying to find. You have already seen solution maps for simple unit conversion problems. Each arrow in a solution map represents a computational step. On the left side of the arrow is the quantity (or quantities) you had before the step; on the right side of the arrow is the quantity (or quantities) you will have after the step; and below the arrow is the information you need to get from one to the other—the relationship between the quantities.

   Often such relationships will take the form of conversion factors or equations. These may be given in the problem, in which case you will have written them down under "Given" in Step 1. Usually, however, you will need other information—such as physical constants, formulas, or conversion factors—to help get you from what you are given to what you must find. You may recall this information from what you have learned, or you can look it up in the chapters or tables within the book.

   In some cases, you may get stuck at the strategize step. If you cannot figure out how to get from the given information to the information you are asked to find, you might try working backwards. For example, you may want to look at the units of the quantity you are trying to find and look for conversion factors to get to the units of the given quantity. You may even try a combination of strategies; work forward, backward, or some of both. If you persist, you will develop a strategy to solve the problem.

3. **Solve.** This is the most straightforward part of solving a problem. Once you set up the problem properly and devise a solution map, you follow the map to solve the problem. Carry out mathematical operations (paying attention to the rules for significant figures in calculations) and cancel units as needed.

4. **Check.** This step is often overlooked by beginning students. Experienced problem solvers always ask, Does this answer make physical sense? Are the units correct? Is the number of significant figures correct? When solving multistep problems, errors easily creep into the solution. You can catch most of these errors by simply checking the answer. For example, suppose you are calculating the number of atoms in a gold coin and end up with an answer of 1.1×10^{-6} atoms. Could the gold coin really be composed of one-millionth of one atom?

In Examples 2.8 and 2.9, you will find this problem-solving procedure applied to unit conversion problems. The procedure is summarized in the left column, and two examples of applying the procedure are shown in the middle and right columns. You will encounter this three-column format in selected examples throughout this text. It allows you to see how a particular procedure can be applied to two different problems. Work through one problem first (from top to bottom) and then examine how the same procedure is applied to the other problem. Recognizing the commonalities and differences between problems is a key part of problem solving.

PROBLEM-SOLVING PROCEDURE	EXAMPLE 2.8 UNIT CONVERSION Convert 7.8 km to miles.	EXAMPLE 2.9 UNIT CONVERSION Convert 0.825 m to millimeters.
SORT Begin by sorting the information in the problem into *given* and *find*.	**GIVEN:** 7.8 km **FIND:** mi	**GIVEN:** 0.825 m **FIND:** mm
STRATEGIZE Draw a *solution map* for the problem. Begin with the *given* quantity and symbolize each step with an arrow. Below the arrow, write the conversion factor for that step. The solution map ends at the *find* quantity. (In these examples, the relationships used in the conversions are below the solution map.)	**SOLUTION MAP** km ➝ mi $\dfrac{0.6214 \text{ mi}}{1 \text{ km}}$ **RELATIONSHIPS USED** $1 \text{ km} = 0.6214 \text{ mi}$ (This conversion factor is from Table 2.3.)	**SOLUTION MAP** m ➝ mm $\dfrac{1 \text{ mm}}{10^{-3} \text{ m}}$ **RELATIONSHIPS USED** $1 \text{ mm} = 10^{-3} \text{ m}$ (This conversion factor is from Table 2.2.)
SOLVE Follow the *solution map* to solve the problem. Begin with the *given* quantity and its units. Multiply by the appropriate conversion factor, canceling units to arrive at the *find* quantity. Round the answer to the correct number of significant figures. (If possible, obtain conversion factors to enough significant figures so that they do not limit the number of significant figures in the answer.)	**SOLUTION** $7.8 \text{ km} \times \dfrac{0.6214 \text{ mi}}{1 \text{ km}} = 4.84692 \text{ mi}$ $4.84692 \text{ mi} = 4.8 \text{ mi}$ Round the answer to two significant figures, because the quantity given has two significant figures.	**SOLUTION** $0.825 \text{ m} \times \dfrac{1 \text{ mm}}{10^{-3} \text{ m}} = 825 \text{ mm}$ $825 \text{ mm} = 825 \text{ mm}$ Leave the answer with three significant figures, because the quantity given has three significant figures and the conversion factor is a definition and therefore does not limit the number of significant figures in the answer.

CHECK Check your answer. Are the units correct? Does the answer make sense?	The units, mi, are correct. The magnitude of the answer is reasonable. A mile is longer than a kilometer, so the value in miles should be smaller than the value in kilometers.	The units, mm, are correct and the magnitude is reasonable. A millimeter is shorter than a meter, so the value in millimeters should be larger than the value in meters.
	▶ **SKILLBUILDER 2.8 | Unit Conversion** Convert 56.0 cm to inches.	▶ **SKILLBUILDER 2.9 | Unit Conversion** Convert 5678 m to kilometers.
	▶ **FOR MORE PRACTICE** Example 2.25; Problems 73, 74, 75, 76.	▶ **FOR MORE PRACTICE** Problems 69, 70, 71, 72.

✓ **CONCEPTUAL CHECKPOINT 2.6**

Which conversion factor should you use to convert a distance in meters to kilometers?

(a) $\dfrac{1\text{ m}}{10^3\text{ km}}$ (b) $\dfrac{10^3\text{ m}}{1\text{ km}}$ (c) $\dfrac{1\text{ km}}{10^3\text{ m}}$ (d) $\dfrac{10^3\text{ km}}{1\text{ m}}$

2.7   Solving Multistep Unit Conversion Problems

LO: Convert between units.

When solving multistep unit conversion problems, follow the preceding procedure, but add more steps to the solution map. Each step in the solution map should have a conversion factor, with the units of the previous step in the denominator and the units of the following step in the numerator. For example, suppose you want to convert 194 cm to feet. The solution map begins with cm, and you use the relationship 2.54 cm = 1 in. to convert to in. Then use the relationship 12 in. = 1 ft to convert to ft.

SOLUTION MAP

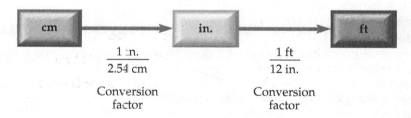

Once the solution map is complete, follow it to solve the problem.

SOLUTION

$$194 \text{ cm} \times \frac{1\text{ in.}}{2.54\text{ cm}} \times \frac{1\text{ ft}}{12\text{ in.}} = 6.3648 \text{ ft}$$

You then round to the correct number of significant figures—in this case, three (from 194 cm, which has three significant figures).

$$6.3648 \text{ ft} = 6.36 \text{ ft}$$

Because 1 foot is defined as 12 in., it does not limit significant figures.

Finally, check the answer. The units of the answer, feet, are the correct ones, and the magnitude seems about right. A foot is larger than a centimeter, so it is reasonable that the value in feet is smaller than the value in centimeters.

EXAMPLE 2.10   SOLVING MULTISTEP UNIT CONVERSION PROBLEMS

A recipe for making creamy pasta sauce calls for 0.75 L of cream. Your measuring cup measures only in cups. How many cups of cream should you use? (4 cups = 1 quart)

SORT Begin by sorting the information in the problem into given and find.	**GIVEN:** 0.75 L **FIND:** cups
STRATEGIZE Draw a solution map for the problem. Begin with the *given* quantity and symbolize each step with an arrow. Below the arrow, write the conversion factor for that step. The solution map ends at the *find* quantity.	**SOLUTION MAP** $$\frac{1.057 \text{ qt}}{1 \text{ L}} \qquad \frac{4 \text{ cups}}{1 \text{ qt}}$$ **RELATIONSHIPS USED** 1.057 qt = 1 L (from Table 2.3) 4 cups = 1 qt (given in problem statement)
SOLVE Follow the solution map to solve the problem. Begin with 0.75 L and multiply by the appropriate conversion factor, canceling units to arrive at qt. Then, use the second conversion factor to arrive at cups. Round the answer to the correct number of significant figures. In this case, you round the answer to two significant figures, because the quantity given has two significant figures.	**SOLUTION** $$0.75 \,\cancel{L} \times \frac{1.057 \,\cancel{qt}}{1 \,\cancel{L}} \times \frac{4 \text{ cups}}{1 \,\cancel{qt}} = 3.171 \text{ cups}$$ $$3.171 \text{ cups} = 3.2 \text{ cups}$$
CHECK Check your answer. Are the units correct? Does the answer make physical sense?	The answer has the right units (cups) and seems reasonable. A cup is smaller than a liter, so the value in cups should be larger than the value in liters.

▶**SKILLBUILDER 2.10 | Solving Multistep Unit Conversion Problems**

A recipe calls for 1.2 cups of oil. How many liters of oil is this?

▶**FOR MORE PRACTICE**   Problems 85, 86.

EXAMPLE 2.11   SOLVING MULTISTEP UNIT CONVERSION PROBLEMS

One lap of a running track measures 255 m. To run 10.0 km, how many laps should you run?

SORT Begin by sorting the information in the problem into given and find. You are given a distance in km and asked to find the distance in laps. You are also given the quantity 255 m per lap, which is a conversion factor between m and laps.	**GIVEN:** 10.0 km 255 m = 1 lap **FIND:** number of laps
STRATEGIZE Build the solution map beginning with km and ending at laps. Focus on the units.	**SOLUTION MAP** $$\frac{10^3 \text{ m}}{1 \text{ km}} \qquad \frac{1 \text{ lap}}{255 \text{ m}}$$ **RELATIONSHIPS USED** 1 km = 10^3 m (from Table 2.2) 1 lap = 255 m (given in problem)

SOLVE	SOLUTION
Follow the solution map to solve the problem. Begin with 10.0 km and multiply by the appropriate conversion factor, canceling units to arrive at m. Then, use the second conversion factor to arrive at laps. Round the intermediate answer (in blue) to three significant figures, because it is limited by the three significant figures in the given quantity, 10.0 km.	$10.0 \text{ km} \times \dfrac{10^3 \text{ m}}{1 \text{ km}} \times \dfrac{1 \text{ lap}}{255 \text{ m}} = 39.216 \text{ laps} = 39.2 \text{ laps}$
CHECK Check your answer. Are the units correct? Does the answer make physical sense?	The units of the answer are correct, and the value of the answer makes sense. If a lap is 255 m, there are about 4 laps to each km (1000 m), so it seems reasonable that you would have to run about 40 laps to cover 10 km.

▶**SKILLBUILDER 2.11 | Solving Multistep Unit Conversion Problems**

A running track measures 1056 ft per lap. To run 15.0 km, how many laps should you run? (1 mi = 5280 ft)

▶**SKILLBUILDER PLUS**

An island is 5.72 nautical mi from the coast. How far away is the island in meters? (1 nautical mi = 1.151 mi)

▶**FOR MORE PRACTICE**   Problems 83, 84.

2.8   Units Raised to a Power

LO: Convert units raised to a power.

I The unit cm³ is often abbreviated as cc.

2.54 cm = 1 in. is an exact conversion factor. After cubing, you retain five significant figures so that the conversion factor does not limit the four significant figures of your original quantity (1255 cm³).

When converting quantities with units raised to a power, such as cubic centimeters (cm^3), *you must raise the conversion factor to that power.* For example, suppose you want to convert the size of a motorcycle engine reported as 1255 cm^3 to cubic inches. You know that:

$$2.54 \text{ cm} = 1 \text{ in.}$$

Most tables of conversion factors do not include conversions between cubic units, but you can derive them from the conversion factors for the basic units. You cube both sides of the preceding equality to obtain the proper conversion factor.

$$(2.54 \text{ cm})^3 = (1 \text{ in.})^3$$
$$(2.54)^3 \text{ cm}^3 = 1^3 \text{ in.}^3$$
$$16.387 \text{ cm}^3 = 1 \text{ in.}^3$$

You can do the same thing in fractional form.

$$\frac{1 \text{ in.}}{2.54 \text{ cm}} = \frac{(1 \text{ in.})^3}{(2.54 \text{ cm})^3} = \frac{1 \text{ in.}^3}{16.387 \text{ cm}^3}$$

You then proceed with the conversion in the usual manner.

SOLUTION MAP

$$\frac{1 \text{ in.}^3}{16.387 \text{ cm}^3}$$

SOLUTION

$$1255 \text{ cm}^3 \times \frac{1 \text{ in.}^3}{16.387 \text{ cm}^3} = 76.5851 \text{ in.}^3 = 76.59 \text{ in.}^3$$

CHEMISTRY AND HEALTH

▶ Drug Dosage

The unit of choice in specifying drug dosage is the milligram (mg). A bottle of aspirin, Tylenol, or any other common drug lists the number of milligrams of the active ingredient contained in each tablet, as well as the number of tablets to take per dose. The following table shows the mass of the active ingredient per pill in several common pain relievers, all reported in milligrams. The remainder of each tablet is composed of inactive ingredients such as cellulose (or fiber) and starch.

The recommended adult dose for many of these pain relievers is one or two tablets every 4 to 8 hours (depending on the specific pain reliever). Notice that the extra-strength version of each pain reliever just contains a higher dose of the same compound found in the regular-strength version. For the pain relievers listed, three regular-strength tablets are the equivalent of two extra-strength tablets (and probably cost less).

The dosages given in the table are fairly standard for each drug, regardless of the brand.

On most drugstore shelves, there are many different brands of regular-strength ibuprofen, some sold under the generic name and others sold under their brand names (such as Advil). However, if you look closely at the labels, you will find that they all contain the same thing: 200 mg of the compound ibuprofen. There is no difference in the compound or in the amount of the compound. Yet these pain relievers will most likely all have different prices. Choose the least expensive. Why pay more for the same thing?

B2.2 CAN YOU ANSWER THIS? *Convert each of the doses in the table to ounces. Why are drug dosages not listed in ounces?*

Drug Mass per Pill for Common Pain Relievers

Pain Reliever	Mass of Active Ingredient per Pill
aspirin	325 mg
aspirin, extra strength	500 mg
ibuprofen (Advil)	200 mg
ibuprofen, extra strength	300 mg
acetaminophen (Tylenol)	325 mg
acetaminophen, extra strength	500 mg

EXAMPLE 2.12 CONVERTING QUANTITIES INVOLVING UNITS RAISED TO A POWER

A circle has an area of 2659 cm². What is its area in square meters?

SORT You are given an area in square centimeters and asked to convert the area to square meters.	**GIVEN:** 2659 cm^2 **FIND:** m^2
STRATEGIZE Build a solution map beginning with cm² and ending with m². Remember that you must square the conversion factor.	**SOLUTION MAP** $$\frac{(0.01 \text{ m})^2}{(1 \text{ cm})^2}$$ **RELATIONSHIPS USED** $1 \text{ cm} = 0.01 \text{ m}$ (from Table 2.2)
SOLVE Follow the solution map to solve the problem. Square the conversion factor (both the units and the number) as you carry out the calculation. Round the answer to four significant figures to reflect the four significant figures in the given quantity. The conversion factor is exact and therefore does not limit the number of significant figures.	**SOLUTION** $$2659 \text{ cm}^2 \times \frac{(0.01 \text{ m})^2}{(1 \text{ cm})^2}$$ $$= 2659 \text{ cm}^2 \times \frac{10^{-4} \text{ m}^2}{1 \text{ cm}^2}$$ $$= 0.265900 \text{ m}^2$$ $$= 0.2659 \text{ m}^2$$

CHECK	
Check your answer. Are the units correct? Does the answer make physical sense?	The units of the answer are correct, and the magnitude makes physical sense. A square meter is much larger than a square centimeter, so the value in square meters should be much smaller than the value in square centimeters.

▶**SKILLBUILDER 2.12** | **Converting Quantities Involving Units Raised to a Power**

An automobile engine has a displacement (a measure of the size of the engine) of 289.7 in.³ What is its displacement in cubic centimeters?

▶**FOR MORE PRACTICE** Example 2.26; Problems 87, 88, 89, 90, 91, 92.

EXAMPLE 2.13 **SOLVING MULTISTEP CONVERSION PROBLEMS INVOLVING UNITS RAISED TO A POWER**

The average annual per person crude oil consumption in the United States is 15,615 dm³. What is this value in cubic inches?

SORT	
You are given a volume in cubic decimeters and asked to convert it to cubic inches.	GIVEN: 15,615 dm³ FIND: in.³

STRATEGIZE	

Build a solution map beginning with dm³ and ending with in.³ You must cube each of the conversion factors, because the quantities involve cubic units.	SOLUTION MAP
	
	 RELATIONSHIPS USED
	    1 dm = 0.1 m (from Table 2.2)
	    1 cm = 0.01 m (from Table 2.2)
	 2.54 cm = 1 in. (from Table 2.3)

SOLVE	
Follow the solution map to solve the problem. Begin with the given value in dm³ and multiply by the string of conversion factors to arrive at in.³ Be sure to cube each conversion factor as you carry out the calculation. Round the answer to five significant figures to reflect the five significant figures in the least precisely known quantity (15,615 dm³). The conversion factors are all exact and therefore do not limit the number of significant figures.	SOLUTION $15,615 \ \cancel{dm^3} \times \dfrac{(0.1 \ \cancel{m})^3}{(1 \ \cancel{dm})^3} \times \dfrac{(1 \ \cancel{cm})^3}{(0.01 \ \cancel{m})^3} \times \dfrac{(1 \ in.)^3}{(2.54 \ \cancel{cm})^3}$ $= 9.5289 \times 10^5 \ in.^3$

CHECK	
Check your answer. Are the units correct? Does the answer make physical sense?	The units of the answer are correct, and the magnitude makes sense. A cubic inch is smaller than a cubic decimeter, so the value in cubic inches should be larger than the value in cubic decimeters.

▶**SKILLBUILDER 2.13** | **Solving Multistep Problems Involving Units Raised to a Power**

How many cubic inches are there in 3.25 yd³?

▶**FOR MORE PRACTICE** Problems 93, 94.

✓ **CONCEPTUAL CHECKPOINT 2.7**

You know that there are 3 ft in a yard. How many cubic feet are there in a cubic yard?

(a) 3
(b) 6
(c) 9
(d) 27

2.9 Density

LO: Calculate the density of a substance.

LO: Use density as a conversion factor.

▲ Top-end bicycle frames are made of titanium because of titanium's low density and high relative strength. Titanium has a density of 4.50 g/cm³, while iron, for example, has a density of 7.86 g/cm³.

TABLE 2.4 Densities of Some Common Substances

Substance	Density (g/cm³)
charcoal, oak	0.57
ethanol	0.789
ice	0.92
water	1.0
glass	2.6
aluminum	2.7
titanium	4.50
iron	7.86
copper	8.96
lead	11.4
gold	19.3
platinum	21.4

Remember that cubic centimeters and milliliters are equivalent units.

Why do some people pay over $3000 for a bicycle made of titanium? A steel frame would be just as strong for a fraction of the cost. The difference between the two bikes is their masses—the titanium bike is lighter. For a given volume of metal, titanium has less mass than steel. Titanium is said to be *less dense* than steel. The **density** of a substance is the ratio of its mass to its volume.

$$\text{Density} = \frac{\text{Mass}}{\text{Volume}} \quad \text{or} \quad d = \frac{m}{V}$$

Density is a fundamental property of a substance and differs from one substance to another. The units of density are those of mass divided by those of volume, most conveniently expressed in grams per cubic centimeter (g/cm³) or grams per milliliter (g/mL). Table 2.4 lists the densities of some common substances. Aluminum is among the least dense structural metals with a density of 2.70 g/cm³, while platinum is among the densest with a density of 21.4 g/cm³. Titanium has a density of 4.50 g/cm³.

Calculating Density

You can calculate the density of a substance by dividing the mass of a given amount of the substance by its volume. For example, a sample of liquid has a volume of 22.5 mL and a mass of 27.2 g. To find its density, use the equation $d = m/V$.

$$d = \frac{m}{V} = \frac{27.2 \text{ g}}{22.5 \text{ mL}} = 1.21 \text{ g/mL}$$

You can use a solution map for solving problems involving equations, but the solution map takes a slightly different form than one for a pure conversion problem. In a problem involving an equation, the solution map shows how the *equation* takes you from the *given* quantities to the *find* quantity. The solution map for this problem is:

$$d = \frac{m}{V}$$

The solution map illustrates that the values of m and V, when substituted into the equation $d = \frac{m}{V}$, give the desired result, d.

EXAMPLE 2.14 CALCULATING DENSITY

A jeweler offers to sell a ring to a woman and tells her that it is made of platinum. Noting that the ring feels a little light, the woman decides to perform a test to determine the ring's density. She places the ring on a balance and finds that it has a mass of 5.84 g. She also finds that the ring *displaces* 0.556 cm^3 of water. Is the ring made of platinum? The density of platinum is 21.4 g/cm^3. (The displacement of water is a common way to measure the volume of irregularly shaped objects. To say that an object *displaces* 0.556 cm^3 of water means that when the object is submerged in a container of water filled to the brim, 0.556 cm^3 overflows. Therefore, the volume of the object is 0.556 cm^3.)

SORT	
You are given the mass and volume of the ring and asked to find the density.	GIVEN: $m = 5.84$ g $V = 0.556$ cm^3 FIND: density in g/cm^3

STRATEGIZE

If the ring is platinum, its density should match that of platinum. Build a solution map that represents how you get from the given quantities (mass and volume) to the find quantity (density). Unlike in conversion problems, where you write a conversion factor beneath the arrow, here you write the equation for density beneath the arrow.

SOLUTION MAP

$$d = \frac{m}{V}$$

RELATIONSHIPS USED

$d = \dfrac{m}{V}$ (equation for density)

SOLVE

Follow the solution map. Substitute the given values into the density equation and calculate the density.

Round the answer to three significant figures to reflect the three significant figures in the given quantities.

SOLUTION

$$d = \frac{m}{V} = \frac{5.84 \text{ g}}{0.556 \text{ cm}^3} = 10.5 \text{ g/cm}^3$$

The density of the ring is much too low to be platinum; therefore the ring is a fake.

CHECK

Check your answer. Are the units correct? Does the answer make physical sense?

The units of the answer are correct, and the magnitude seems like it could be an actual density. As you can see from Table 2.4, the densities of liquids and solids range from below 1 g/cm^3 to just over 20 g/cm^3.

▶**SKILLBUILDER 2.14 | Calculating Density**

The woman takes the ring back to the jewelry shop, where she is met with endless apologies. The jeweler had accidentally made the ring out of silver rather than platinum. The jeweler gives her a new ring that she promises is platinum. This time when the customer checks the density, she finds the mass of the ring to be 9.67 g and its volume to be 0.452 cm^3. Is this ring genuine?

▶**FOR MORE PRACTICE** Example 2.27; Problems 95, 96, 97, 98, 99, 100.

68.4 g liquid

d = 1.32 g/cm^3

Density as a Conversion Factor

You can use the density of a substance as a conversion factor between the mass of the substance and its volume. For example, suppose you need 68.4 g of a liquid with a density of 1.32 g/cm^3 and want to measure the correct amount with a graduated cylinder (a piece of laboratory glassware used to measure volume). How much volume should you measure?

Start with the mass of the liquid and use the density as a conversion factor to convert mass to volume. However, you must use the inverted density expression

$1 \text{ cm}^3/1.32 \text{ g}$ because you want g, the unit you are converting from, to be on the bottom (in the denominator) and cm^3, the unit you are converting to, on the top (in the numerator). The solution map takes this form:

SOLUTION MAP

$$\frac{1 \text{ cm}^3}{1.32 \text{ g}} \qquad \frac{1 \text{ mL}}{1 \text{ cm}^3}$$

SOLUTION

$$68.4 \text{ g} \times \frac{1 \text{ cm}^3}{1.32 \text{ g}} \times \frac{1 \text{ mL}}{1 \text{ cm}^3} = 51.8 \text{ mL}$$

You must measure 51.8 mL to obtain 68.4 g of the liquid.

EXAMPLE 2.15 DENSITY AS A CONVERSION FACTOR

▶ The gasoline in an automobile gas tank has a mass of 60.0 kg and a density of 0.752 g/cm^3. What is its volume in cm^3?

SORT You are given the mass in kilograms and asked to find the volume in cubic centimeters. Density is the conversion factor between mass and volume.	**GIVEN:** 60.0 kg Density $= 0.752 \text{ g/cm}^3$ **FIND:** volume in cm^3
STRATEGIZE Build the solution map starting with kg and ending with cm^3. Use the density (inverted) to convert from g to cm^3.	**SOLUTION MAP** $$\frac{1000 \text{ g}}{1 \text{ kg}} \qquad \frac{1 \text{ cm}^3}{0.752 \text{ g}}$$ **RELATIONSHIPS USED** 0.752 g/cm^3 (given in problem) $1000 \text{ g} = 1 \text{ kg}$ (from Table 2.2)
SOLVE Follow the solution map to solve the problem. Round the answer to three significant figures to reflect the three significant figures in the given quantities.	**SOLUTION** $$60.0 \text{ kg} \times \frac{1000 \text{ g}}{1 \text{ kg}} \times \frac{1 \text{ cm}^3}{0.752 \text{ g}} = 7.98 \times 10^4 \text{ cm}^3$$
CHECK Check your answer. Are the units correct? Does the answer make physical sense?	The units of the answer are those of volume, so they are correct. The magnitude seems reasonable because the density is somewhat less than 1 g/cm^3; therefore the volume of 60.0 kg should be somewhat more than $60.0 \times 10^3 \text{ cm}^3$.

▶**SKILLBUILDER 2.15 | Density as a Conversion Factor**

A drop of acetone (nail polish remover) has a mass of 35 mg and a density of 0.788 g/cm^3. What is its volume in cubic centimeters?

▶**SKILLBUILDER PLUS** | A steel cylinder has a volume of 246 cm^3 and a density of 7.93 g/cm^3. What is its mass in kilograms?

▶**FOR MORE PRACTICE** Example 2.28; Problems 101, 102.

CHEMISTRY **AND HEALTH**

▶ Density, Cholesterol, and Heart Disease

Cholesterol is the fatty substance found in animal-derived foods such as beef, eggs, fish, poultry, and milk products. The body uses cholesterol for several purposes. However, excessive amounts of cholesterol in the blood—which can be caused by both genetic factors and diet—may result in the deposition of cholesterol in arterial walls, leading to a condition called atherosclerosis, or blocking of the arteries. These blockages are dangerous because they inhibit blood flow to important organs, causing heart attacks and strokes. The risk of stroke and heart attack increases with

Clogged
artery

▲ Too many low-density lipoproteins in the blood can lead to the blocking of arteries.

increasing blood cholesterol levels (Table 2.5). Cholesterol is carried in the bloodstream by a class of substances known as lipoproteins. Lipoproteins are often separated and classified according to their density.

The main carriers of blood cholesterol are low-density lipoproteins (LDLs). LDLs, also called bad cholesterol, have a density of $1.04\ \text{g/cm}^3$. They are bad because they tend to deposit cholesterol on arterial walls, increasing the risk of stroke and heart attack. Cholesterol is also carried by high-density lipoproteins (HDLs). HDLs, called good cholesterol, have a density of $1.13\ \text{g/cm}^3$. HDLs transport cholesterol to the liver for processing and excretion and therefore have a tendency to reduce cholesterol on arterial walls. Too low a level of HDLs (below 35 mg/100 mL) is considered a risk factor for heart disease. Exercise, along with a diet low in saturated fats, is believed to raise HDL levels in the blood while lowering LDL levels.

B2.3 CAN YOU ANSWER THIS?   *What mass of low-density lipoprotein is contained in a cylinder that is 1.25 cm long and 0.50 cm in diameter? (The volume of a cylinder, V, is given by $V = \pi r^2 \ell$, where r is the radius of the cylinder and ℓ is its length.)*

TABLE 2.5   Risk of Stroke and Heart Attack versus Blood Cholesterol Level

Risk Level	Total Blood Cholesterol (mg/100 mL)	LDL (mg/100 mL)
low	< 200	< 130
borderline	200–239	130–159
high	> 240	> 160

2.10   Numerical Problem-Solving Strategies and the Solution Map

In this chapter, you have seen a few examples of how to solve numerical problems. In Section 2.6, you encountered a procedure to solve simple unit conversion problems. You then learned how to modify that procedure to work with multistep unit conversion problems and problems involving an equation. This section summarizes and generalizes these procedures and includes two additional examples. Just as was done in Section 2.6, the general procedure for solving numerical problems is shown in the left column and the application of the procedure to the two examples is in the center and right columns.

SOLVING NUMERICAL PROBLEMS

EXAMPLE 2.16

UNIT CONVERSION

A chemist needs a 23.5-kg sample of ethanol for a large-scale reaction. What volume in liters of ethanol should the chemist use? The density of ethanol is 0.789 g/cm³.

EXAMPLE 2.17

UNIT CONVERSION WITH EQUATION

A 55.9-kg person displaces 57.2 L of water when submerged in a water tank. What is the density of the person in grams per cubic centimeter?

---

1. SORT

- Scan the problem for one or more numbers and their associated units. This number (or numbers) is (are) the starting point(s) of the calculation. Write them down as given.
- Scan the problem to determine what you are asked to find. Sometimes the units of this quantity are implied; other times they are specified. Write down the quantity and/or units you are asked to find.

GIVEN: 23.5 kg ethanol
            density = 0.789 g/cm³

FIND: volume in L

GIVEN: $m = 55.9$ kg
            $V = 57.2$ L

FIND: density in g/cm³

---

2. STRATEGIZE

- For problems involving only conversions, focus on units. The solution map shows how to get from the units in the given quantity to the units in the quantity you are asked to find.
- For problems involving equations, focus on the equation. The solution map shows how the equation takes you from the given quantity (or quantities) to the quantity you are asked to find.
- Some problems may involve both unit conversions and equations, in which case the solution map employs both of the above points.

SOLUTION MAP

$$\frac{1000\ g}{1\ kg} \quad \frac{1\ cm^3}{0.789\ g} \quad \frac{1\ mL}{1\ cm^3} \quad \frac{1\ L}{1000\ mL}$$

RELATIONSHIPS USED

  0.789 g/cm³ (given in problem)

  1000 g = 1 kg (Table 2.2)

  1000 mL = 1 L   (Table 2.2)

  1 mL = 1 cm³ (Table 2.3)

SOLUTION MAP

$$d = \frac{m}{V}$$

RELATIONSHIPS USED

$d = \dfrac{m}{V}$ (definition of density)

---

3. SOLVE

- For problems involving only conversions, begin with the given quantity and its units. Multiply by the appropriate conversion factor(s), canceling units, to arrive at the quantity you are asked to find.

SOLUTION

$$23.5\ \cancel{kg} \times \frac{1000\ \cancel{g}}{1\ \cancel{kg}} \times \frac{1\ \cancel{cm^3}}{0.789\ \cancel{g}} \times$$

$$\frac{1\ \cancel{mL}}{1\ \cancel{cm^3}} \times \frac{1\ L}{1000\ \cancel{mL}} = 29.7845\ L$$

$$29.7845\ L = 29.8\ L$$

The equation is already solved for the find quantity. Convert mass from kilograms to grams.

$$m = 55.9\ \cancel{kg} \times \frac{1000\ g}{1\ \cancel{kg}}$$

$$= 5.59 \times 10^4\ g$$

- For problems involving equations, solve the equation to arrive at the quantity you are asked to find. (Use algebra to rearrange the equation so that the quantity you are asked to find is isolated on one side.) Gather each of the quantities that must go into the equation in the correct units. (Convert to the correct units using additional solution maps if necessary.) Finally, substitute the numerical values and their units into the equation and calculate the answer.
- Round the answer to the correct number of significant figures. Use the significant figure rules from Sections 2.3 and 2.4.

Convert volume from liters to cubic centimeters.

$$V = 57.2 \; \cancel{L} \times \frac{1000 \; \cancel{mL}}{1 \; \cancel{L}} \times \frac{1 \; cm^3}{1 \; \cancel{mL}}$$
$$= 57.2 \times 10^3 \; cm^3$$

Calculate density.

$$d = \frac{m}{V} = \frac{55.9 \times 10^3}{57.2 \times 10^3 \; cm^3}$$
$$= 0.9772727 \frac{g}{cm^3}$$
$$= 0.977 \frac{g}{cm^3}$$

4. CHECK		
- Does the magnitude of the answer make physical sense? Are the units correct?	The units are correct (L) and the magnitude is reasonable. Because the density is less than 1 g/cm³, the calculated volume (29.8 L) should be greater than the mass (23.5 kg).	The units are correct. Because the mass in kilograms and the volume in liters are very close to each other in magnitude, it makes sense that the density is close to 1 g/cm³.

▶**SKILLBUILDER 2.16**

Unit Conversion

A pure gold metal bar displaces 0.82 L of water. What is its mass in kilograms? (The density of gold is 19.3 g/cm³.)

▶**SKILLBUILDER 2.17**

Unit Conversion with Equation

A gold-colored pebble is found in a stream. Its mass is 23.2 mg and its volume is 1.20 mm³. What is its density in grams per cubic centimeter? Is it gold? (The density of gold = 19.3 g/cm³.)

▶**FOR MORE PRACTICE** Problems 103, 109, 110, 111, 112.

▶**FOR MORE PRACTICE** Problems 103, 104, 105, 106.

CHAPTER IN REVIEW

Self-Assessment Quiz

Q1. Express the number 0.000042 in scientific notation.
(a) 0.42×10^{-4}
(b) 4.2×10^{-5}
(c) 4.2×10^{-4}
(d) 4×10^{-5}

Q2. A graduated cylinder has markings every milliliter. Which measurement is accurately reported for this graduated cylinder?
(a) 21 mL
(b) 21.2 mL
(c) 21.23 mL
(d) 21.232 mL

Q3. How many significant figures are in the number 0.00620?
(a) 2   (b) 3   (c) 4   (d) 5

Q4. Round the number 89.04997 to three significant figures.
(a) 89.03   (b) 89.04   (c) 89.1   (d) 89.0

Q5. Perform this multiplication to the correct number of significant figures: $65.2 \times 0.0015 \times 12.02$
(a) 1.17   (b) 1.18   (c) 1.2   (d) 1.176

Q6. Perform this addition to the correct number of significant figures: $8.32 + 12.148 + 0.02$
(a) 20.488   (b) 20.49   (c) 20.5   (d) 21

Q7. Perform this calculation to the correct number of significant figures: $78.222 \times (12.02 - 11.52)$

(a) 39   (b) 39.1   (c) 39.11   (d) 39.111

Q8. Convert 76.8 cm to m.

(a) 0.0768 m

(b) 7.68 m

(c) 0.768 m

(d) 7.68×10^{-2} m

Q9. Convert 2855 mg to kg.

(a) 2.855×10^{-3} kg

(b) 2.855 kg

(c) 0.02855 kg

(d) 3.503×10^{-4} kg

Q10. A runner runs 4875 ft in 6.85 minutes. What is the runner's average speed in miles per hour?

(a) 1.34 mi/hr

(b) 0.0022 mi/hr

(c) 8.09 mi/hr

(d) 8.087 mi/hr

Q11. An automobile travels 97.2 km on 7.88 L of gasoline. What is the gas mileage for the automobile in miles per gallon?

(a) 2.02 mi/gal

(b) 7.67 mi/gal

(c) 0.034 mi/gal

(d) 29.0 mi/gal

Q12. Convert 876.9 in.^{3} to m^3.

(a) 0.01437 m^3

(b) 22.27 m^3

(c) 5.351×10^7 m^3

(d) 0.014 m^3

Q13. A cube measures 2.5 cm on each edge and has a mass of 66.9 g. Calculate the density of the material that composes the cube. (The volume of a cube is equal to the edge length cubed.)

(a) 10.7 g/cm^3

(b) 4.3 g/cm^3

(c) 0.234 g/cm^3

(d) 26.7 g/cm^3

Q14. What is the mass of 225 mL of a liquid that has a density of 0.880 g/mL?

(a) 198 g   (b) 0.0039 g   (c) 0.198 g   (d) 0.256 g

Q15. What is the edge length of a 155-g iron cube? (The density of iron is 7.86 g/cm^3, and the volume of a cube is equal to the edge length cubed.)

(a) 0.0197 cm

(b) 19.7 cm

(c) 1218 cm

(d) 2.70 cm

Answers: 1:b, 2:b, 3:b, 4:d, 5:c, 6:b, 7:a, 8:c, 9:a, 10:c, 11:d, 12:a, 13:b, 14:a, 15:d

Chemical Principles	Relevance
Uncertainty: Scientists report measured quantities so that the number of digits reflects the certainty in the measurement. Write measured quantities so that every digit is certain except the last, which is estimated.	**Uncertainty:** Measurement is a hallmark of science, and you must communicate the precision of a measurement with the measurement so that others know how reliable the measurement is. When you write or manipulate measured quantities, you must show and retain the precision with which the original measurement was made.
Units: Measured quantities usually have units associated with them. The SI unit for length is the meter; for mass, the kilogram; and for time, the second. Prefix multipliers such as *kilo-* or *milli-* are often used in combination with these basic units. The SI units of volume are units of length raised to the third power; liters or milliliters are often used as well.	**Units:** The units in a measured quantity communicate what the quantity actually is. Without an agreed-on system of units, scientists could not communicate their measurements. Units are also important in calculations, and the tracking of units throughout a calculation is essential.
Density: The density of a substance is its mass divided by its volume, $d = m/V$, and is usually reported in units of grams per cubic centimeter or grams per milliliter. Density is a fundamental property of all substances and generally differs from one substance to another.	**Density:** The density of substances is an important consideration in choosing materials for manufacturing and production. Airplanes, for example, are made of low-density materials, while bridges are made of higher-density materials. Density is important as a conversion factor between mass and volume and vice versa.

Chemical Skills

Examples

LO: Express very large and very small numbers using scientific notation (Section 2.2).

To express a number in scientific notation:

- Move the decimal point to obtain a number between 1 and 10.

- Write the decimal part multiplied by 10 raised to the number of places you moved the decimal point.

- The exponent is positive if you moved the decimal point to the left and negative if you moved the decimal point to the right.

| EXAMPLE 2.18 | SCIENTIFIC NOTATION |

Express the number 45,000,000 in scientific notation.

$$45,000,000$$
$$\overset{\frown\frown\frown\frown\frown\frown\frown}{7\ 6\ 5\ 4\ 3\ 2\ 1}$$

$$4.5 \times 10^7$$

LO: Report measured quantities to the right number of digits (Section 2.3).

Report measured quantities so that every digit is certain except the last, which is estimated.

| EXAMPLE 2.19 | REPORTING MEASURED QUANTITIES TO THE RIGHT NUMBER OF DIGITS |

Record the volume of liquid in the graduated cylinder to the correct number of digits. Laboratory glassware is calibrated (and should therefore be read) from the bottom of the meniscus, the curved surface at the top of a column of liquid (see figure).

Meniscus

Because the graduated cylinder has markings every 0.1 mL, you should record the measurement to the nearest 0.01 mL. In this case, that is 4.57 mL.

LO: Determine which digits in a number are significant (Section 2.3).

Always count the following as significant:

- nonzero digits
- interior zeros
- trailing zeros after a decimal point
- trailing zeros before a decimal point but after a nonzero number

Never count the following digits as significant:

- zeros to the left of the first nonzero number

The following digits are ambiguous, and you should avoid them by using scientific notation:

- zeros at the end of a number but before a decimal point

| EXAMPLE 2.20 | COUNTING SIGNIFICANT DIGITS |

How many significant figures are in the following numbers?

1.0050	five significant figures
0.00870	three significant figures
100.085	six significant digits
5400	It is not possible to tell in its current form.

The number must be written as 5.4×10^3, 5.40×10^3, or 5.400×10^3, depending on the number of significant figures intended.

LO: Round numbers to the correct number of significant figures (Section 2.4).

When rounding numbers to the correct number of significant figures, round down if the last digit dropped is 4 or less; round up if the last digit dropped is 5 or more.

| EXAMPLE 2.21 | **ROUNDING** |

Round 6.442 and 6.456 to two significant figures each.

6.442 rounds to 6.4
6.456 rounds to 6.5

LO: Determine the correct number of significant figures in the results of multiplication and division calculations (Section 2.4).

The result of a multiplication or division should carry the same number of significant figures as the factor with the least number of significant figures.

| EXAMPLE 2.22 | **SIGNIFICANT FIGURES IN MULTIPLICATION AND DIVISION** |

Perform the calculation and report the answer to the correct number of significant figures.

$$8.54 \times 3.589 \div 4.2$$
$$= 7.2976$$
$$= 7.3$$

Round the final result to two significant figures to reflect the two significant figures in the factor with the least number of significant figures (4.2).

LO: Determine the correct number of significant figures in the results of addition and subtraction calculations (Section 2.4).

The result of an addition or subtraction should carry the same number of decimal places as the quantity carrying the least number of decimal places.

| EXAMPLE 2.23 | **SIGNIFICANT FIGURES IN ADDITION AND SUBTRACTION** |

Perform the operation and report the answer to the correct number of significant figures.

$$\begin{array}{r} 3.098 \\ +0.67 \\ -0.9452 \\ \hline 2.8228 = 2.82 \end{array}$$

Round the final result to two decimal places to reflect the two decimal places in the quantity with the least number of decimal places (0.67).

LO: Determine the correct number of significant figures in the results of calculations involving both addition/subtraction and multiplication/division (Section 2.4).

In calculations involving both addition/subtraction and multiplication/division, do the steps in parentheses first, keeping track of how many significant figures are in the answer by underlining the least significant figure, then proceeding with the remaining steps. Do not round off until the very end.

| EXAMPLE 2.24 | **SIGNIFICANT FIGURES IN CALCULATIONS INVOLVING BOTH ADDITION/ SUBTRACTION AND MULTIPLICATION/DIVISION** |

Perform the operation and report the answer to the correct number of significant figures.

$$8.16 \times (5.4323 - 5.411)$$
$$= 8.16 \times 0.02\underline{1}3$$
$$= 0.1738 = 0.1\underline{7}$$

LO: Convert between units (Sections 2.6, 2.7).

Solve unit conversion problems by following these steps.

1. **Sort** Write down the given quantity and its units and the quantity you are asked to find and its units.

2. **Strategize** Draw a solution map showing how to get from the given quantity to the quantity you are asked to find.

3. **Solve** Follow the solution map. Starting with the given quantity and its units, multiply by the appropriate conversion factor(s), canceling units, to arrive at the quantity to find in the desired units. Round the final answer to the correct number of significant figures.

4. **Check** Are the units correct? Does the answer make physical sense?

EXAMPLE 2.25	**UNIT CONVERSION**

Convert 108 ft to meters.

GIVEN: 108 ft

FIND: m

SOLUTION MAP

$$\frac{12 \text{ in.}}{1 \text{ ft}} \qquad \frac{1 \text{ m}}{39.37 \text{ in.}}$$

RELATIONSHIPS USED

$$1 \text{ m} = 39.37 \text{ in. (Table 2.3)}$$
$$1 \text{ ft} = 12 \text{ in. (by definition)}$$

SOLUTION

$$108 \text{ ft} \times \frac{12 \text{ in.}}{1 \text{ ft}} \times \frac{1 \text{ m}}{39.37 \text{ in.}}$$
$$= 32.918 \text{ m}$$
$$= 32.9 \text{ m}$$

The answer has the right units (meters), and it makes sense; because a meter is longer than a foot, the number of meters should be less than the number of feet.

LO: Convert units raised to a power (Section 2.8).

When working problems involving units raised to a power, raise the conversion factors to the same power.

1. **Sort** Write down the given quantity and its units and the quantity you are asked to find and its units.

2. **Strategize** Draw a solution map showing how to get from the given quantity to the quantity you are asked to find. Because the units are squared, you must square the conversion factor.

3. **Solve** Follow the solution map. Starting with the given quantity and its units, multiply by the appropriate conversion factor(s), canceling units, to arrive at the quantity you are asked to find in the desired units. Don't forget to square the conversion factor for squared units.

4. **Check** Are the units correct? Does the answer make physical sense?

EXAMPLE 2.26	**UNIT CONVERSION INVOLVING UNITS RAISED TO A POWER**

How many square meters are in 1.0 km²?

GIVEN: 1.0 km^2

FIND: m^2

SOLUTION MAP

$$\frac{(1000 \text{ m})^2}{(1 \text{ km})^2}$$

RELATIONSHIPS USED

1 km = 1000 m (Table 2.2)

SOLUTION

$$1.0 \text{ km}^2 \times \frac{(1000 \text{ m})^2}{(1 \text{ km})^2}$$
$$= 1.0 \text{ km}^2 \times \frac{1 \times 10^6 \text{ m}^2}{1 \text{ km}^2}$$
$$= 1.0 \times 10^6 \text{ m}^2$$

The units are correct. The answer makes physical sense. A square meter is much smaller than a square kilometer, so the number of square meters should be much larger than the number of square kilometers.

LO: Calculate the density of a substance (Section 2.9).

The density of an object or substance is its mass divided by its volume.

$$d = \frac{m}{V}$$

1. **Sort** Write down the given quantity and its units and the quantity you are asked to find and its units.

2. **Strategize** Draw a solution map showing how to get from the given quantity to the quantity you are asked to find. Use the definition of density as the equation that takes you from the mass and the volume to the density.

3. **Solve** Substitute the correct values into the equation for density.

4. **Check** Are the units correct? Does the answer make physical sense?

EXAMPLE 2.27   **CALCULATING DENSITY**

An object has a mass of 23.4 g and displaces 5.7 mL of water. Determine its density in grams per milliliter.

GIVEN:
$$m = 23.4 \text{ g}$$
$$V = 5.7 \text{ mL}$$

FIND: density in g/mL

SOLUTION MAP

$$d = \frac{m}{V}$$

RELATIONSHIPS USED

$$d = \frac{m}{V} \text{ (definition of density)}$$

SOLUTION

$$d = \frac{m}{V}$$
$$= \frac{23.4 \text{ g}}{5.7 \text{ mL}}$$
$$= 4.11 \text{ g/mL}$$
$$= 4.1 \text{ g/mL}$$

The units (g/mL) are units of density. The answer is in the range of values for the densities of liquids and solids (see Table 2.4).

LO: Use density as a conversion factor (Section 2.9).

You can use density as a conversion factor from mass to volume or from volume to mass. To convert between volume and mass, use density directly. To convert between mass and volume, invert the density.

1. **Sort** Write down the given quantity and its units and the quantity you are asked to find and its units.

2. **Strategize** Draw a solution map showing how to get from the given quantity to the quantity you are asked to find. Use the inverse of the density to convert from g to mL.

3. **Solve** Begin with the given quantity and multiply by the appropriate conversion factors to arrive at the quantity you are asked to find. Round to the correct number of significant figures.

4. **Check** Are the units correct? Does the answer make physical sense?

EXAMPLE 2.28   **DENSITY AS A CONVERSION FACTOR**

What is the volume in liters of 321 g of a liquid with a density of 0.84 g/mL?

GIVEN: 321 g

FIND: volume in L

SOLUTION MAP

$$\frac{1 \text{ mL}}{0.84 \text{ g}} \qquad \frac{1 \text{ L}}{1000 \text{ mL}}$$

RELATIONSHIPS USED
0.84 g/mL (given in the problem)
1 L = 1000 mL (Table 2.2)

SOLUTION

$$321 \text{ g} \times \frac{1 \text{ mL}}{0.84 \text{ g}} \times \frac{1 \text{ L}}{1000 \text{ mL}}$$
$$= 0.382 \text{ L} = 0.38 \text{ L}$$

The answer is in the correct units. The magnitude seems right because the density is slightly less than 1; therefore the volume (382 mL) should be slightly greater than the mass (321 g).

KEY TERMS

conversion factor **[2.6]**
decimal part **[2.2]**
density **[2.9]**
English system **[2.5]**
exponent **[2.2]**

exponential part **[2.2]**
International System **[2.5]**
kilogram (kg) **[2.5]**
liter (L) **[2.5]**
mass **[2.5]**

meter (m) **[2.5]**
metric system **[2.5]**
prefix multipliers **[2.5]**
scientific notation **[2.2]**
second (s) **[2.5]**

SI units **[2.5]**
significant figures (digits) **[2.3]**
solution map **[2.6]**
units **[2.5]**
volume **[2.5]**

EXERCISES

QUESTIONS

Answers to all questions numbered in blue appear in the Answers section at the back of the book.

1. Why is it necessary to include units when reporting scientific measurements?
2. Why are the number of digits reported in scientific measurements important?
3. Why is scientific notation useful?
4. If a measured quantity is written correctly, which digits are certain? Which are uncertain?
5. When do zeros count as significant digits and when don't they count?
6. How many significant digits are there in exact numbers? What kinds of numbers are exact?
7. What limits the number of significant digits in a calculation involving only multiplication and division?
8. What limits the number of significant digits in a calculation involving only addition and subtraction?
9. How do we determine significant figures in calculations involving both addition/subtraction and multiplication/division?
10. What are the rules for rounding numbers?
11. What are the basic SI units of length, mass, and time?
12. List the common units of volume.
13. Suppose you are trying to measure the diameter of a Frisbee. What unit and prefix multiplier should you use?
14. What is the difference between mass and weight?
15. Using a metric ruler, measure these objects to the correct number of significant figures.
    (a) quarter (diameter)
    (b) dime (diameter)
    (c) notebook paper (width)
    (d) this book (width)
16. Using a stopwatch, measure each time to the correct number of significant figures.
    (a) time between your heartbeats
    (b) time it takes you to do the next problem
    (c) time between your breaths

17. Explain why units are important in calculations.
18. How are units treated in a calculation?
19. What is a conversion factor?
20. Why does the fundamental value of a quantity not change when you multiply the quantity by a conversion factor?
21. Write the conversion factor that converts a measurement in inches to feet. How does the conversion factor change for converting a measurement in feet to inches?
22. Write conversion factors for each.
    (a) miles to kilometers   (c) gallons to liters
    (b) kilometers to miles   (d) liters to gallons
23. This book outlines a four-step problem-solving strategy. Describe each step and its significance.
    (a) Sort   (c) Solve
    (b) Strategize (d) Check
24. Experienced problem solvers always consider both the value and units of their answer to a problem. Why?
25. Draw a solution map to convert a measurement in grams to pounds.
26. Draw a solution map to convert a measurement in milliliters to gallons.
27. Draw a solution map to convert a measurement in meters to feet.
28. Draw a solution map to convert a measurement in ounces to grams. (1 lb = 16 oz)
29. What is density? Explain why density can work as a conversion factor. Between what quantities does it convert?
30. Explain how you would calculate the density of a substance. Include a solution map in your explanation.

PROBLEMS

Note: The exercises in the Problems section are paired, and the answers to the odd-numbered exercises (numbered in blue) appear in the Answers section at the back of the book.

SCIENTIFIC NOTATION

31. Express each number in scientific notation.
    (a) 37,692,000 (population of California)
    (b) 1,360,000 (population of Hawaii)
    (c) 19,306,000 (population of New York)
    (d) 568,000 (population of Wyoming)

32. Express each number in scientific notation.
    (a) 6,974,000,000 (population of the world)
    (b) 1,344,000,000 (population of China)
    (c) 11,254,000 (population of Cuba)
    (d) 4,487,000 (population of Ireland)

33. Express each number in scientific notation.
(a) 0.00000000007461 m (length of a hydrogen–hydrogen chemical bond)
(b) 0.0000158 mi (number of miles in an inch)
(c) 0.000000632 m (wavelength of red light)
(d) 0.000015 m (diameter of a human hair)

34. Express each number in scientific notation.
(a) 0.000000001 s (time it takes light to travel 1 ft)
(b) 0.143 s (time it takes light to travel around the world)
(c) 0.000000000001 s (time it takes a chemical bond to undergo one vibration)
(d) 0.000001 m (approximate size of a dust particle)

35. Express each number in decimal notation (i.e., express the number without using scientific notation).
(a) 6.022×10^{23} (number of carbon atoms in 12.01 g of carbon)
(b) 1.6×10^{-19} C (charge of a proton in coulombs)
(c) 2.99×10^8 m/s (speed of light)
(d) 3.44×10^2 m/s (speed of sound)

36. Express each number in decimal notation (i.e., express the number without using scientific notation).
(a) 450×10^{-9} m (wavelength of blue light)
(b) 13.7×10^9 years (approximate age of the universe)
(c) 5×10^9 years (approximate age of Earth)
(d) 5.0×10^1 years (approximate age of this author)

37. Express each number in decimal notation (i.e., express the number without using scientific notation).
(a) 3.22×10^7
(b) 7.2×10^{-3}
(c) 1.18×10^{11}
(d) 9.43×10^{-6}

38. Express each number in decimal notation (i.e., express the number without using scientific notation).
(a) 1.30×10^6
(b) 1.1×10^{-4}
(c) 1.9×10^2
(d) 7.41×10^{-10}

39. Complete the table.

Decimal Notation	Scientific Notation
2,000,000,000	_____
_____	1.211×10^9
0.000874	_____
_____	3.2×10^{11}

40. Complete the table.

Decimal Notation	Scientific Notation
_____	4.2×10^{-3}
315,171,000	_____
_____	1.8×10^{-11}
1,232,000	_____

SIGNIFICANT FIGURES

41. Read each instrument to the correct number of significant figures. Laboratory glassware should always be read from the bottom of the *meniscus* (the curved surface at the top of the liquid column).

(a)   (b) Celsius

(c) Celsius

(d)

42. Read each instrument to the correct number of significant figures. Laboratory glassware should always be read from the bottom of the meniscus (the curved surface at the top of the liquid column).

(a)

Note: A burette reads from the top down.

(b)

Note: A pipette reads from the top down.

(c)

Note: Digital balances normally display mass to the correct number of significant figures for that
(d) particular balance.

---

43. For each measured quantity, underline the zeros that are significant and draw an X through the zeros that are not.
(a) 0.005050 m
(b) 0.0000000000000060 s
(c) 220,103 kg
(d) 0.00108 in.

44. For each measured quantity, underline the zeros that are significant and draw an X through the zeros that are not.
(a) 0.00010320 s
(b) 1,322,600,324 kg
(c) 0.0001240 in.
(d) 0.02061 m

45. How many significant figures are in each measured quantity?
(a) 0.001125 m
(b) 0.1125 m
(c) 1.12500×10^4 m
(d) 11205 m

46. How many significant figures are in each measured quantity?
(a) 13001 kg
(b) 13111 kg
(c) 1.30×10^4 kg
(d) 0.00013 kg

47. Correct any entries in the table that are wrong.

Quantity	Significant Figures
(a) 895675 m	6
(b) 0.000869 kg	6
(c) 0.5672100 s	5
(d) 6.022×10^{23} atoms	4

48. Correct any entries in the table that are wrong.

Quantity	Significant Figures
(a) 24 days	2
(b) 5.6×10^{-12} s	3
(c) 3.14 m	3
(d) 0.00383 g	5

ROUNDING

49. Round each number to four significant figures.
(a) 255.98612
(b) 0.0004893222
(c) 2.900856×10^{-4}
(d) 2,231,479

50. Round each number to three significant figures.
(a) 10,776.522
(b) 4.999902×10^6
(c) 1.3499999995
(d) 0.0000344988

51. Round each number to two significant figures.
(a) 2.34
(b) 2.35
(c) 2.349
(d) 2.359

52. Round each number to three significant figures.
(a) 65.74
(b) 65.749
(c) 65.75
(d) 65.750

53. Each number is supposed to be rounded to three significant figures. Correct the ones that are incorrectly rounded.
(a) 42.3492 to 42.4
(b) 56.9971 to 57.0
(c) 231.904 to 232
(d) 0.04555 to 0.046

54. Each number is supposed to be rounded to two significant figures. Correct the ones that are incorrectly rounded.
(a) 1.249×10^3 to 1.3×10^3
(b) 3.999×10^2 to 40
(c) 56.21 to 56.2
(d) 0.009964 to 0.010

55. Round the number on the left to the number of significant figures indicated by the example in the first row. (Use scientific notation as needed to avoid ambiguity.)

Number	Rounded to 4 Significant Figures	Rounded to 2 Significant Figures	Rounded to 1 Significant Figure
1.45815	1.458	1.5	1
8.32466			
84.57225			
132.5512			

56. Round the number on the left to the number of significant figures indicated by the example in the first row. (Use scientific notation as needed to avoid ambiguity.)

Number	Rounded to 4 Significant Figures	Rounded to 2 Significant Figures	Rounded to 1 Significant Figure
94.52118	94.52	95	9×10^1
105.4545			
0.455981			
0.009999991			

SIGNIFICANT FIGURES IN CALCULATIONS

57. Perform each calculation to the correct number of significant figures.
(a) $4.5 \times 0.03060 \times 0.391$
(b) $5.55 \div 8.97$
(c) $(7.890 \times 10^{12}) \div (6.7 \times 10^4)$
(d) $67.8 \times 9.8 \div 100.04$

58. Perform each calculation to the correct number of significant figures.
(a) $89.3 \times 77.0 \times 0.08$
(b) $(5.01 \times 10^5) \div (7.8 \times 10^2)$
(c) $4.005 \times 74 \times 0.007$
(d) $453 \div 2.031$

59. Correct any answers that have the incorrect number of significant figures.
  (a) $34.00 \times 567 \div 4.564 = 4.2239 \times 10^3$
  (b) $79.3 \div 0.004 \times 35.4 = 7 \times 10^5$
  (c) $89.763 \div 22.4581 = 3.997$
  (d) $(4.32 \times 10^{12}) \div (3.1 \times 10^{-4}) = 1.4 \times 10^{16}$

60. Correct any answers that have the incorrect number of significant figures.
  (a) $45.3254 \times 89.00205 = 4034.05$
  (b) $0.00740 \times 45.0901 = 0.334$
  (c) $49857 \div 904875 = 0.05510$
  (d) $0.009090 \times 6007.2 = 54.605$

61. Perform each calculation to the correct number of significant figures.
  (a) $87.6 + 9.888 + 2.3 + 10.77$
  (b) $43.7 - 2.341$
  (c) $89.6 + 98.33 - 4.674$
  (d) $6.99 - 5.772$

62. Perform each calculation to the correct number of significant figures.
  (a) $1459.3 + 9.77 + 4.32$
  (b) $0.004 + 0.09879$
  (c) $432 + 7.3 - 28.523$
  (d) $2.4 + 1.777$

63. Correct any answers that have the incorrect number of significant figures.
  (a) $(3.8 \times 10^5) - (8.45 \times 10^5) = -4.7 \times 10^5$
  (b) $0.00456 + 1.0936 = 1.10$
  (c) $8475.45 - 34.899 = 8440.55$
  (d) $908.87 - 905.34095 = 3.5291$

64. Correct any answers that have the incorrect number of significant figures.
  (a) $78.9 + 890.43 - 23 = 9.5 \times 10^2$
  (b) $9354 - 3489.56 + 34.3 = 5898.74$
  (c) $0.00407 + 0.0943 = 0.0984$
  (d) $0.00896 - 0.007 = 0.00196$

65. Perform each calculation to the correct number of significant figures.
  (a) $(78.4 - 44.889) \div 0.0087$
  (b) $(34.6784 \times 5.38) + 445.56$
  (c) $(78.7 \times 10^5 \div 88.529) + 356.99$
  (d) $(892 \div 986.7) + 5.44$

66. Perform each calculation to the correct number of significant figures.
  (a) $(1.7 \times 10^6 \div 2.63 \times 10^5) + 7.33$
  (b) $(568.99 - 232.1) \div 5.3$
  (c) $(9443 + 45 - 9.9) \times 8.1 \times 10^6$
  (d) $(3.14 \times 2.4367) - 2.34$

67. Correct any answers that have the incorrect number of significant figures.
  (a) $(78.56 - 9.44) \times 45.6 = 3152$
  (b) $(8.9 \times 10^5 \div 2.348 \times 10^2) + 121 = 3.9 \times 10^3$
  (c) $(45.8 \div 3.2) - 12.3 = 2$
  (d) $(4.5 \times 10^3 - 1.53 \times 10^3) \div 34.5 = 86$

68. Correct any answers that have the incorrect number of significant figures.
  (a) $(908.4 - 3.4) \div 3.52 \times 10^4 = 0.026$
  (b) $(1206.7 - 0.904) \times 89 = 1.07 \times 10^5$
  (c) $(876.90 + 98.1) \div 56.998 = 17.11$
  (d) $(4.55 \div 407859) + 1.00098 = 1.00210$

UNIT CONVERSION

69. Perform each conversion.
  (a) 3.55 kg to grams
  (b) 8944 mm to meters
  (c) 4598 mg to kilograms
  (d) 0.0187 L to milliliters

70. Perform each conversion.
  (a) 155.5 cm to meters
  (b) 2491.6 g to kilograms
  (c) 248 cm to millimeters
  (d) 6781 mL to liters

71. Perform each conversion.
  (a) 5.88 dL to liters
  (b) 3.41×10^{-5} g to micrograms
  (c) 1.01×10^{-8} s to nanoseconds
  (d) 2.19 pm to meters

72. Perform each conversion.
  (a) 1.08 Mm to kilometers
  (b) 4.88 fs to picoseconds
  (c) 7.39×10^{11} m to gigameters
  (d) 1.15×10^{-10} m to picometers

73. Perform each conversion.
  (a) 22.5 in. to centimeters
  (b) 126 ft to meters
  (c) 825 yd to kilometers
  (d) 2.4 in. to millimeters

74. Perform each conversion.
  (a) 78.3 in. to centimeters
  (b) 445 yd to meters
  (c) 336 ft to centimeters
  (d) 45.3 in. to millimeters

75. Perform each conversion.
  (a) 40.0 cm to inches
  (b) 27.8 m to feet
  (c) 10.0 km to miles
  (d) 3845 kg to pounds

76. Perform each conversion.
  (a) 254 cm to inches
  (b) 89 mm to inches
  (c) 7.5 L to quarts
  (d) 122 kg to pounds

77. Complete the table.

m	km	Mm	Gm	Tm
5.08×10^8 m	____	508 Mm	____	____
____	____	27,976 Mm	____	____
____	____	____	____	1.77 Tm
____	1.5×10^5 km	____	____	____
____	____	____	423 Gm	____

78. Complete the table.

s	ms	μs	ns	ps
1.31×10^{-4} s	____	131μs	____	____
____	____	____	____	12.6 ps
____	____	____	155 ns	____
____	1.99×10^{-3} ms	____	____	____
____	____	8.66×10^{-5} μs	____	____

79. Convert 2.255×10^{10} g to each unit.
(a) kg
(b) Mg
(c) mg
(d) metric tons (1 metric ton = 1000 kg)

80. Convert 1.88×10^{-6} g to each unit.
(a) mg
(b) cg
(c) ng
(d) μg

81. A student loses 3.3 lb in one month. How many grams did he lose?

82. A student gains 1.9 lb in two weeks. How many grams did he gain?

83. A runner wants to run 10.0 km. She knows that her running pace is 7.5 mi/h. How many minutes must she run? *Hint:* Use 7.5 mi/h as a conversion factor between distance and time.

84. A cyclist rides at an average speed of 24 mi/h. If he wants to bike 195 km, how long (in hours) must he ride?

85. A recipe calls for 5.0 qt of milk. What is this quantity in cubic centimeters?

86. A gas can holds 2.0 gal of gasoline. What is this quantity in cubic centimeters?

UNITS RAISED TO A POWER

87. Fill in the blanks.
(a) $1.0 \text{ km}^2 = $ ____ m^2
(b) $1.0 \text{ cm}^3 = $ ____ m^3
(c) $1.0 \text{ mm}^3 = $ ____ m^3

88. Fill in the blanks.
(a) $1.0 \text{ ft}^2 = $ ____ in.^2
(b) $1.0 \text{ yd}^2 = $ ____ ft^2
(c) $1.0 \text{ m}^2 = $ ____ yd^2

89. The hydrogen atom has a volume of approximately 6.2×10^{-31} m^3. What is this volume in each unit?
(a) cubic picometers
(b) cubic nanometers
(c) cubic angstroms (1 angstrom = 10^{-10} m)

90. Earth has a surface area of 197 million square miles. What is its area in each unit?
(a) square kilometers
(b) square megameters
(c) square decimeters

91. A house has an area of 215 m^2. What is its area in each unit?
(a) km^2
(b) dm^2
(c) cm^2

92. A classroom has a volume of 285 m^3. What is its volume in each unit?
(a) km^3
(b) dm^3
(c) cm^3

93. Total U.S. farmland occupies 954 million acres. How many square miles is this?
(1 acre = 43,560 ft^2; 1 mi = 5280 ft)

94. The average U.S. farm occupies 435 acres. How many square miles is this?
(1 acre = 43,560 ft^2; 1 mi = 5280 ft)

DENSITY

95. A sample of an unknown metal has a mass of 35.4 g and a volume of 3.11 cm^3. Calculate its density and identify the metal by comparison to Table 2.4.

96. A new penny has a mass of 2.49 g and a volume of 0.349 cm^3. Is the penny pure copper?

97. Glycerol is a syrupy liquid often used in cosmetics and soaps. A 2.50-L sample of pure glycerol has a mass of 3.15×10^3 g. What is the density of glycerol in grams per cubic centimeter?

98. An aluminum engine block has a volume of 4.77 L and a mass of 12.88 kg. What is the density of the aluminum in grams per cubic centimeter?

99. A supposedly gold crown is tested to determine its density. It displaces 10.7 mL of water and has a mass of 206 g. Could the crown be made of gold?

100. A vase is said to be solid platinum. It displaces 18.65 mL of water and has a mass of 157 g. Could the vase be solid platinum?

101. Ethylene glycol (antifreeze) has a density of 1.11 g/cm^3.
   (a) What is the mass in grams of 387 mL of ethylene glycol?
   (b) What is the volume in liters of 3.46 kg of ethylene glycol?

102. Acetone (fingernail-polish remover) has a density of 0.7857 g/cm^3.
   (a) What is the mass in grams of 17.56 mL of acetone?
   (b) What is the volume in milliliters of 7.22 g of acetone?

CUMULATIVE PROBLEMS

103. A thief uses a bag of sand to replace a gold statue that sits on a weight-sensitive, alarmed pedestal. The bag of sand and the statue have exactly the same volume, 1.75 L. (Assume that the mass of the bag is negligible.)
   (a) Calculate the mass of each object. (density of gold = 19.3 g/cm^3; density of sand = 3.00 g/cm^3)
   (b) Did the thief set off the alarm? Explain.

104. One of the particles in an atom is the proton. A proton has a radius of approximately 1.0×10^{-13} cm and a mass of 1.7×10^{-24} g. Determine the density of a proton.

$$\left(\text{volume of a sphere} = \frac{4}{3}\pi r^3; \pi = 3.14 \right)$$

105. A block of metal has a volume of 13.4 in.^{3} and weighs 5.14 lb. What is its density in grams per cubic centimeter?

106. A log is either oak or pine. It displaces 2.7 gal of water and weighs 19.8 lb. Is the log oak or pine? (density of oak = 0.9 g/cm^3; density of pine = 0.4 g/cm^3)

107. The density of aluminum is 2.7 g/cm^3. What is its density in kilograms per cubic meter?

108. The density of platinum is 21.4 g/cm^3. What is its density in pounds per cubic inch?

109. A typical backyard swimming pool holds 150 yd^3 of water. What is the mass in pounds of the water?

110. An iceberg has a volume of 8975 ft^3. What is the mass in kilograms of the iceberg? The density of ice is 0.917 g/cm^3.

111. The mass of fuel in an airplane must be determined before takeoff. If a 747 contains 155,211 L of fuel, what is the mass of the fuel in kilograms? Assume the density of the fuel to be 0.768 g/cm^3.

112. A backpacker carries 2.5 L of white gas as fuel for her stove. How many pounds does the fuel add to her load? Assume the density of white gas to be 0.79 g/cm^3.

113. Honda produces a hybrid electric car called the Honda Insight. The Insight has both a gasoline-powered engine and an electric motor and has an EPA gas mileage rating of 43 mi per gallon on the highway. What is the Insight's rating in kilometers per liter?

114. You rent a car in Germany with a gas mileage rating of 12.8 km/L. What is its rating in miles per gallon?

115. A car has a mileage rating of 38 mi per gallon of gasoline. How many miles can the car travel on 76.5 L of gasoline?

116. A hybrid SUV consumes fuel at a rate of 12.8 km/L. How many miles can the car travel on 22.5 gal of gasoline?

117. Block A of an unknown metal has a volume of 125 cm^3. Block B of a different metal has a volume of 145 cm^3. If block A has a greater mass than block B, what can be said of the relative densities of the two metals? (Assume that both blocks are solid.)

118. Block A of an unknown metal has a volume of 125 cm^3. Block B of a different metal has a volume of 105 cm^3. If block A has a greater mass than block B, what can be said of the relative densities of the two metals? (Assume that both blocks are solid.)

119. You measure the masses and volumes of two cylinders. The mass of cylinder 1 is 1.35 times the mass of cylinder 2. The volume of cylinder 1 is 0.792 times the volume of cylinder 2. If the density of cylinder 1 is 3.85 g/cm³, what is the density of cylinder 2?

120. A bag contains a mixture of copper and lead BBs. The average density of the BBs is 9.87 g/cm³. Assuming that the copper and lead are pure, determine the relative amounts of each kind of BB.

121. An aluminum sphere has a mass of 25.8 g. Find the radius of the sphere. (The density of aluminum is 2.7 g/cm³, and the volume of a sphere is given by the equation $V = \frac{4}{3}\pi r^3$.)

122. A copper cube has a mass of 87.2 g. Find the edge length of the cube. (The density of copper is 8.96 g/cm³, and the volume of a cube is equal to the edge length cubed.)

HIGHLIGHT PROBLEMS

123. In 1999, NASA lost a $94 million orbiter because one group of engineers used metric units in their calculations while another group used English units. Consequently, the orbiter descended too far into the Martian atmosphere and burned up. Suppose that the orbiter was to have established orbit at 155 km and that one group of engineers specified this distance as 1.55×10^5 m. Suppose further that a second group of engineers programmed the orbiter to go to 1.55×10^5 ft. What was the difference in kilometers between the two altitudes? How low did the probe go?

124. A NASA satellite showed that in 2012 the ozone hole over Antarctica had a maximum surface area of 21.2 million km². The largest ozone hole on record occurred in 2006 and had a surface area of 29.6 million km². Calculate the difference in diameter (in meters) between the ozone hole in 2012 and in 2006.

▲ A layer of ozone gas (a form of oxygen) in the upper atmosphere protects Earth from harmful ultraviolet radiation in sunlight. Human-made chemicals react with the ozone and deplete it, especially over the Antarctic at certain times of the year (the so-called ozone hole). The region of low ozone concentration in 2006 (represented here by the dark purple color) was the largest on record.

▲ The $94 million Mars Climate Orbiter was lost in the Martian atmosphere in 1999 because two groups of engineers failed to communicate with each other about the units in their calculations.

125. In 1999, scientists discovered a new class of black holes with masses 100 to 10,000 times the mass of our sun, but occupying less space than our moon. Suppose that one of these black holes has a mass of 1×10^3 suns and a radius equal to one-half the radius of our moon. What is its density in grams per cubic centimeter? The mass of the sun is 2.0×10^{30} kg, and the radius of the moon is 2.16×10^3 mi. (Volume of a sphere = $\frac{4}{3}\pi r^3$.)

126. A titanium bicycle frame contains the same amount of titanium as a titanium cube measuring 6.8 cm on a side. Use the density of titanium to calculate the mass in kilograms of titanium in the frame. What would be the mass of a similar frame composed of iron?

Titanium

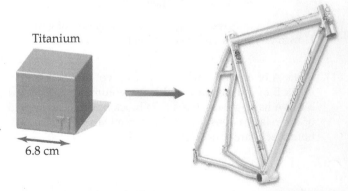

6.8 cm

▲ A titanium bicycle frame contains the same amount of titanium as a titanium cube measuring 6.8 cm on a side.

QUESTIONS FOR GROUP WORK

Discuss these questions with the group and record your consensus answer.

127. Look up the thickness of a human hair.
  (a) Convert it to an SI standard unit (if it isn't already).
  (b) Write it in scientific notation.
  (c) Write it without scientific notation (you may need some zeros!).
  (d) Write it with an appropriate prefix on a base unit.
  Now complete the same exercises with the distance from the Earth to the sun.

128. The following statements are all true.
  (a) Jessica's house is 5 km from the grocery store.
  (b) Jessica's house is 4.73 km from the grocery store.
  (c) Jessica's house is 4.73297 km from the grocery store.
  How can they all be true? What does the number of digits communicate? What sort of device would Jessica need to make the claim in each statement?

139. Convert the height of each group member from feet and inches into meters. Once you determine your heights in meters, calculate the sum of all your heights. Use appropriate rules for significant figures at each step.

►Answers to Skillbuilder Exercises

Skillbuilder 2.1 $\$1.6342 \times 10^{13}$

Skillbuilder 2.2 3.8×10^{-5}

Skillbuilder 2.3   103.4 °F

Skillbuilder 2.4
  (a) four significant figures
  (b) three significant figures
  (c) two significant figures
  (d) unlimited significant figures
  (e) three significant figures
  (f) ambiguous

Skillbuilder 2.5
  (a) 0.001 or 1×10^{-3}
  (b) 0.204

Skillbuilder 2.6
  (a) 7.6
  (b) 131.11

Skillbuilder 2.7
  (a) 1288
  (b) 3.12

Skillbuilder 2.8   22.0 in.

Skillbuilder 2.9   5.678 km

Skillbuilder 2.10   0.28 L

Skillbuilder 2.11   46.6 laps

Skillbuilder Plus, p. 33 1.06×10^4 m

Skillbuilder 2.12   4747 cm^3

Skillbuilder 2.13 1.52×10^5 $in.^3$

Skillbuilder 2.14   Yes, the density is 21.4 g/cm^3 and matches that of platinum.

Skillbuilder 2.15 4.4×10^{-2} cm^3

Skillbuilder Plus, p. 38   1.95 kg

Skillbuilder 2.16   16 kg

Skillbuilder 2.17 $d = 19.3$ g/cm^3; yes, the density is consistent with that of gold.

►Answers to Conceptual Checkpoints

2.1 (c)   Multiplying by 10^{-3} is equivalent to moving the decimal point three places to the left.

2.2 (b)   The last digit is considered to be uncertain by ±1.

2.3 (b)   The result of the calculation in **(a)** would be reported as 4; the result of the calculation in **(b)** would be reported as 1.5.

2.4 (d)   The diameter would be expressed as 28 nm.

2.5 (a)   The unit of ft should be in the denominator, and the conversion factor in **(c)** is incorrect (because 1 in. ≠ 12 ft).

2.6 (c)   Kilometers must appear in the numerator and meters in the denominator, and the conversion factor in **(d)** is incorrect (10^3 km ≠ 1 m).

2.7 (d)   (3 ft) × (3 ft) × (3 ft) = 27 ft^3

Everything that you can see in this room is made of matter. As students of chemistry, we are interested in how the differences between different kinds of matter are related to the differences between the molecules and atoms that compose the matter. The molecular structures shown here are water molecules on the left and carbon atoms in graphite on the right.

Matter and Energy 3

"Thus, the task is, not so much to see what no one has yet seen; but to think what nobody has yet thought, about that which everybody sees." —Erwin Schrödinger (1887–1961)

CHAPTER OUTLINE

3.1 In Your Room

Look around the room you are in—what do you see? You might see your desk, your bed, or a glass of water. Maybe you have a window and can see trees, grass, or mountains. You can certainly see this book and possibly the table it sits on. What are these things made of? They are all made of *matter*, which we will define more carefully shortly. For now, know that all you see is matter—your desk, your bed, the glass of water, the trees, the mountains, and this book. Some of what you don't see is matter as well. For example, you are constantly breathing air, which is also matter, into and out of your lungs. You feel the matter in air when you feel wind on your skin. Virtually everything is made of matter.

Think about the differences between different kinds of matter. Air is different from water, and water is different from wood. One of our first tasks as we learn about matter is to identify the similarities and differences among different kinds of matter. How are sugar and salt similar? How are air and water different? Why are they different? Why is a mixture of sugar and water similar to a mixture of salt and water but different from a mixture of sand and water? As students of chemistry, we are particularly interested in the similarities and differences between various kinds of matter and how these reflect the similarities and differences between their component atoms and molecules. We strive to understand the connection between the macroscopic world and the molecular one.

3.2 What Is Matter?

LO: Define matter, atoms, and molecules.

We define **matter** as anything that occupies space and has mass. Some types of matter—such as steel, water, wood, and plastic—are readily visible to our eyes. Other types of matter—such as air or microscopic dust—are not visible

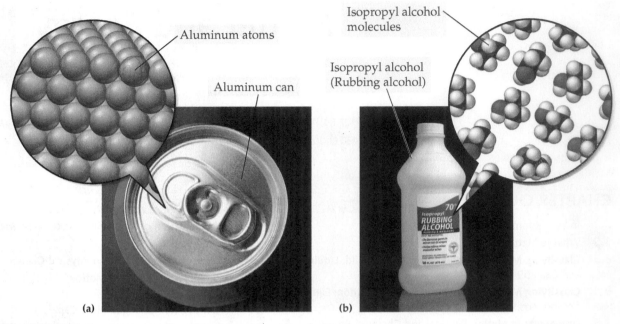

Isopropyl alcohol molecules

Aluminum atoms

Isopropyl alcohol (Rubbing alcohol)

Aluminum can

(a)

(b)

▲ **FIGURE 3.1** **Atoms and molecules** All matter is ultimately composed of atoms. **(a)** In some substances, such as aluminum, the atoms exist as independent particles. **(b)** In other substances, such as rubbing alcohol, several atoms bond together in well-defined structures called molecules.

to our naked eyes. Matter may sometimes appear smooth and continuous, but actually it is not. Matter is ultimately composed of **atoms**, submicroscopic particles that are the fundamental building blocks of matter (▲ Figure 3.1a). In many cases, these atoms are bonded together to form **molecules**, two or more atoms joined to one another in specific geometric arrangements (Figure 3.1b). Recent advances in microscopy have allowed us to image the atoms (▼ Figure 3.2) and molecules (▼ Figure 3.3) that compose matter, sometimes with stunning clarity.

▲ **FIGURE 3.2** **Scanning tunneling microscope image of nickel atoms** A scanning tunneling microscope (STM) creates an image by scanning a surface with a tip of atomic dimensions. It can distinguish individual atoms, seen as blue bumps, in this image. (*Source:* Reprint Courtesy of International Business Machines Corporation, copyright © International Business Machines Corporation.)

▲ **FIGURE 3.3** **Scanning tunneling microscope image of a DNA molecule** DNA is the hereditary material that encodes the operating instructions for most cells in living organisms. In this image, the DNA molecule is yellow, and the double-stranded structure of DNA is discernible.

3.3   Classifying Matter According to Its State: Solid, Liquid, and Gas

LO: Classify matter as solid, liquid, or gas.

The common **states of matter** are **solid**, **liquid**, and **gas** (▼ Figure 3.4). In solid matter, atoms or molecules pack close to each other in fixed locations. Although neighboring atoms or molecules in a solid may vibrate or oscillate, they do not move around each other, giving solids their familiar fixed volume and rigid shape.

▶ **FIGURE 3.4   Three states of matter**   Water exists as ice (solid), water (liquid), and steam (gas). In ice, the water molecules are closely spaced and, although they vibrate about a fixed point, they do not generally move relative to one another. In liquid water, the water molecules are also closely spaced but are free to move around and past each other. In steam, water molecules are separated by large distances and do not interact significantly with one another.

Ice, diamond, quartz, and iron are examples of solid matter. Solid matter may be **crystalline**, in which case its atoms or molecules arrange in geometric patterns with long-range, repeating order (◀ Figure 3.5a), or it may be **amorphous**, in which case its atoms or molecules do not have long-range order (◀ Figure 3.5b). Examples of *crystalline* solids include salt (▼ Figure 3.6) and diamond; the well-ordered, geometric shapes of salt and diamond crystals reflect the well-ordered geometric arrangement of their atoms. Examples of *amorphous* solids include glass, rubber, and plastic.

(a) Crystalline solid

(b) Amorphous solid

▲ **FIGURE 3.5   Types of solid matter**   **(a)** In a crystalline solid, atoms or molecules occupy specific positions to create a well-ordered, three-dimensional structure. **(b)** In an amorphous solid, atoms do not have any long-range order.

▲ **FIGURE 3.6   Salt: a crystalline solid**   Sodium chloride is an example of a crystalline solid. The well-ordered, cubic shape of salt crystals is due to the well-ordered, cubic arrangement of its atoms.

Solid—not compressible

Gas—compressible

▲ **FIGURE 3.7   Gases are compressible**   Because the atoms or molecules that compose gases are not in contact with one another, we can compress gases.

In liquid matter, atoms or molecules are close to each other (about as close as molecules in a solid), but they are free to move around and by each other. Like solids, liquids have a fixed volume because their atoms or molecules are in close contact. Unlike solids, however, liquids assume the shape of their container because the atoms or molecules are free to move relative to one another. Water, gasoline, alcohol, and mercury are examples of liquid matter.

In gaseous matter, atoms or molecules are separated by large distances and are free to move relative to one another. Because the atoms or molecules that compose gases are not in contact with one another, gases are **compressible** (◄ Figure 3.7). When we inflate a bicycle tire, for example, we push more atoms and molecules into the same space, compressing them and making the tire harder. Gases always assume the shape and volume of their containers. Oxygen, helium, and carbon dioxide are all good examples of gases. Table 3.1 summarizes the properties of solids, liquids, and gases.

TABLE 3.1   Properties of Liquids, Solids, and Gases

State	Atomic/ Molecular Motion	Atomic/ Molecular Spacing	Shape	Volume	Compressibility
Solid	Oscillation/ vibration about fixed point	Close together	Definite	Definite	Incompressible
Liquid	Free to move relative to one another	Close together	Indefinite	Definite	Incompressible
Gas	Free to move relative to one another	Far apart	Indefinite	Indefinite	Compressible

✓ **CONCEPTUAL CHECKPOINT 3.1**

Which image best represents matter in the gas state?

(a)   (b)   (c)

Note: You can find the answers to all Conceptual Checkpoints at the end of the chapter.

3.4   Classifying Matter According to Its Composition: Elements, Compounds, and Mixtures

LO: Classify matter as element, compound, or mixture.

In addition to classifying matter according to its state, we can classify it according to its composition (► Figure 3.8). Matter may be either a **pure substance**, composed of only one type of atom or molecule, or a **mixture**, composed of two or more different types of atoms or molecules combined in variable proportions.

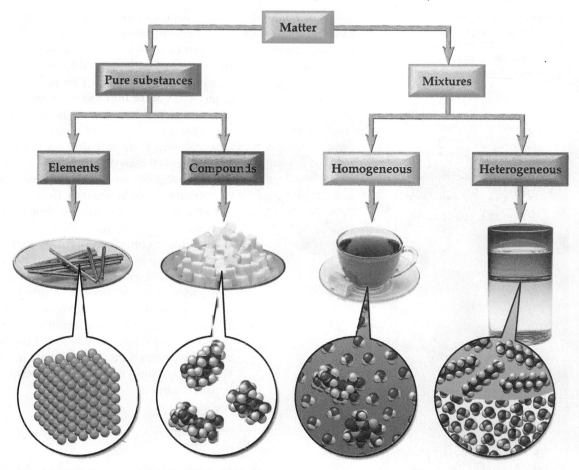

▲ **FIGURE 3.8   Classification of matter**   Matter may be a pure substance or a mixture. A pure substance may be either an element (such as copper) or a compound (such as sugar), and a mixture may be either homogeneous (such as sweetened tea) or heterogeneous (such as gasoline and water).

Pure substances are composed of only one type of atom or molecule. Helium and water are both pure substances. The atoms that compose helium are all helium atoms, and the molecules that compose water are all water molecules—no other atoms or molecules are mixed in.

Pure substances can themselves be divided into two types: elements and compounds. Copper is an example of an **element**, a substance that cannot be broken down into simpler substances. The graphite in pencils is also an element—carbon. No chemical transformation can decompose graphite into simpler substances; it is pure carbon. All known elements are listed in the periodic table in the inside front cover of this book and in alphabetical order on the inside back cover of this book.

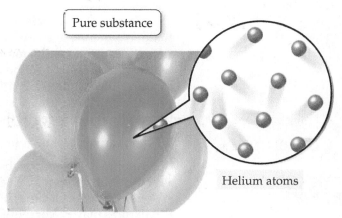

Pure substance

Helium atoms

▲ Helium is a pure substance composed only of helium atoms.

A compound is composed of different atoms that are chemically united (bonded). A mixture is composed of different substances that are not chemically united, but simply mixed together.

A pure substance can also be a **compound**, a substance composed of two or more elements in fixed definite proportions. Compounds are more common than pure elements because most elements are chemically reactive and combine with other elements to form compounds. Water, table salt, and sugar are examples of compounds; they can all be decomposed into simpler substances. If you heat sugar on a pan over a flame, you decompose it into several substances including carbon (an element) and gaseous water (a different compound). The black substance left on your pan after burning is the carbon; the water escapes into the air as steam.

The majority of matter that we encounter is in the form of mixtures. Apple juice, a flame, salad dressing, and soil are all examples of mixtures; they each contain several substances with proportions that vary from one sample to another. Other common mixtures include air, seawater, and brass. Air is a mixture composed primarily of nitrogen and oxygen gas, seawater is a mixture composed primarily of salt and water, and brass is a mixture composed of copper and zinc. Each of these mixtures can have different proportions of its constituent components. For example, metallurgists vary the relative amounts of copper and zinc in brass to tailor the metal's properties to its intended use—the higher the zinc content relative to the copper content, the more brittle the brass.

Pure substance

Water molecules

▲ Water is a pure substance composed only of water molecules.

Air and seawater are mixtures

Oxygen

Nitrogen

Water

Salt

▲ Air and seawater are examples of mixtures. Air contains primarily nitrogen and oxygen. Seawater contains primarily salt and water.

We can also classify mixtures according to how uniformly the substances within them mix. In a **heterogeneous mixture**, such as oil and water, the composition varies from one region to another. In a **homogeneous mixture**, such as salt water or sweetened tea, the composition is the same throughout. Homogeneous mixtures have uniform compositions because the atoms or molecules that compose them mix uniformly. Remember that the properties of matter are determined by the atoms or molecules that compose it.

To summarize, as shown in Figure 3.8 (on p.61):

- Matter may be a pure substance, or it may be a mixture.
- A pure substance may be either an element or a compound.
- A mixture may be either homogeneous or heterogeneous.
- Mixtures may be composed of two or more elements, two or more compounds, or a combination of both.

| EXAMPLE 3.1 | **CLASSIFYING MATTER** |

Classify each type of matter as a pure substance or a mixture. If it is a pure substance, classify it as an element or a compound; if it is a mixture, classify it as homogeneous or heterogeneous.

(a) a lead weight
(b) seawater
(c) distilled water
(d) Italian salad dressing

SOLUTION

Begin by examining the alphabetical listing of pure elements inside the back cover of this text. If the substance appears in that table, it is a pure substance and an element. If it is not in the table but is a pure substance, then it is a compound. If the substance is not a pure substance, then it is a mixture. Think about your everyday experience with each mixture to determine if it is homogeneous or heterogeneous.

(a) Lead is listed in the table of elements. It is a pure substance and an element.
(b) Seawater is composed of several substances, including salt and water; it is a mixture. It has a uniform composition, so it is a homogeneous mixture.
(c) Distilled water is not listed in the table of elements, but it is a pure substance (water); therefore, it is a compound.
(d) Italian salad dressing contains a number of substances and is therefore a mixture. It usually separates into at least two distinct regions with different composition and is therefore a heterogeneous mixture.

▶ **SKILLBUILDER 3.1 | Classifying Matter**

Classify each type of matter as a pure substance or a mixture. If it is a pure substance, classify it as an element or a compound. If it is a mixture, classify it as homogeneous or heterogeneous.

(a) mercury in a thermometer
(b) exhaled air
(c) chicken noodle soup
(d) sugar

▶ **FOR MORE PRACTICE**   Example 3.12; Problems 31, 32, 33, 34, 35, 36.

Note: The answers to all Skillbuilders appear at the end of the chapter.

3.5   Differences in Matter: Physical and Chemical Properties

LO: Distinguish between physical and chemical properties.

The characteristics that distinguish one substance from another are called **properties**. Different substances have unique properties that characterize them and distinguish them from other substances. For example, we can distinguish water from alcohol based on their different smells, or we can distinguish gold from silver based on their different colors.

In chemistry, we categorize properties into two different types: physical and chemical. A **physical property** is one that a substance displays without changing its composition. A **chemical property** is one that a substance displays only through changing its composition. For example, the characteristic odor of gasoline is a physical property—gasoline does not change its composition when it exhibits its odor. On the other hand, the flammability of gasoline is a chemical property—gasoline does change its composition when it burns.

The atomic or molecular composition of a substance does not change when the substance displays its physical properties. For example, the boiling point of water—a physical property—is 100 °C. When water boils, it changes from a liquid to a gas, but the gas is still water (◀ Figure 3.9). On the other hand, the

◀ FIGURE 3.9   **A physical property**   The boiling point of water is a physical property, and boiling is a physical change. When water boils, it turns into a gas, but the water molecules are the same in both the liquid water and the gaseous steam.

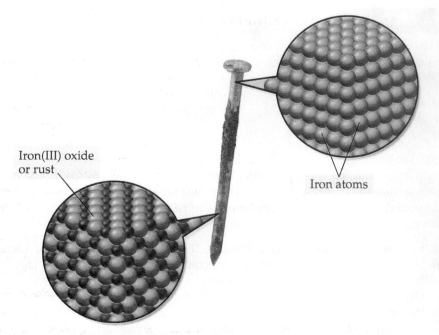

Iron(III) oxide or rust

Iron atoms

▲ **FIGURE 3.10** **A chemical property** The susceptibility of iron to rusting is a chemical property, and rusting is a chemical change. When iron rusts, it turns from iron to iron(III) oxide.

susceptibility of iron to rust is a chemical property—iron must change into iron(III) oxide to display this property (▲ Figure 3.10). Physical properties include odor, taste, color, appearance, melting point, boiling point, and density. Chemical properties include corrosiveness, flammability, acidity, and toxicity.

EXAMPLE 3.2   **PHYSICAL AND CHEMICAL PROPERTIES**

Classify each property as physical or chemical.

(a) the tendency of copper to turn green when exposed to air *Physical*
(b) the tendency of automobile paint to dull over time
(c) the tendency of gasoline to evaporate quickly when spilled
(d) the low mass (for a given volume) of aluminum relative to other metals

SOLUTION

(a) Copper turns green because it reacts with gases in air to form compounds; this is a chemical property.
(b) Automobile paint dulls over time because it can fade (decompose) due to sunlight or it can react with oxygen in air. In either case, this is a chemical property.
(c) Gasoline evaporates quickly because it has a low boiling point; this is a physical property.
(d) Aluminum's low mass (for a given volume) relative to other metals is due to its low density; this is a physical property.

▶**SKILLBUILDER 3.2** | **Physical and Chemical Properties**

Classify each property as physical or chemical.

(a) the explosiveness of hydrogen gas
(b) the bronze color of copper
(c) the shiny appearance of silver
(d) the ability of dry ice to sublime (change from solid directly to vapor)

▶**FOR MORE PRACTICE**   Example 3.13; Problems 37, 38, 39, 40.

3.6   Changes in Matter: Physical and Chemical Changes

LO: Distinguish between physical and chemical changes.

Every day, we witness changes in matter: Ice melts, iron rusts, and fruit ripens, for example. What happens to the atoms and molecules that make up these substances during these changes? The answer depends on the kind of change. In a **physical change**, matter changes its appearance but not its composition. For example, when ice melts, it looks different—water looks different from ice—but its composition is the same. Solid ice and liquid water are both composed of water molecules, so melting is a physical change. Similarly, when glass shatters, it looks different, but its composition remains the same—it is still glass. Again, this is a physical change. On the other hand, in a **chemical change**, matter *does* change its composition. For example, copper turns green upon continued exposure to air because it reacts with gases in air to form new compounds. This is a chemical change. Matter undergoes a chemical change when it undergoes a **chemical reaction**. In a chemical reaction, the substances present before the chemical change are called **reactants**, and the substances present after the change are called **products**:

$$\text{Reactants} \xrightarrow[\substack{\text{Chemical}\\\text{Change}}]{} \text{Products}$$

We will cover chemical reactions in much more detail in Chapter 7.

The differences between physical and chemical changes are not always apparent. Only chemical examination of the substances before and after the change can verify whether the change is physical or chemical. For many cases, however, we can identify chemical and physical changes based on what we know about the changes. Changes in state, such as melting or boiling, or changes that involve merely appearance, such as those produced by cutting or crushing, are always physical changes. Changes involving chemical reactions—often evidenced by heat exchange or color changes—are always chemical changes.

The main difference between chemical and physical changes is related to the changes at the molecular and atomic level. In physical changes, the atoms that compose the matter *do not* change their fundamental associations, even though the matter may change its appearance. In chemical changes, atoms do change their fundamental associations, resulting in matter with a new identity. *A physical change results in a different form of the same substance, while a chemical change results in a completely new substance.*

Consider physical and chemical changes in liquid butane, the substance used to fuel butane lighters. In many lighters, you can see the liquid butane through the plastic case of the lighter. If you push the fuel button on the lighter without turning the flint, some of the liquid butane *vaporizes* (changes from liquid to gas). You cannot see the gaseous butane, but if you listen carefully you can usually hear hissing as it leaks out (◀ Figure 3.11). Since the liquid butane and the gaseous butane are both composed of butane molecules, the change is physical. On the other hand, if you push the button *and* turn the flint to create a spark, a chemical change occurs. The butane molecules react with oxygen molecules in air to form new molecules, carbon dioxide and water (◀ Figure 3.12). The change is chemical because the molecular composition changes upon burning.

> State changes—transformations from one state of matter (such as solid or liquid) to another—are always physical changes.

▼ **FIGURE 3.11   Vaporization: a physical change**   If you push the button on a lighter without turning the flint, some of the liquid butane vaporizes to gaseous butane. Since the liquid butane and the gaseous butane are both composed of butane molecules, this is a physical change.

Physical change

Gaseous butane

Liquid butane

Chemical change

Carbon dioxide and water molecules

Liquid butane

◀ **FIGURE 3.12   Burning: a chemical change**   If you push the button *and* turn the flint to create a spark, you produce a flame. The butane molecules react with oxygen molecules in air to form new molecules, carbon dioxide and water. This is a chemical change.

EXAMPLE 3.3   PHYSICAL AND CHEMICAL CHANGES

Classify each change as physical or chemical.

(a) the rusting of iron *chemical*
(b) the evaporation of fingernail-polish remover (acetone) from the skin *physical*
(c) the burning of coal *chemical*
(d) the fading of a carpet upon repeated exposure to sunlight

SOLUTION

(a) Iron rusts because it reacts with oxygen in air to form iron(III) oxide; therefore, this is a chemical change.
(b) When fingernail-polish remover (acetone) evaporates, it changes from liquid to gas, but it remains acetone; therefore, this is a physical change.
(c) Coal burns because it reacts with oxygen in air to form carbon dioxide; this is a chemical change.
(d) A carpet fades on repeated exposure to sunlight because the molecules that give the carpet its color are decomposed by sunlight; this is a chemical change.

▶**SKILLBUILDER 3.3 | Physical and Chemical Changes**

Classify each change as physical or chemical.

(a) copper metal forming a blue solution when it is dropped into colorless nitric acid
(b) a train flattening a penny placed on a railroad track
(c) ice melting into liquid water
(d) a match igniting a firework

▶**FOR MORE PRACTICE**   Example 3.14; Problems 41, 42, 43, 44.

 CONCEPTUAL CHECKPOINT 3.2

In this figure liquid water is vaporizing into steam.

$H_2O(l)$

Which diagram best represents the molecules in the steam?

(a)

(b)

(c)

► FIGURE 3.13 **Separating a mixture of two liquids by distillation** The liquid with the lower boiling point vaporizes first. The vapors are collected and cooled (with cold water) until they condense back into liquid form.

Distillation

Filtration

Stirring rod

Mixture of liquid and solid

Funnel

Filter paper traps solid

Liquid component of mixture

▲ FIGURE 3.14   **Separating a solid from a liquid by filtration**

Separating Mixtures Through Physical Changes

Chemists often want to separate mixtures into their components. Such separations can be easy or difficult, depending on the components in the mixture. In general, mixtures are separable because the different components have different properties. We can use various techniques that exploit these differences to achieve separation. For example, oil and water are immiscible (do not mix) and have different densities. For this reason, oil floats on top of water and we can separate it from water by **decanting**—carefully pouring off—the oil into another container. We can separate mixtures of miscible liquids by **distillation**, in which we heat the mixture to boil off the more **volatile**—the more easily vaporizable—liquid. We then recondense the volatile liquid in a condenser and collect it in a separate flask (▲ Figure 3.13). If a mixture is composed of a solid and a liquid, we can separate the two by **filtration**, in which we pour the mixture through filter paper usually held in a funnel (◄ Figure 3.14).

3.7   Conservation of Mass: There Is No New Matter

LO: Apply the law of conservation of mass.

This law is a slight oversimplification. In nuclear reactions, covered in Chapter 17, significant changes in mass can occur. In chemical reactions, however, the changes are so minute that they can be ignored.

We will examine the quantitative relationships in chemical reactions in Chapter 8.

As we have seen, our planet, our air, and even our own bodies are composed of matter. Physical and chemical changes do not destroy matter, nor do they create new matter. Recall from Chapter 1 that Antoine Lavoisier, by studying combustion, established the law of conservation of mass, which states:

Matter is neither created nor destroyed in a chemical reaction.

During physical and chemical changes, the total amount of matter remains constant even though it may not initially appear that it has. When we burn butane in a lighter, for example, the butane slowly disappears. Where does it go? It combines with oxygen to form carbon dioxide and water that travel into the surrounding air. The mass of the carbon dioxide and water that forms, however, exactly equals the mass of the butane and oxygen that combined.

Suppose that we burn 58 g of butane in a lighter. It will react with 208 g of oxygen to form 176 g of carbon dioxide and 90 g of water.

$$\underbrace{\text{Butane} + \text{Oxygen}}_{\begin{array}{c}58\,\text{g} + 208\,\text{g}\\266\,\text{g}\end{array}} \longrightarrow \underbrace{\text{Carbon Dioxide} + \text{Water}}_{\begin{array}{c}176\,\text{g} + 90\,\text{g}\\266\,\text{g}\end{array}}$$

The sum of the masses of the butane and oxygen, 266 g, is equal to the sum of the masses of the carbon dioxide and water, which is also 266 g. In this chemical reaction, as in all chemical reactions, matter is conserved.

EXAMPLE 3.4   **CONSERVATION OF MASS**

A chemist forms 16.6 g of potassium iodide by combining 3.9 g of potassium with 12.7 g of iodine. Show that these results are consistent with the law of conservation of mass.

SOLUTION

The sum of the masses of the potassium and iodine is:

$$3.9 \text{ g} + 12.7 \text{ g} = 16.6 \text{ g}$$

The sum of the masses of potassium and iodine equals the mass of the product, potassium iodide. The results are consistent with the law of conservation of mass.

▶**SKILLBUILDER 3.4 | Conservation of Mass**

Suppose 12 g of natural gas combines with 48 g of oxygen in a flame. The chemical change produces 33 g of carbon dioxide. How many grams of water form?

▶**FOR MORE PRACTICE**   Example 3.15; Problems 45, 46, 47, 48, 49, 50.

 CONCEPTUAL CHECKPOINT 3.3

Consider a drop of water that is put into a flask, sealed with a cap, and heated until the droplet vaporizes. Is the mass of the container and water different after heating?

3.8   Energy

LO: Recognize the different forms of energy.

LO: Identify and convert among energy units.

Matter is one of the two major components of our universe. The other major component is **energy**, *the capacity to do work.* **Work** is defined as the result of a force acting on a distance. For example, if you push this book across your desk, you have done work. You may at first think that in chemistry we are only concerned with matter, but the behavior of matter is driven in large part by energy, so understanding energy is critical to understanding chemistry. Like matter, energy is conserved. The **law of conservation of energy** states that *energy is neither created nor destroyed.* The total amount of energy is constant; energy can be changed from one form to another or transferred from one object to another, but it cannot be created out of nothing, and it does not vanish into nothing.

Virtually all samples of matter have energy. The total energy of a sample of matter is the sum of its **kinetic energy**, the energy associated with its motion, and its **potential energy**, the energy associated with its position or composition. For example, a moving billiard ball contains *kinetic energy*, because it is *moving* at some speed across the billiard table. Water behind a dam contains *potential energy*, because it is held at a high *position* in the Earth's gravitational field by the dam. When the water flows through the dam from a higher position to a lower position, it can turn a turbine and produce electrical energy. **Electrical energy** is the energy associated with the flow of electrical charge. **Thermal energy** is the energy associated with the random motions of atoms and molecules in matter. The hotter an object, the more thermal energy it contains.

▲ Water behind a dam contains potential energy.

CHEMISTRY IN THE ENVIRONMENT

▶ Getting Energy out of Nothing?

The law of conservation of energy has significant implications for energy use. The best we can do with energy is break even (and even that is not really possible); we can't continually draw energy from a device without putting energy into it. A device that supposedly produces energy without the need for energy input is sometimes called a *perpetual motion machine* (▶ Figure 3.15). According to the law of conservation of energy, such a machine cannot exist. Occasionally, the media report or speculate on the discovery of a system that appears to produce more energy than it consumes. For example, I once heard a radio talk show on the subject of energy and gasoline costs. The reporter suggested that we simply design an electric car that recharges itself while being driven. The battery in the electric car would charge during operation in the same way that the battery in a conventional car recharges, except the electric car would run with energy from the battery. Although people have dreamed of machines such as this for decades, such ideas violate the law of conservation of energy because they produce energy without any energy input. In the case of the perpetually moving electric car, the fault lies in the idea that driving the electric car can recharge the battery—it can't.

The battery in a conventional car recharges because energy from gasoline combustion is converted into electrical energy that then charges the battery. The electric car needs

◀ **FIGURE 3.15**
A proposed perpetual motion machine The rolling balls supposedly keep the wheel perpetually spinning.
Question: Can you explain why this would not work?

energy to move forward, and the battery eventually discharges as it provides that energy. Hybrid cars (electric and gasoline-powered) such as the Toyota Prius can capture some limited energy from braking and use that energy to recharge the battery. However, they could never run indefinitely without the addition of fuel. Our society has a continual need for energy, and as our current energy resources dwindle, new energy sources are required. Unfortunately, those sources must also follow the law of conservation of energy—energy must be conserved.

B3.1 CAN YOU ANSWER THIS? *A friend asks you to invest in a new flashlight he invented that never needs batteries. What questions should you ask before writing a check?*

Chemical systems contain **chemical energy**, a form of potential energy associated with the positions of the particles that compose the chemical system. For example, the molecules that compose gasoline contain a substantial amount of chemical energy. They are a bit like the water behind a dam. Burning the gasoline is analogous to releasing the water from the dam. The chemical energy present in the gasoline is released upon burning. When we drive a car, we use that chemical energy to move the car forward. When we heat a home, we use chemical energy stored in natural gas to produce heat and warm the air in the house.

Units of Energy

Several different energy units are in common use. The SI unit of energy is the joule (J), named after the English scientist James Joule (1818–1889), who demonstrated that energy could be converted from one type to another as long as the total energy was conserved. A second unit of energy is the **calorie (cal)**, the amount of energy required to raise the temperature of 1 g of water by 1 °C. A calorie is a larger unit than a joule: 1 cal = 4.184 J. A related energy unit is the nutritional or *capital C* **Calorie (Cal)**, equivalent to 1000 *little c* calories. Electricity bills usually come in yet another energy unit, the **kilowatt-hour (kWh)**. The average cost of residential electricity in the United States is about $0.12 per kilowatt-hour. Table 3.2 lists various energy units and their conversion factors. Table 3.3 shows the amount of energy required for various processes in each of these units.

TABLE 3.2   Energy Conversion Factors

1 calorie (cal)	=	4.184 joules (J)
1 Calorie (Cal)	=	1000 calories (cal)
1 kilowatt-hour (kWh)	=	3.60×10^6 joules (J)

TABLE 3.3   Energy Use in Various Units

Unit	Energy Required to Raise Temperature of 1 g of Water by 1 °C	Energy Required to Light 100-W Bulb for 1 Hour	Total Energy Used by Average U.S. Citizen in 1 Day
joule (J)	4.18	3.6×10^5	9.0×10^8
calorie (cal)	1.00	8.60×10^4	2.2×10^8
Calorie (Cal)	0.00100	86.0	2.2×10^5
kilowatt-hour (kWh)	1.16×10^{-6}	0.100	2.50×10^2

EXAMPLE 3.5   CONVERSION OF ENERGY UNITS

A candy bar contains 225 Cal of nutritional energy. How many joules does it contain?

SORT
Begin by sorting the information in the problem. Here you are *given* energy in Calories and asked to *find* energy in joules.

GIVEN: 225 Cal

FIND: J

STRATEGIZE
Draw a solution map. Begin with Cal, convert to cal, and then convert to J.

SOLUTION MAP

$$\frac{1000\ cal}{1\ Cal} \qquad \frac{4.184\ J}{1\ cal}$$

RELATIONSHIPS USED
1000 calories = 1 Cal (Table 3.2)
4.184 J = 1 cal (Table 3.2)

SOLVE
Follow the solution map to solve the problem. Begin with 225 Cal and multiply by the appropriate conversion factors to arrive at J. Round the answer to the correct number of significant figures (in this case, three because of the three significant figures in 225 Cal).

SOLUTION

$$225\ \cancel{Cal} \times \frac{1000\ \cancel{cal}}{1\ \cancel{Cal}} \times \frac{4.184\ J}{1\ \cancel{cal}} = 9.41 \times 10^5\ J$$

CHECK
Check your answer. Are the units correct? Does the answer make physical sense?

The units of the answer (J) are the desired units. The magnitude of the answer makes sense because the J is a smaller unit than the Cal; therefore the quantity of energy in J should be greater than the quantity in Cal.

▶**SKILLBUILDER 3.5 | Conversion of Energy Units**
The complete combustion of a small wooden match produces approximately 512 cal of heat. How many kilojoules are produced?

▶**SKILLBUILDER PLUS**   Convert 2.75×10^4 kJ to calories.

▶**FOR MORE PRACTICE**   Example 3.16; Problems 51, 52, 53, 54, 55, 56, 57, 58.

 CONCEPTUAL CHECKPOINT 3.4

Suppose a salesperson wants to make an appliance seem as efficient as possible. In which units does the yearly energy consumption of the appliance have the lowest numerical value and therefore seem most efficient?

(a) J   (b) cal
(c) Cal   (d) kWh

3.9   Energy and Chemical and Physical Change

LO: Distinguish between exothermic and endothermic reactions.

When discussing energy transfer, we often define the object of our study (such as a flask in which a chemical reaction is occurring) as the *system*. The system then exchanges energy with its *surroundings*. In other words, we view energy changes as an exchange of energy between the system and the surroundings.

The physical and chemical changes that we discussed in Section 3.6 are usually accompanied by energy changes. For example, when water evaporates from skin (a physical change), the water molecules absorb energy, cooling the skin. When we burn natural gas on a stove (a chemical change), energy is released, heating the food we are cooking.

The release of energy during a chemical reaction is analogous to the release of energy that occurs when a weight falls to the ground. When you lift a weight, you raise its potential energy; when you drop it, you release the potential energy (◄ Figure 3.16). *Systems with high potential energy—like the raised weight—have a tendency to change in a way that lowers their potential energy.* For this reason, objects or systems with high potential energy tend to be *unstable*. A weight lifted several meters from the ground is unstable because it contains a significant amount of localized potential energy. Unless restrained, the weight will fall, lowering its potential energy.

Some chemical substances are like a raised weight. For example, the molecules that compose TNT (trinitrotoluene) have a relatively high potential energy—energy is concentrated in them just as energy is concentrated in the raised weight. TNT molecules therefore tend to undergo rapid chemical changes that lower their potential energy, which is why TNT is explosive. Chemical reactions that *release* energy, like the explosion of TNT, are **exothermic**.

Some chemical reactions behave in just the opposite way—they *absorb* energy from their surroundings as they occur. Such reactions are **endothermic**. The reaction that occurs in a chemical cold pack is a good example of an endothermic reaction. When you break the barrier separating the reactants in the chemical cold pack, the substances mix, react, and absorb heat from the surroundings. The surroundings—possibly including your bruised ankle—get colder.

We can represent the energy changes that occur during a chemical reaction with an energy diagram, as shown in Figure 3.17. In an exothermic reaction (▼ Figure 3.17a), the reactants have greater energy than the products, and energy is released as the reaction occurs. In an endothermic reaction (▼ Figure 3.17b), the products have more energy than the reactants, and energy is absorbed as the reaction occurs.

If a particular reaction or process is exothermic, then the reverse process must be endothermic. For example, the evaporation of water from skin is endothermic (and therefore cools you off), but the condensation of water onto skin is exothermic (which is why steam burns can be so painful).

▲ FIGURE 3.16   Potential energy of raised weight   A weight lifted off the ground has a high potential and will tend to fall toward the ground to lower its potential energy.

◄ FIGURE 3.17   Exothermic and endothermic reactions   (a) In an exothermic reaction, energy is released. (b) In an endothermic reaction, energy is absorbed.

EXAMPLE 3.6	EXOTHERMIC AND ENDOTHERMIC PROCESSES

Classify each change as exothermic or endothermic.

(a) wood burning in a fire

(b) ice melting

SOLUTION

(a) When wood burns, it emits heat into the surroundings. Therefore, the process is exothermic.

(b) When ice melts, it absorbs heat from the surroundings. For example, when ice melts in a glass of water, it cools the water as the melting ice absorbs heat from the water. Therefore, the process is endothermic.

▶**SKILLBUILDER 3.6** | Exothermic and Endothermic Processes

Classify each change as exothermic or endothermic.

(a) water freezing into ice

(b) natural gas burning

▶**FOR MORE PRACTICE** Problems 61, 62, 63, 64.

3.10 Temperature: Random Motion of Molecules and Atoms

LO: Convert between Fahrenheit, Celsius, and Kelvin temperature Scales.

The atoms and molecules that compose matter are in constant random motion—they contain *thermal energy*. The **temperature** of a substance is a measure of its thermal energy. The hotter an object, the greater the random motion of the atoms and molecules that compose it, and the higher its temperature. We must be careful to not confuse *temperature* with *heat*. **Heat**, which has units of energy, is the *transfer* or *exchange* of thermal energy caused by a temperature difference. For example, when a cold ice cube is dropped into a warm cup of water, energy is transferred as heat from the water to the ice, resulting in the cooling of the water. Temperature, by contrast, is a *measure* of the thermal energy of matter (not the exchange of thermal energy).

Three different temperature scales are in common use. The most familiar in the United States is the **Fahrenheit (°F) scale**. On the Fahrenheit scale, water freezes at 32 °F and boils at 212 °F. Room temperature is approximately 72 °F. The Fahrenheit scale was initially set up by assigning 0 °F to the freezing point of a concentrated saltwater solution and 96 °F to normal body temperature (although body temperature is now known to be 98.6 °F).

The scale scientists use is the **Celsius (°C) scale**. On this scale, water freezes at 0 °C and boils at 100 °C. Room temperature is approximately 22 °C.

The Fahrenheit and Celsius scales differ in both the size of their respective degrees and the temperature each calls "zero" (▶ Figure 3.18). Both the Fahrenheit and Celsius scales contain negative temperatures. A third temperature scale, called the **Kelvin (K) scale**, avoids negative temperatures by assigning 0 K to the coldest temperature possible, absolute zero. Absolute zero (−273.15 °C or −459.7 °F) is the temperature at which molecular motion virtually stops. There is no lower temperature. The kelvin degree, or kelvin (K), is the same size as the Celsius degree—the only difference is the temperature that each scale designates as zero.

We can convert between these temperature scales using the following formulas.

$$K = {}^{\circ}C + 273.15$$

$$^{\circ}C = \frac{{}^{\circ}F - 32}{1.8}$$

The degree symbol is used with the Celsius and Fahrenheit scales, but not with the Kelvin scale.

▶ **FIGURE 3.18 Comparison of the Fahrenheit, Celsius, and Kelvin temperature scales** The Fahrenheit degree is five-ninths the size of a Celsius degree. The Celsius degree and the kelvin degree are the same size.

For example, suppose we want to convert 212 K to Celsius. Following the procedure for solving numerical problems (Section 2.6), we first sort the information in the problem statement:

GIVEN: 212 K

FIND: °C

We then strategize by building a solution map.

In a solution map involving a formula, the formula establishes the relationship between the variables. However, the formula under the arrow is not necessarily solved for the correct variable until later, as is the case here.

SOLUTION MAP

K = °C + 273.15

RELATIONSHIPS USED

K = °C + 273.15 (This equation relates the *given* quantity (K) to the *find* quantity (°C) and is given in this section.)

SOLUTION

Finally, we follow the solution map to solve the problem. The equation below the arrow shows the relationship between K and °C, but it is not solved for the correct variable. Before using the equation, we must solve it for °C.

$$K = °C + 273.15$$

$$°C = K - 273.15$$

We can now substitute the given value for K and calculate the answer to the correct number of significant figures.

$$°C = 212 - 273.15$$

$$= -61 \, °C$$

EXAMPLE 3.7 **CONVERTING BETWEEN CELSIUS AND KELVIN TEMPERATURE SCALES**

Convert −25 °C to kelvins.

SORT You are given a temperature in degrees Celsius and asked to find the value of the temperature in kelvins.	**GIVEN:** −25 °C **FIND:** K
STRATEGIZE Draw a solution map. Use the equation that relates the temperature in kelvins to the temperature in Celsius to convert from the given quantity to the quantity you want to find.	**SOLUTION MAP** $K = °C + 273.15$ **RELATIONSHIPS USED** $K = °C + 273.15$ (presented in this section)
SOLVE Follow the solution map by substituting the correct value for °C and calculating the answer to the correct number of significant figures.	**SOLUTION** $K = °C + 273.15$ $K = -25 °C + 273.15 = 248 \text{ K}$ The significant figures are limited to the ones place because the given temperature (−25 °C) is only given to the ones place. Remember that for addition and subtraction, the number of *decimal places* in the least precisely known quantity determines the number of *decimal places* in the result.
CHECK Check your answer. Are the units correct? Does the answer make physical sense?	The units (K) are correct. The answer makes sense because the value in kelvins should be a more positive number than the value in degrees Celsius.

▶**SKILLBUILDER 3.7** | **Converting between Celsius and Kelvin Temperature Scales**

Convert 358 K to Celsius.

▶**FOR MORE PRACTICE** Example 3.17; Problems 65c, 66d.

EXAMPLE 3.8 **CONVERTING BETWEEN FAHRENHEIT AND CELSIUS TEMPERATURE SCALES**

Convert 55 °F to Celsius.

SORT You are given a temperature in degrees Fahrenheit and asked to find the value of the temperature in degrees Celsius.	**GIVEN:** 55 °F **FIND:** °C
STRATEGIZE Draw the solution map. Use the equation that shows the relationship between the *given* quantity (°F) and the *find* quantity (°C).	**SOLUTION MAP** $°C = \dfrac{(°F - 32)}{1.8}$ **RELATIONSHIPS USED** $°C = \dfrac{(°F - 32)}{1.8}$ (presented in this section)
SOLVE Substitute the given value into the equation and calculate the answer to the correct number of significant figures.	**SOLUTION** $°C = \dfrac{(°F - 32)}{1.8}$ $°C = \dfrac{(55 - 32)}{1.8} = 12.778 °C = 13 °C$

CHECK	The units (°C) are correct. The value of the answer (13 °C) is smaller than the value in degrees Fahrenheit. For positive temperatures, the value of a temperature in degrees Celsius will always be smaller than the value in degrees Fahrenheit because the Fahrenheit degree is smaller than the Celsius degree and the Fahrenheit scale is offset by 32 degrees (see Figure 3.17).
Check your answer. Are the units correct? Does the answer make physical sense?	

▶**SKILLBUILDER 3.8 | Converting between Fahrenheit and Celsius Temperature Scales**

Convert 139 °C to Fahrenheit.

▶**FOR MORE PRACTICE** Example 3.18; Problems 65a, 66a, c.

EXAMPLE 3.9	**CONVERTING BETWEEN FAHRENHEIT AND KELVIN TEMPERATURE SCALES**

Convert 310 K to Fahrenheit.

SORT You are given a temperature in kelvins and asked to find the value of the temperature in degrees Fahrenheit.	**GIVEN:** 310 K **FIND:** °F
STRATEGIZE Build the solution map, which requires two steps: one to convert kelvins to degrees Celsius and one to convert degrees Celsius to degrees Fahrenheit.	**SOLUTION MAP** $$K = °C + 273.15 \quad °C = \frac{(°F - 32)}{1.8}$$ **RELATIONSHIPS USED** $K = °C + 273.15$ (presented in this section) $°C = \dfrac{(°F - 32)}{1.8}$ (presented in this section)
SOLVE Solve the first equation for °C and substitute the given quantity in K to convert it to °C. Solve the second equation for °F. Substitute the value of the temperature in °C (from the previous step) to convert it to °F and round the answer to the correct number of significant figures.	**SOLUTION** $K = °C + 273.15$ $°C = K - 273.15$ $°C = 310 - 273.15 = 36.85 °C$ $°C = \dfrac{(°F - 32)}{1.8}$ $1.8 \,(°C) = (°F - 32)$ $°F = 1.8 \,(°C) + 32$ $°F = 1.8 \,(36.85) + 32 = 98.33 \,°F = 98 \,°F$
CHECK Check your answer. Are the units correct? Does the answer make physical sense?	The units (°F) are correct. The magnitude of the answer is a bit trickier to judge. In this temperature range, a temperature in Fahrenheit should indeed be smaller than a temperature in kelvins. However, because the Fahrenheit degree is smaller, temperatures in Fahrenheit become larger than temperatures in kelvins above 575 °F.

▶**SKILLBUILDER 3.9 | Converting between Fahrenheit and Kelvin Temperature Scales**

Convert −321 °F to kelvins.

▶**FOR MORE PRACTICE** Problems 65b, d, 66b.

CONCEPTUAL CHECKPOINT 3.5

Which temperature is identical on both the Celsius and the Fahrenheit scales?

(a) 100°

(b) 32°

(c) 0°

(d) −40°

3.11   Temperature Changes: Heat Capacity

LO: Relate energy, temperature change, and heat capacity.

TABLE 3.4   Specific Heat Capacities of Some Common Substances

Substance	Specific Heat Capacity (J/g °C)
Lead	0.128
Gold	0.128
Silver	0.235
Copper	0.385
Iron	0.449
Aluminum	0.903
Ethanol	2.42
Water	4.184

All substances change temperature when they are heated, but how much they change for a given amount of heat varies significantly from one substance to another. For example, if you put a steel skillet on a flame, its temperature rises rapidly. However, if you put some water in the skillet, the temperature increases more slowly. Why? One reason is that when you add water, the same amount of heat energy must warm more matter, so the temperature rise is slower. The second and more interesting reason is that water is more resistant to temperature change than steel because water has a higher *heat capacity*. The **heat capacity** of a substance is the quantity of heat (usually in joules) required to change the temperature of a given amount of the substance by 1 °C. When the amount of the substance is expressed in grams, the heat capacity is called the **specific heat capacity** (or simply the **specific heat**) and has units of joules per gram per degree Celsius (J/g °C). Table 3.4 lists the values of the specific heat capacity for several substances.

Notice that water has the highest specific heat capacity on the list—changing the temperature of water requires a lot of heat. If you have traveled from an inland geographical region to a coastal one and have felt a drop in temperature, you have experienced the effects of water's high specific heat capacity. On a summer day in California, for example, the temperature difference between Sacramento (an inland city) and San Francisco (a coastal city) can be 30 °F (17 °C); San Francisco enjoys a cool 68 °F (20 °C), while Sacramento bakes at near 100 °F (37 °C). Yet the intensity of sunlight falling on these two cities is the same. Why the large temperature difference? The difference is due to the presence of the Pacific Ocean, which practically surrounds San Francisco. Water, with its high heat capacity, absorbs much of the sun's heat without undergoing a large increase in temperature, keeping San Francisco cool. The land surrounding Sacramento, on the other hand, with its low heat capacity, cannot absorb a lot of heat without a large increase in temperature—it has a lower *capacity* to absorb heat without a large temperature increase.

Similarly, only two U.S. states have never recorded a temperature above 100 °F (37 °C). One of them is obvious: Alaska. It is too far north to get that hot. The other one,

▲ San Francisco enjoys cool weather even in summer months because of the high heat capacity of the surrounding ocean.

EVERYDAY CHEMISTRY

▶ Coolers, Camping, and the Heat Capacity of Water

Have you ever loaded a cooler with ice and then added room-temperature drinks? If you have, you know that the ice quickly melts. In contrast, if you load your cooler with chilled drinks, the ice lasts for hours. Why the difference? The answer is related to the high heat capacity of the water within the drinks. As you just learned, water must absorb a lot of heat to raise its temperature, and it must also release a lot of heat to lower its temperature. When the warm drinks are placed into the ice, they release heat, which then melts the ice. The chilled drinks, on the other hand, are already cold, so they do not release much heat. It is always better to load your cooler with chilled drinks—that way, the ice will last the rest of the day.

B3.2 CAN YOU ANSWER THIS?   *Suppose you are cold-weather camping and decide to heat some objects to bring into your sleeping bag for added warmth. You place a large water jug and a rock of equal mass close to the fire. Over time, both the rock and the water jug warm to about 38 °C (100 °F). If you could bring only one into your sleeping bag, which one would keep you warmer? Why?*

▲ The ice in a cooler loaded with cold drinks lasts much longer than the ice in a cooler loaded with warm drinks.
QUESTION: Can you explain why?

however, may come as a surprise. It is Hawaii. The water that surrounds America's only island state moderates the temperature, preventing Hawaii from ever getting too hot.

 CONCEPTUAL CHECKPOINT 3.6

If you want to heat a metal plate to as high a temperature as possible for a given energy input, what metal should you use? (Assume all the plates have the same mass.)

(a) copper

(b) iron

(c) aluminum

(d) it would make no difference

3.12   Energy and Heat Capacity Calculations

LO: Relate energy, temperature change, and heat capacity.

When a substance absorbs heat (which we represent with the symbol q), its temperature change (which we represent as ΔT) is in direct proportion to the amount of heat absorbed.

$$\xrightarrow{\;\;q\;\;} \text{System}$$
$$\Delta T$$

In other words, the more heat absorbed, the greater the temperature change. We can use the specific heat capacity of the substance to *quantify* the relationship between the amount of heat added to a given amount of the substance and the corresponding temperature increase. The equation that relates these quantities is:

$$\text{Heat} = \text{Mass} \times \text{Specific Heat Capacity} \times \text{Temperature Change}$$
$$q = m \qquad \times \qquad C \qquad \times \qquad \Delta T$$

ΔT in °C is equal to ΔT in K but is not equal to ΔT in °F.

where q is the amount of heat in joules, m is the mass of the substance in grams, C is the specific heat capacity in joules per gram per degree Celsius, and ΔT is the temperature change in Celsius. The symbol Δ means *the change in*, so ΔT means *the change in temperature*. For example, suppose we are making a cup of tea and want to know how much heat energy will warm 235 g of water (about 8 oz) from 25 °C to 100.0 °C (boiling).

We begin by sorting the information in the problem statement.

GIVEN: 235 g water (m)
25 °C initial temperature (T_i)
100.0 °C final temperature (T_f)

FIND: amount of heat needed (q)

Then we strategize by building a solution map.

SOLUTION MAP

$$q = m \cdot C \cdot \Delta T$$

In addition to m and ΔT, the equation requires C, the specific heat capacity of water. The next step is to gather all of the required quantities for the equation (C, m, and ΔT) in the correct units. These are:

$$C = 4.18 \, \text{J/g} \, °C$$
$$m = 235 \, \text{g}$$

The other quantity we require is ΔT. The change in temperature is the difference between the final temperature (T_f) and the initial temperature (T_i).

$$\Delta T = T_f - T_i$$
$$= 100.0 \, °C - 25 \, °C = 75 \, °C$$

SOLUTION
Finally, we solve the problem. We substitute the correct values into the equation and calculate the answer to the correct number of significant figures.

$$q = m \cdot C \cdot \Delta T$$
$$= 235 \, \text{g} \times 4.18 \, \frac{\text{J}}{\text{g} \, °C} \times 75 \, °C$$
$$= 7.367 \times 10^4 \, \text{J} = 7.4 \times 10^4 \, \text{J}$$

It is critical that we substitute each of the correct variables into the equation in the correct units and cancel units as we calculate the answer. If, during this process, we learn that one of our variables is not in the correct units, we convert it to the correct units using the skills presented in Chapter 2. Notice that the sign of q is positive (+) if the substance is increasing in temperature (heat entering the substance) and negative (−) if the substance is decreasing in temperature (heat leaving the substance).

EXAMPLE 3.10 RELATING HEAT ENERGY TO TEMPERATURE CHANGES

Gallium is a solid metal at room temperature but melts at 29.9 °C. If you hold gallium in your hand, it melts from your body heat. How much heat must 2.5 g of gallium absorb from your hand to raise the temperature of the gallium from 25.0 °C to 29.9 °C? The specific heat capacity of gallium is 0.372 J/g °C.

SORT You are given the mass of gallium, its initial and final temperatures, and its specific heat capacity, and are asked to find the amount of heat absorbed by the gallium.	**GIVEN:** 2.5 g gallium (m) $T_i = 25.0 \,°C$ $T_f = 29.9 \,°C$ $C = 0.372 \, J/g \,°C$ **FIND:** q
STRATEGIZE The equation that relates the *given* and *find* quantities is the specific heat capacity equation. The solution map indicates that this equation takes you from the *given* quantities to the quantity you are asked to *find*.	**SOLUTION MAP** $q = m \cdot C \cdot \Delta T$ **RELATIONSHIPS USED** $q = m \cdot C \cdot \Delta T$ (presented in this section)
SOLVE Before solving the problem, you must gather the necessary quantities—C, m, and ΔT—in the correct units. Substitute C, m, and ΔT into the equation, canceling units, and calculate the answer to the correct number of significant figures.	**SOLUTION** $C = 0.372 \, J/g \,°C$ $m = 2.5 \, g$ $\Delta T = T_f - T_i$ $\quad = 29.9 \,°C - 25.0 \,°C$ $\quad = 4.9 \,°C$ $q = m \cdot C \cdot \Delta T$ $\quad = 2.5 \, \cancel{g} \times 0.372 \dfrac{1}{\cancel{g} \,°\cancel{C}} \times 4.9° \cancel{C} = 4.557 \, J = 4.6 \, J^*$
CHECK Check your answer. Are the units correct? Does the answer make physical sense?	The units (J) are correct. The magnitude of the answer makes sense because it takes almost 1 J to heat the 2.5 g sample of the metal by 1 °C; therefore, it should take about 5 J to heat the sample by 5 °C.

▶**SKILLBUILDER 3.10 | Relating Heat Energy to Temperature Changes**

You find a 1979 copper penny (pre-1982 pennies are pure copper) in the snow and pick it up. How much heat does the penny absorb as it warms from the temperature of the snow, −5.0 °C, to the temperature of your body, 37.0 °C? Assume the penny is pure copper and has a mass of 3.10 g. You can find the heat capacity of copper in Table 3.4.

▶**SKILLBUILDER PLUS** The temperature of a lead fishing weight rises from 26 °C to 38 °C as it absorbs 11.3 J of heat. What is the mass of the fishing weight in grams?

▶**FOR MORE PRACTICE** Example 3.19; Problems 75, 76, 77, 78

---

* This is the amount of heat required to raise the temperature to the melting point. Actually melting the gallium requires additional heat.

EXAMPLE 3.11   RELATING HEAT CAPACITY TO TEMPERATURE CHANGES

A chemistry student finds a shiny rock that she suspects is gold. She weighs the rock on a balance and determines that its mass is 14.3 g. She then finds that the temperature of the rock rises from 25 °C to 52 °C upon absorption of 174 J of heat. Find the heat capacity of the rock and determine whether the value is consistent with the heat capacity of gold (which is listed in Table 3.4).

SORT You are given the mass of the "gold" rock, the amount of heat absorbed, and the initial and final temperatures. You are asked to find the heat capacity of the rock.	**GIVEN:** 14.3 g 174 J of heat absorbed $T_i = 25\,°C$ $T_f = 52\,°C$ **FIND:** C
STRATEGIZE The solution map shows how the heat capacity equation relates the *given* and *find* quantities.	**SOLUTION MAP** $$q = m \cdot C \cdot \Delta T$$ **RELATIONSHIPS USED** $q = m \cdot C \cdot \Delta T$ (presented in this section)
SOLVE First, gather the necessary quantities—m, q, and ΔT—in the correct units. Then solve the equation for C and substitute the correct variables into the equation. Finally, calculate the answer to the right number of significant figures.	**SOLUTION** $$m = 14.3\ g$$ $$q = 174\ J$$ $$\Delta T = 52\,°C - 25\,°C = 27\,°C$$ $$q = m \cdot C \cdot \Delta T$$ $$C = \frac{q}{m \cdot \Delta T}$$ $$C = \frac{174\ J}{14.3\ g \times 27\,°C}$$ $$= 0.4507\ \frac{J}{g\,°C} = 0.45\ \frac{J}{g\,°C}$$ By comparing the calculated value of the specific heat capacity (0.45 J/g °C) with the specific heat capacity of gold from Table 3.4 (0.128 J/g °C), you conclude that the rock is not pure gold.
CHECK Check your answer. Are the units correct? Does the answer make physical sense?	The units of the answer are those of specific heat capacity, so they are correct. The magnitude of the answer falls in the range of specific heat capacities given in Table 3.4. A value of heat capacity that falls far outside this range would immediately be suspect.

▶**SKILLBUILDER 3.11 | Relating Heat Capacity to Temperature Changes**

A 328-g sample of water absorbs 5.78×10^3 J of heat. Calculate the change in temperature for the water. If the water is initially at 25.0 °C, what is its final temperature?

▶**FOR MORE PRACTICE**   Problems 85, 86, 87, 88.

   CONCEPTUAL CHECKPOINT 3.7

The heat capacity of substance A is twice that of substance B. If samples of equal mass of the two substances absorb the same amount of heat, which substance undergoes the larger change in temperature?

CHAPTER IN REVIEW

Self-Assessment Quiz

Q1. Which substance is a pure compound?
- (a) Gold
- (b) Water
- (c) Milk
- (d) Fruit cake

Q2. Which property of trinitrotoluene (TNT) is most likely a chemical property?
- (a) Yellow color
- (b) Melting point is 80.1 °C
- (c) Explosive
- (d) None of the above

Q3. Which change is a chemical change?
- (a) The condensation of dew on a cold night
- (b) A forest fire
- (c) The smoothening of rocks by ocean waves
- (d) None of the above

Q4. Which process is endothermic?
- (a) The burning of natural gas in a stove
- (b) The metabolism of glucose by your body
- (c) The melting of ice in soft drink
- (d) None of the above

Q5. A 35-g sample of potassium completely reacts with chlorine to form 67 g of potassium chloride. How many grams of chlorine must have reacted?
- (a) 67 g
- (b) 35 g
- (c) 32 g
- (d) 12 g

Q6. A runner burns 2.56×10^3 kJ during a five-mile run. How many nutritional Calories did the runner burn?
- (a) 1.07×10^1 Cal
- (b) 612 Cal
- (c) 6.12×10^5 Cal
- (d) 1.07×10^4 Cal

Q7. Convert the boiling point of water (100.00 °C) to K.
- (a) −173.15 K
- (b) 0 K
- (c) 100.00 K
- (d) 373.15 K

Q8. A European doctor reports that you have a fever of 39.2 °C. What is your fever in degrees Fahrenheit?
- (a) 102.6 °F
- (b) 128.26 °F
- (c) 71.2 °F
- (d) 4 °F

Q9. How much heat must be absorbed by 125 g of ethanol to change its temperature from 21.5 °C to 34.8 °C?
- (a) 6.95 kJ
- (b) 4.02×10^3 kJ
- (c) 86.6 kJ
- (d) 4.02 kJ

Q10. Substance A has a heat capacity that is much greater than that of substance B. If 10.0 g of substance A initially at 25.0 °C is brought into thermal contact with 10.0 g of B initially at 75.0 °C, what can you conclude about the final temperature of the two substances once the exchange of heat between the substances is complete?
- (a) The final temperature will be between 25.0 °C and 50.0 °C.
- (b) The final temperature will be between 50.0 °C and 75.0 °C.
- (c) The final temperature will be 50.0 °C.
- (d) You can conclude nothing about the final temperature without more information.

Answers: 1:b, 2:c, 3:b, 4:c, 5:c, 6:b, 7:d, 8:a, 9:d, 10:a

Chemical Principles

Matter: Matter is anything that occupies space and has mass. It is composed of atoms, which are often bonded together as molecules. Matter can exist as a solid, a liquid, or a gas. Solid matter can be either amorphous or crystalline.

Classification of Matter: We can classify matter according to its composition. Pure matter is composed of only one type of substance; that substance may be an element (a substance that cannot be decomposed into simpler substances), or it may be a compound (a substance composed of two or more elements in fixed definite proportions). Mixtures are composed of two or more different substances, the proportions of which may vary from one sample to the next. Mixtures can be either homogeneous, having the same composition throughout, or heterogeneous, having a composition that varies from region to region.

Relevance

Matter: Everything is made of matter—you, me, the chair you sit on, and the air we breathe. The physical universe basically contains only two things: matter and energy. We begin our study of chemistry by defining and classifying these two building blocks of the universe.

Classification of Matter: Since ancient times, humans have tried to understand matter and harness it for their purposes. The earliest humans shaped matter into tools and used the transformation of matter—especially fire—to keep warm and to cook food. To manipulate matter, we must understand it. Fundamental to this understanding is the connection between the properties of matter and the molecules and atoms that compose it.

Properties and Changes of Matter: We can divide the properties of matter into two types: physical and chemical. The physical properties of matter do not involve a change in composition. The chemical properties of matter involve a change in composition. We can divide changes in matter into physical and chemical. In a physical change, the appearance of matter may change, but its composition does not. In a chemical change, the composition of matter changes.

Properties and Changes of Matter: The physical and chemical properties of matter make the world around us the way it is. For example, a physical property of water is its boiling point at sea level—100 °C. The physical properties of water—and all matter—are determined by the atoms and molecules that compose it. If water molecules were different—even slightly different—water would boil at a different temperature. Imagine a world where water boiled at room temperature.

Conservation of Mass: Whether the changes in matter are chemical or physical, matter is always conserved. In a chemical change, the masses of the matter undergoing the chemical change must equal the sum of the masses of matter resulting from the chemical change.

Conservation of Mass: The conservation of matter is relevant to, for example, pollution. We often think that humans create pollution, but, actually, we are powerless to create anything. Matter cannot be created. So, pollution is simply misplaced matter—matter that we have put into places where it does not belong.

Energy: Besides matter, energy is the other major component of our universe. Like matter, energy is conserved—it can be neither created nor destroyed. Energy exists in various different types, and these can be converted from one to another. Some common units of energy are the joule (J), the calorie (cal), the nutritional Calorie (Cal), and the kilowatt-hour (kWh). Chemical reactions that emit energy are exothermic; those that absorb energy are endothermic.

Energy: Our society's energy sources will not last forever because as we burn fossil fuels—our primary energy source—we convert chemical energy, stored in molecules, to kinetic and thermal energy. The kinetic and thermal energy is not readily available to be used again. Consequently, our energy resources are dwindling, and the conservation of energy implies that we will not be able simply to create new energy—it must come from somewhere. All of the chemical reactions that we use for energy are exothermic.

Temperature: The temperature of matter is related to the random motions of the molecules and atoms that compose it—the greater the motion, the higher the temperature. To measure temperature we use three scales: Fahrenheit (°F), Celsius (°C), and Kelvin (K).

Temperature: The temperature of matter and its measurement are relevant to many everyday phenomena. Humans are understandably interested in the weather, and air temperature is a fundamental part of weather. We use body temperature as one measure of human health and global temperature as one measure of the planet's health.

Heat Capacity: The temperature change that a sample of matter undergoes upon absorption of a given amount of heat relates to the heat capacity of the substance composing the matter. Water has one of the highest heat capacities, meaning that it is most resistant to rapid temperature changes.

Heat Capacity: The heat capacity of water explains why it is cooler in coastal areas, which are near large bodies of high-heat-capacity water, than in inland areas, which are surrounded by low-heat-capacity land. It also explains why it takes longer to cool a refrigerator filled with liquids than an empty one.

Chemical Skills

LO: Classify matter as element, compound, or mixture (Section 3.4).

Begin by examining the alphabetical listing of elements in the back of this book. If the substance is listed in that table, it is a pure substance and an element.

If the substance is not listed in that table, refer to your everyday experience with the substance to determine whether it is a pure substance. If it is a pure substance not listed in the table, then it is a compound.

If it is not a pure substance, then it is a mixture. Refer to your everyday experience with the mixture to determine whether it has uniform composition (homogeneous) or nonuniform composition (heterogeneous).

Examples

EXAMPLE 3.12   CLASSIFYING MATTER

Classify each type of matter as a pure substance or a mixture. If it is a pure substance, classify it as an element or a compound. If it is a mixture, classify it as homogeneous or heterogeneous.

(a) pure silver
(b) swimming-pool water
(c) dry ice (solid carbon dioxide)
(d) blueberry muffin

SOLUTION

(a) Pure element; silver appears in the element table.
(b) Homogeneous mixture; pool water contains at least water and chlorine, and it is uniform throughout.
(c) Compound; dry ice is a pure substance (carbon dioxide), but it is not listed in the table.
(d) Heterogeneous mixture; a blueberry muffin is a mixture of several things and has nonuniform composition.

LO: Distinguish between physical and chemical properties (Section 3.5).

To distinguish between physical and chemical properties, consider whether the substance changes composition while displaying the property. If it *does not* change composition, the property is physical; if it *does*, the property is chemical.

| EXAMPLE 3.13 | DISTINGUISHING BETWEEN PHYSICAL AND CHEMICAL PROPERTIES |

Classify each property as physical or chemical.

(a) the tendency for platinum jewelry to scratch easily
(b) the ability of sulfuric acid to burn the skin
(c) the ability of hydrogen peroxide to bleach hair
(d) the density of lead relative to other metals

SOLUTION

(a) Physical; scratched platinum is still platinum.
(b) Chemical; the acid chemically reacts with the skin to produce the burn.
(c) Chemical; the hydrogen peroxide chemically reacts with hair to change the hair.
(d) Physical; you can determine the density of lead by measuring the volume and mass of a lead sample.

LO: Distinguish between physical and chemical changes (Section 3.6).

To distinguish between physical and chemical changes, consider whether the substance changes composition during the change. If it *does not* change composition, the change is physical; if it *does*, the change is chemical.

| EXAMPLE 3.14 | DISTINGUISHING BETWEEN PHYSICAL AND CHEMICAL CHANGES |

Classify each change as physical or chemical.

(a) the explosion of gunpowder in the barrel of a gun
(b) the melting of gold in a furnace
(c) the bubbling that occurs when you mix baking soda and vinegar
(d) the bubbling that occurs when water boils

SOLUTION

(a) Chemical; the gunpowder reacts with oxygen during the explosion.
(b) Physical; the liquid gold is still gold.
(c) Chemical; the bubbling is a result of a chemical reaction between the two substances to form new substances, one of which is carbon dioxide released as bubbles.
(d) Physical; the bubbling is due to liquid water turning into gaseous water, but it is still water.

LO: Apply the law of conservation of mass (Section 3.7).

The sum of the masses of the substances involved in a chemical change must be the same before and after the change.

| EXAMPLE 3.15 | APPLYING THE LAW OF CONSERVATION OF MASS |

An automobile runs for 10 minutes and burns 47 g of gasoline. The gasoline combines with oxygen from air and forms 132 g of carbon dioxide and 34 g of water. How much oxygen is consumed in the process?

SOLUTION

The total mass after the chemical change is:

$$132 \text{ g} + 34 \text{ g} = 166 \text{ g}$$

The total mass before the change must also be 166 g.

$$47 \text{ g} + \text{oxygen} = 166 \text{ g}$$

So, the mass of oxygen consumed is the total mass (166 g) minus the mass of gasoline (47 g).

$$\text{grams of oxygen} = 166 \text{ g} - 47 \text{ g} = 119 \text{ g}$$

LO: Identify and convert among energy units (Section 3.8).

Solve unit conversion problems using the problem-solving strategies outlined in Section 2.6.

SORT

You are given an amount of energy in kilowatt-hours and asked to find the amount in calories.

STRATEGIZE

Draw a solution map. Begin with kilowatt-hours and determine the conversion factors to get to calories.

SOLVE

Follow the solution map to solve the problem. Begin with the *given* quantity and multiply by the conversion factors to arrive at calories. Round the answer to the correct number of significant figures.

CHECK

Are the units correct? Does the answer make physical sense?

LO: Convert between Fahrenheit, Celsius, and Kelvin temperature Scales (Section 3.10).

Solve temperature conversion problems using the problem-solving procedure in Sections 2.6 and 2.10. Take the steps appropriate for equations.

SORT

You are given the temperature in kelvins and asked to convert it to degrees Celsius.

STRATEGIZE

Draw a solution map. Use the equation that relates the *given* quantity to the *find* quantity.

SOLVE

Solve the equation for the *find* quantity (°C) and substitute the temperature in K into the equation. Calculate the answer to the correct number of significant figures.

CHECK

Are the units correct? Does the answer make physical sense?

EXAMPLE 3.16 — CONVERTING ENERGY UNITS

Convert 1.7×10^3 kWh (the amount of energy the average U.S. citizen uses in one week) into calories.

GIVEN: 1.7×10^3 kWh

FIND: cal

SOLUTION MAP

$$\frac{3.60 \times 10^6 \text{ J}}{1 \text{ kWh}} \qquad \frac{1 \text{ cal}}{4.18 \text{ J}}$$

RELATIONSHIPS USED

$1 \text{ kWh} = 3.60 \times 10^6$ J (Table 3.2)
$1 \text{ cal} = 4.18$ J (Table 3.2)

SOLUTION

$$1.7 \times 10^3 \text{ kWh} \times \frac{3.60 \times 10^6 \text{ J}}{1 \text{ kWh}} \times \frac{1 \text{ cal}}{4.18 \text{ J}}$$
$$= 1.464 \times 10^9 \text{ cal}$$

$$1.464 \times 10^9 \text{ cal} = 1.5 \times 10^9 \text{ cal}$$

The unit of the answer, cal, is correct. The magnitude of the answer makes sense because cal is a smaller unit than kWh; therefore, the value in cal should be larger than the value in kWh.

EXAMPLE 3.17 — CONVERTING BETWEEN CELSIUS AND KELVIN TEMPERATURE SCALES

Convert 257 K to Celsius.

GIVEN: 257 K

FIND: °C

SOLUTION MAP

$$K = {}^\circ C + 273.15$$

RELATIONSHIPS USED

$$K = {}^\circ C + 273.15 \text{ (Section 3.10)}$$

SOLUTION

$$K = {}^\circ C + 273.15$$
$${}^\circ C = K - 273.15$$
$${}^\circ C = 257 - 273.15 = -16\,{}^\circ C$$

The answer has the correct unit, and its magnitude seems correct (see Figure 3.17).

LO: Convert between Fahrenheit, Celsius, and Kelvin temperature Scales (Section 3.10)

Solve temperature conversion problems using the problem-solving procedure in Sections 2.6 and 2.10. Take the steps appropriate for equations.

SORT

You are given the temperature in degrees Celsius and asked to convert it to degrees Fahrenheit.

STRATEGIZE

Draw a solution map. Use the equation that relates the *given* quantity to the *find* quantity.

SOLVE

Solve the equation for the *find* quantity (°F) and substitute the temperature in °C into the equation. Calculate the answer to the correct number of significant figures.

CHECK

Are the units correct? Does the answer make physical sense?

EXAMPLE 3.18	**CONVERTING BETWEEN FAHRENHEIT AND CELSIUS TEMPERATURE SCALES**

Convert 62.0 °C to Fahrenheit.

GIVEN: 62.0 °C

FIND: °F

SOLUTION MAP

$$°C = \frac{(°F - 32)}{1.8}$$

RELATIONSHIPS USED

$$°C = \frac{(°F - 32)}{1.8}$$

SOLUTION

$$°C = \frac{(°F - 32)}{1.8}$$
$$1.8\,(°C) = °F - 32$$
$$°F = 1.8\,(°C) + 32$$
$$°F = 1.8\,(62.0) + 32 = 143.60\,°F = 144\,°F$$

The answer is in the correct units, and its magnitude seems correct (see Figure 3.17).

LO: Relate energy, temperature change, and heat capacity (Sections 3.12).

Solve heat capacity problems using the problem-solving procedure in Sections 2.6 and 2.10. Take the steps appropriate for equations.

SORT

You are given the volume of water and the amount of heat absorbed. You are asked to find the change in temperature.

STRATEGIZE

The solution map shows how the heat capacity equation relates the *given* and *find* quantities.

SOLVE

First, gather the necessary quantities—m, q, and ΔT—in the correct units. You must convert the value for q from kJ to J.

You also must convert the value for m from milliliters to grams; use the density of water, 1.0 g/mL, to convert milliliters to grams.

Look up the heat capacity for water in Table 3.4.

EXAMPLE 3.19	**RELATING ENERGY, TEMPERATURE CHANGE, AND HEAT CAPACITY**

What is the temperature change in 355 mL of water upon absorption of 34 kJ of heat?

GIVEN: 355 mL water
34 kJ of heat

$q = mC\Delta T$
$q =$

FIND: ΔT

SOLUTION MAP

$$q = m \cdot C \cdot \Delta T$$

RELATIONSHIPS USED

$$q = m \cdot C \cdot \Delta T$$

SOLUTION

$$q = 34\ \text{kJ} \times \frac{1000\ \text{J}}{1\ \text{kJ}} = 3.4 \times 10^4\ \text{J}$$

$$m = 355\ \text{mL} \times \frac{1.0\ \text{g}}{1\ \text{mL}} = 355\ \text{g}$$

$$C = 4.18\ \text{J/g}\,°C$$

$$q = m \cdot C \cdot \Delta T$$

Then solve the equation for ΔT and substitute the correct variables into the equation. Finally, calculate the answer to the right number of significant figures.

$$\Delta T = \frac{q}{mC}$$

$$\Delta T = \frac{3.4 \times 10^4 \, J}{355 \, g \times 4.18 \, J/g \, {}^\circ C}$$

$$= 22.91 \, {}^\circ C = 23 \, {}^\circ C$$

CHECK

Check your answer. Are the units correct? Does the answer make physical sense?

The answer has the correct units, and the magnitude seems correct. If the magnitude of the answer were a huge number—3×10^6, for example—you would need to go back and look for a mistake. Above 100 °C, water boils, so such a large answer would be unlikely.

KEY TERMS

amorphous [3.3]
atoms [3.2]
calorie (cal) [3.8]
Calorie (Cal) [3.8]
Celsius (°C) scale [3.10]
chemical change [3.6]
chemical energy [3.8]
chemical property [3.5]
chemical reaction [3.7]
compound [3.4]
compressible [3.3]
crystalline [3.3]
decanting [3.6]

distillation [3.6]
electrical energy [3.8]
element [3.4]
endothermic [3.9]
energy [3.8]
exothermic [3.9]
Fahrenheit (°F) scale [3.10]
filtration [3.6]
gas [3.3]
heat [3.10]
heat capacity [3.11]
heterogeneous mixture [3.4]
homogeneous mixture [3.4]

Kelvin (K) scale [3.10]
kilowatt-hour (kWh) [3.8]
kinetic energy [3.8]
law of conservation of
    energy [3.8]
liquid [3.3]
matter [3.2]
mixture [3.4]
molecule [3.2]
physical change [3.6]
physical property [3.5]
potential energy [3.8]
product [3.7]

property [3.5]
pure substance [3.4]
reactant [3.7]
solid [3.3]
specific heat capacity
    (specific heat) [3.11]
state of matter [3.3]
temperature [3.10]
thermal energy [3.8]
volatile [3.6]
work [3.8]

EXERCISES

QUESTIONS

Answers to all odd-numbered questions (numbered in blue) appear in the Answers section at the back of the book.

1. Define matter and list some examples.
2. What is matter composed of?
3. What are the three states of matter?
4. What are the properties of a solid?
5. What is the difference between a crystalline solid and an amorphous solid?
6. What are the properties of a liquid?
7. What are the properties of a gas?
8. Why are gases compressible?
9. What is a mixture?
10. What is the difference between a homogeneous mixture and a heterogeneous mixture?
11. What is a pure substance?
12. What is an element? A compound?
13. What is the difference between a mixture and a compound?
14. What is the definition of a physical property? What is the definition of a chemical property?
15. What is the difference between a physical change and a chemical change?

16. What is the law of conservation of mass?
17. What is the definition of energy?
18. What is the law of conservation of energy?
19. Explain the difference between kinetic energy and potential energy.
20. What is chemical energy? List some examples of common substances that contain chemical energy.
21. List three common units for energy.
22. What is an exothermic reaction? Which has greater energy in an exothermic reaction, the reactants or the products?
23. What is an endothermic reaction? Which has greater energy in an endothermic reaction, the reactants or the products?
24. List three common units for measuring temperature.
25. Explain the difference between heat and temperature.
26. How do the three temperature scales differ?
27. What is heat capacity?
28. Why are coastal geographic regions normally cooler in the summer than inland geographic regions?

29. The following equation can be used to convert Fahrenheit temperature to Celsius temperature.

$$°C = \frac{(°F - 32)}{1.8}$$

Use algebra to change the equation to convert Celsius temperature to Fahrenheit temperature.

30. The following equation can be used to convert Celsius temperature to Kelvin temperature.

$$K = °C + 273.15$$

Use algebra to change the equation to convert Kelvin temperature to Celsius temperature.

PROBLEMS

Note: The exercises in the Problems section are paired, and the answers to the odd-numbered exercises (numbered in blue) appear in the Answers section at the back of the book.

CLASSIFYING MATTER

31. Classify each pure substance as an element or a compound.
  (a) aluminum
  (b) sulfur
  (c) methane
  (d) acetone

32. Classify each pure substance as an element or a compound.
  (a) carbon
  (b) baking soda (sodium bicarbonate)
  (c) nickel
  (d) gold

33. Classify each mixture as homogeneous or heterogeneous.
  (a) coffee
  (b) chocolate sundae
  (c) apple juice
  (d) gasoline

34. Classify each mixture as homogeneous or heterogeneous.
  (a) baby oil
  (b) chocolate chip cookie
  (c) water and gasoline
  (d) wine

35. Classify each substance as a pure substance or a mixture. If it is a pure substance, classify it as an element or a compound. If it is a mixture, classify it as homogeneous or heterogeneous.
  (a) helium gas
  (b) clean air
  (c) rocky road ice cream
  (d) concrete

36. Classify each substance as a pure substance or a mixture. If it is a pure substance, classify it as an element or a compound. If it is a mixture, classify it as homogeneous or heterogeneous.
  (a) urine
  (b) pure water
  (c) Snickers™ bar
  (d) soil

PHYSICAL AND CHEMICAL PROPERTIES AND PHYSICAL AND CHEMICAL CHANGES

37. Classify each property as physical or chemical.
  (a) the tendency of silver to tarnish
  (b) the shine of chrome
  (c) the color of gold
  (d) the flammability of propane gas

38. Classify each property as physical or chemical.
  (a) the boiling point of ethyl alcohol
  (b) the temperature at which dry ice sublimes (turns from a solid into a gas).
  (c) the flammability of ethyl alcohol
  (d) the smell of perfume

39. Which of the following properties of ethylene (a ripening agent for bananas) are physical properties, and which are chemical?
  • colorless
  • odorless
  • flammable
  • gas at room temperature
  • 1 L has a mass of 1.260 g under standard conditions
  • mixes with acetone
  • polymerizes to form polyethylene

40. Which of the following properties of ozone (a pollutant in the lower atmosphere but part of a protective shield against UV light in the upper atmosphere) are physical, and which are chemical?
  • bluish color
  • pungent odor
  • very reactive
  • decomposes on exposure to ultraviolet light
  • gas at room temperature

41. Classify each change as physical or chemical.
    (a) A balloon filled with hydrogen gas explodes upon contact with a spark.
    (b) The liquid propane in a barbecue evaporates away because someone left the valve open.
    (c) The liquid propane in a barbecue ignites upon contact with a spark.
    (d) Copper metal turns green on exposure to air and water.

42. Classify each change as physical or chemical.
    (a) Sugar dissolves in hot water.
    (b) Sugar burns in a pot.
    (c) A metal surface becomes dull because of continued abrasion.
    (d) A metal surface becomes dull on exposure to air.

43. A block of aluminum is (a) ground into aluminum powder and then (b) ignited. It then emits flames and smoke. Classify (a) and (b) as chemical or physical changes.

44. Several pieces of graphite from a mechanical pencil are (a) broken into tiny pieces. Then the pile of graphite is (b) ignited with a hot flame. Classify (a) and (b) as chemical or physical changes.

THE CONSERVATION OF MASS

45. An automobile gasoline tank holds 42 kg of gasoline. When the gasoline burns, 168 kg of oxygen are consumed and carbon dioxide and water are produced. What total combined mass of carbon dioxide and water is produced?

46. In the explosion of a hydrogen-filled balloon, 0.50 g of hydrogen reacts with 4.0 g of oxygen. How many grams of water vapor are formed? (Water vapor is the only product.)

47. Are these data sets on chemical changes consistent with the law of conservation of mass?
    (a) A 7.5-g sample of hydrogen gas completely reacts with 60.0 g of oxygen gas to form 67.5 g of water.
    (b) A 60.5-g sample of gasoline completely reacts with 243 g of oxygen to form 206 g of carbon dioxide and 88 g of water.

48. Are these data sets on chemical changes consistent with the law of conservation of mass?
    (a) A 12.8-g sample of sodium completely reacts with 19.6 g of chlorine to form 32.4 g of sodium chloride.
    (b) An 8-g sample of natural gas completely reacts with 32 g of oxygen gas to form 17 g of carbon dioxide and 16 g of water.

49. In a butane lighter, 9.7 g of butane combine with 34.7 g of oxygen to form 29.3 g carbon dioxide and how many grams of water?

50. A 56-g sample of iron reacts with 24 g of oxygen to form how many grams of iron oxide?

CONVERSION OF ENERGY UNITS

51. Perform each conversion.
    (a) 588 cal to joules
    (b) 17.4 J to Calories
    (c) 134 kJ to Calories
    (d) 56.2 Cal to joules

52. Perform each conversion.
    (a) 45.6 J to calories
    (b) 355 cal to joules
    (c) 43.8 kJ to calories
    (d) 215 cal to kilojoules

53. Perform each conversion.
    (a) 25 kWh to joules
    (b) 249 cal to Calories
    (c) 113 cal to kilowatt-hours
    (d) 44 kJ to calories

54. Perform each conversion.
    (a) 345 Cal to kilowatt-hours
    (b) 23 J to calories
    (c) 5.7×10^3 J to kilojoules
    (d) 326 kJ to joules

55. Complete the table:

J	cal	Cal	kWh
225 J	_____	5.38×10^{-2} Cal	_____
_____	8.21×10^5 cal	_____	_____
_____	_____	_____	295 kWh
_____	_____	155 Cal	_____

56. Complete the table:

J	cal	Cal	kWh
7.88×10^6 J	1.88×10^6 cal	_____	_____
_____	_____	1154 Cal	_____
_____	88.4 cal	_____	_____
_____	_____	_____	125 kWh

57. An energy bill indicates that a customer used 1027 kWh in July. How many joules did the customer use?

58. A television uses 32 kWh of energy per year. How many joules does it use?

59. An adult eats food whose nutritional energy totals approximately 2.2×10^3 Cal per day. The adult burns 2.0×10^3 Cal per day. How much excess nutritional energy, in kilojoules, does the adult consume per day? If 1 lb of fat is stored by the body for each 14.6×10^3 kJ of excess nutritional energy consumed, how long will it take this person to gain 1 lb?

60. How many joules of nutritional energy are in a bag of chips with a label that lists 245 Cal? If 1 lb of fat is stored by the body for each 14.6×10^3 kJ of excess nutritional energy consumed, how many bags of chips contain enough nutritional energy to result in 1 lb of body fat?

ENERGY AND CHEMICAL AND PHYSICAL CHANGE

61. A common type of handwarmer contains iron powder that reacts with oxygen to form an oxide of iron. As soon as the handwarmer is exposed to air, the reaction begins and heat is emitted. Is the reaction between the iron and oxygen exothermic or endothermic? Draw an energy diagram showing the relative energies of the reactants and products in the reaction.

62. In a chemical cold pack, two substances are kept separate by a divider. When the divider is broken, the substances mix and absorb heat from the surroundings. The chemical cold pack feels cold. Is the reaction exothermic or endothermic? Draw an energy diagram showing the relative energies of the reactants and products in the reaction.

63. Classify each process as exothermic or endothermic.
   (a) gasoline burning in a car
   (b) isopropyl alcohol evaporating from skin
   (c) water condensing as dew during the night

64. Classify each process as exothermic or endothermic.
   (a) dry ice subliming (changing from a solid directly to a gas)
   (b) the wax in a candle burning
   (c) a match burning

CONVERTING BETWEEN TEMPERATURE SCALES

65. Perform each temperature conversion.
   (a) 212 °F to Celsius (temperature of boiling water)
   (b) 77 K to Fahrenheit (temperature of liquid nitrogen)
   (c) 25 °C to kelvins (room temperature)
   (d) 98.6 °F to kelvins (body temperature)

66. Perform each temperature conversion.
   (a) 102 °F to Celsius
   (b) 0 K to Fahrenheit
   (c) −48 °C to Fahrenheit
   (d) 273 K to Celsius

67. The coldest temperature ever measured in the United States was −80 °F on January 23, 1971, in Prospect Creek, Alaska. Convert that temperature to degrees Celsius and Kelvin. (Assume that −80 °F is accurate to two significant figures.)

68. The warmest temperature ever measured in the United States was 134 °F on July 10, 1913, in Death Valley, California. Convert that temperature to degrees Celsius and Kelvin.

69. Vodka does not freeze in the freezer because it contains a high percentage of ethanol. The freezing point of pure ethanol is −114 °C. Convert that temperature to degrees Fahrenheit and Kelvin.

70. Liquid helium boils at 4.2 K. Convert this temperature to degrees Fahrenheit and Celsius.

71. The temperature in the South Pole during the Antarctic winter is so cold that planes cannot land or take off, effectively leaving the inhabitants of the South Pole isolated for the winter. The average daily temperature at the South Pole in July is −59.7 °C. Convert this temperature to degrees Fahrenheit.

72. The coldest temperature ever recorded in Iowa was −47 °F on February 3, 1998. Convert this temperature to Kelvins and degrees Celsius.

73. Complete the table.

Kelvin	Fahrenheit	Celsius
0.0 K	_____	−273.0 °C
_____	82.5 °F	_____
_____	_____	8.5 °C

74. Complete the table.

Kelvin	Fahrenheit	Celsius
273.0 K	_____	0.0 °C
_____	−40.0 °F	_____
385 K	_____	_____

ENERGY, HEAT CAPACITY, AND TEMPERATURE CHANGES

75. Calculate the amount of heat required to raise the temperature of a 65-g sample of water from 32 °C to 65 °C.

76. Calculate the amount of heat required to raise the temperature of a 22-g sample of water from 7 °C to 18 °C.

77. Calculate the amount of heat required to heat a 45-kg sample of ethanol from 11.0 °C to 19.0 °C.

78. Calculate the amount of heat required to heat a 3.5-kg gold bar from 21 °C to 67 °C.

79. If 89 J of heat are added to a pure gold coin with a mass of 12 g, what is its temperature change?

80. If 57 J of heat are added to an aluminum can with a mass of 17.1 g, what is its temperature change?

81. An iron nail with a mass of 12 g absorbs 15 J of heat. If the nail was initially at 28 °C, what is its final temperature?

82. A 45-kg sample of water absorbs 345 kJ of heat. If the water was initially at 22.1 °C, what is its final temperature?

83. Calculate the temperature change that occurs when 248 cal of heat are added to 24 g of water.

84. A lead fishing weight with a mass of 57 g absorbs 146 cal of heat. If its initial temperature is 47 °C, what is its final temperature?

85. An unknown metal with a mass of 28 g absorbs 58 J of heat. Its temperature rises from 31.1 °C to 39.9 °C. Calculate the heat capacity of the metal and identify it referring to Table 3.4.

86. When 2.8 J of heat are added to 5.6 g of an unknown metal, its temperature rises by 3.9 °C. Are these data consistent with the metal being gold?

87. When 56 J of heat are added to 11 g of a liquid, its temperature rises from 10.4 °C to 12.7 °C. What is the heat capacity of the liquid?

88. When 47.5 J of heat are added to 13.2 g of a liquid, its temperature rises by 1.72 °C. What is the heat capacity of the liquid?

89. Two identical coolers are packed for a picnic. Each cooler is packed with eighteen 12-oz soft drinks and 3 lb of ice. However, the drinks that went into cooler A were refrigerated for several hours before they were packed in the cooler, while the drinks that went into cooler B were at room temperature. When the two coolers are opened three hours later, most of the ice in cooler A is still ice, while nearly all of the ice in cooler B has melted. Explain.

90. A 100-g block of iron metal and 100 g of water are each warmed to 75 °C and placed into two identical insulated containers. Two hours later, the two containers are opened and the temperature of each substance is measured. The iron metal has cooled to 38 °C while the water has cooled only to 69 °C. Explain.

91. How much energy (in J) is lost when a sample of iron with a mass of 25.7 g cools from 75.0 °C to 22.0 °C?

92. A sample of aluminum with mass of 53.2 g is initially at 155 °C. What is the temperature of the aluminum after it loses 2.87×10^3 J?

CUMULATIVE PROBLEMS

93. Calculate the final temperature of 245 mL of water initially at 32 °C upon absorption of 17 kJ of heat.

94. Calculate the final temperature of 32 mL of ethanol initially at 11 °C upon absorption of 562 J of heat. (density of ethanol = 0.789 g/mL)

95. A pure gold ring with a volume of 1.57 cm^3 is initially at 11.4 °C. When it is put on, it warms to 29.5 °C. How much heat does the ring absorb? (density of gold = 19.3 g/cm^3)

96. A block of aluminum with a volume of 98.5 cm^3 absorbs 67.4 J of heat. If its initial temperature is 32.5 °C, what is its final temperature? (density of aluminum = 2.70 g/cm^3)

97. How much heat in kilojoules is required to heat 56 L of water from 85 °F to 212 °F?

98. How much heat in joules is required to heat a 43-g sample of aluminum from 72 °F to 145 °F?

99. What is the temperature change in Celsius when 29.5 L of water absorbs 2.3 kWh of heat?

100. If 1.45 L of water is initially at 25.0 °C, what is its temperature after absorption of 9.4×10^{-2} kWh of heat?

101. A water heater contains 55 gal of water. How many kilowatt-hours of energy are necessary to heat the water in the water heater by 25 °C?

102. A room contains 48 kg of air. How many kilowatt-hours of energy are necessary to heat the air in the house from 7 °C to 28 °C? The heat capacity of air is 1.03 J/g °C.

103. A backpacker wants to carry enough fuel to heat 2.5 kg of water from 25 °C to 100.0 °C. If the fuel she carries produces 36 kJ of heat per gram when it burns, how much fuel should she carry? (For the sake of simplicity, assume that the transfer of heat is 100% efficient.)

104. A cook wants to heat 1.35 kg of water from 32.0 °C to 100.0 °C. If he uses the combustion of natural gas (which is exothermic) to heat the water, how much natural gas will he need to burn? Natural gas produces 49.3 kJ of heat per gram. (For the sake of simplicity, assume that the transfer of heat is 100% efficient.)

105. Evaporating sweat cools the body because evaporation is endothermic and absorbs 2.44 kJ per gram of water evaporated. Estimate the mass of water that must evaporate from the skin to cool a body by 0.50 °C, if the mass of the body is 95 kg and its heat capacity is 4.0 J/g °C. (Assume that the heat transfer is 100% efficient.)

106. When ice melts, it absorbs 0.33 kJ per gram. How much ice is required to cool a 12.0-oz drink from 75 °F to 35 °F, if the heat capacity of the drink is 4.18 J/g °C? (Assume that the heat transfer is 100% efficient.)

107. A 15.7-g aluminum block is warmed to 53.2 °C and plunged into an insulated beaker containing 32.5 g of water initially at 24.5 °C. The aluminum and the water are allowed to come to thermal equilibrium. Assuming that no heat is lost, what is the final temperature of the water and aluminum?

108. A 25.0-mL sample of ethanol (density = 0.789 g/mL) initially at 7.0 °C is mixed with 35.0 mL of water (density = 1.0 g/mL) initially at 25.3 °C in an insulated beaker. Assuming that no heat is lost, what is the final temperature of the mixture?

109. The wattage of an appliance indicates its average power consumption in watts (W), where 1 W = 1 J/s. What is the difference in the number of kJ of energy consumed per month between a refrigeration unit that consumes 625 W and one that consumes 855 W? If electricity costs $0.15 per kWh, what is the monthly cost difference to operate the two refrigerators? (Assume 30.0 days in one month and 24.0 hours per day.)

110. A portable electric water heater transfers 255 watts (W) of power to 5.5 L of water, where 1 W = 1 J/s. How much time (in minutes) does it take for the water heater to heat the 5.5 L of water from 25 °C to 42 °C? (Assume that the water has a density of 1.0 g/mL.)

111. What temperature is the same whether it is expressed in the Celsius or Fahrenheit scale?

112. What temperature on the Celsius scale is equal to twice its value when expressed on the Fahrenheit scale?

HIGHLIGHT PROBLEMS

113. Classify each as a pure substance or a mixture.

(a)

(b)

(c)

(d)

114. Classify each as a pure substance or a mixture. If it is a pure substance, classify it as an element or a compound. If it is a mixture, classify it as homogeneous or heterogeneous.

(a)

(b)

(c)

(d)

115. This molecular drawing shows images of acetone molecules before and after a change. Was the change chemical or physical?

116. This molecular drawing shows images of methane molecules and oxygen molecules before and after a change. Was the change chemical or physical?

117. A major event affecting global climate is the El Niño/La Niña cycle. In this cycle, equatorial Pacific Ocean waters warm by several degrees Celsius above normal (El Niño) and then cool by several degrees Celsius below normal (La Niña). This cycle affects weather not only in North and South America, but also in places as far away as Africa. Why does a seemingly small change in ocean temperature have such a large impact on weather?

◄ Temperature anomaly plot of the world's oceans for July 5–August 1, 2009. The large red-orange section in the middle of the map indicates the El Niño effect, a warming of the Pacific Ocean along the equator.

118. Global warming refers to the rise in average global temperature due to the increased concentration of certain gases, called greenhouse gases, in our atmosphere. Earth's oceans, because of their high heat capacity, absorb heat and therefore act to slow down global warming. How much heat would be required to warm Earth's oceans by 1.0 °C? Assume that the volume of water in Earth's oceans is 137×10^7 km^3 and that the density of seawater is 1.03 g/cm^3. Also assume that the heat capacity of seawater is the same as that of water.

▲ Earth's oceans moderate temperatures by absorbing heat during warm periods.

119. Examine the data for the maximum and minimum average temperatures of San Francisco and Sacramento in the summer and in the winter.

San Francisco (Coastal City)

January		August	
High	Low	High	Low
57.4 °F	43.8 °F	64.4 °F	54.5 °F

Sacramento (Inland City)

January		August	
High	Low	High	Low
53.2 °F	37.7 °F	91.5 °F	57.7 °F

(a) Notice the difference between the August high in San Francisco and Sacramento. Why is it much hotter in the summer in Sacramento?

(b) Notice the difference between the January low in San Francisco and Sacramento. How might the heat capacity of the ocean contribute to this difference?

QUESTIONS FOR GROUP WORK

Discuss the following questions with your group. Record the answer that your group agrees on.

120. Using white and black circles to represent different kinds of atoms, make a drawing that accurately represents each of the following: a solid element, a liquid compound, a homogeneous mixture, and a heterogeneous mixture.

121. Make a drawing (clearly showing *before* and *after*) depicting your liquid compound from Question 120 undergoing a physical change. Make a drawing depicting your solid element undergoing a chemical change.

122. A friend asks you to invest in a new motorbike that he invented that never needs gasoline and does not use batteries. What questions should you ask before investing?

123. In a grammatically correct sentence or two (and in your own words!), describe what heat and temperature have in common and how they are different. Make sure you are using the words correctly with their precise scientific meanings.

▶Answers to Skillbuilder Exercises

Skillbuilder 3.1
  (a) pure substance, element
  (b) mixture, homogeneous
  (c) mixture, heterogeneous
  (d) pure substance, compound

Skillbuilder 3.2
  (a) chemical
  (b) physical
  (c) physical
  (d) physical

Skillbuilder 3.3
  (a) chemical
  (b) physical
  (c) physical
  (d) chemical

Skillbuilder 3.4   27 g
Skillbuilder 3.5   2.14 kJ
Skillbuilder Plus, p. 70 6.57×10^6 cal
Skillbuilder 3.6
  (a) exothermic
  (b) exothermic
Skillbuilder 3.7   85 °C
Skillbuilder 3.8   282 °F
Skillbuilder 3.9   77 K
Skillbuilder 3.10   50.1 J
Skillbuilder Plus, p. 79   7.4 g
Skillbuilder 3.11 $\Delta T = 4.21$ °C; $T_f = 29.2$ °C

▶Answers to Conceptual Checkpoints

3.1 (c) The particles are far apart and moving relative to one another.

3.2 (a) Vaporization is a physical change, so the water molecules are the same before and after the boiling.

3.3 No In the vaporization, the liquid water becomes gaseous, but its mass does not change. Like chemical changes, physical changes also follow the law of conservation of mass.

3.4 (d) kWh is the largest of the four units listed, so the numerical value of the yearly energy consumption is lowest if expressed in kWh.

3.5 (d) You can confirm this by substituting each of the Fahrenheit temperatures into the equation in Section 3.10 and solving for the Celsius temperature.

3.6 (a) Because copper has the lowest specific heat capacity of the three metals, it experiences the greatest temperature change for a given energy input.

3.7 Substance B will undergo a greater change in temperature because it has the lower heat capacity. A substance with a lower heat capacity is less resistant to temperature changes.

Seaside rocks are typically composed of silicates, compounds of silicon and oxygen atoms. Seaside air, like all air, contains nitrogen and oxygen molecules, and it often also contains substances called amines. The amine shown here is triethylamine, which is emitted by decaying fish. Triethylamine is one of the compounds responsible for the fishy smell of the seaside.

Atoms and Elements 4

"Nothing exists except atoms and empty space; everything else is opinion."

—Democritus (460–370 B.C.)

CHAPTER OUTLINE

4.1 Experiencing Atoms at Tiburon

As we learned in Chapter 3, many atoms exist not as free particles but as groups of atoms bound together to form molecules. Nevertheless, all matter is ultimately made of atoms.

My wife and I recently enjoyed a visit to the northern California seaside town of Tiburon. Tiburon sits next to San Francisco Bay and enjoys views of the water, the city of San Francisco, and the surrounding mountains. As we walked along a waterside path, I could feel the wind as it blew over the bay. I could hear the water splashing on the shore, and I could smell the sea air. What was the cause of these sensations? The answer is simple—atoms.

Because all matter is made of atoms, atoms are at the foundation of our sensations. The atom is the fundamental building block of everything you hear, feel, see, and experience. When you feel wind on your skin, you are feeling atoms. When you hear sounds, you are in a sense hearing atoms. When you touch a shoreside rock, you are touching atoms, and when you smell sea air, you are smelling atoms. You eat atoms, you breathe atoms, and you excrete atoms. Atoms are the building blocks of matter; they are the basic units from which nature builds. They are all around us and compose everything, including our own bodies.

Atoms are incredibly small. A single pebble from the shoreline contains more atoms than you could ever count. The number of atoms in a single pebble far exceeds the number of pebbles on the bottom of San Francisco Bay. To get an idea of how small atoms are, imagine this: If every atom within a small pebble were the size of the pebble itself, the pebble would be larger than Mount Everest (▶ Figure 4.1). Atoms are small—yet they compose everything.

The key to connecting the submicroscopic world with the macroscopic world is the atom. Atoms compose matter; the properties of atoms determine the properties of matter. An **atom** is the smallest identifiable unit of an element. Recall from Section 3.4 that an *element* is a substance that cannot be broken down into simpler substances. There are about 91 different elements in nature, and consequently about 91 different kinds of atoms. In addition, scientists have succeeded in making over 20 synthetic elements (not found in nature). In this chapter, we examine atoms: what they are made of, how they differ from one another, and how they are structured. We also examine the elements that atoms compose and some of the properties of those elements.

The exact number of naturally occurring elements is controversial because some elements previously considered only synthetic may actually occur in nature in very small quantities.

▲ **FIGURE 4.1** **The size of the atom** If every atom within a pebble were the size of the pebble itself, then the pebble would be larger than Mount Everest.

4.2 Indivisible: The Atomic Theory

LO: Recognize that all matter is composed of atoms.

▲ Diogenes and Democritus, as imagined by a medieval artist. Democritus is the first person on record to have postulated that matter was composed of atoms.

If we look at matter, even under a microscope, it is not obvious that matter is composed of tiny particles. In fact, it appears to be just the opposite. If we divide a sample of matter into smaller and smaller pieces, it seems that we could divide it forever. From our perspective, matter seems continuous. The first people recorded as thinking otherwise were Leucippus (fifth century B.C.E., exact dates unknown) and Democritus (460–370 B.C.E.). These Greek philosophers theorized that matter was ultimately composed of small, indivisible particles. Democritus suggested that if you divided matter into smaller and smaller pieces, you would eventually end up with tiny, indestructible particles called *atomos,* or "atoms." The word *atomos* means "indivisible."

The ideas of Leucippus and Democritus were not widely accepted. It was not until 1808—over 2000 years later—that John Dalton formalized a theory of atoms that gained broad acceptance. Dalton's atomic theory has three parts:

1. Each element is composed of tiny indestructible particles called atoms.
2. All atoms of a given element have the same mass and other properties that distinguish them from the atoms of other elements.
3. Atoms combine in simple, whole-number ratios to form compounds.

Today, the evidence for the atomic theory is overwhelming. Recent advances in microscopy have allowed scientists not only to image individual atoms but also to pick them up and move them (▼ Figure 4.2). Matter is indeed composed of atoms.

▶ **FIGURE 4.2** **Writing with atoms** Scientists at IBM used a special microscope, called a scanning tunneling microscope (STM), to move xenon atoms to form the letters I, B, and M. The cone shape of these atoms is due to the peculiarities of the instrumentation. Atoms are, in general, spherical in shape.

Xenon atoms

EVERYDAY CHEMISTRY

▶ Atoms and Humans

All matter is composed of atoms. What does that mean? What does it imply? It means that everything before you is composed of tiny particles too small to see. It means that even you and I are composed of these same particles. We acquired those particles from the food we have eaten over the years. The average carbon atom in your body has been used by 20 other living organisms before you get to it and will be used by other organisms when you are done with it. In fact, it is likely that at this moment, your body contains over 1 trillion carbon atoms that were at one time part of your chemistry professor.*

The idea that all matter is composed of atoms has far-reaching implications. It implies that our bodies, our hearts, and even our brains are composed of atoms acting according to the laws of chemistry and physics. Some people view this as a devaluation of human life. We have always wanted to distinguish ourselves from everything else, and the idea that we are made of the same basic particles as all other matter takes something away from that distinction . . . or does it?

B4.1 CAN YOU ANSWER THIS? *Do you find the idea that you are made of atoms disturbing? Why or why not?*

* This calculation assumes that all of the carbon atoms your professor has metabolized over the last 40 years have been uniformly distributed into atmospheric carbon dioxide and subsequently incorporated into plants that you eat.

4.3   The Nuclear Atom

LO: Explain how the experiments of Thomson and Rutherford led to the development of the nuclear theory of the atom.

Electric charge is more fully defined in Section 4.4. For now, think of it as an inherent property of electrons that causes them to interact with other charged particles.

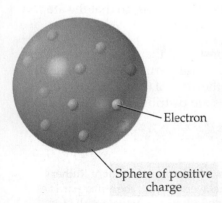

▲ **FIGURE 4.3   Plum pudding model of the atom**   In the model suggested by J. J. Thomson, negatively charged electrons (yellow) are held in a sphere of positive charge (red).

By the end of the nineteenth century, scientists were convinced that matter was composed of atoms, the permanent, indestructible building blocks from which all substances are constructed. However, an English physicist named J. J. Thomson (1856–1940) complicated the picture by discovering an even smaller and more fundamental particle called the **electron**. Thomson discovered that electrons are negatively charged, that they are much smaller and lighter than atoms, and that they are uniformly present in many different kinds of substances. His experiments proved that the indestructible building block called the atom could apparently be "chipped."

The discovery of negatively charged particles within atoms raised the question of a balancing positive charge. Atoms are known to be charge-neutral, so it was believed that they must contain positive charge that balanced the negative charge of electrons. But how do the positive and negative charges within the atom fit together? Are atoms just a jumble of even more fundamental particles? Are they solid spheres, or do they have some internal structure? Thomson proposed that the negatively charged electrons were small particles held within a positively charged sphere. This model, the most popular of the time, became known as the plum pudding model (plum pudding is an English dessert) (◀ Figure 4.3). The picture suggested by Thomson was—to those of us not familiar with plum pudding—like a blueberry muffin, where the blueberries are the electrons and the muffin is the positively charged sphere.

In 1909, Ernest Rutherford (1871–1937), who had worked under Thomson and adhered to his plum pudding model, performed an experiment in an attempt to confirm it. His experiment instead proved the plum pudding model wrong. In his experiment, Rutherford directed tiny, positively charged particles—called alpha-particles—at an ultrathin sheet of gold foil (▶ Figure 4.4). Alpha-particles are about 7000 times more massive than electrons and carry a positive charge. These particles were to act as probes of the gold atoms' structure. If the gold atoms were indeed like blueberry muffins or plum pudding—with their mass and charge spread throughout the entire volume of the atom—these speeding probes should pass right through the gold foil with minimum deflection. Rutherford's results were not as he expected. A majority of the particles did pass directly through the

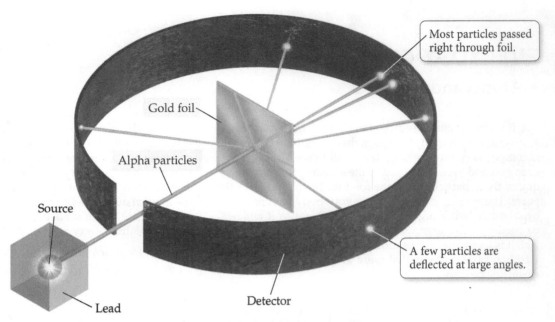

Most particles passed right through foil.

Gold foil

Alpha particles

Source

A few particles are deflected at large angles.

Lead

Detector

▲ **FIGURE 4.4** **Rutherford's gold foil experiment** Rutherford directed tiny particles called alpha-particles at a thin sheet of gold foil. Most of the particles passed directly through the foil. A few, however, were deflected—some of them at sharp angles.

foil, but some particles were deflected, and some (1 in 20,000) even bounced back. The results puzzled Rutherford, who found them "about as credible as if you had fired a 15-inch shell at a piece of tissue paper and it came back and hit you." What must the structure of the atom be in order to explain this odd behavior?

Rutherford created a new model to explain his results (◄ Figure 4.5). He concluded that matter must not be as uniform as it appears. It contains large regions of empty space dotted with small regions of very dense matter. In order to explain the deflections he observed, the mass and positive charge of an atom must all be concentrated in a space much smaller than the size of the atom itself. Based on this idea, he developed the **nuclear theory of the atom**, which has three basic parts:

1. Most of the atom's mass and all of its positive charge are contained in a small core called the *nucleus*.
2. Most of the volume of the atom is empty space through which the tiny, negatively charged electrons are dispersed.
3. There are as many negatively charged electrons outside the nucleus as there are positively charged particles (*protons*) inside the nucleus, so that the atom is electrically neutral.

Later work by Rutherford and others demonstrated that the atom's **nucleus** contains both positively charged **protons** and neutral particles called **neutrons**. The dense nucleus makes up more than 99.9% of the mass of the atom, but occupies only a small fraction of its volume. The electrons are distributed through a much

Plum pudding model

Alpha-particles

(a) Rutherford's expected result

Nuclear model

Nucleus ● Proton
● Neutron

(b) Rutherford's actual result

◄ **FIGURE 4.5** **Discovery of the atomic nucleus** **(a)** Expected result of Rutherford's gold foil experiment. If the plum pudding model were correct, the alpha-particles would pass right through the gold foil with minimal deflection. **(b)** Actual result of Rutherford's gold foil experiment. A small number of alpha-particles were deflected or bounced back. The only way to explain the deflections was to suggest that most of the mass and all of the positive charge of an atom must be concentrated in a space much smaller than the size of the atom itself—the nucleus. The nucleus itself is composed of positively charged particles (protons) and neutral particles (neutrons).

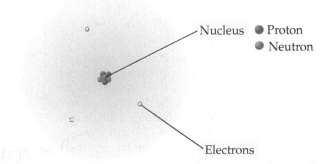

Nuclear model—volume of atom is mostly empty space.

Nucleus   ● Proton
           ● Neutron

Electrons

▶ **FIGURE 4.6   The nuclear atom**   In this model, 99.9% of the atom's mass is concentrated in a small, dense nucleus that contains protons and neutrons. The rest of the volume of the atom is mostly empty space occupied by negatively charged electrons. The number of electrons outside the nucleus is equal to the number of protons inside the nucleus. In this image, the nucleus is greatly enlarged and the electrons are portrayed as particles.

larger region, but don't have much mass (▲ Figure 4.6). For now, you can think of these electrons as akin to the water droplets that make up a cloud—they are dispersed throughout a large volume but weigh almost nothing.

Rutherford's nuclear theory is still valid today. The revolutionary part of this theory is the idea that matter—at its core—is much less uniform than it appears. If the nucleus of the atom were the size of this dot ·, the average electron would be about 10 m away. Yet the dot would contain almost the entire mass of the atom. What if matter were composed of atomic nuclei piled on top of each other like marbles? Such matter would be incredibly dense; a single grain of sand composed of solid atomic nuclei would have a mass of 5 million kg (or a weight of about 10 million lb). Astronomers believe that black holes and neutron stars are composed of this kind of incredibly dense matter.

4.4   The Properties of Protons, Neutrons, and Electrons

LO: Describe the respective properties and charges of electrons, neutrons, and protons.

Protons and neutrons have very similar masses. In SI units, the mass of the proton is 1.67262×10^{-27} kg, and the mass of the neutron is a close 1.67493×10^{-27} kg. A more common unit to express these masses, however, is the **atomic mass unit (amu)**, defined as one-twelfth of the mass of a carbon atom containing 6 protons and 6 neutrons. A proton has a mass of 1.0073 amu, and a neutron has a mass of 1.0087 amu. Electrons, by contrast, have an almost negligible mass of 0.00091×10^{-27} kg, or approximately 0.00055 amu.

The proton and the electron both have electrical **charge**. The proton's charge is 1+ and the electron's charge is 1−. The charges of the proton and the electron are equal in magnitude but opposite in sign, so that when the two particles are paired, the charges exactly cancel. The neutron has no charge.

What is electrical charge? Electrical charge is a fundamental property of protons and electrons, just as mass is a fundamental property of matter. Most matter is charge-neutral because protons and electrons occur together and their charges cancel. However, you may have experienced excess electrical charge when brushing your hair on a dry day. The brushing action results in the accumulation of electrical charge on the hair strands, which then repel each other, causing your hair to stand on end.

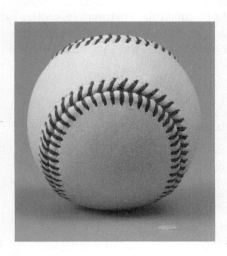

◀ If a proton had the mass of a baseball, an electron would have the mass of a rice grain. The proton is nearly 2000 times as massive as an electron.

EVERYDAY CHEMISTRY

▶ Solid Matter?

If matter really is mostly empty space as Rutherford suggested, then why does it appear so solid? Why can you tap your knuckles on the table and feel a solid thump? Matter appears solid because the variation in the density is on such a small scale that our eyes can't see it. Imagine a jungle gym 100 stories high and the size of a football field. It is mostly empty space. Yet if you were to view it from an airplane, it would appear as a solid mass. Matter is similar. When you tap your knuckles on the table, it is much like one giant jungle gym (your finger) crashing into another (the table). Even though they are both primarily empty space, one does not fall into the other.

B4.2 CAN YOU ANSWER THIS? *Use the jungle gym analogy to explain why most of Rutherford's alpha-particles went right through the gold foil and why a few bounced back. Remember that his gold foil was extremely thin.*

▲ Matter appears solid and uniform because the variation in density is on a scale too small for our eyes to see. Just as this scaffolding appears solid at a distance, so matter appears solid to us.

Positive (red) and negative (yellow) charges attract.

Positive–positive and negative–negative charges repel.

Positive and negative charges cancel.

▲ **FIGURE 4.7 The properties of electrical charge**

We can summarize the nature of electrical charge as follows (◀ Figure 4.7).

- Electrical charge is a fundamental property of protons and electrons.
- Positive and negative electrical charges attract each other.
- Positive–positive and negative–negative charges repel each other.
- Positive and negative charges cancel each other so that a proton and an electron, when paired, are charge-neutral.

Note that matter is usually charge-neutral due to the canceling effect of protons and electrons. When matter does acquire charge imbalances, these imbalances usually equalize quickly, often in dramatic ways. For example, the shock you receive when touching a doorknob during dry weather is the equalization of a charge imbalance that developed as you walked across the carpet. Lightning is an equalization of charge imbalances that develop during electrical storms.

If you had a sample of matter—even a tiny sample, such as a sand grain—that was composed of only protons or only electrons, the forces around that matter would be extraordinary, and the matter would be unstable. Fortunately, matter is not that way—protons and electrons exist together, canceling each other's charge and making matter charge-neutral. Table 4.1 summarizes the properties of protons, neutrons, and electrons.

TABLE 4.1 Subatomic Particles

	Mass (kg)	Mass (amu)	Charge
proton	1.67262×10^{-27}	1.0073	1+
neutron	1.67493×10^{-27}	1.0087	0
electron	0.00091×10^{-27}	0.00055	1−

▶ Matter is normally charge-neutral, having equal numbers of positive and negative charges that exactly cancel. When the charge balance of matter is disturbed, as in an electrical storm, it quickly rebalances, often in dramatic ways such as lightning.

Negative charge buildup

Charge equalization

Positive charge buildup

 CONCEPTUAL CHECKPOINT 4.1

An atom composed of which of these particles would have a mass of approximately 12 amu and be charge-neutral?

(a) 6 protons and 6 electrons

(b) 3 protons, 3 neutrons, and 6 electrons

(c) 6 protons, 6 neutrons, and 6 electrons

(d) 12 neutrons and 12 electrons

4.5   Elements: Defined by Their Numbers of Protons

LO: Determine the atomic symbol and atomic number for an element using the periodic table.

We have seen that atoms are composed of protons, neutrons, and electrons. However, it is the number of protons in the nucleus of an atom that identifies it as a particular element. For example, atoms with 2 protons in their nucleus are helium atoms, atoms with 13 protons in their nucleus are aluminum atoms, and atoms with 92 protons in their nucleus are uranium atoms. The number of protons in an atom's nucleus defines the element (▼ Figure 4.8). Every aluminum atom has

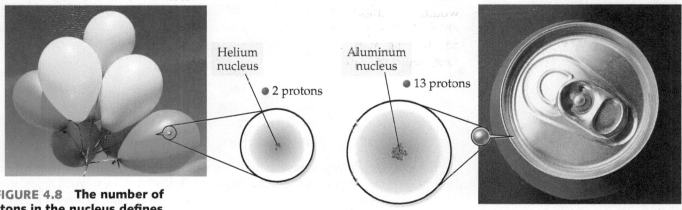

Helium
nucleus

● 2 protons

Aluminum
nucleus

● 13 protons

▲ **FIGURE 4.8   The number of protons in the nucleus defines the element**

▲ FIGURE 4.9 The periodic table of the elements

Key:
- Atomic number (Z): 4
- Chemical symbol: Be
- Atomic mass (defined in Section 4.9): 9.01
- Name: beryllium

1A (1)	2A (2)	3B (3)	4B (4)	5B (5)	6B (6)	7B (7)	8B (8)	8B (9)	8B (10)	1B (11)	2B (12)	3A (13)	4A (14)	5A (15)	6A (16)	7A (17)	8A (18)
1 H 1.01 hydrogen																	2 He 4.00 helium
3 Li 6.94 lithium	4 Be 9.01 beryllium											5 B 10.81 boron	6 C 12.01 carbon	7 N 14.01 nitrogen	8 O 16.00 oxygen	9 F 19.00 fluorine	10 Ne 20.18 neon
11 Na 22.99 sodium	12 Mg 24.31 magnesium											13 Al 26.98 aluminum	14 Si 28.09 silicon	15 P 30.97 phosphorus	16 S 32.06 sulfur	17 Cl 35.45 chlorine	18 Ar 39.95 argon
19 K 39.10 potassium	20 Ca 40.08 calcium	21 Sc 44.96 scandium	22 Ti 47.88 titanium	23 V 50.94 vanadium	24 Cr 52.00 chromium	25 Mn 54.94 manganese	26 Fe 55.85 iron	27 Co 58.93 cobalt	28 Ni 58.69 nickel	29 Cu 63.55 copper	30 Zn 65.39 zinc	31 Ga 69.72 gallium	32 Ge 72.63 germanium	33 As 74.92 arsenic	34 Se 78.96 selenium	35 Br 79.90 bromine	36 Kr 83.80 krypton
37 Rb 85.47 rubidium	38 Sr 87.62 strontium	39 Y 88.91 yttrium	40 Zr 91.22 zirconium	41 Nb 92.91 niobium	42 Mo 95.94 molybdenum	43 Tc (99) technetium	44 Ru 101.07 ruthenium	45 Rh 102.91 rhodium	46 Pd 106.42 palladium	47 Ag 107.87 silver	48 Cd 112.41 cadmium	49 In 114.82 indium	50 Sn 118.71 tin	51 Sb 121.75 antimony	52 Te 127.60 tellurium	53 I 126.90 iodine	54 Xe 131.29 xenon
55 Cs 132.91 cesium	56 Ba 137.33 barium	57 La 138.91 lanthanum	72 Hf 178.49 hafnium	73 Ta 180.95 tantalum	74 W 183.85 tungsten	75 Re 186.21 rhenium	76 Os 190.2 osmium	77 Ir 192.22 iridium	78 Pt 195.08 platinum	79 Au 196.97 gold	80 Hg 200.59 mercury	81 Tl 204.38 thallium	82 Pb 207.2 lead	83 Bi 208.98 bismuth	84 Po (209) polonium	85 At (210) astatine	86 Rn (222) radon
87 Fr (223) francium	88 Ra (226) radium	89 Ac (227) actinium	104 Rf (261) rutherfordium	105 Db (262) dubnium	106 Sg (263) seaborgium	107 Bh (262) bohrium	108 Hs (265) hassium	109 Mt (266) meitnerium	110 Ds (281) darmstadtium	111 Rg (280) roentgenium	112 Cn (285)	113 — (284)	114 Fl (289)	115 — (288)	116 Lv (292)	117 ** (292)	118 — (294)

Lanthanides:

58 Ce 140.12 cerium	59 Pr 140.91 praseodymium	60 Nd 144.24 neodymium	61 Pm (147) promethium	62 Sm 150.36 samarium	63 Eu 151.97 europium	64 Gd 157.25 gadolinium	65 Tb 158.93 terbium	66 Dy 162.50 dysprosium	67 Ho 164.93 holmium	68 Er 167.26 erbium	69 Tm 168.93 thulium	70 Yb 173.04 ytterbium	71 Lu 174.97 lutetium

Actinides:

90 Th (232) thorium	91 Pa (231) protactinium	92 U (238) uranium	93 Np (237) neptunium	94 Pu (244) plutonium	95 Am (243) americium	96 Cm (247) curium	97 Bk (247) berkelium	98 Cf (251) californium	99 Es (252) einsteinium	100 Fm (257) fermium	101 Md (258) mendelevium	102 No (259) nobelium	103 Lr (260) lawrencium

Periods 1–7 (left margin).

**Element 117 is currently under review by IUPAC.

13 protons in its nucleus; if it had a different number of protons, it would be a different element. The number of protons in the nucleus of an atom is its **atomic number** and is represented with the symbol Z.

The periodic table of the elements (▲ Figure 4.9) lists all known elements according to their atomic numbers. Each element is represented by a unique **chemical symbol**, a one- or two-letter abbreviation for the element that appears directly below its atomic number on the periodic table. The chemical symbol for helium is He; for aluminum, Al; and for uranium, U. The chemical symbol and the atomic number always go together. If the atomic number is 13, the chemical symbol must be Al. If the atomic number is 92, the chemical symbol must be U. This is just another way of saying that the number of protons defines the element.

Most chemical symbols are based on the English name of the element. For example, the symbol for carbon is C; for silicon, Si; and for bromine, Br. Some elements, however, have symbols based on their Latin names. For example, the symbol for potassium is K, from the Latin *kalium*, and the symbol for sodium is Na, from the Latin *natrium*. Additional elements with symbols based on their Greek or Latin names include:

lead	Pb	*plumbum*
mercury	Hg	*hydrargyrum*
iron	Fe	*ferrum*
silver	Ag	*argentum*
tin	Sn	*stannum*
copper	Cu	*cuprum*

Early scientists often gave newly discovered elements names that reflected their properties. For example, *argon* originates from the Greek word *argos*, meaning "inactive," referring to argon's chemical inertness (it does not react with other elements). *Bromine* originates from the Greek word *bromos*, meaning "stench," referring to bromine's strong odor. Scientists named other elements after countries.

▲ The name *bromine* originates from the Greek word *bromos*, meaning "stench." Bromine vapor, seen as the red-brown gas in this photograph, has a strong odor.

Curium
96
Cm
(247)

▲ Curium is named after Marie Curie (1867–1934), a chemist who helped discover radioactivity and also discovered two new elements. Curie won two Nobel Prizes for her work.

For example, polonium was named after Poland, francium after France, and americium after the United States of America. Still other elements were named after scientists. Curium was named after Marie Curie, and mendelevium after Dmitri Mendeleev. You can find every element's name, symbol, and atomic number in the periodic table (inside front cover) and in an alphabetical listing (inside back cover) in this book.

EXAMPLE 4.1   **ATOMIC NUMBER, ATOMIC SYMBOL, AND ELEMENT NAME**

List the atomic symbol and atomic number for each element.

(a) silicon
(b) potassium
(c) gold
(d) antimony

SOLUTION

As you become familiar with the periodic table, you will be able to quickly locate elements on it. At first you may find it easier to locate them in the alphabetical listing on the inside back cover of this book, but you should become familiar with their positions in the periodic table.

Element	Symbol	Atomic Number
silicon	Si	14
potassium	K	19
gold	Au	79
antimony	Sb	51

**Element 117 is currently under review by IUPAC.

▶**SKILLBUILDER 4.1** | **Atomic Number, Atomic Symbol, and Element Name**

Find the name and atomic number for each element.

(a) Na
(b) Ni
(c) P
(d) Ta

▶**FOR MORE PRACTICE**   Problems 41, 42, 45, 46, 47, 48, 49, 50.

4.6 Looking for Patterns: The Periodic Law and the Periodic Table

LO: Use the periodic table to classify elements by group.

▲ Dmitri Mendeleev, a Russian chemistry professor who arranged early versions of the periodic table.

┃ *Periodic* means "recurring regularly."

1								2
H								He

3	4	5	6	7	8	9	10
Li	Be	B	C	N	O	F	Ne
11	12	13	14	15	16	17	18
Na	Mg	Al	Si	P	S	Cl	Ar
19	20						
K	Ca						

▲ **FIGURE 4.11 Making a periodic table** If we place the elements from Figure 4.10 in a table, we can arrange them in rows so that similar properties align in the same vertical columns. This is similar to Mendeleev's first periodic table.

The organization of the periodic table has its origins in the work of Dmitri Mendeleev (1834–1907), a nineteenth-century Russian chemistry professor. In his time, about 65 different elements had been discovered. Thanks to the work of a number of chemists, much was known about each of these elements, including their relative masses, chemical activity, and some of their physical properties. However, there was no systematic way of organizing them.

1	2	3	4	5	6	7	8	9	10	11	12	13	14	15	16	17	18	19	20
H	He	Li	Be	B	C	N	O	F	Ne	Na	Mg	Al	Si	P	S	Cl	Ar	K	Ca

▲ **FIGURE 4.10 Recurring properties** These elements are listed in order of increasing atomic number (Mendeleev used relative mass, which is similar). The color of each element represents its properties. Notice that the properties (colors) of these elements form a repeating pattern.

In 1869, Mendeleev noticed that certain groups of elements had similar properties. He found that if he listed the elements in order of increasing relative mass, those similar properties recurred in a regular pattern (▲ Figure 4.10). Mendeleev summarized these observations in the **periodic law**:

When the elements are arranged in order of increasing relative mass, certain sets of properties recur periodically.

Mendeleev organized all the known elements in a table in which relative mass increased from left to right and elements with similar properties were aligned in the same vertical columns (◄ Figure 4.11). Because many elements had not yet been discovered, Mendeleev's table contained some gaps, which allowed him to predict the existence of yet-undiscovered elements. For example, Mendeleev predicted the existence of an element he called *eka-silicon*, which fell below silicon on the table and between gallium and arsenic. In 1886, eka-silicon was discovered by German chemist Clemens Winkler (1838–1904) and was found to have almost exactly the properties that Mendeleev had anticipated. Winkler named the element germanium, after his home country.

Mendeleev's original listing has evolved into the modern **periodic table**. In the modern table, elements are listed in order of increasing atomic number rather than increasing relative mass. The modern periodic table also contains more elements than Mendeleev's original table because many more have been discovered since his time.

Mendeleev's periodic law was based on observation. Like all scientific laws, the periodic law summarized many observations but did not give the underlying reason for the observation—only theories do that. For now, we accept the periodic law as it is, but in Chapter 9 we will examine a powerful theory that explains the law and gives the underlying reasons for it.

We can broadly classify the elements in the periodic table as metals, nonmetals, and metalloids (▶ Figure 4.12). **Metals** occupy the left side of the periodic table and have similar properties: They are good conductors of heat and electricity; they can be pounded into flat sheets (malleability); they can be drawn into wires (ductility); they are often shiny; and they tend to lose electrons when they undergo chemical changes. Good examples of metals are iron, magnesium, chromium, and sodium.

Nonmetals occupy the upper right side of the periodic table. The dividing line between metals and nonmetals is the zigzag diagonal line running from boron to astatine in Figure 4.12. Nonmetals have more varied properties—some are solids at room temperature, others are gases—but as a whole they tend to be poor conductors of heat and electricity, and they all tend to gain electrons when they undergo chemical changes. Good examples of nonmetals are oxygen, nitrogen, chlorine, and iodine.

Most of the elements that lie along the zigzag diagonal line dividing metals and nonmetals are **metalloids**, or semimetals, and display mixed properties.

1A 1																	8A 18
1 1 H	2A 2												3A 13	4A 14	5A 15	6A 16	7A 17	2 He
2 3 Li	4 Be												5 B	6 C	7 N	8 O	9 F	10 Ne
3 11 Na	12 Mg	3B 3	4B 4	5B 5	6B 6	7B 7	8	8B 9	10	1B 11	2B 12		13 Al	14 Si	15 P	16 S	17 Cl	18 Ar
4 19 K	20 Ca	21 Sc	22 Ti	23 V	24 Cr	25 Mn	26 Fe	27 Co	28 Ni	29 Cu	30 Zn		31 Ga	32 Ge	33 As	34 Se	35 Br	36 Kr
5 37 Rb	38 Sr	39 Y	40 Zr	41 Nb	42 Mo	43 Tc	44 Ru	45 Rh	46 Pd	47 Ag	48 Cd		49 In	50 Sn	51 Sb	52 Te	53 I	54 Xe
6 55 Cs	56 Ba	57 La	72 Hf	73 Ta	74 W	75 Re	76 Os	77 Ir	78 Pt	79 Au	80 Hg		81 Tl	82 Pb	83 Bi	84 Po	85 At	86 Rn
7 87 Fr	88 Ra	89 Ac	104 Rf	105 Db	106 Sg	107 Bh	108 Hs	109 Mt	110 Ds	111 Rg	112 Cn		113	114 Fl	115	116 Lv	117 **	118

Metals
Nonmetals
Metalloids

Lanthanides	58 Ce	59 Pr	60 Nd	61 Pm	62 Sm	63 Eu	64 Gd	65 Tb	66 Dy	67 Ho	68 Er	69 Tm	70 Yb	71 Lu
Actinides	90 Th	91 Pa	92 U	93 Np	94 Pu	95 Am	96 Cm	97 Bk	98 Cf	99 Es	100 Fm	101 Md	102 No	103 Lr

**Element 117 is currently under review by IUPAC.

▲ **FIGURE 4.12 Metals, nonmetals, and metalloids**
The elements in the periodic table can be broadly classified as metals, nonmetals, or metalloids.

▲ Silicon is a metalloid used extensively in the computer and electronics industries.

We also call metalloids **semiconductors** because of their intermediate electrical conductivity, which can be changed and controlled. This property makes semiconductors useful in the manufacture of the electronic devices that are central to computers, cell phones, and many other technological gadgets. Silicon, arsenic, and germanium are good examples of metalloids.

EXAMPLE 4.2	**CLASSIFYING ELEMENTS AS METALS, NONMETALS, OR METALLOIDS**

Classify each element as a metal, nonmetal, or metalloid.

(a) Ba   **(b)** I   **(c)** O   **(d)** Te

SOLUTION

(a) Barium is on the left side of the periodic table; it is a metal.
(b) Iodine is on the right side of the periodic table; it is a nonmetal.
(c) Oxygen is on the right side of the periodic table; it is a nonmetal.
(d) Tellurium is in the middle-right section of the periodic table, along the line that divides the metals from the nonmetals; it is a metalloid.

▶**SKILLBUILDER 4.2 | Classifying Elements as Metals, Nonmetals, or Metalloids**

Classify each element as a metal, nonmetal, or metalloid.

(a) S   **(b)** Cl   **(c)** Ti   **(d)** Sb

▶**FOR MORE PRACTICE** Problems 51, 52, 53, 54.

We can also broadly divide the periodic table into **main-group elements**, whose properties tend to be more predictable based on their position in the periodic table, and **transition elements** or **transition metals**, whose properties are less easily

▶ **FIGURE 4.13 Main-group and transition elements** We can broadly divide the periodic table into main-group elements, whose properties we can generally predict based on their position, and transition elements, whose properties tend to be less predictable based on their position.

Main-group elements | Transition elements | Main-group elements

	1A																	8A
1	1 H	2A											3A	4A	5A	6A	7A	2 He
2	3 Li	4 Be											5 B	6 C	7 N	8 O	9 F	10 Ne
3	11 Na	12 Mg	3B	4B	5B	6B	7B		8B		1B	2B	13 Al	14 Si	15 P	16 S	17 Cl	18 Ar
4	19 K	20 Ca	21 Sc	22 Ti	23 V	24 Cr	25 Mn	26 Fe	27 Co	28 Ni	29 Cu	30 Zn	31 Ga	32 Ge	33 As	34 Se	35 Br	36 Kr
5	37 Rb	38 Sr	39 Y	40 Zr	41 Nb	42 Mo	43 Tc	44 Ru	45 Rh	46 Pd	47 Ag	48 Cd	49 In	50 Sn	51 Sb	52 Te	53 I	54 Xe
6	55 Cs	56 Ba	57 La	72 Hf	73 Ta	74 W	75 Re	76 Os	77 Ir	78 Pt	79 Au	80 Hg	81 Tl	82 Pb	83 Bi	84 Po	85 At	86 Rn
7	87 Fr	88 Ra	89 Ac	104 Rf	105 Db	106 Sg	107 Bh	108 Hs	109 Mt	110 Ds	111 Rg	112 Cn	113	114 Fl	115	116 Lv	117 **	118

Periods (axis label)

Group number (label)

**Element 117 is currently under review by IUPAC.

predictable based simply on their position in the periodic table (▲ Figure 4.13). Main-group elements are in columns labeled with a number and the letter A. Transition elements are in columns labeled with a number and the letter B. A competing numbering system does not use letters, but only the numbers 1–18. We show both numbering systems in the periodic table in the inside front cover of this book.

✓ CONCEPTUAL CHECKPOINT 4.2

Which element is a main-group metal?

(a) O   **(b)** Ag   **(c)** P   **(d)** Pb

Each column within the periodic table is a **family** or **group** of elements. The elements within a family of main-group elements usually have similar properties, and some have a group name. For example, the Group 8A elements, the **noble gases**, are chemically inert gases. The most familiar noble gas is probably helium, used to fill balloons. Helium, like the other noble gases, is chemically stable—it won't combine with other elements to form compounds—and is therefore safe to put into balloons. Other noble gases include neon, often used in neon signs; argon, which makes up a small percentage of our atmosphere; krypton; and xenon. The Group 1A elements, the **alkali metals**, are all very reactive metals. A marble-sized piece of sodium can explode when dropped into water. Other alkali metals include lithium, potassium, and rubidium. The Group 2A elements, the **alkaline earth metals**, are also fairly reactive, although not quite as reactive as the alkali metals. Calcium, for example, reacts fairly vigorously when dropped into water but does not explode as readily as sodium. Other alkaline earth metals are magnesium, a common low-density structural metal; strontium; and barium. The Group 7A elements, the **halogens**, are very reactive nonmetals. Chlorine, a greenish-yellow gas with a pungent odor is probably the most familiar halogen. Because of its reactivity, people often use chlorine as a sterilizing and disinfecting agent (it reacts with and kills bacteria and other microscopic organisms). Other halogens include bromine, a red-brown liquid that readily evaporates into a gas; iodine, a purple solid; and fluorine, a pale yellow gas.

The noble gases are inert (unreactive) compared to other elements. However, some noble gases, especially the heavier ones, form a limited number of compounds with other elements under special conditions.

Noble gases

| He |
| Ne |
| Ar |
| Kr |
| Xe |

▲ The noble gases include helium (used in balloons), neon (used in neon signs), argon, krypton, and xenon.

Alkali metals

| Li |
| Na |
| K |
| Rb |
| Cs |

▲ The alkali metals include lithium, sodium (shown in the second photo reacting with water), potassium, rubidium, and cesium.

► The periodic table with Groups 1A, 2A, 7A, and 8A highlighted.

Alkali metals

Alkaline earth metals

Noble gases

Halogens

Group numbers

1A																	8A
1 H	2A											3A	4A	5A	6A	7A	2 He
3 Li	4 Be											5 B	6 C	7 N	8 O	9 F	10 Ne
11 Na	12 Mg				Transition metals							13 Al	14 Si	15 P	16 S	17 Cl	18 Ar
19 K	20 Ca	21 Sc	22 Ti	23 V	24 Cr	25 Mn	26 Fe	27 Co	28 Ni	29 Cu	30 Zn	31 Ga	32 Ge	33 As	34 Se	35 Br	36 Kr
37 Rb	38 Sr	39 Y	40 Zr	41 Nb	42 Mo	43 Tc	44 Ru	45 Rh	46 Pd	47 Ag	48 Cd	49 In	50 Sn	51 Sb	52 Te	53 I	54 Xe
55 Cs	56 Ba	57 La	72 Hf	73 Ta	74 W	75 Re	76 Os	77 Ir	78 Pt	79 Au	80 Hg	81 Tl	82 Pb	83 Bi	84 Po	85 At	86 Rn
87 Fr	88 Ra	89 Ac	104 Rf	105 Db	106 Sg	107 Bh	108 Hs	109 Mt	110 Ds	111 Rg	112 Cn	113	114 Fl	115	116 Lv	117 **	118

Lanthanides

58 Ce	59 Pr	60 Nd	61 Pm	62 Sm	63 Eu	64 Gd	65 Tb	66 Dy	67 Ho	68 Er	69 Tm	70 Yb	71 Lu

Actinides

90 Th	91 Pa	92 U	93 Np	94 Pu	95 Am	96 Cm	97 Bk	98 Cf	99 Es	100 Fm	101 Md	102 No	103 Lr

**Element 117 is currently under review by IUPAC.

EXAMPLE 4.3 | GROUPS AND FAMILIES OF ELEMENTS

To which group or family of elements does each element belong?

(a) Mg **(b)** N **(c)** K **(d)** Br

SOLUTION

(a) Mg is in Group 2A; it is an alkaline earth metal.
(b) N is in Group 5A.
(c) K is in Group 1A; it is an alkali metal.
(d) Br is in Group 7A; it is a halogen.

► **SKILLBUILDER 4.3 | Groups and Families of Elements**

To which group or family of elements does each element belong?

(a) Li **(b)** B **(c)** I **(d)** Ar

► **FOR MORE PRACTICE** Problems 57, 58, 59, 60, 61, 62, 63, 64.

Alkaline earth metals

◄ The alkaline earth metals include beryllium, magnesium (shown burning in the first photo), calcium (shown reacting with water in the second photo), strontium, and barium.

Be
Mg
Ca
Sr
Ba

Halogens

F
Cl
Br
I
At

► The halogens include fluorine, chlorine, bromine, iodine, and astatine.

CONCEPTUAL CHECKPOINT 4.3

Which statement is NEVER true?

(a) An element can be both a transition element and a metal.

(b) An element can be both a transition element and a metalloid.

(c) An element can be both a metalloid and a halogen.

(d) An element can be both a main-group element and a halogen.

4.7 Ions: Losing and Gaining Electrons

LO: Determine ion charge from numbers of protons and electrons.

LO: Determine the number of protons and electrons in an ion.

| The charge of an ion is indicated in the upper right corner of the symbol.

In chemical reactions, atoms often lose or gain electrons to form charged particles called **ions**. For example, a neutral lithium (Li) atom contains 3 protons and 3 electrons; however, in reactions, a lithium atom loses one electron (e^-) to form a Li^+ ion.

$$Li \longrightarrow Li^+ + e^-$$

The Li^+ *ion* contains 3 protons but only 2 electrons, resulting in a net charge of 1+. We usually write ion charges with the magnitude of the charge first followed by the sign of the charge. For example, we write a positive two charge as 2+ and a negative two charge as 2−. The charge of an ion depends on how many electrons were gained or lost and is given by the formula:

$$Ion\ charge = number\ of\ protons - number\ of\ electrons$$
$$= \#p^+ - \#e^-$$

where p^+ stands for *proton* and e^- stands for *electron*.

For the Li^+ ion with 3 protons and 2 electrons the charge is:

$$Ion\ charge = 3 - 2 = 1+$$

A neutral fluorine (F) atom contains 9 protons and 9 electrons; however, in chemical reactions a fluorine atom gains 1 electron to form F^- ions:

$$F + e^- \longrightarrow F^-$$

The F^- *ion* contains 9 protons and 10 electrons, resulting in a 1− charge.

$$Ion\ charge = 9 - 10$$
$$= 1-$$

Positively charged ions, such as Li^+, are **cations**, and negatively charged ions, such as F^-, are **anions**. Ions behave very differently than the atoms from which they are formed. Neutral sodium atoms, for example, are extremely reactive, interacting violently with most things they contact. Sodium cations (Na^+), on the other hand, are relatively inert—we eat them all the time in sodium chloride (table salt). In nature, cations and anions always occur together so that, again, matter is charge-neutral. For example, in table salt, the sodium cation occurs together with the chloride anion (Cl^-).

EXAMPLE 4.4	**DETERMINING ION CHARGE FROM NUMBERS OF PROTONS AND ELECTRONS**

Determine the charge of each ion.

(a) a magnesium ion with 10 electrons
(b) a sulfur ion with 18 electrons
(c) an iron ion with 23 electrons

SOLUTION

To determine the charge of each ion, use the ion charge equation.

Ion charge $= \#p^+ - \#e^-$

You are given the number of electrons in the problem. You can obtain the number of protons from the element's atomic number in the periodic table.

(a) Magnesium's atomic number is 12.

Ion charge $= 12 - 10 = 2+ (Mg^{2+})$

(b) Sulfur's atomic number is 16.

Ion charge $= 16 - 18 = 2- (S^{2-})$

(c) Iron's atomic number is 26.

Ion charge $= 26 - 23 = 3+ (Fe^{3+})$

▶SKILLBUILDER 4.4 | **Determining Ion Charge from Numbers of Protons and Electrons**

Determine the charge of each ion.
(a) a nickel ion with 26 electrons
(b) a bromine ion with 36 electrons
(c) a phosphorus ion with 18 electrons

▶**FOR MORE PRACTICE**   Example 4.10; Problems 75, 76.

EXAMPLE 4.5	**DETERMINING THE NUMBER OF PROTONS AND ELECTRONS IN AN ION**

Determine the number of protons and electrons in the Ca^{2+} ion.

The periodic table indicates that the atomic number for calcium is 20, so calcium has 20 protons. You can find the number of electrons using the ion charge equation.	**SOLUTION** Ion charge $= \#p^+ - \#e^-$ $2+ = 20 - \#e^-$ $\#e^- = 20 - 2 = 18$ The number of electrons is 18. The Ca^{2+} ion has 20 protons and 18 electrons.

▶SKILLBUILDER 4.5 | **Determining the Number of Protons and Electrons in an Ion**

Determine the number of protons and electrons in the S^{2-} ion.

▶**FOR MORE PRACTICE**   Example 4.11; Problems 77, 78.

Ions and the Periodic Table

For many main-group elements, we can use the periodic table to predict how many electrons tend to be lost or gained when an atom of that particular element ionizes. The number associated with the letter A above each *main-group* column in the periodic table—1 through 8—gives the number of *valence electrons* for the elements in

▲ FIGURE 4.14 **Elements that form predictable ions**

that column. We will discuss the concept of valence electrons more fully in Chapter 9; for now, you can think of valence electrons as the outermost electrons in an atom. Because oxygen is in column 6A, we can deduce that it has 6 valence electrons; because magnesium is in column 2A, it has 2 valence electrons, and so on. An important exception to this rule is helium—it is in column 8A, but has only 2 valence electrons. Valence electrons are particularly important because, as we shall see in Chapter 10, these electrons are the ones that are most important in chemical bonding.

We can predict the charge acquired by a particular element when it ionizes from its position in the periodic table relative to the noble gases.

Main-group elements tend to form ions that have the same number of valence electrons as the nearest noble gas.

For example, the closest noble gas to oxygen is neon. When oxygen ionizes, it *acquires* two additional electrons for a total of 8 valence electrons—the same number as neon. When determining the closest noble gas, we can move either forward or backward on the periodic table. For example, the closest noble gas to magnesium is also neon, even though neon (atomic number 10) falls before magnesium (atomic number 12) in the periodic table. Magnesium *loses* its 2 valence electrons to attain the same number of valence electrons as neon.

In accordance with this principle, the alkali metals (Group 1A) tend to lose 1 electron and form 1+ ions, while the alkaline earth metals (Group 2A) tend to lose 2 electrons and form 2+ ions. The halogens (Group 7A) tend to gain 1 electron and form 1− ions. The groups in the periodic table that form predictable ions are shown in ▲ Figure 4.14. Become familiar with these groups and the ions they form. In Chapter 9, we will examine a theory that more fully explains why these groups form ions as they do.

EXAMPLE 4.6 | CHARGE OF IONS FROM POSITION IN PERIODIC TABLE

Based on their position in the periodic table, what ions do barium and iodine tend to form?

SOLUTION

Because barium is in Group 2A, it tends to form a cation with a 2+ charge (Ba^{2+}). Because iodine is in Group 7A, it tends to form an anion with a 1− charge (I^-).

▶**SKILLBUILDER 4.6 | Charge of Ions from Position in Periodic Table**

Based on their position in the periodic table, what ions do potassium and selenium tend to form?

▶**FOR MORE PRACTICE**   Problems 81, 82.

CONCEPTUAL CHECKPOINT 4.4

Which pair of ions has the same total number of electrons?

(a) Na^+ and Mg^{2+} $11-x=1$ $x=10$ $12-x=2$

 Na ions $x=10$ Mg 10 ele s

(b) F^- and Cl^-

(c) O^- and O^{2-}

(d) Ga^{3+} and Fe^{3+}

4.8   Isotopes: When the Number of Neutrons Varies

LO: Determine atomic numbers, mass numbers, and isotope symbols for an isotope.

LO: Determine number of protons and neutrons from isotope symbols.

Recent studies have shown that for some elements, the relative amounts of each different isotope vary depending on the history of the sample. However, these variations are usually small and beyond the scope of this book.

Percent means "per hundred." 90.48% means that 90.48 atoms out of 100 are the isotope with 10 neutrons.

All atoms of a given element have the same number of protons; however, they do not necessarily have the same number of neutrons. Because neutrons and protons have nearly the same mass (approximately 1 amu), and the number of neutrons in the atoms of a given element can vary, all atoms of a given element *do not* have the same mass (contrary to what John Dalton originally proposed in his atomic theory). For example, all neon atoms in nature contain 10 protons, but they may have 10, 11, or 12 neutrons (▼ Figure 4.15). All three types of neon atoms exist, and each has a slightly different mass. Atoms with the same number of protons but different numbers of neutrons are **isotopes**. Some elements, such as beryllium (Be) and aluminum (Al), have only one naturally occurring isotope, while other elements, such as neon (Ne) and chlorine (Cl), have two or more.

For a given element, the relative amounts of each different isotope in a naturally occurring sample of that element are always the same. For example, in any natural sample of neon atoms, 90.48% of the atoms are the isotope with 10 neutrons, 0.27% are the isotope with 11 neutrons, and 9.25% are the isotope with 12 neutrons as summarized in Table 4.2. This means that in a sample of 10,000 neon atoms, 9048 have 10 neutrons, 27 have 11 neutrons, and 925 have 12 neutrons. These percentages are the **percent natural abundance** of the isotopes. The preceding numbers are for neon only; each element has its own unique percent natural abundance of isotopes.

TABLE 4.2   Neon Isotopes

Symbol	Number of Protons	Number of Neutrons	A (Mass Number)	Percent Natural Abundance
Ne-20 or $^{20}_{10}$Ne	10	10	20	90.48%
Ne-21 or $^{21}_{10}$Ne	10	11	21	0.27%
Ne-22 or $^{22}_{10}$Ne	10	12	22	9.25%

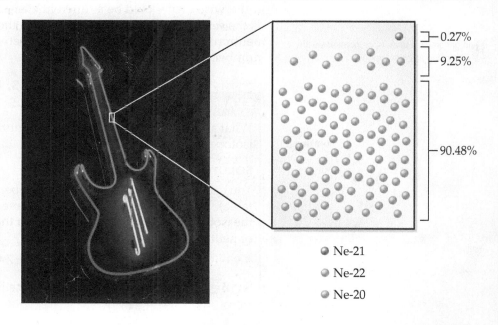

▶ **FIGURE 4.15   Isotopes of neon**   Naturally occurring neon contains three different isotopes: Ne-20 (with 10 neutrons), Ne-21 (with 11 neutrons), and Ne-22 (with 12 neutrons).

The sum of the number of neutrons and protons in an atom is its **mass number** and is given the symbol **A**.

$$A = \text{Number of protons} + \text{Number of neutrons}$$

For neon, which has 10 protons, the mass numbers of the three different naturally occurring isotopes are 20, 21, and 22, corresponding to 10, 11, and 12 neutrons, respectively.

We often symbolize isotopes in the following way:

where X is the chemical symbol, A is the mass number, and Z is the atomic number.

For example, the symbols for the neon isotopes are:

$$^{20}_{10}\text{Ne} \quad ^{21}_{10}\text{Ne} \quad ^{22}_{10}\text{Ne}$$

Notice that the chemical symbol, Ne, and the atomic number, 10, are redundant. If the atomic number is 10, the symbol must be Ne, and vice versa. The mass numbers, however, are different, reflecting the different number of neutrons in each isotope.

 ✓ CONCEPTUAL CHECKPOINT 4.5

Carbon has two naturally occurring isotopes: $^{12}_{6}\text{C}$ and $^{13}_{6}\text{C}$. Using circles to represent protons and squares to represent neutrons, draw the nucleus of each isotope.

A second common notation for isotopes is the chemical symbol (or chemical name) followed by a hyphen and the mass number of the isotope:

$$X\text{-}A$$

Chemical symbol or name ⟶ ⟵ Mass number

In this notation, the neon isotopes are:

Ne-20	neon-20
Ne-21	neon-21
Ne-22	neon-22

Notice that all isotopes of a given element have the same number of protons (otherwise they would be a different element). Notice also that the mass number is the *sum* of the number of protons and the number of neutrons. The number of neutrons in an isotope is the difference between the mass number and the atomic number.

In general, mass number increases with increasing atomic number.

EXAMPLE 4.7 ATOMIC NUMBERS, MASS NUMBERS, AND ISOTOPE SYMBOLS

What are the atomic number (Z), mass number (A), and symbols of the carbon isotope that has 7 neutrons?

SOLUTION

You can determine that the atomic number (Z) of carbon is 6 (from the periodic table). This means that carbon atoms have 6 protons. The mass number (A) for the isotope with 7 neutrons is the sum of the number of protons and the number of neutrons.

$$A = 6 + 7 = 13$$

So, Z = 6, A = 13, and the symbols for the isotope are C-13 and $^{13}_{6}\text{C}$.

▶SKILLBUILDER 4.7 | **Atomic Numbers, Mass Numbers, and Isotope Symbols**

▶SKILLBUILDER 4.7 | **Atomic Numbers, Mass Numbers, and Isotope Symbols**

What are the atomic number, mass number, and symbols for the chlorine isotope with 18 neutrons?

▶**FOR MORE PRACTICE**   Example 4.12; Problems 87, 89, 91, 92.

| EXAMPLE 4.8 | **NUMBERS OF PROTONS AND NEUTRONS FROM ISOTOPE SYMBOLS** |

How many protons and neutrons are in the chromium isotope $^{52}_{24}Cr$? *28·*

The number of protons is equal to Z (lower left number).	**SOLUTION** $\#p^+ = Z = 24$
The number of neutrons is equal to A (upper left number) $-Z$ (lower left number).	$\#n = A - Z$ $= 52 - 24$ $= 28$

▶**SKILLBUILDER 4.8** | **Numbers of Protons and Neutrons from Isotope Symbols**

How many protons and neutrons are in the potassium isotope $^{39}_{19}K$?

▶**FOR MORE PRACTICE**   Example 4.13; Problems 93, 94.

CONCEPTUAL CHECKPOINT 4.6

If an atom with a mass number of 27 has 14 neutrons, it is an isotope of which element?

(a) silicon
(b) aluminum
(c) cobalt
(d) niobium

CONCEPTUAL CHECKPOINT 4.7

Throughout this book, we represent atoms as spheres. For example, we represent a carbon atom by a black sphere as shown here. In light of the nuclear theory of the atom, when represented this way, would C-12 and C-13 look different? Why or why not?

Carbon

4.9   Atomic Mass: The Average Mass of an Element's Atoms

LO: Calculate atomic mass from percent natural abundances and isotopic masses.

An important part of Dalton's atomic theory was that all atoms of a given element have the same mass. But as we just learned, the atoms of a given element may have different masses (because of isotopes). So Dalton was not completely correct. We can, however, calculate an average mass—called the **atomic mass**—for each element. You can find the atomic mass of each element in the periodic table directly beneath the element's symbol; it represents the average mass of the atoms that compose that element. For example, the periodic table lists the atomic mass of chlorine as 35.45 amu. Naturally occurring chlorine consists of 75.77% chlorine-35 (mass 34.97 amu) and 24.23% chlorine-37 (mass 36.97 amu). Its atomic mass is:

> Some books use the terms *average atomic mass* or atomic weight instead of simply *atomic mass*.

$$\text{Atomic mass} = (0.7577 \times 34.97 \text{ amu}) + (0.2423 \times 36.97 \text{ amu})$$
$$= 35.45 \text{ amu}$$

$(0.7577 \times 36.97) + (0.2623 \times 36.97)$

CHEMISTRY IN THE ENVIRONMENT

▶ Radioactive Isotopes at Hanford, Washington

The nuclei of the isotopes of a given element are not all equally stable. For example, naturally occurring lead is composed primarily of Pb-206, Pb-207, and Pb-208. Other isotopes of lead also exist, but their nuclei are unstable. Scientists can make some of these other isotopes, such as Pb-185, in the laboratory. However, within seconds Pb-185 atoms emit a few energetic subatomic particles from their nuclei and change into different isotopes of different elements (which are themselves unstable). These emitted subatomic particles are called **nuclear radiation**, and we call the isotopes that emit them **radioactive**. Nuclear radiation, always associated with unstable nuclei, can be harmful to humans and other living organisms because the emitted energetic particles interact with and damage biological molecules. Some isotopes, such as Pb-185, emit significant amounts of radiation only for a very short time. Others remain radioactive for a long time—in some cases millions or even billions of years.

The nuclear power and nuclear weapons industries produce by-products containing unstable isotopes of several different elements. Many of these isotopes emit nuclear radiation for a long time, and their disposal is an environmental problem. For example, in Hanford, Washington, which

for 50 years produced fuel for nuclear weapons, 177 underground storage tanks contain 55 million gallons of highly radioactive nuclear waste. Certain radioactive isotopes within that waste will produce nuclear radiation for the foreseeable future. Unfortunately, some of the underground storage tanks in Hanford are aging, and leaks have allowed some of the waste to seep into the environment. While the danger from short-term external exposure to this waste is minimal, ingestion of the waste through contamination of drinking water or food supplies would pose significant health risks. Consequently, Hanford is now the site of the largest environmental cleanup project in U.S. history, involving 11,000 workers. The U.S. government expects the project to last for decades, and current costs are about $2 billion per year.

Radioactive isotopes are not always harmful, however, and many have beneficial uses. For example, physicians give technetium-99 (Tc-99) to patients to diagnose disease. The radiation emitted by Tc-99 helps doctors image internal organs or detect infection.

B4.3 CAN YOU ANSWER THIS? *Give the number of neutrons in each of the following isotopes: Pb-206, Pb-207, Pb-208, Pb-185, Tc-99.*

◀ Storage tanks at Hanford, Washington, contain 55 million gallons of high-level nuclear waste. Each tank pictured here holds 1 million gallons.

Notice that the atomic mass of chlorine is closer to 35 than 37 because naturally occurring chlorine contains more chlorine-35 atoms than chlorine-37 atoms. Notice also that when we use percentages in these calculations, we must always convert them to their decimal value. To convert a percentage to its decimal value, we divide by 100. For example:

$$75.77\% = 75.77/100 = 0.7577$$
$$24.23\% = 24.23/100 = 0.2423$$

In general, we calculate atomic mass according to the following equation:

Atomic mass = (Fraction of isotope 1 × Mass of isotope 1) +
(Fraction of isotope 2 × Mass of isotope 2) +
(Fraction of isotope 3 × Mass of isotope 3) + . . .

where the fractions of each isotope are the percent natural abundances converted to their decimal values. Atomic mass is useful because it allows us to assign a characteristic mass to each element and, as we will see in Chapter 6, it allows us to quantify the number of atoms in a sample of that element.

EXAMPLE 4.9   CALCULATING ATOMIC MASS

 Gallium has two naturally occurring isotopes: Ga-69 with mass 68.9256 amu and a natural abundance of 60.11%, and Ga-71 with mass 70.9247 amu and a natural abundance of 39.89%. Calculate the atomic mass of gallium.

Remember to convert the percent natural abundances into decimal form by dividing by 100.	**SOLUTION** $\left(0.6011 \times 68.9256\right) + \left(0.3989 \times 70.9247\right)$ $$\text{Fraction Ga-69} = \frac{60.11}{100} = 0.6011$$ $$\text{Fraction Ga-71} = \frac{39.89}{100} = 0.3989$$
Use the fractional abundances and the atomic masses of the isotopes to calculate the atomic mass according to the atomic mass definition.	Atomic mass = (0.6011 × 68.9256 amu) + (0.3989 × 70.9247 amu) = 41.4312 amu + 28.2919 amu = 69.7231 = 69.72 amu

▶**SKILLBUILDER 4.9 | Calculating Atomic Mass**

Magnesium has three naturally occurring isotopes with masses of 23.99, 24.99, and 25.98 amu and natural abundances of 78.99%, 10.00%, and 11.01%. Calculate the atomic mass of magnesium.

▶**FOR MORE PRACTICE**   Example 4.14; Problems 97, 98.

 CONCEPTUAL CHECKPOINT 4.8

A fictitious element is composed of isotopes A and B with masses of 61.9887 and 64.9846 amu, respectively. The atomic mass of the element is 64.52. What can you conclude about the natural abundances of the two isotopes?

(a) The natural abundance of isotope A must be greater than the natural abundance of isotope B.

(b) The natural abundance of isotope B must be greater than the natural abundance of isotope A.

(c) The natural abundances of both isotopes must be about equal.

(d) Nothing can be concluded about the natural abundances of the two isotopes from the given information.

CHAPTER IN REVIEW

Self-Assessment Quiz

Q1. Which statement is not part of Dalton's atomic theory?

(a) Each element is composed of indestructible particles called atoms.

(b) All atoms of a given element have the same mass and other properties.

(c) Atoms are themselves composed of protons, neutrons, and electrons.

(d) Atoms combine in simple whole-number ratios to form compounds.

Q2. Which statement best summarizes the nuclear model of the atom that emerged from Rutherford's gold foil experiment?

(a) The atom is composed of a dense core that contains most of its mass and all of its positive charge, while low-mass negatively charged particles compose most of its volume.

(b) The atom is composed of a sphere of positive charge with many negatively charged particles within the sphere.

(c) Most of the mass of the atom is evenly distributed throughout its volume.

(d) All of the particles that compose an atom have exactly the same mass.

Q3. An ion composed of which of these particles would have a mass of approximately 16 amu and a charge of 2–?

(a) 8 protons and 8 electrons

(b) 8 protons, 8 neutrons, and 10 electrons

(c) 8 protons, 8 neutrons, and 8 electrons

(d) 8 protons, 8 neutrons, and 6 electrons

Q4. Which element is a main-group metal with an even atomic number?

(a) K (b) Ca (c) Cr (d) Se

Q5. Which element is a halogen?

(a) Ne (b) O (c) Ca (d) I

Q6. Which pair of elements has the most similar properties?

(a) Sr and Ba (b) S and Ar
(c) H and He (d) K and Se

Q7. Which element is a row 4 noble gas?

(a) Ne (b) Br (c) Zr (d) Kr

Q8. How many electrons does the predictable (most common) ion of fluorine contain?

(a) 1 (b) 4 (c) 9 (d) 10

Q9. How many neutrons does the Fe-56 isotope contain?

(a) 26 (b) 30 (c) 56 (d) 112

Q10. Determine the number of protons, neutrons, and electrons in $^{32}_{16}S^{2-}$.

(a) 16 protons; 32 neutrons; and 18 electrons

(b) 16 protons; 16 neutrons; and 18 electrons

(c) 32 protons; 16 neutrons; and 2 electrons

(d) 16 protons; 48 neutrons; and 16 electrons

Q11. What is the charge of the Cr ion that contains 21 electrons?

(a) 2– (b) 3– (c) 2+ (d) 3+

Q12. An element has four naturally occurring isotopes; the table lists the mass and natural abundance of each isotope. Find the atomic mass of the element.

Isotope	Mass (amu)	Natural abundance
A	203.9730	1.4%
B	205.9744	24.1 %
C	206.9758	22.1 %
D	207.9766	52.4%

(a) 207.2 amu

(b) 2.072×10^4 amu

(c) 206.2 amu

(d) 206.5 amu

Chemical Principles

The Atomic Theory: Democritus and Leucippus, ancient Greek philosophers, were the first to assert that matter is ultimately composed of small, indestructible particles. It was not until 2000 years later, however, that John Dalton introduced a formal atomic theory stating that matter is composed of atoms; atoms of a given element have unique properties that distinguish them from atoms of other elements; and atoms combine in simple, whole-number ratios to form compounds.

Relevance

The Atomic Theory: The concept of atoms is important because it explains the physical world. Humans and everything we see are made of atoms. To understand the physical world, we must begin by understanding atoms. Atoms are the key concept—they determine the properties of matter.

Discovery of the Atom's Nucleus: Rutherford's gold foil experiment probed atomic structure, and his results led to the nuclear model of the atom, which, with minor modifications to accommodate neutrons, is still valid today. According to this model, the atom is composed of protons and neutrons—which compose most of the atom's mass and are grouped together in a dense nucleus—and electrons, which compose most of the atom's volume. Protons and neutrons have similar masses (1 amu), while electrons have a much smaller mass (0.00055 amu).

Discovery of the Atom's Nucleus: We can understand why this is relevant by asking, what if it were otherwise? What if matter were *not* mostly empty space? While we cannot know for certain, it seems probable that such matter would not form the diversity of substances required for life—and then, of course, we would not be around to ask the question.

Charge: Protons and electrons both have electrical charge; the charge of the proton is 1+ and the charge of the electron is 1−. The neutron has no charge. When protons and electrons combine in atoms, their charges cancel.

Charge: Electrical charge is relevant to much of our modern world. Many of the machines and computers we depend on are powered by electricity, which is the movement of electrical charge.

The Periodic Table: The periodic table tabulates all known elements in order of increasing atomic number. The periodic table is arranged so that similar elements are grouped in columns. Columns of elements in the periodic table have similar properties and are called groups or families. Elements on the left side of the periodic table are metals and tend to lose electrons in their chemical changes. Elements on the upper right side of the periodic table are nonmetals and tend to gain electrons in their chemical changes. Elements between the two are metalloids.

The Periodic Table: The periodic table helps us organize the elements in ways that allow us to predict their properties. Helium, for example, is not toxic in small amounts because it is an inert gas—it does not react with anything. The gases in the column below it on the periodic table are also inert gases and form a family or group of elements called the noble gases. By tabulating the elements and grouping similar ones together, we begin to understand their properties.

Atomic Number: The characteristic that defines an element is the number of protons in the nuclei of its atoms; this number is the atomic number (Z).

Atomic Number: Elements are the fundamental building blocks from which all compounds are made.

Ions: When an atom gains or loses electrons, it becomes an ion. Positively charged ions are cations, and negatively charged ions are anions. Cations and anions occur together so that matter is ordinarily charge-neutral.

Ions: Ions occur in many common compounds, such as sodium chloride.

Isotopes: While all atoms of a given element have the same number of protons, they do not necessarily have the same number of neutrons. Atoms of the same element with different numbers of neutrons are isotopes. Isotopes are characterized by their mass number (A), the sum of the number of protons and the number of neutrons in the nucleus.

Each naturally occurring sample of an element has the same percent natural abundance of each isotope. We can use these percentages, together with the mass of each isotope, to calculate the atomic mass of the element, a weighted average of the masses of the individual isotopes.

Isotopes: Isotopes are relevant because they influence atomic masses. To understand these masses, we must understand the presence and abundance of isotopes. In nuclear processes—processes in which the nuclei of atoms actually change—the presence of different isotopes becomes even more important.

Some isotopes are not stable—they lose subatomic particles and transform into other elements. The emission of subatomic particles by unstable nuclei is called radioactive decay. In many situations, such as in diagnosing and treating certain diseases, nuclear radiation is extremely useful. In other situations, such as in the disposal of radioactive waste, it can pose environmental problems.

Chemical Skills

Examples

LO: Determine ion charge from numbers of protons and electrons (Section 4.7).

- Refer to the periodic table or the alphabetical list of elements to find the atomic number of the element; this number is equal to the number of protons.
- Use the ion charge equation to calculate charge.

$$\text{Ion charge} = \#p^+ - \#e^-$$

EXAMPLE 4.10   **DETERMINING ION CHARGE FROM NUMBERS OF PROTONS AND ELECTRONS**

Determine the charge of a selenium ion with 36 electrons.

SOLUTION

Selenium is atomic number 34; therefore, it has 34 protons.

$$\text{Ion charge} = 34 - 36 = 2-$$

LO: Determine the number of protons and electrons in an ion (Section 4.7).

- Refer to the periodic table or the alphabetical list of elements to find the atomic number of the element; this number is equal to the number of protons.
- Use the ion charge equation and substitute in the known values.

$$\text{Ion charge} = \#p^+ - \#e^-$$

- Solve the equation for the number of electrons.

EXAMPLE 4.11   **DETERMINING THE NUMBER OF PROTONS AND ELECTRONS IN AN ION**

Find the number of protons and electrons in the O^{2-} ion.

SOLUTION

The atomic number of O is 8; therefore, it has 8 protons.

$$\text{Ion charge} = \#p^+ - \#e^-$$
$$2- = 8 - \#e^-$$
$$\#e^- = 8 + 2 = 10$$

The ion has 8 protons and 10 electrons.

LO: Determine atomic numbers, mass numbers, and isotope symbols for an isotope (Section 4.8).

- Refer to the periodic table or the alphabetical list of elements to find the atomic number of the element.
- The mass number (A) is equal to the atomic number plus the number of neutrons.
- Write the symbol for the isotope by writing the symbol for the element with the mass number in the upper left corner and the atomic number in the lower left corner.
- The other symbol for the isotope is simply the chemical symbol followed by a hyphen and the mass number.

EXAMPLE 4.12   **DETERMINING ATOMIC NUMBERS, MASS NUMBERS, AND ISOTOPE SYMBOLS FOR AN ISOTOPE**

What are the atomic number (Z), mass number (A), and symbols for the iron isotope with 30 neutrons?

SOLUTION

The atomic number of iron is 26.

$$A = 26 + 30 = 56$$

The mass number is 56.

$$^{56}_{26}Fe$$
$$Fe-56$$

LO: Determine number of protons and neutrons from isotope symbols (Section 4.8).

- The number of protons is equal to Z (lower left number).
- The number of neutrons is equal to

  A (upper left number) − Z (lower left number.)

EXAMPLE 4.13   **DETERMINING NUMBER OF PROTONS AND NEUTRONS FROM ISOTOPE SYMBOLS**

How many protons and neutrons are in $^{62}_{28}Ni$?

SOLUTION

28 protons

$$\#n = 62 - 28 = 34 \text{ neutrons}$$

LO: Calculate atomic mass from percent natural abundances and isotopic masses (Section 4.9).

- Convert the natural abundances from percent to decimal values by dividing by 100.
- Find the atomic mass by multiplying the fractions of each isotope by its respective mass and summing them.
- Round to the correct number of significant figures.
- Check your work.

EXAMPLE 4.14	CALCULATING ATOMIC MASS FROM PERCENT NATURAL ABUNDANCES AND ISOTOPIC MASSES

Copper has two naturally occurring isotopes: Cu-63 with mass 62.9395 amu and a natural abundance of 69.17%, and Cu-65 with mass 64.9278 amu and a natural abundance of 30.83%. Calculate the atomic mass of copper.

SOLUTION

$$\text{Fraction Cu-63} = \frac{69.17}{100} = 0.6917$$

$$\text{Fraction Cu-65} = \frac{30.83}{100} = 0.3083$$

$$\begin{aligned}
\text{Atomic mass} &= (0.6917 \times 62.9395 \text{ amu}) + \\
&\quad (0.3083 \times 64.9278) \\
&= 43.5353 \text{ amu} + 20.0172 \text{ amu} \\
&= 63.5525 \text{ amu} \\
&= 63.55 \text{ amu}
\end{aligned}$$

KEY TERMS

alkali metals [4.6]	chemical symbol [4.5]	metalloids [4.6]	percent natural
alkaline earth metals [4.6]	electron [4.3]	metals [4.6]	abundance [4.8]
anions [4.7]	family (of elements) [4.6]	neutron [4.3]	periodic law [4.6]
atom [4.1]	group (of elements) [4.6]	noble gases [4.6]	periodic table [4.6]
atomic mass [4.9]	halogens [4.6]	nonmetals [4.6]	proton [4.3]
atomic mass unit (amu) [4.4]	ion [4.7]	nuclear radiation [4.9]	radioactive [4.9]
atomic number (Z) [4.5]	isotope [4.8]	nuclear theory of the	semiconductor [4.6]
cation [4.7]	main-group elements [4.6]	atom [4.3]	transition elements [4.6]
charge [4.4]	mass number (A) [4.8]	nucleus [4.3]	transition metals [4.6]

EXERCISES

QUESTIONS

1. What did Democritus contribute to our modern understanding of matter?
2. What are three main ideas in Dalton's atomic theory?
3. Describe Rutherford's gold foil experiment and the results of that experiment. How did these results refute the plum pudding model of the atom?
4. What are the main ideas in the nuclear theory of the atom?
5. List the three subatomic particles and their properties.
6. What is electrical charge?
7. Is matter usually charge-neutral? How would matter be different if it were not charge-neutral?
8. What does the atomic number of an element specify?
9. What is a chemical symbol?
10. List some examples of how elements were named.
11. What was Dmitri Mendeleev's main contribution to our modern understanding of chemistry?

12. What is the main idea in the periodic law?
13. How is the periodic table organized?
14. What are the properties of metals? Where are metals found on the periodic table?
15. What are the properties of nonmetals? Where are nonmetals found on the periodic table?
16. Where on the periodic table are metalloids found?
17. What is a family or group of elements?
18. Locate each group of elements on the periodic table and list its group number.
    (a) alkali metals
    (b) alkaline earth metals
    (c) halogens
    (d) noble gases
19. What is an ion?
20. What is an anion? What is a cation?

21. Locate each group on the periodic table and list the charge of the ions it tends to form.
  (a) Group 1A
  (b) Group 2A
  (c) Group 3A
  (d) Group 6A
  (e) Group 7A

22. What are isotopes?
23. What is the percent natural abundance of isotopes?
24. What is the mass number of an isotope?
25. What notations are commonly used to specify isotopes? What do each of the numbers in these symbols mean?
26. What is the atomic mass of an element?

PROBLEMS

ATOMIC AND NUCLEAR THEORY

27. Which statements are *inconsistent* with Dalton's atomic theory as it was originally stated? Explain your answers.
  (a) All carbon atoms are identical.
  (b) Helium atoms can be split into two hydrogen atoms.
  (c) An oxygen atom combines with 1.5 hydrogen atoms to form water molecules.
  (d) Two oxygen atoms combine with a carbon atom to form carbon dioxide molecules.

28. Which statements are *consistent* with Dalton's atomic theory as it was originally stated? Explain your answers.
  (a) Calcium and titanium atoms have the same mass.
  (b) Neon and argon atoms are the same.
  (c) All cobalt atoms are identical.
  (d) Sodium and chlorine atoms combine in a 1:1 ratio to form sodium chloride.

29. Which statements are *inconsistent* with Rutherford's nuclear theory as it was originally stated? Explain your answers.
  (a) Helium atoms have two protons in the nucleus and two electrons outside the nucleus.
  (b) Most of the volume of hydrogen atoms is due to the nucleus.
  (c) Aluminum atoms have 13 protons in the nucleus and 22 electrons outside the nucleus.
  (d) The majority of the mass of nitrogen atoms is due to their 7 electrons.

30. Which statements are *consistent* with Rutherford's nuclear theory as it was originally stated? Explain your answers.
  (a) Atomic nuclei are small compared to the size of atoms.
  (b) The volume of an atom is mostly empty space.
  (c) Neutral potassium atoms contain more protons than electrons.
  (d) Neutral potassium atoms contain more neutrons than protons.

31. If atoms are mostly empty space and atoms compose all ordinary matter, why does solid matter seem to have no space within it?

32. Rutherford's experiment indicated that matter was not as uniform as it appears. What part of his experimental results implied this idea? Explain.

PROTONS, NEUTRONS, AND ELECTRONS

33. Which statements about electrons are true?
  (a) Electrons repel each other.
  (b) Electrons are attracted to protons.
  (c) Some electrons have a charge of 1− and some have no charge.
  (d) Electrons are much lighter than neutrons.

34. Which statements about electrons are false?
  (a) Most atoms have more electrons than protons.
  (b) Electrons have a charge of 1−.
  (c) If an atom has an equal number of protons and electrons, it will be charge-neutral.
  (d) Electrons experience an attraction to protons.

35. Which statements about protons are true?
  (a) Protons have twice the mass of neutrons.
  (b) Protons have the same magnitude of charge as electrons but are opposite in sign.
  (c) Most atoms have more protons than electrons.
  (d) Protons have a charge of 1+.

36. Which statements about protons are false?
  (a) Protons have about the same mass as neutrons.
  (b) Protons have about the same mass as electrons.
  (c) Some atoms don't have any protons.
  (d) Protons have the same magnitude of charge as neutrons but are opposite in sign.

37. How many electrons would it take to equal the mass of a proton?

38. A helium nucleus has two protons and two neutrons. How many electrons would it take to equal the mass of a helium nucleus?

39. What mass of electrons is required to neutralize the charge of 1.0 g of protons?

40. What mass of protons is required to neutralize the charge of 1.0 g of electrons?

ELEMENTS, SYMBOLS, AND NAMES

41. Find the atomic number (Z) for each element.
(a) Fr
(b) Kr
(c) Pa
(d) Ge
(e) Al

42. Find the atomic number (Z) for each element.
(a) Si
(b) W
(c) Ni
(d) Rn
(e) Sr

43. How many protons are in the nucleus of an atom of each element?
(a) Ar
(b) Sn
(c) Xe
(d) O
(e) Tl

44. How many protons are in the nucleus of an atom of each element?
(a) Ti
(b) Li
(c) U
(d) Br
(e) F

45. List the symbol and atomic number of each element.
(a) carbon
(b) nitrogen
(c) sodium
(d) potassium
(e) copper

46. List the symbol and atomic number of each element.
(a) boron
(b) neon
(c) silver
(d) mercury
(e) curium

47. List the name and the atomic number of each element.
(a) Mn
(b) Ag
(c) Au
(d) Pb
(e) S

48. List the name and the atomic number of each element.
(a) Y
(b) N
(c) Ne
(d) K
(e) Mo

49. Fill in the blanks to complete the table.

Element Name	Element Symbol	Atomic Number
_____	Au	79
Tin	_____	_____
_____	As	_____
Copper	_____	29
_____	Fe	_____
_____	_____	80

50. Fill in the blanks to complete the table.

Element Name	Element Symbol	Atomic Number
_____	Al	13
Iodine	_____	_____
_____	Sb	_____
Sodium	_____	_____
_____	Rn	86
_____	_____	82

THE PERIODIC TABLE

51. Classify each element as a metal, nonmetal, or metalloid.
(a) Sr
(b) Mg
(c) F
(d) N
(e) As

52. Classify each element as a metal, nonmetal, or metalloid.
(a) Na
(b) Ge
(c) Si
(d) Br
(e) Ag

53. Which elements would you expect to lose electrons in chemical changes?
(a) potassium
(b) sulfur
(c) fluorine
(d) barium
(e) copper

54. Which elements would you expect to gain electrons in chemical changes?
(a) nitrogen
(b) iodine
(c) tungsten
(d) strontium
(e) gold

55. Which elements are main-group elements?
(a) Te
(b) K
(c) V
(d) Re
(e) Ag

56. Which elements are *not* main-group elements?
(a) Al
(b) Br
(c) Mo
(d) Cs
(e) Pb

57. Which elements are alkaline earth metals?
(a) sodium
(b) aluminum
(c) calcium
(d) barium
(e) lithium

58. Which elements are alkaline earth metals?
(a) rubidium
(b) tungsten
(c) magnesium
(d) cesium
(e) beryllium

59. Which elements are alkali metals?
(a) barium
(b) sodium
(c) gold
(d) tin
(e) rubidium

60. Which elements are alkali metals?
(a) scandium
(b) iron
(c) potassium
(d) lithium
(e) cobalt

61. Classify each element as a halogen, a noble gas, or neither.
(a) Cl
(b) Kr
(c) F
(d) Ga
(e) He

62. Classify each element as a halogen, a noble gas, or neither.
(a) Ne
(b) Br
(c) S
(d) Xe
(e) I

63. To what group number does each element belong?
(a) oxygen
(b) aluminum
(c) silicon
(d) tin
(e) phosphorus

64. To what group number does each element belong?
(a) germanium
(b) nitrogen
(c) sulfur
(d) carbon
(e) boron

65. Which element do you expect to be most like sulfur? Why?
(a) nitrogen
(b) oxygen
(c) fluorine
(d) lithium
(e) potassium

66. Which element do you expect to be most like magnesium? Why?
(a) potassium
(b) silver
(c) bromine
(d) calcium
(e) lead

67. Which pair of elements do you expect to be most similar? Why?
(a) Si and P
(b) Cl and F
(c) Na and Mg
(d) Mo and Sn
(e) N and Ni

68. Which pair of elements do you expect to be most similar? Why?
(a) Ti and Ga
(b) N and O
(c) Li and Na
(d) Ar and Br
(e) Ge and Ga

69. Which element is a main-group nonmetal?
(a) K
(b) Fe
(c) Sn
(d) S

70. Which element is a row 5 transition element?
(a) Sr
(b) Pd
(c) P
(d) V

71. Fill in the blanks to complete the table.

Chemical Symbol	Group Number	Group Name	Metal or Nonmetal
K	____	____	metal
Br	____	halogens	____
Sr	____	____	____
He	8A	____	____
Ar	____	____	____

72. Fill in the blanks to complete the table.

Chemical Symbol	Group Number	Group Name	Metal or Nonmetal
Cl	7A	____	____
Ca	____	____	metal
Xe	____	____	nonmetal
Na	____	alkali metal	____
F	____	____	____

IONS

73. Complete each ionization equation.
(a) $Na \longrightarrow Na^+ + $ ____
(b) $O + 2e^- \longrightarrow$ ____
(c) $Ca \longrightarrow Ca^{2+} + $ ____
(d) $Cl + e^- \longrightarrow$ ____

74. Complete each ionization equation.
(a) $Mg \longrightarrow$ ____ $+ 2e^-$
(b) $Ba \longrightarrow Ba^{2+} + $ ____
(c) $I + e^- \longrightarrow$ ____
(d) $Al \longrightarrow$ ____ $+ 3e^-$

75. Determine the charge of each ion.
(a) oxygen ion with 10 electrons
(b) aluminum ion with 10 electrons
(c) titanium ion with 18 electrons
(d) iodine ion with 54 electrons

76. Determine the charge of each ion.
(a) tungsten ion with 68 electrons
(b) tellurium ion with 54 electrons
(c) nitrogen ion with 10 electrons
(d) barium ion with 54 electrons

77. Determine the number of protons and electrons in each ion.
(a) Na^+
(b) Ba^{2+}
(c) O^{2-}
(d) Co^{3+}

78. Determine the number of protons and electrons in each ion.
(a) Al^{3+}
(b) S^{2-}
(c) I^-
(d) Ag^+

79. Determine whether each statement is true or false. If false, correct it.
(a) The Ti^{2+} ion contains 22 protons and 24 electrons.
(b) The I^- ion contains 53 protons and 54 electrons.
(c) The Mg^{2+} ion contains 14 protons and 12 electrons.
(d) The O^{2-} ion contains 8 protons and 10 electrons.

80. Determine whether each statement is true or false. If false, correct it.
(a) The Fe^{2+} ion contains 29 protons and 26 electrons.
(b) The Cs^+ ion contains 55 protons and 56 electrons.
(c) The Se^{2-} ion contains 32 protons and 34 electrons.
(d) The Li^+ ion contains 3 protons and 2 electrons.

81. Predict the ion formed by each element.
(a) Rb
(b) K
(c) Al
(d) O

82. Predict the ion formed by each element.
(a) F
(b) N
(c) Mg
(d) Na

83. Predict how many electrons each element will most likely gain or lose.
(a) Ga
(b) Li
(c) Br
(d) S

84. Predict how many electrons each element will most likely gain or lose.
(a) I
(b) Ba
(c) Cs
(d) Se

85. Fill in the blanks to complete the table.

Symbol	Ion Commonly Formed	Number of Electrons in Ion	Number of Protons in Ion
Te	____	54	____
In	____	____	49
Sr	Sr^{2+}	____	____
____	Mg^{2+}	____	12
Cl	____	____	____

86. Fill in the blanks to complete the table.

Symbol	Ion Commonly Formed	Number of Electrons in Ion	Number of Protons in Ion
F	____	____	9
____	Be^{2+}	2	____
Br	____	36	____
Al	____	____	13
O	____	____	____

ISOTOPES

87. Determine the atomic number and mass number for each isotope.
  (a) the hydrogen isotope with 2 neutrons
  (b) the chromium isotope with 28 neutrons
  (c) the calcium isotope with 22 neutrons
  (d) the tantalum isotope with 109 neutrons

88. How many neutrons are in an atom with each atomic number and mass number?
  (a) $Z = 28, A = 59$
  (b) $Z = 92, A = 235$
  (c) $Z = 21, A = 46$
  (d) $Z = 18, A = 42$

89. Write isotopic symbols in the form $_Z^A X$ for each isotope.
  (a) the oxygen isotope with 8 neutrons
  (b) the fluorine isotope with 10 neutrons
  (c) the sodium isotope with 12 neutrons
  (d) the aluminum isotope with 14 neutrons

90. Write isotopic symbols in the form X-A (for example, C-13) for each isotope.
  (a) the iodine isotope with 74 neutrons
  (b) the phosphorus isotope with 16 neutrons
  (c) the uranium isotope with 234 neutrons
  (d) the argon isotope with 22 neutrons

91. Write the symbol for each isotope in the form $_Z^A X$.
  (a) cobalt-60
  (b) neon-22
  (c) iodine-131
  (d) plutonium-244

92. Write the symbol for each isotope in the form $_Z^A X$.
  (a) U-235
  (b) V-52
  (c) P-32
  (d) Xe-144

93. Determine the number of protons and neutrons in each isotope.
  (a) $_{11}^{23}Na$
  (b) $_{88}^{266}Ra$
  (c) $_{82}^{208}Pb$
  (d) $_{7}^{14}N$

94. Determine the number of protons and neutrons in each isotope.
  (a) $_{15}^{33}P$
  (b) $_{19}^{40}K$
  (c) $_{86}^{222}Rn$
  (d) $_{43}^{99}Tc$

95. Carbon-14, present within living organisms and substances derived from living organisms, is often used to establish the age of fossils and artifacts. Determine the number of protons and neutrons in a carbon-14 isotope and write its symbol in the form $_Z^A X$.

96. Plutonium-239 is used in nuclear bombs. Determine the number of protons and neutrons in plutonium-239 and write its symbol in the form $_Z^A X$.

ATOMIC MASS

97. Rubidium has two naturally occurring isotopes: Rb-85 with mass 84.9118 amu and a natural abundance of 72.17%, and Rb-87 with mass 86.9092 amu and a natural abundance of 27.83%. Calculate the atomic mass of rubidium.

98. Silicon has three naturally occurring isotopes: Si-28 with mass 27.9769 amu and a natural abundance of 92.21%, Si-29 with mass 28.9765 amu and a natural abundance of 4.69%, and Si-30 with mass 29.9737 amu and a natural abundance of 3.10%. Calculate the atomic mass of silicon.

99. Bromine has two naturally occurring isotopes (Br-79 and Br-81) and an atomic mass of 79.904 amu.
  (a) If the natural abundance of Br-79 is 50.69%, what is the natural abundance of Br-81?
  (b) If the mass of Br-81 is 80.9163 amu, what is the mass of Br-79?

100. Silver has two naturally occurring isotopes (Ag-107 and Ag-109).
  (a) Use the periodic table to find the atomic mass of silver.
  (b) If the natural abundance of Ag-107 is 51.84%, what is the natural abundance of Ag-109?
  (c) If the mass of Ag-107 is 106.905 amu, what is the mass of Ag-109?

101. An element has two naturally occurring isotopes. Isotope 1 has a mass of 120.9038 amu and a relative abundance of 57.4%, and isotope 2 has a mass of 122.9042 amu and a relative abundance of 42.6%. Find the atomic mass of this element and, referring to the periodic table, identify it.

102. Copper has two naturally occurring isotopes. Cu-63 has a mass of 62.939 amu and relative abundance of 69.17%. Use the atomic weight of copper to determine the mass of the other copper isotope.

CUMULATIVE PROBLEMS

103. Electrical charge is sometimes reported in coulombs (C). On this scale, 1 electron has a charge of -1.6×10^{-19} C. Suppose your body acquires -125 mC (millicoulombs) of charge on a dry day. How many excess electrons has it acquired? (*Hint:* Use the charge of an electron in coulombs as a conversion factor between charge and electrons.)

104. How many excess protons are in a positively charged object with a charge of $+398$ mC (millicoulombs)? The charge of 1 proton is $+1.6 \times 10^{-19}$ C. (*Hint:* See previous problem.)

105. The hydrogen atom contains 1 proton and 1 electron. The radius of the proton is approximately 1.0 fm (femtometer), and the radius of the hydrogen atom is approximately 53 pm (picometers). Calculate the volume of the nucleus and the volume of the atom for hydrogen. What percentage of the hydrogen atom's volume does the nucleus occupy?

106. Carbon-12 contains 6 protons and 6 neutrons. The radius of the nucleus is approximately 2.7 fm, and the radius of the atom is approximately 70 pm. Calculate the volume of the nucleus and the volume of the atom. What percentage of the carbon atom's volume does the nucleus occupy?

107. Prepare a table like Table 4.2 for the four different isotopes of Sr that have the natural abundances and masses listed here.

Sr-84	0.56%	83.9134 amu
Sr-86	9.86%	85.9093 amu
Sr-87	7.00%	86.9089 amu
Sr-88	82.58%	87.9056 amu

Use your table and the listed atomic masses to calculate the atomic mass of strontium.

108. Determine the number of protons and neutrons in each isotope of chromium and use the listed natural abundances and masses to calculate its atomic mass.

Cr-50	4.345%	49.9460 amu
Cr-52	83.79%	51.9405 amu
Cr-53	9.50%	52.9407 amu
Cr-54	2.365%	53.9389 amu

109. Fill in the blanks to complete the table.

Symbol	Z	A	Number of Protons	Number of Electrons	Number of Neutrons	Charge
Zn^{2+}	___	___	___	___	34	2+
___	25	55	___	22	___	___
___	___	___	15	15	16	___
O^{2-}	___	16	___	___	___	2−
___	___	___	16	18	18	___

110. Fill in the blanks to complete the table.

Symbol	Z	A	Number of Protons	Number of Electrons	Number of Neutrons	Charge
Mg^{2+}	___	25	___	___	13	2+
___	22	48	___	18	___	___
___	16	___	___	___	16	2−
Ga^{3+}	___	71	___	___	___	___
___	___	___	82	80	125	___

111. Europium has two naturally occurring isotopes: Eu-151 with a mass of 150.9198 amu and a natural abundance of 47.8%, and Eu-153. Use the atomic mass of europium to find the mass and natural abundance of Eu-153.

112. Rhenium has two naturally occurring isotopes: Re-185 with a natural abundance of 37.40% and Re-187 with a natural abundance of 62.60%. The sum of the masses of the two isotopes is 371.9087 amu. Find the masses of the individual isotopes.

113. Chapter 1 describes the difference between observations, laws, and theories. Cite two examples of theories from this chapter and explain why they are theories.

114. Chapter 1 describes the difference between observations, laws, and theories. Cite one example of a law from this chapter and explain why it is a law.

115. The atomic mass of fluorine is 19.00 amu, and all fluorine atoms in a naturally occurring sample of fluorine have this mass. The atomic mass of chlorine is 35.45 amu, but no chlorine atoms in a naturally occurring sample of chlorine have this mass. Provide an explanation for the difference.

116. The atomic mass of germanium is 72.61 amu. Is it likely that any individual germanium atoms have a mass of 72.61 amu?

117. Copper has only two naturally occurring isotopes, Cu-63 and Cu-65. The mass of Cu-63 is 62.9396 amu, and the mass of Cu-65 is 64.9278 amu. Use the atomic mass of copper to determine the relative abundance of each isotope in a naturally occurring sample.

118. Gallium has only two naturally occurring isotopes, Ga-69 and Ga-71. The mass of Ga-69 is 68.9256 amu, and the mass of Ga-71 is 70.9247 amu. Use the atomic mass of gallium to determine the relative abundance of each isotope in a naturally occurring sample.

HIGHLIGHT PROBLEMS

119. The figure shown here is a representation of 50 atoms of a fictitious element with the symbol Nt and atomic number 120. Nt has three isotopes represented by the following colors: Nt-304 (red), Nt-305 (blue), and Nt-306 (green).

   (a) Assuming that the figure is statistically representative of naturally occurring Nt, what is the percent natural abundance of each Nt isotope?

   (b) Use the listed masses of each isotope to calculate the atomic mass of Nt. Then draw a box for the element similar to the boxes for each element shown in the periodic table in the inside front cover of this book. Make sure your box includes the atomic number, symbol, and atomic mass. (Assume that the percentages from part (a) are correct to four significant figures.)

Nt-304	303.956 amu
Nt-305	304.962 amu
Nt-306	305.978 amu

120. Neutron stars are believed to be composed of solid nuclear matter, primarily neutrons.

   (a) If the radius of a neutron is 1.0×10^{-13} cm, calculate its density in g/cm^3.

$$\left(\text{volume of a sphere} = \tfrac{4}{3}\pi r^3\right)$$

   (b) Assuming that a neutron star has the same density as a neutron, calculate the mass in kilograms of a small piece of a neutron star the size of a spherical pebble with a radius of 0.10 mm.

QUESTIONS FOR GROUP WORK

Discuss these questions with the group and record your consensus answer.

121. Complete the following table.

Particle	Mass (amu)	Charge	In the nucleus? (yes/no)	# in ^{32}S atom	# in $^{79}Br^-$ ion
Proton					
Neutron					
Electron					

122. Make a sketch of an oxygen atom. Include the correct number of protons, electrons, and neutrons for the most abundant isotope. Use the following symbols: proton = •, neutron = o, electron = •.

123. The table at right includes data similar to that used by Mendeleev when he made the periodic table. Write on a small card the symbol, atomic mass, and a stable compound formed by each element. Arrange your cards in order of increasing atomic mass. Do you observe any repeating patterns? Describe any patterns you observe. (*Hint*: There is one missing element somewhere in the pattern.)

Element	Atomic Mass	Stable Compound	Element	Atomic Mass	Stable Compound
Be	9	$BeCl_2$	O	16	H_2O
S	32	H_2S	Ga	69.7	GaH_3
F	19	F_2	As	75	AsF_3
Ca	40	$CaCl_2$	C	12	CH_4
Li	7	$LiCl$	K	39	KCl
Si	28	SiH_4	Mg	24.3	$MgCl_2$
Cl	35.4	Cl_2	Se	79	H_2Se
B	10.8	BH_3	Al	27	AlH_3
Ge	72.6	GeH_4	Br	80	Br_2
N	14	NF_3	Na	23	$NaCl$

124. Arrange the cards from Question 123 so that mass increases from left to right and elements with similar properties are above and below each other. Copy the periodic table you have invented onto a piece of paper. There is one element missing. Predict its mass and a stable compound it might form.

▶Answers to Skillbuilder Exercises

Skillbuilder 4.1
- (a) sodium, 11
- (b) nickel, 28
- (c) phosphorus, 15
- (d) tantalum, 73

Skillbuilder 4.2
- (a) nonmetal
- (b) nonmetal
- (c) metal
- (d) metalloid

Skillbuilder 4.3
- (a) alkali metal, Group 1A
- (b) Group 3A
- (c) halogen, Group 7A
- (d) noble gas, Group 8A

Skillbuilder 4.4
- (a) 2+
- (b) 1−
- (c) 3−

Skillbuilder 4.5 16 protons, 18 electrons

Skillbuilder 4.6 K^+ and Se^{2-}

Skillbuilder 4.7 Z = 17, A = 35, Cl-35, and $^{35}_{17}Cl$

Skillbuilder 4.8 19 protons, 20 neutrons

Skillbuilder 4.9 24.31 amu

▶Answers to Conceptual Checkpoints

4.1 (c) The mass in amu is approximately equal to the number of protons plus the number of neutrons. In order to be charge-neutral, the number of protons must equal the number of electrons.

4.2 (d) Lead is a metal (see Figure 4.12) and a main-group element (see Figure 4.13).

4.3 (b) All of the metalloids are main-group elements (see Figures 4.12 and 4.13).

4.4 (a) Both of these ions have 10 electrons.

4.5

C-12 nucleus

C-13 nucleus

4.6 (b) This atom must have (27 − 14) = 13 protons; the element with an atomic number of 13 is Al.

4.7 The isotopes C-12 and C-13 would not look different in this representation of atoms because the only difference between the two isotopes is that C-13 has an extra neutron in the nucleus. The illustration represents the whole atom and does not attempt to illustrate its nucleus. Because the nucleus of an atom is miniscule compared to the size of the atom itself, the extra neutron would not affect the size of the atom.

4.8 (b) The natural abundance of isotope B must be greater than the natural abundance of isotope A because the atomic mass is closer to the mass of isotope B than to the mass of isotope A.

▲ Ordinary table sugar is a compound called sucrose. A sucrose molecule, such as the one shown here, contains carbon, hydrogen, and oxygen atoms. The properties of sucrose are, however, very different from those of carbon (also shown in the form of graphite), hydrogen, and oxygen. The properties of a compound are, in general, different from the properties of the elements that compose it.

Molecules and Compounds 5

"Almost all aspects of life are engineered at the molecular level, and without understanding molecules, we can only have a very sketchy understanding of life itself."

—Francis Harry Compton Crick (1916–2004)

CHAPTER OUTLINE

5.1 Sugar and Salt

Sodium, a shiny metal (◄ Figure 5.1) that dulls almost instantly upon exposure to air, is extremely reactive and poisonous. If you were to consume any appreciable amount of elemental sodium, you would need immediate medical help. Chlorine, a pale yellow gas (▼ Figure 5.2), is equally reactive and poisonous. Yet the compound formed from these two elements, sodium chloride, is the relatively harmless flavor enhancer that we call table salt (▼ Figure 5.3). When elements combine to form compounds, their properties completely change.

Consider also ordinary sugar. Sugar is a compound composed of carbon, hydrogen, and oxygen. Each of these elements has its own unique properties. Carbon is most familiar to us as the graphite found in pencils or as the diamonds in jewelry. Hydrogen is an extremely flammable gas used as a fuel for rocket engines, and oxygen is one of the gases that compose air. When these three elements combine to form sugar, however, a sweet, white, crystalline solid results.

▲ FIGURE 5.1 **Elemental sodium** Sodium is an extremely reactive metal that dulls almost instantly upon exposure to air.

▶ FIGURE 5.2 **Elemental chlorine** Chlorine is a yellow gas with a pungent odor. It is highly reactive and poisonous.

▲ FIGURE 5.3 **Sodium chloride** The compound formed by sodium and chlorine is table salt.

In Chapter 4, you learned how protons, neutrons, and electrons combine to form different elements, each with its own properties and its own chemistry, each different from the other. In this chapter, you learn how these elements combine with each other to form different compounds, each with its own properties and its own chemistry, each different from all the others and different from the elements that compose it. This is the great wonder of nature: how from such simplicity— protons, neutrons, and electrons—we get such great complexity. It is exactly this complexity that makes life possible. Life could not exist with just 91 different elements if they did not combine to form compounds. It takes compounds in all of their diversity to make living organisms.

5.2 Compounds Display Constant Composition

LO: Restate and apply the law of constant composition.

Although some of the substances you encounter in everyday life are elements, most are not—they are compounds. Free atoms are rare in nature. As you learned in Chapter 3, a compound is different from a mixture of elements. In a compound, the elements combine in fixed, definite proportions, whereas in a mixture, they can have any proportions whatsoever. Consider the difference between a mixture of hydrogen and oxygen gas (▼ Figure 5.4) and the compound water (▼ Figure 5.5). A mixture of hydrogen and oxygen gas can contain any proportions of hydrogen and oxygen. Water, on the other hand, is composed of water molecules that consist of two hydrogen atoms bonded to one oxygen atom. Consequently, water has a definite proportion of hydrogen to oxygen.

The first chemist to formally state the idea that elements combine in fixed proportions to form compounds was Joseph Proust (1754–1826) in the **law of constant composition**, which states:

> All samples of a given compound have the same proportions of their constituent elements.

The ratio of hydrogen to oxygen in a mixture is variable.

Hydrogen molecule

Oxygen molecule

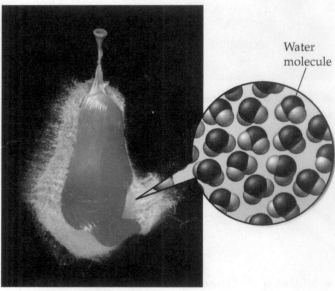

The ratio of hydrogen to oxygen in water is fixed.

Water molecule

2 H atoms (◗) to every 1 O atom (●)

▲ **FIGURE 5.4   A mixture**   This balloon is filled with a mixture of hydrogen and oxygen gas. The relative amounts of hydrogen and oxygen are variable. We could easily add either more hydrogen or more oxygen to the balloon.

▲ **FIGURE 5.5   A chemical compound**   This balloon is filled with water, composed of molecules that have a fixed ratio of hydrogen to oxygen. (*Source*: JoLynn E. Funk.)

For example, if we decompose an 18.0 g sample of water, we get 16.0 g of oxygen and 2.0 g of hydrogen, or an oxygen-to-hydrogen mass ratio of

$$\text{Mass ratio} = \frac{16.0 \text{ g O}}{2.0 \text{ g H}} = 8.0 \quad \text{or} \quad 8.0{:}1$$

This is true of any sample of pure water, no matter what its origin. The law of constant composition applies not only to water, but to every compound. If we decompose a 17.0 g sample of ammonia, a compound composed of nitrogen and hydrogen, we get 14.0 g of nitrogen and 3.0 g of hydrogen, or a nitrogen-to-hydrogen mass ratio of:

$$\text{Mass ratio} = \frac{14.0 \text{ g N}}{3.0 \text{ g H}} = 4.7 \quad \text{or} \quad 4.7{:}1$$

Again, this ratio is the same for every sample of ammonia—the composition of each compound is constant.

> Even though atoms combine in whole-number ratios, their mass ratios are not necessarily whole numbers.

EXAMPLE 5.1   CONSTANT COMPOSITION OF COMPOUNDS

Two samples of carbon dioxide, obtained from different sources, are decomposed into their constituent elements. One sample produces 4.8 g of oxygen and 1.8 g of carbon, and the other sample produces 17.1 g of oxygen and 6.4 g of carbon. Show that these results are consistent with the law of constant composition.

Calculate the mass ratio of one element to the other by dividing the larger mass by the smaller one. For the first sample:	**SOLUTION** $\dfrac{\text{Mass oxygen}}{\text{Mass carbon}} = \dfrac{4.8 \text{ g}}{1.8 \text{ g}} = 2.7$
For the second sample:	$\dfrac{\text{Mass oxygen}}{\text{Mass carbon}} = \dfrac{17.1 \text{ g}}{6.4 \text{ g}} = 2.7$

Because the ratios are the same for the two samples, these results are consistent with the law of constant composition.

▶**SKILLBUILDER 5.1 | Constant Composition of Compounds**

Two samples of carbon monoxide, obtained from different sources, are decomposed into their constituent elements. One sample produces 4.3 g of oxygen and 3.2 g of carbon, and the other sample produces 7.5 g of oxygen and 5.6 g of carbon. Are these results consistent with the law of constant composition?

▶**FOR MORE PRACTICE**   Example 5.16; Problems 25, 26.

 CONCEPTUAL CHECKPOINT 5.1

A compound composed of two elements A and B has a ratio of $\dfrac{\text{Mass A}}{\text{Mass B}} = 3.0$.

Decomposition of the compound produces 9.0 g of element A. What mass of element B is produced?

(a) 27.0 g B   (b) 9.0 g B   (c) 3.0 g B   (d) 1.0 g B

5.3   Chemical Formulas: How to Represent Compounds

LO: Write chemical formulas.

LO: Determine the total number of each type of atom in a chemical formula.

We represent a compound with a **chemical formula**, which indicates the elements present in the compound and the relative number of atoms of each element. For example, H_2O is the chemical formula for water; it indicates that water consists of hydrogen and oxygen atoms in a 2:1 ratio. (Note that the ratio in a chemical formula is a ratio of atoms, not a ratio of masses.) The formula contains the symbol

Compounds have constant composition with respect to mass (as you learned in the previous section) because they are composed of atoms in fixed ratios.

for each element, accompanied by a subscript indicating the number of atoms of that element. By convention, a subscript of 1 is omitted.

symbol for hydrogen · · · → H_2O ← · · · symbol for oxygen

subscript indicating 2 hydrogen atoms

implied subscript of 1 indicating 1 oxygen atom

Other common chemical formulas include NaCl for table salt, indicating sodium and chlorine atoms in a 1:1 ratio; CO_2 for carbon dioxide, indicating carbon and oxygen atoms in a 1:2 ratio; and $C_{12}H_{22}O_{11}$ for table sugar (sucrose), indicating carbon, hydrogen, and oxygen atoms in a 12:22:11 ratio. The subscripts in a chemical formula are part of the compound's definition—if the subscripts change, the formula no longer specifies the same compound. For example, CO is the chemical formula for carbon monoxide, an air pollutant with adverse health effects on humans. When inhaled, carbon monoxide interferes with the blood's ability to carry oxygen, which can be fatal. CO is the primary substance responsible for the deaths of people who inhale too much automobile exhaust. If we change the subscript of the O in CO from 1 to 2, however, we get the formula for a totally different compound. CO_2 is the chemical formula for carbon dioxide, the relatively harmless product of combustion and human respiration. We breathe small amounts of CO_2 all the time with no harmful effects. So, remember that:

CO CO_2

The subscripts in a chemical formula represent the relative numbers of each type of atom in a chemical compound; they never change for a given compound.

Chemical formulas normally list the most metallic elements first. Therefore, the formula for table salt is NaCl, not ClNa. In compounds that do not include a metal, we list the more metal-like element first. Recall from Chapter 4 that metals occupy the left side of the periodic table and nonmetals the upper right side. Among nonmetals, those to the left in the periodic table are more metal-like than those to the right and are normally listed first. Therefore, we write CO_2 and NO, not O_2C and ON. Within a single column in the periodic table, elements toward the bottom are more metal-like than elements toward the top. So, we write SO_2, not O_2S. Table 5.1 lists the specific order for listing nonmetal elements in a chemical formula.

TABLE 5.1   Order of Listing Nonmetal Elements in a Chemical Formula

There are a few historical exceptions in which the most metallic element is not listed first, such as the hydroxide ion, which we write as OH^-.

C	P	N	H	S	I	Br	Cl	O	F

Elements on the left are generally listed before elements on the right.

EXAMPLE 5.2   WRITING CHEMICAL FORMULAS

Write a chemical formula for each compound.

(a) the compound containing two aluminum atoms to every three oxygen atoms
(b) the compound containing three oxygen atoms to every sulfur atom
(c) the compound containing four chlorine atoms to every carbon atom

	SOLUTION
Aluminum is the metal, so list it first.	(a) Al_2O_3
Sulfur is below oxygen on the periodic table and it occurs before oxygen in Table 5.1, so list it first.	(b) SO_3
Carbon is to the left of chlorine on the periodic table and it occurs before chlorine in Table 5.1, so list it first.	(c) CCl_4

Polyatomic Ions in Chemical Formulas

Some chemical formulas contain groups of atoms that act as a unit. When more than one group of the same kind are present, we set their formula off in parentheses with a subscript to indicate the number of units of that group. Many of these groups of atoms have a charge associated with them and are called **polyatomic ions**. For example, NO_3^- is a polyatomic ion with a 1− charge. We describe polyatomic ions in more detail in Section 5.5.

To determine the total number of each type of atom in a compound containing a group within parentheses, we multiply the subscript outside the parentheses by the subscript for each atom inside the parentheses. For example, $Mg(NO_3)_2$ indicates a compound containing one magnesium atom (present as the Mg^{2+} ion) and two NO_3^- groups.

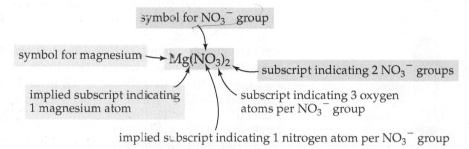

Therefore, the formula $Mg(NO_3)_2$ has the following numbers of each type of atom.

Mg: 1 Mg
N: $1 \times 2 = 2$ N (implied 1 inside parentheses times 2 outside parentheses)
O: $3 \times 2 = 6$ O (3 inside parentheses times 2 outside parentheses)

| **EXAMPLE 5.3** | **TOTAL NUMBER OF EACH TYPE OF ATOM IN A CHEMICAL FORMULA** |

Determine the number of each type of atom in $Mg_3(PO_4)_2$.

SOLUTION
Mg: There are three Mg atoms (present as Mg^{2+} ions), as indicated by the subscript 3.
P: There are two P atoms. We determine this by multiplying the subscript outside the parentheses (2) by the subscript for P inside the parentheses, which is 1 (implied).
O: There are eight O atoms. We determine this by multiplying the subscript outside the parentheses (2) by the subscript for O inside the parentheses (4).

▶**SKILLBUILDER 5.3** | **Total Number of Each Type of Atom in a Chemical Formula**
Determine the number of each type of atom in K_2SO_4.

▶**SKILLBUILDER PLUS**
Determine the number of each type of atom in $Al_2(SO_4)_3$.

▶**FOR MORE PRACTICE** Example 5.18; Problems 35, 36, 37, 38.

✓ **CONCEPTUAL CHECKPOINT 5.2**

Which formula represents the greatest total number of atoms?

(a) $Al(C_2H_3O_2)_3$ **(b)** $Al_2(Cr_2O_7)_3$ **(c)** $Pb(HSO_4)_4$

(d) $Pb_3(PO_4)_4$ **(e)** $(NH_4)_3 PO_4$

Types of Chemical Formulas

We categorize chemical formulas into three types: empirical, molecular, and structural. An **empirical formula** is the simplest whole-number ratio of atoms of each element in a compound. A **molecular formula** is the *actual* number of atoms of each element in a molecule of the compound. For example, the molecular formula for hydrogen peroxide is H_2O_2, and its empirical formula is HO. The molecular formula is always a whole-number multiple of the empirical formula. For many compounds, the molecular and empirical formulas are the same. For example, the empirical and molecular formula for water is H_2O because water molecules contain two hydrogen atoms and one oxygen atom; no simpler whole-number ratio can express the number of hydrogen atoms relative to oxygen atoms.

A **structural formula** uses lines to represent chemical bonds and shows how the atoms in a molecule are connected to each other. The structural formula for hydrogen peroxide is H—O—O—H. We can also use **molecular models**—three-dimensional representations of molecules—to represent compounds. In this book, we use two types of molecular models: ball-and-stick and space-filling. In **ball-and-stick models**, we represent atoms as balls and chemical bonds as sticks. The balls and sticks are connected to represent the molecule's shape. The balls are color coded, and we assign each element a color as shown in the margin.

In **space-filling models**, atoms fill the space between each other to more closely represent our best idea for how a molecule might appear if we could scale it to a visible size. Consider the following ways to represent a molecule of methane, the main component of natural gas:

○ Hydrogen

● Carbon

● Nitrogen

● Oxygen

○ Fluorine

● Phosphorus

○ Sulfur

● Chlorine

CH_4

Molecular formula

$$H—\overset{\displaystyle H}{\underset{\displaystyle H}{C}}—H$$

Structural formula

Ball-and-stick model   Space-filling model

The molecular formula of methane indicates that methane has one carbon atom and four hydrogen atoms. The structural formula shows how the atoms are connected: Each hydrogen atom is bonded to the central carbon atom. The ball-and-stick model and the space-filling model illustrate the *geometry* of the molecule: how the atoms are arranged in three dimensions.

Throughout this book, you have seen and will continue to see images that show the connection between the *macroscopic world* (what we see), the *atomic and molecular world* (the particles that compose matter), and the *symbolic way* that chemists represent the atomic and molecular world. For example, at left is a representation of water using this kind of image.

The main goal of these images is to help you visualize the main theme of this book: *the connection between the world around us and the world of atoms and molecules.*

Macroscopic   Molecular

H_2O

Symbolic

5.4   A Molecular View of Elements and Compounds

LO: Classify elements as atomic or molecular.

LO: Classify compounds as ionic or molecular.

Recall from Chapter 3 that we can categorize pure substances as either elements or compounds. We can further subcategorize elements and compounds according to the basic units that compose them (▼ Figure 5.6). Pure substances may be elements, or they may be compounds. Elements may be either atomic or molecular. Compounds may be either molecular or ionic.

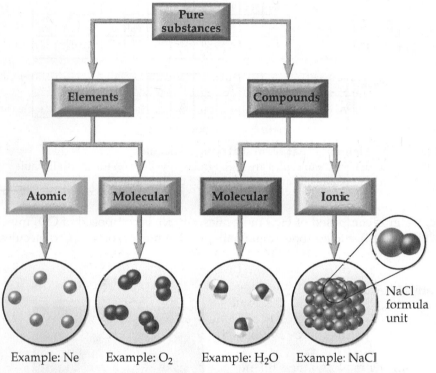

Example: Ne   Example: O_2 Example: H_2O Example: NaCl

▲ **FIGURE 5.6   A molecular view of elements and compounds**

Mercury atoms

Hg

▲ **FIGURE 5.7   An atomic element**
The basic units that compose mercury, an atomic element and a metal, are single mercury atoms.

A few molecular elements, such as S_8 and P_4, are composed of molecules containing several atoms.

Chlorine molecule

Cl_2

Atomic Elements

Atomic elements have single atoms as their basic units. Most elements fall into this category. For example, helium is composed of helium atoms, copper is composed of copper atoms, and mercury of mercury atoms (▲ Figure 5.7).

Molecular Elements

Molecular elements do not normally exist in nature with single atoms as their basic units. Instead, these elements exist as *diatomic molecules*—two atoms of that element bonded together—as their basic units. For example, hydrogen is composed of H_2 molecules, oxygen is composed of O_2 molecules, and chlorine of Cl_2 molecules (◄ Figure 5.8). Table 5.2 and ▶ Figure 5.9 list elements that exist as diatomic molecules.

Molecular Compounds

Molecular compounds are composed of two or more nonmetals. The basic units of molecular compounds are molecules composed of the constituent atoms. For

◄ **FIGURE 5.8   A molecular element**   The basic units that compose chlorine, a molecular element, are diatomic chlorine molecules; each molecule is composed of two chlorine atoms.

TABLE 5.2   Elements That Occur as Diatomic Molecules

Name of Element	Formula of Basic Unit
hydrogen	H_2
nitrogen	N_2
oxygen	O_2
fluorine	F_2
chlorine	Cl_2
bromine	Br_2
iodine	I_2

▲ FIGURE 5.9   Elements that form diatomic molecules   Elements that normally exist as diatomic molecules are highlighted in yellow on this periodic table. Note that they are all nonmetals and include four of the halogens.

example, water is composed of H_2O molecules, dry ice is composed of CO_2 molecules (▼ Figure 5.10), and acetone (finger nail–polish remover) of C_3H_6O molecules.

Carbon dioxide molecule

CO_2

▶ FIGURE 5.10   A molecular compound   The basic units that compose dry ice, a molecular compound, are CO_2 molecules.

Ionic Compounds

Ionic compounds are composed of one or more cations paired with one or more anions. In most cases, the cations are metals and the anions are nonmetals. When a metal, which has a tendency to lose electrons (see Section 4.6), combines with a nonmetal, which has a tendency to gain electrons, one or more electrons transfer from the metal to the nonmetal, creating positive and negative ions that are then attracted to each other. We can assume that a compound composed of a metal and a nonmetal is ionic. The basic unit of ionic compounds is the **formula unit**, the smallest electrically neutral collection of ions. Formula units are different from molecules in that they do not exist as discrete entities, but rather as part of a larger three

Sodium chloride formula unit

NaCl

▲ **FIGURE 5.11 An ionic compound** The basic units that compose table salt, an ionic compound, are NaCl formula units. Unlike molecular compounds, ionic compounds do not contain individual molecules but rather sodium and chloride ions in an alternating three-dimensional array.

dimensional array. For example, salt (NaCl) is composed of Na⁺ and Cl⁻ ions in a 1:1 ratio. In table salt, Na⁺ and Cl⁻ ions exist in an alternating three-dimensional array (◄ Figure 5.11). However, any one Na⁺ ion does not pair with one specific Cl⁻ ion. Sometimes chemists refer to formula units as molecules, but this is not strictly correct since ionic compounds do not contain distinct molecules.

EXAMPLE 5.4 CLASSIFYING SUBSTANCES AS ATOMIC ELEMENTS, MOLECULAR ELEMENTS, MOLECULAR COMPOUNDS, OR IONIC COMPOUNDS

Classify each substance as an atomic element, molecular element, molecular compound, or ionic compound.

(a) krypton (b) $CoCl_2$ (c) nitrogen (d) SO_2 (e) KNO_3

SOLUTION

(a) Krypton is an element that is not listed as diatomic in Table 5.2; therefore, it is an atomic element.

(b) $CoCl_2$ is a compound composed of a metal (left side of periodic table) and nonmetal (right side of the periodic table); therefore, it is an ionic compound.

(c) Nitrogen is an element that is listed as diatomic in Table 5.2; therefore, it is a molecular element.

(d) SO_2 is a compound composed of two nonmetals; therefore, it is a molecular compound.

(e) KNO_3 is a compound composed of a metal and two nonmetals; therefore, it is an ionic compound.

▶**SKILLBUILDER 5.4 | Classifying Substances as Atomic Elements, Molecular Elements, Molecular Compounds, or Ionic Compounds**

Classify each substance as an atomic element, molecular element, molecular compound, or ionic compound.

(a) chlorine (b) NO (c) Au (d) Na_2O (e) $CrCl_3$

▶**FOR MORE PRACTICE** Example 5.19, Example 5.20; Problems 43, 44, 45, 46.

✓ CONCEPTUAL CHECKPOINT 5.3

Which image represents a molecular compound?

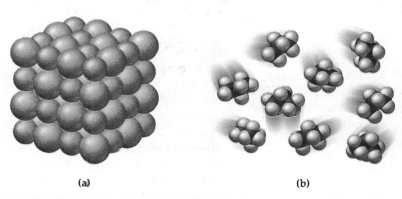

(a) (b)

5.5 Writing Formulas for Ionic Compounds

LO: Write formulas for ionic compounds.

Because ionic compounds must be charge-neutral, and many elements form only one type of ion with a predictable charge, we can determine the formulas for many ionic compounds based on their constituent elements. For example, the formula for the ionic compound composed of sodium and chlorine must be NaCl and not anything else because in ionic compounds Na always forms 1+ cations and Cl always forms 1− anions. In order for the compound to be charge-neutral, it must contain one Na^+ cation to every Cl^- anion. The formula for the ionic compound composed of magnesium and chlorine, on the other hand, must be $MgCl_2$, because Mg always forms 2+ cations and Cl always forms 1− anions. In order for the compound to be charge-neutral, it must contain one Mg^{2+} cation to every two Cl^- anions. In general:

• Ionic compounds always contain positive and negative ions.
• In the chemical formula, the sum of the charges of the positive ions (cations) must always exactly cancel the sum of the charges of the negative ions (anions).

Writing Formulas for Ionic Compounds Containing Only Monoatomic Ions

To write the formula for an ionic compound containing monoatomic ions (no polyatomic ions), follow the procedure in the left column of the following examples. Two examples of how to apply the procedure are provided in the center and right columns.

Revisit Section 4.7 and Figure 4.14 to review the elements that form ions with a predictable charge.

WRITING FORMULAS FOR IONIC COMPOUNDS	EXAMPLE 5.5 Write a formula for the ionic compound that forms from aluminum and oxygen.	EXAMPLE 5.6 Write a formula for the ionic compound that forms from magnesium and oxygen.
1. Write the symbol for the metal and its charge followed by the symbol of the nonmetal and its charge. For many elements, you can determine these charges from their group number in the periodic table (refer to Figure 4.14).	**SOLUTION** Al^{3+} O^{2-}	**SOLUTION** Mg^{2+} O^{2-}
2. Use the magnitude of the charge on each ion (without the sign) as the subscript for the other ion.	Al^{3+} O^{2-} Al_2O_3	Mg^{2+} O^{2-} Mg_2O_2
3. If possible, reduce the subscripts to give a ratio with the smallest whole numbers.	In this case, you cannot reduce the numbers any further; the correct formula is Al_2O_3.	To reduce the subscripts, divide both subscripts by 2. $Mg_2O_2 \div 2 = MgO$
4. Check to make sure that the sum of the charges of the cations exactly cancels the sum of the charges of the anions.	Cations: $2(3+) = 6+$ Anions: $3(2-) = 6-$ The charges cancel.	Cations: $2+$ Anions: $2-$ The charges cancel.
	▶**SKILLBUILDER 5.5** | Write a formula for the compound that forms from strontium and chlorine.	▶**SKILLBUILDER 5.6** | Write a formula for the compound that forms from aluminum and nitrogen. ▶**FOR MORE PRACTICE** Problems 53, 54, 57.

Writing Formulas for Ionic Compounds Containing Polyatomic Ions

As noted previously, some ionic compounds contain **polyatomic ions** (ions that are themselves composed of a group of atoms with an overall charge). Table 5.3 lists the most common polyatomic ions. You need to be able to recognize polyatomic ions in a chemical formula, so it is good idea to become familiar with Table 5.3. To write a formula for ionic compounds containing polyatomic ions, use the formula and charge of the polyatomic ion as demonstrated in Example 5.7.

TABLE 5.3 Some Common Polyatomic Ions

Name	Formula	Name	Formula
acetate	$C_2H_3O_2^-$	hypochlorite	ClO^-
carbonate	CO_3^{2-}	chlorite	ClO_2^-
hydrogen carbonate (or bicarbonate)	HCO_3^-	chlorate	ClO_3^-
hydroxide	OH^-	perchlorate	ClO_4^-
nitrate	NO_3^-	permanganate	MnO_4^-
nitrite	NO_2^-	sulfate	SO_4^{2-}
chromate	CrO_4^{2-}	sulfite	SO_3^{2-}
dichromate	$Cr_2O_7^{2-}$	hydrogen sulfite (or bisulfite)	HSO_3^-
phosphate	PO_4^{3-}	hydrogen sulfate (or bisulfate)	HSO_4^-
hydrogen phosphate	HPO_4^{2-}	peroxide	O_2^{2-}
ammonium	NH_4^+	cyanide	CN^-

EXAMPLE 5.7

WRITING FORMULAS FOR IONIC COMPOUNDS CONTAINING POLYATOMIC IONS

Write a formula for the compound that forms from calcium and nitrate ions.

1. Write the symbol for the metal ion followed by the symbol for the polyatomic ion and their charges. You can deduce these charges from the group numbers in the periodic table. For polyatomic ions, look up the charges and names in Table 5.3.	**SOLUTION** Ca^{2+} NO_3^-
2. Use the magnitude of the charge on each ion as the subscript for the other ion.	$Ca_1(NO_3)_2$
3. Check to see if the subscripts can be reduced to simpler whole numbers. You should drop subscripts of 1 because they are implied.	In this case, you cannot further reduce the subscripts, but you can drop the subscript of 1. $Ca(NO_3)_2$
4. Confirm that the sum of the charges of the cations exactly cancels the sum of the charges of the anions.	Cations Anions 2+ $2(1-) = 2-$

▶**SKILLBUILDER 5.7** | Write the formula for the compound that forms between aluminum and phosphate ions.

▶**SKILLBUILDER PLUS** | Write the formula for the compound that forms between sodium and sulfite ions.

▶**FOR MORE PRACTICE**   Example 5.21; Problems 55, 56, 58.

CONCEPTUAL CHECKPOINT 5.4

Some metals can form ions of different charges in different compounds. Deduce the charge of the Cr ion in the compound $Cr(NO_3)_3$.

(a) 1+

(b) 2+

(c) 3+

(d) 1−

5.6 Nomenclature: Naming Compounds

LO: Distinguish between common and systematic names for compounds.

Because there are so many different compounds, chemists have developed systematic ways to name them. These naming rules can help you examine a compound's formula and determine its name, or vice versa. Many compounds also have a common name. For example, H_2O has the common name *water* and the systematic name *dihydrogen monoxide*. A common name is like a nickname for a compound, used by those who are familiar with it. Since water is such a familiar compound, everyone uses its common name and not its systematic name. In the sections that follow, you learn how to systematically name simple ionic and molecular compounds. Keep in mind, however, that some compounds also have common names that are often used instead of the systematic name. Common names can be learned only through familiarity.

5.7 Naming Ionic Compounds

LO: Name binary ionic compounds containing a metal that forms only one type of ion.

LO: Name binary ionic compounds containing a metal that forms more than one type of ion.

LO: Name ionic compounds containing a polyatomic ion.

The first step in naming an ionic compound is identifying it as one. Remember, any time we have a metal and one or more nonmetals together in a chemical formula, we can assume the compound is ionic. Ionic compounds are categorized into two types (▼ Figure 5.12) depending on the metal in the compound. The first type (sometimes called Type I) contains a metal with an invariant charge—one that does not vary from one compound to another. Sodium, for instance, has a 1+ charge in all of its compounds. Table 5.4 lists examples of metals whose charge is invariant from one compound to another. The charge of most of these metals can be inferred from their group number in the periodic table (see Figure 4.14).

▲ **FIGURE 5.12 Classification of ionic compounds** We classify ionic compounds into two types, depending on the metal in the compound.

TABLE 5.4 Metals Whose Charge Is Invariant from One Compound to Another

Metal	Ion	Name	Group Number
Li	Li^+	lithium	1A
Na	Na^+	sodium	1A
K	K^+	potassium	1A
Rb	Rb^+	rubidium	1A
Cs	Cs^+	cesium	1A
Mg	Mg^{2+}	magnesium	2A
Ca	Ca^{2+}	calcium	2A
Sr	Sr^{2+}	strontium	2A
Ba	Ba^{2+}	barium	2A
Al	Al^{3+}	aluminum	3A
Zn	Zn^{2+}	zinc	*
Ag	Ag^+	silver	*

*The charge of these metals cannot be inferred from their group number.

TABLE 5.5   Some Metals That Form More Than One Type of Ion and Their Common Charges

Metal	Symbol Ion	Name	Older Name*
chromium	Cr^{2+}	chromium(II)	chromous
	Cr^{3+}	chromium(III)	chromic
iron	Fe^{2+}	iron(II)	ferrous
	Fe^{3+}	iron(III)	ferric
cobalt	Co^{2+}	cobalt(II)	cobaltous
	Co^{3+}	cobalt(III)	cobaltic
copper	Cu^{+}	copper(I)	cuprous
	Cu^{2+}	copper(II)	cupric
tin	Sn^{2+}	tin(II)	stannous
	Sn^{4+}	tin(IV)	stannic
mercury	Hg_2^{2+}	mercury(I)	mercurous
	Hg^{2-}	mercury(II)	mercuric
lead	Pb^{2-}	lead(II)	plumbous
	Pb^{4-}	lead(IV)	plumbic

* An older naming system substitutes the names found in this column for the name of the metal and its charge. Under this system, chromium(II) oxide is named chromous oxide. We do *not* use this older system in this text.

▲ **FIGURE 5.13   The transition metals** The metals that form more than one type of ion are usually (but not always) transition metals.

The second type of ionic compound (sometimes called Type II) contains a metal with a charge that can differ in different compounds. In other words, the metal in this second type of ionic compound can form more than one kind of cation (depending on the compound). Iron, for instance, has a 2+ charge in some of its compounds and a 3+ charge in others. Table 5.5 lists additional examples of metals that form more than one type of cation. Such metals are usually (but not always) found in the **transition metals** section of the periodic table (◀ Figure 5.13). However, some transition metals, such as Zn and Ag, form cations with the same charge in all of their compounds, and some main group metals, such as Pb and Sn, form more than one type of cation.

Naming Binary Ionic Compounds Containing a Metal That Forms Only One Type of Cation

Binary compounds contain only two different elements. The names for binary ionic compounds containing a metal that forms only one type of ion have the form:

name of cation (metal)	base name of anion (nonmetal) + -*ide*

Because the charge of the metal is always the same for these types of compounds, we do not need to specify it in the compound's name. For example, the name for NaCl consists of the name of the cation, *sodium*, followed by the base name of the anion, *chlor*, with the ending -*ide*. The full name is *sodium chloride*.

| | The name of the cation in ionic compounds is the same as the name of the metal. |

NaCl   sodium chloride

The name for MgO consists of the name of the cation, *magnesium*, followed by the base name of the anion, *ox*, with the ending -*ide*. The full name is *magnesium oxide*.

MgO   magnesium oxide

Table 5.6 contains the base names for various nonmetals and their most common charges in ionic compounds.

TABLE 5.6   Some Common Anions

Nonmetal	Symbol for Ion	Base Name	Anion Name
fluorine	F^-	fluor-	fluoride
chlorine	Cl^-	chlor-	chloride
bromine	Br^-	brom-	bromide
iodine	I^-	iod-	iodide
oxygen	O^{2-}	ox-	oxide
sulfur	S^{2-}	sulf-	sulfide
nitrogen	N^{3-}	nitr-	nitride

EXAMPLE 5.8 | NAMING IONIC COMPOUNDS CONTAINING A METAL THAT FORMS ONLY ONE TYPE OF CATION

Name the compound MgF_2.

SOLUTION

The cation is magnesium. The anion is fluorine, which becomes *fluoride*. Its correct name is *magnesium fluoride*.

▶ **SKILLBUILDER 5.8 | Naming Ionic Compounds Containing a Metal That Forms Only One Type of Ion**

Name the compound KBr.

▶ **SKILLBUILDER PLUS**   Name the compound Zn_3N_2.

▶ **FOR MORE PRACTICE**   Example 5.22; Problems 59, 60.

Naming Binary Ionic Compounds Containing a Metal That Forms More Than One Type of Cation

Because the charge of the metal cation in these types of compounds is not always the same, we must specify the charge in the metal's name. We specify the charge with a roman numeral (in parentheses) following the name of the metal. For example, we distinguish between Cu^+ and Cu^{2+} by writing a (I) to indicate the 1+ ion or a (II) to indicate the 2+ ion:

$$Cu^+ \quad Copper(I)$$

$$Cu^{2+} \quad Copper(II)$$

The full names for these types of compounds have the form:

name of cation (metal)	(charge of cation (metal) in roman numerals in parentheses)	base name of anion (nonmetal) + *-ide*

We can determine the charge of the metal from the chemical formula of the compound—remember that the sum of all the charges must be zero. For example, the charge of iron in $FeCl_3$ must be 3+ in order for the compound to be charge-neutral with the three Cl^- anions. The name for $FeCl_3$ is therefore the name of the cation, *iron*, followed by the charge of the cation in parentheses *(III)*, followed by the base name of the anion, *chlor*, with the ending *-ide*. The full name is *iron(III) chloride*.

$$FeCl_3 \qquad iron(III) \ chloride$$

Likewise, the name for CrO consists of the name of the cation, *chromium*, followed by the charge of the cation in parentheses *(II)*, followed by the base name of the anion, *ox-*, with the ending *-ide*. The full name is *chromium(II) oxide*.

CrO   chromium(II) oxide   *chromium (I) oxide*

The charge of chromium must be 2+ in order for the compound to be charge-neutral with one O^{2-} anion.

EXAMPLE 5.9 | NAMING IONIC COMPOUNDS CONTAINING A METAL THAT FORMS MORE THAN ONE TYPE OF CATION

Name the compound $PbCl_4$.

SOLUTION

The name for $PbCl_4$ consists of the name of the cation, *lead*, followed by the charge of the cation in parentheses *(IV)*, followed by the base name of the anion, *chlor-*, with the ending *-ide*. The full name is *lead(IV) chloride*. We know the charge on Pb is 4+ because the charge on Cl is 1−. Since there are 4 Cl^- anions, the Pb cation must be Pb^{4+}.

$PbCl_4$ lead(IV) chloride

▶**SKILLBUILDER 5.9 | Naming Ionic Compounds Containing a Metal That Forms More Than One Type of Cation**

Name the compound PbO.

▶**FOR MORE PRACTICE**   Example 5.23; Problems 61, 62.

  CONCEPTUAL CHECKPOINT 5.5

Explain why CaO is NOT named calcium(II) oxide.

Naming Ionic Compounds Containing a Polyatomic Ion

We name ionic compounds containing polyatomic ions using the same procedure we apply to other ionic compounds, except that we use the name of the polyatomic ion whenever it occurs (see Table 5.3). For example, we name KNO_3 using its cation, K^+, *potassium*, and its polyatomic anion, NO_3^-, *nitrate*. The full name is *potassium nitrate*.

KNO₃   potassium nitrate

We name $Fe(OH)_2$ according to its cation, *iron*, its charge *(II)*, and its polyatomic ion, *hydroxide*. Its full name is *iron(II) hydroxide*.

$Fe(OH)_2$ iron(II) hydroxide

If the compound contains both a polyatomic cation and a polyatomic anion, we use the names of both polyatomic ions. For example, NH_4NO_3 is *ammonium nitrate*.

NH_4NO_3 ammonium nitrate

Most polyatomic ions are **oxyanions**, anions containing oxygen. Notice in Table 5.3 that when a series of oxyanions contain different numbers of oxygen atoms, we name them systematically according to the number of oxygen atoms in the ion. If there are two ions in the series, we give the one with more oxygen atoms the ending *-ate* and we give the one with fewer oxygen atoms the ending *-ite*. For example, NO_3^- is *nitrate* and NO_2^- is *nitrite*.

NO_3^- nitrate
NO_2^- nitrite

If there are more than two ions in the series, then we use the prefixes *hypo-*, meaning "less than," and *per-*, meaning "more than." So we call ClO^- *hypochlorite*, meaning "less oxygen than chlorite," and we call ClO_4^- *perchlorate*, meaning "more oxygen than chlorate."

ClO^-	hypochlorite
ClO_2^-	chlorite
ClO_3^-	chlorate
ClO_4^-	perchlorate

EXAMPLE 5.10 | **NAMING IONIC COMPOUNDS CONTAINING A POLYATOMIC ION**

Name the compound K_2CrO_4.   *potassium (   )   chromate.*

SOLUTION

The name for K_2CrO_4 consists of the name of the cation, *potassium*, followed by the name of the polyatomic ion, *chromate*.

$$K_2CrO_4 \text{ potassium chromate}$$

▶**SKILLBUILDER 5.10 | Naming Ionic Compounds Containing a Polyatomic Ion**

Name the compound $Mn(NO_3)_2$.

▶**FOR MORE PRACTICE**   Example 5.24; Problems 65, 66.

 CONCEPTUAL CHECKPOINT 5.6

We just saw that the anion ClO_3^- is named chlorate. What is the name of the anion IO_3^-?

EVERYDAY CHEMISTRY

▶ Polyatomic Ions

A glance at the labels of household products reveals the importance of polyatomic ions in everyday compounds. For example, the active ingredient in household bleach is sodium hypochlorite, which acts to decompose color-causing molecules in clothes (bleaching action) and to kill bacteria (disinfection). A box of baking soda contains sodium bicarbonate (sodium hydrogen carbonate), which acts as an antacid when consumed in small quantities and as a source of carbon dioxide gas in baking. The pockets of carbon dioxide gas make baked goods fluffy rather than flat.

Calcium carbonate is the active ingredient in many antacids such as Tums™ and Alka-Mints™. It neutralizes stomach acids, relieving the symptoms of indigestion and heartburn. Too much calcium carbonate, however, can cause constipation, so Tums should not be overused. Sodium nitrite is a common food additive used to preserve packaged meats such as ham, hot dogs, and bologna. Sodium nitrite inhibits the growth of bacteria, especially those that cause botulism, an often fatal type of food poisoning.

▲ Compounds containing polyatomic ions are present in many consumer products.

▲ The active ingredient in bleach is sodium hypochlorite.

B5.1 CAN YOU ANSWER THIS?   *Write a formula for each of these compounds that contain polyatomic ions: sodium hypochlorite, sodium bicarbonate, calcium carbonate, sodium nitrite.*

5.8   Naming Molecular Compounds

LO: Name molecular compounds.

The first step in naming a molecular compound is identifying it as one. Remember, nearly all molecular compounds form from two or more nonmetals. In this section, we discuss how to name binary (two-element) molecular compounds. Their names have the form:

When writing the name of a molecular compound, as when writing the formula, the first element is the more metal-like one (see Table 5.1). The prefixes given to each element indicate the number of atoms present.

mono- 1	*hexa-* 6
di- 2	*hepta-* 7
tri- 3	*octa-* 8
tetra- 4	*nona-* 9
penta- 5	*deca-* 10

If there is only one atom of the *first element* in the formula, the prefix *mono-* is normally omitted. For example, the name for CO_2 begins with *carbon*, without a prefix because *mono-* is omitted for the first element, followed by the prefix *di-*, to indicate two oxygen atoms, followed by the base name of the second element, *ox*, with the ending *-ide*.

carbon   di- ox -ide

The full name is *carbon dioxide*.

CO_2 carbon dioxide

> When the prefix ends with a vowel and the base name starts with a vowel, we sometimes drop the first vowel, especially in the case of mono oxide, which becomes monoxide.

The name for the compound N_2O, also called laughing gas, begins with the first element, *nitrogen*, with the prefix *di-*, to indicate that there are two of them, followed by the base name of the second element, *ox*, prefixed by *mono-*, to indicate one, and the suffix *-ide*. Because *mono-* ends with a vowel and *oxide* begins with one, we drop an *o* and combine the two as *monoxide*. The entire name is *dinitrogen monoxide*.

N_2O dinitrogen monoxide

EXAMPLE 5.11   NAMING MOLECULAR COMPOUNDS

Name each compound.

(a) CCl_4 (b) BCl_3 (c) SF_6

SOLUTION

(a) The name of the compound is the name of the first element, *carbon*, followed by the base name of the second element, *chlor*, prefixed by *tetra-* to indicate four, and the suffix *-ide*.

   CCl_4 carbon tetrachloride

(b) The name of the compound is the name of the first element, *boron*, followed by the base name of the second element, *chlor*, prefixed by *tri-* to indicate three, and the suffix *-ide*.

   BCl_3 boron trichloride

(c) The name of the compound is the name of the first element, *sulfur*, followed by the base name of the second element, *fluor*, prefixed by *hexa-* to indicate six, and the suffix *-ide*. The entire name is *sulfur hexafluoride*.

   SF_6 sulfur hexafluoride

▶**SKILLBUILDER 5.11 | Naming Molecular Compounds**

Name the compound N_2O_4.

▶**FOR MORE PRACTICE**   Example 5.25; Problems 71, 72.

5.9 Naming Acids

LO: Name binary acids.

LO: Name oxyacids containing an oxyanion ending in *-ate*.

LO: Name oxyacids containing an oxyanion ending in *-ite*.

| HCl(*g*) refers to HCl molecules in the gas state.

Acids are molecular compounds that produce H⁺ ions when dissolved in water. They are composed of hydrogen, which we usually write first in their formula, and one or more nonmetals, which we usually write second. Acids are characterized by their sour taste and their ability to dissolve some metals. For example, HCl(*aq*) is an acid—the (*aq*) indicates that the compound is "aqueous" or "dissolved in water." HCl(*aq*) has a characteristically sour taste. Since HCl(*aq*) is present in stomach fluids, its sour taste becomes painfully obvious during vomiting. HCl(*aq*) also dissolves some metals. If we drop a strip of zinc into a beaker of HCl(*aq*), it will slowly disappear as the acid converts the zinc metal into dissolved Zn^{2+} cations.

Acids are present in many foods, such as lemons and limes, and they are used in some household products such as toilet bowl cleaners and Lime-A-Way. In this section, we only learn how to name them, but in Chapter 14 we will learn more about the properties of acids. We categorize acids into two groups: **binary acids**, those containing only hydrogen and a nonmetal, and **oxyacids**, those containing hydrogen, a nonmetal, and oxygen (▼ Figure 5.14).

$$\left[\begin{array}{l} HX \\ HXO \end{array} \right.$$

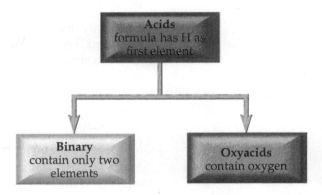

▶ **FIGURE 5.14 Classification of acids** We classify acids into two types, depending on the number of elements in the acid. If the acid contains only two elements, it is a binary acid. If it contains oxygen, it is an oxyacid.

Naming Binary Acids

Binary acids are composed of hydrogen and a nonmetal. The names for binary acids have the following form:

For example, HCl(*aq*) is hydro*chlor*ic acid and HBr(*aq*) is hydro*brom*ic acid.

| HCl(*aq*) hydrochloric acid | HBr(*aq*) hydrobromic acid |

EXAMPLE 5.12 **NAMING BINARY ACIDS**

Give the name of H_2S(*aq*).

| The base name of S is *sulfur*, so the name is *hydrosulfuric acid*. | **SOLUTION** H_2S(*aq*) hydrosulfuric acid |

▶**SKILLBUILDER 5.12 | Naming Binary Acids**

Name HF(*aq*).

▶**FOR MORE PRACTICE** Example 5.26; Problems 77b, 78d.

▲ **FIGURE 5.15** **Classification of oxyacids**
Oxyacids are classified into two types, depending on the endings of the oxyanions that they contain.

You can use the saying, "*ic* I *ate* an acid" to remember the association of *-ic* with *-ate*.

Naming Oxyacids

Oxyacids are acids that contain oxyanions, which are listed in the table of polyatomic ions (Table 5.3). For example, $HNO_3(aq)$ contains the nitrate (NO_3^-) ion, $H_2SO_3(aq)$ contains the sulfite (SO_3^{2-}) ion, and $H_2SO_4(aq)$ contains the sulfate (SO_4^{2-}) ion. All of these acids are a combination of one or more H^+ ions with an oxyanion. The number of H^+ ions depends on the charge of the oxyanion, so that the formula is always charge-neutral. The names of oxyacids depend on the ending of the oxyanion (◄ Figure 5.15).

The names of acids containing oxyanions ending with *-ite* take this form:

base name of oxyanion + *-ous* acid

The names of acids containing oxyanions ending with *-ate* take this form:

base name of oxyanion + *-ic* acid

So H_2SO_3 is *sulfurous acid* (oxyanion is sulfite), and HNO_3 is *nitric acid* (oxyanion is nitrate).

$H_2SO_3(aq)$ sulfurous acid $HNO_3(aq)$ nitric acid

Table 5.7 lists some common oxyacids and their oxyanions.

EXAMPLE 5.13	NAMING OXYACIDS

Name $HC_2H_3O_2(aq)$.

The oxyanion is acetate, which ends in *-ate*; therefore, the name of the acid is *acetic acid*.	**SOLUTION** $HC_2H_3O_2(aq)$ acetic acid

▶**SKILLBUILDER 5.13 | Naming Oxyacids**
Name $HNO_2(aq)$.

▶**FOR MORE PRACTICE** Examples 5.27, 5.28; Problems 77acd, 78abc.

TABLE 5.7 Names of Some Common Oxyacids and Their Oxyanions

Acid Formula	Acid Name	Oxyanion Name	Oxyanion Formula
HNO_2	nitrous acid	nitrite	NO_2^-
HNO_3	nitric acid	nitrate	NO_3^-
H_2SO_3	sulfurous acid	sulfite	SO_3^{2-}
H_2SO_4	sulfuric acid	sulfate	SO_4^{2-}
$HClO_2$	chlorous acid	chlorite	ClO_2^-
$HClO_3$	chloric acid	chlorate	ClO_3^-
$HC_2H_3O_2$	acetic acid	acetate	$C_2H_3O_2^-$
H_2CO_3	carbonic acid	carbonate	CO_3^{2-}

CHEMISTRY IN THE ENVIRONMENT
▶ Acid Rain

Acid rain occurs when rainwater mixes with air pollutants—such as NO, NO_2, and SO_2—that form acids. NO and NO_2, primarily from vehicular emission, combine with water to form $HNO_3(aq)$. SO_2, primarily from coal-powered electricity generation, combines with water and oxygen in air to form $H_2SO_4(aq)$. $HNO_3(aq)$ and $H_2SO_4(aq)$ both cause rainwater to become acidic. The problem is greatest in the northeastern United States, where pollutants from midwestern electrical power plants combine with rainwater to produce rain with acid levels that are 10 times higher than normal.

When acid rain falls or flows into lakes and streams, it makes them more acidic. Some species of aquatic animals—such as trout, bass, snails, salamanders, and clams—cannot tolerate the increased acidity and die. These deaths disturb the ecosystem of the lake, resulting in imbalances that may lead in turn to the deaths of other aquatic species. Acid rain also weakens trees by dissolving nutrients in the soil and by damaging leaves. Appalachian red spruce trees have been the hardest hit, with many forests showing significant acid rain damage.

Acid rain also damages building materials. Acids dissolve $CaCO_3$ (limestone), a component of marble and concrete, and iron, the main component of steel. Consequently, many statues, buildings, and bridges in the northeastern United States show significant deterioration, and some historical gravestones made of limestone are barely legible due to acid rain damage.

Although acid rain has been a problem for many years, innovative legislation has offered hope for change. In 1990, Congress passed several amendments to the Clean Air Act that included provisions requiring electrical utilities to reduce SO_2 emissions. Since then, SO_2 emissions have decreased, and rain in the northeastern United States has become somewhat less acidic. For example, according to the U.S. Environmental Protection Agency, average U.S. atmospheric SO_2 concentrations were 0.012 ppm in 1980, but have decreased to less than 0.003 ppm today. With time, and continued enforcement of the acid rain program, lakes, streams, and forests damaged by acid rain should recover. However, acid rain continues to worsen in countries such as China, where industrial growth is outpacing environmental controls. International cooperation is essential to solving environmental problems such as acid rain.

B5.2 CAN YOU ANSWER THIS? *Name each compound, given here as formulas:*

$$NO, NO_2, SO_2, HNO_3(aq), CaCO_3$$

▲ Acid rain harms many materials, including the limestone often used for tombstones, buildings, and statues.

▲ A forest damaged by acid rain.

5.10 Nomenclature Summary

LO: Recognize and name chemical compounds.

Acids are technically a subclass of molecular compounds; that is, they are molecular compounds that form H^+ ions when dissolved in water.

Naming compounds requires several steps. The flowchart in ▶ Figure 5.16 summarizes the different categories of compounds that we have covered in the chapter and how to identify and name them. The first step is to decide whether the compound is ionic, molecular, or an acid. We can recognize ionic compounds by the presence of a metal and a nonmetal, molecular compounds by two or more nonmetals, and acids by the presence of hydrogen (written first) and one or more nonmetals.

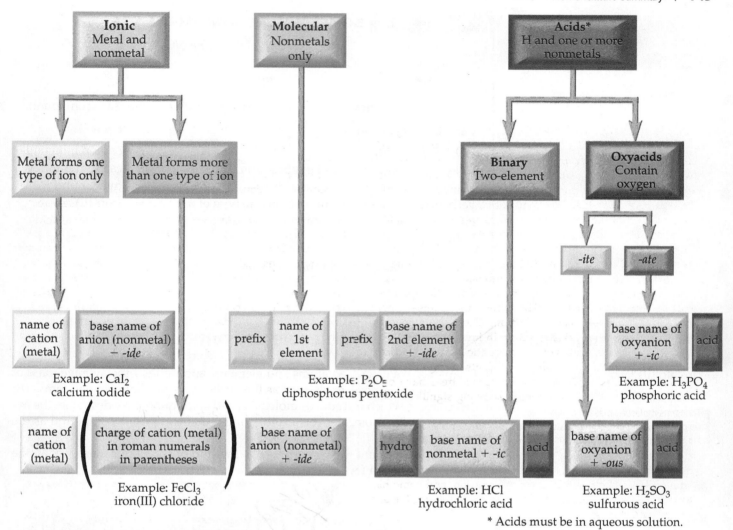

▲ **FIGURE 5.16 Nomenclature flowchart**

Ionic Compounds

For an ionic compound, we must next decide whether the metal forms only one type of ion or more than one type of ion. Group 1A (alkali) metals, Group 2A (alkaline earth) metals, and aluminum always form only one type of ion (Figure 4.14). Most of the transition metals form more than one type of ion. Once we have identified the type of ionic compound, we name it according to the scheme in the chart. If the ionic compound contains a polyatomic ion—something we must learn to recognize by familiarity—we insert the name of the polyatomic ion in place of the metal (positive polyatomic ion) or the nonmetal (negative polyatomic ion).

Zinc (Zn^{2+}), scandium (Sc^{3+}), and silver (Ag^{+}) also form only one type of ion.

Molecular Compounds

We have learned how to name only one type of molecular compound, the binary (two-element) compound. If we identify a compound as molecular, we name it according to the scheme in Figure 5.16.

Acids

To name an acid, we must first decide whether it is a binary (two-element) acid or an oxyacid (an acid containing oxygen). We name binary acids according to the scheme in Figure 5.16. We must further subdivide oxyacids based on the name of their corresponding oxyanion. If the oxyanion ends in -*ite*, we use one scheme; if it ends with -*ate*, we use the other.

EXAMPLE 5.14 **NOMENCLATURE USING FIGURE 5.16**

 Name each compound: CO, CaF₂, HF(*aq*), Fe(NO₃)₃, HClO₄(*aq*).
H₂SO₃(*aq*)

SOLUTION

The table illustrates how to use Figure 5.16 to arrive at a name for each compound.

Formula	Flowchart Path			Name
CO	molecular			carbon monoxide
CaF₂	ionic ⟶	one type of ion ⟶		calcium fluoride
HF(*aq*)	acid ⟶	binary ⟶		hydrofluoric acid
Fe(NO₃)₃	ionic ⟶	more than one type of ion ⟶		iron(III) nitrate
HClO₄(*aq*)	acid ⟶	oxyacid ⟶	-*ate* ⟶	perchloric acid
H₂SO₃(*aq*)	acid ⟶	oxyacid ⟶	-*ite* ⟶	sulfurous acid

▶**FOR MORE PRACTICE** Problems 93, 94.

5.11 Formula Mass: The Mass of a Molecule or Formula Unit

LO: Calculate formula mass.

The terms *molecular mass* and *molecular weight*, which are also commonly used, have the same meaning as formula mass.

In Chapter 4, we discussed atoms and elements and defined the average mass of the atoms that compose an element as the *atomic mass* for that element. Similarly, in this chapter, which introduces molecules and compounds, we designate the average mass of the molecules (or formula units) that compose a compound as the **formula mass**.

For any compound, the *formula mass* is the sum of the atomic masses of all the atoms in its chemical formula:

$$\text{Formula mass} = \left(\begin{array}{c} \text{\# atoms of 1st} \\ \text{element in} \\ \text{chemical formula} \end{array} \times \begin{array}{c} \text{Atomic mass} \\ \text{of} \\ \text{1st element} \end{array} \right) + \left(\begin{array}{c} \text{\# atoms of 2nd} \\ \text{element in} \\ \text{chemical formula} \end{array} \times \begin{array}{c} \text{Atomic mass} \\ \text{of} \\ \text{2nd element} \end{array} \right) + \dots$$

Like atomic mass for atoms, formula mass characterizes the average mass of a molecule or formula unit. For example, the formula mass of water, H₂O, is:

$$\text{Formula mass} = 2(1.01 \text{ amu}) + 16.00 \text{ amu}$$
$$= 18.02 \text{ amu}$$

and that of sodium chloride, NaCl, is:

$$\text{Formula mass} = 22.99 \text{ amu} + 35.45 \text{ amu}$$
$$= 58.44 \text{ amu}$$

In addition to giving a characteristic mass to the molecules or formula units of a compound, formula mass—as we will discuss in Chapter 6—allows us to quantify the number of molecules or formula units in a sample of a given mass.

EXAMPLE 5.15 **CALCULATING FORMULA MASS**

Calculate the formula mass of carbon tetrachloride, CCl_4.

SOLUTION

To find the formula mass, sum the atomic masses of each atom in the chemical formula.

$$\text{Formula mass} = 1 \times (\text{Atomic mass C}) + 4 \times (\text{Atomic mass Cl})$$
$$= 12.01 \text{ amu} + 4(35.45 \text{ amu})$$
$$= 12.01 \text{ amu} + 141.\underline{8}0 \text{ amu}$$
$$= 153.8 \text{ amu}$$

▶**SKILLBUILDER 5.15 | Calculating Formula Masses**

Calculate the formula mass of dinitrogen monoxide, N_2O, also called laughing gas.

▶**FOR MORE PRACTICE** Example 5.29; Problems 83, 84.

 CONCEPTUAL CHECKPOINT 5.7

Which substance has the greatest formula mass?
(a) O_2 **(b)** O_3 **(c)** H_2O **(d)** H_2O_2

CHAPTER IN REVIEW

Self-Assessment Quiz

Q1. Carbon tetrachloride has a chlorine-to-carbon mass ratio of 11.8:1. If a sample of carbon tetrachloride contains 35 g of chlorine, what mass of carbon does it contain?
(a) 0.34 g C
(b) 1.0 g C
(c) 3.0 g C
(d) 11.8 g C

Q2. Write a chemical formula for a compound that contains two chlorine atoms to every one oxygen atom.
(a) Cl_2O
(b) ClO_2
(c) $2ClO$
(d) $Cl(O_2)_2$

Q3. How many oxygen atoms are in the chemical formula $Fe_2(SO_4)_3$?
(a) 2   (b) 3   (c) 4   (d) 12

Q4. Which element is a molecular element?
(a) copper   (b) iodine   (c) krypton   (d) potassium

Q5. Which compound is ionic?
(a) BrF_5 (b) HNO_3 (c) $MgSO_4$ (d) NI_3

Q6. Write a formula for the compound that forms between Sr and Br.
(a) SrBr   (b) Sr_2Br (c) $SrBr_2$ (d) Sr_2Br_2

Q7. Write a formula for the compound that forms between sodium and chlorite ions.
(a) $NaClO_2$
(b) Na_2ClO_2
(c) $Na(ClO)_2$
(d) $NaClO_3$

Q8. Name the compound Li_3N.
(a) Trilithium mononitride
(b) Trilithium nitride
(c) Lithium(I) nitride
(d) Lithium nitride

Q9. Name the compound $CrCl_3$.
(a) Monochromium trichloride
(b) Chromium trichloride
(c) Chromium chloride
(d) Chromium(III) chloride

Q10. Name the compound $BaSO_4$.
(a) Barium sulfate
(b) Barium(II) sulfate
(c) Barium monosulfur tetraoxygen
(d) Barium tetrasulfate

Q11. Name the compound PF_5.

(a) Monophosphorus pentafluoride

(b) Phosphorus pentafluoride

(c) Phosphorus fluoride

(d) Phosphorus(III) fluoride

Q12. What is the formula for manganese(III) oxide?

(a) MnO

(b) Mn_3O

(c) Mn_2O_3

(d) MnO_3

Q13. Name the acid $H_3PO_4(aq)$.

(a) Hydrogen phosphate

(b) Phosphoric acid

(c) Phosphorus acid

(d) Hydrophosphic acid

Q14. What is the formula for hydrobromic acid?

(a) HBr

(b) HBrO

(c) $HBrO_2$

(d) $HBrO_3$

Q15. Determine the formula mass of CCl_2F_2.

(a) 66.46 amu

(b) 108.9 amu

(c) 132.92 amu

(d) 120.91 amu

Answers 1:c, 2:a, 3:d, 4:b, 5:c, 6:c, 7:a, 8:d, 9:d, 10:a, 11:b, 12:c, 13:b, 14:a, 15:d

Chemical Principles

Compounds: Matter is ultimately composed of atoms, and those atoms are often combined in compounds. The most important characteristic of a compound is its constant composition. The elements that make up a particular compound are in fixed, definite proportions in all samples of the compound.

Chemical Formulas: Chemical formulas represent compounds. Formulas indicate the elements present in the compound and the relative number of atoms of each. These formulas represent the basic units that make up a compound. Pure substances can be categorized according to the basic units that compose them. Elements can be composed of atoms or molecules. Compounds can be molecular, in which case their basic units are molecules, or ionic, in which case their basic units are formula units (composed of cations and anions). We can write the formulas for many ionic compounds simply by knowing the elements in the compound.

Chemical Nomenclature: We can write the names of simple ionic compounds, molecular compounds, and acids, by examining their chemical formulas. The nomenclature flowchart (Figure 5.16) shows the basic procedure for determining these names.

Formula Mass: The formula mass of a compound is the sum of the atomic masses of all the atoms in the chemical formula for the compound. Like atomic mass for elements, formula mass characterizes the average mass of a molecule or formula unit.

Relevance

Compounds: Most of the matter you encounter is in the form of compounds. Water, salt, and carbon dioxide are all examples of common simple compounds. More complex compounds include caffeine, aspirin, acetone, and testosterone.

Chemical Formulas: To understand compounds, you must understand their composition, which is represented by a chemical formula. The connection between the microscopic world and the macroscopic world hinges on the particles that compose matter. Since most matter is in the form of compounds, the properties of most matter depend on the molecules or ions that compose it. Molecular matter does what its molecules do; ionic matter does what its ions do. The world you see and experience is governed by what these particles are doing.

Chemical Nomenclature: Because there are so many compounds, there must be a systematic way to name them. By learning these few simple rules, you will be able to name thousands of different compounds. The next time you look at the label on a consumer product, try to identify as many of the compounds as you can by examining their names.

Formula Mass: Besides being the characteristic mass of a molecule or formula unit, formula mass is important in many calculations involving the composition of compounds and quantities in chemical reactions.

Chemical Skills

Examples

LO: Restate and apply the law of constant composition (Section 5.2).

The law of constant composition states that all samples of a given compound have the same ratio of their constituent elements.

To determine whether experimental data are consistent with the law of constant composition, calculate the ratios of the masses of each element in all samples. When calculating these ratios, it is most convenient to put the larger number in the numerator (top) and the smaller one in the denominator (bottom); that way, the ratio is greater than 1. If the ratios are the same, then the data are consistent with the law of constant composition.

EXAMPLE 5.16 CONSTANT COMPOSITION OF COMPOUNDS

Two samples said to be carbon disulfide (CS_2) are decomposed into their constituent elements. One sample produces 8.08 g S and 1.51 g C, while the other produces 31.3 g S and 3.85 g C. Are these results consistent with the law of constant composition?

SOLUTION
Sample 1

$$\frac{\text{Mass S}}{\text{Mass C}} = \frac{8.08 \text{ g}}{1.51 \text{ g}} = 5.35$$

Sample 2

$$\frac{\text{Mass S}}{\text{Mass C}} = \frac{31.3 \text{ g}}{3.85 \text{ g}} = 8.13$$

These results are not consistent with the law of constant composition, so the information that the two samples are the same substance must therefore be in error.

LO: Write chemical formulas (Section 5.3).

Chemical formulas indicate the elements present in a compound and the relative number of atoms of each. When writing formulas, put the more metallic element first.

EXAMPLE 5.17 WRITING CHEMICAL FORMULAS

Write a chemical formula for the compound containing one nitrogen atom for every two oxygen atoms.

SOLUTION
NO_2

LO: Determine the total number of each type of atom in a chemical formula (Section 5.3).

The numbers of atoms not enclosed in parentheses are given directly by their subscript.

Find the numbers of atoms within parentheses by multiplying their subscript within the parentheses by their subscript outside the parentheses.

EXAMPLE 5.18 DETERMINING THE TOTAL NUMBER OF EACH TYPE OF ATOM IN A CHEMICAL FORMULA

Determine the number of each type of atom in $Pb(ClO_3)_2$.

SOLUTION
One Pb atom

Two Cl atoms

Six O atoms

LO: Classify elements as atomic or molecular (Section 5.4).

Most elements exist as atomic elements; their basic units in nature are individual atoms. However, several elements (H_2, N_2, O_2, F_2, Cl_2, Br_2, and I_2) exist as molecular elements; their basic units in nature are diatomic molecules.

EXAMPLE 5.19 CLASSIFYING ELEMENTS AS ATOMIC OR MOLECULAR

Classify each element as atomic or molecular: sodium, iodine, and nitrogen.

SOLUTION
sodium: atomic

iodine: molecular (I_2)

nitrogen: molecular (N_2)

LO: Classify compounds as ionic or molecular (Section 5.4).

Compounds containing a metal and a nonmetal are ionic. If the metal is a transition metal, it is likely to form more than one type of ion (see exceptions in Tables 5.4 and 5.5). If the metal is not a transition metal, it is likely to form only one type of ion (see exceptions in Tables 5.4 and 5.5).

Compounds composed of nonmetals are molecular.

EXAMPLE 5.20 CLASSIFYING COMPOUNDS AS IONIC OR MOLECULAR

Classify each compound as ionic or molecular. If they are ionic, determine whether the metal forms only one type of ion or more than one type of ion.

$$FeCl_3, K_2SO_4, CCl_4$$

SOLUTION

$FeCl_3$: ionic, metal forms more than one type of ion

K_2SO_4: ionic, metal forms only one type of ion

CCl_4: molecular

LO: Write formulas for ionic compounds (Section 5.5).

1. Write the symbol for the metal ion followed by the symbol for the nonmetal ion (or polyatomic ion) and their charges. These charges can be deduced from the group numbers in the periodic table. (In the case of polyatomic ions, the charges come from Table 5.3.)

2. Use the magnitude of the charge on each ion as the subscript for the other ion.

3. Check to see if you can reduce the subscripts to simpler whole numbers. Drop subscripts of 1; they are implied.

4. Confirm that the sum of the charges of the cations exactly cancels the sum of the charges of the anions.

EXAMPLE 5.21 WRITING FORMULAS FOR IONIC COMPOUNDS

Write a formula for the compound that forms from lithium and sulfate ions.

SOLUTION

$$Li^+ \quad SO_4^{2-}$$
$$Li_2(SO_4)$$

In this case, the subscripts cannot be further reduced.

$$Li_2SO_4$$

Cations	Anions
$2(1+) = 2+$	$2-$

LO: Name binary ionic compounds containing a metal that forms only one type of ion (Section 5.7).

The name of the metal is unchanged. The name of the nonmetal is its base name with the ending -ide.

EXAMPLE 5.22 NAMING BINARY IONIC COMPOUNDS CONTAINING A METAL THAT FORMS ONLY ONE TYPE OF ION

Name the compound Al_2O_3.

SOLUTION

aluminum oxide

LO: Name binary ionic compounds containing a metal that forms more than one type of ion (Section 5.7).

Because the names of these compounds include the charge of the metal ion, first determine that charge by calculating the total charge of the nonmetal ions.

The total charge of the metal ions must equal the total charge of the nonmetal ions, but have the opposite sign.

The name of the compound is the name of the metal ion, followed by the charge of the metal ion, followed by the base name of the nonmetal + -ide.

EXAMPLE 5.23 NAMING BINARY IONIC COMPOUNDS CONTAINING A METAL THAT FORMS MORE THAN ONE TYPE OF ION

Name the compound Fe_2S_3.

SOLUTION

3 sulfide ions $\times$ $(2-) = 6-$

2 iron ions $\times$ (*ion charge*) $= 6+$

ion charge $= 3+$

Charge of each iron ion $= 3+$

iron(III) sulfide

LO: Name compounds containing a polyatomic ion (Section 5.7).

Name ionic compounds containing a polyatomic ion in the normal way, except substitute the name of the polyatomic ion (from Table 5.3) in place of the nonmetal.

Because the metal in this example forms more than one type of ion, you need to determine the charge on the metal ion. The charge of the metal ion must be equal in magnitude to the sum of the charges of the polyatomic ions but opposite in sign.

The name of the compound is the name of the metal ion, followed by the charge of the metal ion, followed by the name of the polyatomic ion.

| EXAMPLE 5.24 | NAMING COMPOUNDS CONTAINING A POLYATOMIC ION |

Name the compound $Co(ClO_4)_2$.

SOLUTION

2 perchlorate ions × (1−) = 2−

Charge of cobalt ion = 2+

cobalt(II) perchlorate

LO: Name molecular compounds (Section 5.8).

The name consists of a prefix indicating the number of atoms of the first element, followed by the name of the first element, and a prefix for the number of atoms of the second element, followed by the base name of the second element plus the suffix *-ide*. The prefix *-mono* is normally dropped on the first element.

| EXAMPLE 5.25 | NAMING MOLECULAR COMPOUNDS |

Name the compound NO_2.

SOLUTION

nitrogen dioxide

LO: Name binary acids (Section 5.9).

The name begins with *hydro-*, followed by the base name of the nonmetal, plus the suffix *–ic*, and the word *acid*.

| EXAMPLE 5.26 | NAMING BINARY ACIDS |

Name the acid $HI(aq)$.

SOLUTION

hydroiodic acid

LO: Name oxyacids containing an oxyanion ending in *–ate* (Section 5.9).

The name is the base name of the oxyanion + *-ic*, followed by the word *acid* (sulfate violates the rule somewhat; in strict terms, the base name would be *sulf*).

| EXAMPLE 5.27 | NAMING OXYACIDS CONTAINING AN OXYANION ENDING IN *-ATE* |

Name the acid $H_2SO_4(aq)$.

SOLUTION

The oxyanion is sulfate. The name of the acid is *sulfuric acid*.

LO: Name oxyacids containing an oxyanion ending in *–ite* (Section 5.9).

The name is the base name of the oxyanion + *-ous*, followed by the word *acid*.

| EXAMPLE 5.28 | NAMING OXYACIDS CONTAINING AN OXYANION ENDING IN *-ITE* |

Name the acid $HClO_2(aq)$.

SOLUTION

The oxyanion is chlorite. The name of the acid is *chlorous acid*.

LO: Calculate formula mass (Section 5.11).

The formula mass is the sum of the atomic masses of all the atoms in the chemical formula. In determining the number of each type of atom, multiply subscripts inside parentheses by subscripts outside parentheses.

| EXAMPLE 5.29 | CALCULATING FORMULA MASS |

Calculate the formula mass of $Mg(NO_3)_2$.

SOLUTION

Formula mass = 24.31 + 2(14.01) + 6(16.00)

= 148.33 amu

KEY TERMS

acid **[5.9]**	empirical formula **[5.3]**	molecular compound **[5.4]**	polyatomic ion **[5.3]**
atomic element **[5.4]**	formula mass **[5.11]**	molecular element **[5.4]**	space-filling
ball-and-stick model **[5.3]**	formula unit **[5.4]**	molecular formula **[5.3]**	model **[5.3]**
binary acid **[5.9]**	ionic compound **[5.4]**	molecular model **[5.3]**	structural formula **[5.3]**
binary compound **[5.7]**	law of constant	oxyacid **[5.9]**	transition metals **[5.7]**
chemical formula **[5.3]**	composition **[5.2]**	oxyanion **[5.7]**	

EXERCISES

QUESTIONS

1. Do the properties of an element change when it combines with another element to form a compound? Explain.

2. How might the world be different if elements did not combine to form compounds?

3. What is the law of constant composition? Who discovered it?

4. What is a chemical formula? List some examples.

5. In a chemical formula, which element is listed first?

6. In a chemical formula, how do you calculate the number of atoms of an element within parentheses? Provide an example.

7. Explain the difference between a molecular formula and an empirical formula.

8. What is a structural formula? What is the difference between a structural formula and a molecular model?

9. What is the difference between a molecular element and an atomic element? List the elements that occur as diatomic molecules.

10. What is the difference between an ionic compound and a molecular compound?

11. What is the difference between a common name for a compound and a systematic name?

12. List the metals that form only one type of ion (that is, metals whose charge is invariant from one compound to another). What are the group numbers of these metals?

13. Identify the block in the periodic table of metals that tend to form more than one type of ion.

14. What is the basic form for the names of ionic compounds containing a metal that forms only one type of ion?

15. What is the basic form for the names of ionic compounds containing a metal that forms more than one type of ion?

16. Why are roman numerals needed in the names of ionic compounds containing a metal that forms more than one type of ion?

17. How are compounds containing a polyatomic ion named?

18. Which polyatomic ions have a 2– charge? Which polyatomic ions have a 3– charge?

19. What is the basic form for the names of molecular compounds?

20. How many atoms does each prefix specify? *mono-, di-, tri-, tetra-, penta-, hexa-*.

21. What is the basic form for the names of binary acids?

22. What is the basic form for the name of oxyacids whose oxyanions end with *-ate*?

23. What is the basic form for the name of oxyacids whose oxyanions end with *-ite*?

24. What is the formula mass of a compound?

PROBLEMS

CONSTANT COMPOSITION OF COMPOUNDS

25. Two samples of sodium chloride are decomposed into their constituent elements. One sample produces 4.65 g of sodium and 7.16 g of chlorine, and the other sample produces 7.45 g of sodium and 11.5 g of chlorine. Are these results consistent with the law of constant composition? Explain your answer.

26. Two samples of carbon tetrachloride are decomposed into their constituent elements. One sample produces 32.4 g of carbon and 373 g of chlorine, and the other sample produces 12.3 g of carbon and 112 g of chlorine. Are these results consistent with the law of constant composition? Explain your answer.

27. Upon decomposition, one sample of magnesium fluoride produced 1.65 kg of magnesium and 2.57 kg of fluorine. A second sample produced 1.32 kg of magnesium. How much fluorine (in grams) did the second sample produce?

28. The mass ratio of sodium to fluorine in sodium fluoride is 1.21:1. A sample of sodium fluoride produces 34.5 g of sodium upon decomposition. How much fluorine (in grams) forms?

29. Use the law of constant composition to complete the table summarizing the amounts of nitrogen and oxygen produced upon the decomposition of several samples of dinitrogen monoxide.

	Mass N_2O	Mass N	Mass O
Sample A	2.85 g	1.82 g	1.03 g
Sample B	4.55 g	——	——
Sample C	——	——	1.35 g
Sample D	——	1.11 g	——

30. Use the law of constant composition to complete the table summarizing the amounts of iron and chlorine produced upon the decomposition of several samples of iron(III) chloride.

	Mass $FeCl_3$	Mass Fe	Mass Cl
Sample A	3.785 g	1.302 g	2.483 g
Sample B	2.175 g	——	——
Sample C	——	2.012 g	——
Sample D	——	——	2.329 g

CHEMICAL FORMULAS

31. Write a chemical formula for the compound containing one nitrogen atom for every three iodine atoms.

32. Write a chemical formula for the compound containing one carbon atom for every four bromine atoms.

33. Write chemical formulas for compounds containing:
 (a) three iron atoms for every four oxygen atoms
 (b) one phosphorus atom for every three chlorine atoms
 (c) one phosphorus atom for every five chlorine atoms
 (d) two silver atoms for every oxygen atom

34. Write chemical formulas for compounds containing:
 (a) one calcium atom for every two iodine atoms
 (b) two nitrogen atoms for every four oxygen atoms
 (c) one silicon atom for every two oxygen atoms
 (d) one zinc atom for every two chlorine atoms

35. How many oxygen atoms are in each chemical formula?
 (a) H_3PO_4
 (b) Na_2HPO_4
 (c) $Ca(HCO_3)_2$
 (d) $Ba(C_2H_3O_2)_2$

36. How many hydrogen atoms are in each of the formulas in Question 35?

37. Determine the number of each type of atom in each formula.
 (a) $MgCl_2$
 (b) $NaNO_3$
 (c) $Ca(NO_2)_2$
 (d) $Sr(OH)_2$

38. Determine the number of each type of atom in each formula.
 (a) NH_4Cl
 (b) $Mg_3(PO_4)_2$
 (c) $NaCN$
 (d) $Ba(HCO_3)_2$

39. Complete the table.

Formula	Number of $C_2H_3O_2^-$ Units	Number of Carbon Atoms	Number of Hydrogen Atoms	Number of Oxygen Atoms	Number of Metal Atoms
$Mg(C_2H_3O_2)_2$	——	——	——	——	——
$NaC_2H_3O_2$	——	——	——	——	——
$Cr_2(C_2H_3O_2)_4$	——	——	——	——	——

40. Complete the table.

Formula	Number of SO_4^{2-} Units	Number of Sulfur Atoms	Number of Oxygen Atoms	Number of Metal Atoms
$CaSO_4$	——	——	——	——
$Al_2(SO_4)_3$	——	——	——	——
K_2SO_4	——	——	——	——

41. Give the empirical formula that corresponds to each molecular formula.
 (a) C_2H_6
 (b) N_2O_4
 (c) $C_4H_6O_2$
 (d) NH_3

42. Give the empirical formula that corresponds to each molecular formula.
 (a) C_2H_2
 (b) CO_2
 (c) $C_6H_{12}O_6$
 (d) B_2H_6

MOLECULAR VIEW OF ELEMENTS AND COMPOUNDS

43. Classify each element as atomic or molecular.
  (a) chlorine
  (b) argon
  (c) cobalt
  (d) hydrogen

44. Which elements have molecules as their basic units?
  (a) helium
  (b) oxygen
  (c) iron
  (d) bromine

45. Classify each compound as ionic or molecular.
  (a) CS_2
  (b) CuO
  (c) KI
  (d) PCl_3

46. Classify each compound as ionic or molecular.
  (a) PtO_2
  (b) CF_2Cl_2
  (c) CO
  (d) SO_3

47. Match the substances on the left with the basic units that compose them on the right.
  helium   molecules
  CCl_4 formula units
  K_2SO_4 diatomic molecules
  bromine   single atoms

48. Match the substances on the left with the basic units that compose them on the right.
  NI_3 molecules
  copper metal   single atoms
  $SrCl_2$ diatomic molecules
  nitrogen   formula units

49. What are the basic units—single atoms, molecules, or formula units—that compose each substance?
  (a) $BaBr_2$
  (b) Ne
  (c) I_2
  (d) CO

50. What are the basic units—single atoms, molecules, or formula units—that compose each substance?
  (a) Rb_2O
  (b) N_2
  (c) $Fe(NO_3)_2$
  (d) N_2F_4

51. Classify each compound as ionic or molecular. If it is ionic, determine whether the metal forms only one type of ion or more than one type of ion.
  (a) KCl
  (b) CBr_4
  (c) NO_2
  (d) $Sn(SO_4)_2$

52. Classify each compound as ionic or molecular. If it is ionic, determine whether the metal forms only one type of ion or more than one type of ion.
  (a) $CoCl_2$
  (b) CF_4
  (c) $BaSO_4$
  (d) NO

WRITING FORMULAS FOR IONIC COMPOUNDS

53. Write a formula for the ionic compound that forms from each pair of elements.
  (a) sodium and sulfur
  (b) strontium and oxygen
  (c) aluminum and sulfur
  (d) magnesium and chlorine

54. Write a formula for the ionic compound that forms from each pair of elements.
  (a) aluminum and oxygen
  (b) beryllium and iodine
  (c) calcium and sulfur
  (d) calcium and iodine

55. Write a formula for the compound that forms from potassium and
  (a) acetate
  (b) chromate
  (c) phosphate
  (d) cyanide

56. Write a formula for the compound that forms from calcium and
  (a) hydroxide
  (b) carbonate
  (c) phosphate
  (d) hydrogen phosphate

57. Write formulas for the compounds formed from the element on the left and each of the elements on the right.
  (a) Li   N, O, F
  (b) Ba   N, O, F
  (c) Al   N, O, F

58. Write formulas for the compounds formed from the element on the left and each polyatomic ion on the right.
  (a) Rb NO_3^-, SO_4^{2-}, PO_4^{3-}
  (b) Sr NO_3^-, SO_4^{2-}, PO_4^{3-}
  (c) In NO_3^-, SO_4^{2-}, PO_4^{3-}
  (Assume In charge is 3+.)

NAMING IONIC COMPOUNDS

59. Name each ionic compound. In each of these compounds, the metal forms only one type of ion.
  (a) $CsCl$
  (b) $SrBr_2$
  (c) K_2O
  (d) LiF

60. Name each ionic compound. In each of these compounds, the metal forms only one type of ion.
  (a) LiI
  (b) MgS
  (c) BaF_2
  (d) NaF

61. Name each ionic compound. In each of these compounds, the metal forms more than one type of ion.
  (a) $CrCl_2$
  (b) $CrCl_3$
  (c) SnO_2
  (d) PbI_2

62. Name each ionic compound. In each of these compounds, the metal forms more than one type of ion.
  (a) $HgBr_2$
  (b) Fe_2O_3
  (c) CuI_2
  (d) $SnCl_4$

63. Determine whether the metal in each ionic compound forms only one type of ion or more than one type of ion and name the compound accordingly.
  (a) Cr_2O_3
  (b) NaI
  (c) $CaBr_2$
  (d) SnO

64. Determine whether the metal in each ionic compound forms only one type of ion or more than one type of ion and name the compound accordingly.
  (a) FeI_3
  (b) $PbCl_4$
  (c) SrI_2
  (d) BaO

65. Name each ionic compound containing a polyatomic ion.
  (a) $Ba(NO_3)_2$
  (b) $Pb(C_2H_3O_2)_2$
  (c) NH_4I
  (d) $KClO_3$
  (e) $CoSO_4$
  (f) $NaClO_4$

66. Name each ionic compound containing a polyatomic ion.
  (a) $Ba(OH)_2$
  (b) $Fe(OH)_3$
  (c) $Cu(NO_2)_2$
  (d) $PbSO_4$
  (e) $KClO$
  (f) $Mg(C_2H_3O_2)_2$

67. Name each polyatomic ion.
  (a) BrO^-
  (b) BrO_2^-
  (c) BrO_3^-
  (d) BrO_4^-

68. Name each polyatomic ion.
  (a) IO^-
  (b) IO_2^-
  (c) IO_3^-
  (d) IO_4^-

69. Write a formula for each ionic compound.
  (a) copper(II) bromide
  (b) silver nitrate
  (c) potassium hydroxide
  (d) sodium sulfate
  (e) potassium hydrogen sulfate
  (f) sodium hydrogen carbonate

70. Write a formula for each ionic compound.
  (a) copper(I) chlorate
  (b) potassium permanganate
  (c) lead(II) chromate
  (d) calcium fluoride
  (e) iron(II) phosphate
  (f) lithium hydrogen sulfite

NAMING MOLECULAR COMPOUNDS

71. Name each molecular compound.
- **(a)** SO_2
- **(b)** NI_3
- **(c)** BrF_5
- **(d)** NO
- **(e)** N_4Se_4

72. Name each molecular compound.
- **(a)** XeF_4
- **(b)** PI_3
- **(c)** SO_3
- **(d)** $SiCl_4$
- **(e)** I_2O_5

73. Write a formula for each molecular compound.
- **(a)** carbon monoxide
- **(b)** disulfur tetrafluoride
- **(c)** dichlorine monoxide
- **(d)** phosphorus pentafluoride
- **(e)** boron tribromide
- **(f)** diphosphorus pentasulfide

74. Write a formula for each molecular compound.
- **(a)** chlorine monoxide
- **(b)** xenon tetroxide
- **(c)** xenon hexafluoride
- **(d)** carbon tetrabromide
- **(e)** diboron tetrachloride
- **(f)** tetraphosphorus triselenide

75. Determine whether the name shown for each molecular compound is correct. If not, provide the compound's correct name.
- **(a)** PBr_5 phosphorus(V) pentabromide
- **(b)** P_2O_3 phosphorus trioxide
- **(c)** SF_4 monosulfur hexafluoride
- **(d)** NF_4 nitrogen trifluoride

76. Determine whether the name shown for each molecular compound is correct. If not, provide the compound's correct name.
- **(a)** NCl_3 nitrogen chloride
- **(b)** CI_4 carbon(IV) iodide
- **(c)** CO carbon oxide
- **(d)** SCl_4 sulfur tetrachloride

NAMING ACIDS

77. Determine whether each acid is a binary acid or an oxyacid and name each acid. If the acid is an oxyacid, provide the name of the oxyanion.
- **(a)** $HNO_2(aq)$
- **(b)** $HI(aq)$
- **(c)** $H_2SO_4(aq)$
- **(d)** $HNO_3(aq)$

78. Determine whether each acid is a binary acid or an oxyacid and name each acid. If the acid is an oxyacid, provide the name of the oxyanion.
- **(a)** $H_2CO_3(aq)$
- **(b)** $HC_2H_3O_2(aq)$
- **(c)** $H_3PO_4(aq)$
- **(d)** $HCl(aq)$

79. Name each acid.
- **(a)** $HClO$
- **(b)** $HClO_2$
- **(c)** $HClO_3$
- **(d)** $HClO_4$

80. Name each acid. (*Hint*: The names of the oxyanions are analogous to the names of the oxyanions of chlorine.)
- **(a)** $HBrO_3$
- **(b)** HIO_3

81. Write a formula for each acid.
- **(a)** phosphoric acid
- **(b)** hydrobromic acid
- **(c)** sulfurous acid

82. Write a formula for each acid.
- **(a)** hydrofluoric acid
- **(b)** hydrocyanic acid
- **(c)** chlorous acid

FORMULA MASS

83. Calculate the formula mass for each compound.
- **(a)** HNO_3
- **(b)** $CaBr_2$
- **(c)** CCl_4
- **(d)** $Sr(NO_3)_2$

84. Calculate the formula mass for each compound.
- **(a)** CS_2
- **(b)** $C_6H_{12}O_6$
- **(c)** $Fe(NO_3)_3$
- **(d)** C_7H_{16}

85. Arrange the compounds in order of decreasing formula mass.

Ag_2O, PtO_2, $Al(NO_3)_3$, PBr_3

86. Arrange the compounds in order of decreasing formula mass.

WO_2, Rb_2SO_4, $Pb(C_2H_3O_2)_2$, RbI

CUMULATIVE PROBLEMS

87. Write a molecular formula for each molecular model. (White = hydrogen; red = oxygen; black = carbon; blue = nitrogen; yellow = sulfur)

(a)

(b)

(c)

88. Write a molecular formula for each molecular model. (White = hydrogen; red = oxygen; black = carbon; blue = nitrogen; yellow = sulfur)

(a)

(b)

(c)

89. How many chlorine atoms are in each set?
(a) three carbon tetrachloride molecules
(b) two calcium chloride formula units
(c) four phosphorus trichloride molecules
(d) seven sodium chloride formula units

90. How many oxygen atoms are in each set?
(a) four dinitrogen monoxide molecules
(b) two calcium carbonate formula units
(c) three sulfur dioxide molecules
(d) five perchlorate ions

91. Specify the number of hydrogen atoms (white) represented in each set of molecular models:

(a)

(b)

(c)

92. Specify the number of oxygen atoms (red) represented in each set of molecular models:

(a)

(b)

(c)

93. Complete the table:

Formula	Type of Compound (Ionic, Molecular, Acid)	Name
N_2H_4	molecular	_____
_____	_____	potassium chloride
$H_2CrO_4(aq)$	_____	_____
_____	_____	cobalt(III) cyanide

94. Complete the table:

Formula	Type of Compound (Ionic, Molecular, Acid)	Name
$K_2Cr_2O_7$	ionic	_____
$HBr(aq)$	_____	hydrobromic acid
_____	_____	dinitrogen pentoxide
PbO_2	_____	_____

95. Is each name correct for the given formula? If not, provide the correct name.
(a) $Ca(NO_2)_2$ calcium nitrate
(b) K_2O dipotassium monoxide
(c) PCl_3 phosphorus chloride
(d) $PbCO_3$ lead(II) carbonate
(e) KIO_2 potassium hypoiodite

96. Is each name correct for the given formula? If not, provide the correct name.
(a) $HNO_3(aq)$ hydrogen nitrate
(b) $NaClO$ sodium hypochlorite
(c) CaI_2 calcium diiodide
(d) $SnCrO_4$ tin chromate
(e) $NaBrO_3$ sodium bromite

97. For each compound, list the correct formula and calculate the formula mass.
   (a) tin(IV) sulfate
   (b) nitrous acid
   (c) sodium bicarbonate
   (d) phosphorus pentafluoride

98. For each compound, list the correct formula and calculate the formula mass.
   (a) barium bromide
   (b) dinitrogen trioxide
   (c) copper(I) sulfate
   (d) hydrobromic acid

99. Name each compound and calculate its formula mass.
   (a) PtO_2
   (b) N_2O_5
   (c) $Al(ClO_3)_3$
   (d) PBr_5

100. Name each compound and calculate its formula mass.
   (a) $Al_2(SO_4)_3$
   (b) P_2O_3
   (c) $HClO(aq)$
   (d) $Cr(C_2H_3O_2)_3$

101. A compound contains only carbon and hydrogen and has a formula mass of 28.06 amu. What is its molecular formula?

102. A compound contains only nitrogen and oxygen and has a formula mass of 44.02 amu. What is its molecular formula?

103. Carbon has two naturally occurring isotopes: carbon-12 (mass = 12.00 amu) and carbon-13 (mass = 13.00 amu). Chlorine also has two naturally occurring isotopes: chlorine-35 (mass = 34.97 amu) and chlorine-37 (mass = 36.97 amu). How many CCl_4 molecules of different masses can exist? Determine the mass (in amu) of each of them.

104. Nitrogen has two naturally occurring isotopes: nitrogen-14 (mass = 14.00 amu) and nitrogen-15 (mass = 15.00 amu). Bromine also has two naturally occurring isotopes: bromine-79 (mass = 78.92 amu) and bromine-81 (mass = 80.92 amu). How many types of NBr_3 molecules of different masses can exist? Determine the mass (in amu) of each of them.

HIGHLIGHT PROBLEMS

105. Examine each substance and the corresponding molecular view and classify it as an atomic element, a molecular element, a molecular compound, or an ionic compound.

(a)

(b)

(c)

METHANOL
CH₃CH

(d)

106. Molecules can be as small as two atoms or as large as thousands of atoms. In 1962, Max F. Perutz and John C. Kendrew were awarded the Nobel Prize for their discovery of the structure of hemoglobin, a very large molecule that transports oxygen from the lungs to cells through the bloodstream. The chemical formula of hemoglobin is $C_{2952}H_{4664}O_{832}N_{812}S_8Fe_4$. Calculate the formula mass of hemoglobin.

▲ Max Perutz and John C. Kendrew won a Nobel Prize in 1962 for determining the structure of hemoglobin by X-ray diffraction.

▲ Computer-generated model of hemoglobin.

107. Examine each consumer product label. Write chemical formulas for as many of the compounds as possible based on what you have learned in this chapter.

(a)

Active Ingredient:
Sodium Hypochlorite 6.0%
Other Ingredients: 94.0%
Total: 100.0%
(Yields 5.7% available chlorine)

KEEP OUT OF REACH OF CHILDREN
DANGER: CORROSIVE.

FIRST AID: IF IN EYES: Hold eye open and rinse slowly and gently with water for 15-20 minutes. Remove contact lenses, if present, after the first 5 minutes, then continue rinsing eye. IF ON SKIN OR CLOTHING: Take off contaminated clothing. Rinse skin immediately with plenty of water for 15-20 minutes. IN EITHER CASE, CALL A POISON CONTROL CENTER OR DOCTOR IMMEDIATELY FOR TREATMENT ADVICE. See back panel for additional precautionary labeling.

Kills Methicillin Resistant Staphylococcus aureus (MRSA)
* Staphylococcus aureus, Streptococcus pyogenes, Salmonella enterica, Escherichia coli O157:H7 and Influenza A2

3 QT (96 FL OZ) 2.83 L

(c)

Drug Facts

Active ingredients (in each 5 mL teaspoon)	Purposes
Aluminum hydroxide (equivalent to dried gel, USP) 400 mg	Antacid
Magnesium hydroxide 400 mg	Antacid
Simethicone 40 mg	Antigas

Use relieves: ■ heartburn ■ acid indigestion ■ sour stomach ■ upset stomach due to these symptoms ■ pressure and bloating commonly referred to as gas

Warnings
Ask a doctor before use if you have
■ kidney disease ■ a magnesium-restricted diet

Ask a doctor or pharmacist if you are taking a prescription drug. Antacids may interact with certain prescription drugs.

Stop use and ask a doctor if symptoms last more than 2 weeks.

Keep out of reach of children.

Directions ■ shake well ■ adults/children 12 years and older: take 2-4 teaspoonfuls between meals, at bedtime, or as directed by a doctor ■ do not take more than 12 teaspoonfuls in a 24-hour period, or use the maximum dosage for more than 2 weeks ■ children under 12 years: ask a doctor

Other information ■ each teaspoon contains: magnesium 171 mg ■ do not use if breakaway band on plastic cap is broken or missing ■ does not meet USP requirements for preservative effectiveness ■ do not freeze

Inactive ingredients butylparaben, carboxymethylcellulose sodium, flavors, hypromellose, microcrystalline cellulose, propylparaben, purified water, sodium saccharin, sorbitol

Questions or comments?
1-800-469-5268 (English) or
1-888-466-8746 (Spanish)

Johnson-Johnson · MERCK
Consumer Pharmaceuticals Co.
FORT WASHINGTON, PA 19034 USA

(b)

NOTICE! PROTECTIVE INNER SEAL BENEATH CAP.
IF MISSING OR DAMAGED, DO NOT USE CONTENTS.

Drug Facts

Active ingredients (in each tablet)	Purpose
Calcium carbonate 1000 mg	Antacid
Simethicone 60 mg	Antigas

Uses for the relief of
• acid indigestion
• heartburn
• sour stomach
• upset stomach associated with these symptoms
• bloating and pressure commonly referred to as gas

Warning
Do not take more than 8 tablets in a 24-hour period or use the maximum dosage for more than 2 weeks except under the advice and supervision of a physician

Ask a doctor before use if you have
• kidney stones   • a calcium-restricted diet

Ask a doctor or pharmacist before use if your are presently taking a prescription drug. Antacids may interact with certain prescription drugs.

When using this product
• at maximum dose, constipation may occur

Stop use and ask a doctor if
• symptoms last more than two weeks

Keep out of reach of children.

Directions

(d)

Nutrition Facts
Serving Size 1/8 tsp (0.6g)
Servings Per Container about 472

Amount Per Serving

Calories 0

	% Daily Value*
Total Fat 0g	0%
Sodium 65mg	3%
Total Carb. 0g	0%
Protein 0g	
Calcium 2%	

Not a significant source of calories from fat, saturated fat, trans fat, cholesterol, dietary fiber, sugars, vitamin A, vitamin C and iron.

*Percent Daily Values are based on a 2,000 calorie diet.

Ingredients: Cornstarch, Sodium Bicarbonate, Sodium Aluminum Sulfate, Monocalcium Phosphate.

CLABBER GIRL CORPORATION
TERRE HAUTE, IN 47808

davisbakingpowder.com
MADE IN USA

QUESTIONS FOR GROUP WORK

Discuss these questions with the group and record your consensus answer.

108. Write the correct formula for each species: carbon monoxide, carbon dioxide, the carbonate ion. List as many similarities and differences between these three species as you can. Try to get at least one contribution from each group member.

109. What questions do you need to ask about a substance in order to determine whether it is (1) an atomic element, (2) a molecular element, (3) a molecular compound, or (4) an ionic compound? Write a detailed set of instructions describing how to determine the classification of a substance based on the answers to your questions.

110. Name each compound: $Ca(NO_3)_2$, N_2O, NaS, $CrCl_3$. For each compound, include a detailed step-by-step description of the process you used to determine the name. (*Tip:* Each group member could name one compound and present it to the whole group.)

111. Calculate the formula mass for each compound in Group Work Question 110.

▶Answers to Skillbuilder Exercises

Skillbuilder 5.1 Yes, because in both cases

$$\frac{\text{Mass O}}{\text{Mass C}} = 1.3$$

Skillbuilder 5.2 (a) Ag_2S (b) N_2O (c) TiO_2

Skillbuilder 5.3 two K atoms, one S atom, four O atoms

Skillbuilder Plus, p. 133

two Al atoms, three S atoms, twelve O atoms

Skillbuilder 5.4
  (a) molecular element
  (b) molecular compound
  (c) atomic element
  (d) ionic compound
  (e) ionic compound

Skillbuilder 5.5 $SrCl_2$
Skillbuilder 5.6   AlN
Skillbuilder 5.7 $AlPO_4$
Skillbuilder Plus, p. 139 Na_2SO_3
Skillbuilder 5.8   potassium bromide
Skillbuilder Plus, p. 142 zinc nitride
Skillbuilder 5.9   lead(II) oxide
Skillbuilder 5.10 manganese(II) nitrate
Skillbuilder 5.11 dinitrogen tetroxide
Skillbuilder 5.12 hydrofluoric acid
Skillbuilder 5.13 nitrous acid
Skillbuilder 5.15 44.02 amu

▶Answers to Conceptual Checkpoints

5.1 (c) The ratio of A/B is 3.0, and A is 9.0 g, so B must be 3.0 g.

5.2 (b) This formula represents 2 Al atoms + 3(2 Cr atoms +7 O atoms) = 29 atoms.

5.3 (b) The figure represents a molecular compound because the compound exists as individual molecules. Figure (a) represents an ionic compound with formula units in a lattice structure.

5.4 (c) Because the nitrate ion has a charge of 1−, the three nitrate ions together have a charge of 3−. Because the compound must be charge-neutral, Cr must have a charge of 3+.

5.5 Because calcium forms only one type of ion (Ca^{2+}); therefore, the charge of the ion is not included in the name (it is always the same, 2+).

5.6 Iodate

5.7 (b)

Moonlight Diner
Specials

Breakfast Special
Two eggs, Three strips
of bacon, Sausage link,
Toast NaCl $5.95

Lunch Special

1500 milligrams a day

142/93 mmHg

Omelettes
Served with side of NaCl
Denver Omelette
BP Delight
Atherosclerosis
Sodium Chloride
Hypertension

Symptoms:

Chest pain
Confusion
Ear noise or buzzing
Irregular heartbeat
Nosebleed
Tiredness

On the Healthy Side
120/80 mmHg

▲ Ordinary table salt is a compound called
sodium chloride. The sodium within sodium
chloride has been linked to high blood
pressure. In this chapter, we learn how to
determine how much sodium is in a given
amount of sodium chloride.

Chemical Composition 6

"In science, you don't ask why, you ask how much." —Erwin Chargaff (1905–2002)

CHAPTER OUTLINE

6.1 How Much Sodium?

Sodium is an important dietary mineral that we eat in food, primarily as sodium chloride (table salt). Sodium is involved in the regulation of body fluids, and eating too much of it can lead to high blood pressure. High blood pressure, in turn, increases the risk of stroke and heart attack. Consequently, people with high blood pressure should limit their sodium intake. The FDA recommends that a person consume less than 2.4 g (2400 mg) of sodium per day. However, sodium is usually consumed as sodium chloride, so the mass of sodium that we eat is not the same as the mass of sodium chloride that we eat. How many grams of sodium chloride can we consume and still stay below the FDA recommendation for sodium?

To answer this question, we need to know the *chemical composition* of sodium chloride. From Chapter 5, we are familiar with its formula, NaCl, which indicates that there is one sodium ion to every chloride ion. However, because the masses of sodium and chlorine are different, the relationship between the mass of sodium and the mass of sodium chloride is not clear from the chemical formula alone.

In this chapter , we learn how to use the information in a chemical formula, together with atomic and formula masses, to calculate the amount of a constituent element in a given amount of a compound (or vice versa).

Chemical composition is important not just for assessing dietary sodium intake, but for addressing many other questions as well. A company that mines iron, for example, wants to know how much iron it can extract from a given amount of iron ore; an organization interested in developing hydrogen as a potential fuel would want to know how much hydrogen it can extract from a given amount of water. Many environmental issues also require knowledge of chemical composition. An estimate of the threat of ozone depletion requires knowing how much chlorine is in a given amount of a particular chlorofluorocarbon such as freon-12.

▲ The mining of iron requires knowing how much iron is in a given amount of iron ore.

Freon-12

▲ Estimating the threat of ozone depletion requires knowing the amount of chlorine in a given amount of a chlorofluorocarbon.

To determine these kinds of quantities, we must understand the relationships inherent in a chemical formula and the relationship between numbers of atoms or molecules and their masses. In this chapter, we examine these relationships.

6.2 Counting Nails by the Pound

LO: Recognize that we use the mass of atoms to count them because they are too small and numerous to count individually.

3.4 lb nails

8.25 grams carbon

▲ Asking how many nails are in a given weight of nails is similar to asking how many atoms are in a given mass of an element. In both cases, we count the objects by weighing them.

Some hardware stores sell nails by the pound, which is easier than selling them by the nail because customers often need hundreds of nails and counting them takes too long. However, a customer may still want to know the number of nails contained in a given weight of nails. This problem is similar to asking how many atoms are in a given mass of an element. With atoms, we *must* use their mass as a way to count them because atoms are too small and too numerous to count individually. Even if you could see atoms and counted them 24 hours a day for as long as you lived, you would barely begin to count the number of atoms in something as small as a grain of sand. However, just as the hardware store customer wants to know the number of nails in a given weight, we want to know the number of atoms in a given mass. How do we do that?

Suppose the hardware store customer buys 2.60 lb of medium-sized nails and a dozen nails weigh 0.150 lb. How many nails did the customer buy? This calculation requires two conversions: one between pounds and dozens and another between dozens and number of nails. The conversion factor for the first part is the weight per dozen nails.

$$0.150 \text{ lb nails} = 1 \text{ doz nails}$$

The conversion factor for the second part is the number of nails in one dozen.

$$1 \text{ doz nails} = 12 \text{ nails}$$

The solution map for the problem is:

$$\frac{1 \text{ doz nails}}{0.150 \text{ lb nails}} \qquad \frac{12 \text{ nails}}{1 \text{ doz nails}}$$

Beginning with 2.60 lb and using the solution map as a guide, we convert from lb to number of nails.

$$2.60 \text{ lb nails} \times \frac{1 \text{ doz nails}}{0.150 \text{ lb nails}} \times \frac{12 \text{ nails}}{1 \text{ doz nails}} = 208 \text{ nails}$$

The customer who bought 2.60 lb of nails has 208 nails. She counted the nails by weighing them. If the customer purchased a different size of nail, the first conversion factor—relating pounds to dozens—would change, but the second conversion factor would not. One dozen corresponds to 12 nails, regardless of their size.

✓ **CONCEPTUAL CHECKPOINT 6.1**

A certain type of nail weighs 0.50 lb per dozen. How many nails are contained in 3.5 lb of these nails?

(a) 84   (b) 21   (c) 0.58   (d) 12

6.3   Counting Atoms by the Gram

LO: Convert between moles and number of atoms.

LO: Convert between grams and moles.

LO: Convert between grams and number of atoms.

Determining the number of atoms in a sample with a certain mass is similar to determining the number of nails in a sample with a certain weight. With nails, we used a dozen as a convenient number in our conversions, but a dozen is too small to use with atoms. We need a larger number because atoms are so small. The chemist's "dozen" is called the **mole (mol)** and has a value of 6.022×10^{23}.

$$1 \text{ mol} = 6.022 \times 10^{23}$$

This is **Avogadro's number**, named after Amadeo Avogadro (1776–1856).

The first thing to understand about the mole is that it can specify Avogadro's number of anything. *One mole of anything is 6.022×10^{23} units of that thing.* For example, one mole of marbles corresponds to 6.022×10^{23} marbles, and one mole of sand grains corresponds to 6.022×10^{23} sand grains. One mole of atoms, ions, or molecules generally makes up objects of reasonable size. For example, 22 *copper* pennies contain approximately 1 mol of copper (Cu) atoms, and a couple of large helium balloons contain approximately 1 mol of helium (He) atoms.

The second thing to understand about the mole is how it gets its specific value. *The numerical value of the mole is defined as being equal to the number of atoms in exactly 12 g of pure carbon-12.*

This definition of the mole establishes a relationship between mass (grams of carbon) and number of atoms (Avogadro's number). This relationship, as we will see shortly, allows us to count atoms by weighing them.

1 mole of copper atoms

▲ Twenty-two *copper* pennies contain approximately 1 mol of copper atoms. Pennies were mostly copper until 1982, at which point the U.S. Mint started making them out of zinc with a copper coating (because copper became too valuable).

Converting between Moles and Number of Atoms

Converting between moles and number of atoms is similar to converting between dozens and number of nails. To convert between moles of atoms and number of atoms, we use these conversion factors:

$$\frac{1 \text{ mol}}{6.022 \times 10^{23} \text{ atoms}} \quad \text{or} \quad \frac{6.022 \times 10^{23} \text{ atoms}}{1 \text{ mol}}$$

For example, suppose we want to convert 3.5 mol of helium to a number of helium atoms. We set up the problem in the standard way.

GIVEN: 3.5 mol He

FIND: He atoms

RELATIONSHIPS USED   1 mol He $=$ 6.022×10^{23} He atoms

SOLUTION MAP   We draw a solution map showing the conversion from moles of He to He atoms.

$$\frac{6.022 \times 10^{23} \text{ He atoms}}{1 \text{ mol He}}$$

1 mole of helium atoms

▲ Two large helium balloons contain approximately 1 mol of helium atoms.

SOLUTION

Beginning with 3.5 mol He, we use the conversion factor to get to He atoms.

$$3.5 \text{ mol He} \times \frac{6.022 \times 10^{23} \text{ He atoms}}{1 \text{ mol He}} = 2.1 \times 10^{24} \text{ He atoms}$$

	CONVERTING BETWEEN MOLES AND NUMBER
EXAMPLE 6.1	**OF ATOMS**

A silver ring contains 1.1×10^{22} silver atoms. How many moles of silver are in the ring?

SORT You are given the number of silver atoms and asked to find the number of moles.	**GIVEN:** 1.1×10^{22} Ag atoms **FIND:** mol Ag
STRATEGIZE Draw a solution map, beginning with silver atoms and ending at moles. The conversion factor is Avogadro's number.	**SOLUTION MAP** $$\frac{1 \text{ mol Ag}}{6.022 \times 10^{23} \text{ Ag atoms}}$$ **RELATIONSHIPS USED** $$1 \text{ mol Ag} = 6.022 \times 10^{23} \text{ Ag atoms}$$ (Avogadro's number)
SOLVE Follow the solution map to solve the problem. Beginning with 1.1×10^{22} Ag atoms, use the conversion factor to determine the moles of Ag.	**SOLUTION** $$1.1 \times 10^{22} \text{ Ag atoms} \times \frac{1 \text{ mol Ag}}{6.022 \times 10^{23} \text{ Ag atoms}}$$ $$= 1.8 \times 10^{-2} \text{ mol Ag}$$
CHECK Are the units correct? Does the answer make physical sense?	The units, mol Ag, are the desired units. The magnitude of the answer is orders of magnitude smaller than the given quantity because it takes many atoms to make a mole, so you expect the answer to be orders of magnitude smaller than the given quantity.

▶**SKILLBUILDER 6.1** | **Converting between Moles and Number of Atoms**

How many gold atoms are in a pure gold ring containing 8.83×10^{-2} mol Au?

▶**FOR MORE PRACTICE** Example 6.14, Problems 17, 18, 19, 20.

Converting between Grams and Moles of an Element

We just explained how to convert between moles and number of atoms, which is like converting between dozens and number of nails. We need one more conversion factor to convert from the mass of a sample to the number of atoms in the sample. For nails, we used the weight of one dozen nails; for atoms, we use the mass of one mole of atoms.

> The mass of 1 mol of atoms of an element is its **molar mass**. The value of an element's molar mass in grams per mole is numerically equal to the element's atomic mass in atomic mass units.

Recall that Avogadro's number, the number of atoms in a mole, is defined as the number of atoms in exactly 12 g of carbon-12. The atomic mass unit is defined as one-twelfth of the mass of a carbon-12 atom, so it follows that the molar mass of any element—the mass of 1 mol of atoms in grams of that element—is equal to the atomic mass of that element expressed in atomic mass units. For example, copper has an atomic mass of 63.55 amu; therefore, 1 mol of copper atoms has a mass of 63.55 g, and the molar mass of copper is 63.55 g/mol. Just as the weight of 1 doz nails changes for different types of nails, so the mass of 1 mol of atoms changes for different elements: 1 mol of sulfur atoms (sulfur atoms are lighter than copper atoms) has a mass of 32.07 g; 1 mol of carbon atoms (lighter than sulfur) has a mass of 12.01 g; and 1 mol of lithium atoms (lighter yet) has a mass of 6.94 g.

$$32.07 \text{ g sulfur} = 1 \text{ mol sulfur} = 6.022 \times 10^{23} \text{ S atoms}$$

$$12.01 \text{ g carbon} = 1 \text{ mol carbon} = 6.022 \times 10^{23} \text{ C atoms}$$

$$6.94 \text{ g lithium} = 1 \text{ mol lithium} = 6.022 \times 10^{23} \text{ Li atoms}$$

The lighter the atom, the less mass in one mole of that atom (▼ Figure 6.1).

The molar mass of any element is a conversion factor between grams of that element and moles of that element. For carbon:

$$12.01 \text{ g C} = 1 \text{ mol C} \quad \text{or} \quad \frac{12.01 \text{ g C}}{1 \text{ mol C}} \quad \text{or} \quad \frac{1 \text{ mol C}}{12.01 \text{ g C}}$$

1 dozen large nails

1 dozen small nails

(a)

1 mole S (32.07 g)

1 mole C (12.01 g)

▶ **FIGURE 6.1   The mass of 1 mol** (a) Each of these pictures shows the same number of nails: 12. As you can see, 12 large nails have more weight and occupy more space than 12 small nails. The same is true for atoms. (b) Each of these samples has the same number of atoms: 6.022×10^{23}. Because sulfur atoms are more massive and larger than carbon atoms, 1 mol of S atoms is heavier and occupies more space than 1 mol of C atoms.

(b)

A 0.58-g diamond is about a three-carat diamond.

Suppose we want to calculate the number of moles of carbon in a 0.58-g diamond (pure carbon).

We first sort the information in the problem.

GIVEN: 0.58 g C

FIND: mol C

SOLUTION MAP We then strategize by drawing a solution map showing the conversion from grams of C to moles of C. The conversion factor is the molar mass of carbon.

$$\frac{1 \text{ mol}}{12.01 \text{ g}}$$

RELATIONSHIPS USED

12.01 g C = 1 mol C (molar mass of carbon, from periodic table)

SOLUTION

Finally, we solve the problem by following the solution map.

$$0.58 \text{ g C} \times \frac{1 \text{ mol C}}{12.01 \text{ g C}} = 4.8 \times 10^{-2} \text{ mol C}$$

EXAMPLE 6.2 **THE MOLE CONCEPT—CONVERTING BETWEEN GRAMS AND MOLES**

Calculate the number of moles of sulfur in 57.8 g of sulfur.

SORT Begin by sorting the information in the problem. You are given the mass of sulfur and asked to find the number of moles.	**GIVEN:** 57.8 g S **FIND:** mol S
STRATEGIZE Draw a solution map showing the conversion from g S to mol S. The conversion factor is the molar mass of sulfur.	**SOLUTION MAP** g S → mol S $$\frac{1 \text{ mol S}}{32.07 \text{ g S}}$$ **RELATIONSHIPS USED** 32.07 g S = 1 mol S (molar mass of sulfur, from periodic table)
SOLVE Follow the solution map to solve the problem. Begin with 57.8 g S and use the conversion factor to determine mol S.	**SOLUTION** $$57.8 \text{ g S} \times \frac{1 \text{ mol S}}{32.07 \text{ g S}} = 1.80 \text{ mol S}$$
CHECK Check your answer. Are the units correct? Does the answer make physical sense?	The units (mol S) are correct. The magnitude of the answer makes sense because 1 mole of S has a mass of 32.07 g; therefore, 57.8 g of S should be close to 2 moles.

▶**SKILLBUILDER 6.2 | The Mole Concept—Converting between Grams and Moles**

Calculate the number of grams of sulfur in 2.78 mol of sulfur.

▶**FOR MORE PRACTICE** Example 6.15; Problems 25, 26, 27, 28, 29, 30.

Converting between Grams of an Element and Number of Atoms

Suppose we want to know the number of carbon *atoms* in the 0.58-g diamond. We first convert from grams to moles and then from moles to number of atoms. The solution map is:

Notice the similarity between this solution map and the one we used for nails:

Beginning with 0.58 g carbon and using the solution map as a guide, we convert to the number of carbon atoms.

$$0.58 \text{ g C} \times \frac{1 \text{ mol C}}{12.01 \text{ g C}} \times \frac{6.022 \times 10^{23} \text{ C atoms}}{1 \text{ mol C}} = 2.9 \times 10^{22} \text{ C atoms}$$

EXAMPLE 6.3 **THE MOLE CONCEPT—CONVERTING BETWEEN GRAMS AND NUMBER OF ATOMS**

How many aluminum atoms are in an aluminum can with a mass of 16.2 g?

SORT	GIVEN: 16.2 g Al
You are given the mass of aluminum and asked to find the number of aluminum atoms.	FIND: Al atoms

STRATEGIZE	SOLUTION MAP
The solution map has two steps. In the first step, convert from g Al to mol Al. In the second step, convert from mol Al to the number of Al atoms. The required conversion factors are the molar mass of aluminum and the number of atoms in a mole.	 **RELATIONSHIPS USED** 26.98 g Al = 1 mol Al (molar mass of aluminum, from periodic table) 6.022×10^{23} = 1 mol (Avogadro's number)

SOLVE	SOLUTION
Follow the solution map to solve the problem, beginning with 16.2 g Al and multiplying by the appropriate conversion factors to arrive at Al atoms.	$16.2 \text{ g Al} \times \dfrac{1 \text{ mol Al}}{26.98 \text{ g Al}} \times \dfrac{6.022 \times 10^{23} \text{ Al atoms}}{1 \text{ mol Al}} = 3.62 \times 10^{23} \text{ Al atoms}$

CHECK	
Are the units correct? Does the answer make physical sense?	The units, Al atoms, are correct. The answer makes sense because the number of atoms in any macroscopic-sized sample of matter is very large.

▶**SKILLBUILDER 6.3 | The Mole Concept—Converting between Grams and Number of Atoms**

Calculate the mass of 1.23×10^{24} helium atoms.

▶**FOR MORE PRACTICE** Example 6.16; Problems 35, 36, 37, 38, 39, 40, 41, 42.

Before we move on, notice that numbers with large exponents, such as 6.022×10^{23}, are almost unimaginably large. Twenty-two copper pennies contain 6.022×10^{23} or 1 mol of copper atoms; 6.022×10^{23} pennies would cover Earth's entire surface to a depth of 300 m. Even objects that are small by everyday standards occupy a huge space when we have a mole of them. For example, one crystal of granulated sugar has a mass of less than 1 mg and a diameter of less than 0.1 mm, yet 1 mol of sugar crystals would cover the state of Texas to a depth of several feet. For every increase of 1 in the exponent of a number, the number increases by 10. So a number with an exponent of 23 is incredibly large. A mole has to be a large number because atoms are so small.

 CONCEPTUAL CHECKPOINT 6.2

Which statement is *always* true for samples of atomic elements, regardless of the type of element present in the samples?

(a) If two samples of different elements contain the same number of atoms, they contain the same number of moles.

(b) If two samples of different elements have the same mass, they contain the same number of moles.

(c) If two samples of different elements have the same mass, they contain the same number of atoms.

 CONCEPTUAL CHECKPOINT 6.3

Without doing any calculations, determine which sample contains the most atoms.

(a) one gram of cobalt

(b) one gram of carbon

(c) one gram of lead

6.4 Counting Molecules by the Gram

LO: Convert between grams and moles of a compound.

LO: Convert between mass of a compound and number of molecules.

The calculations we just performed for atoms can also be applied to molecules for covalent compounds or formula units for ionic compounds. We first convert between the mass of a compound and moles of the compound, and then we calculate the number of molecules (or formula units) from moles.

Converting between Grams and Moles of a Compound

Remember, ionic compounds do not contain individual molecules. In loose language, the smallest electrically neutral collection of ions is sometimes called a molecule but is a formula unit.

For elements, the molar mass is the mass of 1 mol of atoms of that element. For compounds, the molar mass is the mass of 1 mol of molecules or formula units of that compound. The molar mass of a compound in grams per mole is numerically equal to the formula mass of the compound in atomic mass units. For example, the formula mass of CO_2 is:

Remember, the formula mass for a compound is the sum of the atomic masses of all of the atoms in a chemical formula.

$$\begin{aligned} \text{Formula mass} &= 1(\text{Atomic mass of C}) + 2(\text{Atomic mass of O}) \\ &= 1(12.01 \text{ amu}) + 2(16.00 \text{ amu}) \\ &= 44.01 \text{ amu} \end{aligned}$$

The molar mass of CO_2 is therefore:

$$\text{Molar mass} = 44.01 \text{ g/mol}$$

Just as the molar mass of an element serves as a conversion factor between grams and moles of that element, the molar mass of a compound serves as a conversion factor between grams and moles of that compound. For example, suppose we want to find the number of moles in a 22.5-g sample of dry ice (solid CO_2). We begin by sorting the information.

GIVEN: 22.5 g CO_2

FIND: mol CO_2

SOLUTION MAP

We then strategize by drawing a solution map that shows how the molar mass converts grams of the compound to moles of the compound.

$$\frac{1 \text{ mol } CO_2}{44.01 \text{ g } CO_2}$$

RELATIONSHIPS USED

44.01 g CO_2 = 1 mol CO_2 (molar mass of CO_2)

SOLUTION

Finally, we solve the problem.

$$22.5 \text{ g} \times \frac{1 \text{ mol } CO_2}{44.01 \text{ g}} = 0.511 \text{ mol } CO_2$$

EXAMPLE 6.4	THE MOLE CONCEPT—CONVERTING BETWEEN GRAMS AND MOLES FOR COMPOUNDS
Calculate the mass (in grams) of 1.75 mol of water.	

SORT You are given moles of water and asked to find the mass.	GIVEN: 1.75 mol H_2O FIND: g H_2O
STRATEGIZE Draw a solution map showing the conversion from mol H_2O to g H_2O. The conversion factor is the molar mass of water, which you can determine by summing the atomic masses of all the atoms in the chemical formula.	**SOLUTION MAP** mol H_2O ⟶ g H_2O $$\frac{18.02 \text{ g } H_2O}{1 \text{ mol } H_2O}$$ RELATIONSHIPS USED H_2O molar mass = 2(Atomic mass H) + 1(Atomic mass O) = 2(1.01) + 1(16.00) = 18.02 g/mol
SOLVE Follow the solution map to solve the problem. Begin with 1.75 mol of water and use the molar mass to convert to grams of water.	**SOLUTION** $$1.75 \text{ mol } H_2O \times \frac{18.02 \text{ g } H_2O}{\text{mol } H_2O} = 31.5 \text{ g } H_2O$$
CHECK Check your answer. Are the units correct? Does the answer make physical sense?	The units (g H_2O) are the desired units. The magnitude of the answer makes sense because 1 mole of water has a mass of 18.02 g; therefore, 1.75 moles should have a mass that is slightly less than 36 g.

▶**SKILLBUILDER 6.4 | The Mole Concept—Converting between Grams and Moles**

Calculate the number of moles of NO_2 in 1.18 g of NO_2.

▶**FOR MORE PRACTICE**   Problems 47, 48, 49, 50.

Converting between Grams of a Compound and Number of Molecules

Suppose that we want to find the *number of CO_2 molecules* in a sample of dry ice (solid CO_2) with a mass of 22.5 g. The solution map for the problem is:

Notice that the first part of the solution map is identical to calculating the number of moles of CO_2 in 22.5 g of dry ice. The second part of the solution map shows the conversion from moles to number of molecules. Following the solution map, we calculate:

$$22.5 \ \cancel{g \ CO_2} \times \frac{1 \ \cancel{mol \ CO_2}}{44.01 \ \cancel{g \ CO_2}} \times \frac{6.022 \times 10^{23} \ CO_2 \ \text{molecules}}{\cancel{mol \ CO_2}}$$

$$= 3.08 \times 10^{23} \ CO_2 \ \text{molecules}$$

EXAMPLE 6.5	**THE MOLE CONCEPT—CONVERTING BETWEEN MASS OF A COMPOUND AND NUMBER OF MOLECULES**

What is the mass of 4.78×10^{24} NO_2 molecules?

SORT You are given the number of NO_2 molecules and asked to find the mass.	**GIVEN:** 4.78×10^{24} NO_2 molecules **FIND:** g NO_2
STRATEGIZE The solution map has two steps. In the first step, convert from molecules of NO_2 to moles of NO_2. In the second step, convert from moles of NO_2 to mass of NO_2. The required conversion factors are the molar mass of NO_2 and the number of molecules in a mole.	**SOLUTION MAP** **RELATIONSHIPS USED** 6.022×10^{23} molecules $= 1$ mol (Avogadro's number) NO_2 molar mass $= 1$(Atomic mass N) $+ 2$(Atomic mass O) $\qquad\qquad = 14.01 + 2(16.00)$ $\qquad\qquad = 46.01$ g/mol
SOLVE Using the solution map as a guide, begin with molecules of NO_2 and multiply by the appropriate conversion factors to arrive at g NO_2.	**SOLUTION** $4.78 \times 10^{24} \ \cancel{NO_2 \ \text{molecules}} \times \dfrac{1 \ \cancel{mol \ NO_2}}{6.022 \times 10^{23} \ \cancel{NO_2 \ \text{molecules}}}$ $\qquad\qquad \times \dfrac{46.01 \ g \ NO_2}{1 \ \cancel{mol \ NO_2}} = 365 \ g \ NO_2$
CHECK Check your answer. Are the units correct? Does the answer make physical sense?	The units, g NO_2, are correct. Because the number of NO_2 molecules is more than one mole, the answer should be more than one molar mass (more than 46.01 g), which it is; therefore, the magnitude of the answer is reasonable.

▶**SKILLBUILDER 6.5 | The Mole Concept—Converting between Mass and Number of Molecules**

How many H_2O molecules are in a sample of water with a mass of 3.64 g?

▶**FOR MORE PRACTICE**   Problems 51, 52, 53, 54.

✓ CONCEPTUAL CHECKPOINT 6.4

Compound A has a molar mass of 100 g/mol and Compound B has a molar mass of 200 g/mol. If you have samples of equal mass of both compounds, which sample contains the greater number of molecules?

6.5   Chemical Formulas as Conversion Factors

LO: Convert between moles of a compound and moles of a constituent element.

LO: Convert between grams of a compound and grams of a constituent element.

3 leaves : 1 clover

▲ We know that each clover has three leaves. We can express that as a ratio: 3 leaves : 1 clover.

Chemical formulas are discussed in Chapter 5.

We are almost ready to address the sodium problem posed in Section 6.1. To determine how much of a particular element (such as sodium) is in a given amount of a particular compound (such as sodium chloride), we must understand the numerical relationships inherent in a chemical formula. We can understand these relationships with a straightforward analogy: Asking how much sodium is in a given amount of sodium chloride is similar to asking how many leaves are on a given number of clovers. For example, suppose we want to know the number of leaves on 14 clovers. We need a conversion factor between leaves and clovers. For clovers, the conversion factor comes from our everyday knowledge about them—we know that each clover has three leaves. We can express that relationship as a ratio between clovers and leaves.

3 leaves : 1 clover

Like other conversion factors, this ratio gives the relationship between leaves and clovers. With this ratio, we can write a conversion factor to determine the number of leaves in 14 clovers. The solution map is:

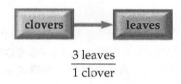

$$\frac{3 \text{ leaves}}{1 \text{ clover}}$$

We solve the problem by beginning with clovers and converting to leaves.

$$14 \text{ clovers} \times \frac{3 \text{ leaves}}{1 \text{ clover}} = 42 \text{ leaves}$$

Similarly, a chemical formula gives us ratios between elements and molecules for a particular compound. For example, the formula for carbon dioxide (CO_2) indicates that there are two O atoms per CO_2 molecule. We write this as:

2 O atoms : 1 CO_2 molecule

Just as 3 leaves : 1 clover can also be written as 3 dozen leaves : 1 dozen clovers, for molecules we can write:

2 doz O atoms : 1 doz CO_2 molecules

However, for atoms and molecules, we normally work in moles.

2 mol O : 1 mol CO_2

With conversion factors such as these—which come directly from the chemical formula—we can determine the amounts of the constituent elements present in a given amount of a compound.

8 legs : 1 spider   4 legs : 1 chair   2 H atoms : 1 H$_2$O molecule

▲ Each of these shows a ratio.

Converting between Moles of a Compound and Moles of a Constituent Element

Suppose we want to know the number of moles of O in 18 mol of CO$_2$. Our solution map is:

$$\frac{2 \text{ mol O}}{1 \text{ mol CO}_2}$$

We can then calculate the moles of O.

$$18 \text{ mol CO}_2 \times \frac{2 \text{ mol O}}{1 \text{ mol CO}_2} = 36 \text{ mol O}$$

EXAMPLE 6.6 CHEMICAL FORMULAS AS CONVERSION FACTORS—CONVERTING BETWEEN MOLES OF A COMPOUND AND MOLES OF A CONSTITUENT ELEMENT

Determine the number of moles of O in 1.7 mol of CaCO$_3$.

SORT You are given the number of moles of CaCO$_3$ and asked to find the number of moles of O.	**GIVEN:** 1.7 mol CaCO$_3$ **FIND:** mol O
STRATEGIZE The solution map begins with moles of calcium carbonate and ends with moles of oxygen. Determine the conversion factor from the chemical formula, which indicates three O atoms for every CaCO$_3$ unit.	**SOLUTION MAP** mol CaCO$_3$ ⟶ mol O $$\frac{3 \text{ mol O}}{1 \text{ mol CaCO}_3}$$ **RELATIONSHIPS USED** 3 mol O : 1 mol CaCO$_3$ (from chemical formula)
SOLVE Follow the solution map to solve the problem. The subscripts in a chemical formula are exact, so they never limit significant figures.	**SOLUTION** $$1.7 \text{ mol CaCO}_3 \times \frac{3 \text{ mol O}}{1 \text{ mol CaCO}_3} = 5.1 \text{ mol O}$$
CHECK Check your answer. Are the units correct? Does the answer make physical sense?	The units (mol O) are correct. The magnitude is reasonable as the number of moles of oxygen should be larger than the number of moles of CaCO$_3$ (because each CaCO$_3$ unit contains 3 O atoms).

▶**SKILLBUILDER 6.6** | **Chemical Formulas as Conversion Factors—Converting between Moles of a Compound and Moles of a Constituent Element**

Determine the number of moles of O in 1.4 mol of H_2SO_4.

▶**FOR MORE PRACTICE**   Example 6.17; Problems 63, 64.

Converting between Grams of a Compound and Grams of a Constituent Element

Now, we have the tools we need to solve our sodium problem from the beginning of the chapter. Suppose we want to know the mass of sodium in 15 g of NaCl. The chemical formula gives us the relationship between moles of Na and moles of NaCl:

$$1 \text{ mol Na} : 1 \text{ mol NaCl}$$

To use this relationship, we need *mol* NaCl, but we have *g* NaCl. We can use the *molar mass* of NaCl to convert from g NaCl to mol NaCl. Then we use the conversion factor from the chemical formula to convert to mol Na. Finally, we use the molar mass of Na to convert to g Na. The solution map is:

$$\frac{1 \text{ mol NaCl}}{58.44 \text{ g NaCl}} \qquad \frac{1 \text{ mol Na}}{1 \text{ mol NaCl}} \qquad \frac{22.99 \text{ g Na}}{1 \text{ mol Na}}$$

Notice that we must convert from g NaCl to mol NaCl *before* we can use the chemical formula as a conversion factor.

> *The chemical formula gives us a relationship between moles of substances, not between grams.*

We follow the solution map to solve the problem.

$$15 \text{ g NaCl} \times \frac{1 \text{ mol NaCl}}{58.44 \text{ g NaCl}} \times \frac{1 \text{ mol Na}}{1 \text{ mol NaCl}} \times \frac{22.99 \text{ g Na}}{1 \text{ mol Na}} = 5.9 \text{ g Na}$$

The general form for solving problems where you are asked to find the mass of an element present in a given mass of a compound is:

Mass compound ⟶ **Moles** compound ⟶ **Moles** element ⟶ **Mass** element

Use the atomic or molar mass to convert between mass and moles, and use the relationships inherent in the chemical formula to convert between moles and moles (▼Figure 6.2).

▶ **FIGURE 6.2   Mole relationships from a chemical formula**   The relationships inherent in a chemical formula allow us to convert between moles of the compound and moles of a constituent element (or vice versa).

1 mol CCl_4 : 4 mol Cl

CHEMICAL FORMULAS AS CONVERSION FACTORS—CONVERTING BETWEEN GRAMS OF A COMPOUND AND GRAMS OF A CONSTITUENT ELEMENT

EXAMPLE 6.7

 Carvone ($C_{10}H_{14}O$) is the main component of spearmint oil. It has a pleasant aroma and mint flavor. Carvone is added to chewing gum, liqueurs, soaps, and perfumes. Calculate the mass of carbon in 55.4 g of carvone.

SORT	GIVEN: 55.4 g $C_{10}H_{14}O$
You are given the mass of carvone and asked to find the mass of one of its constituent elements.	FIND: g C

STRATEGIZE

Base the solution map on:

Grams ⟶ Mole ⟶ Mole ⟶ Grams

SOLUTION MAP

$$\frac{1 \text{ mol } C_{10}H_{14}O}{150.2 \text{ g } C_{10}H_{14}O} \qquad \frac{10 \text{ mol } C}{1 \text{ mol } C_{10}H_{14}O} \qquad \frac{12.01 \text{ g } C}{1 \text{ mol } C}$$

You need three conversion factors. The first is the molar mass of carvone.

RELATIONSHIPS USED

$$\text{Molar mass carvone} = 10(12.01) + 14(1.01) + 1(16.00)$$
$$= 120.1 + 14.14 + 16.00$$
$$= 150.2 \text{ g/mol}$$

The second conversion factor is the relationship between moles of carbon and moles of carvone from the molecular formula.

10 mol C : 1 mol $C_{10}H_{14}O$ (from chemical formula)

The third conversion factor is the molar mass of carbon.

1 mol C = 12.01 g C (molar mass C, from periodic table)

SOLVE

Follow the solution map to solve the problem, beginning with g $C_{10}H_{14}O$ and multiplying by the appropriate conversion factors to arrive at g C.

SOLUTION

$$55.4 \text{ g } C_{10}H_{14}O \times \frac{1 \text{ mol } C_{10}H_{14}O}{150.2 \text{ g } C_{10}H_{14}O} \times$$

$$\frac{10 \text{ mol } C}{1 \text{ mol } C_{10}H_{14}O} \times \frac{12.01 \text{ g } C}{1 \text{ mol } C} = 44.3 \text{ g C}$$

CHECK

Check your answer. Are the units correct? Does the answer make physical sense?

The units, g C, are correct. The magnitude of the answer is reasonable because the mass of carbon with the compound must be less than the mass of the compound itself. If you had arrived at a mass of carbon that was greater than the mass of the compound, you would know that you had made a mistake; the mass of a constituent element can never be greater than the mass of the compound itself.

▶**SKILLBUILDER 6.7** | **Chemical Formulas as Conversion Factors—Converting between Grams of a Compound and Grams of a Constituent Element**

Determine the mass of oxygen in a 5.8-g sample of sodium bicarbonate ($NaHCO_3$).

▶**SKILLBUILDER PLUS** Determine the mass of oxygen in a 7.20-g sample of $Al_2(SO_4)_3$.

▶**FOR MORE PRACTICE** Example 6.18; Problems 67, 68, 69, 70.

 CONCEPTUAL CHECKPOINT 6.5

Without doing any detailed calculations, determine which sample contains the most fluorine atoms.

(a) 25 g of HF

(b) 1.5 mol of CH_3F

(c) 1.0 mol of F_2

CHEMISTRY IN THE ENVIRONMENT

▶ Chlorine in Chlorofluorocarbons

About 40 years ago, scientists began to suspect that synthetic compounds known as chlorofluorocarbons (CFCs) were destroying a vital compound called ozone (O_3) in Earth's upper atmosphere. Upper atmospheric ozone is important because it acts as a shield to protect life on Earth from harmful ultraviolet light (▶ Figure 6.3). CFCs are chemically inert molecules (they do not readily react with other substances) used primarily as refrigerants and industrial solvents. Their inertness has allowed them to leak into the atmosphere and stay there for many years. In the upper atmosphere, however, sunlight eventually breaks bonds within CFCs, resulting in the release of chlorine atoms. The chlorine atoms then react with ozone and destroy it by converting it from O_3 into O_2.

In 1985, scientists discovered a large hole in the ozone layer over Antarctica that has since been attributed to CFCs. The amount of ozone over Antarctica had depleted by a startling 50%. The ozone hole is transient, existing only in the Antarctic spring, from late August to November. Examination of data from previous years showed that this gradually expanding ozone hole has formed each spring and had been growing bigger each year (▼ Figure 6.4). A similar hole has been observed during some years over the North Pole, and a smaller, but still significant, drop in ozone has been observed over more populated areas such as the northern United States and Canada. The thinning of ozone over these areas is dangerous because ultraviolet light can harm living things and induce skin cancer in humans. Based on this evidence, most developed nations banned the production of CFCs on January 1, 1996. The ozone hole

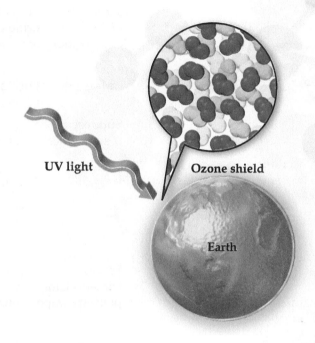

▲ **FIGURE 6.3 The ozone shield** Atmospheric ozone shields life on Earth from harmful ultraviolet light.

continues to form today, but has reached a maximum and is starting to contract. The contraction of the ozone hole is attributed to the CFC ban.

B6.1 CAN YOU ANSWER THIS? *Suppose a car air conditioner contains 2.5 kg of freon-12 (CCl_2F_2), a CFC. How many kilograms of Cl are contained within the freon?*

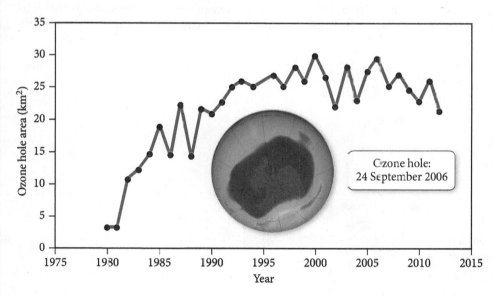

Ozone hole: 24 September 2006

◀ **FIGURE 6.4 Growth of the ozone hole** Antarctic ozone levels from 1980 to 2012.

6.6 Mass Percent Composition of Compounds

LO: Use mass percent composition as a conversion factor.

Another way to express how much of an element is in a given compound is to use the element's mass percent composition for that compound. The **mass percent composition** or simply **mass percent** of an element is the element's percentage of the total mass of the compound. For example, the mass percent composition of sodium in sodium chloride is 39%. This information tells us that a 100-g sample of sodium chloride contains 39 g of sodium. We can determine the mass percent composition for a compound from experimental data using the formula:

$$\text{Mass percent of element } X = \frac{\text{Mass of } X \text{ in a sample of the compound}}{\text{Mass of the sample of the compound}} \times 100\%$$

Suppose a 0.358-g sample of chromium reacts with oxygen to form 0.523 g of the metal oxide. Then the mass percent of chromium is:

$$\text{Mass percent Cr} = \frac{\text{Mass Cr}}{\text{Mass metal oxide}} \times 100\%$$

$$= \frac{0.358 \text{ g}}{0.523 \text{ g}} \times 100\% = 68.5\%$$

We can use mass percent composition as a conversion factor between grams of a constituent element and grams of the compound. For example, we just saw that the mass percent composition of sodium in sodium chloride is 39%. This can be written as:

39 g sodium : 100 g sodium chloride

or in fractional form:

$$\frac{39 \text{ g Na}}{100 \text{ g NaCl}} \quad \text{or} \quad \frac{100 \text{ g NaCl}}{39 \text{ g Na}}$$

These fractions are conversion factors between g Na and g NaCl, as shown in Example 6.8.

EXAMPLE 6.8 **USING MASS PERCENT COMPOSITION AS A CONVERSION FACTOR**

The FDA recommends that adults consume less than 2.4 g of sodium per day. How many grams of sodium chloride can you consume and still be within the FDA guidelines? Sodium chloride is 39% sodium by mass.

SORT	
You are given the mass of sodium and the mass percent of sodium in sodium chloride. When mass percent is given, write it as a fraction. *Percent means per hundred*, so 39% sodium indicates that there are 39 g Na per 100 g NaCl. You are asked to find the mass of sodium chloride that contains the given mass of sodium.	**GIVEN:** 2.4 g Na $$\frac{39 \text{ g Na}}{100 \text{ g NaCl}}$$ **FIND:** g NaCl

STRATEGIZE	
Draw a solution map that starts with the mass of sodium and uses the mass percent as a conversion factor to get to the mass of sodium chloride.	**SOLUTION MAP** $$\frac{100 \text{ g NaCl}}{39 \text{ g Na}}$$ **RELATIONSHIPS USED** 39 g Na : 100 g NaCl (given in the problem)

SOLVE

Follow the solution map to solve the problem, beginning with grams Na and ending with grams of NaCl. The amount of salt you can consume and still be within the FDA guideline is 6.2 g NaCl.

SOLUTION

$$2.4 \ \text{g Na} \times \frac{100 \ \text{g NaCl}}{39 \ \text{g Na}} = 6.2 \ \text{g NaCl}$$

CHECK

Check your answer. Are the units correct? Does the answer make physical sense?

The units, g NaCl, are correct. The answer makes physical sense because the mass of NaCl should be *larger* than the mass of Na. The mass of a compound containing a given mass of a particular element is always larger than the mass of the element itself.

▲ Twelve and a half packets of salt contain 6.2 g NaCl.

▶**SKILLBUILDER 6.8 | Using Mass Percent Composition as a Conversion Factor**

If a woman consumes 22 g of sodium chloride, how much sodium does she consume? Sodium chloride is 39% sodium by mass.

▶**FOR MORE PRACTICE** Example 6.19; Problems 75, 76, 77, 78.

6.7 Mass Percent Composition from a Chemical Formula

LO: Determine mass percent composition from a chemical formula.

In the previous section, we demonstrated how to calculate mass percent composition from experimental data and how to use mass percent composition as a conversion factor. We can also calculate the mass percent of any element in a compound from the chemical formula for the compound. Based on the chemical formula, the mass percent of element X in a compound is:

$$\text{Mass percent of element } X = \frac{\text{Mass of element } X \text{ in 1 mol of compound}}{\text{Mass of 1 mol of compound}} \times 100\%$$

Suppose, for example, that we want to calculate the mass percent composition of Cl in the chlorofluorocarbon CCl_2F_2. The mass percent of Cl is given by:

$$\text{Mass percent Cl} = \frac{2 \times \text{Molar mass Cl}}{\text{Molar mass } CCl_2F_2} \times 100\%$$

We must multiply the molar mass of Cl by 2 because the chemical formula has a subscript of 2 for Cl, meaning that 1 mol of CCl_2F_2 contains 2 mol of Cl atoms. We calculate the molar mass of CCl_2F_2 as follows:

$$\text{Molar mass} = 1(12.01) + 2(35.45) + 2(19.00) = 120.91 \ \text{g/mol}$$

So the mass percent of Cl in CCl_2F_2 is:

$$\text{Mass percent Cl} = \frac{2 \times \text{Molar mass Cl}}{\text{Molar mass } CCl_2F_2} \times 100\% = \frac{2 \times 35.45 \ \text{g}}{120.91 \ \text{g}} \times 100\%$$

$$= 58.64\%$$

EXAMPLE 6.9 **MASS PERCENT COMPOSITION**

Calculate the mass percent of Cl in freon-114 ($C_2Cl_4F_2$).

SORT You are given the molecular formula of freon-114 and asked to find the mass percent of Cl.	**GIVEN:** $C_2Cl_4F_2$ **FIND:** Mass % Cl
STRATEGIZE You can use the information in the chemical formula to substitute into the mass percent equation and obtain the mass percent Cl.	**SOLUTION MAP** $$\text{Mass \% Cl} = \frac{4 \times \text{Molar mass Cl}}{\text{Molar mass } C_2Cl_4F_2} \times 100\%$$ **RELATIONSHIPS USED** Mass percent of element X = $$\frac{\text{Mass of element } X \text{ in 1 mol of compound}}{\text{Mass of 1 mol of compound}} \times 100\%$$ (mass percent equation, introduced in this section)
SOLVE Calculate the molar mass of freon-114 and substitute the values into the equation to find mass percent Cl.	**SOLUTION** $4 \times$ Molar mass Cl $= 4(35.45 \text{ g}) = 141.8 \text{ g}$ Molar mass $C_2Cl_4F_2 = 2(12.01) + 4(35.45) + 2(19.00)$ $= 24.02 + 141.8 + 38.00$ $= \dfrac{203.8 \text{ g}}{\text{mol}}$ $$\text{Mass \% Cl} = \frac{4 \times \text{Molar mass Cl}}{\text{Molar mass } C_2Cl_4F_2} \times 100\%$$ $$= \frac{141.8 \text{ g}}{203.8 \text{ g}} \times 100\%$$ $= 69.58\%$
CHECK Check your answer. Are the units correct? Does the answer make physical sense?	The units (%) are correct. The answer makes physical sense. Mass percent composition should never exceed 100%. If your answer is greater than 100%, you have made an error.

▶**SKILLBUILDER 6.9 | Mass Percent Composition**

Acetic acid ($HC_2H_3O_2$) is the active ingredient in vinegar. Calculate the mass percent composition of O in acetic acid.

▶**FOR MORE PRACTICE** Example 6.20; Problems 79, 80, 81, 82, 85, 86.

 CONCEPTUAL CHECKPOINT 6.6

Which compound has the highest mass percent of O? (You should not have to perform any detailed calculations to answer this question.)

(a) CrO

(b) CrO_2

(c) Cr_2O_3

CHEMISTRY **AND HEALTH**
▶ **Fluoridation of Drinking Water**

In the early 1900s, scientists discovered that people whose drinking water naturally contained fluoride (F^-) ions had fewer cavities than people whose water did not. At appropriate levels, fluoride strengthens tooth enamel, which prevents tooth decay. In an effort to improve public health, fluoride has been artificially added to drinking water supplies since 1945. In the United States today, about 62% of the population drinks artificially fluoridated drinking water. The American Dental Association and public health agencies estimate that water fluoridation reduces tooth decay by 40 to 65%.

The fluoridation of public drinking water, however, is often controversial. Some opponents argue that fluoride is available from other sources—such as toothpaste, mouthwash, drops, and pills—and therefore should not be added to drinking water. Anyone who wants fluoride can get it from these optional sources, they argue, and the government should not impose fluoride on the population. Other opponents argue that the risks associated with fluoridation are too

great. Indeed, too much fluoride can cause teeth to become brown and spotted, a condition known as dental fluorosis. Extremely high levels can lead to skeletal fluorosis, a condition in which the bones become brittle and arthritic.

The scientific consensus is that, like many minerals, fluoride shows some health benefits at certain levels—about 1–4 mg/day for adults—but can have detrimental effects at higher levels. Consequently, most major cities fluoridate their drinking water at a level of about 1 mg/L. Most adults drink between 1 and 2 L of water per day, so they receive beneficial amounts of fluoride from the water. Bottled water does not normally contain fluoride. Fluoridated bottled water can sometimes be found in the infant section of supermarkets.

B6.2 CAN YOU ANSWER THIS? *Fluoride is often added to water as sodium fluoride (NaF). What is the mass percent composition of F^- in NaF? How many grams of NaF must be added to 1500 L of water to fluoridate it at a level of 1.0 mg F^-/L?*

6.8 Calculating Empirical Formulas for Compounds

LO: Determine an empirical formula from experimental data.

LO: Calculate an empirical formula from reaction data.

In Section 6.7, we learned how to calculate mass percent composition from a chemical formula. But can we go the other way? Can we calculate a chemical formula from mass percent composition? This is important because laboratory analyses of compounds do not often give chemical formulas directly; rather, they give the relative masses of each element present in a compound. For example, if we decompose water into hydrogen and oxygen in the laboratory, we could measure the masses of hydrogen and oxygen produced. Can we determine the chemical formula for water from this kind of data?

▶ We just learned how to go from the chemical formula of a compound to its mass percent composition. Can we also go the other way?

The answer is a qualified yes. We can determine a chemical formula, but it is the **empirical formula**, not the molecular formula. As we saw in Section 5.3, an empirical formula gives the smallest whole-number ratio of each type of atom in a compound, not the specific number of each type of atom in a molecule. Recall that the **molecular formula** is always a whole-number multiple of the empirical formula: Molecular formula = Empirical × n, where $n = 1, 2, 3 \ldots$

For example, the molecular formula for hydrogen peroxide is H_2O_2, and its empirical formula is HO.

▌ A chemical formula represents a ratio of atoms or moles of atoms, not a ratio of masses.

$$HO \times 2 \longrightarrow H_2O_2$$

Calculating an Empirical Formula from Experimental Data

Suppose we decompose a sample of water in the laboratory and find that it produces 3.0 g of hydrogen and 24 g of oxygen. How do we determine an empirical formula from these data?

oxygen gas   hydrogen gas

▲ Water can be decomposed by an electric current into hydrogen and oxygen. How can we find the empirical formula for water from the masses of its component elements?

We know that an empirical formula represents a ratio of atoms or a ratio of moles of atoms, but it *does not* represent a ratio of masses. So the first thing we must do is convert our data from grams to moles. How many moles of each element formed during the decomposition? To convert to moles, we divide each mass by the molar mass of that element.

$$\text{Moles H} = 3.0 \ \text{g H} \times \frac{1 \ \text{mol H}}{1.01 \ \text{g H}} = 3.0 \ \text{mol H}$$

$$\text{Moles O} = 24 \ \text{g O} \times \frac{1 \ \text{mol O}}{16.00 \ \text{g O}} = 1.5 \ \text{mol O}$$

From these data, we know there are 3 mol of H for every 1.5 mol of O. We can now write a pseudoformula for water:

$$H_3O_{1.5}$$

To get whole-number subscripts in our formula, we divide all the subscripts by the smallest one, in this case 1.5.

$$H_{\frac{3}{1.5}}O_{\frac{1.5}{1.5}} = H_2O$$

Our empirical formula for water, which in this case also happens to be the molecular formula, is H_2O. The following procedure can be used to obtain the empirical formula of any compound from experimental data. The left column outlines the procedure, and the center and right columns contain two examples of how to apply the procedure.

	EXAMPLE 6.10	**EXAMPLE 6.11**
OBTAINING AN EMPIRICAL FORMULA FROM EXPERIMENTAL DATA	You decompose a compound containing nitrogen and oxygen in the laboratory and produce 24.5 g of nitrogen and 70.0 g of oxygen. Calculate the empirical formula of the compound.	A laboratory analysis of aspirin determines the following mass percent composition: C 60.00% H 4.48% O 35.53% Find the empirical formula.
1. Write down (or calculate) the masses of each element present in a sample of the compound. If you are given mass percent composition, assume a 100-g sample and calculate the masses of each element from the given percentages.	**GIVEN:** 24.5 g N 70.0 g O **FIND:** empirical formula	**GIVEN:** In a 100-g sample: 60.00 g C 4.48 g H 35.53 g O **FIND:** empirical formula
2. Convert each of the masses in Step 1 to moles by using the appropriate molar mass for each element as a conversion factor.	**SOLUTION** $24.5 \ \cancel{g \ N} \times \dfrac{1 \ mol \ N}{14.01 \ \cancel{g \ N}}$ $= 1.75 \ mol \ N$ $70.0 \ \cancel{g \ O} \times \dfrac{1 \ mol \ O}{16.00 \ \cancel{g \ O}}$ $= 4.38 \ mol \ O$	**SOLUTION** $60.00 \ \cancel{g \ C} \times \dfrac{1 \ mol \ C}{12.01 \ \cancel{g \ C}}$ $= 4.996 \ mol \ C$ $4.48 \ \cancel{g \ H} \times \dfrac{1 \ mol \ H}{1.01 \ \cancel{g \ H}}$ $= 4.44 \ mol \ H$ $35.53 \ \cancel{g \ O} \times \dfrac{1 \ mol \ O}{16.00 \ \cancel{g \ O}}$ $= 2.221 \ mol \ O$
3. Write down a pseudoformula for the compound, using the moles of each element (from Step 2) as subscripts.	$N_{1.75}O_{4.38}$	$C_{4.996}H_{4.44}O_{2.221}$
4. Divide all the subscripts in the formula by the smallest subscript.	$N_{\frac{1.75}{1.75}} O_{\frac{4.38}{1.75}} \longrightarrow N_1 O_{2.5}$	$C_{\frac{4.996}{2.221}} H_{\frac{4.44}{2.221}} O_{\frac{2.221}{2.221}} \longrightarrow C_{2.25}H_2O_1$
5. If the subscripts are not whole numbers, multiply all the subscripts by a small whole number (see the following table) to arrive at whole-number subscripts.	$N_1O_{2.5} \times 2 \longrightarrow N_2O_5$ The correct empirical formula is N_2O_5.	$C_{2.25}H_2O_1 \times 4 \longrightarrow C_9H_8O_4$ The correct empirical formula is $C_9H_8O_4$.

Fractional Subscript	Multiply by This Number to Get Whole-Number Subscripts
_.10	10
_.20	5
_.25	4
_.33	3
_.50	2
_.66	3
_.75	4

▶**SKILLBUILDER 6.10** | A sample of a compound is decomposed in the laboratory and produces 165 g of carbon, 27.8 g of hydrogen, and 220.2 g O. Calculate the empirical formula of the compound.

▶**FOR MORE PRACTICE**
Problems 87, 88, 89, 90.

▶**SKILLBUILDER 6.11** | Ibuprofen, an aspirin substitute, has the mass percent composition: C 75.69%; H 8.80%; O 15.51%. Calculate the empirical formula of the ibuprofen.

▶**FOR MORE PRACTICE**
Example 6.21; Problems 91, 92, 93, 94.

EXAMPLE 6.12	CALCULATING AN EMPIRICAL FORMULA FROM REACTION DATA

A 3.24-g sample of titanium reacts with oxygen to form 5.40 g of the metal oxide. What is the empirical formula of the metal oxide?

You are given the mass of titanium and the mass of the metal oxide that forms. You are asked to find the empirical formula. You need to recognize this problem as one requiring a special procedure and apply that procedure, which is outlined below.	**GIVEN:** 3.24 g Ti 5.40 g metal oxide **FIND:** empirical formula
1. Write down (or calculate) the masses of each element present in a sample of the compound. In this case, you are given the mass of the initial Ti sample and the mass of its oxide after the sample reacts with oxygen. The mass of oxygen is the difference between the mass of the oxide and the mass of titanium.	**SOLUTION** 3.24 g Ti Mass O = Mass oxide − Mass titanium $\quad\quad$ = 5.40 g − 3.24 g $\quad\quad$ = 2.16 g O
2. Convert each of the masses in Step 1 to moles by using the appropriate molar mass for each element as a conversion factor.	$3.24 \text{ g Ti} \times \dfrac{1 \text{ mol Ti}}{47.88 \text{ g Ti}} = 0.0677 \text{ mol Ti}$ $2.16 \text{ g O} \times \dfrac{1 \text{ mol O}}{16.00 \text{ g O}} = 0.135 \text{ mol O}$
3. Write down a pseudoformula for the compound, using the moles of each element obtained in Step 2 as subscripts.	$Ti_{0.0677}O_{0.135}$
4. Divide all the subscripts in the formula by the smallest subscript.	$Ti_{\frac{0.0677}{0.0677}} O_{\frac{0.135}{0.0677}} \longrightarrow TiO_2$
5. If the subscripts are not whole numbers, multiply all the subscripts by a small whole number to arrive at whole-number subscripts.	As the subscripts are already whole numbers, this last step is unnecessary. The correct empirical formula is TiO_2.

▶**SKILLBUILDER 6.12** | **Calculating an Empirical Formula from Reaction Data**

A 1.56-g sample of copper reacts with oxygen to form 1.95 g of the metal oxide. What is the formula of the metal oxide?

▶**FOR MORE PRACTICE**   Problems 95, 96, 97, 98.

6.9   Calculating Molecular Formulas for Compounds

LO: Calculate a molecular formula from an empirical formula and molar mass.

▲ Fructose, a sugar found in fruit.

We can determine the *molecular* formula of a compound from the empirical formula if we also know the molar mass of the compound. Recall from Section 6.8 that the molecular formula is always a whole-number multiple of the empirical formula.

$$\text{Molecular formula} = \text{Empirical formula} \times n, \text{ where } n = 1, 2, 3 \dots$$

Suppose we want to find the molecular formula for fructose (a sugar found in fruit) from its empirical formula, CH_2O, and its molar mass, 180.2 g/mol. We know that the molecular formula is a whole-number multiple of CH_2O.

$$\text{Molecular formula} = CH_2O \times n$$

We also know that the molar mass is a whole-number multiple of the **empirical formula molar mass**, the sum of the masses of all the atoms in the empirical formula.

$$\text{Molar mass} = \text{Empirical formula molar mass} \times n$$

For a particular compound, the value of n in both cases is the same. Therefore, we can find n by calculating the ratio of the molar mass to the empirical formula molar mass.

$$n = \frac{\text{Molar mass}}{\text{Empirical formula molar mass}}$$

For fructose, the empirical formula molar mass is:

Empirical formula molar mass = $1(12.01) + 2(1.01) + 16.00 = 30.03$ g/mol

Therefore, n is:

$$n = \frac{180.2 \text{ g/mol}}{30.03 \text{ g/mol}} = 6$$

We can then use this value of n to find the molecular formula.

Molecular formula = $CH_2O \times 6 = C_6H_{12}O_6$

EXAMPLE 6.13	CALCULATING MOLECULAR FORMULA FROM EMPIRICAL FORMULA AND MOLAR MASS

Naphthalene is a compound containing carbon and hydrogen that is used in mothballs. Its empirical formula is C_5H_4 and its molar mass is 128.16 g/mol. What is its molecular formula?

SORT
You are given the empirical formula and the molar mass of a compound and asked to find its molecular formula.

GIVEN: empirical formula = C_5H_4
molar mass = 128.16 g/mol

FIND: molecular formula

STRATEGIZE
In the first step, use the molar mass (which is given) and the empirical formula molar mass (which you can calculate based on the empirical formula) to determine n (the integer by which you must multiply the empirical formula to determine the molecular formula).

In the second step, multiply the subscripts in the empirical formula by n to arrive at the molecular formula.

SOLUTION MAP

$$n = \frac{\text{Molar mass}}{\text{Empirical formula molar mass}}$$

| n, empirical formula | → | molecular formula |

Molecular formula = Empirical formula $\times n$

SOLVE
First find the empirical formula molar mass. Next follow the solution map. Find n by dividing the molar mass by the empirical formula molar mass (which you just calculated). Multiply the empirical formula by n to determine the molecular formula.

SOLUTION
Empirical formula molar mass = $5(12.01) + 4(1.01)$
= 64.09 g/mol

$$n = \frac{\text{Molar mass}}{\text{Empirical formula mass}} = \frac{128.16 \text{ g/mol}}{64.09 \text{ g/mol}} = 2$$

Molecular formula = $C_5H_4 \times 2 = C_{10}H_8$

CHECK
Check your answer. Does the answer make physical sense?

The answer makes physical sense because it is a whole-number multiple of the empirical formula. Any answer containing fractional subscripts would be an error.

▶**SKILLBUILDER 6.13 | Calculating Molecular Formula from Empirical Formula and Molar Mass**

Butane is a compound containing carbon and hydrogen used as a fuel in butane lighters. Its empirical formula is C_2H_5, and its molar mass is 58.12 g/mol. Find its molecular formula.

▶**SKILLBUILDER PLUS** A compound with the following mass percent composition has a molar mass of 60.10 g/mol. Find its molecular formula.
C 39.97%   H 13.41%   N 46.62%

▶**FOR MORE PRACTICE** Example 6.22; Problems 99, 100, 101, 102.

CHAPTER IN REVIEW

Self-Assessment Quiz

Q1. How many atoms are there in 5.8 mol helium?
(a) 23.2 atoms
(b) 9.6×10^{-24} atoms
(c) 5.8×10^{23} atoms
(d) 3.5×10^{24} atoms

Q2. A sample of pure silver has a mass of 155 g. How many moles of silver are in the sample?
(a) 1.44 mol
(b) 1.67×10^4 mol
(c) 0.696 mol
(d) 155 mol

Q3. How many carbon atoms are there in a 12.5 kg sample of carbon?
(a) 6.27×10^{20} atoms
(b) 9.04×10^{28} atoms
(c) 6.27×10^{26} atoms
(d) 1.73×10^{-21} atoms

Q4. Which sample contains the greatest number of atoms?
(a) 15 g Ne
(b) 15 g Ar
(c) 15 g Kr
(d) None of the above (all contain the same number of atoms).

Q5. What is the average mass (in grams) of a single carbon dioxide molecule?
(a) 3.8×10^{-26} g
(b) 7.31×10^{-23} g
(c) 2.65×10^{25} g
(d) 44.01 g

Q6. How many moles of O are in 1.6 mol of $Ca(NO_3)_2$?
(a) 1.6 mol O
(b) 3.2 mol O
(c) 4.8 mol O
(d) 9.6 mol O

Q7. How many grams of Cl are in 25.8 g CF_2Cl_2?
(a) 7.56 g
(b) 3.78 g
(c) 15.1 g
(d) 0.427 g

Q8. Which sample contains the greatest number of F atoms?
(a) 2.0 mol HF
(b) 1.5 mol F_2
(c) 1.0 mol CF_4
(d) 0.5 mol CH_2F_2

Q9. The compound A_2X is 35.8% A by mass. What mass of the compound contains 55.1 g A?
(a) 308 g
(b) 154 g
(c) 19.7 g
(d) 35.8 g

Q10. Which compound has the highest mass percent C?
(a) CO
(b) CO_2
(c) H_2CO_3
(d) H_2CO

Q11. What is the mass percent N in $C_2H_8N_2$?
(a) 23.3% N
(b) 16.6% N
(c) 215% N
(d) 46.6% N

Q12. A compound is 52.14% C, 13.13% H, and 34.73% O by mass. What is the empirical formula of the compound?
(a) C_4HO_3
(b) C_2H_6O
(c) $C_2H_8O_3$
(d) C_3HO_6

Q13. A compound has the empirical formula CH_2O and a formula mass of 120.10 amu. What is the molecular formula of the compound?
(a) CH_2O
(b) $C_2H_4O_2$
(c) $C_3H_6O_3$
(d) $C_4H_8O_4$

Q14. A compound is decomposed in the laboratory and produces 1.40 g N and 0.20 g H. What is the empirical formula of the compound?
(a) NH   (c) NH_2
(b) N_2H (d) N_7H

Answers: 1d; 2a; 3c; 4a; 5b; 6d; 7c; 8c; 9b; 10a; 11d; 12b; 13d; 14c

Chemical Principles

The Mole Concept: The mole is a specific number (6.022×10^{23}) that allows us to count atoms or molecules by weighing them. One mole of any element has a mass equivalent to its atomic mass in grams, and a mole of any compound has a mass equivalent to its formula mass in grams. The mass of 1 mol of an element or compound is its molar mass.

Chemical Formulas and Chemical Composition: Chemical formulas indicate the relative number of each kind of element in a compound. These numbers are based on atoms or moles. By using molar masses, we can use the information in a chemical formula to determine the relative masses of each kind of element in a compound. We can then relate the mass of a sample of a compound to the masses of the elements contained in the compound.

Empirical and Molecular Formulas from Laboratory Data: The relative masses of the elements within a compound allow us to determine the empirical formula of the compound. If we know the molar mass of the compound, we can also determine its molecular formula.

Relevance

The Mole Concept: The mole concept allows us to determine the number of atoms or molecules in a sample from its mass. Just as a hardware store customer wants to know the number of nails in a certain weight of nails, we want to know the number of atoms in a certain mass of atoms. Because atoms are too small to count, we use their mass.

Chemical Formulas and Chemical Composition: The chemical composition of compounds is important because it lets us determine how much of a particular element is contained within a particular compound. For example, to assess the threat to the Earth's ozone layer from chlorofluorocarbons (CFCs), we need to know how much chlorine is in a particular CFC.

Empirical and Molecular Formulas from Laboratory Data: The first thing we want to know about an unknown compound is its chemical formula, because the formula reveals the compound's composition. Chemists often arrive at formulas by analyzing compounds in the laboratory—either by decomposing them or by synthesizing them—to determine the relative masses of the elements they contain.

Chemical Skills

LO: Convert between moles and number of atoms (Section 6.3).

SORT
You are given moles of copper and asked to find the number of copper atoms.

STRATEGIZE
To convert between moles and number of atoms, use Avogadro's number, 6.022×10^{23} atoms $= 1$ mol, as a conversion factor.

SOLVE
Follow the solution map to solve the problem.

CHECK
Check your answer. Are the units correct? Does the answer make physical sense?

Examples

EXAMPLE 6.14	CONVERTING BETWEEN MOLES AND NUMBER OF ATOMS

Calculate the number of atoms in 4.8 mol of copper.

GIVEN: 4.8 mol Cu

FIND: Cu atoms

SOLUTION MAP

$$\frac{6.022 \times 10^{23} \text{ Cu atoms}}{1 \text{ mol Cu}}$$

RELATIONSHIPS USED
1 mol Cu $= 6.022 \times 10^{23}$ Cu atoms (Avogadro's number, from inside back cover)

SOLUTION

$$4.8 \text{ mol Cu} \times \frac{6.022 \times 10^{23} \text{ Cu atoms}}{1 \text{ mol Cu}} =$$
$$2.9 \times 10^{24} \text{ Cu atoms}$$

The units, Cu atoms, are correct. The answer makes physical sense because the number is very large, as you would expect for nearly 5 moles of atoms.

LO: Convert between grams and moles (Section 6.3).

EXAMPLE 6.15 **CONVERTING BETWEEN GRAMS AND MOLES**

Calculate the mass of aluminum (in grams) of 6.73 moles of aluminum.

SORT
You are given the number of moles of aluminum and asked to find the mass of aluminum in grams.

GIVEN: 6.73 mol Al

FIND: g Al

STRATEGIZE
Use the molar mass of aluminum to convert between moles and grams.

SOLUTION MAP

$$\frac{26.98 \text{ g Al}}{1 \text{ mol Al}}$$

RELATIONSHIPS USED
26.98 g Al = 1 mol Al (molar mass of Al from periodic table)

SOLVE
Follow the solution map to solve the problem.

SOLUTION

$$6.73 \text{ mol Al} \times \frac{26.98 \text{ g Al}}{1 \text{ mol Al}} = 182 \text{ g Al}$$

CHECK
Check your answer. Are the units correct? Does the answer make physical sense?

The units, g Al, are correct. The answer makes physical sense because each mole has a mass of about 27 g; therefore, nearly 7 moles should have a mass of nearly 190 g.

LO: Convert between grams and number of atoms or molecules (Section 6.3).

EXAMPLE 6.16 **CONVERTING BETWEEN GRAMS AND NUMBER OF ATOMS OR MOLECULES**

Determine the number of atoms in a 48.3-g sample of zinc.

SORT
You are given the mass of a zinc sample and asked to find the number of Zn atoms that it contains.

GIVEN: 48.3 g Zn

FIND: Zn atoms

STRATEGIZE
Use the molar mass of the element to convert from grams to moles, and then use Avogadro's number to convert moles to number of atoms.

SOLUTION MAP

$$\frac{1 \text{ mol Zn}}{65.39 \text{ g Zn}} \qquad \frac{6.022 \times 10^{23} \text{ Zn atoms}}{1 \text{ mol Zn}}$$

RELATIONSHIPS USED
65.39 g Zn = 1 mol Zn (molar mass of Zn from periodic table)

1 mol = 6.022 × 10²³ atoms (Avogadro's number, from inside back cover)

SOLVE
Follow the solution map to solve the problem.

SOLUTION

$$48.3 \text{ g Zn} \times \frac{1 \text{ mol Zn}}{65.39 \text{ g Zn}} \times \frac{6.022 \times 10^{23} \text{ Zn atoms}}{1 \text{ mol Zn}}$$
$$= 4.45 \times 10^{23} \text{ Zn atoms}$$

CHECK
Check your answer. Are the units correct? Does the answer make physical sense?

The units, Zn atoms, are correct. The answer makes physical sense because the number of atoms in any macroscopic-sized sample should be very large.

LO: Convert between moles of a compound and moles of a constituent element (Section 6.5).

SORT
You are given the number of moles of sulfuric acid and asked to find the number of moles of oxygen.

STRATEGIZE
To convert between moles of a compound and moles of a constituent element, use the chemical formula of the compound to determine a ratio between the moles of the element and the moles of the compound.

SOLVE
Follow the solution map to solve the problem.

CHECK
Check your answer. Are the units correct? Does the answer make physical sense?

LO: Convert between grams of a compound and grams of a constituent element (Section 6.5).

SORT
You are given the mass of iron(III) oxide and asked to find the mass of iron contained within it.

STRATEGIZE
Use the molar mass of the compound to convert from grams of the compound to moles of the compound. Then use the chemical formula to obtain a conversion factor to convert from moles of the compound to moles of the constituent element. Finally, use the molar mass of the constituent element to convert from moles of the element to grams of the element.

SOLVE
Follow the solution map to solve the problem.

CHECK
Check your answer. Are the units correct? Does the answer make physical sense?

EXAMPLE 6.17 **CONVERTING BETWEEN MOLES OF A COMPOUND AND MOLES OF A CONSTITUENT ELEMENT**

Determine the number of moles of oxygen in 7.20 mol of H_2SO_4.

GIVEN: 7.20 mol H_2SO_4

FIND: mol O

SOLUTION MAP

$$\frac{4\ mol\ O}{1\ mol\ H_2SO_4}$$

RELATIONSHIPS USED
4 mol O : 1 mol H_2SO_4

SOLUTION
$$7.20\ mol\ H_2SO_4 \times \frac{4\ mol\ O}{1\ mol\ H_2SO_4} = 28.8\ mol\ O$$

The units, mol O, are correct. The answer makes physical sense because the number of moles of an element in a compound is equal to or greater than the number of moles of the compound itself.

EXAMPLE 6.18 **CONVERTING BETWEEN GRAMS OF A COMPOUND AND GRAMS OF A CONSTITUENT ELEMENT**

Find the grams of iron in 79.2 g of Fe_2O_3.

GIVEN: 79.2 g Fe_2O_3

FIND: g Fe

SOLUTION MAP

$$\frac{1\ mol\ Fe_2O_3}{159.70\ g\ Fe_2O_3} \qquad \frac{2\ mol\ Fe}{1\ mol\ Fe_2O_3} \qquad \frac{55.85\ g\ Fe}{1\ mol\ Fe}$$

RELATIONSHIPS USED
Molar mass Fe_2O_3
$$= 2(55.85) + 3(16.00)$$
$$= 159.70\ g/mol$$
2 mol Fe : 1 mol Fe_2O_3 (from given chemical formula)

SOLUTION
$$79.2\ g\ Fe_2O_3 \times \frac{1\ mol\ Fe_2O_3}{159.70\ g\ Fe_2O_3} \times \frac{2\ mol\ Fe}{1\ mol\ Fe_2O_3} \times \frac{55.85\ g\ Fe}{1\ mol\ Fe} = 55.4\ g\ Fe$$

The units, g Fe, are correct. The answer makes physical sense because the mass of a constituent element within a compound should be less than the mass of the compound itself.

LO: Use mass percent composition as a conversion factor (Section 6.6).

SORT
You are given the mass of titanium(IV) oxide and the mass percent titanium in the oxide. You are asked to find the mass of titanium in the sample.

STRATEGIZE
Use the percent composition as a conversion factor between grams of titanium(IV) oxide and grams of titanium.

SOLVE
Follow the solution map to solve the problem.

CHECK
Check your answer. Are the units correct? Does the answer make physical sense?

LO: Determine mass percent composition from a chemical formula (Section 6.7).

SORT
You are given the formula of potassium oxide and asked to determine the mass percent of potassium within it.

STRATEGIZE
The solution map shows how you can substitute the information derived from the chemical formula into the mass percent equation to yield the mass percent of the element.

EXAMPLE 6.19	USING MASS PERCENT COMPOSITION AS A CONVERSION FACTOR

Determine the mass of titanium in 57.2 g of titanium(IV) oxide. The mass percent of titanium in titanium(IV) oxide is 59.9%.

GIVEN: 57.2 g TiO_2

$$\frac{59.9 \text{ g Ti}}{100 \text{ g TiO}_2}$$

FIND: g Ti

SOLUTION MAP

$$\frac{59.9 \text{ g Ti}}{100 \text{ g TiO}_2}$$

RELATIONSHIPS USED
59.9 g Ti : 100 g TiO_2

SOLUTION

$$57.2 \text{ g TiO}_2 \times \frac{59.9 \text{ g Ti}}{100 \text{ g TiO}_2} = 34.3 \text{ g Ti}$$

The units, g Ti, are correct. The answer makes physical sense because the mass of an element within a compound should be less than the mass of the compound itself.

EXAMPLE 6.20	DETERMINING MASS PERCENT COMPOSITION FROM A CHEMICAL FORMULA

Calculate the mass percent composition of potassium in potassium oxide (K_2O).

GIVEN: K_2O

FIND: Mass % K

SOLUTION MAP

$$\text{Mass \% K} = \frac{2 \times \text{Molar mass K}}{\text{Molar mass K}_2\text{O}} \times 100\%$$

RELATIONSHIPS USED
Mass percent of element X

$$= \frac{\text{Mass of element } X \text{ in 1 mol of compound}}{\text{Mass of 1 mol of compound}} \times 100\%$$

(mass percent equation, from Section 6.6)

SOLVE

Calculate the molar mass of potassium oxide and follow the solution map to solve the problem.

SOLUTION

Molar mass $K_2O = 2(39.10) + 16.00$

$$= 94.20 \text{ g/mol}$$

$$\text{Mass \% } K = \frac{2(39.10 \text{ g K})}{94.20 \text{ g K}_2\text{O}} \times 100\% = 83.01\% \text{ K}$$

CHECK

Check your answer. Are the units correct? Does the answer make physical sense?

The units, % K, are correct. The answer makes physical sense because it should be below 100%.

LO: Determine an empirical formula from experimental data (Section 6.8).

You need to recognize this problem as one requiring a special procedure. Follow these steps to solve the problem.

1. Write down (or calculate) the masses of each element present in a sample of the compound. If you are given mass percent composition, assume a 100-g sample and calculate the masses of each element from the given percentages.

2. Convert each of the masses in Step 1 to moles by using the appropriate molar mass for each element as a conversion factor.

3. Write down a pseudoformula for the compound using the moles of each element (from Step 2) as subscripts.

4. Divide all the subscripts in the formula by the smallest subscript.

5. If the subscripts are not whole numbers, multiply all the subscripts by a small whole number to arrive at whole-number subscripts.

EXAMPLE 6.21   DETERMINING AN EMPIRICAL FORMULA FROM EXPERIMENTAL DATA

A laboratory analysis of vanillin, the flavoring agent in vanilla, determined the mass percent composition: C, 63.15%; H, 5.30%; O, 31.55%. Determine the empirical formula of vanillin.

GIVEN: 63.15% C, 5.30% H, and 31.55% O.

FIND: empirical formula

SOLUTION

In a 100 g sample:

63.15 g C

5.30 g H

31.55 g O

$$63.15 \text{ g C} \times \frac{1 \text{ mol C}}{12.01 \text{ g C}} = 5.258 \text{ mol C}$$

$$5.30 \text{ g H} \times \frac{1 \text{ mol H}}{1.01 \text{ g H}} = 5.25 \text{ mol H}$$

$$31.55 \text{ g O} \times \frac{1 \text{ mol O}}{16.00 \text{ g O}} = 1.972 \text{ mol O}$$

$$C_{5.258}H_{5.25}O_{1.972}$$

$$C_{\frac{5.258}{1.972}} H_{\frac{5.25}{1.972}} O_{\frac{1.972}{1.972}} \longrightarrow C_{2.67}H_{2.66}O_1$$

$$C_{2.67}H_{2.66}O_1 \times 3 \longrightarrow C_8H_8O_3$$

The correct empirical formula is $C_8H_8O_3$.

LO: Calculate a molecular formula from an empirical formula and molar mass (Section 6.9).

EXAMPLE 6.22   CALCULATING A MOLECULAR FORMULA FROM AN EMPIRICAL FORMULA AND MOLAR MASS

Acetylene, a gas used in welding torches, has the empirical formula CH and a molar mass of 26.04 g/mol. Find its molecular formula.

SORT

You are given the empirical formula and molar mass of acetylene and asked to find the molecular formula.

GIVEN: empirical formula = CH

molar mass = 26.04 g/mol

FIND: molecular formula

STRATEGIZE

In the first step, use the molar mass (which is given) and the empirical formula molar mass (which you can calculate based on the empirical formula) to determine n (the integer by which you must multiply the empirical formula to arrive at the molecular formula).

In the second step, multiply the coefficients in the empirical formula by n to arrive at the molecular formula.

SOLVE

Follow the solution map to solve the problem. Calculate the empirical formula molar mass, which is the sum of the masses of all the atoms in the empirical formula.

Next, find n, the ratio of the molar mass to empirical mass.

Finally, multiply the empirical formula by n to get the molecular formula.

CHECK

Check your answer. Does the answer make physical sense?

SOLUTION MAP

$$n = \frac{\text{Molar mass}}{\text{Empirical formula molar mass}}$$

Molecular formula = Empirical formula $\times n$

SOLUTION

Empirical formula molar mass

$$= 12.01 + 1.01$$

$$= 13.02 \text{ g/mol}$$

$$n = \frac{\text{Molar mass}}{\text{Empirical formula molar mass}}$$

$$= \frac{26.04 \text{ g/mol}}{13.02 \text{ g/mol}} = 2$$

Molecular formula = CH $\times$ 2 $\longrightarrow$ C_2H_2

The answer makes physical sense because the formula subscripts are all integers. Any answer with fractional integers is incorrrect.

KEY TERMS

Avogadro's number [6.3]
empirical formula [6.8]

empirical formula molar
mass [6.9]

mass percent (composition)
[6.6]

molar mass [6.3]
mole (mol) [6.3]
molecular formula [6.8]

EXERCISES

QUESTIONS

1. Why is chemical composition important?
2. How can you efficiently determine the number of atoms in a sample of an element? Why is counting them not an option?
3. How many atoms are in 1 mol of atoms?
4. How many molecules are in 1 mol of molecules?
5. What is the mass of 1 mol of atoms for an element?
6. What is the mass of 1 mol of molecules for a compound?
7. What is the mass of 1 mol of atoms of each element?
   (a) P   (b) Pt   (c) C   (d) Cr
8. What is the mass of 1 mol of molecules of each compound?
   (a) CO_2 (b) CH_2Cl_2 (c) $C_{12}H_{22}O_{11}$ (d) SO_2
9. The subscripts in a chemical formula give relationships between moles of the constituent elements and moles of the compound. Explain why these subscripts *do not* give

relationships between grams of the constituent elements and grams of the compound.
10. Write the conversion factors between moles of each constituent element and moles of the compound for $C_{12}H_{22}O_{11}$.
11. You can use mass percent composition as a conversion factor between grams of a constituent element and grams of the compound. Write the conversion factor (including units) inherent in each mass percent composition.
   (a) Water is 11.19% hydrogen by mass.
   (b) Fructose, also known as fruit sugar, is 53.29% oxygen by mass.
   (c) Octane, a component of gasoline, is 84.12% carbon by mass.
   (d) Ethanol, the alcohol in alcoholic beverages, is 52.14% carbon by mass.

12. What is the mathematical formula for calculating mass percent composition from a chemical formula?

13. How are the empirical formula and the molecular formula of a compound related?

14. Why is it important to be able to calculate an empirical formula from experimental data?

15. What is the empirical formula mass of a compound?

16. How are the molar mass and empirical formula mass for a compound related?

PROBLEMS

THE MOLE CONCEPT

17. How many mercury atoms are in 5.8 mol of mercury?

18. How many moles of gold atoms do 3.45×10^{24} gold atoms constitute?

19. How many atoms are in each elemental sample?
  (a) 3.4 mol Cu   **(b)** 9.7×10^{-3} mol C
  (c) 22.9 mol Hg   **(d)** 0.215 mol Na

20. How many moles of atoms are in each elemental sample?
  (a) 4.6×10^{24} Pb atoms   **(b)** 2.87×10^{22} He atoms
  (c) 7.91×10^{23} K atoms   **(d)** 4.41×10^{21} Ca atoms

21. Complete the table.

Element	Moles	Number of Atoms
Ne	0.552	_____
Ar	_____	3.25×10^{24}
Xe	1.78	_____
He	_____	1.08×10^{20}

22. Complete the table.

Element	Moles	Number of Atoms
Cr	_____	9.61×10^{23}
Fe	1.52×10^{-5}	_____
Ti	0.0365	_____
Hg	_____	1.09×10^{23}

23. Consider these definitions.
  1 doz = 12   1 gross = 144
  1 ream = 500   1 mol = 6.022×10^{23}

Suppose you have 872 sheets of paper. How many _____ of paper sheets do you have?
  (a) dozens   **(b)** gross   **(c)** reams   **(d)** moles

24. A pure copper penny contains approximately 3.0×10^{22} copper atoms. Use the definitions in the previous problem to determine how many _____ of copper atoms are in a penny.
  (a) dozens   **(b)** gross   **(c)** reams   **(d)** moles

25. How many moles of tin atoms are in a pure tin cup with a mass of 38.1 g?

26. A lead fishing weight contains 0.12 mol of lead atoms. What is its mass?

27. A pure gold coin contains 0.145 mol of gold. What is its mass?

28. A helium balloon contains 0.46 g of helium. How many moles of helium does it contain?

29. How many moles of atoms are in each elemental sample?
  (a) 1.34 g Zn   **(b)** 24.9 g Ar
  (c) 72.5 g Ta   **(d)** 0.0223 g Li

30. What is the mass in grams of each elemental sample?
  (a) 6.64 mol W   **(b)** 0.581 mol Ba
  (c) 68.1 mol Xe   **(d)** 1.57 mol S

31. Complete the table.

Element	Moles	Mass
Ne	_____	22.5 g
Ar	0.117	_____
Xe	_____	1.00 kg
He	1.44×10^{-4}	_____

32. Complete the table.

Element	Moles	Mass
Cr	0.00442	_____
Fe	_____	73.5 mg
Ti	1.009×10^{-3}	_____
Hg	_____	1.78 kg

33. A pure silver ring contains 0.0134 mmol (millimol) Ag. How many silver atoms does it contain?

34. A pure gold ring contains 0.0102 mmol (millimol) Au. How many gold atoms does it contain?

35. How many aluminum atoms are in 3.78 g of aluminum?

36. What is the mass of 4.91×10^{21} platinum atoms?

37. How many atoms are in each elemental sample?
(a) 16.9 g Sr
(b) 26.1 g Fe
(c) 8.55 g Bi
(d) 38.2 g P

38. Calculate the mass in grams of each elemental sample.
(a) 1.32×10^{20} uranium atoms
(b) 2.55×10^{22} zinc atoms
(c) 4.11×10^{23} lead atoms
(d) 6.59×10^{24} silicon atoms

39. How many carbon atoms are in a diamond (pure carbon) with a mass of 38 mg?

40. How many helium atoms are in a helium blimp containing 495 kg of helium?

41. How many titanium atoms are in a pure titanium bicycle frame with a mass of 1.28 kg?

42. How many copper atoms are in a pure copper statue with a mass of 133 kg?

43. Complete the table.

Element	Mass	Moles	Number of Atoms
Na	38.5 mg	___	___
C	___	1.12	___
V	___	___	214
Hg	1.44 kg	___	___

44. Complete the table.

Element	Mass	Moles	Number of Atoms
Pt	___	0.0449	___
Fe	___	___	1.14×10^{25}
Ti	23.8 mg	___	___
Hg	___	2.05	___

45. Which sample contains the greatest number of atoms?
(a) 27.2 g Cr   (b) 55.1 g Ti   (c) 205 g Pb

46. Which sample contains the greatest number of atoms?
(a) 10.0 g He   (b) 25.0 g Ne   (c) 115 g Xe

47. Determine the number of moles of molecules (or formula units) in each sample.
(a) 38.2 g sodium chloride
(b) 36.5 g nitrogen monoxide
(c) 4.25 kg carbon dioxide
(d) 2.71 mg carbon tetrachloride

48. Determine the mass of each sample.
(a) 1.32 mol carbon tetrafluoride
(b) 0.555 mol magnesium fluoride
(c) 1.29 mmol carbon disulfide
(d) 1.89 kmol sulfur trioxide

49. Complete the table.

Compound	Mass	Moles	Number of Molecules
H_2O	112 kg	___	___
N_2O	6.33 g	___	___
SO_2	___	2.44	___
CH_2Cl_2	___	0.0643	___

50. Complete the table.

Compound	Mass	Moles	Number of Molecules
CO_2	___	0.0153	___
CO	___	0.0150	___
BrI	23.8 mg	___	___
CF_2Cl_2	1.02 kg	___	___

51. A mothball, composed of naphthalene ($C_{10}H_8$), has a mass of 1.32 g. How many naphthalene molecules does it contain?

52. Calculate the mass in grams of a single water molecule.

53. How many molecules are in each sample?
(a) 3.5 g H_2O
(b) 56.1 g N_2
(c) 89 g CCl_4
(d) 19 g $C_6H_{12}O_6$

54. Calculate the mass in grams of each sample.
(a) 5.94×10^{20} H_2O_2 molecules
(b) 2.8×10^{22} SO_2 molecules
(c) 4.5×10^{25} O_3 molecules
(d) 9.85×10^{19} CH_4 molecules

55. A sugar crystal contains approximately 1.8×10^{17} sucrose ($C_{12}H_{22}O_{11}$) molecules. What is its mass in milligrams?

56. A salt crystal has a mass of 0.12 mg. How many NaCl formula units does it contain?

57. How much money, in dollars, does one mole of pennies represent? If this amount of money were evenly distributed to the entire world's population (about 7.1 billion people), how much would each person get? Would each person be a millionaire? Billionaire? Trillionaire?

58. A typical dust particle has a diameter of about 10.0 μm. If 1.0 mol of dust particles were laid end to end along the equator, how many times would they encircle the planet? The circumference of the Earth at the equator is 40,076 km.

CHEMICAL FORMULAS AS CONVERSION FACTORS

59. Determine the number of moles of Cl in 2.7 mol $CaCl_2$.

60. How many moles of O are in 12.4 mol $Fe(NO_3)_3$?

61. Which sample contains the greatest number of moles of O?
(a) 2.3 mol H_2O (b) 1.2 mol H_2O_2
(c) 0.9 mol $NaNO_3$ (d) 0.5 mol $Ca(NO_3)_2$

62. Which sample contains the greatest number of moles of Cl?
(a) 3.8 mol HCl   (b) 1.7 mol CH_2Cl_2
(c) 4.2 mol $NaClO_3$ (d) 2.2 mol $Mg(ClO_4)_2$

63. Determine the number of moles of C in each sample.
(a) 2.5 mol CH_4 (b) 0.115 mol C_2H_6
(c) 5.67 mol C_4H_{10} (d) 25.1 mol C_8H_{18}

64. Determine the number of moles of H in each sample.
(a) 4.67 mol H_2O (b) 8.39 mol NH_3
(c) 0.117 mol N_2H_4 (d) 35.8 mol $C_{10}H_{22}$

65. For each set of molecular models, write a relationship between moles of hydrogen and moles of molecules. Then determine the total number of hydrogen atoms present. (H—white; O—red; C—black; N—blue)

(a)   (b)   (c)

66. For each set of molecular models, write a relationship between moles of oxygen and moles of molecules. Then determine the total number of oxygen atoms present. (H—white; O—red; C—black; S—yellow)

(a)   (b)   (c)

67. How many grams of Cl are in 38.0 g of each sample of chlorofluorocarbons (CFCs)?
(a) CF_2Cl_2
(b) $CFCl_3$
(c) $C_2F_3Cl_3$
(d) CF_3Cl

68. Calculate the number of grams of sodium in 1.00 g of each sodium-containing food additive.
(a) NaCl (table salt)
(b) Na_3PO_4 (sodium phosphate)
(c) $NaC_7H_5O_2$ (sodium benzoate)
(d) $Na_2C_6H_6O_7$ (sodium hydrogen citrate)

69. Iron is found in Earth's crust as several different iron compounds. Calculate the mass (in kg) of each compound that contains 1.0×10^3 kg of iron.
(a) Fe_2O_3 (hematite)
(b) Fe_3O_4 (magnetite)
(c) $FeCO_3$ (siderite)

70. Lead is found in Earth's crust as several lead compounds. Calculate the mass (in kg) of each compound that contains 1.0×10^3 kg of lead.
(a) PbS (galena)
(b) $PbCO_3$ (cerussite)
(c) $PbSO_4$ (anglesite)

MASS PERCENT COMPOSITION

71. A 2.45-g sample of strontium completely reacts with oxygen to form 2.89 g of strontium oxide. Use this data to calculate the mass percent composition of strontium in strontium oxide.

72. A 4.78-g sample of aluminum completely reacts with oxygen to form 6.67 g of aluminum oxide. Use this data to calculate the mass percent composition of aluminum in aluminum oxide.

73. A 1.912-g sample of calcium chloride is decomposed into its constituent elements and found to contain 0.690 g Ca and 1.222 g Cl. Calculate the mass percent composition of Ca and Cl in calcium chloride.

74. A 0.45-g sample of aspirin is decomposed into its constituent elements and found to contain 0.27 g C, 0.020 g H, and 0.16 g O. Calculate the mass percent composition of C, H, and O in aspirin.

75. Copper(II) fluoride contains 37.42% F by mass. Use this percentage to calculate the mass of fluorine in grams contained in 28.5 g of copper(II) fluoride.

76. Silver chloride, used in silver plating, contains 75.27% Ag. Calculate the mass of silver chloride in grams required to make 4.8 g of silver plating.

77. In small amounts, the fluoride ion (often consumed as NaF) prevents tooth decay. According to the American Dental Association, an adult female should consume 3.0 mg of fluorine per day. Calculate the amount of sodium fluoride (45.24% F) that a woman should consume to get the recommended amount of fluorine.

78. The iodide ion, usually consumed as potassium iodide, is a dietary mineral essential to good nutrition. In countries where potassium iodide is added to salt, iodine deficiency or goiter has been almost completely eliminated. The recommended daily allowance (RDA) for iodine is 150 μg/day. How much potassium iodide (76.45% I) should you consume to meet the RDA?

MASS PERCENT COMPOSITION FROM CHEMICAL FORMULA

79. Calculate the mass percent composition of nitrogen in each compound.
(a) N_2O (b) NO (c) NO_2 (d) N_2O_5

80. Calculate the mass percent composition of carbon in each compound.
(a) C_2H_2 (b) C_3H_6 (c) C_2H_6 (d) C_2H_6O

81. Calculate the mass percent composition of each element in each compound.
(a) $C_2H_4O_2$ (b) CH_2O_2 (c) C_3H_9N (d) $C_4H_{12}N_2$

82. Calculate the mass percent composition of each element in each compound.
(a) $FeCl_3$ (b) TiO_2 (c) H_3PO_4 (d) HNO_3

83. Calculate the mass percent composition of O in each compound.
(a) calcium nitrate   (b) iron(II) sulfate
(c) carbon dioxide CO_2

84. Calculate the mass percent composition of Cl in each compound.
(a) carbon tetrachloride   (b) calcium hypochlorite
(c) perchloric acid

85. Various iron ores have different amounts of iron per kilogram of ore. Calculate the mass percent composition of iron for each iron ore: Fe_2O_3 (hematite), Fe_3O_4 (magnetite), $FeCO_3$ (siderite). Which ore has the highest iron content?

86. Plants need nitrogen to grow, so many fertilizers consist of nitrogen-containing compounds. Calculate the mass percent composition of nitrogen in each fertilizer: NH_3, $CO(NH_2)_2$, NH_4NO_3, $(NH_4)_2SO_4$. Which fertilizer has the highest nitrogen content?

CALCULATING EMPIRICAL FORMULAS

87. A compound containing nitrogen and oxygen is decomposed in the laboratory and produces 1.78 g of nitrogen and 4.05 g of oxygen. Calculate the empirical formula of the compound.

88. A compound containing selenium and fluorine is decomposed in the laboratory and produces 2.231 g of selenium and 3.221 g of fluorine. Calculate the empirical formula of the compound.

89. Samples of several compounds are decomposed, and the masses of their constituent elements are measured. Calculate the empirical formula for each compound.
(a) 1.245 g Ni, 5.381 g I   (b) 1.443 g Se, 5.841 g Br
(c) 2.128 g Be, 7.557 g S, 15.107 g O

90. Samples of several compounds are decomposed, and the masses of their constituent elements are measured. Calculate the empirical formula for each compound.
(a) 2.677 g Ba, 3.115 g Br   (b) 1.651 g Ag, 0.1224 g O
(c) 0.672 g Co, 0.569 g As, 0.486 g O

91. The rotten smell of a decaying animal carcass is partially due to a nitrogen-containing compound called putrescine. Elemental analysis of putrescine indicates that it consists of 54.50% C, 13.73% H, and 31.77% N. Calculate the empirical formula of putrescine.

92. Citric acid, the compound responsible for the sour taste of lemons, has the elemental composition: C, 37.51%; H, 4.20%; O, 58.29%. Calculate the empirical formula of citric acid.

93. These compounds are found in many natural flavors and scents. Calculate the empirical formula for each compound.
(a) ethyl butyrate (pineapple oil): C, 62.04%; H, 10.41%; O, 27.55%
(b) methyl butyrate (apple flavor): C, 58.80%; H, 9.87%; O, 31.33%
(c) benzyl acetate (oil of jasmine): C, 71.98%; H, 6.71%; O, 21.31%

94. Calculate the empirical formula for each over-the-counter pain reliever
(a) acetaminophen (Tylenol): C, 63.56%; H, 6.00%; N, 9.27%; O, 21.17%
(b) naproxen (Aleve): C, 73.03%; H, 6.13%; O, 20.84%

95. A 1.45-g sample of phosphorus burns in air and forms 2.57 g of a phosphorus oxide. Calculate the empirical formula of the oxide.

96. A 2.241-g sample of nickel reacts with oxygen to form 2.852 g of the metal oxide. Calculate the empirical formula of the oxide.

97. A 0.77-mg sample of nitrogen reacts with chlorine to form 6.61 mg of the chloride. What is the empirical formula of the nitrogen chloride?

98. A 45.2-mg sample of phosphorus reacts with selenium to form 131.6 mg of the selenide. What is the empirical formula of the phosphorus selenide?

CALCULATING MOLECULAR FORMULAS

99. A compound containing carbon and hydrogen has a molar mass of 56.11 g/mol and an empirical formula of CH_2. Determine its molecular formula.

100. A compound containing phosphorus and oxygen has a molar mass of 219.9 g/mol and an empirical formula of P_2O_3. Determine its molecular formula.

101. The molar masses and empirical formulas of several compounds containing carbon and chlorine are listed here. Find the molecular formula of each compound.
(a) 284.77 g/mol, CCl (b) 131.39 g/mol, C_2HCl_3
(c) 181.44 g/mol, C_2HCl

102. The molar masses and empirical formulas of several compounds containing carbon and nitrogen are listed here. Find the molecular formula of each compound.
(a) 163.26 g/mol, $C_{11}H_{17}N$ (b) 186.24 g/mol, C_6H_7N
(c) 312.29 g/mol, C_3H_2N

CUMULATIVE PROBLEMS

103. A pure copper cube has an edge length of 1.42 cm. How many copper atoms does it contain? (volume of a cube = (edge length)^3; density of copper = 8.96 g/cm^3)

104. A pure silver sphere has a radius of 0.886 cm. How many silver atoms does it contain? (volume of a sphere = $\frac{4}{3}\pi r^3$; density of silver = 10.5 g/cm^3)

105. A drop of water has a volume of approximately 0.05 mL. How many water molecules does it contain? (density of water = 1.0 g/cm^3)

106. Fingernail–polish remover is primarily acetone (C_3H_6O). How many acetone molecules are in a bottle of acetone with a volume of 325 mL? (density of acetone = 0.788 g/cm^3)

107. Complete the table.

Substance	Mass	Moles	Number of Particles (atoms or molecules)
Ar	——	4.5×10^{-4}	——
NO_2	——	——	1.09×10^{20}
K	22.4 mg	——	——
C_8H_{18}	3.76 kg	——	——

108. Complete the table.

Substance	Mass	Moles	Number of Particles (atoms or molecules)
$C_6H_{12}O_6$	15.8 g	——	——
Pb	——	——	9.04×10^{21}
CF_4	22.5 mg	——	——
C	——	0.0388	

109. Determine the chemical formula of each compound and refer to the formula to calculate the mass percent composition of each constituent element.
(a) copper(II) iodide (b) sodium nitrate
(c) lead(II) sulfate (d) calcium fluoride

110. Determine the chemical formula of each compound and refer to the formula to calculate the mass percent composition of each constituent element.
(a) nitrogen triiodide (b) xenon tetrafluoride
(c) phosphorus trichloride (d) carbon monoxide

111. The rock in a particular iron ore deposit contains 78% Fe_2O_3 by mass. How many kilograms of the rock must a mining company process to obtain 1.0×10^3 kg of iron?

112. The rock in a lead ore deposit contains 84% PbS by mass. How many kilograms of the rock must a mining company process to obtain 1.0 kg of Pb?

113. A leak in the air conditioning system of an office building releases 12 kg of CHF_2Cl per month. If the leak continues, how many kilograms of Cl are emitted into the atmosphere each year?

114. A leak in the air conditioning system of an older car releases 55 g of CF_2Cl_2 per month. How much Cl is emitted into the atmosphere each year by this car?

115. Hydrogen is a possible future fuel. However, elemental hydrogen is rare, so it must be obtained from a hydrogen-containing compound such as water. If hydrogen were obtained from water, how much hydrogen, in grams, could be obtained from 1.0 L of water? (density of water = 1.0 g/cm^3)

116. Hydrogen, a possible future fuel mentioned in Problem 115, can also be obtained from ethanol. Ethanol can be made from the fermentation of crops such as corn. How much hydrogen, in grams, could be obtained from 1.0 kg of ethanol (C_2H_5OH)?

117. Complete the table of compounds that contain only carbon and hydrogen.

Formula	Molar Mass	% C (by mass)	% H (by mass)
C_2H_4	___	___	___
___	58.12	82.66%	___
C_4H_8	___	___	___
___	44.09	___	18.29%

118. Complete the table of compounds that contain only chromium and oxygen.

Formula	Name	Molar Mass	% Cr (by mass)	% O (by mass)
___	Chromium (III) oxide	___	___	___
___	___	84.00	61.90%	___
___	___	100.00	___	48.00%

119. Butanedione, a component of butter and body odor, has a cheesy smell. Elemental analysis of butanedione gave the mass percent composition: C, 55.80%; H, 7.03%; O, 37.17%. The molar mass of butanedione is 86.09 g/mol. Determine the molecular formula of butanedione.

120. Caffeine, a stimulant found in coffee and soda, has the mass percent composition: C, 49.48%; H, 5.19%; N, 28.85%; O, 16.48%. The molar mass of caffeine is 194.19 g/mol. Find the molecular formula of caffeine.

121. Nicotine, a stimulant found in tobacco, has the mass percent composition: C, 74.03%; H, 8.70%; N, 17.27%. The molar mass of nicotine is 162.26 g/mol. Find the molecular formula of nicotine.

122. Estradiol is a female sexual hormone that causes maturation and maintenance of the female reproductive system. Elemental analysis of estradiol gave the mass percent composition: C, 79.37%; H, 8.88%; O, 11.75%. The molar mass of estradiol is 272.37 g/mol. Find the molecular formula of estradiol.

123. A sample contains both KBr and KI in unknown quantities. If the sample has a total mass of 5.00 g and contains 1.51 g K, what are the percentages of KBr and KI in the sample by mass?

124. A sample contains both CO_2 and Ne in unknown quantities. If the sample contains a combined total of 1.75 mol and has a total mass of 65.3 g, what are the percentages of CO_2 and Ne in the sample by mole?

125. Ethanethiol (C_2H_6S) is a compound with a disagreeable odor that is used to impart an odor to natural gas. When ethanethiol is burned, the sulfur reacts with oxygen to form SO_2. What mass of SO_2 forms upon the complete combustion of 28.7 g of ethanethiol?

126. Methanethiol (CH_4S) has a disagreeable odor and is often a component of bad breath. When methanethiol is burned, the sulfur reacts with oxygen to form SO_2. What mass of SO_2 forms upon the complete combustion of 1.89 g of methanethiol?

127. An iron ore contains 38% Fe_2O_3 by mass. What is the maximum mass of iron that can be recovered from 10.0 kg of this ore?

128. Seawater contains approximately 3.5% NaCl by mass and has a density of 1.02 g/mL. What volume of seawater contains 1.0 g of sodium?

HIGHLIGHT PROBLEMS

129. You can use the concepts in this chapter to obtain an estimate of the number of atoms in the universe. These steps will guide you through this calculation.
   (a) Begin by calculating the number of atoms in the sun. Assume that the sun is pure hydrogen with a density of 1.4 g/cm³. The radius of the sun is 7×10^8 m, and the volume of a sphere is $V = \frac{4}{3}\pi r^3$.
   (b) The sun is an average–sized star, and stars are believed to compose most of the mass of the visible universe (planets are so small they can be ignored), so we can estimate the number of atoms in a galaxy by assuming that every star in the galaxy has the same number of atoms as our sun. The Milky Way galaxy is believed to contain 1×10^{11} stars. Use your answer from part (a) to calculate the number of atoms in the Milky Way galaxy.

   (c) Astronomers estimate that the universe contains approximately 1×10^{11} galaxies. If each of these galaxies contains the same number of atoms as the Milky Way galaxy, what is the total number of atoms in the universe?

▲ Our sun is one of the 100 billion stars in the Milky Way galaxy. The universe is estimated to contain about 100 billion galaxies.

130. Because of increasing evidence of damage to the ozone layer, chlorofluorocarbon (CFC) production was banned in 1996. However, there are about 100 million auto air conditioners that still use CFC-12 (CF_2Cl_2). These air conditioners are recharged from stockpiled supplies of CFC-12. If each of the 100 million automobiles contains 1.1 kg of CFC-12 and leaks 25% of its CFC-12 into the atmosphere per year, how much Cl in kilograms is added to the atmosphere each year by auto air conditioners? (Assume two significant figures in your calculations.)

▲ The ozone hole over Antarctica on September 24, 2009. The dark blue and purple areas over the South Pole represent depressed ozone concentrations.

131. In 1996, the media reported that possible evidence of life on Mars was found on a meteorite called Allan Hills 84001 (AH 84001). The meteorite was discovered in Antarctica in 1984 and is believed to have originated on Mars. Elemental analysis of substances within its crevices revealed carbon-containing compounds that normally derive only from living organisms. Suppose that one of those compounds had a molar mass of 202.23 g/mol and the mass percent composition: C, 95.02%; H, 4.98%. What is the molecular formula for the carbon-containing compound?

▲ The Allan Hills 84001 meteorite. Elemental analysis of the substances within the crevices of this meteorite revealed carbon-containing compounds that normally originate from living organisms.

QUESTIONS FOR GROUP WORK

Discuss these questions with the group and record your consensus answer.

132. Using grammatically correct English sentences, describe the relationship between the number 6.022×10^{23} and the gram.

133. Imagine that all our balances displayed mass in units of slugs instead of grams. Would we still want to use the number 6.022×10^{23} for Avogadro's number? Why or why not? If not, what number would we want to use instead? (A slug is equal to 14,954 g.)

134. Amylose is a "polysaccharide" that plants use to store energy. It is made of repeating subunits of $C_6H_{10}O_5$. A particular amylose molecule has 2537 of these subunits, what is its molecular formula? What is its molar mass? What is the empirical formula for amylose?

▶Answers to Skillbuilder Exercises

Skillbuilder 6.1	5.32×10^{22} Au atoms	**Skillbuilder 6.8**	8.6 g Na
Skillbuilder 6.2	89.2 g S	**Skillbuilder 6.9**	53.28% O
Skillbuilder 6.3	8.17 g He	**Skillbuilder 6.10**	CH_2O
Skillbuilder 6.4	2.56×10^{-2} mol NO_2	**Skillbuilder 6.11**	$C_{13}H_{18}O_2$
Skillbuilder 6.5	1.22×10^{23} H_2O molecules	**Skillbuilder 6.12**	CuO
Skillbuilder 6.6	5.6 mol O	**Skillbuilder 6.13**	C_4H_{10}
Skillbuilder 6.7	3.3 g O	**Skillbuilder Plus, p. 189**	$C_2H_8N_2$
Skillbuilder Plus, p. 180	4.04 g O		

▶Answers to Conceptual Checkpoints

6.1 (a) $3.5 \text{ lb} \times \dfrac{1 \text{ doz}}{0.50 \text{ lb}} \times \dfrac{12 \text{ nails}}{\text{doz}} = 84 \text{ nails}$

6.2 (a) The mole is a counting unit; it represents a definite number (Avogadro's number, 6.022×10^{23}). Therefore, a given number of atoms always represents a precise number of moles, regardless of what atom is involved. Atoms of different elements have different masses. So if samples of different elements have the same mass, they *cannot* contain the same number of atoms or moles.

6.3 (b) Because carbon has lower molar mass than cobalt or lead, a one-gram sample of carbon contains more atoms than one gram of cobalt or lead.

6.4 Sample A would have the greatest number of molecules. Sample A has a lower molar mass than sample B, so a given mass of sample A has more moles and therefore more molecules than the same mass of sample B.

6.5 (c) 1.0 mole of F_2 contains 2.0 mol of F atoms. The other two options each contain less than two moles of F atoms.

6.6 (b) This compound has the highest ratio of oxygen atoms to chromium atoms and therefore has the greatest mass percent of oxygen.

▲ A clay volcano can be made to erupt by combining vinegar and baking soda, which react to produce the bubbling and splattering.

Chemical Reactions

7

"Chemistry . . . is one of the broadest branches of science if for no other reason than, when we think about it, everything is chemistry."—Luciano Caglioti (1933–)

CHAPTER OUTLINE

7.1   Grade School Volcanoes, Automobiles, and Laundry Detergents

Did you ever make a clay volcano in grade school that erupted when filled with vinegar and baking soda? Have you pushed the gas pedal of a car and felt the acceleration as the car moved forward? Have you wondered why laundry detergents work better than hand soap to clean your clothes? Each of these processes involves a *chemical reaction*—the transformation of one or more substances into different substances.

In the classic grade school volcano, the baking soda (which is sodium bicarbonate) reacts with acetic acid in the vinegar to form carbon dioxide gas, water, and sodium acetate. The newly formed carbon dioxide bubbles out of the mixture, causing the eruption. Reactions that occur in liquids and form a gas are *gas evolution reactions*. A similar reaction causes the fizzing of antacids such as Alka-Seltzer™.

> Hydrocarbons are covered in detail in Chapter 18.

When you drive a car, hydrocarbons such as octane (in gasoline) react with oxygen from the air to form carbon dioxide gas and water (▼ Figure 7.1). This reaction

Octane
(a component of gasoline)

Oxygen

Auto engine

Carbon dioxide

Water

▲ **FIGURE 7.1   A combustion reaction**   In an automobile engine, hydrocarbons such as octane (C_8H_{18}) from gasoline combine with oxygen from the air and react to form carbon dioxide and water.

Soap in
pure water

Soap in
hard water

▲ **FIGURE 7.2 Soap and water**
Soap forms suds with pure water
(left), but reacts with the ions in hard
water (right) to form a gray residue
that adheres to clothes.

produces heat, which expands the gases in the car's cylinders, accelerating it forward. Reactions such as this one—in which a substance reacts with oxygen, emitting heat and forming one or more oxygen-containing compounds—are *combustion reactions*. Combustion reactions are a subcategory of *oxidation–reduction reactions*, in which electrons are transferred from one substance to another. The formation of rust and the dulling of automobile paint are other examples of oxidation–reduction reactions.

Laundry detergent works better than hand soap to wash clothes because it contains substances that soften hard water. Hard water contains dissolved calcium (Ca^{2+}) and magnesium (Mg^{2+}) ions. These ions interfere with the cleaning action of soap by reacting with it to form a gray, slimy substance called *curd* or *soap scum* (◄ Figure 7.2). If you have ever washed your clothes in ordinary soap, you may have noticed gray soap scum residue on your clothes.

Laundry detergents inhibit curd formation because they contain substances such as sodium carbonate (Na_2CO_3) that remove calcium and magnesium ions from the water. When sodium carbonate dissolves in water, it *dissociates*, or separates into sodium ions (Na^+) and carbonate ions (CO_3^{2-}). The dissolved carbonate ions react with calcium and magnesium ions in the hard water to form solid calcium carbonate ($CaCO_3$) and solid magnesium carbonate ($MgCO_3$). These solids simply settle to the bottom of the laundry mixture, resulting in the removal of the ions from the water. In other words, laundry detergents contain substances that react with the ions in hard water to immobilize them. Reactions such as these—that form solid substances in water—are *precipitation reactions*. Precipitation reactions are also used to remove dissolved toxic metals in industrial wastes.

Chemical reactions take place all around us and even inside us. They are involved in many of the products we use daily and in many of our experiences. Chemical reactions can be relatively simple, like the combination of hydrogen and oxygen to form water, or they can be complex, like the synthesis of a protein molecule from thousands of simpler molecules. In some cases, such as the neutralization reaction that occurs in a swimming pool when acid is added to adjust the water's acidity level, chemical reactions are not noticeable to the naked eye. In other cases, such as the combustion reaction that produces a pillar of smoke and fire under a rocket during liftoff, chemical reactions are very obvious. In all cases, however, chemical reactions produce changes in the arrangements of the molecules and atoms that compose matter. Often, these molecular changes cause macroscopic changes that we can directly experience.

7.2 Evidence of a Chemical Reaction

LO: Identify a chemical reaction.

If we could see the atoms and molecules that compose matter, we could easily identify a chemical reaction. Do atoms combine with other atoms to form compounds? Do new molecules form? Do the original molecules decompose? Do atoms in one molecule change places with atoms in another? If the answer to one or more of these questions is yes, a chemical reaction has occurred.

Although we can't see atoms, many chemical reactions do produce easily detectable changes as they occur. For example, when the color-causing molecules in a brightly colored shirt decompose with repeated exposure to sunlight, the color of the shirt fades. Similarly, when the molecules embedded in the plastic of a child's temperature-sensitive spoon transform upon warming, the color of the spoon changes. These *color changes* are evidence that a chemical reaction has occurred.

Other changes that identify chemical reactions include the *formation of a solid* (► Figure 7.3) or *the formation of a gas* (► Figure 7.4). Dropping Alka-Seltzer tablets into water or combining baking soda and vinegar (as in our opening example of the grade school volcano) are both good examples of chemical reactions that produce a gas—the gas is visible as bubbles in the liquid.

Solid formation

▲ **FIGURE 7.3   A precipitation reaction**   The formation of a solid in a previously clear solution is evidence of a chemical reaction.

Gas formation

▲ **FIGURE 7.4   A gas evolution reaction**   The formation of a gas is evidence of a chemical reaction.

Recall from Section 3.9 that a reaction that emits heat is an *exothermic* reaction and one that absorbs heat is an *endothermic* reaction.

Heat absorption or *emission*, as well as *light emission*, are also evidence of reactions. For example, a natural gas flame produces heat and light. A chemical cold pack becomes cold when the plastic barrier separating two substances is broken. Both of these changes suggest that a chemical reaction is occurring.

Color change

▲ A child's temperature-sensitive spoon changes color upon warming due to a reaction induced by the higher temperature.

Heat absorption

▲ A change in temperature due to absorption or emission of heat is evidence of a chemical reaction. This chemical cold pack becomes cold when the barrier separating two substances is broken.

▲ **FIGURE 7.5   Boiling: A physical change**   When water boils, bubbles are formed and a gas is evolved. However, no chemical change has occurred because the gas, like the liquid water, is also composed of water molecules.

While these changes provide evidence of a chemical reaction, they are not *definitive* evidence. Only chemical analysis showing that the initial substances have changed into other substances conclusively proves that a chemical reaction has occurred. We can be fooled. For example, when water boils, bubbles form but no chemical reaction has occurred. Boiling water forms gaseous steam, but both water and steam are composed of water molecules—no chemical change has occurred (◀ Figure 7.5). On the other hand, chemical reactions may occur without any obvious signs, yet chemical analysis may show that a reaction has indeed occurred. The changes occurring at the atomic and molecular level determine whether a chemical reaction has taken place.

In summary, each of the following provides evidence of a chemical reaction.

- a *color change*

- the *emission of light*

- the *formation of a solid* in a previously clear (unclouded) solution

- the *emission* or *absorption of heat*

- the *formation of a gas* when we add a substance to a solution

---

EXAMPLE 7.1   **EVIDENCE OF A CHEMICAL REACTION**

Which changes involve a chemical reaction? Explain your answers.

(a) ice melting upon warming
(b) an electric current passing through water, resulting in the formation of hydrogen and oxygen gas that appears as bubbles rising in the water
(c) iron rusting
(d) bubbles forming when a soda can is opened

SOLUTION
(a) not a chemical reaction; melting ice forms water, but both the ice and water are composed of water molecules.
(b) chemical reaction; water decomposes into hydrogen and oxygen, as evidenced by the bubbling.
(c) chemical reaction; iron changes into iron oxide, changing color in the process.
(d) not a chemical reaction; even though there is bubbling, it is just carbon dioxide coming out of the liquid.

▶**SKILLBUILDER 7.1 | Evidence of a Chemical Reaction**

Which changes involve a chemical reaction? Explain your answers.

(a) butane burning in a butane lighter
(b) butane evaporating out of a butane lighter
(c) wood burning
(d) dry ice subliming

▶**FOR MORE PRACTICE**   Example 7.16; Problems 25, 26, 27, 28, 29, 30.

✓ **CONCEPTUAL CHECKPOINT 7.1**

These images portray molecular views of various substances before and after a change. Determine whether a chemical reaction has occurred in each case.

(a)

(b)

(c)

7.3 The Chemical Equation

LO: Identify balanced chemical equations.

Recall from Section 3.6 that we represent chemical reactions with *chemical equations*. For example, the reaction occurring in a natural-gas flame, such as the flame on a kitchen stove, is methane (CH_4) reacting with oxygen (O_2) to form carbon dioxide (CO_2) and water (H_2O). We represent this reaction with the equation:

$$\underset{\text{reactants}}{CH_4 + O_2} \longrightarrow \underset{\text{products}}{CO_2 + H_2O}$$

The substances on the left side of the equation are the *reactants*, and the substances on the right side are the *products*. We often specify the state of each reactant or product in parentheses next to the formula. If we add states to our equation, it becomes:

$$CH_4(g) + O_2(g) \longrightarrow CO_2(g) + H_2O(g)$$

The (g) indicates that these substances are gases in the reaction. Table 7.1 summarizes the common states of reactants and products and the symbols used in chemical reactions.

Let's look more closely at the equation for the burning of natural gas. How many oxygen atoms are on each side of the equation?

TABLE 7.1 Abbreviations Indicating the States of Reactants and Products in Chemical Equations

Abbreviation	State
(*g*)	gas
(*l*)	liquid
(*s*)	solid
(*aq*)	aqueous (water solution)*

*The (*aq*) designation stands for *aqueous*, which indicates that a substance is dissolved in water. When a substance dissolves in water, the mixture is called a *solution* (see Section 7.5).

$$CH_4(g) + O_2(g) \longrightarrow CO_2(g) + H_2O(g)$$

In chemical equations, atoms cannot change from one type to another—hydrogen atoms cannot change into oxygen atoms, for example. Nor can atoms disappear (recall the law of conservation of mass from Section 3.7).

The left side of the equation has two oxygen atoms, and the right side has three. Since chemical equations represent real chemical reactions, atoms cannot simply appear or disappear in chemical equations because, as we know, atoms don't simply appear or disappear in nature. We must account for the atoms on both sides of the equation. Notice that the left side of the equation has four hydrogen atoms and the right side only two.

$$CH_4(g) + O_2(g) \longrightarrow CO_2(g) + H_2O(g)$$

To correct these problems, we must create a **balanced equation**, one in which the numbers of each type of atom on both sides of the equation are equal. To balance an equation, we insert coefficients—not subscripts—in front of the chemical formulas as needed to make the number of each type of atom in the reactants equal to the number of each type of atom in the products. New atoms do not form during a reaction, nor do atoms vanish—matter must be conserved.

When we balance chemical equations by inserting coefficients as needed in front of the formulas of the reactants and products, it changes the number of molecules in the equation, but it does not change the *kinds* of molecules. To balance the preceding equation, for example, we put the coefficient 2 before O_2 in the reactants, and the coefficient 2 before H_2O in the products.

$$CH_4(g) + 2\,O_2(g) \longrightarrow CO_2(g) + 2\,H_2O(g)$$

The equation is now balanced because the numbers of each type of atom on both sides of the equation are equal. We can verify this by summing the number of each type of atom.

We determine the number of a particular type of atom within a chemical formula in an equation by multiplying the subscript for the atom by the coefficient for the chemical formula. If there is no coefficient or subscript, a 1 is implied. So the balanced equation for the combustion of natural gas is:

$$CH_4(g) + 2\,O_2(g) \longrightarrow CO_2(g) + 2\,H_2O(g)$$

Reactants	Products
1 C atom (1 × C$\underline{H}_4$)	1 C atom (1 × $\underline{C}O_2$)
4 H atoms (1 × $\underline{CH}_4$)	4 H atoms (2 × $\underline{H}_2O$)
4 O atoms (2 × $\underline{O}_2$)	4 O atoms (1 × C$\underline{O}_2$ + 2 × H$_2\underline{O}$)

The numbers of each type of atom on both sides of the equation are equal—the equation is balanced.

$$CH_4(g) - 2\,O_2(g) \longrightarrow CO_2(g) + 2\,H_2O(g)$$

▶ A balanced chemical equation represents a chemical reaction. In this equation, methane molecules combine with oxygen to form carbon dioxide and water. The photo shows a stove burning methane and the balanced equation for the reaction above it.

 CONCEPTUAL CHECKPOINT 7.2

In photosynthesis, plants make the sugar glucose, $C_6H_{12}O_6$, from carbon dioxide and water. The equation for the reaction is:

$$6\,CO_2 + 6\,H_2O \longrightarrow C_6H_{12}O_6 + x\,O_2$$

In order for this equation to be balanced, the coefficient x must be

(a) 3 (b) 6 (c) 9 (d) 12

7.4 How to Write Balanced Chemical Equations

LO: Write balanced chemical equations.

The following procedure box details the steps for writing balanced chemical equations. As in other procedures in the book, we show the steps in the left column and examples of applying each step in the center and right columns. Remember, change only the *coefficients* to balance a chemical equation; *never change the subscripts because changing the subscripts changes the kinds of molecules, not the number of molecules.*

WRITING BALANCED CHEMICAL EQUATIONS	**EXAMPLE 7.2** Write a balanced equation for the reaction between solid silicon dioxide and solid carbon to produce solid silicon carbide and carbon monoxide gas.	**EXAMPLE 7.3** Write a balanced equation for the combustion reaction between liquid octane (C_8H_{18}), a component of gasoline, and gaseous oxygen to form gaseous carbon dioxide and gaseous water.
1. Write the unbalanced equation by writing chemical formulas for each of the reactants and products. Review Chapter 5 for nomenclature rules. (If the unbalanced equation is provided in the problem, skip this step and go to Step 2.)	**SOLUTION** $SiO_2(s) + C(s) \longrightarrow SiC(s) + CO(g)$	**SOLUTION** $C_8H_{18}(l) + O_2(g) \longrightarrow$ $\qquad\qquad CO_2(g) + H_2O(g)$
2. If an element occurs in only one compound on both sides of the equation, balance it first. If there is more than one such element, balance metals before nonmetals.	**BEGIN WITH SI** $SiO_2(s) + C(s) \longrightarrow SiC(s) + CO(g)$ **1 Si atom $\longrightarrow$ 1 Si atom** Si is already balanced. **BALANCE O NEXT** $SiO_2(s) + C(s) \longrightarrow SiC(s) + CO(g)$ **2 O atoms $\longrightarrow$ 1 O atom** To balance O, put a 2 before $CO(g)$. $SiO_2(s) + C(s) \longrightarrow SiC(s) + 2\,CO(g)$ **2 O atoms $\longrightarrow$ 2 O atoms**	**BEGIN WITH C** $C_8H_{18}(l) + O_2(g) \longrightarrow$ $\qquad\qquad CO_2(g) + H_2O(g)$ **8 C atoms $\longrightarrow$ 1 C atom** To balance C, put an 8 before $CO_2(g)$. $C_8H_{18}(l) + O_2(g) \longrightarrow$ $\qquad\qquad 8\,CO_2(g) + H_2O(g)$ **8 C atoms $\longrightarrow$ 8 C atoms** **BALANCE H NEXT** $C_8H_{18}(l) + O_2(g) \longrightarrow$ $\qquad\qquad 8\,CO_2(g) + H_2O(g)$ **18 H atoms $\longrightarrow$ 2 H atoms** To balance H, put a 9 before $H_2O(g)$. $C_8H_{18}(l) + O_2(g) \longrightarrow$ $\qquad\qquad 8\,CO_2(g) + 9\,H_2O(g)$ **18 H atoms $\longrightarrow$ 18 H atoms**
3. If an element occurs as a free element on either side of the chemical equation, balance it last. Always balance free elements by adjusting the coefficient *on the free element*.	**BALANCE C** $SiO_2(s) + C(s) \longrightarrow SiC(s) + 2\,CO(g)$ **1 C atom $\longrightarrow$ 1 C + 2 C = 3 C atoms** To balance C, put a 3 before $C(s)$. $SiO_2(s) + 3\,C(s) \longrightarrow SiC(s) + 2\,CO(g)$ **3 C atoms $\longrightarrow$ 1 C + 2 C = 3 C atoms**	**BALANCE O** $C_8H_{18}(l) + O_2(g) \longrightarrow$ $\qquad\qquad 8\,CO_2(g) + 9\,H_2O(g)$ **2 O atoms $\longrightarrow$ 16 O + 9 O** $\qquad\qquad\qquad$ **= 25 O atoms** To balance O, put a $\frac{25}{2}$ before $O_2(g)$. $C_8H_{18}(l) + \frac{25}{2}\,O_2(g) \longrightarrow$ $\qquad\qquad 8\,CO_2(g) + 9\,H_2O(g)$ **25 O atoms $\longrightarrow$ 16 O + 9 O** $\qquad\qquad\qquad$ **= 25 O atoms**
4. If the balanced equation contains coefficient fractions, change these into whole numbers by multiplying the entire equation by the appropriate factor.	This step is not necessary in this example. Proceed to Step 5.	$[C_8H_{18}(l) + \frac{25}{2}\,O_2(g) \longrightarrow$ $\qquad\qquad 8\,CO_2(g) + 9\,H_2O(g)] \times 2$ $2\,C_8H_{18}(l) + 25\,O_2(g) \longrightarrow$ $\qquad\qquad 16\,CO_2(g) + 18\,H_2O(g)$

5. Check to make certain the equation is balanced by summing the total number of each type of atom on both sides of the equation.

$$SiO_2(s) + 3\,C(s) \longrightarrow SiC(s) + 2\,CO(g)$$

Reactants		Products
1 Si atom	$\longrightarrow$	1 Si atom
2 O atoms	$\longrightarrow$	2 O atoms
3 C atoms	$\longrightarrow$	3 C atoms

The equation is balanced.

▶**SKILLBUILDER 7.2** | Write a balanced equation for the reaction between solid chromium(III) oxide and solid carbon to produce solid chromium and carbon dioxide gas.

$$2\,C_8H_{18}(l) + 25\,O_2(g) \longrightarrow$$
$$16\,CO_2(g) + 18\,H_2O(g)$$

Reactants		Products
16 C atoms	$\longrightarrow$	16 C atoms
36 H atoms	$\longrightarrow$	36 H atoms
50 O atoms	$\longrightarrow$	50 O atoms

The equation is balanced.

▶**SKILLBUILDER 7.3** | Write a balanced equation for the combustion reaction of gaseous C_4H_{10} and gaseous oxygen to form gaseous carbon dioxide and gaseous water.

▶**FOR MORE PRACTICE** Example 7.17; Problems 35, 36, 37, 38, 39, 40.

EXAMPLE 7.4   **BALANCING CHEMICAL EQUATIONS**

Write a balanced equation for the reaction of solid aluminum with aqueous sulfuric acid to form aqueous aluminum sulfate and hydrogen gas.

Use your knowledge of chemical nomenclature from Chapter 5 to write a skeletal equation containing formulas for each of the reactants and products. The formulas for each compound MUST BE CORRECT before you begin to balance the equation.	**SOLUTION** $Al(s) + H_2SO_4(aq) \longrightarrow Al_2(SO_4)_3(aq) + H_2(g)$
Since both aluminum and hydrogen occur as pure elements, balance those last. Sulfur and oxygen occur in only one compound on each side of the equation, so balance these first. Sulfur and oxygen are also part of a polyatomic ion that stays intact on both sides of the equation. *Balance polyatomic ions such as these as a unit.* There are $3\,SO_4^{2-}$ ions on the right side of the equation, so put a 3 in front of H_2SO_4.	$Al(s) + 3\,H_2SO_4(aq) \longrightarrow Al_2(SO_4)_3(aq) + H_2(g)$
Balance Al next. Since there are 2 Al atoms on the right side of the equation, place a 2 in front of Al on the left side of the equation.	$2\,Al(s) + 3\,H_2SO_4(aq) \longrightarrow Al_2(SO_4)_3(aq) + H_2(g)$
Balance H next. Since there are 6 H atoms on the left side, place a 3 in front of $H_2(g)$ on the right side.	$2\,Al(s) + 3\,H_2SO_4(aq) \longrightarrow Al_2(SO_4)_3(aq) + 3\,H_2(g)$
Finally, sum the number of atoms on each side to make sure that the equation is balanced.	$2\,Al(s) + 3\,H_2SO_4(aq) \longrightarrow Al_2(SO_4)_3(aq) + 3\,H_2(g)$

Reactants		Products
2 Al atoms	$\longrightarrow$	2 Al atoms
6 H atoms	$\longrightarrow$	6 H atoms
3 S atoms	$\longrightarrow$	3 S atoms
12 O atoms	$\longrightarrow$	12 O atoms

▶**SKILLBUILDER 7.4** | **Balancing Chemical Equations**

Write a balanced equation for the reaction of aqueous lead(II) acetate with aqueous potassium iodide to form solid lead(II) iodide and aqueous potassium acetate.

▶**FOR MORE PRACTICE** Problems 41, 42, 43, 44, 45, 46.

EXAMPLE 7.5 BALANCING CHEMICAL EQUATIONS

Balance the chemical equation.

$$Fe(s) + HCl(aq) \longrightarrow FeCl_3(aq) + H_2(g)$$

Since Cl occurs in only one compound on each side of the equation, balance it first. There are 1 Cl atom on the left side of the equation and 3 Cl atoms on the right side. To balance Cl, place a 3 in front of HCl.	**SOLUTION** $Fe(s) + 3\,HCl(aq) \longrightarrow FeCl_3(aq) + H_2(g)$
Since H and Fe occur as free elements, balance them last. There is 1 Fe atom on the left side of the equation and 1 Fe atom on the right, so Fe is balanced. There are 3 H atoms on the left and 2 H atoms on the right. Balance H by placing a $\frac{3}{2}$ in front of H_2. (That way you don't alter other elements that are already balanced.)	$Fe(s) + 3\,HCl(aq) \longrightarrow FeCl_3(aq) + \frac{3}{2}\,H_2(g)$
The equation now contains a coefficient fraction; clear it by multiplying the entire equation (both sides) by 2.	$[Fe(s) + 3\,HCl(aq) \longrightarrow FeCl_3(aq) + \frac{3}{2}\,H_2(g)] \times 2$ $2\,Fe(s) + 6\,HCl(aq) \longrightarrow 2\,FeCl_3(aq) + 3\,H_2(g)$
Finally, sum the number of atoms on each side to check that the equation is balanced.	$2\,Fe(s) + 6\,HCl(aq) \longrightarrow 2\,FeCl_3(aq) + 3\,H_2(g)$

Reactants		Products
2 Fe atoms	$\longrightarrow$	2 Fe atoms
6 Cl atoms	$\longrightarrow$	6 Cl atoms
6 H atoms	$\longrightarrow$	6 H atoms

▶**SKILLBUILDER 7.5 | Balancing Chemical Equations**

Balance the chemical equation.

$$HCl(g) + O_2(g) \longrightarrow H_2O(l) + Cl_2(g)$$

▶**FOR MORE PRACTICE** Problems 47, 48, 49, 50, 51, 52.

 CONCEPTUAL CHECKPOINT 7.3

Which quantity must always be the same on both sides of a balanced chemical equation?

(a) the number of each type of atom
(b) the number of each type of molecule
(c) the sum of all of the coefficients

7.5 Aqueous Solutions and Solubility: Compounds Dissolved in Water

LO: Determine whether a compound is soluble.

In the previous section, we learned how to balance chemical equations. We now turn to investigating several types of reactions. Since many of these occur in water, we must first understand *aqueous solutions*. Reactions occurring in aqueous solution are among the most common and important. An **aqueous solution** is a homogeneous mixture of a substance with water. For example, a sodium chloride (NaCl) solution (also called a saline solution) is composed of sodium chloride dissolved in water. Sodium chloride solutions are common both in the oceans and in living cells. You can form a sodium chloride solution yourself by adding table salt to water. As you stir the salt into the water, it seems to disappear. However, you

Strong electrolyte solution

Battery   Battery

Pure water   NaCl solution
(a)   (b)

▲ **FIGURE 7.6   Ions as conductors** **(a)** Pure water does not conduct electricity. **(b)** Ions in a sodium chloride solution conduct electricity, causing the bulb to light. Solutions such as NaCl are called strong electrolyte solutions.

Cl⁻

Na⁺

A sodium chloride solution contains independent **Na⁺** and **Cl⁻** ions.

NO₃⁻

Ag⁺

A silver nitrate solution contains independent **Ag⁺** and **NO₃⁻** ions.

Ag⁺   Cl⁻

When silver chloride is added to water, it remains as solid AgCl—it does not dissolve into independent ions.

know the salt is still there because if you taste the water, it has a salty flavor. How does sodium chloride dissolve in water?

When ionic compounds such as NaCl dissolve in water, they usually dissociate into their component ions. A sodium chloride solution, represented as $NaCl(aq)$, does not contain any NaCl units; only dissolved Na^+ ions and Cl^- ions are present.

We know that NaCl is present as independent sodium and chloride ions in solution because sodium chloride solutions conduct electricity, which requires the presence of freely moving charged particles. Substances (such as NaCl) that completely dissociate into ions in solution are called *strong electrolytes*, and the resultant solutions are called **strong electrolyte solutions** (▲ Figure 7.6). Similarly, a silver nitrate solution, represented as $AgNO_3(aq)$, does not contain any $AgNO_3$ units, but only dissolved Ag^+ ions and NO_3^- ions. It, too, is a strong electrolyte solution. When compounds containing polyatomic ions such as NO_3^- dissolve, the polyatomic ions dissolve as intact units.

Not all ionic compounds, however, dissolve in water. AgCl, for example, does not. If we add AgCl to water, it remains as solid AgCl and appears as a white solid at the bottom of the beaker.

Solubility

A compound is **soluble** in a particular liquid if it dissolves in that liquid; a compound is **insoluble** if it does not dissolve in the liquid. NaCl, for example, is soluble in water. If we mix solid sodium chloride into water, it dissolves and forms a strong electrolyte solution. AgCl, on the other hand, is insoluble in water. If we mix solid silver chloride into water, it remains as a solid within the liquid water.

There is no easy way to predict whether a particular compound will be soluble or insoluble in water. For ionic compounds, however, empirical rules have been deduced from observations of many compounds. These **solubility rules** are summarized in Table 7.2 and ▼ Figure 7.7. For example, the solubility rules indicate that compounds containing the lithium ion are *soluble*. That means that compounds such as $LiBr$, $LiNO_3$, Li_2SO_4, $LiOH$, and Li_2CO_3 all dissolve in water to form strong electrolyte solutions. If a compound contains Li^+, it is soluble. Similarly, the solubility rules state that compounds containing the NO_3^- ion are soluble. Compounds such as $AgNO_3$, $Pb(NO_3)_2$, $NaNO_3$, $Ca(NO_3)_2$, and $Sr(NO_3)_2$ all dissolve in water to form strong electrolyte solutions.

The solubility rules also state that, with some exceptions, compounds containing the CO_3^{2-} ion are *insoluble*. Compounds such as $CuCO_3$, $CaCO_3$, $SrCO_3$, and $FeCO_3$ do not dissolve in water. Note that the solubility rules contain many exceptions. For example, compounds containing CO_3^{2-} are *soluble when paired with* Li^+, Na^+, K^+, or NH_4^+. Thus Li_2CO_3, Na_2CO_3, K_2CO_3, and $(NH_4)_2CO_3$ are all soluble.

| The solubility rules apply only to the solubility of the compounds in water.

▲ **FIGURE 7.7** Solubility rules flowchart.

TABLE 7.2   Solubility Rules

Compounds Containing the Following Ions Are Mostly Soluble	Exceptions
Li^+, Na^+, K^+, NH_4^+	None
NO_3^-, $C_2H_3O_2^-$	None
Cl^-, Br^-, I^-	When any of these ions pairs with Ag^+, Hg_2^{2+}, or Pb^{2+}, the compound is insoluble.
SO_4^{2-}	When SO_4^{2-} pairs with Ca^{2+}, Sr^{2+}, Ba^{2+}, or Pb^{2+}, the compound is insoluble.

Compounds Containing the Following Ions Are Mostly Insoluble	Exceptions
OH^-, S^{2-}	When either of these ions pairs with Li^+, Na^+, K^+, or NH_4^+, the compound is soluble.
	When S^{2-} pairs with Ca^{2+}, Sr^{2+}, or Ba^{2+}, the compound is soluble.
	When OH^- pairs with Ca^{2+}, Sr^{2+}, or Ba^{2+}, the compound is slightly soluble.*
CO_3^{2-}, PO_4^{3-}	When either of these ions pairs with Li^+, Na^+, K^+, or NH_4^+, the compound is soluble.

*For many purposes these can be considered insoluble.

EXAMPLE 7.6   DETERMINING WHETHER A COMPOUND IS SOLUBLE

Is each compound soluble or insoluble?

(a) AgBr   **(b)** $CaCl_2$ **(c)** $Pb(NO_3)_2$ **(d)** $PbSO_4$

SOLUTION

(a) Insoluble; compounds containing Br^- are normally soluble, but Ag^+ is an exception.
(b) Soluble; compounds containing Cl^- are normally soluble, and Ca^{2+} is not an exception.
(c) Soluble; compounds containing NO_3^- are always soluble.
(d) Insoluble; compounds containing SO_4^{2-} are normally soluble, but Pb^{2+} is an exception.

▶**SKILLBUILDER 7.6 | Determining Whether a Compound Is Soluble**

Is each compound soluble or insoluble?

(a) CuS   **(b)** $FeSO_4$ **(c)** $PbCO_3$ **(d)** NH_4Cl

▶**FOR MORE PRACTICE**   Example 7.18; Problems 59, 60, 61, 62, 63, 64.

✓ **CONCEPTUAL CHECKPOINT 7.4**

Which image best depicts a mixture of $BaCl_2$ and water?

(a)   (b)   (c)

7.6 Precipitation Reactions: Reactions in Aqueous Solution That Form a Solid

LO: Predict and write equations for precipitation reactions.

Recall from Section 7.1 that sodium carbonate in laundry detergent reacts with dissolved Mg^{2+} and Ca^{2+} ions to form solids that precipitate (come out of) solution. These reactions are examples of **precipitation reactions**—reactions that form a solid, called a **precipitate**, upon mixing two aqueous solutions.

Precipitation reactions are common in chemistry. Potassium iodide and lead nitrate, for example, both form colorless, strong electrolyte solutions when dissolved in water (see the solubility rules). When the two solutions are combined, however, a brilliant yellow precipitate forms (▼ Figure 7.8). We describe this precipitation reaction with the chemical equation:

$$2\ KI(aq) + Pb(NO_3)_2(aq) \longrightarrow PbI_2(s) + 2\ KNO_3(aq)$$

Precipitation reactions do not always occur when mixing two aqueous solutions. For example, when we combine solutions of $KI(aq)$ and $NaCl(aq)$, nothing happens (▼ Figure 7.9).

$$KI(aq) + NaCl(aq) \longrightarrow \text{NO REACTION}$$

$$\boxed{2\ KI(aq) + Pb(NO_3)_2(aq) \longrightarrow PbI_2(s) + 2\ KNO_3(aq)}$$

▲ **FIGURE 7.8 Precipitation** When we mix a potassium iodide solution with a lead(II) nitrate solution, a brilliant yellow precipitate of $PbI_2(s)$ forms.

$$\boxed{KI(aq) + NaCl(aq) \longrightarrow \text{NO REACTION}}$$

▲ **FIGURE 7.9 No reaction** When we mix a potassium iodide solution with a sodium chloride solution, no reaction occurs.

Predicting Precipitation Reactions

The key to predicting precipitation reactions is understanding that *only insoluble compounds form precipitates*. In a precipitation reaction, two solutions containing soluble compounds combine and an insoluble compound precipitates. Consider the precipitation reaction from Figure 7.8 shown here:

$$2\ KI(aq) + Pb(NO_3)_2(aq) \longrightarrow PbI_2(s) + 2\ KNO_3(aq)$$

soluble   soluble   insoluble   soluble

KI and $Pb(NO_3)_2$ are both soluble, but the precipitate, PbI_2, is *insoluble*. Before mixing, KI(*aq*) and $Pb(NO_3)_2$(*aq*) are both dissociated in their respective solutions.

The instant that the solutions are mixed, all four ions are present.

KI(*aq*) and $Pb(NO_3)_2$(*aq*)

However, new compounds—potentially insoluble ones—are now possible. Specifically, the cation from one compound can pair with the anion from the other compound to form new (and potentially insoluble) products.

Original compounds	*Potentially insoluble products*
K I (*aq*)	KNO_3
Pb $(NO_3)_2$(*aq*)	PbI_2

If the *potentially insoluble products* are both *soluble*, no reaction occurs. If, on the other hand, one or both of the potentially insoluble products are *indeed insoluble*, a precipitation reaction occurs. In this case, KNO_3 is soluble, but PbI_2 is insoluble. Consequently, PbI_2 precipitates.

PbI_2(*s*) and KNO_3(*aq*)

To predict whether a precipitation reaction will occur when two solutions are mixed and to write an equation for the reaction, we follow the steps in the procedure box that accompanies Examples 7.7 and 7.8. As usual, the steps are shown in the left column, and two examples of applying the procedure are shown in the center and right columns.

WRITING EQUATIONS FOR PRECIPITATION REACTIONS	EXAMPLE 7.7 ▶ Write an equation for the precipitation reaction that occurs (if any) when solutions of sodium carbonate and copper(II) chloride are mixed.	EXAMPLE 7.8 Write an equation for the precipitation reaction that occurs (if any) when solutions of lithium nitrate and sodium sulfate are mixed.
1. Write the formulas of the two compounds being mixed as reactants in a chemical equation.	**SOLUTION** $Na_2CO_3(aq) + CuCl_2(aq) \longrightarrow$	**SOLUTION** $LiNO_3(aq) + Na_2SO_4(aq) \longrightarrow$
2. Below the equation, write the formulas of the potentially insoluble products that could form from the reactants. Obtain these by combining the cation from one reactant with the anion from the other. Make sure to write correct (charge-neutral) formulas for these ionic compounds as described in Section 5.5.	$Na_2CO_3(aq) + CuCl_2(aq) \longrightarrow$ **Potentially Insoluble Products** NaCl $CuCO_3$	$LiNO_3(aq) + Na_2SO_4(aq) \longrightarrow$ **Potentially Insoluble Products** $NaNO_3$ Li_2SO_4
3. Use the solubility rules to determine whether any of the potential new products are indeed insoluble.	NaCl is *soluble* (compounds containing Cl^- are usually soluble, and Na^+ is not an exception). $CuCO_3$ is *insoluble* (compounds containing CO_3^{2-} are usually insoluble, and Cu^{2+} is not an exception).	$NaNO_3$ is *soluble* (compounds containing NO_3^- are soluble, and Na^+ is not an exception). Li_2SO_4 is *soluble* (compounds containing SO_4^{2-} are soluble and Li^+ is not an exception).
4. If all of the potentially insoluble products are soluble, there will be no precipitate. Write NO REACTION next to the arrow.	Because this example has an insoluble product, you proceed to the next step.	$LiNO_3(aq) + Na_2SO_4(aq) \longrightarrow$ NO REACTION
5. If one or both of the potentially insoluble products are insoluble, write their formula(s) as the product(s) of the reaction, using (s) to indicate solid. Follow any soluble products with (aq) to indicate aqueous.	$Na_2CO_3(aq) + CuCl_2(aq) \longrightarrow$ $CuCO_3(s) + NaCl(aq)$	
6. Balance the equation. Remember to adjust only coefficients, not subscripts.	$Na_2CO_3(aq) + CuCl_2(aq) \longrightarrow$ $CuCO_3(s) + 2\,NaCl(aq)$	
	▶**SKILLBUILDER 7.7**	Write an equation for the precipitation reaction that occurs (if any) when solutions of potassium hydroxide and nickel(II) bromide are mixed.	▶**SKILLBUILDER 7.8**	Write an equation for the precipitation reaction that occurs (if any) when solutions of ammonium chloride and iron(III) nitrate are mixed. ▶**FOR MORE PRACTICE** Example 7.19; Problems 65, 66, 67, 68.

EXAMPLE 7.9	**PREDICTING AND WRITING EQUATIONS FOR PRECIPITATION REACTIONS**

Write an equation for the precipitation reaction (if any) that occurs when solutions of lead(II) acetate and sodium sulfate are mixed. If no reaction occurs, write *NO REACTION*

1. Write the formulas of the two compounds being mixed as reactants in a chemical equation.	**SOLUTION** $Pb(C_2H_3O_2)_2(aq) + Na_2SO_4(aq) \longrightarrow$
2. Below the equation, write the formulas of the potentially insoluble products that could form from the reactants. Determine these by combining the cation from one reactant with the anion from the other. Make sure to adjust the subscripts so that all formulas are charge-neutral.	$Pb(C_2H_3O_2)_2(aq) + Na_2SO_4(aq) \longrightarrow$ **Potentially insoluble products** $NaC_2H_3O_2 \qquad PbSO_4$
3. Use the solubility rules to determine whether any of the potentially insoluble products are indeed insoluble.	$NaC_2H_3O_2$ is *soluble* (compounds containing Na^+ are always soluble). $PbSO_4$ is *insoluble* (compounds containing SO_4^{2-} are normally soluble, but Pb^{2+} is an exception).
4. If all of the potentially insoluble products are soluble, there will be no precipitate. Write *NO REACTION* next to the arrow.	This reaction has an insoluble product so you proceed to the next step.
5. If one or both of the potentially insoluble products are indeed insoluble, write their formula(s) as the product(s) of the reaction, using (s) to indicate solid. Follow any soluble products with (aq) to indicate aqueous.	$Pb(C_2H_3O_2)_2(aq) + Na_2SO_4(aq) \longrightarrow PbSO_4(s) + NaC_2H_3O_2(aq)$
6. Balance the equation.	$Pb(C_2H_3O_2)_2(aq) + Na_2SO_4(aq) \longrightarrow PbSO_4(s) + 2\,NaC_2H_3O_2(aq)$

▶**SKILLBUILDER 7.9 | Predicting and Writing Equations for Precipitation Reactions**

Write an equation for the precipitation reaction (if any) that occurs when solutions of potassium sulfate and strontium nitrate are mixed. If no reaction occurs, write *NO REACTION*.

▶**FOR MORE PRACTICE** Problems 69, 70.

 CONCEPTUAL CHECKPOINT 7.5

Which of these reactions results in the formation of a precipitate?
(a) $NaNO_3(aq) + CaS(aq)$
(b) $MgSO_4(aq) + CaS(aq)$
(c) $NaNO_3(aq) + MgSO_4(aq)$

7.7 Writing Chemical Equations for Reactions in Solution: Molecular, Complete Ionic, and Net Ionic Equations

LO: Write molecular, complete ionic, and net ionic equations.

Consider the following equation for a precipitation reaction:

$$AgNO_3(aq) + NaCl(aq) \longrightarrow AgCl(s) + NaNO_3(aq)$$

This equation is written as a **molecular equation**, an equation showing the complete neutral formulas for every compound in the reaction. We can also write equations for reactions occurring in aqueous solution to show that aqueous ionic compounds normally dissociate in solution. For example, we can write the previous equation as:

$$Ag^+(aq) + NO_3^-(aq) + Na^+(aq) + Cl^-(aq) \longrightarrow AgCl(s) + Na^+(aq) + NO_3^-(aq)$$

> When writing complete ionic equations, separate only aqueous ionic compounds into their constituent ions. Do NOT separate solid, liquid, or gaseous compounds.

Equations such as this one, which show the reactants and products as they are actually present in solution, are called **complete ionic equations**.

Notice that in the complete ionic equation, some of the ions in solution appear unchanged on both sides of the equation. These ions are called **spectator ions** because they do not participate in the reaction.

$$Ag^+(aq) + NO_3^-(aq) + Na^+(aq) + Cl^-(aq) \longrightarrow AgCl(s) + Na^+(aq) + NO_3^-(aq)$$

Spectator ions

To simplify the equation, and to more clearly show what is happening, spectator ions can be omitted.

$$Ag^+(aq) + Cl^-(aq) \longrightarrow AgCl(s)$$

> Species refers to a kind or sort of thing. In this case, the species are the different molecules and ions that are present during the reaction.

Equations such as this one, which show only the *species* that actually participate in the reaction, are called **net ionic equations**.

As another example, consider the reaction between HCl(*aq*) and NaOH(*aq*).

$$HCl(aq) + NaOH(aq) \longrightarrow H_2O(l) + NaCl(aq)$$

HCl, NaOH, and NaCl exist in solution as independent ions. The *complete ionic equation* for this reaction is:

$$H^+(aq) + Cl^-(aq) + Na^+(aq) + OH^-(aq) \longrightarrow H_2O(l) + Na^+(aq) + Cl^-(aq)$$

To write the *net ionic equation*, we remove the spectator ions, those that are unchanged on both sides of the equation.

$$H^+(aq) + Cl^-(aq) + Na^+(aq) + OH^-(aq) \longrightarrow H_2O(l) + Na^+(aq) + Cl^-(aq)$$

Spectator ions

The net ionic equation is $H^+(aq) + OH^-(aq) \longrightarrow H_2O(l)$.

To summarize:

- A molecular equation is a chemical equation showing the complete, neutral formulas for every compound in a reaction.
- A complete ionic equation is a chemical equation showing all of the species as they are actually present in solution.
- A net ionic equation is an equation showing only the species that actually participate in the reaction.

EXAMPLE 7.10	**WRITING COMPLETE IONIC AND NET IONIC EQUATIONS**

Consider this precipitation reaction occurring in aqueous solution.

$$Pb(NO_3)_2(aq) + 2\,LiCl(aq) \longrightarrow PbCl_2(s) + 2\,LiNO_3(aq)$$

Write a complete ionic equation and a net ionic equation for the reaction.

Write the complete ionic equation by separating aqueous ionic compounds into their constituent ions. The $PbCl_2(s)$ remains as one unit.	**SOLUTION** **Complete ionic equation** $Pb^{2+}(aq) + 2\,NO_3^-(aq) + 2\,Li^+(aq) + 2\,Cl^-(aq) \longrightarrow$ $\qquad\qquad\qquad\qquad PbCl_2(s) + 2\,Li^+(aq) + 2\,NO_3^-(aq)$
Write the net ionic equation by eliminating the spectator ions, those that do not change during the reaction.	**Net ionic equation** $Pb^{2+}(aq) + 2\,Cl^-(aq) \longrightarrow PbCl_2(s)$

▶**SKILLBUILDER 7.10 | Writing Complete Ionic and Net Ionic Equations**

Consider this reaction occurring in aqueous solution.

$$2\,HBr(aq) + Ca(OH)_2(aq) \longrightarrow 2\,H_2O(l) + CaBr_2(aq)$$

Write a complete ionic equation and a net ionic equation for the reaction.

▶**FOR MORE PRACTICE**   Example 7.20; Problems 71, 72, 73, 74.

7.8 Acid–Base and Gas Evolution Reactions

LO: Identify and write equations for acid–base reactions.

LO: Identify and write equations for gas evolution reactions.

Two other kinds of reactions that occur in solution are **acid–base reactions**—reactions that form water upon mixing of an acid and a base—and **gas evolution reactions**—reactions that evolve a gas. Like precipitation reactions, these reactions occur when the cation of one reactant combines with the anion of another. As we will see in the next section, many gas evolution reactions also happen to be acid–base reactions.

Acid–Base (Neutralization) Reactions

As we saw in Chapter 5, an acid is a compound characterized by its sour taste, its ability to dissolve some metals, and its tendency to form H^+ ions in solution. A base is a compound characterized by its bitter taste, its slippery feel, and its tendency to form OH^- ions in solution. Table 7.3 lists some common acids and bases. Acids and bases are also found in many everyday substances. Foods such as lemons, limes, and vinegar contain acids. Soap, coffee, and milk of magnesia all contain bases.

When an acid and a base are mixed, the $H^+(aq)$ from the acid combines with the $OH^-(aq)$ from the base to form $H_2O(l)$. Consider the reaction between hydrochloric acid and sodium hydroxide mentioned earlier.

$$\underset{\text{Acid}}{HCl(aq)} + \underset{\text{Base}}{NaOH(aq)} \longrightarrow \underset{\text{Water}}{H_2O(l)} + \underset{\text{Salt}}{NaCl(aq)}$$

▲ Milk of magnesia is basic and tastes bitter.

Even though coffee is acidic overall, it contains some naturally occurring bases (such as caffeine) that give it a bitter taste.

TABLE 7.3 Some Common Acids and Bases

Acid	Formula	Base	Formula
hydrochloric acid	HCl	sodium hydroxide	$NaOH$
hydrobromic acid	HBr	lithium hydroxide	$LiOH$
nitric acid	HNO_3	potassium hydroxide	KOH
sulfuric acid	H_2SO_4	calcium hydroxide	$Ca(OH)_2$
perchloric acid	$HClO_4$	barium hydroxide	$Ba(OH)_2$
acetic acid	$HC_2H_3O_2$		

▲ Common foods and everyday substances such as oranges, lemons, vinegar, and vitamin C contain acids.

Acid–base reactions (also called **neutralization reactions**) generally form water and an ionic compound—called a **salt**—that usually remains dissolved in the solution. The net ionic equation for many acid–base reactions is:

$$H^+(aq) + OH^-(aq) \longrightarrow H_2O(l)$$

Another example of an acid–base reaction is the reaction that occurs between sulfuric acid and potassium hydroxide.

$$\underset{\text{acid}}{H_2SO_4(aq)} + \underset{\text{base}}{2\,KOH} \longrightarrow \underset{\text{water}}{2\,H_2O(l)} + \underset{\text{salt}}{K_2SO_4(aq)}$$

Notice the pattern of acid and base reacting to form water and a salt.

$$\text{Acid} + \text{Base} \longrightarrow \text{Water} + \text{Salt} \quad \text{(acid–base reactions)}$$

When writing equations for acid–base reactions, write the formula of the salt using the procedure for writing formulas of ionic compounds presented in Section 5.5.

EXAMPLE 7.11	**WRITING EQUATIONS FOR ACID–BASE REACTIONS**

Write a molecular and a net ionic equation for the reaction between aqueous HNO_3 and aqueous $Ca(OH)_2$.

You must recognize these substances as an acid and a base. Write the skeletal reaction following the general pattern of acid plus base goes to water plus salt.	**SOLUTION** $$\underset{\text{acid}}{HNO_3(aq)} + \underset{\text{base}}{Ca(OH)_2(aq)} \longrightarrow \underset{\text{water}}{H_2O(l)} + \underset{\text{salt}}{Ca(NO_3)_3(aq)}$$
Next, balance the equation.	$$2\,HNO_3(aq) + Ca(OH)_2(aq) \longrightarrow 2\,H_2O(l) + Ca(NO_3)_2(aq)$$
Write the net ionic equation by eliminating those ions that remain the same on both sides of the equation.	$$2\,H^+(aq) + 2\,OH^-(aq) \longrightarrow 2\,H_2O(l)$$ or simply $$H^+(aq) + OH^-(aq) \longrightarrow H_2O(l)$$

▶**SKILLBUILDER 7.11** | **Writing Equations for Acid–Base Reactions**

Write a molecular and a net ionic equation for the reaction that occurs between aqueous H_2SO_4 and aqueous KOH.

▶**FOR MORE PRACTICE**   Example 7.21; Problems 79, 80, 81, 82.

Gas Evolution Reactions

Some aqueous reactions form a gas as a product. These reactions, as we learned in the opening section of this chapter, are called gas evolution reactions. Some gas evolution reactions form a gaseous product directly when the cation of one reactant reacts with the anion of the other. For example, when sulfuric acid reacts with lithium sulfide, dihydrogen sulfide gas is formed:

$$H_2SO_4(aq) + Li_2S(aq) \longrightarrow \underset{\text{Gas}}{H_2S(g)} + Li_2SO_4(aq)$$

Many gas evolution reactions such as this one are also acid–base reactions. In Chapter 14 we learn how ions such as HCO_3^- act as bases in aqueous solution.

Other gas evolution reactions form an intermediate product that then decomposes into a gas. For example, when aqueous hydrochloric acid is mixed with aqueous sodium bicarbonate, the following reaction occurs:

$$HCl(aq) + NaHCO_3(aq) \longrightarrow H_2CO_3(aq) + NaCl(aq) \longrightarrow H_2O(l) + CO_2(g) + NaCl(aq)$$
Gas

Gas evolution reaction

▲ In this gas evolution reaction, vinegar (a dilute solution of acetic acid) and baking soda (sodium bicarbonate) produce carbon dioxide.

The intermediate product, H_2CO_3, is not stable and decomposes to form H_2O and gaseous CO_2. This reaction is almost identical to the reaction in the grade school volcano of Section 7.1, which involves the mixing of acetic acid and sodium bicarbonate:

$$HC_2H_3O_2(aq) + NaHCO_3(aq) \longrightarrow H_2CO_3(aq) + NaC_2H_3O_2(aq) \longrightarrow$$
$$H_2O(l) + CO_2(g) + NaC_2H_3O_2(aq)$$

The bubbling of the classroom volcano is caused by the newly formed carbon dioxide gas. Other important gas evolution reactions form either H_2SO_3 or NH_4OH as intermediate products:

$$HCl(aq) + NaHSO_3(aq) \longrightarrow H_2SO_3(aq) + NaCl(aq) \longrightarrow$$
$$H_2O(l) + SO_2(g) + NaCl(aq)$$

$$NH_4Cl(aq) + NaOH(aq) \longrightarrow NH_4OH(aq) + NaCl(aq) \longrightarrow$$
$$H_2O(l) + NH_3(g) + NaCl(aq)$$

Table 7.4 lists the main types of compounds that form gases in aqueous reactions, as well as the gases that they form.

TABLE 7.4 Types of Compounds That Undergo Gas Evolution Reactions

Reactant Type	Intermediate Product	Gas Evolved	Example
sulfides	none	H_2S	$2\,HCl(aq) + K_2S(aq) \longrightarrow H_2S(g) + 2\,KCl(aq)$
carbonates and bicarbonates	H_2CO_3	CO_2	$2\,HCl(aq) + K_2CO_3(aq) \longrightarrow H_2O(l) + CO_2(g) + 2\,KCl(aq)$
sulfites and bisulfites	H_2SO_3	SO_2	$2\,HCl(aq) + K_2SO_3(aq) \longrightarrow H_2O(l) + SO_2(g) + 2\,KCl(aq)$
ammonium	NH_4OH	NH_3	$NH_4Cl(aq) + KOH(aq) \longrightarrow H_2O(l) + NH_3(g) + KCl(aq)$

EXAMPLE 7.12 WRITING EQUATIONS FOR GAS EVOLUTION REACTIONS

Write a molecular equation for the gas evolution reaction that occurs when you mix aqueous nitric acid and aqueous sodium carbonate.

Begin by writing a skeletal equation that includes the reactants and products that form when the cation of each reactant combines with the anion of the other.	**SOLUTION** $HNO_3(aq) + Na_2CO_3(aq) \longrightarrow H_2CO_3(aq) + NaNO_3(aq)$
You must recognize that $H_2CO_3(aq)$ decomposes into $H_2O(l)$ and $CO_2(g)$ and write the corresponding equation.	$HNO_3(aq) + Na_2CO_3(aq) \longrightarrow H_2O(l) + CO_2(g) + NaNO_3(aq)$
Finally, balance the equation.	$2\,HNO_3(aq) - Na_2CO_3(aq) \longrightarrow H_2O(l) + CO_2(g) + 2\,NaNO_3(aq)$

▶**SKILLBUILDER 7.12 | Writing Equations for Gas Evolution Reactions**

Write a molecular equation for the gas evolution reaction that occurs when you mix aqueous hydrobromic acid and aqueous potassium sulfite.

▶**SKILLBUILDER PLUS |** Write a net ionic equation for the previous reaction.

▶**FOR MORE PRACTICE** Example 7.22; Problems 83, 84.

CHEMISTRY **AND HEALTH**

▶ Neutralizing Excess Stomach Acid

Your stomach normally contains acids that are involved in food digestion. Certain foods and stress, however, can increase the acidity of your stomach to uncomfortable levels, causing acid stomach or heartburn. Antacids are over-the-counter medicines that work by reacting with and neutralizing stomach acid. Antacids employ different bases as neutralizing agents. Tums™, for example, contains $CaCO_3$; milk of magnesia contains $Mg(OH)_2$; and Mylanta™ contains $Al(OH)_3$. They all, however, have the same effect of neutralizing stomach acid and relieving heartburn.

B7.1 CAN YOU ANSWER THIS? *Assume that stomach acid is HCl and write equations showing how each of these antacids neutralizes stomach acid.*

▲ The base in an antacid neutralizes excess stomach acid, relieving heartburn and acid stomach.

▲ Antacids contain bases such as $Mg(OH)_2$, $Al(OH)_3$, and $NaHCO_3$.

7.9 Oxidation–Reduction Reactions

LO: Identify redox reactions.

LO: Identify and write equations for combustion reactions.

Reactions involving the transfer of electrons are called **oxidation–reduction reactions** or **redox reactions**. Redox reactions are responsible for the rusting of iron, the bleaching of hair, and the production of electricity in batteries. Many redox reactions involve the reaction of a substance with oxygen.

We will cover oxidation–reduction reactions in more detail in Chapter 16.

$$2\,H_2(g) + O_2(g) \longrightarrow 2\,H_2O(g)$$
(reaction that powers the space shuttle)

$$4\,Fe(s) + 3\,O_2(g) \longrightarrow 2\,Fe_2O_3(s)$$
(rusting of iron)

$$CH_4(g) + 2\,O_2(g) \longrightarrow CO_2(g) + 2\,H_2O(g)$$
(combustion of natural gas)

However, redox reactions need not involve oxygen. Consider, for example, the reaction between sodium and chlorine to form table salt (NaCl).

$$2\,Na(s) + Cl_2(g) \longrightarrow 2\,NaCl(s)$$

This reaction is similar to the reaction between sodium and oxygen, which can form sodium oxide.

$$4 \, Na(s) + O_2(g) \longrightarrow 2 \, Na_2O(s)$$

What do these two reactions have in common? In both cases, sodium (a metal with a tendency to lose electrons) reacts with a nonmetal (that has a tendency to gain electrons). In both cases, sodium atoms lose electrons to nonmetal atoms. A fundamental definition of oxidation is *the loss of electrons*, and a fundamental definition of reduction is *the gain of electrons*.

Notice that oxidation and reduction must occur together. If one substance loses electrons (oxidation), then another substance must gain electrons (reduction). For now, you simply need to be able to identify redox reactions. In Chapter 16 we will examine them more thoroughly.

Redox reactions are those in which:

- A substance reacts with elemental oxygen.
- A metal reacts with a nonmetal.
- More generally, one substance transfers electrons to another substance.

> The reaction between sodium and oxygen also forms other oxides besides Na_2O.

> Helpful mnemonics: CIL RIG—**O**xidation **I**s **L**oss; **R**eduction **I**s **G**ain. LEO GER—**L**ose **E**lectrons **O**xidation; **G**ain **E**lectrons **R**eduction.

> A reaction can be classified as a redox reaction if it meets any one of these requirements.

EXAMPLE 7.13 **IDENTIFYING REDOX REACTIONS**

Which of these are redox reactions?

(a) $2 \, Mg(s) + O_2(g) \longrightarrow 2 \, MgO(s)$
(b) $2 \, HBr(aq) + Ca(OH)_2(aq) \longrightarrow 2 \, H_2O(l) + CaBr_2(aq)$
(c) $Ca(s) + Cl_2(g) \longrightarrow CaCl_2(s)$
(d) $Zn(s) + Fe^{2+}(aq) \longrightarrow Zn^{2+}(aq) + Fe(s)$

SOLUTION

(a) Redox reaction; Mg reacts with elemental oxygen.
(b) Not a redox reaction; it is an acid–base reaction.
(c) Redox reaction; a metal reacts with a nonmetal.
(d) Redox reaction; Zn transfers two electrons to Fe^{2+}.

▶**SKILLBUILDER 7.13 | Identifying Redox Reactions**

Which of these are redox reactions?

(a) $2 \, Li(s) + Cl_2(g) \longrightarrow 2 \, LiCl(s)$
(b) $2 \, Al(s) + 3 \, Sn^{2+}(aq) \longrightarrow 2 \, Al^{3+}(aq) + 3 \, Sn(s)$
(c) $Pb(NO_3)_2(aq) + 2 \, LiCl(aq) \longrightarrow PbCl_2(s) + 2 \, LiNO_3(aq)$
(d) $C(s) + O_2(g) \longrightarrow CO_2(g)$

▶**FOR MORE PRACTICE** Example 7.23; Problems 85, 86.

Combustion Reactions

Combustion reactions are a type of redox reaction. They are important because most of our society's energy is derived from combustion reactions. Combustion reactions are characterized by the reaction of a substance with O_2 to form one or more oxygen-containing compounds, often including water. Combustion reactions are exothermic (they emit heat). For example, as we saw in Section 7.3, natural gas (CH_4) reacts with oxygen to form carbon dioxide and water.

$$CH_4(g) + 2 \, O_2(g) \longrightarrow CO_2(g) + 2 \, H_2O(g)$$

As mentioned in the opening section of this chapter, combustion reactions power automobiles. For example, octane, a component of gasoline, reacts with oxygen to form carbon dioxide and water.

$$2 \, C_8H_{18}(l) + 25 \, O_2(g) \longrightarrow 16 \, CO_2(g) + 18 \, H_2O(g)$$

> The water formed in combustion reactions may be gaseous (g) or liquid (l) depending on the reaction conditions.

Combustion

▲ Combustion of octane occurs in the cylinders of an automobile engine.

Ethanol, the alcohol in alcoholic beverages, also reacts with oxygen in a combustion reaction to form carbon dioxide and water.

$$C_2H_5OH(l) + 3\,O_2(g) \longrightarrow 2\,CO_2(g) + 3\,H_2O(g)$$

Compounds containing carbon and hydrogen—or carbon, hydrogen, and oxygen—always form carbon dioxide and water upon combustion. Other combustion reactions include the reaction of carbon with oxygen to form carbon dioxide:

$$C(s) + O_2(g) \longrightarrow CO_2(g)$$

and the reaction of hydrogen with oxygen to form water:

$$2\,H_2(g) + O_2(g) \longrightarrow 2\,H_2O(g)$$

EXAMPLE 7.14 **WRITING COMBUSTION REACTIONS**

Write a balanced equation for the combustion of liquid methyl alcohol (CH_3OH).

Begin by writing a skeletal equation showing the reaction of CH_3OH with O_2 to form CO_2 and H_2O.	**SOLUTION** $$CH_3OH(l) + O_2(g) \longrightarrow CO_2(g) + H_2O(g)$$
Balance the skeletal equation using the rules in Section 7.4.	$$2\,CH_3OH(l) + 3\,O_2(g) \longrightarrow 2\,CO_2(g) + 4\,H_2O(g)$$

▶**SKILLBUILDER 7.14** | **Writing Combustion Reactions**

Write a balanced equation for the combustion of liquid pentane (C_5H_{12}), a component of gasoline.

▶**SKILLBUILDER PLUS** | Write a balanced equation for the combustion of liquid propanol (C_3H_7OH).

▶**FOR MORE PRACTICE** Example 7.24; Problems 87, 88.

7.10 Classifying Chemical Reactions

LO: Classify chemical reactions.

Throughout this chapter, we have examined different types of chemical reactions. We have seen examples of precipitation reactions, acid–base reactions, gas evolution reactions, oxidation–reduction reactions, and combustion reactions. We can organize these different types of reactions with the following flowchart:

*Many gas evolution reactions are also acid–base reactions.

This classification scheme focuses on the type of chemistry or phenomenon that is occurring during the reaction (such as the formation of a precipitate or the transfer of electrons). However, an alternative way to classify chemical reactions is by what atoms or groups of atoms do during the reaction.

Classifying Chemical Reactions by What Atoms Do

In an alternative way of classifying reactions, we focus on the pattern of the reaction by classifying it into one of the following four categories. In this classification scheme, the letters (A, B, C, D) represent atoms or groups of atoms.

Type of Reaction	Generic Equation
synthesis or combination	$A + B \longrightarrow AB$
decomposition	$AB \longrightarrow A + B$
single-displacement	$A + BC \longrightarrow AC + B$
double-displacement	$AB + CD \longrightarrow AD + CB$

SYNTHESIS OR COMBINATION REACTIONS. In a **synthesis** or **combination reaction**, simpler substances combine to form more complex substances. The simpler substances may be elements, such as sodium and chlorine combining to form sodium chloride.

$$2\,Na(s) + Cl_2(g) \longrightarrow 2\,NaCl(s)$$

The simpler substances may also be compounds, such as calcium oxide and carbon dioxide combining to form calcium carbonate.

$$CaO(s) + CO_2(g) \longrightarrow CaCO_3(s)$$

In either case, a synthesis reaction follows the general equation:

$$A + B \longrightarrow AB$$

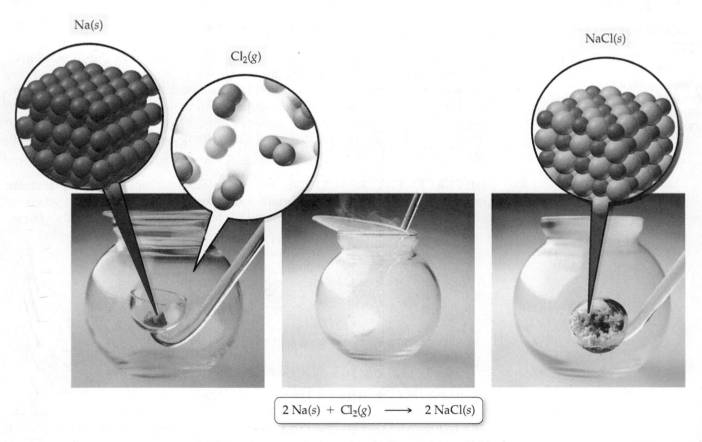

Na(s)   Cl₂(g)   NaCl(s)

$$2\,Na(s) + Cl_2(g) \longrightarrow 2\,NaCl(s)$$

▲ In a synthesis reaction, two simpler substances combine to make a more complex substance. In this series of photographs we see sodium metal and chlorine gas. When they combine, a chemical reaction occurs that forms sodium chloride.

Note that the first two of these reactions are also redox reactions.

Other examples of synthesis reactions include:

$$2\,H_2(g) + O_2(g) \longrightarrow 2\,H_2O(l)$$

$$2\,Mg(s) + O_2(g) \longrightarrow 2\,MgO(s)$$

$$SO_3(g) + H_2O(l) \longrightarrow H_2SO_4(aq)$$

DECOMPOSITION REACTIONS. In a **decomposition reaction**, a complex substance decomposes to form simpler substances. The simpler substances may be elements, such as the hydrogen and oxygen gases that form upon the decomposition of water when electrical current passes through it.

$$2\,H_2O(l) \xrightarrow{\text{electrical current}} 2\,H_2(g) + O_2(g)$$

The simpler substances may also be compounds, such as the calcium oxide and carbon dioxide that form upon heating calcium carbonate.

$$CaCO_3(s) \xrightarrow{\text{heat}} CaO(s) + CO_2(g)$$

In either case, a decomposition reaction follows the general equation:

$$AB \longrightarrow A + B$$

Other examples of decomposition reactions include:

$$2\,HgO(s) \xrightarrow{\text{heat}} 2\,Hg(l) + O_2(g)$$

$$2\,KClO_3(s) \xrightarrow{\text{heat}} 2\,KCl(s) + 3\,O_2(g)$$

$$CH_3I(g) \xrightarrow{\text{light}} CH_3(g) + I(g)$$

$$2\,H_2O(l) \longrightarrow 2\,H_2(g) + O_2(g)$$

▲ When electrical current is passed through water, the water undergoes a decomposition reaction to form hydrogen gas and oxygen gas.

Notice that these decomposition reactions require energy in the form of heat, electrical current, or light to make them happen. This is because compounds are normally stable and energy is required to decompose them. A number of decomposition reactions require *ultraviolet* or *UV light*, which is light in the ultraviolet region of the spectrum. UV light carries more energy than visible light and can therefore initiate the decomposition of many compounds. (We will discuss light in more detail in Chapter 9.)

DISPLACEMENT REACTIONS. In a **displacement** or **single-displacement reaction**, one element displaces another in a compound. For example, when we add metallic zinc to a solution of copper(II) chloride, the zinc replaces the copper.

$$Zn(s) + CuCl_2(aq) \longrightarrow ZnCl_2(aq) + Cu(s)$$

A displacement reaction follows the general equation:

$$A + BC \longrightarrow AC + B$$

Other examples of displacement reactions include:

$$Mg(s) + 2\,HCl(aq) \longrightarrow MgCl_2(aq) + H_2(g)$$

$$2\,Na(s) + 2\,H_2O(l) \longrightarrow 2\,NaOH(aq) + H_2(g)$$

The last reaction can be identified more easily as a displacement reaction if we write water as HOH(l).

$$2\,Na(s) + 2\,HOH(l) \longrightarrow 2\,NaOH(aq) + H_2(g)$$

▶ In a single-displacement reaction, one element displaces another in a compound. When zinc metal is immersed in a copper(II) chloride solution, the zinc atoms displace the copper ions in solution.

Zn(s)

Cu(s)

CuCl$_2$(aq)

ZnCl$_2$(aq)

(a)   (b)

DOUBLE-DISPLACEMENT REACTIONS. In a **double-displacement reaction**, two elements or groups of elements in two different compounds exchange places to form two new compounds. For example, in aqueous solution, the silver in silver nitrate changes places with the sodium in sodium chloride and solid silver chloride and aqueous sodium nitrate form.

This double-displacement reaction is also a precipitation reaction.

$$AgNO_3(aq) + NaCl(aq) \longrightarrow AgCl(s) + NaNO_3(aq)$$

A double-displacement reaction follows the general form:

$$AB + CD \longrightarrow AD + CB$$

Other examples of double-displacement reactions include:

These double-displacement reactions are also acid–base reactions.

$$HCl(aq) + NaOH(aq) \longrightarrow H_2O(l) + NaCl(aq)$$
$$2\,HCl(aq) + Na_2CO_3(aq) \longrightarrow H_2CO_3(aq) + 2\,NaCl(aq)$$

As we learned in Section 7.8, $H_2CO_3(aq)$ is not stable and decomposes to form $H_2O(l) + CO_2(g)$, so the overall equation is:

This double-displacement reaction is also a gas evolution reaction and an acid–base reaction.

$$2\,HCl(aq) + Na_2CO_3(aq) \longrightarrow H_2O(l) + CO_2(g) + 2\,NaCl(aq)$$

Classification Flowchart

A flowchart for this classification scheme of chemical reactions is as follows:

No single classification scheme is perfect because all chemical reactions are unique in some sense. However, both classification schemes—one that focuses on the type of chemistry occurring and the other that focuses on what atoms or groups of atoms are doing—are helpful because they help us see differences and similarities among chemical reactions.

EXAMPLE 7.15 | CLASSIFYING CHEMICAL REACTIONS ACCORDING TO WHAT ATOMS DO

Classify each reaction as a synthesis, decomposition, single-displacement, or double-displacement reaction.

(a) $Na_2O(s) + H_2O(l) \longrightarrow 2\,NaOH(aq)$
(b) $Ba(NO_3)_2(aq) + K_2SO_4(aq) \longrightarrow BaSO_4(s) + 2\,KNO_3(aq)$
(c) $2\,Al(s) + Fe_2O_3(s) \longrightarrow Al_2O_3(s) + 2\,Fe(l)$
(d) $2\,H_2O_2(aq) \longrightarrow 2\,H_2O(l) + O_2(g)$
(e) $Ca(s) + Cl_2(g) \longrightarrow CaCl_2(s)$

SOLUTION

(a) Synthesis; a more complex substance forms from two simpler ones.
(b) Double-displacment; Ba and K switch places to form two new compounds.
(c) Single-displacement; Al displaces Fe in Fe_2O_3.
(d) Decomposition; a complex substance decomposes into simpler ones.
(e) Synthesis; a more complex substance forms from two simpler ones.

▶SKILLBUILDER 7.15 | Classifying Chemical Reactions According to What Atoms Do

Classify each reaction as a synthesis, decomposition, single-displacement, or double-displacement reaction.

(a) $2\,Al(s) + 2\,H_3PO_4(aq) \longrightarrow 2\,AlPO_4(aq) + 3\,H_2(g)$
(b) $CuSO_4(aq) + 2\,KOH(aq) \longrightarrow Cu(OH)_2(s) + K_2SO_4(aq)$
(c) $2\,K(s) + Br_2(l) \longrightarrow 2\,KBr(s)$
(d) $CuCl_2(aq) \xrightarrow[\text{electrical current}]{} Cu(s) + Cl_2(g)$

▶FOR MORE PRACTICE   Example 7.25; Problems 91, 92, 93, 94.

 CONCEPTUAL CHECKPOINT 7.6

Precipitation reactions and acid–base reactions can both also be classified as:
(a) synthesis reactions
(b) decomposition reactions
(c) single-displacement reactions
(d) double-displacement reactions

CHEMISTRY IN THE ENVIRONMENT
▶ The Reactions Involved in Ozone Depletion

Chemistry in the Environment: Chlorine in Chlorofluorocarbons in Chapter 6 explained that chlorine atoms from chlorofluorocarbons deplete the ozone layer, which protects life on Earth from harmful ultraviolet light. Through research, chemists have discovered the reactions by which this depletion occurs.

Ozone normally forms in the upper atmosphere according to this reaction:

(a) $O_2(g) + O(g) \longrightarrow O_3(g)$

When chlorofluorocarbons drift to the upper atmosphere, they are exposed to ultraviolet light and undergo this reaction:

(b) $CF_2Cl_2(g) \xrightarrow{\text{UV light}} CF_2Cl(g) + Cl(g)$

Atomic chlorine then reacts with and depletes ozone according to this cycle of reactions:

(c) $Cl(g) + O_3(g) \longrightarrow ClO(g) + O_2(g)$

(d) $O_3(g) \xrightarrow{\text{UV light}} O_2(g) + O(g)$

(e) $O(g) + ClO(g) \longrightarrow O_2(g) + Cl(g)$

Notice that in the final reaction, atomic chlorine is regenerated and can go through the cycle again to deplete more ozone. Through this cycle of reactions, a single chlorofluorocarbon molecule can deplete thousands of ozone molecules.

B7.2 CAN YOU ANSWER THIS? *Classify each of the reactions involved in ozone depletion (a–e) as a synthesis, decomposition, single-displacement, or double-displacement reaction.*

CHAPTER IN REVIEW

Self-Assessment Quiz

Q1. Which process is a chemical reaction?
(a) Gasoline evaporating from a gasoline tank
(b) Iron rusting when left outdoors
(c) Dew condensing on grass during the night
(d) Water boiling on a stove top

Q2. How many oxygen atoms are on the reactant side of this chemical equation?
$K_2CO_3(aq) + Pb(NO_3)_2(aq) \longrightarrow 2\ KNO_3(aq) + PbCO_3(s)$
(a) 3
(b) 6
(c) 9
(d) 12

Q3. What is the coefficient for hydrogen in the balanced equation for the reaction of solid iron(III) oxide with gaseous hydrogen to form solid iron and liquid water?
(a) 2
(b) 3
(c) 4
(d) 6

Q4. Determine the correct set of coefficients to balance the chemical equation.
$\_C_6H_6(l) + \_O_2(g) \longrightarrow \_CO_2(g) + \_H_2O(g)$
(a) 2, 15, 12, 6
(b) 1, 15, 6, 3
(c) 2, 15, 12, 12
(d) 1, 7, 6, 3

Q5. Which compound is soluble in water?

(a) $Fe(OH)_2$

(b) CuS

(c) $AgCl$

(d) $CuCl_2$

Q6. Name the precipitate that forms (if any) when aqueous solutions of barium nitrate and potassium sulfate are mixed.

(a) $BaK(s)$

(b) $NO_3SO_4(s)$

(c) $BaSO_4(s)$

(d) $KNO_3(s)$

Q7. Which set of reactants forms a solid precipitate when mixed?

(a) $NaNO_3(aq)$ and $KCl(aq)$

(b) $KOH(aq)$ and $Na_2CO_3(aq)$

(c) $CuCl_2(aq)$ and $NaC_2H_3O_2(aq)$

(d) $Na_2CO_3(aq)$ and $CaCl_2(aq)$

Q8. What is the net ionic equation for the reaction between $Pb(C_2H_3O_2)_2(aq)$ and $KBr(aq)$?

(a) $Pb(C_2H_3O_2)_2(aq) + 2\,KBr(aq) \longrightarrow PbBr_2(s) + 2\,KC_2H_3O_2(aq)$

(b) $Pb^{2+}(aq) + 2\,Br^-(aq) \longrightarrow PbBr_2(s)$

(c) $K^+(aq) + C_2H_3O_2^-(aq) \longrightarrow KC_2H_3O_2(s)$

(d) $Pb(C_2H_3O_2)_2(aq) + 2\,KBr(aq) \longrightarrow 2\,KC_2H_3O_2(s) + PbBr_2(aq)$

Q9. Complete the equation:
$HBr(aq) + NaOH(aq) \longrightarrow$ _____

(a) $NaH(s) + BrOH(aq)$

(b) $NaBr(s) + NaOH(aq)$

(c) $H_2O(l) + NaBr(aq)$

(d) No Reaction occurs

Q10. Complete the equation:
$HNO_3(aq) + KHCO_3(aq) \longrightarrow$ _____

(a) $H_2O(l) + CO_2(g) + KNO_3(aq)$

(b) $KNO_3(s) + H_2CO_3(aq)$

(c) $HK(aq) + NO_3HCO_3$

(d) No Reaction occurs

Q11. What are the products of the balanced equation for the combustion of C_4H_9OH?

(a) $C_4H_9(s) + NaOH(aq)$

(b) $4\,CO_2(g) + 5\,H_2O(l)$

(c) $4\,O_2(g) + 5\,H_2O(l)$

(d) $2\,C_2H_4(g) + H_2O(l)$

Q12. Precipitation reactions are best classified as which type of reaction?

(a) Single displacement

(b) Double displacement

(c) Decomposition

(d) None of the above

Answers: 1:b, 2:c, 3:b, 4:a, 5:d, 6:c, 7:d, 8:b, 9:c, 10:a, 11:b, 12:b

Chemical Principles

Chemical Reactions: In a chemical reaction, one or more substances—either elements or compounds—change into a different substance.

Evidence of a Chemical Reaction: The only absolute evidence for a chemical reaction is chemical analysis showing that one or more substances have changed into another substance. However, one or more of the following often accompany a chemical reaction: a color change; the formation of a solid or precipitate; the formation of a gas; the emission of light; and the emission or absorption of heat.

Chemical Equations: Chemical equations represent chemical reactions. They include formulas for the reactants (the substances present before the reaction) and for the products (the new substances formed by the reaction). Chemical equations must be balanced to reflect the conservation of matter in nature; atoms do not spontaneously appear or disappear.

Relevance

Chemical Reactions: Chemical reactions are central to many processes, including transportation, energy generation, manufacture of household products, vision, and life itself.

Evidence of a Chemical Reaction: We can often perceive the changes that accompany chemical reactions. In fact, we often employ chemical reactions for the changes they produce. For example, we use the heat emitted by the combustion of fossil fuels to heat our homes, drive our cars, and generate electricity.

Chemical Equations: Chemical equations allow us to represent and understand chemical reactions. For example, the equations for the combustion reactions of fossil fuels let us see that carbon dioxide, a gas that contributes to global warming, is one of the products of these reactions.

Aqueous Solutions and Solubility: Aqueous solutions are mixtures of a substance dissolved in water. If a substance dissolves in water it is soluble; otherwise, it is insoluble.

Aqueous Solutions and Solubility: Aqueous solutions are common. Oceans, lakes, and most of the fluids in our bodies are aqueous solutions.

Some Specific Types of Reactions:

Precipitation reaction: A solid or precipitate forms upon mixing two aqueous solutions.

Acid–base reaction: Water forms upon mixing an acid and a base.

Gas evolution reaction: A gas forms upon mixing two aqueous solutions.

Redox reaction: Electrons transfer from one substance to another.

Combustion reaction: A substance reacts with oxygen, emitting heat, and forming an oxygen-containing compound and, in many cases, water.

Some Specific Types of Reactions: Many of the specific types of reactions discussed in this chapter occur in aqueous solutions and are therefore important to living organisms. Acid–base reactions, for example, constantly occur in the blood of living organisms to maintain constant blood acidity levels. In humans, a small change in blood acidity levels would result in death, so our bodies carry out chemical reactions to prevent this. Combustion reactions are important because they are the main energy source for our society.

Classifying Chemical Reactions: We can classify many chemical reactions into one of the following four categories according to what atoms or groups of atoms do:

- synthesis: $(A + B \longrightarrow AB)$
- decomposition: $(AB \longrightarrow A + B)$
- single-displacement: $(A + BC \longrightarrow AC + B)$
- double-displacement: $(AB + CD \longrightarrow AD + CB)$

Classifying Chemical Reactions: We classify chemical reactions to better understand them and to recognize similarities and differences among reactions.

Chemical Skills

Examples

LO: Identify a chemical reaction (Section 7.2).

To identify a chemical reaction, determine whether one or more of the initial substances changed into a different substance. If so, a chemical reaction occurred. One or more of the following often accompanies a chemical reaction: a color change; the formation of a solid or precipitate; the formation of a gas; the emission of light; and the emission or absorption of heat.

EXAMPLE 7.16 IDENTIFYING A CHEMICAL REACTION

Which of these are chemical reactions?

(a) Copper turns green on exposure to air.
(b) When sodium bicarbonate is combined with hydrochloric acid, bubbling is observed.
(c) Liquid water freezes to form solid ice.
(d) A pure copper penny forms bubbles of a dark brown gas when dropped into nitric acid. The nitric acid solution turns blue.

SOLUTION

(a) Chemical reaction, as evidenced by the color change.
(b) Chemical reaction, as evidenced by the evolution of a gas.
(c) Not a chemical reaction; solid ice is still water.
(d) Chemical reaction, as evidenced by the evolution of a gas and by a color change.

LO: Write balanced chemical equations (Section 7.3, 7.4).

To write balanced chemical equations, follow these steps.

1. Write a skeletal equation by writing chemical formulas for each of the reactants and products. (If a skeletal equation is provided, proceed to Step 2.)
2. If an element occurs in only one compound on both sides of the equation, balance that element first. If there is more than one such element, and the equation contains both metals and nonmetals, balance metals before nonmetals.
3. If an element occurs as a free element on either side of the chemical equation, balance that element last.
4. If the balanced equation contains coefficient fractions, clear these by multiplying the entire equation by the appropriate factor.
5. Check to make certain the equation is balanced by summing the total number of each type of atom on both sides of the equation.

Reminders

- Change only the *coefficients* to balance a chemical equation, *never the subscripts*. Changing the subscripts would change the compound itself.
- If the equation contains polyatomic ions that stay intact on both sides of the equation, balance the polyatomic ions as a group.

EXAMPLE 7.17 **WRITING BALANCED CHEMICAL EQUATIONS**

Write a balanced chemical equation for the reaction of solid vanadium(V) oxide with hydrogen gas to form solid vanadium(III) oxide and liquid water.

$$V_2O_5(s) + H_2(g) \longrightarrow V_2O_3(s) + H_2O(l)$$

SOLUTION
A skeletal equation is given. Proceed to Step 2.

Vanadium occurs in only one compound on both sides of the equation. However, it is balanced, so you can proceed and balance oxygen by placing a 2 in front of H_2O on the right side.

$$V_2O_5(s) + H_2(g) \longrightarrow V_2O_3(s) + 2\,H_2O(l)$$

Hydrogen occurs as a free element; balance it last by placing a 2 in front of H_2 on the left side.

$$V_2O_5(s) + 2\,H_2(g) \longrightarrow V_2O_3(s) + 2\,H_2O(l)$$

Equation does not contain coefficient fractions. Proceed to Step 5.

Check the equation.

$$V_2O_5(s) + 2\,H_2(g) \longrightarrow V_2O_3(s) + 2\,H_2O(l)$$

Reactants		Products
2 V atoms	$\longrightarrow$	2 V atoms
5 O atoms	$\longrightarrow$	5 O atoms
4 H atoms	$\longrightarrow$	4 H atoms

LO: Determine whether a compound is soluble (Section 7.5).

To determine whether a compound is soluble or not, refer to the solubility rules in Table 7.2. It is simplest to begin by looking for those ions that always form soluble compounds (Li^+, Na^+, K^+, NH_4^+, NO_3^-, and $C_2H_3O_2^-$). If a compound contains one of those, it is soluble. If it does not, determine if the anion is mostly soluble (Cl^-, Br^-, I^-, or SO_4^{2-}) or mostly insoluble (OH^-, S^{2-}, CO_3^{2-}, or PO_4^{3-}). Look at the cation as well to determine whether it is one of the exceptions.

EXAMPLE 7.18 **DETERMINING WHETHER A COMPOUND IS SOLUBLE**

Is each compound soluble or insoluble?

(a) $CuCO_3$
(b) $BaSO_4$
(c) $Fe(NO_3)_3$

SOLUTION

(a) Insoluble; compounds containing CO_3^{2-} are insoluble, and Cu^{2+} is not an exception.
(b) Insoluble; compounds containing SO_4^{2-} are usually soluble, but Ba^{2+} is an exception.
(c) Soluble; all compounds containing NO_3^- are soluble.

LO: Predict and write equations for precipitation reactions (Section 7.6).

To predict whether a precipitation reaction occurs when two solutions are mixed and to write an equation for the reaction, follow these steps.

1. Write the formulas of the two compounds being mixed as reactants in a chemical equation.
2. Below the equation, write the formulas of the potentially insoluble products that could form from the reactants. These are obtained by combining the cation from one reactant with the anion from the other. Make sure to adjust the subscripts so that all formulas are charge-neutral.
3. Use the solubility rules to determine whether any of the potentially insoluble products are indeed insoluble.
4. If all of the potentially insoluble products are soluble, there will be no precipitate. Write *NO REACTION* next to the arrow.
5. If one or both of the potentially insoluble products are insoluble, write their formula(s) as the product(s) of the reaction using (s) to indicate *solid*. Write any soluble products with (aq) to indicate *aqueous*.
6. Balance the equation.

EXAMPLE 7.19 **PREDICTING PRECIPITATION REACTIONS**

Write an equation for the precipitation reaction that occurs, if any, when solutions of sodium phosphate and cobalt(II) chloride are mixed.

SOLUTION

$$Na_3PO_4(aq) + CoCl_2(aq) \longrightarrow$$

Potentially Insoluble Products:

$$NaCl \qquad Co_3(PO_4)_2$$

NaCl is soluble.
$Co_3(PO_4)_2$ is insoluble.
   Reaction contains an insoluble product; proceed to Step 5.

$$Na_3PO_4(aq) + CoCl_2(aq) \longrightarrow Co_3(PO_4)_2(s) + NaCl(aq)$$

$$2 Na_3PO_4(aq) + 3 CoCl_2(aq) \longrightarrow Co_3(PO_4)_2(s) + 6 NaCl(aq)$$

LO: Write molecular, complete ionic, and net ionic equations (Section 7.7).

To write a molecular equation, include the complete, neutral formulas for every compound in the reaction.
   To write a complete ionic equation from a molecular equation, separate all aqueous ionic compounds into independent ions. Do not separate solid, liquid, or gaseous compounds.
   To write a net ionic equation from a complete ionic equation, eliminate all species that do not change (spectator ions) in the course of the reaction.

EXAMPLE 7.20 **WRITING COMPLETE IONIC AND NET IONIC EQUATIONS**

Write a complete ionic and a net ionic equation for the reaction.

$$2 NH_4Cl(aq) + Hg_2(NO_3)_2(aq) \longrightarrow$$
$$Hg_2Cl_2(s) + 2 NH_4NO_3(aq)$$

SOLUTION
Complete ionic equation:

$$2 NH_4^+(aq) + 2 Cl^-(aq) + Hg_2^{2+}(aq) + 2 NO_3^-(aq) \longrightarrow$$
$$Hg_2Cl_2(s) + 2 NH_4^+(aq) + 2 NO_3^-(aq)$$

   Net ionic equation:

$$2 Cl^-(aq) - Hg_2^{2+}(aq) \longrightarrow Hg_2Cl_2(s)$$

LO: Identify and write equations for acid–base reactions (Section 7.8).

When you see an acid and a base (see Table 7.3) as reactants in an equation, write a reaction in which the acid and the base react to form water and a salt.

EXAMPLE 7.21 **WRITING EQUATIONS FOR ACID–BASE REACTIONS**

Write an equation for the reaction that occurs when aqueous hydroiodic acid is mixed with aqueous barium hydroxide.

SOLUTION

$$\underset{\text{acid}}{2 HI(aq)} + \underset{\text{base}}{Ba(OH)_2(aq)} \longrightarrow \underset{\text{water}}{2 H_2O(l)} + \underset{\text{salt}}{BaI_2(aq)}$$

LO: Identify and write equations for gas evolution reactions (Section 7.8).

Refer to Table 7.4 to identify gas evolution reactions.

LO: Identify redox reactions (Section 7.9).

Redox reactions are those in which any of the following occurs:

- a substance reacts with elemental oxygen
- a metal reacts with a nonmetal
- one substance transfers electrons to another substance

LO: Identify and write equations for combustion reactions (Section 7.9).

In a combustion reaction, a substance reacts with O_2 to form one or more oxygen-containing compounds and, in many cases, water.

LO: Classify chemical reactions (Section 7.10).

You can can classify chemical reactions by inspection. The four major categories are:

Synthesis or combination

$$A + B \longrightarrow AB$$

Decomposition

$$AB \longrightarrow A + B$$

Single-displacement

$$A + BC \longrightarrow AC + B$$

Double-displacement

$$AB + CD \longrightarrow AD + CB$$

EXAMPLE 7.22 WRITING EQUATIONS FOR GAS EVOLUTION REACTIONS

Write an equation for the reaction that occurs when aqueous hydrobromic acid is mixed with aqueous potassium bisulfite.

SOLUTION

$$HBr(aq) + KHSO_3(aq) \longrightarrow H_2SO_3(aq) + KBr(aq) \longrightarrow$$
$$H_2O(l) + SO_2(g) + KBr(aq)$$

EXAMPLE 7.23 IDENTIFYING REDOX REACTIONS

Which of these reactions is a redox reaction?

(a) $4\,Fe(s) + 3\,O_2(g) \longrightarrow 2\,Fe_2O_3(s)$
(b) $CaO(s) + CO_2(g) \longrightarrow CaCO_3(s)$
(c) $AgNO_3(aq) + NaCl(aq) \longrightarrow AgCl(s) + NaNO_3(aq)$

SOLUTION
Only (a) is a redox reaction.

EXAMPLE 7.24 WRITING EQUATIONS FOR COMBUSTION REACTIONS

Write a balanced equation for the combustion of gaseous ethane (C_2H_6), a minority component of natural gas.

SOLUTION
The skeletal equation is:

$$C_2H_6(g) + O_2(g) \longrightarrow CO_2(g) + H_2O(g)$$

The balanced equation is:

$$2\,C_2H_6(g) + 7\,O_2(g) \longrightarrow 4\,CO_2(g) + 6\,H_2O(g)$$

EXAMPLE 7.25 CLASSIFYING CHEMICAL REACTIONS

Classify each chemical reaction as a synthesis, decomposition, single-displacement, or double-displacement reaction.

(a) $2\,K(s) + Br_2(g) \longrightarrow 2\,KBr(s)$
(b) $Fe(s) + 2\,AgNO_3(aq) \longrightarrow Fe(NO_3)_2(aq) + 2\,Ag(s)$
(c) $CaSO_3(s) \longrightarrow CaO(s) + SO_2(g)$
(d) $CaCl_2(aq) + Li_2SO_4(aq) \longrightarrow CaSO_4(s) + 2\,LiCl(aq)$

SOLUTION
(a) Synthesis; KBr, a more complex substance, is formed from simpler substances.
(b) Single-displacement; Fe displaces Ag in $AgNO_3$.
(c) Decomposition; $CaSO_3$ decomposes into simpler substances.
(d) Double-displacement; Ca and Li switch places to form new compounds.

KEY TERMS

acid–base reaction **[7.8]**
aqueous solution **[7.5]**
balanced equation **[7.3]**
combination reaction **[7.10]**
combustion reaction **[7.9]**
complete ionic equation **[7.7]**
decomposition reaction
   [7.10]

displacement reaction **[7.10]**
double-displacement reac-
   tion **[7.10]**
gas evolution reaction **[7.8]**
insoluble **[7.5]**
molecular equation **[7.7]**
net ionic equation **[7.7]**
neutralization reaction **[7.8]**

oxidation–reduction (redox)
   reaction **[7.9]**
precipitate **[7.6]**
precipitation reaction **[7.6]**
salt **[7.8]**
single-displacement reaction
   [7.10]
solubility rules **[7.5]**

soluble **[7.5]**
spectator ion **[7.7]**
strong electrolyte solution
   [7.5]
synthesis reaction **[7.10]**

EXERCISES

QUESTIONS

1. What is a chemical reaction? List some examples.
2. If you could observe atoms and molecules with the naked eye, what would you look for as conclusive evidence of a chemical reaction?
3. What are the main indications that a chemical reaction has occurred?
4. What is a chemical equation? Provide an example and identify the reactants and products.
5. What does each abbreviation, often used in chemical equations, represent?
   (a) (g) (b) (l) (c) (s) (d) (aq)
6. To balance a chemical equation, adjust the _____ as necessary to make the numbers of each type of atom on both sides of the equation equal. Never adjust the _____ to balance a chemical equation.
7. Is the chemical equation balanced? Why or why not?

$$2\, Ag_2O(s) + C(s) \longrightarrow CO_2(g) + 4\, Ag(s)$$

8. What is an aqueous solution? List two examples.
9. What does it mean if a compound is referred to as soluble? Insoluble?
10. Explain what happens to an ionic substance when it dissolves in water.
11. Do polyatomic ions dissociate when they dissolve in water, or do they remain intact?
12. What is a strong electrolyte solution?
13. What are the solubility rules, and how are they useful?
14. What is a precipitation reaction? Provide an example and identify the precipitate.
15. Is the precipitate in a precipitation reaction always a compound that is soluble or insoluble? Explain.
16. Describe the differences between a molecular equation, a complete ionic equation, and net ionic equation. Give an example of each to illustrate the differences.
17. What is an acid–base reaction? List an example and identify the acid and the base.
18. What are the distinguishing properties of acids and bases?
19. What is a gas evolution reaction? Give an example.
20. What is a redox reaction? Give an example.
21. What is a combustion reaction? Give an example.
22. What are two different ways to classify chemical reactions presented in Section 7.10? Explain the differences between the two methods.
23. Explain the difference between a synthesis reaction and a decomposition reaction and provide an example of each.
24. Explain the difference between a single-displacement reaction and a double-displacement reaction and provide an example of each.

PROBLEMS

EVIDENCE OF CHEMICAL REACTIONS

25. Which observation is consistent with a chemical reaction occurring? Why?
   (a) Solid copper deposits on a piece of aluminum foil when the foil is placed in a blue copper nitrate solution. The blue color of the solution fades.
   (b) Liquid ethyl alcohol turns into a solid when placed in a low-temperature freezer.
   (c) A white precipitate forms when solutions of barium nitrate and sodium sulfate are mixed.
   (d) A mixture of sugar and water bubbles when yeasts are added. After several days, the sugar is gone and ethyl alcohol is found in the water.

26. Which observation is consistent with a chemical reaction occurring? Why?
   (a) Propane forms a flame and emits heat as it burns.
   (b) Acetone feels cold as it evaporates from the skin.
   (c) Bubbling occurs when potassium carbonate and hydrochloric acid solutions are mixed.
   (d) Heat is felt when a warm object is placed in your hand.

27. Vinegar forms bubbles when it is poured onto the calcium deposits on a faucet, and some of the calcium dissolves. Has a chemical reaction occurred? Explain your answer.

28. When a chemical drain opener is added to a clogged sink, bubbles form and the water in the sink gets warmer. Has a chemical reaction occurred? Explain your answer.

29. When a commercial hair bleaching mixture is applied to brown hair, the hair turns blond. Has a chemical reaction occurred? Explain your answer.

30. When water is boiled in a pot, it bubbles. Has a chemical reaction occurred? Explain your answer.

WRITING AND BALANCING CHEMICAL EQUATIONS

31. For each chemical equation (which may or may not be balanced), list the number of each type of atom on each side of the equation, and determine if the equation is balanced.
  (a) $Pb(NO_3)_2(aq) + 2\,NaCl(aq) \longrightarrow$
  $$PbCl_2(s) + 2\,NaNO_3(aq)$$
  (b) $C_3H_8(g) + O_2(g) \longrightarrow 3\,CO_2(g) + 4\,H_2O(g)$

32. For each chemical equation (which may or may not be balanced), list the number of each type of atom on each side of the equation, and determine if the equation is balanced.
  (a) $MgS(aq) + 2\,CuCl_2(aq) \longrightarrow 2\,CuS(s) + MgCl_2(aq)$
  (b) $2\,C_6H_{14}(l) + 19\,O_2(g) \longrightarrow 12\,CO_2(g) + 14\,H_2O(g)$

33. Consider the unbalanced chemical equation.

$$H_2O(l) \xrightarrow{\text{electrical current}} H_2(g) + O_2(g)$$

A chemistry student tries to balance the equation by placing the subscript 2 after the oxygen atom in H_2O. Explain why this is not correct. What is the correct balanced equation?

34. Consider the unbalanced chemical equation.

$$Al(s) + Cl_2(g) \longrightarrow AlCl_3(s)$$

A student tries to balance the equation by changing the subscript 2 on Cl to a 3. Explain why this is not correct. What is the correct balanced equation?

35. Write a balanced chemical equation for each chemical reaction.
  (a) Solid lead(II) sulfide reacts with aqueous hydrochloric acid to form solid lead(II) chloride and dihydrogen sulfide gas.
  (b) Gaseous carbon monoxide reacts with hydrogen gas to form gaseous methane (CH_4) and liquid water.
  (c) Solid iron(III) oxide reacts with hydrogen gas to form solid iron and liquid water.
  (d) Gaseous ammonia (NH_3) reacts with gaseous oxygen to form gaseous nitrogen monoxide and gaseous water.

36. Write a balanced chemical equation for each chemical reaction.
  (a) Solid copper reacts with solid sulfur to form solid copper(I) sulfide.
  (b) Sulfur dioxide gas reacts with oxygen gas to form sulfur trioxide gas.
  (c) Aqueous hydrochloric acid reacts with solid manganese(IV) oxide to form aqueous manganese(II) chloride, liquid water, and chlorine gas.
  (d) Liquid benzene (C_6H_6) reacts with gaseous oxygen to form carbon dioxide and liquid water.

37. Write a balanced chemical equation for each chemical reaction.
  (a) Solid magnesium reacts with aqueous copper(I) nitrate to form aqueous magnesium nitrate and solid copper.
  (b) Gaseous dinitrogen pentoxide decomposes to form nitrogen dioxide and oxygen gas.
  (c) Solid calcium reacts with aqueous nitric acid to form aqueous calcium nitrate and hydrogen gas.
  (d) Liquid methanol (CH_3OH) reacts with oxygen gas to form gaseous carbon dioxide and gaseous water.

38. Write a balanced chemical equation for each chemical reaction.
  (a) Gaseous acetylene (C_2H_2) reacts with oxygen gas to form gaseous carbon dioxide and gaseous water.
  (b) Chlorine gas reacts with aqueous potassium iodide to form solid iodine and aqueous potassium chloride.
  (c) Solid lithium oxide reacts with liquid water to form aqueous lithium hydroxide.
  (d) Gaseous carbon monoxide reacts with oxygen gas to form carbon dioxide gas.

39. Hydrogen has been proposed as a alternative fuel to replace fossil fuels. Some scientists are trying to anticipate any potential problems that might be associated with a hydrogen-based economy. One group of scientists has calculated that the amount of atmospheric hydrogen could increase by a factor of four due to leaks in hydrogen transport and storage. Upper atmospheric hydrogen gas reacts with oxygen gas to form liquid water. An increase in upper atmospheric water would enhance processes that release atmospheric chlorine atoms. The gaseous chlorine atoms would then react with gaseous ozone (O_3) to form gaseous chlorine monoxide and gaseous oxygen, resulting in the depletion of ozone. Write balanced chemical equations for the two reactions described in this problem.

40. Waste water from certain industrial chemical processes contains aqueous Hg_2^{2+} ions. Because the mercury ion is toxic, it is removed from the waste water by reaction with aqueous sodium sulfide. The products of the reaction are solid mercury(I) sulfide and aqueous sodium ions. Write a balanced equation for this reaction.

41. When solid sodium is added to liquid water, it reacts with the water to produce hydrogen gas and aqueous sodium hydroxide. Write a balanced chemical equation for this reaction.

42. When iron rusts, solid iron reacts with gaseous oxygen to form solid iron(III) oxide. Write a balanced chemical equation for this reaction.

43. Sulfuric acid in acid rain forms when gaseous sulfur dioxide pollutant reacts with gaseous oxygen and liquid water to form aqueous sulfuric acid. Write a balanced chemical equation for this reaction.

44. Nitric acid in acid rain forms when gaseous nitrogen dioxide pollutant reacts with gaseous oxygen and liquid water to form aqueous nitric acid. Write a balanced chemical equation for this reaction.

45. Write a balanced chemical equation for the reaction of solid vanadium(V) oxide with hydrogen gas to form solid vanadium(III) oxide and liquid water.

46. Write a balanced chemical equation for the reaction of gaseous nitrogen dioxide with hydrogen gas to form gaseous ammonia and liquid water.

47. Write a balanced chemical equation for the fermentation of sugar ($C_{12}H_{22}O_{11}$) by yeasts in which the aqueous sugar reacts with water to form aqueous ethyl alcohol (C_2H_5OH) and carbon dioxide gas.

48. Write a balanced chemical equation for the photosynthesis reaction in which gaseous carbon dioxide and liquid water react in the presence of chlorophyll to produce aqueous glucose ($C_6H_{12}O_6$) and oxygen gas.

49. Balance each chemical equation.
(a) $Na_2S(aq) + Cu(NO_3)_2(aq) \longrightarrow NaNO_3(aq) + CuS(s)$
(b) $HCl(aq) + O_2(g) \longrightarrow H_2O(l) + Cl_2(g)$
(c) $H_2(g) + O_2(g) \longrightarrow H_2O(l)$
(d) $FeS(s) + HCl(aq) \longrightarrow FeCl_2(aq) + H_2S(g)$

50. Balance each chemical equation.
(a) $N_2H_4(l) \longrightarrow NH_3(g) + N_2(g)$
(b) $H_2(g) + N_2(g) \longrightarrow NH_3(g)$
(c) $Cu_2O(s) + C(s) \longrightarrow Cu(s) + CO(g)$
(d) $H_2(g) + Cl_2(g) \longrightarrow HCl(g)$

51. Balance each chemical equation.
(a) $BaO_2(s) + H_2SO_4(aq) \longrightarrow BaSO_4(s) + H_2O_2(aq)$
(b) $Co(NO_3)_3(aq) + (NH_4)_2S(aq) \longrightarrow$ $Co_2S_3(s) + NH_4NO_3(aq)$
(c) $Li_2O(s) + H_2O(l) \longrightarrow LiOH(aq)$
(d) $Hg_2(C_2H_3O_2)_2(aq) + KCl(aq) \longrightarrow$ $Hg_2Cl_2(s) + KC_2H_3O_2(aq)$

52. Balance each chemical equation.
(a) $MnO_2(s) + HCl(aq) \longrightarrow$ $Cl_2(g) + MnCl_2(aq) + H_2O(l)$
(b) $CO_2(g) + CaSiO_3(s) + H_2O(l) \longrightarrow$ $SiO_2(s) + Ca(HCO_3)_2(aq)$
(c) $Fe(s) + S(l) \longrightarrow Fe_2S_3(s)$
(d) $NO_2(g) + H_2O(l) \longrightarrow HNO_3(aq) + NO(g)$

53. Is each chemical equation correctly balanced? If not, correct it.
(a) $Rb(s) + H_2O(l) \longrightarrow RbOH(aq) + H_2(g)$
(b) $2 N_2H_4(g) + N_2O_4(g) \longrightarrow 3 N_2(g) + 4 H_2O(g)$
(c) $NiS(s) + O_2(g) \longrightarrow NiO(s) + SO_2(g)$
(d) $PbO(s) + 2 NH_3(g) \longrightarrow Pb(s) + N_2(g) + H_2O(l)$

54. Is each chemical equation correctly balanced? If not, correct it.
(a) $SiO_2(s) + 4 HF(aq) \longrightarrow SiF_4(g) + 2 H_2O(l)$
(b) $2 Cr(s) + 3 O_2(g) \longrightarrow Cr_2O_3(s)$
(c) $Al_2S_3(s) + H_2O(l) \longrightarrow 2 Al(OH)_3(s) + 3 H_2S(g)$
(d) $Fe_2O_3(s) + CO(g) \longrightarrow 2 Fe(s) + CO_2(g)$

55. Human cells obtain energy from a reaction called cellular respiration. Balance the skeletal equation for cellular respiration.

$$C_6H_{12}O_6(aq) + O_2(g) \longrightarrow CO_2(g) + H_2O(l)$$

56. Propane camping stoves produce heat by the combustion of gaseous propane (C_3H_8). Balance the skeletal equation for the combustion of propane.

$$C_3H_8(g) + O_2(g) \longrightarrow CO_2(g) + H_2O(g)$$

57. Catalytic converters work to remove nitrogen oxides and carbon monoxide from exhaust. Balance the skeletal equation for one of the reactions that occurs in a catalytic converter.

$$NO(g) + CO(g) \longrightarrow N_2(g) + CO_2(g)$$

58. Billions of pounds of urea are produced annually for use as fertilizer. Balance the skeletal equation for the synthesis of urea.

$$NH_3(g) + CO_2(g) \longrightarrow CO(NH_2)_2(s) + H_2O(l)$$

SOLUBILITY

59. Is each compound soluble or insoluble? For the soluble compounds, identify the ions present in solution.
(a) $NaC_2H_3O_2$
(b) $Sn(NO_3)_2$
(c) AgI
(d) $Na_3(PO_4)$

60. Is each compound soluble or insoluble? For the soluble compounds, identify the ions present in solution.
(a) $(NH_4)_2S$
(b) $CuCO_3$
(c) ZnS
(d) $Pb(C_2H_3O_2)_2$

61. Pair each cation on the left with an anion on the right that will form an *insoluble* compound with it and write a formula for the insoluble compound. Use each anion only once.

Ag^+ SO_4^{2-}
Ba^{2+} Cl^-
Cu^{2+} CO_3^{2-}
Fe^{3+} S^{2-}

62. Pair each cation on the left with an anion on the right that will form a *soluble* compound with it and write a formula for the soluble compound. Use each anion only once.

Na^+ NO_3^-
Sr^{2+} SO_4^{2-}
Co^{2+} S^{2-}
Pb^{2+} CO_3^{2-}

63. Move any misplaced compounds to the correct column.

Soluble	Insoluble
K_2S	K_2SO_4
$PbSO_4$	Hg_2I_2
BaS	$Cu_3(PO_4)_2$
$PbCl_2$	MgS
Hg_2Cl_2	$CaSO_4$
NH_4Cl	SrS
Na_2CO_3	Li_2S

64. Move any misplaced compounds to the correct column.

Soluble	Insoluble
$LiOH$	$CaCl_2$
Na_2CO_3	$Cu(OH)_2$
$AgCl$	$Ca(C_2H_3O_2)_2$
K_3PO_4	$SrSO_4$
CuI_2	Hg_2Br_2
$Pb(NO_3)_2$	$PbBr_2$
$CoCO_3$	PbI_2

PRECIPITATION REACTIONS

65. Complete and balance each equation. If no reaction occurs, write *NO REACTION*.
(a) $KI(aq) + BaS(aq) \longrightarrow$
(b) $K_2SO_4(aq) + BaBr_2(aq) \longrightarrow$
(c) $NaCl(aq) + Hg_2(C_2H_3O_2)_2(aq) \longrightarrow$
(d) $NaC_2H_3O_2(aq) + Pb(NO_3)_2(aq) \longrightarrow$

66. Complete and balance each equation. If no reaction occurs, write *NO REACTION*.
(a) $NaOH(aq) + FeBr_3(aq) \longrightarrow$
(b) $BaCl_2(aq) + AgNO_3(aq) \longrightarrow$
(c) $Na_2CO_3(aq) + CoCl_2(aq) \longrightarrow$
(d) $K_2S(aq) + BaCl_2(aq) \longrightarrow$

67. Write a molecular equation for the precipitation reaction that occurs (if any) when each pair of solutions is mixed. If no reaction occurs, write *NO REACTION*.
(a) sodium carbonate and lead(II) nitrate
(b) potassium sulfate and lead(II) acetate
(c) copper(II) nitrate and barium sulfide
(d) calcium nitrate and sodium iodide

68. Write a molecular equation for the precipitation reaction that occurs (if any) when each pair of solutions is mixed. If no reaction occurs, write *NO REACTION*.
(a) potassium chloride and lead(II) acetate
(b) lithium sulfate and strontium chloride
(c) potassium bromide and calcium sulfide
(d) chromium(III) nitrate and potassium phosphate

69. Correct any incorrect equations. If no reaction occurs, write *NO REACTION*.
(a) $Ba(NO_3)_2(aq) + (NH_4)_2SO_4(aq) \longrightarrow$
$\qquad\qquad BaSO_4(s) + 2\,NH_4NO_3(aq)$
(b) $BaS(aq) + 2\,KCl(aq) \longrightarrow BaCl_2(s) + K_2S(aq)$
(c) $2\,KI(aq) + Pb(NO_3)_2(aq) \longrightarrow PbI_2(s) + 2\,KNO_3(aq)$
(d) $Pb(NO_3)_2(aq) + 2\,LiCl(aq) \longrightarrow$
$\qquad\qquad 2\,LiNO_3(s) + PbCl_2(aq)$

70. Correct any incorrect equations. If no reaction occurs, write *NO REACTION*.
(a) $AgNO_3(aq) + NaCl(aq) \longrightarrow NaCl(s) + AgNO_3(aq)$
(b) $K_2SO_4(aq) + Co(NO_3)_2(aq) \longrightarrow$
$\qquad\qquad CoSO_4(s) + 2\,KNO_3(aq)$
(c) $Cu(NO_3)_2(aq) + (NH_4)_2S(aq) \longrightarrow$
$\qquad\qquad CuS(s) + 2\,NH_4NO_3(aq)$
(d) $Hg_2(NO_3)_2(aq) + 2\,LiCl(aq) \longrightarrow$
$\qquad\qquad Hg_2Cl_2(s) + 2\,LiNO_3(aq)$

IONIC AND NET IONIC EQUATIONS

71. Identify the spectator ions in the complete ionic equation.

$$2\,K^+(aq) + S^{2-}(aq) + Pb^{2+}(aq) + 2\,NO_3^-(aq) \longrightarrow$$
$$PbS(s) + 2\,K^+(aq) + 2\,NO_3^-(aq)$$

72. Identify the spectator ions in the complete ionic equation.

$$Ba^{2+}(aq) + 2\,I^-(aq) + 2\,Na^+(aq) + SO_4^{2-}(aq) \longrightarrow$$
$$BaSO_4(s) + 2\,I^-(aq) + 2\,Na^+(aq)$$

73. Write balanced complete ionic and net ionic equations for each reaction.
 (a) $AgNO_3(aq) + KCl(aq) \longrightarrow AgCl(s) + KNO_3(aq)$
 (b) $CaS(aq) + CuCl_2(aq) \longrightarrow CuS(s) + CaCl_2(aq)$
 (c) $NaOH(aq) + HNO_3(aq) \longrightarrow H_2O(l) + NaNO_3(aq)$
 (d) $2\,K_3PO_4(aq) + 3\,NiCl_2(aq) \longrightarrow$
$$Ni_3(PO_4)_2(s) + 6\,KCl(aq)$$

74. Write balanced complete ionic and net ionic equations for each reaction.
 (a) $HI(aq) + KOH(aq) \longrightarrow H_2O(l) + KI(aq)$
 (b) $Na_2SO_4(aq) + CaI_2(aq) \longrightarrow CaSO_4(s) + 2\,NaI(aq)$
 (c) $2\,HC_2H_3O_2(aq) + Na_2CO_3(aq) \longrightarrow$
$$H_2O(l) + CO_2(g) + 2\,NaC_2H_3O_2(aq)$$
 (d) $NH_4Cl(aq) + NaOH(aq) \longrightarrow$
$$H_2O(l) + NH_3(g) + NaCl(aq)$$

75. Mercury(I) ions (Hg_2^{2+}) can be removed from solution by precipitation with Cl^-. Suppose a solution contains aqueous $Hg_2(NO_3)_2$. Write complete ionic and net ionic equations to show the reaction of aqueous $Hg_2(NO_3)_2$ with aqueous sodium chloride to form solid Hg_2Cl_2 and aqueous sodium nitrate.

76. Lead ions can be removed from solution by precipitation with sulfate ions. Suppose a solution contains lead(II) nitrate. Write a complete ionic and net ionic equation to show the reaction of aqueous lead(II) nitrate with aqueous potassium sulfate to form solid lead(II) sulfate and aqueous potassium nitrate.

77. Write complete ionic and net ionic equations for each of the reactions in Problem 67.

78. Write complete ionic and net ionic equations for each of the reactions in Problem 68.

ACID–BASE AND GAS EVOLUTION REACTIONS

79. When a hydrochloric acid solution is combined with a potassium hydroxide solution, an acid–base reaction occurs. Write a balanced molecular equation and a net ionic equation for this reaction.

80. A beaker of nitric acid is neutralized with calcium hydroxide. Write a balanced molecular equation and a net ionic equation for this reaction.

81. Complete and balance each acid–base reaction.
 (a) $HCl(aq) + Ba(OH)_2(aq) \longrightarrow$
 (b) $H_2SO_4(aq) + KOH(aq) \longrightarrow$
 (c) $HClO_4(aq) + NaOH(aq) \longrightarrow$

82. Complete and balance each acid–base reaction.
 (a) $HC_2H_3O_2(aq) + Ca(OH)_2(aq) \longrightarrow$
 (b) $HBr(aq) + LiOH(aq) \longrightarrow$
 (c) $H_2SO_4(aq) + Ba(OH)_2(aq) \longrightarrow$

83. Complete and balance each gas evolution reaction.
 (a) $HBr(aq) + NaHCO_3(aq) \longrightarrow$
 (b) $NH_4I(aq) + KOH(aq) \longrightarrow$
 (c) $HNO_3(aq) + K_2SO_3(aq) \longrightarrow$
 (d) $HI(aq) + Li_2S(aq) \longrightarrow$

84. Complete and balance each gas evolution reaction.
 (a) $HClO_4(aq) + K_2CO_3(aq) \longrightarrow$
 (b) $HC_2H_3O_2(aq) + LiHSO_3(aq) \longrightarrow$
 (c) $(NH_4)_2SO_4(aq) + Ca(OH)_2(aq) \longrightarrow$
 (d) $HCl(aq) + ZnS(s) \longrightarrow$

OXIDATION–REDUCTION AND COMBUSTION

85. Which reactions are redox reactions?
 (a) $Ba(NO_3)_2(aq) + K_2SO_4(aq) \longrightarrow$
$$BaSO_4(s) + 2\,KNO_3(aq)$$
 (b) $Ca(s) + Cl_2(g) \longrightarrow CaCl_2(s)$
 (c) $HCl(aq) + NaOH(aq) \longrightarrow H_2O(l) + NaCl(aq)$
 (d) $Zn(s) + Fe^{2+}(aq) \longrightarrow Zn^{2+}(aq) + Fe(s)$

86. Which reactions are redox reactions?
 (a) $Al(s) + 3\,Ag^+(aq) \longrightarrow Al^{3+}(aq) + 3\,Ag(s)$
 (b) $4\,K(s) + O_2(g) \longrightarrow 2\,K_2O(s)$
 (c) $SO_3(g) + H_2O(l) \longrightarrow H_2SO_4(aq)$
 (d) $Mg(s) + Br_2(l) \longrightarrow MgBr_2(s)$

87. Complete and balance each combustion reaction.
  (a) $C_2H_6(g) + O_2(g) \longrightarrow$
  (b) $Ca(s) + O_2(g) \longrightarrow$
  (c) $C_3H_8O(l) + O_2(g) \longrightarrow$
  (d) $C_4H_{10}S(l) + O_2(g) \longrightarrow$

88. Complete and balance each combustion reaction.
  (a) $S(s) + O_2(g) \longrightarrow$
  (b) $C_7H_{16}(l) + O_2(g) \longrightarrow$
  (c) $C_4H_{10}O(l) + O_2(g) \longrightarrow$
  (d) $CS_2(l) + O_2(g) \longrightarrow$

89. Write a balanced chemical equation for the synthesis reaction of $Br_2(g)$ with each metal.
  (a) $Ag(s)$
  (b) $K(s)$
  (c) $Al(s)$
  (d) $Ca(s)$

90. Write a balanced chemical equation for the synthesis reaction of $Cl_2(g)$ with each metal.
  (a) $Zn(s)$
  (b) $Ga(s)$
  (c) $Rb(s)$
  (d) $Mg(s)$

CLASSIFYING CHEMICAL REACTIONS BY WHAT ATOMS DO

91. Classify each chemical reaction as a synthesis, decomposition, single-displacement, or double-displacement reaction.
  (a) $K_2S(aq) + Co(NO_3)_2(aq) \longrightarrow 2\,KNO_3(aq) + CoS(s)$
  (b) $3\,H_2(g) + N_2(g) \longrightarrow 2\,NH_3(g)$
  (c) $Zn(s) + CoCl_2(aq) \longrightarrow ZnCl_2(aq) + Co(s)$
  (d) $CH_3Br(g) \xrightarrow{\text{UV light}} CH_3(g) + Br(g)$

92. Classify each chemical reaction as a synthesis, decomposition, single-displacement, or double-displacement reaction.
  (a) $CaSO_4(g) \xrightarrow{\text{heat}} CaO(s) + SO_3(g)$
  (b) $2\,Na(s) + O_2(g) \longrightarrow Na_2O_2(s)$
  (c) $Pb(s) + 2\,AgNO_3(aq) \longrightarrow Pb(NO_3)_2(aq) + 2\,Ag(s)$
  (d) $HI(aq) + NaOH(aq) \longrightarrow H_2O(l) + NaI(aq)$

93. NO is a pollutant emitted by motor vehicles. It is formed by the reaction:
  (a) $N_2(g) + O_2(g) \longrightarrow 2\,NO(g)$
  Once in the atmosphere, NO (through a series of reactions) adds one oxygen atom to form NO_2. NO_2 then interacts with UV light according to the reaction:
  (b) $NO_2(g) \xrightarrow{\text{UV light}} NO(g) + O(g)$

  These freshly formed oxygen atoms then react with O_2 in the air to form ozone (O_3), a main component of smog:
  (c) $O(g) + O_2(g) \longrightarrow O_3(g)$
  Classify each of the preceding reactions (a, b, c) as a synthesis, decomposition, single-displacement, or double-displacement reaction.

94. A main source of sulfur oxide pollutants are smelters where sulfide ores are converted into metals. The first step in this process is the reaction of the sulfide ore with oxygen in reactions such as:
  (a) $2\,PbS(s) + 3\,O_2(g) \longrightarrow 2\,PbO(s) + 2\,SO_2(g)$
  Sulfur dioxide can then react with oxygen in air to form sulfur trioxide:
  (b) $2\,SO_2(g) + O_2(g) \longrightarrow 2\,SO_3(g)$
  Sulfur trioxide can then react with water from rain to form sulfuric acid that falls as acid rain:
  (c) $SO_3(g) + H_2O(l) \longrightarrow H_2SO_4(aq)$
  Classify each of the preceding reactions (a, b, c) as a synthesis, decomposition, single-displacement, or double-displacement reaction.

CUMULATIVE PROBLEMS

95. Predict the products of each reaction and write balanced complete ionic and net ionic equations for each. If no reaction occurs, write *NO REACTION*.
  (a) $NaI(aq) + Hg_2(NO_3)_2(aq) \longrightarrow$
  (b) $HClO_4(aq) + Ba(OH)_2(aq) \longrightarrow$
  (c) $Li_2CO_3(aq) + NaCl(aq) \longrightarrow$
  (d) $HCl(aq) + Li_2CO_3(aq) \longrightarrow$

96. Predict the products of each reaction and write balanced complete ionic and net ionic equations for each. If no reaction occurs, write *NO REACTION*.
  (a) $LiCl(aq) + AgNO_3(aq) \longrightarrow$
  (b) $H_2SO_4(aq) + Li_2SO_3(aq) \longrightarrow$
  (c) $HC_2H_3O_2(aq) + Ca(OH)_2(aq) \longrightarrow$
  (d) $HCl(aq) + KBr(aq) \longrightarrow$

97. Predict the products of each reaction and write balanced complete ionic and net ionic equations for each. If no reaction occurs, write *NO REACTION*.
  (a) $BaS(aq) + NH_4Cl(aq) \longrightarrow$
  (b) $NaC_2H_3O_2(aq) + KCl(aq) \longrightarrow$
  (c) $KHSO_3(aq) + HNO_3(aq) \longrightarrow$
  (d) $MnCl_3(aq) + K_3PO_4(aq) \longrightarrow$

98. Predict the products of each reaction and write balanced complete ionic and net ionic equations for each. If no reaction occurs, write *NO REACTION*.
  (a) $H_2SO_4(aq) + HNO_3(aq) \longrightarrow$
  (b) $NaOH(aq) + LiOH(aq) \longrightarrow$
  (c) $Cr(NO_3)_3(aq) + LiOH(aq) \longrightarrow$
  (d) $HCl(aq) + Hg_2(NO_3)_2(aq) \longrightarrow$

99. Predict the type of reaction (if any) that occurs between each pair of substances. Write balanced molecular equations for each. If no reaction occurs, write *NO REACTION*.
  (a) aqueous potassium hydroxide and aqueous acetic acid
  (b) aqueous hydrobromic acid and aqueous potassium carbonate
  (c) gaseous hydrogen and gaseous oxygen
  (d) aqueous ammonium chloride and aqueous lead(II) nitrate

100. Predict the type of reaction (if any) that occurs between each pair of substances. Write balanced molecular equations for each. If no reaction occurs, write *NO REACTION*.
  (a) aqueous hydrochloric acid and aqueous copper(II) nitrate
  (b) liquid pentanol ($C_5H_{12}O$) and gaseous oxygen
  (c) aqueous ammonium chloride and aqueous calcium hydroxide
  (d) aqueous strontium sulfide and aqueous copper(II) sulfate

101. Classify each reaction in as many ways as possible.
  (a) $2\,Al(s) + 3\,Cu(NO_3)_2(aq) \longrightarrow$
  $$2\,Al(NO_3)_3(aq) + 3\,Cu(s)$$
  (b) $HBr(aq) + KHSO_3(aq) \longrightarrow$
  $$H_2O(l) + SO_2(g) + NaBr(aq)$$
  (c) $2\,HI(aq) + Na_2S(aq) \longrightarrow H_2S(g) + 2\,NaI(aq)$
  (d) $K_2CO_3(aq) + FeBr_2(aq) \longrightarrow FeCO_3(s) + 2\,KBr(aq)$

102. Classify each reaction in as many ways as possible.
  (a) $NaCl(aq) + AgNO_3(aq) \longrightarrow$
  $$AgCl(s) + NaNO_3(aq)$$
  (b) $2\,Rb(s) + Br_2(g) \longrightarrow 2\,RbBr(s)$
  (c) $Zn(s) + NiBr_2(aq) \longrightarrow Ni(s) + ZnBr_2(aq)$
  (d) $Ca(s) + 2\,H_2O(l) \longrightarrow Ca(OH)_2(aq) + H_2(g)$

103. Hard water often contains dissolved Ca^{2+} and Mg^{2+} ions. One way to soften water is to add phosphates. The phosphate ion forms insoluble precipitates with calcium and magnesium ions, removing them from solution. Suppose that a solution contains aqueous calcium chloride and aqueous magnesium nitrate. Write molecular, complete ionic, and net ionic equations showing how the addition of sodium phosphate precipitates the calcium and magnesium ions.

104. Lakes that have been acidified by acid rain (HNO_3 and H_2SO_4) can be neutralized by a process called *liming*, in which limestone ($CaCO_3$) is added to the acidified water. Write ionic and net ionic equations to show how limestone reacts with HNO_3 and H_2SO_4 to neutralize them. How would you be able to tell if the neutralization process was working?

105. What solution can you add to each cation mixture to precipitate one cation while keeping the other cation in solution? Write a net ionic equation for the precipitation reaction that occurs.
  (a) $Fe^{2+}(aq)$ and $Pb^{2+}(aq)$
  (b) $K^+(aq)$ and $Ca^{2+}(aq)$
  (c) $Ag^+(aq)$ and $Ba^{2+}(aq)$
  (d) $Cu^{2+}(aq)$ and $Hg_2^{2+}(aq)$

106. What solution can you add to each cation mixture to precipitate one cation while keeping the other cation in solution? Write a net ionic equation for the precipitation reaction that occurs.
  (a) $Sr^{2+}(aq)$ and $Hg_2^{2+}(aq)$
  (b) $NH_4^+(aq)$ and $Ca^{2+}(aq)$
  (c) $Ba^{2+}(aq)$ and $Mg^{2+}(aq)$
  (d) $Ag^+(aq)$ and $Zn^{2+}(aq)$

107. A solution contains one or more of the following ions: Ag^+, Ca^{2+}, and Cu^{2+}. When sodium chloride is added to the solution, no precipitate occurs. When sodium sulfate is added to the solution, a white precipitate occurs. The precipitate is filtered off and sodium carbonate is added to the remaining solution, producing a precipitate. Which ions were present in the original solution? Write net ionic equations for the formation of each of the precipitates observed.

108. A solution contains one or more of the following ions: Hg_2^{2+}, Ba^{2+}, and Fe^{2+}. When potassium chloride is added to the solution, a precipitate forms. The precipitate is filtered off and potassium sulfate is added to the remaining solution, producing no precipitate. When potassium carbonate is added to the remaining solution, a precipitate occurs. Which ions were present in the original solution? Write net ionic equations for the formation of each of the precipitates observed.

109. A solution contains an unknown amount of dissolved calcium. Addition of 0.112 mol of K_3PO_4 causes complete precipitation of all of the calcium. How many moles of calcium were dissolved in the solution? What mass of calcium was dissolved in the solution?

110. A solution contains an unknown amount of dissolved magnesium. Addition of 0.0877 mol of Na_2CO_3 causes complete precipitation of all of the magnesium. What mass of magnesium was dissolved in the solution?

111. A solution contains 0.133 g of dissolved lead. How many moles of sodium chloride must be added to the solution to completely precipitate all of the dissolved lead? What mass of sodium chloride must be added?

112. A solution contains 1.77 g of dissolved silver. How many moles of potassium chloride must be added to the solution to completely precipitate all of the silver? What mass of potassium chloride must be added?

HIGHLIGHT PROBLEMS

113. Shown here are molecular views of two different possible mechanisms by which an automobile airbag might function. One of these mechanisms involves a chemical reaction and the other does not. By looking at the molecular views, can you tell which mechanism operates via a chemical reaction?

▲ When an airbag is detonated, the bag inflates. These figures show two possible ways in which the inflation may happen.

114. Precipitation reactions often produce brilliant colors. Look at the photographs of each precipitation reaction and write molecular, complete ionic, and net ionic equations for each one.

(a)   (b)

(c)

▲ **(a)** The precipitation reaction that occurs when aqueous iron(III) nitrate is added to aqueous sodium hydroxide. **(b)** The precipitation reaction that occurs when aqueous cobalt(II) chloride is added to aqueous potassium hydroxide. **(c)** The precipitation reaction that occurs when aqueous $AgNO_3$ is added to aqueous sodium iodide.

QUESTIONS FOR GROUP WORK

Discuss these questions with the group and record your consensus answer.

115. Using group members to represent atoms or ions, act out a specific balanced chemical reaction.
116. Memorize the solubility rules. Without referring back to the rules, have each group member list two ionic compounds that are expected to be soluble and two that are expected to be insoluble. Include at least one exception. Check the work of the other members of your group.

117. Define and give an example of each of the following classes of reactions: precipitation, acid–base, gas evolution, redox (noncombustion), and combustion. Have each group member define one type and provide an example, and then present his or her reaction to the group.

▶Answers to Skillbuilder Exercises

Skillbuilder 7.1
  (a) Chemical reaction; heat and light are emitted.
  (b) Not a chemical reaction; gaseous and liquid butane are both butane.
  (c) Chemical reaction; heat and light are emitted.
  (d) Not a chemical reaction; solid dry ice is made of carbon dioxide, which sublimes (evaporates) as carbon dioxide gas.

Skillbuilder 7.2
  $2 Cr_2O_3(s) + 3 C(s) \longrightarrow 4 Cr(s) + 3 CO_2(g)$

Skillbuilder 7.3
  $2 C_4H_{10}(g) + 13 O_2(g) \longrightarrow 8 CO_2(g) + 10 H_2O(g)$

Skillbuilder 7.4
  $Pb(C_2H_3O_2)_2(aq) + 2 KI(aq) \longrightarrow PbI_2(s) + 2 KC_2H_3O_2(aq)$

Skillbuilder 7.5
  $4 HCl(g) + O_2(g) \longrightarrow 2 H_2O(l) + 2 Cl_2(g)$

Skillbuilder 7.6
  (a) insoluble
  (b) soluble
  (c) insoluble
  (d) soluble

Skillbuilder 7.7
  $2 KOH(aq) + NiBr_2(aq) \longrightarrow Ni(OH)_2(s) + 2 KBr(aq)$

Skillbuilder 7.8
  $NH_4Cl(aq) + Fe(NO_3)_3(aq) \longrightarrow$ NO REACTION

Skillbuilder 7.9

$$K_2SO_4(aq) + Sr(NO_3)_2(aq) \longrightarrow SrSO_4(s) + 2\,KNO_3(aq)$$

Skillbuilder 7.10

Complete ionic equation:

$$2\,H^+(aq) + 2\,Br^-(aq) + Ca^{2+}(aq) + 2\,OH^-(aq) \longrightarrow$$
$$2\,H_2O(l) + Ca^{2+}(aq) + 2\,Br^-(aq)$$

Net ionic equation:

$$2\,H^+(aq) + 2\,OH^-(aq) \longrightarrow 2\,H_2O(l),\ \text{or simply}$$
$$H^+(aq) + OH^-(aq) \longrightarrow H_2O(l)$$

Skillbuilder 7.11

Molecular equation:

$$H_2SO_4(aq) + 2\,KOH(aq) \longrightarrow 2\,H_2O(l) + K_2SO_4(aq)$$

Net ionic equation:

$$H^+(aq) + OH^-(aq) \longrightarrow H_2O(l)$$

Skillbuilder 7.12

$$2\,HBr(aq) + K_2SO_3(aq) \longrightarrow H_2O(l) + SO_2(g) + 2\,KBr(aq)$$

Skillbuilder Plus, p. 225

$$2\,H^+(aq) + SO_3^{2-}(aq) \longrightarrow H_2O(l) + SO_2(g)$$

Skillbuilder 7.13

(a), (b), and (d) are all redox reactions; (c) is a precipitation reaction.

Skillbuilder 7.14

$$C_5H_{12}(l) + 8\,O_2(g) \longrightarrow 5\,CO_2(g) + 6\,H_2O(g)$$

Skillbuilder Plus, p. 228

$$2\,C_3H_7OH(l) + 9\,O_2(g) \longrightarrow 6\,CO_2(g) + 8\,H_2O(g)$$

Skillbuilder 7.15

(a) single-displacement (b) double-displacement (c) synthesis (d) decomposition

▶Answers to Conceptual Checkpoints

7.1 (a) No reaction occurred. The molecules are the same before and after the change.

(b) A reaction occurred; the molecules have changed.

(c) A reaction occurred; the molecules have changed.

7.2 (b) There are 18 oxygen atoms on the left side of the equation, so the same number is needed on the right: $6 + 6(2) = 18$.

7.3 (a) (a) The number of each type of atom must be the same on both sides of a balanced chemical equation. Since molecules change during a chemical reaction, their number is not the same on both sides (b), nor is the sum of all of the coefficients the same (c).

7.4 (a) Since chlorides are usually soluble and Ba^{2+} is not an exception, $BaCl_2$ is soluble and will dissolve in water. When it dissolves, it dissociates into its component ions, as shown in (a).

7.5 (b) Both of the possible products, MgS and $CaSO_4$, are insoluble. The possible products of the other reactions—Na_2S, $Ca(NO_3)_2$, Na_2SO_4, and $Mg(NO_3)_2$—are all soluble.

7.6 (d) In a precipitation reaction, cations and anions "exchange partners" to produce at least one product. In an acid–base reaction, H^+ and OH^- combine to form water, and their partners pair off to a salt.

▲ The combustion of fossil fuels such as octane (shown here) produces water and carbon dioxide as products. Carbon dioxide is a greenhouse gas that is believed to be responsible for climate change.

Quantities in Chemical Reactions 8

> *"Man masters nature not by force but by understanding. That is why science
> has succeeded where magic failed: because it has looked for no spell to cast."*
>
> —Jacob Bronowski (1908–1974)

CHAPTER OUTLINE

8.1 Climate Change: Too Much Carbon Dioxide

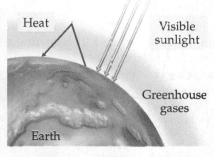

Outgoing heat is trapped by atmospheric greenhouse gases.

Heat

Visible sunlight

Greenhouse gases

Earth

▲ FIGURE 8.1 **The greenhouse effect** Greenhouse gases act like glass in a greenhouse, allowing visible-light energy to enter the atmosphere but preventing heat energy from escaping.

Average global temperatures depend on the balance between incoming sunlight, which warms Earth, and outgoing heat lost to space, which cools it. Certain gases in Earth's atmosphere, called **greenhouse gases**, affect that balance by acting like glass in a greenhouse. They allow sunlight into the atmosphere to warm Earth but prevent heat from escaping (◄ Figure 8.1). Without greenhouse gases, more heat would escape, and Earth's average temperature would be about 60 °F colder. Caribbean tourists would freeze at an icy 21 °F (−6 °C), instead of baking at a tropical 81 °F (27 °C). On the other hand, if the concentration of greenhouse gases in the atmosphere were to increase, Earth's average temperature would rise.

In recent decades, scientists have become concerned because the atmospheric concentration of carbon dioxide (CO_2)—Earth's most significant greenhouse gas in terms of its contribution to climate—is rising. This rise in CO_2 concentration enhances the atmosphere's ability to hold heat and may therefore lead to **climate change**, seen most clearly as an increase in Earth's average temperature. Since 1860, atmospheric CO_2 levels have risen by 25%, and Earth's average temperature has increased by 0.7 °C (about 1.3 °F) (► Figure 8.2).

The primary cause of rising atmospheric CO_2 concentration is the burning of fossil fuels. Fossil fuels—natural gas, petroleum, and coal—provide approximately 90% of our society's energy. Combustion of fossil fuels, however, produces CO_2. As an example, consider the combustion of octane (C_8H_{18}), a component of gasoline.

$$2 \, C_8H_{13}(l) + 25 \, O_2(g) \longrightarrow 16 \, CO_2(g) + 18 \, H_2O(g)$$

The balanced chemical equation shows that 16 mol of CO_2 are produced for every 2 mol of octane burned. Because we know the world's annual fossil fuel consumption, we can estimate the world's annual CO_2 production. A simple calculation shows that the world's annual CO_2 production—from fossil fuel combustion—matches the measured annual atmospheric CO_2 increase. This implies that fossil fuel combustion is indeed responsible for increased atmospheric CO_2 levels.

▶ **FIGURE 8.2 Climate change**
Yearly temperature differences from the 120-year average temperature. Earth's average temperature has increased by about 0.7 °C since 1880. (*Source*: NASA GISS Surface Temperature Analysis)

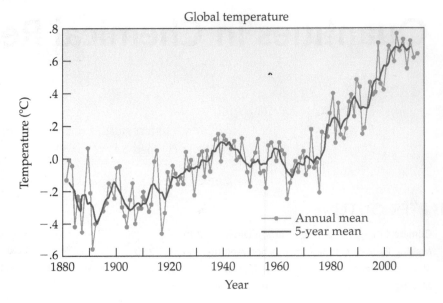

The numerical relationship between chemical quantities in a balanced chemical equation is called reaction **stoichiometry**. Stoichiometry allows us to predict the amounts of products that form in a chemical reaction based on the amounts of reactants. Stoichiometry also allows us to predict how much of the reactants is necessary to form a given amount of product, or how much of one reactant is required to completely react with another reactant. These calculations are central to chemistry, allowing chemists to plan and carry out chemical reactions to obtain products in desired quantities.

8.2 Making Pancakes: Relationships between Ingredients

LO: Recognize the numerical relationship between chemical quantities in a balanced chemical equation.

| For the sake of simplicity, this recipe omits liquid ingredients.

The concepts of stoichiometry are similar to the concepts we use in following a cooking recipe. Calculating the amount of carbon dioxide produced by the combustion of a given amount of a fossil fuel is similar to calculating the number of pancakes that can be made from a given number of eggs. For example, suppose we use the following pancake recipe:

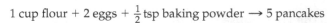

$$\text{1 cup flour} + \text{2 eggs} + \tfrac{1}{2}\text{ tsp baking powder} \longrightarrow \text{5 pancakes}$$

1 cup flour   2 eggs $\frac{1}{2}$ tsp baking powder   5 pancakes

▲ A recipe gives numerical relationships between the ingredients and the number of pancakes.

The recipe shows the numerical relationships between the pancake ingredients. It says that if we have 2 eggs—and enough of everything else—we can make 5 pancakes. We can write this relationship as a ratio:

2 eggs   5 pancakes

2 eggs:5 pancakes

What if we have 8 eggs? Assuming that we have enough of everything else, how many pancakes can we make? Using the preceding ratio as a conversion factor, we can determine that 8 eggs are sufficient to make 20 pancakes.

8 eggs   20 pancakes

$$8 \text{ eggs} \times \frac{5 \text{ pancakes}}{2 \text{ eggs}} = 20 \text{ pancakes}$$

The pancake recipe contains numerical conversion factors between the pancake ingredients and the number of pancakes. Other conversion factors from this recipe include:

1 cup flour:5 pancakes

$\frac{1}{2}$ tsp baking powder:5 pancakes

The recipe also gives us relationships among the ingredients themselves. For example, how much baking powder is required to go with 3 cups of flour? From the recipe:

1 cup flour:$\frac{1}{2}$ tsp baking powder

With this ratio, we can form the conversion factor to calculate the appropriate amount of baking powder.

$$3 \text{ cups flour} \times \frac{\frac{1}{2} \text{ tsp baking powder}}{1 \text{ cup flour}} = \tfrac{3}{2} \text{ tsp baking powder}$$

8.3 Making Molecules: Mole-to-Mole Conversions

LO: Carry out mole-to-mole conversions between reactants and products based on the numerical relationship between chemical quantities in a balanced chemical equation.

In a balanced chemical equation, we have a "recipe" for how reactants combine to form products. For example, the following equation shows how hydrogen and nitrogen combine to form ammonia (NH_3):

$$3 H_2(g) + N_2(g) \longrightarrow 2 NH_3(g)$$

The balanced equation shows that 3 H_2 molecules react with 1 N_2 molecule to form 2 NH_3 molecules. We can express these relationships as the following ratios:

3 H_2 molecules:1 N_2 molecule:2 NH_3 molecules

Since we do not ordinarily deal with individual molecules, we can express the same ratios in moles.

$$3 \text{ mol } H_2 : 1 \text{ mol } N_2 : 2 \text{ mol } NH_3$$

If we have 3 mol of N_2, and more than enough H_2, how much NH_3 can we make? We first sort the information in the problem.

GIVEN: 3 mol N_2

FIND: mol NH_3

SOLUTION MAP

We then strategize by drawing a solution map that begins with mol N_2 and ends with mol NH_3. The conversion factor comes from the balanced chemical equation.

$$\frac{2 \text{ mol } NH_3}{1 \text{ mol } N_2}$$

RELATIONSHIPS USED

1 mol N_2:2 mol NH_3 (from balanced equation)

SOLUTION

We can then do the conversion.

$$3 \text{ mol } N_2 \times \frac{2 \text{ mol } NH_3}{1 \text{ mol } N_2} = 6 \text{ mol } NH_3$$

We have enough N_2 to make 6 mol of NH_3.

EXAMPLE 8.1 MOLE-TO-MOLE CONVERSIONS

Sodium chloride, NaCl, forms by this reaction between sodium and chlorine.

$$2 \text{ Na}(s) + Cl_2(g) \longrightarrow 2 \text{ NaCl}(s)$$

How many moles of NaCl result from the complete reaction of 3.4 mol of Cl_2? Assume that there is more than enough Na.

SORT You are given the number of moles of a reactant (Cl_2) and asked to find the number of moles of product (NaCl) that will form if the reactant completely reacts.	**GIVEN:** 3.4 mol Cl_2 **FIND:** mol NaCl
STRATEGIZE Draw the solution map beginning with moles of chlorine and using the stoichiometric conversion factor to calculate moles of sodium chloride. The conversion factor comes from the balanced chemical equation.	**SOLUTION MAP** $\dfrac{2 \text{ mol NaCl}}{1 \text{ mol } Cl_2}$ **RELATIONSHIPS USED** 1 mol Cl_2:2 mol NaCl (from balanced chemical equation)
SOLVE Follow the solution map to solve the problem.	**SOLUTION** $3.4 \text{ mol } Cl_2 \dfrac{2 \text{ mol NaCl}}{1 \text{ mol } Cl_2} = 6.8 \text{ mol NaCl}$ There is enough Cl_2 to produce 6.8 mol of NaCl.

CHECK
Check your answer. Are the units correct? Does the answer make physical sense?

The answer has the correct units, moles. The answer is reasonable because each mole of Cl_2 makes two moles of NaCl.

▶**SKILLBUILDER 8.1** | **Mole-to-Mole Conversions**

Water forms when hydrogen gas reacts explosively with oxygen gas according to the balanced equation:

$$O_2(g) + 2 H_2(g) \longrightarrow 2 H_2O(g)$$

How many moles of H_2O result from the complete reaction of 24.6 mol of O_2? Assume that there is more than enough H_2.

▶**FOR MORE PRACTICE** Example 8.8; Problems 15, 16, 17, 18

 CONCEPTUAL CHECKPOINT 8.1

Methane (CH_4) undergoes combustion according to this reaction.

$$CH_4(g) + 2 O_2(g) \longrightarrow CO_2(g) + 2 H_2O(g)$$

If the figure shown in the left margin represents the amount of oxygen available to react, which of the following figures best represents the amount of CH_4 required to completely react with all of the oxygen?

(a)   (b)   (c)

8.4 Making Molecules: Mass-to-Mass Conversions

LO: Carry out mass-to-mass conversions between reactants and products based on the numerical relationship between chemical quantities in a balanced chemical equation and molar masses.

In Chapter 6, we learned how a chemical *formula* contains conversion factors for converting between moles of a compound and moles of its constituent elements. In this chapter, we have seen how a chemical *equation* contains conversion factors between moles of reactants and moles of products. However, we are often interested in relationships between *mass* of reactants and *mass* of products. For example, we might want to know the mass of carbon dioxide emitted by an automobile per kilogram of gasoline used. Or we might want to know the mass of each reactant required to obtain a certain mass of a product in a synthesis reaction. These calculations are similar to calculations covered in Section 6.5, where we converted between mass of a compound and mass of a constituent element. The general outline for these types of calculations is:

| Mass A | Moles A | Moles B | Mass B |

Molar mass A   Ratio from   Molar mass B
                    balanced equation

where A and B are two different substances involved in the reaction. We use the molar mass of A to convert from mass of A to moles of A. We use the ratio from the balanced equation to convert from moles of A to moles of B, and we use the molar mass of B to convert moles of B to mass of B. For example, suppose we want to calculate the mass of CO_2 emitted upon the combustion of 5.0×10^2 g of pure octane. The balanced chemical equation for octane combustion is:

$$2\ C_8H_{18}(l) + 25\ O_2(g) \longrightarrow 16\ CO_2(g) + 18\ H_2O(g)$$

We begin by sorting the information in the problem.

GIVEN: 5.0×10^2 g C_8H_{18}

FIND: g CO_2

Notice that we are given g C_8H_{18} and asked to find g CO_2. The balanced chemical equation, however, gives us a relationship between moles of C_8H_{18} and moles of CO_2. Consequently, before using that relationship, we must convert from grams to moles.

CHEMISTRY **IN THE MEDIA**

▶ The Controversy over Oxygenated Fuels

We have seen that the balanced chemical equation for the combustion of octane, a component of gasoline, is:

$$2\ C_8H_{18}(l) + 25\ O_2(g) \longrightarrow 16\ CO_2(g) + 18\ H_2O(g)$$

We have also learned how balanced chemical equations give numerical relationships between reactants. This equation shows that 25 mol of O_2 are required to completely react with 2 mol of C_8H_{18}. What if there is not enough O_2 in the cylinders of an automobile engine to fully react with the amount of octane flowing into them? For many reactions, a shortage of one reactant simply means that less product forms, something we will learn more about later in this chapter. However, for some reactions, a shortage of one reactant causes other reactions—called *side reactions*—to occur along with the desired reaction. In the case of octane and the other major components of gasoline, those side reactions result in pollutants such as carbon monoxide (CO) and ozone (O_3).

In 1990, the U.S. Congress, in efforts to lower air pollution levels, passed amendments to the Clean Air Act requiring oil companies to add substances to gasoline that prevent these side reactions. Because these additives increase the amount of oxygen during combustion, the resulting gasoline is called oxygenated fuel. The additive of choice

▲ At one time, MTBE was the gasoline additive of choice.

among oil companies used to be a compound called MTBE (methyl tertiary butyl ether). The immediate results were positive: Carbon monoxide and ozone levels in many major cities decreased significantly.

Over time, however, MTBE—a compound that does not readily biodegrade—began to appear in drinking-water supplies across the nation. MTBE made its way into drinking water through gasoline spills at gas stations, from boat motors, and from leaking underground storage tanks. The consequences have been significant. MTBE, even at low levels, imparts a turpentine-like odor and foul taste to drinking water. It is also a suspected carcinogen.

Public response was swift and dramatic. Several multimillion dollar class-action lawsuits were filed and settled against the manufacturers of MTBE, against gas stations suspected of leaking it, and against the oil companies that put the additive into gasoline. Most states have completely banned MTBE from gasoline. Ethanol, made from the fermentation of grains, has been used as a substitute for MTBE because it has many of the same pollution-reducing effects without the associated health hazards. Oil companies did not use ethanol originally because it was more expensive than MTBE, but now ethanol has become the additive of choice.

B8.1 CAN YOU ANSWER THIS? *How many moles of oxygen (O_2) are required to completely react with 425 mol of octane (approximate capacity of a 15-gal automobile gasoline tank)?*

▲ The 1990 amendments to the Clean Air Act required oil companies to put additives in gasoline that increased its oxygen content.

The solution map uses the general outline:

Mass A $\longrightarrow$ Moles A $\longrightarrow$ Moles B $\longrightarrow$ Mass B

where A is octane and B is carbon dioxide.

SOLUTION MAP

We strategize by drawing the solution map, which begins with mass of octane and ends with mass of carbon dioxide.

$$\frac{1 \text{ mol } C_8H_{18}}{114.3 \text{ g } C_8H_{18}} \qquad \frac{16 \text{ mol } CO_2}{2 \text{ mol } C_8H_{18}} \qquad \frac{44.01 \text{ g } CO_2}{1 \text{ mol } CO_2}$$

RELATIONSHIPS USED

2 mol C_8H_{18}:16 mol CO_2 (from chemical equation)

Molar mass C_8H_{18} = 114.3 g/mol

Molar mass CO_2 = 44.01 g/mol

SOLUTION

We then follow the solution map to solve the problem, beginning with g C_8H_{18} and canceling units to arrive at g CO_2.

$$5.0 \times 10^2 \text{ g } C_8H_{18} \times \frac{1 \text{ mol } C_8H_{18}}{114.3 \text{ g } C_8H_{18}} \times \frac{16 \text{ mol } CO_2}{2 \text{ mol } C_8H_{18}} \times \frac{44.01 \text{ g } CO_2}{1 \text{ mol } CO_2} = 1.5 \times 10^3 \text{ g } CO_2$$

Upon combustion, 5.0×10^2 g of octane produces 1.5×10^3 g of carbon dioxide.

EXAMPLE 8.2   MASS-TO-MASS CONVERSIONS

In photosynthesis, plants convert carbon dioxide and water into glucose ($C_6H_{12}O_6$) according to the reaction:

$$6 \text{ CO}_2(g) + 6 \text{ H}_2O(l) \xrightarrow[\text{sunlight}]{} 6 \text{ O}_2(g) + C_6H_{12}O_6(aq)$$

How many grams of glucose can be synthesized from 58.5 g of CO_2? Assume that there is more than enough water present to react with all of the CO_2.

SORT You are given the mass of carbon dioxide and asked to find the mass of glucose that can form if the carbon dioxide completely reacts.	**GIVEN:** 58.5 g CO_2 **FIND:** g $C_6H_{12}O_6$
STRATEGIZE The solution map uses the general outline: Mass A $\longrightarrow$ Moles A $\longrightarrow$ Moles B $\longrightarrow$ Mass B where A is carbon dioxide and B is glucose. The main conversion factor is the stoichiometric relationship between moles of carbon dioxide and moles of glucose. This conversion factor comes from the balanced equation. The other conversion factors are the molar masses of carbon dioxide and glucose.	**SOLUTION MAP** $$\frac{1 \text{ mol } CO_2}{44.01 \text{ g } CO_2} \qquad \frac{1 \text{ mol } C_6H_{12}O_6}{6 \text{ mol } CO_2} \qquad \frac{180.2 \text{ g } C_6H_{12}O_6}{1 \text{ mol } C_6H_{12}O_6}$$ **RELATIONSHIPS USED** 6 mol CO_2:1 mol $C_6H_{12}O_6$ (from balanced chemical equation) Molar mass CO_2 = 44.01 g/mol Molar mass $C_6H_{12}O_6$ = 180.2 g/mol

SOLVE	SOLUTION
Follow the solution map to solve the problem. Begin with grams of carbon dioxide and multiply by the appropriate factors to arrive at grams of glucose.	$58.5 \text{ g CO}_2 \times \dfrac{1 \text{ mol CO}_2}{44.01 \text{ g CO}_2} \times \dfrac{1 \text{ mol C}_6\text{H}_{12}\text{O}_6}{6 \text{ mol CO}_2} \times \dfrac{180.2 \text{ g C}_6\text{H}_{12}\text{O}_6}{1 \text{ mol C}_6\text{H}_{12}\text{O}_6}$ $= 39.9 \text{ g C}_6\text{H}_{12}\text{O}_6$
CHECK Are the units correct? Does the answer make physical sense?	The units, g $C_6H_{12}O_6$, are correct. The magnitude of the answer seems reasonable because it is of the same order of magnitude as the given mass of carbon dioxide. An answer that is orders of magnitude different would immediately be suspect.

▶SKILLBUILDER 8.2 | **Mass-to-Mass Conversions**

Magnesium hydroxide, the active ingredient in milk of magnesia, neutralizes stomach acid, primarily HCl, according to the reaction:

$$Mg(OH)_2(aq) + 2 \text{ HCl}(aq) \longrightarrow 2 \text{ H}_2O(l) + MgCl_2(aq)$$

How much HCl in grams can be neutralized by 5.50 g of $Mg(OH)_2$?

▶FOR MORE PRACTICE   Example 8.9; Problems 31, 32, 33, 34.

EXAMPLE 8.3   MASS-TO-MASS CONVERSIONS

One of the components of acid rain is nitric acid, which forms when NO_2, a pollutant, reacts with oxygen and rainwater according to the following simplified reaction:

$$4 \text{ NO}_2(g) + O_2(g) + 2 \text{ H}_2O(l) \longrightarrow 4 \text{ HNO}_3(aq)$$

Assuming that there is more than enough O_2 and H_2O, how much HNO_3 in kilograms forms from 1.5×10^3 kg of NO_2 pollutant?

SORT You are given the mass of nitrogen dioxide (a reactant) and asked to find the mass of nitric acid that can form if the nitrogen dioxide completely reacts.	GIVEN: 1.5×10^3 kg NO_2 FIND: kg HNO_3
STRATEGIZE The solution map follows the general format of: Mass $\longrightarrow$ Moles $\longrightarrow$ Moles $\longrightarrow$ Mass However, because the original quantity of NO_2 is given in kilograms, you must first convert to grams. The final quantity is requested in kilograms, so you must convert back to kilograms at the end. The main conversion factor is the stoichiometric relationship between moles of nitrogen dioxide and moles of nitric acid. This conversion factor comes from the balanced equation. The other conversion factors are the molar masses of nitrogen dioxide and nitric acid and the relationship between kilograms and grams.	SOLUTION MAP RELATIONSHIPS USED 4 mol NO_2 : 4 mol HNO_3 (from balanced chemical equation) Molar mass NO_2 = 46.01 g/mol Molar mass HNO_3 = 63.02 g/mol 1 kg = 1000 g

SOLVE	SOLUTION
Follow the solution map to solve the problem. Begin with kilograms of nitrogen dioxide and multiply by the appropriate conversion factors to arrive at kilograms of nitric acid.	$1.5 \times 10^3 \text{ kg NO}_2 \times \dfrac{1000 \text{ g}}{1 \text{ kg}} \times \dfrac{1 \text{ mol NO}_2}{46.01 \text{ g NO}_2} \times \dfrac{4 \text{ mol HNO}_3}{4 \text{ mol NO}_2} \times$ $\dfrac{63.02 \text{ g HNO}_3}{1 \text{ mol HNO}_3} \times \dfrac{1 \text{ kg}}{1000 \text{ g}} = 2.1 \times 10^3 \text{ kg HNO}_3$
CHECK	
Are the units correct? Does the answer make physical sense?	The units, kg HNO_3 are correct. The magnitude of the answer seems reasonable because it is of the same order of magnitude as the given mass of nitrogen dioxide. An answer that is orders of magnitude different would immediately be suspect.

▶SKILLBUILDER 8.3 | **Mass-to-Mass Conversions**

Another component of acid rain is sulfuric acid, which forms when SO_2, also a pollutant, reacts with oxygen and rainwater according to the following reaction:

$$2\,SO_2(g) + O_2(g) + 2\,H_2O(l) \longrightarrow 2\,H_2SO_4(aq)$$

Assuming that there is more than enough O_2 and H_2O, how much H_2SO_4 in kilograms forms from 2.6×10^3 kg of SO_2?

▶**FOR MORE PRACTICE**   Problems 35, 36, 37, 38.

8.5   More Pancakes: Limiting Reactant, Theoretical Yield, and Percent Yield

LO: Calculate limiting reactant, theoretical yield, and percent yield for a given amount of reactants in a balanced chemical equation.

Let's return to our pancake analogy to understand two more concepts important in reaction stoichiometry: limiting reactant and percent yield. Recall our pancake recipe:

$$1 \text{ cup flour} + 2 \text{ eggs} + \tfrac{1}{2} \text{ tsp baking powder} \longrightarrow 5 \text{ pancakes}$$

Suppose we have 3 cups flour, 10 eggs, and 4 tsp baking powder. How many pancakes can we make? We have enough flour to make:

$$3 \text{ cups flour} \times \frac{5 \text{ pancakes}}{1 \text{ cup flour}} = 15 \text{ pancakes}$$

We have enough eggs to make:

$$10 \text{ eggs} \times \frac{5 \text{ pancakes}}{2 \text{ eggs}} = 25 \text{ pancakes}$$

We have enough baking powder to make:

$$4 \text{ tsp baking powder} \times \frac{5 \text{ pancakes}}{\tfrac{1}{2} \text{ tsp baking powder}} = 40 \text{ pancakes}$$

We have enough flour for 15 pancakes, enough eggs for 25 pancakes, and enough baking powder for 40 pancakes. Consequently, unless we get more ingredients, *we can make only 15 pancakes*. The amount of flour we have *limits* the number of pancakes we can make. If this were a chemical reaction, the flour would be the *limiting reactant*, the reactant that limits the amount of product in a chemical reaction. Notice that the **limiting reactant** is simply the reactant that makes *the least amount of product*. If this were a chemical reaction, 15 pancakes would be the **theoretical yield**, the amount of product that can be made in a chemical reaction based on the amount of limiting reactant.

The term *limiting reagent* is sometimes used in place of limiting reactant.

Limiting reactant

Theoretical yield

15 pancakes   25 pancakes   40 pancakes

▲ If this were a chemical reaction, the flour would be the limiting reactant and 15 pancakes would be the theoretical yield.

The actual yield of a chemical reaction, which must be determined experimentally, often depends in various ways on the reaction conditions. We will explore some of the factors involved in Chapter 15.

Let us carry this analogy one step further. Suppose we go on to make our pancakes. We accidentally burn three of them and one falls on the floor. So even though we had enough flour for 15 pancakes, we finished with only 11 pancakes. If this were a chemical reaction, the 11 pancakes would be our **actual yield**, the amount of product actually produced by a chemical reaction. Finally, our **percent yield**, the percentage of the theoretical yield that was actually attained, would be:

$$\text{Percent yield} = \frac{11 \text{ pancakes}}{15 \text{ pancakes}} \times 100\% = 73\%$$

Since four of the pancakes were ruined, we ended up with only 73% of our theoretical yield. In a chemical reaction, the actual yield is almost always less than 100% because at least some of the product does not form or is lost in the process of recovering it (in analogy to some of the pancakes being burned).

To summarize:

- **Limiting reactant (or limiting reagent)**—the reactant that is completely consumed in a chemical reaction.
- **Theoretical yield**—the amount of product that can be made in a chemical reaction based on the amount of limiting reactant.
- **Actual yield**—the amount of product actually produced by a chemical reaction.
- **Percent yield $= \dfrac{\textbf{Actual yield}}{\textbf{Theoretical yield}} \times \textbf{100\%}$**

Consider this reaction:

$$\text{Ti}(s) + 2\,\text{Cl}_2(g) \longrightarrow \text{TiCl}_4(s)$$

If we begin with 1.8 mol of titanium and 3.2 mol of chlorine, what is the limiting reactant and theoretical yield of TiCl_4 in moles? We begin by sorting the information in the problem according to our standard problem-solving procedure.

GIVEN: 1.8 mol Ti
3.2 mol Cl_2

FIND: limiting reactant
theoretical yield

SOLUTION MAP

As in our pancake analogy, we determine the limiting reactant by calculating how much product can be made from each reactant. The reactant that makes the *least amount of product* is the limiting reactant.

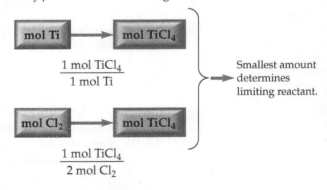

mol Ti → mol TiCl₄

$$\frac{1 \text{ mol TiCl}_4}{1 \text{ mol Ti}}$$

mol Cl₂ → mol TiCl₄

$$\frac{1 \text{ mol TiCl}_4}{2 \text{ mol Cl}_2}$$

Smallest amount determines limiting reactant.

RELATIONSHIPS USED

The conversion factors come from the balanced chemical equation and give the relationships between moles of each of the reactants and moles of product.

$$1 \text{ mol Ti} : 1 \text{ mol TiCl}_4$$

$$2 \text{ mol Cl}_2 : 1 \text{ mol TiCl}_4$$

SOLUTION

$$1.8 \text{ mol Ti} \times \frac{1 \text{ mol TiCl}_4}{1 \text{ mol Ti}} = 1.8 \text{ mol TiCl}_4$$

$$3.2 \text{ mol Cl}_2 \times \frac{1 \text{ mol TiCl}_4}{2 \text{ mol Cl}_2} = 1.6 \text{ mol TiCl}_4$$

Limiting reactant   Least amount of product

In many industrial applications, the more costly reactant or the reactant that is most difficult to remove from the product mixture is chosen to be the limiting reactant.

Since the 3.2 mol of Cl_2 make the least amount of $TiCl_4$, Cl_2 is the limiting reactant. Notice that we began with more moles of Cl_2 than Ti, but because the reaction requires 2 Cl_2 for each Ti, Cl_2 is still the limiting reactant. The theoretical yield is 1.6 mol of $TiCl_4$.

EXAMPLE 8.4   LIMITING REACTANT AND THEORETICAL YIELD FROM INITIAL MOLES OF REACTANTS

Consider this reaction:

$$2 \text{ Al}(s) + 3 \text{ Cl}_2(g) \longrightarrow 2 \text{ AlCl}_3(s)$$

If you begin with 0.552 mol of aluminum and 0.887 mol of chlorine, what is the limiting reactant and theoretical yield of $AlCl_3$ in moles?

SORT
You are given the number of moles of aluminum and chlorine and asked to find the limiting reactant and theoretical yield of aluminum chloride.
	GIVEN: 0.552 mol Al
	    0.887 mol Cl_2
	
	FIND: limiting reactant
	    theoretical yield of $AlCl_3$

STRATEGIZE Draw a solution map that shows how to get from moles of each reactant to moles of $AlCl_3$. The reactant that makes the *least amount of $AlCl_3$* is the limiting reactant. The conversion factors are the stoichiometric relationships (from the balanced equation).	**SOLUTION MAP** **RELATIONSHIPS USED** 2 mol Al : 2 mol $AlCl_3$ (from balanced equation) 3 mol Cl_2 : 2 mol $AlCl_3$ (from balanced equation)

SOLVE	SOLUTION
Follow the solution map to solve the problem.	$$0.552 \text{ mol Al} \times \frac{2 \text{ mol AlCl}_3}{2 \text{ mol Al}} = 0.552 \text{ mol AlCl}_3$$ Limiting reactant · Least amount of product $$0.887 \text{ mol Cl}_2 \times \frac{2 \text{ mol AlCl}_3}{3 \text{ mol Cl}_2} = 0.591 \text{ mol AlCl}_3$$ Because the 0.552 mol of Al makes the least amount of AlCl$_3$, Al is the limiting reactant. The theoretical yield is 0.552 mol of AlCl$_3$.
CHECK Are the units correct? Does the answer make physical sense?	The units, mol AlCl$_3$, are correct. The magnitude of the answer seems reasonable because it is of the same order of magnitude as the given number of moles of Al and Cl$_2$. An answer that is orders of magnitude different would immediately be suspect.

▶**SKILLBUILDER 8.4 | Limiting Reactant and Theoretical Yield from Initial Moles of Reactants**

Consider the reaction:

$$2 \text{ Na}(s) + \text{F}_2(g) \longrightarrow 2 \text{ NaF}(s)$$

If you begin with 4.8 mol of sodium and 2.6 mol of fluorine, what is the limiting reactant and theoretical yield of NaF in moles?

▶**FOR MORE PRACTICE**   Problems 43, 44, 45, 46, 47, 48, 49, 50.

 CONCEPTUAL CHECKPOINT 8.2

Consider the reaction:

$$\text{N}_2(g) + 3 \text{ H}_2(g) \longrightarrow 2 \text{ NH}_3(g)$$

If the flask in the left margin represents the mixture before the reaction, which flask represents the products after the limiting reactant has completely reacted?

H$_2$ N$_2$

NH$_3$

(a)   (b)   (c)

8.6 Limiting Reactant, Theoretical Yield, and Percent Yield from Initial Masses of Reactants

LO: Calculate limiting reactant, theoretical yield, and percent yield for a given amount of reactants in a balanced chemical equation.

When working in the laboratory, we normally measure the initial amounts of reactants in grams. To find limiting reactants and theoretical yields from initial masses, we must add two steps to our calculations. Consider, for example, the synthesis reaction:

$$2 \text{ Na}(s) + \text{Cl}_2(g) \longrightarrow 2 \text{ NaCl}(s)$$

If we have 53.2 g of Na and 65.8 g of Cl_2, what is the limiting reactant and theoretical yield? We begin by sorting the information in the problem.

GIVEN: 53.2 g Na

65.8 g Cl_2

FIND: limiting reactant

theoretical yield

SOLUTION MAP

Again, we find the limiting reactant by calculating how much product can be made from each reactant. Since we are given the initial amounts in grams, we must first convert to moles. After we convert to moles of product, we convert back to grams of product. The reactant that makes the *least amount of product* is the limiting reactant.

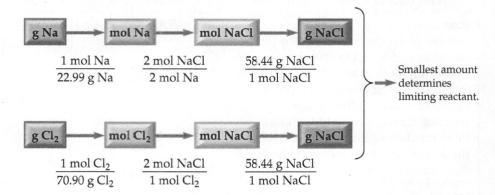

Smallest amount determines limiting reactant.

RELATIONSHIPS USED

From the balanced chemical equation, we know:

2 mol Na : 2 mol NaCl

1 mol Cl_2 : 2 mol NaCl

We also use these molar masses:

$$\text{Molar mass Na} = \frac{22.99 \text{ g Na}}{1 \text{ mol Na}}$$

$$\text{Molar mass Cl}_2 = \frac{70.90 \text{ g Cl}_2}{1 \text{ mol Cl}_2}$$

$$\text{Molar mass NaCl} = \frac{58.44 \text{ g NaCl}}{1 \text{ mol NaCl}}$$

SOLUTION

Beginning with the actual amounts of each reactant, we follow the solution map to calculate how much product can be made from each.

We can also find the limiting reactant by calculating the number of moles of NaCl (rather than grams) that can be made from each reactant. However, since theoretical yields are normally calculated in grams, we take the calculation all the way to grams to determine limiting reactant.

$$53.2 \text{ g Na} \times \frac{1 \text{ mol Na}}{22.99 \text{ g Na}} \times \frac{2 \text{ mol NaCl}}{2 \text{ mol Na}} \times \frac{58.44 \text{ g NaCl}}{1 \text{ mol NaCl}} = 135 \text{ g NaCl}$$

$$65.8 \text{ g Cl}_2 \times \frac{1 \text{ mol Cl}_2}{70.90 \text{ g Cl}_2} \times \frac{2 \text{ mol NaCl}}{1 \text{ mol Cl}_2} \times \frac{58.44 \text{ g NaCl}}{1 \text{ mol NaCl}} = 108 \text{ g NaCl}$$

Limiting reactant

Least amount of product

The limiting reactant is not necessarily the reactant with the least mass.

Since Cl_2 makes the least amount of product, it is the limiting reactant. Notice that the limiting reactant is not necessarily the reactant with the least mass. In this case, we had fewer grams of Na than Cl_2, yet Cl_2 was the limiting reactant because it made less NaCl. The theoretical yield is therefore 108 g of NaCl, the amount of product possible based on the limiting reactant.

Now suppose that when the synthesis is carried out, the actual yield of NaCl is 86.4 g. What is the percent yield? The percent yield is:

The actual yield is always less than the theoretical yield because at least a small amount of product is usually lost or does not form during a reaction.

$$\text{Percent yield} = \frac{\text{Actual yield}}{\text{Theoretical yield}} \times 100\% = \frac{86.4 \text{ g}}{108 \text{ g}} \times 100\% = 80.0\%$$

EXAMPLE 8.5 FINDING LIMITING REACTANT AND THEORETICAL YIELD

 Ammonia, NH_3, can be synthesized by this reaction:

$$2 \, NO(g) + 5 \, H_2(g) \longrightarrow 2 \, NH_3(g) + 2 \, H_2O(g)$$

What maximum amount of ammonia in grams can be synthesized from 45.8 g of NO and 12.4 g of H_2?

SORT You are given the masses of two reactants and asked to find the maximum mass of ammonia that forms. Although this problem does not specifically ask for the limiting reactant, it must be found to determine the theoretical yield, which is the maximum amount of ammonia that can be synthesized.	**GIVEN:** 45.8 g NO, 12.4 g H_2 **FIND:** maximum amount of NH_3 in g (this is the theoretical yield)
STRATEGIZE Identify the limiting reactant by calculating how much product can be made from each reactant. The reactant that makes the *least amount of product* is the limiting reactant. The mass of ammonia formed by the limiting reactant is the maximum amount of ammonia that can be synthesized.	**SOLUTION MAP**
The main conversion factors come from the stoichiometric relationship between moles of each reactant and moles of ammonia. The other conversion factors are the molar masses of nitrogen monoxide, hydrogen gas, and ammonia.	**RELATIONSHIPS USED** 2 mol NO : 2 mol NH_3 5 mol H_2 : 2 mol NH_3 Molar mass NO = $\dfrac{30.01 \text{ g NO}}{1 \text{ mol NO}}$ Molar mass H_2 = $\dfrac{2.02 \text{ g } H_2}{1 \text{ mol } H_2}$ Molar mass NH_3 = $\dfrac{17.04 \text{ g } NH_3}{1 \text{ mol } NH_3}$

SOLVE
Follow the solution map, beginning with the actual amount of each reactant given, to calculate the amount of product that can be made from each reactant.

SOLUTION

$$45.8 \text{ g NO} \times \frac{1 \text{ mol NO}}{30.01 \text{ g NO}} \times \frac{2 \text{ mol } NH_3}{2 \text{ mol NO}} \times \frac{17.04 \text{ g } NH_3}{1 \text{ mol } NH_3} = 26.0 \text{ g } NH_3$$

Limiting reactant   Least amount of product

$$12.4 \text{ g } H_2 \times \frac{1 \text{ mol } H_2}{2.02 \text{ g } H_2} \times \frac{2 \text{ mol } NH_3}{5 \text{ mol } H_2} \times \frac{17.04 \text{ g } NH_3}{1 \text{ mol } NH_3} = 41.8 \text{ g } NH_3$$

There is enough NO to make 26.0 g of NH_3 and enough H_2 to make 41.8 g of NH_3. Therefore, NO is the limiting reactant, and the maximum amount of ammonia that can possibly be made is 26.0 g, which is the theoretical yield.

CHECK	The units of the answer, g NH_3, are correct. The magnitude of the answer
Are the units correct? Does the answer make physical sense?	seems reasonable because it is of the same order of magnitude as the given masses of NO and H_2. An answer that is orders of magnitude different would immediately be suspect.

▶**SKILLBUILDER 8.5 | Finding Limiting Reactant and Theoretical Yield**

Ammonia can also be synthesized by this reaction:

$$3 H_2(g) + N_2(g) \longrightarrow 2 NH_3(g)$$

What maximum amount of ammonia in grams can be synthesized from 25.2 g of N_2 and 8.42 g of H_2?

▶**SKILLBUILDER PLUS**   What maximum amount of ammonia in kilograms can be synthesized from 5.22 kg of H_2 and 31.5 kg of N_2?

▶**FOR MORE PRACTICE**   Problems 55, 56, 57, 58.

EXAMPLE 8.6   FINDING LIMITING REACTANT, THEORETICAL YIELD, AND PERCENT YIELD

Consider this reaction:

$$Cu_2O(s) + C(s) \longrightarrow 2 Cu(s) + CO(g)$$

When 11.5 g of C are allowed to react with 114.5 g of Cu_2O, 87.4 g of Cu are obtained. Determine the limiting reactant, theoretical yield, and percent yield.

SORT	GIVEN: 11.5 g C
You are given the mass of the reactants, carbon and copper(I) oxide, as well as the mass of copper formed by the reaction. You are asked to find the limiting reactant, theoretical yield, and percent yield.	114.5 g Cu_2O 87.4 g Cu produced FIND: limiting reactant theoretical yield percent yield

STRATEGIZE	SOLUTION MAP
The solution map shows how to find the mass of Cu formed by the initial masses of Cu_2O and C. The reactant that makes the *least amount of product* is the limiting reactant and determines the theoretical yield.	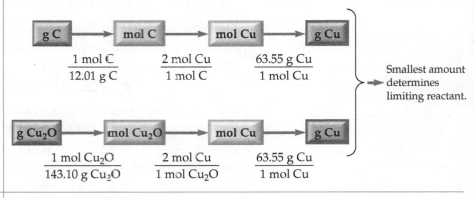

The main conversion factors are the stoichiometric relationships between moles of each reactant and moles of copper. The other conversion factors are the molar masses of copper(I) oxide, carbon, and copper.	RELATIONSHIPS USED
	1 mol Cu_2O:2 mol Cu 1 mol C:2 mol Cu Molar mass Cu_2O = 143.10 g/mol Molar mass C = 12.01 g/mol Molar mass Cu = 63.55 g/mol

SOLVE

Follow the solution map, beginning with the actual amount of each reactant given, to calculate the amount of product that can be made from each reactant.

Since Cu_2O makes the least amount of product, Cu_2O is the limiting reactant. The theoretical yield is then the amount of product made by the limiting reactant. The percent yield is the actual yield (87.4 g Cu) divided by the theoretical yield (101.7 g Cu) multiplied by 100%.

SOLUTION

$$11.5 \text{ g C} \times \frac{1 \text{ mol C}}{12.01 \text{ g C}} \times \frac{2 \text{ mol Cu}}{1 \text{ mol C}} \times \frac{63.55 \text{ g Cu}}{1 \text{ mol Cu}} = 122 \text{ g Cu}$$

$$114.5 \text{ g Cu}_2\text{O} \times \frac{1 \text{ mol Cu}_2\text{O}}{143.10 \text{ g Cu}_2\text{O}} \times \frac{2 \text{ mol Cu}}{1 \text{ mol Cu}_2\text{O}} \times \frac{63.55 \text{ g Cu}}{1 \text{ mol Cu}} = 101.7 \text{ g Cu}$$

Limiting reactant

Least amount of product

Theoretical yield = 101.7 g Cu

$$\text{Percent yield} = \frac{\text{Actual yield}}{\text{Theoretical yield}} \times 100\%$$

$$= \frac{87.4 \text{ g}}{101.7 \text{ g}} \times 100\% = 85.9\%$$

CHECK

Are the units correct? Does the answer make physical sense?

The theoretical yield has the right units (g Cu). The magnitude of the theoretical yield seems reasonable because it is of the same order of magnitude as the given masses of C and Cu_2O. The theoretical yield is reasonable because it is less than 100%. Any calculated theoretical yield above 100% is incorrect.

▶**SKILLBUILDER 8.6** | **Finding Limiting Reactant, Theoretical Yield, and Percent Yield**

This reaction is used to obtain iron from iron ore:

$$Fe_2O_3(s) + 3 CO(g) \longrightarrow 2 Fe(s) + 3 CO_2(g)$$

The reaction of 185 g of Fe_2O_3 with 95.3 g of CO produces 87.4 g of Fe. Determine the limiting reactant, theoretical yield, and percent yield.

▶**FOR MORE PRACTICE**   Example 8.10; Problems 61, 62, 63, 64, 65, 66.

   CONCEPTUAL CHECKPOINT 8.3

Limiting Reactant and Theoretical Yield

Ammonia can be synthesized by the reaction of nitrogen monoxide and hydrogen gas.

$$2 NO(g) + 5 H_2(g) \longrightarrow 2 NH_3(g) + 2 H_2O(g)$$

A reaction vessel initially contains 4.0 mol of NO and 15.0 mol of H_2. What is in the reaction vessel once the reaction has occurred to the fullest extent possible?

(a) 2 mol NO; 5 mol H_2; 2 mol NH_3; and 2 mol H_2O

(b) 0 mol NO; 0 mol H_2; 6 mol NH_3; and 6 mol H_2O

(c) 2 mol NO; 0 mol H_2; 4 mol NH_3; and 2 mol H_2O

(d) 0 mol NO; 5 mol H_2; 4 mol NH_3; and 4 mol H_2O

8.7   Enthalpy: A Measure of the Heat Evolved or Absorbed in a Reaction

LO: Calculate the amount of thermal energy emitted or absorbed by a chemical reaction.

Chapter 3 (see Section 3.9) describes how chemical reactions can be *exothermic* (in which case they *emit* thermal energy when they occur) or *endothermic* (in which case they *absorb* thermal energy when they occur). The *amount* of thermal energy emitted or absorbed by a chemical reaction, under conditions of constant pressure (which are common for most everyday reactions), can be quantified with a

EVERYDAY CHEMISTRY

▶ Bunsen Burners

In the laboratory, we often use Bunsen burners as heat sources. These burners are normally fueled by methane. The balanced equation for methane (CH_4) combustion is:

$$CH_4(g) + 2 O_2(g) \longrightarrow CO_2(g) + 2 H_2O(g)$$

Most Bunsen burners have a mechanism to adjust the amount of air (and therefore of oxygen) that is mixed with the methane. If you light the burner with the air completely closed off, you get a yellow, smoky flame that is not very hot. As you increase the amount of air going into the burner, the flame becomes bluer, less smoky, and hotter. When you reach the optimum adjustment, the flame has a sharp, inner blue triangle, no smoke, and is hot enough to melt glass easily. Continuing to increase the air beyond this point causes the flame to become cooler again and may actually extinguish it.

B8.2 CAN YOU ANSWER THIS? *Can you use the concepts from this chapter to explain the changes in the Bunsen burner as the air intake is adjusted?*

(a) No air   **(b)** Small amount of air   **(c)** Optimum   **(d)** Too much air

▲ Bunsen burner at various stages of air-intake adjustment.

function called **enthalpy**. Specifically, we define a quantity called the **enthalpy of reaction** (ΔH_{rxn}) as the amount of thermal energy (or heat) that flows when a reaction occurs at constant pressure.

Sign of ΔH_{rxn}

The *sign* of ΔH_{rxn} (positive or negative) depends on the *direction* in which thermal energy flows when the reaction occurs. If thermal energy flows out of the reaction and into the surroundings (as in an exothermic reaction), then ΔH_{rxn} is negative. For example, we can specify the enthalpy of reaction for the combustion of CH_4, the main component in natural gas, as:

$$CH_4(g) + 2 O_2(g) \longrightarrow CO_2(g) + 2 H_2O(g) \qquad \Delta H_{rxn} = -802.3 \text{ kJ}$$

This reaction is exothermic and therefore has a negative enthalpy of reaction. The magnitude of ΔH_{rxn} tells us that 802.3 kJ of heat are emitted when 1 mol of CH_4 reacts with 2 mol of O_2.

If, by contrast, thermal energy flows into the reaction and out of the surroundings (as in an endothermic reaction), then ΔH_{rxn} is positive. For example, we specify the enthalpy of reaction for the reaction between nitrogen and oxygen gas to form nitrogen monoxide as:

$$N_2(g) + O_2(g) \longrightarrow 2 NO(g) \qquad \Delta H_{rxn} = +182.6 \text{ kJ}$$

▶ **FIGURE 8.3 Exothermic and endothermic reactions** **(a)** In an exothermic reaction, energy is released into the surroundings. **(b)** In an endothermic reaction, energy is absorbed from the surroundings.

This reaction is endothermic and therefore has a positive enthalpy of reaction. When 1 mol of N_2 reacts with 1 mol of O_2, 182.6 kJ of heat are absorbed from the surroundings.

We can think of the energy of a chemical system in the same way that you think about the balance in a checking account. Energy flowing *out* of the chemical system is like a withdrawal and carries a negative sign as shown in ▲Figure 8.3a. Energy flowing *into* the system is like a deposit and carries a positive sign as shown in Figure 8.3b.

Stoichiometry of ΔH_{rxn}

The amount of heat emitted or absorbed when a chemical reaction occurs depends on the *amounts* of reactants that actually react. As we have just seen, we usually specify ΔH_{rxn} in combination with the balanced chemical equation for the reaction. The magnitude of ΔH_{rxn} is for the stoichiometric amounts of reactants and products for the reaction *as written*. For example, the balanced equation and ΔH_{rxn} for the combustion of propane (the fuel used in LP gas) is:

$$C_3H_8(g) + 5\,O_2(g) \longrightarrow 3\,CO_2(g) + 4\,H_2O(g) \qquad \Delta H_{rxn} = -2044 \text{ kJ}$$

This means that when 1 mole of C_3H_8 reacts with 5 moles of O_2 to form 3 moles of CO_2 and 4 moles of H_2O, 2044 kJ of heat are emitted. We can write these relationships in the same way that we express stoichiometric relationships: as ratios between two quantities. For the reactants in this reaction, we write:

$$1 \text{ mol } C_3H_8 : -2044 \text{ kJ} \quad \text{or} \quad 5 \text{ mol } O_2 : -2044 \text{ kJ}$$

The ratios mean that 2044 kJ of thermal energy are evolved when 1 mole of C_3H_8 and 5 moles of O_2 completely react. We can use these ratios to construct conversion factors between amounts of reactants or products and the quantity of heat emitted (for exothermic reactions) or absorbed (for endothermic reactions). To find out how much heat is emitted upon the combustion of a certain mass in grams of C_3H_8, we use the following solution map:

We use the molar mass to convert between grams and moles, and the stoichiometric relationship between moles of C_3H_8 and kJ to convert between moles and kJ, as shown in Example 8.7.

EXAMPLE 8.7 STOICHIOMETRY INVOLVING ΔH_{rxn}

An LP gas tank in a home barbecue contains 11.8×10^3 g of propane (C_3H_8). Calculate the heat (in kJ) associated with the complete combustion of all of the propane in the tank.

$$C_3H_8(g) + 5\,O_2(g) \longrightarrow 3\,CO_2(g) + 4\,H_2O(g) \qquad \Delta H_{rxn} = -2044\ kJ$$

SORT You are given the mass of propane and asked to find the heat evolved (in kJ) in its combustion.	**GIVEN:** 11.8×10^3 g C_3H_8 **FIND:** kJ
STRATEGIZE Start with the given mass of propane and use its molar mass to find the number of moles. Use the stoichiometric relationship between moles of propane and kilojoules of heat to find the heat evolved.	**SOLUTION MAP** **RELATIONSHIPS USED** 1 mol C_3H_8 : -2044 kJ (from balanced equation) Molar mass $C_3H_8 = 44.11$ g/mol
SOLVE Follow the solution map to solve the problem. Begin with 11.8×10^3 g C_3H_8 and multiply by the appropriate conversion factors to arrive at kJ.	**SOLUTION** $11.8 \times 10^3 \ g\,C_3H_8 \times \dfrac{1\ mol\,C_3H_8}{44.11\ g\,C_3H_8} \times \dfrac{-2044\ kJ}{1\ mol\,C_3H_8} = -5.47 \times 10^5$ kJ
CHECK Check your answer. Are the units correct? Does the answer make physical sense?	The units, kJ, are correct. The answer is negative, as it should be when heat is evolved by a reaction.

▶**SKILLBUILDER 8.7 | Stoichiometry Involving ΔH**

Ammonia reacts with oxygen according to the equation:

$$4\,NH_3(g) + 5\,O_2(g) \longrightarrow 4\,NO(g) + 6\,H_2O \qquad \Delta H_{rxn} = -906\ kJ$$

Calculate the heat (in kJ) associated with the complete reaction of 155 g of NH_3.

▶**SKILLBUILDER PLUS** What mass of butane in grams is necessary to produce 1.5×10^3 kJ of heat? What mass of CO_2 is produced?

$$C_4H_{10}(g) + \tfrac{13}{2}\,O_2(g) \longrightarrow 4\,CO_2(g) + 5\,H_2O(g) \qquad \Delta H_{rxn} = -2658\ kJ$$

▶**FOR MORE PRACTICE**   Example 8.11; Problems 71, 72, 73, 74, 75, 76.

 CONCEPTUAL CHECKPOINT 8.4

Stoichiometry Involving ΔH_{rxn}

Consider the generic reaction:

$$2A + 3B \longrightarrow 2C \qquad \Delta H_{rxn} = -100\ kJ$$

If a reaction mixture initially contains 5 mol of A and 6 mol of B, how much heat (in kJ) will have evolved once the reaction has occurred to the greatest extent possible?

(a) 100 kJ   **(b)** 150 kJ   **(c)** 200 kJ   **(d)** 300 kJ

CHAPTER IN REVIEW

Self-Assessment Quiz

Q1. Sulfur and fluorine react to form sulfur hexafluoride according to the reaction shown here. How many moles of F_2 are required to react completely with 2.55 mol of S?

$$S(s) + 3\,F_2(g) \longrightarrow SF_6(g)$$

(a) 0.85 mol F_2 (b) 2.55 mol F_2
(c) 7.65 mol F_2 (d) 15.3 mol F_2

Q2. Hydrogen chloride gas and oxygen gas react to form gaseous water and chlorine gas according to the reaction shown here.

$$4\,HCl(g) + O_2(g) \longrightarrow 2\,H_2O(g) + 2\,Cl_2(g)$$

If the first image below represents the amount of HCl available for the reaction, which image represents the amount of oxygen required to react completely with the amount of available HCl?

(a)   (b)   (c)

Q3. Sodium reacts with fluorine to form sodium fluoride. What mass of sodium fluoride forms from the complete reaction of 12.5 g of fluorine with enough sodium to completely react with it?

$$2\,Na(s) + F_2(g) \longrightarrow 2\,NaF(s)$$

(a) 0.658 g NaF (b) 13.8 g NaF
(c) 6.91 g NaF (d) 27.6 g NaF

Q4. Consider the hypothetical reaction shown here. If 11 moles of A are combined with 16 moles of B and the reaction occurs to the greatest extent possible, how many moles of C form?

$$3\,A + 4\,B \longrightarrow 2\,C$$

(a) 7.3 mol C (b) 8.0 mol C
(c) 17 mol C (d) 32 mol C

Q5. Consider the generic reaction:

$$2\,A + 3\,B + C \longrightarrow 2\,D$$

A reaction mixture contains 6 mol A; 8 mol B; and 10 mol C. What is the limiting reactant?

(a) A   (b) B
(c) C   (d) D

Q6. Methanol (CH_3OH) reacts with oxygen to form carbon dioxide and water according to the reaction shown here.

$$2\,CH_3OH(g) + 3\,O_2(g) \longrightarrow 2\,CO_2(g) + 4\,H_2O(g)$$

If the first image below represents a reaction mixture of methanol and oxygen, which image represents the reaction mixture after the reaction has occurred to the maximum extent possible?

(a)   (b)

(c)   (d)

Q7. Sodium and chlorine react to form sodium chloride.

$$2\,Na(s) + Cl_2(g) \longrightarrow 2\,NaCl(s)$$

What is the theoretical yield of sodium chloride for the reaction of 55.0 g Na with 67.2 g Cl_2?

(a) 1.40×10^2 g NaCl
(b) 111 g NaCl
(c) 55.4 g NaCl
(d) 222 g NaCl

Q8. A reaction has a theoretical yield of 22.8 g. When the reaction is carried out, 15.1 g of the product is obtained. What is the percent yield?

(a) 151%   (b) 66.2%   (c) 344%   (d) 88.2%

Q9. Titanium can be obtained from its oxide by the reaction shown here. When 42.0 g of TiO_2 react with 11.5 g C, 18.7 g Ti are obtained. What is the percent yield for the reaction?

$$TiO_2(s) + 2\,C(s) \longrightarrow Ti(s) + CO(g)$$

(a) 74.2%   (b) 81.6%
(c) 122%   (d) 41%

Q10. Which statement best describes an exothermic reaction?

(a) An exothermic reaction gives off heat.

(b) An exothermic reaction absorbs heat.

(c) An exothermic reaction produces only small amounts of products.

(d) None of the above.

Q11. Consider the generic reaction:

$$A + 2B \longrightarrow AB_2 \qquad \Delta H_{rxn} = -155 \text{ kJ}$$

If a reaction mixture contains 5 mol A and 8 mol B, how much heat is emitted or absorbed once the reaction has occurred to the greatest extent possible?

(a) 775 kJ emitted

(b) 775 kJ absorbed

(c) 620 kJ emitted

(d) 620 kJ absorbed

Q12. Hydrogen gas reacts with oxygen to form water.

$$2 H_2(g) + O_2(g) \longrightarrow 2 H_2O(g) \quad \Delta H = -483.5 \text{ kJ}$$

Determine the minimum mass of hydrogen gas required to produce 226 kJ of heat.

(a) 8.63 g (c) 0.942 g

(b) 1.88 g (d) 0.935 g

Chemical Principles

Stoichiometry: A balanced chemical equation indicates quantitative relationships between the amounts of reactants and products. For example, the reaction $2 H_2 + O_2 \longrightarrow 2 H_2O$ tells us that 2 mol of H_2 reacts with 1 mol of O_2 to form 2 mol of H_2O. We can use these relationships to calculate quantities such as the amount of product possible with a certain amount of reactant, or the amount of one reactant required to completely react with a certain amount of another reactant. The quantitative relationship between reactants and products in a chemical reaction is reaction stoichiometry.

Limiting Reactant, Theoretical Yield, and Percent Yield: The limiting reactant in a chemical reaction is the reactant that limits the amount of product that can be made. The theoretical yield in a chemical reaction is the amount of product that can be made based on the amount of the limiting reactant. The actual yield in a chemical reaction is the amount of product actually produced. The percent yield in a chemical reaction is the actual yield divided by theoretical yield times 100%.

Enthalpy of Reaction: The amount of heat released or absorbed by a chemical reaction under conditions of constant pressure is the enthalpy of reaction (ΔH_{rxn}).

Relevance

Stoichiometry: Reaction stoichiometry is important because we often want to know the numerical relationship between the reactants and products in a chemical reaction. For example, we might want to know how much carbon dioxide, a greenhouse gas, is formed when a certain amount of a particular fossil fuel burns.

Limiting Reactant, Theoretical Yield, and Percent Yield: Calculations of limiting reactant, theoretical yield, and percent yield are central to chemistry because they allow for quantitative understanding of chemical reactions. Just as we need to know relationships between ingredients to follow a recipe, so we must know relationships between reactants and products to carry out a chemical reaction. The percent yield in a chemical reaction is often used as a measure of the success of the reaction. Imagine following a recipe and making only 1% of the final product—your cooking would be a failure. Similarly, low percent yields in chemical reactions are usually considered poor, and high percent yields are considered good.

Enthalpy of Reaction: The enthalpy of reaction describes the relationship between the amount of reactant that undergoes reaction and the amount of thermal energy produced. This is important, for example, in determining quantities such as the amount of fuel needed to produce a given amount of energy.

Chemical Skills

Examples

LO: Carry out mole-to-mole conversions between reactants and products based on the numerical relationship between chemical quantities in a balanced chemical equation (Section 8.3).

EXAMPLE 8.8   MOLE-TO-MOLE CONVERSIONS

How many moles of sodium oxide can be synthesized from 4.8 mol of sodium? Assume that more than enough oxygen is present. The balanced equation is:

$$4\,Na(s) + O_2(g) \longrightarrow 2\,Na_2O(s)$$

SORT
You are given the number of moles of sodium and asked to find the number of moles of sodium oxide formed by the reaction.

GIVEN: 4.8 mol Na

FIND: mol Na_2O

STRATEGIZE
Draw a solution map beginning with the number of moles of the given substance and then use the conversion factor from the balanced chemical equation to determine the number of moles of the substance you are trying to find.

SOLUTION MAP

$$\frac{2\ \text{mol Na}_2\text{O}}{4\ \text{mol Na}}$$

RELATIONSHIPS USED

$$4\ \text{mol Na}:2\ \text{mol Na}_2\text{O}$$

SOLVE
Follow the solution map to get to the number of moles of the substance you are trying to find.

SOLUTION

$$4.8\ \text{mol Na} \times \frac{2\ \text{mol Na}_2\text{O}}{4\ \text{mol Na}} = 2.4\ \text{mol Na}_2\text{O}$$

CHECK
Are the units correct? Does the answer make physical sense?

The units of the answer, mol Na_2O, are correct. The magnitude of the answer seems reasonable because it is of the same order of magnitude as the given number of moles of Na.

LO: Carry out mass-to-mass conversions between reactants and products based on the numerical relationship between chemical quantities in a balanced chemical equation and molar masses (Section 8.4).

EXAMPLE 8.9   MASS-TO-MASS CONVERSIONS

How many grams of sodium oxide can be synthesized from 17.4 g of sodium? Assume that more than enough oxygen is present. The balanced equation is:

$$4\,Na(s) + O_2(g) \longrightarrow 2\,Na_2O(s)$$

SORT
You are given the mass of sodium and asked to find the mass of sodium oxide that forms upon reaction.

GIVEN: 17.4 g Na

FIND: g Na_2O

STRATEGIZE
Draw the solution map by beginning with the mass of the given substance. Convert to moles using the molar mass and then convert to moles of the substance you are trying to find, using the conversion factor obtained from the balanced chemical equation.

Finally, convert to the mass of the substance you are trying to find, using its molar mass.

SOLUTION MAP

RELATIONSHIPS USED

4 mol Na:2 mol Na_2O (from balanced equation)

Molar mass Na = 22.99 g/mol

Molar mass Na_2O = 61.98 g/mol

SOLVE

Follow the solution map and calculate the answer by beginning with the mass of the given substance and multiplying by the appropriate conversion factors to determine the mass of the substance you are trying to find.

CHECK

Are the units correct? Does the answer make physical sense?

SOLUTION

$$174 \text{ g Na} \times \frac{1 \text{ mol Na}}{22.99 \text{ g Na}} \times \frac{2 \text{ mol Na}_2\text{O}}{4 \text{ mol Na}} \times$$

$$\frac{61.98 \text{ g Na}_2\text{O}}{1 \text{ mol Na}_2\text{O}} = 23.5 \text{ g Na}_2\text{O}$$

The units of the answer, g Na_2O, are correct. The magnitude of the answer seems reasonable because it is of the same order of magnitude as the given mass of Na.

LO: Calculate limiting reactant, theoretical yield, and percent yield for a given amount of reactants in a balanced chemical equation (Sections 8.5, 8.6).

EXAMPLE 8.10   LIMITING REACTANT, THEORETICAL YIELD, AND PERCENT YIELD

10.4 g of As reacts with 11.8 g of S to produce 14.2 g of As_2S_3. Find the limiting reactant, theoretical yield, and percent yield for this reaction. The balanced chemical equation is:

$$2 \text{ As}(s) + 3 \text{ S}(l) \longrightarrow \text{As}_2\text{S}_3(s)$$

SORT

You are given the masses of arsenic and sulfur as well as the mass of arsenic sulfide formed by the reaction. You are asked to find the limiting reactant, theoretical yield, and percent yield.

GIVEN: 10.4 g As
        11.8 g S
        14.2 g As_2S_3

FIND: limiting reactant
        theoretical yield
        percent yield

SOLUTION MAP

STRATEGIZE

The solution map for limiting-reactant problems shows how to convert from the mass of each of the reactants to the mass of the product for each reactant. These are mass-to-mass conversions with the basic outline of

$$\text{Mass} \longrightarrow \text{Moles} \longrightarrow \text{Moles} \longrightarrow \text{Mass}$$

The reactant that forms the least amount of product is the limiting reactant.

The conversion factors you need are the stoichiometric relationships between each of the reactants and the product. You also need the molar masses of each reactant and product.

RELATIONSHIPS USED

2 mol As:1 mol As_2S_3

3 mol S:1 mol As_2S_3

Molar mass As = 74.92 g/mol

Molar mass S = 32.07 g/mol

Molar mass As_2S_3 = 246.05 g/mol

SOLVE

To calculate the amount of product formed by each reactant, begin with the given amount of each reactant and multiply by the appropriate conversion factors, as shown in the solution map, to arrive at the mass of product for each reactant. The reactant that forms the least amount of product is the limiting reactant.

SOLUTION

$$10.4 \text{ g As} \times \frac{1 \text{ mol As}}{74.92 \text{ g As}} \times \frac{1 \text{ mol As}_2\text{S}_3}{2 \text{ mol As}} \times \frac{246.05 \text{ g As}_2\text{S}_3}{1 \text{ mol As}_2\text{S}_3}$$

Limiting reactant

$$= 17.1 \text{ g As}_2\text{S}_3$$

Least amount of product

$$11.8 \text{ g S} \times \frac{1 \text{ mol S}}{32.07 \text{ g S}} \times \frac{1 \text{ mol As}_2\text{S}_3}{3 \text{ mol S}} \times \frac{246.05 \text{ g As}_2\text{S}_3}{1 \text{ mol As}_2\text{S}_3}$$

$$= 30.2 \text{ g As}_2\text{S}_3$$

The theoretical yield is the amount of product formed by the limiting reactant.

The percent yield is the actual yield divided by the theoretical yield times 100%.

The limiting reactant is As.

The theoretical yield is 17.1 g of As_2S_3.

$$\text{Percent yield} = \frac{\text{Actual yield}}{\text{Theoretical yield}} \times 100\%$$

$$= \frac{14.2 \text{ g}}{17.1 \text{ g}} \times 100\% = 83.0\%$$

The percent yield is 83.0%.

CHECK

Check your answer. Are the units correct? Does the answer make physical sense?

The theoretical yield has the right units (g As_2S_3). The magnitude of the theoretical yield seems reasonable because it is of the same order of magnitude as the given masses of As and S. The theoretical yield is reasonable because it is less than 100%. Any calculated theoretical yield above 100% would be suspect.

LO: Calculate the amount of thermal energy emitted or absorbed by a chemical reaction (Section 8.7).

EXAMPLE 8.11 STOICHIOMETRY INVOLVING ΔH_{rxn}

Calculate the heat evolved (in kJ) upon complete combustion of 25.0 g of methane (CH_4).

$$CH_4(g) + 2\,O_2(g) \longrightarrow CO_2(g) + 2\,H_2O(g)$$

$$\Delta H_{rxn} = -802 \text{ kJ}$$

SORT

You are given the mass of methane and asked to find the quantity of heat in kJ emitted upon combustion.

Draw the solution map by beginning with the mass of the given substance. Convert to moles using molar mass and to kJ using ΔH_{rxn}.

GIVEN: 25 g CH_4

FIND: kJ

SOLUTION MAP

$$\frac{1 \text{ mol CH}_4}{16.05 \text{ g CH}_4} \qquad \frac{-802 \text{ kJ}}{1 \text{ mol CH}_4}$$

RELATIONSHIPS USED

1 mol CH_4 : −802 kJ (from balanced equation)

Molar mass CH_4 = 16.05 g/mol

SOLVE

Follow the solution map to solve the problem. Begin with the mass of the given substance and multiply by the appropriate conversion factors to arrive at kJ. A negative answer indicates that heat is evolved into the surroundings. A positive answer indicates that heat is absorbed from the surroundings.

SOLUTION

$$25.0 \text{ g CH}_4 \times \frac{1 \text{ mol CH}_4}{16.05 \text{ g CH}_4} \times \frac{-802 \text{ kJ}}{1 \text{ mol CH}_4} = -1.25 \times 10^3 \text{ kJ}$$

CHECK

Are the units correct? Does the answer make physical sense?

The units, kJ, are correct. The answer is negative, as it should be since heat is evolved by the reaction.

KEY TERMS

actual yield **[8.5]**

climate change **[8.1]**

enthalpy **[8.7]**

enthalpy of reaction (ΔH_{rxn}) **[8.7]**

greenhouse gases **[8.1]**

limiting reactant **[8.5]**

percent yield **[8.5]**

stoichiometry **[8.1]**

theoretical yield **[8.5]**

EXERCISES

QUESTIONS

1. Why is reaction stoichiometry important? Cite some examples in your answer.

2. Nitrogen and hydrogen can react to form ammonia:

$$N_2(g) + 3 H_2(g) \longrightarrow 2 NH_3(g)$$

   (a) Write ratios showing the relationships between moles of each of the reactants and products in the reaction.
   (b) How many molecules of H_2 are required to completely react with two molecules of N_2?
   (c) How many moles of H_2 are required to completely react with 2 mol of N_2?

3. Write the conversion factor that you would use to convert from moles of Cl_2 to moles of NaCl in the reaction:

$$2 Na(s) + Cl_2(g) \longrightarrow 2 NaCl(s)$$

4. What is wrong with this statement in reference to the reaction in the previous problem? "2 g of Na react with 1 g of Cl_2 to form 2 g of NaCl." Correct the statement to make it true.

5. What is the general form of the solution map for problems in which you are given the mass of a reactant in a chemical reaction and asked to find the mass of the product that can be made from the given amount of reactant?

6. Consider the recipe for making tomato and garlic pasta.

   2 cups noodles + 12 tomatoes + 3 cloves garlic
   $\longrightarrow$ 4 servings pasta

   If you have 7 cups of noodles, 27 tomatoes, and 9 cloves of garlic, how many servings of pasta can you make? Which ingredient limits the amount of pasta that it is possible to make?

7. In a chemical reaction, what is the limiting reactant?

8. In a chemical reaction, what is the theoretical yield?

9. In a chemical reaction, what are the actual yield and percent yield?

10. If you are given a chemical equation and specific amounts for each reactant in grams, how do you determine the maximum amount of product that can be made?

11. Consider the generic chemical reaction:

$$A + 2 B \longrightarrow C + D$$

   Suppose you have 12 g of A and 24 g of B. Which statement is true?
   (a) A will definitely be the limiting reactant.
   (b) B will definitely be the limiting reactant.
   (c) A will be the limiting reactant if its molar mass is less than B.
   (d) A will be the limiting reactant if its molar mass is greater than B.

12. Consider the generic chemical equation:

$$A + B \longrightarrow C$$

   Suppose 25 g of A were allowed to react with 8 g of B. Analysis of the final mixture showed that A was completely used up and 4 g of B remained. What was the limiting reactant?

13. What is the enthalpy of reaction (ΔH_{rxn})? Why is this quantity important?

14. Explain the relationship between the sign of ΔH_{rxn} and whether a reaction is exothermic or endothermic.

PROBLEMS

MOLE-TO-MOLE CONVERSIONS

15. Consider the generic chemical reaction:

$$A + 2 B \longrightarrow C$$

   How many moles of C are formed upon complete reaction of:
   (a) 2 mol of A
   (b) 2 mol of B
   (c) 3 mol of A
   (d) 3 mol of B

16. Consider the generic chemical reaction:

$$2 A + 3 B \longrightarrow 3 C$$

   How many moles of B are required to completely react with:
   (a) 6 mol of A
   (b) 2 mol of A
   (c) 7 mol of A
   (d) 11 mol of A

17. For the reaction shown, calculate how many moles of NO_2 form when each amount of reactant completely reacts.

$$2 N_2O_5(g) \longrightarrow 4 NO_2(g) + O_2(g)$$

   (a) 1.3 mol N_2O_5
   (b) 5.8 mol N_2O_5
   (c) 4.45×10^3 mol N_2O_5
   (d) 1.006×10^{-3} mol N_2O_5

18. For the reaction shown, calculate how many moles of NH_3 form when each amount of reactant completely reacts.

$$3 N_2H_4(l) \longrightarrow 4 NH_3(g) + N_2(g)$$

   (a) 5.3 mol N_2H_4
   (b) 2.28 mol N_2H_4
   (c) 5.8×10^{-2} mol N_2H_4
   (d) 9.76×10^7 mol N_2H_4

19. Dihydrogen monosulfide reacts with sulfur dioxide according to the balanced equation:

$$2\,H_2S(g) + SO_2(g) \longrightarrow 3\,S(s) + 2\,H_2O(g)$$

$$\bigcirc = SO_2$$

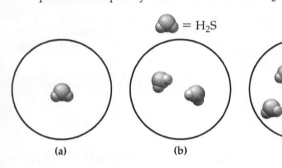

If the first figure represents the amount of SO_2 available to react, which figure best represents the amount of H_2S required to completely react with all of the SO_2?

$$\bigcirc = H_2S$$

(a)   (b)   (c)

20. Chlorine gas reacts with fluorine gas according to the balanced equation:

$$Cl_2(g) + 3\,F_2(g) \longrightarrow 2\,ClF_3(g)$$

$$\bigcirc = F_2$$

If the first figure represents the amount of fluorine available to react, and assuming that there is more than enough chlorine, which figure best represents the amount of chlorine trifluoride that would form upon complete reaction of all of the fluorine?

$$\bigcirc = ClF_3$$

(a)   (b)   (c)

21. For each reaction, calculate how many moles of product form when 1.75 mol of the reactant in color completely reacts. Assume there is more than enough of the other reactant.
(a) $H_2(g) + Cl_2(g) \longrightarrow 2\,HCl(g)$
(b) $2\,H_2(g) + O_2(g) \longrightarrow 2\,H_2O(l)$
(c) $2\,Na(s) + O_2(g) \longrightarrow Na_2O_2(s)$
(d) $2\,S(s) + 3\,O_2(g) \longrightarrow 2\,SO_3(g)$

22. For each reaction, calculate how many moles of the product form when 0.112 mol of the reactant in color completely reacts. Assume there is more than enough of the other reactant.
(a) $2\,Ca(s) + O_2(g) \longrightarrow 2\,CaO(s)$
(b) $4\,Fe(s) + 3\,O_2(g) \longrightarrow 2\,Fe_2O_3(s)$
(c) $4\,K(s) + O_2(g) \longrightarrow 2\,K_2O(s)$
(d) $4\,Al(s) + 3\,O_2(g) \longrightarrow 2\,Al_2O_3(s)$

23. For the reaction shown, calculate how many moles of each product form when the given amount of each reactant completely reacts. Assume there is more than enough of the other reactant.

$$2\,PbS(s) + 3\,O_2(g) \longrightarrow 2\,PbO(s) + 2\,SO_2(g)$$

(a) 2.4 mol PbS
(b) 2.4 mol O_2
(c) 5.3 mol PbS
(d) 5.3 mol O_2

24. For the reaction shown, calculate how many moles of each product form when the given amount of each reactant completely reacts. Assume there is more than enough of the other reactant.

$$C_3H_8(g) + 5\,O_2(g) \longrightarrow 3\,CO_2(g) + 4\,H_2O(g)$$

(a) 4.6 mol C_3H_8
(b) 4.6 mol O_2
(c) 0.0558 mol C_3H_8
(d) 0.0558 mol O_2

25. Consider the balanced equation:

$$2\,N_2H_4(g) + N_2O_4(g) \longrightarrow 3\,N_2(g) + 4\,H_2O(g)$$

Complete the table with the appropriate number of moles of reactants and products. If the number of moles of a reactant is provided, fill in the required amount of the other reactant, as well as the moles of each product formed. If the number of moles of a product is provided, fill in the required amount of each reactant to make that amount of product, as well as the amount of the other product that is made.

mol N_2H_4	mol N_2O_4	mol N_2	mol H_2O
___	2	___	___
6	___	___	___
___	___	___	8
___	5.5	___	___
3	___	___	___
___	___	12.4	___

26. Consider the balanced equation:

$$SiO_2(s) + 3\,C(s) \longrightarrow SiC(s) + 2\,CO(g)$$

Complete the table with the appropriate number of moles of reactants and products. If the number of moles of a reactant is provided, fill in the required amount of the other reactant, as well as the moles of each product formed. If the number of moles of a product is provided, fill in the required amount of each reactant to make that amount of product, as well as the amount of the other product that is made.

mol SiO$_2$	mol C	mol SiC	mol CO
	6		
3			
			10
	9.5		
3.2			

27. Consider the unbalanced equation for the combustion of butane:

$$C_4H_{10}(g) + O_2(g) \longrightarrow CO_2(g) + H_2O(g)$$

Balance the equation and determine how many moles of O_2 are required to react completely with 4.9 mol of C_4H_{10}.

28. Consider the unbalanced equation for the neutralization of acetic acid:

$$2\,HC_2H_3O_2(aq) + Ca(OH)_2(aq) \longrightarrow$$
$$2\,H_2O(l) + Ca(C_2H_3O_2)_2(aq)$$

Balance the equation and determine how many moles of $Ca(OH)_2$ are required to completely neutralize 1.07 mol of $HC_2H_3O_2$.

29. Consider the unbalanced equation for the reaction of solid lead with silver nitrate:

$$Pb(s) + AgNO_3(aq) \longrightarrow Pb(NO_3)_2(aq) + Ag(s)$$

(a) Balance the equation.
(b) How many moles of silver nitrate are required to completely react with 9.3 mol of lead?
(c) How many moles of Ag are formed by the complete reaction of 28.4 mol of Pb?

30. Consider the unbalanced equation for the reaction of aluminum with sulfuric acid:

$$Al(s) + H_2SO_4(aq) \longrightarrow Al_2(SO_4)_3(aq) + H_2(g)$$

(a) Balance the equation.
(b) How many moles of H_2SO_4 are required to completely react with 8.3 mol of Al?
(c) How many moles of H_2 are formed by the complete reaction of 0.341 mol of Al?

MASS-TO-MASS CONVERSIONS

31. For the reaction shown, calculate how many grams of oxygen form when each quantity of reactant completely reacts.

$$2\,HgO(s) \longrightarrow 2\,Hg(l) + O_2(g)$$

(a) 2.13 g HgO
(b) 6.77 g HgO
(c) 1.55 kg HgO
(d) 3.87 mg HgO

32. For the reaction shown, calculate how many grams of oxygen form when each quantity of reactant completely reacts.

$$2\,KClO_3(s) \longrightarrow 2\,KCl(s) + 3\,O_2(g)$$

(a) 2.72 g KClO$_3$
(b) 0.361g KClO$_3$
(c) 83.6 kg KClO$_3$
(d) 22.4 mg KClO$_3$

33. For each of the reactions, calculate how many grams of the product form when 2.4 g of the reactant in color completely reacts. Assume there is more than enough of the other reactant.

(a) $2\,Na(s) + Cl_2(g) \longrightarrow 2\,NaCl(s)$
(b) $CaO(s) + CO_2(g) \longrightarrow CaCO_3(s)$
(c) $2\,Mg(s) + O_2(g) \longrightarrow 2\,MgO(s)$
(d) $Na_2O(s) + H_2O(l) \longrightarrow 2\,NaOH(aq)$

34. For each of the reactions, calculate how many grams of the product form when 17.8 g of the reactant in color completely reacts. Assume there is more than enough of the other reactant.

(a) $Ca(s) + Cl_2(g) \longrightarrow CaCl_2(s)$
(b) $2\,K(s) + Br_2(l) \longrightarrow 2\,KBr(s)$
(c) $4\,Cr(s) + 3\,O_2(g) \longrightarrow 2\,Cr_2O_3(s)$
(d) $2\,Sr(s) + O_2(g) \longrightarrow 2\,SrO(s)$

35. For the reaction shown, calculate how many grams of each product form when the given amount of each reactant completely reacts to form products. Assume there is more than enough of the other reactant.

$$2\,Al(s) + Fe_2O_3(s) \longrightarrow Al_2O_3(s) + 2\,Fe(l)$$

(a) 4.7 g Al
(b) 4.7 g Fe$_2$O$_3$

36. For the reaction shown, calculate how many grams of each product form when the given amount of each reactant completely reacts to form products. Assume there is more than enough of the other reactant.

$$2\,HCl(aq) + Na_2CO_3(aq) \longrightarrow$$
$$2\,NaCl(aq) + H_2O(l) + CO_2(g)$$

(a) 10.8 g HCl
(b) 10.8 g Na$_2$CO$_3$

37. Consider the balanced equation for the combustion of methane, a component of natural gas:

$$CH_4(g) + 2\,O_2(g) \longrightarrow CO_2(g) + 2\,H_2O(g)$$

Complete the table with the appropriate masses of reactants and products. If the mass of a reactant is provided, fill in the mass of other reactants required to completely react with the given mass, as well as the mass of each product formed. If the mass of a product is provided, fill in the required masses of each reactant to make that amount of product, as well as the mass of the other product that forms.

Mass CH₄	Mass O₂	Mass CO₂	Mass H₂O
_____	2.57 g	_____	_____
22.32 g	_____	_____	_____
_____	_____	_____	11.32 g
_____	_____	2.94 g	_____
3.18 kg	_____	_____	_____
_____	_____	2.35 × 10³ kg	_____

38. Consider the balanced equation for the combustion of butane, a fuel often used in lighters:

$$2\,C_4H_{10}(g) + 13\,O_2(g) \longrightarrow 8\,CO_2(g) + 10\,H_2O(g)$$

Complete the table showing the appropriate masses of reactants and products. If the mass of a reactant is provided, fill in the mass of other reactants required to completely react with the given mass, as well as the mass of each product formed. If the mass of a product is provided, fill in the required masses of each reactant to make that amount of product, as well as the mass of the other product that forms.

Mass C₄H₁₀	Mass O₂	Mass CO₂	Mass H₂O
_____	1.11 g	_____	_____
5.22 g	_____	_____	_____
_____	_____	10.12 g	_____
_____	_____	_____	9.04 g
232 mg	_____	_____	_____
_____	_____	118 mg	_____

39. For each acid–base reaction, calculate how many grams of acid are necessary to completely react with and neutralize 2.5 g of the base.
(a) $HCl(aq) + NaOH(aq) \longrightarrow H_2O(l) + NaCl(aq)$
(b) $2\,HNO_3(aq) + Ca(OH)_2(aq) \longrightarrow$
$\qquad\qquad\qquad 2\,H_2O(l) + Ca(NO_3)_2(aq)$
(c) $H_2SO_4(aq) + 2\,KOH(aq) \longrightarrow 2\,H_2O(l) + K_2SO_4(aq)$

40. For each precipitation reaction, calculate how many grams of the first reactant are necessary to completely react with 17.3 g of the second reactant.
(a) $2\,KI(aq) + Pb(NO_3)_2(aq) \longrightarrow PbI_2(s) + 2\,KNO_3(aq)$
(b) $Na_2CO_3(aq) + CuCl_2(aq) \longrightarrow CuCO_3(s) + 2\,NaCl(aq)$
(c) $K_2SO_4(aq) + Sr(NO_3)_2(aq) \longrightarrow$
$\qquad\qquad\qquad SrSO_4(s) + 2\,KNO_3(aq)$

41. Sulfuric acid can dissolve aluminum metal according to the reaction:

$$2\,Al(s) + 3\,H_2SO_4(aq) \longrightarrow Al_2(SO_4)_3(aq) + 3\,H_2(g)$$

Suppose you wanted to dissolve an aluminum block with a mass of 22.5 g. What minimum amount of H_2SO_4 in grams do you need? How many grams of H_2 gas will be produced by the complete reaction of the aluminum block?

42. Hydrochloric acid can dissolve solid iron according to the reaction:

$$Fe(s) + 2\,HCl(aq) \longrightarrow FeCl_2(aq) + H_2(g)$$

What minimum mass of HCl in grams dissolves a 2.8-g iron bar on a padlock? How much H_2 is produced by the complete reaction of the iron bar?

LIMITING REACTANT, THEORETICAL YIELD, AND PERCENT YIELD

43. Consider the generic chemical equation:

$$2\,A + 4\,B \longrightarrow 3\,C$$

What is the limiting reactant when each of the initial quantities of A and B is allowed to react?
(a) 2 mol A; 5 mol B
(b) 1.8 mol A; 4 mol B
(c) 3 mol A; 4 mol B
(d) 22 mol A; 40 mol B

44. Consider the generic chemical equation:

$$A + 3\,B \longrightarrow C$$

What is the limiting reactant when each of the initial quantities of A and B is allowed to react?
(a) 1 mol A; 4 mol B
(b) 2 mol A; 3 mol B
(c) 0.5 mol A; 1.6 mol B
(d) 24 mol A; 75 mol B

45. Determine the theoretical yield of C when each of the initial quantities of A and B is allowed to react in the generic reaction:

$$A + 2\,B \longrightarrow 3\,C$$

(a) 1 mol A; 1 mol B
(b) 2 mol A; 2 mol B
(c) 1 mol A; 3 mol B
(d) 32 mol A; 68 mol B

46. Determine the theoretical yield of C when each of the initial quantities of A and B is allowed to react in the generic reaction:

$$2\,A + 3\,B \longrightarrow 2\,C$$

(a) 2 mol A; 4 mol B
(b) 3 mol A; 3 mol B
(c) 5 mol A; 6 mol B
(d) 4 mol A; 5 mol B

47. For the reaction shown, find the limiting reactant for each of the initial quantities of reactants.

$$2 K(s) + Cl_2(g) \longrightarrow 2 KCl(s)$$

(a) 1 mol K; 1 mol Cl_2
(b) 1.8 mol K; 1 mol Cl_2
(c) 2.2 mol K; 1 mol Cl_2
(d) 14.6 mol K; 7.8 mol Cl_2

48. For the reaction shown, find the limiting reactant for each of the initial quantities of reactants.

$$4 Cr(s) + 3 O_2(g) \longrightarrow 2 Cr_2O_3(s)$$

(a) 1 mol Cr; 1 mol O_2
(b) 4 mol Cr; 2.5 mol O_2
(c) 12 mol Cr; 10 mol O_2
(d) 14.8 mol Cr; 10.3 mol O_2

49. For the reaction shown, calculate the theoretical yield of product in moles for each of the initial quantities of reactants.

$$2 Mn(s) + 3 O_2(g) \longrightarrow 2 MnO_3(s)$$

(a) 2 mol Mn; 2 mol O_2
(b) 4.8 mol Mn; 8.5 mol O_2
(c) 0.114 mol Mn; 0.161 mol O_2
(d) 27.5 mol Mn; 43.8 mol O_2

50. For the reaction shown, calculate the theoretical yield of the product in moles for each of the initial quantities of reactants.

$$Ti(s) + 2 Cl_2(g) \longrightarrow TiCl_4(s)$$

(a) 2 mol Ti; 2 mol Cl_2
(b) 5 mol Ti; 9 mol Cl_2
(c) 0.483 mol Ti; 0.911 mol Cl_2
(d) 12.4 mol Ti; 15.8 mol Cl_2

51. Consider the generic reaction between reactants A and B:

$$3 A + 4 B \longrightarrow 2 C$$

If a reaction vessel initially contains 9 mol A and 8 mol B, how many moles of A, B, and C will be in the reaction vessel after the reactants have reacted as much as possible? (Assume 100% actual yield.)

52. Consider the reaction between reactants S and O_2:

$$2 S(s) + 3 O_2(g) \longrightarrow 2 SO_3(g)$$

If a reaction vessel initially contains 5 mol S and 9 mol O_2, how many moles of S, O_2, and SO_3 will be in the reaction vessel after the reactants have reacted as much as possible? (Assume 100% actual yield.)

53. Consider the reaction:

$$4 HCl(g) + O_2(g) \longrightarrow 2 H_2O(g) + 2 Cl_2(g)$$

Each molecular diagram represents an initial mixture of the reactants. How many molecules of Cl_2 are formed by complete reaction in each case? (Assume 100% actual yield.)

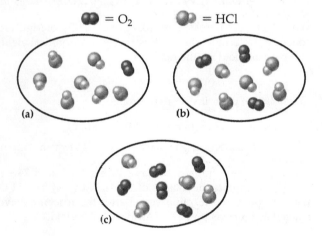

54. Consider the reaction:

$$2 CH_3OH(g) + 3 O_2(g) \longrightarrow 2 CO_2(g) + 4 H_2O(g)$$

Each molecular diagram represents an initial mixture of the reactants. How many CO_2 molecules are formed by complete reaction in each case? (Assume 100% actual yield.)

55. For the reaction shown, find the limiting reactant for each of the initial quantities of reactants.

$$2 Li(s) + F_2(g) \longrightarrow 2 LiF(s)$$

(a) 1.0 g Li; 1.0 g F_2
(b) 10.5 g Li; 37.2 g F_2
(c) 2.85×10^3 g Li; 6.79×10^3 g F_2

56. For the reaction shown, find the limiting reactant for each of the initial quantities of reactants.

$$4 Al(s) + 3 O_2(g) \longrightarrow 2 Al_2O_3(s)$$

(a) 1.0 g Al; 1.0 g O_2
(b) 2.2 g Al; 1.8 g O_2
(c) 0.353 g Al; 0.482 g O_2

57. For the reaction shown, calculate the theoretical yield of the product in grams for each of the initial quantities of reactants.

$$2\,Al(s) + 3\,Cl_2(g) \longrightarrow 2\,AlCl_3(s)$$

(a) 1.0 g Al; 1.0 g Cl_2
(b) 5.5 g Al; 19.8 g Cl_2
(c) 0.439 g Al; 2.29 g Cl_2

58. For the reaction shown, calculate the theoretical yield of the product in grams for each of the initial quantities of reactants.

$$Ti(s) + 2\,F_2(g) \longrightarrow TiF_4(s)$$

(a) 1.0 g Ti; 1.0 g F_2
(b) 4.8 g Ti; 3.2 g F_2
(c) 0.388 g Ti; 0.341 g F_2

59. If the theoretical yield of a reaction is 24.8 g and the actual yield is 18.5 g, what is the percent yield?

60. If the theoretical yield of a reaction is 0.118 g and the actual yield is 0.104 g, what is the percent yield?

61. Consider the reaction between calcium oxide and carbon dioxide:

$$CaO(s) + CO_2(g) \longrightarrow CaCO_3(s)$$

A chemist allows 14.4 g of CaO and 13.8 g of CO_2 to react. When the reaction is finished, the chemist collects 19.4 g of $CaCO_3$. Determine the limiting reactant, theoretical yield, and percent yield for the reaction.

62. Consider the reaction between sulfur trioxide and water:

$$SO_3(g) + H_2O(l) \longrightarrow H_2SO_4(aq)$$

A chemist allows 61.5 g of SO_3 and 11.2 g of H_2O to react. When the reaction is finished, the chemist collects 54.9 g of H_2SO_4. Determine the limiting reactant, theoretical yield, and percent yield for the reaction.

63. Consider the reaction between NiS_2 and O_2:

$$2\,NiS_2(s) + 5\,O_2(g) \longrightarrow 2\,NiO(s) + 4\,SO_2(g)$$

When 11.2 g of NiS_2 react with 5.43 g of O_2, 4.86 g of NiO are obtained. Determine the limiting reactant, theoretical yield of NiO, and percent yield for the reaction.

64. Consider the reaction between HCl and O_2:

$$4\,HCl(g) + O_2(g) \longrightarrow 2\,H_2O(l) + 2\,Cl_2(g)$$

When 63.1 g of HCl react with 17.2 g of O_2, 49.3 g of Cl_2 are collected. Determine the limiting reactant, theoretical yield of Cl_2, and percent yield for the reaction.

65. Lead ions can be precipitated from solution with NaCl according to the reaction:

$$Pb^{2+}(aq) + 2\,NaCl(aq) \longrightarrow PbCl_2(s) + 2\,Na^+(aq)$$

When 135.8 g of NaCl are added to a solution containing 195.7 g of Pb^{2+}, a $PbCl_2$ precipitate forms. The precipitate is filtered and dried and found to have a mass of 252.4 g. Determine the limiting reactant, theoretical yield of $PbCl_2$, and percent yield for the reaction.

66. Magnesium oxide can be produced by heating magnesium metal in the presence of oxygen. The balanced equation for the reaction is:

$$2\,Mg(s) + O_2(g) \longrightarrow 2\,MgO(s)$$

When 10.1 g of Mg react with 10.5 g of O_2, 11.9 g of MgO are collected. Determine the limiting reactant, theoretical yield, and percent yield for the reaction.

67. Consider the reaction between TiO_2 and C:

$$TiO_2(s) + 2\,C(s) \longrightarrow Ti(s) + 2\,CO(g)$$

A reaction vessel initially contains 10.0 g of each of the reactants. Calculate the masses of TiO_2, C, Ti, and CO that will be in the reaction vessel after the reactants have reacted as much as possible. (Assume 100% yield.)

68. Consider the reaction between N_2H_4 and N_2O_4:

$$2\,N_2H_4(g) + N_2O_4(g) \longrightarrow 3\,N_2(g) + 4\,H_2O(g)$$

A reaction vessel initially contains 27.5 g N_2H_4 and 74.9 g of N_2O_4. Calculate the masses of N_2H_4, N_2O_4, N_2, and H_2O that will be in the reaction vessel after the reactants have reacted as much as possible. (Assume 100% yield.)

ENTHALPY AND STOICHIOMETRY OF ΔH_{rxn}

69. Classify each process as exothermic or endothermic and indicate the sign of ΔH_{rxn}.
    (a) butane gas burning in a lighter
    (b) the reaction that occurs in the chemical cold packs used to ice athletic injuries
    (c) the burning of wax in a candle

70. Classify each process as exothermic or endothermic and indicate the sign of ΔH_{rxn}.
    (a) ice melting
    (b) a sparkler burning
    (c) acetone evaporating from skin

71. Consider the generic reaction:

$$A + 2B \longrightarrow C \qquad \Delta H_{rxn} = -55 \text{ kJ}$$

Determine the amount of heat emitted when each amount of reactant completely reacts (assume that there is more than enough of the other reactant).
(a) 1 mol A
(b) 2 mol A
(c) 1 mol B
(d) 2 mol B

72. Consider the generic reaction:

$$2A + 3B \longrightarrow C \qquad \Delta H_{rxn} = -125 \text{ kJ}$$

Determine the amount of heat emitted when each amount of reactant completely reacts (assume that there is more than enough of the other reactant).
(a) 2 mol A
(b) 3 mol A
(c) 3 mol B
(d) 5 mol B

73. Consider the equation for the combustion of acetone (C_3H_6O), the main ingredient in nail polish remover:

$$C_3H_6O(l) + 4 O_2(g) \longrightarrow 3 CO_2(g) + 3 H_2O(g)$$
$$\Delta H_{rxn} = -1790 \text{ kJ}$$

If a bottle of nail polish remover contains 155 g of acetone, how much heat is released by its complete combustion?

74. The equation for the combustion of CH_4 (the main component of natural gas) is shown below. How much heat is produced by the complete combustion of 237 g of CH_4?

$$CH_4(g) + 2 O_2(g) \longrightarrow CO_2(g) + 2 H_2O(g)$$
$$\Delta H_{rxn} = -802.3 \text{ kJ}$$

75. Octane (C_8H_{18}) is a component of gasoline that burns according to the equation:

$$C_8H_{18}(l) + \tfrac{25}{2} O_2(g) \longrightarrow 8 CO_2(g) + 9 H_2O(g)$$
$$\Delta H_{rxn} = -5074.1 \text{ kJ}$$

What mass of octane (in g) is required to produce 1.55×10^3 kJ of heat?

76. The evaporation of water is endothermic:

$$H_2O(l) \longrightarrow H_2O(g) \qquad \Delta H_{rxn} = +44.01 \text{ kJ}$$

What minimum mass of water (in g) has to evaporate to absorb 175 kJ of heat?

CUMULATIVE PROBLEMS

77. Consider the reaction:

$$2 N_2(g) + 5 O_2(g) + 2 H_2O(g) \longrightarrow 4 HNO_3(g)$$

If a reaction mixture contains 28 g of N_2, 150 g of O_2, and 36 g of H_2O, what is the limiting reactant? (Try to do this problem in your head without any written calculations.)

78. Consider the reaction:

$$2 CO(g) + O_2(g) \longrightarrow 2 CO_2(g)$$

If a reaction mixture contains 28 g of CO and 32 g of O_2, what is the limiting reactant? (Try to do this problem in your head without any written calculations.)

79. A solution contains an unknown mass of dissolved barium ions. When sodium sulfate is added to the solution, a white precipitate forms. The precipitate is filtered and dried and found to have a mass of 258 mg. What mass of barium was in the original solution? (Assume that all of the barium was precipitated out of solution by the reaction.)

80. A solution contains an unknown mass of dissolved silver ions. When potassium chloride is added to the solution, a white precipitate forms. The precipitate is filtered and dried and found to have a mass of 212 mg. What mass of silver was in the original solution? (Assume that all of the silver was precipitated out of solution by the reaction.)

81. Sodium bicarbonate is often used as an antacid to neutralize excess hydrochloric acid in an upset stomach. How much hydrochloric acid in grams can be neutralized by 3.5 g of sodium bicarbonate? (*Hint:* Begin by writing a balanced equation for the reaction between aqueous sodium bicarbonate and aqueous hydrochloric acid.)

82. Toilet bowl cleaners often contain hydrochloric acid to dissolve the calcium carbonate deposits that accumulate within a toilet bowl. How much calcium carbonate in grams can be dissolved by 5.8 g of HCl? (*Hint:* Begin by writing a balanced equation for the reaction between hydrochloric acid and calcium carbonate.)

83. The combustion of gasoline produces carbon dioxide and water. Assume gasoline to be pure octane (C_8H_{18}) and calculate how many kilograms of carbon dioxide are added to the atmosphere per 1.0 kg of octane burned. (*Hint:* Begin by writing a balanced equation for the combustion reaction.)

84. Many home barbecues are fueled with propane gas (C_3H_8). How much carbon dioxide in kilograms is produced upon the complete combustion of 18.9 L of propane (approximate contents of one 5-gal tank)? Assume that the density of the liquid propane in the tank is 0.621 g/mL. (*Hint:* Begin by writing a balanced equation for the combustion reaction.)

85. A hard water solution contains 4.8 g of calcium chloride. How much sodium phosphate in grams should be added to the solution to completely precipitate all of the calcium?

86. Magnesium ions can be precipitated from seawater by the addition of sodium hydroxide. How much sodium hydroxide in grams must be added to a sample of seawater to completely precipitate the 88.4 mg of magnesium present?

87. Hydrogen gas can be prepared in the laboratory by a single-displacement reaction in which solid zinc reacts with hydrochloric acid. How much zinc in grams is required to make 14.5 g of hydrogen gas through this reaction?

88. Sodium peroxide (Na_2O_2) reacts with water to form sodium hydroxide and oxygen gas. Write a balanced equation for the reaction and determine how much oxygen in grams is formed by the complete reaction of 35.23 g of Na_2O_2.

89. Ammonium nitrate reacts explosively upon heating to form nitrogen gas, oxygen gas, and gaseous water. Write a balanced equation for this reaction and determine how much oxygen in grams is produced by the complete reaction of 1.00 kg of ammonium nitrate.

90. Pure oxygen gas can be prepared in the laboratory by the decomposition of solid potassium chlorate to form solid potassium chloride and oxygen gas. How much oxygen gas in grams can be prepared from 45.8 g of potassium chlorate?

91. Aspirin can be made in the laboratory by reacting acetic anhydride ($C_4H_6O_3$) with salicylic acid ($C_7H_6O_3$) to form aspirin ($C_9H_8O_4$) and acetic acid ($C_2H_4O_2$). The balanced equation is:

$$C_4H_6O_3 + C_7H_6O_3 \longrightarrow C_9H_8O_4 + C_2H_4O_2$$

In a laboratory synthesis, a student begins with 5.00 mL of acetic anhydride (density = 1.08 g/mL) and 2.08 g of salicylic acid. Once the reaction is complete, the student collects 2.01 g of aspirin. Determine the limiting reactant, theoretical yield of aspirin, and percent yield for the reaction.

92. The combustion of liquid ethanol (C_2H_5OH) produces carbon dioxide and water. After 3.8 mL of ethanol (density = 0.789 g/mL) is allowed to burn in the presence of 12.5 g of oxygen gas, 3.10 mL of water (density = 1.00 g/mL) is collected. Determine the limiting reactant, theoretical yield of H_2O, and percent yield for the reaction. (*Hint:* Write a balanced equation for the combustion of ethanol.)

93. Urea (CH_4N_2O), a common fertilizer, can be synthesized by the reaction of ammonia (NH_3) with carbon dioxide:

$$2\, NH_3(aq) + CO_2(aq) \longrightarrow CH_4N_2O(aq) + H_2O(l)$$

An industrial synthesis of urea produces 87.5 kg of urea upon reaction of 68.2 kg of ammonia with 105 kg of carbon dioxide. Determine the limiting reactant, theoretical yield of urea, and percent yield for the reaction.

94. Silicon, which occurs in nature as SiO_2, is the material from which most computer chips are made. If SiO_2 is heated until it melts into a liquid, it reacts with solid carbon to form liquid silicon and carbon monoxide gas. In an industrial preparation of silicon, 52.8 kg of SiO_2 reacts with 25.8 kg of carbon to produce 22.4 kg of silicon. Determine the limiting reactant, theoretical yield, and percent yield for the reaction.

95. The ingestion of lead from food, water, or other environmental sources can cause lead poisoning, a serious condition that affects the central nervous system, causing symptoms such as distractibility, lethargy, and loss of motor function. Lead poisoning is treated with chelating agents, substances that bind to lead and allow it to be eliminated in the urine. A modern chelating agent used for this purpose is succimer ($C_4H_6O_4S_2$). Suppose you are trying to determine the appropriate dose for succimer treatment of lead poisoning. Assume that a patient's blood lead levels are 0.550 mg/L, that total blood volume is 5.0 L, and that 1 mol of succimer binds 1 mol of lead. What minimum mass of succimer in milligrams is needed to bind all of the lead in this patient's bloodstream?

96. An emergency breathing apparatus placed in mines or caves works via the chemical reaction:

$$4\, KO_2(s) + 2\, CO_2(g) \longrightarrow 2\, K_2CO_3(s) + 3\, O_2(g)$$

If the oxygen supply becomes limited or if the air becomes poisoned, a worker can use the apparatus to breathe while exiting the mine. Notice that the reaction produces O_2, which can be breathed, and absorbs CO_2, a product of respiration. What minimum amount of KO_2 is required for the apparatus to produce enough oxygen to allow the user 15 minutes to exit the mine in an emergency? Assume that an adult consumes approximately 4.4 g of oxygen in 15 minutes of normal breathing.

97. The propane fuel (C_3H_8) used in gas barbecues burns according to the equation:

$$C_3H_8(g) + 5\,O_2(g) \longrightarrow 3\,CO_2(g) + 4\,H_2O(g)$$
$$\Delta H_{rxn} = -2044\ \text{kJ}$$

If a pork roast must absorb 1.6×10^3 kJ to fully cook, and if only 10% of the heat produced by the barbecue is actually absorbed by the roast, what mass of CO_2 is emitted into the atmosphere during the grilling of the pork roast?

98. Charcoal is primarily carbon. Determine the mass of CO_2 produced by burning enough carbon to produce 5.00×10^2 kJ of heat.

$$C(s) + O_2(g) \longrightarrow CO_2(g) \qquad \Delta H_{rxn} = -393.5\ \text{kJ}$$

HIGHLIGHT PROBLEMS

99. A loud classroom demonstration involves igniting a hydrogen-filled balloon. The hydrogen within the balloon reacts explosively with oxygen in the air to form water according to this reaction:

$$2\,H_2(g) + O_2(g) \longrightarrow 2\,H_2O(g)$$

If the balloon is filled with a mixture of hydrogen and oxygen, the explosion is even louder than if the balloon is filled with only hydrogen; the intensity of the explosion depends on the relative amounts of oxygen and hydrogen within the balloon. Consider the molecular views representing different amounts of hydrogen and oxygen in four different balloons. Based on the balanced chemical equation, which balloon will make the loudest explosion?

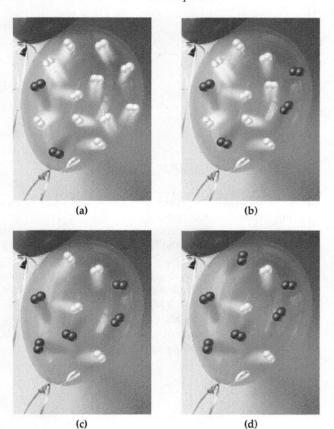

(a) (b)

(c) (d)

● ● O_2 ◯ H_2

100. A hydrochloric acid solution will neutralize a sodium hydroxide solution. Consider the molecular views showing one beaker of HCl and four beakers of NaOH. Which NaOH beaker will just neutralize the HCl beaker? Begin by writing a balanced chemical equation for the neutralization reaction.

(a) (b)

(c) (d)

101. As we have seen, scientists have grown progressively more worried about the potential for climate change caused by increasing atmospheric carbon dioxide levels. The world burns the fossil fuel equivalent of approximately 9.0×10^{12} kg of petroleum per year. Assume that all of this petroleum is in the form of octane (C_8H_{18}) and calculate how much CO_2 in kilograms is produced by world fossil fuel combustion per year. (*Hint:* Begin by writing a balanced equation for the combustion of octane.) If the atmosphere currently contains approximately 3.0×10^{15} kg of CO_2, how long will it take for the world's fossil fuel combustion to double the amount of atmospheric carbon dioxide?

102. Lakes that have been acidified by acid rain can be neutralized by the addition of limestone ($CaCO_3$). How much limestone in kilograms would be required to completely neutralize a 5.2×10^9-L lake containing 5.0×10^{-3} g of H_2SO_4 per liter?

Atmospheric carbon dioxide (CO_2)

Atmospheric CO_2 levels 1750 to present

QUESTIONS FOR GROUP WORK

Discuss these questions with the group and record your consensus answer.

103. What volume of air is needed to burn an entire 55-L (approximately 15-gal) tank of gasoline? Assume that the gasoline is pure octane, C_8H_{18}. *Hint:* Air is 20% oxygen, 1 mol of a gas occupies about 25 L at room temperature, and the density of octane is 0.70 g/cm^3.

104. Have each member of your group choose a precipitation reaction from Chapter 7 and write a limiting reagent problem based on it. Provide the masses of reactants and the product. Trade problems within your group and solve them by determining the limiting reagent, the theoretical yield, and the percent yield.

105. Consider the combustion of propane:

$$C_3H_8(g) + O_2(g) \longrightarrow CO_2(g) + H_2O(g)$$

(a) Balance the reaction.
(b) Divide all coefficients by the coefficient on propane, so that you have the reaction for the combustion of 1 mole of propane.
(c) ΔH_{rxn} for the combustion of one mole of propane is -2219 kJ. What mass of propane would you need to burn to generate 5.0 MJ of heat?
(d) If propane costs about $0.67/L and has a density of 2.01 g/cm^3 how much would it cost to generate 5.0 MJ of heat by burning propane?

▶ Answers to Skillbuilder Exercises

Skillbuilder 8.1	49.2 mol H_2O	**Skillbuilder Plus, p. 263**	29.4 kg NH_3
Skillbuilder 8.2	6.88 g HCl	**Skillbuilder 8.6**	Limiting reactant is CO; theoretical
Skillbuilder 8.3	4.0×10^3 kg H_2SO_4		yield = 127 g Fe; percent yield = 68.8%
Skillbuilder 8.4	Limiting reactant is Na; theoretical yield	**Skillbuilder 8.7**	-2.06×10^3 kJ
	is 4.8 mol of NaF	**Skillbuilder Plus, p. 267**	33 g C_4H_{10} necessary; 99 g CO_2
Skillbuilder 8.5	30.7 g NH_3		produced

▸ Answers to Conceptual Checkpoints

8.1 (a) Because the reaction requires 2 O_2 molecules to react with 1 CH_4 molecule, and there are 4 O_2 molecules available to react, 2 CH_4 molecules are required for complete reaction.

8.2 (c) Hydrogen is the limiting reactant. The reaction mixture contains 3 H_2 molecules; therefore 2 NH_3 molecules will form when the reactants have reacted as completely as possible. Nitrogen is in excess, and there is one leftover nitrogen molecule.

8.3 (d) NO is the limiting reagent. The reaction mixture initially contains 4 mol NO; therefore 10 moles of H_2O will be consumed, leaving 5 mol H_2 unreacted. The products will be 4 mol NH_3 and 4 mol H_2O.

8.4 (c) B is the limiting reactant. If 4 mol B react, then 200 kJ of heat is produced.

▲ Modern blimps are filled with helium, an inert gas. The nucleus of the helium atom (inset) has two protons, so the neutral helium atom has two electrons—a highly stable configuration. In this chapter we learn about models that explain the inertness of helium and the reactivity of other elements.

Electrons in Atoms and the Periodic Table

9

"Anyone who is not shocked by quantum mechanics has not understood it."

—Niels Bohr (1885–1962)

CHAPTER OUTLINE

9.1 Blimps, Balloons, and Models of the Atom

▲ The *Hindenburg* was filled with hydrogen, a reactive and flammable gas. Question: What makes hydrogen reactive?

The periodic law stated here is a modification of Mendeleev's original formulation. Mendeleev listed elements in order of increasing *mass*; today we list them in order of increasing *atomic number*.

You have probably seen one of the Goodyear blimps floating in the sky. A Goodyear blimp is often present at championship sporting events such as the Rose Bowl, the Indy 500, or the U.S. Open golf tournament. One attended the Statue of Liberty's 100th birthday party, and blimps have made appearances in countless movies and television shows. The blimp's inherent stability allows cameras to provide spectacular views of the world below for television and film.

The Goodyear blimp is similar to a large balloon. Unlike airplanes, which must be moving fast to stay in flight, a blimp or *airship* floats in air because it is filled with a gas that is less dense than air. The Goodyear blimp is filled with helium. Other airships in history, however, have used hydrogen for buoyancy. For example, the *Hindenburg*—the largest airship ever constructed—was filled with hydrogen, which turned out to be a poor choice. Hydrogen is a reactive and flammable gas. On May 6, 1937, while landing in New Jersey after its first transatlantic crossing, the *Hindenburg* burst into flames, destroying the airship and killing 36 of its 97 passengers. Apparently, as the *Hindenburg* was landing, leaking hydrogen gas ignited, resulting in an explosion that destroyed the ship. A similar accident cannot happen to the Goodyear blimp because it uses helium—an inert gas—for buoyancy. A spark or even a flame would actually be *extinguished* by helium.

Why is helium inert? What is it about helium *atoms* that makes helium *gas* inert? By contrast, why is hydrogen so reactive? Recall from Chapter 5 that elemental hydrogen exists as a diatomic element. Hydrogen atoms are so reactive that they react with each other to form hydrogen molecules. What is it about hydrogen atoms that makes them so reactive? What is the difference between hydrogen and helium that accounts for their different reactivities?

When we examine the properties of hydrogen and helium, we make observations about nature. Mendeleev's periodic law, first discussed in Chapter 4, summarizes the results of many similar observations on the properties of elements:

When the elements are arranged in order of increasing atomic number, certain sets of properties recur periodically.

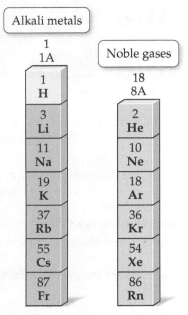

▲ The noble gases are chemically inert, and the alkali metals are chemically reactive. Why? (Hydrogen is a Group 1 element, but it is not considered an alkali metal.)

The reactivity exhibited by hydrogen (the first element in Group 1A) is also seen in other Group 1A elements, such as lithium and sodium. Likewise, the inertness of helium (a Group 8A element) is seen in other Group 8A elements such as neon and argon and the other noble gases. In this chapter, we consider models and theories that help explain the observed behaviors of groups of elements such as the Group 1A metals and the noble gases. We examine two important models in particular—the **Bohr model** and the **quantum-mechanical model**—that propose explanations for the inertness of helium, the reactivity of hydrogen, and the periodic law. These models explain how electrons exist in atoms and how those electrons affect the chemical and physical properties of elements. We have already learned much about the behavior of elements in this book. We know, for example, that sodium tends to form 1+ ions and that fluorine tends to form 1− ions. We know that some elements are metals and that others are nonmetals. And we know that the noble gases are, in genereal, chemically inert and that the alkali metals are chemically reactive. But we have not yet explored *why*. The models in this chapter explain why.

When the Bohr model and the quantum-mechanical model were developed in the early 1900s, they caused a revolution in the physical sciences, changing our fundamental view of matter at its most basic level. The scientists who devised these models—including Niels Bohr, Erwin Schrödinger, and Albert Einstein—were bewildered by their own discoveries. Bohr claimed, "Anyone who is not shocked by quantum mechanics has not understood it." Schrödinger lamented, "I don't like it, and I am sorry I ever had anything to do with it." Einstein disbelieved it, insisting that "God does not play dice with the universe." However, the quantum-mechanical model has such explanatory power that it is rarely questioned today. It forms the basis of the modern periodic table and our understanding of chemical bonding. Its applications include lasers, computers, and semiconductor devices, and it has led us to discover new ways to design drugs that cure disease. The quantum-mechanical model for the atom is, in many ways, the foundation of modern chemistry.

▲ Niels Bohr (left) and Erwin Schrödinger (right), along with Albert Einstein, played a role in the development of quantum mechanics, yet they were bewildered by their own findings.

9.2 Light: Electromagnetic Radiation

LO: Understand and explain the nature of electromagnetic radiation.

Before we explore models of the atom, we must understand a few things about light, because the interaction of light with atoms helped to shape these models. Light is familiar to all of us—we see the world by it—but what is light? Unlike most of what we have encountered so far in this book, light is not matter—it has no mass. Light is

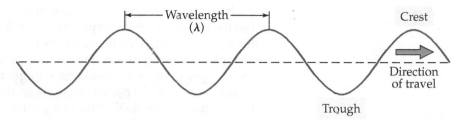

▲ **FIGURE 9.1 Wavelength** The wavelength of light (λ) is the distance between adjacent wave crests.

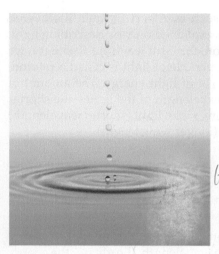

▲ When a water surface is disturbed, waves are created that radiate outward from the site.

The Greek letter *lambda* (λ) is pronounced "lam-duh."

Helpful mnemonic: ROY G BIV—Red, Orange, Yellow, Green, Blue, Indigo, Violet

▶ **FIGURE 9.2 Components of white light** Light is separated into its constituent colors—red, orange, yellow, green, blue, indigo, and violet—when it is passed through a prism.

▲ **FIGURE 9.3 Color in objects** A red shirt appears red because it absorbs all colors except red, which it reflects.

The Greek letter *nu* (ν) is pronounced "noo."

Light is a form of **electromagnetic radiation**, a type of energy that travels through space at a constant speed of 3.0×10^8 m/s (186,000 mi/s). At this speed, a flash of light generated at the equator can travel around the world in one-seventh of a second. This extremely fast speed is part of the reason that we *see* a firework in the sky before we *hear* the sound of its explosion. The light from the exploding firework reaches our eyes almost instantaneously. The sound, traveling much more slowly, takes longer.

Before the advent of quantum mechanics, light was described exclusively as a wave of electromagnetic energy traveling through space. You are probably familiar with water waves (think of the waves created by a rock dropped into a still pond), or you may have created a wave on a rope by moving the end of the rope up and down in a quick motion. In either case, the wave carries energy as it moves through the water or along the rope.

Waves are generally characterized by **wavelength** (λ), the distance between adjacent wave crests (▲ Figure 9.1). For visible light, wavelength determines color. For example, orange light has a longer wavelength than blue light. White light, as produced by the sun or by a lightbulb, contains a spectrum of wavelengths and therefore a spectrum of color. We see these colors—red, orange, yellow, green, blue, indigo, and violet—in a rainbow or when white light is passed through a prism (▼ Figure 9.2). Red light, with a wavelength of 750 nm (nanometers), has the longest wavelength of visible light. Violet light, with a wavelength of 400 nm, has the shortest (1 nm = 10^{-9} m). The presence of color in white light is responsible for the colors we see in our everyday vision. For example, a red shirt is red because it reflects red light (◀ Figure 9.3). Our eyes see only the reflected light, making the shirt appear red.

White light contains the entire spectrum of visible colors.

Light waves are also often characterized by **frequency** (ν), the number of cycles or crests that pass through a stationary point in one second. Wavelength and frequency are inversely related—the shorter the wavelength, the higher the frequency. Blue light, for example, has a higher frequency than red light.

In the early twentieth century, scientists such as Albert Einstein discovered that the results of certain experiments could be explained only by describing light, not as waves, but as particles. In this description, the light leaving a flashlight, for example, is viewed as a stream of particles. A particle of light is called a **photon**, and we can think of a photon as a single packet of light energy. The amount of energy carried in the packet depends on the wavelength of the light—the shorter the wavelength, the greater the energy. Therefore, violet light (shorter wavelength) carries more energy per photon than red light (longer wavelength).

To summarize:

• Electromagnetic radiation is a form of energy that travels through space at a constant speed of 3.0×10^8 m/s and can exhibit wavelike or particle-like properties.

• The wavelength of electromagnetic radiation determines the amount of energy carried by one of its photons. The shorter the wavelength, the greater the energy of each photon.

• The frequency and energy of electromagnetic radiation are inversely related to its wavelength.

 CONCEPTUAL CHECKPOINT 9.1

Which wavelength of light has the highest frequency?
(a) 350 nm   **(b)** 500 nm   **(c)** 750 nm

9.3 The Electromagnetic Spectrum

LO: Predict the relative wavelength, energy, and frequency of different types of light.

Electromagnetic radiation ranges in wavelength from 10^{-16} m (gamma rays) to 10^6 m (radio waves). Visible light composes only a tiny portion of that range. The entire range of electromagnetic radiation is called the **electromagnetic spectrum**. ▼ Figure 9.4 shows the electromagnetic spectrum, with short-wavelength, high-frequency radiation on the right and long-wavelength, low-frequency radiation on the left. Visible light is the small sliver in the middle.

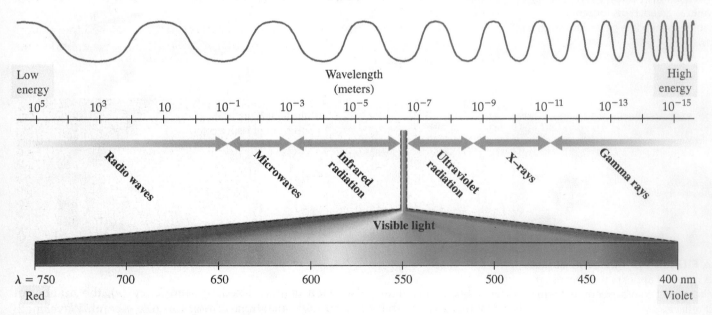

▲ **FIGURE 9.4 The electromagnetic spectrum**

Remember that the energy carried per photon is greater for short-wavelength light than for long-wavelength light. The shortest wavelength (and therefore most energetic) photons are those of **gamma rays**, shown on the far right of Figure 9.4. Gamma rays are produced by the sun, by stars, and by certain unstable atomic nuclei on Earth. Excessive human exposure to gamma rays is dangerous because the high energy of gamma-ray photons can damage biological molecules.

Next on the electromagnetic spectrum (to the left in Figure 9.4), with longer wavelengths (and lower energy) than gamma rays, are **X-rays**, familiar to us from their medical use. X-rays pass through many substances that block visible light and are therefore used to image internal bones and organs. Like gamma-ray photons, X-ray photons carry enough energy to damage biological molecules. While several yearly exposures to X-rays are relatively harmless, excessive exposure to X-rays increases cancer risk.

Sandwiched between X-rays and visible light in the electromagnetic spectrum is **ultraviolet** or **UV light**, most familiar to us as the component of sunlight that produces a sunburn or suntan. Though not as energetic as gamma-ray or X-ray photons, ultraviolet photons still carry enough energy to damage biological molecules. Excessive exposure to ultraviolet light increases the risk of skin cancer and cataracts and causes premature wrinkling of the skin. Next on the spectrum is **visible light**, ranging from violet (shorter wavelength, higher energy) to red (longer wavelength, lower energy). Photons of visible light do not damage biological molecules. They do, however, cause molecules in our eyes to rearrange, which sends a signal to our brains that results in vision.

Infrared light is next, with even longer wavelengths than visible light. The heat we feel when we place a hand near a hot object is infrared light. All warm objects, including human bodies, emit infrared light. While infrared light is invisible to our eyes, infrared sensors can detect it and are often used in night-vision technology to "see" in the dark. In the infrared region of the spectrum, warm objects—such as human bodies—glow, much as a lightbulb glows in the visible region of the spectrum.

Beyond infrared light, at longer wavelengths still, are **microwaves**, used for radar and in microwave ovens. Although microwave light has longer wavelengths—and therefore lower energy per photon—than visible or infrared light, it is efficiently absorbed by water and therefore heats substances that contain water. For this reason substances that contain water, such as food, are warmed when placed in a microwave oven, but substances that do not contain water, such as a plate, are not.

The longest wavelengths of light are **radio waves**, which are used to transmit the signals used by AM and FM radio, cellular telephones, television, and other forms of communication.

Some types of plates contain substances that absorb microwave radiation, but most do not.

Normal photograph　　Infrared photograph

▲ Warm objects, such as human or animal bodies, give off infrared light that is easily detected with an infrared camera. In the infrared photograph, the warmest areas appear as red and the coolest as dark blue. (*Source:* Sierra Pacific Innovations. All rights reserved. SPI CORP, www.x20.org)

CHEMISTRY **AND HEALTH**
▶ Radiation Treatment for Cancer

X-rays and gamma rays are sometimes called ionizing radiation because the high energy in their photons can ionize atoms and molecules. When ionizing radiation interacts with biological molecules, it can permanently change or even destroy them. Consequently, we normally try to limit our exposure to ionizing radiation. However, doctors can use ionizing radiation to destroy molecules within unwanted cells such as cancer cells.

In radiation therapy (or radiotherapy), doctors aim X-ray or gamma-ray beams at cancerous tumors. The ionizing radiation damages the molecules within the tumor's cells that carry genetic information—information necessary for the cell to grow and divide—and the cell dies or stops dividing. Ionizing radiation also damages molecules within healthy cells; however, cancerous cells divide more quickly than healthy cells, making them more susceptible to genetic damage. Nonetheless, healthy cells often inadvertently sustain damage during treatments, resulting in side effects such as fatigue, skin lesions, and hair loss. Doctors try to minimize the exposure of healthy cells by appropriate shielding and by targeting the tumor from multiple directions, minimizing the exposure of healthy cells while maximizing the exposure of cancerous cells (▶ Figure 9.5).

Another side effect of exposing healthy cells to radiation is that they too may become cancerous. So a treatment for cancer may cause cancer. So why do we continue to use it? Radiation therapy, as most other disease therapies, has associated risks. However, we take risks all the time, many for lesser reasons. For example, every time we drive a car, we risk injury or even death. Why? Because we perceive the benefit—such as getting to the grocery store to buy food—to be worth the risk. The situation is similar in cancer therapy or any other therapy for that matter. The benefit of cancer therapy (possibly curing a cancer that will certainly kill) is worth the risk (a slight increase in the chance of developing a future cancer).

B9.1 CAN YOU ANSWER THIS? *Why is visible light not used to destroy cancerous tumors?*

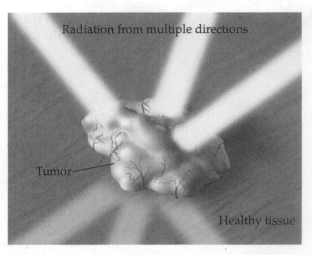

▲ **FIGURE 9.5** **Radiation therapy** By targeting the tumor from various different directions, radiologists attempt to limit damage to healthy tissue.

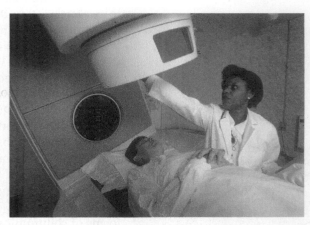

▲ Cancer patient undergoing radiation therapy.

EXAMPLE 9.1   WAVELENGTH, ENERGY, AND FREQUENCY

Arrange the three types of electromagnetic radiation—visible light, X-rays, and microwaves—in order of increasing:

(a) wavelength   **(b)** frequency   **(c)** energy per photon

	SOLUTION
(a) wavelength Figure 9.4 indicates that X-rays have the shortest wavelength, followed by visible light and then microwaves.	X-rays, visible light, microwaves
(b) frequency Since frequency and wavelength are inversely proportional—the longer the wavelength, the shorter the frequency—the ordering with respect to frequency is exactly the reverse of the ordering with respect to wavelength.	microwaves, visible light, X-rays

(c) energy per photon
Energy per photon decreases with increasing wavelength but increases with increasing frequency; therefore, the ordering with respect to energy per photon is the same as frequency.

microwaves, visible light, X-rays

▶ **SKILLBUILDER 9.1 | Wavelength, Energy, and Frequency**
Arrange the colors of visible light—green, red, and blue—in order of increasing:

(a) wavelength   **(b)** frequency   **(c)** energy per photon

▶ **FOR MORE PRACTICE**   Example 9.9; Problems 31, 32, 33, 34, 35, 36, 37, 38.

  CONCEPTUAL CHECKPOINT 9.2

Yellow light has a longer wavelength than violet light. Therefore:
(a) Yellow light has more energy per photon than violet light.
(b) Yellow light has less energy per photon than violet light.
(c) Both yellow light and violet light have the same energy per photon.

9.4   The Bohr Model: Atoms with Orbits

LO: Understand and explain the key characteristics of the Bohr model of the atom.

When an atom absorbs energy—in the form of heat, light, or electricity—it often reemits that energy as light. For example, a neon sign is composed of one or more glass tubes filled with gaseous neon atoms. When an electrical current passes through the tube, the neon atoms absorb some of the electrical energy and reemit it as the familiar red light of a neon sign (◀ Figure 9.6). The absorption and emission of light by atoms is due to the interaction of the light with the electrons in the atom. If the atoms in the tube are different, the electrons have different energies, and the emitted light is a different color. In other words, atoms of each unique element emit light of a unique color (or unique wavelength). Mercury atoms, for example, emit light that appears blue, hydrogen atoms emit light that appears pink (▼ Figure 9.7), and helium atoms emit light that appears yellow-orange.

▲ **FIGURE 9.6   A neon sign** Neon atoms inside a glass tube absorb electrical energy and reemit the energy as light.

▶ **FIGURE 9.7   Light emission by different elements** Light emitted from a mercury lamp (left) appears blue, and light emitted from a hydrogen lamp (right) appears pink.

▶ **FIGURE 9.8 Emission spectra** A white-light spectrum is continuous, with some radiation emitted at every wavelength. The emission spectrum of an individual element, however, includes only certain specific wavelengths. (The different wavelengths appear as *lines* because the light from the source passes through a slit before entering the prism.) Each element produces its own unique and distinctive emission spectrum.

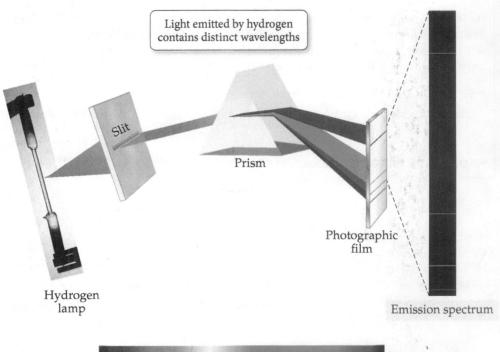

Light emitted by hydrogen contains distinct wavelengths

Slit

Prism

Photographic film

Hydrogen lamp

Emission spectrum

White-light spectrum

Hydrogen light spectrum

Helium light spectrum

Neon light spectrum

Closer inspection of the light emitted by hydrogen, helium, and neon atoms reveals that the light contains several distinct colors or wavelengths. Just as we can separate the white light from a lightbulb into its constituent wavelengths by passing it through a prism, so we can separate the light emitted by glowing hydrogen, helium, or neon into its constituent wavelengths (▲ Figure 9.8) by passing it through a prism. The result is an **emission spectrum**. Notice the differences between a white-light spectrum and the emission spectra of hydrogen, helium, and neon. The white-light spectrum is *continuous*, meaning that the light intensity is uninterrupted or smooth across the entire visible range—there is some radiation at all wavelengths, with no gaps. The emission spectra of hydrogen, helium, and neon, however, are not continuous. They consist of bright spots or lines at specific wavelengths with complete darkness in between. Since the emission of light in atoms is related to the motions of electrons within the atoms, a model for how electrons exist in atoms must account for these spectra.

A major challenge in developing a model for electrons in atoms is the discrete or bright-line nature of the emission spectra. Why do atoms, when excited with energy, emit light only at particular wavelengths? Why do they *not* emit a continuous spectrum? Niels Bohr developed a simple model to explain these results. In his model, now called the Bohr model, electrons travel around the nucleus in circular orbits that are similar to planetary orbits around the sun. However, unlike planets revolving around the sun—which can theoretically orbit at any distance whatsoever from the sun—electrons in the Bohr model can orbit only at *specific, fixed* distances from the nucleus (◀ Figure 9.9).

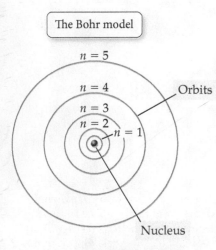

The Bohr model

$n = 5$

$n = 4$

$n = 3$

$n = 2$

$n = 1$

Orbits

Nucleus

▲ **FIGURE 9.9 Bohr orbits**

n = 6
n = 5
n = 4
n = 3
n = 2
n = 1

▲ **FIGURE 9.10** **The Bohr energy ladder** Bohr orbits are like steps on a ladder. It is possible to stand on one step or another, but impossible to stand between steps.

The Bohr model is still important because it provides a logical foundation to the quantum-mechanical model and reveals the historical development of scientific understanding.

The *energy* of each Bohr orbit, specified by a **quantum number** $n = 1, 2, 3 \ldots$, is also fixed, or **quantized**. The energy of each orbit increases with increasing value of n, but the levels become more closely spaced as n increases. Bohr orbits are like steps of a ladder (◄ Figure 9.10), each at a specific distance from the nucleus and each at a specific energy. Just as it is impossible to stand *between steps* on a ladder, so it is impossible for an electron to exist *between orbits* in the Bohr model. An electron in an $n = 3$ orbit, for example, is farther from the nucleus and has more energy than an electron in an $n = 2$ orbit. And an electron cannot exist at an intermediate distance or energy between the two orbits—the orbits are *quantized*. As long as an electron remains in a given orbit, it does not absorb or emit light, and its energy remains fixed and constant.

When an atom absorbs energy, an electron in one of these fixed orbits is *excited* or promoted to an orbit that is farther away from the nucleus (▼ Figure 9.11) and therefore higher in energy (this is analogous to moving up a step on the ladder). However, in this new configuration, the atom is less stable, and the electron quickly falls back or *relaxes* to a lower-energy orbit (this is analogous to moving down a step on the ladder). As it does so, it releases a photon of light containing the precise amount of energy—called a **quantum** of energy—that corresponds to the energy difference between the two orbits.

Since the amount of energy in a photon is directly related to its wavelength, the photon has a specific wavelength. *Consequently, the light emitted by excited atoms consists of specific lines at specific wavelengths, each corresponding to a specific transition between two orbits.* For example, the line at 486 nm in the hydrogen emission spectrum corresponds to an electron relaxing from the $n = 4$ orbit to the $n = 2$ orbit (▼ Figure 9.12). In the same way, the line at 657 nm (longer wavelength and therefore lower energy) corresponds to an electron relaxing from the $n = 3$ orbit to the $n = 2$ orbit. Notice that transitions between orbits that are closer together produce lower-energy (and therefore longer-wavelength) light than transitions between orbits that are farther apart.

The great success of the Bohr model of the atom was that it predicts the lines of the hydrogen emission spectrum. However, it failed to predict the emission spectra of other elements that contained more than one electron. For this, and other reasons, the Bohr model was replaced with a more sophisticated model called the quantum-mechanical or wave-mechanical model.

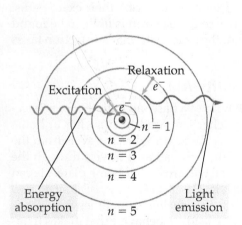

▲ **FIGURE 9.11** **Excitation and emission** When a hydrogen atom absorbs energy, an electron is excited to a higher-energy orbit. The electron then relaxes back to a lower-energy orbit, emitting a photon of light.

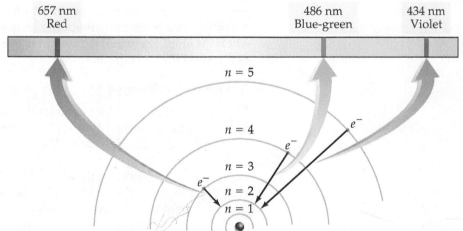

▲ **FIGURE 9.12** **Hydrogen emission lines** The 657-nm line of the hydrogen emission spectrum corresponds to an electron relaxing from the $n = 3$ orbit to the $n = 2$ orbit. The 486-nm line corresponds to an electron relaxing from the $n = 4$ orbit to the $n = 2$ orbit, and the 434-nm line corresponds to an electron relaxing from $n = 5$ to $n = 2$.

To summarize:

- Electrons exist in quantized orbits at specific, fixed energies and specific, fixed distances from the nucleus.

- When energy is put into an atom, electrons are excited to higher-energy orbits.

- When an electron in an atom relaxes (or falls) from a higher-energy orbit to a lower-energy orbit, the atom emits light.

- The energy (and therefore the wavelength) of the emitted light corresponds to the energy difference between the two orbits in the transition. Since these energies are fixed and discrete, the energy (and therefore the wavelength) of the emitted light is fixed and discrete.

CONCEPTUAL CHECKPOINT 9.3

In one transition, an electron in a hydrogen atom falls from the $n = 3$ level to the $n = 2$ level. In a second transition, an electron in a hydrogen atom falls from the $n = 2$ level to the $n = 1$ level. Compared to the radiation emitted by the first of these transitions, the radiation emitted by the second has:

(a) a lower frequency

(b) a smaller energy per photon

(c) a shorter wavelength

(d) a longer wavelength

9.5 The Quantum-Mechanical Model: Atoms with Orbitals

LO: Understand and explain the key characteristics of the quantum-mechanical model of the atom.

The quantum-mechanical model of the atom replaced the Bohr model in the early twentieth century. In the quantum-mechanical model, *Bohr orbits* are replaced with *quantum-mechanical* **orbitals**. Orbitals are different from orbits in that they represent, not specific paths that electrons follow, but probability maps that show a statistical distribution of where the electron is likely to be found. The idea of an orbital is not easy to visualize. Quantum mechanics revolutionized physics and chemistry because in the quantum-mechanical model, electrons *do not* behave like particles flying through space. We cannot, in general, describe their exact paths. An orbital is a probability map that shows where the electron is *likely* to be found when the atom is probed; it does not represent the exact path that an electron takes as it travels through space.

Baseball Paths and Electron Probability Maps

To understand orbitals, let's contrast the behavior of a baseball with that of an electron. Imagine a baseball thrown from the pitcher's mound to a catcher at home plate (▶ Figure 9.13). The baseball's path can easily be traced as it travels from the pitcher to the catcher. The catcher can watch the baseball as it travels through the air, and he can predict exactly where the baseball will cross over home plate. He can even place his mitt in the correct place to catch it. *This would be impossible for an electron.* Like photons, electrons exhibit a *wave–particle duality*; sometimes they act as particles, and other times as waves. This duality leads to behavior that makes it impossible to trace an electron's path. If an electron were "thrown" from the pitcher's mound to home plate, it would land in a different place every time, *even if it were thrown in exactly the same way.* Baseballs have predictable paths—electrons do not.

▶ **FIGURE 9.13   Baseballs follow predictable paths**   A baseball follows a well-defined path as it travels from the pitcher to the catcher.

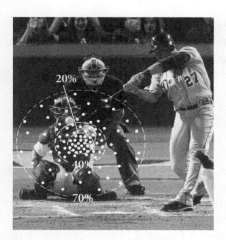

▲ **FIGURE 9.14   Electrons are unpredictable**   To describe the behavior of a "pitched" electron, we would have to construct a probability map of where it would cross home plate.

In the quantum-mechanical world of the electron, the catcher could not know exactly where the electron would cross the plate for any given throw. He would have no way of putting his mitt in the right place to catch it. However, if the catcher kept track of hundreds of electron throws, he could observe a reproducible, statistical pattern of where the electron crosses the plate. He could even draw maps in the strike zone showing the probability of an electron crossing a certain area (◀ Figure 9.14). These maps are called *probability maps*.

From Orbits to Orbitals

In the Bohr model, an *orbit* is a circular path—analogous to a baseball's path—that shows the electron's motion around an atomic nucleus. In the quantum-mechanical model, an *orbital* is a probability map, analogous to the probability map drawn by our catcher. It shows the relative likelihood of the electron being found at various locations when the atom is probed. Just as the Bohr model has different orbits with different radii, the quantum-mechanical model has different orbitals with different shapes.

9.6   Quantum-Mechanical Orbitals and Electron Configurations

LO: Write electron configurations and orbital diagrams for atoms.

In the Bohr model of the atom, a single quantum number (n) specifies each orbit. In the quantum-mechanical model, a number and a letter specify an orbital (or orbitals). In this section, we examine quantum-mechanical orbitals and electron configurations. An electron configuration is a compact way to specify the occupation of quantum-mechanical orbitals by electrons.

▲ FIGURE 9.15 Principal quantum numbers The principal quantum numbers ($n = 1, 2, 3 \ldots$) determine the energy of the hydrogen quantum-mechanical orbitals.

This analogy is purely hypothetical. It is impossible to photograph electrons in this way.

Quantum-Mechanical Orbitals

The lowest-energy orbital in the quantum-mechanical model—analogous to the $n = 1$ orbit in the Bohr model—is the *1s orbital*. We specifiy it by the number 1 and the letter *s*. The number is the **principal quantum number** (*n*) and specifies the **principal shell** of the orbital. The higher the principal quantum number, the higher the energy of the orbital. The possible principal quantum numbers are $n = 1, 2, 3 \ldots$, with energy increasing as *n* increases (◄ Figure 9.15). Because the 1s orbital has the lowest possible principal quantum number, it is in the lowest-energy shell and has the lowest possible energy.

The letter indicates the **subshell** of the orbital and specifies its shape. The possible letters are *s*, *p*, *d*, and *f*, and each letter corresponds to a different shape. For example, orbitals within the *s* subshell have a spherical shape. Unlike the $n = 1$ Bohr orbit, which shows the electron's path, the 1s quantum-mechanical orbital is a three-dimensional probability map. We sometimes represent orbitals with dots (▼ Figure 9.16), where the dot density is proportional to the probability of finding the electron.

We can understand the dot representation of an orbital better with another analogy. Imagine taking a photograph of an electron in an atom every second for 10 or 15 minutes. One second the electron is very close to the nucleus; the next second it is farther away and so on. Each photo shows a dot representing the electron's position relative to the nucleus at that time. If we took hundreds of photos and superimposed all of them, we would have an image like Figure 9.16—a statistical representation of where the electron is found. Notice that the dot density for the 1s orbital is greatest near the nucleus and decreases farther away from the nucleus. This means that the electron is more likely to be found close to the nucleus than far away from it.

Orbitals can also be represented as geometric shapes that encompass most of the volume where the electron is likely to be found. For example, the 1s orbital can be represented as a sphere (▼ Figure 9.17) that encompasses the volume within which the electron is found 90% of the time. If we superimpose the dot representation of the 1s orbital on the shape representation (▼ Figure 9.18), we can see that most of the dots are within the sphere, meaning that the electron is most likely to be found within the sphere when it is in the 1s orbital.

The single electron of an undisturbed hydrogen atom at room temperature is in the 1s orbital. This is the **ground state**, or lowest energy state, of the hydrogen atom. However, like the Bohr model, the quantum-mechanical model allows tran-

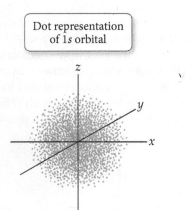

▲ FIGURE 9.16 1s orbital The dot density in this plot is proportional to the probability of finding the electron. The greater dot density near the middle indicates a higher probability of finding the electron near the nucleus.

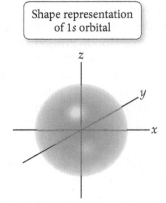

▲ FIGURE 9.17 Shape representation of the 1s orbital Because the distribution of electron density around the nucleus in Figure 9.16 is symmetrical—the same in all directions—we can represent the 1s orbital as a sphere.

▲ FIGURE 9.18 Orbital shape and dot representation for the 1s orbital The shape representation of the 1s orbital superimposed on the dot density representation. We can see that when the electron is in the 1s orbital, it is most likely to be found within the sphere.

▶ **FIGURE 9.19 Subshells** The number of subshells in a given principal shell is equal to the value of n.

Shell	Number of subshells	Letters specifying subshells			
$n = 4$	4	s	p	d	f
$n = 3$	3	s	p	d	
$n = 2$	2	s	p		
$n = 1$	1	s			

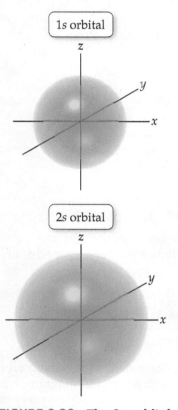

1s orbital

2s orbital

▲ **FIGURE 9.20   The 2s orbital** The 2s orbital is similar to the 1s orbital, but larger in size.

sitions to higher-energy orbitals upon the absorption of energy. What are these higher-energy orbitals? What do they look like?

The next orbitals in the quantum-mechanical model are those with principal quantum number $n = 2$. Unlike the $n = 1$ principal shell, which contains only one subshell (specified by s), the $n = 2$ principal shell contains two subshells, specified by s and p.

The number of subshells in a given principal shell is equal to the value of n. Therefore the $n = 1$ principal shell has one subshell, the $n = 2$ principal shell has two subshells, and so on (▲ Figure 9.19). The s subshell contains the 2s orbital, higher in energy than the 1s orbital and slightly larger (◀ Figure 9.20), but otherwise similar in shape. The p subshell contains three 2p orbitals (▼ Figure 9.21), all with the same dumbbell-like shape but with different orientations.

The next principal shell, $n = 3$, contains three subshells specified by s, p, and d. The s and p subshells contain the 3s and 3p orbitals, similar in shape to the 2s and 2p orbitals, but slightly larger and higher in energy. The d subshell contains the five d orbitals shown in ▶ Figure 9.22. The next principal shell, $n = 4$, contains four subshells specified by s, p, d, and f. The s, p, and d subshells are similar to those in $n = 3$. The f subshell contains seven orbitals (called the 4f orbitals), whose shape we do not consider in this book.

As we have already discussed, hydrogen's single electron is usually in the 1s orbital because electrons generally occupy the lowest-energy orbital available. In hydrogen, the rest of the orbitals are normally empty. However, the absorption of energy by a hydrogen atom can cause the electron to jump (or make a transition) from the 1s orbital to a higher-energy orbital. When the electron is in a higher-energy orbital, we say that the hydrogen atom is in an **excited state**.

Because of their higher energy, excited states are unstable, and the electron will usually fall (or relax) back to a lower-energy orbital. In the process the electron emits energy, often in the form of light. As in the Bohr model, the energy difference between the two orbitals involved in the transition determines the wavelength of the emitted light (the greater the energy difference, the shorter the wavelength). The quantum-mechanical model predicts the bright-line spectrum of hydrogen as well as the Bohr model. However, it also predicts the bright-line spectra of other elements.

The 2p orbitals

(a) p_x (b) p_y (c) p_z

▲ **FIGURE 9.21   The 2p orbitals** This figure shows both the dot representation (left) and shape representation (right) for each p orbital.

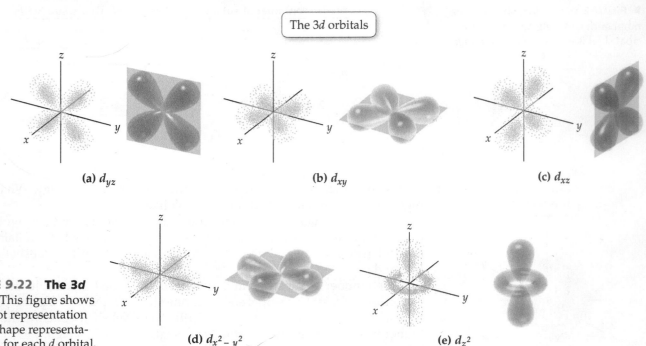

▶ **FIGURE 9.22 The 3d orbitals** This figure shows both the dot representation (left) and shape representation (right) for each d orbital.

(a) d_{yz}

(b) d_{xy}

(c) d_{xz}

(d) $d_{x^2-y^2}$

(e) d_{z^2}

Electron Configurations: How Electrons Occupy Orbitals

An **electron configuration** illustrates the occupation of orbitals by electrons for a particular atom. For example, the electron configuration for a ground-state (or lowest energy) hydrogen atom is:

H $1s^1$ ⟵——— Number of
                electrons in orbital

Orbital

The electron configuration tells us that hydrogen's single electron is in the 1s orbital.

Another way to represent this information is with an **orbital diagram**, which gives similar information but shows the electrons as arrows in a box representing the orbital. The orbital diagram for a ground-state hydrogen atom is:

H   ⬆
     1s

The box represents the 1s orbital, and the arrow within the box represents the electron in the 1s orbital. In orbital diagrams, the direction of the arrow (pointing up or pointing down) represents **electron spin**, a fundamental property of electrons. All electrons have spin. The **Pauli exclusion principle** states that *orbitals may hold no more than two electrons with opposing spins.* We symbolize this as two arrows pointing in opposite directions:

⬆⬇

A helium atom, for example, has two electrons. The electron configuration and orbital diagram for helium are:

Electron configuration	Orbital diagram
He $1s^2$	⬆⬇
1s

▶ **FIGURE 9.23 Energy ordering of orbitals for multi-electron atoms** Different subshells within the same principal shell have different energies.

Since we know that electrons occupy the lowest-energy orbitals available, and since we know that only two electrons (with opposing spins) are allowed in each orbital, we can continue to build ground-state electron configurations for the rest of the elements as long as we know the energy ordering of the orbitals. ▲ Figure 9.23 shows the energy ordering of a number of orbitals for multi-electron atoms.

> In multi-electron atoms, the subshells within a principal shell do not have the same energy because of electron–electron interactions.

Notice that, for multi-electron atoms (in contrast to hydrogen which has only one electron), the subshells within a principal shell *do not* have the same energy. In elements other than hydrogen, the energy ordering is not determined by the principal quantum number alone. For example, in multi-electron atoms, the 4s subshell is lower in energy than the 3d subshell, even though its principal quantum number is higher. Using this relative energy ordering, we can write ground-state electron configurations and orbital diagrams for other elements. For lithium, which has three electrons, the electron configuration and orbital diagram are:

Electron configuration	Orbital diagram
Li $1s^2 2s^1$	

1s   2s

> Remember that the number of electrons in an atom is equal to its atomic number.

For carbon, which has 6 electrons, the electron configuration and orbital diagram are:

Electron configuration	Orbital diagram
C $1s^2 2s^2 2p^2$	

1s   2s   2p

Notice that the 2p electrons occupy the p orbitals (of equal energy) singly rather than pairing in one orbital. This is the result of **Hund's rule**, which states that *when filling orbitals of equal energy, electrons fill them singly first, with parallel spins.*

Before we write electron configurations for other elements, let us summarize what we have learned so far:

▲ **FIGURE 9.24 Orbital filling order** The arrows indicate the order in which orbitals fill.

- Electrons occupy orbitals so as to minimize the energy of the atom; therefore, lower-energy orbitals fill before higher-energy orbitals. Orbitals fill in the following order: 1s 2s 2p 3s 3p 4s 3d 4p 5s 4d 5p 6s (◀ Figure 9.24).

- Orbitals can hold no more than two electrons each. When two electrons occupy the same orbital, they must have opposing spins. This is known as the Pauli exclusion principle.

- When orbitals of identical energy are available, these are first occupied singly with parallel spins rather than in pairs. This is known as Hund's rule.

Consider the electron configurations and orbital diagrams for elements with atomic numbers 3 through 10:

Symbol (#e^-)	Electron configuration	Orbital diagram
Li (3)	$1s^2 2s^1$	$\boxed{\uparrow\downarrow}$ $\boxed{\uparrow}$ $\quad 1s \quad\; 2s$
Be (4)	$1s^2 2s^2$	$\boxed{\uparrow\downarrow}$ $\boxed{\uparrow\downarrow}$ $\quad 1s \quad\; 2s$
B (5)	$1s^2 2s^2 2p^1$	$\boxed{\uparrow\downarrow}$ $\boxed{\uparrow\downarrow}$ $\boxed{\uparrow\;|\;\;|\;\;}$ $\quad 1s \quad\; 2s \qquad 2p$
C (6)	$1s^2 2s^2 2p^2$	$\boxed{\uparrow\downarrow}$ $\boxed{\uparrow\downarrow}$ $\boxed{\uparrow\;|\uparrow|\;\;}$ $\quad 1s \quad\; 2s \qquad 2p$
N (7)	$1s^2 2s^2 2p^3$	$\boxed{\uparrow\downarrow}$ $\boxed{\uparrow\downarrow}$ $\boxed{\uparrow\;|\uparrow|\uparrow}$ $\quad 1s \quad\; 2s \qquad 2p$
O (8)	$1s^2 2s^2 2p^4$	$\boxed{\uparrow\downarrow}$ $\boxed{\uparrow\downarrow}$ $\boxed{\uparrow\downarrow|\uparrow|\uparrow}$ $\quad 1s \quad\; 2s \qquad 2p$
F (9)	$1s^2 2s^2 2p^5$	$\boxed{\uparrow\downarrow}$ $\boxed{\uparrow\downarrow}$ $\boxed{\uparrow\downarrow|\uparrow\downarrow|\uparrow}$ $\quad 1s \quad\; 2s \qquad 2p$
Ne (10)	$1s^2 2s^2 2p^6$	$\boxed{\uparrow\downarrow}$ $\boxed{\uparrow\downarrow}$ $\boxed{\uparrow\downarrow|\uparrow\downarrow|\uparrow\downarrow}$ $\quad 1s \quad\; 2s \qquad 2p$

Notice how the p orbitals fill. As a result of Hund's rule, the p orbitals fill with single electrons before they fill with paired electrons. The electron configuration of neon represents the complete filling of the $n = 2$ principal shell. When writing electron configurations for elements beyond neon—or beyond any other noble gas—we often abbreviate the electron configuration of the previous noble gas by the symbol for the noble gas in brackets. For example, the electron configuration of sodium is:

$$\text{Na} \qquad 1s^2 2s^2 2p^6 3s^1$$

We can write this using the noble gas core notation as:

$$\text{Na} \qquad [\text{Ne}]3s^1$$

where [Ne] represents $1s^2 2s^2 2p^6$, the electron configuration for neon.

To write an electron configuration for an element, we first find its atomic number from the periodic table—this number equals the number of electrons in the neutral atom. Then we use the order of filling from Figure 9.23 or 9.24 to distribute the electrons in the appropriate orbitals. Remember that each orbital can hold a maximum of 2 electrons. Consequently:

- the s subshell has only 1 orbital and therefore can hold only 2 electrons.
- the p subshell has 3 orbitals and therefore can hold 6 electrons.
- the d subshell has 5 orbitals and therefore can hold 10 electrons.
- the f subshell has 7 orbitals and therefore can hold 14 electrons.

EXAMPLE 9.2	ELECTRON CONFIGURATIONS

Write electron configurations for each element.

(a) Mg   **(b)** S   **(c)** Ga

	SOLUTION
(a) Magnesium has 12 electrons. Distribute two of these into the 1s orbital, two into the 2s orbital, six into the 2p orbitals, and two into the 3s orbital. You can also write the electron configuration more compactly using the noble gas core notation. For magnesium, use [Ne] to represent $1s^2 2s^2 2p^6$.	Mg $\quad 1s^2 2s^2 2p^6 3s^2$ *or* Mg $\quad$ [Ne]$3s^2$
(b) Sulfur has 16 electrons. Distribute two of these into the 1s orbital, two into the 2s orbital, six into the 2p orbitals, two into the 3s orbital, and four into the 3p orbitals. You can write the electron configuration more compactly by using [Ne] to represent $1s^2 2s^2 2p^6$.	S $\quad 1s^2 2s^2 2p^6 3s^2 3p^4$ *or* S $\quad$ [Ne]$3s^2 3p^4$
(c) Gallium has 31 electrons. Distribute two of these into the 1s orbital, two into the 2s orbital, six into the 2p orbitals, two into the 3s orbital, six into the 3p orbitals, two into the 4s orbital, ten into the 3d orbitals, and one into the 4p orbitals. Notice that the d subshell has five orbitals and can therefore hold 10 electrons. You can write the electron configuration more compactly by using [Ar] to represent $1s^2 2s^2 2p^6 3s^2 3p^6$.	Ga $\quad 1s^2 2s^2 2p^6 3s^2 3p^6 4s^2 3d^{10} 4p^1$ *or* Ga $\quad$ [Ar]$4s^2 3d^{10} 4p^1$

▶ **SKILLBUILDER 9.2** | **Electron Configurations**

Write electron configurations for each element.

(a) Al   **(b)** Br   **(c)** Sr

▶ **SKILLBUILDER PLUS** | Write electron configurations for each ion. (*Hint:* To determine the number of electrons to include in the electron configuration of an ion, add or subtract electrons as needed to account for the charge of the ion.)

(a) Al^{3+} **(b)** Cl^- **(c)** O^{2-}

▶ **FOR MORE PRACTICE**   Problems 49, 50, 53, 54, 55, 56.

EXAMPLE 9.3	WRITING ORBITAL DIAGRAMS

Write an orbital diagram for silicon.

SOLUTION

Since silicon is atomic number 14, it has 14 electrons. Draw a box for each orbital, putting the lowest-energy orbital (1s) on the far left and proceeding to orbitals of higher energy to the right.

$\qquad$ 1s $\quad$ 2s $\qquad$ 2p $\qquad$ 3s $\qquad$ 3p

Distribute the 14 electrons into the orbitals, allowing a maximum of 2 electrons per orbital and remembering Hund's rule. The complete orbital diagram is:

Si $\quad$ ⇅ $\quad$ ⇅ $\quad$ ⇅ ⇅ ⇅ $\quad$ ⇅ $\quad$ ↑ ↑

$\qquad$ 1s $\quad$ 2s $\qquad$ 2p $\qquad$ 3s $\qquad$ 3p

▶ **SKILLBUILDER 9.3** | **Writing Orbital Diagrams**

Write an orbital diagram for argon.

▶ **FOR MORE PRACTICE**   Example 9.10; Problems 51, 52.

✓ **CONCEPTUAL CHECKPOINT 9.4**

Which pair of elements has the same *total* number of electrons in *p* orbitals?

(a) Na and K

(b) K and Kr

(c) P and N

(d) Ar and Ca

9.7   Electron Configurations and the Periodic Table

LO: Identify valence electrons and core electrons.

LO: Write electron configurations for elements based on their positions in the periodic table.

Valence electrons are the electrons in the outermost principal shell (the principal shell with the highest principal quantum number, n). These electrons are important because, as we will see in the next chapter, they are held most loosely and are most easily lost or shared; therefore they are involved in chemical bonding. Electrons that are *not* in the outermost principal shell are **core electrons**. For example, silicon, with the electron configuration of $1s^2 2s^2 2p^6 3s^2 3p^2$, has 4 valence electrons (those in the $n = 3$ principal shell) and 10 core electrons.

Si $1s^2 2s^2 2p^6\ 3s^2 3p^2$

Core electrons   Valence electrons

EXAMPLE 9.4   **VALENCE ELECTRONS AND CORE ELECTRONS**

Write an electron configuration for selenium and identify the valence electrons and the core electrons.

SOLUTION

Write the electron configuration for selenium by determining the total number of electrons from selenium's atomic number (34) and distributing them into the appropriate orbitals.

Se $1s^2 2s^2 2p^6 3s^2 3p^6 4s^2 3d^{10} 4p^4$

The valence electrons are those in the outermost principal shell. For selenium, the outermost principal shell is the $n = 4$ shell, which contains 6 electrons (2 in the 4s orbital and 4 in the three 4p orbitals). All other electrons, including those in the 3d orbitals, are core electrons.

6 valence electrons

Se $1s^2 2s^2 2p^6\ 3s^2 3p^6\ 4s^2\ 3d^{10}\ 4p^4$

28 core electrons

▶ **SKILLBUILDER 9.4 | Valence Electrons and Core Electrons**

Write an electron configuration for chlorine and identify the valence electrons and core electrons.

▶ **FOR MORE PRACTICE**   Example 9.11; Problems 57, 58, 61, 62.

▶ **FIGURE 9.25   Outer electron configurations of the first 18 elements**

1A	2A	3A	4A	5A	6A	7A	8A
1 H $1s^1$							2 He $1s^2$
3 Li $2s^1$	4 Be $2s^2$	5 B $2s^22p^1$	6 C $2s^22p^2$	7 N $2s^22p^3$	8 O $2s^22p^4$	9 F $2s^22p^5$	10 Ne $2s^22p^6$
11 Na $3s^1$	12 Mg $3s^2$	13 Al $3s^23p^1$	14 Si $3s^23p^2$	15 P $3s^23p^3$	16 S $3s^23p^4$	17 Cl $3s^23p^5$	18 Ar $3s^23p^6$

▲ Figure 9.25 shows the first 18 elements in the periodic table with an outer electron configuration listed below each one. As we move across a row, the orbitals are simply filling in the correct order. As we move down a column, the highest principal quantum number increases, but the number of electrons in each subshell remains the same. Consequently, the elements within a column (or family) all have the same number of valence electrons and similar outer electron configurations.

A similar pattern exists for the entire periodic table (▼ Figure 9.26). Notice that, because of the filling order of orbitals, we can divide the periodic table into blocks representing the filling of particular subshells.

- The first two columns on the left side of the periodic table are the *s* block with outer electron configurations of ns^1 (first column) and ns^2 (second column).
- The six columns on the right side of the periodic table are the *p* block with outer electron configurations of: ns^2np^1, ns^2np^2, ns^2np^3, ns^2np^4, ns^2np^5 (halogens), and ns^2np^6 (noble gases).
- The transition metals are the *d* block.
- The lanthanides and actinides (also called the inner transition metals) are the *f* block.

Figure 9.26

Groups: 1 (1A), 2 (2A), 3 (3B), 4 (4B), 5 (5B), 6 (6B), 7 (7B), 8 (8B), 9 (8B), 10 (8B), 11 (1B), 12 (2B), 13 (3A), 14 (4A), 15 (5A), 16 (6A), 17 (7A), 18 (8A)

s-block elements; *p*-block elements; *d*-block elements; *f*-block elements

Period																		
1	1 H $1s^1$																	2 He $1s^2$
2	3 Li $2s^1$	4 Be $2s^2$											5 B $2s^22p^1$	6 C $2s^22p^2$	7 N $2s^22p^3$	8 O $2s^22p^4$	9 F $2s^22p^5$	10 Ne $2s^22p^6$
3	11 Na $3s^1$	12 Mg $3s^2$											13 Al $3s^23p^1$	14 Si $3s^23p^2$	15 P $3s^23p^3$	16 S $3s^23p^4$	17 Cl $3s^23p^5$	18 Ar $3s^23p^6$
4	19 K $4s^1$	20 Ca $4s^2$	21 Sc $4s^23d^1$	22 Ti $4s^23d^2$	23 V $4s^23d^3$	24 Cr $4s^13d^5$	25 Mn $4s^23d^5$	26 Fe $4s^23d^6$	27 Co $4s^23d^7$	28 Ni $4s^23d^8$	29 Cu $4s^13d^{10}$	30 Zn $4s^23d^{10}$	31 Ga $4s^24p^1$	32 Ge $4s^24p^2$	33 As $4s^24p^3$	34 Se $4s^24p^4$	35 Br $4s^24p^5$	36 Kr $4s^24p^6$
5	37 Rb $5s^1$	38 Sr $5s^2$	39 Y $5s^24d^1$	40 Zr $5s^24d^2$	41 Nb $5s^14d^4$	42 Mo $5s^14d^5$	43 Tc $5s^24d^5$	44 Ru $5s^14d^7$	45 Rh $5s^14d^8$	46 Pd $4d^{10}$	47 Ag $5s^14d^{10}$	48 Cd $5s^24d^{10}$	49 In $5s^25p^1$	50 Sn $5s^25p^2$	51 Sb $5s^25p^3$	52 Te $5s^25p^4$	53 I $5s^25p^5$	54 Xe $5s^25p^6$
6	55 Cs $6s^1$	56 Ba $6s^2$	57 La $6s^25d^1$	72 Hf $6s^25d^2$	73 Ta $6s^25d^3$	74 W $6s^25d^4$	75 Re $6s^25d^5$	76 Os $6s^25d^6$	77 Ir $6s^25d^7$	78 Pt $6s^15d^9$	79 Au $6s^15d^{10}$	80 Hg $6s^25d^{10}$	81 Tl $6s^26p^1$	82 Pb $6s^26p^2$	83 Bi $6s^26p^3$	84 Po $6s^26p^4$	85 At $6s^26p^5$	86 Rn $6s^26p^6$
7	87 Fr $7s^1$	88 Ra $7s^2$	89 Ac $7s^26d^1$	104 Rf $7s^26d^2$	105 Db $7s^26d^3$	106 Sg $7s^26d^4$	107 Bh	108 Hs	109 Mt	110 Ds	111 Rg	112 Cn	113	114	115	116	117 ** (292)	118

Lanthanides

58 Ce $6s^25d\text{-}4f^1$	59 Pr $6s^24f^3$	60 Nd $6s^24f^4$	61 Pm $6s^24f^5$	62 Sm $6s^24f^6$	63 Eu $6s^24f^7$	64 Gd $6s^24f^75d^1$	65 Tb $6s^24f^9$	66 Dy $6s^24f^{10}$	67 Ho $6s^24f^{11}$	68 Er $6s^24f^{12}$	69 Tm $6s^24f^{13}$	70 Yb $6s^24f^{14}$	71 Lu $6s^24f^{14}5d^1$

Actinides

90 Th $7s^26d^2$	91 Pa $7s^25f^26d^1$	92 U $7s^25f^36d^1$	93 Np $7s^25f^46d^1$	94 Pu $7s^25f^6$	95 Am $7s^25f^7$	96 Cm $7s^25f^76d^1$	97 Bk $7s^25f^96d^1$	98 Cf $7s^25f^{10}$	99 Es $7s^25f^{11}$	100 Fm $7s^25f^{12}$	101 Md $7s^25f^{13}$	102 No $7s^25f^{14}$	103 Lr $7s^25f^{14}6d^1$

**Element 117 is currently under review by IUPAC.

▲ **FIGURE 9.26   Outer electron configurations of the elements**

Remember that main-group elements are those in the two far–left columns (1A, 2A) and the six far–right columns (3A–8A) of the periodic table (see Section 4.6).

▲ **FIGURE 9.27** **Electron configuration of phosphorus** Determining the electron configuration for P from its position in the periodic table.

Notice that, except for helium, the number of valence electrons for any main-group element is equal to the group number of its column. For example, we can tell that chlorine has 7 valence electrons because it is in the column with group number 7A. The row number in the periodic table is equal to the number of the highest principal shell (n value). For example, since chlorine is in row 3, its highest principal shell is the $n = 3$ shell.

The transition metals have electron configurations with trends that differ somewhat from main-group elements. As we move across a row in the d block, the d orbitals are filling (Figure 9.26). However, the principal quantum number of the d orbital being filled across each row in the transition series is equal to the row number minus one (in the fourth row, the $3d$ orbitals fill; in the fifth row, the $4d$ orbitals fill; and so on). For the first transition series, the outer configuration is $4s^2 3d^x$ ($x =$ number of d electrons) with two exceptions: Cr is $4s^1 3d^5$ and Cu is $4s^1 3d^{10}$. These exceptions occur because a half-filled d subshell and a completely filled d subshell are particularly stable. Otherwise, the number of outershell electrons in a transition series does not change as we move across a period. In other words, *the transition series represents the filling of core orbitals, and the number of outershell electrons is mostly constant.*

We can now see that the organization of the periodic table allows us to write the electron configuration for any element based simply on its position in the periodic table. For example, suppose we want to write an electron configuration for P. The inner electrons of P are those of the noble gas that precedes P in the periodic table, Ne. So we can represent the inner electrons with [Ne]. We obtain the outer electron configuration by tracing the elements between Ne and P and assigning electrons to the appropriate orbitals (◄ Figure 9.27). Remember that the highest n value is given by the row number (3 for phosphorus). So we begin with [Ne], then add in the two $3s$ electrons as we trace across the s block, followed by three $3p$ electrons as we trace across the p block to P, which is in the third column of the p block. The electron configuration is:

$$P \qquad [Ne]3s^2 3p^3$$

Notice that P is in column 5A and therefore has 5 valence electrons and an outer electron configuration of $ns^2 np^3$.

To summarize writing an electron configuration for an element based on its position in the periodic table:

- The inner electron configuration for any element is the electron configuration of the noble gas that immediately precedes that element in the periodic table. We represent the inner configuration with the symbol for the noble gas in brackets.
- We can determine the outer electrons from the element's position within a particular block (s, p, d, or f) in the periodic table. We trace the elements between the preceding noble gas and the element of interest, and assign electrons to the appropriate orbitals.
- The highest principal quantum number (highest n value) is equal to the row number of the element in the periodic table.
- For any element containing d electrons, the principal quantum number (n value) of the outermost d electrons is equal to the row number of the element minus 1.

WRITING ELECTRON CONFIGURATIONS FROM THE PERIODIC TABLE

EXAMPLE 9.5

 Write an electron configuration for arsenic based on its position in the periodic table.

SOLUTION

The noble gas that precedes arsenic in the periodic table is argon, so the inner electron configuration is [Ar]. Obtain the outer electron configuration by tracing the elements between Ar and As and assigning electrons to the appropriate orbitals.

Remember that the highest n value is given by the row number (4 for arsenic). So, begin with [Ar], then add in the two 4s electrons as you trace across the s block, followed by ten 3d electrons as you trace across the d block (the n value for d subshells is equal to the row number minus one), and finally the three 4p electrons as you trace across the p block to As, which is in the third column of the p block:

The electron configuration is:

$$\text{As} \qquad [\text{Ar}]4s^2 3d^{10} 4p^3$$

▶ **SKILLBUILDER 9.5 | Writing Electron Configurations from the Periodic Table**

Use the periodic table to determine the electron configuration for tin.

▶ **FOR MORE PRACTICE**   Example 9.12; Problems 65, 66, 67, 68.

  CONCEPTUAL CHECKPOINT 9.5

Which element has the *fewest* valence electrons?

(a) B   **(b)** Ca   **(c)** O

(d) K   **(e)** Ga

9.8   The Explanatory Power of the Quantum-Mechanical Model

LO: Recognize that the chemical properties of elements are largely determined by the number of valence electrons they contain.

Noble gases
18 8A
2 **He** $1s^2$
10 **Ne** $2s^2 2p^6$
18 **Ar** $3s^2 3p^6$
36 **Kr** $4s^2 4p^6$
54 **Xe** $5s^2 5p^6$
86 **Rn** $6s^2 6p^6$

▶ **FIGURE 9.28   Electron configurations of the noble gases** The noble gases (except for helium) all have 8 valence electrons and completely full outer principal shells.

At the beginning of this chapter, we asserted that the quantum-mechanical model explains the chemical properties of the elements such as the inertness of helium, the reactivity of hydrogen, and the periodic law. We can now see how: *The chemical properties of elements are largely determined by the number of valence electrons they contain.* The properties of elements vary in a periodic fashion because the number of valence electrons is periodic.

Because elements within a column in the periodic table have the same number of valence electrons, they also have similar chemical properties. The noble gases, for example, all have 8 valence electrons, except for helium, which has 2 (◀ Figure 9.28). Although we don't get into the quantitative (or numerical) aspects of the quantum-mechanical model in this book, calculations show that atoms with 8 valence electrons (or 2 for helium) are particularly low in energy, and therefore stable. The noble gases are indeed chemically stable and thus relatively inert or nonreactive as accounted for by the quantum model.

Elements with electron configurations close to the noble gases are the most reactive because they can attain noble gas electron configurations by losing or gaining a small number of electrons. Alkali metals (Group 1) are among the most reactive metals since their outer electron configuration (ns^1) is 1 electron beyond a noble gas

Alkali metals
1
1A
3
Li
$2s^1$
11
Na
$3s^1$
19
K
$4s^1$
37
Rb
$5s^1$
55
Cs
$6s^1$
87
Fr
$7s^1$

▲ **FIGURE 9.29 Electron configurations of the alkali metals**   The alkali metals all have ns^1 electron configurations and are therefore 1 electron beyond a noble gas configuration. In their reactions, they tend to lose that electron, forming 1+ ions and attaining a noble gas configuration.

Atoms and/or ions that share the same electron configuration are termed isoelectronic.

configuration (◀ Figure 9.29). If they can react to lose the ns^1 electron, they attain a noble gas configuration. This explains why—as we learned in Chapter 4—the Group 1A metals tend to form 1+ cations. As an example, consider the electron configuration of sodium:

$$\text{Na} \qquad 1s^2 2s^2 2p^6 3s^1$$

In reactions, sodium loses its $3s$ electron, forming a 1+ ion with the electron configuration of neon.

$$\text{Na}^+ \qquad 1s^2 2s^2 2p^6$$

$$\text{Ne} \qquad 1s^2 2s^2 2p^6$$

Similarly, alkaline earth metals, with an outer electron configuration of ns^2, also tend to be reactive metals, losing their ns^2 electrons to form 2+ cations (▼ Figure 9.30). For example, consider magnesium:

$$\text{Mg} \qquad 1s^2 2s^2 2p^6 3s^2$$

In reactions, magnesium loses its two $3s$ electrons, forming a 2+ ion with the electron configuration of neon.

$$\text{Mg}^{2+} \qquad 1s^2 2s^2 2p^6$$

On the other side of the periodic table, halogens are among the most reactive nonmetals because of their $ns^2 np^5$ electron configurations (▼ Figure 9.31). They are only one electron away from a noble gas configuration and tend to react to gain that one electron, forming 1− ions. For example, consider fluorine:

$$\text{F} \qquad 1s^2 2s^2 2p^5$$

In reactions, fluorine gains an additional $2p$ electron, forming a 1− ion with the electron configuration of neon.

$$\text{F}^- \qquad 1s^2 2s^2 2p^6$$

The elements that form predictable ions are shown in ▶ Figure 9.32 (first introduced in Chapter 4). Notice how the charge of these ions reflects their electron configurations—these elements form ions with noble gas electron configurations.

Alkaline earth metals
2
2A
4
Be
$2s^2$
12
Mg
$3s^2$
20
Ca
$4s^2$
38
Sr
$5s^2$
56
Ba
$6s^2$
88
Ra
$7s^2$

◀ **FIGURE 9.30   Electron configurations of the alkaline earth metals**   The alkaline earth metals all have ns^2 electron configurations and are therefore 2 electrons beyond a noble gas configuration. In their reactions, they tend to lose 2 electrons, forming 2+ ions and attaining a noble gas configuration.

▶ **FIGURE 9.31   Electron configurations of the halogens**   The halogens all have $ns^2 np^5$ electron configurations and are therefore 1 electron short of a noble gas configuration. In their reactions, they tend to gain 1 electron, forming 1− ions and attaining a noble gas configuration.

Halogens
17
7A
9
F
$2s^2 2p^5$
17
Cl
$3s^2 3p^5$
35
Br
$4s^2 4p^5$
53
I
$5s^2 5p^5$
85
At
$6s^2 6p^5$

1																	8
	2										3	4	5	6	7		
Li⁺													N³⁻	O²⁻	F⁻		
Na⁺	Mg²⁺										Al³⁺			S²⁻	Cl⁻		
K⁺	Ca²⁺										Ga³⁺			Se²⁻	Br⁻		
Rb⁺	Sr²⁺										In³⁺			Te²⁻	I⁻		
Cs⁺	Ba²⁺																

Periodic table fragment — "Elements that form predictable ions":

Row 1: Li^+; N^{3-}, O^{2-}, F^-
Row 2: Na^+, Mg^{2+}; Al^{3+}; S^{2-}, Cl^-
Row 3: K^+, Ca^{2+}; Ga^{3+}; Se^{2-}, Br^-
Row 4: Rb^+, Sr^{2+}; In^{3+}; Te^{2-}, I^-
Row 5: Cs^+, Ba^{2+}

Most transition metals form cations with various charges

▲ **FIGURE 9.32   Elements that form predictable ions**

CONCEPTUAL CHECKPOINT 9.6

Below is the electron configuration of calcium:

$$Ca \qquad 1s^2 2s^2 2p^6 3s^2 3p^6 \underline{4s^2}$$

In its reactions, calcium tends to form the Ca^{2+} ion. Which electrons are lost upon ionization?

(a) the $4s$ electrons

(c) the $3s$ electrons

(b) two of the $3p$ electrons

(d) the $1s$ electrons

9.9   Periodic Trends: Atomic Size, Ionization Energy, and Metallic Character

LO: Identify and understand periodic trends such as atomic size, ionization energy, and metallic character.

The quantum-mechanical model also explains other periodic trends such as atomic size, ionization energy, and metallic character. We examine these trends individually in this section of the chapter.

Atomic Size

The **atomic size** of an atom is determined by the distance between the outermost electrons and the nucleus. As we move across a period in the periodic table, we know that electrons occupy orbitals with the same principal quantum number, n. Since the principal quantum number largely determines the size of an orbital, electrons are therefore filling orbitals of approximately the same size, and we might expect atomic size to remain constant across a period. However, with each step across a period, the number of protons in the nucleus also increases. This increase in the number of protons results in a greater pull on the electrons from the nucleus, causing atomic size to actually decrease. Therefore:

As we move to the right across a period, or row, in the periodic table, atomic size decreases, as shown in ▶Figure 9.33.

As we move down a column in the periodic table, the highest principal quantum number, n, increases. Because the size of an orbital increases with increasing principal quantum number, the electrons that occupy the outermost orbitals are farther from the nucleus as we move down a column. Therefore:

As we move down a column, or family, in the periodic table, atomic size increases, as shown in Figure 9.33.

▶ **FIGURE 9.33 Periodic properties: atomic size** Atomic size decreases as we move to the right across a period and increases as we move down a column in the periodic table.

Relative atomic sizes of the main-group elements

Sizes of atoms tend to increase down a column

Sizes of atoms tend to decrease across a period

(a)

(b)

(c)

(d)

EXAMPLE 9.6 ATOMIC SIZE

Choose the larger atom in each pair.

(a) C or O   (b) Li or K   (c) C or Al   (d) Se or I

SOLUTION

(a) C or O

Carbon atoms are larger than O atoms because, as you trace the path between C and O on the periodic table, you move to the right within the same period. Atomic size decreases as you go to the right.

(b) Li or K

Potassium atoms are larger than Li atoms because, as you trace the path between Li and K on the periodic table, you move down a column. Atomic size increases as you go down a column.

(c) C or Al

Aluminum atoms are larger than C atoms because, as you trace the path between C and Al on the periodic table you move down a column (atomic size increases) and then to the left across a period (atomic size increases). These effects add together for an overall increase.

(d) Se or I

Based on periodic properties alone, you cannot tell which atom is larger because as you trace the path between Se and I, you go down a column (atomic size increases) and then to the right across a period (atomic size decreases). These effects tend to cancel one another.

▶ **SKILLBUILDER 9.6 | Atomic Size**

Choose the larger atom in each pair.

(a) Pb or Po   (b) Rb or Na   (c) Sn or Bi   (d) F or Se

▶ **FOR MORE PRACTICE**   Example 9.13a; Problems 81, 82, 83, 84.

CHEMISTRY **AND HEALTH**

▶ Pumping Ions: Atomic Size and Nerve Impulses

No matter what you are doing at this moment, tiny pumps in each of the trillions of cells that make up your body are hard at work. These pumps, located in the cell membrane, move a number of different ions into and out of the cell. The most important of these ions are sodium (Na^+) and potassium (K^+), which happen to be pumped in opposite directions. Sodium ions are pumped *out of cells*, while potassium ions are pumped *into cells*. The result is a *chemical gradient* for each ion. The concentration of sodium is higher outside the cell than within, while exactly the opposite is true for potassium.

The ion pumps within the cell membrane are analogous to water pumps in a high-rise building that pump water against the force of gravity to a tank on the roof. Other structures within the membrane, called ion channels, are like the building's faucets. When they open momentarily, bursts of sodium and potassium ions, driven by their concentration gradients, flow back across the membrane—sodium flowing in and potassium flowing out. These ion pulses are the basis for the transmission of nerve signals in the brain, heart, and throughout the body. Consequently, every move you make or every thought you have is mediated by the flow of these ions.

How do the pumps and channels differentiate between sodium and potassium ions? How do the ion pumps selectively move sodium out of the cell and potassium into the cell? To answer this question, we must examine the sodium and potassium ions more closely. In what ways do they differ? Both are cations of Group I metals. All Group I metals tend to lose one electron to form cations with 1+ charge, so the magnitude of the charge cannot be the decisive factor. But potassium (atomic number 19) lies directly below sodium in the periodic table (atomic number 11) and based on periodic properties is therefore larger than sodium. The potassium ion has a radius of 133 pm, while the sodium ion has a radius of 95 pm. (Recall from Chapter 2 that 1 pm = 10^{-12} m.) The pumps and channels within cell membranes are so sensitive that they distinguish between the sizes of these two ions and selectively allow only one or the other to pass. The result is the transmission of nerve signals that allows you to read this page.

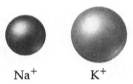

Na^+ K^+

B9.2 CAN YOU ANSWER THIS? *Other ions, including calcium and magnesium, are also important to nerve signal transmission. Arrange these four ions in order of increasing size: K^+, Na^+, Mg^{2+}, and Ca^{2+}.*

Ionization Energy

The **ionization energy** of an atom is the energy required to remove an electron from the atom in the gaseous state. For example, the ionization of sodium can be represented with the equation:

$$Na + \text{Ionization energy} \longrightarrow Na^+ + 1e^-$$

Based on what we know about electron configurations, what can we predict about ionization energy trends? Would it take more or less energy to remove an electron from Na than from Cl? We know that Na has an outer electron configuration of $3s^1$ and Cl has an outer electron configuration of $3s^2 3p^5$. Since removing an electron from Na gives it a noble gas configuration—and removing an electron from Cl does not—we would expect sodium to have a lower ionization energy, and that is the case. It is easier to remove an electron from sodium than it is from chlorine. We can generalize this idea in this statement:

As we move across a period, or row, to the right in the periodic table, ionization energy increases (▶Figure 9.34).

What happens to ionization energy as we move down a column? As we have learned, the principal quantum number, n, increases as we move down a column. Within a given subshell, orbitals with higher principal quantum numbers are larger than orbitals with smaller principal quantum numbers. Consequently, electrons in the outermost principal shell are farther away from the positively charged nucleus—and therefore are held less tightly—as we move down a column. This

▶ **FIGURE 9.34 Periodic properties: ionization energy**
Ionization energy increases as we move to the right across a period and decreases as we move down a column in the periodic table.

Ionization energy trends

Ionization energy decreases

Periods

Ionization energy increases

results in a lower ionization energy (if the electron is held less tightly, it is easier to pull away) as we move down a column. Therefore:

As we move down a column (or family) in the periodic table, ionization energy decreases (Figure 9.34).

Notice that the trends in ionization energy are consistent with the trends in atomic size. Smaller atoms are more difficult to ionize because their electrons are held more tightly. Therefore, as we move across a period, atomic size decreases and ionization energy increases. Similarly, as we move down a column, atomic size increases and ionization energy decreases since electrons are farther from the nucleus and are therefore less tightly held.

(a)

(b)

EXAMPLE 9.7   **IONIZATION ENERGY**

Choose the element with the higher ionization energy from each pair.

(a) Mg or P
(b) As or Sb
(c) N or Si
(d) O or Cl

SOLUTION

(a) Mg or P
P has a higher ionization than Mg because, as you trace the path between Mg and P on the periodic table, you move to the right within the same period. Ionization energy increases as you go to the right.

(b) As or Sb
As has a higher ionization energy than Sb because, as you trace the path between As and Sb on the periodic table, you move down a column. Ionization energy decreases as you go down a column.

(c) N or Si
N has a higher ionization energy than Si because, as you trace the path between N and Si on the periodic table, you move down a column (ionization energy decreases) and then to the left across a period (ionization energy decreases). These effects sum together for an overall decrease.

(c)

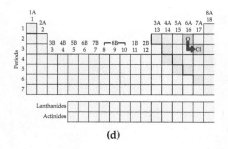

(d)

(d) O or Cl

Based on periodic properties alone, you cannot tell which has a higher ionization energy because, as you trace the path between O and Cl you move down a column (ionization energy decreases) and then to the right across a period (ionization energy increases). These effects tend to cancel.

▶ **SKILLBUILDER 9.7 | Ionization Energy**

Choose the element with the higher ionization energy from each pair.

(a) Mg or Sr
(b) In or Te
(c) C or P
(d) F or S

▶ **FOR MORE PRACTICE**   Example 9.13b; Problems 77, 78, 79, 80.

Metallic Character

As we learned in Chapter 4, metals tend to lose electrons in their chemical reactions, while nonmetals tend to gain electrons. As we move across a period in the periodic table, ionization energy increases, which means that electrons are less likely to be lost in chemical reactions. Consequently:

As we move across a period, or row, to the right in the periodic table, **metallic character** decreases (▼Figure 9.35).

As we move down a column in the periodic table, ionization energy decreases, making electrons more likely to be lost in chemical reactions. Consequently:

As we move down a column, or family, in the periodic table, metallic character increases (Figure 9.35).

These trends, based on the quantum-mechanical model, explain the distribution of metals and nonmetals that we were introduced to in Chapter 4. Metals are found toward the left side of the periodic table and nonmetals (with the exception of hydrogen) toward the upper right.

▲ **FIGURE 9.35 Periodic properties: metallic character** Metallic character decreases as we move to the right across a period and increases as we move down a column in the periodic table.

(a)

(b)

(c)

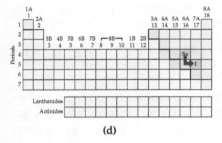

(d)

EXAMPLE 9.8   METALLIC CHARACTER

Choose the more metallic element from each pair.

(a) Sn or Te
(b) Si or Sn
(c) Br or Te
(d) Se or I

SOLUTION

(a) Sn or Te

Sn is more metallic than Te because, as you trace the path between Sn and Te on the periodic table, you move to the right within the same period. Metallic character decreases as you go to the right.

(b) Si or Sn

Sn is more metallic than Si because, as you trace the path between Si and Sn on the periodic table, you move down a column. Metallic character increases as you go down a column.

(c) Br or Te

Te is more metallic than Br because, as you trace the path between Br and Te on the periodic table, you move down a column (metallic character increases) and then to the left across a period (metallic character increases). These effects add together for an overall increase.

(d) Se or I

Based on periodic properties alone, you cannot tell which is more metallic because, as you trace the path between Se and I, you go down a column (metallic character increases) and then to the right across a period (metallic character decreases). These effects tend to cancel.

▶ **SKILLBUILDER 9.8 | Metallic Character**

Choose the more metallic element from each pair.

(a) Ge or In
(b) Ga or Sn
(c) P or Bi
(d) B or N

▶ **FOR MORE PRACTICE**   Example 9.13; Problems 85, 86, 87, 88.

✓ CONCEPTUAL CHECKPOINT 9.7

Which property *increases* as you move from left to right across a row in the periodic table?

(a) Atomic size
(b) Ionization energy
(c) Metallic character

CHAPTER IN REVIEW

Self-Assessment Quiz

Q1. Which set of wavelengths for light are arranged in order of increasing frequency?

(a) 250 nm; 300 nm; 350 nm

(b) 350 nm; 300 nm; 250 nm

(c) 300 nm; 350 nm; 250 nm

(d) 300 nm; 250 nm; 350 nm

Q2. Which of the listed types of electromagnetic radiation has the longest wavelength?

(a) Ultraviolet   (c) Infrared

(b) X-ray   (d) Microwaves

Q3. Which electron transition in the Bohr model would produce light with the longest wavelength?

(a) $n = 2 \longrightarrow n = 1$ (c) $n = 4 \longrightarrow n = 1$

(b) $n = 3 \longrightarrow n = 1$ (d) $n = 5 \longrightarrow n = 1$

Q4. What is the electron configuration of arsenic (As)?

(a) $[Ar]4s^2 4p^3$ (c) $[Ar]4s^2 3d^6 4p^3$

(b) $[Ar]4s^2 4d^{10} 4p^3$ (d) $[Ar]4s^2 3d^{10} 4p^3$

Q5. Which orbital diagram corresponds to phosphorus (P)?

Q6. How many valence electrons does tellurium (Te) have?

(a) 5   (b) 6   (c) 16   (d) 52

Q7. The element sulfur forms an ion with what charge?

(a) 2−   (b) 1−   (c) 1+   (d) 2+

Q8. Order the elements Sr, Ca, and Se in order of decreasing atomic size.

(a) Se > Sr > Ca   (c) Sr > Ca > Se

(b) Ca > Se > Sr   (d) Se > Ca > Sr

Q9. Which element has the highest ionization energy?

(a) Sn   (b) S   (c) Si   (d) F

Q10. Which element is most metallic?

(a) Al   (b) N   (c) P   (d) O

Q11. Which property decreases as you move down a column in the periodic table?

(a) Atomic size

(b) Ionization energy

(c) Metallic character

(d) None of the above (all increase as you move down a column).

Q12. When aluminum forms an ion, it loses electrons. How many electrons does it lose, and which orbitals do the electrons come from?

(a) 1 electron from the 3s orbital

(b) 2 electrons; one from the 3s orbital and one from the 2s orbital

(c) 3 electrons; two from the 3s orbital and one from the 3p orbital

(d) 5 electrons from the 3p orbital

Answers: 1:b; 2:d; 3:a; 4:d; 5:c; 6:b; 7:a; 8:c; 9:d; 10:a; 11:b; 12:c

Chemical Principles

Light: Light is electromagnetic radiation, energy that travels through space at a constant speed of 3.0×10^8 m/s (186,000 mi/s) and exhibits both wavelike and particle-like behavior. Particles of light are called photons. The wave nature of light is characterized by its wavelength, the distance between adjacent crests in the wave. The wavelength of light is inversely proportional to both the frequency—the number of cycles that pass a stationary point in one second—and the energy of a photon. Electromagnetic radiation ranges in wavelength from 10^{-16} m (gamma rays) to 10^6 m (radio waves). In between these lie X-rays, ultraviolet light, visible light, infrared light, and microwaves.

Relevance

Light: Light enables us to see the world. However, we see only visible light, a small sliver in the center of the electromagnetic spectrum. We use other forms of electromagnetic radiation for cancer therapy, X-ray imaging, night vision, microwave cooking, and communications. Light is also important to many chemical processes. We can learn about the electronic structure of atoms, for example, by examining their interaction with light.

The Bohr Model: The emission spectrum of hydrogen, consisting of bright lines at specific wavelengths, is explained by the Bohr model for the hydrogen atom. In this model, electrons occupy circular orbits at specific fixed distances from the nucleus. Each orbit is specified by a quantum number (n), which also specifies the orbit's energy. While an electron is in a given orbit, its energy remains constant. When an electron jumps between orbits, a quantum of energy is absorbed or emitted. Since the difference in energy between orbits is fixed, the energy emitted or absorbed is also fixed. Emitted energy is carried away in the form of a photon of specific wavelength.

The Bohr Model: The Bohr model was a first attempt to explain the bright-line spectra of atoms. While it does predict the spectrum of the hydrogen atom, it fails to predict the spectra of other atoms and was consequently replaced by the quantum-mechanical model.

The Quantum-Mechanical Model: The quantum-mechanical model for the atom describes electron orbitals, which are electron probability maps that show the relative probability of finding an electron in various places surrounding the atomic nucleus. Orbitals are specified with a number (n), called the principal quantum number, and a letter. The principal quantum number ($n = 1, 2, 3 \ldots$) specifies the principal shell, and the letter (s, p, d, or f) specifies the subshell of the orbital. In the hydrogen atom, the energy of orbitals depends only on n. In multi-electron atoms, the energy ordering is $1s$ $2s$ $2p$ $3s$ $3p$ $4s$ $3d$ $4p$ $5s$ $4d$ $5p$ $6s$.

An electron configuration indicates which orbitals are occupied for a particular atom. Orbitals are filled in order of increasing energy and obey the Pauli exclusion principle (each orbital can hold a maximum of two electrons with opposing spins) and Hund's rule (electrons occupy orbitals of identical energy singly before pairing).

The Quantum-Mechanical Model: The quantum-mechanical model changed the way we view nature. Before the quantum-mechanical model, electrons were viewed as small particles, much like any other particle. Electrons were expected to follow the normal laws of motion, just as a baseball does. However, the electron, with its wavelike properties, does not follow these laws. Instead, electron motion is describable only through probabilistic predictions. Quantum theory single-handedly changed the predictability of nature at its most fundamental level.

The quantum-mechanical model of the atom predicts and explains many of the chemical properties we learned about in earlier chapters.

The Periodic Table: Elements within the same column of the periodic table have similar outer electron configurations and the same number of valence electrons (electrons in the outermost principal shell), and therefore similar chemical properties. We divide the periodic table into blocks (s block, p block, d block, and f block) in which particular sublevels are filled. As we move across a period to the right in the periodic table, atomic size decreases, ionization energy increases, and metallic character decreases. As we move down a column in the periodic table, atomic size increases, ionization energy decreases, and metallic character increases.

The Periodic Table: The periodic law exists because the number of valence electrons is periodic, and valence electrons determine chemical properties. Quantum theory also predicts that atoms with 8 outershell electrons (or 2 for helium) are particularly stable, thus explaining the inertness of the noble gases. Atoms without noble gas configurations undergo chemical reactions to attain them, explaining the reactivity of the alkali metals and the halogens as well as the tendency of several families to form ions with certain charges.

Chemical Skills

LO: Predict the relative wavelength, energy, and frequency of different types of light (Section 9.3).

- Relative wavelengths are included in Figure 9.4.
- Energy per photon increases with decreasing (shorter) wavelength.
- Frequency increases with decreasing (shorter) wavelength.

Examples

EXAMPLE 9.9 **PREDICTING RELATIVE WAVELENGTH, ENERGY, AND FREQUENCY OF LIGHT**

Which type of light—infrared or ultraviolet—has the longer wavelength? Higher frequency? Higher energy per photon?

SOLUTION

Infrared light has the longer wavelength (Figure 9.4). Ultraviolet light has the higher frequency and the higher energy per photon.

LO: Write electron configurations and orbital diagrams for atoms (Section 9.6).

To write electron configurations, determine the number of electrons in the atom from the element's atomic number and then follow these rules:

- Electrons occupy orbitals so as to minimize the energy of the atom; therefore, lower-energy orbitals fill before higher-energy orbitals. Orbitals fill in the order: 1s 2s 2p 3s 3p 4s 3d 4p 5s 4d 5p 6s (Figure 9.24). The s subshells hold up to 2 electrons, p subshells hold up to 6, d subshells hold up to 10, and f subshells hold up to 14.
- Orbitals can hold no more than 2 electrons each. When 2 electrons occupy the same orbital, they must have opposing spins.
- When orbitals of identical energy are available, these are first occupied singly with parallel spins rather than in pairs.

EXAMPLE 9.10   WRITING ELECTRON CONFIGURATIONS AND ORBITAL DIAGRAMS

Write an electron configuration and orbital diagram (outer electrons only) for germanium.

SOLUTION
Germanium is atomic number 32; therefore, it has 32 electrons.

Electron Configuration

$$Ge \quad 1s^2 2s^2 2p^6 3s^2 3p^6 4s^2 3d^{10} 4p^2$$
or
$$Ge \quad [Ar]4s^2 3d^{10} 4p^2$$

Orbital Diagram (Outer Electrons)

$$4s \qquad\qquad 3d \qquad\qquad\qquad 4p$$

LO: Identify valence electrons and core electrons (Section 9.7).

- Valence electrons are the electrons in the outermost principal energy shell (the principal shell with the highest principal quantum number).
- Core electrons are electrons that are not in the outermost principal shell.

EXAMPLE 9.11   IDENTIFYING VALENCE ELECTRONS AND CORE ELECTRONS

Identify the valence electrons and core electrons in the electron configuration of germanium (given in Example 9.10).

SOLUTION

$$Ge \quad 1s^2 2s^2 2p^6 3s^2 3p^6\ 4s^2\ 3d^{10}\ 4p^2$$

28 core electrons   4 valence electrons

LO: Write electron configurations for elements based on their positions in the periodic table (Section 9.7).

- The inner electron configuration for any element is the electron configuration of the noble gas that immediately precedes that element in the periodic table. Represent the inner configuration with the symbol for the noble gas in brackets.
- The outer electrons can be determined from the element's position within a particular block (s, p, d, or f) in the periodic table. Trace the elements between the preceding noble gas and the element of interest and assign electrons to the appropriate orbitals. Figure 9.26 shows the outer electron configuration based on the position of an element in the periodic table.
- The highest principal quantum number (highest n value) is equal to the row number of the element in the periodic table.
- The principal quantum number (n value) of the outermost d electrons for any element containing d electrons is equal to the row number of the element minus 1.

EXAMPLE 9.12   WRITING AN ELECTRON CONFIGURATION FOR AN ELEMENT BASED ON ITS POSITION IN THE PERIODIC TABLE

Write an electron configuration for iodine based on its position in the periodic table.

SOLUTION
The inner configuration for I is [Kr].
Begin with the [Kr] inner electron configuration. As you trace from Kr to I, add two 5s electrons, ten 4d electrons, and five 5p electrons. The overall configuration is:

$$I \quad [Kr]5s^2 4d^{10} 5p^5$$

LO: Identify and understand periodic trends such as atomic size, ionization energy, and metallic character (Section 9.9).

On the periodic table:

- Atomic size decreases as you move to the right and increases as you move down.

- Ionization energy increases as you move to the right and decreases as you move down.

- Metallic character decreases as you move to the right and increases as you move down.

EXAMPLE 9.13	PERIODIC TRENDS: ATOMIC SIZE, IONIZATION ENERGY, AND METALLIC CHARACTER

Arrange Si, In, and S in order of **(a)** increasing atomic size, **(b)** increasing ionization energy, and **(c)** increasing metallic character.

SOLUTION

(a) S, Si, In
(b) In, Si, S
(c) S, Si, In

KEY TERMS

atomic size **[9.9]**
Bohr model **[9.1]**
core electrons **[9.7]**
electromagnetic radiation **[9.2]**
electromagnetic spectrum **[9.3]**
electron configuration **[9.6]**
electron spin **[9.6]**
emission spectrum (plural, emission *spectra*) **[9.4]**

excited state **[9.6]**
frequency (*v*) **[9.2]**
gamma rays **[9.3]**
ground state **[9.6]**
Hund's rule **[9.6]**
infrared light **[9.3]**
ionization energy **[9.9]**
metallic character **[9.9]**
microwaves **[9.3]**
orbital **[9.5]**
orbital diagram **[9.6]**

Pauli exclusion principle **[9.6]**
photon **[9.2]**
principal quantum number **[9.6]**
principal shell **[9.6]**
quantized **[9.4]**
quantum (plural, *quanta*) **[9.4]**
quantum-mechanical model **[9.1]**

quantum number **[9.4]**
radio waves **[9.3]**
subshell **[9.6]**
ultraviolet (UV) light **[9.3]**
valence electron **[9.7]**
visible light **[9.3]**
wavelength (λ) **[9.2]**
X-rays **[9.3]**

EXERCISES

QUESTIONS

1. When were the Bohr model and the quantum-mechanical model for the atom developed? What purpose do these models serve?
2. What is light? How fast does light travel?
3. What is white light? Colored light?
4. Explain, in terms of absorbed and reflected light, why a blue object appears blue.
5. What is the relationship between the wavelength of light and the amount of energy carried by its photons? How are wavelength and frequency of light related?
6. List some sources of gamma rays.
7. How are X-rays used?
8. Why should excess exposure to gamma rays and X-rays be avoided?
9. Why should excess exposure to ultraviolet light be avoided?
10. What objects emit infrared light? What technology exploits this?
11. Why do microwave ovens heat food, but tend not to heat the dish the food is on?
12. What type of electromagnetic radiation is used in communications devices such as cellular telephones?
13. Describe the Bohr model for the hydrogen atom.

14. What is an emission spectrum? Use the Bohr model to explain why the emission spectrum of the hydrogen atom consists of distinct lines at specific wavelengths.
15. Explain the difference between a Bohr orbit and a quantum-mechanical orbital.
16. What is the difference between the ground state of an atom and an excited state of an atom?
17. Explain how the motion of an electron is different from the motion of a baseball. What is a probability map?
18. Why do quantum-mechanical orbitals have "fuzzy" boundaries?
19. List the four possible subshells in the quantum-mechanical model, the number of orbitals in each subshell, and the maximum number of electrons that can be contained in each subshell.
20. List the quantum-mechanical orbitals through 5s, in the correct energy order for multi-electron atoms.
21. What is the Pauli exclusion principle? Why is it important when writing electron configurations?
22. What is Hund's rule? Why is it important when writing orbital diagrams?
23. Within an electron configuration, what do symbols such as [Ne] and [Kr] represent?

24. Explain the difference between valence electrons and core electrons.

25. Identify each block in the blank periodic table.
 (a) s block
 (b) p block
 (c) d block
 (d) f block

26. List some examples of the explanatory power of the quantum-mechanical model.

27. Explain why Group 1 elements tend to form 1+ ions and Group 7 elements tend to form 1− ions.

28. Explain the periodic trends in each chemical property.
 (a) ionization energy
 (b) atomic size
 (c) metallic character

PROBLEMS

WAVELENGTH, ENERGY, AND FREQUENCY OF ELECTROMAGNETIC RADIATION

29. How long does it take light to travel in:
 (a) 1.0 ft (report answer in nanoseconds)
 (b) 2462 mi, the distance between Los Angeles and New York (report answer in milliseconds)
 (c) 4.5 billion km, the average separation between the sun and Neptune (report answer in hours and minutes)

30. How far does light travel in each time period?
 (a) 1.0 s
 (b) 1.0 day
 (c) 1.0 yr

31. Which type of electromagnetic radiation has the longest wavelength?
 (a) visible
 (b) ultraviolet
 (c) infrared
 (d) X-ray

32. Which type of electromagnetic radiation has the shortest wavelength?
 (a) radio waves
 (b) microwaves
 (c) infrared
 (d) ultraviolet

33. List the types of electromagnetic radiation in order of increasing energy per photon.
 (a) radio waves
 (b) microwaves
 (c) infrared
 (d) ultraviolet

34. List the types of electromagnetic radiation in order of decreasing energy per photon.
 (a) gamma rays
 (b) radio waves
 (c) microwaves
 (d) visible light

35. List two types of electromagnetic radiation with frequencies higher than visible light.

36. List two types of electromagnetic radiation with frequencies lower than infrared light.

37. List these three types of radiation—infrared, X-ray, and radio waves—in order of:
 (a) increasing energy per photon
 (b) increasing frequency
 (c) increasing wavelength

38. List these three types of electromagnetic radiation—visible, gamma rays, and microwaves—in order of:
 (a) decreasing energy per photon
 (b) decreasing frequency
 (c) decreasing wavelength

THE BOHR MODEL

39. Bohr orbits have fixed _____ and fixed _____.

40. In the Bohr model, what happens when an electron makes a transition between orbits?

41. Two of the emission wavelengths in the hydrogen emission spectrum are 410 nm and 434 nm. One of these is due to the $n = 6$ to $n = 2$ transition, and the other is due to the $n = 5$ to $n = 2$ transition. Which wavelength corresponds to which transition?

42. Two of the emission wavelengths in the hydrogen emission spectrum are 656 nm and 486 nm. One of these is due to the $n = 4$ to $n = 2$ transition, and the other is due to the $n = 3$ to $n = 2$ transition. Which wavelength corresponds to which transition?

THE QUANTUM-MECHANICAL MODEL

43. Sketch the $1s$ and $2p$ orbitals. How do the $2s$ and $3p$ orbitals differ from the $1s$ and $2p$ orbitals?

44. Sketch the $3d$ orbitals. How do the $4d$ orbitals differ from the $3d$ orbitals?

45. Which electron is, on average, closer to the nucleus: an electron in a $2s$ orbital or an electron in a $3s$ orbital?

46. Which electron is, on average, farther from the nucleus: an electron in a $3p$ orbital or an electron in a $4p$ orbital?

47. According to the quantum-mechanical model for the hydrogen atom, which electron transition produces light with longer wavelength: $2p$ to $1s$ or $3p$ to $1s$?

48. According to the quantum-mechanical model for the hydrogen atom, which transition produces light with longer wavelength: $3p$ to $2s$ or $4p$ to $2s$?

ELECTRON CONFIGURATIONS

49. Write full electron configurations for each element.
   (a) Sr
   (b) Ge
   (c) Li
   (d) Kr

50. Write full electron configurations for each element.
   (a) N
   (b) Mg
   (c) Ar
   (d) Se

51. Write full orbital diagrams and indicate the number of unpaired electrons for each element.
   (a) He
   (b) B
   (c) Li
   (d) N

52. Write full orbital diagrams and indicate the number of unpaired electrons for each element.
   (a) F
   (b) C
   (c) Ne
   (d) Be

53. Write electron configurations for each element. Use the symbol of the previous noble gas in brackets to represent the core electrons.
   (a) Ga
   (b) As
   (c) Rb
   (d) Sn

54. Write electron configurations for each element. Use the symbol of the previous noble gas in brackets to represent the core electrons.
   (a) Te
   (b) Br
   (c) I
   (d) Cs

55. Write electron configurations for each transition metal.
   (a) Zn
   (b) Cu
   (c) Zr
   (d) Fe

56. Write electron configurations for each transition metal.
   (a) Mn
   (b) Ti
   (c) Cd
   (d) V

VALENCE ELECTRONS AND CORE ELECTRONS

57. Write full electron configurations and indicate the valence electrons and the core electrons for each element.
   (a) Kr
   (b) Ge
   (c) Cl
   (d) Sr

58. Write full electron configurations and indicate the valence electrons and the core electrons for each element.
   (a) Sb
   (b) N
   (c) B
   (d) K

59. Write orbital diagrams for the valence electrons and indicate the number of unpaired electrons for each element.
   (a) Br
   (b) Kr
   (c) Na
   (d) In

60. Write orbital diagrams for the valence electrons and indicate the number of unpaired electrons for each element.
   (a) Ne
   (b) I
   (c) Sr
   (d) Ge

61. How many valence electrons are in each element?
   (a) O
   (b) S
   (c) Br
   (d) Rb

62. How many valence electrons are in each element?
   (a) Ba
   (b) Al
   (c) Be
   (d) Se

ELECTRON CONFIGURATIONS AND THE PERIODIC TABLE

63. List the outer electron configuration for each column in the periodic table.
   (a) 1A
   (b) 2A
   (c) 5A
   (d) 7A

64. List the outer electron configuration for each column in the periodic table.
   (a) 3A
   (b) 4A
   (c) 6A
   (d) 8A

65. Use the periodic table to write electron configurations for each element.
   (a) Al
   (b) Be
   (c) In
   (d) Zr

66. Use the periodic table to write electron configurations for each element.
   (a) Tl
   (b) Co
   (c) Ba
   (d) Sb

67. Use the periodic table to write electron configurations for each element.
   (a) Sr
   (b) Y
   (c) Ti
   (d) Te

68. Use the periodic table to write electron configurations for each element.
   (a) Se
   (b) Sn
   (c) Pb
   (d) Cd

69. How many $2p$ electrons are in an atom of each element?
   (a) C
   (b) N
   (c) F
   (d) P

70. How many $3d$ electrons are in an atom of each element?
   (a) Fe
   (b) Zn
   (c) K
   (d) As

71. List the number of elements in periods 1 and 2 of the periodic table. Why does each period have a different number of elements?

72. List the number of elements in periods 3 and 4 of the periodic table. Why does each period have a different number of elements?

73. Name the element in the third period (row) of the periodic table with:
   (a) 3 valence electrons
   (b) a total of four $3p$ electrons
   (c) six $3p$ electrons
   (d) two $3s$ electrons and no $3p$ electrons

74. Name the element in the fourth period of the periodic table with:
   (a) 5 valence electrons
   (b) a total of four $4p$ electrons
   (c) a total of three $3d$ electrons
   (d) a complete outer shell

75. Use the periodic table to identify the element with each electron configuration.
   (a) $[Ne]3s^23p^5$
   (b) $[Ar]4s^23d^{10}4p^1$
   (c) $[Ar]4s^23d^6$
   (d) $[Kr]5s^1$

76. Use the periodic table to identify the element with each electron configuration.
   (a) $[Ne]3s^1$
   (b) $[Kr]5s^24d^{10}$
   (c) $[Xe]6s^2$
   (d) $[Kr]5s^24d^{10}5p^3$

PERIODIC TRENDS

77. Choose the element with the higher ionization energy from each pair.
(a) As or Bi
(b) As or Br
(c) S or I
(d) S or Sb

78. Choose the element with the higher ionization energy from each pair.
(a) Al or In
(b) Cl or Sb
(c) K or Ge
(d) S or Se

79. Arrange the elements in order of increasing ionization energy: Te, Pb, Cl, S, Sn.

80. Arrange the elements in order of increasing ionization energy: Ga, In, F, Si, N.

81. Choose the element with the larger atoms from each pair.
(a) Al or In
(b) Si or N
(c) P or Pb
(d) C or F

82. Choose the element with the larger atoms from each pair.
(a) Sn or Si
(b) Br or Ga
(c) Sn or Bi
(d) Se or Sn

83. Arrange these elements in order of increasing atomic size: Ca, Rb, S, Si, Ge, F.

84. Arrange these elements in order of increasing atomic size: Cs, Sb, S, Pb, Se.

85. Choose the more metallic element from each pair.
(a) Sr or Sb
(b) As or Bi
(c) Cl or O
(d) S or As

86. Choose the more metallic element from each pair.
(a) Sb or Pb
(b) K or Ge
(c) Ge or Sb
(d) As or Sn

87. Arrange these elements in order of increasing metallic character: Fr, Sb, In, S, Ba, Se.

88. Arrange these elements in order of increasing metallic character: Sr, N, Si, P, Ga, Al.

CUMULATIVE PROBLEMS

89. What is the maximum number of electrons that can occupy the $n = 3$ quantum shell?

90. What is the maximum number of electrons that can occupy the $n = 4$ quantum shell?

91. Use the electron configurations of the alkaline earth metals to explain why they tend to form 2+ ions.

92. Use the electron configuration of oxygen to explain why it tends to form a 2− ion.

93. Write the electron configuration for each ion. What do all of the electron configurations have in common?
(a) Ca^{2+}
(b) K^+
(c) S^{2-}
(d) Br^-

94. Write the electron configuration for each ion. What do all of the electron configurations have in common?
(a) F^-
(b) P^{3-}
(c) Li^+
(d) Al^{3+}

95. Examine Figure 4.12, which shows the division of the periodic table into metals, nonmetals, and metalloids. Use what you know about electron configurations to explain these divisions.

96. Examine Figure 4.14, which shows the elements that form predictable ions. Use what you know about electron configurations to explain these trends.

97. Identify what is wrong with each electron configuration and write the correct ground state (or lowest energy) configuration based on the number of electrons.
(a) $1s^3 2s^3 2p^9$
(b) $1s^2 2s^2 2p^6 2d^4$
(c) $1s^2 1p^5$
(d) $1s^2 2s^2 2p^8 3s^2 3p^1$

98. Identify what is wrong with each electron configuration and write the correct ground state (or lowest energy) configuration based on the number of electrons.
(a) $1s^4 2s^4 2p^{12}$
(b) $1s^2 2s^2 2p^6 3s^2 3p^6 3d^{10}$
(c) $1s^2 2p^6 3s^2$
(d) $1s^2 2s^2 2p^6 3s^2 3p^6 4s^2 4d^{10} 4p^3$

99. Bromine is a highly reactive liquid, while krypton is an inert gas. Explain this difference based on their electron configurations.

100. Potassium is a highly reactive metal, while argon is an inert gas. Explain this difference based on their electron configurations.

101. Based on periodic trends, which one of these elements would you expect to be most easily oxidized: Ge, K, S, or N?

102. Based on periodic trends, which one of these elements would you expect to be most easily reduced: Ca, Sr, P, or Cl?

103. When an electron makes a transition from the $n = 3$ to the $n = 2$ hydrogen atom Bohr orbit, the energy difference between these two orbits (3.0×10^{-19} J) is emitted as a photon of light. The relationship between the energy of a photon and its wavelength is given by $E = hc/\lambda$, where E is the energy of the photon in J, h is Planck's constant (6.626×10^{-34} J $\cdot$ s), and c is the speed of light (3.00×10^8 m/s). Find the wavelength of light emitted by hydrogen atoms when an electron makes this transition.

104. When an electron makes a transition from the $n = 4$ to the $n = 2$ hydrogen atom Bohr orbit, the energy difference between these two orbits (4.1×10^{-19} J) is emitted as a photon of light. The relationship between the energy of a photon and its wavelength is given by $E = hc/\lambda$, where E is the energy of the photon in J, h is Planck's constant (6.626×10^{-34} J $\cdot$ s), and c is the speed of light (3.00×10^8 m/s). Find the wavelength of light emitted by hydrogen atoms when an electron makes this transition.

105. The distance from the sun to Earth is 1.496×10^8 km. How long does it take light to travel from the sun to Earth?

106. The nearest star is Alpha Centauri, at a distance of 4.3 light-years from Earth. A light-year is the distance that light travels in one year (365 days). How far away, in kilometers, is Alpha Centauri from Earth?

107. In the beginning of this chapter, you learned that the quantum-mechanical model for the atom is the foundation for modern chemical understanding. Explain why this is so.

108. Niels Bohr said, "Anyone who is not shocked by quantum mechanics has not understood it." What do you think he meant by this statement?

109. The wave nature of matter was first proposed by Louis de Broglie, who suggested that the wavelength (λ) of a particle was related to its mass (m) and its velocity (v) by the equation: $\lambda = h/mv$, where h is Planck's constant (6.626×10^{-34} J $\cdot$ s). Calculate the de Broglie wavelength of: (a) a 0.0459 kg golf ball traveling at 95 m/s; (b) an electron traveling at 3.88×10^6 m/s. Can you explain why the wave nature of matter is significant for the electron but not for the golf ball? (*Hint:* Express mass in kilograms.)

110. The particle nature of light was first proposed by Albert Einstein, who suggested that light could be described as a stream of particles called photons. A photon of wavelength λ has an energy (E) given by the equation: $E = hc/\lambda$, where E is the energy of the photon in J, h is Planck's constant (6.626×10^{-34} J $\cdot$ s), and c is the speed of light (3.00×10^8 m/s). Calculate the energy of 1 mol of photons with a wavelength of 632 nm.

111. You learned in this chapter that ionization generally increases as you move from left to right across the periodic table. However, consider the data below, which shows the ionization energies of the period 2 and 3 elements:

Group	Period 2 Elements	Ionization Energy (kJ/mol)	Period 3 Elements	Ionization Energy (kJ/mol)
1A	Li	520	Na	496
2A	Be	899	Mg	738
3A	B	801	Al	578
4A	C	1086	Si	786
5A	N	1402	P	1012
6A	O	1314	S	1000
7A	F	1681	Cl	1251
8A	Ne	2081	Ar	1521

Notice that the increase is not uniform. In fact, ionization energy actually decreases a bit in going from elements in group 2A to 3A and then again from 5A to 6A. Use what you know about electron configurations to explain why these dips in ionization energy exist.

112. When atoms lose more than one electron, the ionization energy to remove the second electron is always more than the ionization energy to remove the first. Similarly, the ionization energy to remove the third electron is more than the second and so on. However, the increase in ionization energy upon the removal of subsequent electrons is not necessarily uniform. For example, consider the first three ionization energies of magnesium:

First ionization energy	738 kJ/mol
Second ionization energy	1450 kJ/mol
Third ionization energy	7730 kJ/mol

The second ionization energy is roughly twice the first ionization energy, but then the third ionization energy is over five times the second. Use the electron configuration of magnesium to explain why this is so. Would you expect the same behavior in sodium? Why or why not?

HIGHLIGHT PROBLEMS

113. Excessive exposure to sunlight increases the risk of skin cancer because some of the photons have enough energy to break chemical bonds in biological molecules. These bonds require approximately 250–800 kJ/mol of energy to break. The energy of a single photon is given by $E = hc/\lambda$, where E is the energy of the photon in J, h is Planck's constant (6.626×10^{-34} J·s), and c is the speed of light (3.00×10^8 m/s). Determine which kinds of light contain enough energy to break chemical bonds in biological molecules by calculating the total energy in 1 mol of photons for light of each wavelength.

(a) infrared light (1500 nm)
(b) visible light (500 nm)
(c) ultraviolet light (150 nm)

114. The quantum-mechanical model, besides revolutionizing chemistry, shook the philosophical world because of its implications regarding determinism. Determinism is the idea that the outcomes of future events are determined by preceding events. The trajectory of a baseball, for example, is deterministic; that is, its trajectory—and therefore its landing place—is determined by its position, speed, and direction of travel. Before quantum mechanics, most scientists thought that fundamental particles—such as electrons and protons—also behaved deterministically. The implication of this belief was that the entire universe must behave deterministically—the future must be determined by preceding events. Quantum mechanics challenged this reasoning because fundamental particles do not behave deterministically—their future paths are not determined by preceding events. Some scientists struggled with this idea. Einstein himself refused to believe it, stating, "God does not play dice with the universe." Explain what Einstein meant by this statement.

▲ "God does not play dice with the universe."

QUESTIONS FOR GROUP WORK

Discuss these questions with the group and record your consensus answer.

115. Sketch the following orbitals (including the x, y, and z axes): $1s$, $2p_x$, $3d_{xy}$, $3d_{z^2}$.

116. Draw the best periodic table you can from memory (do not look at a table to do this). You do not need to label the elements, but you should put the correct number of elements in each block. After your group agrees that the group has done its best, spend exactly three minutes comparing your table with Figure 9.26. Make a second periodic table from memory. Is it better than your first one?

117. Play the following game to memorize the order in which orbitals fill. Go around your group and have each group member say the name of the next orbital to fill and the maximum number of electrons it can hold ("$1s$ two," "$2s$ two," "$2p$ six,"...). If a group member gets stuck, other members can help, referring to Figure 9.24 or 9.26 if necessary. However, when anyone gets stuck, the next player starts back at "$1s$ two." Keep going until each group member can list the correct sequence up to "$6s$ two."

118. Using grammatically correct sentences, describe the periodic trends for atomic size, ionization energy, and metallic character.

►Answers to Skillbuilder Exercises

Skillbuilder 9.1
- (a) blue, green, red
- (b) red, green, blue
- (c) red, green, blue

Skillbuilder 9.2
- (a) Al $1s^2 2s^2 2p^6 3s^2 3p^1$ or [Ne]$3s^2 3p^1$
- (b) Br $1s^2 2s^2 2p^6 3s^2 3p^6 4s^2 3d^{10} 4p^5$ or [Ar]$4s^2 3d^{10} 4p^5$
- (c) Sr $1s^2 2s^2 2p^6 3s^2 3p^6 4s^2 3d^{10} 4p^6 5s^2$ or [Kr]$5s^2$

Skillbuilder Plus, p. 301

Subtract 1 electron for each unit of positive charge. Add 1 electron for each unit of negative charge.
- (a) Al^{3+} $1s^2 2s^2 2p^6$
- (b) Cl^- $1s^2 2s^2 2p^6 3s^2 3p^6$
- (c) O^{2-} $1s^2 2s^2 2p^6$

Skillbuilder 9.3

Ar

$\quad\quad 1s \quad\quad 2s \quad\quad\quad 2p \quad\quad\quad 3s \quad\quad\quad 3p$

Skillbuilder 9.4

Cl $\quad 1s^2 2s^2 2p^6\ 3s^2 3p^5$

10 core electrons   7 valence electrons

Skillbuilder 9.5 [Kr]$5s^2 4d^{10} 5p^2$

Skillbuilder 9.6
- (a) Pb
- (b) Rb
- (c) cannot determine based on periodic properties
- (d) Se

Skillbuilder 9.7
- (a) Mg
- (b) Te
- (c) cannot determine based on periodic properties
- (d) F

Skillbuilder 9.8
- (a) In
- (b) cannot determine based on periodic properties
- (c) Bi
- (d) B

►Answers to Conceptual Checkpoints

9.1 (a) Wavelength and frequency are inversely related. Therefore, the shortest wavelength has the highest frequency.

9.2 (b) Wavelength and energy per photon are inversely related. Since yellow light has a longer wavelength, it has less energy per photon than violet light.

9.3 (c) The higher energy levels are more closely spaced than the lower ones, so the difference in energy between $n = 2$ and $n = 1$ is greater than the difference in energy between $n = 3$ and $n = 2$. The photon emitted when an electron falls from $n = 2$ to $n = 1$ therefore carries more energy, corresponding to radiation with a shorter wavelength and higher frequency.

9.4 (d) Both have 6 electrons in $2p$ orbitals and 6 electrons in $3p$ orbitals.

9.5 (d) The outermost principal shell for K is $n = 4$, which contains only a single valence electron, $4s^1$.

9.6 (a) Calcium loses its $4s$ electron and attains a noble gas configuration (that of Ar).

9.7 (b) Ionization energy increases as you move from left to right across a row in the periodic table. Both atomic size and metallic character decrease as you move from left to right across a row.

Chemical Bonding

"The fascination of a growing science lies in the work of the pioneers at the very borderland of the unknown, but to reach this frontier one must pass over well traveled roads."—Gilbert N. Lewis (1875–1946)

CHAPTER OUTLINE

10.1 Bonding Models and AIDS Drugs

We will discuss proteins in more detail in Chapter 19.

In 1989, researchers discovered the structure of a molecule called HIV-protease. HIV-protease is a protein (a class of biological molecules) synthesized by the human immunodeficiency virus (HIV), which causes AIDS. HIV-protease is crucial to the virus's ability to replicate itself. Without HIV-protease, HIV could not spread in the human body because the virus could not copy itself, and AIDS would not develop.

With knowledge of the HIV-protease structure, drug companies set out to design a molecule that would disable the protease by sticking to the working part of the molecule (called the *active site*). To design such a molecule, researchers used **bonding theories**—models that predict how atoms bond together to form molecules—to simulate how potential drug molecules would interact with the protease molecule. By the early 1990s, these companies had developed several effective drug molecules. Since these molecules inhibit the action of HIV-protease, they are called *protease inhibitors*. In human trials, protease inhibitors in combination with other drugs have decreased the viral count in HIV-infected individuals to undetectable levels. Although these drugs do not cure AIDS, HIV-infected individuals who regularly take their medication can now expect nearly normal life spans.

Bonding theories are central to chemistry because they predict how atoms bond together to form compounds. They predict what combinations of atoms form compounds and what combinations do not. Bonding theories predict why salt is $NaCl$ and not $NaCl_2$ and why water is H_2O and not H_3O. Bonding theories also explain the shapes of molecules, which in turn determine many of their physical and chemical properties. The bonding theory you will learn in this chapter is the **Lewis model**, named after G. N. Lewis (1875–1946), the American chemist who developed it. In this model, we represent electrons as dots and draw *dot structures* or *Lewis structures* to represent molecules. These structures, which are fairly simple to draw, have tremendous predictive power. It takes just a few minutes to apply the Lewis model to determine whether a particular set of atoms will form a stable molecule and what that molecule might look like. Although modern chemists also use more advanced bonding theories to better predict molecular properties, the Lewis model remains the simplest method for making quick, everyday predictions about molecules.

10.2 Representing Valence Electrons with Dots

LO: Write Lewis structures for elements.

As we discussed in Chapter 9, valence electrons are those electrons in the outermost principal shell. Since valence electrons are most important in bonding, the Lewis model focuses on these. In the Lewis model, the valence electrons of main-group elements are represented as dots surrounding the symbol of the element. The result is a **Lewis structure**, or **dot structure**. For example, the electron configuration of O is:

and its Lewis structure is:

Each dot represents a valence electron. We place the dots around the element's symbol with a maximum of two dots per side. Although the exact location of dots is not critical, in this book we fill in the dots singly first and then pair them (with the exception of helium, described shortly).

The Lewis structures for the period 2 elements are:

$$\text{Li}\cdot \quad \cdot\text{Be}\cdot \quad \cdot\overset{\cdot}{\text{B}}\cdot \quad \cdot\overset{\cdot}{\text{C}}\cdot \quad \cdot\overset{\cdot}{\underset{\cdot}{\text{N}}}: \quad \cdot\overset{\cdot\cdot}{\underset{\cdot\cdot}{\text{O}}}: \quad :\overset{\cdot\cdot}{\underset{\cdot\cdot}{\text{F}}}: \quad :\overset{\cdot\cdot}{\underset{\cdot\cdot}{\text{Ne}}}:$$

> Remember, the number of valence electrons for any main-group element is equal to the group number of the element (except helium, which has 2 valence electrons but is in Group 8A).

Lewis structures allow us to easily see the number of valence electrons in an atom. Atoms with 8 valence electrons—which are particularly stable—are easily identified because they have eight dots, an **octet**.

Helium is somewhat of an exception. Its electron configuration and Lewis structure are:

$$1s^2 \quad \text{He:}$$

The Lewis structure of helium contains two paired dots (a **duet**). For helium, a duet represents a stable electron configuration.

In the Lewis model, a **chemical bond** involves the sharing or transfer of electrons to attain stable electron configurations for the bonding atoms. If the electrons are transferred, the bond is an **ionic bond**. If the electrons are shared, the bond is a **covalent bond**. In either case, the bonding atoms attain stable electron configurations. As we have seen, a stable configuration usually consists of eight electrons in the outermost or valence shell. This observation leads to the **octet rule**:

> In chemical bonding, atoms transfer or share electrons to obtain outer shells with eight electrons.

The octet rule generally applies to all main-group elements except hydrogen and lithium. Each of these elements achieves stability when it has two electrons (a duet) in its outermost shell.

EXAMPLE 10.1	**WRITING LEWIS STRUCTURES FOR ELEMENTS**

Write the Lewis structure of phosphorus.

Since phosphorus is in Group 5A in the periodic table, it has 5 valence electrons. Represent these as five dots surrounding the symbol for phosphorus.	**SOLUTION** ·P̈:

▶**SKILLBUILDER 10.1 | Writing Lewis Structures for Elements**

Write the Lewis structure of Mg.

▶**FOR MORE PRACTICE**   Example 10.12; Problems 25, 26.

✓   **CONCEPTUAL CHECKPOINT 10.1**

Which two elements have the most similar Lewis structures?

(a) C and Si   **(b)** O and P   **(c)** Li and F   **(d)** S and Br

---

10.3   Lewis Structures of Ionic Compounds: Electrons Transferred

LO: Write Lewis structures for ionic compounds.

LO: Use the Lewis model to predict the chemical formula of an ionic compound.

Recall from Chapter 5 that when metals bond with nonmetals, electrons are transferred from the metal to the nonmetal. The metal becomes a cation and the nonmetal becomes an anion. The attraction between the cation and the anion results in an ionic compound. In the Lewis model, we represent this by moving electron dots from the metal to the nonmetal. For example, the Lewis structures for potassium and chlorine are:

$$K· \quad :\ddot{C}l:$$

When potassium and chlorine bond, potassium transfers its valence electron to chlorine.

$$K· \quad :\ddot{C}l: \quad \longrightarrow \quad K^+ \ [:\ddot{C}l:]^-$$

Recall from Section 4.7 that atoms that lose electrons become positively charged and atoms that gain electrons become negatively charged.

The transfer of the electron gives chlorine an octet (shown as eight dots around chlorine) and leaves potassium with an octet in the previous principal shell, which is now the valence shell. Because the potassium lost an electron, it becomes positively charged, while the chlorine, which gained an electron, becomes negatively charged. The Lewis structure of an anion is usually written within brackets with the charge in the upper right corner (outside the brackets). The positive and negative charges attract one another, forming the compound KCl.

EXAMPLE 10.2	**WRITING IONIC LEWIS STRUCTURES**

Write the Lewis structure of the compound MgO.

Draw the Lewis structures of magnesium and oxygen by drawing two dots around the symbol for magnesium and six dots around the symbol for oxygen.	**SOLUTION** ·Mg· ·Ö:
In MgO, magnesium loses its 2 valence electrons, resulting in a 2+ charge, and oxygen gains two electrons, attaining a 2− charge and an octet.	$Mg^{2+}\ [:\ddot{O}:]^{2-}$

▶**SKILLBUILDER 10.2 | Writing Ionic Lewis Structures**

Write the Lewis structure of the compound NaBr.

▶**FOR MORE PRACTICE**   Example 10.13; Problems 37, 38.

Recall from Section 5.4 that ionic compounds do not exist as distinct molecules, but rather as part of a large lattice of alternating cations and anions.

The Lewis model predicts the correct chemical formulas for ionic compounds. For the compound that forms between K and Cl, for example, the Lewis model predicts one potassium cation to every chlorine anion, KCl. As another example, consider the ionic compound formed between sodium and sulfur. The Lewis structures for sodium and sulfur are:

$$Na\cdot \quad \cdot \overset{\cdot\cdot}{\underset{\cdot\cdot}{S}}:$$

Notice that sodium must lose its one valence electron to obtain an octet (in the previous principal shell), while sulfur must gain two electrons to obtain an octet. Consequently, the compound that forms between sodium and sulfur requires two sodium atoms to every one sulfur atom. The Lewis structure is:

$$Na^+ \; [:\overset{\cdot\cdot}{\underset{\cdot\cdot}{S}}:]^{2-} \; Na^+$$

The two sodium atoms each lose their single valence electron, while the sulfur atom gains two electrons and obtains an octet. The correct chemical formula is Na_2S.

EXAMPLE 10.3	**USING THE LEWIS MODEL TO PREDICT THE CHEMICAL FORMULA OF AN IONIC COMPOUND**

Use the Lewis model to predict the formula of the compound that forms between calcium and chlorine.

Draw the Lewis structures of calcium and chlorine by drawing two dots around the symbol for calcium and seven dots around the symbol for chlorine.	**SOLUTION** $\cdot Ca\cdot \quad :\overset{\cdot\cdot}{\underset{\cdot\cdot}{Cl}}:$
Calcium must lose its 2 valence electrons (to effectively attain an octet in its previous principal shell), while chlorine needs to gain only 1 electron to obtain an octet. Consequently, the compound that forms between Ca and Cl has two chlorine atoms to every one calcium atom.	$[:\overset{\cdot\cdot}{\underset{\cdot\cdot}{Cl}}:]^- \; Ca^{2+} \; [:\overset{\cdot\cdot}{\underset{\cdot\cdot}{Cl}}:]^-$ The formula is therefore $CaCl_2$.

▶ **SKILLBUILDER 10.3 | Using the Lewis Model to Predict the Chemical Formula of an Ionic Compound**

Use the Lewis model to predict the formula of the compound that forms between magnesium and nitrogen.

▶ **FOR MORE PRACTICE**   Example 10.14; Problems 39, 40, 41, 42.

✓ **CONCEPTUAL CHECKPOINT 10.2**

Which nonmetal forms an ionic compound with aluminum that has the formula Al_2X_3 (where X represents the nonmetal)?

(a) Cl   **(b)** S   **(c)** N   **(d)** C

10.4   Covalent Lewis Structures: Electrons Shared

LO: Write Lewis structures for covalent compounds.

Recall from Chapter 5 that when nonmetals bond with other nonmetals, a molecular compound results. Molecular compounds contain covalent bonds in which electrons are shared between atoms rather than transferred. In the Lewis model, we represent covalent bonding by allowing neighboring atoms to share some of their valence electrons in order to attain octets (or duets for hydrogen). For example, hydrogen and oxygen have the Lewis structures:

$$H\cdot \quad \cdot \overset{\cdot\cdot}{\underset{\cdot\cdot}{O}}:$$

In water, hydrogen and oxygen share their electrons so that each hydrogen atom gets a duet and the oxygen atom gets an octet.

$$H:\overset{\cdot\cdot}{\underset{\cdot\cdot}{O}}:H$$

The shared electrons—those that appear in the space between the two atoms—count toward the octets (or duets) of *both of the atoms*.

Duet   Octet   Duet

Electrons that are shared between two atoms are **bonding pair** electrons, while those that are only on one atom are **lone pair** (or nonbonding) electrons.

Bonding pair   H:Ö:H   Lone pair

Bonding pair electrons are often represented by dashes to emphasize that they are a chemical bond.

$$H—\ddot{O}—H$$

The Lewis model also explains why the halogens form diatomic molecules. Consider the Lewis structure of chlorine:

$$:\ddot{C}l:$$

If two Cl atoms pair, they can each attain an octet.

$$:\ddot{C}l:\ddot{C}l: \quad or \quad :\ddot{C}l—\ddot{C}l:$$

When we examine elemental chlorine, we find that it indeed exists as a diatomic molecule, just as the Lewis model predicts. The same is true for the other halogens.

Similarly, the Lewis model predicts that hydrogen, which has this Lewis structure:

$$H·$$

should exist as H_2. When two hydrogen atoms share their valence electrons, they each get a duet, a stable configuration for hydrogen.

$$H:H \quad or \quad H—H$$

Again, the Lewis model prediction is correct. In nature, elemental hydrogen exists as H_2 molecules.

Double and Triple Bonds

In the Lewis model, atoms can share more than one electron pair to attain an octet. For example, we know from Chapter 5 that oxygen exists as the diatomic molecule, O_2. The Lewis structure of an oxygen atom is:

$$·\ddot{O}:$$

If we pair two oxygen atoms together and then try to write the Lewis structure, we do not have enough electrons to give each O atom an octet.

$$:\ddot{O}:\ddot{O}:$$

However, we can convert a lone pair into an additional bonding pair by moving it into the bonding region.

$$:\ddot{O}:\ddot{O}: \longrightarrow :\ddot{O}::\ddot{O}: \quad or \quad :\ddot{O}=\ddot{O}:$$

Remember that each dash represents a *pair* of shared electrons.

Each oxygen atom now has an octet because the additional bonding pair counts toward the octet of both oxygen atoms.

Octet —————→ :Ö⬡⬡Ö: ←————— Octet

When two electron pairs are shared between two atoms, the resulting bond is a **double bond**. In general, double bonds are shorter and stronger than single bonds. For example, the distance between oxygen nuclei in an oxygen–oxygen double bond is 121 pm. In a single bond, it is 148 pm.

| 1 pm = 10^{-12} m

Atoms can also share three electron pairs. Consider the Lewis structure of N_2. Since each N atom has 5 valence electrons, the Lewis structure for N_2 has 10 electrons. A first attempt at writing the Lewis structure looks like this:

$$:\ddot{N}:\ddot{N}:$$

As with O_2, we do not have enough electrons to satisfy the octet rule for both N atoms. However, if we convert two additional lone pairs into bonding pairs, each nitrogen atom can get an octet.

:N̈:N̈: ⟶ :N:::N: *or* :N≡N:

The resulting bond is a **triple bond**. Triple bonds are even shorter and stronger than double bonds. The distance between nitrogen nuclei in a nitrogen–nitrogen triple bond is 110 pm. In a double bond, the distance is 124 pm. When we examine nitrogen in nature, we find that it exists as a diatomic molecule with a very strong short bond between the two nitrogen atoms. The bond is so strong that it is difficult to break, making N_2 a relatively unreactive molecule.

✓ **CONCEPTUAL CHECKPOINT 10.3**

How many bonding electrons are in the Lewis structure of O_2?
(a) 2   (b) 4   (c) 6

10.5 Writing Lewis Structures for Covalent Compounds

LO: Write Lewis structures for covalent compounds.

When guessing at skeletal structures, put the less metallic elements in terminal positions and the more metallic elements in central positions. Halogens, which are among the least metallic elements, are nearly always terminal.

Nonterminal hydrogen atoms exist in some compounds. However, they are rare and beyond the scope of this text.

To write the Lewis structure for a covalent compound, follow these steps:

1. **Write the correct skeletal structure for the molecule.** The skeletal structure shows the relative positions of the atoms and does not include electrons, but it must have the atoms in the correct positions. For example, you could *not* write the Lewis structure for water if you started with the hydrogen atoms next to each other and the oxygen atom at the end (H H O). In nature, oxygen is the central atom, and the hydrogen atoms are **terminal atoms** (at the ends). The correct skeletal structure is H O H.

   The only way to absolutely know the correct skeletal structure for any molecule is to examine its structure in nature. However, you can write likely skeletal structures by remembering two guidelines. First, *hydrogen atoms are always terminal*. Since hydrogen requires only a duet, it is never a central atom because central atoms must be able to form at least two bonds and hydrogen can form only one. Second, *many molecules tend to be symmetrical*, so when a molecule contains several atoms of the same type, these tend to be in terminal positions. *This second guideline, however, has many exceptions*. In cases where the skeletal structure is unclear, this text provides you with the correct skeletal structure.

2. **Calculate the total number of electrons for the Lewis structure by summing the valence electrons of each atom in the molecule.** Remember that the number of valence electrons for any main-group element is equal to its group number

in the periodic table. **If you are writing a Lewis structure for a polyatomic ion, you must consider the charge of the ion when calculating the total number of electrons.** Add one electron for each negative charge and subtract one electron for each positive charge.

3. **Distribute the electrons among the atoms, giving octets (or duets for hydrogen) to as many atoms as possible.** Begin by placing two electrons between each pair of atoms. These are the minimal number of bonding electrons. Then distribute the remaining electrons, first to terminal atoms and then to the central atom, giving octets to as many atoms as possible.

4. **If any atoms lack an octet, form double or triple bonds as necessary to give them octets.** Do this by moving lone electron pairs from terminal atoms into the bonding region with the central atom.

A brief version of this procedure is presented in the left column. In the center and right columns, Examples 10. 4 and 10.5 demonstrate the procedure.

WRITING LEWIS STRUCTURES FOR COVALENT COMPOUNDS	EXAMPLE 10.4 ▶ Write the Lewis structure for CO_2.	EXAMPLE 10.5 Write the Lewis structure for CCl_4.
1. Write the correct skeletal structure for the molecule.	**SOLUTION** Following the symmetry guideline, write: O C O	**SOLUTION** Following the symmetry guideline, write: Cl Cl C Cl Cl
2. Calculate the total number of electrons for the Lewis structure by summing the valence electrons of each atom in the molecule.	Total number of electrons for Lewis structure = $\left(\begin{smallmatrix}\#\text{ valence}\\e^-\text{ for C}\end{smallmatrix}\right)+2\left(\begin{smallmatrix}\#\text{ valence}\\e^-\text{for O}\end{smallmatrix}\right)$ $= 4 + 2(6)$ $= 16$	Total number of electrons for Lewis structure = $\left(\begin{smallmatrix}\#\text{ valence}\\e^-\text{ for C}\end{smallmatrix}\right)+4\left(\begin{smallmatrix}\#\text{ valence}\\e^-\text{ for Cl}\end{smallmatrix}\right)$ $= 4 + 4(7)$ $= 32$
3. Distribute the electrons among the atoms, giving octets (or duets for hydrogen) to as many atoms as possible. Begin with the bonding electrons, and proceed to lone pairs on terminal atoms, and finally to lone pairs on the central atom.	Work with bonding electrons first. O:C:O (4 of 16 electrons used) Proceed to lone pairs on terminal atoms next. :Ö:C:Ö: (16 of 16 electrons used)	Work with bonding electrons first. Cl Cl:C:Cl Cl (8 of 32 electrons used) Proceed to lone pairs on terminal atoms next. :Cl: :Cl:C:Cl: :Cl: (32 of 32 electrons used)
4. If any atoms lack octets, form double or triple bonds as necessary to give them octets.	Move lone pairs from the oxygen atoms to bonding regions to form double bonds. :Ö:C:Ö: ⟶ :Ö::C::Ö: ▶**SKILLBUILDER 10.4**	Write the Lewis structure for CO.	Since all of the atoms have octets, the Lewis structure is complete. ▶**SKILLBUILDER 10.5**	Write the Lewis structure for H_2CO. ▶**FOR MORE PRACTICE** Example 10.15; Problems 47, 48, 49, 50, 51, 52.

Writing Lewis Structures for Polyatomic Ions

We write Lewis structures for polyatomic ions by following the same procedure, but we pay special attention to the charge of the ion when calculating the number of electrons for the Lewis structure. We add one electron for each negative charge and subtract one electron for each positive charge. We normally show the Lewis structure for a polyatomic ion within brackets and write the charge of the ion in the upper right corner. For example, suppose we want to write the Lewis structure for the CN^- ion. We begin by writing the skeletal structure:

CN

Next we calculate the total number of electrons for the Lewis structure by summing the number of valence electrons for each atom and adding one for the negative charge.

Total number of electrons
for Lewis structure = (# valence e⁻ in C) + (# valence e⁻ in N) + 1

= 4 + 5 + 1

= 10

Add one e⁻ to account for 1− charge of ion.

We then place 2 electrons between each pair of atoms

C:N   (2 of 10 electrons used)

and distribute the remaining electrons.

:C̈:N̈:   (10 of 10 electrons used)

Since neither of the atoms has octets, we move two lone pairs into the bonding region to form a triple bond, giving both atoms octets. We also enclose the Lewis structure in brackets and write the charge of the ion in the upper right corner.

$[:C:::N:]^-$ or $[:C{\equiv}N:]^-$

✓ CONCEPTUAL CHECKPOINT 10.4

What is the total number of electrons in the Lewis structure of OH^-?

(a) 6   **(b)** 7   **(c)** 8   **(d)** 9

EXAMPLE 10.6   WRITING LEWIS STRUCTURES FOR POLYATOMIC IONS

Write the Lewis structure for the NH_4^+ ion.

Begin by writing the skeletal structure. Hydrogen atoms must be terminal, and following the guideline of symmetry, the nitrogen atom should be in the middle surrounded by four hydrogen atoms.	**SOLUTION** H H N H H
Calculate the total number of electrons for the Lewis structure by summing the number of valence electrons for each atom and subtracting 1 for the positive charge.	4 × (# valence e⁻ in H) Total number of electrons for Lewis structure = 5 + 4 − 1 = 8 # valence e⁻ in N Subtract 1 e⁻ to account for 1+ charge of ion.
Next, place 2 electrons between each pair of atoms.	H H:N̈:H (8 of 8 electrons used) H

Since the nitrogen atom has an octet and all of the hydrogen atoms have duets, the placement of electrons is complete. Write the entire Lewis structure in brackets indicating the charge of the ion in the upper right corner.

$$\left[\begin{array}{c} H \\ H:\overset{\displaystyle\cdot\cdot}{N}:H \\ H \end{array}\right]^{+} \quad or \quad \left[\begin{array}{c} H \\ | \\ H-N-H \\ | \\ H \end{array}\right]^{+}$$

▶**SKILLBUILDER 10.6 | Writing Lewis Structures for Polyatomic Ions**

Write the Lewis structure for the ClO^{-} ion.

▶**FOR MORE PRACTICE**   Problems 55bcd, 56abc, 57, 58.

   CONCEPTUAL CHECKPOINT 10.5

Which two species have the same number of lone electron pairs in their Lewis structures?

(a) H_2O and H_3O^{+}

(b) NH_3 and H_3O^{+}

(c) NH_3 and CH_4

(d) NH_3 and NH_4^{+}

Exceptions to the Octet Rule

Lewis model predictions are often correct, but exceptions exist. For example, if we try to write the Lewis structure for NO, which has 11 electrons, the best we can do is:

$$:\overset{\cdot}{N}::\overset{\cdot\cdot}{O}: \quad or \quad :\overset{\cdot}{N}=\overset{\cdot\cdot}{O}:$$

The nitrogen atom does not have an octet, so this is not a great Lewis structure. However, NO exists in nature. Why does the Lewis model not account for the existence of NO? As with any simple theory, the Lewis model is not sophisticated enough to be correct every time. It is impossible to write good Lewis structures for molecules with odd numbers of electrons, yet some of these molecules exist in nature. In such cases, we write the best Lewis structure that we can. Another significant exception to the octet rule is boron, which tends to form compounds with only 6 electrons around B, rather than 8. For example, BF_3 and BH_3—which both exist in nature—each lack an octet for B.

$$\begin{array}{cc} :\overset{\cdot\cdot}{F}: & H \\ :\overset{\cdot\cdot}{F}:B:\overset{\cdot\cdot}{F}: & H:B:H \\ \quad & \end{array}$$

A third type of exception to the octet rule is also common. A number of molecules, such as SF_6 and PCl_5, have more than 8 electrons around a central atom in their Lewis structures.

$$\begin{array}{cc} :\overset{\cdot\cdot}{F}: & :\overset{\cdot\cdot}{Cl}: \\ :F\diagdown\overset{|}{S}\diagup F: & :\overset{\cdot\cdot}{Cl}-\overset{|}{P}-\overset{\cdot\cdot}{Cl}: \\ :F\diagup^{|}\diagdown F: & :\overset{\cdot\cdot}{Cl}.\ .\overset{\cdot\cdot}{Cl}: \\ :\overset{\cdot\cdot}{F}: & \end{array}$$

We often refer to these as *expanded octets*. Expanded octets can form for period 3 elements and beyond. Beyond mentioning them, we do not cover expanded octets in this book. In spite of these exceptions, the Lewis model remains a powerful and simple way to understand chemical bonding.

10.6   Resonance: Equivalent Lewis Structures for the Same Molecule

LO: Write resonance structures.

When writing Lewis structures, we may find that, for some molecules, we can write more than one good Lewis structure. For example, consider writing a Lewis structure for SO_2. We begin with the skeletal structure:

$$O\ S\ O$$

We then sum the valence electrons.

$$\text{Total number of electrons for Lewis structure}$$
$$= (\# \text{ valence } e^- \text{ in S}) + 2(\# \text{ valence } e^- \text{ in O})$$
$$= 6 + 2(6)$$
$$= 18$$

We next place 2 electrons between each pair of atoms

$$O{:}S{:}O \quad \text{(4 of 18 electrons used)}$$

and distribute the remaining electrons, first to terminal atoms

$$:\!\ddot{O}{:}S{:}\ddot{O}\!: \quad \text{(16 of 18 electrons used)}$$

and finally to the central atom.

$$:\!\ddot{O}{:}\ddot{S}{:}\ddot{O}\!: \quad \text{(18 of 18 electrons used)}$$

Since the central atom lacks an octet, we move one lone pair from an oxygen atom into the bonding region to form a double bond, giving all of the atoms octets.

$$:\!\ddot{O}{::}\ddot{S}{:}\ddot{O}\!: \quad or \quad :\!\ddot{O}{=}\ddot{S}{-}\ddot{O}\!:$$

However, we could have formed the double bond with the other oxygen atom.

$$:\!\ddot{O}{-}\ddot{S}{=}\ddot{O}\!:$$

These two Lewis structures are equally correct. In cases such as this—where we can write two or more equivalent (or nearly equivalent) Lewis structures for the same molecule—we find that the molecule exists in nature as an average or intermediate between the two Lewis structures. Both of the two Lewis structures for SO_2 predict that SO_2 would contain two different kinds of bonds (one double bond and one single bond). However, when we examine SO_2 in nature, we find that both of the bonds are equivalent and intermediate in strength and length between a double bond and single bond. We address this in the Lewis model by representing the molecule with both structures, called **resonance structures**, with a double-headed arrow between them.

$$:\!\ddot{O}{=}\ddot{S}{-}\ddot{O}\!: \quad \longleftrightarrow \quad :\!\ddot{O}{-}\ddot{S}{=}\ddot{O}\!:$$

The true structure of SO_2 is intermediate between these two resonance structures.

EXAMPLE 10.7	WRITING RESONANCE STRUCTURES

Write the Lewis structure for the NO_3^- ion. Include resonance structures.

	SOLUTION
Begin by writing the skeletal structure. Applying the guideline of symmetry, make the three oxygen atoms terminal.	O O N O
Sum the valence electrons (adding one electron to account for the 1– charge) to determine the total number of electrons in the Lewis structure.	Total number of electrons for Lewis structure = 5 + 3(6) + 1 = 24 3 × (# valence e⁻ in O) # valence e⁻ in N Add one e⁻ to account for negative charge of ion.
Place 2 electrons between each pair of atoms.	O O:N:O (6 of 24 electrons used)
Distribute the remaining electrons, first to terminal atoms.	:Ö: :Ö:N:Ö: (24 of 24 electrons used)
Since there are no electrons remaining to complete the octet of the central atom, form a double bond by moving a lone pair from one of the oxygen atoms into the bonding region with nitrogen. Enclose the structure in brackets and write the charge at the upper right.	$\left[\begin{array}{c} :\ddot{O}: \\ :\ddot{O}:N::\ddot{O}: \end{array}\right]^-$ or $\left[\begin{array}{c} :\ddot{O}: \\ \| \\ :\ddot{O}-N=\ddot{O}: \end{array}\right]^-$
Notice that you can form the double bond with either of the other two oxygen atoms as well.	$\left[\begin{array}{c} :\ddot{O}: \\ \| \\ :O=N-\ddot{O}: \end{array}\right]^-$ or $\left[\begin{array}{c} :\ddot{O} \\ \| \\ :\ddot{O}-N-\ddot{O}: \end{array}\right]^-$
Since the three Lewis structures are equally correct, write the three structures as resonance structures.	$\left[\begin{array}{c} :\ddot{O}: \\ \| \\ :O=N-\ddot{O}: \end{array}\right]^- \longleftrightarrow \left[\begin{array}{c} :\ddot{O} \\ \| \\ :\ddot{O}-N-\ddot{O}: \end{array}\right]^- \longleftrightarrow \left[\begin{array}{c} :\ddot{O}: \\ \| \\ :\ddot{O}-N=O: \end{array}\right]^-$

▶SKILLBUILDER 10.7 | **Writing Resonance Structures**
Write the Lewis structure for the NO_2^- ion. Include resonance structures.

▶**FOR MORE PRACTICE**   Example 10.16; Problems 55, 56, 57, 58.

10.7   Predicting the Shapes of Molecules

LO: Predict the shapes of molecules.

We can use the Lewis model, in combination with **valence shell electron pair repulsion (VSEPR) theory**, to predict the shapes of molecules. VSEPR theory is based on the idea that **electron groups**—lone pairs, single bonds, or multiple bonds—repel each other. This repulsion between the negative charges of electron groups on the central atom determines the geometry of the molecule. For example, consider CO_2, which has the Lewis structure:

$$:\ddot{O}=C=\ddot{O}:$$

CHEMISTRY IN THE ENVIRONMENT

▶ The Lewis Structure of Ozone

Ozone is a form of oxygen in which three oxygen atoms bond together. The Lewis structure for O_3 consists of two resonance structures:

$$:\ddot{O}=\ddot{O}-\ddot{O}: \longleftrightarrow :\ddot{O}-\ddot{O}=\ddot{O}:$$

Compare the Lewis structure of ozone to the Lewis structure of O_2:

$$:\ddot{O}=\ddot{O}:$$

Which molecule, O_3 or O_2, do you think has the stronger oxygen–oxygen bond? If you deduced O_2, you are correct. O_2 has a stronger bond because it is a pure double bond. Ozone, on the other hand, has bonds that are intermediate between single and double, so O_3 has weaker bonds. The effects of this are significant. As discussed in the *Chemistry in the Environment* box in Chapter 6, O_3 shields us from harmful ultraviolet light entering Earth's atmosphere. O_3 is ideally suited to do this because photons at wavelengths of 280–320 nm (the most dangerous components of sunlight to humans) are just strong enough to break ozone's bonds. In the process, the photons are absorbed.

$$:\ddot{O}-\ddot{O}=\ddot{O}: + \text{UV light} \longrightarrow :\ddot{O}=\ddot{O}: + \cdot\ddot{O}\cdot$$

The same wavelengths of UV light, however, do not have sufficient energy to break the stronger double bond of O_2, which is therefore transparent to UV. Consequently, it is important that we continue, and even strengthen, the ban on ozone-depleting compounds.

B10.1 CAN YOU ANSWER THIS? *Why are these Lewis structures for ozone incorrect?*

$$:\ddot{O}-\ddot{O}-\ddot{O}: \qquad :\ddot{O}=O=\ddot{O}:$$

The geometry of CO_2 is determined by the repulsion between the two electron groups (the two double bonds) on the central carbon atom. These two electron groups get as far away from each other as possible, resulting in a bond angle of 180° and a **linear** geometry for CO_2.

180°

As another example, consider the molecule H_2CO. Its Lewis structure is:

$$\begin{array}{c} :O: \\ \| \\ H-C-H \end{array}$$

This molecule has three electron groups around the central atom. These three electron groups get as far away from each other as possible, resulting in a bond angle of 120° and a **trigonal planar** geometry.

The angles shown here for H_2CO are approximate. The C=O double bond contains more electron density than do C—H single bonds, resulting in a slightly greater repulsion; thus the HCH bond angle is actually 116°, and the HCO bond angles are actually 122°.

~120°   ~120°

~120°

A tetrahedron is a geometric shape with four triangular faces.

CH_4 is shown here with both a ball-and-stick model (left) and a space-filling model (right). Although space-filling models more closely portray molecules, ball-and-stick models are often used to clearly illustrate molecular geometries.

If a molecule has four electron groups around the central atom, as CH_4 does, it has a **tetrahedral** geometry with bond angles of 109.5°.

The mutual repulsion of the four electron groups causes the tetrahedral shape; the tetrahedron allows the maximum separation among the four groups. When we write the structure of CH_4 on paper, it may seem that the molecule should be square planar, with bond angles of 90°. However, in three dimensions the electron groups can get farther away from each other by forming the tetrahedral geometry.

Each of the molecules in the preceding examples has only bonding groups of electrons around the central atom. What happens in molecules with lone pairs around the central atom? These lone pairs also repel other electron groups. For example, consider the NH_3 molecule:

$$H-\overset{\overset{\displaystyle H}{|}}{N}-H$$

The four electron groups (one lone pair and three bonding pairs) get as far away from each other as possible. If we look only at the electrons, we find that the **electron geometry**—the geometrical arrangement of the electron groups—is tetrahedral.

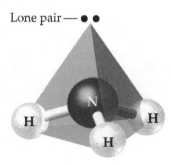

However, the **molecular geometry**—the geometrical arrangement of the atoms—is **trigonal pyramidal**.

Trigonal pyramidal structure

Notice that, although the electron geometry and the molecular geometry are different, the electron geometry is relevant to the molecular geometry. In other words, the lone pair exerts its influence on the bonding pairs.

Consider one last example, H_2O. Its Lewis structure is:

$$H-\overset{\displaystyle \cdot\cdot}{\underset{\displaystyle \cdot\cdot}{O}}-H$$

The bond angles in NH_3 and H_2O are actually a few degrees smaller than the ideal tetrahedral angles.

Since it has four electron groups, its electron geometry is also tetrahedral.

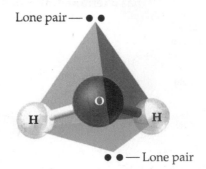

Lone pair — ●●

O

H   H

●● —Lone pair

However, its molecular geometry is **bent**.

Bent structure

Table 10.1 summarizes the electron and molecular geometry of a molecule based on the total number of electron groups, the number of bonding groups, and the number of lone pairs.

To determine the geometry of any molecule, we use the procedure presented in the left column of Examples 10.8 and 10.9. As usual, the two examples of applying the steps are in the center and right columns.

TABLE 10.1 Electron and Molecular Geometries

Electron Groups*	Bonding Groups	Lone Pairs	Electron Geometry	Angle between Electron Groups**	Molecular Geometry	Example
2	2	0	linear	180°	linear	:Ö=C=Ö:
3	3	0	trigonal planar	120°	trigonal planar	Ö: ‖ H—C—H
3	2	1	trigonal planar	120°	bent	:Ö=S—Ö:
4	4	0	tetrahedral	109.5°	tetrahedral	H—C—H (H top, H bottom)
4	3	1	tetrahedral	109.5°	trigonal pyramidal	H—N̈—H H
4	2	2	tetrahedral	109.5°	bent	H—Ö—H

* Count only electron groups around the *central* atom. Each of the following is considered one electron group: a lone pair, a single bond, a double bond, and a triple bond.

** Angles listed here are idealized. Actual angles in specific molecules may vary by several degrees.

	EXAMPLE 10.8	EXAMPLE 10.9
PREDICTING GEOMETRY USING VSEPR THEORY	▶ Predict the electron and molecular geometry of PCl_3.	Predict the electron and molecular geometry of the $[NO_3]^-$ ion.
1. Draw a Lewis structure for the molecule.	**SOLUTION** PCl_3 has 26 electrons. $$:\ddot{C}l:$$ $$:\ddot{C}l:\ddot{P}:\ddot{C}l:$$	**SOLUTION** $[NO_3]^-$ has 24 electrons. $$\left[:\ddot{O}:\ddot{N}::\ddot{O}:\right]^-$$
2. Determine the total number of electron groups around the central atom. Lone pairs, single bonds, double bonds, and triple bonds each count as one group.	The central atom (P) has four electron groups.	The central atom (N) has three electron groups (the double bond counts as one group).

3. Determine the number of bonding groups and the number of lone pairs around the central atom.
    These should sum to the result from Step 2. Bonding groups include single bonds, double bonds, and triple bonds.
	$$:\ddot{C}l:$$ $$:\ddot{C}l:\ddot{P}:\ddot{C}l:$$
	  Lone pair
	 Three of the four electron groups around P are bonding groups, and one is a lone pair.
		$$\left[:\ddot{O}:\ddot{N}::\ddot{O}:\right]^-$$
		 No lone pairs
		 All three of the electron groups around N are bonding groups.

4. Refer to Table 10.1 to determine the electron geometry and molecular geometry.	The electron geometry is tetrahedral (four electron groups), and the molecular geometry—the shape of the molecule—is trigonal pyramidal (four electron groups, three bonding groups, and one lone pair).	The electron geometry is trigonal planar (three electron groups), and the molecular geometry—the shape of the molecule—is trigonal planar (three electron groups, three bonding groups, and no lone pairs).
	▶**SKILLBUILDER 10.8**	Predict the molecular geometry of ClNO (N is the central atom)	▶**SKILLBUILDER 10.9**	Predict the molecular geometry of the SO_3^{2-} ion. ▶**FOR MORE PRACTICE** Example 10.17; Problems 65, 66, 69, 70, 73, 74.

✓ **CONCEPTUAL CHECKPOINT 10.6**

Which condition necessarily leads to a molecular geometry that is identical to the electron geometry?

(a) The presence of a double bond between the central atom and a terminal atom.

(b) The presence of two or more identical terminal atoms bonded to the central atom.

(c) The presence of one or more lone pairs on the central atom.

(d) The absence of any lone pairs on the central atom.

Representing Molecular Geometries on Paper

Because molecular geometries are three-dimensional, they are often difficult to represent on two-dimensional paper. Many chemists use this notation for bonds to indicate three-dimensional structures on two-dimensional paper:

—	‖···	◄
Straight line	*Hashed lines*	*Wedge*
Bond in plane of paper	Bond projecting into the paper	Bond projecting out of the paper

CHEMISTRY AND HEALTH
▶Fooled by Molecular Shape

Artificial sweeteners, such as aspartame (Nutrasweet™), taste sweet but have few or no calories. Why? Because taste and caloric value are entirely separate properties of foods. The caloric value of a food depends on the amount of energy released when the food is metabolized. Sucrose (table sugar) is metabolized by oxidation to carbon dioxide and water:

$$C_{12}H_{22}O_{11} + 6\,O_2 \longrightarrow 12\,CO_2 + 11\,H_2O$$
$$\Delta H = -5644 \text{ kJ}$$

When your body metabolizes one mole of sucrose, it obtains 5644 kJ of energy. Some artificial sweeteners, such as saccharin, are not metabolized at all—they just pass through the body unchanged—and therefore have no caloric value. Other artificial sweeteners, such as aspartame, are metabolized but have a much lower caloric content (for a given amount of sweetness) than sucrose.

The *taste* of a food, however, is independent of its metabolism. The sensation of taste originates in the tongue, where specialized cells called taste cells act as highly sensitive and specific molecular detectors. These cells can distinguish the sugar molecules from the thousands of different types of molecules present in a mouthful of food. The main basis for this discrimination is the molecule's *shape*.

The surface of a taste cell contains specialized protein molecules called taste receptors. Each particular *tastant*—a molecule that you can taste—fits snugly into a special pocket on the taste receptor protein called the *active site*, just as a key fits into a lock (see Section 15.12). For example, a sugar molecule fits only into the active site of the sugar receptor protein called Tlr3. When the sugar molecule (the key) enters the active site (the lock), the different subunits of the Tlr3 protein split apart. This split causes a series of events that results in transmission of a nerve signal, which reaches the brain and registers a sweet taste.

Artificial sweeteners taste sweet because they fit into the receptor pocket that normally binds sucrose. In fact, both aspartame and saccharin bind to the active site in the Tlr3 protein more strongly than sugar does! For this reason, artificial sweeteners are "sweeter than sugar." It takes 200 times as much sucrose as aspartame to trigger the same amount of nerve signal transmission from taste cells.

This type of lock-and-key fit between the active site of a protein and a particular molecule is important not only to taste but to many other biological functions as well. For example, immune response, the sense of smell, and many types of drug action all depend on shape-specific interactions between molecules and proteins. The ability of scientists to determine the shapes of key biological molecules is largely responsible for the revolution in biology that has occurred over the last 50 years.

B10.2 CAN YOU ANSWER THIS? *Proteins are long-chain molecules in which each link is an amino acid. The simplest amino acid is glycine, which has this structure:*

Determine the geometry around each interior atom in the glycine structure and make a three-dimensional sketch of the molecule.

The major molecular geometries used in this book are shown here using this notation:

X—A—X Linear Trigonal planar Bent Tetrahedral Trigonal pyramidal

10.8 Electronegativity and Polarity: Why Oil and Water Don't Mix

LO: Determine whether a molecule is polar.

▲ **FIGURE10.1 Oil and water don't mix** Question: Why not?

> The representation for depicting electron density in this figure is introduced in Section 9.6.

> The value of electronegativity is assigned using a relative scale on which fluorine, the most electronegative element, has an electronegativity of 4.0. All other electronegativities are defined relative to fluorine.

If we combine oil and water in a container, they separate into distinct regions (◄ Figure 10.1). Why? Something about water molecules causes them to bunch together into one region, expelling the oil molecules into a separate region. What is that something? We can begin to understand the answer by examining the Lewis structure of water.

$$H—\ddot{O}—H$$

The two bonds between O and H each consist of an electron pair—2 electrons shared between the oxygen atom and the hydrogen atom. The oxygen and hydrogen atoms each donate one electron to this electron pair; however, like most children, they don't share them equally. The oxygen atom takes more than its fair share of the electron pair.

Electronegativity

The ability of an element to attract electrons within a covalent bond is called **electronegativity.** Oxygen is more electronegative than hydrogen, which means that, on average, the shared electrons are more likely to be found near the oxygen atom than near the hydrogen atom. Consider one of the two OH bonds:

Dipole moment

Since the electron pair is unequally shared (with oxygen getting the larger share), the oxygen atom has a partial negative charge, symbolized by δ− (delta minus). The hydrogen atom (which gets the smaller share) has a partial positive charge, symbolized by δ+ (delta plus). The result of this uneven electron sharing is a **dipole moment**, a separation of charge within the bond. We call covalent bonds that have a dipole moment **polar covalent bonds.** The magnitude of the dipole moment, and therefore the degree of polarity of the bond, depend on the electronegativity difference between the two elements in the bond and the length of the bond. For a fixed bond length, the greater the electronegativity difference, the greater the dipole moment and the more polar the bond.

▼ Figure 10.2 shows the relative electronegativities of the elements. Notice that electronegativity increases as we move toward the right across a period in the periodic table and decreases as we move down a column in the periodic table. If

▶ **FIGURE 10.2**
Electronegativity of the elements
Linus Pauling introduced the scale shown in this figure. He arbitrarily set the electronegativity of fluorine at 4.0 and calculated all other values relative to fluorine.

▲ FIGURE 10.3 **Pure covalent bonding** In Cl₂, the two Cl atoms share the electrons evenly. This is a pure covalent bond.

▲ FIGURE 10.4 **Ionic bonding** In NaCl, Na completely transfers an electron to Cl. This is an ionic bond.

> The degree of bond polarity is a continuous function. The guidelines given here are approximate.

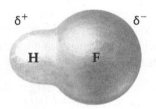

▲ FIGURE 10.5 **Polar covalent bonding** In HF, the electrons are shared, but the shared electrons are more likely to be found on F than on H. The bond is polar covalent.

two elements with identical electronegativities form a covalent bond, they share the electrons equally, and there is no dipole moment. For example, the chlorine molecule, composed of two chlorine atoms (which of course have identical electronegativities), has a pure covalent bond in which electrons are evenly shared (◄ Figure 10.3). The bond has no dipole moment, and the molecule is **nonpolar**.

If there is a large electronegativity difference between the two elements in a bond, such as normally occurs between a metal and a nonmetal, the electron is completely transferred and the bond is ionic. For example, sodium and chlorine form an ionic bond (◄ Figure 10.4).

If there is an intermediate electronegativity difference between the two elements, such as between two different nonmetals, the bond is polar covalent. For example, HF forms a polar covalent bond (◄ Figure 10.5).

These concepts are summarized in Table 10.2 and ▼ Figure 10.6.

TABLE 10.2 **The Effect of Electronegativity Difference on Bond Type**

Electronegativity Difference (ΔEN)	Bond Type	Example
zero (0–0.4)	pure covalent	Cl₂
intermediate (0.4–2.0)	polar covalent	HF
large (2.0+)	ionic	NaCl

▲ FIGURE 10.6 **The continuum of bond types** The electronegativity difference between two bonded atoms determines the type of bond (pure covalent, polar covalent, or ionic).

EXAMPLE 10.10 CLASSIFYING BONDS AS PURE COVALENT, POLAR COVALENT, OR IONIC

Is the bond formed between each pair of atoms pure covalent, polar covalent, or ionic?

(a) Sr and F   (b) N and Cl   (c) N and O

SOLUTION

(a) In Figure 10.2, find the electronegativity of Sr (1.0) and of F (4.0). The electronegativity difference (ΔEN) is:

$$\Delta EN = 4.0 - 1.0 = 3.0$$

Refer to Table 10.2 and classify this bond as ionic.

(b) In Figure 10.2, find the electronegativity of N (3.0) and of Cl (3.0). The electronegativity difference (ΔEN) is:

$$\Delta EN = 3.0 - 3.0 = 0$$

Refer to Table 10.2 and classify this bond as pure covalent.

(c) In Figure 10.2, find the electronegativity of N (3.0) and of O (3.5). The electronegativity difference (ΔEN) is:

$$\Delta EN = 3.5 - 3.0 = 0.5$$

Refer to Table 10.2 and classify this bond as polar covalent.

> ▶**SKILLBUILDER 10.10 | Classifying Bonds as Pure Covalent, Polar Covalent, or Ionic**
>
> Is the bond formed between each pair of atoms pure covalent, polar covalent, or ionic?
>
> (a) I and I   (b) Cs and Br   (c) P and O
>
> ▶**FOR MORE PRACTICE**   Problems 81, 82.

 CONCEPTUAL CHECKPOINT 10.7

Which bond would you expect to be more polar: the bond in HCl or the bond in HBr?

Polar Bonds and Polar Molecules

Does the presence of one or more polar bonds in a molecule always result in a polar molecule? The answer is no. A **polar molecule** is one with polar bonds that add together—they do not cancel each other—to form a net dipole moment. For diatomic molecules, we can readily tell polar molecules from nonpolar ones. If a diatomic molecule contains a polar bond, then the molecule is polar. However, for molecules with more than two atoms, it is more difficult to tell polar molecules from nonpolar ones because two or more polar bonds may cancel one another. For example, consider carbon dioxide:

$$:\ddot{O}{=}C{=}\ddot{O}:$$

Each C=O *bond* is polar because the difference in electronegativity between oxygen and carbon is 1.0. However, since CO_2 has a linear geometry, the dipole moment of one bond completely cancels the dipole moment of the other and the *molecule* is nonpolar. We can understand this with an analogy. Imagine each polar bond to be a rope pulling on the central atom. In CO_2 we can see how the two ropes pulling in opposing directions cancel each other's effect:

We can also represent polar bonds with arrows (or *vectors*) that point in the direction of the negative pole and have a plus sign at the positive pole (as we just saw for carbon dioxide). If the arrows (or vectors) point in exactly opposing directions as in carbon dioxide, the dipole moments cancel.

Water, on the other hand, has two dipole moments that do not cancel. If we imagine each bond as a rope pulling on oxygen, we see that, because of the angle between the bonds, the pulls of the two ropes do not cancel:

In the vector representation of a dipole moment, the vector points in the direction of the atom with the partial negative charge.

$$\xrightarrow{\;+\;}$$
$$\delta^+ \qquad\qquad \delta^-$$

Nonpolar

Two identical polar bonds pointing in opposite directions will cancel. The molecule is nonpolar.

Nonpolar

Three identical polar bonds at 120° from each other will cancel. The molecule is nonpolar.

Polar

Three polar bonds in a trigonal pyramidal arrangement (109.5°) will not cancel. The molecule is polar.

Polar

Two polar bonds with an angle of less than 180° between them will not cancel. The molecule is polar.

Nonpolar

Four identical polar bonds in a tetrahedral arrangement (109.5° from each other) will cancel. The molecule is nonpolar.

Note: In all cases where the polar bonds cancel, the bonds are assumed to be identical. If one or more of the bonds are different than the other(s), the bonds will not cancel and the molecule is polar.

Consequently, water is a polar molecule. We can use symmetry as a guide to determine whether a molecule containing polar bonds is indeed polar. Highly symmetric molecules tend to be nonpolar even if they have polar bonds because the bond dipole moments (or the pulls of the ropes) tend to cancel. Asymmetric molecules that contain polar bonds tend to be polar because the bond dipole moments (or the pulls of the ropes) tend not to cancel. Table 10.3 summarizes some common cases.

In summary, to determine whether a molecule is polar:

- **We determine whether the molecule contains polar bonds.** A bond is polar if the two bonding atoms have different electronegativities. If there are no polar bonds, the molecule is nonpolar.

- **We determine whether the polar bonds add together to form a net dipole moment.** We must first use VSEPR to determine the geometry of the molecule. Then we visualize each bond as a rope pulling on the central atom. Is the molecule highly symmetrical? Do the pulls of the ropes cancel? If so, there is no net dipole moment and the molecule is nonpolar. If the molecule is asymmetrical and the pulls of the rope do not cancel, the molecule is polar.

EXAMPLE 10.11	**DETERMINING WHETHER A MOLECULE IS POLAR**

Is NH_3 polar?

	SOLUTION
Begin by drawing the Lewis structure of NH_3. Since N and H have different electronegativities, the bonds are polar.	
The geometry of NH_3 is trigonal pyramidal (four electron groups, three bonding groups, one lone pair). Draw a three-dimensional picture of NH_3 and imagine each bond as a rope that is being pulled. The pulls of the ropes do not cancel and the molecule is polar.	NH_3 is polar

▶**SKILLBUILDER 10.11** | **Determining Whether a Molecule Is Polar**
Determine whether CH_4 is polar.

▶**FOR MORE PRACTICE**   Example 10.18; Problems 89, 90, 91, 92.

Polarity is important because polar molecules tend to behave differently than nonpolar molecules. Water and oil do not mix, for example, because water molecules are polar and the molecules that compose oil are generally nonpolar. Polar molecules interact strongly with other polar molecules because the positive end of one molecule is attracted to the negative end of another, just as the south pole of a

EVERYDAY CHEMISTRY

▶ How Soap Works

Imagine eating a greasy cheeseburger without flatware or napkins. By the end of the meal, your hands are coated with grease and oil. If you try to wash them with only water, they remain greasy. However, if you add a little soap, the grease washes away. Why? As we learned previously, water molecules are polar and the molecules that compose grease and oil are nonpolar. As a result, water and grease repel each other.

The molecules that compose soap, however, have a special structure that allows them to interact strongly with both water and grease. One end of a soap molecule is polar, while the other end is nonpolar.

Soap molecule

Polar head   Nonpolar tail
attracts water   attracts grease

The polar head of a soap molecule strongly attracts water molecules, while the nonpolar tail strongly attracts grease and oil molecules. Soap is a sort of molecular liaison, one end interacting with water and the other end interacting with grease. Soap therefore allows water and grease to mix, removing the grease from your hands and washing it down the drain.

B10.3 CAN YOU ANSWER THIS? *Consider this detergent molecule. Which end do you think is polar? Which end is nonpolar?*

$$CH_3(CH_2)_{11}OCH_2CH_2OH$$

▶ **FIGURE 10.7 Dipole–dipole attraction** Just as the north pole of one magnet is attracted to the south pole of another, so the positive end of one molecule with a dipole is attracted to the negative end of another molecule with a dipole.

magnet is attracted to the north pole of another magnet (▲ Figure 10.7). A mixture of polar and nonpolar molecules is similar to a mixture of small magnetic and nonmagnetic particles. The magnetic particles clump together, excluding the nonmagnetic ones and separating into distinct regions (◀ Figure 10.8). Similarly, the polar water molecules attract one another, forming regions from which the nonpolar oil molecules are excluded (▼ Figure 10.9).

▲ **FIGURE 10.8 Magnetic and nonmagnetic particles** Magnetic particles (the colored marbles) attract one another, excluding nonmagnetic particles (the clear marbles). This behavior is analogous to that of polar and nonpolar molecules.

◀ **FIGURE 10.9 Polar and nonpolar molecules** A mixture of polar and nonpolar molecules, like a mixture of magnetic and nonmagnetic particles, separates into distinct regions because the polar molecules attract one another, excluding the nonpolar ones. **Question:** Can you think of some examples of this behavior?

CHAPTER IN REVIEW

Self-Assessment Quiz

Q1. Which pair of elements has the most similar Lewis structures?

(a) N and S   (b) F and Ar

(c) Cl and Ar   (d) O and S

Q2. What is the Lewis structure for the compound that forms between K and S?

(a) $K-\ddot{\underset{..}{S}}-K$ (b) $K^+[:\ddot{\underset{..}{S}}:]^-$

(c) $K^+[:\ddot{\underset{..}{S}}:]^{2-}K^+$ (d) $[:\ddot{\underset{..}{S}}:]^{2-}K^+[:\ddot{\underset{..}{S}}:]^{2-}$

Q3. Use the Lewis model to predict the correct formula for the compound that forms between K and S.

(a) KS   (b) K_2S (c) KS_2 (d) K_2S_2

Q4. What is the correct Lewis structure for H_2CS?

(a) $H-H-\ddot{\underset{..}{C}}-\ddot{\underset{..}{S}}:$ (b) $H-\underset{\overset{|}{:\ddot{S}:}}{C}-H$

(c) $H=\underset{\overset{|}{:\ddot{S}:}}{C}-H$ (d) $H-\underset{\overset{||}{:\ddot{S}}}{C}-H$

Q5. How many electron dots are in the Lewis structure of NO_2^-?

(a) 17   (b) 18   (c) 19   (d) 20

Q6. Which compound has two or more resonance structures?

(a) NO_2^- (b) CO_2 (c) NH_4^+ (d) CCl_4

Q7. What is the molecular geometry of PBr_3?

(a) Bent   (b) Tetrahedral

(c) Trigonal pyramidal   (d) Linear

Q8. What is the molecular geometry of N_2O (Nitrogen is the central atom.)?

(a) Bent   (b) Tetrahedral

(c) Trigonal pyramidal   (d) Linear

Q9. Which bond is polar?

(a) A bond between C and S

(b) A bond between Br and Br

(c) A bond between C and O

(d) A bond between B and H

Q10. Which molecule is polar?

(a) SCl_2 (b) CS_2 (c) CF_4 (d) $SiCl_4$

Answers: 1:d, 2:c, 3:b, 4:d, 5:b, 6:a, 7:c, 8:d, 9:c, 10:a

Chemical Principles

The Lewis Model: The Lewis model is a model for chemical bonding. According to the Lewis model, chemical bonds form when atoms transfer valence electrons (ionic bonding) or share valence electrons (covalent bonding) to attain noble gas electron configurations. In the Lewis model, we represent valence electrons as dots surrounding the symbol for an element. When two or more elements bond together, the dots are transferred or shared so that every atom attains eight dots (an octet), or two dots (a duet) in the case of hydrogen.

Molecular Shapes: We can predict the shapes of molecules by combining the Lewis model with valence shell electron pair repulsion (VSEPR) theory. In this model, electron groups—lone pairs, single bonds, double bonds, and triple bonds—around the central atom repel one another and determine the geometry of the molecule.

Electronegativity and Polarity: Electronegativity refers to the relative ability of elements to attract electrons within a chemical bond. Electronegativity increases as we move to the right across a period in the periodic table and decreases as we move down a column. When two nonmetal atoms of different electronegativities form a covalent bond, the electrons in the bond are not evenly shared and the bond is polar. In diatomic molecules, a polar bond results in a polar molecule. In molecules with more than two atoms, polar bonds may cancel, forming a nonpolar molecule, or they may sum, forming a polar molecule.

Relevance

The Lewis Model: Bonding theories predict what combinations of elements will form stable compounds, and we can use them to predict the properties of those compounds. For example, pharmaceutical companies use bonding theories when they are designing drug molecules to interact with a specific part of a protein molecule.

Molecular Shapes: Molecular shapes determine many of the properties of compounds. Water's bent geometry, for example, causes it to be a liquid at room temperature instead of a gas. It is also the reason ice floats on water and snowflakes have hexagonal patterns.

Electronegativity and Polarity: The polarity of a molecule influences many of its properties such as whether it is a solid, liquid, or gas at room temperature and whether it mixes with other compounds. Oil and water, for example, do not mix because water is polar while oil is nonpolar.

Chemical Skills

Examples

LO: Write Lewis structures for elements (Section 10.2).

The Lewis structure of any element is the symbol for the element with the valence electrons represented as dots drawn around the element. The number of valence electrons is equal to the group number of the element (for main-group elements).

| EXAMPLE 10.12 | LEWIS STRUCTURES FOR ELEMENTS |

Draw the Lewis structure of sulfur.

SOLUTION

Since S is in Group 6A, it has 6 valence electrons. Draw these as dots surrounding its symbol, S.

$$\cdot \ddot{\underset{\cdot\cdot}{S}} :$$

LO: Write Lewis structures for ionic compounds (Section 10.3).

In an ionic Lewis structure, the metal loses all of its valence electrons to the nonmetal, which attains an octet. We place the nonmetal in brackets with the charge in the upper right corner.

| EXAMPLE 10.13 | WRITING LEWIS STRUCTURES OF IONIC COMPOUNDS |

Write the Lewis structure for lithium bromide.

SOLUTION

$$\text{Li}^+ \ [:\ddot{\underset{\cdot\cdot}{Br}}:]^-$$

LO: Use the Lewis model to predict the chemical formula of an ionic compound (Section 10.3).

To determine the chemical formula of an ionic compound, write the Lewis structures of each of the elements. Then choose the correct number of each type of atom so that the metal atom(s) lose all of their valence electrons and the nonmetal atom(s) attain an octet.

| EXAMPLE 10.14 | USING THE LEWIS MODEL TO PREDICT THE CHEMICAL FORMULA OF AN IONIC COMPOUND |

Use the Lewis model to predict the formula for the compound that forms between potassium and sulfur.

SOLUTION

The Lewis structures of K and S are:

$$\text{K}\cdot \qquad \cdot\ddot{\underset{\cdot\cdot}{S}}:$$

Potassium must lose 1 electron, and sulfur must gain 2. Consequently, there are two potassium atoms for every sulfur atom. The Lewis structure is:

$$\text{K}^+[:\ddot{\underset{\cdot\cdot}{S}}:]^{2-}\text{K}^+$$

The correct formula is K_2S.

LO: Write Lewis structures for covalent compounds (Sections 10.4, 10.5).

To write covalent Lewis structures, follow these steps:

1. **Write the correct skeletal structure for the molecule.** Hydrogen atoms are always terminal, halogens are usually terminal, and many molecules tend to be symmetrical.

2. **Calculate the total number of electrons for the Lewis structure by summing the valence electrons of each atom in the molecule.** Remember that the number of valence electrons for any main-group element is equal to its group number in the periodic table. For polyatomic ions, add one electron for each negative charge and subtract one electron for each positive charge.

| EXAMPLE 10.15 | WRITING LEWIS STRUCTURES FOR COVALENT COMPOUNDS |

Write the Lewis structure for CS_2.

SOLUTION

S C S

$$\begin{aligned}\text{Total e}^- &= 1 \times (\text{\# valence e}^- \text{ in C}) \\ &\quad + 2 \times (\text{\# valence e}^- \text{ in S}) \\ &= 4 + 2(6) \\ &= 16\end{aligned}$$

3. **Distribute the electrons among the atoms, giving octets (or duets for hydrogen) to as many atoms as possible.** Begin by placing 2 electrons between each pair of atoms. These are the bonding electrons. Then distribute the remaining electrons, first to terminal atoms and then to the central atom.

4. **If any atoms lack an octet, form double or triple bonds as necessary to give them octets.** Do this by moving lone electron pairs from terminal atoms into the bonding region with the central atom.

S:C:S   (4 of 16 e⁻ used)

:S̈:C:S̈:   (16 of 16 e⁻ used)

:S̈::C::S̈:   or   :S̈=C=S̈:

LO: Write resonance structures (Section 10.6).

When you can write two or more equivalent (or nearly equivalent) Lewis structures for a molecule, the true structure is an average between these. Represent this by writing all of the correct structures (called resonance structures) with double-headed arrows between them.

EXAMPLE 10.16   WRITING RESONANCE STRUCTURES

Write resonance structures for SeO_2.

SOLUTION

You can write the Lewis structure for SeO_2 by following the steps for writing covalent Lewis structures. You can write two equally correct structures, so draw them both as resonance structures.

:Ö—S̈e=Ö: ⟷   :Ö=S̈e—Ö:

LO: Predict the shapes of molecules (Section 10.7).

To determine the shape of a molecule, follow these steps:

1. **Draw the Lewis structure for the molecule.**

2. **Determine the total number of electron groups around the central atom.** Lone pairs, single bonds, double bonds, and triple bonds each count as one group.

3. **Determine the number of bonding groups and the number of lone pairs around the central atom.** These should sum to the result from Step 2. Bonding groups include single bonds, double bonds, and triple bonds.

4. Refer to Table 10.1 to determine the electron geometry and molecular geometry.

EXAMPLE 10.17   PREDICTING THE SHAPES OF MOLECULES

Predict the geometry of SeO_2.

SOLUTION

The Lewis structure for SeO_2 (as you determined in Example 10.16) is composed of the following two resonance structures.

:Ö—S̈e=Ö: ⟷   :Ö=S̈e—Ö:

Either of the resonance structures will give the same geometry.

    Total number of electron groups = 3
    Number of bonding groups = 2
    Number of lone pairs = 1

    Electron geometry = Trigonal planar
    Molecular geometry = Bent

LO: Determine whether a molecule is polar (Section 10.8).

• **Determine whether the molecule contains polar bonds.** A bond is polar if the two bonding atoms have different electronegativities. If there are no polar bonds, the molecule is nonpolar.

• **Determine whether the polar bonds add together to form a net dipole moment.** Use VSEPR theory to determine the geometry of the molecule. Then visualize each bond as a rope pulling on the central atom. Is the molecule highly symmetrical? Do the pulls of the ropes cancel? If so, there is no net dipole moment and the molecule is nonpolar. If the molecule is asymmetrical and the pulls of the rope do not cancel, the molecule is polar.

EXAMPLE 10.18   DETERMINING WHETHER A MOLECULE IS POLAR

Determine whether SeO_2 is polar.

SOLUTION

Se and O are nonmetals with different electronegativities (2.4 for Se and 3.5 for O). Therefore, the Se–O bonds are polar.

    As you determined in Example 10.17, the geometry of SeO_2 is bent.

The polar bonds do not cancel but rather sum to give a net dipole moment. Therefore the molecule is polar.

2-105

KEY TERMS

bent **[10.7]**	duet **[10.2]**	lone pair **[10.4]**	terminal atom **[10.5]**
bonding pair **[10.4]**	electron geometry **[10.7]**	molecular geometry **[10.7]**	tetrahedral **[10.7]**
bonding theory **[10.1]**	electron group **[10.7]**	nonpolar **[10.8]**	trigonal planar **[10.7]**
chemical bond **[10.2]**	electronegativity **[10.8]**	octet **[10.2]**	trigonal pyramidal **[10.7]**
covalent bond **[10.2]**	ionic bond **[10.2]**	octet rule **[10.2]**	triple bond **[10.4]**
dipole moment **[10.8]**	Lewis model **[10.1]**	polar covalent bond **[10.8]**	valence shell electron pair
dot structure **[10.2]**	Lewis structure **[10.2]**	polar molecule **[10.8]**	repulsion (VSEPR) theory
double bond **[10.4]**	linear **[10.7]**	resonance structures **[10.6]**	**[10.7]**

EXERCISES

QUESTIONS

1. Why are bonding theories important? Cite some examples of what bonding theories can predict.
2. Write the electron configurations for Ne and Ar. How many valence electrons does each element have?
3. In the Lewis model, what is an octet? What is a duet? What is a chemical bond?
4. What is the difference between ionic bonding and covalent bonding?
5. How can the Lewis model be used to determine the formula of ionic compounds? You may explain this with an example.
6. What is the difference between lone pair and bonding pair electrons?
7. How are double and triple bonds physically different from single bonds?
8. What is the procedure for writing a covalent Lewis structure?
9. How do you determine the number of electrons that go into the Lewis structure of a molecule?
10. How do you determine the number of electrons that go into the Lewis structure of a polyatomic ion?
11. Why does the octet rule have exceptions? List some examples.

12. What are resonance structures? Why are they necessary?
13. Explain how VSEPR theory predicts the shapes of molecules.
14. If all of the electron groups around a central atom are bonding groups (that is, there are no lone pairs), what is the molecular geometry for:
    (a) two electron groups
    (b) three electron groups
    (c) four electron groups
15. Give the bond angles for each of the geometries in the preceding question.
16. What is the difference between electron geometry and molecular geometry in VSEPR theory?
17. What is electronegativity?
18. What is the most electronegative element on the periodic table?
19. What is a polar covalent bond?
20. What is a dipole moment?
21. What happens if you try to mix a polar liquid with a nonpolar one?
22. If a molecule has polar bonds, is the molecule itself polar? Why or why not?

PROBLEMS

WRITING LEWIS STRUCTURES FOR ELEMENTS

23. Write an electron configuration for each element and the corresponding Lewis structure. Indicate which electrons in the electron configuration are included in the Lewis structure.
    (a) N
    (b) C
    (c) Cl
    (d) Ar

24. Write an electron configuration for each element and the corresponding Lewis structure. Indicate which electrons in the electron configuration are included in the Lewis structure.
    (a) Li
    (b) P
    (c) F
    (d) Ne

25. Write the Lewis structure for each element.
    (a) I
    (b) S
    (c) Ge
    (d) Ca

26. Write the Lewis structure for each element.
    (a) Kr
    (b) P
    (c) B
    (d) Na

27. Write a generic Lewis structure for the halogens. Do the halogens tend to gain or lose electrons in chemical reactions? How many?

28. Write a generic Lewis structure for the alkali metals. Do the alkali metals tend to gain or lose electrons in chemical reactions? How many?

29. Write a generic Lewis structure for the alkaline earth metals. Do the alkaline earth metals tend to gain or lose electrons in chemical reactions? How many?

30. Write a generic Lewis structure for the elements in the oxygen family (Group 6A). Do the elements in the oxygen family tend to gain or lose electrons in chemical reactions? How many?

31. Write the Lewis structure for each ion.
(a) Al^{3+}
(b) Mg^{2+}
(c) Se^{2-}
(d) N^{3-}

32. Write the Lewis structure for each ion.
(a) Sr^{2+}
(b) S^{2-}
(c) Li^+
(d) Cl^-

33. Indicate the noble gas that has the same Lewis structure as each ion.
(a) Br^-
(b) O^{2-}
(c) Rb^+
(d) Ba^{2+}

34. Indicate the noble gas that has the same Lewis structure as each ion.
(a) Se^{2-}
(b) I^-
(c) Sr^{2+}
(d) F^-

LEWIS STRUCTURES FOR IONIC COMPOUNDS

35. Is each compound best represented by an ionic or a covalent Lewis structure?
(a) SF_6
(b) $MgCl_2$
(c) $BrCl$
(d) K_2S

36. Is each compound best represented by an ionic or a covalent Lewis structure?
(a) NO
(b) CO_2
(c) Rb_2O
(d) Al_2S_3

37. Write the Lewis structure for each ionic compound.
(a) NaF
(b) CaO
(c) $SrBr_2$
(d) K_2O

38. Write the Lewis structure for each ionic compound.
(a) SrO
(b) Li_2S
(c) CaI_2
(d) RbF

39. Use the Lewis model to determine the formula for the compound that forms from each pair of atoms.
(a) Ca and S
(b) Mg and Br
(c) Cs and I
(d) Ca and N

40. Use the Lewis model to determine the formula for the compound that forms from each pair of atoms.
(a) Al and S
(b) Na and S
(c) Sr and Se
(d) Ba and F

41. Draw the Lewis structure for the ionic compound that forms from Mg and each atom.
(a) F
(b) O
(c) N

42. Draw the Lewis structure for the ionic compound that forms from Al and each atom.
(a) F
(b) O
(c) N

43. Determine what is wrong with each ionic Lewis structure and write the correct structure.
(a) $[Cs:]^+ [:\ddot{C}l:]^-$
(b) $Ba^+ [:\ddot{O}:]^-$
(c) $Ca^{2+} [:\ddot{I}:]^-$

44. Determine what is wrong with each ionic Lewis structure and write the correct structure.
(a) $[:\ddot{O}:]^{2-} Na^+ [:\ddot{O}:]^{2-}$
(b) $Mg:\ddot{O}:$
(c) $[Li:]^+ [:\ddot{S}:]^-$

LEWIS STRUCTURES FOR COVALENT COMPOUNDS

45. Use the Lewis model to explain why each element exists as a diatomic molecule.
  (a) hydrogen
  (b) iodine
  (c) nitrogen
  (d) oxygen

46. Use the Lewis model to explain why the compound that forms between hydrogen and sulfur has the formula H_2S. Would you expect HS to be stable? H_3S?

47. Write the Lewis structure for each molecule.
  (a) PH_3
  (b) SCl_2
  (c) F_2
  (d) HI

48. Write the Lewis structure for each molecule.
  (a) CH_4
  (b) NF_3
  (c) OF_2
  (d) H_2O

49. Write the Lewis structure for each molecule.
  (a) O_2
  (b) CO
  (c) HONO (N is central; H bonded to one of the O atoms.)
  (d) SO_2

50. Write the Lewis structure for each molecule.
  (a) N_2O (oxygen is terminal)
  (b) SiH_4
  (c) CI_4
  (d) Cl_2CO (carbon is central)

51. Write the Lewis structure for each molecule.
  (a) C_2H_2
  (b) C_2H_4
  (c) N_2H_2
  (d) N_2H_4

52. Write the Lewis structure for each molecule.
  (a) H_2CO (carbon is central)
  (b) H_3COH (carbon and oxygen are both central)
  (c) H_3COCH_3 (oxygen is between the two carbon atoms)
  (d) H_2O_2

53. Determine what is wrong with each Lewis structure and write the correct structure.
  (a) $:\ddot{N}=\ddot{N}:$

  (b) $:\ddot{S}-Si-\ddot{S}:$

  (c) $H-H-\ddot{O}:$

  (d) $:\ddot{I}-N-\ddot{I}:$
  $\qquad\quad |$
  $\qquad\quad :\ddot{I}:$

54. Determine what is wrong with each Lewis structure and write the correct structure.
  (a) $H-H-H-\ddot{N}:$

  (b) $:\ddot{C}l=O=\ddot{C}l:$

  (c) $\qquad\quad :\ddot{O}:$
  $\qquad\qquad |$
  $\quad H-C-\ddot{O}-H$

  (d) $H=\ddot{B}r:$

55. Write the Lewis structure for each molecule or ion. Include resonance structures if necessary.
  (a) SeO_2
  (b) CO_3^{2-}
  (c) ClO^-
  (d) ClO_2^-

56. Write the Lewis structure for each molecule or ion. Include resonance structures if necessary.
  (a) ClO_3^-
  (b) ClO_4^-
  (c) NO_3^-
  (d) SO_3

57. Write the Lewis structure for each ion. Include resonance structures if necessary.
  (a) PO_4^{3-}
  (b) CN^-
  (c) NO_2^-
  (d) SO_3^{2-}

58. Write the Lewis structure for each ion. Include resonance structures if necessary.
  (a) SO_4^{2-}
  (b) HSO_4^- (S is central; H is attached to one of the O atoms)
  (c) NH_4^+
  (d) BrO_2^- (Br is central)

59. Write the Lewis structure for each molecule. These molecules do not follow the octet rule.
  (a) BCl_3
  (b) NO_2
  (c) BH_3

60. Write the Lewis structure for each molecule. These molecules do not follow the octet rule.
  (a) BBr_3
  (b) NO

PREDICTING THE SHAPES OF MOLECULES

61. Determine the number of electron groups around the central atom for each molecule.
(a) OF_2
(b) NF_3
(c) CS_2
(d) CH_4

62. Determine the number of electron groups around the central atom for each molecule.
(a) CH_2Cl_2
(b) SBr_2
(c) H_2S
(d) PCl_3

63. Determine the number of bonding groups and the number of lone pairs for each of the molecules in Problem 61. The sum of these should equal your answers to Problem 61.

64. Determine the number of bonding groups and the number of lone pairs for each of the molecules in Problem 62. The sum of these should equal your answers to Problem 62.

65. Determine the molecular geometry of each molecule.
(a) CBr_4
(b) H_2CO
(c) CS_2
(d) BH_3

66. Determine the molecular geometry of each molecule.
(a) SiO_2
(b) BF_3
(c) $CFCl_3$ (carbon is central)
(d) H_2CS (carbon is central)

67. Determine the bond angles for each molecule in Problem 65.

68. Determine the bond angles for each molecule in Problem 66.

69. Determine the electron and molecular geometries of each molecule.
(a) N_2O (oxygen is terminal)
(b) SO_2
(c) H_2S
(d) PF_3

70. Determine the electron and molecular geometries of each molecule. (*Hint:* Determine the geometry around each of the two central atoms.)
(a) C_2H_2 (skeletal structure HCCH)
(b) C_2H_4 (skeletal structure H_2CCH_2)
(c) C_2H_6 (skeletal structure H_3CCH_3)

71. Determine the bond angles for each molecule in Problem 69.

72. Determine the bond angles for each molecule in Problem 70.

73. Determine the electron and molecular geometries of each molecule. For molecules with two central atoms, indicate the geometry about each central atom.
(a) N_2
(b) N_2H_2 (skeletal structure HNNH)
(c) N_2H_4 (skeletal structure H_2NNH_2)

74. Determine the electron and molecular geometries of each molecule. For molecules with more than one central atom, indicate the geometry about each central atom.
(a) CH_3OH (skeletal structure H_3COH)
(b) H_3COCH_3 (skeletal structure H_3COCH_3)
(c) H_2O_2 (skeletal structure HOOH)

75. Determine the molecular geometry of each polyatomic ion.
(a) CO_3^{2-}
(b) ClO_2^-
(c) NO_3^-
(d) NH_4^+

76. Determine the molecular geometry of each polyatomic ion.
(a) ClO_4^-
(b) BrO_2^-
(c) NO_2^-
(d) SO_4^{2-}

ELECTRONEGATIVITY AND POLARITY

77. Refer to Figure 10.2 to determine the electronegativity of each element.
(a) Mg
(b) Si
(c) Br

78. Refer to Figure 10.2 to determine the electronegativity of each element.
(a) F
(b) C
(c) S

79. List these elements in order of decreasing electronegativity: Rb, Si, Cl, Ca, Ga.

80. List these elements in order of increasing electronegativity: Ba, N, F, Si, Cs.

81. Refer to Figure 10.2 to find the electronegativity difference between each pair of elements; then refer to Table 10.2 to classify the bonds that occur between them as pure covalent, polar covalent, or ionic.
 (a) Mg and Br
 (b) Cr and F
 (c) Br and Br
 (d) Si and O

82. Refer to Figure 10.2 to find the electronegativity difference between each pair of elements; then refer to Table 10.2 to classify the bonds that occur between them as pure covalent, polar covalent, or ionic.
 (a) K and Cl
 (b) N and N
 (c) C and S
 (d) C and Cl

83. Arrange these diatomic molecules in order of increasing bond polarity: ICl, HBr, H_2, CO

84. Arrange these diatomic molecules in order of decreasing bond polarity: HCl, NO, F_2, HI

85. Classify each diatomic molecule as polar or nonpolar.
 (a) CO
 (b) O_2
 (c) F_2
 (d) HBr

86. Classify each diatomic molecule as polar or nonpolar.
 (a) I_2
 (b) NO
 (c) HCl
 (d) N_2

87. For each polar molecule in Problem 85 draw the molecule and indicate the positive and negative ends of the dipole moment.

88. For each polar molecule in Problem 86 draw the molecule and indicate the positive and negative ends of the dipole moment.

89. Classify each molecule as polar or nonpolar.
 (a) CS_2
 (b) SO_2
 (c) CH_4
 (d) CH_3Cl

90. Classify each molecule as polar or nonpolar.
 (a) H_2CO
 (b) CH_3OH
 (c) CH_2Cl_2
 (d) CO_2

91. Classify each molecule as polar or nonpolar.
 (a) BH_3
 (b) $CHCl_3$
 (c) C_2H_2
 (d) NH_3

92. Classify each molecule as polar or nonpolar.
 (a) N_2H_2
 (b) H_2O_2
 (c) CF_4
 (d) NO_2

CUMULATIVE PROBLEMS

93. Write electron configurations and Lewis structures for each element. Indicate which of the electrons in the electron configuration are shown in the Lewis structure.
 (a) Ca
 (b) Ga
 (c) As
 (d) I

94. Write electron configurations and Lewis structures for each element. Indicate which of the electrons in the electron configuration are shown in the Lewis structure.
 (a) Rb
 (b) Ge
 (c) Kr
 (d) Se

95. Determine whether each compound is ionic or covalent and write the appropriate Lewis structure.
 (a) K_2S
 (b) CHFO (carbon is central)
 (c) MgSe
 (d) PBr_3

96. Determine whether each compound is ionic or covalent and write the appropriate Lewis structure.
 (a) HCN
 (b) ClF
 (c) MgI_2
 (d) CaS

97. Write the Lewis structure for OCCl₂ (carbon is central) and determine whether the molecule is polar. Draw the three-dimensional structure of the molecule.

98. Write the Lewis structure for CH₃COH and determine whether the molecule is polar. Draw the three-dimensional structure of the molecule. The skeletal structure is:

$$
\begin{array}{ccc}
 & \text{H} & \text{O} \\
\text{H} & \text{C} & \text{C} \quad \text{H} \\
 & \text{H} &
\end{array}
$$

99. Write the Lewis structure for acetic acid (a component of vinegar) CH₃COOH, and draw the three-dimensional sketch of the molecule. Its skeletal structure is:

$$
\begin{array}{ccccc}
 & \text{H} & \text{O} & & \\
\text{H} & \text{C} & \text{C} & \text{O} & \text{H} \\
 & \text{H} & & &
\end{array}
$$

100. Write the Lewis structure for benzene, C₆H₆, and draw a three-dimensional sketch of the molecule. The skeletal structure is the ring shown here. (*Hint:* The Lewis structure consists of two resonance structures.)

$$
\begin{array}{ccc}
 & \text{H} & \\
 & \text{C} & \\
\text{HC} & & \text{CH} \\
\text{HC} & & \text{CH} \\
 & \text{C} & \\
 & \text{H} &
\end{array}
$$

101. Consider the neutralization reaction.

$$\text{HCl}(aq) + \text{NaOH}(aq) \longrightarrow \text{H}_2\text{O}(l) + \text{NaCl}(aq)$$

Write the reaction showing the Lewis structures of each of the reactants and products.

102. Consider the precipitation reaction.

$$\text{Pb(NO}_3)_2(aq) + 2\,\text{LiCl}(aq) \longrightarrow \text{PbCl}_2(s) + 2\,\text{LiNO}_3(aq)$$

Write the reaction showing the Lewis structures of each of the reactants and products.

103. Consider the redox reaction.

$$2\,\text{K}(s) + \text{Cl}_2(g) \longrightarrow 2\,\text{KCl}(s)$$

Draw the Lewis structure for each reactant and product and determine which reactant was oxidized and which one was reduced.

104. Consider the redox reaction.

$$\text{Ca}(s) + \text{Br}_2(g) \longrightarrow \text{CaBr}_2(s)$$

Draw the Lewis structure for each reactant and product and determine which reactant was oxidized and which one was reduced.

105. Each compound listed contains both ionic and covalent bonds. Write the ionic Lewis structure for each one including the covalent structure for the polyatomic ion. Write resonance structures if necessary.
(a) KOH
(b) KNO₃
(c) LiIO
(d) BaCO₃

106. Each of the compounds listed contains both ionic and covalent bonds. Write an ionic Lewis structure for each one, including the covalent structure for the polyatomic ion. Write resonance structures if necessary.
(a) RbIO₂
(b) Ca(OH)₂
(c) NH₄Cl
(d) Sr(CN)₂

107. Each molecule listed contains an expanded octet (10 or 12 electrons) around the central atom. Write the Lewis structure for each molecule.
(a) PF₅
(b) SF₄
(c) SeF₄

108. Each molecule listed contains an expanded octet (10 or 12 electrons) around the central atom. Write the Lewis structure for each molecule.
(a) ClF₅
(b) SF₆
(c) IF₅

109. Formic acid is responsible for the sting you feel when stung by fire ants. By mass, formic acid is 26.10% C, 4.38% H, and 69.52% O. The molar mass of formic acid is 46.02 g/mol. Find the molecular formula of formic acid and draw its Lewis structure.

110. Diazomethane has the following composition by mass: 28.57% C, 4.80% H, and 66.64% N. The molar mass of diazomethane is 42.04 g/mol. Find the molecular formula of diazomethane and draw its Lewis structure.

111. Free radicals are molecules that contain an odd number of valence electrons and therefore contain an unpaired electron in their Lewis structure. Write the best possible Lewis structure for the free radical HOO. Does the Lewis model predict that HOO is stable? Predict its geometry.

112. Free radicals (as explained in the previous problem) are molecules that contain an odd number of valence electrons. Write the best possible Lewis structure for the free radical CH_3. Predict its geometry.

HIGHLIGHT PROBLEMS

113. Some theories on aging suggest that free radicals cause a variety of diseases and aging. Free radicals (as explained in Problems 111 and 112) are molecules or ions containing an unpaired electron. As you know from the Lewis model, such molecules are not chemically stable and quickly react with other molecules. Free radicals may attack molecules within the cell, such as DNA, changing them and causing cancer or other diseases. Free radicals may also attack molecules on the surfaces of cells, making them appear foreign to the body's immune system. The immune system then attacks the cell and destroys it, weakening the body. Draw the Lewis structure for each of these free radicals, which have been implicated in theories of aging.
(a) O_2^-
(b) O^-
(c) OH
(d) CH_3OO (unpaired electron on terminal oxygen)

114. Free radicals (see Problem 113) are important in many environmentally significant reactions. For example, photochemical smog, which forms as a result of the action of sunlight on air pollutants, is formed in part by these two steps:

$$NO_2 \xrightarrow{\text{UV light}} NO + O$$
$$O + O_2 \longrightarrow O_3$$

The product of this reaction, ozone, is a pollutant in the lower atmosphere. Ozone is an eye and lung irritant and also accelerates the weathering of rubber products. Write Lewis structures for each of the reactants and products in the preceding reactions.

▲ Ozone damages rubber products.

▲ Free radicals, molecules containing unpaired electrons (represented here as X·), may attack biological molecules such as the DNA molecule depicted here.

115. Examine the formulas and space-filling models of the molecules shown here. Determine whether the structure is correct. If the structure is incorrect, sketch the correct structure.

(a) H₂Se

(b) CSe₂

(c) PCl₃

(d) CF₂Cl₂

QUESTIONS FOR GROUP WORK

Discuss these questions with the group and record your consensus answer.

116. Draw the Lewis dot structure for the atoms Al and O. Use the Lewis model to determine the formula for the compound formed from these atoms.
117. Draft a list of step-by-step instructions for writing a correct Lewis dot structure for any molecule or polyatomic ion.

118. For each of the following molecules:

$$CS_2 \quad NCl_3 \quad CF_4 \quad CH_2F_2$$

(a) Draw the Lewis dot structure.
(b) Determine the molecular geometry and draw it as accurately as you can.
(c) Indicate the polarity of any polar bonds with the δ symbol.
(d) Classify the molecule as polar or nonpolar.

▶ Answers to Skillbuilder Exercises

Skillbuilder 10.1 ·Mg·

Skillbuilder 10.2 Na⁺ [:B̈r̈:]⁻

Skillbuilder 10.3 Mg₃N₂

Skillbuilder 10.4 :C≡O:

Skillbuilder 10.5
$$\overset{\displaystyle \ddot{O}:}{\underset{\displaystyle }{\|}}$$
H—C—H

Skillbuilder 10.6 [:C̈l—Ö:]⁻

Skillbuilder 10.7

[:Ö=N̈—Ö:]⁻ ⟷ [:Ö—N̈=Ö:]⁻

Skillbuilder 10.8 bent
Skillbuilder 10.9 trigonal pyramidal
Skillbuilder 10.10
(a) pure covalent
(b) ionic
(c) polar covalent
Skillbuilder 10.11 CH₄ is nonpolar

▶ Answers to Conceptual Checkpoints

10.1 (a) C and Si both have four dots in their Lewis structure because they are both in the same column in the periodic table.

10.2 (b) Aluminum must lose its 3 valence electrons to obtain an octet. Sulfur must gain 2 electrons to obtain an octet. Therefore, two Al atoms are required for every three S atoms.

10.3 (b) The Lewis structure of O_2 has one double bond that contains 4 electrons (all of them bonding electrons); therefore, the number of bonding electrons is four.

10.4 (c) The Lewis structure of OH^- has eight electrons: six from oxygen, one from hydrogen, and one from the negative charge.

10.5 (b) Both NH_3 and H_3O^+ have one lone electron pair.

10.6 (d) If there are no lone pairs on the central atom, all of its valence electrons are involved in bonds, so the molecular geometry must be the same as the electron geometry.

10.7 The bond in H—Cl is more polar than the bond in H—Br because Cl is more electronegative than Br, so the electronegativity difference between H and Cl is greater than the difference between H and Br.

▲ When we drink from a straw, we remove some of the molecules from inside the straw. This creates a pressure difference between the inside of the straw and the outside of the straw that results in the liquid being pushed up the straw. The pushing is done by molecules in the atmosphere—primarily nitrogen and oxygen—as shown here.

Gases 11

> *"The generality of men are so accustomed to judge of things by their senses that, because the air is invisible, they ascribe but little to it, and think it but one removed from nothing."*—Robert Boyle (1627–1691)

CHAPTER OUTLINE

11.1 Extra-Long Straws

Like too many kids, I grew up preferring fast-food restaurants to home cooking. My favorite stunt at the burger restaurant was drinking my orange soda from an extra-long straw that I pieced together from several smaller straws. I would pinch the end of one straw and squeeze it into the end of another. By attaching several straws together in this way, I could put my orange soda on the floor and drink it while standing on my chair (for some reason, my parents did not appreciate my scientific curiosity). I sometimes planned ahead and brought duct tape to the restaurant to form extra-tight seals between adjacent straws. My brother and I would compete to see who could make the longest working straw. Since I was older, I usually won.

I often wondered how long the straw could be if I made perfect seals between the straws. Could I drink my orange soda from a cup on the ground while I sat in my tree house? Could I drink it from the top of a 10-story building? It seemed to me that I could; but I was wrong. Even if the extended straw had perfect seals and rigid walls, and even if I could create a perfect vacuum (the absence of all air), I could never suck my orange soda from a straw longer than about 10.3 m (34 ft). Why?

Straws work because sucking creates a *pressure* difference between the inside of the straw and the outside. We define pressure and its units more thoroughly later in this chapter; for now think of pressure as the force exerted per unit area by gas molecules as they collide with the surfaces around them (◄ Figure 11.1). Just as a ball exerts a force when it bounces against a wall, so a molecule exerts a force when it collides with a surface. The result of many of these collisions is pressure. The total amount of pressure exerted by a gas sample depends on several factors, including the concentration of gas molecules in the sample. On Earth at sea level, the gas molecules in our atmosphere exert an average pressure of 101,325 N/m^2 or, in English units, 14.7 lb/in^2.

Pressure is the result of collisions between gas molecules and the surfaces around them.

Gas molecules

Surface

▲ FIGURE 11.1 **Gas pressure** Pressure is the force exerted by gas molecules as they collide with the surfaces around them.

When we put a straw in a glass of soda, the pressure inside and outside the straw are the same, so the soda does not rise within the straw (▼ Figure 11.2a). When we suck on the straw, we remove some of the air molecules from inside the straw, lowering the number of collisions that occur and therefore lowering the pressure inside the straw (▼ Figure 11.2b). However, the pressure outside the straw remains the same. The result is a pressure differential—the pressure outside the straw becomes greater than the pressure inside the straw. This greater external pressure pushes the liquid up the straw.

How high can this greater external pressure push the liquid up the straw? If we formed a perfect vacuum within the straw, the pressure outside of the straw at sea level would be enough to push the orange soda (which is mostly water) to a total height of about 10.3 m (▼ Figure 11.3). This is because a 10.3-m column of water exerts the same pressure—101,325 N/m² or 14.7 lb/in.²—as the gas molecules in our atmosphere. In other words, the orange soda can rise up the straw until the pressure exerted by its weight equals the pressure exerted by the molecules in our atmosphere.

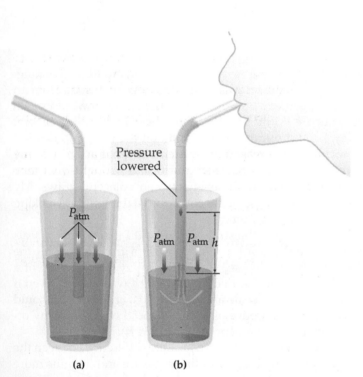

(a)   (b)

▲ **FIGURE 11.2   Sipping soda**   (a) When a straw is put into a glass of orange soda, the pressure inside and outside the straw is the same, so the liquid levels inside and outside the straw are the same. (b) When a person sucks on the straw, the pressure inside the straw is lowered. The greater pressure on the surface of the liquid outside the straw pushes the liquid up the straw.

The pressure exerted by the atmosphere is equal to the pressure exerted by a 10.3-m column of water

Valve

Vacuum

Vacuum pump

Pressure exerted by 10.3-m column of orange soda: 14.7 pounds per square inch

Pressure exerted by our atmosphere: 14.7 pounds per square inch

10.3 m

▲ **FIGURE 11.3   Atmospheric pressure**   Even if we form a perfect vacuum, atmospheric pressure can only push orange soda to a total height of about 10 m. This is because a column of water (or soda) 10.3 m high exerts the same pressure (14.7 lb/in.²) as the gas molecules in our atmosphere.

11.2   Kinetic Molecular Theory: A Model for Gases

LO: Describe how the main properties of a gas are predicted by kinetic molecular theory.

In prior chapters we have seen the importance of models or theories in understanding nature. A simple model for understanding the behavior of gases is the **kinetic molecular theory**. This model predicts the correct behavior for most gases under many conditions. Like other models, the kinetic molecular theory is not

▶ **FIGURE 11.4 Simplified representation of an ideal gas** In reality, the spaces between the gas molecules would be larger in relation to the size of the molecules than shown here.

Kinetic molecular theory

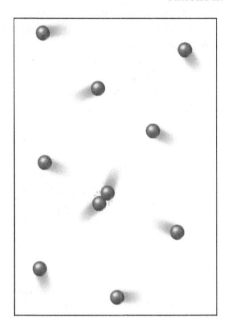

1. Collection of particles in constant motion

2. No attractions or repulsions between particles; collisions like billiard ball collisions

3. A lot of space between the particles compared to the size of the particles themselves

4. The speed of the particles increases with increasing temperature

Gases are compressible.

Gas

▲ **FIGURE 11.5 Compressibility of gases** Gases are compressible because there is so much empty space between gas particles.

Liquids are not compressible.

Liquid

▲ **FIGURE 11.6 Incompressibility of liquids** Liquids are not compressible because there is so little space between the liquid particles.

perfect and breaks down under certain conditions. In this book, however, we focus on conditions where it works well.

Kinetic molecular theory makes the following assumptions (▲ Figure 11.4):

1. A gas is a collection of particles (molecules or atoms) in constant, straight-line motion.

2. Gas particles do not attract or repel each other—they do not interact. The particles collide with each other and with the surfaces around them, but they bounce back from these collisions like idealized billiard balls.

3. There is a lot of space between gas particles compared with the size of the particles themselves.

4. The average kinetic energy—energy due to motion—of gas particles is proportional to the temperature of the gas in kelvins. This means that as the temperature increases, the particles move faster and therefore have more energy.

Kinetic molecular theory is consistent with, and indeed predicts, the properties of gases. Recall from Section 3.3 that gases:

• are compressible
• assume the shape and volume of their container
• have low densities in comparison with liquids and solids

Gases are compressible because the atoms or molecules that compose them have a lot of space between them. By applying external pressure to a gas sample, the atoms or molecules are forced closer together, compressing the gas. Liquids and solids, in contrast, are not compressible because the atoms or molecules composing them are already in close contact—they cannot be forced any closer together. We can witness the compressibility of a gas, for example, by pushing a piston into a cylinder containing a gas. The piston goes down (◀ Figure 11.5) in response to the external pressure. If the cylinder were filled with a liquid or a solid, the piston would not move when pushed (◀ Figure 11.6).

Gases assume the shape and volume of their container because gaseous atoms or molecules are in constant, straight-line motion. In contrast to a solid or liquid, whose atoms or molecules interact with one another, the atoms or molecules in

▲ **FIGURE 11.7 A gas assumes the shape of its container** Since the attractions between molecules in a gas are negligible, and since the particles are in constant motion, a gas expands to fill the volume of its container.

a gas do not interact with one another (or more precisely, their interactions are negligible). They simply move in straight lines, colliding with each other and with the walls of their container. As a result, they fill the entire container, collectively assuming its shape (◀ Figure 11.7).

Gases have a low density in comparison with solids and liquids because there is so much empty space between the atoms or molecules in a gas. For example, if the water in a 350-mL (12-oz) can of soda were converted to steam (gaseous water), the steam would occupy a volume of 595 L (the equivalent of 1700 soda cans).

Convert liquid to gas

(1 can of soda)   (1700 cans of soda)

▲ If all of the water in a 12-oz (350-mL) can of orange soda were converted to gaseous steam (at 1 atm pressure and 100 °C), the steam would occupy a volume equal to 1700 soda cans.

11.3 Pressure: The Result of Constant Molecular Collisions

LO: Identify and understand the relationship between pressure, force, and area.

LO: Convert among pressure units.

A prediction of kinetic molecular theory—which we already encountered in explaining how straws work—is the very existence of pressure. **Pressure** is the result of the constant collisions between the atoms or molecules in a gas and the surfaces around them. Because of pressure, we can drink from straws, inflate basketballs, and move air into and out of our lungs. Variation in pressure in Earth's atmosphere creates wind, and changes in pressure help predict weather. Pressure is all around us and even inside us. The pressure exerted by a gas sample is defined as the force per unit area that results from the collisions of gas particles with surrounding surfaces.

$$\text{Pressure} = \frac{\text{Force}}{\text{Area}}$$

The pressure exerted by a gas depends on several factors, including the number of gas particles in a given volume (◀ Figure 11.8). The fewer the gas particles, the lower the pressure. Pressure decreases, for example, with increasing altitude. As we climb a mountain or ascend in an airplane, there are fewer molecules per unit volume in air and the pressure consequently drops. For this reason, most airplane cabins are artificially pressurized (see the *Everyday Chemistry* box on page 366.)

You may feel the effect of a drop in pressure as a pain in your ears. This pain is caused by air-containing cavities within your ear (▶ Figure 11.9). When you climb a mountain, for example, the external pressure (that pressure that surrounds you) drops while the pressure within your ear cavities (the internal pressure) remains the same. This creates an imbalance—the lower external pressure causes your eardrum to bulge outward, causing pain. With time and a yawn or two, the excess air within your ears' cavities escapes, equalizing the internal and external pressure and relieving the pain.

Lower pressure

Higher pressure

◀ **FIGURE 11.8 Pressure** Since pressure is a result of collisions between gas particles and the surfaces around them, the amount of pressure increases when the number of particles in a given volume increases (assuming constant temperature).

▶ FIGURE 11.9 **Pressure imbalance** The pain you feel in your ears upon climbing a mountain or ascending in an airplane is caused by an imbalance of pressure between the cavities inside your ear and the outside air.

Higher pressure

Lower pressure

✓ **CONCEPTUAL CHECKPOINT 11.1**

Which sample of an ideal gas has the *lowest* pressure? Assume that all of the particles are identical and that the three samples are at the same temperature.

(a)   (b)   (c)

Vacuum

Glass tube

760 mm
(29.92 in.)

Atmospheric pressure

Mercury

▶ FIGURE 11.10 **The mercury barometer** Average atmospheric pressure at sea level pushes a column of mercury to a height of 760 mm (29.92 in.). **Question:** What happens to the height of the mercury column if the external pressure decreases? increases?

Pressure Units

The simplest unit of pressure is the **atmosphere (atm)**, the average pressure at sea level. The SI unit of pressure is the **pascal (Pa)**, defined as 1 newton (N) per square meter.

$$1 \, \text{Pa} = 1 \, \text{N/m}^2$$

The pascal is a much smaller unit of pressure; 1 atm is equal to 101,325 Pa.

$$1 \, \text{atm} = 101{,}325 \, \text{Pa}$$

The pressure in a fully inflated mountain bike tire is about 6 atm, and the pressure on top of Mount Everest is about 0.31 atm.

A third unit of pressure, the **millimeter of mercury (mm Hg)**, originates from how pressure is measured with a barometer (◀ Figure 11.10). A barometer is an evacuated glass tube whose tip is submerged in a pool of mercury. As described in Section 11.1, liquid is pushed up an evacuated tube by the atmospheric pressure on the liquid's surface. We learned that water is pushed up to a height of 10.3 m by the average pressure at sea level. Mercury, however, with its higher density, is

Since mercury is 13.5 times as dense as water, it is pushed up 1/13.5 times as high as water by atmospheric pressure.

pushed up to a height of only 0.760 m, or 760 mm, by the average pressure at sea level. This shorter length—0.760 m instead of 10.3 m—makes a column of mercury a convenient way to measure pressure.

In a barometer, the mercury column rises or falls with changes in atmospheric pressure. If the pressure increases, the level of mercury within the column rises. If the pressure decreases, the level of mercury within the column falls. Since 1 atm of pressure pushes a column of mercury to a height of 760 mm, 1 atm and 760 mm Hg are equal.

$$1 \text{ atm} = 760 \text{ mm Hg}$$

A millimeter of mercury is also called a **torr**, after Italian physicist Evangelista Torricelli (1608–1647), who invented the barometer.

$$1 \text{ mm Hg} = 1 \text{ torr}$$

Other common units of pressure include inches of mercury (in. Hg) and **pounds per square inch (psi)**.

$$1 \text{ atm} = 29.92 \text{ in. Hg} \qquad 1 \text{ atm} = 14.7 \text{ psi}$$

Inches of mercury is still a widely used unit in weather reports. You have probably heard a weather forecaster say, "The barometer is 30.07 and rising," meaning that the atmospheric pressure is currently 30.07 in. Hg.

Table 11.1 lists the common units of pressure.

TABLE 11.1 Common Units of Pressure

Unit	Average Air Pressure at Sea Level
pascal (Pa)	101,325 Pa
atmosphere (atm)	1 atm
millimeter of mercury (mm Hg)	760 mm Hg (exact)
torr (torr)	760 torr (exact)
pounds per square inch (psi)	14.7 psi
inches of mercury (in. Hg)	29.92 in. Hg

 CONCEPTUAL CHECKPOINT 11.2

A liquid that is about twice as dense as water is used in a barometer. With this barometer, normal atmospheric pressure would be about:
(a) 0.38 m   **(b)** 1.52 m   **(c)** 5.15 m   **(d)** 20.6 m

See Section 2.6 for a review on converting between units.

Pressure Unit Conversion

We convert one pressure unit to another in the same way that we converted between other units in Chapter 2. For example, suppose we want to convert 0.311 atm (the approximate average pressure at the top of Mount Everest) to millimeters of mercury. We begin by sorting the information in the problem statement.

GIVEN: 0.311 atm

FIND: mm Hg

SOLUTION MAP
We then strategize by building a solution map that shows how to convert from atm to mm Hg.

$$\frac{760 \text{ mm Hg}}{1 \text{ atm}}$$

RELATIONSHIPS USED

$$1 \text{ atm} = 760 \text{ mm Hg (from Table 11.1)}$$

SOLUTION
The solution begins with the given value (0.311 atm) and converts it to mm Hg.

$$0.311 \text{ atm} \times \frac{760 \text{ mm Hg}}{1 \text{ atm}} = 236 \text{ mm Hg}$$

| EXAMPLE 11.1 | CONVERTING BETWEEN PRESSURE UNITS |

A high-performance road bicycle tire is inflated to a total pressure of 125 psi. What is this pressure in millimeters of mercury?

SORT You are given a pressure in psi and asked to convert it to mm Hg.	**GIVEN:** 125 psi **FIND:** mm Hg
STRATEGIZE Begin the solution map with the given units of psi. Use the conversion factors to convert first to atm and then to mm Hg.	**SOLUTION MAP** $$\frac{1\ atm}{14.7\ psi} \qquad \frac{760\ mm\ Hg}{1\ atm}$$ **RELATIONSHIPS USED** 1 atm = 14.7 psi (Table 11.1) 760 mm Hg = 1 atm (Table 11.1)
SOLVE Follow the solution map to solve the problem.	**SOLUTION** $$125\ \text{psi} \times \frac{1\ \text{atm}}{14.7\ \text{psi}} \times \frac{760\ \text{mm Hg}}{1\ \text{atm}} = 6.46 \times 10^3\ \text{mm Hg}$$
CHECK Check your answer. Are the units correct? Does the answer make physical sense?	The answer has the correct units, mm Hg. The answer is reasonable because the mm Hg is a smaller unit than psi; therefore the value of the pressure in mm Hg should be greater than the value of the same pressure in psi.

▶**SKILLBUILDER 11.1 | Converting between Pressure Units**

Convert a pressure of 173 in. Hg into pounds per square inch.

▶**SKILLBUILDER PLUS** Convert a pressure of 23.8 in. Hg into kilopascals.

▶**FOR MORE PRACTICE**   Example 11.13; Problems 23, 24, 25, 26, 29, 30, 31, 32.

11.4 Boyle's Law: Pressure and Volume

LO: Restate and apply Boyle's law.

The pressure of a gas sample depends, in part, on its volume. If the temperature and the amount of gas are constant, the pressure of a gas sample *increases* for a *decrease* in volume and *decreases* for an *increase* in volume. A simple hand pump, for example, works on this principle. A hand pump is basically a cylinder equipped with a moveable piston (▶ Figure 11.11). The volume in the cylinder increases when you pull the handle up (the upstroke) and decreases when you push the handle down (the downstroke). On the upstroke, the *increasing* volume causes a *decrease* in the internal pressure (the pressure within the pump's cylinder). This, in turn, draws air into the pump's cylinder through a one-way valve. On the downstroke, the *decreasing* volume causes an *increase* in the internal pressure. This increase forces the air out of the pump, through a different one-way valve, and into the tire or whatever else is being inflated.

The relationships between gas properties—such as the relationship between pressure and volume—are described by gas laws. These laws show how a change in one of these properties affects one or more of the others. The relationship between volume and pressure was discovered by Robert Boyle (1627–1691) and is called **Boyle's law**.

Boyle's law: The volume of a gas and its pressure are inversely proportional.

Boyle's law assumes constant temperature and a constant number of gas particles.

$$V \propto \frac{1}{P} \qquad \propto \text{ means ``proportional to''}$$

EVERYDAY CHEMISTRY

▶ Airplane Cabin Pressurization

Most commercial airplanes fly at elevations between 25,000 and 40,000 ft. At these elevations, atmospheric pressure is below 0.50 atm, much less than the normal atmospheric pressure to which our bodies are accustomed. The physiological effects of these lowered pressures—and the correspondingly lowered oxygen levels (see Section 11.9)—include dizziness, headache, shortness of breath, and even unconsciousness. Consequently, commercial airplanes pressurize the air in their cabins. If, for some reason, an airplane cabin should lose its pressurization, passengers are directed to breathe oxygen through an oxygen mask.

Cabin air pressurization is accomplished as part of the cabin's overall air circulation system. As air flows into the plane's jet engines, the large turbines at the front of the engines compress it. Most of this compressed (or pressurized) air exits out the back of the engines, creating the thrust that drives the plane forward. However, some of the pressurized air is directed into the cabin, where it is cooled and mixed with existing cabin air. This air is then circulated through the cabin through the overhead vents. The air leaves the cabin through ducts that direct it into the lower portion of the airplane. About half of this exiting air is mixed with incoming, pressurized air to circulate again. The other half is vented out of the plane through an outflow valve. This valve is adjusted to maintain the desired cabin pressure. Federal regulations require that cabin pressure in commercial airliners be greater than the equivalent of outside air pressure at 8000 ft. Some newer jets, such as the Boeing 787 Dreamliner, pressurize their cabins at an equivalent pressure of 6000 ft for greater passenger comfort.

B11.1 CAN YOU ANSWER THIS? *Atmospheric pressure at elevations of 8000 ft averages about 0.72 atm. Convert this pressure to millimeters of mercury, inches of mercury, and pounds per square inch. Would a cabin pressurized at 500 mm Hg meet federal standards?*

◀ Commercial airplane cabins must be pressurized to a pressure greater than the equivalent atmospheric pressure at an elevation of 8000 ft.

One-way valve

Upstroke	Downstroke
Volume increases	Volume decreases
Pressure decreases	Pressure increases

If two quantities are inversely proportional, increasing one decreases the other (▶ Figure 11.12). As we saw for the hand pump, when the volume of a gas sample is decreased, its pressure increases and vice versa. Kinetic molecular theory explains the observed change in pressure. If the volume of a gas sample is decreased, the same number of gas particles is crowded into a smaller volume, causing more collisions with the walls of the container and therefore increasing the pressure (▶ Figure 11.13).

Scuba divers learn about Boyle's law during certification courses because it explains why ascending too quickly toward the surface is dangerous. For every 10 m of depth that a diver descends in water, he experiences an additional 1 atm of pressure due to the weight of the water above him (▶ Figure 11.14). The pressure regulator used in scuba diving delivers air at a pressure that matches the external pressure;

◀ **FIGURE 11.11 Operation of a hand pump**

► **FIGURE 11.12 Volume versus pressure** (a) We can use a J-tube to measure the volume of a gas at different pressures. Adding mercury to the J-tube causes the pressure on the gas sample to increase and its volume to decrease. (b) A plot of the volume of a gas as a function of pressure.

As pressure increases, volume decreases

Added mercury increases pressure on gas sample

As pressure increases, volume decreases

(a) (b)

► **FIGURE 11.13 Volume versus pressure: a molecular view** As the volume of a sample of gas is decreased, the number of collisions between the gas molecules and each square meter of the container increases. This raises the pressure exerted by the gas.

$P = 1$ atm $P = 2$ atm

$V = 1$ L $V = 0.5$ L

Depth = 0 m
$P = 1$ atm

Depth = 20 m
$P = 3$ atm

otherwise the diver could not inhale the air (see the *Everyday Chemistry* box on page 370). For example, when a diver is at 20 m of depth, the regulator delivers air at a pressure of 3 atm to match the 3 atm of pressure around the diver—1 atm due to normal atmospheric pressure and 2 additional atmospheres due to the weight of the water at 20 m (► Figure 11.15).

Suppose that a diver inhales a lungful of 3-atm air and swims quickly to the surface (where the pressure drops to 1 atm) while holding his breath. What happens to the volume of air in his lungs? Since the pressure decreases by a factor of 3, the volume of the air in his lungs increases by a factor of 3, severely damaging his lungs and possibly killing him. The volume increase in the diver's lungs would be so great that the diver would not be able to hold his breath all the way to the surface—the air would force itself out of his mouth. So the most important rule in diving is *never hold your breath*. Divers must ascend slowly

◄ **FIGURE 11.14 Pressure at depth** For every 10 m of depth, a diver experiences an additional 1 atm of pressure due to the weight of the water surrounding him. At 20 m, the diver experiences a total pressure of 3 atm (1 atm from atmospheric pressure plus an additional 2 atm from the weight of the water).

▶ **FIGURE 11.15**
The dangers of decompression (a) A diver at 20 m experiences an external pressure of 3 atm and breathes air pressurized at 3 atm.
(b) If the diver shoots toward the surface with lungs full of 3 atm air, his lungs will expand as the external pressure drops to 1 atm.

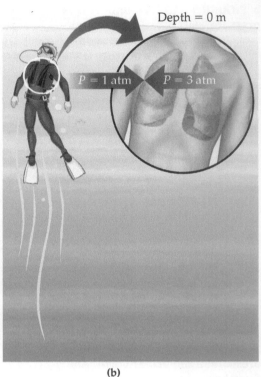

(a)   (b)

and breathe continuously, allowing the regulator to bring the air pressure in their lungs back to 1 atm by the time they reach the surface.

We can use Boyle's law to calculate the volume of a gas following a pressure change or the pressure of a gas following a volume change *as long as the temperature and the amount of gas remain constant*. For these calculations, we write Boyle's law in a slightly different way.

$$\text{Since } V \propto \frac{1}{P}, \text{ then } V = \frac{\text{Constant}}{P}$$

If we multiply both sides by P, we get:

$$PV = \text{Constant}$$

This relationship is true because if the pressure increases, the volume decreases, but the product $P \times V$ is always equal to the same constant. For two different sets of conditions, we can say that

$$P_1V_1 = \text{Constant} = P_2V_2, \text{ or}$$

$$P_1V_1 = P_2V_2$$

where P_1 and V_1 are the initial pressure and volume of the gas, and P_2 and V_2 are the final volume and pressure. For example, suppose we want to calculate the pressure of a gas that was initially at 765 mm Hg and 1.78 L and later compressed to 1.25 L. We first sort the information in the problem.

GIVEN: $P_1 = 765$ mm Hg
$V_1 = 1.78$ L
$V_2 = 1.25$ L

FIND: P_2

Based on Boyle's law, and before doing any calculations, do you expect P_2 to be greater than or less than P_1?

SOLUTION MAP

We then draw a solution map showing how the equation takes us from the given quantities (what we have) to the find quantity (what we want to find).

$$P_1V_1 = P_2V_2 \quad \text{Equation relating them}$$

RELATIONSHIPS USED

$$P_1V_1 = P_2V_2 \text{ (Boyle's law, presented in this section)}$$

SOLUTION

We then solve the equation for the quantity we are trying to find (P_2).

$$P_1V_1 = P_2V_2$$

$$P_2 = \frac{P_1V_1}{V_2}$$

Lastly, we substitute the numerical values into the equation and calculate the answer.

$$P_2 = \frac{P_1V_1}{V_2} = \frac{(765 \text{ mm Hg})(1.78 \text{ L})}{1.25 \text{ L}}$$

$$= 1.09 \times 10^3 \text{ mm Hg}$$

EXAMPLE 11.2   BOYLE'S LAW

A cylinder equipped with a moveable piston has an applied pressure of 4.0 atm and a volume of 6.0 L. What is the volume of the cylinder if the applied pressure is decreased to 1.0 atm?

SORT	
You are given an initial pressure, an initial volume, and a final pressure. You are asked to find the final volume.	**GIVEN:** $P_1 = 4.0$ atm $V_1 = 6.0$ L $P_2 = 1.0$ atm **FIND:** V_2

STRATEGIZE	
Draw a solution map beginning with the given quantities. Boyle's law shows the relationship necessary to get to the find quantity.	**SOLUTION MAP** $$P_1V_1 = P_2V_2$$ **RELATIONSHIPS USED** $P_1V_1 = P_2V_2$ (Boyle's law, presented in this section)

SOLVE	
Solve the equation for the quantity you are trying to find (V_2), and substitute the numerical quantities into the equation to calculate the answer.	**SOLUTION** $$P_1V_1 = P_2V_2$$ $$V_2 = \frac{V_1P_1}{P_2}$$ $$= \frac{(6.0 \text{ L})(4.0 \text{ atm})}{1.0 \text{ atm}}$$ $$= 24 \text{ L}$$

CHECK	
Check your answer. Are the units correct? Does the answer make physical sense?	The answer has units of volume (L) as expected. The answer is reasonable because you expect the volume to increase as the pressure decreases.

▶SKILLBUILDER 11.2 | Boyle's Law

A snorkeler takes a syringe filled with 16 mL of air from the surface, where the pressure is 1.0 atm, to an unknown depth. The volume of the air in the syringe at this depth is 7.5 mL. What is the pressure at this depth? If pressure increases by an additional 1 atm for every 10 m of depth, how deep is the snorkeler?

▶FOR MORE PRACTICE   Example 11.14; Problems 33, 34, 35, 36.

✓ CONCEPTUAL CHECKPOINT 11.3

A flask contains a gas sample at pressure x. If the volume of the container triples at constant temperature and constant amount of gas, the pressure becomes:

(a) $3x$ (b) $\frac{1}{3}x$ (c) $9x$

EVERYDAY CHEMISTRY

▶ Extra-long Snorkels

Several episodes of *The Flintstones* featured Fred Flintstone and Barney Rubble snorkeling. Their snorkels, however, were not the modern kind, but long reeds that stretched from the surface of the water down to many meters of depth. Fred and Barney swam around in deep water while breathing air provided to them by these extra-long snorkels. Would this work? Why do people bother with scuba diving equipment if they could simply use 10-m snorkels like Fred and Barney did?

When we breathe, we expand the volume of our lungs, lowering the pressure within them (Boyle's law). Air from outside our lungs then flows into them. Extra-long snorkels, such as those used by Fred and Barney, do not work because of the pressure caused by water at depth. A diver at 10 m experiences a pressure of 2 atm that compresses the air in his lungs to a pressure of 2 atm. If the diver had a snorkel that went to the surface—where the air pressure is 1 atm—air would flow out of his lungs, not into them. It would be impossible to breathe.

B11.2 CAN YOU ANSWER THIS? *Suppose a diver takes a balloon with a volume of 2.5 L from the surface, where the pressure is 1.0 atm, to a depth of 20 m, where the pressure is 3.0 atm. What would happen to the volume of the balloon? What if the end of the balloon was on a long tube that went to the surface and was attached to another balloon, as shown in the drawing below? Which way would air flow as the diver descends?*

◀ Fred and Barney used reeds to breathe air from the surface, even when they were at depth. This would not work because the pressure at depth would push air out of their lungs, preventing them from breathing.

▶ If one end of a long tube with balloons tied on both ends is submerged in water, in which direction does air flow?

11.5   Charles's Law: Volume and Temperature

LO: Restate and apply Charles's law.

Recall from Section 2.9 that Density = Mass/Volume. If the volume increases and the mass remains constant, the density must decrease.

Have you ever noticed that hot air rises? You may have walked upstairs in your house and noticed it getting warmer. Or you may have witnessed a hot-air balloon take flight. The air that fills a hot-air balloon is warmed with a burner, which causes the balloon to rise in the cooler air around it. Why does hot air rise? Hot air rises because the volume of a gas sample at constant pressure increases with increasing temperature. As long as the amount of gas (and therefore its mass) remains constant, warming decreases its density because density is mass divided by volume. A lower-density gas floats in a higher-density gas just as wood floats in water.

Suppose we keep the pressure of a gas sample constant and measure its volume at a number of different temperatures. The results of a number of such measurements are shown in ▼ Figure 11.16. The plot reveals the relationship between volume and temperature: The volume of a gas increases with increasing temperature. Note also that temperature and volume are *linearly related*. If two variables are linearly related, plotting one against the other produces a straight line.

▲ Heating the air in a balloon makes it expand (Charles's law). As the volume occupied by the hot air increases, its density decreases, allowing the balloon to float in the cooler, denser air that surrounds it.

The extrapolated line cannot be measured experimentally because all gases condense into liquids before −273 °C is reached.

Section 3.10 summarizes the three different temperature scales.

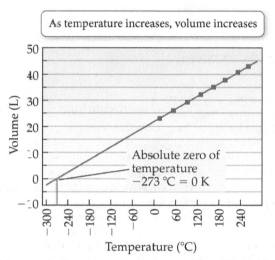

▲ **FIGURE 11.16   Volume versus temperature** The volume of a gas increases linearly with increasing temperature. **Question: How does this graph demonstrate that −273 °C is the coldest possible temperature?**

We can predict an important property of matter by extending the line on our plot backward from the lowest measured point—a process called *extrapolation*. Our extrapolated line shows that the gas should have a zero volume at −273 °C. Recall from Chapter 3 that −273 °C corresponds to 0 K, the coldest possible temperature. Our extrapolated line shows that below −273 °C, our gas would have a negative volume, which is physically impossible. For this reason, we refer to 0 K as **absolute zero**—colder temperatures do not exist.

The first person to carefully quantify the relationship between the volume of a gas and its temperature was J. A. C. Charles (1746–1823), a French mathematician and physicist. Charles was interested in gases and was among the first people to ascend in a hydrogen-filled balloon. The law he formulated is called **Charles's law.**

Charles's law assumes constant pressure and a constant amount of gas.

Charles's law: The volume (V) of a gas and its Kelvin temperature (T) are directly proportional.

$$V \propto T$$

If two variables are directly proportional, increasing one by some factor increases the other by the same factor. For example, when the temperature of a gas sample (in kelvins) is doubled, its volume doubles; when the temperature is tripled, its volume triples; and so on. The observed relationship between the temperature and volume of a gas follows from kinetic molecular theory. If the temperature of a gas sample increases, the gas particles move faster (they have more kinetic energy), and if the pressure is to remain constant, the volume must increase (▼ Figure 11.17).

You can experience Charles's law directly by holding a partially inflated balloon over a warm toaster. As the air in the balloon warms, you can feel the balloon expanding. Alternatively, you can put an inflated balloon in the freezer or take it outside on a very cold day (below freezing) and see that it becomes smaller as it cools.

We can use Charles's law to calculate the volume of a gas following a temperature change or the temperature of a gas following a volume change as *long as the pressure and the amount of gas are constant*. For these calculations, we express Charles's law in a different way.

▲ If you hold a partially inflated balloon over a warm toaster, the balloon will expand as the air within the balloon warms.

Since $V \propto T$, then $V = \text{Constant} \times T$

If we divide both sides by T, we get:

$$\frac{V}{T} = \text{Constant}$$

If the temperature increases, the volume increases in direct proportion so that the quotient, V/T, is always equal to the same constant. So, for two different measurements, we can say that

$$\frac{V_1}{T_1} = \text{Constant} = \frac{V_2}{T_2}, \text{ or}$$

$$\frac{V_1}{T_1} = \frac{V_2}{T_2}$$

As temperature increases, the volume of the balloon increases

Ice water

Boiling water

▲ **FIGURE 11.17 Volume versus temperature: a molecular view** If a balloon is moved from an ice-water bath into a boiling-water bath, the gas molecules inside it move faster (they have more kinetic energy) due to the increased temperature. If the external pressure remains constant, the molecules will expand the balloon and collectively occupy a larger volume.

where V_1 and T_1 are the initial volume and temperature of the gas and V_2 and T_2 are the final volume and temperature. *All temperatures must be expressed in kelvins.*

For example, suppose we have a 2.37-L sample of a gas at 298 K that is then heated to 354 K with no change in pressure. To determine the final volume of the gas, we begin by sorting the information in the problem statement.

Based on Charles's law, and before doing any calculations, do you expect V_2 to be greater than or less than V_1?

GIVEN: $T_1 = 298 \text{ K}$

$V_1 = 2.37 \text{ L}$

$T_2 = 354 \text{ K}$

FIND: V_2

SOLUTION MAP

We then strategize by building a solution map that shows how the equation takes us from the given quantities to the unknown quantity.

RELATIONSHIPS USED

$$\frac{V_1}{T_1} = \frac{V_2}{T_2} \text{ (Charles's law, presented in this section)}$$

SOLUTION

We then solve the equation for the quantity we are trying to find (V_2).

$$\frac{V_1}{T_1} = \frac{V_2}{T_2}$$

$$V_2 = \frac{V_1}{T_1} T_2$$

Lastly, we substitute the numerical values into the equation and calculate the answer.

$$V_2 = \frac{V_1}{T_1} T_2$$

$$= \frac{2.37 \text{ L}}{298 \text{ K}} 354 \text{ K}$$

$$= 2.82 \text{ L}$$

EXAMPLE 11.3 CHARLES'S LAW

A sample of gas has a volume of 2.80 L at an unknown temperature. When the sample is submerged in ice water at $t = 0\,°C$, its volume decreases to 2.57 L. What was its initial temperature (in kelvins and in Celsius)? Assume a constant pressure. (To distinguish between the two temperature scales, use t for temperature in °C and T for temperature in K.)

SORT You are given an initial volume, a final volume, and a final temperature. You are asked to find the intitial temperature in both kelvins (T_1) and degrees Celsius (t_1).	**GIVEN:** $V_1 = 2.80\text{ L}$ $\qquad\quad V_2 = 2.57\text{ L}$ $\qquad\quad t_2 = 0\,°C$ **FIND:** T_1 and t_1
STRATEGIZE Draw a solution map beginning with the given quantities. Charles's law shows the relationship necessary to get to the find quantity.	**SOLUTION MAP** 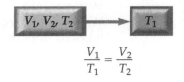 $$\frac{V_1}{T_1} = \frac{V_2}{T_2}$$ **RELATIONSHIPS USED** $$\frac{V_1}{T_1} = \frac{V_2}{T_2} \quad \text{(Charles's law, presented in this section)}$$
SOLVE Solve the equation for the quantity you are trying to find (T_1). Before you substitute in the numerical values, you need to convert the temperature to kelvins. *Remember, you must always work gas law problems using Kelvin temperatures.* Once you have converted the temperature to kelvins, substitute into the equation to find T_1. Convert the temperature to degrees Celsius to find t_1.	**SOLUTION** $$\frac{V_1}{T_1} = \frac{V_2}{T_2}$$ $$T_1 = \frac{V_1}{V_2}\,T_2$$ $$T_2 = 0 + 273 = 273\text{ K}$$ $$T_1 = \frac{V_1}{V_2}\,T_2$$ $$= \frac{2.80\text{ L}}{2.57\text{ L}}\,273\text{ K}$$ $$= 297\text{ K}$$ $$t_1 = 297 - 273 = 24\,°C$$
CHECK Check your answer. Are the units correct? Does the answer make physical sense?	The answers have the correct units, K and °C. The answer is reasonable because the initial volume was larger than the final volume; therefore the initial temperature must be higher than the final temperature.

▶**SKILLBUILDER 11.3 | Charles's Law**

A gas in a cylinder with a moveable piston has an initial volume of 88.2 mL and is heated from 35 °C to 155 °C. What is the final volume of the gas in milliliters?

▶**FOR MORE PRACTICE**   Problems 39, 40, 41, 42.

CONCEPTUAL CHECKPOINT 11.4

A volume of gas is confined to a cylinder with a freely moveable piston at one end. If you apply enough heat to double the Kelvin temperature of the gas, what happens? (Assume constant pressure.)

(a) the volume doubles

(b) the volume remains the same

(c) the volume falls to half of the initial volume

11.6   The Combined Gas Law: Pressure, Volume, and Temperature

LO: Restate and apply the combined gas law.

Boyle's law shows how P and V are related at constant temperature, and Charles's law shows how V and T are related at constant pressure. But what if two of these variables change at once? For example, what happens to the volume of a gas if both its pressure and its temperature are changed?

Since volume is inversely proportional to pressure ($V \propto 1/P$) and directly proportional to temperature ($V \propto T$), we can write:

$$V \propto \frac{T}{P} \quad \text{or} \quad \frac{PV}{T} = \text{Constant}$$

For a sample of gas under two different sets of conditions we use the **combined gas law**.

The combined gas law encompasses both Boyle's law and Charles's law, and we can use it in place of them. If one physical property (P, V, or T) is constant, it cancels out of our calculations when we use the combined gas law.

The combined gas law: $\dfrac{P_1 V_1}{T_1} = \dfrac{P_2 V_2}{T_2}$

The combined gas law applies only when the *amount* of gas is constant. We must express the temperature (as with Charles's law) in kelvins.

Suppose a person carries a cylinder with a moveable piston that has an initial volume of 3.65 L up a mountain. The pressure at the bottom of the mountain is 755 mm Hg, and the temperature is 302 K. The pressure at the top of the mountain is 687 mm Hg, and the temperature is 291 K. What is the volume of the cylinder at the top of the mountain? We begin by sorting the information in the problem statement.

GIVEN: $P_1 = 755$ mm Hg $T_2 = 291$ K

$V_1 = 3.65$ L $P_2 = 687$ mm Hg

$T_1 = 302$ K

FIND: V_2

SOLUTION MAP

We strategize by building a solution map that shows how the combined gas law equation takes us from the given quantities to the find quantity.

RELATIONSHIPS USED

$\dfrac{P_1 V_1}{T_1} = \dfrac{P_2 V_2}{T_2}$ (combined gas law, presented in this section)

SOLUTION

We then solve the equation for the quantity we are trying to find (V_2).

$$\frac{P_1 V_1}{T_1} = \frac{P_2 V_2}{T_2}$$

$$V_2 = \frac{P_1 V_1 T_2}{T_1 P_2}$$

Lastly, we substitute in the appropriate values and calculate the answer.

$$V_2 = \frac{P_1 V_1 T_2}{T_1 P_2}$$

$$= \frac{755 \text{ mm Hg} \times 3.65 \text{ L} \times 291 \text{ K}}{302 \text{ K} \times 687 \text{ mm Hg}}$$

$$= 3.87 \text{ L}$$

EXAMPLE 11.4 THE COMBINED GAS LAW

A sample of gas has an initial volume of 158 mL at a pressure of 735 mm Hg and a temperature of 34 °C. If the gas is compressed to a volume of 108 mL and heated to a temperature of 85 °C, what is its final pressure in millimeters of mercury?

SORT You are given an initial pressure, temperature, and volume as well as a final temperature and volume. You are asked to find the final pressure.	**GIVEN:** $P_1 = 735$ mm Hg $\qquad\quad t_1 = 34\,°C \qquad\quad t_2 = 85\,°C$ $\qquad\quad V_1 = 158$ mL $\quad V_2 = 108$ mL **FIND:** P_2
STRATEGIZE Draw a solution map beginning with the given quantities. The combined gas law shows the relationship necessary to get to the find quantity.	**SOLUTION MAP** $$\frac{P_1 V_1}{T_1} = \frac{P_2 V_2}{T_2}$$ **RELATIONSHIPS USED** $\dfrac{P_1 V_1}{T_1} = \dfrac{P_2 V_2}{T_2}$ (combined gas law, presented in this section)
SOLVE Solve the equation for the quantity you are trying to find (P_2). Before you substitute in the numerical values, you must convert the temperatures to kelvins. Once you have converted the temperature to kelvins, substitute into the equation to find P_2.	**SOLUTION** $$\frac{P_1 V_1}{T_1} = \frac{P_2 V_2}{T_2}$$ $$P_2 = \frac{P_1 V_1 T_2}{T_1 V_2}$$ $T_1 = 34 + 273 = 307$ K $T_2 = 85 + 273 = 358$ K $$P_2 = \frac{735 \text{ mm Hg} \times 158 \text{ mL} \times 358 \text{ K}}{307 \text{ K} \times 108 \text{ mL}}$$ $$= 1.25 \times 10^3 \text{ mm Hg}$$
CHECK Check your answer. Are the units correct? Does the answer make physical sense?	The answer has the correct units, mm Hg. The answer is reasonable because the decrease in volume and the increase in temperature should result in a pressure that is higher than the initial pressure.

▶**SKILLBUILDER 11.4 | The Combined Gas Law**

A balloon has a volume of 3.7 L at a pressure of 1.1 atm and a temperature of 30°C. If the balloon is submerged in water to a depth where the pressure is 4.7 atm and the temperature is 15°C, what will its volume be (assume that any changes in pressure caused by the skin of the balloon are negligible)?

▶**FOR MORE PRACTICE** Example 11.15; Problems 51, 52, 53, 54, 55, 56.

  CONCEPTUAL CHECKPOINT 11.5

A volume of gas is confined to a container. If you apply enough heat to double the Kelvin temperature of the gas and expand the size of the container to double its initial volume, what happens to the pressure?

(a) the pressure doubles

(b) the pressure falls to half of its initial value

(c) the pressure is the same as its initial value

11.7 Avogadro's Law: Volume and Moles

LO: Restate and apply Avogadro's law.

So far, we have learned how V, P, and T are interrelated, but we have considered only a constant amount of a gas. What happens when the amount of gas changes? If we make several measurements of the volume of a gas sample (at constant temperature and pressure) while varying the number of moles in the sample, we get results similar to those shown in ▼ Figure 11.18. We can see that the relationship between volume and number of moles is linear. An extrapolation to zero moles shows a zero volume, as we might expect. This relationship was first stated formally by Amedeo Avogadro (1776–1856) and is called **Avogadro's law**.

> Avogadro's law assumes constant temperature and pressure.

Avogadro's law: The volume of a gas and the amount of the gas in moles (n) are directly proportional.

$$V \propto n$$

> Since $V \propto n$, then $V/n =$ Constant. If the number of moles increases, then the volume increases in direct proportion so that the quotient, V/n, is always equal to the same constant. Thus, for two different measurements, we can say that
> $$\frac{V_1}{n_1} = \text{Constant} = \frac{V_2}{n_2} \text{ or } \frac{V_1}{n_1} = \frac{V_2}{n_2}.$$

When the amount of gas in a sample increases, its volume increases in direct proportion, which is yet another prediction of kinetic molecular theory. If the number of gas particles increases at constant pressure and temperature, the particles must occupy more volume.

We experience Avogadro's law when we inflate a balloon, for example. With each exhaled breath, we add more gas particles to the inside of the balloon, increasing its volume (▼ Figure 11.19). We can use Avogadro's law to calculate the volume of a gas following a change in the amount of the gas *as long as the pressure and temperature of the gas are constant*. For these calculations, Avogadro's law is expressed as

$$\frac{V_1}{n_1} = \frac{V_2}{n_2}$$

◀ **FIGURE 11.18 Volume versus number of moles** The volume of a gas sample increases linearly with the number of moles in the sample.

As number of moles increases, volume increases

▶ **FIGURE 11.19 Blow-up** As you exhale into a balloon, you add gas molecules to the inside of the balloon, increasing its volume.

where V_1 and n_1 are the initial volume and number of moles of the gas and V_2 and n_2 are the final volume and number of moles. In calculations, we use Avogadro's law in a manner similar to the other gas laws, as shown in Example 11.5.

EXAMPLE 11.5 | AVOGADRO'S LAW

A 4.8-L sample of helium gas contains 0.22 mol of helium. How many additional moles of helium gas should you add to the sample to obtain a volume of 6.4 L? Assume constant temperature and pressure.

SORT You are given an initial volume, an initial number of moles, and a final volume. You are (essentially) asked to find the final number of moles.	**GIVEN:** $V_1 = 4.8 \text{ L}$ $n_1 = 0.22 \text{ mol}$ $V_2 = 6.4 \text{ L}$ **FIND:** n_2
STRATEGIZE Draw a solution map beginning with the given quantities. Avogadro's law addresses the relationship necessary to get to the find quantity.	**SOLUTION MAP** $$\frac{V_1}{n_1} = \frac{V_2}{n_2}$$ **RELATIONSHIPS USED** $$\frac{V_1}{n_1} = \frac{V_2}{n_2}$$ (Avogadro's law, presented in this section)
SOLVE Solve the equation for the quantity you are trying to find (n_2) and substitute the appropriate quantities to calculate n_2. Since the balloon already contains 0.22 mol, subtract this quantity from the final number of moles to determine how much you must add.	**SOLUTION** $$\frac{V_1}{n_1} = \frac{V_2}{n_2}$$ $$n_2 = \frac{V_2}{V_1} n_1$$ $$= \frac{6.4 \text{ L}}{4.8 \text{ L}} 0.22 \text{ mol}$$ $$= 0.29 \text{ mol}$$ mol to add $= 0.29 \text{ mol} - 0.22 \text{ mol} = 0.07 \text{ mol}$
CHECK Check your answer. Are the units correct? Does the answer make physical sense?	The answer has the correct units, moles. The answer is reasonable because the increase in the number of moles is proportional to the given increase in the volume.

▶**SKILLBUILDER 11.5 | Avogadro's Law**

A chemical reaction occurring in a cylinder equipped with a moveable piston produces 0.58 mol of a gaseous product. If the cylinder contained 0.11 mol of gas before the reaction and had an initial volume of 2.1 L, what was its volume after the reaction?

▶**FOR MORE PRACTICE**   Problems 45, 46, 47, 48.

 CONCEPTUAL CHECKPOINT 11.6

If each gas sample has the same temperature and pressure, which has the greatest volume?

(a) 1 g O_2

(b) 1 g Ar

(c) 1 g H_2

11.8   The Ideal Gas Law: Pressure, Volume, Temperature, and Moles

LO: Restate and apply the ideal gas law.

The relationships covered so far can be combined into a single law that encompasses all of them. So far, we know that:

$$V \propto \frac{1}{P} \quad \text{(Boyle's law)}$$
$$V \propto T \quad \text{(Charles's law)}$$
$$V \propto n \quad \text{(Avogadro's law)}$$

Combining these three expressions, we arrive at:

$$V \propto \frac{nT}{P}$$

The volume of a gas is directly proportional to the number of moles of gas and the temperature of the gas and is inversely proportional to the pressure of the gas. We can replace the proportional sign with an equal sign by adding R, a proportionality constant called the **ideal gas constant**.

$$V = \frac{RnT}{P}$$

Rearranging, we get the **ideal gas law**:

The ideal gas law: $PV = nRT$

The value of R, the ideal gas constant, is:

R can also be expressed in other units, but its numerical value will be different.

$$R = 0.0821 \frac{L \cdot atm}{mol \cdot K}$$

The ideal gas law contains within it the simple gas laws. For example, recall that Boyle's law states that $V \propto 1/P$ when the amount of gas (n) and the temperature of the gas (T) are kept constant. To derive Boyle's law, we can rearrange the ideal gas law as follows:

$$PV = nRT$$

First, divide both sides by P.

$$V = \frac{nRT}{P}$$

Then put the variables that are constant in parentheses.

$$V = (nRT)\frac{1}{P}$$

Since n and T are constant in this case and since R is always a constant,

$$V = (\text{Constant}) \times \frac{1}{P}$$

which gives us Boyle's law $\left(V \propto \frac{1}{P} \right)$.

The ideal gas law also shows how other pairs of variables are related. For example, from Charles's law we know that volume is proportional to temperature at constant pressure and a constant number of moles. But what if we heat a sample of gas at constant *volume* and a constant number of moles? This question applies to the warning labels on aerosol cans such as hair spray or deodorants. These labels warn the user against excessive heating or incineration of the can, even after the contents are used up. Why? An aerosol can that appears empty actually contains a fixed amount of gas trapped in a fixed volume. What would happen if we heated the can? Let's rearrange the ideal gas law to clearly see the relationship between pressure and temperature at constant volume and a constant number of moles.

$$PV = nRT$$

If we divide both sides by V, we get:

$$P = \frac{nRT}{V}$$

$$P = \left(\frac{nR}{V}\right)T$$

The relationship between pressure and temperature is also known as Gay-Lussac's law.

Since n and V are constant and since R is always a constant:

$$P = \text{Constant} \times T$$

As the temperature of a fixed amount of gas in a fixed volume increases, the pressure increases. In an aerosol can, this pressure increase can cause the can to explode, which is why aerosol cans should not be heated or incinerated. Table 11.2 summarizes the relationships between all of the simple gas laws and the ideal gas law.

TABLE 11.2 Relationships between Simple Gas Laws and Ideal Gas Law

Variable Quantities	Constant Quantities	Ideal Gas Law in Form of Variables-Constant	Simple Gas Law	Name of Simple Law
V and P	n and T	$PV = nRT$	$P_1V_1 = P_2V_2$	Boyle's law
V and T	n and P	$\frac{V}{T} = \frac{nR}{P}$	$\frac{V_1}{T_1} = \frac{V_2}{T_2}$	Charles's law
P and T	n and V	$\frac{P}{T} = \frac{nR}{V}$	$\frac{P_1}{T_1} = \frac{P_2}{T_2}$	Gay-Lussac's law
P and n	V and T	$\frac{P}{n} = \frac{RT}{V}$	$\frac{P_1}{n_1} = \frac{P_2}{n_2}$	
V and n	T and P	$\frac{V}{n} = \frac{RT}{P}$	$\frac{V_1}{n_1} = \frac{V_2}{n_2}$	Avogadro's law

We can use the ideal gas law to determine the value of any one of the four variables (P, V, n, or T) given the other three. However, each of the quantities in the ideal gas law *must be expressed* in the units within R.

- Pressure (**P**) must be expressed in atmospheres.
- Volume (**V**) must be expressed in liters.
- Amount of gas (**n**) must be expressed in moles.
- Temperature (**T**) must be expressed in kelvins.

For example, suppose we want to know the pressure of 0.18 mol of a gas in a 1.2-L flask at 298 K. We begin by sorting the information in the problem statement.

GIVEN: $n = 0.18$ mol
$V = 1.2$ L
$T = 298$ K

FIND: P

SOLUTION MAP
We then strategize by drawing a solution map that shows how the ideal gas law takes us from the given quantities to the find quantity.

$PV = nRT$

RELATIONSHIPS USED

$$PV = nRT \text{ (ideal gas law, presented in this section)}$$

SOLUTION

We then solve the equation for the quantity we are trying to find (in this case, P).

$$PV = nRT$$

$$P = \frac{nRT}{V}$$

Next we substitute in the numerical values and calculate the answer.

$$P = \frac{0.18 \text{ mol} \times 0.0821 \dfrac{L \cdot atm}{mol \cdot K} \times 298 \text{ K}}{1.2 \text{ L}}$$

$$= 3.7 \text{ atm}$$

Notice that all units cancel except the units of the quantity we need (atm).

EXAMPLE 11.6   THE IDEAL GAS LAW

▶   Calculate the volume occupied by 0.845 mol of nitrogen gas at a pressure of 1.37 atm and a temperature of 315 K.

SORT You are given the number of moles, the pressure, and the temperature of a gas sample. You are asked to find the volume.	**GIVEN:** $n = 0.845 \text{ mol}$ $P = 1.37 \text{ atm}$ $T = 315 \text{ K}$ **FIND:** V
STRATEGIZE Draw a solution map beginning with the given quantities. The ideal gas law shows the relationship necessary to get to the find quantity.	**SOLUTION MAP** $PV = nRT$ **RELATIONSHIPS USED** $PV = nRT$ (ideal gas law, presented in this section)
SOLVE Solve the equation for the quantity you are trying to find (V) and substitute the appropriate quantities to calculate V.	**SOLUTION** $PV = nRT$ $V = \dfrac{nRT}{P}$ $V = \dfrac{0.845 \text{ mol} \times 0.0821 \dfrac{L \cdot atm}{mol \cdot K} \times 315 \text{ K}}{1.37 \text{ atm}} = 16.0 \text{ L}$
CHECK Check your answer. Are the units correct? Does the answer make physical sense?	The answer has the correct units for volume, liters. The *value* of the answer is a bit more difficult to judge. However, at standard temperature and pressure ($T = 0 \text{ °C}$ or 273.15 K and $P = 1$ atm), 1 mol gas occupies 22.4 L (see Section 11.10). Therefore your answer of 16.0 L seems reasonable for the volume of 0.85 mol of gas under conditions that are not too far from standard temperature and pressure.

▶**SKILLBUILDER 11.6 | The Ideal Gas Law**

An 8.5-L tire is filled with 0.55 mol of gas at a temperature of 305 K. What is the pressure of the gas in the tire?

▶**FOR MORE PRACTICE**   Example 11.16; Problems 59, 60, 61, 62.

If the units given in an ideal gas law problem are different from those of the ideal gas constant (atm, L, mol, and K), we must convert to the correct units before we substitute into the ideal gas equation, as demonstrated in Example 11.7.

EXAMPLE 11.7	THE IDEAL GAS LAW REQUIRING UNIT CONVERSION

Calculate the number of moles of gas in a basketball inflated to a total pressure of 24.2 psi with a volume of 3.2 L at 25 °C.

SORT You are given the pressure, the volume, and the temperature of a gas sample. You are asked to find the number of moles.	**GIVEN:** $P = 24.2$ psi $V = 3.2$ L $t = 25$ °C **FIND:** n
STRATEGIZE Draw a solution map beginning with the given quantities. The ideal gas law shows the relationship necessary to get to the find quantity.	**SOLUTION MAP** $$PV = nRT$$ **RELATIONSHIPS USED** $PV = nRT$ (ideal gas law, presented in this section)
SOLVE Solve the equation for the quantity you are trying to find (n). Before substituting into the equation, convert P and t into the correct units. (Since 1.6462 atm is an intermediate answer, mark the least significant digit, but don't round until the end.) Finally, substitute into the equation to calculate n.	**SOLUTION** $$PV = nRT$$ $$n = \frac{PV}{RT}$$ $$P = 24.2 \text{ psi} \times \frac{1 \text{ atm}}{14.7 \text{ psi}} = 1.6\underline{4}62 \text{ atm}$$ $$T = t + 273$$ $$= 25 + 273 = 298 \text{ K}$$ $$n = \frac{1.6\underline{4}62 \text{ atm} \times 3.2 \text{ L}}{0.0821 \dfrac{\text{L} \cdot \text{atm}}{\text{mol} \cdot \text{K}} \times 298 \text{ K}}$$ $$= 0.22 \text{ mol}$$
CHECK Check your answer. Are the units correct? Does the answer make physical sense?	The answer has the correct units, moles. The *value* of the answer is a bit more difficult to judge. Again, it is helpful to know that at standard temperature and pressure ($T = 0$ °C or 273.15 K and $P = 1$ atm), 1 mol of gas occupies 22.4 L (see Check step in Example 11.6). A 3.2 L sample of gas at standard temperature and pressure (STP) would contain about 0.15 mol; therefore at a greater pressure, the sample should contain a bit more than 0.15 mol, which is consistent with the answer.

▶**SKILLBUILDER 11.7 | The Ideal Gas Law Requiring Unit Conversion**

How much volume does 0.556 mol of gas occupy when its pressure is 715 mm Hg and its temperature is 58 °C?

▶**SKILLBUILDER PLUS**

Find the pressure in millimeters of mercury of a 0.133-g sample of helium gas at 32 °C contained in a 648-mL container.

▶**FOR MORE PRACTICE** Problems 63, 64, 67, 68.

Molar Mass of a Gas from the Ideal Gas Law

We can use the ideal gas law in combination with mass measurements to calculate the molar mass of a gas. For example, a sample of gas has a mass of 0.136 g. Its volume is 0.112 L at a temperature of 298 K and a pressure of 1.06 atm. With this information, we can find its molar mass.

We begin by sorting the information given in the problem.

GIVEN: $m = 0.136$ g $V = 0.112$ L

$T = 298$ K $P = 1.06$ atm

FIND: molar mass (g/mol)

SOLUTION MAP

We strategize by drawing a solution map, which in this case has two parts. In the first part, we use P, V, and T to find the number of moles of gas. In the second part, we use the number of moles of gas and the given mass to find the molar mass.

$$PV = nRT$$

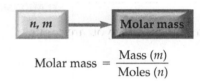

$$\text{Molar mass} = \frac{\text{Mass } (m)}{\text{Moles } (n)}$$

RELATIONSHIPS USED

$$PV = nRT \text{ (ideal gas law, presented in this section)}$$

$$\text{Molar mass} = \frac{\text{Mass}}{\text{Moles}} \text{(definition of molar mass from Section 6.3)}$$

SOLUTION

$$PV = nRT$$

$$n = \frac{PV}{RT}$$

$$= \frac{1.06 \text{ atm} \times 0.112 \text{ L}}{0.0821 \dfrac{\text{L} \cdot \text{atm}}{\text{mol} \cdot \text{K}} \times 298 \text{ K}}$$

$$= 4.8525 \times 10^{-3} \text{ mol}$$

$$\text{Molar mass} = \frac{\text{Mass } (m)}{\text{Moles } (n)}$$

$$= \frac{0.136 \text{ g}}{4.8525 \times 10^{-3} \text{ mol}}$$

$$= 28.0 \text{ g/mol}$$

EXAMPLE 11.8 **MOLAR MASS USING THE IDEAL GAS LAW AND MASS MEASUREMENT**

A sample of gas has a mass of 0.311 g. Its volume is 0.225 L at a temperature of 55 °C and a pressure of 886 mm Hg. Determine its molar mass.

SORT You are given the mass, the volume, the temperature, and the pressure of a gas sample. You are asked to find the molar mass of the gas.	**GIVEN:** $m = 0.311$ g $V = 0.225$ L $t = 55\,°C$ $P = 886$ mm Hg **FIND:** Molar mass (g/mol)
STRATEGIZE In the first part of the solution map, use the ideal gas law to find the number of moles of gas from the other given quantities. In the second part, use the number of moles from the first part, as well as the given mass, to find the molar mass.	**SOLUTION MAP** $$PV = nRT$$ $$\text{Molar mass} = \frac{\text{Mass }(m)}{\text{Moles }(n)}$$ **RELATIONSHIPS USED** $PV = nRT$ (ideal gas law, presented in this section) $\text{Molar mass} = \dfrac{\text{Mass }(m)}{\text{Moles }(n)}$ (definition of molar mass from Section 6.3)
SOLVE First, solve the ideal gas law for n. Before substituting into the equation, convert the pressure to atm and temperature to K. Now, substitute into the equation to calculate n, the number of moles. Finally, use the number of moles just found and the given mass (m) to find the molar mass.	**SOLUTION** $$PV = nRT$$ $$n = \frac{PV}{RT}$$ $$P = 886 \text{ mm Hg} \times \frac{1 \text{ atm}}{760 \text{ mm Hg}} = \underline{1.1658} \text{ atm}$$ $$T = 55\,°C + 273 = 328 \text{ K}$$ $$n = \frac{1.1658 \text{ atm} \times 0.225 \text{ L}}{0.0821 \frac{\text{L} \cdot \text{atm}}{\text{mol} \cdot \text{K}} \times 328 \text{ K}}$$ $$= 9.7\underline{4}06 \times 10^{-3} \text{ mol}$$ $$\text{Molar mass} = \frac{\text{Mass }(m)}{\text{Moles }(n)}$$ $$= \frac{0.311 \text{ g}}{9.7\underline{4}06 \times 10^{-3} \text{ mol}}$$ $$= 31.9 \text{ g/mol}$$
CHECK Check your answer. Are the units correct? Does the answer make physical sense?	The answer has the correct units, g/mol. The answer is reasonable because its value is within the range of molar masses for common compounds.

▶**SKILLBUILDER 11.8** | **Molar Mass Using the Ideal Gas Law and Mass Measurement**

A sample of gas has a mass of 827 mg. Its volume is 0.270 L at a temperature of 88 °C and a pressure of 975 mm Hg. Find its molar mass.

▶**FOR MORE PRACTICE**   Problems 69, 70, 71, 72.

Ideal gas conditions
•High temperature
•Low pressure

•Particle size is small compared to space between particles.
•Interactions between particles are insignificant.

▲ **FIGURE 11.20   Conditions for ideal gas behavior**   At high temperatures and low pressures, the assumptions of the kinetic molecular theory apply.

Although a complete derivation is beyond the scope of this book, the ideal gas law follows directly from the kinetic molecular theory of gases. Consequently, the ideal gas law holds only under conditions where the kinetic molecular theory holds. The ideal gas law works exactly only for gases that are acting ideally (◀ Figure 11.20), which means that (a) the volume of the gas particles is small compared to the space between them and (b) the forces between the gas particles are not significant. These assumptions break down (▼ Figure 11.21) under conditions of high pressure (because the space between particles is no longer much larger than the size of the particles themselves) or low temperatures (because the gas particles move so slowly that their interactions become significant). For all of the problems encountered in this book, you may assume ideal gas behavior.

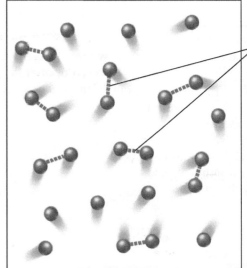

Nonideal gas conditions
•Low temperature
•High pressure

Intermolecular interactions

•Particle size is significant compared to space between particles.
•Interactions between particles are significant.

▶ **FIGURE 11.21   Conditions for nonideal gas behavior**   At low temperatures and high pressures, the assumptions of the kinetic molecular theory do not apply.

11.9   Mixtures of Gases: Why Deep-Sea Divers Breathe a Mixture of Helium and Oxygen

LO: Restate and apply Dalton's law of partial pressures.

Many gas samples are not pure but consist of mixtures of gases. The air in our atmosphere, for example, is a mixture containing 78% nitrogen, 21% oxygen, 0.9% argon, 0.04% carbon dioxide (Table 11.3), and a few other gases in smaller amounts.

According to the kinetic molecular theory, each of the components in a gas mixture acts independently of the others. For example, the nitrogen molecules in air exert a certain pressure—78% of the total pressure—that is independent of the

TABLE 11.3 Composition of Dry Air

Gas	Percent by Volume (%)
nitrogen (N_2)	78
oxygen (O_2)	21
argon (Ar)	0.9
carbon dioxide (CO_2)	0.04

| The fractional composition is the percent composition divided by 100.

Gas mixture (80% He ●, 20% Ne ●)
$P_{tot} = 1.0$ atm
$P_{He} = 0.80$ atm
$P_{Ne} = 0.20$ atm

▲ **FIGURE 11.22 Partial pressures** A gas mixture at a total pressure of 1.0 atm consisting of 80% helium and 20% neon has a helium partial pressure of 0.80 atm and a neon partial pressure of 0.20 atm.

presence of the other gases in the mixture. Likewise, the oxygen molecules in air exert a certain pressure—21% of the total pressure—that is also independent of the presence of the other gases in the mixture. The pressure due to any individual component in a gas mixture is called the **partial pressure** of that component. The partial pressure of any component is that component's fractional composition times the total pressure of the mixture (◄ Figure 11.22).

Partial pressure of component:

= Fractional composition of component × Total pressure

For example, the partial pressure of nitrogen (P_{N_2}) in air at 1.0 atm is:

$$P_{N_2} = 0.78 \times 1.0 \text{ atm}$$

$$= 0.78 \text{ atm}$$

Similarly, the partial pressure of oxygen in air at 1.0 atm is:

$$P_{O_2} = 0.21 \times 1.0 \text{ atm}$$

$$= 0.21 \text{ atm}$$

The sum of the partial pressures of each of the components in a gas mixture must equal the total pressure, as expressed by **Dalton's law of partial pressures**:

Dalton's law of partial pressures:

$$P_{tot} = P_a + P_b + P_c + \dots$$

where P_{tot} is the total pressure and $P_a, P_b, P_c, \dots$ are the partial pressures of the components.

For 1 atm air:

$$P_{tot} = P_{N_2} + P_{O_2} + P_{Ar}$$

$$P_{tot} = 0.78 \text{ atm} + 0.21 \text{ atm} + 0.01 \text{ atm}$$

$$= 1.00 \text{ atm}$$

EXAMPLE 11.9 TOTAL PRESSURE AND PARTIAL PRESSURE

A mixture of helium, neon, and argon has a total pressure of 558 mm Hg. If the partial pressure of helium is 341 mm Hg and the partial pressure of neon is 112 mm Hg, what is the partial pressure of argon?

You are given the total pressure of a gas mixture and the partial pressures of two (of its three) components. You are asked to find the partial pressure of the third component.	**GIVEN:** $P_{tot} = 558$ mm Hg $P_{He} = 341$ mm Hg $P_{Ne} = 112$ mm Hg **FIND:** P_{Ar}
To solve this problem, solve Dalton's law for the partial pressure of argon and substitute the correct values to calculate it.	**SOLUTION** $P_{tot} = P_{He} + P_{Ne} + P_{Ar}$ $P_{Ar} = P_{tot} - P_{He} - P_{Ne}$ $\quad = 558$ mm Hg $- 341$ mm Hg $- 112$ mm Hg $\quad = 105$ mm Hg

> **SKILLBUILDER 11.9 | Total Pressure and Partial Pressure**

A sample of hydrogen gas is mixed with water vapor. The mixture has a total pressure of 745 torr, and the water vapor has a partial pressure of 24 torr. What is the partial pressure of the hydrogen gas?

> **FOR MORE PRACTICE**   Example 11.17; Problems 73, 74, 75, 76.

Deep-Sea Diving and Partial Pressure

Our lungs have evolved to breathe oxygen at a partial pressure of $P_{O_2} = 0.21$ atm. If the total pressure decreases—as happens when we climb a mountain, for example—the partial pressure of oxygen also decreases. For example, on top of Mount Everest, where the total pressure is 0.311 atm, the partial pressure of oxygen is only 0.065 atm. As we learned earlier, low oxygen levels can have negative physiological effects, a condition called **hypoxia**, or oxygen starvation. Mild hypoxia causes dizziness, headache, and shortness of breath. Severe hypoxia, which occurs when P_{O_2} drops below 0.1 atm, may cause unconsciousness or even death. For this reason, climbers hoping to make the summit of Mount Everest usually carry oxygen to breathe.

High oxygen levels can also have negative physiological effects. Scuba divers, as we have learned, breathe pressurized air. At 30 m, a scuba diver breathes air at a total pressure of 4.0 atm, making P_{O_2} about 0.84 atm. This increased partial pressure of oxygen causes a higher density of oxygen molecules in the lungs (▼ Figure 11.23), which results in a higher concentration of oxygen in body tissues. When P_{O_2} increases beyond 1.4 atm, the increased oxygen concentration in body tissues causes a condition called **oxygen toxicity**, which is characterized by muscle twitching, tunnel vision, and convulsions (▶ Figure 11.24). Divers who venture too deep without proper precautions have drowned because of oxygen toxicity.

▲ Mountain climbers on Mount Everest require oxygen because the pressure is so low that the lack of oxygen causes hypoxia, a condition that in severe cases can be fatal.

Surface
$P_{tot} = 1$ atm
$P_{N_2} = 0.78$ atm
$P_{O_2} = 0.21$ atm

30 m
$P_{tot} = 4$ atm
$P_{N_2} = 3.12$ atm
$P_{O_2} = 0.84$ atm

▲ **FIGURE 11.23   Too much of a good thing**   When a person is breathing compressed air, there is a larger partial pressure of oxygen in the lungs. A large oxygen partial pressure in the lungs results in a larger amount of oxygen in bodily tissues. When the oxygen partial pressure increases beyond 1.4 atm, oxygen toxicity results. (In this figure, the red molecules are oxygen and the blue ones are nitrogen.)

▶ **FIGURE 11.24   Oxygen partial pressure limits**   The partial pressure of oxygen in air at sea level is 0.21 atm. If this pressure drops by 50%, fatal hypoxia can result. High oxygen levels can also be harmful, but only if the partial pressure of oxygen increases by a factor of 7 or more.

A second problem associated with breathing pressurized air is the increase in nitrogen in the lungs. At 30 m a scuba diver breathes nitrogen at $P_{N_2} = 3.1$ atm, which causes an increase in nitrogen concentration in bodily tissues and fluids. When P_{N_2} increases beyond about 4 atm, a condition called **nitrogen narcosis**, which is referred to as *rapture of the deep*, results. Divers describe this condition as a feeling of being tipsy. A diver breathing compressed air at 60 m feels as if he has had too much wine.

To avoid oxygen toxicity and nitrogen narcosis, deep-sea divers—those venturing beyond 50 m—breathe specialized mixtures of gases. One common mixture is called heliox, a mixture of helium and oxygen. These mixtures usually contain a smaller percentage of oxygen than would be found in air, thereby lowering the risk of oxygen toxicity. Heliox also contains helium instead of nitrogen, eliminating the risk of nitrogen narcosis.

EXAMPLE 11.10	**PARTIAL PRESSURE, TOTAL PRESSURE, AND PERCENT COMPOSITION**

Calculate the partial pressure of oxygen that a diver breathes with a heliox mixture containing 2.0% oxygen at a depth of 100 m where the total pressure is 10.0 atm.

You are given the percent oxygen in the mixture and the total pressure. You are asked to find the partial pressure of oxygen.

GIVEN: O_2 percent = 2.0%
$P_{tot} = 10.0$ atm

FIND: P_{O_2}

The partial pressure of a component in a gas mixture is equal to the fractional composition of the component multiplied by the total pressure. Calculate the fractional composition of O_2 by dividing the percent composition by 100. Calculate the partial pressure of O_2 by multiplying the fractional composition by the total pressure.

SOLUTION

Partial pressure of component

= Fractional composition of component × Total pressure

Fractional composition of $O_2 = \dfrac{2.0}{100} = 0.020$

$P_{O_2} = 0.020 \times 10.0$ atm $= 0.20$ atm

▶**SKILLBUILDER 11.10 | Partial Pressure, Total Pressure, and Percent Composition**

A diver breathing heliox with an oxygen composition of 5.0% wants to adjust the total pressure so that $P_{O_2} = 0.21$ atm. What must the total pressure be?

▶**FOR MORE PRACTICE**   Problems 79, 80, 81, 82.

Collecting Gases over Water

When the product of a chemical reaction is gaseous, it is often collected by the displacement of water. For example, suppose the following reaction is used as a source of hydrogen gas:

$$Zn(s) + 2\,HCl(aq) \longrightarrow ZnCl_2(aq) + H_2(g)$$

Hydrogen plus
water vapor

Zn

HCl

▲ FIGURE 11.25   **Vapor pressure**   When a gas from a chemical reaction
is collected through water, water molecules mix with the gas molecules. The
pressure of water vapor in the final mixture is the vapor pressure of water at the
temperature at which the gas is collected.

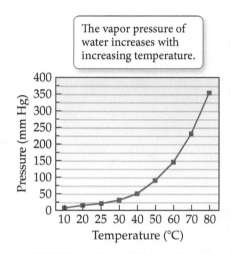

The vapor pressure of
water increases with
increasing temperature.

▲ FIGURE 11.26   **Vapor pressure of
water as a function of temperature**
Vapor pressure increases with increasing
temperature.

| We will cover vapor pressure in detail in Chapter 12. |

**TABLE 11.4   Vapor Pressure of
Water versus Temperature**

Temperature (°C)	Pressure (mm Hg)
10 °C	9.2
20 °C	17.5
25 °C	23.8
30 °C	31.8
40 °C	55.3
50 °C	92.5
60 °C	149.4
70 °C	233.7
80 °C	355.1

As the hydrogen gas forms, it bubbles through the water and gathers in the collection flask (▲ Figure 11.25). However, the hydrogen gas collected in this way is not pure but is mixed with water vapor because some water molecules evaporate and become mixed with the hydrogen molecules. The partial pressure of water in the mixture is called its **vapor pressure** (Table 11.4 and ▲ Figure 11.26). Vapor pressure depends on temperature. It increases with increasing temperature because higher temperatures cause more water molecules to evaporate.

Suppose we collect the hydrogen gas over water at a total pressure of 758 mm Hg and a temperature of 25 °C. What is the partial pressure of the hydrogen gas? We know that the total pressure is 758 mm Hg and that the partial pressure of water is 23.8 mm Hg (its vapor pressure at 25 °C).

$$P_{tot} = P_{H_2} + P_{H_2O}$$
$$758 \text{ mm Hg} = P_{H_2} + 23.8 \text{ mm Hg}$$

Therefore,

$$P_{H_2} = 758 \text{ mm Hg} - 23.8 \text{ mm Hg}$$
$$= 734 \text{ mm Hg}$$

The partial pressure of the hydrogen in the mixture will be 734 mm Hg.

11.10   Gases in Chemical Reactions

**LO: Apply the principles of
stoichiometry to chemical
reactions involving gases.**

Chapter 8 describes how we can use the coefficients in chemical equations as conversion factors between moles of reactants and moles of products in a chemical reaction. We can use these conversion factors to determine, for example, the amount of product obtained in a chemical reaction based on a given amount of reactant or the amount of one reactant we need to completely react with a given amount of another reactant. The general solution map for these kinds of calculations is:

$$\text{Moles A} \longrightarrow \text{Moles B}$$

where A and B are two different substances involved in the reaction and the conversion factor between them comes from the stoichiometric coefficients in the balanced chemical equation.

In reactions involving gaseous reactants or products, the amount of gas is often specified in terms of its volume at a given temperature and pressure. In cases like this, we can use the ideal gas law to convert pressure, volume, and temperature to moles.

$$n = \frac{PV}{RT}$$

We can then use the stoichiometric coefficients to convert to other quantities in the reaction. For example, consider the reaction for the synthesis of ammonia.

$$3\,H_2(g) + N_2(g) \longrightarrow 2\,NH_3(g)$$

How many moles of NH_3 are formed by the complete reaction of 2.5 L of hydrogen at 381 K and 1.32 atm? Assume that there is more than enough N_2.

We begin by sorting the information in the problem statement.

GIVEN: $V = 2.5\,L$

$T = 381\,K$

$P = 1.32\,atm\ (of\ H_2)$

FIND: mol NH_3

SOLUTION MAP

We strategize by drawing a solution map. The solution map for this problem is similar to the solution maps for other stoichiometric problems (see Sections 8.3 and 8.4). However, we first use the ideal gas law to find mol H_2 from P, V, and T. Then we use the stoichiometric coefficients from the equation to convert mol H_2 to mol NH_3.

RELATIONSHIPS USED

$PV = nRT$ (ideal gas law, Section 11.8)

3 mol H_2:2 mol NH_3 (from balanced equation given in problem)

SOLUTION

We first solve the ideal gas equation for n.

$$PV = nRT$$

$$n = \frac{PV}{RT}$$

Then we substitute in the appropriate values.

$$n = \frac{1.32\ \text{atm} \times 2.5\ \text{L}}{0.0821\ \dfrac{\text{L}\cdot\text{atm}}{\text{mol}\cdot\text{K}} \times 381\ \text{K}}$$

$$= 0.1\underline{0}55\ \text{mol}\ H_2$$

Next, we convert mol H_2 to mol NH_3.

$$0.1055 \text{ mol } H_2 \times \frac{2 \text{ mol } NH_3}{3 \text{ mol } H_2} = 0.070 \text{ mol } NH_3$$

There is enough H_2 to form 0.070 mol NH_3.

EXAMPLE 11.11   GASES IN CHEMICAL REACTIONS

How many liters of oxygen gas form when 294 g of $KClO_3$ completely react in this reaction (which is used in the ignition of fireworks)?

$$2 \, KClO_3(s) \longrightarrow 2 \, KCl(s) + 3 \, O_2(g)$$

Assume that the oxygen gas is collected at $P = 755$ mm Hg and $T = 305$ K.

SORT You are given the mass of a reactant in a chemical reaction. You are asked to find the volume of a gaseous product at a given pressure and temperature.	**GIVEN:** 294 g $KClO_3$ $P = 755$ mm Hg (of oxygen gas) $T = 305$ K **FIND:** Volume of O_2 in liters

STRATEGIZE The solution map has two parts. In the first part, convert from g $KClO_3$ to mol $KClO_3$ and then to mol O_2. In the second part, use mol O_2 as n in the ideal gas law to find the volume of O_2. You need the molar mass of $KClO_3$ and the stoichiometric relationship between $KClO_3$ and O_2 (from the balanced chemical equation). You also use the ideal gas law.	**SOLUTION MAP** $PV = nRT$ **RELATIONSHIPS USED** 1 mol $KClO_3$ = 122.55 g (molar mass of $KClO_3$) 2 mol $KClO_3$: 3 mol O_2 (from balanced equation given in problem) $PV = nRT$ (ideal gas law, Section 11.8)

SOLVE Begin by converting mass $KClO_3$ to mol $KClO_3$ and then to mol O_2. Then solve the ideal gas equation for V. Before substituting the values into this equation, convert the pressure to atm. Finally, substitute the given quantities along with the number of moles just calculated to calculate the volume.	**SOLUTION** $294 \text{ g } KClO_3 \times \dfrac{1 \text{ mol } KClO_3}{122.55 \text{ g } KClO_3} \times \dfrac{3 \text{ mol } O_2}{2 \text{ mol } KClO_3} = 3.60 \text{ mol } O_2$ $PV = nRT$ $V = \dfrac{nRT}{P}$ $P = 755 \text{ mm Hg} \times \dfrac{1 \text{ atm}}{760 \text{ mm Hg}} = 0.99342 \text{ atm}$ $V = \dfrac{3.60 \text{ mol} \times 0.0821 \dfrac{L \cdot atm}{mol \cdot K} \times 305 \text{ K}}{0.99342 \text{ atm}}$ $= 90.7 \text{ L}$

CHECK
Check your answer. Are the units correct? Does the answer make physical sense?

The answer has the correct units, liters. The *value* of the answer is a bit more difficult to judge. Again, it is helpful to know that at standard temperature and pressure ($T = 0$ °C or 273.15 K and $P = 1$ atm), 1 mol of gas occupies 22.4 L (see Check step in Example 11.6). A 90.7 L sample of gas at STP would contain about 4 mol; since we started with a little more than 2 mol $KClO_3$, and since 2 mol $KClO_3$ forms 3 mol O_2, an answer that corresponds to about 4 mol O_2 is reasonable.

▶**SKILLBUILDER 11.11** | **Gases in Chemical Reactions**

In this reaction, 4.58 L of O_2 were formed at 745 mm Hg and 308 K. How many grams of Ag_2O decomposed?

$$2\,Ag_2O(s) \longrightarrow 4\,Ag(s) + O_2(g)$$

▶**FOR MORE PRACTICE**   Problems 89, 90, 91, 92, 93, 94.

Molar Volume at Standard Temperature and Pressure

Recall from the Check step of Example 11.6 that the volume occupied by 1 mol of gas at 0 °C (273.15 K) and 1 atm is 22.4 L. These conditions are called **standard temperature and pressure (STP)**, and the volume occupied by 1 mol of gas under these conditions is called the **molar volume** of an ideal gas at STP. Using the ideal gas law, we can confirm that the molar volume at STP is 22.4 L.

$$V = \frac{nRT}{P}$$

$$= \frac{1.00\ \text{mol} \times 0.0821\ \dfrac{\text{L} \cdot \text{atm}}{\text{mol} \cdot \text{K}} \times 273\ \text{K}}{1.00\ \text{atm}}$$

$$= 22.4\ \text{L}$$

Under standard conditions, therefore, we can use this ratio as a conversion factor.

The molar volume of 22.4 L applies only at STP.

$$1\ \text{mol} : 22.4\ \text{L}$$

One mole of any gas at standard temperature and pressure (STP) occupies 22.4 L.

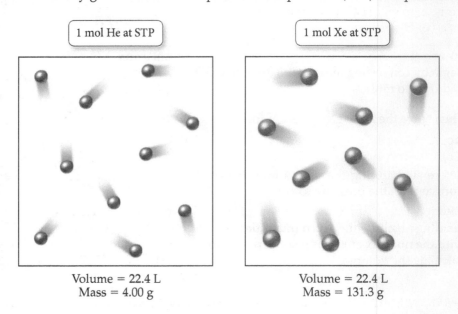

| 1 mol He at STP | 1 mol Xe at STP |

Volume = 22.4 L
Mass = 4.00 g

Volume = 22.4 L
Mass = 131.3 g

For example, suppose we wanted to calculate the number of liters of CO_2 gas that forms at STP when 0.879 moles of $CaCO_3$ undergoes this reaction:

$$CaCO_3(s) \longrightarrow CaO(s) + CO_2(g)$$

We begin by sorting the information in the problem statement.

GIVEN: 0.879 mol $CaCO_3$

FIND: $CO_2(g)$ in liters

SOLUTION MAP

We strategize by drawing a solution map that shows how to convert from mol $CaCO_3$ to mol CO_2 to L CO_2 using the molar volume at STP.

$$\frac{1 \text{ mol } CO_2}{1 \text{ mol } CaCO_3} \qquad \frac{22.4 \text{ L } CO_2}{1 \text{ mol } CO_2}$$

RELATIONSHIPS USED

1 mol $CaCO_3$:1 mol CO_2 (from balanced equation given in problem)

1 mol = 22.4 L (at STP) (molar volume at STP, presented in this section)

SOLUTION

$$0.879 \text{ mol } CaCO_3 \times \frac{1 \text{ mol } CO_2}{1 \text{ mol } CaCO_3} \times \frac{22.4 \text{ L } CO_2}{1 \text{ mol } CO_2} = 19.7 \text{ L } CO_2$$

EXAMPLE 11.12   USING MOLAR VOLUME IN CALCULATIONS

How many grams of water form when 1.24 L of H_2 gas at STP completely reacts with O_2?

$$2 H_2(g) + O_2(g) \longrightarrow 2 H_2O(g)$$

SORT You are given the volume of a reactant at STP and asked to find the mass of the product formed.	GIVEN: 1.24 L H_2 FIND: g H_2O
STRATEGIZE In the solution map, use the molar volume to convert from volume H_2 to mol H_2. Then use the stoichiometric relationship to convert to mol H_2O and finally the molar mass of H_2O to get to mass H_2O.	SOLUTION MAP $$\frac{1 \text{ mol } H_2}{22.4 \text{ L } H_2} \qquad \frac{2 \text{ mol } H_2O}{2 \text{ mol } H_2} \qquad \frac{18.02 \text{ g } H_2O}{1 \text{ mol } H_2O}$$ RELATIONSHIPS USED 1 mol = 22.4 L (molar volume at STP, presented in this section) 2 mol H_2 : 2 mol H_2O (from balanced equation given in problem) 18.02 g H_2O = 1 mol H_2O (molar mass of H_2O)
SOLVE Begin with the volume of H_2 and follow the solution map to arrive at mass H_2O in grams.	SOLUTION $$1.24 \text{ L } H_2 \times \frac{1 \text{ mol } H_2}{22.4 \text{ L } H_2} \times \frac{2 \text{ mol } H_2O}{2 \text{ mol } H_2} \times \frac{18.02 \text{ g } H_2O}{1 \text{ mol } H_2O} = 0.998 \text{ g } H_2O$$
CHECK Check your answer. Are the units correct? Does the answer make physical sense?	The answer has the correct units, g H_2O. The answer is reasonable because 1.24 L of a gas is about 0.05 mol of reactant (at STP) and 1 g H_2O is about 0.05 mol product (1 g/18 g/mol ≈ 0.05 mol). Since the reaction produces 1 mol H_2O to 1 mol H_2, you expect the number of moles of H_2O produced to be equal to the number of moles of H_2 that react.

▶**SKILLBUILDER 11.12** | **Using Molar Volume in Calculations**

How many liters of oxygen (at STP) are required to form 10.5 g of H_2O?

$$2 H_2(g) + O_2(g) \longrightarrow 2 H_2O(g)$$

▶**FOR MORE PRACTICE**   Problems 95, 96, 97, 98.

CHEMISTRY IN THE ENVIRONMENT

▶ Air Pollution

All major cities in the world have polluted air. This pollution comes from a number of sources, including electricity generation, motor vehicles, and industrial waste. While there are many different kinds of air pollutants, the major gaseous air pollutants include the following:

Sulfur dioxide (SO_2)—Sulfur dioxide is primarily a by-product of electricity generation and industrial metal refining. SO_2 is a lung and eye irritant that affects the respiratory system. SO_2 is also one of the main precursors of acid rain.

Carbon monoxide (CO)—Carbon monoxide is formed by the incomplete combustion of fossil fuels (petroleum, natural gas, and coal). It is emitted mainly by motor vehicles. CO displaces oxygen in the blood and causes the heart and lungs to work harder. At high levels, CO can cause sensory impairment, decreased thinking ability, unconsciousness, and even death.

Ozone (O_3)—Ozone in the upper atmosphere is a normal part of our environment. Upper atmospheric ozone filters out part of the harmful UV light contained in sunlight. Lower-atmospheric or *ground-level ozone*, on the other hand, is a pollutant that results from the action of sunlight on motor vehicle emissions. Ground-level ozone is an eye and lung irritant. Prolonged exposure to ozone has been shown to permanently damage the lungs.

Nitrogen dioxide (NO_2)—Nitrogen dioxide is emitted by motor vehicles and by electricity generation plants. It is an orange-brown gas that causes the dark haze often seen over polluted cities. NO_2 is an eye and lung irritant and a precursor of acid rain.

In the United States, the U.S. Environmental Protection Agency (EPA) has set standards for these pollutants. Beginning in the 1970s, the U.S. Congress passed the Clean Air Act and its amendments, requiring U.S. cities to reduce their pollution and maintain levels below the limits set by the EPA. As a result of this legislation, pollutant levels in U.S. cities have decreased significantly over the last 30 years, even as the number of vehicles has increased. For example, according to the EPA, the levels of all four of the previously mentioned pollutants in major U.S cities decreased during 1980–2010. Table 11.5 lists the amounts of these decreases.

TABLE 11.5   CHANGES IN POLLUTANT LEVELS FOR MAJOR U.S. CITIES, 1980–2010

Pollutant	Change, 1980–2010
SO_2	−76%
CO	−82%
O_3	−28%
NO_2	−52%

(*Source:* U.S. EPA)

Although the levels of pollutants (especially ozone) in many cities are still above what the EPA considers safe, much progress has been made. These trends demonstrate that good legislation can clean up our environment.

B11.3 CAN YOU ANSWER THIS?   *Calculate the amount (in grams) of SO_2 emitted when 1.0 kg of coal containing 4.0% S by mass is completely burned. Under standard conditions, what volume in liters does this SO_2 occupy?*

▲ Air pollution plagues most large cities.

CHAPTER IN REVIEW

Self-Assessment Quiz

Q1. According to kinetic molecular theory, the particles that compose a gas:

(a) attract one another strongly

(b) are packed closely together—nearly touching one another

(c) have an average kinetic energy proportional to the temperature in kelvins

(d) All of the above

Q2. Convert 558 mm Hg to atm.

(a) 0.734 atm (c) 38.0 atm

(b) 4.24×10^5 atm (d) 18.6 atm

Q3. If you double the volume of a constant amount of gas at a constant temperature, what happens to the pressure?

(a) The pressure doubles.

(b) The pressure quadruples.

(c) The pressure does not change.

(d) The pressure is one-half the initial pressure.

Q4. A 2.55-L gas sample in a cylinder with a freely moveable piston is initially at 25.0 °C. What is the volume of the gas when it is heated to 145 °C (at constant pressure)?

(a) 1.82 L (b) 3.58 L (c) 0.440 L (d) 14.8 L

Q5. A gas sample has an initial volume of 55.2 mL, an initial temperature of 35.0 °C, and an initial pressure of 735 mm Hg. The volume is decreased to 48.8 mL and the temperature is increased to 72.5 °C. What is the final pressure?

(a) 933 mm Hg (c) 1.72×10^3 mm Hg

(b) 186 mm Hg (d) 401 mm Hg

Q6. Each gas sample has the same temperature and pressure. Which sample occupies the greatest volume?

(a) 4.0 g He (c) 40.0 g Ar

(b) 40.0 g Ne (d) 84.0 g Kr

Q7. Find the volume occupied by 22.0 g of helium gas at 25.0 °C and 1.18 atm of pressure.

(a) 123 L (c) 114 L

(b) 9.57 L (d) 159 L

Q8. A 2.82 g sample of an unknown gas occupies 525 mL at 25.0 °C and a pressure of 1.00 atm. Find the molar mass of the gas.

(a) 11.0 g/mol (c) 90.9 g/mol

(b) 0.011 g/mol (d) 131 g/mol

Q9. A mixture of three gases containing an equal number of moles of each gas has a total pressure of 9.0 atm. What is the partial pressure of each gas?

(a) 1.0 atm (c) 9.0 atm

(b) 3.0 atm (d) 27.0 atm

Q10. A gas mixture containing only helium and neon is 22.1% neon (by volume) and has a total pressure of 748 mm Hg. What is the partial pressure of neon?

(a) 165 mm Hg (c) 583 mm Hg

(b) 1.69×10^4 mm Hg (d) 22.1 mm Hg

Q11. Aluminum reacts with chlorine gas to form aluminum chloride.

$$2 Al(s) + 3 Cl_2(g) \longrightarrow 2 AlCl_3(s)$$

What minimum volume of chlorine gas (at 298 K and 225 mm Hg) is required to completely react with 7.85 g of aluminum?

(a) 36.0 L (c) 0.0474 L

(b) 24.0 L (d) 16.0 L

Q12. A gas sample at STP contains 1.15 g oxygen and 1.55 g nitrogen. What is the volume of the gas sample?

(a) 1.26 L (c) 4.08 L

(b) 2.04 L (d) 61.0 L

Answers: 1:c, 2:a, 3:d, 4:b, 5:a, 6:b, 7:c, 8:d, 9:b, 10:a, 11:a, 12:b

Chemical Principles

Kinetic Molecular Theory: The kinetic molecular theory is a model for gases. In this model, gases are composed of widely spaced, noninteracting particles whose average kinetic energy depends on temperature.

Pressure: Pressure is the force per unit area that results from the collision of gas particles with surfaces. The SI unit of pressure is the pascal, but we often express pressure in other units such as atmospheres, millimeters of mercury, torr, pounds per square inch, and inches of mercury.

Relevance

Kinetic Molecular Theory: The kinetic molecular theory predicts many of the properties of gases, including their low density in comparison to solids, their compressibility, and their tendency to assume the shape and volume of their container. The kinetic molecular theory also predicts the ideal gas law.

Pressure: Pressure is a fundamental property of a gas. It allows tires to be inflated and makes it possible to drink from straws.

Simple Gas Laws: The simple gas laws show how one of the properties of a gas varies with another property of the same gas.

Volume (V) and Pressure (P)

$$V \propto \frac{1}{P} \quad \text{(Boyle's law)}$$

Volume (V) and Temperature (T)

$$V \propto T \quad \text{(Charles's law)}$$

Volume (V) and Moles (n)

$$V \propto n \quad \text{(Avogadro's law)}$$

Simple Gas Laws: Each of the simple gas laws allows us to see how two properties of a gas are interrelated. They are also useful in calculating how one of the properties of a gas changes when another does. We can use Boyle's law, for example, to calculate how the volume of a gas will change in response to a change in pressure, or vice versa.

The Combined Gas Law: The combined gas law joins Boyle's law and Charles's law.

$$\frac{P_1 V_1}{T_1} = \frac{P_2 V_2}{T_2}$$

The Combined Gas Law: We use the combined gas law to calculate how a property of a gas (pressure, volume, or temperature) changes when two other properties change at the same time.

The Ideal Gas Law: The ideal gas law combines the four properties of a gas—pressure, volume, temperature, and number of moles—in a single equation showing their interrelatedness.

$$PV = nRT$$

The Ideal Gas Law: We can use the ideal gas law to find any one of the four properties of a gas if we know the other three.

Mixtures of Gases: The pressure due to an individual component in a mixture of gases is its partial pressure, and we define it as the fractional composition of the component multiplied by the total pressure:

Partial pressure of component = Fractional composition of component × Total pressure

Dalton's law states that the total pressure of a mixture of gases is equal to the sum of the partial pressures of its components.

$$P_{tot} = P_a + P_b + P_c + \ldots$$

Mixtures of Gases: Since many gases are not pure but mixtures of several components, it is useful to know how each component contributes to the properties of the entire mixture. The concepts of partial pressure are relevant to deep-sea diving, for example, and to collecting gases over water, where water vapor mixes with the gas being collected.

Gases in Chemical Reactions: Stoichiometric calculations involving gases are similar to those that do not involve gases in that the coefficients in a balanced chemical equation provide conversion factors among moles of reactants and products in the reaction. For gases, the amount of a reactant or product is often specified by the volume of reactant or product at a given temperature and pressure. The ideal gas law is then used to convert from these quantities to moles of reactant or product. Alternatively, at standard temperature and pressure, volume can be converted directly to moles with the equality:

$$1 \text{ mol} = 22.4 \text{ L (at STP)}$$

Gases in Chemical Reactions: Reactions involving gases are common in chemistry. For example, many atmospheric reactions—some of which are important to the environment—occur as gaseous reactions.

Chemical Skills

Examples

EXAMPLE 11.13	PRESSURE UNIT CONVERSION

Convert 18.4 in. Hg to torr.

GIVEN: 18.4 in. Hg

FIND: torr

SOLUTION MAP

$$\frac{1 \text{ atm}}{29.92 \text{ in. Hg}} \qquad \frac{760 \text{ torr}}{1 \text{ atm}}$$

SORT
You are given a pressure in inches of mercury and asked to convert the units to torr.

STRATEGIZE
Begin with the quantity you are given and multiply by the appropriate conversion factor(s) to determine the quantity you are trying to find.

RELATIONSHIPS USED

$$1 \text{ atm} = 29.92 \text{ in. Hg (Table 11.1)}$$
$$760 \text{ torr} = 1 \text{ atm} \qquad \text{(Table 11.1)}$$

SOLUTION

SOLVE
Follow the solution map to solve the problem.

$$18.4 \text{ in. Hg} \times \frac{1 \text{ atm}}{29.92 \text{ in. Hg}} \times \frac{760 \text{ torr}}{1 \text{ atm}} = 467 \text{ torr}$$

CHECK
Are the units correct? Does the answer make physical sense?

The units (torr) are correct. The value of the answer is reasonable because the torr is a smaller unit than in. Hg; therefore the value of a pressure in torr should be larger than in in. Hg.

EXAMPLE 11.14	SIMPLE GAS LAWS

A gas has a volume of 5.7 L at a pressure of 3.2 atm. What is its volume at 4.7 atm? (Assume constant temperature.)

GIVEN: $P_1 = 3.2 \text{ atm}$
$V_1 = 5.7 \text{ L}$
$P_2 = 4.7 \text{ atm}$

FIND: V_2

SORT
You are given the initial and final pressures and the initial volume. You are asked to find the final volume.

SOLUTION MAP

$$P_1 V_1 = P_2 V_2$$

STRATEGIZE
Calculations involving the simple gas laws usually consist of finding one of the initial or final conditions given the other initial and final conditions. In this case, use Boyle's law to find V_2 given P_1, V_1, and V_2.

RELATIONSHIPS USED

$$P_1 V_1 = P_2 V_2 \text{ (Boyle's law, Section 11.4)}$$

SOLUTION

SOLVE
Solve Boyle's law for V_2 and substitute the correct variables to calculate its value.

$$P_1 V_1 = P_2 V_2$$
$$V_2 = \frac{P_1}{P_2} V_1$$
$$= \frac{3.2 \text{ atm}}{4.7 \text{ atm}} 5.7 \text{ L}$$
$$= 3.9 \text{ L}$$

CHECK
Are the units correct? Does the answer make physical sense?

The units (L) are correct. The value is reasonable because as pressure increases volume should decrease.

LO: Restate and apply the combined gas law (Section 11.6).

| EXAMPLE 11.15 | THE COMBINED GAS LAW |

A sample of gas has an initial volume of 2.4 L at a pressure of 855 mm Hg and a temperature of 298 K. If the gas is heated to a temperature of 387 K and expanded to a volume of 4.1 L, what is its final pressure in millimeters of mercury?

SORT
You are given the initial and final volume and temperature, and you are given the initial pressure. You are asked to find the final pressure.

GIVEN: $P_1 = 855$ mm Hg

$V_1 = 2.4$ L

$T_1 = 298$ K

$V_2 = 4.1$ L

$T_2 = 387$ K

FIND: P_2

STRATEGIZE
Problems involving the combined gas law usually consist of finding one of the initial or final conditions given the other initial and final conditions. In this case, you can use the combined gas law to find the unknown quantity, P_2.

SOLUTION MAP

$$\frac{P_1 V_1}{T_1} = \frac{P_2 V_2}{T_2}$$

RELATIONSHIPS USED

$$\frac{P_1 V_1}{T_1} = \frac{P_2 V_2}{T_2} \quad \text{(combined gas law, Section 11.6)}$$

SOLVE
Solve the combined gas law for the quantity you are trying to find, in this case P_2, and substitute the known quantities to calculate the value of P_2.

SOLUTION

$$\frac{P_1 V_1}{T_1} = \frac{P_2 V_2}{T_2}$$

$$P_2 = \frac{P_1 V_1 T_2}{T_1 V_2}$$

$$= \frac{855 \text{ mm Hg} \times 2.4 \text{ L} \times 387 \text{ K}}{298 \text{ K} \times 4.1 \text{ L}}$$

$$= 6.5 \times 10^2 \text{ mm Hg}$$

CHECK
Are the units correct? Does the answer make physical sense?

The units, mm Hg, are correct. The value of the answer makes sense because the volume increase was proportionally more than the temperature decrease; therefore you would expect the pressure to decrease.

LO: Restate and apply the ideal gas law (Section 11.8).

| EXAMPLE 11.16 | THE IDEAL GAS LAW |

Calculate the pressure exerted by 1.2 mol of gas in a volume of 28.2 L and at a temperature of 334 K.

SORT
You are given the number of moles of a gas, its volume, and its temperature. You are asked to find its pressure.

GIVEN: $n = 1.2$ mol

$V = 28.2$ L

$T = 334$ K

FIND: P

STRATEGIZE

Calculations involving the ideal gas law often involve finding one of the four variables (P, V, n, or T) given the other three. In this case, you are asked to find P. Use the given variables and the ideal gas law to arrive at P.

SOLVE

Solve the ideal gas law equation for P and substitute the given variables to calculate P.

SOLUTION MAP

$$PV = nRT$$

RELATIONSHIPS USED

$$PV = nRT \text{ (ideal gas law, Section 11.8)}$$

SOLUTION

$$PV = nRT$$

$$P = \frac{nRT}{V}$$

$$= \frac{1.2 \ \text{mol} \times 0.0821 \ \frac{\text{L} \cdot \text{atm}}{\text{mol} \cdot \text{K}} \times 334 \ \text{K}}{28.2 \ \text{L}}$$

$$= 1.2 \ \text{atm}$$

CHECK

Are the units correct? Does the answer make physical sense?

The units (atm) are correct units for pressure. The *value* of the answer is a bit more difficult to judge. However, knowing that at standard temperature and pressure ($T = 0 \ °\text{C}$ or 273.15 K and $P = 1$ atm) 1 mol of gas occupies 22.4 L, you can see that the answer is reasonable because you have a bit more than one mole of a gas at a temperature not too far from standard temperature. The volume of the gas is a bit higher than 22.4 L; therefore you might expect the pressure to be a bit higher than 1 atm.

LO: Restate and apply Dalton's law of partial pressures (Section 11.9).

EXAMPLE 11.17 **TOTAL PRESSURE AND PARTIAL PRESSURE**

A mixture of three gases has the partial pressures:

$$P_{CO_2} = 289 \ \text{mm Hg}$$

$$P_{O_2} = 342 \ \text{mm Hg}$$

$$P_{N_2} = 122 \ \text{mm Hg}$$

What is the total pressure of the mixture?

You are given the partial pressures of three gases in a mixture and asked to find the total pressure.

GIVEN: $P_{CO_2} = 289 \ \text{mm Hg}$
$P_{O_2} = 342 \ \text{mm Hg}$
$P_{N_2} = 122 \ \text{mm Hg}$

FIND: P_{tot}

Use Dalton's law of partial pressures ($P_{tot} = P_a + P_b + P_c + \ldots$) to solve the problem. Sum the partial pressures to obtain the total pressure.

SOLUTION

$$P_{tot} = P_{CO_2} + P_{O_2} + P_{N_2}$$

$$= 289 \ \text{mm Hg} + 342 \ \text{mm Hg} + 122 \ \text{mm Hg}$$

$$= 753 \ \text{mm Hg}$$

KEY TERMS

absolute zero [11.5]
atmosphere (atm) [11.3]
Avogadro's law [11.7]
Boyle's law [11.4]
Charles's law [11.5]
combined gas
   law [11.6]

Dalton's law of partial
   pressures [11.9]
hypoxia [11.9]
ideal gas constant (R) [11.8]
ideal gas law [11.8]
kinetic molecular theory
   [11.2]

millimeter of mercury
   (mm Hg) [11.3]
molar volume [11.10]
nitrogen narcosis [11.9]
oxygen toxicity [11.9]
partial pressure [11.9]
pascal (Pa) [11.3]

pounds per square inch
   (psi) [11.3]
pressure [11.3]
standard temperature and
   pressure (STP) [11.10]
torr [11.3]
vapor pressure [11.9]

EXERCISES

QUESTIONS

1. What is pressure?
2. Explain how drinking from a straw works. What causes the beverage to go up the straw? Is there an upper limit to how long a straw can theoretically be and still work as a drinking straw?
3. What are the main assumptions of kinetic molecular theory?
4. Describe the main properties of a gas. How are these predicted by kinetic molecular theory?
5. Why do we experience pain in our ears during changes in altitude?
6. What units are used to measure pressure?
7. What is Boyle's law? Explain Boyle's law from the perspective of kinetic molecular theory.
8. Explain why scuba divers should not hold their breath as they ascend to the surface.
9. Why would it be impossible to breathe air through an extra-long snorkel (greater than a couple of meters) while swimming underwater?

10. What is Charles's law? Explain Charles's law from the perspective of kinetic molecular theory.
11. Explain why hot-air balloons float above the ground.
12. What is the combined gas law? When is it useful?
13. What is Avogadro's law? Explain Avogadro's law from the perspective of kinetic molecular theory.
14. What is the ideal gas law? When is it useful?
15. Under what conditions is the ideal gas law most accurate? Under what conditions does the ideal gas law break down? Why?
16. What is partial pressure?
17. What is Dalton's law?
18. Describe hypoxia and oxygen toxicity.
19. Why do deep-sea divers breathe a mixture of helium and oxygen?
20. When a gas is collected over water, is the gas pure? Why or why not?
21. What is vapor pressure?
22. What is standard temperature and pressure (STP)? What is the molar volume of a gas at STP?

PROBLEMS

CONVERTING BETWEEN PRESSURE UNITS

23. Convert each measurement to atm.
    (a) 1277 mm Hg
    (b) 2.38×10^5 Pa
    (c) 127 psi
    (d) 455 torr

24. Convert each measurement to atm.
    (a) 921 torr
    (b) 4.8×10^4 Pa
    (c) 87.5 psi
    (d) 34.22 in. Hg

25. Perform each conversion.
    (a) 2.3 atm to torr
    (b) 4.7×10^{-2} atm to millimeters of mercury
    (c) 24.8 psi to millimeters of mercury
    (d) 32.84 in. Hg to torr

26. Perform each conversion.
    (a) 1.06 atm to millimeters of mercury
    (b) 95,422 Pa to millimeters of mercury
    (c) 22.3 psi to torr
    (d) 35.78 in. Hg to millimeters of mercury

27. Complete the table.

Pascals	Atmospheres	Millimeters of Mercury	Torr	Pounds per Square Inch
882 Pa	___	6.62 mm Hg	___	___
___	0.558 atm	___	___	___
___	___	___	___	24.8 psi
___	___	___	764 torr	___
___	___	249 mm Hg	___	___

28. Complete the table.

Pascals	Atmospheres	Millimeters of Mercury	Torr	Pounds per Square Inch
___	1.91 atm	___	1.45×10^3 torr	___
1.15×10^4 Pa	___	___	___	___
___	___	___	721 torr	___
___	___	109 mm Hg	___	___
___	___	___	___	38.9 psi

29. The pressure in Denver, Colorado (5280-ft elevation), averages about 24.9 in. Hg. Convert this pressure to:
(a) atmospheres
(b) millimeters of mercury
(c) pounds per square inch
(d) pascals

30. The pressure on top of Mount Everest averages about 235 mm Hg. Convert this pressure to:
(a) torr
(b) pounds per square inch
(c) inches of mercury
(d) atmospheres

31. The North American record for highest recorded barometric pressure is 31.85 in. Hg, set in 1989 in Northway, Alaska. Convert this pressure to:
(a) millimeters of mercury
(b) atmospheres
(c) torr
(d) kilopascals

32. The world record for lowest pressure (at sea level) was 652 mm Hg, inside of Typhoon Tip, 300 miles west of Guam on October 12, 1979. Convert this pressure to:
(a) torr
(b) atmospheres
(c) inches of mercury
(d) pounds per square inch

SIMPLE GAS LAWS

33. A sample of gas has an initial volume of 3.95 L at a pressure of 705 mm Hg. If the volume of the gas is increased to 5.38 L, what is the pressure? (Assume constant temperature.)

34. A sample of gas has an initial volume of 22.8 L at a pressure of 1.65 atm. If the sample is compressed to a volume of 10.7 L, what is its pressure? (Assume constant temperature.)

35. A snorkeler with a lung capacity of 6.3 L inhales a lungful of air at the surface, where the pressure is 1.0 atm. The snorkeler then descends to a depth of 25 m, where the pressure increases to 3.5 atm. What is the capacity of the snorkeler's lungs at this depth? (Assume constant temperature.)

36. A scuba diver with a lung capacity of 5.2 L inhales at a depth of 45 m and a pressure of 5.5 atm. If the diver were to ascend to the surface (where the pressure is 1.0 atm) while holding her breath, to what volume would the air in her lungs expand? (Assume constant temperature.)

37. Use Boyle's law to complete the table (assume temperature and number of moles of gas to be constant).

P_1	V_1	P_2	V_2
755 mm Hg	2.85 L	885 mm Hg	___
___	1.33 L	4.32 atm	2.88 L
192 mm Hg	382 mL	___	482 mL
2.11 atm	___	3.82 atm	125 mL

38. Use Boyle's law to complete the table (assume temperature and number of moles of gas to be constant).

P_1	V_1	P_2	V_2
___	1.90 L	4.19 atm	1.09 L
755 mm Hg	118 mL	709 mm Hg	___
2.75 atm	6.75 mL	___	49.8 mL
343 torr	___	683 torr	8.79 L

39. A balloon with an initial volume of 3.2 L at a temperature of 299 K is warmed to 376 K. What is its volume at 376 K?

40. A dramatic classroom demonstration involves cooling a balloon from room temperature (298 K) to liquid nitrogen temperature (77 K). If the initial volume of the balloon is 2.7 L, what is its volume after it cools? (Ignore the effect of any gases that might liquefy upon cooling.)

41. A 48.3-mL sample of gas in a cylinder equipped with a piston is warmed from 22 °C to 87 °C. What is its volume at the final temperature?

42. A syringe containing 1.55 mL of oxygen gas is cooled from 95.3 °C to 0.0 °C. What is the final volume of oxygen gas?

43. Use Charles's law to complete the table (assume pressure and number of moles of gas to be constant).

V_1	T_1	V_2	T_2
1.08 L	25.4 °C	1.33 L	_____
_____	77 K	228 mL	298 K
115 cm³	_____	119 cm³	22.4 °C
232 L	18.5 °C	_____	96.2 °C

44. Use Charles's law to complete the table (assume pressure and number of moles of gas to be constant).

V_1	T_1	V_2	T_2
119 L	10.5 °C	_____	112.3 °C
_____	135 K	176 mL	315 K
2.11 L	15.4 °C	2.33 L	_____
15.4 cm³	_____	19.2 cm³	10.4 °C

45. A 0.12-mole sample of nitrogen gas occupies a volume of 2.55 L. What is the volume of 0.32 mol of nitrogen gas under the same conditions?

46. A 0.48-mole sample of helium gas occupies a volume of 11.7 L. What is the volume of 0.72 mol of helium gas under the same conditions?

47. A balloon contains 0.128 mol of gas and has a volume of 2.76 L. If an additional 0.073 mol of gas is added to the balloon, what is its final volume?

48. A cylinder with a moveable piston contains 0.87 mol of gas and has a volume of 334 mL. What will its volume be if an additional 0.22 mol of gas is added to the cylinder?

49. Use Avogadro's law to complete the table (assume pressure and temperature to be constant).

V_1	n_1	V_2	n_2
38.5 mL	1.55×10^{-3} mol	49.4 mL	_____
_____	1.37 mol	26.8 L	4.57 mol
11.2 L	0.628 mol	_____	0.881 mol
422 mL	_____	671 mL	0.0174 mol

50. Use Avogadro's law to complete the table (assume pressure and temperature to be constant).

V_1	n_1	V_2	n_2
25.2 L	5.05 mol	_____	3.03 mol
_____	1.10 mol	414 mL	0.913 mol
8.63 L	0.0018 mol	10.9 L	_____
53 mL	_____	13 mL	2.61×10^{-4} mol

THE COMBINED GAS LAW

51. A sample of gas with an initial volume of 28.4 L at a pressure of 725 mm Hg and a temperature of 305 K is compressed to a volume of 14.8 L and warmed to a temperature of 375 K. What is the final pressure of the gas?

52. A cylinder with a moveable piston contains 218 mL of nitrogen gas at a pressure of 1.32 atm and a temperature of 298 K. What must the final volume be for the pressure of the gas to be 1.55 atm at a temperature of 335 K?

53. A scuba diver takes a 2.8-L balloon from the surface, where the pressure is 1.0 atm and the temperature is 34 °C, to a depth of 25 m, where the pressure is 3.5 atm and the temperature is 18 °C. What is the volume of the balloon at this depth?

54. A bag of potato chips contains 585 mL of air at 25 °C and a pressure of 765 mm Hg. Assuming the bag does not break, what will be its volume at the top of a mountain where the pressure is 442 mm Hg and the temperature is 5.0 °C?

55. A gas sample with a volume of 5.3 L has a pressure of 735 mm Hg at 28 °C. What is the pressure of the sample if the volume remains at 5.3 L but the temperature rises to 86 °C?

56. The total pressure in a 11.7-L automobile tire is 44 psi at 11 °C. How much does the pressure in the tire rise if its temperature increases to 37 °C and the volume remains at 11.7 L?

57. Use the combined gas law to complete the table (assume the number of moles of gas to be constant).

P_1	V_1	T_1	P_2	V_2	T_2
1.21 atm	1.58 L	12.2 °C	1.54 atm	_____	32.3 °C
721 torr	141 mL	135 K	801 torr	152 mL	_____
5.51 atm	0.879 L	22.1 °C	_____	1.05 L	38.3 °C

58. Use the combined gas law to complete the table (assume the number of moles of gas to be constant).

P_1	V_1	T_1	P_2	V_2	T_2
1.01 atm	_____	2.7 °C	0.54 atm	0.58 L	42.3 °C
123 torr	41.5 mL	_____	626 torr	36.5 mL	205 K
_____	1.879 L	20.8 °C	0.412 atm	2.05 L	48.1 °C

THE IDEAL GAS LAW

59. What is the volume occupied by 0.255 mol of helium gas at 1.25 atm and 305 K?

60. What is the pressure in a 20.0-L cylinder filled with 0.683 mol of nitrogen gas at 325 K?

61. A cylinder contains 28.5 L of oxygen gas at a pressure of 1.8 atm and a temperature of 298 K. How many moles of gas are in the cylinder?

62. What is the temperature of 0.52 mol of gas at a pressure of 1.3 atm and a volume of 11.8 L?

63. A cylinder contains 11.8 L of air at a total pressure of 43.2 psi and a temperature of 25 °C. How many moles of gas does the cylinder contain?

64. What is the pressure in millimeters of mercury of 0.0115 mol of helium gas with a volume of 214 mL at 45 °C?

65. Use the ideal gas law to complete the table.

P	V	n	T
1.05 atm	1.19 L	0.112 mol	_____
112 torr	_____	0.241 mol	304 K
_____	28.5 mL	1.74×10^{-3} mol	25.4 °C
0.559 atm	0.439 L	_____	255 K

66. Use the ideal gas law to complete the table.

P	V	n	T
2.39 atm	1.21 L	_____	205 K
512 torr	_____	0.741 mol	298 K
0.433 atm	0.192 L	0.0131 mol	_____
_____	20.2 mL	5.71×10^{-3} mol	20.4 °C

67. How many moles of gas must be forced into a 3.5-L ball to give it a gauge pressure of 9.4 psi at 25 °C? The gauge pressure is relative to atmospheric pressure. Assume that atmospheric pressure is 14.7 psi so that the total pressure in the ball is 24.1 psi.

68. How many moles of gas must be forced into a 4.8-L tire to give it a gauge pressure of 32.4 psi at 25 °C? The gauge pressure is relative to atmospheric pressure. Assume that atmospheric pressure is 14.7 psi so that the total pressure in the tire is 47.1 psi.

69. An experiment shows that a 248-mL gas sample has a mass of 0.433 g at a pressure of 745 mm Hg and a temperature of 28 °C. What is the molar mass of the gas?

70. An experiment shows that a 113-mL gas sample has a mass of 0.171 g at a pressure of 721 mm Hg and a temperature of 32 °C. What is the molar mass of the gas?

71. A sample of gas has a mass of 38.8 mg. Its volume is 224 mL at a temperature of 55 °C and a pressure of 886 torr. Find the molar mass of the gas.

72. A sample of gas has a mass of 0.555 g. Its volume is 117 mL at a temperature of 85 °C and a pressure of 753 mm Hg. Find the molar mass of the gas.

PARTIAL PRESSURE

73. A gas mixture contains each gas at the indicated partial pressure.

N_2	217 torr
O_2	106 torr
He	248 torr

What is the total pressure of the mixture?

74. A gas mixture contains each gas at the indicated partial pressure.

CO_2	422 mm Hg
Ar	102 mm Hg
O_2	165 mm Hg
H_2	52 mm Hg

What is the total pressure of the mixture?

75. A heliox deep-sea diving mixture delivers an oxygen partial pressure of 0.30 atm when the total pressure is 11.0 atm. What is the partial pressure of helium in this mixture?

76. A mixture of helium, nitrogen, and oxygen has a total pressure of 752 mm Hg. The partial pressures of helium and nitrogen are 234 mm Hg and 197 mm Hg, respectively. What is the partial pressure of oxygen in the mixture?

77. The hydrogen gas formed in a chemical reaction is collected over water at 30 °C at a total pressure of 732 mm Hg. What is the partial pressure of the hydrogen gas collected in this way?

78. The oxygen gas emitted from an aquatic plant during photosynthesis is collected over water at 25 °C and a total pressure of 753 torr. What is the partial pressure of the oxygen gas?

79. A gas mixture contains 78% nitrogen and 22% oxygen. If the total pressure is 1.12 atm, what are the partial pressures of each component?

80. An air sample contains 0.038% CO_2. If the total pressure is 758 mm Hg, what is the partial pressure of CO_2?

81. A heliox deep-sea diving mixture contains 4.0% oxygen and 96.0% helium. What is the partial pressure of oxygen when this mixture is delivered at a total pressure of 8.5 atm?

82. A scuba diver breathing normal air descends to 100 m of depth, where the total pressure is 11 atm. What is the partial pressure of oxygen that the diver experiences at this depth? Is the diver in danger of experiencing oxygen toxicity?

MOLAR VOLUME

83. Calculate the volume of each gas sample at STP.
(a) 22.5 mol Cl_2
(b) 3.6 mol nitrogen
(c) 2.2 mol helium
(d) 27 mol CH_4

84. Calculate the volume of each gas sample at STP.
(a) 21.2 mol N_2O
(b) 0.215 mol CO
(c) 0.364 mol CO_2
(d) 8.6 mol C_2H_6

85. Calculate the volume of each gas sample at STP.
(a) 73.9 g N_2
(b) 42.9 g O_2
(c) 148 g NO_2
(d) 245 mg CO_2

86. Calculate the volume of each gas sample at STP.
(a) 48.9 g He
(b) 45.2 g Xe
(c) 48.2 mg Cl_2
(d) 3.83 kg SO_2

87. Calculate the mass of each gas sample at STP.
(a) 178 mL CO_2
(b) 155 mL O_2
(c) 1.25 L SF_6

88. Calculate the mass of each gas sample at STP.
(a) 5.82 L NO
(b) 0.324 L N_2
(c) 139 cm^3 Ar

GASES IN CHEMICAL REACTIONS

89. Consider the chemical reaction:

$$C(s) + H_2O(g) \longrightarrow CO(g) + H_2(g)$$

How many liters of hydrogen gas are formed from the complete reaction of 1.07 mol of C? Assume that the hydrogen gas is collected at 1.0 atm and 315 K.

90. Consider the chemical reaction:

$$2\,H_2O(l) \longrightarrow 2\,H_2(g) + O_2(g)$$

How many moles of H_2O are required to form 1.3 L of O_2 at 325 K and 0.988 atm?

91. CH_3OH can be synthesized by the reaction:

$$CO(g) + 2\,H_2(g) \longrightarrow CH_3OH(g)$$

How many liters of H_2 gas, measured at 748 mm Hg and 86 °C, are required to synthesize 0.55 mol of CH_3OH? How many liters of CO gas, measured under the same conditions, are required?

92. Oxygen gas reacts with powdered aluminum according to the reaction:

$$4\,Al(s) + 3\,O_2(g) \longrightarrow 2\,Al_2O_3(s)$$

How many liters of O_2 gas, measured at 782 mm Hg and 25 °C, are required to completely react with 2.4 mol of Al?

93. Nitrogen reacts with powdered aluminum according to the reaction:

$$2\,Al(s) + N_2(g) \longrightarrow 2\,AlN(s)$$

How many liters of N_2 gas, measured at 892 torr and 95 °C, are required to completely react with 18.5 g of Al?

94. Sodium reacts with chlorine gas according to the reaction:

$$2\,Na(s) + Cl_2(g) \longrightarrow 2\,NaCl(s)$$

What volume of Cl_2 gas, measured at 687 torr and 35 °C, is required to form 28 g of NaCl?

95. How many grams of NH_3 form when 24.8 L of $H_2(g)$ (measured at STP) reacts with N_2 to form NH_3 according to this reaction?

$$N_2(g) + 3\,H_2(g) \longrightarrow 2\,NH_3(g)$$

96. Lithium reacts with nitrogen gas according to the reaction:

$$6\,Li(s) + N_2(g) \longrightarrow 2\,Li_3N(s)$$

How many grams of lithium are required to completely react with 58.5 mL of N_2 gas measured at STP?

97. How many grams of calcium are consumed when 156.8 mL of oxygen gas, measured at STP, reacts with calcium according to this reaction?

$$2\,Ca(s) + O_2(g) \longrightarrow 2\,CaO(s)$$

98. How many grams of magnesium oxide form when 14.8 L of oxygen gas, measured at STP, completely reacts with magnesium metal according to this reaction?

$$2\,Mg(s) + O_2(g) \longrightarrow 2\,MgO(s)$$

CUMULATIVE PROBLEMS

99. Use the ideal gas law to show that the molar volume of a gas at STP is 22.4 L.

100. Use the ideal gas law to show that 28.0 g of nitrogen gas and 4.00 g of helium gas occupy the same volume at any temperature and pressure.

101. The mass of an evacuated 255-mL flask is 143.187 g. The mass of the flask filled with 267 torr of an unknown gas at 25 °C is 143.289 g. Calculate the molar mass of the unknown gas.

102. A 118-mL flask is evacuated, and its mass is measured as 97.129 g. When the flask is filled with 768 torr of helium gas at 35 °C, it is found to have a mass of 97.171 g. Is the gas pure helium?

103. A gaseous compound containing hydrogen and carbon is decomposed and found to contain 82.66% carbon and 17.34% hydrogen by mass. The mass of 158 mL of the gas, measured at 556 mm Hg and 25 °C, is 0.275 g. What is the molecular formula of the compound?

104. A gaseous compound containing hydrogen and carbon is decomposed and found to contain 85.63% C and 14.37% H by mass. The mass of 258 mL of the gas, measured at STP, is 0.646 g. What is the molecular formula of the compound?

105. The reaction between zinc and hydrochloric acid is carried out as a source of hydrogen gas in the laboratory:

$$Zn(s) + 2\,HCl(aq) \longrightarrow ZnCl_2(aq) + H_2(g)$$

If 325 mL of hydrogen gas is collected over water at 25 °C at a total pressure of 748 mm Hg, how many grams of Zn reacted?

106. Consider the reaction:

$$2\,NiO(s) \longrightarrow 2\,Ni(s) + O_2(g)$$

If O_2 is collected over water at 40 °C and a total pressure of 745 mm Hg, what volume of gas will be collected for the complete reaction of 24.78 g of NiO?

107. How many grams of hydrogen are collected in a reaction where 1.78 L of hydrogen gas is collected over water at a temperature of 40 °C and a total pressure of 748 torr?

108. How many grams of oxygen are collected in a reaction where 235 mL of oxygen gas is collected over water at a temperature of 25 °C and a total pressure of 697 torr?

109. The decomposition of a silver oxide sample forms 15.8 g of Ag(s):

$$2\,Ag_2O(s) \longrightarrow 4\,Ag(s) + O_2(g)$$

What total volume of O_2 gas forms if it is collected over water at a temperature of 25 °C and a total pressure of 752 mm Hg?

110. The following reaction consumes 2.45 kg of CO(g):

$$CO(g) + H_2O(g) \longrightarrow CO_2(g) + H_2(g)$$

How many total liters of gas are formed if the products are collected at STP?

111. When hydrochloric acid is poured over a sample of sodium bicarbonate, 28.2 mL of carbon dioxide gas is produced at a pressure of 0.954 atm and a temperature of 22.7 °C. Write an equation for the gas evolution reaction and determine how much sodium bicarbonate reacted.

112. When hydrochloric acid is poured over potassium sulfide, 42.9 mL of hydrogen sulfide gas is produced at a pressure of 752 torr and a temperature of 25.8 °C. Write an equation for the gas evolution reaction and determine how much potassium sulfide (in grams) reacted.

113. Consider the reaction:

$$2\,SO_2(g) + O_2(g) \longrightarrow 2\,SO_3(s)$$

(a) If 285.5 mL of SO_2 is allowed to react with 158.9 mL of O_2 (both measured at STP), what is the limiting reactant and the theoretical yield of SO_3?
(b) If 2.805 g of SO_3 is collected (measured at STP), what is the percent yield for the reaction?

114. Consider the reaction:

$$P_4(s) + 6\,H_2(g) \longrightarrow 4\,PH_3(g)$$

(a) If 88.6 L of $H_2(g)$, measured at STP, is allowed to react with 158.3 g of P_4, what is the limiting reactant?
(b) If 48.3 L of PH_3, measured at STP, forms, what is the percent yield?

115. Consider the reaction for the synthesis of nitric acid:

$$3 NO_2(g) + H_2O(l) \longrightarrow 2 HNO_3(aq) + NO(g)$$

(a) If 12.8 L of $NO_2(g)$, measured at STP, is allowed to react with 14.9 g of water, find the limiting reagent and the theoretical yield of HNO_3 in grams.
(b) If 14.8 g of HNO_3 forms, what is the percent yield?

116. Consider the reaction for the production of NO_2 from NO:

$$2 NO(g) + O_2(g) \longrightarrow 2 NO_2(g)$$

(a) If 84.8 L of $O_2(g)$, measured at 35 °C and 632 mm Hg, is allowed to react with 158.2 g of NO, find the limiting reagent.
(b) If 97.3 L of NO_2 forms, measured at 35 °C and 632 mm Hg, what is the percent yield?

117. Ammonium carbonate decomposes upon heating according to the balanced equation:

$$(NH_4)_2CO_3(s) \longrightarrow 2 NH_3(g) + CO_2(g) + H_2O(g)$$

Calculate the total volume of gas produced at 22 °C and 1.02 atm by the complete decomposition of 11.83 g of ammonium carbonate.

118. Ammonium nitrate decomposes explosively upon heating according to the balanced equation:

$$2 NH_4NO_3(s) \longrightarrow 2 N_2(g) + O_2(g) + 4 H_2O(g)$$

Calculate the total volume of gas (at 25 °C and 748 mm Hg) produced by the complete decomposition of 1.55 kg of ammonium nitrate.

119. A mixture containing 235 mg of helium and 325 mg of neon has a total pressure of 453 torr. What is the partial pressure of helium in the mixture?

120. A mixture containing 4.33 g of CO_2 and 3.11 g of CH_4 has a total pressure of 1.09 atm. What is the partial pressure of CO_2 in the mixture?

121. Consider the reaction:

$$2 SO_2(g) + O_2(g) \longrightarrow 2 SO_3(g)$$

A reaction flask initially contains 0.10 atm of SO_2 and 0.10 atm of O_2. What is the total pressure in the flask once the limiting reactant is completely consumed? Assume a constant temperature and volume and a 100% reaction yield.

122. Consider the reaction:

$$CO(g) + 2 H_2(g) \longrightarrow CH_3OH(g)$$

A reaction flask initially contains 112 torr of CO and 282 torr of H_2. The reaction is allowed to proceed until the pressure stops changing, at which point the total pressure is 196 torr. Determine the percent yield for the reaction. Assume a constant temperature and that no other reactions occur other than the one indicated.

HIGHLIGHT PROBLEMS

123. Which gas sample has the greatest pressure? Assume they are all at the same temperature. Explain.

(a)

(b)

(c)

124. This image represents a sample of gas at a pressure of 1 atm, a volume of 1 L, and a temperature of 25 °C. Draw a similar picture showing what happens if the volume is reduced to 0.5 L and the temperature is increased to 250 °C. What happens to the pressure?

$V = 1.0$ L
$T = 25$ °C
$P = 1.0$ atm

125. Automobile air bag inflate following a serious impact. The impact triggers the chemical reaction:

$$2\,NaN_3(s) \longrightarrow 2\,Na(s) + 3\,N_2(g)$$

If an automobile air bag has a volume of 11.8 L, how much NaN_3 in grams is required to fully inflate the air bag upon impact? Assume STP conditions.

FO4305OZ02

126. Olympic cyclists fill their tires with helium to make them lighter. Calculate the mass of air in an air-filled tire and the mass of helium in a helium-filled tire. What is the mass difference between the two? Assume that the volume of the tire is 855 mL, that it is filled with a total pressure of 125 psi, and that the temperature is 25 °C. Also, assume an average molar mass for air of 28.8 g/mol.

127. In a common classroom demonstration, a balloon is filled with air and submerged into liquid nitrogen. The balloon contracts as the gases within the balloon cool. Suppose the balloon initially contains 2.95 L of air at 25.0 °C and a pressure of 0.998 atm. Calculate the expected volume of the balloon upon cooling to −196 °C (the boiling point of liquid nitrogen). When the demonstration is carried out, the actual volume of the balloon decreases to 0.61 L. How well does the observed volume of the balloon compare to your calculated value? Can you explain the difference?

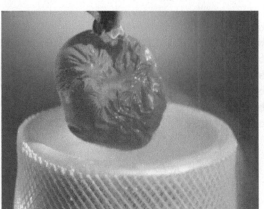

128. Aerosol cans carry clear warnings against incineration because of the high pressures that can develop upon heating. Suppose a can contains a residual amount of gas at a pressure of 755 mm Hg and 25 °C. What would the pressure be if the can were heated to 1155 °C?

QUESTIONS FOR GROUP WORK

Discuss these questions with the group and record your consensus answer.

129. Complete the table.

Variables Related	Name of Law	Proportionality Expression	Equality Expression	Held Constant
V, P	Boyle's law	$V \propto 1/P$	$P_1V_1 = P_2V_2$	n, T
_____	_____	$V \propto T$	$V_1/T_1 = V_2/T_2$	n, P
V, n	Avogadro's law	_____	_____	P, T
_____	Gay-Lussac's law	_____	$P_1/T_1 = P_2/T_2$	_____
P, V, T	_____	_____	_____	_____

130. A chemical reaction produces 10.4 g of CO_2. What volume does this gas occupy at 1.2 atm and 29 °C? Assign one member of your group to check all units and another to check all significant figures.

131. A 14.22-g aluminum soda can reacts with hydrochloric acid according to the reaction:

$$2 \, Al(s) + 6 \, HCl(aq) \longrightarrow 3 \, H_2(g) + 2 \, AlCl_3(aq)$$

The hydrogen gas is collected by the displacement of water. What volume of hydrogen is collected if the external pressure is 749 mm Hg and the temperature is 31°C, assuming that there is no water vapor present? What is the vapor pressure of water at this temperature? What volume do the hydrogen and water vapor occupy under these conditions?

▶ Answers to Skillbuilder Exercises

Skillbuilder 11.1	85.0 psi	**Skillbuilder 11.7**	16.1 L
Skillbuilder Plus, p. 365	80.6 kPa	**Skillbuilder Plus, p. 382**	977 mm Hg
Skillbuilder 11.2	P_2 = 2.1 atm; depth is approximately 11 m	**Skillbuilder 11.8**	70.8 g/mol
		Skillbuilder 11.9	721 torr
Skillbuilder 11.3	123 mL	**Skillbuilder 11.10**	P_{tot} = 4.2 atm
Skillbuilder 11.4	0.82 L	**Skillbuilder 11.11**	82.3 g
Skillbuilder 11.5	13 L	**Skillbuilder 11.12**	6.53 L O_2
Skillbuilder 11.6	1.6 atm		

▶ Answers to Conceptual Checkpoints

11.1 (a) Since all the particles are identical and since (a) has the smallest number of particles per unit volume, it will have the lowest pressure.

11.2 (c) Atmospheric pressure will support a column of water 10.3 m in height. If the liquid in a barometer were twice as dense as water, a column of it would be twice as heavy and the pressure it exerted at its base would be twice as great. Therefore, atmospheric pressure would be able to support a column only half as high.

11.3 (b) Since the volume triples, and since according to Boyle's law the volume and pressure are inversely proportional, the pressure will fall by a factor of 3.

11.4 (a) At constant pressure, the volume of the gas will be proportional to the temperature—if the Kelvin temperature doubles, the volume will double.

11.5 (c) Doubling the temperature in kelvins doubles the pressure, but doubling the volume halves the pressure. The net result is that the pressure is the same as its initial value.

11.6 (c) Since hydrogen gas has the lowest molar mass of the set, 1 g will have the greatest number of moles and therefore the greatest volume.

▲ Flavors are caused by the interactions of molecules in foods or drinks with molecular receptors on the surface of the tongue. This image shows a caffeine molecule, one of the substances responsible for the sometimes bitter flavors in coffee.

Liquids, Solids, and Intermolecular Forces

12

"It will be found that everything depends on the composition of the forces with which the particles of matter act upon one another; and from these forces ... all phenomena of nature take their origin." —Roger Joseph Boscovich (1711–1787)

CHAPTER OUTLINE

12.1 Interactions between Molecules

Bite into a candy bar and taste its sweetness. Drink a cup of strong coffee and experience its bitterness. What causes these flavors? Most tastes originate from interactions between molecules. Certain molecules in coffee, for example, interact with molecular receptors on the surface of specialized cells on the tongue. The receptors are highly specific, recognizing only certain types of molecules. The interaction between the molecule and the receptor triggers a signal that goes to the brain, which we interpret as a bitter taste. Bitter tastes are usually unpleasant because many of the molecules that cause them are poisons. Our response to the bitterness of these molecules is probably an evolutionary adaptation that helps us avoid these poisons.

The interaction between the molecules in coffee that taste bitter and the taste receptors on the tongue is caused by **intermolecular forces**—attractive forces that exist *between* molecules. Living organisms depend on intermolecular forces not only for taste but also for many other physiological processes. For example, in Chapter 19, we will see how intermolecular forces help determine the shapes of protein molecules—the workhorse molecules in living organisms. Later in this chapter—in the *Chemistry and Health* box in Section 12.6—we learn how intermolecular forces are central to DNA, the inheritable molecules that serve as blueprints for life.

The interactions between bitter molecules in coffee and molecular receptors on the tongue are highly specific. However, less specific intermolecular forces exist between all molecules and atoms. These intermolecular forces are responsible for the very existence of liquids and solids. The state of a sample of matter—solid, liquid, or gas—depends on the magnitude of intermolecular forces relative to the amount of thermal energy in the sample. Recall from Section 3.10 that the molecules and atoms that compose matter are in constant random motion that increases with increasing temperature. The energy associated with this motion is called **thermal energy**. The weaker the intermolecular forces relative to thermal energy, the more likely the sample will be gaseous. The stronger the intermolecular forces relative to thermal energy, the more likely the sample will be liquid or solid.

12.2   Properties of Liquids and Solids

LO: Describe the properties of solids and liquids and relate them to their constituent atoms and molecules.

We are all familiar with solids and liquids. Water, gasoline, rubbing alcohol, and fingernail-polish remover are all common liquids. Ice, dry ice, and diamond are familiar solids. In contrast to gases—in which molecules or atoms are separated by large distances—the molecules or atoms that compose liquids and solids are in close contact with one another (▼ Figure 12.1).

The difference between solids and liquids is in the freedom of movement of the constituent molecules or atoms. In liquids, even though the atoms or molecules are in close contact, they are still free to move around each other. In solids, the atoms or molecules are fixed in their positions, although thermal energy causes them to vibrate about a fixed point. These molecular properties of solids and liquids result in characteristic macroscopic properties.

| Gas | Liquid | Solid |

▶ **FIGURE 12.1   Gas, liquid, and solid states**

Properties of Liquids

- High densities in comparison to gases.
- Indefinite shape; liquids assume the shape of their container.
- Definite volume; liquids are not easily compressed.

Properties of Solids

- High densities in comparison to gases.
- Definite shape; solids do not assume the shape of their container.
- Definite volume; solids are not easily compressed.
- May be crystalline (ordered) or amorphous (disordered).

Table 12.1 summarizes these properties, as well as the properties of gases for comparison.

TABLE 12.1   Properties of the States of Matter

Phase	Density	Shape	Volume	Strength of Intermolecular Forces[a]	Example
gas	low	indefinite	indefinite	weak	carbon dioxide gas (CO_2)
liquid	high	indefinite	definite	moderate	liquid water (H_2O)
solid	high	definite	definite	strong	sugar ($C_{12}H_{22}O_{11}$)

[a]Relative to thermal energy.

Liquids have high densities in comparison to gases because the atoms or molecules that compose liquids are much closer together. The density of liquid water, for example, is 1.0 g/cm³ (at 25 °C), while the density of gaseous water at 100 °C and 1 atm is 0.59 g/L, or 5.9×10^{-4} g/cm³. Liquids assume the shape of their containers because the atoms or molecules that compose them are free to flow. When we pour water into a flask, the water flows and assumes the shape of the flask (◀ Figure 12.2). Liquids are not easily compressed because the molecules or atoms that compose them are in close contact—they cannot be pushed closer together.

Like liquids, solids have high densities in comparison to gases because the atoms or molecules that compose solids are also close together. The densities of solids are usually just slightly greater than those of the corresponding liquids. A major exception is water, whose solid (ice) is slightly less dense than liquid water. Solids have a definite shape because, in contrast to liquids or gases, the molecules or atoms that compose solids are fixed in place (▼ Figure 12.3). Each molecule or atom in a solid only vibrates about a fixed point. Like liquids, solids have a definite volume and cannot be compressed because the molecules or atoms composing them are in close contact. As described in Section 3.3, solids may be *crystalline*, in which case the atoms or molecules that compose them arrange themselves in a well-ordered, three-dimensional array, or they may be *amorphous*, in which case the atoms or molecules that compose them have no long-range order.

As we will see in Section 12.8, ice is less dense than liquid water because water expands when it freezes due to its unique crystalline structure.

▲ **FIGURE 12.2   A liquid assumes the shape of its container** Because the molecules in liquid water are free to move around each other, they flow and assume the shape of their container.

▲ **FIGURE 12.3   Solids have a definite shape**   In a solid such as ice, the molecules are fixed in place. However, they vibrate about fixed points.

  CONCEPTUAL CHECKPOINT 12.1

A substance has a definite shape and definite volume. What is the state of the substance?

(a) Solid   **(b)** Liquid   **(c)** Gas

12.3   Intermolecular Forces in Action: Surface Tension and Viscosity

LO: Describe how surface tension and viscosity are manifestations of the intermolecular forces in liquids.

The most important manifestation of intermolecular forces is the very existence of molecular liquids and solids. Without intermolecular forces, molecular solids and liquids would not exist (they would be gaseous). In liquids, we can observe several other manifestations of intermolecular forces including surface tension and viscosity.

▲ **FIGURE 12.4 Floating flies** Even though they are denser than water, fly-fishing lures float on the surface of a stream or lake because of surface tension.

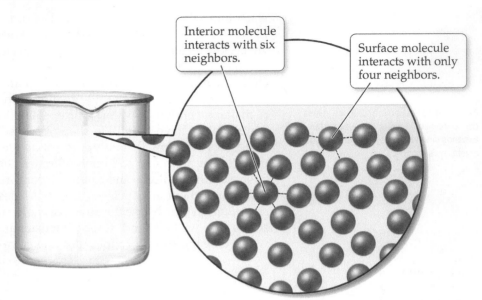

▲ **FIGURE 12.5 Origin of surface tension** Molecules at the surface of a liquid interact with fewer molecules than those in the interior; the lower number of interactions makes the surface molecules less stable.

▲ **FIGURE 12.6 Surface tension at work** A paper clip will float on water if it is carefully placed on the surface of the water. It is held up by surface tension.

Surface Tension

A fly fisherman delicately casts a small metal hook (with a few feathers and strings attached to make it look like an insect) onto the surface of a moving stream. The hook floats on the surface of the water and attracts trout (◀ Figure 12.4). The hook floats because of **surface tension**, the tendency of liquids to minimize their surface area. This tendency causes liquids to have a sort of "skin" that resists penetration. For the fisherman's hook to sink into the water, the water's surface area would have to increase slightly. The increase is resisted because molecules at the surface interact with fewer neighbors than those in the interior of the liquid (▲ Figure 12.5). Since molecules at the surface have fewer interactions with other molecules, they are inherently less stable than those in the interior; consequently, liquids have a tendency to minimize the number of the molecules at the surface, which results in surface tension. You can observe surface tension by carefully placing a paper clip on the surface of water (◀ Figure 12.6). The paper clip, even though it is denser than water, will float on the surface of the water. A slight tap on the clip overcomes surface tension and causes the clip to sink. Surface tension increases with increasing intermolecular forces. You can't float a paper clip on gasoline, for example, because the intermolecular forces among the molecules composing gasoline are weaker than the intermolecular forces among water molecules; they are not under as much tension, so they do not form a "skin."

Viscosity

Another manifestation of intermolecular forces is **viscosity**, the resistance of a liquid to flow. Liquids that are viscous flow more slowly than liquids that are not viscous. For example, motor oil is more viscous than gasoline, and maple syrup is more viscous than water (◀ Figure 12.7). Viscosity is greater in substances with stronger intermolecular forces because molecules cannot move around each other as freely, hindering flow. Long molecules, such as the hydrocarbons in motor oil, also tend to form viscous liquids because of molecular entanglement (the long chainlike molecules get tangled together).

◀ **FIGURE 12.7 Viscosity** Maple syrup is more viscous than water because its molecules interact strongly and so cannot flow past one another easily.

EVERYDAY CHEMISTRY

▶ Why Are Water Drops Spherical?

Have you ever seen a close-up photograph of tiny water droplets (▼ Figure 12.8) or carefully watched water in free fall? In both cases, the distorting effects of gravity are diminished, and the water forms nearly perfect spheres. On the space shuttle, the complete absence of gravity results in floating spheres of water (▼ Figure 12.9). Why? Water drops are spherical because of the surface tension caused by the attractive forces between water molecules. Just as gravity pulls matter within a planet or star inward to form a sphere, so intermolecular forces pull water molecules inward to form a sphere. The sphere minimizes the surface-area-to-volume ratio, thereby minimizing the number of molecules at the surface.

A collection of magnetic marbles provides a good physical model of a water drop. Each magnetic marble is like a water molecule, attracted to the marbles around it. If you agitate these marbles slightly, so that they can find their preferred configuration, they tend toward a spherical shape (▼ Figure 12.10) because the attractions between the marbles cause them to minimize the number of marbles at the surface.

▲ **FIGURE 12.8   An almost perfect sphere**   If a water droplet is small enough, it will largely be free of the distorting effects of gravity and be almost perfectly spherical.

▲ **FIGURE 12.9   A perfect sphere**   In the absence of gravity, as in this picture taken on the space shuttle, water assumes the shape of a sphere.

▲ **FIGURE 12.10   An analogy for surface tension**   Magnetic marbles tend to arrange themselves in a spherical shape.

B12 1 CAN YOU ANSWER THIS?   *How does the tendency of a liquid to form spherical drops depend on the strength of intermolecular forces? Do liquids with weaker intermolecular forces have a higher or lower tendency to form spherical drops?*

12.4   Evaporation and Condensation

LO: Describe and explain the processes of evaporation and condensation.

LO: Use the heat of vaporization in calculations.

Leave a glass of water in the open for several days and the water level within the glass slowly drops. Why? The first reason is that water molecules at the surface of the liquid—which experience fewer attractions to neighboring molecules and are therefore held less tightly—can break away from the rest of the liquid. The second reason is that all of the molecules in the liquid have a *distribution of kinetic energy*

▶ **FIGURE 12.11** **Energy distribution** At a given temperature, a sample of molecules or atoms will have a distribution of kinetic energies, as shown here. Only a small fraction of molecules has enough energy to escape. At a higher temperature, the fraction of molecules with enough energy to escape increases.

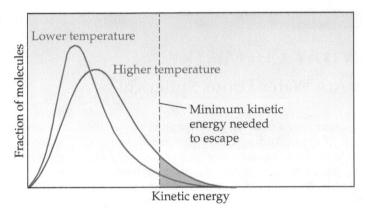

at any given temperature (▲ Figure 12.11). At any given moment, some molecules in the liquid are moving faster than the average (higher energy), and others are moving more slowly (lower energy). Some of the molecules that are moving faster have enough energy to break free from the surface, resulting in **evaporation** or **vaporization**, a physical change in which a substance converts from its liquid state to its gaseous state (◀ Figure 12.12).

If we spill the same amount of water (as was in the glass) on a table, it evaporates more quickly, probably within a few hours. Why? The surface area of the spilled water is greater, leaving more molecules susceptible to evaporation. If we warm the glass of water, it also evaporates more quickly because the greater thermal energy causes a greater fraction of molecules to have enough energy to break away from the surface (see Figure 12.11). If we fill the glass with rubbing alcohol instead of water, the liquid again evaporates more quickly because the intermolecular forces between the alcohol molecules are weaker than the intermolecular forces between water molecules. In general, the rate of vaporization increases with:

| In evaporation or vaporization, a substance is converted from its liquid state into its gaseous state.

▲ **FIGURE 12.12** **Evaporation** Because molecules on the surface of a liquid are held less tightly than those in the interior, the most energetic among them can break away into the gas state in the process called *evaporation*.

- Increasing surface area
- Increasing temperature
- Decreasing strength of intermolecular forces

Liquids that evaporate easily are termed **volatile**, while those that do not vaporize easily are termed **nonvolatile**. Rubbing alcohol, for example, is more volatile than water. Motor oil at room temperature is virtually nonvolatile.

If we leave water in a *closed* container, its level remains constant because the molecules that leave the liquid are trapped in the air space above the water. These gaseous molecules bounce off the walls of the container and eventually hit the surface of the water again and recondense. **Condensation** is a physical change in which a substance converts from its gaseous state to its liquid state.

Evaporation and condensation are opposites: Evaporation is a liquid turning into a gas, and condensation is a gas turning into a liquid. When we initially put liquid water into a closed container, more evaporation happens than condensation because there are so few gaseous water molecules in the space above the water (▶ Figure 12.13a). However, as the number of gaseous water molecules increases, the rate of condensation also increases (▶ Figure 12.13b). At the point where the rates of condensation and evaporation become equal (▶ Figure 12.13c), **dynamic equilibrium** is reached and the number of gaseous water molecules above the liquid remains constant. The **vapor pressure** of a liquid is the partial pressure of its vapor in dynamic equilibrium with its liquid. At 25 °C, water's vapor pressure is 23.8 mm Hg. Vapor pressure increases with:

| *Dynamic equilibrium* is so named because both condensation and evaporation of individual molecules continue, but at the same rate.

- Increasing temperature
- Decreasing strength of intermolecular forces

| Table 11.4 lists the vapor pressure of water at different temperatures.

Vapor pressure is independent of surface area because an increase in surface area at equilibrium equally affects the rate of evaporation and the rate of condensation.

▶ **FIGURE 12.13   Evaporation and condensation   (a)** When water is first put into a closed container, water molecules begin to evaporate. **(b)** As the number of gaseous molecules increases, some of the molecules begin to collide with the liquid and are recaptured—that is, they recondense into liquid. **(c)** When the rate of evaporation equals the rate of condensation, dynamic equilibrium occurs, and the number of gaseous molecules remains constant.

Evaporation begins to occur.

Evaporation continues, but condensation also begins to occur.

Dynamic equilibrium: rate of evaporation = rate of condensation

(a)   (b)   (c)

Boiling

Sometimes you see bubbles begin to form in hot water below 100 °C. These bubbles are dissolved air—not gaseous water—leaving the liquid. Dissolved air comes out of water as you heat it because the solubility of a gas in a liquid decreases with increasing temperature (Section 13.4).

As you increase the temperature of water in an open container, the increasing thermal energy causes molecules to leave the surface and vaporize at a faster and faster rate. At the **boiling point**—the temperature at which the vapor pressure of a liquid is equal to the pressure above it—the thermal energy is enough for molecules within the *interior* of the liquid (not just those at the surface) to break free into the gas phase (▼ Figure 12.14). Water's **normal boiling point**—its boiling point at a pressure of 1 atmosphere—is 100 °C. When a sample of water reaches 100 °C, you can see bubbles form within the liquid. These bubbles are pockets of gaseous water. The bubbles quickly rise to the surface of the liquid, and the water molecules that were in the bubble leave as gaseous water, or steam. Once the boiling point of a liquid is reached, additional heating only causes more rapid boiling, it does not raise the temperature of the liquid above its boiling point (▶ Figure 12.15). A mixture of boiling water *and* steam always has a temperature of 100 °C (at 1 atm pressure). Only after all the water has been converted to steam can the temperature of the steam rise beyond 100 °C.

▶ **FIGURE 12.14   Boiling**   During boiling, thermal energy is enough to cause water molecules in the interior of the liquid to become gaseous, forming bubbles containing gaseous water molecules.

► **FIGURE 12.15 Heating curve during boiling** The temperature of water as it is heated from room temperature through boiling. During boiling, the temperature remains at 100 °C until all the liquid is evaporated.

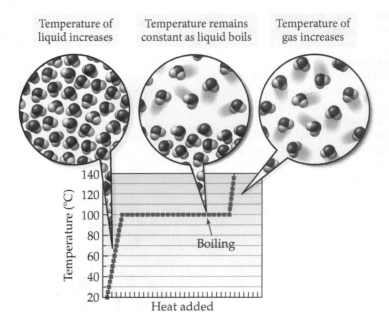

Temperature of liquid increases

Temperature remains constant as liquid boils

Temperature of gas increases

Boiling

Temperature (°C)

Heat added

 CONCEPTUAL CHECKPOINT 12.2

The gas over a rapidly boiling pot of water is sampled and analyzed. Which substance composes a large fraction of the gas sample?

(a) $H_2(g)$ **(b)** $H_2O(g)$ **(c)** $O_2(g)$ **(d)** $H_2O_2(g)$

Energetics of Evaporation and Condensation

In an endothermic process, heat is absorbed; in an exothermic process, heat is released.

Evaporation is *endothermic*—when a liquid is converted into a gas, it absorbs heat because energy is required to break molecules away from the rest of the liquid. Imagine a collection of water molecules in the liquid state. As the water evaporates, it cools—typical of endothermic processes—because only the fastest-moving molecules break away, which leaves the slower-moving molecules behind. Under ordinary conditions, the slight decrease in temperature of water as it evaporates is counteracted by thermal energy transfer from the surroundings, which warms the water back up. However, if the evaporating water were thermally isolated from the surroundings, it would continue to cool down as it evaporated.

You can observe the endothermic nature of evaporation by turning off the heat beneath a boiling pot of water; it quickly stops boiling as the heat lost due to vaporization causes the water to cool below its boiling point. Our bodies use the endothermic nature of evaporation for cooling. When we overheat, we sweat, causing our skin to be covered with liquid water. As this water evaporates it absorbs heat from our bodies, cooling us down. A fan intensifies the cooling effect because it blows newly vaporized water away from the skin, allowing more sweat to vaporize and cause even more cooling. High humidity, however, slows down evaporation, preventing cooling. When the air already contains high amounts of water vapor, sweat does not evaporate as easily, making our cooling system less efficient.

Condensation, the opposite of evaporation, is *exothermic*—heat is released when a gas condenses to a liquid. If you have ever accidentally put your hand above a steaming kettle, you may have experienced a *steam burn*. As the steam condenses to a liquid on your skin, it releases heat, causing a severe burn. The exothermic nature of condensation is also the reason that winter overnight temperatures in coastal cities, which tend to have water vapor in the air, do not get as low as in deserts, which tend to have dry air. As the air temperature in a coastal city drops, water condenses out of the air, releasing heat and preventing the temperature from dropping further. In deserts, there is little moisture in the air to condense, so the temperature drop is greater.

Heat of Vaporization

The amount of heat required to vaporize one mole of liquid is the **heat of vaporization** (ΔH_{vap}). The heat of vaporization of water at its normal boiling point (100 °C) is 40.7 kJ/mole.

$$H_2O(l) \longrightarrow H_2O(g) \quad \Delta H = +40.7 \text{ kJ (at } 100\,°C)$$

ΔH is positive because vaporization is endothermic; energy must be added to the water to vaporize it.

The same amount of heat is involved when 1 mol of gas condenses, but *the heat is emitted* rather than absorbed.

$$H_2O(g) \longrightarrow H_2O(l) \quad \Delta H = -40.7 \text{ kJ (at } 100\,°C)$$

ΔH is negative because condensation is exothermic; energy is given off as the water condenses.

Different liquids have different heats of vaporization (Table 12.2). Heats of vaporization are also *temperature dependent* (they change with temperature). The higher the temperature, the easier it is to vaporize a given liquid and therefore the lower the heat of vaporization.

TABLE 12.2   Heats of Vaporization of Several Liquids at Their Boiling Points and at 25 °C

Liquid	Chemical Formula	Normal Boiling Point (°C)	Heat of Vaporization (kJ/mol) at Boiling Point	Heat of Vaporization (kJ/mol) at 25 °C
water	H_2O	100.0	40.7	44.0
isopropyl alcohol (rubbing alcohol)	C_3H_8O	82.3	39.9	45.4
acetone	C_3H_6O	56.1	29.1	31.0
diethyl ether	$C_4H_{10}O$	34.5	26.5	27.1

We can use the heat of vaporization of a liquid to calculate the amount of heat energy required to vaporize a given amount of that liquid. To do so, we use the heat of vaporization as a conversion factor between moles of the liquid and the amount of heat required to vaporize it. For example, suppose we want to calculate the amount of heat required to vaporize 25.0 g of water at its boiling point. We begin by sorting the information in the problem statement.

GIVEN: 25.0 g H_2O

FIND: heat (kJ)

SOLUTION MAP
We then strategize by building a solution map that begins with the mass of water and ends with the energy required to vaporize it.

$$\boxed{\text{g } H_2O} \longrightarrow \boxed{\text{mol } H_2O} \longrightarrow \boxed{\text{kJ}}$$

$$\frac{1 \text{ mol } H_2O}{18.02 \text{ g } H_2O} \qquad \frac{40.7 \text{ kJ}}{1 \text{ mol } H_2O}$$

RELATIONSHIPS USED

$$\Delta H_{vap} = 40.7 \text{ kJ/mol at } 100\,°C \text{ (Table 12.2)}$$

$$1 \text{ mol } H_2O = 18.02 \text{ g } H_2O \text{ (molar mass of water)}$$

SOLUTION

$$25.0 \text{ g } H_2O \times \frac{1 \text{ mol } H_2O}{18.02 \text{ g } H_2O} \times \frac{40.7 \text{ kJ}}{1 \text{ mol } H_2O} = 56.5 \text{ kJ}$$

EXAMPLE 12.1   USING THE HEAT OF VAPORIZATION IN CALCULATIONS

▶ Calculate the amount of water in grams that can be vaporized at its boiling point with 155 kJ of heat.

SORT	
You are given the number of kilojoules of heat energy and asked to find the mass of water that can be vaporized with the given amount of energy.	**GIVEN:** 155 kJ **FIND:** g H_2O

STRATEGIZE	
Draw the solution map beginning with the energy in kilojoules and converting to moles of water and then to grams of water.	**SOLUTION MAP** $\dfrac{1 \text{ mol } H_2O}{40.7 \text{ kJ}}$ $\dfrac{18.02 \text{ g } H_2O}{1 \text{ mol } H_2O}$ **RELATIONSHIPS USED** $\Delta H_{vap} = 40.7 \text{ kJ/mol at } 100\,°C$ (Table 12.2) $18.02 \text{ g } H_2O = 1 \text{ mol } H_2O$ (molar mass of water)

SOLVE	
Follow the solution map to solve the problem.	**SOLUTION** $155 \text{ kJ} \times \dfrac{1 \text{ mol } H_2O}{40.7 \text{ kJ}} \times \dfrac{18.02 \text{ g}}{1 \text{ mol } H_2O} = 68.6 \text{ g}$

CHECK	
Check your answer. Are the units correct? Does the answer make physical sense?	The units (g) are correct. The magnitude of the answer makes sense because each mole of water absorbs about 40 kJ of energy upon vaporization. Therefore 155 kJ should vaporize close to 4 mol of water, which is consistent with the answer (4 mol of water has a mass of about 72 g).

▶**SKILLBUILDER 12.1 | Using the Heat of Vaporization in Calculations**

Calculate the amount of heat in kilojoules required to vaporize 2.58 kg of water at its boiling point.

▶**SKILLBUILDER PLUS** A drop of water weighing 0.48 g condenses on the surface of a 55-g block of aluminum that is initially at 25 °C. If the heat released during condensation goes only toward heating the metal, what is the final temperature in Celsius of the metal block? (The specific heat capacity of aluminum is listed in Table 3.4 and is 0.903 J/g °C.)

▶**FOR MORE PRACTICE**   Example 12.7; Problems 49, 50, 51, 52, 53, 54.

 CONCEPTUAL CHECKPOINT 12.3

When water condenses on a small metal block, what would you expect to happen to the temperature of the metal block?

12.5   Melting, Freezing, and Sublimation

LO: Describe and explain the processes of melting, freezing, and sublimation.

LO: Use the heat of fusion in calculations.

As the temperature of a solid increases, thermal energy causes the molecules and atoms composing the solid to vibrate faster. At the **melting point**, atoms and molecules have enough thermal energy to overcome the intermolecular forces that hold them at their stationary points, and the solid turns into a liquid. The melting point of ice, for example, is 0 °C. Once the melting point of a solid is reached, additional heating only causes more rapid melting; it does not raise the temperature of the solid above its melting point (▶ Figure 12.16). Only after all of the ice has melted does additional heating raise the temperature of the liquid water past 0 °C. A mixture of water *and* ice always has a temperature of 0 °C (at 1 atm pressure).

Temperature of solid increases | Temperature remains constant as solid melts | Temperature of liquid increases

▲ **FIGURE 12.16 Heating curve during melting** A graph of the temperature of ice as it is heated from −20 °C to 35 °C. During melting, the temperature of the solid and the liquid remains at 0 °C until the entire solid is melted.

Energetics of Melting and Freezing

The most common way to cool down a drink is to drop several ice cubes into it. As the ice melts, the drink cools because melting is endothermic—heat is absorbed when a solid is converted into a liquid. The melting ice absorbs heat from the liquid in the drink and cools the liquid. Melting is endothermic because energy is required to partially overcome the attractions between molecules in the solid and free them into the liquid state.

Freezing, the opposite of melting, is exothermic—heat is released when a liquid freezes into a solid. For example, as water in your freezer turns into ice, it releases heat, which must be removed by the refrigeration system of the freezer. If the refrigeration system did not remove the heat, the water would not completely freeze into ice. The heat released as it began to freeze would warm the freezer, preventing further freezing.

Heat of Fusion

The amount of heat required to melt 1 mol of a solid is the **heat of fusion** (ΔH_{fus}). The heat of fusion for water is 6.02 kJ/mol.

$$H_2O(s) \longrightarrow H_2O(l) \quad \Delta H = +6.02 \text{ kJ}$$

ΔH is positive because melting is endothermic; energy must be added to the ice to melt it.

The same amount of heat is involved when 1 mol of liquid water freezes, but the heat is emitted rather than absorbed.

$$H_2O(l) \longrightarrow H_2O(s) \quad \Delta H = -6.02 \text{ kJ}$$

ΔH is negative because freezing is exothermic; energy is given off as the water freezes.

Different substances have different heats of fusion (Table 12.3 on page 422). Notice that, in general, the heat of fusion is significantly less than the heat of vaporization. It takes less energy to melt 1 mol of ice than it does to vaporize 1 mol

▶ When ice melts, water molecules break free from the solid structure and become liquid. As long as ice and water are both present, the temperature is 0.0 °C.

TABLE 12.3   Heats of Fusion of Several Substances

Liquid	Chemical Formula	Melting Point (°C)	Heat of Fusion (kJ/mol)
water	H_2O	0.00	6.02
isopropyl alcohol (rubbing alcohol)	C_3H_8O	−89.5	5.37
acetone	C_3H_6O	−94.8	5.69
diethyl ether	$C_4H_{10}O$	−116.3	7.27

of liquid water. Why? Vaporization requires complete separation of one molecule from another, so the intermolecular forces must be completely overcome. Melting, on the other hand, requires that intermolecular forces be only partially overcome, allowing molecules to move around one another while still remaining in contact.

We can use the heat of fusion to calculate the amount of heat energy required to melt a given amount of a solid. The heat of fusion is a conversion factor between moles of a solid and the amount of heat required to melt it. For example, suppose we want to calculate the amount of heat required to melt 25.0 g of ice (at 0 °C). We first sort the information in the problem statement.

GIVEN: 25.0 g H_2O

FIND: heat (kJ)

SOLUTION MAP
We then draw the solution map, beginning with the mass of water and ending with the energy required to melt it.

$$\frac{1 \text{ mol } H_2O}{18.02 \text{ g } H_2O} \qquad \frac{6.02 \text{ kJ}}{1 \text{ mol } H_2O}$$

RELATIONSHIPS USED
$$\Delta H_{fus} = 6.02 \text{ kJ/mol (Table 12.3)}$$
$$1 \text{ mol } H_2O = 18.02 \text{ g } H_2O \text{ (molar mass of water)}$$

SOLUTION
$$25.0 \text{ g } H_2O \times \frac{1 \text{ mol } H_2O}{18.02 \text{ g } H_2O} \times \frac{6.02 \text{ kJ}}{1 \text{ mol } H_2O} = 8.35 \text{ kJ}$$

EXAMPLE 12.2   USING THE HEAT OF FUSION IN CALCULATIONS

Calculate the amount of ice in grams that, upon melting (at 0 °C), absorbs 237 kJ of heat.

SORT You are given the number of kJ of heat energy and asked to find the mass of ice that absorbs the given amount of energy upon melting.	**GIVEN:** 237 kJ **FIND:** g H_2O (ice)
STRATEGIZE Draw the solution map beginning with the energy in kilojoules and converting to moles of water and then to grams of water.	**SOLUTION MAP** $$\frac{1 \text{ mol } H_2O}{6.02 \text{ kJ}} \qquad \frac{18.02 \text{ g}}{1 \text{ mol } H_2O}$$

	RELATIONSHIPS USED
	$\Delta H_{fus} = 6.02 \text{ kJ/mol}$ (Table 12.3) $1 \text{ mol } H_2O = 18.02 \text{ g } H_2O$ (molar mass of water)
SOLVE Follow the solution map to solve the problem.	**SOLUTION** $237 \text{ kJ} \times \dfrac{1 \text{ mol } H_2O}{6.02 \text{ kJ}} \times \dfrac{18.02 \text{ g}}{1 \text{ mol } H_2O} = 709 \text{ g}$
CHECK Check your answer. Are the units correct? Does the answer make physical sense?	The units (g) are correct. The magnitude of the answer makes sense because each mole of water absorbs about 6 kJ of energy upon melting. Therefore 237 kJ should melt close to 40 mol of water, which is consistent with the answer (40 mol of water has a mass of about 720 g).

▶**SKILLBUILDER 12.2 | Using the Heat of Fusion in Calculations**

Calculate the amount of heat absorbed when a 15.5-g ice cube melts (at 0 °C).

▶**SKILLBUILDER PLUS** A 5.6-g ice cube (at 0 °C) is placed into 195 g of water initially at 25 °C. If the heat absorbed for melting the ice comes only from the 195 g of water, what is the temperature change of the 195 g of water?

▶**FOR MORE PRACTICE** Example 12.8; Problems 57, 58, 59, 60.

CONCEPTUAL CHECKPOINT 12.4

This diagram shows a heating curve for ice beginning at −25 °C and ending at 125 °C. Correlate sections i, ii, and iii with the correct states of water.

(a) i—solid, ii—liquid, iii—gas
(b) i—solid and liquid, ii—liquid, iii—liquid and gas
(c) i—liquid, ii—liquid and gas, iii—gas
(d) i—solid and liquid, ii—liquid and gas , iii—gas

Sublimation

Sublimation is a physical change in which a substance changes from its solid state directly to its gaseous state. When a substance sublimes, molecules leave

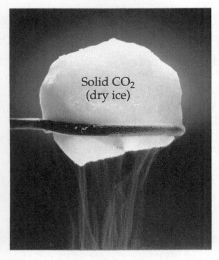

Solid CO₂
(dry ice)

▲ Dry ice is solid carbon dioxide. The solid does not melt but rather sublimes. It transforms directly from solid carbon dioxide to gaseous carbon dioxide.

the surface of the solid, where they are held less tightly than in the interior, and become gaseous. For example, dry ice, which is solid carbon dioxide, does not melt under atmospheric pressure (at any temperature). At $-78\,°C$, the CO_2 molecules have enough energy to leave the surface of the dry ice and become gaseous. Regular ice slowly sublimes at temperatures below $0\,°C$. You can observe the sublimation of ice in cold climates; ice or snow laying on the ground gradually disappears, even if the temperature remains below $0\,°C$. Similarly, ice cubes left in the freezer for a long time slowly become smaller, even though the freezer is always below $0\,°C$. In both cases, the ice is subliming, turning directly into water vapor.

Ice also sublimes out of frozen foods. You can clearly see this in food that is frozen in an airtight plastic bag for a long time. The ice crystals that form in the bag are water that has sublimed out of the food and redeposited on the surface of the bag. For this reason, food that remains frozen for too long becomes dried out. This can be avoided to some degree by freezing foods to colder temperatures (further below $0\,°C$), a process called deep-freezing. The colder temperature lowers the rate of sublimation and preserves the food longer.

✓ CONCEPTUAL CHECKPOINT 12.5

Solid carbon dioxide (dry ice) can be depicted as follows:

Which image best represents the dry ice after it has sublimed?

(a)   (b)   (c)

12.6   Types of Intermolecular Forces: Dispersion, Dipole–Dipole, Hydrogen Bonding, and Ion–Dipole

LO: Compare and contrast four types of intermolecular forces: dispersion, dipole–dipole, hydrogen bonds, and ion–dipole.

LO: Determine the types of intermolecular forces in compounds.

LO: Use intermolecular forces to determine relative melting and/or boiling points.

The strength of the intermolecular forces between the molecules or atoms that compose a substance determines the state—solid, liquid, or gas—of the substance at room temperature. Strong intermolecular forces tend to result in liquids and solids (with high melting and boiling points). Weak intermolecular forces tend to result in gases (with low melting and boiling points). In this book, we focus on four fundamental types of intermolecular forces. In order of increasing strength, they are the dispersion force, the dipole–dipole force, the hydrogen bond, and the ion–dipole force.

Dispersion Force

The default intermolecular force, present in all molecules and atoms, is the **dispersion force** (also called the *London force*). Dispersion forces are caused by fluctuations in the electron distribution within molecules or atoms. Since all atoms and molecules have electrons, they all have dispersion forces. The electrons in an atom or a molecule may, at any one instant, be unevenly distributed. For example, imagine a frame-by-frame movie of a helium atom in which each "frame" captures the position of the helium atom's two electrons (▼ Figure 12.17). In any one frame, the electrons are not symmetrically arranged around the nucleus. In Frame 3, for example, helium's two electrons are on the left side of the helium atom. The left side then acquires a slightly negative charge (δ^-). The right side of the atom, which is void of electrons, acquires a slightly positive charge (δ^+).

> The nature of dispersion forces was first recognized by Fritz W. London (1900–1954), a German-American physicist.

▶ **FIGURE 12.17 Instantaneous dipoles** Random fluctuations in the electron distribution of a helium atom cause instantaneous dipoles to form.

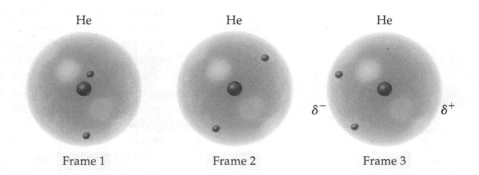

He	He	He

Frame 1   Frame 2   Frame 3

This fleeting charge separation is called an **instantaneous dipole** (or *temporary dipole*). An instantaneous dipole on one helium atom induces an instantaneous dipole on its neighboring atoms because the positive end of the instantaneous dipole attracts electrons in the neighboring atoms (▼ Figure 12.18). The dispersion force occurs as neighboring atoms attract one another—the positive end of one instantaneous dipole attracts the negative end of another. The dipoles responsible for the dispersion force are transient, constantly appearing and disappearing in response to fluctuations in electron clouds.

▶ **FIGURE 12.18 Dispersion force** An instantaneous dipole on any one helium atom induces instantaneous dipoles on neighboring atoms. The neighboring atoms then attract one another. This attraction is called the dispersion force.

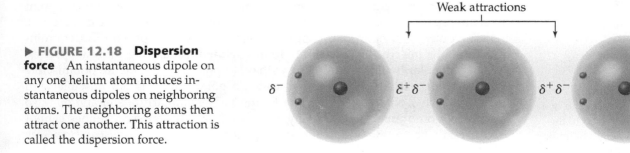

Weak attractions

| To *polarize* means to form a dipole moment.

TABLE 12.4   Noble Gas Boiling Points

Noble Gas	Molar Mass (g/mol)	Boiling Point (K)
He	4.00	4.2 K
Ne	20.18	27 K
Ar	39.95	87 K
Kr	83.80	120 K
Xe	131.29	165 K

The magnitude of the dispersion force depends on how easily the electrons in the atom or molecule move or *polarize* in response to an instantaneous dipole, which in turn depends on the size of the electron cloud. A larger electron cloud results in a greater dispersion force because the electrons are held less tightly by the nucleus and therefore can polarize more easily. If all other variables are constant, the dispersion force increases with increasing molar mass. For example, consider the boiling points of the noble gases displayed in Table 12.4. As the molar mass of the noble gases increases, their boiling points increase. While molar mass alone does not determine the magnitude of the dispersion force, it can be useful as a guide when comparing dispersion forces within a family of similar elements or compounds.

EXAMPLE 12.3   DISPERSION FORCES

Which halogen, Cl_2 or I_2, has the higher boiling point?

SOLUTION
The molar mass of Cl_2 is 70.90 g/mol, and the molar mass of I_2 is 253.80 g/mol. Since I_2 has the higher molar mass, it has stronger dispersion forces and therefore the higher boiling point.

▶SKILLBUILDER 12.3 | Dispersion Forces
Which hydrocarbon, CH_4 or C_2H_6, has the higher boiling point?

▶FOR MORE PRACTICE   Problems 69, 70.

Dipole–Dipole Force

| See Section 10.8 to review how to determine whether a molecule is polar.

The **dipole–dipole force** exists in all polar molecules. Polar molecules have **permanent dipoles** (Section 10.8) that interact with the permanent dipoles of neighboring molecules (◀ Figure 12.19). The positive end of one permanent dipole is attracted to the negative end of another; this attraction is the dipole–dipole force (◀ Figure 12.20). Polar molecules, therefore, have higher melting and boiling points than nonpolar molecules of similar molar mass. Remember that all molecules (including polar ones) have dispersion forces. In addition, polar molecules have dipole–dipole forces. These additional attractive forces raise their melting and boiling points relative to nonpolar molecules of similar molar mass. For example, consider the compounds formaldehyde and ethane:

▲ **FIGURE 12.19   A permanent dipole**   Molecules such as formaldehyde are polar and therefore have a permanent dipole.

Name	Formula	Molar mass (g/mol)	Structure	bp (°C)	mp (°C)
Formaldehyde	CH_2O	30.0	H—C—H with O double bond	−19.5	−92
Ethane	C_2H_6	30.1	H—C—C—H (with H's)	−88	−172

Formaldehyde is polar and therefore has a higher melting point and boiling point than nonpolar ethane, even though the two compounds have the same molar mass.

The polarity of molecules composing liquids is also important in determining a liquid's **miscibility**—its ability to mix without separating into two phases. In general, polar liquids are miscible with other polar liquids but are not miscible with nonpolar liquids. For example, water, a polar liquid, is not miscible with pentane (C_5H_{12}), a nonpolar liquid (▶ Figure 12.21). Similarly, water and oil (also nonpolar) do not mix. Consequently, oily hands or oily stains on clothes cannot be washed away with plain water (see Chapter 10, *Everyday Chemistry: How Soap Works*).

▲ **FIGURE 12.20   Dipole–dipole attraction**   The positive end of a polar molecule is attracted to the negative end of its neighbor, giving rise to the dipole–dipole force.

(a)   (b)   (c)

◀ **FIGURE 12.21 Polar and nonpolar compounds** (a) Pentane, a nonpolar compound, does not mix with water, a polar compound. **(b)** For the same reason, the oil and vinegar (vinegar is largely a water solution of acetic acid) in salad dressing tend to separate into distinct layers. **(c)** An oil spill from a tanker demonstrates dramatically that petroleum and seawater are not miscible.

EXAMPLE 12.4   DIPOLE–DIPOLE FORCES

Determine whether each molecule has dipole–dipole forces.

(a) CO_2 (b) CH_2Cl_2 (c) CH_4

SOLUTION

A molecule has dipole–dipole forces if it is polar. To find out whether a molecule is polar, you must:

1. determine whether the molecule contains polar bonds, and
2. determine whether the polar bonds add together to form a net dipole moment (Section 10.8).

(a) The electronegativities of carbon and oxygen are 2.5 and 3.5, respectively (Figure 10.2), so CO_2 has polar bonds. The geometry of CO_2 is linear. Consequently, the polar bonds cancel; the molecule is not polar and does not have dipole–dipole forces.	$O=C=O$ Nonpolar; no dipole–dipole forces
(b) The electronegativities of C, H, and Cl are 2.5, 2.1, and 3.5, respectively. Consequently, CH_2Cl_2 has two polar bonds (C—Cl) and two bonds that are nearly nonpolar (C—H). The geometry of CH_2Cl_2 is tetrahedral. Since the C—Cl bonds and the C—H bonds are different, they do not cancel, but sum to a net dipole moment. Therefore the molecule is polar and has dipole–dipole forces.	 Polar; dipole-dipole forces
(c) Since the electronegativities of C and H are 2.5 and 2.1, respectively, the C—H bonds are nearly nonpolar. In addition, because the geometry of the molecule is tetrahedral, any slight polarities that the bonds might have will cancel. CH_4 is therefore nonpolar and does not have dipole–dipole forces.	 Nonpolar; no dipole-dipole forces

---

▶**SKILLBUILDER 12.4 | Dipole–Dipole Forces**

Determine whether or not each molecule has dipole–dipole forces.

(a) CI_4 (b) CH_3Cl (c) HCl

▶**FOR MORE PRACTICE**   Problems 61, 62, 65, 66.

Hydrogen Bonding

Polar molecules containing hydrogen atoms bonded directly to fluorine, oxygen, or nitrogen exhibit an additional intermolecular force called a **hydrogen bond**. HF, NH_3, and H_2O, for example, all undergo hydrogen bonding. A hydrogen bond is a sort of *super* dipole–dipole force. The large electronegativity difference between hydrogen and these electronegative elements, as well as the small size of these atoms (which allows neighboring molecules to get very close to each other), gives rise to a strong attraction between the hydrogen in each of these molecules and the F, O, or N on neighboring molecules. This attraction between a hydrogen atom and an electronegative atom is the hydrogen bond. For example, in HF the hydrogen is strongly attracted to the fluorine on neighboring molecules (◄ Figure 12.22).

Do not confuse hydrogen bonds with chemical bonds. Chemical bonds occur between *individual atoms within a molecule* and are generally much stronger than hydrogen bonds. A hydrogen bond has only 2 to 5% the strength of a typical covalent chemical bond. Hydrogen bonds—like dispersion forces and dipole–dipole forces—are intermolecular forces that occur *between molecules*. In liquid water, for example, the hydrogen bonds are transient, constantly forming, breaking, and reforming as water molecules move within the liquid. Hydrogen bonds are, however, strong intermolecular forces. Substances composed of molecules that form hydrogen bonds have much higher melting and boiling points than you would predict based on molar mass. For example, consider the two compounds, methanol and ethane:

$\delta^+ \ \delta^- \quad \delta^+ \ \delta^- \quad \delta^+ \ \delta^-$

H—F ⋯⋯ H—F ⋯⋯ H—F

▲ **FIGURE 12.22 The hydrogen bond** In HF, the hydrogen on each molecule is strongly attracted to the fluorine on its neighbor. The intermolecular attraction of a hydrogen atom to an electronegative atom is called a *hydrogen bond*.

Name	Formula	Molar mass (g/mol)	Structure	bp (°C)	mp (°C)
Methanol	CH_3OH	32.0	H—C—O—H (with H above and H below C)	64.7	−97.8
Ethane	C_2H_6	30.1	H—C—C—H (with H's above and below each C)	−88	−172

Since methanol contains hydrogen directly bonded to oxygen, its molecules have hydrogen bonding as an intermolecular force. The hydrogen that is directly bonded to oxygen is strongly attracted to the oxygen on neighboring molecules (◄ Figure 12.23). This strong attraction makes the boiling point of methanol 64.7 °C. Consequently, methanol is a liquid at room temperature. Water is another good example of a molecule with hydrogen bonding as an intermolecular force (▼ Figure 12.24). The boiling point of water (100 °C) is remarkably high for a molecule with such a low molar mass (18.02 g/mol). Hydrogen bonding is important in biological molecules. The shapes of proteins and nucleic acids are largely influenced by hydrogen bonding; for example, the two halves of DNA are held together by hydrogen bonds (see the *Chemistry and Health* box later in this section).

▲ **FIGURE 12.23 Hydrogen bonding in methanol** Since methanol contains hydrogen atoms directly bonded to oxygen, methanol molecules form hydrogen bonds to one another. The hydrogen atom on each methanol molecule is attracted to the oxygen atom of its neighbor.

◄ **FIGURE 12.24 Hydrogen bonding in water** Water molecules form strong hydrogen bonds with one another.

EXAMPLE 12.5   **HYDROGEN BONDING**

One of these compounds is a liquid at room temperature. Which one and why?

| Formaldehyde | Fluoromethane | Hydrogen peroxide |

SOLUTION

The three compounds have similar molar masses.

formaldehyde	30.03 g/mol
fluoromethane	34.04 g/mol
hydrogen peroxide	34.02 g/mol

Therefore, the strengths of their dispersion forces are similar. All three compounds are also polar, so they have dipole–dipole forces. Hydrogen peroxide, however, is the only compound that also contains H bonded directly to F, O, or N. Therefore it also has hydrogen bonding and is most likely to have the highest boiling point of the three. Since the problem stated that only one of the compounds was a liquid, we can safely assume that hydrogen peroxide is the liquid. Note that although fluoromethane *contains* both H and F, H is not *directly bonded* to F, so fluoromethane does not have hydrogen bonding as an intermolecular force. Similarly, although formaldehyde *contains* both H and O, H is not *directly bonded* to O, so formaldehyde does not have hydrogen bonding either.

▶**SKILLBUILDER 12.5** | **Hydrogen Bonding**

Which has the higher boiling point, HF or HCl? Why?

▶**FOR MORE PRACTICE**   Examples 12.9, 12.10; Problems 71, 72, 73, 74, 75, 76.

> In some cases, hydrogen bonding can occur between one molecule in which H is directly bonded to F, O, or N and another molecule containing an electronegative atom. (See the box, *Chemistry and Health*, in this section for an example.)

✓   **CONCEPTUAL CHECKPOINT 12.6**

Three molecular compounds A, B, and C have nearly identical molar masses. Substance A is nonpolar, substance B is polar, and substance C undergoes hydrogen bonding. What is most likely to be the relative order of their boiling points?

(a) A < B < C

(b) C < B < A

(c) B < C < A

▲ **FIGURE 12.25   Ion–dipole forces.**   Ion–dipole forces exist between Na⁺ and the negative ends of H_2O molecules and between Cl⁻ and the positive ends of H_2O molecules.

Ion–Dipole Force

The **ion–dipole force** occurs in mixtures of ionic compounds and polar compounds; it is especially important in aqueous solutions of ionic compounds. For example, when sodium chloride is mixed with water, the sodium and chloride ions interact with water molecules via ion–dipole forces, as shown in ◀ Figure 12.25. The positive sodium ions interact with the negative poles of water molecules, while the negative chloride ions interact with the positive poles. Ion–dipole forces are the strongest of the four types of intermolecular forces discussed and are responsible for the ability of ionic substances to form solutions with water. We will discuss aqueous solutions more thoroughly in Chapter 13.

Table 12.5 summarizes the different types of intermolecular forces. Remember that dispersion forces, the weakest kind of intermolecular force, are present in all molecules and atoms and increase with increasing molar mass. These forces are weak in small molecules, but they become substantial in molecules with high molar masses. Dipole–dipole forces are present only in polar molecules. Hydrogen bonds are present in molecules containing hydrogen bonded directly to fluorine, oxygen, or nitrogen, and ion–dipole forces occur in mixtures of ionic compounds and polar compounds.

TABLE 12.5 Types of Intermolecular Forces

Type of Force	Relative Strength	Present in	Example
dispersion force (or London force)	weak, but increases with increasing molar mass	all atoms and molecules	H_2 ... H_2
dipole–dipole force	moderate	only polar molecules	HCl ... HCl
hydrogen bond	strong	molecules containing H bonded directly to F, O, or N	HF ... HF
ion–dipole	very strong	mixtures of ionic compounds and polar compounds	

CHEMISTRY AND HEALTH
▶ Hydrogen Bonding in DNA

DNA is a long chainlike molecule that acts as a blueprint for living organisms. Copies of DNA are passed from parent to offspring, which is why we inherit traits from our parents. A DNA molecule is composed of thousands of repeating units called *nucleotides* (▶ Figure 12.26). Each nucleotide contains one of four different bases: adenine, thymine, cytosine, and guanine (abbreviated A, T, C, and G, respectively). The order of these bases in DNA encodes the instructions that specify how proteins—the workhorse molecules in living organisms—are made in each cell of the body. Proteins determine virtually all human characteristics, including how

we look, how we fight infections, and even how we behave. Consequently, human DNA is a blueprint for how humans are made.

Each time a human cell divides, it must copy the blueprint—which means replicating its DNA. The replicating mechanism is related to the structure of DNA, discovered in 1953 by James Watson and Francis Crick. DNA consists of two complementary strands wrapped around each other in the now famous double helix. Each strand is held to the other by hydrogen bonds that occur between the bases on each strand. DNA replicates because each base (A, T, C, and G)

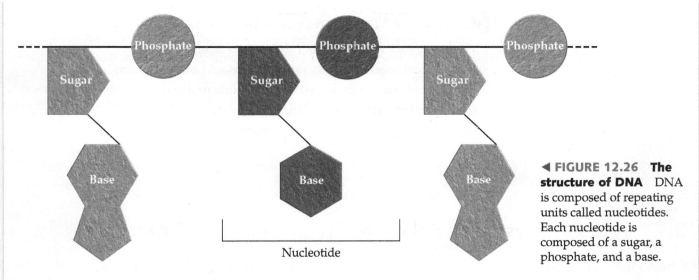

◀ **FIGURE 12.26 The structure of DNA** DNA is composed of repeating units called nucleotides. Each nucleotide is composed of a sugar, a phosphate, and a base.

has a complementary partner with which it hydrogen-bonds (▼ Figure 12.27). Adenine (A) hydrogen-bonds with thymine (T), and cytosine (C) hydrogen-bonds with guanine (G). The hydrogen bonds are so specific that each base will pair only with its complementary partner. When a cell is going to divide, the DNA unzips across the hydrogen bonds that run along its length. Then new nucleotides, containing bases complementary to the bases in each half, add along each of the halves, forming hydrogen bonds with their complement. The result is two identical copies of the original DNA (see Chapter 19).

B12.2 CAN YOU ANSWER THIS? *Why would dispersion forces not work as a way to hold the two halves of DNA together? Why would covalent bonds not work?*

▶ **FIGURE 12.27 Hydrogen bonding in DNA** The two halves of the DNA double helix are held together by hydrogen bonds.

CONCEPTUAL CHECKPOINT 12.7

When dry ice sublimes, what forces are overcome?

(a) chemical bonds between carbon atoms and oxygen atoms

(b) hydrogen bonds between carbon dioxide molecules

(c) dispersion forces between carbon dioxide molecules

(d) dipole–dipole forces between carbon dioxide molecules

12.7   Types of Crystalline Solids: Molecular, Ionic, and Atomic

LO: Identify types of crystalline solids.

As we learned in Section 12.2, solids may be crystalline (showing a well-ordered array of atoms or molecules) or amorphous (having no long-range order). We divide crystalline solids into three categories—molecular, ionic, and atomic—based on the individual units that compose the solid (▼ Figure 12.28).

Molecular Solids

Molecular solids are solids whose composite units are *molecules*. Ice (solid H_2O) and dry ice (solid CO_2) are examples of molecular solids. Molecular solids are held together by the kinds of intermolecular forces—dispersion forces, dipole–dipole forces, and hydrogen bonding—that we just discussed in Section 12.6. For example,

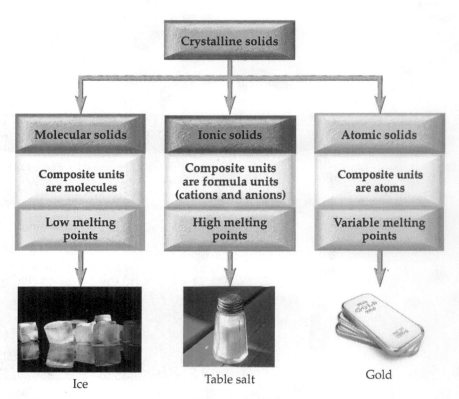

▲ **FIGURE 12.28   A classification scheme for crystalline solids**

ice is held together by hydrogen bonds, and dry ice is held together by dispersion forces. Molecular solids as a whole tend to have low to moderately low melting points; ice melts at 0 °C and dry ice sublimes at −78.5 °C.

Ionic Solids

See Section 5.4 for a complete description of the formula unit.

Ionic solids are solids whose composite units are *formula units*, the smallest electrically neutral collection of cations and anions that compose the compound. Table salt (NaCl) and calcium fluoride (CaF_2) are good examples of ionic solids. Ionic solids are held together by electrostatic attractions between cations and anions. For example, in NaCl, the attraction between the Na^+ cation and the Cl^- anion holds the solid lattice together because the lattice is composed of alternating Na^+ cations and Cl^- anions in a three-dimensional array. In other words, the forces that hold ionic solids together are actual ionic bonds. Since ionic bonds are much stronger than any of the intermolecular forces discussed previously, ionic solids tend to have much higher melting points than molecular solids. For example, sodium chloride melts at 801 °C, while carbon disulfide CS_2—a molecular solid with a higher molar mass—melts at −110 °C.

Atomic Solids

Atomic solids are solids whose composite units are *individual atoms*. Diamond (C), iron (Fe), and solid xenon (Xe) are good examples of atomic solids. We can divide atomic solids into three categories—**covalent atomic solids**, **nonbonding atomic solids**, and **metallic atomic solids**—each held together by a different kind of force (▼ Figure 12.29).

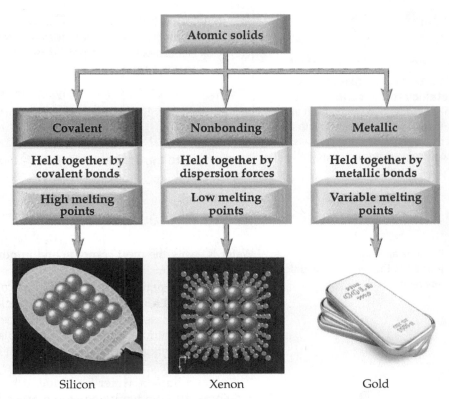

▲ **FIGURE 12.29   A classification scheme for atomic solids**

▲ **FIGURE 12.30 Diamond: a covalent atomic solid** In diamond, carbon atoms form covalent bonds in a three-dimensional hexagonal pattern.

▲ **FIGURE 12.31 Structure of a metallic atomic solid** In the simplest model of a metal, each atom donates one or more electrons to an "electron sea." The metal consists of the metal cations in a negatively charged electron sea.

Covalent atomic solids, such as diamond, are held together by covalent bonds. In diamond (◀ Figure 12.30), each carbon atom forms four covalent bonds to four other carbon atoms in a tetrahedral geometry. This structure extends throughout the entire crystal, so that a diamond crystal can be thought of as a giant molecule held together by these covalent bonds. Since covalent bonds are very strong, covalent atomic solids have high melting points. Diamond is estimated to melt at about 3800 °C.

Nonbonding atomic solids, such as solid xenon, are held together by relatively weak dispersion forces. Xenon atoms have stable electron configurations and therefore do not form covalent bonds with each other. Consequently, solid xenon, like other nonbonding atomic solids, has a very low melting point (about −112 °C).

Metallic atomic solids, such as iron, have variable melting points. Metals are held together by metallic bonds that, in the simplest model, consist of positively charged ions in a sea of electrons (◀ Figure 12.31). Metallic bonds are of varying strengths, with some metals, such as mercury, having melting points below room temperature, and other metals, such as iron, having relatively high melting points (iron melts at 1809 °C).

| EXAMPLE 12.6 | IDENTIFYING TYPES OF CRYSTALLINE SOLIDS |

Identify each solid as molecular, ionic, or atomic.

(a) $CaCl_2(s)$ **(b)** $Co(s)$ **(c)** $CS_2(s)$

SOLUTION

(a) $CaCl_2$ is an ionic compound (metal and nonmetal) and therefore forms an ionic solid ($CaCl_2$ melts at 772 °C).

(b) Co is a metal and therefore forms a metallic atomic solid (Co melts at 1768 °C).

(c) CS_2 is a molecular compound (nonmetal bonded to a nonmetal) and therefore forms a molecular solid (CS_2 melts at −110 °C).

▶**SKILLBUILDER 12.6 | Identifying Types of Crystalline Solids**

Identify each solid as molecular, ionic, or atomic.

(a) $NH_3(s)$ **(b)** $CaO(s)$ **(c)** $Kr(s)$

▶**FOR MORE PRACTICE** Problems 79, 80, 81, 82.

12.8 Water: A Remarkable Molecule

LO: Describe and explain the properties that make water unique among molecules.

Water is easily the most common and important liquid on Earth. It fills our oceans, lakes, and streams. In its solid form, it covers nearly an entire continent (Antarctica), as well as large regions around the North Pole, and caps our tallest mountains. In its gaseous form, it humidifies our air. We drink water, we sweat water, and we excrete bodily wastes dissolved in water. Indeed, the majority of our body mass *is* water. Life is impossible without water, and in most places on Earth where liquid water exists, life exists. Evidence of water on Mars—that existed either in the past or exists in the present—has fueled hopes of finding life or evidence of life there. Water is remarkable.

Among liquids, water is unique. It has a low molar mass (18.02 g/mol), yet is a liquid at room temperature. No other compound of similar molar mass even comes close to being a liquid at room temperature. For example, nitrogen (28.02 g/mol) and carbon dioxide (44.01 g/mol) are both gases at room temperature. Water's relatively high boiling point (for its low molar mass) can be understood by examining the structure of the water molecule (◀ Figure 12.32). The bent geometry

▲ **FIGURE 12.32 The water molecule**

of the water molecule and the highly polar nature of the O—H bonds result in a molecule with a significant dipole moment. Water's two O—H bonds (hydrogen directly bonded to oxygen) allow water molecules to form strong hydrogen bonds with other water molecules, resulting in a relatively high boiling point. Water's high polarity also allows it to dissolve many other polar and ionic compounds. Consequently, water is the main solvent of living organisms, transporting nutrients and other important compounds throughout the body.

The way water freezes is also unique. Unlike other substances, which contract upon freezing, water expands upon freezing. This seemingly trivial property has significant consequences. Because liquid water expands when it freezes, ice is less dense than liquid water. Consequently, ice cubes and icebergs both float. The frozen layer of ice at the surface of a winter lake insulates the water in the lake from further freezing. If this ice layer were to sink, it would kill bottom-dwelling aquatic life and possibly allow the lake to freeze solid, eliminating virtually all aquatic life in the lake.

The expansion of water upon freezing, however, is one reason that most organisms do not survive freezing. When the water within a cell freezes, it expands and often ruptures the cell, just as water freezing within a pipe bursts the pipe. Many foods, especially those with high water content, do not survive freezing very well either. Have you ever tried, for example, to freeze a vegetable? Try putting lettuce or spinach in the freezer. When you defrost it, it will be limp and damaged. The frozen food industry gets around this problem by *flash-freezing* vegetables and other foods. In this process, foods are frozen instantaneously, preventing water molecules from settling into their preferred crystalline structure. Consequently, the water does not expand very much, and the food remains largely undamaged.

Water reaches its maximum density at 4.0 °C.

▲ Lettuce does not survive freezing because the expansion of water upon freezing ruptures the cells within the lettuce leaf.

CHEMISTRY IN THE ENVIRONMENT
▶ Water Pollution

Water quality is critical to human health. Many human diseases—especially in developing nations—are caused by poor water quality. Several kinds of pollutants, including biological and chemical contaminants, can get into water supplies. Biological contaminants are microorganisms that cause diseases such as hepatitis, cholera, dysentery, and typhoid. Drinking water in developed nations is usually treated to kill microorganisms. Most biological contaminants can be eliminated from untreated water by boiling. Water containing biological contaminants poses an immediate danger to human health and should not be consumed.

Chemical contaminants get into drinking water from sources such as industrial dumping, pesticide and fertilizer use, and household dumping. These contaminants include organic compounds, such as carbon tetrachloride and dioxin, and inorganic elements and compounds such as mercury, lead, and nitrates. Since many chemical contaminants are neither volatile nor alive like biological contaminants, they are *not* eliminated through boiling.

The Environmental Protection Agency (EPA), under the Safe Drinking Water Act of 1974 and its amendments, sets standards that specify the maximum contamination level (MCL) for nearly 100 biological and chemical contaminants in water. Water providers that serve more than 25 people must periodically test the water they deliver to their consumers for these contaminants. If levels exceed the standards set by the EPA, the water provider must notify the consumer and take appropriate measures to remove the contaminant

from the water. According to the EPA, if water comes from a provider that serves more than 25 people, it should be safe to consume over a lifetime. If it is not safe to drink for a short period of time, consumers are notified.

▲ Safe drinking water has a major effect on public health and the spread of disease. In many parts of the world, the water supply is unsafe to drink. In the United States the Environmental Protection Agency (EPA) is charged with maintaining water safety.

B12.3 CAN YOU ANSWER THIS? *Suppose a sample of water is contaminated by a nonvolatile contaminant such as lead. Why doesn't boiling eliminate the contaminant?*

CHAPTER IN REVIEW

Self-Assessment Quiz

Q1. The first diagram shown here represents liquid water. Which of the diagrams that follow best represents the water after it has boiled?

(a)

(b)

(c)

Q2. Which change affects the vapor pressure of a liquid?

(a) Pouring the liquid into a different container

(b) Increasing the surface area of the liquid

(c) Increasing the temperature of the liquid

(d) All of the above

Q3. How much heat is required to vaporize 38.5 g of acetone (C_3H_6O) at 25 °C? The heat of vaporization for acetone at this temperature is 31.0 kJ/mol.

(a) 31.0 kJ   (b) 1194 kJ

(c) 0.0214 kJ   (d) 20.5 kJ

Q4. How many 20.0-g ice cubes are required to absorb 47.0 kJ from a glass of water upon melting?

(a) 6   (b) 7   (c) 127   (d) 140

Q5. A sample of ice is heated past its melting point, and its temperature is monitored. The graph below shows the results. What is the first point on the graph where the sample contains no solid ice?

(a) A   (b) B   (c) C   (d) D

Q6. Which halogen has the highest boiling point?

(a) F_2 (b) Cl_2 (c) Br_2 (d) I_2

Q7. Which substance has dipole–dipole forces?

(a) OF_2 (b) CBr_4 (c) CS_2 (d) Br_2

Q8. Which substance exhibits hydrogen bonding?

(a) CF_4 (b) CH_3OH (c) H_2 (d) PH_3

Q9. Which substance is an ionic solid?

(a) $Ti(s)$ (b) $CaO(s)$

(c) $CO_2(s)$ (d) $H_2O(s)$

Q10. Which substance would you expect to have the highest melting point?

(a) CH_3CH_3 (b) CH_3CH_2Cl

(c) CH_4 (d) CH_3CH_2OH

Answers: 1:a, 2:c, 3:d, 4:b, 5:c, 6:d, 7:a, 8:b, 9:b, 10:d

Chemical Principles

Properties of Liquids:

- High densities in comparison to gases.

- Indefinite shape; they assume the shape of their container.

- Definite volume; they are not easily compressed.

Properties of Solids:

- High densities in comparison to gases.

- Definite shape; they do not assume the shape of their container.

- Definite volume; they are not easily compressed.

- May be crystalline (ordered) or amorphous (disordered).

Relevance

Properties of Liquids: Common liquids include water, acetone (fingernail-polish remover), and rubbing alcohol. Water is the most common and most important liquid on Earth. It is difficult to imagine life without water.

Properties of Solids: Much of the matter we encounter is solid. Common solids include ice, dry ice, and diamond. Understanding the properties of solids involves understanding the particles that compose them and how those particles interact.

Manifestations of Intermolecular Forces: Surface tension—the tendency for liquids to minimize their surface area—is a direct result of intermolecular forces. Viscosity—the resistance of liquids to flow—is another result of intermolecular forces. Both surface tension and viscosity increase with greater intermolecular forces.

Manifestations of Intermolecular Forces: Many insects can walk on water due to surface tension. The viscosity of a liquid is one of its defining properties and is important in applications such as automobile lubrication; the viscosity of a motor oil must be high enough to coat an engine's surfaces, but not so high that it can't flow to remote parts of the engine.

Evaporation and Condensation: Evaporation or vaporization—an endothermic physical change—is the conversion of a liquid to a gas. Condensation—an exothermic physical change—is the conversion of a gas to a liquid. When the rates of evaporation and condensation in a liquid/gas sample are equal, dynamic equilibrium is reached and the partial pressure of the gas at that point is its vapor pressure. When the vapor pressure equals the external pressure, the boiling point is reached. At the boiling point, thermal energy causes molecules in the interior of the liquid, as well as those at the surface, to convert to gas, resulting in the bubbling. We can calculate the heat absorbed or emitted during evaporation and condensation (respectively) using the heat of vaporization.

Evaporation and Condensation: Evaporation is the body's natural cooling system. When we get overheated, we sweat; the sweat then evaporates and cools us. Evaporation and condensation both play roles in moderating climate. Humid areas, for example, cool less at night because as the temperature drops, water condenses out of the air, releasing heat and preventing a further temperature drop.

Melting and Freezing: Melting—an endothermic physical change—is the conversion of a solid to a liquid, and freezing—an exothermic physical change—is the conversion of a liquid to a solid. We can calculate the heat absorbed or emitted during melting and freezing (respectively) using the heat of fusion.

Melting and Freezing: We use the melting of solid ice, for example, to cool drinks when we place ice cubes in them. Since melting is endothermic, it absorbs heat from the liquid and cools it.

Types of Intermolecular Forces: The four main types of intermolecular forces are:

Dispersion forces—Dispersion forces occur between all molecules and atoms due to instantaneous fluctuations in electron charge distribution. The strength of the dispersion force increases with increasing molar mass.

Dipole–dipole forces—Dipole–dipole forces exist between molecules that are polar. Consequently, polar molecules have higher melting and boiling points than nonpolar molecules of similar molar mass.

Hydrogen bonding—Hydrogen bonding exists between molecules that have H bonded directly to F, O, or N. Hydrogen bonds are stronger than dispersion forces or dipole–dipole forces.

Ion–dipole forces—The ion–dipole force occurs in mixtures of ionic compound and polar compounds.

Types of Intermolecular Forces: The type of intermolecular force present in a substance determines many of the properties of the substance. The stronger the intermolecular force, for example, the greater the melting and boiling points of the substance. In addition, the miscibility of liquids—their ability to mix without separating—depends on the relative kinds of intermolecular forces present within them. In general, polar liquids are miscible with other polar liquids, but not with nonpolar liquids. Hydrogen bonding is important in many biological molecules such as proteins and DNA. Ion–dipole forces are important in mixtures of ionic compounds and water.

Types of Crystalline Solids: We divide crystalline solids into three categories based on the individual units composing the solid:

Molecular solids—Molecules are the composite units of molecular solids, which are held together by dispersion forces, dipole–dipole forces, or hydrogen bonding.

Ionic solids—Formula units (the smallest electrically neutral collection of cations and anions) are the composite units of ionic solids. They are held together by the electrostatic attractions that occur between cations and anions.

Atomic solids—Atoms are the composite units of atomic solids, which are held together by different forces depending on the particular solid.

Types of Crystalline Solids: Solids have different properties depending on their individual units and the forces that hold those units together. Molecular solids tend to have low melting points. Ionic solids tend to have intermediate to high melting points. Atomic solids have varied melting points, depending on the particular solid.

Water: Water is a unique molecule. Because of its strong hydrogen bonding, water is a liquid at room temperature. Unlike most liquids, water expands when it freezes. In addition, water is highly polar, making it a good solvent for many polar substances.

Water: Water is critical to life. On Earth, wherever there is water, there is life. Water acts as a solvent and transport medium, and virtually all the chemical reactions on which life depends take place in aqueous solution. The expansion of water upon freezing allows life within frozen lakes to survive the winter. The ice on top of the lake acts as insulation, protecting the rest of the lake (and the life within it) from freezing.

Chemical Skills

Examples

LO: Use the heat of vaporization in calculations (Section 12.4).

EXAMPLE 12.7	HEAT OF VAPORIZATION IN CALCULATIONS

Calculate the amount of heat required to vaporize 84.8 g of water at its boiling point.

SORT

You are given the mass of water and asked to find the amount of heat required to vaporize it.

GIVEN: 84.8 g H_2O

FIND: heat (kJ)

STRATEGIZE

To calculate the amount of heat required to vaporize a given amount of a substance, first convert the given amount of the substance to moles and then use the heat of vaporization as a conversion factor to get to kilojoules. For vaporization, the heat is always absorbed. For condensation, follow the same procedure, but the heat is always emitted.

SOLUTION MAP

$$\frac{1 \text{ mol } H_2O}{18.02 \text{ g } H_2O} \qquad \frac{40.7 \text{ kJ}}{1 \text{ mol } H_2O}$$

RELATIONSHIPS USED

ΔH_{vap} = 40.7 kJ/mol   at 100 °C   (Table 12.2)

1 mol H_2O = 18.02 g H_2O (molar mass of water)

SOLVE

Follow the solution map to solve the problem.

SOLUTION

$$84.8 \text{ g } H_2O \times \frac{1 \text{ mol } H_2O}{18.02 \text{ g } H_2O} \times \frac{40.7 \text{ kJ}}{1 \text{ mol } H_2O} = 192 \text{ kJ}$$

CHECK

Check your answer. Are the units correct? Does the answer make physical sense?

The units (kJ) are correct. The magnitude of the answer makes sense because each mole of water absorbs about 40 kJ of energy upon vaporization. Therefore 84.8 g (between 4 and 5 mol) should absorb between 160 and 200 kJ upon vaporization.

LO: Use the heat of fusion in calculations (Section 12.5).

EXAMPLE 12.8	USING HEAT OF FUSION IN CALCULATIONS

Calculate the amount of heat emitted when 12.4 g of water freezes to solid ice.

SORT

You are given the mass of water and asked to find the amount of heat emitted when it freezes.

GIVEN: 12.4 g H_2O

FIND: heat (kJ)

STRATEGIZE

Use the heat of fusion as a conversion factor between moles of a substance and the amount of heat required to melt it. To calculate the amount of heat required to melt a given amount of a substance, first convert the given amount of the substance to moles and then use the heat of fusion as a conversion factor to get to kilojoules. For melting, the heat is always absorbed. For freezing, follow the same procedure, but the heat is always emitted.

SOLUTION MAP

$$\frac{1 \text{ mol } H_2O}{18.02 \text{ g } H_2O} \qquad \frac{6.02 \text{ kJ}}{1 \text{ mol } H_2O}$$

RELATIONSHIPS USED

$\Delta H_{fus} = 6.02 \text{ kJ/mol}$ (Table 12.3)

$1 \text{ mol } H_2O = 18.02 \text{ g } H_2O$ (molar mass of water)

SOLVE

Follow the solution map to solve the problem.

SOLUTION

$$12.4 \text{ g } H_2O \times \frac{1 \text{ mol } H_2O}{18.02 \text{ g } H_2O} \times \frac{6.02 \text{ kJ}}{1 \text{ mol } H_2O} = 4.14 \text{ kJ}$$

The heat emitted is 4.14 kJ.

CHECK

Check your answer. Are the units correct? Does the answer make physical sense?

The units (kJ) are correct. The magnitude of the answer makes sense because each mole of water emits about 6 kJ of energy upon freezing. Therefore 12.2 g (less than 1 mol) should emit less than 6 kJ upon freezing.

LO: Determine the types of intermolecular forces in compounds (Section 12.6).

All substances exhibit dispersion forces. Polar substances—those whose molecules have polar bonds that add to net dipole moment—also exhibit dipole–dipole forces. Substances whose molecules contain H bonded directly to F, O, or N exhibit hydrogen bonding as well.

EXAMPLE 12.9 **DETERMINING THE TYPE OF INTERMOLECULAR FORCES IN A COMPOUND**

Determine the types of intermolecular forces present in each substance.

(a) N_2
(b) CO
(c) NH_3

SOLUTION

(a) N_2 is nonpolar and therefore has only dispersion forces.
(b) CO is polar and therefore has dipole–dipole forces (in addition to dispersion forces).
(c) NH_3 has hydrogen bonding (in addition to dispersion forces and dipole–dipole forces).

LO: Use intermolecular forces to determine melting and/or boiling points (Section 12.6).

To determine relative boiling points and melting points among compounds, you must evaluate the types of intermolecular forces that each compound exhibits. Dispersion forces are the weakest kind of intermolecular force, but they increase with increasing molar mass. Dipole–dipole forces are stronger than dispersion forces. If two compounds have similar molar mass, but one is polar, it will have higher melting and boiling points. Hydrogen bonds are a stronger type of intermolecular force. Substances that exhibit hydrogen bonding will have much higher boiling and melting points than substances without hydrogen bonding, even if the substance without hydrogen bonding is of higher molar mass.

EXAMPLE 12.10 **USING INTERMOLECULAR FORCES TO DETERMINE MELTING AND/OR BOILING POINTS**

Arrange each group of compounds in order of increasing boiling point.

(a) F_2, Cl_2, Br_2
(b) HF, HCl, HBr

SOLUTION

(a) Since these all have only dispersion forces, and since they are similar substances (all halogens), the strength of the dispersion force will increase with increasing molar mass. Therefore, the correct order is $F_2 < Cl_2 < Br_2$.
(b) Since HF has hydrogen bonding, it has the highest boiling point. Between HCl and HBr, HBr (because of its higher molar mass) has a higher boiling point. Therefore the correct order is HCl < HBr < HF.

KEY TERMS

atomic solid **[12.7]**	heat of vaporization (ΔH_{vap})	metallic atomic solid **[12.7]**	surface tension **[12.3]**
boiling point **[12.4]**	**[12.4]**	miscibility **[12.6]**	thermal energy **[12.1]**
condensation **[12.4]**	hydrogen bond **[12.6]**	molecular solid **[12.7]**	vaporization **[12.4]**
covalent atomic solid **[12.7]**	instantaneous (temporary)	nonbonding atomic solid	vapor pressure **[12.4]**
dipole–dipole force **[12.6]**	dipole **[12.6]**	**[12.7]**	viscosity **[12.3]**
dispersion force **[12.6]**	intermolecular forces **[12.1]**	nonvolatile **[12.4]**	volatile **[12.4]**
dynamic equilibrium **[12.4]**	ion–dipole force **[12.6]**	normal boiling point **[12.4]**	
evaporation **[12.4]**	ionic solid **[12.7]**	permanent dipole **[12.6]**	
heat of fusion (ΔH_{fus}) **[12.5]**	melting point **[12.5]**	sublimation **[12.5]**	

EXERCISES

QUESTIONS

1. What are intermolecular forces? Why are intermolecular forces important?
2. Why are water droplets spherical?
3. What determines whether a substance is a solid, liquid, or gas?
4. What are the properties of liquids? Explain the properties of liquids in terms of the molecules or atoms that compose them.
5. What are the properties of solids? Explain the properties of solids in terms of the molecules or atoms that compose them.
6. What is the difference between a crystalline solid and an amorphous solid?
7. What is surface tension? How does it depend on intermolecular forces?
8. What is viscosity? How does it depend on intermolecular forces?
9. What is evaporation? Condensation?
10. Why does a glass of water evaporate more slowly in the glass than if you spilled the same amount of water on a table?
11. Explain the difference between evaporation below the boiling point of a liquid and evaporation at the boiling point of a liquid.
12. What is the boiling point of a liquid? What is the normal boiling point?
13. Acetone evaporates more quickly than water at room temperature. What can you say about the relative strength of the intermolecular forces in the two compounds? Which substance is more volatile?
14. Explain condensation and dynamic equilibrium.
15. What is the vapor pressure of a substance? How does it depend on the temperature and strength of intermolecular forces?
16. Explain how sweat cools the body.
17. Explain why a steam burn from gaseous water at 100 °C is worse than a water burn involving the same amount of liquid water at 100 °C.

18. Explain what happens when a liquid boils.
19. Explain why the water in a cup placed in a small ice chest (without a refrigeration mechanism) initially at −5 °C does *not* freeze.
20. Explain how ice cubes cool down beverages.
21. Is the melting of ice endothermic or exothermic? What is the sign of ΔH for the melting of ice? For the freezing of water?
22. Is the boiling of water endothermic or exothermic? What is the sign of ΔH for the boiling of water? For the condensation of steam?
23. What are dispersion forces? How does the strength of dispersion forces relate to molar mass?
24. What are dipole–dipole forces? How can you tell whether a compound has dipole–dipole forces?
25. What is hydrogen bonding? How can you tell whether a compound has hydrogen bonding?
26. What are ion–dipole forces? What kinds of substances contain ion–dipole forces?
27. List the four types of intermolecular forces discussed in this chapter in order of increasing relative strength.
28. What is a molecular solid? What kinds of forces hold molecular solids together?
29. How do the melting points of molecular solids relate to those of other types of solids?
30. What is an ionic solid? What kinds of forces hold ionic solids together?
31. How do the melting points of ionic solids relate to those of other types of solids?
32. What is an atomic solid? What are the properties of atomic solids?
33. In what ways is water unique?
34. How would ice be different if it were denser than water? How would that affect aquatic life in cold-climate lakes?

PROBLEMS

EVAPORATION, CONDENSATION, MELTING, AND FREEZING

35. Which evaporates more quickly: 55 mL of water in a beaker with a diameter of 4.5 cm or 55 mL of water in a dish with a diameter of 12 cm? Why?

36. Two samples of pure water of equal volume are put into separate dishes and kept at room temperature for several days. The water in the first dish is completely vaporized after 2.8 days, while the water in the second dish takes 8.3 days to completely evaporate. What can you conclude about the two dishes?

37. One milliliter of water is poured onto one hand, and one milliliter of acetone (fingernail-polish remover) is poured onto the other. As they evaporate, they both feel cool. Which one feels cooler and why? (*Hint:* Which substance is more volatile?)

38. Spilling water over your skin on a hot day will cool you down. Spilling vegetable oil over your skin on a hot day will not. Explain the difference.

39. Several ice cubes are placed in a beaker on a lab bench, and their temperature, initially at −5.0 °C, is monitored. Explain what happens to the temperature as a function of time. Make a sketch of how the temperature might change with time. (Assume that the lab is at 25 °C.)

40. Water is put into a beaker and heated with a Bunsen burner. The temperature of the water, initially at 25 °C, is monitored. Explain what happens to the temperature as a function of time. Make a sketch of how the temperature might change with time. (Assume that the Bunsen burner is hot enough to heat the water to its boiling point.)

41. Which causes a more severe burn: spilling 0.50 g of 100 °C water on your hand or allowing 0.50 g of 100 °C steam to condense on your hand? Why?

42. The nightly winter temperature drop in a seaside town is usually less than that in nearby towns that are farther inland. Explain.

43. When a plastic bag containing a water and ice mixture is placed in an ice chest initially at −8 °C, the temperature of the ice chest goes up. Why?

44. The refrigeration mechanism in a freezer with an automatic ice maker runs extensively each time ice forms from liquid water in the freezer. Why?

45. An ice chest is filled with 3.5 kg of ice at 0 °C. A second ice chest is filled with 3.5 kg of water at 0 °C. After several hours, which ice chest is colder? Why?

46. Why does 50 g of water initially at 0 °C warm more quickly than 50 g of an ice/water mixture initially at 0 °C?

47. In Denver, Colorado, water boils at 95 °C. Explain.

48. At the top of Mount Everest, water boils at 70 °C. Explain.

HEAT OF VAPORIZATION AND HEAT OF FUSION

49. How much heat is required to vaporize 33.8 g of water at 100 °C?

50. How much heat is required to vaporize 43.9 g of acetone at its boiling point?

51. How much heat does your body lose when 2.8 g of sweat evaporates from your skin at 25 °C? (Assume that the sweat is only water.)

52. How much heat does your body lose when 4.86 g of sweat evaporates from your skin at 25 °C? (Assume that the sweat is only water.)

53. How much heat is emitted when 4.25 g of water condenses at 25 °C?

54. How much heat is emitted when 65.6 g of isopropyl alcohol condenses at 25 °C?

55. The human body obtains 835 kJ of energy from a chocolate chip cookie. If this energy were used to vaporize water at 100 °C, how many grams of water could be vaporized? (Assume that the density of water is 1.0 g/mL.)

56. The human body obtains 1078 kJ from a candy bar. If this energy were used to vaporize water at 100 °C, how much water in liters could be vaporized? (Assume that the density of water is 1.0 g/mL.)

57. How much heat is required to melt 37.4 g of ice at 0 °C?

58. How much heat is required to melt 23.9 g of solid diethyl ether (at its melting point)?

59. How much energy is released when 34.2 g of water freezes?

60. How much energy is released when 2.55 kg of diethyl ether freezes?

61. How much heat is required to convert 2.55 g of water at 28.0 °C to steam at 100.0 °C?

62. How much heat is required to convert 5.88 g of ice at −12.0 °C to water at 25.0 °C? (The heat capacity of ice is 2.09 J/g °C.)

INTERMOLECULAR FORCES

63. What kinds of intermolecular forces are present in each substance?
  (a) Kr
  (b) N_2
  (c) CO
  (d) HF

64. What kinds of intermolecular forces are present in each substance?
  (a) HCl
  (b) H_2O
  (c) Br_2
  (d) He

65. What kinds of intermolecular forces are present in each substance?
  (a) NCl_3 (trigonal pyramidal)
  (b) NH_3 (trigonal pyramidal)
  (c) SiH_4 (tetrahedral)
  (d) CCl_4 (tetrahedral)

66. What kinds of intermolecular forces are present in each substance?
  (a) O_3
  (b) HBr
  (c) CH_3OH
  (d) I_2

67. What kinds of intermolecular forces are present in a mixture of potassium chloride and water?

68. What kinds of intermolecular forces are present in a mixture of calcium bromide and water?

69. Which substance has the highest boiling point? Why? *Hint:* They are all nonpolar.
  (a) CH_4
  (b) CH_3CH_3
  (c) $CH_3CH_2CH_3$
  (d) $CH_3CH_2CH_2CH_3$

70. Which noble gas has the highest boiling point? Why?
  (a) Kr
  (b) Xe
  (c) Rn

71. One of these two substances is a liquid at room temperature and the other one is a gas. Which one is the liquid and why?

$$CH_3OH \quad CH_3SH$$

72. One of these two substances is a liquid at room temperature and the other one is a gas. Which one is the liquid and why?

$$CH_3OCH_3 \quad CH_3CH_2OH$$

73. A flask containing a mixture of $NH_3(g)$ and $CH_4(g)$ is cooled. At $-33.3\,°C$ a liquid begins to form in the flask. What is the liquid?

74. Explain why CS_2 is a liquid at room temperature while CO_2 is a gas.

75. Are $CH_3CH_2CH_2CH_2CH_3$ and H_2O miscible?

76. Are CH_3OH and H_2O miscible?

77. Determine whether a homogeneous solution forms when each pair of substances is mixed.
  (a) CCl_4 and H_2O
  (b) Br_2 and CCl_4
  (c) CH_3CH_2OH and H_2O

78. Determine whether a homogeneous solution forms when each pair of substances is mixed.
  (a) $CH_3CH_2CH_2CH_2CH_3$ and $CH_3CH_2CH_2CH_2CH_2CH_3$
  (b) CBr_4 and H_2O
  (c) Cl_2 and H_2O

TYPES OF SOLIDS

79. Identify each solid as molecular, ionic, or atomic.
  (a) $Ar(s)$
  (b) $H_2O(s)$
  (c) $K_2O(s)$
  (d) $Fe(s)$

80. Identify each solid as molecular, ionic, or atomic.
  (a) $CaCl_2(s)$
  (b) $CO_2(s)$
  (c) $Ni(s)$
  (d) $I_2(s)$

81. Identify each solid as molecular, ionic, or atomic.
  (a) $H_2S(s)$
  (b) $KCl(s)$
  (c) $N_2(s)$
  (d) $NI_3(s)$

82. Identify each solid as molecular, ionic, or atomic.
  (a) $SF_6(s)$
  (b) $C(s)$
  (c) $MgCl_2(s)$
  (d) $Ti(s)$

83. Which solid has the highest melting point? Why?
(a) Ar(s)
(b) CCl$_4$(s)
(c) LiCl(s)
(d) CH$_3$OH(s)

84. Which solid has the highest melting point? Why?
(a) C (s, diamond)
(b) Kr(s)
(c) NaCl(s)
(d) H$_2$O(s)

85. For each pair of solids, determine which solid has the higher melting point and explain why.
(a) Ti(s) and Ne(s)
(b) H$_2$O(s) and H$_2$S(s)
(c) Kr(s) and Xe(s)
(d) NaCl(s) and CH$_4$(s)

86. For each pair of solids, determine which solid has the higher melting point and explain why.
(a) Fe(s) and CCl$_4$(s)
(b) KCl(s) or HCl(s)
(c) TiO$_2$(s) or HOOH(s)

87. List these substances in order of increasing boiling point:

H$_2$O, Ne, NH$_3$, NaF, SO$_2$

88. List these substances in order of decreasing boiling point:

CO$_2$, Ne, CH$_3$OH, KF

CUMULATIVE PROBLEMS

89. Ice actually has negative caloric content. How much energy, in each of the following units, does your body lose from eating (and therefore melting) 78 g of ice?
(a) joules
(b) kilojoules
(c) calories (1 cal = 4.18 J)
(d) nutritional Calories or capital "C" Calories (1000 cal = 1 Cal)

90. Ice has negative caloric content. How much energy, in each of the following units, does your body lose from eating (and therefore melting) 145 g of ice?
(a) joules
(b) kilojoules
(c) calories (1 cal = 4.18 J)
(d) nutritional Calories or capital "C" calories (1000 cal = 1 Cal)

91. An 8.5-g ice cube is placed into 255 g of water. Calculate the temperature change in the water upon the complete melting of the ice. *Hint:* Determine how much heat is absorbed by the melting ice and then use $q = mC\Delta T$ to calculate the temperature change of the 255 g of water.

92. A 14.7-g ice cube is placed into 324 g of water. Calculate the temperature change in the water upon complete melting of the ice. *Hint:* Determine how much heat is absorbed by the melting ice and then use $q = mC\Delta T$ to calculate the temperature change of the 324 g of water.

93. How much ice in grams would have to melt to lower the temperature of 352 mL of water from 25 °C to 0 °C? (Assume that the density of water is 1.0 g/mL.)

94. How much ice in grams would have to melt to lower the temperature of 55.8 g of water from 55.0 °C to 0 °C? (Assume that the density of water is 1.0 g/mL.)

95. How much heat in kilojoules is evolved in converting 1.00 mol of steam at 145 °C to ice at −50.0 °C? The heat capacity of steam is 1.84 J/g °C and that of ice is 2.09 J/g °C.

96. How much heat in kilojoules is required to warm 10.0 g of ice, initially at −10.0 °C, to steam at 110.0 °C. The heat capacity of ice is 2.09 J/g °C and that of steam is 1.84 J/g °C.

97. Draw a Lewis structure for each molecule and determine its molecular geometry. What kind of intermolecular forces are present in each substance?
(a) H$_2$Se
(b) SO$_2$
(c) CHCl$_3$
(d) CO$_2$

98. Draw a Lewis structure for each molecule and determine its molecular geometry. What kind of intermolecular forces are present in each substance?
(a) BCl$_3$ (remember that B is a frequent exception to the octet rule)
(b) HCOH (carbon is central; each H and O bonded directly to C)
(c) CS$_2$
(d) NCl$_3$

99. The melting point of ionic solids depends on the magnitude of the electrostatic attractions that hold the solid together. Draw ionic Lewis structures for NaF and MgO. Which do you think has the higher melting point?

100. Draw ionic Lewis structures for KF and CaO. Use the information and the method in the previous problem to predict which of these two ionic solids has the higher melting point.

101. Explain the observed trend in the melting points of the alkyl halides. Why is HF atypical?

Compound	Melting Point
HI	−50.8 °C
HBr	−88.5 °C
HCl	−114.8 °C
HF	−83.1 °C

102. Explain the observed trend in the boiling points of the compounds listed. Why is H₂O atypical?

Compound	Boiling Point
H_2Te	−2 °C
H_2Se	−41.5 °C
H_2S	−60.7 °C
H_2O	+100 °C

103. An ice cube at 0.00 °C with a mass of 23.5 g is placed into 550.0 g of water, initially at 28.0 °C, in an insulated container. Assuming that no heat is lost to the surroundings, what is the temperature of the entire water sample after all of the ice has melted?

104. If 1.10 g of steam at 100.0 °C condenses into 38.5 g of water, initially at 27.0 °C, in an insulated container, what is the final temperature of the entire water sample? Assume no loss of heat into the surroundings.

HIGHLIGHT PROBLEMS

105. Consider the molecular view of water shown here. Pick a molecule in the interior and draw a line to each of its direct neighbors. Pick a molecule near the edge (analogous to a molecule on the surface in three dimensions) and do the same. Which molecule has the most neighbors? Which molecule is more likely to evaporate?

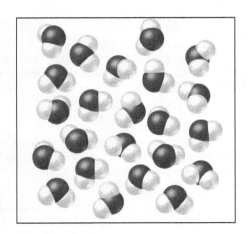

106. Water does not easily remove grease from dirty hands because grease is nonpolar and water is polar; therefore they are immiscible. The addition of soap, however, results in the removal of the grease. Examine the structure of soap shown here and explain how soap works.

$$CH_3(CH_2)_{16}\overset{\overset{\displaystyle O}{\|}}{C}-O^-Na^+$$

Nonpolar tail   Polar head

Sodium stearate
a soap

107. One prediction of global warming is the melting of global ice, which may result in coastal flooding. A criticism of this prediction is that the melting of icebergs does not increase ocean levels any more than the melting of ice in a glass of water increases the level of liquid in the glass.

   (a) Is this a valid criticism? Does the melting of an ice cube in a cup of water raise the level of the liquid in the cup? Why or why not?
   A response to this criticism is that scientists are not worried about rising ocean levels due to melting icebergs; rather, scientists are worried about rising ocean levels due to melting ice sheets that sit on the continent of Antarctica.

   (b) Would the melting of the ice sheets increase ocean levels? Why or why not?

108. Explain why rubbing alcohol feels cold when applied to the skin.

QUESTIONS FOR GROUP WORK

Discuss these questions with the group and record your consensus answer.

109. Consider the following compounds.

Acetone   Butane   1–propanol

(a) Calculate the molar mass of each compound.
(b) Redraw each Lewis structure and indicate polar bonds with δ+ and δ−.
(c) Indicate which of these molecules would be considered polar, and why.
(d) Indicate which of these molecules can hydrogen-bond, and why.
(e) Identify the predominant intermolecular force in each molecule.
(f) Rank the molecules in order of increasing boiling point.
(g) Why is your answer to part a important in answering part f?

110. Look up the boiling points of carbon monoxide and carbon dioxide. Which intermolecular force would you cite to account for the difference? Explain.

111. The existence of "triads" of elements was a big clue that eventually led to the discovery of the periodic table. A triad is a group of three elements for which the middle element has properties that are the average of the properties of the first and third elements. Some triads include: (O, S, Se); (Cl, Br, I); and (Li, Na, K). Verify that the atomic weight of the middle element in each triad is approximately the average of the other two. Explain why the melting points of the compounds formed by combining each element with hydrogen (e.g., HCl, HBr, and HI) might be expected to show the same trend.

112. How much sweat (in mL) would you have to evaporate per hour to remove the same amount of heat a 100 W light bulb produces? (1 W = 1 J/s.)

▶Answers to Skillbuilder Exercises

Skillbuilder 12.1 5.83×10^3 kJ
Skillbuilder Plus, p. 420   47 °C
Skillbuilder 12.2   5.18 kJ
Skillbuilder Plus, p. 423   −2.3 °C
Skillbuilder 12.3 C_2H_6
Skillbuilder 12.4
(a) no dipole–dipole forces
(b) yes, it has dipole–dipole forces
(c) yes, it has dipole–dipole forces

Skillbuilder 12.5
HF, because it has hydrogen bonding as an intermolecular force
Skillbuilder 12.6
(a) molecular
(b) ionic
(c) atomic

▶Answers to Conceptual Checkpoints

12.1 (a) The substance has definite volume *and* a definite shape, so it must be a solid.

12.2 (b) Since boiling is a physical rather than a chemical change, the water molecules (H_2O) undergo no chemical alteration—they merely change from the liquid to the gaseous state.

12.3 The temperature of the metal block increases. Condensation is exothermic, so it would give off heat to the metal block and raise its temperature.

12.4 (b) The temperature remains flat during a state transition; therefore, since the water starts as ice, the first flat section (i) is the melting of the ice to liquid water. The increasing temperature section (ii) is the water warming to its boiling point. The subsequent flat section (iii) is the boiling of the liquid water to gaseous steam.

12.5 (c) Since sublimation is a physical change, the carbon dioxide molecules do not decompose into other molecules or atoms; they simply change state from the solid to the gaseous state.

12.6 (a) All three compounds have nearly identical molar masses, so the strength of the dispersion forces should be similar in all three. A is nonpolar; it has only dispersion forces and will have the lowest boiling point. B is polar; it has dipole–dipole forces in addition and therefore has the next highest boiling point. C has hydrogen bonding in addition; it therefore has the highest boiling point.

12.7 (c) The chemical bonds between carbon and oxygen atoms are not broken by changes of state such as sublimation. Because carbon dioxide contains no hydrogen atoms, it cannot undergo hydrogen bonding, and because the molecule is nonpolar, it does not experience dipole–dipole interactions.

Late in the summer of 1986, carbon dioxide bubbled out of Lake Nyos and flowed into the adjacent valley. The carbon dioxide came from the bottom of the lake where it was held in a mixture with water by the pressure above it. When the layers in the lake were disturbed, the carbon dioxide came out of the water due to the decrease in pressure—with lethal consequences.

Solutions 13

"The goal of science is to make sense of the diversity of nature."
—John Barrow (b. 1952)

CHAPTER OUTLINE

13.1 Tragedy in Cameroon

▲ Cameroon is in West Africa.

Carbon dioxide, a colorless and odorless gas, displaced the air in low-lying regions surrounding Lake Nyos, leaving no oxygen for the inhabitants to breathe. The rotten-egg smell was an indication of the presence of additional sulfur-containing gases.

On August 22, 1986, most people living near Lake Nyos in Cameroon, West Africa, began their day in an ordinary way. Unfortunately, the day ended in tragedy. On that evening, a large cloud of carbon dioxide gas, burped up from the depths of Lake Nyos, killed more than 1700 people and about 3000 head of cattle. Survivors tell of smelling rotten eggs, feeling a warm sensation, and then losing consciousness. Two years before that, a similar tragedy occurred in Lake Monoun, just 60 miles away, killing 37 people. Today, scientists have taken steps to prevent these lakes from burping again.

Lake Nyos is a water-filled volcanic crater. Some 50 miles beneath the surface of the lake, molten volcanic rock (magma) produces carbon dioxide gas that seeps into the lake through the volcano's plumbing system. The carbon dioxide then mixes with the lake water. However, as we will see later in this chapter, the concentration of a gas (such as carbon dioxide) that can build up in water increases with increasing pressure. The great pressure at the bottom of the deep lake allows the concentration of carbon dioxide to become very high (just as the pressure in a soda can allows the concentration of carbon dioxide in soda to be very high). Over time, the carbon dioxide and water mixture at the bottom of the lake became so concentrated that—either because of the high concentration itself or because of some other natural trigger, such as a landslide—some gaseous carbon dioxide escaped. The rising bubbles disrupted the lake water, causing the highly concentrated carbon dioxide and water mixture at the bottom of the lake to rise, which lowered the pressure on it. The drop in pressure on the mixture released more carbon dioxide bubbles just as the drop in pressure upon opening a soda can releases carbon dioxide bubbles. This in turn caused further churning and more carbon dioxide release. Since carbon dioxide is more dense than air, once freed from the lake, it traveled down the sides of the volcano and into the nearby valley, displacing air and asphyxiating many of the local residents.

In efforts to prevent these events from occurring again—by 2001, carbon dioxide concentrations had already returned to dangerously high levels—scientists built a piping system to slowly vent carbon dioxide from the lake bottom. Since 2001, this system has gradually been releasing the carbon dioxide into the atmosphere, preventing a repeat of the tragedy.

▶ Engineers watch as the carbon dioxide vented from the bottom of Lake Nyos creates a geyser. The controlled release of carbon dioxide from the lake bed is designed to prevent future catastrophes like the one that killed more than 1700 people in 1986.

13.2   Solutions: Homogeneous Mixtures

LO: Define solution, solute, and solvent.

The carbon dioxide and water mixture at the bottom of Lake Nyos is an example of a **solution**, a homogeneous mixture of two or more substances. Solutions are common—most of the liquids and gases that we encounter every day are actually solutions. When most people think of a solution, they think of a solid dissolved in water. The ocean, for example, is a solution of salt and other solids dissolved in water. Blood plasma (blood that has had blood cells removed from it) is a solution of several solids (as well as some gases) dissolved in water. In addition to these, many other kinds of solutions exist. A solution may be composed of a gas and a liquid (like the carbon dioxide and water of Lake Nyos), a liquid and another liquid, a solid and a gas, or other combinations (see Table 13.1).

Aqueous comes from the Latin word *aqua*, which means "water."

The most common solutions are those containing a solid, a liquid, or a gas and water. These are *aqueous solutions*—they are critical to life and are the main focus of this chapter. Common examples of aqueous solutions include sugar water and salt water, both solutions of solids and water. Similarly, ethyl alcohol—the alcohol in alcoholic beverages—readily mixes with water to form a solution of a liquid with water, and we have already seen an example of a gas-and-water solution in Lake Nyos.

In a solid/liquid solution, the liquid is usually considered the solvent, regardless of the relative proportions of the components.

A solution has at least two components. The majority component is usually called the **solvent**, and the minority component is called the **solute**. In our carbon-dioxide-and-water solution, carbon dioxide is the solute and water is the solvent. In a salt-and-water solution, salt is the solute and water is the solvent. Because water is so abundant on Earth, it is a common solvent. However, other solvents are often used in the laboratory, in industry, and even in the home, especially to

TABLE 13.1   Common Types of Solutions

Solution Phase	Solute Phase	Solvent Phase	Example
gaseous solutions	gas	gas	air (mainly oxygen and nitrogen)
liquid solutions	gas	liquid	soda water (CO_2 and water)
	liquid	liquid	vodka (ethanol and water)
	solid	liquid	seawater (salt and water)
solid solutions	solid	solid	brass (copper and zinc) and other alloys

form solutions with nonpolar solutes. For example, you may use paint thinner, a nonpolar solvent, to remove grease from a dirty bicycle chain or from ball bearings. The paint thinner dissolves (or forms a solution with) the grease, removing it from the metal.

In general, polar solvents dissolve polar or ionic solutes, and nonpolar solvents dissolve nonpolar solutes. This tendency is described by the rule *like dissolves like*. Thus, similar kinds of solvents dissolve similar kinds of solutes. Table 13.2 lists some common polar and nonpolar laboratory solvents.

See Sections 10.8 and 12.6 to review the concept of polarity.

TABLE 13.2   Common Laboratory Solvents

Common Polar Solvents	Common Nonpolar Solvents
water (H_2O)	hexane (C_6H_{14})
acetone (CH_3COCH_3)	diethyl ether ($CH_3CH_2OCH_2CH_3$)
methyl alcohol (CH_3OH)	toluene (C_7H_8)

CONCEPTUAL CHECKPOINT 13.1

Which compound would you expect to be *least* soluble in water?

(a) CCl_4

(b) CH_3Cl

(c) NH_3

(d) KF

13.3   Solutions of Solids Dissolved in Water: How to Make Rock Candy

LO: Relate the solubility of solids in water to temperature.

We have already seen several examples of solutions of a solid dissolved in water. The ocean, for example, is a solution of salt and other solids dissolved in water. A sweetened cup of coffee is a solution of sugar and other solids dissolved in water. Blood plasma is a solution of several solids (and some gases) dissolved in water. Not all solids, however, dissolve in water. We already know that nonpolar solids—such as lard and shortening—do not dissolve in water. Solids such as calcium carbonate and sand do not dissolve either.

When a solid is put into water, there is competition between the attractive forces that hold the solid together (the solute–solute interactions) and the attractive forces occurring between the water molecules and the particles that compose the solid (the solvent–solute interactions). The solvent–solute interactions are usually intermolecular forces of the type discussed in Chapter 12. For example, when sodium chloride is put into water, there is competition between the mutual attraction of Na^+ cations and Cl^- anions and the ion–dipole forces between Na^+ or Cl^- and water molecules as shown in the margin. For sodium ions, the attraction is between the positive charge of the sodium ion and the negative side of water's dipole moment as shown in ▶ Figure 13.1 (see Section 10.8 to review dipole moment). For chloride ions, the attraction is between the negative charge of the chloride ion and the positive side of water's dipole moment. In the case of NaCl, the

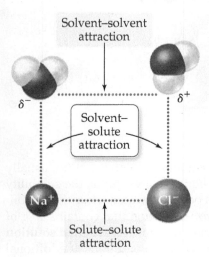

◀ When NaCl is put into water, the attraction between water molecules and Na^+ and Cl^- ions (solvent–solute attraction) overcomes the attraction between Na^+ and Cl^- ions (solute–solute attraction).

▶ **FIGURE 13.1 How a solid dissolves in water** The positive ends of the water dipoles are attracted to the negatively charged Cl^- ions, and the negative ends of the water dipoles are attracted to the positively charged Na^+ ions via ion–dipole forces. The water molecules surround the ions of NaCl and disperse them in the solution.

attraction to water wins, and sodium chloride dissolves (▼ Figure 13.2). However, in the case of calcium carbonate ($CaCO_3$), the attraction between Ca^{2+} ions and CO_3^{2-} ions wins and calcium carbonate does not dissolve in water.

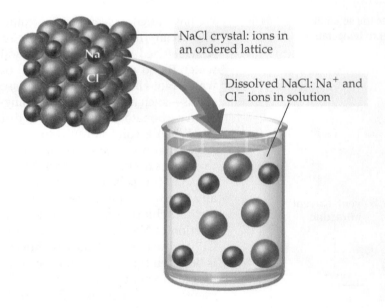

NaCl crystal: ions in an ordered lattice

Dissolved NaCl: Na^+ and Cl^- ions in solution

▶ **FIGURE 13.2 A sodium chloride solution** In a solution of NaCl, the Na^+ and Cl^- ions are dispersed in the water.

Solubility and Saturation

The **solubility** of a compound is defined as the amount of the compound, usually in grams, that dissolves in a certain amount of liquid. For example, the solubility of sodium chloride in water at 25 °C is 36 g NaCl per 100 g water, while the solubility of calcium carbonate in water is close to zero. A solution that contains 36 g of NaCl per 100 g water is a *saturated* sodium chloride solution. A **saturated solution** holds the maximum amount of solute under the solution conditions. If additional solute is added to a saturated solution, it will not dissolve. An **unsaturated solution** is holding less than the maximum amount of solute. If additional solute is added to an unsaturated solution, it will dissolve. A **supersaturated solution** is one holding more than the normal maximum amount of solute. The solute will normally *precipitate* from (or come out of) a supersaturated solution. As the carbon dioxide and water solution rose from the bottom of Lake Nyos, for example, it became supersaturated because of the drop in pressure. The excess gas came out of the solution and rose to the surface of the lake, where it was emitted into the surrounding air.

Supersaturated solutions can form under special circumstances, such as the sudden release in pressure that occurs in a soda can when it is opened.

▶ A supersaturated solution holds more than the normal maximum amount of solute. In some cases, such as the sodium acetate solution pictured here, a supersaturated solution may be temporarily stable. Any disturbance, however, such as dropping in a small piece of solid sodium acetate **(a)**, causes the solid to come out of solution **(b, c)**.

(a)   (b)   (c)

Chapter 7 introduced the solubility rules (Section 7.5, Table 7.2), which give us a qualitative description of the solubility of ionic solids. Molecular solids may also be soluble in water depending on whether the solid is polar. Table sugar ($C_{12}H_{22}O_{11}$), for example, is polar and soluble in water. Nonpolar solids, such as lard and vegetable shortening, are usually insoluble in water.

Electrolyte Solutions: Dissolved Ionic Solids

A sugar solution (containing a molecular solid) and a salt solution (containing an ionic solid) are very different, as shown in ▼ Figure 13.3. In a salt solution the dissolved particles are ions, while in a sugar solution the dissolved particles are molecules. The ions in the salt solution are mobile charged particles and can therefore conduct electricity. As described in Section 7.5, a solution containing a solute that dissociates into ions is an **electrolyte solution**. The sugar solution contains dissolved sugar molecules and cannot conduct electricity; it is a **nonelectrolyte solution**. In general, soluble ionic solids form electrolyte solutions, while soluble molecular solids form nonelectrolyte solutions.

NaCl forms a strong electrolyte solution (Section 7.5). Weak electrolyte solutions are covered in Chapter 14.

Dissolved ions (NaCl)   Dissolved molecules (sugar)

▶ **FIGURE 13.3 Electrolyte and nonelectrolyte solutions** Electrolyte solutions contain dissolved ions (charged particles) and therefore conduct electricity. Nonelectrolyte solutions contain dissolved molecules (neutral particles) and therefore do not conduct electricity.

Electrolyte solution   Nonelectrolyte solution

▶ **FIGURE 13.4 Solubility of some ionic solids as a function of temperature**

How Solubility Varies with Temperature

Have you ever noticed how much easier it is to dissolve sugar in hot tea than in cold tea? The solubility of solids in water can be highly dependent on temperature. In general, the solubility of *solids* in water increases with increasing temperature (▲ Figure 13.4). For example, the solubility of potassium nitrate (KNO_3) at 20 °C is about 30 g KNO_3 per 100 g of water. However, at 50 °C, the solubility rises to 88 g KNO_3 per 100 g of water. A common way to purify a solid is **recrystallization**. Recrystallization involves putting the solid into water (or some other solvent) at an elevated temperature. Enough solid is added to the solvent to create a saturated solution at the elevated temperature. As the solution cools, the solubility decreases, causing some of the solid to precipitate from solution. If the solution cools slowly, the solid will form crystals as it comes out. The crystalline structure tends to reject impurities, resulting in a purer solid.

▲ Rock candy is composed of sugar crystals that form through recrystallization.

Rock Candy

We can use recrystallization to make rock candy. To make rock candy, we prepare a saturated sucrose (table sugar) solution at an elevated temperature. We dangle a string in the solution, and leave it to cool and stand for several days. As the solution cools, it becomes supersaturated and sugar crystals grow on the string. After several days, beautiful and sweet crystals, or "rocks," of sugar cover the string, ready to be admired and eaten.

13.4   Solutions of Gases in Water: How Soda Pop Gets Its Fizz

LO: Relate the solubility of gases in liquids to temperature and pressure.

The water at the bottom of Lake Nyos and a can of soda pop are both examples of solutions in which a gas (carbon dioxide) is dissolved in a liquid (water). Most liquids exposed to air contain some dissolved gases. Lake water and seawater, for example, contain dissolved oxygen necessary for the survival of fish. Our blood contains dissolved nitrogen, oxygen, and carbon dioxide. Even tap water contains dissolved atmospheric gases.

   We can see the dissolved gases in ordinary tap water when we heat it it on a stove. Before the water reaches its boiling point, small bubbles develop in the water. These bubbles are dissolved air (mostly nitrogen and oxygen) coming out of solution. Once the water boils, the bubbling becomes more vigorous—these larger bubbles are composed of water vapor. The dissolved air comes out of solution upon heating because—unlike solids, whose solubility *increases* with increasing temperature—the solubility of gases in water *decreases* with increasing

Cold soda pop: carbon dioxide more likely to stay in solution | Warm soda pop: carbon dioxide more likely to bubble out of solution

▲ Warm soda pop fizzes more than cold soda pop because the solubility of the dissolved carbon dioxide decreases with increasing temperature.

temperature. As the temperature of the water rises, the solubility of the dissolved nitrogen and oxygen decreases and these gases come out of solution, forming small bubbles around the bottom of the pot.

The decrease in the solubility of gases with increasing temperature is the reason that warm soda pop bubbles more than cold soda pop and also the reason that warm soda goes flat faster than cold soda. The carbon dioxide comes out of solution faster (bubbles more) at room temperature than at cooler temperature because the gas is less soluble at room temperature.

The solubility of gases also depends on pressure. The higher the pressure above a liquid, the more soluble the gas is in the liquid (▼ Figure 13.5), a relationship known as **Henry's law**.

The solubility of a gas in a liquid increases with increasing pressure.

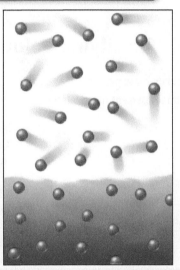

Gas molecules

Dissolved gas

Gas at low pressure over a liquid   Gas at high pressure over a liquid

▶ **FIGURE 13.5 Pressure and solubility** The higher the pressure above a liquid, the more soluble the gas is in the liquid.

In a can of soda pop and at the bottom of Lake Nyos, high pressure maintains the carbon dioxide in solution. In soda pop, the pressure is provided by a large amount of carbon dioxide gas that is pumped into the can before sealing it. When we open the can, we release the pressure and the solubility of carbon dioxide decreases, resulting in bubbling (▼ Figure 13.6). The bubbles are formed by the carbon dioxide gas as it escapes. In Lake Nyos, the mass of the lake water provides

▶ **FIGURE 13.6 Pop! Fizz!** A can of soda pop is pressurized with carbon dioxide. When the can is opened, the pressure is released, lowering the solubility of carbon dioxide in the solution and causing it to come out of solution as bubbles.

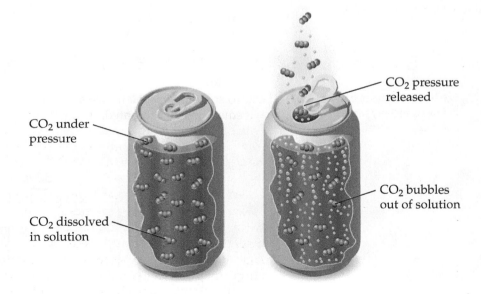

CO_2 under pressure

CO_2 dissolved in solution

CO_2 pressure released

CO_2 bubbles out of solution

the pressure by pushing down on the carbon-dioxide–rich water at the bottom of the lake. When the stratification (or layering) of the lake is disturbed, the pressure on the carbon dioxide solution is lowered and the solubility of carbon dioxide decreases, resulting in the release of excess carbon dioxide gas.

 CONCEPTUAL CHECKPOINT 13.2

A solution is saturated in both nitrogen gas (N_2) and potassium chloride (KCl) at 75 °C. What happens when the solution is cooled to room temperature?

(a) Some nitrogen gas bubbles out of solution.

(b) Some potassium chloride precipitates out of solution.

(c) Both (a) and (b).

(d) Nothing happens.

13.5 Specifying Solution Concentration: Mass Percent

LO: **Calculate mass percent.**

LO: **Use mass percent in calculations.**

As we have seen, the amount of solute in a solution is an important property of the solution. For example, the amount of carbon dioxide in the water at the bottom of Lake Nyos is an important predictor of when the deadly event may repeat itself. A **dilute solution** is one containing small amounts of solute relative to solvent. If the water at the bottom of Lake Nyos were a dilute carbon dioxide solution, it would pose little threat. A **concentrated solution** is one containing large amounts of solute relative to solvent. If the carbon dioxide in the water at the bottom of Lake Nyos becomes concentrated (through the continual feeding of carbon dioxide from magma into the lake), it becomes a threat. A common method of reporting solution concentration is *mass percent*.

Mass Percent

Also in common use are *parts per million* (ppm), the number of grams of solute per 1 million g of solution, and *parts per billion* (ppb), the number of grams of solute per 1 billion g of solution.

Note that the denominator is the mass of *solution*, not the mass of solvent.

Mass percent is the number of grams of solute per 100 g of solution. A solution with a concentration of 14% by mass, for example, contains 14 g of solute per 100 g of solution. To calculate mass percent, we divide the mass of the solute by the mass of the solution (solute *and* solvent) and multiply by 100%.

$$\text{Mass percent} = \frac{\text{Mass solute}}{\text{Mass solute} + \text{Mass solvent}} \times 100\%$$

Suppose we want to calculate the mass percent of NaCl in a solution containing 15.3 g of NaCl and 155.0 g of water. We begin by sorting the information in the problem statement.

GIVEN: 15.3 g NaCl
155.0 g H_2O

FIND: mass percent

SOLUTION

To solve this problem, we substitute the correct values into the mass percent equation just presented.

$$\text{Mass percent} = \frac{\text{Mass solute}}{\text{Mass solute} + \text{Mass solvent}} \times 100\%$$

$$= \frac{15.3 \text{ g}}{15.3 \text{ g} + 155.0 \text{ g}} \times 100\%$$

$$= \frac{15.3 \text{ g}}{170.3 \text{ g}} \times 100\%$$

$$= 8.98\%$$

The solution is 8.98% NaCl by mass.

EXAMPLE 13.1   **CALCULATING MASS PERCENT**

Calculate the mass percent of a solution containing 27.5 g of ethanol (C_2H_6O) and 175 mL of H_2O. (Assume that the density of water is 1.00 g/mL.)

Begin by setting up the problem. You are given the mass of ethanol and the volume of water and asked to find the mass percent of the solution.	**GIVEN:** 27.5 g C_2H_6O 175 mL H_2O $d_{H_2O} = \dfrac{1.00\ g}{mL}$ **FIND:** mass percent
To find the mass percent, substitute into the equation for mass percent. You need the mass of ethanol and the mass of water. Obtain the mass of water from the volume of water by using the density as a conversion factor. Finally, substitute the correct quantities into the equation and calculate the mass percent.	**SOLUTION** $\text{Mass percent} = \dfrac{\text{Mass solute}}{\text{Mass solute + Mass solvent}} \times 100\%$ $\text{Mass } H_2O = 175\ \cancel{mL}\ H_2O \times \dfrac{1.00\ g}{\cancel{mL}} = 175\ g$ $\text{Mass percent} = \dfrac{\text{Mass solute}}{\text{Mass solute + Mass solvent}} \times 100\%$ $\quad = \dfrac{27.5\ g}{27.5\ g + 175\ g}$ $\quad = \dfrac{27.5\ g}{202.5\ g} \times 100\%$ $\quad = 13.6\%$

▶**SKILLBUILDER 13.1 | Calculating Mass Percent**

Calculate the mass percent of a sucrose solution containing 11.3 g of sucrose and 412.1 mL of water. (Assume that the density of water is 1.00 g/mL.)

▶**FOR MORE PRACTICE**   Example 13.11; Problems 41, 42, 43, 44, 45, 46.

Using Mass Percent in Calculations

We can use the mass percent of a solution as a conversion factor between mass of the solute and mass of the solution. The key to using mass percent in this way is writing it as a fraction.

$$\text{Mass percent} = \frac{\text{g solute}}{100\ \text{g solution}}$$

A solution containing 3.5% sodium chloride, for example, has the following conversion factor:

$$\frac{3.5\ \text{g NaCl}}{100\ \text{g solution}} \qquad \text{converts g solution} \longrightarrow \text{g NaCl}$$

This conversion factor converts from grams of solution to grams of NaCl. If we want to go the other way, we invert the conversion factor:

$$\frac{100\ \text{g solution}}{3.5\ \text{g NaCl}} \qquad \text{converts g NaCl} \longrightarrow \text{g solution}$$

For example, to use mass percent as a conversion factor, let's consider a water sample from the bottom of Lake Nyos containing 8.5% carbon dioxide by mass. We can determine how much carbon dioxide in grams is contained in 28.6 L of the water solution. (Assume that the density of the solution is 1.03 g/mL.) We begin by sorting the information in the problem statement.

GIVEN: 8.5% CO_2 by mass

28.6 L solution

$$d = \frac{1.03 \text{ g}}{\text{mL}}$$

FIND: g CO_2

SOLUTION MAP

We strategize by drawing a solution map that begins with L solution and shows the conversion to mL solution and then to g solution using density. Then we proceed from g solution to g CO_2, using the mass percent (expressed as a fraction) as a conversion factor.

$$\frac{1 \text{ mL}}{10^{-3} \text{ L}} \qquad \frac{1.03 \text{ g}}{\text{mL}} \qquad \frac{8.5 \text{ g } CO_2}{100 \text{ g solution}}$$

RELATIONSHIPS USED

$$\frac{8.5 \text{ g } CO_2}{100 \text{ g solution}} \text{ (given mass percent, written as a fraction)}$$

$$\frac{1.03 \text{ g}}{\text{mL}} \text{ (given density of the solution)}$$

$$1 \text{ mL} = 10^{-3} \text{ L} \quad \text{(from Table 2.2)}$$

SOLUTION

We follow the solution map to calculate the answer.

$$28.6 \text{ L solution} \times \frac{1 \text{ mL}}{10^{-3} \text{ L}} \times \frac{1.03 \text{ g}}{\text{mL}} \times \frac{8.5 \text{ g } CO_2}{100 \text{ g solution}} = 2.5 \times 10^3 \text{ g } CO_2$$

In this example, we used mass percent to convert from a given amount of *solution* to the amount of *solute* present in the solution. In Example 13.2, you use mass percent to convert from a given amount of *solute* to the amount of *solution* containing that solute.

EXAMPLE 13.2   USING MASS PERCENT IN CALCULATIONS

A soft drink contains 11.5% sucrose ($C_{12}H_{22}O_{11}$) by mass. What volume of the soft drink solution in milliliters contains 85.2 g of sucrose? (Assume a density of 1.04 g/mL.)

SORT You are given the concentration of sucrose in a soft drink and a mass of sucrose. You are asked to find the volume of the soft drink that contains the given mass of sucrose.	**GIVEN:** 11.5% $C_{12}H_{22}O_{11}$ by mass 85.2 g $C_{12}H_{22}O_{11}$ $d = \dfrac{1.04 \text{ g}}{\text{mL}}$ **FIND:** mL solution (soft drink)
STRATEGIZE Draw a solution map to convert from g solute ($C_{12}H_{22}O_{11}$) to g solution using the mass percent in fractional form as the conversion factor. Convert to mL using the density.	**SOLUTION MAP** $\dfrac{100 \text{ g solution}}{11.5 \text{ g } C_{12}H_{22}O_{11}} \qquad \dfrac{1 \text{ mL}}{1.04 \text{ g}}$ **RELATIONSHIPS USED** $\dfrac{11.5 \text{ g } C_{12}H_{22}O_{11}}{100 \text{ g solution}}$ (given mass percent, written as a fraction) $\dfrac{1.04 \text{ g}}{\text{mL}}$ (given density of solution)

SOLVE	SOLUTION
Follow the solution map to solve the problem.	$$85.2 \text{ g } C_{12}H_{22}O_{11} \times \frac{100 \text{ g solution}}{11.5 \text{ g } C_{12}H_{22}O_{11}} \times \frac{1 \text{ mL}}{1.04 \text{ g}} = 712 \text{ mL solution}$$
CHECK Check your answer. Are the units correct? Does the answer make physical sense?	The units (mL solution) are correct. The magnitude of the answer makes sense because each 100 mL of solution contains 11.5 g sucrose; therefore 712 mL should contain a bit more than 77 g, which is close to the given amount of 85.2 g.

▶**SKILLBUILDER 13.2 | Using Mass Percent in Calculations**

How much sucrose ($C_{12}H_{22}O_{11}$) in grams is contained in 355 mL (12 oz) of the soft drink in Example 13.2?

▶**FOR MORE PRACTICE**   Example 13.12; Problems 47, 48, 49, 50, 51, 52.

13.6   Specifying Solution Concentration: Molarity

LO: Calculate molarity.

LO: Use molarity in calculations.

LO: Calculate ion concentration.

| Note that molarity is abbreviated with a capital M.

A second way to express solution concentration is **molarity** (M), defined as the number of moles of solute per liter of solution. We calculate the molarity of a solution as follows:

$$\textbf{Molarity (M)} = \frac{\text{Moles solute}}{\text{Liters solution}}$$

Note that molarity is moles of solute per liter of *solution*, not per liter of solvent. To make a solution of a specified molarity, we usually put the solute into a flask and then add water to the desired volume of solution. For example, to make 1.00 L of a 1.00 M NaCl solution, we add 1.00 mol of NaCl to a flask and then add water to make 1.00 L of solution (▼ Figure 13.7). We *do not* combine 1.00 mol of NaCl with 1.00 L of water because that would result in a total volume exceeding 1.00 L and therefore a molarity of less than 1.00 M.

How to prepare a 1.00 molar NaCl solution.

1.00 mol NaCl (58.44 g)

First add 1.00 mol of NaCl.

Water

Add water until solid is dissolved. Then add additional water until the 1-liter mark is reached.

Mix

A 1.00 molar NaCl solution

▶ **FIGURE 13.7   Making a solution of specific molarity**   To make 1.00 L of a 1.00 M NaCl solution, we add 1.00 mol (58.44 g) of sodium chloride to a flask and then dilute to 1.00 L of total volume.
Question: What would happen if we added 1 L of water to 1 mol of sodium chloride? Would the resulting solution be 1 M?

CHEMISTRY IN THE ENVIRONMENT
▶ The Dirty Dozen

A number of potentially harmful chemicals—such as DDT, dioxin, and polychlorinated biphenyls (PCBs)—make their way into water sources from industrial dumping, atmospheric emissions, agriculture, and household dumping. Since crops, livestock, and fish all rely on water, they too can accumulate these chemicals from water. Human consumption of food or water contaminated with these chemicals leads to a number of diseases and adverse health effects such as increased cancer risk, liver damage, or central nervous system damage. Governments around the world have joined forces to ban a number of these chemicals—called persistent organic pollutants or POPs—from production. The original treaty (known as the Stockholm Convention on Persistent Organic Pollutants) targeted 12 such substances called the dirty dozen (Table 13.3).

TABLE 13.3 The Dirty Dozen

1. aldrin (insecticide)
2. chlordane (insecticide by-product)
3. DDT (insecticide)
4. dieldrin (insecticide)
5. dioxin (industrial by-product)
6. eldrin (insecticide)
7. furan (industrial by-product)
8. heptachlor (insecticide)
9. hexachlorobenzene (fungicide, industrial by-product)
10. mirex (insecticide, fire retardant)
11. polychlorinated biphenyls (PCBs) (electrical insulators)
12. toxaphene (insecticide)

A difficult problem posed by these chemicals is their persistence. Once they get into the environment, they stay there for a long time. A second problem is their tendency to undergo *bioamplification*. Because these chemicals are nonpolar, they are stored and concentrated in the fatty tissues of the organisms that consume them. As larger organisms eat smaller ones that have consumed the chemical, the larger organisms consume even more of the stored chemicals. The result is an increase in the concentrations of these chemicals as they move up the food chain.

Under the treaty, nearly all intentional production of these chemicals is banned. In the United States, the presence of these contaminants in water supplies is monitored under supervision of the Environmental Protection Agency (EPA). The EPA has set limits, called maximum contaminant levels (MCLs), for each of the dirty dozen in food and drinking water. Some MCLs for selected compounds in water supplies are listed in Table 13.4.

▲ Potentially dangerous chemicals can leak into the environment and contaminate water and food supplies.

TABLE 13.4 EPA Maximum Contaminant Level (MCL) for Several "Dirty Dozen" Chemicals

chlordane	0.002 mg/L
dioxin	0.00000003 mg/L
heptachlor	0.0004 mg/L
hexachlorobenzene	0.001 mg/L

Notice the units that the EPA uses to express the concentration of the contaminants: milligrams per liter. This unit is a conversion factor between liters of water consumed and the mass in milligrams of the pollutant. According to the EPA, as long as the contaminant concentrations are below these levels, the water is safe to drink.

B13.1 CAN YOU ANSWER THIS? *Using what you know about conversion factors, calculate how much of each of the chemicals in Table 13.4 (at their MCL) is present in 715 L of water, the approximate amount of water consumed by an adult in one year.*

To calculate molarity, we divide the number of moles of the solute by the volume of the solution (solute *and* solvent) in liters. For example, to calculate the molarity of a sucrose ($C_{12}H_{22}O_{11}$) solution made with 1.58 mol of sucrose diluted to a total volume of 5.0 L of solution, we begin by sorting the information in the problem statement.

GIVEN: 1.58 mol $C_{12}H_{22}O_{11}$
5.0 L solution

FIND: molarity (M)

SOLUTION

We substitute the correct values into the equation for molarity and calculate the answer.

$$\text{Molarity (M)} = \frac{\text{Moles solute}}{\text{Liters solution}}$$

$$= \frac{1.58 \text{ mol } C_{12}H_{22}O_{11}}{5.0 \text{ L solution}}$$

$$= 0.32 \text{ M}$$

EXAMPLE 13.3 | **CALCULATING MOLARITY**

Calculate the molarity of a solution made by putting 15.5 g NaCl into a beaker and adding water to make 1.50 L of NaCl solution.

You are given the mass of sodium chloride (the solute) and the volume of solution. You are asked to find the molarity of the solution.	GIVEN: 15.5 g NaCl 1.50 L solution FIND: molarity (M)
To calculate molarity, substitute the correct values into the equation and calculate the answer. You must first convert the amount of NaCl from grams to moles using the molar mass of NaCl.	**SOLUTION** $\text{mol NaCl} = 15.5 \text{ g NaCl} \times \dfrac{1 \text{ mol NaCl}}{58.44 \text{ g NaCl}} = 0.2652 \text{ mol NaCl}$ $\text{Molarity (M)} = \dfrac{\text{Moles solute}}{\text{Liters solution}}$ $= \dfrac{0.2652 \text{ mol NaCl}}{1.50 \text{ L solution}}$ $= 0.177 \text{ M}$

▶**SKILLBUILDER 13.3** | **Calculating Molarity**

Calculate the molarity of a solution made by putting 55.8 g of $NaNO_3$ into a beaker and diluting to 2.50 L.

▶**FOR MORE PRACTICE** Example 13.13; Problems 59, 60, 61, 62, 63, 64.

Using Molarity in Calculations

We can use the molarity of a solution as a conversion factor between moles of the solute and liters of the solution. For example, a 0.500 M NaCl solution contains 0.500 mol NaCl for every liter of solution.

$$\frac{0.500 \text{ mol NaCl}}{\text{L solution}} \qquad \text{converts L solution} \longrightarrow \text{mol NaCl}$$

This conversion factor converts from liters of solution to moles of NaCl. If we want to go the other way, we invert the conversion factor.

$$\frac{\text{L solution}}{0.500 \text{ mol NaCl}} \qquad \text{converts mol NaCl} \longrightarrow \text{L solution}$$

For example, to determine how many grams of sucrose ($C_{12}H_{22}O_{11}$) are contained in 1.72 L of 0.758 M sucrose solution, we begin by sorting the information in the problem statement.

GIVEN: 0.758 M $C_{12}H_{22}O_{11}$
1.72 L solution

FIND: g $C_{12}H_{22}O_{11}$

SOLUTION MAP

We strategize by drawing a solution map that begins with L solution and shows the conversion to moles of sucrose using the molarity, and then the conversion to mass of sucrose using the molar mass.

$$\frac{0.758 \text{ mol } C_{12}H_{22}O_{11}}{\text{L solution}} \qquad \frac{342.34 \text{ g}}{\text{mol}}$$

RELATIONSHIPS USED

$$\frac{0.758 \text{ mol } C_{12}H_{22}O_{11}}{\text{L solution}} \text{ (given molarity of solution, written out as a fraction)}$$

$1 \text{ mol } C_{12}H_{22}O_{11} = 342.34 \text{ g (molar mass of sucrose)}$

SOLUTION

We then follow the solution map to calculate the answer.

$$1.72 \text{ L solution} \times \frac{0.758 \text{ mol } C_{12}H_{22}O_{11}}{\text{L solution}}$$

$$\times \frac{342.34 \text{ g } C_{12}H_{22}O_{11}}{\text{mol } C_{12}H_{22}O_{11}} = 446 \text{ g } C_{12}H_{22}O_{11}$$

In this example, we used molarity to convert from a given amount of *solution* to the amount of *solute* in that solution. In Example 13.4, we use molarity to convert from a given amount of *solute* to the amount of *solution* containing that solute.

EXAMPLE 13.4	USING MOLARITY IN CALCULATIONS

How many liters of a 0.114 M NaOH solution contains 1.24 mol of NaOH?

SORT You are given the molarity of an NaOH solution and the number of moles of NaOH. You are asked to find the volume of solution that contains the given number of moles.	**GIVEN:** 0.114 M NaOH 1.24 mol NaOH **FIND:** L solution
STRATEGIZE The solution map begins with mol NaOH and shows the conversion to liters of solution using the molarity as a conversion factor.	**SOLUTION MAP** $$\frac{1 \text{ L solution}}{0.114 \text{ mol NaOH}}$$ **RELATIONSHIP USED** $\dfrac{0.114 \text{ mol NaOH}}{\text{L solution}}$ (given molarity of solution, written out as a fraction)
SOLVE Solve the problem by following the solution map.	**SOLUTION** $$1.24 \text{ mol NaOH} \times \frac{1 \text{ L solution}}{0.114 \text{ mol NaOH}} = 10.9 \text{ L solution}$$

CHECK Check your answer. Are the units correct? Does the answer make physical sense?	The units (L solution) are correct. The magnitude of the answer makes sense because each L of solution contains a little more than 0.10 moles; therefore about 10 L contains a little more than 1 mole.

▶**SKILLBUILDER 13.4 | Using Molarity in Calculations**

How much of a 0.225 M KCl solution contains 55.8 g of KCl?

▶**FOR MORE PRACTICE** Example 13.14; Problems 65, 66, 67, 68, 69, 70.

Ion Concentrations

When an ionic compound dissolves in solution, some of the cations and anions may pair up, so that the actual concentrations of the ions are lower than what you would expect if you assume complete dissociation occurred.

The reported concentration of a solution containing a *molecular* compound usually reflects the concentration of the solute as it actually exists in solution. For example, a 1.0 M glucose ($C_6H_{12}O_6$) solution indicates that the solution contains 1.0 mol of $C_6H_{12}O_6$ per liter of solution. However, the reported concentration of solution containing an *ionic* compound reflects the concentration of the solute *before it is dissolved in solution*. For example, a 1.0 M $CaCl_2$ solution contains 1.0 mol of Ca^{2+} per liter and 2.0 mol of Cl^- per liter. The concentration of the individual ions present in a solution containing an ionic compound can usually be approximated from the overall concentration as shown by the following example.

EXAMPLE 13.5 **CALCULATING ION CONCENTRATION**

Determine the molar concentrations of Na^+ and PO_4^{3-} in a 1.50 M Na_3PO_4 solution.

You are given the concentration of an ionic solution and asked to find the concentrations of the component ions.	**GIVEN:** 1.50 M Na_3PO_4 **FIND:** molarity (M) of Na^+ and PO_4^{3-}
A formula unit of Na_3PO_4 contains 3 Na^+ ions (as indicated by the subscript), so the concentration of Na^+ is three times the concentration of Na_3PO_4. Since the same formula unit contains one PO_4^{3-} ion, the concentration of PO_4^{3-} is equal to the concentration of Na_3PO_4.	**SOLUTION** molarity of Na^+ = 3(1.50 M) = 4.50 M molarity of PO_4^{3-} = 1.50 M

▶**SKILLBUILDER 13.5 | Ion Concentration**

Determine the molar concentrations of Ca^{2+} and Cl^- in a 0.75 M $CaCl_2$ solution.

▶**FOR MORE PRACTICE** Problems 77, 78, 79, 80.

 CONCEPTUAL CHECKPOINT 13.3

A solution is 0.15 M in K_2SO_4. What is the concentration of K^+ in solution?

(a) 0.075 M

(b) 0.15 M

(c) 0.30 M

(d) 0.45 M

13.7 Solution Dilution

LO: Use the dilution equation in calculations.

To save space in laboratory storerooms, solutions are often stored in concentrated forms called **stock solutions**. For example, hydrochloric acid is typically stored as a 12 M stock solution. However, many lab procedures call for much less concentrated hydrochloric acid solutions, so chemists must dilute the stock solution to the required concentration. This is normally done by diluting a certain amount of

When diluting acids, always add the concentrated acid to the water. *Never add water to concentrated acid solutions.*

the stock solution with water. How do we determine how much of the stock solution to use? The easiest way to solve this problem is to use the dilution equation:

$$M_1V_1 = M_2V_2$$

where M_1 and V_1 are the molarity and volume of the initial concentrated solution and M_2 and V_2 are the molarity and volume of the final diluted solution. This equation works because the molarity multiplied by the volume gives the number of moles of solute ($M \times V = $ mol), which is the same in both solutions. For example, suppose a laboratory procedure calls for 5.00 L of a 1.50 M KCl solution. How should we prepare this solution from a 12.0 M stock solution? We begin by sorting the information in the problem statement.

The equation $M_1V_1 = M_2V_2$ applies only to solution dilution, NOT to stoichiometry.

GIVEN: $M_1 = 12.0$ M
$M_2 = 1.50$ M
$V_2 = 5.00$ L

FIND: V_1

SOLUTION
We solve the solution dilution equation for V_1 (the volume of the stock solution required for the dilution) and substitute in the correct values to calculate it.

$$M_1V_1 = M_2V_2$$

$$V_1 = \frac{M_2V_2}{M_1}$$

$$= \frac{1.50\frac{\text{mol}}{\text{L}} \times 5.00 \text{ L}}{12.0\frac{\text{mol}}{\text{L}}}$$

$$= 0.625 \text{ L}$$

We can therefore make the solution by diluting 0.625 L of the stock solution to a total volume of 5.00 L (V_2). The resulting solution is 1.50 M in KCl (▶ Figure 13.8).

EXAMPLE 13.6 SOLUTION DILUTION

To what volume should you dilute 0.100 L of a 15 M NaOH solution to obtain a 1.0 M NaOH solution?

You are given the initial volume and concentration of an NaOH solution and a final concentration. You are asked to find the volume required to dilute the initial solution to the given final concentration.	**GIVEN:** $V_1 = 0.100$ L $M_1 = 15$ M $M_2 = 1.0$ M **FIND:** V_2
Solve the solution dilution equation for V_2 (the volume of the final solution) and substitute the required quantities to calculate V_2. You can make the solution by diluting 0.100 L of the stock solution to a total volume of 1.5 L (V_2). The resulting solution has a concentration of 1.0 M.	**SOLUTION** $M_1V_1 = M_2V_2$ $V_2 = \dfrac{M_1V_1}{M_2}$ $= \dfrac{15\frac{\text{mol}}{\text{L}} \times 0.100 \text{ L}}{1.0\frac{\text{mol}}{\text{L}}}$ $= 1.5$ L

▶**SKILLBUILDER 13.6 | Solution Dilution**

How much 6.0 M NaNO₃ solution should you use to make 0.585 L of a 1.2 M NaNO₃ solution?

▶**FOR MORE PRACTICE** Example 13.15; Problems 81, 82, 83, 84, 85, 86, 87, 88.

► FIGURE 13.8   **Making a solution by dilution of a more concentrated solution**

How to make 5.00 L of a 1.50 M KCl solution from a 12.0 M stock solution.

First add 0.625 L of 12.0 M stock solution

Dilute with water to total volume of 5.00 L

1.50 M KCl

$$M_1 V_1 = M_2 V_2$$

$$\frac{12.0 \text{ mol}}{\not{L}} \times 0.625 \not{L} = \frac{1.50 \text{ mol}}{\not{L}} \times 5.00 \not{L}$$

$$7.50 \text{ mol} = 7.50 \text{ mol}$$

 CONCEPTUAL CHECKPOINT 13.4

What is the molarity of a solution in which 100.0 mL of 1.0 M KCl is diluted to 1.0 L?

(a) 0.10 M

(b) 1.0 M

(c) 10.0 M

13.8   Solution Stoichiometry

LO: Use volume and concentration to calculate the number of moles of reactants or products and then use stoichiometric coefficients to convert to other quantities in a reaction.

See Sections 8.2 through 8.4 for a review of reaction stoichiometry.

As we discussed in Chapter 7, many chemical reactions take place in aqueous solutions. Precipitation reactions, neutralization reactions, and gas evolution reactions, for example, all occur in aqueous solutions. Chapter 8 described how we use the coefficients in chemical equations as conversion factors between moles of reactants and moles of products in stoichiometric calculations. We often use these conversion factors to determine, for example, the amount of product obtained in a chemical reaction based on a given amount of reactant or the amount of one reactant needed to completely react with a given amount of another reactant. The general solution map for these kinds of calculations is:

Moles A → Moles B

where A and B are two different substances involved in the reaction and the conversion factor between them comes from the stoichiometric coefficients in the balanced chemical equation.

In reactions involving aqueous reactant and products, it is often convenient to specify the amount of reactants or products in terms of their volume and concentration. We can use the volume and concentration to calculate the number of moles of reactants or products, and then use the stoichiometric coefficients to convert to other quantities in the reaction. The general solution map for these kinds of calculations is:

where the conversions between volume and moles are achieved using the molarities of the solutions. For example, consider the reaction for the neutralization of sulfuric acid.

$$H_2SO_4(aq) + 2\,NaOH(aq) \longrightarrow Na_2SO_4(aq) + 2\,H_2O(l)$$

How much 0.125 M NaOH solution do we need to completely neutralize 0.225 L of 0.175 M H_2SO_4 solution? We begin by sorting the information in the problem statement.

GIVEN: 0.225 L H_2SO_4 solution
0.175 M H_2SO_4
0.125 M NaOH

FIND: L NaOH solution

SOLUTION MAP
We strategize by drawing a solution map, which is similar to those for other stoichiometric problems. We first use the volume and molarity of H_2SO_4 solution to get mol H_2SO_4. Then we use the stoichiometric coefficients from the equation to convert mol H_2SO_4 to mol NaOH. Finally, we use the molarity of NaOH to get to L NaOH solution.

RELATIONSHIPS USED

$$M(H_2SO_4) = \frac{0.175\ \text{mol}\ H_2SO_4}{L\ H_2SO_4\ \text{solution}} \quad \text{(given molarity of } H_2SO_4 \text{ solution, written out as a fraction)}$$

$$M(NaOH) = \frac{0.125\ \text{mol}\ NaOH}{L\ NaOH\ \text{solution}} \quad \text{(given molarity of NaOH solution, written out as a fraction)}$$

1 mol H_2SO_4:2 mol NaOH   (stoichiometric relationship between H_2SO_4 and NaOH, from balanced chemical equation)

SOLUTION
To solve the problem, we follow the solution map and calculate the answer.

$$0.225\ \text{L}\ H_2SO_4\ \text{solution} \times \frac{0.175\ \text{mol}\ H_2SO_4}{\text{L}\ H_2SO_4\ \text{solution}} \times \frac{2\ \text{mol}\ NaOH}{1\ \text{mol}\ H_2SO_4}$$
$$\times \frac{1\ \text{L}\ NaOH\ \text{solution}}{0.125\ \text{mol}\ NaOH} = 0.630\ \text{L}\ NaOH\ \text{solution}$$

It will take 0.630 L of the NaOH solution to completely neutralize the H_2SO_4.

EXAMPLE 13.7   SOLUTION STOICHIOMETRY

 Consider the precipitation reaction.

$$2 \text{ KI}(aq) + \text{Pb(NO}_3)_2(aq) \longrightarrow \text{PbI}_2(s) + 2 \text{ KNO}_3(aq)$$

How much 0.115 M KI solution in liters will completely precipitate the Pb^{2+} in 0.104 L of 0.225 M $Pb(NO_3)_2$ solution?

SORT You are given the concentration of a reactant, KI, in a chemical reaction. You are also given the volume and concentration of a second reactant, $Pb(NO_3)_2$. You are asked to find the volume of the first reactant that completely reacts with the given amount of the second.	**GIVEN:** 0.115 M KI 0.104 L $Pb(NO_3)_2$ solution 0.225 M $Pb(NO_3)_2$ **FIND:** L KI solution
STRATEGIZE The solution map for this problem is similar to the solution maps for other stoichiometric problems. First use the volume and molarity of $Pb(NO_3)_2$ solution to determine mol $Pb(NO_3)_2$. Then use the stoichiometric coefficients from the equation to convert mol $Pb(NO_3)_2$ to mol KI. Finally, use mol KI to find L KI solution.	**SOLUTION MAP** $$\frac{0.225 \text{ mol Pb(NO}_3)_2}{\text{L Pb(NO}_3)_2 \text{ solution}} \quad \frac{2 \text{ mol KI}}{1 \text{ mol Pb(NO}_3)_2} \quad \frac{1 \text{ L KI solution}}{0.115 \text{ mol KI}}$$ **RELATIONSHIP USED** $\text{M KI} = \dfrac{0.115 \text{ mol KI}}{\text{L KI solution}}$ (given molarity of KI solution, written out as a fraction) $\text{M Pb(NO}_3)_2 = \dfrac{0.225 \text{ mol Pb(NO}_3)_2}{\text{L Pb(NO}_3)_2 \text{ solution}}$ (given molarity of $Pb(NO_3)_2$ solution, written out as a fraction) 2 mol KI : 1 mol $Pb(NO_3)_2$ (stoichiometric relationship between KI and $Pb(NO_3)_2$, from balanced chemical equation)
SOLVE Follow the solution map to solve the problem. Begin with volume of $Pb(NO_3)_2$ solution and cancel units to arrive at volume of KI solution.	**SOLUTION** $0.104 \text{ L Pb(NO}_3)_2 \text{ solution} \times \dfrac{0.225 \text{ mol Pb(NO}_3)_2}{\text{L Pb(NO}_3)_2 \text{ solution}} \times \dfrac{2 \text{ mol KI}}{\text{mol Pb(NO}_3)}$ $\times \dfrac{\text{L KI solution}}{0.115 \text{ mol KI}} = 0.407 \text{ KI solution}$
CHECK Check your answer. Are the units correct? Does the answer make physical sense?	The units (L KI solution) are correct. The magnitude of the answer makes sense because the lead nitrate solution is about twice as concentrated as the potassium iodide solution and 2 mol of potassium iodide are required to react with 1 mol of lead(II) nitrate. Therefore you would expect the volume of the potassium solution required to completely react with a given volume of the $Pb(NO_3)_2$ solution to be about four times as much.

▶**SKILLBUILDER 13.7** | **Solution Stoichiometry**

How many milliliters of 0.112 M Na_2CO_3 will completely react with 27.2 mL of 0.135 M HNO_3 according to the reaction?

$$2 \text{ HNO}_3(aq) + \text{Na}_2\text{CO}_3(aq) \longrightarrow \text{H}_2\text{O}(l) + \text{CO}_2(g) + 2 \text{ NaNO}_3(aq)$$

▶**SKILLBUILDER PLUS** A 25.0-mL sample of HNO_3 solution requires 35.7 mL of 0.108 M Na_2CO_3 to completely react with all of the HNO_3 in the solution. What is the concentration of the HNO_3 solution?

▶**FOR MORE PRACTICE** Example 13.16; Problems 89, 90, 91, 92.

✓ **CONCEPTUAL CHECKPOINT 13.5**

Consider the following reaction occurring in aqueous solution.

$$A(aq) + 2\,B(aq) \longrightarrow \text{Products}$$

What volume of a 0.100 M solution of B is required to completely react with 50.0 mL of a 0.200 M solution of A?

(a) 25.0 mL

(b) 50.0 mL

(c) 100.0 mL

(d) 200.0 mL

13.9   Freezing Point Depression and Boiling Point Elevation: Making Water Freeze Colder and Boil Hotter

LO: Calculate molality.

LO: Calculate freezing points and boiling points for solutions.

Have you ever wondered why salt is added to ice in an ice-cream maker? Or why salt is scattered on icy roads in cold climates? Salt actually lowers the melting point of ice. A salt-and-water solution remains a liquid even below 0 °C. By adding salt to ice in the ice-cream maker, you form a mixture of ice, salt, and water that can reach a temperature of about −10 °C, cold enough to freeze the cream. On the road, salt allows the ice to melt, even if the ambient temperature is below freezing.

Adding a nonvolatile solute—one that does not readily evaporate—to a liquid extends the temperature range over which the liquid remains a liquid. The solution has a lower melting point and a higher boiling point than the pure liquid; these effects are called **freezing point depression** and **boiling point elevation**. Freezing point depression and boiling point elevation depend only on the number of solute particles *in solution*, not on the type of solute particles. Properties such as these—which depend on the number of dissolved solute particles and not on the type of solute particles—are called **colligative properties**.

▲ Sprinkling salt on icy roads lowers the freezing point of water, so the ice melts even if the temperature is below 0 °C.

Freezing Point Depression

The freezing point of a solution containing a nonvolatile solute is lower than the freezing point of the pure solvent. For example, antifreeze, which is added to engine coolant to prevent it from freezing in cold climates, is an aqueous solution of ethylene glycol ($C_2H_6O_2$). The ethylene glycol lowers the freezing point of the aqueous solution. The more concentrated the solution is, the lower the freezing point becomes. For freezing point depression and boiling point elevation, the concentration of the solution is usually expressed in **molality (*m*)**, the number of moles of solute per kilogram of solvent.

Molality is abbreviated with a lowercase *m*, while molarity is abbreviated with a capital M.

$$\text{Molality } (m) = \frac{\text{Moles solute}}{\text{Kilograms solvent}}$$

Notice that molality is defined with respect to kilograms of *solvent*, not kilograms of *solution*.

EXAMPLE 13.8	**CALCULATING MOLALITY**

Calculate the molality of a solution containing 17.2 g of ethylene glycol ($C_2H_6O_2$) dissolved in 0.500 kg of water.

You are given the mass of ethylene glycol in grams and the mass of the solvent in kilograms. You are asked to find the molality of the resulting solution.	**GIVEN:** 17.2 g $C_2H_6O_2$ 0.500 kg H_2O **FIND:** molality (*m*)

To calculate molality, substitute the correct values into the equation and calculate the answer. You must first convert the amount of $C_2H_6O_2$ from grams to moles using the molar mass of $C_2H_6O_2$.

SOLUTION

$$mol\ C_2H_6O_2 = 17.2\ g\ C_2H_6O_2 \times \frac{1\ mol\ C_2H_6O_2}{62.08\ g\ C_2H_6O_2}$$

$$= 0.2771\ mol\ C_2H_6O_2$$

$$Molality\ (m) = \frac{Moles\ solute}{Kilograms\ solvent}$$

$$= \frac{0.2771\ mol\ C_2H_6O_2}{0.500\ kg\ H_2O}$$

$$= 0.554\ m$$

▶**SKILLBUILDER 13.8 | Calculating Molality**

Calculate the molality (m) of a sucrose ($C_{12}H_{22}O_{11}$) solution containing 50.4 g sucrose and 0.332 kg of water.

▶**FOR MORE PRACTICE**   Example 13.17; Problems 97, 98, 99, 100.

▲ Ethylene glycol is the chief component of antifreeze, which keeps engine coolant from freezing in winter or boiling over in summer.

 CONCEPTUAL CHECKPOINT 13.6

A laboratory procedure calls for a 2.0 molal aqueous solution. A student accidentally makes a 2.0 molar solution. The solution made by the student is:

(a) too concentrated

(b) too dilute

(c) just right

(d) it depends on the molar mass of the solute

With an understanding of molality, we can now quantify freezing point depression. The amount that the freezing point of a solution is lowered by a particular amount of solute is given by the following equation:

The freezing point depression of a solution

$$\Delta T_f = m \times K_f$$

where

- ΔT_f is the change in temperature of the freezing point in °C (from the freezing point of the pure solvent).
- m is the molality of the solution in $\frac{mol\ solute}{kg\ solvent}$.
- K_f is the freezing point depression constant for the solvent.

For water:

The equations for freezing point depression and boiling point elevation given in this section apply only to nonelectrolyte solutions.

Different solvents have different values of K_f.

$$K_f = 1.86\ \frac{°C\ kg\ solvent}{mol\ solute}$$

Calculating the freezing point of a solution involves substituting into the given equation, as Example 13.9 demonstrates.

EVERYDAY CHEMISTRY

▶ Antifreeze in Frogs

Wood frogs (*Rana sylvatica*) look like most other frogs. They are a few inches long and have characteristic greenish-brown skin. However, wood frogs survive cold winters in a remarkable way—they partially freeze. In its frozen state, the frog has no heartbeat, no blood circulation, no breathing, and no brain activity. Within 1 to 2 hours of thawing, however, these vital functions return, and the frog hops off to find food. How is this possible?

Most cold-blooded animals cannot survive freezing temperatures because the water within their cells freezes. As described in Section 12.8, when water freezes, it expands, irreversibly damaging cells. When the wood frog hibernates for the winter, however, it secretes large amounts of glucose into its blood and into the interior of its cells. When the temperature drops below freezing, extracellular bodily fluids, such as those in the abdominal cavity, freeze solid. Fluids within the frogs' cells, however, remain liquid because the high glucose concentration lowers their freezing point. In other words, the concentrated glucose solution within the cells acts as antifreeze, preventing the water within from freezing and allowing the frog to survive.

▲ The wood frog survives cold winters by partially freezing. The fluids in frog cells are protected by a high concentration of glucose that acts as antifreeze, lowering their freezing point so the intracellular fluids remain liquid to temperatures as low as −8 °C.

B13.2 CAN YOU ANSWER THIS? *The wood frog can survive at body temperatures as low as −8.0 °C. Calculate the molality of a glucose solution ($C_6H_{12}O_6$) required to lower the freezing point of water to −8.0 °C.*

EXAMPLE 13.9 **FREEZING POINT DEPRESSION**

Calculate the freezing point of a 1.7 *m* ethylene glycol solution.

You are given the molality of an aqueous solution and asked to find the freezing point depression. You will need the freezing point depression equation provided in this section.	**GIVEN:** 1.7 *m* solution **FIND:** ΔT_f
To solve this problem, substitute the values into the equation for freezing point depression and calculate ΔT_f.	**SOLUTION** $$\Delta T_f = m \times K_f$$ $$= 1.7 \,\frac{\text{mol solute}}{\text{kg solvent}} \times 1.86 \,\frac{°\text{C kg solvent}}{\text{mol solute}}$$ $$= 3.2 \,°\text{C}$$
The actual freezing point is the freezing point of pure water (0.00 °C) − ΔT_f.	$$\text{Freezing point} = 0.00 \,°\text{C} - 3.2 \,°\text{C}$$ $$= -3.2 \,°\text{C}$$

▶**SKILLBUILDER 13.9 | Freezing Point Depression**

Calculate the freezing point of a 2.6 *m* sucrose solution.

▶**FOR MORE PRACTICE** Example 13.18; Problems 101, 102.

Boiling Point Elevation

The boiling point of a solution containing a nonvolatile solute is higher than the boiling point of the pure solvent. In automobiles, antifreeze not only prevents the freezing of coolant within engine blocks in cold climates, but it also prevents the boiling of engine coolant in hot climates. The amount that the boiling point is raised for solutions is given by the following equation:

The boiling point elevation of a solution:

$$\Delta T_b = m \times K_b$$

where

- ΔT_b is change in temperature of the boiling point in °C (from the boiling point of the pure solvent).
- m is the molality of the solution in $\dfrac{\text{mol solute}}{\text{kg solvent}}$.
- K_b is the boiling point elevation constant for the solvent.

For water:

$$K_b = 0.512 \, \dfrac{\text{°C kg solvent}}{\text{mol solute}}$$

Different solvents have different values of K_b.

The boiling point of solutions is calculated by substituting into the preceding equation, as Example 13.10 demonstrates.

EXAMPLE 13.10   BOILING POINT ELEVATION

Calculate the boiling point of a 1.7 m ethylene glycol solution.

You are given the molality of an aqueous solution and asked to find the boiling point.	**GIVEN:** 1.7 m solution **FIND:** boiling point
To solve this problem, substitute the values into the equation for boiling point elevation and calculate ΔT_b.	**SOLUTION** $\Delta T_b = m \times K_b$ $= 1.7 \, \dfrac{\text{mol solute}}{\text{kg solvent}} \times 0.512 \, \dfrac{\text{°C kg solvent}}{\text{mol solute}}$ $= 0.87 \, \text{°C}$
The actual boiling point of the solution is the boiling point of pure water (100.00 °C) plus ΔT_b.	Boiling point $= 100.00 \, \text{°C} + 0.87 \, \text{°C}$ $= 100.87 \, \text{°C}$

▶**SKILLBUILDER 13.10 | Boiling Point Elevation**

Calculate the boiling point of a 3.5 m glucose solution.

▶**FOR MORE PRACTICE** Problems 103, 104, 105, 106.

CONCEPTUAL CHECKPOINT 13.7

Which solution has the highest boiling point?
(a) 0.50 m $C_{12}H_{22}O_{11}$
(b) 0.50 m $C_6H_{12}O_6$
(c) 0.50 m $C_2H_6O_2$
(d) All of these solutions will have the same boiling point.

13.10   Osmosis: Why Drinking Salt Water Causes Dehydration

LO: Summarize and explain the process of osmosis.

Humans adrift at sea are surrounded by water, yet drinking that water only accelerates their dehydration. Why? Salt water causes dehydration because of **osmosis**, the flow of solvent from a less concentrated solution to a more concentrated solution. Solutions containing a high concentration of solute draw solvent from solutions containing a lower concentration of solute. In other words, aqueous solutions with high concentrations of solute, such as seawater, are actually *thirsty solutions*—they draw water away from other, less concentrated solutions, including those in the human body (▼ Figure 13.9).

▶ **FIGURE 13.9   Seawater is a *thirsty* solution**   As it flows through the stomach and intestine, seawater draws water *out of* bodily tissues, promoting dehydration.

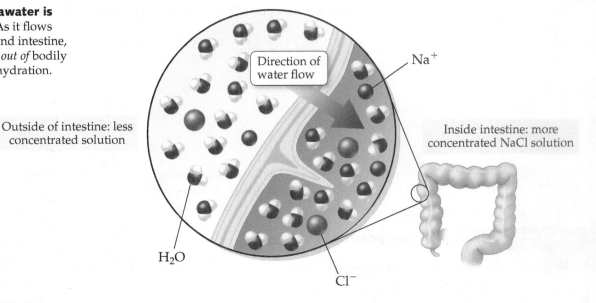

Outside of intestine: less concentrated solution

Direction of water flow

Na⁺

Inside intestine: more concentrated NaCl solution

H_2O

Cl^-

▼ Figure 13.10 shows an osmosis cell. The left side of the cell contains a concentrated saltwater solution, and the right side of the cell contains pure water. A **semipermeable membrane**—a membrane that allows some substances to pass

Osmotic Cell: Water flows toward the more concentrated solution

At first

At equilibrium

Osmotic pressure

Semipermeable membrane

Water molecules

Solute particles

▲ **FIGURE 13.10   An osmosis cell**   In an osmosis cell, water flows through a semipermeable membrane from a less concentrated solution into a more concentrated solution. As a result, fluid rises in one side of the tube until the weight of the excess fluid creates enough pressure to stop the flow. This pressure is the osmotic pressure of the solution.

through but not others—separates the two halves of the cell. Through osmosis, water flows from the pure-water side of the cell through the semipermeable membrane into the saltwater side. Over time, the water level on the left side of the cell rises while the water level on the right side of the cell falls. This continues until the pressure created by the weight of the water on the left side is enough to stop the osmotic flow. The pressure required to stop the osmotic flow is the **osmotic pressure** of the solution. Osmotic pressure—like freezing point depression and boiling point elevation—is a colligative property; it depends only on the concentration of the solute particles, not on the type of solute. The more concentrated the solution, the greater its osmotic pressure.

The **membranes** of living cells act as semipermeable membranes. Consequently, if you put a living cell into seawater, it loses water through osmosis and

CHEMISTRY **AND HEALTH**
▶ Solutions in Medicine

Doctors and others working in health fields often administer solutions to patients. The osmotic pressure of these solutions is controlled for the desired effect on the patient. Solutions having osmotic pressures less than that of bodily fluids are called *hypoosmotic*. These solutions tend to pump water into cells. When a human cell is placed in a hypoosmotic solution—such as pure water—water enters the cell, sometimes causing it to burst (Figure 13.11b). Solutions having osmotic pressures greater than that of bodily fluids are called *hyperosmotic*. These solutions tend to take water out of cells and tissues. When a human cell is placed in a hyperosmotic solution, it typically shrivels as it loses water to the surrounding solution (Figure 13.11c).

Intravenous solutions—those that are administered directly into a patient's veins—must have osmotic pressure equal to that of bodily fluids. These solutions are called *isoosmotic*. When a patient is given an IV in a hospital, the majority of the fluid is usually an isoosmotic saline solution—a solution containing 0.9 g NaCl per 100 mL of solution. In medicine and in other health-related fields, solution concentrations are often reported in units that indicate the mass of the solute in a given volume of solution. Also common is *percent mass to volume*—which is the mass of the solute in grams divided by volume of the solution in milliliters times 100%. In these units, the concentration of an isoosmotic saline solution is 0.9% mass/volume.

B13.3 CAN YOU ANSWER THIS?   *An isoosmotic sucrose ($C_{12}H_{22}O_{11}$) solution has a concentration of 0.30 M. Calculate its concentration in percent mass to volume.*

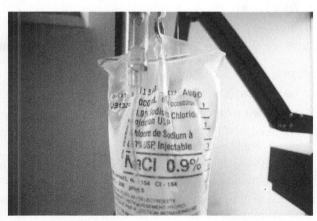

▲ Intravenous fluids consist mostly of isoosmotic saline solutions with an osmotic pressure equal to that of bodily fluids.
Question: Why would it be dangerous to administer intravenous fluids that do not have an osmotic pressure comparable to that of bodily fluids?

▶ **FIGURE 13.11   Red blood cells in solutions of different concentration**   (a) When the solute concentration of the surrounding fluid is equal to that within the cell, there is no net osmotic flow, and the red blood cell exhibits its typical shape. (b) When a cell is placed in pure water, osmotic flow of water into the cell causes it to swell up. Eventually it may burst. (c) When a cell is placed in a concentrated solution, osmosis draws water out of the cell, distorting its normal shape.

Normal red blood cell

(a)

Red blood cell in pure water: water flows into cell

(b)

Red blood cell in concentrated solution: water flows out of cell

(c)

becomes dehydrated. ▲ Figure 13.11 shows red blood cells in solutions of various concentrations. The cells in Figure 13.11a, immersed in a solution with the same solute concentration as the cell interior, have the normal red blood cell shape. The cells in Figure 13.11b, in pure water, are swollen. Because the solute concentration within the cells is higher than that of the surrounding fluid, osmosis has pulled water across the membrane *into* the cells. The cells in Figure 13.11c, in a solution more concentrated than the cell interior, are starting to shrivel as osmosis draws water *out of* the cells. Similarly, if you drink seawater, the seawater actually draws water out of your body as it passes through your stomach and intestines. All of that extra water in your intestine promotes dehydration of bodily tissues and diarrhea. Consequently, seawater should never be consumed.

CHAPTER IN REVIEW

Self-Assessment Quiz

Q1. Which compound forms an electrolyte solution when dissolved in water?

(a) KBr

(b) Br_2

(c) CH_3OH

(d) $C_6H_{12}O_6$ (glucose)

Q2. A solution is saturated in O_2 gas and KNO_3 at room temperature. What happens if the solution is warmed to 75 °C?

(a) Solid KNO_3 precipitates out of solution.

(b) Gaseous O_2 bubbles out of solution.

(c) Solid KNO_3 precipitates out of solution *and* gaseous O_2 bubbles out of solution.

(d) Nothing happens (both O_2 and KNO_3 remain in solution).

Q3. What is the mass percent concentration of a solution containing 25.0 g NaCl and 155.0 mL of water? Assume a density of 1.00 g/mL for water.

(a) 2.76%

(b) 6.20%

(c) 13.9%

(d) 16.1%

Q4. A glucose solution is 3.25% glucose by mass and has a density of 1.03 g/mL. What mass of glucose is contained in 58.2 mL of this solution?

(a) 18.4 g   (b) 184 g

(c) 195 g   (d) 1.95 g

Q5. What is the molarity of a solution containing 11.2 g $Ca(NO_3)_2$ in 175 mL of solution?

(a) 64.0 M   (b) 0.390 M

(c) 0.064 M   (d) 1.96×10^3 M

Q6. What mass of glucose ($C_6H_{12}O_6$) is contained in 75.0 mL of a 1.75 M glucose solution?

(a) 23.6 g   (b) 7.72 g

(c) 0.131 g   (d) 75.0 g

Q7. What is the molar concentration of potassium ions in a 0.250 M K_2SO_4 solution?

(a) 0.125 M   (b) 0.250 M

(c) 0.500 M   (d) 0.750 M

Q8. What volume of a 3.50 M Na_3PO_4 solution should you use to make 1.50 L of a 2.55 M Na_3PO_4 solution?

(a) 0.917 L   (b) 13.4 L

(c) 2.06 L   (d) 1.09 L

Q9. Potassium iodide reacts with lead(II) nitrate in the following precipitation reaction:

$$2\,KI(aq) + Pb(NO_3)_2(aq) \longrightarrow 2\,KNO_3(aq) + PbI_2(s)$$

What minimum volume of 0.200 M potassium iodide solution is required to completely precipitate all of the lead in 155.0 mL of a 0.112 M lead(II) nitrate solution?

(a) 348 mL   (b) 86.8 mL

(c) 43.4 mL   (d) 174 mL

Q10. A solution contains 22.4 g glucose ($C_6H_{12}O_6$) dissolved in 500.0 g of water. What is the molality of the solution?

(a) 0.238 m (b) 0.249 m

(c) 44.8 m (d) 4.03 m

Q11. Calculate the freezing point of a 1.30 m sucrose ($C_{12}H_{22}O_{11}$) solution.

(a) 2.42 °C

(b) −2.42 °C

(c) 0.472 °C

(d) −0.472 °C

Q12. What mass of ethylene glycol ($C_2H_6O_2$) must be added to 250.0 g of water to obtain a solution with a boiling point of 102.5 °C?

(a) 75.7 g

(b) 3.11 × 10³ g

(c) 1.22 g

(d) 0.0197 g

Answers: 1:a, 2:b, 3:c, 4:d, 5:b, 6:a, 7:c, 8:d, 9:d, 10:b, 11:b, 12:a

Chemical Principles

Solutions: A solution is a homogeneous mixture with two or more components. The solvent is the majority component, and the solute is the minority component. Water is the solvent in aqueous solutions.

Solid-and-Liquid Solutions: The solubility—the amount of solute that dissolves in a certain amount of solvent—of solids in liquids increases with increasing temperature. Recrystallization involves dissolving a solid into hot solvent to saturation and then allowing it to cool. As the solution cools, it becomes supersaturated and the solid crystallizes.

Gas-and-Liquid Solutions: The solubility of gases in liquids decreases with increasing temperature but increases with increasing pressure.

Solution Concentration: We use solution concentration to specify how much of the solute is present in a given amount of solution. Three common ways to express solution concentration are mass percent, molarity, and molality.

$$\text{Mass percent} = \frac{\text{Mass solute}}{\text{Mass solute} + \text{Mass solvent}} \times 100\%$$

$$\text{Molarity (M)} = \frac{\text{Moles solute}}{\text{Liters solution}}$$

$$\text{Molality } (m) = \frac{\text{Moles solute}}{\text{Kilograms solvent}}$$

Solution Dilution: We can solve solution dilution problems using the following equation:

$$M_1V_1 = M_2V_2$$

Relevance

Solutions: Solutions are all around us—most of the fluids that we encounter every day are solutions. Common solutions include seawater (solid and liquid), soda pop (gas and liquid), alcoholic spirits such as vodka (liquid and liquid), air (gas and gas), and blood (solid, gas, and liquid).

Solid-and-Liquid Solutions: Solutions of solids dissolved in liquids, such as seawater, coffee, and sugar water, are important both in chemistry and in everyday life. Recrystallization is used extensively in the laboratory to purify solids.

Gas-and-Liquid Solutions: The temperature and pressure dependence of gas solubility is the reason that soda pop fizzes when opened and the reason that warm soda goes flat.

Solution Concentration: Solution concentration is useful in converting between amounts of solute and solution. Mass percent and molarity are the most common concentration units. We use molality to quantify colligative properties such as freezing point depression and boiling point elevation.

Solution Dilution: Since many solutions are stored in concentrated form, it is often necessary to dilute them to a desired concentration.

Freezing Point Depression and Boiling Point Elevation: A nonvolatile solute will extend the liquid temperature range of a solution relative to the pure solvent. The freezing point of a solution is lower than the freezing point of the pure solvent, and the boiling point of a solution is higher than the boiling point of the pure solvent. These relationships are quantified by the following equations:

Freezing point depression:

$$\Delta T_f = m \times K_f$$

Boiling point elevation:

$$\Delta T_b = m \times K_b$$

Freezing Point Depression and Boiling Point Elevation: We add salt to ice in ice-cream makers and use it to melt ice on roads in frigid weather. The salt lowers the freezing point of water, allowing the cream within the ice-cream maker to freeze and the ice on icy roads to melt. We use antifreeze in the cooling systems of cars both to lower the freezing point of the coolant in winter and to raise its boiling point in summer.

Osmosis: Osmosis is the flow of water from a low-concentration solution to a high-concentration solution through a semipermeable membrane.

Osmosis: Osmosis is the reason drinking seawater causes dehydration. As seawater goes through the stomach and intestines, it draws water away from the body through osmosis, resulting in diarrhea and dehydration. To avoid damage to body tissues, transfused fluids must always be isoosmotic with body fluids. Most transfused fluids consist in whole or part of 0.9% mass/volume saline solution.

Chemical Skills

Examples

LO: Calculate mass percent (Section 13.5).

You are given the mass of the solute and the solvent and asked to find the concentration of the solution in mass percent.

EXAMPLE 13.11 **CALCULATING MASS PERCENT**

Find the mass percent concentration of a solution containing 19 g of solute and 158 g of solvent.

GIVEN: 19 g solute
158 g solvent

FIND: mass percent

SOLUTION

To calculate mass percent concentration, divide the mass of the solute by the mass of the solution (solute and solvent) and multiply by 100%.

$$\text{Mass percent} = \frac{\text{mass solute}}{\text{mass solute} + \text{mass solvent}} \times 100\%$$

$$\text{Mass percent} = \frac{19\text{ g}}{19\text{ g} + 158\text{ g}} \times 100\%$$

$$\text{Mass percent} = \frac{19\text{ g}}{177\text{ g}} \times 100\%$$

$$= 11\%$$

LO: Use mass percent in calculations (Section 13.5).

EXAMPLE 13.12 **USING MASS PERCENT IN CALCULATIONS**

How much KCl in grams is in 0.337 L of a 5.80% mass percent KCl solution? (Assume that the density of the solution is 1.05 g/mL.)

SORT

You are given the volume of a potassium chloride solution and its mass percent concentration. You are asked to find the mass of potassium chloride.

GIVEN: 5.80% KCl by mass
0.337 L solution

$$d = \frac{1.05\text{ g}}{\text{mL}}$$

FIND: g KCl

STRATEGIZE

Draw a solution map. Begin with the given volume of the solution in L and convert to mL. Use the density to find the mass of the solution. Finally, use the mass percent to get to the mass of potassium chloride.

SOLUTION MAP

$$\frac{1\ mL}{10^{-3}\ L} \qquad \frac{1.05\ g}{mL} \qquad \frac{5.80\ g\ KCl}{100\ g\ solution}$$

RELATIONSHIPS USED

$\frac{5.80\ g\ KCl}{100\ g\ solution}$ (given mass percent, written as a fraction)

$\frac{1.05\ g}{mL}$ (given density)

$1\ mL = 10^{-3}\ L$ (Table 2.2)

SOLUTION

$$0.337\ L\ solution \times \frac{1\ mL}{10^{-3}\ L} \times \frac{1.05\ g}{mL} \times \frac{5.80\ g\ KCl}{100\ g\ solution}$$

$$= 20.5\ g\ KCl$$

SOLVE

Follow your solution map to calculate the answer.

CHECK

Check your answer. Are the units correct? Does the answer make physical sense?

The units (g KCl) are correct. The magnitude of the answer makes sense because 0.337 L is a bit more than 300 g of solution. Each 100 g of solution contains about 6 g KCl. Therefore the answer should be a bit more than 18 g.

LO: Calculate molarity (Section 13.6).

You are given the number of moles of potassium chloride and the volume of solution. You are asked to find the molarity.

To calculate molarity, divide the number of moles of solute by the volume of the solution in liters.

EXAMPLE 13.13 **CALCULATING MOLARITY**

Calculate the molarity of a KCl solution containing 0.22 mol of KCl in 0.455 L of solution.

GIVEN: 0.22 mol KCl
0.455 L solution

FIND: molarity (M)

SOLUTION

$$Molarity\ (M) = \frac{0.22\ mol\ KCl}{0.455\ L\ solution}$$

$$= 0.48\ M$$

LO: Use molarity in calculations (Section 13.6).

EXAMPLE 13.14 **USING MOLARITY IN CALCULATIONS**

How much KCl in grams is contained in 0.488 L of 1.25 M KCl solution?

GIVEN: 1.25 M KCl
0.488 L solution

FIND: g KCl

SORT

You are given the volume and molarity of a potassium chloride solution and asked to find the mass of potassium chloride contained in the solution.

STRATEGIZE

Draw a solution map beginning with liters of solution and converting to moles of solute using the molarity as a conversion factor. Then convert to grams using the molar mass.

SOLUTION MAP

$$\frac{1.25\ mol\ KCl}{L\ solution} \qquad \frac{74.55\ g\ KCl}{mol\ KCl}$$

RELATIONSHIPS USED

$$\frac{1.25 \text{ mol KCl}}{\text{L solution}} \text{ (given molarity, written as a fraction)}$$

$$1 \text{ mol} = 74.55 \text{ g (molar mass KCl)}$$

SOLVE

Follow your solution map to calculate the answer.

SOLUTION

$$0.488 \text{ L solution} \times \frac{1.25 \text{ mol KCl}}{\text{L solution}} \times \frac{74.55 \text{ g KCl}}{\text{mol KCl}}$$

$$= 45.5 \text{ g KCl}$$

CHECK

Check your answer. Are the units correct? Does the answer make physical sense?

The units (g KCl) are correct. The magnitude of the answer makes sense because if each liter of solution contains 1.25 mol, then the given amount of solution (which is about 0.5 L) should contain a bit more than 0.5 mol, which would have a mass that is bit more than about 37 g.

LO: Use the dilution equation in calculations (Section 13.7).

You are given the initial molarity and final molarity of a solution as well as the final volume. You are asked to find the initial volume.

Most solution dilution problems will use equation $M_1V_1 = M_2V_2$.

Solve the equation for the quantity you are trying to find (in this case, V_1) and substitute in the correct values to calculate it.

EXAMPLE 13.15   **SOLUTION DILUTION**

How much of an 8.0 M HCl solution should be used to make 0.400 L of a 2.7 M HCl solution?

GIVEN: $M_1 = 8.0 \text{ M}$
$M_2 = 2.7 \text{ M}$
$V_2 = 0.400 \text{ L}$

FIND: V_1

SOLUTION

$$M_1V_1 = M_2V_2$$

$$V_1 = \frac{M_2V_2}{M_1}$$

$$= \frac{2.7 \frac{\text{mol}}{\text{L}} \times 0.400 \text{ L}}{8.0 \frac{\text{mol}}{\text{L}}}$$

$$= 0.14 \text{ L}$$

LO: Use volume and concentration to calculate the number of moles of reactants or products and then use stoichiometric coefficients to convert to other quantities in a reaction (Section 13.8).

EXAMPLE 13.16   **SOLUTION STOICHIOMETRY**

Consider the reaction:

$$HCl(aq) + NaOH(aq) \longrightarrow NaCl(aq) + H_2O(l)$$

How much 0.113 M NaOH solution will completely neutralize 1.25 L of 0.228 M HCl solution?

SORT

You are given the volume and concentration of a hydrochloric acid solution as well as the concentration of a sodium hydroxide solution with which it reacts. You are asked to find the volume of the sodium hydroxide solution that will completely react with the hydrochloric acid.

GIVEN: 1.25 L HCl solution
0.228 M HCl
0.113 M NaOH

FIND: L NaOH solution

STRATEGIZE

Draw a solution map. Use the volume and molarity of HCl to get to mol HCl. Then use the stoichiometric coefficients to convert to mole NaOH. Finally, convert back to volume of NaOH using the molarity of NaOH.

SOLUTION MAP

$$\frac{0.228 \text{ mol HCl}}{\text{L HCl solution}} \quad \frac{1 \text{ mol NaOH}}{1 \text{ mol HCl}} \quad \frac{1 \text{ L NaOH solution}}{0.113 \text{ mol NaOH}}$$

RELATIONSHIPS USED

$$M\,(HCl) = \frac{0.228 \text{ mol HCl}}{\text{L HCl solution}} \text{ (given concentration of HCl solution, written as a fraction)}$$

$$M\,(NaOH) = \frac{0.113 \text{ mol NaOH}}{\text{L NaOH solution}} \text{ (given concentration of NaOH solution, written as a fraction)}$$

1 mol HCl:1 mol NaOH (stoichiometric relationship between HCl and NaOH, from balanced equation)

SOLVE

Follow the solution map to calculate the answer.

SOLUTION

$$1.25 \text{ L HCl solution} \times \frac{0.228 \text{ mol HCl}}{\text{L HCl solution}}$$

$$\times \frac{1 \text{ mol NaOH}}{1 \text{ mol HCl}} \times \frac{\text{L NaOH solution}}{0.113 \text{ mol NaOH}}$$

$$= 2.52 \text{ L NaOH solution}$$

CHECK

Check your answer. Are the units correct? Does the answer make physical sense?

The units (L NaOH solution) are correct. The magnitude of the answer makes sense because the sodium hydroxide solution is about half as concentrated as the hydrochloric acid. Since the reaction stoichiometry is 1:1, the volume of the sodium hydroxide solution should be about twice the volume of the hydrochloric acid.

LO: Calculate molality (Section 13.9).

You are given the number of moles of sucrose and the mass of water into which it is dissolved. You are asked to find the molality of the resulting solution.

Substitute the correct values into the definition of molality and calculate the answer. If any of the quantities are not in the correct units, convert them into the correct units before substituting into the equation.

EXAMPLE 13.17 CALCULATING MOLALITY

Calculate the molality of a solution containing 0.183 mol of sucrose dissolved in 1.10 kg of water.

GIVEN: 0.183 mol of sucrose
1.10 kg H_2O

FIND: molality (m)

SOLUTION

$$\text{Molality } (m) = \frac{\text{Moles solute}}{\text{Kilograms solvent}}$$

$$\text{Molality } (m) = \frac{0.183 \text{ mol sucrose}}{1.10 \text{ kg } H_2O}$$

$$= 0.166 \, m$$

LO: Calculate freezing points and boiling points for solutions (Section 13.9).

You are given the molality of the solution and asked to find its freezing point.

To find ΔT_f or ΔT_b, simply substitute the values into the equation and calculate the answer.

The freezing point is the freezing point of pure water $(0.00\,°C) - \Delta T_f$.

EXAMPLE 13.18   FREEZING POINT DEPRESSION

Calculate the freezing point of a 2.5 m aqueous sucrose solution.

GIVEN: 2.5 m solution

FIND: ΔT_f

SOLUTION

$$\Delta T_f = m \times K_f$$

$$= 2.5\,\frac{\text{mol solute}}{\text{kg solvent}} \times 1.86\,\frac{°C\,\text{kg solvent}}{\text{mol solute}}$$

$$= 4.7\,°C$$

$$\text{Freezing point} = 0.00\,°C - 4.7\,°C$$

$$= -4.7\,°C$$

KEY TERMS

boiling point elevation
  [13.9]
colligative properties **[13.9]**
concentrated solution **[13.5]**
dilute solution **[13.5]**
electrolyte solution **[13.3]**
freezing point depression
  [13.9]

Henry's law **[13.4]**
mass percent **[13.5]**
membranes **[13.10]**
molality (m) **[13.9]**
molarity (M) **[13.6]**
nonelectrolyte solution
  [13.3]
osmosis **[13.10]**

osmotic pressure **[13.10]**
recrystallization **[13.3]**
saturated solution **[13.3]**
semipermeable membrane
  [13.10]
solubility **[13.3]**
solute **[13.2]**
solution **[13.2]**

solvent **[13.2]**
stock solution **[13.7]**
supersaturated solution
  [13.3]
unsaturated solution **[13.3]**

EXERCISES

QUESTIONS

1. What is a solution? List some examples.
2. What is an aqueous solution?
3. In a solution, what is the solvent? What is the solute? List some examples.
4. Explain what "like dissolves like" means.
5. What is solubility?
6. Describe what happens when additional solute is added to:
   (a) a saturated solution
   (b) an unsaturated solution
   (c) a supersaturated solution
7. Explain the difference between a strong electrolyte solution and a nonelectrolyte solution. What kinds of solutes form strong electrolyte solutions?
8. How does gas solubility depend on temperature?
9. Explain recrystallization.
10. How is rock candy made?
11. When you heat water on a stove, bubbles form on the bottom of the pot *before* the water boils. What are these bubbles? Why do they form?
12. Explain why warm soda pop goes flat faster than cold soda pop.

13. How does gas solubility depend on pressure? How does this relationship explain why a can of soda pop fizzes when opened?
14. What is the difference between a dilute solution and a concentrated solution?
15. Define the concentration units mass percent and molarity.
16. What is a stock solution?
17. How does the presence of a nonvolatile solute affect the boiling point and melting point of a solution relative to the boiling point and melting point of the pure solvent?
18. What are colligative properties?
19. Define molality.
20. What is osmosis?
21. Two shipwreck survivors were rescued from a life raft. One had drunk seawater while the other had not. The one who had drunk the seawater was more severely dehydrated than the one who did not. Explain.
22. Why are intravenous fluids always isoosmotic saline solutions? What would happen if pure water were administered intravenously?

PROBLEMS

SOLUTIONS

23. Determine whether or not each mixture is a solution.
(a) sand and water mixture
(b) oil and water mixture
(c) salt and water mixture
(d) sterling silver cup

24. Determine whether or not each mixture is a solution.
(a) air
(b) carbon dioxide and water mixture
(c) a blueberry muffin
(d) a brass buckle

25. Identify the solute and solvent in each solution.
(a) salt water
(b) sugar water
(c) soda water

26. Identify the solute and solvent in each solution.
(a) 80-proof vodka (40% ethyl alcohol)
(b) oxygenated water
(c) antifreeze (ethylene glycol and water)

27. Pick an appropriate solvent from Table 13.2 to dissolve:
(a) motor oil (nonpolar)
(b) sugar (polar)
(c) lard (nonpolar)
(d) potassium chloride (ionic)

28. Pick an appropriate solvent from Table 13.2 to dissolve:
(a) glucose (polar)
(b) salt (ionic)
(c) vegetable oil (nonpolar)
(d) sodium nitrate (ionic)

SOLIDS DISSOLVED IN WATER

29. What are the dissolved particles in a solution containing an ionic solute? What is the name for this kind of solution?

30. What are the dissolved particles in a solution containing a molecular solute? What is the name for this kind of solution?

31. A solution contains 35 g of $NaCl$ per 100 g of water at 25 °C. Is the solution unsaturated, saturated, or supersaturated? (See Figure 13.4.)

32. A solution contains 28 g of KNO_3 per 100 g of water at 25 °C. Is the solution unsaturated, saturated, or supersaturated? (See Figure 13.4.)

33. A KNO_3 solution containing 45 g of KNO_3 per 100 g of water is cooled from 40 °C to 0 °C. What happens during cooling? (See Figure 13.4.)

34. A KCl solution containing 42 g of KCl per 100 g of water is cooled from 60 °C to 0 °C. What happens during cooling? (See Figure 13.4.)

35. Refer to Figure 13.4 to determine whether each of the given amounts of solid will completely dissolve in the given amount of water at the indicated temperature.
(a) 30.0 g $KClO_3$ in 85.0 g of water at 35 °C
(b) 65.0 g $NaNO_3$ in 125 g of water at 15 °C
(c) 32.0 g KCl in 70.0 g of water at 82 °C

36. Refer to Figure 13.4 to determine whether each of the given amounts of solid will completely dissolve in the given amount of water at the indicated temperature.
(a) 45.0 g $CaCl_2$ in 105 g of water at 5 °C
(b) 15.0 g $KClO_3$ in 115 g of water at 25 °C
(c) 50.0 g $Pb(NO_3)_2$ in 95.0 g of water at 10 °C

GASES DISSOLVED IN WATER

37. Some laboratory procedures involving oxygen-sensitive reactants or products call for using preboiled (and then cooled) water. Explain why this is so.

38. A person preparing a fish tank uses preboiled (and then cooled) water to fill it. When the fish is put into the tank, it dies. Explain.

39. Scuba divers breathing air at increased pressure can suffer from nitrogen narcosis—a condition resembling drunkenness—when the partial pressure of nitrogen exceeds about 4 atm. What property of gas/water solutions causes this to happen? How could the diver reverse this effect?

40. Scuba divers breathing air at increased pressure can suffer from oxygen toxicity—too much oxygen in the bloodstream—when the partial pressure of oxygen exceeds about 1.4 atm. What happens to the amount of oxygen in a diver's bloodstream when he or she breathes oxygen at elevated pressures? How can this be reversed?

MASS PERCENT

41. Calculate the concentration of each solution in mass percent.
 (a) 41.2 g $C_{12}H_{22}O_{11}$ in 498 g H_2O
 (b) 178 mg $C_6H_{12}O_6$ in 4.91 g H_2O
 (c) 7.55 g NaCl in 155 g H_2O

42. Calculate the concentration of each solution in mass percent.
 (a) 132 g KCl in 598 g H_2O
 (b) 22.3 mg KNO_3 in 2.84 g H_2O
 (c) 8.72 g C_2H_6O in 76.1 g H_2O

43. A soft drink contains 42 g of sugar in 311 g of H_2O. What is the concentration of sugar in the soft drink in mass percent?

44. A soft drink contains 32 mg of sodium in 309 g of H_2O. What is the concentration of sodium in the soft drink in mass percent?

45. Complete the table.

Mass Solute	Mass Solvent	Mass Solution	Mass Percent
15.5 g	238.1 g	____	
22.8 g	____	____	12.0%
____	183.3 g	212.1 g	____
____	315.2 g		15.3%

46. Complete the table.

Mass Solute	Mass Solvent	Mass Solution	Mass Percent
2.55 g	25.0 g	____	
____	45.8 g	____	3.8%
1.38 g	____	27.2 g	____
23.7 g	____		5.8%

47. Ocean water contains 3.5% NaCl by mass. How much salt can be obtained from 254 g of seawater?

48. A saline solution contains 1.1% NaCl by mass. How much NaCl is present in 96.3 g of this solution?

49. Determine the amount of sucrose in each solution.
 (a) 48 g of a solution containing 3.7% sucrose by mass
 (b) 103 mg of a solution containing 10.2% sucrose by mass
 (c) 3.2 kg of a solution containing 14.3% sucrose by mass

50. Determine the amount of potassium chloride in each solution.
 (a) 19.7 g of a solution containing 1.08% KCl by mass
 (b) 23.2 kg of a solution containing 18.7% KCl by mass
 (c) 38 mg of a solution containing 12% KCl by mass

51. Determine the mass (in g) of each NaCl solution that contains 1.5 g of NaCl.
 (a) 0.058% NaCl by mass
 (b) 1.46% NaCl by mass
 (c) 8.44% NaCl by mass

52. Determine the mass (in g) of each sucrose solution that contains 12 g of sucrose.
 (a) 4.1% sucrose by mass
 (b) 3.2% sucrose by mass
 (c) 12.5% sucrose by mass

53. $AgNO_3$ solutions are often used to plate silver onto other metals. What is the maximum amount of silver in grams that can be plated out of 4.8 L of an $AgNO_3$ solution containing 3.4% Ag by mass? (Assume that the density of the solution is 1.01 g/mL.)

54. A dioxin-contaminated water source contains 0.085% dioxin by mass. How much dioxin is present in 2.5 L of this water? (Assume that the density of the solution is 1.01 g/mL.)

55. Ocean water contains 3.5% NaCl by mass. What mass of ocean water in grams contains 45.8 g of NaCl?

56. A hard water sample contains 0.0085% Ca by mass (in the form of Ca^{2+} ions). What mass of water in grams contains 1.2 g of Ca? (1.2 g of Ca is the recommended daily allowance of calcium for 19- to 24-year-olds.)

57. Lead is a toxic metal that affects the central nervous system. A Pb-contaminated water sample contains 0.0011% Pb by mass. What volume of the water in milliliters contains 115 mg of Pb? (Assume that the density of the solution is 1.0 g/mL.)

58. Benzene is a carcinogenic (cancer-causing) compound. A benzene-contaminated water sample contains 0.000037% benzene by mass. What volume of the water in liters contains 175 mg of benzene? (Assume that the density of the solution is 1.0 g/mL.)

MOLARITY

59. Calculate the molarity of each solution.
 (a) 0.127 mol of sucrose in 655 mL of solution
 (b) 0.205 mol of KNO_3 in 0.875 L of solution
 (c) 1.1 mol of KCl in 2.7 L of solution

60. Calculate the molarity of each solution.
 (a) 1.54 mol of LiCl in 22.2 L of solution
 (b) 0.101 mol of $LiNO_3$ in 6.4 L of solution
 (c) 0.0323 mol of glucose in 76.2 mL of solution

61. Calculate the molarity of each solution.
  (a) 22.6 g of $C_{12}H_{22}O_{11}$ in 0.442 L of solution
  (b) 42.6 g of NaCl in 1.58 L of solution
  (c) 315 mg of $C_5H_{12}O_6$ in 58.2 mL of solution

62. Calculate the molarity of each solution.
  (a) 33.2 g of KCl in 0.895 L of solution
  (b) 61.3 g of C_2H_6O in 3.4 L of solution
  (c) 38.2 mg of KI in 112 mL of solution

63. A 205-mL sample of ocean water contains 6.8 g of NaCl. What is the molarity of the solution with respect to NaCl?

64. A 355-mL can of soda pop contains 41 g of sucrose ($C_{12}H_{22}O_{11}$). What is the molarity of the solution with respect to sucrose?

65. How many moles of NaCl are contained in each solution?
  (a) 1.5 L of a 1.2 M NaCl solution
  (b) 0.448 L of a 0.85 M NaCl solution
  (c) 144 mL of a 1.65 M NaCl solution

66. How many moles of sucrose are contained in each solution?
  (a) 3.4 L of a 0.100 M sucrose solution
  (b) 0.952 L of a 1.88 M sucrose solution
  (c) 21.5 mL of a 0.528 M sucrose solution

67. What volume of each solution contains 0.15 mol of KCl?
  (a) 0.255 M KCl
  (b) 1.8 M KCl
  (c) 0.995 M KCl

68. What volume of each solution contains 0.325 mol of NaI?
  (a) 0.152 M NaI
  (b) 0.982 M NaI
  (c) 1.76 M NaI

69. Complete the table.

Solute	Solute Mass	Mol Solute	Volume Solution	Molarity
KNO_3	22.5 g	_____	125.0 mL	_____
$NaHCO_3$	_____	_____	250.0 mL	0.100 M
$C_{12}H_{22}O_{11}$	55.38 g	_____	_____	0.150 M

70. Complete the table.

Solute	Solute Mass	Mol Solute	Volume Solution	Molarity
$MgSO_4$	0.588 g	_____	25.0 mL	_____
NaOH	_____	_____	0.100 mL	1.75 M
CH_3OH	12.5 g	_____	_____	0.500 M

71. Calculate the mass of NaCl in a 35-mL sample of a 1.3 M NaCl solution.

72. Calculate the mass of glucose ($C_6H_{12}O_6$) in a 105-mL sample of a 1.02 M glucose solution.

73. A chemist wants to make 2.5 L of a 0.100 M KCl solution. How much KCl in grams should the chemist use?

74. A laboratory procedure calls for making 500.0 mL of a 1.4 M KNO_3 solution. How much KNO_3 in grams is needed?

75. How many liters of a 0.500 M sucrose ($C_{12}H_{22}O_{11}$) solution contain 1.5 kg of sucrose?

76. What volume of a 0.35 M $Mg(NO_3)_2$ solution contains 87 g of $Mg(NO_3)_2$?

77. Determine the concentration of Cl^- in each aqueous solution. (Assume complete dissociation of each compound.)
  (a) 0.15 M NaCl
  (b) 0.15 M $CuCl_2$
  (c) 0.15 M $AlCl_3$

78. Determine the concentration of NO_3^- in each aqueous solution. (Assume complete dissociation of each compound.)
  (a) 0.10 M KNO_3
  (b) 0.10 M $Ca(NO_3)_2$
  (c) 0.10 M $Cr(NO_3)_3$

79. Determine the concentration of the cation and anion in each aqueous solution. (Assume complete dissociation of each compound.)
  (a) 0.12 M Na_2SO_4
  (b) 0.25 M K_2CO_3
  (c) 0.11 M RbBr

80. Determine the concentration of the cation and anion in each aqueous solution. (Assume complete dissociation of each compound.)
  (a) 0.20 M $SrSO_4$
  (b) 0.15 M $Cr_2(SO_4)_3$
  (c) 0.12 M SrI_2

SOLUTION DILUTION

81. A 122-mL sample of a 1.2 M sucrose solution is diluted to 500.0 mL. What is the molarity of the diluted solution?

82. A 3.5-L sample of a 5.8 M NaCl solution is diluted to 55 L. What is the molarity of the diluted solution?

83. Describe how you would make 2.5 L of a 0.100 M KCl solution from a 5.5 M stock KCl solution.

84. Describe how you would make 500.0 mL of a 0.200 M NaOH solution from a 15.0 M stock NaOH solution.

85. To what volume should you dilute 25 mL of a 12 M stock HCl solution to obtain a 0.500 M HCl solution?

86. To what volume should you dilute 75 mL of a 10.0 M H_2SO_4 solution to obtain a 1.75 M H_2SO_4 solution?

87. How much of a 12.0 M HNO_3 solution should you use to make 850.0 mL of a 0.250 M HNO_3 solution?

88. How much of a 5.0 M sucrose solution should you use to make 85.0 mL of a 0.040 M solution?

SOLUTION STOICHIOMETRY

89. Determine the volume of 0.150 M NaOH solution required to neutralize each sample of hydrochloric acid. The neutralization reaction is:

$$NaOH(aq) + HCl(aq) \longrightarrow H_2O(l) + NaCl(aq)$$

   (a) 25 mL of a 0.150 M HCl solution
   (b) 55 mL of a 0.055 M HCl solution
   (c) 175 mL of a 0.885 M HCl solution

90. Determine the volume of 0.225 M KOH solution required to neutralize each sample of sulfuric acid. The neutralization reaction is:

$$H_2SO_4(aq) + 2 KOH(aq) \longrightarrow K_2SO_4(aq) + 2 H_2O(l)$$

   (a) 45 mL of 0.225 M H_2SO_4
   (b) 185 mL of 0.125 M H_2SO_4
   (c) 75 mL of 0.100 M H_2SO_4

91. Consider the reaction:

$$2 K_3PO_4(aq) + 3 NiCl_2(aq) \longrightarrow Ni_3(PO_4)_2(s) + 6 KCl(aq)$$

What volume of 0.225 M K_3PO_4 solution is necessary to completely react with 134 mL of 0.0112 M $NiCl_2$?

92. Consider the reaction:

$$K_2S(aq) + Co(NO_3)_2(aq) \longrightarrow 2 KNO_3(aq) + CoS(s)$$

What volume of 0.225 M K_2S solution is required to completely react with 175 mL of 0.115 M $Co(NO_3)_2$?

93. A 10.0-mL sample of an unknown H_3PO_4 solution requires 112 mL of 0.100 M KOH to completely react with the H_3PO_4. What was the concentration of the unknown H_3PO_4 solution?

$$H_3PO_4(aq) + 3 KOH(aq) \longrightarrow 3 H_2O(l) + K_3PO_4(aq)$$

94. A 25.0-mL sample of an unknown $HClO_4$ solution requires 45.3 mL of 0.101 M NaOH for complete neutralization. What was the concentration of the unknown $HClO_4$ solution? The neutralization reaction is:

$$HClO_4(aq) + NaOH(aq) \longrightarrow H_2O(l) + NaClO_4(aq)$$

95. What is the minimum amount of 6.0 M H_2SO_4 necessary to produce 15.0 g of $H_2(g)$ according to the reaction:

$$2 Al(s) + 3 H_2SO_4(aq) \longrightarrow Al_2(SO_4)_3(aq) + 3 H_2(g)$$

96. What is the molarity of $ZnCl_2(aq)$ that forms when 15.0 g of zinc completely reacts with $CuCl_2(aq)$ according to the following reaction? (Assume a final volume of 175 mL.)

$$Zn(s) + CuCl_2(aq) \longrightarrow ZnCl_2 + Cu(s)$$

MOLALITY, FREEZING POINT DEPRESSION, AND BOILING POINT ELEVATION

97. Calculate the molality of each solution.
   (a) 0.25 mol solute; 0.250 kg solvent
   (b) 0.882 mol solute; 0.225 kg solvent
   (c) 0.012 mol solute; 23.1 g solvent

98. Calculate the molality of each solution.
   (a) 0.455 mol solute; 1.97 kg solvent
   (b) 0.559 mol solute; 1.44 kg solvent
   (c) 0.119 mol solute; 488 g solvent

99. Calculate the molality of a solution containing 12.5 g of ethylene glycol ($C_2H_6O_2$) dissolved in 135 g of water.

100. Calculate the molality of a solution containing 257 g glucose ($C_6H_{12}O_6$) dissolved in 1.62 L of water. (Assume a density of 1.00 g/mL for water.)

101. Calculate the freezing point of a water solution at each concentration.
   (a) 0.85 m
   (b) 1.45 m
   (c) 4.8 m
   (d) 2.35 m

102. Calculate the freezing point of a water solution at each concentration.
   (a) 0.100 m
   (b) 0.469 m
   (c) 1.44 m
   (d) 5.89 m

103. Calculate the boiling point of a water solution at each concentration.
   (a) 0.118 m
   (b) 1.94 m
   (c) 3.88 m
   (d) 2.16 m

104. Calculate the boiling point of a water solution at each concentration.
   (a) 0.225 m
   (b) 2.58 m
   (c) 4.33 m
   (d) 6.77 m

105. A glucose solution contains 55.8 g of glucose $(C_6H_{12}O_6)$ in 455 g of water. Calculate the freezing point and boiling point of the solution. (Assume a density of 1.00 g/mL for water.)

106. An ethylene glycol solution contains 21.2 g of ethylene glycol $(C_2H_6O_2)$ in 85.4 mL of water. Calculate the freezing point and boiling point of the solution. (Assume a density of 1.00 g/mL for water.)

CUMULATIVE PROBLEMS

107. An NaCl solution is made using 133 g of NaCl and diluting to a total solution volume of 1.00 L. Calculate the molarity and mass percent of the solution. (Assume a density of 1.08 g/mL for the solution.)

108. A KNO_3 solution is made using 88.4 g of KNO_3 and diluting to a total solution volume of 1.50 L. Calculate the molarity and mass percent of the solution. (Assume a density of 1.05 g/mL for the solution.)

109. A 125-mL sample of an 8.5 M NaCl solution is diluted to 2.5 L. What volume of the diluted solution contains 10.8 g of NaCl?

110. A 45.8-mL sample of a 5.8 M KNO_3 solution is diluted to 1.00 L. What volume of the diluted solution contains 15.0 g of KNO_3?

111. To what final volume should you dilute 50.0 mL of a 5.00 M KI solution so that 25.0 mL of the diluted solution contains 3.25 g of KI?

112. To what volume should you dilute 125 mL of an 8.00 M $CuCl_2$ solution so that 50.0 mL of the diluted solution contains 5.9 g $CuCl_2$?

113. What is the molarity of an aqueous solution that is 5.88% NaCl by mass? (Assume a density of 1.02 g/mL for the solution.)

114. What is the molarity of an aqueous solution that is 6.75% glucose $(C_6H_{12}O_6)$ by mass? (Assume a density of 1.03 g/mL for the solution.)

115. Consider the reaction:

$$2 Al(s) + 3 H_2SO_4(aq) \longrightarrow Al_2(SO_4)_3(aq) + 3 H_2(g)$$

What minimum volume of 4.0 M H_2SO_4 is required to produce 15.0 L of H_2 at STP?

116. Consider the reaction:

$$Mg(s) + 2 HCl(aq) \longrightarrow MgCl_2(aq) + H_2(g)$$

What minimum amount of 1.85 M HCl is necessary to produce 28.5 L of H_2 at STP?

117. How much of a 1.25 M sodium chloride solution in milliliters is required to completely precipitate all of the silver in 25.0 mL of a 0.45 M silver nitrate solution?

118. How much of a 1.50 M sodium sulfate solution in milliliters is required to completely precipitate all of the barium in 150.0 mL of a 0.250 M barium nitrate solution?

119. Nitric acid is usually purchased in concentrated form with a 70.3% HNO_3 concentration by mass and a density of 1.41 g/mL. How much of the concentrated stock solution in milliliters should you use to make 2.5 L of 0.500 M HNO_3?

120. Hydrochloric acid is usually purchased in concentrated form with a 37.0% HCl concentration by mass and a density of 1.20 g/mL. How much of the concentrated stock solution in milliliters should you use to make 2.5 L of 0.500 M HCl?

121. An ethylene glycol solution is made using 58.5 g of ethylene glycol $(C_2H_6O_2)$ and diluting to a total volume of 500.0 mL. Calculate the freezing point and boiling point of the solution. (Assume a density of 1.09 g/mL for the solution.)

122. A sucrose solution is made using 144 g of sucrose $(C_{12}H_{22}O_{11})$ and diluting to a total volume of 1.00 L. Calculate the freezing point and boiling point of the solution. (Assume a density of 1.06 g/mL for the final solution.)

123. A 250.0-mL sample of a 5.00 M glucose $(C_6H_{12}O_6)$ solution is diluted to 1.40 L. What are the freezing and boiling points of the final solution? (Assume a density of 1.06 g/mL for the final solution.)

124. A 135-mL sample of a 10.0 M ethylene glycol $(C_2H_6O_2)$ solution is diluted to 1.50 L. What are the freezing and boiling points of the final solution? (Assume a density of 1.05 g/mL for the final solution.)

125. An aqueous solution containing 17.5 g of an unknown molecular (nonelectrolyte) compound in 100.0 g of water has a freezing point of −1.8 °C. Calculate the molar mass of the unknown compound.

126. An aqueous solution containing 35.9 g of an unknown molecular (nonelectrolyte) compound in 150.0 g of water has a freezing point of −1.3 °C. Calculate the molar mass of the unknown compound.

127. What is the boiling point of an aqueous solution that freezes at −6.7 °C?

128. What is the freezing point of an aqueous solution that boils at 102.1 °C?

129. A 125-g sample contains only glucose ($C_6H_{12}O_6$) and sucrose ($C_{12}H_{22}O_{11}$). When the sample is added to 0.500 kg of pure water, the resulting solution has a freezing point of −1.75 °C. What were the masses of glucose and sucrose in the original sample?

130. A 13.03-g sample contains only ethylene glycol ($C_2H_6O_2$) and propylene glycol ($C_3H_8O_2$). When the sample is added to 100.0 g of pure water, the resulting solution has a freezing point of −3.50 °C. What was the percent composition of ethylene glycol and propylene glycol in the original sample?

HIGHLIGHT PROBLEMS

131. Consider the molecular views of osmosis cells. For each cell, determine the direction of water flow.

(a)

(b)

(c)

132. What is wrong with this molecular view of a sodium chloride solution? What would make the picture correct?

133. The Safe Drinking Water Act (SDWA) sets a limit for mercury—a toxin to the central nervous system—at 0.002 mg/L. Water suppliers must periodically test their water to ensure that mercury levels do not exceed 0.002 mg/L. Suppose water is contaminated with mercury at twice the legal limit (0.004 mg/L). How much of this water would a person have to consume to ingest 0.100 g of mercury?

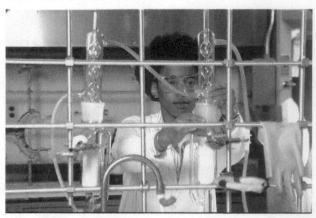

▲ Drinking water must be tested for the presence of various pollutants, including mercury compounds that can damage the nervous system.

134. Water softeners often replace calcium ions in hard water with sodium ions. Since sodium compounds are soluble, the presence of sodium ions in water does not result in the white, scaly residues caused by calcium ions. However, calcium is more beneficial to human health than sodium. Calcium is a necessary part of the human diet, while high levels of sodium intake are linked to increases in blood pressure. The Food and Drug Administration (FDA) recommends that adults ingest less than 2.4 g of sodium per day. How many liters of softened water, containing a sodium concentration of 0.050% sodium by mass, have to be consumed to exceed the FDA recommendation? (Assume a density of 1.0 g/mL for water.)

QUESTIONS FOR GROUP WORK

Discuss these questions with the group and record your consensus answer.

135. 13.62 g (about one tablespoon) of table sugar (sucrose, $C_{12}H_{22}O_{11}$) is dissolved in 241.5 mL of water (density 0.997 g/mL). The final volume is 250.0 mL (about one cup). Have each group member calculate one of the following, and present their answer to the group.
 (a) mass percent
 (b) molarity
 (c) molality

136. Calculate the expected boiling and freezing point for the solution in Question 135. If you boil this syrup for a recipe, would you expect it to take more time to come to a boil than it takes to boil the same amount of pure water? Why or why not? Would the syrup freeze in a typical freezer (−18 °C)? Why or why not?

137. 1 L of a 4 M solution of compound X is diluted to a final volume of 4 L. What is the final concentration? Draw a detailed diagram (including before and after) to illustrate the dilution process. In your diagram, indicate one mole of compound X with an "X" symbol.

138. It has been proposed that uranium be extracted from seawater to fuel nuclear power plants. If the concentration of uranium in seawater is 3.2 µg/L, how much seawater must be processed to generate one pound of uranium?

▶Answers to Skillbuilder Exercises

Skillbuilder 13.1	2.67%	Skillbuilder 13.7	16.4 mL
Skillbuilder 13.2	42.5 g sucrose	Skillbuilder Plus, p. 465	0.308 M
Skillbuilder 13.3	0.263 M	Skillbuilder 13.8	0.443 *m*
Skillbuilder 13.4	3.33 L	Skillbuilder 13.9	−4.8 °C
Skillbuilder 13.5	0.75 M Ca^{2+} and 1.5 M Cl^-	Skillbuilder 13.10	101.8 °C
Skillbuilder 13.6	0.12 L		

▶Answers to Conceptual Checkpoints

13.1 (a) CH_3Cl and NH_3 are both polar compounds, and KF is ionic. All three would therefore interact more strongly with water molecules (which are polar) than CCl_4, which is nonpolar.

13.2 (b) Some potassium chloride precipitates out of solution. The solubility of most solids decreases with decreasing temperature. However, the solubility of gases increases with decreasing temperature. Therefore, the nitrogen becomes more soluble and will not bubble out of solution.

13.3 (c) The solution is 0.30 M in K^+ because the compound K_2SO_4 forms two moles of K^+ in solution for each mole of K_2SO_4 that dissolves.

13.4 (a) The original 100.0 mL solution contains 0.10 mol, which is present in 1.0 L after the dilution. Therefore the molarity of the diluted solution is 0.10 M.

13.5 (d) You need twice as many moles of B as you have moles of A. But since the solution of A is twice as concentrated, you need four times the volume of B as you have of A.

13.6 (a) A 2.0 *m* solution would be made by adding 2 mol of solute to 1 kg of solvent. 1 kg of water has a volume of 1 L, but because of the dissolved solute, the final solution would have a volume of slightly *more than* 1 L. A 2.0 M solution, by contrast, would consist of 2 mol of solute in a solution of *exactly* 1 L. Therefore, a 2 M aqueous solution would be slightly more concentrated than a 2 *m* solution.

13.7 (d) Since boiling point elevation depends only on the *concentration* of the dissolved particles, and not on the *kind* of dissolved particles, all of these solutions have the same boiling point.

Acids have been used in spy movies and other thrillers to dissolve the metal bars of a prison cell.

Acids and Bases 14

"The differences between the various acid–base concepts are not concerned with which is 'right,' but which is most convenient to use in a particular situation." —James E. Huheey

CHAPTER OUTLINE

14.1 Sour Patch Kids and International Spy Movies

Gummy candies have a sweet taste and chewy texture that both children and adults can enjoy. From the original classic gummy bear to the gummy worm to the gummy just-about-any-shape-you-can-imagine, these candies are incredibly popular. A common variation is the *sour* gummy candy, whose best-known incarnation is the Sour Patch Kid. Sour Patch Kids are gummy candies shaped like children and coated with a white powder. When you first put a Sour Patch Kid in your mouth, it tastes incredibly sour. The taste is caused by the white powder coating, a mixture of citric acid and tartaric acid. Like all acids, citric and tartaric acid taste sour.

A number of other foods contain acids as well. Acids are responsible for the sour taste of lemons and limes, the bite of sourdough bread, and the tang of a tomato. Acids are substances that—by one definition that we will elaborate on later—produce H^+ ions in solution. When the citric and tartaric acids from a Sour Patch Kid combine with saliva in the mouth, they produce H^+ ions. Those H^+ ions react with protein molecules on the tongue. The protein molecules then change shape, sending an electrical signal to the brain that we experience as a sour taste (▶ Figure 14.1).

Acids have also been made famous by their use in spy movies. James Bond, for example, has been known to carry an acid-filled gold pen. When captured and imprisoned—as inevitably happens at least one time in each movie—Bond can squirt the acid out of his pen and onto the iron bars of his cell. The acid quickly dissolves the metal, allowing Bond to escape. Although acids do not dissolve iron bars with the ease depicted in movies, they do dissolve metals. A small piece of aluminum placed in hydrochloric acid, for example, dissolves away in about 10 minutes (▶ Figure 14.2). With enough acid, it would be possible to dissolve the iron bars of a prison cell, but it would take more acid than the amount that fits in a pen.

When we say that acids dissolve metals, we mean that acids react with metals in a way that causes them to go into solution as metal cations. Bond's pen is made of gold because gold is one of the few metals that is not dissolved by most acids (see Section 16.5).

488 | CHAPTER 14 Acids and Bases

◄ **FIGURE 14.1 Acids taste sour**
When a person eats a sour food, H^+ ions from the acid in the food react with protein molecules in the taste cells of the tongue. This interaction causes the protein molecules to change shape, triggering a nerve impulse to the brain that the person experiences as a sour taste.

▶ **FIGURE 14.2 Acids dissolve many metals** When aluminum is put into hydrochloric acid, the aluminum dissolves. Question: What happens to the aluminum atoms? Where do they go?

14.2 Acids: Properties and Examples

LO: Identify common acids and describe their key characteristics.

❚ NEVER taste or touch laboratory chemicals.

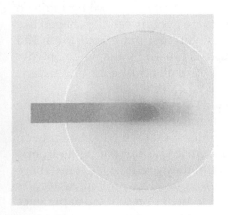

▲ **FIGURE 14.3 Acids turn blue litmus paper red.**

❚ For a review of naming acids, see Section 5.9.

Acids have the following properties:

- Acids have a sour taste.
- Acids dissolve many metals.
- Acids turn blue litmus paper red.

We just discussed examples of the sour taste of acids and their ability to dissolve metals. Acids also turn blue litmus paper red. Litmus paper contains a dye that turns red in acidic solutions (◄ Figure 14.3). In the laboratory, litmus paper is used routinely to test the acidity of solutions.

Table 14.1 lists some common acids. Hydrochloric acid is found in most chemistry laboratories. It is used in industry to clean metals, to prepare and process foods, and to refine metal ores.

HCl

Hydrochloric acid

Hydrochloric acid is also the main component of stomach acid. In the stomach, hydrochloric acid breaks down food and kills harmful bacteria that might enter the body through food. The sour taste sometimes associated with indigestion

TABLE 14.1 Some Common Acids

Name	Uses
hydrochloric acid (HCl)	metal cleaning; food preparation; ore refining; main component of stomach acid
sulfuric acid (H_2SO_4)	fertilizer and explosive manufacturing; dye and glue production; automobile batteries
nitric acid (HNO_3)	fertilizer and explosive manufacturing; dye and glue production
acetic acid ($HC_2H_3O_2$)	plastic and rubber manufacturing; food preservation; component of vinegar
carbonic acid (H_2CO_3)	component of carbonated beverages due to the reaction of carbon dioxide with water
hydrofluoric acid (HF)	metal cleaning; glass frosting and etching

is caused by the stomach's hydrochloric acid refluxing up into the esophagus (the tube that joins the stomach and the mouth) and throat.

Sulfuric acid—the most widely produced chemical in the United States—and nitric acid are commonly used in the laboratory. In addition, they are used in the manufacture of fertilizers, explosives, dyes, and glue. Sulfuric acid is contained in most automobile batteries.

H_2SO_4

Sulfuric acid

HNO_3

Nitric acid

Acetic acid is present in vinegar and is also produced in improperly stored wines. The word *vinegar* originates from the French *vin aigre*, which means "sour wine." The presence of vinegar in wines is considered a serious fault, making the wine taste like salad dressing.

$HC_2H_3O_2$

Acetic acid

▲ Vinegar is a solution of acetic acid and water.

Acetic acid is an example of a **carboxylic acid**, an acid containing the grouping of atoms known as the carboxylic acid group.

$-COOH$

Carboxylic acid group

We often find carboxylic acids (covered in more detail in Chapter 18, Section 18.15) in substances derived from living organisms. Other carboxylic acids include citric acid, the main acid in lemons and limes, and malic acid, an acid found in apples, grapes, and wine.

$HC_6H_7O_7$ $HC_4H_5O_5$

Citric acid   Malic acid

14.3   Bases: Properties and Examples

LO: Identify common bases and describe their key characteristics.

■ NEVER taste or touch laboratory chemicals.

Bases have the following properties:

• Bases have a bitter taste.
• Bases have a slippery feel.
• Bases turn red litmus paper blue.

Coffee is acidic overall, but bases present in coffee—such as caffeine—impart a bitter flavor.

▲ All these consumer products contain bases.

▲ **FIGURE 14.4   Bases turn red litmus paper blue.**

Bases are less common in foods than acids because of their bitter taste. A Sour Patch Kid coated with a base would never sell. Our aversion to the taste of bases is probably an adaptation to protect us against **alkaloids**, organic bases found in plants (see the Chemistry and Health box, p. 512). Alkaloids are often poisonous—the toxic component of hemlock, for example, is the alkaloid coniine—and their bitter taste warns us against eating them. Nonetheless, some foods, such as coffee, contain small amounts of base (caffeine is a base). Many people enjoy the bitterness, but only after acquiring the taste over time.

$C_8H_{17}N$

Coniine

$C_8H_{10}N_4O_2$

Caffeine

Bases feel slippery because they react with oils on our skin to form soaplike substances. Soap itself is basic, and its slippery feel is characteristic of bases. Some household cleaning solutions, such as ammonia, are also basic and have the typical slippery feel of a base. Bases turn red litmus paper blue (◀ Figure 14.4). In the laboratory, litmus paper is routinely used to test the basicity of solutions.

Table 14.2 lists some common bases. Sodium hydroxide and potassium hydroxide are found in most chemistry laboratories. They are also used in processing petroleum and cotton and in soap and plastic manufacturing. Sodium hydroxide is the active ingredient in products such as Drano that work to unclog drains. Sodium bicarbonate can be found in most homes as baking soda and is also an active ingredient in many antacids. When taken as an antacid, sodium bicarbonate neutralizes stomach acid (see Section 14.5), relieving heartburn and sour stomach.

TABLE 14.2   Some Common Bases

Name	Uses
sodium hydroxide (NaOH)	petroleum processing; soap and plastic manufacturing
potassium hydroxide (KOH)	cotton processing; electroplating; soap production
sodium bicarbonate (NaHCO₃)*	antacid; ingredient of baking soda; source of CO_2
ammonia (NH₃)	detergent; fertilizer and explosive manufacturing; synthetic fiber production

*Sodium bicarbonate is a salt whose anion (HCO_3^-) is the conjugate base of a weak acid (see Section 14.4) and acts as a base.

✓ **CONCEPTUAL CHECKPOINT 14.1**

Which substance is most likely to have a sour taste?
(a) HCl(aq)   **(b)** NH₃(aq)   **(c)** KOH(aq)

14.4   Molecular Definitions of Acids and Bases

LO: **Identify Arrhenius acids and bases.**

LO: **Identify Brønsted–Lowry acids and bases and their conjugates.**

We have just seen some of the properties of acids and bases. In this section we examine two different models that explain the molecular basis for acid and base behavior: the Arrhenius model and the Brønsted–Lowry model. The Arrhenius model, which was developed earlier, is more limited in its scope. The Brønsted–Lowry model was developed later and is more broadly applicable.

The Arrhenius Definition

In the 1880s, the Swedish chemist Svante Arrhenius proposed the following molecular definitions of acids and bases:

HCl

HCl(aq) $\longrightarrow$
$\qquad$ H$^+$(aq) + Cl$^-$(aq)

▲ **FIGURE 14.5   Arrhenius definition of an acid**   The Arrhenius definition states that an acid is a substance that produces H$^+$ ions in solution. These H$^+$ ions associate with H$_2$O to form H$_3$O$^+$ ions.

NaOH

NaOH(aq) $\longrightarrow$
$\qquad$ Na$^+$(aq) + OH$^-$(aq)

▲ **FIGURE 14.6   Arrhenius definition of a base**   The Arrhenius definition states that a base is a substance that produces OH$^-$ ions in solution.

Ionic compounds such as NaOH are composed of positive and negative ions. In solution, soluble ionic compounds dissociate into their component ions. Molecular compounds containing an OH group, such as methanol CH$_3$OH, do not dissociate and therefore do not act as bases.

ARRHENIUS DEFINITION

Acid—An acid produces H$^+$ ions in aqueous solution.
Base—A base produces OH$^-$ ions in aqueous solution.

For example, according to the **Arrhenius definition**, HCl is an **Arrhenius acid** because it produces H$^+$ ions in solution (◀ Figure 14.5).

$$HCl(aq) \longrightarrow H^+(aq) + Cl^-(aq)$$

HCl is a covalent compound and does not contain ions. However, in water it **ionizes** to form H$^+$(aq) ions and Cl$^-$(aq) ions. The H$^+$ ions are highly reactive. In aqueous solution, they bond to water molecules according to this reaction:

The H$_3$O$^+$ ion is the **hydronium ion**. In water, H$^+$ ions *always* associate with H$_2$O molecules. Chemists often use H$^+$(aq) and H$_3$O$^+$(aq) interchangeably, however, to refer to the same thing—a hydronium ion.

In the molecular formula for an acid, we often write the ionizable hydrogen first. For example, we write the formula for formic acid as follows:

HCHO$_2$
Ionizable hydrogen   Non-ionizable hydrogen

The structure of formic acid, however, is not indicated by the molecular formula in the preceding figure. We represent the *structure* of formic acid with its structural formula:

O
‖
HC—OH   Ionizable hydrogen

Notice that the structural formula indicates how the atoms are bonded together; the molecular formula, by contrast, indicates only the number of each type of atom.

NaOH is an **Arrhenius base** because it produces OH$^-$ ions in solution (◀ Figure 14.6).

$$NaOH(aq) \longrightarrow Na^+(aq) + OH^-(aq)$$

NaOH is an ionic compound and therefore contains Na$^+$ and OH$^-$ ions. When NaOH is added to water, it **dissociates**, or breaks apart into its component ions.

Under the Arrhenius definition, acids and bases naturally combine to form water, neutralizing each other in the process.

$$H^+(aq) + OH^-(aq) \longrightarrow H_2O(l)$$

The Brønsted–Lowry Definition

Although the Arrhenius definition of acids and bases works in many cases, it cannot easily explain why some substances act as bases even though they do not contain OH$^-$. The Arrhenius definition also does not apply to nonaqueous solvents. A second definition of acids and bases, called the **Brønsted–Lowry definition**, introduced in 1923, applies to a wider range of acid–base phenomena. This definition focuses on the *transfer* of H$^+$ ions in an acid–base reaction. Since an H$^+$ ion is a proton—a hydrogen atom with its electron taken away—this definition focuses on the idea of a proton donor and a proton acceptor.

BRØNSTED–LOWRY DEFINITION

Acid—An acid is a proton (H^+ ion) *donor*.
Base—A base is a proton (H^+ ion) *acceptor*.

According to this definition, HCl is a **Brønsted–Lowry acid** because, in solution, it donates a proton to water.

$$HCl(aq) + H_2O(l) \longrightarrow H_3O^+(aq) + Cl^-(aq)$$

This definition more clearly accounts for what happens to the H^+ ion from an acid: It associates with a water molecule to form H_3O^+ (a hydronium ion). The Brønsted–Lowry definition also works well with bases (such as NH_3) that do not inherently contain OH^- ions but that still produce OH^- ions in solution. NH_3 is a **Brønsted–Lowry base** because it accepts a proton from water.

$$NH_3(aq) + H_2O(l) \rightleftharpoons NH_4^+(aq) + OH^-(aq)$$

According to the Brønsted–Lowry definition, acids (proton donors) and bases (proton acceptors) always occur together. In the reaction between HCl and H_2O, HCl is the proton donor (acid), and H_2O is the proton acceptor (base).

$$\underset{\substack{\text{Acid} \\ \text{(Proton donor)}}}{HCl(aq)} + \underset{\substack{\text{Base} \\ \text{(Proton acceptor)}}}{H_2O(l)} \longrightarrow H_3O^+(aq) + Cl^-(aq)$$

In the reaction between NH_3 and H_2O, H_2O is the proton donor (acid) and NH_3 is the proton acceptor (base).

$$\underset{\substack{\text{Base} \\ \text{(Proton acceptor)}}}{NH_3(aq)} + \underset{\substack{\text{Acid} \\ \text{(Proton donor)}}}{H_2O(l)} \rightleftharpoons NH_4^+(aq) + OH^-(aq)$$

Notice that under the Brønsted–Lowry definition, some substances—such as water in the previous two equations—can act as acids *or* bases. Substances that can act as acids or bases are **amphoteric**. Notice also what happens when an equation representing Brønsted–Lowry acid–base behavior is reversed.

$$\underset{\substack{\text{Base} \\ \text{(Proton acceptor)}}}{NH_4^+(aq)} + \underset{\substack{\text{Acid} \\ \text{(Proton donor)}}}{OH^-(aq)} \rightleftharpoons NH_3(aq) + H_2O(l)$$

In this reaction, NH_4^+ is the proton donor (acid) and OH^- is the proton acceptor (base). The substance that was the base (NH_3) becomes the acid (NH_4^+), and vice versa. NH_4^+ and NH_3 are often referred to as a **conjugate acid–base pair**, two substances related to each other by the transfer of a proton (◀ Figure 14.7). Going back to the original forward reaction, we can identify the conjugate acid–base pairs as follows:

$$\underset{\substack{\text{Base}}}{NH_3(aq)} + \underset{\substack{\text{Acid}}}{H_2O(l)} \rightleftharpoons \underset{\substack{\text{Conjugate} \\ \text{acid}}}{NH_4^+(aq)} + \underset{\substack{\text{Conjugate} \\ \text{base}}}{OH^-(aq)}$$

In an acid–base reaction, a base accepts a proton and becomes a conjugate acid. An acid donates a proton and becomes a conjugate base.

Johannes Brønsted, working in Denmark, and Thomas Lowry, working in England, developed the concept of proton transfer in acid–base behavior independently and simultaneously.

The double arrows in this equation indicate that the reaction does not go to completion. We discuss this concept in more detail in Section 14.7.

▲ **FIGURE 14.7 A conjugate acid–base pair** Any two substances related to each other by the transfer of a proton can be considered a conjugate acid–base pair.

EXAMPLE 14.1 **IDENTIFYING BRØNSTED–LOWRY ACIDS AND BASES AND THEIR CONJUGATES**

In each reaction, identify the Brønsted–Lowry acid, the Brønsted–Lowry base, the conjugate acid, and the conjugate base.

(a) $H_2SO_4(aq) + H_2O(l) \longrightarrow H_3O^+(aq) + HSO_4^-(aq)$
(b) $HCO_3^-(aq) + H_2O(l) \rightleftharpoons H_2CO_3(aq) + OH^-(aq)$

SOLUTION

(a) Since H_2SO_4 donates a proton to H_2O in this reaction, it is the acid (the proton donor). After H_2SO_4 donates the proton, it becomes HSO_4^-, the conjugate base. Since H_2O accepts a proton, it is the base (the proton acceptor). After H_2O accepts the proton, it becomes H_3O^+, the conjugate acid.

$$H_2SO_4(aq) + H_2O(l) \longrightarrow HSO_4^-(aq) + H_3O^+(aq)$$

Acid   Base   Conjugate base   Conjugate acid

(b) Since H_2O donates a proton to HCO_3^- in this reaction, it is the acid (the proton donor). After H_2O donates the proton, it becomes OH^-, the conjugate base. Since HCO_3^- accepts a proton, it is the base (the proton acceptor). After HCO_3^- accepts the proton, it becomes H_2CO_3, the conjugate acid.

$$HCO_3^-(aq) + H_2O(l) \rightleftharpoons H_2CO_3(aq) + OH^-(aq)$$

Base   Acid   Conjugate acid   Conjugate base

▶**SKILLBUILDER 14.1** | **Identifying Brønsted–Lowry Acids and Bases and Their Conjugates**

In each reaction, identify the Brønsted–Lowry acid, the Brønsted–Lowry base, the conjugate acid, and the conjugate base.

(a) $C_5H_5N(aq) + H_2O(l) \rightleftharpoons C_5H_5NH^+(aq) + OH^-(aq)$
(b) $HNO_3(aq) + H_2O(l) \longrightarrow NO_3^-(aq) + H_3O^+(aq)$

▶**FOR MORE PRACTICE** Example 14.11; Problems 31, 32, 33, 34.

  CONCEPTUAL CHECKPOINT 14.2

Which species is the conjugate base of H_2SO_3?
(a) $H_3SO_3^+$ (b) HSO_3^- (c) SO_3^{2-}

14.5 Reactions of Acids and Bases

LO: Write equations for neutralization reactions.

LO: Write equations for the reactions of acids with metals and with metal oxides.

Acids and bases are typically reactive substances. In this section, we examine how they react with one another, as well as with other substances.

Neutralization Reactions

The reaction between HCl and KOH is also a double-displacement reaction (see Section 7.10).

One of the most important reactions of acids and bases is **neutralization**, first introduced in Chapter 7. When we mix an acid and a base, the $H^+(aq)$ from the acid combines with the $OH^-(aq)$ from the base to form $H_2O(l)$. For example, consider the reaction between hydrochloric acid and potassium hydroxide:

Neutralization reactions are covered in Section 7.8.

$$HCl(aq) + KOH(aq) \longrightarrow H_2O(l) + KCl(aq)$$

Acid   Base   Water   Salt

Acid–base reactions generally form water and a **salt**—an ionic compound—that usually remains dissolved in the solution. The salt contains the cation from the base and the anion from the acid.

Ionic compound that contains the cation from the base and the anion from the acid

Acid + Base $\longrightarrow$ Water + Salt

Net ionic equations are explained in Section 7.7.

The net ionic equation for many neutralization reactions is:

$$H^+(aq) + OH^-(aq) \longrightarrow H_2O(l)$$

A slightly different but common type of neutralization reaction involves an acid reacting with carbonates or bicarbonates (compounds containing CO_3^{2-} or HCO_3^-). This type of neutralization reaction produces water, gaseous carbon dioxide, and a salt. As an example, consider the reaction of hydrochloric acid and sodium bicarbonate.

$$HCl(aq) + NaHCO_3(aq) \longrightarrow H_2O(l) + CO_2(g) + NaCl(aq)$$

Since this reaction produces gaseous CO_2, it is also called a *gas evolution reaction* (Section 7.8).

$$HCl(aq) + NaHCO_3(aq) \longrightarrow$$

$$H_2O(l) + CO_2(g) + NaCl(aq)$$

▲ The reaction of carbonates or bicarbonates with acids produces water, gaseous carbon dioxide, and a salt.

EXAMPLE 14.2	WRITING EQUATIONS FOR NEUTRALIZATION REACTIONS

Write a molecular equation for the reaction between aqueous HCl and aqueous $Ca(OH)_2$.

SOLUTION First identify the acid and the base and write the skeletal reaction showing the production of water and the salt. The formulas for the ionic compounds in the equation must be charge neutral (see Section 5.5).	$HCl(aq) + Ca(OH)_2(aq) \longrightarrow H_2O(l) + CaCl_2(aq)$
Balance the equation. Notice that $Ca(OH)_2$ contains 2 mol of OH^- for every 1 mol of $Ca(OH)_2$ and therefore requires 2 mol of H^+ to neutralize it.	$2\,HCl(aq) + Ca(OH)_2(aq) \longrightarrow 2\,H_2O(l) + CaCl_2(aq)$

▶**SKILLBUILDER 14.2 | Writing Equations for Neutralization Reactions**

Write a molecular equation for the reaction that occurs between aqueous H_3PO_4 and aqueous NaOH. *Hint:* H_3PO_4 is a triprotic acid, meaning that 1 mol of H_3PO_4 requires 3 mol of OH^- to completely react with it.

▶**FOR MORE PRACTICE** Example 14.12; Problems 39, 40.

Acid Reactions

Recall from Section 14.1 that acids dissolve metals, or more precisely, that acids react with metals in a way that causes metals to go into solution. The reaction between an acid and a metal usually produces hydrogen gas and a dissolved salt containing the metal ion as the cation. For example, hydrochloric acid reacts with magnesium metal to form hydrogen gas and magnesium chloride.

$$2\,HCl(aq) + Mg(s) \longrightarrow$$

$$H_2(g) + MgCl_2(aq)$$

▲ The reaction between an acid and a metal usually produces hydrogen gas and a dissolved salt containing the metal ion.

$$\underset{\text{Acid}}{2\,HCl(aq)} + \underset{\text{Metal}}{Mg(s)} \longrightarrow \underset{\substack{\text{Hydrogen} \\ \text{gas}}}{H_2(g)} + \underset{\text{Salt}}{MgCl_2(aq)}$$

Similarly, sulfuric acid reacts with zinc to form hydrogen gas and zinc sulfate.

$$\underset{\text{Acid}}{H_2SO_4(aq)} + \underset{\text{Metal}}{Zn(s)} \longrightarrow \underset{\substack{\text{Hydrogen} \\ \text{gas}}}{H_2(g)} + \underset{\text{Salt}}{ZnSO_4(aq)}$$

It is through reactions such as these that the acid from James Bond's pen (discussed in Section 14.1) dissolves the metal bars that imprison him. If the bars were made of iron and the acid in the pen were hydrochloric acid, the reaction would be:

$$\underset{\text{Acid}}{2\,HCl(aq)} + \underset{\text{Metal}}{Fe(s)} \longrightarrow \underset{\substack{\text{Hydrogen} \\ \text{gas}}}{H_2(g)} + \underset{\text{Salt}}{FeCl_2(aq)}$$

Some metals, however, do not readily react with acids. If the bars that imprisoned James Bond were made of gold, for example, a pen filled with hydrochloric acid would not dissolve the bars. We will discuss the way to determine whether a particular metal dissolves in an acid in Section 16.5.

Acids also react with metal oxides to produce water and a dissolved salt. For example, hydrochloric acid reacts with potassium oxide to form water and potassium chloride.

$$\underset{\text{Acid}}{2\,HCl(aq)} + \underset{\text{Metal oxide}}{K_2O(s)} \longrightarrow \underset{\text{Water}}{H_2O(l)} + \underset{\text{Salt}}{2\,KCl(aq)}$$

Similarly, hydrobromic acid reacts with magnesium oxide to form water and magnesium bromide.

$$\underset{\text{Acid}}{2\,HBr(aq)} + \underset{\text{Metal oxide}}{MgO(s)} \longrightarrow \underset{\text{Water}}{H_2O(l)} + \underset{\text{Salt}}{MgBr_2(aq)}$$

EXAMPLE 14.3	WRITING EQUATIONS FOR ACID REACTIONS

Write an equation for each reaction.

(a) The reaction of hydroiodic acid with potassium metal
(b) The reaction of hydrobromic acid with sodium oxide

SOLUTION

(a) The reaction of hydroiodic acid with potassium metal forms hydrogen gas and a salt. The salt contains the ionized form of the metal (K^+) as the cation and the anion of the acid (I^-). Write the skeletal equation and then balance it.	$HI(aq) + K(s) \longrightarrow H_2(g) + KI(aq)$ $2\,HI(aq) + 2\,K(s) \longrightarrow H_2(g) + 2\,KI(aq)$
(b) The reaction of hydrobromic acid with sodium oxide forms water and a salt. The salt contains the cation from the metal oxide (Na^+) and the anion of the acid (Br^-). Write the skeletal equation and then balance it.	$HBr(aq) + Na_2O(s) \longrightarrow H_2O(l) + NaBr(aq)$ $2\,HBr(aq) + Na_2O(s) \longrightarrow H_2O(l) + 2\,NaBr(aq)$

▶SKILLBUILDER 14.3 | **Writing Equations for Acid Reactions**

Write an equation for each reaction.

(a) The reaction of hydrochloric acid with strontium metal
(b) The reaction of hydroiodic acid with barium oxide

▶FOR MORE PRACTICE   Example 14.13; Problems 41, 42. 43, 44.

EVERYDAY CHEMISTRY

▶ What Is in My Antacid?

Heartburn, a burning sensation in the lower throat and above the stomach, is caused by the reflux or back-flow of stomach acid into the esophagus (the tube that joins the stomach to the throat). In most individuals, this occurs only occasionally, typically after large meals. Physical activity—such as bending, stooping, or lifting—after meals also aggravates heartburn. In some people, the flap between the esophagus and the stomach that normally prevents acid

Drug Facts

Active ingredients (in each 5 mL teaspoon) **Purposes**
Aluminum hydroxide (equivalent to dried gel, USP) 200 mg.........Antacid
Magnesium hydroxide 200 mg...Antacid
Simethicone 20 mg..Antigas

Use relieves:
■ heartburn ■ acid indigestion ■ sour stomach
■ upset stomach due to these symptoms ■ overindulgence in food and drink

Warnings
Ask a doctor before use if you have kidney disease.
Ask a doctor or pharmacist if you are taking a prescription drug. Antacids may interact with certain prescription drugs.
Stop use and ask a doctor if symptoms last more than 2 weeks.
Keep out of reach of children.

Directions ■ shake well ■ take 2-4 teaspoonfuls between meals, at bedtime, or as directed by a doctor ■ do not take more than 24 teaspoonfuls in a 24-hour period, or use the maximum dosage for more than 2 weeks

Other information ■ does not meet USP requirements for preservative effectiveness ■ do not use if breakaway band on plastic cap is broken or missing

reflux becomes damaged, in which case heartburn becomes a regular occurrence.

Drugstores carry many products that either reduce the secretion of stomach acid or neutralize the acid that is produced. Antacids such as Mylanta or Phillips' milk of magnesia contain bases that neutralize the refluxed stomach acid, alleviating heartburn.

B14.1 CAN YOU ANSWER THIS? *Look at the label of Mylanta shown in the photograph. Can you identify the bases responsible for the antacid action? Write chemical equations showing the reactions of these bases with stomach acid (HCl).*

Base Reactions

The most important base reactions are those in which a base neutralizes an acid (see the beginning of this section). The only other kind of base reaction that we cover in this book is the reaction of sodium hydroxide with aluminum and water.

$$2\,NaOH(aq) + 2\,Al(s) + 6\,H_2O(l) \longrightarrow 2\,NaAl(OH)_4(aq) + 3\,H_2(g)$$

Aluminum is one of the few metals that dissolves in a base. Consequently, it is safe to use NaOH (the main ingredient in many drain-opening products) to unclog your drain as long as your pipes are not made of aluminum, which is generally the case as the use of aluminum pipe is forbidden by most building codes.

14.6 Acid–Base Titration: A Way to Quantify the Amount of Acid or Base in a Solution

LO: Use acid–base titration to determine the concentration of an unknown solution.

We can apply the principles we learned in Chapter 13 (Section 13.8) on solution stoichiometry to a common laboratory procedure called a titration. In a **titration**, we react a substance in a solution of known concentration with another substance in a solution of unknown concentration. For example, consider the acid–base reaction between hydrochloric acid and sodium hydroxide:

$$HCl(aq) + NaOH(aq) \longrightarrow H_2O(l) + NaCl(aq)$$

The net ionic equation for this reaction is:

$$H^+(aq) + OH^-(aq) \longrightarrow H_2O(l)$$

Suppose we have an HCl solution represented by the molecular diagram at left. (The Cl^- ions and the H_2O molecules not involved in the reaction have been omitted from this representation for clarity.)

In titrating this sample, we slowly add a solution of known OH^- concentration. This process is represented by the following molecular diagrams:

● H^+

● OH^-

The OH⁻ solution also contains Na⁺ cations that we do not show in this figure for clarity.

Beginning of titration   Equivalence point

At the equivalence point, neither reactant is present in excess, and both are limiting. The number of moles of the reactants are related by the reaction stoichiometry (see Chapter 8).

As we add the OH^-, it reacts with and neutralizes the H^+, forming water. At the **equivalence point**—*the point in the titration when the number of moles of OH^- added equals the number of moles of H^+ originally in solution*—the titration is complete. The equivalence point is usually signaled by an **indicator**, a dye whose color depends on the acidity of the solution (▶ Figure 14.8). In most laboratory titrations, the concentration of one of the reactant solutions is unknown, and the concentration of the other is precisely known. By carefully measuring the volume of each solution required to reach the equivalence point, we can determine the concentration of the unknown solution, as demonstrated in Example 14.4.

▶ **FIGURE 14.8   Acid–base titration**   In this titration, NaOH is added to an HCl solution. When the NaOH and HCl reach stoichiometric proportions (1 mol of OH^- for every 1 mol of H^+), the indicator (phenolphthalein) changes to pink, signaling the equivalence point of the titration. (Phenolphthalein is an indicator that is colorless in acidic solution and pink in basic solution.)

EXAMPLE 14.4   ACID–BASE TITRATION

 The titration of 10.00 mL of an HCl solution of unknown concentration requires 12.54 mL of a 0.100 M NaOH solution to reach the equivalence point. What is the concentration of the unknown HCl solution?

SORT You are given the volume of an unknown HCl solution and the volume of a known NaOH solution required to titrate the unknown solution. You are asked to find the concentration of the unknown solution.	**GIVEN:** 10.00 mL HCl solution 12.54 mL of a 0.100 M NaOH solution **FIND:** concentration of HCl solution (mol/L)

STRATEGIZE

First write the balanced chemical equation for the reaction between the acid and the base (see Example 14.2).

The solution map has two parts. In the first part, use the volume of NaOH required to reach the equivalence point to calculate the number of moles of HCl in the solution. The final conversion factor comes from the balanced neutralization equation.

In the second part, use the number of moles of HCl and the volume of HCl solution to determine the molarity of the HCl solution.

SOLUTION MAP

$$HCl(aq) + NaOH(aq) \longrightarrow H_2O(l) + NaCl(aq)$$

mL NaOH	→	L NaOH	→	mol NaOH	→	mol HCl

$$\frac{1\ L}{1000\ mL} \qquad \frac{0.100\ mol\ NaOH}{1\ L\ NaOH} \qquad \frac{1\ mol\ HCl}{1\ mol\ NaOH}$$

mol HCl, volume HCl solution	→	molarity

$$M = \frac{mol}{L}$$

RELATIONSHIPS USED

1 mol HCl : 1 mol NaOH (from balanced chemical equation)

$$Molarity\ (M) = \frac{mol\ solute}{L\ solution}\ (\text{definition of molarity, from Section 13.6})$$

SOLVE

Calculate the moles of HCl in the unknown solution by following the first part of the solution map.

To find the concentration of the solution, divide the number of moles of HCl by the volume of the HCl solution in L. (Note that 10.00 mL is equivalent to 0.01000 L.)

The unknown HCl solution therefore has a concentration of 0.125 M.

SOLUTION

$$12.54\ \cancel{mL\ NaOH} \times \frac{1\ \cancel{L}}{1000\ \cancel{mL}} \times \frac{0.100\ \cancel{mol\ NaOH}}{1\ \cancel{L\ NaOH}} \times \frac{1\ mol\ HCl}{1\ \cancel{mol\ NaOH}}$$

$$= 1.25 \times 10^{-3}\ mol\ HCl$$

$$Molarity = \frac{1.25 \times 10^{-3}\ mol\ HCl}{0.01000\ L} = 0.125\ M$$

CHECK

Check your answer. Are the units correct? Does the answer make physical sense?

The units (M) are correct. The magnitude of the answer makes sense because the reaction has a one-to-one stoichiometry and the volumes of the two solutions are similar; therefore, their concentrations should also be similar.

▶**SKILLBUILDER 14.4 | Acid–Base Titration**

The titration of a 20.0-mL sample of an H_2SO_4 solution of unknown concentration requires 22.87 mL of a 0.158 M KOH solution to reach the equivalence point. What is the concentration of the unknown H_2SO_4 solution?

▶**FOR MORE PRACTICE**   Example 14.14; Problems 47, 48, 49, 50, 51, 52.

 CONCEPTUAL CHECKPOINT 14.3

The flask shown here represents a sample or acid to be titrated.

Which of the beakers contains the amount of OH^- required to reach the equivalence point in the titration?

(a)   (b)   (c)

14.7   Strong and Weak Acids and Bases

LO: Identify strong and weak acids and strong and weak bases.

LO: Determine $[H_3O^+]$ in acid solutions.

LO: Determine $[OH^-]$ in base solutions.

Acids and bases can each be categorized as strong or weak, depending on how much they ionize or dissociate in aqueous solution. In this section, we first look at strong and weak acids, and then turn to strong and weak bases.

Strong Acids

Hydrochloric acid (HCl) and hydrofluoric acid (HF) appear to be similar, but there is an important difference between these two acids. HCl is an example of a **strong acid**, one that completely ionizes in solution.

Single arrow indicates complete ionization

$$HCl(aq) + H_2O(l) \longrightarrow H_3O^+(aq) + Cl^-(aq)$$

| [X] means "molar concentration of X."

We show the *complete* ionization of HCl with a single arrow pointing to the right in the equation. An HCl solution contains almost no intact HCl; virtually all the HCl has reacted with water to form $H_3O^+(aq)$ and $Cl^-(aq)$ (◄ Figure 14.9). A 1.0 M HCl solution therefore has an H_3O^+ concentration of 1.0 M. We often abbreviate the concentration of H_3O^+ as $[H_3O^+]$. Using this notation, a 1.0-M HCl solution has $[H_3O^+] = 1.0$ M.

A strong acid is also a **strong electrolyte** (first defined in Section 7.5), a substance whose aqueous solutions are good conductors of electricity (▼ Figure 14.10). Aqueous solutions require the presence of charged particles to conduct electricity. Strong acid solutions are also strong electrolyte solutions because each acid molecule ionizes into positive and negative ions. These mobile ions are good conductors of electricity. Pure water is not a good conductor of electricity because it has relatively few charged particles. The danger of using electrical devices—such as a hair dryer—while sitting in the bathtub is that water is seldom pure and often contains dissolved ions. If the device were to come in contact with the water, dangerously high levels of electricity could flow through the water and through your body.

▲ **FIGURE 14.9** **A strong acid** When HCl dissolves in water, it completely ionizes into H_3O^+ and Cl^- ions. The solution contains no intact HCl.

| An ionizable proton is one that becomes an
| H^+ ion in solution.

Table 14.3 lists the six strong acids. The first five acids in the table are **monoprotic acids**, acids containing only one ionizable proton. Sulfuric acid is an example of a **diprotic acid**, an acid that contains two ionizable protons.

TABLE 14.3 Strong Acids

hydrochloric acid (HCl)	nitric acid (HNO_3)
hydrobromic acid (HBr)	perchloric acid ($HClO_4$)
hydroiodic acid (HI)	sulfuric acid (H_2SO_4) (*diprotic*)

| (a) Pure water | (b) HCl solution |

▲ **FIGURE 14.10** **Conductivity of a strong electrolyte solution** **(a)** Pure water does not conduct electricity. **(b)** The presence of ions in an HCl solution results in the conduction of electricity, causing the lightbulb to light. Solutions such as these are strong electrolyte solutions.

Weak Acids

| It is a common mistake to confuse the
| terms *strong* and *weak acids* with the terms
| *concentrated* and *dilute acids*. Can you state
| the difference between these terms?

In contrast to HCl, HF is a **weak acid**, one that does not completely ionize in solution.

Double arrow indicates
partial ionization

$$HF(aq) + H_2O(l) \rightleftharpoons H_3O^+(aq) + F^-(aq)$$

Calculating exact [H₃O⁺] for weak acids is beyond the scope of this text.

▲ **FIGURE 14.11 A weak acid** When HF dissolves in water, only a fraction of the dissolved molecules ionize into H₃O⁺ and F⁻ ions. The solution contains many intact HF molecules.

To show that HF does not completely ionize in solution, the equation for its ionization has two opposing arrows, indicating that the reverse reaction occurs to some degree. An HF solution contains a lot of intact HF; it also contains some $H_3O^+(aq)$ and $F^-(aq)$ (◄ Figure 14.11). In other words, a 1.0 M HF solution has $[H_3O^+] < 1.0$ M because only some of the HF molecules ionize to form H_3O^+.

A weak acid is also a **weak electrolyte**, a substance whose aqueous solutions are poor conductors of electricity (▼ Figure 14.12). Weak acid solutions contain few charged particles because only a small fraction of the acid molecules ionize into positive and negative ions.

The degree to which an acid is strong or weak depends in part on the attraction between the anion of the acid (the conjugate base) and the hydrogen ion. Suppose HA is a generic formula for an acid. Then, the degree to which the following reaction proceeds in the forward direction depends in part on the strength of the attraction between H⁺ and A⁻.

$$HA(aq) + H_2O(l) \longrightarrow H_3O^+(aq) + A^-(aq)$$
Acid   Conjugate base

(a) Pure water   (b) HF solution

▲ **FIGURE 14.12 Conductivity of a weak electrolyte solution** (a) Pure water does not conduct electricity. (b) An HF solution contains some ions, but most of the HF is intact. The light glows only dimly. Solutions such as these are weak electrolyte solutions.

(a) Strong acid

Weak attraction
Complete ionization

(b) Weak acid

H⁺ ◄► A⁻

Strong attraction
Partial ionization

◄ **FIGURE 14.13 Strong and weak acids** (a) In a strong acid, the attraction between H⁺ and A⁻ is low, resulting in complete ionization. **(b)** In a weak acid, the attraction between H⁺ and A⁻ is high, resulting in partial ionization.

If the attraction between H⁺ and A⁻ is *weak*, the reaction favors the forward direction and the acid is *strong* (◄ Figure 14.13a). If the attraction between H⁺ and A⁻ is *strong*, the reaction favors the reverse direction and the acid is *weak* (Figure 14.13b). For example, in HCl, the conjugate base (Cl⁻) has a relatively weak attraction to H⁺, meaning that the reverse reaction does not occur to any significant extent. In HF, on the other hand, the conjugate base (F⁻) has a greater attraction to H⁺, meaning that the reverse reaction occurs to a significant degree. *In general, the stronger the acid, the weaker the conjugate base and vice versa.* This means that if the forward reaction (that of the acid) has a high tendency to occur, then the reverse reaction (that of the conjugate base) has a low tendency to occur. Table 14.4 lists some common weak acids.

TABLE 14.4 Weak Acids

hydrofluoric acid (HF)	sulfurous acid (H_2SO_3) *(diprotic)*
acetic acid ($HC_2H_3O_2$)	carbonic acid (H_2CO_3) *(diprotic)*
formic acid ($HCHO_2$)	phosphoric acid (H_3PO_4) *(triprotic)*

Notice that two of the weak acids in Table 14.4 are diprotic (they have two ionizable protons) and one is triprotic (it has three ionizable protons). Let us return to sulfuric acid (Table 14.3) for a moment. Sulfuric acid is a diprotic acid that is strong in its first ionizable proton:

$$H_2SO_4(aq) + H_2O(l) \longrightarrow H_3O^+(aq) + HSO_4^-(aq)$$

but weak in its second ionizable proton:

$$HSO_4^-(aq) + H_2O(l) \rightleftharpoons H_3O^+(aq) + SO_4^{2-}(aq)$$

Sulfurous acid and carbonic acid are weak in both of their ionizable protons, and phosphoric acid is weak in all three of its ionizable protons.

EXAMPLE 14.5 **DETERMINING [H₃O⁺] IN ACID SOLUTIONS**

Determine the H_3O^+ concentration in each solution.

(a) 1.5 M HCl   (b) 3.0 M $HC_2H_3O_2$ (c) 2.5 M HNO_3

SOLUTION

(a) Since HCl is a strong acid, it completely ionizes. The concentration of H_3O^+ will be 1.5 M.

$$[H_3O^+] = 1.5 \text{ M}$$

(b) Since $HC_2H_3O_2$ is a weak acid, it partially ionizes. The calculation of the exact concentration of H_3O^+ is beyond the scope of this text, but we know that it will be less than 3.0 M.

$$[H_3O^+] < 3.0 \text{ M}$$

(c) Since HNO_3 is a strong acid, it completely ionizes. The concentration of H_3O^+ will be 2.5 M.

$$[H_3O^+] = 2.5 \text{ M}$$

▶**SKILLBUILDER 14.5** | **Determining [H₃O⁺] in Acid Solutions**

Determine the H_3O^+ concentration in each solution.

(a) 0.50 M $HCHO_2$ (b) 1.25 M HI   (c) 0.75 M HF

▶**FOR MORE PRACTICE** Example 14.15; Problems 55, 56.

 CONCEPTUAL CHECKPOINT 14.4

Examine these molecular views of three different acid solutions. Which of these acids is a weak acid?

(a)   (b)   (c)

Strong Bases

By analogy to the definition of a strong acid, a **strong base** is one that completely dissociates in solution. NaOH, for example, is a strong base.

$$NaOH(aq) \longrightarrow Na^+(aq) + OH^-(aq)$$

An NaOH solution contains no intact NaOH—it has all dissociated to form $Na^+(aq)$ and $OH^-(aq)$ (▼ Figure 14.14), and a 1.0 M NaOH solution has $[OH^-] = 1.0$ M and $[Na^+] = 1.0$ M. Table 14.5 lists some common strong bases.

NaOH

▶ **FIGURE 14.14   A strong base**
When NaOH dissolves in water, it completely dissociates into Na^+ and OH^-. Question: The solution contains no intact NaOH. Is NaOH a strong or weak electrolyte?

TABLE 14.5   Strong Bases

lithium hydroxide (LiOH)	strontium hydroxide ($Sr(OH)_2$)
sodium hydroxide (NaOH)	calcium hydroxide ($Ca(OH)_2$)
potassium hydroxide (KOH)	barium hydroxide ($Ba(OH)_2$)

| Unlike diprotic acids, which ionize in two steps, bases containing 2 OH^- ions dissociate in one step.

Some strong bases, such as $Sr(OH)_2$, contain two OH^- ions. These bases completely dissociate, producing two moles of OH^- per mole of base. For example, $Sr(OH)_2$ dissociates as follows:

$$Sr(OH)_2(aq) \longrightarrow Sr^{2+}(aq) + 2 OH^-(aq)$$

Weak Bases

A **weak base** is analogous to a weak acid. In contrast to strong bases that contain OH^- and dissociate in water, the most common weak bases produce OH^- by accepting a proton from water, ionizing water to form OH^-.

| Calculating exact $[OH^-]$ for weak bases is beyond the scope of this text.

$$B(aq) + H_2O(l) \rightleftharpoons BH^+(aq) + OH^-(aq)$$

In this equation, B is generic for a weak base. Ammonia, for example, ionizes water according to the reaction:

$$NH_3(aq) + H_2O(l) \rightleftharpoons NH_4^+(aq) + OH^-(aq)$$

The double arrow indicates that the ionization is not complete. An NH_3 solution contains NH_3, NH_4^+, and OH^- (◀ Figure 14.15). A 1.0 M NH_3 solution has $[OH^-] < 1.0$ M. Table 14.6 lists some common weak bases.

NH₃

◀ **FIGURE 14.15   A weak base**   When NH_3 dissolves in water, it partially ionizes to form NH_4^+ and OH^-. However, only a fraction of the molecules ionize. Most NH_3 molecules remain as NH_3.
Question: Is NH_3 a strong or weak electrolyte?

TABLE 14.6 Some Weak Bases

Base	Ionization Reaction
ammonia (NH_3)	$NH_3(aq) + H_2O(l) \rightleftharpoons NH_4^+(aq) + OH^-(aq)$
pyridine (C_5H_5N)	$C_5H_5N(aq) + H_2O(l) \rightleftharpoons C_5H_5NH^+(aq) + OH^-(aq)$
methylamine (CH_3NH_2)	$CH_3NH_2(aq) + H_2O(l) \rightleftharpoons CH_3NH_3^+(aq) + OH^-(aq)$
ethylamine ($C_2H_5NH_2$)	$C_2H_5NH_2(aq) + H_2O(l) \rightleftharpoons C_2H_5NH_3^+(aq) + OH^-(aq)$
bicarbonate ion (HCO_3^-)*	$HCO_3^-(aq) + H_2O(l) \rightleftharpoons H_2CO_3(aq) + OH^-(aq)$

*The bicarbonate ion must occur with a positively charged ion such as Na^+ that serves to balance the charge but does not have any part in the ionization reaction. It is the bicarbonate ion that makes sodium bicarbonate ($NaHCO_3$) basic.

EXAMPLE 14.6 **DETERMINING [OH$^-$] IN BASE SOLUTIONS**

Determine the OH^- concentration in each solution.

(a) 2.25 M KOH   **(b)** 0.35 M CH_3NH_2 **(c)** 0.025 M $Sr(OH)_2$

SOLUTION

(a) Since KOH is a strong base, it completely dissociates into K^+ and OH^- in solution. The concentration of OH^- is 2.25 M.

$$[OH^-] = 2.25 \text{ M}$$

(b) Since CH_3NH_2 is a weak base, it only partially ionizes water. We cannot calculate the exact concentration of OH^-, but we know it is less than 0.35 M.

$$[OH^-] < 0.35 \text{ M}$$

(c) Since $Sr(OH)_2$ is a strong base, it completely dissociates into $Sr^{2+}(aq)$ and $2\,OH^-(aq)$. $Sr(OH)_2$ forms 2 mol of OH^- for every 1 mol of $Sr(OH)_2$. Consequently, the concentration of OH^- is twice the concentration of $Sr(OH)_2$.

$$[OH^-] = 2(0.025 \text{ M}) = 0.050 \text{ M}$$

▶**SKILLBUILDER 14.6** | **Determining [OH$^-$] in Base Solutions**

Determine the OH^- concentration in each solution.

(a) 0.055 M $Ba(OH)_2$ **(b)** 1.05 M C_5H_5N **(c)** 0.45 M NaOH

▶**FOR MORE PRACTICE** Example 14.16; Problems 59, 60.

14.8 Water: Acid and Base in One

LO: Calculate [H$_3$O$^+$] or [OH$^-$] from K_w (Section 14.8).

Recall that water acts as a base when it reacts with HCl and as an acid when it reacts with NH_3.

Water acting as a base

$$HCl(aq) + H_2O(l) \longrightarrow H_3O^+(aq) + Cl^-(aq)$$

Acid (Proton donor)   Base (Proton acceptor)

Water acting as an acid

$$NH_3(aq) + H_2O(l) \rightleftharpoons NH_4^+(aq) + OH^-(aq)$$

Base (Proton acceptor)   Acid (Proton donor)

Water is *amphoteric*; it can act as either an acid or a base. Even in pure water, water acts as an acid and a base with itself, a process called self-ionization.

Water acting as both an acid and a base

$$H_2O(l) \; + \; H_2O(l) \; \rightleftharpoons \; H_3O^+(aq) + OH^-(aq)$$

Acid   Base
(Proton donor)   (Proton acceptor)

In pure water, at 25 °C, the preceding reaction occurs only to a very small extent, resulting in equal and small concentrations of H_3O^+ and OH^-.

$$[H_3O^+] = [OH^-] = 1.0 \times 10^{-7} \, M \quad \text{(in pure water at 25 °C)}$$

where $[H_3O^+]$ = the concentration of H_3O^+ in M
and $[OH^-]$ = the concentration of OH^- in M

So all samples of water contain some hydronium ions and some hydroxide ions. The *product* of the concentration of these two ions in aqueous solutions is called the **ion product constant for water (K_w)**.

$$K_w = [H_3O^+][OH^-]$$

| The units of K_w are normally dropped.

We can find the value of K_w at 25 °C by multiplying the hydronium and hydroxide concentrations for pure water listed earlier.

$$\begin{aligned} K_w &= [H_3O^+][OH^-] \\ &= (1.0 \times 10^{-7})(1.0 \times 10^{-7}) \\ &= (1.0 \times 10^{-7})^2 \\ &= 1.0 \times 10^{-14} \end{aligned}$$

The preceding equation holds true for all aqueous solutions at 25 °C. The concentration of H_3O^+ times the concentration of OH^- is 1.0×10^{-14}. In pure water, since H_2O is the only source of these ions, there is one H_3O^+ ion for every OH^- ion. Consequently, the concentrations of H_3O^+ and OH^- are equal. Such a solution is a **neutral solution**.

| In a neutral solution, $[H_3O^+] = [OH^-]$.

$$[H_3O^+] = [OH^-] = \sqrt{K_w} = 1.0 \times 10^{-7} \, M \text{ (in pure water)}$$

An **acidic solution** contains an acid that creates additional H_3O^+ ions, causing $[H_3O^+]$ to increase. However, the *ion product constant still applies.*

$$[H_3O^+][OH^-] = K_w = 1.0 \times 10^{-14}$$

| In an acidic solution, $[H_3O^+] > [OH^-]$.

If $[H_3O^+]$ increases, then $[OH^-]$ must decrease for the ion product to remain 1.0×10^{-14}. For example, suppose $[H_3O^+] = 1.0 \times 10^{-3} \, M$; then $[OH^-]$ can be found by solving the ion product expression for $[OH^-]$.

$$(1.0 \times 10^{-3})[OH^-] = 1.0 \times 10^{-14}$$

$$[OH^-] = \frac{1.0 \times 10^{-14}}{1.0 \times 10^{-3}} = 1.0 \times 10^{-11} \, M$$

In an acidic solution, $[H_3O^+]$ is greater than $1.0 \times 10^{-7} \, M$, and $[OH^-]$ is less than $1.0 \times 10^{-7} \, M$.

| In a basic solution, $[H_3O^+] < [OH^-]$.

A **basic solution** contains a base that creates additional OH^- ions, causing the $[OH^-]$ to increase and the $[H_3O^+]$ to decrease. For example, suppose

$[OH^-] = 1.0 \times 10^{-2}$ M; $[H_3O^+]$ can be found by solving the ion product expression for $[H_3O^+]$.

$$[H_3O^+](1.0 \times 10^{-2}) = 1.0 \times 10^{-14}$$

$$[H_3O^+] = \frac{1.0 \times 10^{-14}}{1.0 \times 10^{-2}} = 1.0 \times 10^{-12} \text{ M}$$

In a basic solution, $[OH^-]$ is greater than 1.0×10^{-7} M and $[H_3O^+]$ is less than 1.0×10^{-7} M.

▶ **FIGURE 14.16 Acidic and basic solutions**

To summarize, at 25 °C (▲ Figure 14.16):

- In a neutral solution, $[H_3O^+] = [OH^-] = 1.0 \times 10^{-7}$ M
- In an acidic solution, $[H_3O^+] > 1.0 \times 10^{-7}$ M $[OH^-] < 1.0 \times 10^{-7}$ M
- In a basic solution, $[H_3O^+] < 1.0 \times 10^{-7}$ M $[OH^-] > 1.0 \times 10^{-7}$ M
- In all aqueous solutions, $[H_3O^+][OH^-] = K_w = 1.0 \times 10^{-14}$

EXAMPLE 14.7   USING K_w IN CALCULATIONS

Calculate $[OH^-]$ for each solution and determine whether the solution is acidic, basic, or neutral.

(a) $[H_3O^+] = 7.5 \times 10^{-5}$ M
(b) $[H_3O^+] = 1.5 \times 10^{-9}$ M
(c) $[H_3O^+] = 1.0 \times 10^{-7}$ M

To find $[OH^-]$ use the ion product constant, K_w. Substitute the given value for $[H_3O^+]$ and solve the equation for $[OH^-]$. Since $[H_3O^+] > 1.0 \times 10^{-7}$ M and $[OH^-] < 1.0 \times 10^{-7}$ M, the solution is acidic.	**SOLUTION** **(a)** $[H_3O^+][OH^-] = K_w = 1.0 \times 10^{-14}$ $[7.5 \times 10^{-5}][OH^-] = K_w = 1.0 \times 10^{-14}$ $[OH^-] = \dfrac{1.0 \times 10^{-14}}{7.5 \times 10^{-5}} = 1.3 \times 10^{-10}$ M acidic solution
Substitute the given value for $[H_3O^+]$ into the ion product constant equation and solve the equation for $[OH^-]$. Since $[H_3O^+] < 1.0 \times 10^{-7}$ M and $[OH^-] > 1.0 \times 10^{-7}$ M, the solution is basic.	**(b)** $[H_3O^+][OH^-] = K_w = 1.0 \times 10^{-14}$ $[1.5 \times 10^{-9}][OH^-] = 1.0 \times 10^{-14}$ $[OH^-] = \dfrac{1.0 \times 10^{-14}}{1.5 \times 10^{-9}} = 6.7 \times 10^{-6}$ M basic solution

Substitute the given value for $[H_3O^+]$ into the ion product constant equation and solve the equation for $[OH^-]$. Since $[H_3O^+] = 1.0 \times 10^{-7}$ M and $[OH^-] = 1.0 \times 10^{-7}$ M, the solution is neutral.

(c) $[H_3O^+][OH^-] = K_w = 1.0 \times 10^{-14}$

$[1.0 \times 10^{-7}][OH^-] = 1.0 \times 10^{-14}$

$$[OH^-] = \frac{1.0 \times 10^{-14}}{1.0 \times 10^{-7}} = 1.0 \times 10^{-7} \text{ M}$$

neutral solution

▶**SKILLBUILDER 14.7 | Using K_w in Calculations**

Calculate $[H_3O^+]$ in each solution and determine whether the solution is acidic, basic, or neutral.

(a) $[OH^-] = 1.5 \times 10^{-2}$ M
(b) $[OH^-] = 1.0 \times 10^{-7}$ M
(c) $[OH^-] = 8.2 \times 10^{-10}$ M

▶**FOR MORE PRACTICE**   Example 14.17; Problems 63, 64, 65, 66.

  CONCEPTUAL CHECKPOINT 14.5

Which substance is least likely to act as a base?
(a) H_2O
(b) OH^-
(c) NH_3
(d) NH_4^+

14.9   The pH and pOH Scales: Ways to Express Acidity and Basicity

LO: Calculate pH from $[H_3O^+]$.

LO: Calculate $[H_3O^+]$ from pH.

LO: Calculate $[OH^-]$ from pOH.

LO: Compare and contrast the pOH scale and the pH scale.

| Notice that an increase of 1 in pH corresponds to a tenfold *decrease* in $[H_3O^+]$.

Chemists have devised a scale, called the **pH** scale, based on hydrogen ion concentration to express the acidity or basicity of solutions. At 25 °C according to the pH scale, a solution has these general characteristics:

• pH < 7 *acidic* solution
• pH > 7 *basic* solution
• pH = 7 *neutral* solution

TABLE 14.7   The pH of Some Common Substances

Substance	pH
gastric (human stomach) acid	1.0–3.0
limes	1.8–2.0
lemons	2.2–2.4
soft drinks	2.0–4.0
plums	2.8–3.0
wine	2.8–3.8
apples	2.9–3.3
peaches	3.4–3.6
cherries	3.2–4.0
beer	4.0–5.0
rainwater (unpolluted)	5.6
human blood	7.3–7.4
egg whites	7.6–8.0
milk of magnesia	10.5
household ammonia	10.5–11.5
4% NaOH solution	14

Table 14.7 lists the pH of some common substances. Notice that, as we discussed in Section 14.1, many foods, especially fruits, are acidic and therefore have low pH values. The foods with the lowest pH values are limes and lemons, and they are among the sourest. Relatively few foods, however, are basic.

The pH scale is a **logarithmic scale**; a change of 1 pH unit corresponds to a tenfold change in H_3O^+ concentration. For example, a lime with a pH of 2.0 is 10 times more acidic than a plum with a pH of 3.0 and 100 times more acidic than a cherry with a pH of 4.0. Each change of 1 in pH scale corresponds to a change of 10 in $[H_3O^+]$ (▶ Figure 14.17).

▶ **FIGURE 14.17 The pH scale is a logarithmic scale** A *decrease* of 1 unit on the pH scale corresponds to an *increase* in [H_3O^+] concentration by a factor of 10. Each circle stands for 10^{-4} mol H^+/L, or 6.022×10^{19} H^+ ions per liter.
Question: How much of an increase in H_3O^+ concentration corresponds to a decrease of 2 pH units?

pH	[H_3O^+]	[H_3O^+] Representation	
4	10^{-4}		$\left(\begin{array}{l}\text{Each circle}\\ \text{represents}\end{array} \dfrac{10^{-4}\,\text{mol}\,H^+}{L}\right)$
3	10^{-3}		
2	10^{-2}		

Calculating pH from [H_3O^+]

We define the pH of a solution as the negative of the log of the hydronium ion concentration:

$$pH = -\log[H_3O^+]$$

Note that pH is defined using the log function (base ten), which is different from the natural log (abbreviated ln).

To calculate pH, we must use logarithms. Recall that the log of a number is the exponent to which 10 must be raised to obtain that number, as shown in these examples:

$$\log 10^1 = 1; \log 10^2 = 2; \log 10^3 = 3$$

$$\log 10^{-1} = -1; \log 10^{-2} = -2; \log 10^{-3} = -3$$

In the next example, we calculate the log of 1.5×10^{-7}. A solution having an [H_3O^+] = 1.5×10^{-7} M (acidic) has a pH of:

$$\begin{aligned} pH &= -\log[H_3O^+] \\ &= -\log(1.5 \times 10^{-7}) \\ &= -(-6.82) \\ &= 6.82 \end{aligned}$$

Notice that the pH is reported to two decimal places here. This is because only the numbers to the right of the decimal place are significant in a log. Because our original value for the concentration had two significant figures, the log of that number has two decimal places:

2 decimal places

$$\log(1.0 \times 10^{-3}) = 3.00$$

When we take the log of a quantity, the result should have the same number of decimal places as the number of significant figures in the original quantity.

If the original number has three significant figures, we report the log to three decimal places:

3 decimal places

$$-\log(1.00 \times 10^{-3}) = 3.000$$

A solution having $[H_3O^+] = 1.0 \times 10^{-7}$ M (neutral) has a pH of:

$$pH = -\log[H_3O^+]$$
$$= -\log(1.0 \times 10^{-7})$$
$$= -(-7.00)$$
$$= 7.00$$

EXAMPLE 14.8   **CALCULATING PH FROM $[H_3O^+]$**

Calculate the pH of each solution and indicate whether the solution is acidic or basic.

(a) $[H_3O^+] = 1.8 \times 10^{-4}$ M
(b) $[H_3O^+] = 7.2 \times 10^{-9}$ M

SOLUTION To calculate pH, substitute the given $[H_3O^+]$ into the pH equation.	(a) $pH = -\log[H_3O^+]$ $= -\log(1.8 \times 10^{-4})$ $= -(-3.74)$
Since the pH < 7, this solution is acidic.	$= 3.74$
Again, substitute the given $[H_3O^+]$ into the pH equation.	(b) $pH = -\log[H_3O^+]$ $= -\log(7.2 \times 10^{-9})$ $= -(-8.14)$
Since the pH > 7, this solution is basic.	$= 8.14$

▶SKILLBUILDER 14.8 | Calculating pH from $[H_3O^+]$

Calculate the pH of each solution and indicate whether the solution is acidic or basic.

(a) $[H_3O^+] = 9.5 \times 10^{-9}$ M
(b) $[H_3O^+] = 6.1 \times 10^{-3}$ M

▶SKILLBUILDER PLUS

Calculate the pH of a solution with $[OH^-] = 1.3 \times 10^{-2}$ M and indicate whether the solution is acidic or basic. *Hint:* Begin by using K_w to find $[H_3O^+]$.

▶FOR MORE PRACTICE   Example 14.18; Problems 69, 70.

Calculating $[H_3O^-]$ from pH

Ten raised to the log of a number is equal to that number: $10^{\log x} = x$.

To calculate $[H_3O^+]$ from a pH value, we *undo* the log. The log can be undone using the inverse log function (*Method 1*) on most calculators or using the 10^x key (*Method 2*). Both methods do the same thing; the one you use depends on your calculator.

Method 1: Inverse Log Function	Method 2: 10^x Function
$pH = -\log[H_3O^+]$	$pH = -\log[H_3O^+]$
$-pH = \log[H_3O^+]$	$-pH = \log[H_3O^+]$
$\text{invlog}(-pH) = \text{invlog}(\log[H_3O^+])$	$10^{-pH} = 10^{\log[H_3O^+]}$
$\text{invlog}(-pH) = [H_3O^+]$	$10^{-pH} = [H_3O^+]$

The invlog function "undoes" log: $\text{invlog}(\log x) = x$.

The inverse log is sometimes called the antilog.

So, to calculate $[H_3O^+]$ from a pH value, we take the inverse log of the negative of the pH value (*Method 1*) or raise 10 to the negative of the pH value (*Method 2*).

The number of significant figures in the inverse log of a number is equal to the number of decimal places in the number.

EXAMPLE 14.9 CALCULATING [H₃O⁺] FROM pH

Calculate the H_3O^+ concentration for a solution with a pH of 4.80.

SOLUTION

To find the $[H_3O^+]$ from pH, undo the log function. Use either Method 1 or Method 2.

Method 1: Inverse Log Function	Method 2: 10ˣ Function
$pH = -\log[H_3O^+]$	$pH = -\log[H_3O^+]$
$4.80 = -\log[H_3O^+]$	$4.80 = -\log[H_3O^+]$
$-4.80 = \log[H_3O^+]$	$-4.80 = \log[H_3O^+]$
$\text{invlog}(-4.80) = \text{invlog}(\log[H_3O^+])$	$10^{-4.80} = 10^{\log[H_3O^+]}$
$\text{invlog}(-4.80) = [H_3O^+]$	$10^{-4.80} = [H_3O^+]$
$[H_3O^+] = 1.6 \times 10^{-5}$ M	$[H_3O^+] = 1.6 \times 10^{-5}$ M

▶**SKILLBUILDER 14.9 | Calculating [H₃O⁺] from pH**

Calculate the H_3O^+ concentration for a solution with a pH of 8.37.

▶**SKILLBUILDER PLUS**

Calculate the OH^- concentration for a solution with a pH of 3.66.

▶**FOR MORE PRACTICE** Example 14.19; Problems 71, 72.

CONCEPTUAL CHECKPOINT 14.6

Solution A has a pH of 13. Solution B has a pH of 10. The concentration of H_3O^+ in solution B is _____ times that in solution A.

(a) 0.001

(b) $\frac{1}{3}$

(c) 3

(d) 1000

The pOH Scale

The **pOH** scale is analogous to the pH scale but is defined with respect to $[OH^-]$ instead of $[H_3O^+]$.

Notice that p is the mathematical function; $-\log$; thus, $pX = -\log X$.

$$pOH = -\log[OH^-]$$

A solution with an $[OH^-]$ of 1.0×10^{-3} M (basic) has a pOH of 3.00. On the pOH scale, a pOH less than 7 is basic and a pOH greater than 7 is acidic. A pOH of 7 is neutral. We can find the $[OH^-]$ concentration from the pOH just as the $[H_3O^+]$ concentration is found from the pH, as shown in Example 14.10.

EXAMPLE 14.10 CALCULATING [OH⁻] FROM pOH

Calculate the $[OH^-]$ concentration for a solution with a pOH of 8.55.

SOLUTION

To find the $[OH^-]$ from pOH, undo the log function. Use either Method 1 or Method 2.

Method 1: Inverse Log Function	Method 2: 10^x Function
$pOH = -\log[OH^-]$	$pOH = -\log[OH^-]$
$8.55 = -\log[OH^-]$	$8.55 = -\log[OH^-]$
$-8.55 = \log[OH^-]$	$-8.55 = \log[OH^-]$
$invlog(-8.55) = invlog(\log[OH^-])$	$10^{-8.55} = 10^{\log[OH^-]}$
$invlog(-8.55) = [OH^-]$	$10^{-8.55} = [OH^-]$
$[OH^-] = 2.8 \times 10^{-9}$ M	$[OH^-] = 2.8 \times 10^{-9}$ M

▶**SKILLBUILDER 14.10 | Calculating [OH⁻] from pOH**

Calculate the OH^- concentration for a solution with a pOH of 4.25.

▶**SKILLBUILDER PLUS**

Calculate the H_3O^+ concentration for a solution with a pOH of 5.68.

▶**FOR MORE PRACTICE** Problems 79, 80, 81, 82.

We can derive a relationship between pH and pOH at 25 °C from the expression for K_w.

$$[H_3O^+][OH^-] = 1.0 \times 10^{-14}$$

| $\log(AB) = \log A + \log B$

Taking the log of both sides, we get:

$$\log\{[H_3O^+][OH^-]\} = \log(1.0 \times 10^{-14})$$
$$\log[H_3O^+] + \log[OH^-] = -14.00$$
$$-\log[H_3O^+] - \log[OH^-] = 14.00$$
$$pH + pOH = 14.00$$

The sum of pH and pOH is always equal to 14.00 at 25 °C. Therefore, a solution with a pH of 3 has a pOH of 11.

  CONCEPTUAL CHECKPOINT 14.7

A solution has a pH of 5. What is the pOH of the solution?

(a) 5

(b) 10

(c) 14

(d) 9

14.10 Buffers: Solutions That Resist pH Change

LO: Describe how buffers resist pH change.

Most solutions rapidly become more acidic (lower pH) upon addition of an acid or more basic (higher pH) upon addition of a base. A **buffer**, however, resists pH change by neutralizing added acid or added base. Human blood, for example, is a buffer. Acid or base that is added to blood gets neutralized by components within blood, resulting in a nearly constant pH. In healthy individuals, blood pH is between 7.36 and 7.40. If blood pH drops below 7.0 or rises above 7.8, death results.

How does blood maintain such a narrow pH range? Like all buffers, blood contains *significant* amounts of *both a weak acid and its conjugate base*. When additional base is added to blood, the weak acid reacts with the base, neutralizing it. When additional acid is added to blood, the conjugate base reacts with the acid, neutralizing it. In this way, blood maintains a constant pH.

| Buffers can also be composed of a weak base and its conjugate acid.

CHEMISTRY **AND HEALTH**

▶ Alkaloids

Alkaloids are organic bases that occur naturally in many plants (see Section 14.3) that often have medicinal qualities. Morphine, for example, is a powerful alkaloid drug that occurs in the opium poppy (▶ Figure 14.18) and is used to relieve severe pain. Morphine is an example of a *narcotic*, a drug that dulls the senses and induces sleep. It produces relief from and indifference to pain. Morphine can also produce feelings of euphoria and contentment, which leads to its abuse. Morphine is highly addictive, both psychologically and physically. A person who abuses morphine over long periods of time becomes physically dependent on the drug and suffers severe withdrawal symptoms upon termination of use.

▲ **FIGURE 14.18 Opium poppy** The opium poppy contains the alkaloids morphine and codeine.

Morphine

Amphetamine is another powerful drug related to the alkaloid ephedrine. Whereas morphine slows down nerve signal transmissions, amphetamine enhances them. Amphetamine is an example of a *stimulant*, a drug that increases alertness and wakefulness. Amphetamine is widely used to treat Attention-Deficit Hyperactivity Disorder (ADHD) and is prescribed under the trade name Adderall. Patients suffering from ADHD find that amphetamine helps them to focus and concentrate more effectively. However, because amphetamine produces alertness and increased stamina, it, too, is often abused.

Amphetamine

Other common alkaloids include caffeine and nicotine, both of which are stimulants. Caffeine is found in the coffee bean, and nicotine is found in tobacco. Although both have some addictive qualities, nicotine is by far the most addictive. A nicotine addiction is among the most difficult to break, as any smoker can attest.

B14.2 CAN YOU ANSWER THIS? *What part of the amphetamine and morphine molecules makes them bases?*

We can make a simple buffer by mixing acetic acid ($HC_2H_3O_2$) and its conjugate base, sodium acetate ($NaC_2H_3O_2$), in water (▶ Figure 14.19). (The sodium in sodium acetate is just a spectator ion and does not contribute to buffering action.) Because $HC_2H_3O_2$ is a weak acid and $C_2H_3O_2^-$ is its conjugate base, a solution containing both of these is a buffer. Note that a weak acid by itself, even though it partially ionizes to form some of its conjugate base, does not contain sufficient base to be a buffer. A buffer must contain *significant* amounts of *both* a weak acid and its conjugate base. If we add more base, in the form of NaOH, to the buffer solution containing acetic acid and sodium acetate, the acetic acid neutralizes the base according to the reaction:

$$NaOH(aq) + HC_2H_3O_2(aq) \longrightarrow H_2O(l) + NaC_2H_3O_2(aq)$$

Base   Acid

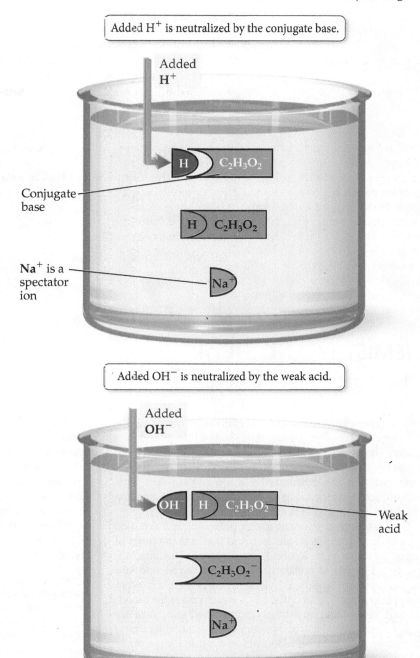

▲ **FIGURE 14.19   How buffers resist pH change**   A buffer contains significant amounts of a weak acid and its conjugate base. The acid consumes any added base, and the base consumes any added acid. In this way, a buffer resists pH change.

As long as the amount of NaOH that we add is less than the amount of $HC_2H_3O_2$ in solution, the solution neutralizes the NaOH, and the resulting pH change is small. Suppose, on the other hand, that we add more acid, in the form of HCl, to the solution. In this case, the conjugate base, $NaC_2H_3O_2$, neutralizes the added HCl according to the reaction:

$$\underset{\text{Acid}}{HCl(aq)} + \underset{\text{Base}}{NaC_2H_3O_2(aq)} \longrightarrow HC_2H_3O_2(aq) + NaCl(aq)$$

As long as the amount of HCl that we add is less than the amount of $NaC_2H_3O_2$ in solution, the solution neutralizes the HCl and the resulting pH change is small.

To summarize:

- Buffers resist pH change.
- Buffers contain significant amounts of both a weak acid and its conjugate base.
- The weak acid in a buffer neutralizes added base.
- The conjugate base in a buffer neutralizes added acid.

 CONCEPTUAL CHECKPOINT 14.8

Which of the following is a buffer solution?

(a) $H_2SO_4(aq)$ and $H_2SO_3(aq)$

(b) $HF(aq)$ and $NaF(aq)$

(c) $HCl(aq)$ and $NaCl(aq)$

(d) $NaCl(aq)$ and $NaOH(aq)$

CHEMISTRY AND HEALTH
▶ The Danger of Antifreeze

Most types of antifreeze used in cars are solutions of ethylene glycol. Every year, thousands of dogs and cats die from ethylene glycol poisoning because they consume improperly stored antifreeze or antifreeze that has leaked out of a radiator. The antifreeze has a somewhat sweet taste, which attracts a curious dog or cat. Young children are also at risk for ethylene glycol poisoning.

The first stage of ethylene glycol poisoning is a drunken state. Ethylene glycol is an alcohol, and it affects the brain of a dog or cat much as an alcoholic beverage would. Once ethylene glycol begins to metabolize, however, the second and more deadly stage begins. Ethylene glycol is metabolized in the liver into glycolic acid ($HC_2H_3O_3$), which enters the bloodstream. If the original quantities of consumed antifreeze are significant, the glycolic acid overwhelms the blood's natural buffering system, causing blood pH to drop to dangerously low levels. At this point, the cat or dog may begin hyperventilating in an effort to overcome the acidic blood's reduced ability to carry oxygen. If no treatment is administered, the animal will eventually go into a coma and die.

One treatment for ethylene glycol poisoning is the administration of ethyl alcohol (the alcohol found in alcoholic beverages). The liver enzyme that metabolizes ethylene glycol is the same one that metabolizes ethyl alcohol, but it has a higher affinity for ethyl alcohol than for ethylene glycol. Consequently, the enzyme preferentially metabolizes ethyl alcohol, allowing the unmetabolized ethylene glycol to escape through the urine. If administered early, this treatment can save the life of a dog or cat that has consumed ethylene glycol.

B14.3 CAN YOU ANSWER THIS? *One of the main buffering systems found in blood consists of carbonic acid (H_2CO_3) and bicarbonate ion (HCO_3^-). Write an equation showing how this buffering system could neutralize glycolic acid ($HC_2H_3O_3$) that might enter the blood from ethylene glycol poisoning. Suppose a cat has 0.15 mol of HCO_3^- and 0.15 mol of H_2CO_3 in its bloodstream. How many grams of $HC_2H_3O_3$ could be neutralized before the buffering system in the cat's blood is overwhelmed?*

CHAPTER IN REVIEW

Self-Assessment Quiz

Q1. Which substance is most likely to have a bitter taste?

(a) $HCl(aq)$ **(b)** $NaCl(aq)$

(c) $NaOH(aq)$ **(d)** None of the above

Q2. Identify the Brønsted–Lowry base in the reaction.

$$HClO_2(aq) + H_2O(aq) \rightleftharpoons H_3O^+(aq) + ClO_2^-(aq)$$

(a) $HClO_2$ **(b)** H_2O

(c) H_3O^+ **(d)** ClO_2^-

Q3. What is the conjugate base of the acid $HClO_4$?

(a) HCl

(b) HO_3^+

(c) ClO_3^-

(d) ClO_4^-

Q4. What are the products of the reaction between HBr(*aq*) and KOH(*aq*)?

(a) HK(*aq*) and BrOH(*aq*)

(b) H_2(*g*) and KBr(*aq*)

(c) H_2O(*l*) and KBr(*aq*)

(d) H_2O(*l*) and BrOH(*aq*)

Q5. What are the products of the reaction between HCl and Sn?

(a) $SnCl_2$(*aq*) and H_2(*g*)

(b) SnH(*aq*) and Cl_2(*g*)

(c) H_2O(*l*) and SnCl(*aq*)

(d) H_2(*g*), Cl_2(*g*) and Sn(*s*)

Q6. A 25.00-mL sample of an HNO_3 solution is titrated with 0.102 M NaOH. The titration requires 28.52 mL to reach the equivalence point. What is the concentration of the HNO_3 solution?

(a) 0.116 M

(b) 8.89 M

(c) 0.0894 M

(d) 0.102 M

Q7. In which solution is $[H_3O^+]$ less than 0.100 M?

(a) 0.100 M H_2SO_4(*aq*)

(b) 0.100 M $HCHO_2$(*aq*)

(c) 0.100 M $HClO_4$(*aq*)

(d) None of the above (all have $[H_3O^+]$ less than 0.100 M.)

Q8. In which solution is $[OH^-]$ equal to 0.100 M?

(a) 0.100 M NH_3(*aq*)

(b) 0.100 M $Ba(OH)_2$(*aq*)

(c) 0.100 M NaOH(*aq*)

(d) All of the above (all have $[OH^-]$ equal to 0.100 M).

Q9. What is $[H_3O^+]$ in a solution with $[OH^-] = 2.5 \times 10^{-4}$ M?

(a) 2.5×10^{10} M

(b) 4.0×10^{-11} M

(c) 1.0×10^{-7} M

(d) 1.0×10^{-14} M

Q10. What is the pH of a solution with $[H_3O^+] = 2.8 \times 10^{-5}$ M?

(a) −4.55

(b) 4.55

(c) 10.48

(d) 1.00

Q11. What is $[OH^-]$ in a solution with a pH of 9.55?

(a) 2.82×10^{-10} M

(b) 4.45 M

(c) 2.82×10^4 M

(d) 3.55×10^{-5} M

Q12. A buffer contains $HCHO_2$(*aq*) and $KCHO_2$(*aq*). Which statement correctly summarizes the action of this buffer?

(a) $HCHO_2$(*aq*) neutralizes added acid, and $KCHO_2$(*aq*) neutralizes added base.

(b) Both $HCHO_2$(*aq*) and $KCHO_2$(*aq*) neutralize added acid.

(c) Both $HCHO_2$(*aq*) and $KCHO_2$(*aq*) neutralize added base.

(d) $HCHO_2$(*aq*) neutralizes added base, and $KCHO_2$(*aq*) neutralizes added acid.

Answers: 1:c, 2:b, 3:d, 4:c, 5:a, 6:a, 7:b, 8:c, 9:b, 10:b, 11:d, 12:d

Chemical Principles

Acid Properties:

• Acids have a sour taste.

• Acids dissolve many metals.

• Acids turn blue litmus paper red.

Base Properties:

• Bases have a bitter taste.

• Bases have a slippery feel.

• Bases turn red litmus paper blue.

Relevance

Acid Properties: Acids are responsible for the sour taste in foods such as lemons, limes, and vinegar. Acids are also frequently used in the laboratory and in industry.

Base Properties: Bases are less common in foods, but their presence in some foods—such as coffee and beer—is enjoyed by many as an acquired taste. Bases are also frequently used in the laboratory and in industry.

Molecular Definitions of Acids and Bases: Arrhenius definition

Acid—substance that produces H^+ ions in solution

Base—substance that produces OH^- ions in solution

Brønsted–Lowry definition

Acid—proton donor

Base—proton acceptor

Molecular Definitions of Acids and Bases: The Arrhenius definition is simpler and easier to use. It also shows how an acid and a base neutralize each other to form water ($H^+ + OH^- \longrightarrow H_2O$). The more generally applicable Brønsted–Lowry definition helps us see that, in water, H^+ ions usually associate with water molecules to form H_3O^+. It also shows how bases that do not contain OH^- ions can still act as bases by accepting a proton from water.

Reactions of Acids and Bases: Neutralization Reactions An acid and a base react to form water and a salt.

$$\underset{\text{Acid}}{HCl(aq)} + \underset{\text{Base}}{KOH(aq)} \longrightarrow \underset{\text{Water}}{H_2O(l)} + \underset{\text{Salt}}{KCl(aq)}$$

Acid–Metal Reactions Acids react with many metals to form hydrogen gas and a salt.

$$\underset{\text{Acid}}{2\ HCl(aq)} + \underset{\text{Metal}}{Mg(s)} \longrightarrow \underset{\substack{\text{Hydrogen}\\\text{gas}}}{H_2(g)} + \underset{\text{Salt}}{MgCl_2(aq)}$$

Acid–Metal Oxide Reactions Acids react with many metal oxides to form water and a salt.

$$\underset{\text{Acid}}{2\ HCl(aq)} + \underset{\text{Metal oxide}}{K_2O(s)} \longrightarrow \underset{\text{Water}}{H_2O(l)} + \underset{\text{Salt}}{2\ KCl(aq)}$$

Reactions of Acids and Bases: Neutralization reactions are common in our everyday lives. Antacids, for example, are bases that react with acids from the stomach to alleviate heartburn and sour stomach.

Acid–metal and acid–metal oxide reactions show the corrosive nature of acids. In both of these reactions, the acid dissolves the metal or the metal oxide. Some of the effects of these kinds of reactions can be seen in the damage to building materials caused by acid rain. Acids dissolve metals and metal oxides, so building materials composed of these substances are susceptible to acid rain.

Acid–Base Titration: In an acid–base titration, we add an acid (or base) of known concentration to a base (or acid) of unknown concentration. We combine the two reactants until they are in exact stoichiometric proportions (moles of H^+ = moles of OH^-), which marks the equivalence point of the titration. In titration, since we know the moles of H^+ (or OH^-) that we added, we can determine the moles of OH^- (or H^+) in the unknown solution.

Acid–Base Titration: An acid–base titration is a laboratory procedure often used to determine the unknown concentration of an acid or a base.

Strong and Weak Acids and Bases: Strong acids completely ionize, and strong bases completely dissociate in aqueous solutions. For example:

$$HCl(aq) + H_2O(l) \longrightarrow H_3O^+(aq) + Cl^-(aq)$$
$$NaOH(aq) \longrightarrow Na^+(aq) + OH^-(aq)$$

A 1 M HCl solution has $[H_3O^+]$ = 1 M and a 1 M NaOH solution has $[OH^-]$ = 1 M.

Weak acids only partially ionize in solution. Most weak bases partially ionize water in solution. For example:

$$HF(aq) + H_2O(l) \rightleftharpoons H_3O^+(aq) + F^-(aq)$$
$$NH_3(aq) + H_2O(l) \rightleftharpoons NH_4^+(aq) + OH^-(aq)$$

A 1 M HF solution has $[H_3O^+]$ < 1 M, and a 1 M NH_3 solution has $[OH^-]$ < 1 M.

Strong and Weak Acids and Bases: Whether an acid is strong or weak depends on the conjugate base: The stronger the conjugate base, the weaker the acid. Since the acidity or basicity of a solution depends on $[H_3O^+]$ and $[OH^-]$, we must know whether an acid is strong or weak to know the degree of acidity or basicity.

Self-Ionization of Water: Water can act as both an acid and a base with itself.

$$\underset{\text{Acid}}{H_2O(l)} + \underset{\text{Base}}{H_2O(l)} \rightleftharpoons H_3O^+(aq) + OH^-(aq)$$

The product of $[H_3O^+]$ and $[OH^-]$ in aqueous solutions is always equal to the ion product constant, $K_w(10^{-14})$.

$$[H_3O^+][OH^-] = K_w = 1.0 \times 10^{-14}$$

Self-Ionization of Water: The self-ionization of water occurs because aqueous solutions always contain some H_3O^+ and some OH^-. In a neutral solution, the concentrations of these are equal (1.0×10^{-7} M). When an acid is added to water, $[H_3O^+]$ increases and $[OH^-]$ decreases. When a base is added to water, the opposite happens. The ion product constant, however, still equals 1.0×10^{-14}, allowing us to calculate $[H_3O^+]$ given $[OH^-]$ and vice versa.

pH and pOH Scales:

$$pH = -\log[H_3O^+]$$
$$pH > 7 \text{ (basic)}$$
$$pH < 7 \text{ (acidic)}$$
$$pH = 7 \text{ (neutral)}$$
$$pOH = -\log[OH^-]$$

pH and pOH Scales: pH is a convenient way to specify acidity or basicity. Since the pH scale is logarithmic, a change of one on the pH scale corresponds to a tenfold change in the $[H_3O^+]$. The pOH scale, defined with respect to $[OH^-]$ instead of $[H_3O^+]$, is less commonly used.

Buffers: Buffers are solutions containing significant amounts of both a weak acid and its conjugate base. Buffers resist pH change by neutralizing added acid or base.

Buffers: Buffers are important in blood chemistry because blood must stay within a narrow pH range in order to carry oxygen.

Chemical Skills

Examples

LO: Identify Brønsted–Lowry acids and bases and their conjugates (Section 14.4).

The substance that donates the proton is the acid (proton donor) and becomes the conjugate base (as a product). The substance that accepts the proton (proton acceptor) is the base and becomes the conjugate acid (as a product).

EXAMPLE 14.11 IDENTIFYING BRØNSTED–LOWRY ACIDS AND BASES AND THEIR CONJUGATES

Identify the Brønsted–Lowry acid, the Brønsted–Lowry base, the conjugate acid, and the conjugate base in this reaction:

$$HNO_3(aq) + H_2O(l) \longrightarrow H_3O^+(aq) + NO_3^-(aq)$$

SOLUTION

$$\underset{\text{Acid}}{HNO_3(aq)} + \underset{\text{Base}}{H_2O(l)} \longrightarrow \underset{\text{Conjugate acid}}{H_3O^+(aq)} + \underset{\text{Conjugate base}}{NO_3^-(aq)}$$

LO: Write equations for neutralization reactions (Section 14.5).

In a neutralization reaction, an acid and a base usually react to form water and a salt (ionic compound).

$$\text{Acid + Base} \longrightarrow \text{Water + Salt}$$

Write the skeletal equation first, making sure to write the formula of the salt so that it is charge-neutral. Then balance the equation.

EXAMPLE 14.12 WRITING EQUATIONS FOR NEUTRALIZATION REACTIONS

Write a molecular equation for the reaction between aqueous HBr and aqueous $Ca(OH)_2$.

SOLUTION
Skeletal equation:

$$HBr(aq) + Ca(OH)_2(aq) \longrightarrow H_2O(l) + CaBr_2(aq)$$

Balanced equation:

$$2\,HBr(aq) + Ca(OH)_2(aq) \longrightarrow 2\,H_2O(l) + CaBr_2(aq)$$

LO: Write equations for the reactions of acids with metals and with metal oxides (Section 14.5).

Acids react with many metals to form hydrogen gas and a salt.

$$\text{Acid + Metal} \longrightarrow \text{Hydrogen gas + Salt}$$

Write the skeletal equation first, making sure to write the formula of the salt so that it is charge-neutral. Then balance the equation.

EXAMPLE 14.13 WRITING EQUATIONS FOR THE REACTIONS OF ACIDS WITH METALS AND WITH METAL OXIDES

Write equations for the reaction of hydrobromic acid with calcium metal and for the reaction of hydrobromic acid with calcium oxide.

SOLUTION
Skeletal equation:

$$HBr(aq) + Ca(s) \longrightarrow H_2(g) + CaBr_2(aq)$$

Balanced equation:

$$2\,HBr(aq) + Ca(s) \longrightarrow H_2(g) + CaBr_2(aq)$$

Acids react with many metal oxides to form water and a salt.

Acid + Metal oxide ⟶ Water + Salt

Write the skeletal equation first, making sure to write the formula of the salt so that it is charge-neutral. Then balance the equation.

Skeletal equation:

$$HBr(aq) + CaO(s) \longrightarrow H_2O(l) + CaBr_2(aq)$$

Balanced equation:

$$2\ HBr(aq) + CaO(s) \longrightarrow H_2O(l) + CaBr_2(aq)$$

LO: Use acid–base titration to determine the concentration of an unknown solution (Section 14.6).

EXAMPLE 14.14 ACID–BASE TITRATIONS

A 15.00-mL sample of a NaOH solution of unknown concentration requires 17.88 mL of a 0.1053 M H_2SO_4 solution to reach the equivalence point in a titration. What is the concentration of the NaOH solution?

SORT
You are given the volume of a sodium hydroxide solution and the volume and concentration of the sulfuric acid solution required for its titration. You are asked to find the concentration of the sodium hydroxide solution.

GIVEN: 15.00-mL NaOH
17.88 mL of a 0.1053 M H_2SO_4 solution

FIND: concentration of NaOH solution mol/L

STRATEGIZE
Begin by writing the balanced equation for the neutralization reaction (see Example 14.12).

Next draw a solution map. Use the volume and concentration of the known reactant to determine moles of the known reactant. (You have to convert from milliliters to liters first.) Then use the stoichiometric ratio from the balanced equation to get moles of the unknown reactant.

Then add a second part to the solution map indicating how to use moles and volume to determine molarity.

SOLUTION MAP

$$H_2SO_4(aq) + 2NaOH(aq) \longrightarrow 2\ H_2O(l) + Na_2SO_4(aq)$$

mL H_2SO_4	L H_2SO_4	mol H_2SO_4	mol NaOH

$$\frac{1\ L}{1000\ mL} \qquad \frac{0.1053\ mol\ H_2SO_4}{1\ L\ H_2SO_4} \qquad \frac{2\ mol\ NaOH}{1\ mol\ H_2SO_4}$$

mol NaOH, volume NaOH solution	molarity

$$M = \frac{mol}{L}$$

RELATIONSHIPS USED

2 mol NaOH:1 mol H_2SO_4 (from balanced equation)

$$Molarity(M) = \frac{mol\ solute}{L\ solution}$$

SOLVE
Follow the solution map to solve the problem. The first part of the solution gives you moles of the unknown reactant. In the second part of the solution, divide the moles from the first part by the volume to obtain molarity.

SOLUTION

$$17.88\ mL\ H_2SO_4 \times \frac{1\ L}{1000\ mL} \times \frac{0.1053\ mol\ H_2SO_4}{L\ H_2SO_4}$$

$$\times \frac{2\ mol\ NaOH}{1\ mol\ H_2SO_4} = 3.7655 \times 10^{-3}\ mol\ NaOH$$

$$M = \frac{mol}{L} = \frac{3.7655 \times 10^{-3}\ mol\ NaOH}{0.01500\ L\ NaOH} = 0.2510\ M$$

CHECK
Check your answer. Are the units correct? Does the answer make physical sense?

The unknown NaOH solution has a concentration of 0.2510 M.
The units (M) are correct. The magnitude of the answer makes sense because the reaction has a two-to-one stoichiometry and the volumes of the two solutions are similar; therefore, the concentration of the NaOH solution must be approximately twice the concentration of the H_2SO_4 solution.

LO: Determine [H_3O^+] in acid solutions (Section 14.7).

In a strong acid, [H_3O^+] is equal to the concentration of the acid. In a weak acid, [H_3O^+] is less than the concentration of the acid.

EXAMPLE 14.15   DETERMINING [H_3O^+] IN ACID SOLUTIONS

What is the H_3O^+ concentration in a 0.25 M HCl solution and in a 0.25 M HF solution?

SOLUTION
In the 0.25 M HCl solution (strong acid), [H_3O^+] = 0.25 M.
In the 0.25 M HF solution (weak acid), [H_3O^+] < 0.25 M.

LO: Determine [OH^-] in base solutions (Section 14.7).

In a strong base, [OH^-] is equal to the concentration of the base times the number of hydroxide ions in the base. In a weak base, [OH^-] is less than the concentration of the base.

EXAMPLE 14.16   DETERMINING [OH^-] IN BASE SOLUTIONS

What is the OH^- concentration in a 0.25 M NaOH solution, in a 0.25 M $Sr(OH)_2$ solution, and in a 0.25 M NH_3 solution?

SOLUTION
In the 0.25 M NaOH solution (strong base), [OH^-] = 0.25 M. In the 0.25 M $Sr(OH)_2$ solution (strong base), [OH^-] = 0.50 M. In the 0.25 M NH_3 solution (weak base), [OH^-] < 0.25 M.

LO: Calculate [H_3O^+] or [OH^-] from K_w (Section 14.8).

To find [H_3O^+] or [OH^-], use the ion product constant expression.

$$[H_3O^+][OH^-] = 1.0 \times 10^{-14}$$

Substitute the known quantity into the equation ([H_3O^+] or [OH^-]) and solve for the unknown quantity.

EXAMPLE 14.17   FINDING [H_3O^+] OR [OH^-] FROM K_w

Calculate [OH^-] in a solution with
$$[H_3O^+] = 1.5 \times 10^{-4} \text{ M.}$$

SOLUTION
$$[H_3O^+][OH^-] = 1.0 \times 10^{-14}$$
$$[1.5 \times 10^{-4}][OH^-] = 1.0 \times 10^{-14}$$
$$[OH^-] = \frac{1.0 \times 10^{-14}}{1.5 \times 10^{-4}} = 6.7 \times 10^{-11} \text{ M}$$

LO: Calculate pH from [H_3O^+] (Section 14.9).

To calculate the pH of a solution from [H_3O^+], take the negative log of [H_3O^+].

$$pH = -\log[H_3O^+]$$

EXAMPLE 14.18   CALCULATING pH FROM [H_3O^+]

Calculate the pH of a solution with [H_3O^+] = 2.4 × 10^{-5} M.

SOLUTION
$$pH = -\log[H_3O^+]$$
$$= -\log(2.4 \times 10^{-5})$$
$$= -(-4.62)$$
$$= 4.62$$

LO: Calculate [H_3O^+] from pH (Section 14.9).

Calculate [H_3O^+] from pH by taking the inverse log of the negative of the pH value (Method 1):

$$[H_3O^+] = \text{invlog}(-pH)$$

EXAMPLE 14.19   CALCULATING [H_3O^+] FROM pH

Calculate [H_3O^+] for a solution with a pH of 6.22.

SOLUTION
Method 1: Inverse Log Function
$$[H_3O^+] = \text{invlog}(-pH)$$
$$= \text{invlog}(-6.22)$$
$$= 6.0 \times 10^{-7}$$

You can also calculate $[H_3O^+]$ from pH by raising 10 to the negative of the pH (Method 2):

$$[H_3O^+] = 10^{-pH}$$

KEY TERMS

acid [14.2]	Brønsted–Lowry base [14.4]	hydronium ion [14.4]	pOH [14.9]
acidic solution [14.8]	Brønsted–Lowry definition	indicator [14.6]	salt [14.5]
alkaloid [14.3]	[14.4]	ion product constant for water	strong acid [14.7]
amphoteric [14.4]	buffer [14.10]	(K_w) [14.8]	strong base [14.7]
Arrhenius acid [14.4]	carboxylic acid [14.2]	ionize [14.4]	strong electrolyte [14.7]
Arrhenius base [14.4]	conjugate acid–base pair	logarithmic scale [14.9]	titration [14.6]
Arrhenius definition [14.4]	[14.4]	monoprotic acid [14.7]	weak acid [14.7]
base [14.3]	diprotic acid [14.7]	neutral solution [14.8]	weak base [14.7]
basic solution [14.8]	dissociation [14.4]	neutralization [14.5]	weak electrolyte [14.7]
Brønsted–Lowry acid [14.4]	equivalence point [14.6]	pH [14.9]	

EXERCISES

QUESTIONS

1. What makes tart gummy candies, such as Sour Patch Kids, sour?
2. What are the properties of acids? List some foods that contain acids.
3. What is the main component of stomach acid? Why do we have stomach acid?
4. What are organic acids? List two examples of organic acids.
5. What are the properties of bases? Provide some examples of common substances that contain bases.
6. What are alkaloids?
7. Restate the Arrhenius definition of an acid and demonstrate the definition with a chemical equation.
8. Restate the Arrhenius definition of a base and demonstrate the definition with a chemical equation.
9. Restate the Brønsted–Lowry definitions of acids and bases and demonstrate the definitions with a chemical equation.
10. According to the Brønsted–Lowry definition of acids and bases, what is a conjugate acid–base pair? Provide an example.
11. What is an acid–base neutralization reaction? Provide an example.
12. Provide an example of a reaction between an acid and a metal.
13. List an example of a reaction between an acid and a metal oxide.
14. Name a metal that a base can dissolves and write an equation for the reaction.

15. What is a titration? What is the equivalence point?
16. If a solution contains 0.85 mol of OH^-, how many moles of H^+ are required to reach the equivalence point in a titration?
17. What is the difference between a strong acid and a weak acid?
18. How is the strength of an acid related to the strength of its conjugate base?
19. What are monoprotic and diprotic acids?
20. What is the difference between a strong base and a weak base?
21. Does pure water contain any H_3O^+ ions? Explain your answer.
22. What happens to $[OH^-]$ in an aqueous solution when $[H_3O^+]$ increases?
23. Give a possible value of $[OH^-]$ and $[H_3O^+]$ in a solution that is:
    (a) acidic   (b) basic   (c) neutral
24. How is pH defined? A change of 1.0 pH unit corresponds to how much of a change in $[H_3O^+]$?
25. How is pOH defined? A change of 2.0 pOH units corresponds to how much of a change in $[OH^-]$?
26. In any aqueous solution at 25 °C, the sum of pH and pOH is 14.0. Explain why this is so.
27. What is a buffer?
28. What are the main components in a buffer?

PROBLEMS

ACID AND BASE DEFINITIONS

29. Identify each substance as an acid or a base and write a chemical equation showing how it is an acid or a base according to the Arrhenius definition.
    (a) $H_2SO_4(aq)$
    (b) $Sr(OH)_2(aq)$
    (c) $HBr(aq)$
    (d) $NaOH(aq)$

30. Identify each substance as an acid or a base and write a chemical equation showing how it is an acid or a base according to the Arrhenius definition.
    (a) $Ca(OH)_2(aq)$
    (b) $HC_2H_3O_2(aq)$
    (c) $KOH(aq)$
    (d) $HNO_3(aq)$

31. For each reaction, identify the Brønsted–Lowry acid, the Brønsted–Lowry base, the conjugate acid, and the conjugate base.
(a) $HBr(aq) + H_2O(l) \longrightarrow H_3O^+(aq) + Br^-(aq)$
(b) $NH_3(aq) + H_2O(l) \rightleftharpoons NH_4^+(aq) + OH^-(aq)$
(c) $HNO_3(aq) + H_2O(l) \longrightarrow H_3O^+(aq) + NO_3^-(aq)$
(d) $C_2H_5N(aq) + H_2O(l) \rightleftharpoons C_2H_5NH^+(aq) + OH^-(aq)$

32. For each reaction, identify the Brønsted–Lowry acid, the Brønsted–Lowry base, the conjugate acid, and the conjugate base.
(a) $HI(aq) + H_2O(l) \longrightarrow H_3O^+(aq) + I^-(aq)$
(b) $CH_3NH_2(aq) + H_2O(l) \rightleftharpoons CH_3NH_3^+(aq) + OH^-(aq)$
(c) $CO_3^{2-}(aq) + H_2O(l) \rightleftharpoons HCO_3^-(aq) + OH^-(aq)$
(d) $H_2CO_3(aq) + H_2O(l) \rightleftharpoons H_3O^+(aq) + HCO_3^-(aq)$

33. Determine whether each pair is a conjugate acid–base pair.
(a) NH_3, NH_4^+
(b) HCl, HBr
(c) $C_2H_3O_2^-$, $HC_2H_3O_2$
(d) HCO_3^-, NO_3^-

34. Determine whether each pair is a conjugate acid–base pair.
(a) HI, I^-
(b) $HCHO_2$, SO_4^{2-}
(c) PO_4^{3-}, HPO_4^{2-}
(d) CO_3^{2-}, HCl

35. Write the formula for the conjugate base of each acid.
(a) HCl
(b) H_2SO_3
(c) $HCHO_2$
(d) HF

36. Write the formula for the conjugate base of each acid.
(a) HBr
(b) H_2CO_3
(c) $HClO_4$
(d) $HC_2H_3O_2$

37. Write the formula for the conjugate acid of each base.
(a) NH_3
(b) ClO_4^-
(c) HSO_4^-
(d) CO_3^{2-}

38. Write the formula for the conjugate acid of each base.
(a) CH_3NH_2
(b) C_5H_5N
(c) Cl^-
(d) F^-

ACID–BASE REACTIONS

39. Write a neutralization reaction for each acid and base pair.
(a) $HI(aq)$ and $NaOH(aq)$
(b) $HBr(aq)$ and $KOH(aq)$
(c) $HNO_3(aq)$ and $Ba(OH)_2(aq)$
(d) $HClO_4(aq)$ and $Sr(OH)_2(aq)$

40. Write a neutralization reaction for each acid and base pair.
(a) $HF(aq)$ and $Ba(OH)_2(aq)$
(b) $HClO_4(aq)$ and $NaOH(aq)$
(c) $HBr(aq)$ and $Ca(OH)_2(aq)$
(d) $HCl(aq)$ and $KOH(aq)$

41. Write a balanced chemical equation showing how each metal reacts with HBr.
(a) Rb
(b) Mg
(c) Ba
(d) Al

42. Write a balanced chemical equation showing how each metal reacts with HCl.
(a) K
(b) Ca
(c) Na
(d) Sr

43. Write a balanced chemical equation showing how each metal oxide reacts with HI.
(a) MgO
(b) K_2O
(c) Rb_2O
(d) CaO

44. Write a balanced chemical equation showing how each metal oxide reacts with HCl.
(a) SrO
(b) Na_2O
(c) Li_2O
(d) BaO

45. Predict the products of each reaction.
(a) $HClO_4(aq) + Fe_2O_3(s) \longrightarrow$
(b) $H_2SO_4(aq) + Sr(s) \longrightarrow$
(c) $H_3PO_4(aq) + KOH(aq) \longrightarrow$

46. Predict the products of each reaction.
(a) $HI(aq) + Al(s) \longrightarrow$
(b) $H_2SO_4(aq) + TiO_2(s) \longrightarrow$
(c) $H_2CO_3(aq) + LiOH(aq) \longrightarrow$

ACID–BASE TITRATIONS

47. Four solutions of unknown HCl concentration are titrated with solutions of NaOH. The following table lists the volume of each unknown HCl solution, the volume of NaOH solution required to reach the equivalence point, and the concentration of each NaOH solution. Calculate the concentration (in M) of the unknown HCl solution in each case.

HCl Volume (mL)	NaOH Volume (mL)	[NaOH] (M)
(a) 25.00 mL	28.44 mL	0.1231 M
(b) 15.00 mL	21.22 mL	0.0972 M
(c) 20.00 mL	14.88 mL	0.1178 M
(d) 5.00 mL	6.88 mL	0.1325 M

48. Four solutions of unknown NaOH concentration are titrated with solutions of HCl. The following table lists the volume of each unknown NaOH solution, the volume of HCl solution required to reach the equivalence point, and the concentration of each HCl solution. Calculate the concentration (in M) of the unknown NaOH solution in each case.

NaOH Volume (mL)	HCl Volume (mL)	[HCl] (M)
(a) 5.00 mL	9.77 mL	0.1599 M
(b) 15.00 mL	11.34 mL	0.1311 M
(c) 10.00 mL	10.55 mL	0.0889 M
(d) 30.00 mL	36.18 mL	0.1021 M

49. A 25.00-mL sample of an H_2SO_4 solution of unknown concentration is titrated with a 0.1322 M KOH solution. A volume of 41.22 mL of KOH is required to reach the equivalence point. What is the concentration of the unknown H_2SO_4 solution?

50. A 5.00-mL sample of an H_3PO_4 solution of unknown concentration is titrated with a 0.1090 M NaOH solution. A volume of 7.12 mL of the NaOH solution is required to reach the equivalence point. What is the concentration of the unknown H_3PO_4 solution?

51. What volume in milliliters of a 0.121 M sodium hydroxide solution is required to reach the equivalence point in the complete titration of a 10.0-mL sample of 0.102 M sulfuric acid?

52. What volume in milliliters of 0.0985 M sodium hydroxide solution is required to reach the equivalence point in the complete titration of a 15.0-mL sample of 0.124 M phosphoric acid?

STRONG AND WEAK ACIDS AND BASES

53. Classify each acid as strong or weak.
(a) HCl
(b) HF
(c) HBr
(d) H_2SO_3

54. Classify each acid as strong or weak.
(a) $HCHO_2$
(b) H_2SO_4
(c) HNO_3
(d) H_2CO_3

55. Determine $[H_3O^+]$ in each acid solution. If the acid is weak, indicate the value that $[H_3O^+]$ is less than.
(a) 1.7 M HBr
(b) 1.5 M HNO_3
(c) 0.38 M H_2CO_3
(d) 1.75 M $HCHO_2$

56. Determine $[H_3O^+]$ in each acid solution. If the acid is weak, indicate the value that $[H_3O^+]$ is less than.
(a) 0.125 M $HClO_2$
(b) 1.25 M H_3PO_4
(c) 2.77 M HCl
(d) 0.95 M H_2SO_3

57. Classify each base as strong or weak.
(a) LiOH
(b) NH_4OH
(c) $Ca(OH)_2$
(d) NH_3

58. Classify each base as strong or weak.
(a) C_5H_5N
(b) NaOH·
(c) $Ba(OH)_2$
(d) KOH

59. Determine $[OH^-]$ in each base solution. If the acid is weak, indicate the value that $[OH^-]$ is less than.
(a) 0.25 M NaOH
(b) 0.25 M NH_3
(c) 0.25 M $Sr(OH)_2$
(d) 1.25 M KOH

60. Determine $[OH^-]$ in each base solution. If the acid is weak, indicate the value that $[OH^-]$ is less than.
(a) 2.5 M KOH
(b) 1.95 M NH_3
(c) 0.225 M $Ba(OH)_2$
(d) 1.8 M C_5H_5N

ACIDITY, BASICITY, AND K_W

61. Determine if each solution is acidic, basic, or neutral.
   (a) $[H_3O^+] = 1 \times 10^{-5}$ M; $[OH^-] = 1 \times 10^{-9}$ M
   (b) $[H_3O^+] = 1 \times 10^{-6}$ M; $[OH^-] = 1 \times 10^{-8}$ M
   (c) $[H_3O^+] = 1 \times 10^{-7}$ M; $[OH^-] = 1 \times 10^{-7}$ M
   (d) $[H_3O^+] = 1 \times 10^{-8}$ M; $[OH^-] = 1 \times 10^{-6}$ M

62. Determine if each solution is acidic, basic, or neutral.
   (a) $[H_3O^+] = 1 \times 10^{-9}$ M; $[OH^-] = 1 \times 10^{-5}$ M
   (b) $[H_3O^+] = 1 \times 10^{-10}$ M; $[OH^-] = 1 \times 10^{-4}$ M
   (c) $[H_3O^+] = 1 \times 10^{-2}$ M; $[OH^-] = 1 \times 10^{-12}$ M
   (d) $[H_3O^+] = 1 \times 10^{-13}$ M; $[OH^-] = 1 \times 10^{-1}$ M

63. Calculate $[OH^-]$ given $[H_3O^+]$ in each aqueous solution and classify the solution as acidic or basic.
   (a) $[H_3O^+] = 1.5 \times 10^{-9}$ M
   (b) $[H_3O^+] = 9.3 \times 10^{-9}$ M
   (c) $[H_3O^+] = 2.2 \times 10^{-6}$ M
   (d) $[H_3O^+] = 7.4 \times 10^{-4}$ M

64. Calculate $[OH^-]$ given $[H_3O^+]$ in each aqueous solution and classify the solution as acidic or basic.
   (a) $[H_3O^+] = 1.3 \times 10^{-3}$ M
   (b) $[H_3O^+] = 9.1 \times 10^{-12}$ M
   (c) $[H_3O^+] = 5.2 \times 10^{-4}$ M
   (d) $[H_3O^+] = 6.1 \times 10^{-9}$ M

65. Calculate $[H_3O^+]$ given $[OH^-]$ in each aqueous solution and classify each solution as acidic or basic.
   (a) $[OH^-] = 2.7 \times 10^{-12}$ M
   (b) $[OH^-] = 2.5 \times 10^{-2}$ M
   (c) $[OH^-] = 1.1 \times 10^{-10}$ M
   (d) $[OH^-] = 3.3 \times 10^{-4}$ M

66. Calculate $[H_3O^+]$ given $[OH^-]$ in each aqueous solution and classify each solution as acidic or basic.
   (a) $[OH^-] = 2.1 \times 10^{-11}$ M
   (b) $[OH^-] = 7.5 \times 10^{-9}$ M
   (c) $[OH^-] = 2.1 \times 10^{-4}$ M
   (d) $[OH^-] = 1.0 \times 10^{-2}$ M

pH

67. Classify each solution as acidic, basic, or neutral according to its pH value.
   (a) pH = 8.0
   (b) pH = 7.0
   (c) pH = 3.5
   (d) pH = 6.1

68. Classify each solution as acidic, basic, or neutral according to its pH value.
   (a) pH = 4.0
   (b) pH = 3.5
   (c) pH = 13.0
   (d) pH = 0.85

69. Calculate the pH of each solution.
   (a) $[H_3O^+] = 1.7 \times 10^{-8}$ M
   (b) $[H_3O^+] = 1.0 \times 10^{-7}$ M
   (c) $[H_3O^+] = 2.2 \times 10^{-6}$ M
   (d) $[H_3O^+] = 7.4 \times 10^{-4}$ M

70. Calculate the pH of each solution.
   (a) $[H_3O^+] = 2.4 \times 10^{-10}$ M
   (b) $[H_3O^+] = 7.6 \times 10^{-2}$ M
   (c) $[H_3O^+] = 9.2 \times 10^{-13}$ M
   (d) $[H_3O^+] = 3.4 \times 10^{-5}$ M

71. Calculate $[H_3O^+]$ for each solution.
   (a) pH = 8.55
   (b) pH = 11.23
   (c) pH = 2.87
   (d) pH = 1.22

72. Calculate $[H_3O^+]$ for each solution.
   (a) pH = 1.76
   (b) pH = 3.88
   (c) pH = 8.43
   (d) pH = 12.32

73. Calculate the pH of each solution.
   (a) $[OH^-] = 1.9 \times 10^{-7}$ M
   (b) $[OH^-] = 2.6 \times 10^{-8}$ M
   (c) $[OH^-] = 7.2 \times 10^{-11}$ M
   (d) $[OH^-] = 9.5 \times 10^{-2}$ M

74. Calculate the pH of each solution.
   (a) $[OH^-] = 2.8 \times 10^{-11}$ M
   (b) $[OH^-] = 9.6 \times 10^{-3}$ M
   (c) $[OH^-] = 3.8 \times 10^{-12}$ M
   (d) $[OH^-] = 6.4 \times 10^{-4}$ M

75. Calculate $[OH^-]$ for each solution.
   (a) pH = 4.25
   (b) pH = 12.53
   (c) pH = 1.50
   (d) pH = 8.25

76. Calculate $[OH^-]$ for each solution.
   (a) pH = 1.82
   (b) pH = 13.28
   (c) pH = 8.29
   (d) pH = 2.32

77. Calculate the pH of each solution:
(a) 0.0155 M HBr
(b) 1.28×10^{-3} M KOH
(c) 1.89×10^{-3} M HNO_3
(d) 1.54×10^{-4} M $Sr(OH)_2$

78. Calculate the pH of each solution:
(a) 1.34×10^{-3} M $HClO_4$
(b) 0.0211 M NaOH
(c) 0.0109 M HBr
(d) 7.02×10^{-5} M $Ba(OH)_2$

pOH

79. Detemine the pOH of each solution and classify it as acidic, basic, or neutral.
(a) $[OH^-] = 1.5 \times 10^{-9}$ M
(b) $[OH^-] = 7.0 \times 10^{-5}$ M
(c) $[OH^-] = 1.0 \times 10^{-7}$ M
(d) $[OH^-] = 8.8 \times 10^{-3}$ M

80. Detemine the pOH of each solution and classify it as acidic, basic, or neutral.
(a) $[OH^-] = 4.5 \times 10^{-2}$ M
(b) $[OH^-] = 3.1 \times 10^{-12}$ M
(c) $[OH^-] = 5.4 \times 10^{-5}$ M
(d) $[OH^-] = 1.2 \times 10^{-2}$ M

81. Determine the pOH of each solution.
(a) $[H_3O^+] = 1.2 \times 10^{-8}$ M
(b) $[H_3O^+] = 5.5 \times 10^{-2}$ M
(c) $[H_3O^+] = 3.9 \times 10^{-9}$ M
(d) $[H_3O^+] = 1.88 \times 10^{-13}$ M

82. Determine the pOH of each solution.
(a) $[H_3O^+] = 8.3 \times 10^{-10}$ M
(b) $[H_3O^+] = 1.6 \times 10^{-7}$ M
(c) $[H_3O^+] = 7.3 \times 10^{-2}$ M
(d) $[OH^-] = 4.32 \times 10^{-4}$ M

83. Determine the pH of each solution and classify it as acidic, basic, or neutral.
(a) pOH = 8.5
(b) pOH = 4.2
(c) pOH = 1.7
(d) pOH = 7.0

84. Determine the pH of each solution and classify it as acidic, basic, or neutral.
(a) pOH = 12.5
(b) pOH = 5.5
(c) pOH = 0.55
(d) pOH = 7.98

BUFFERS AND ACID RAIN

85. Determine whether or not each mixture is a buffer.
(a) HCl and HF
(b) NaOH and NH_3
(c) HF and NaF
(d) $HC_2H_3O_2$ and $KC_2H_3O_2$

86. Determine whether or not each mixture is a buffer.
(a) HBr and NaCl
(b) $HCHO_2$ and $NaCHO_2$
(c) HCl and HBr
(d) KOH and NH_3

87. Write reactions showing how each of the buffers in Problem 85 would neutralize added HCl.

88. Write reactions showing how each of the buffers in Problem 86 would neutralize added NaOH.

89. What substance could you add to each solution to make it a buffer solution?
(a) 0.100 M $NaC_2H_3O_2$
(b) 0.500 M H_3PO_4
(c) 0.200 M $HCHO_2$

90. What substance could you add to each solution to make it a buffer solution?
(a) 0.050 M $NaHSO_3$
(b) 0.150 M HF
(c) 0.200 M $KCHO_2$

CUMULATIVE PROBLEMS

91. How much 0.100 M HCl is required to completely neutralize 20.0 mL of 0.250 M NaOH?

92. How much 0.200 M KOH is required to completely neutralize 25.0 mL of 0.150 M $HClO_4$?

93. What is the minimum volume of 5.0 M HCl required to completely dissolve 10.0 g of magnesium metal?

94. What is the minimum volume of 3.0 M HBr required to completely dissolve 15.0 g of potassium metal?

95. When 18.5 g of $K_2O(s)$ is completely dissolved by $HI(aq)$, how many grams of $KI(aq)$ form in solution?

96. When 5.88 g of $CaO(s)$ is completely dissolved by $HBr(aq)$, how many grams of $CaBr_2(aq)$ form in solution?

97. A 0.125-g sample of a monoprotic acid of unknown molar mass is dissolved in water and titrated with 0.1003 M NaOH. The equivalence point is reached after adding 20.77 mL of base. What is the molar mass of the unknown acid?

98. A 0.105-g sample of a diprotic acid of unknown molar mass is dissolved in water and titrated with 0.1288 M NaOH. The equivalence point is reached after adding 15.2 mL of base. What is the molar mass of the unknown acid?

99. People take antacids, such as milk of magnesia, to reduce the discomfort of acid stomach or heartburn. The recommended dose of milk of magnesia is 1 teaspoon, which contains 400 mg of $Mg(OH)_2$. What volume of HCl solution with a pH of 1.1 can be neutralized by 1 dose of milk of magnesia? (Assume two significant figures in your calculations.)

100. An antacid tablet requires 25.82 mL of 0.200 M HCl to titrate to its equivalence point. What volume in milliliters of stomach acid can be neutralized by the antacid tablet? Assume that stomach acid has a pH of 1.1. (Assume two significant figures in your calculations.)

101. For each $[H_3O^+]$, determine the pH and state whether the solution is acidic or basic.
(a) $[H_3O^+] = 0.0025$ M
(b) $[H_3O^+] = 1.8 \times 10^{-12}$ M
(c) $[H_3O^+] = 9.6 \times 10^{-9}$ M
(d) $[H_3O^+] = 0.0195$ M

102. For each $[OH^-]$, determine the pH and state whether the solution is acidic or basic.
(a) $[OH^-] = 1.8 \times 10^{-5}$ M
(b) $[OH^-] = 8.9 \times 10^{-12}$ M
(c) $[OH^-] = 3.1 \times 10^{-2}$ M
(d) $[OH^-] = 1.96 \times 10^{-9}$ M

103. Complete the table. (The first row is completed for you.)

$[H_3O^+]$	$[OH^-]$	pOH	pH	Acidic or Basic
1.0×10^{-4}	1.0×10^{-10}	10.00	4.00	acidic
5.5×10^{-3}	___	___	___	___
___	3.2×10^{-6}	___	___	___
4.8×10^{-9}	___	___	___	___
___	___	___	7.55	___

104. Complete the table. (The first row is completed for you.)

$[H_3O^+]$	$[OH^-]$	pOH	pH	Acidic or Basic
1.0×10^{-8}	1.0×10^{-6}	6.00	8.00	basic
___	___	___	3.55	___
1.7×10^{-9}	___	___	___	___
___	___	___	13.5	___
___	8.6×10^{-11}	___	___	___

105. For each strong acid solution, determine $[H_3O^+]$, $[OH^-]$, and pH.
(a) 0.0088 M $HClO_4$
(b) 1.5×10^{-3} M HBr
(c) 9.77×10^{-4} M HI
(d) 0.0878 M HNO_3

106. For each strong acid solution, determine $[H_3O^+]$, $[OH^-]$, and pH.
(a) 0.0150 M HCl
(b) 1.9×10^{-4} M HI
(c) 0.0226 M HBr
(d) 1.7×10^{-3} M HNO_3

107. For each strong base solution, determine $[OH^-]$, $[H_3O^+]$, pH, and pOH.
(a) 0.15 M NaOH
(b) 1.5×10^{-3} M $Ca(OH)_2$
(c) 4.8×10^{-4} M $Sr(OH)_2$
(d) 8.7×10^{-5} M KOH

108. For each strong base solution, determine $[OH^-]$, $[H_3O^+]$, pH, and pOH.
(a) 8.77×10^{-3} M LiOH
(b) 0.0112 M $Ba(OH)_2$
(c) 1.9×10^{-4} M KOH
(d) 5.0×10^{-4} M $Ca(OH)_2$

109. As described in Section 14.1, jailed spies on the big screen have been known to use acid stored in a pen to dissolve jail bars and escape. What minimum volume of 12.0 M hydrochloric acid would be required to completely dissolve a 500.0-g iron bar? Would this amount of acid fit into a pen?

110. A popular classroom demonstration consists of filing notches into a new penny and soaking the penny in hydrochloric acid overnight. Because new pennies are made of zinc coated with copper, and hydrochloric acid dissolves zinc and not copper, the inside of the penny is dissolved by the acid, while the outer copper shell remains. Suppose a penny contains 2.5 g of zinc and is soaked in 20.0 mL of 6.0 M HCl. Calculate the concentration of the HCl solution after all of the zinc has dissolved. *Hint:* The Zn from the penny is oxidized to Zn^{2+}.

111. What is the pH of a solution formed by mixing 125.0 mL of 0.0250 M HCl with 75.0 mL of 0.0500 M NaOH?

112. What is the pH of a solution formed by mixing 175.0 mL of 0.0880 M HI with 125.0 mL of 0.0570 M KOH?

113. How many H^+ (or H_3O^+) ions are present in one drop (0.050 mL) of pure water at 25 °C?

114. Calculate the number of H^+ (or H_3O^+) ions and OH^- ions in 1.0 mL of 0.100 M HCl.

115. A 4.00-L base solution contains 0.100 mol total of NaOH and $Sr(OH)_2$. The pOH of the solution is 1.51. Determine the amounts (in moles) of NaOH and $Sr(OH)_2$ in the solution.

116. A 1.50-L acid solution contains 0.35 g total of HCl and HBr. The pH of the solution is 2.40. What are the masses of HCl and HBr in the solution?

HIGHLIGHT PROBLEMS

117. Based on the molecular view of each acid solution, determine whether the acid is weak or strong.

(a)

(b)

(c)

(d)

118. Lakes that have been acidified by acid rain (see Chemistry in the Environment box in Section 5.9) can be neutralized by liming, the addition of limestone ($CaCO_3$). How much limestone in kilograms is required to completely neutralize a 3.8×10^9 L lake with a pH of 5.5?

119. Acid rain (see Chemistry in the Environment box in Section 5.9) over the Great Lakes has a pH of about 4.5. Calculate the $[H_3O^+]$ of this rain and compare that value to the $[H_3O^+]$ of rain over the West Coast that has a pH of 5.4. How many times more concentrated is the acid in rain over the Great Lakes?

QUESTIONS FOR GROUP WORK

Discuss these questions with the group and record your consensus answer.

120. Choose an example of a reaction featuring a chemical acting as an Arrhenius base. With group members representing atoms or ions, act out the reaction. Now repeat the process for a chemical acting as a Brønstead–Lowry acid. Write a script for a narrator to describe the processes that occur.

121. Divide your group in two. Have each half of your group write a quiz related to an acid–base titration. Make an answer key for your problem. Trade problems with the other half of your group and solve each other's problems.

122. Each group member needs to have the calculator that they will use for homework and exams in this class. For each

member of your group, write out the specific instructions (the order in which you press the buttons) for using his or her calculator to verify the following:
(a) a solution with $[H_3O^+] = 2.8 \times 10^{-4}$ M has a pH of 3.55
(b) a solution with pOH = 6.83 has $[OH^-] = 1.47 \times 10^{-7}$ M

123. With group members acting as atoms or ions, act out the reaction that occurs when HCl is added to a buffer solution composed of $HC_2H_3O_2$ and $NaC_2H_3O_2$. Write a script for a narrator to describe the processes that occur, including how the buffer keeps the pH approximately the same, even though a strong acid is added.

▸Answers to Skillbuilder Exercises

Skillbuilder 14.1

(a) $C_5H_5N(aq) + H_2O(l) \rightleftharpoons C_5H_5NH^+(aq) + OH^-(aq)$
   Base   Acid   Conjugate acid   Conjugate base

(b) $HNO_3(aq) + H_2O(l) \longrightarrow H_3O^+(aq) + NO_3^-(aq)$
   Acid   Base   Conjugate acid   Conjugate base

Skillbuilder 14.2

$H_3PO_4(aq) + 3\,NaOH(aq) \longrightarrow 3\,H_2O(l) + Na_3PO_4(aq)$

Skillbuilder 14.3

(a) $2\,HCl(aq) + Sr(s) \longrightarrow H_2(g) + SrCl_2(aq)$

(b) $2\,HI(aq) + BaO(s) \longrightarrow H_2O(l) + BaI_2(aq)$

Skillbuilder 14.4 9.03×10^{-2} M H_2SO_4

Skillbuilder 14.5

(a) $[H_3O^+] < 0.50$ M

(b) $[H_3O^+] = 1.25$ M

(c) $[H_3O^+] < 0.75$ M

Skillbuilder 14.6

(a) $[OH^-] = 0.11$ M

(b) $[OH^-] < 1.05$ M

(c) $[OH^-] = 0.45$ M

Skillbuilder 14.7

(a) $[H_3O^+] = 6.7 \times 10^{-13}$ M; basic

(b) $[H_3O^+] = 1.0 \times 10^{-7}$ M; neutral

(c) $[H_3O^+] = 1.2 \times 10^{-5}$ M; acidic

Skillbuilder 14.8

(a) pH = 8.02; basic

(b) pH = 2.21; acidic

Skillbuilder Plus, p. 509   pH = 12.11; basic

Skillbuilder 14.9 4.3×10^{-9} M

Skillbuilder Plus, p. 510 4.6×10^{-11} M

Skillbuilder 14.10 5.6×10^{-5} M

Skillbuilder Plus, p. 511 4.8×10^{-9} M

▸Answers to Conceptual Checkpoints

14.1 (a) HCl is an acid. Acids have a sour taste. The other two compounds are bases.

14.2 (b) The conjugate base of an acid always has one fewer proton and is one charge unit lower (more negative) than the acid.

14.3 (c) The acid solution contains 7 H^+ ions; therefore, 7 OH^- ions are required to reach the equivalence point.

14.4 (c) Both **(a)** and **(b)** show complete ionization and are therefore strong acids. Only the acid depicted in **(c)** undergoes partial ionization and is therefore a weak acid.

14.5 (d) Each of the others can accept a proton and thus acts as a base. NH_4^+, however, is the conjugate acid of NH_3 and therefore acts as an acid and not as a base.

14.6 (d) Because pH is the *negative* log of the H_3O^+ concentration, a higher pH corresponds to a lower $[H_3O^+]$, and each unit of pH represents a tenfold change in concentration.

14.7 (d) Since the pH is 5, the pOH = 14 − 5 = 9.

14.8 (b) A buffer solution consists of a weak acid and its conjugate base. Of the compounds listed, HF is the only weak acid, and F^- (from NaF in solution) is its conjugate base.

Appendix: Mathematics Review

Basic Algebra

In chemistry, you often have to solve an equation for a particular variable. For example, suppose you want to solve the following equation for V:

$$PV = nRT$$

To solve an equation for a particular variable, you must isolate that variable on one side of the equation. The rest of the variables or numbers will then be on the other side of the equation. To solve the above equation for V, divide both sides by P.

$$\frac{PV}{P} = \frac{nRT}{P}$$

$$V = \frac{nRT}{P}$$

The Ps cancel, and you are left with an expression for V. For another example, consider solving the following equation for °F:

$$°C = \frac{(°F - 32)}{1.8}$$

First, eliminate the 1.8 in the denominator of the right side by multiplying both sides by 1.8.

$$(1.8) \, °C = \frac{(°F - 32)}{1.8}(1.8)$$

$$(1.8) \, °C = (°F - 32)$$

Then eliminate the -32 on the right by adding 32 to both sides.

$$(1.8) \, °C + 32 = (°F - 32) + 32$$

$$(1.8) \, °C + 32 = °F$$

You are now left with an expression for °F.

In general, solve equations by following these guidelines:

- Cancel numbers or symbols in the denominator (bottom part of a fraction) by multiplying by the number or symbol to be canceled.
- Cancel numbers or symbols in the numerator (upper part of a fraction) by dividing by the number or symbol to be canceled.
- Eliminate numbers or symbols that are added by subtracting the same number or symbol.
- Eliminate numbers or symbols that are subtracted by adding the same number or symbol.
- Whether you add, subtract, multiply, or divide, **always perform the same operation for both sides of a mathematical equation**. (Otherwise, the two sides will no longer be equal.)

For a final example, solve the following equation for x:

$$\frac{67x - y + 3}{6} = 2z$$

Cancel the 6 in the denominator by multiplying both sides by 6.

$$(6) \frac{67x - y + 3}{6} = (6)2z$$

$$67x - y + 3 = 12z$$

Eliminate the +3 by subtracting 3 from both sides.

$$67x - y + 3 - 3 = 12z - 3$$
$$67x - y = 12z - 3$$

Eliminate the $-y$ by adding y to both sides.

$$67x - y + y = 12z - 3 + y$$
$$67x = 12z - 3 + y$$

Cancel the 67 by dividing both sides by 67.

$$\frac{67x}{67} = \frac{12z - 3 + y}{67}$$

$$x = \frac{12z - 3 + y}{67}$$

FOR PRACTICE   **Using Algebra to Solve Equations**

Solve each of the following for the indicated variable:

(a) $P_1V_1 = P_2V_2$; solve for V_2

(b) $\frac{V_1}{T_1} = \frac{V_2}{T_2}$; solve for T_1

(c) $PV = nRT$; solve for n

(d) $K = °C + 273$; solve for °C

(e) $\frac{3x + 7}{2} = y$; solve for x

(f) $\frac{32}{y + 3} = 8$; solve for y

ANSWERS

(a) $V_2 = \frac{P_1V_1}{P_2}$

(b) $T_1 = \frac{V_1T_2}{V_2}$

(c) $n = \frac{PV}{RT}$

(d) $°C = K - 273$

(e) $x = \frac{2y - 7}{3}$

(f) $y = 1$

Mathematical Operations with Scientific Notation

Writing numbers in scientific notation is covered in detail in Section 2.2. Briefly, a number written in scientific notation consists of a **decimal part**, a number that is usually between 1 and 10, and an **exponential part**, 10 raised to an **exponent**, n.

Each of the following numbers is written in both scientific and decimal notation:

$$1.0 \times 10^5 = 100,000 \qquad 1.0 \times 10^{-6} = 0.000001$$

$$6.7 \times 10^3 = 6700 \qquad 6.7 \times 10^{-3} = 0.0067$$

Multiplication and Division

To multiply numbers expressed in scientific notation, multiply the decimal parts and add the exponents.

$$(A \times 10^m)(B \times 10^n) = (A \times B) \times 10^{m+n}$$

To divide numbers expressed in scientific notation, divide the decimal parts and subtract the exponent in the denominator from the exponent in the numerator.

$$\frac{(A \times 10^m)}{(B \times 10^n)} = \left(\frac{A}{B}\right) \times 10^{m-n}$$

Consider the following example involving multiplication:

$$(3.5 \times 10^4)(1.8 \times 10^6) = (3.5 \times 1.8) \times 10^{4+6}$$
$$= 6.3 \times 10^{10}$$

Consider the following example involving division:

$$\frac{(5.6 \times 10^7)}{(1.4 \times 10^3)} = \left(\frac{5.6}{1.4}\right) \times 10^{7-3}$$
$$= 4.0 \times 10^4$$

Addition and Subtraction

To add or subtract numbers expressed in scientific notation, rewrite all the numbers so that they have the same exponent, and then add or subtract the decimal parts of the numbers. The exponents remain unchanged.

$$A \times 10^n$$
$$\pm B \times 10^n$$
$$\underline{(A \pm B) \times 10^n}$$

Notice that the numbers *must have* the same exponent.
Consider the following example involving addition:

$$4.82 \times 10^7$$
$$\underline{+3.4 \times 10^6}$$

First, express both numbers with the same exponent. In this case, rewrite the lower number and perform the addition as follows:

$$4.82 \times 10^7$$
$$\underline{+0.34 \times 10^7}$$
$$5.16 \times 10^7$$

Consider the following example involving subtraction:

$$7.33 \times 10^5$$
$$\underline{-1.9 \times 10^4}$$

First, express both numbers with the same exponent. In this case, rewrite the lower number and perform the subtraction as follows:

$$7.33 \times 10^5$$
$$-0.19 \times 10^5$$
$$\overline{7.14 \times 10^5}$$

FOR PRACTICE   **Mathematical Operations with Scientific Notation**

Perform each of the following operations:

(a) $(2.1 \times 10^7)(9.3 \times 10^5)$

(b) $(5.58 \times 10^{12})\,(7.84 \times 10^{-8})$

(c) $\dfrac{(1.5 \times 10^{14})}{(5.9 \times 10^8)}$

(d) $\dfrac{(2.69 \times 10^7)}{(8.44 \times 10^{11})}$

(e) $\begin{array}{r} 1.823 \times 10^9 \\ +1.11 \times 10^7 \\ \hline \end{array}$

(f) $\begin{array}{r} 3.32 \times 10^{-5} \\ +3.400 \times 10^{-7} \\ \hline \end{array}$

(g) $\begin{array}{r} 6.893 \times 10^9 \\ -2.44 \times 10^8 \\ \hline \end{array}$

(h) $\begin{array}{r} 1.74 \times 10^4 \\ -2.9 \times 10^3 \\ \hline \end{array}$

ANSWERS

(a) 2.0×10^{13}

(b) 4.37×10^5

(c) 2.5×10^5

(d) 3.19×10^{-5}

(e) 1.834×10^9

(f) 3.35×10^{-5}

(g) 6.649×10^9

(h) 1.45×10^4

Logarithms

The logarithm (or log) of a number is the exponent to which 10 must be raised to obtain that number. For example, the log of 100 is 2 because 10 must be raised to the second power to get 100. Similarly, the log of 1000 is 3 because 10 must be raised to the third power to get 1000. The logs of several multiples of 10 are shown as follows:

$$\log 10 = 1$$
$$\log 100 = 2$$
$$\log 1000 = 3$$
$$\log 10{,}000 = 4$$

Because $10^0 = 1$ by definition, $\log 1 = 0$.

The log of a number smaller than 1 is negative because 10 must be raised to a negative exponent to get a number smaller than 1. For example, the log of 0.01 is -2 because 10 must be raised to the power of -2 to get 0.01. Similarly, the log of 0.001 is -3 because 10 must be raised to the power of -3 to get 0.001. The logs of several fractional numbers are as follows:

$$\log 0.1 = -1$$
$$\log 0.01 = -2$$
$$\log 0.001 = -3$$
$$\log 0.0001 = -4$$

The logs of numbers that are not multiples of 10 can be computed on your calculator. See your calculator manual for specific instructions.

Inverse Logarithms

The inverse logarithm or invlog function (sometimes called antilog) is exactly the opposite of the log function. For example, the log of 100 is 2 and the inverse log of 2 is 100. The log function and the invlog function undo one another.

$$\log\ 100 = 3$$
$$\text{invlog } 3 = 1000$$
$$\text{invlog } (\log\ 1000) = 1000$$

The inverse log of a number is simply 10 raised to that number.

$$\text{invlog } x = 10^x$$
$$\text{invlog } 3 = 10^3 = 1000$$

The inverse logs of numbers can be computed on your calculator. See your calculator manual for specific instructions.

FOR PRACTICE **Logarithms and Inverse Logarithms**

Perform each of the following operations:

(a) $\log\ 1.0 \times 10^5$

(b) $\log\ 59$

(c) $\log\ 1.0 \times 10^{-5}$

(d) $\log\ 0.068$

(e) invlog 7.0

(f) invlog 1.44

(g) invlog -6.0

(h) invlog -0.250

(i) invlog (log 88)

ANSWERS

(a) 5.00

(b) 1.77

(c) -5.00

(d) -1.17

(e) 1×10^7

(f) 28

(g) 1×10^{-6}

(h) 0.56

(i) 88

Answers to Odd-Numbered Exercises

NOTE: Answers in the Questions section are written as briefly as possible. Student answers may vary and still be correct.

CHAPTER 1
QUESTIONS

1. Soda fizzes due to the interactions between carbon dioxide and water under high pressure. At room temperature, carbon dioxide is a gas and water is a liquid. Through the use of pressure, the makers of soda force the carbon dioxide gas to dissolve in the water. When the can is sealed, the solution remains mixed. When the can is opened, the pressure is released and the carbon dioxide molecules escape in bubbles of gas.

3. Chemists study molecules and interactions at the molecular level to learn about and explain macroscopic events. Chemists attempt to explain why ordinary things are as they are.

5. Chemistry is the science that seeks to understand what matter does by studying what atoms and molecules do.

7. The scientific method is the way chemists investigate the chemical world. The first step consists of observing the natural world. Later observations can be combined to create a scientific law, which summarizes and predicts behavior. Theories are models that strive to explain the cause of the observed phenomenon. Theories are tested through experiment. When a theory is not well established, it is sometimes referred to as a hypothesis.

9. A law is simply a general statement that summarizes and predicts observed behavior. Theories seek to explain the causes of observed behavior.

11. To say "It is just a theory" makes it seem as if theories are easily discardable. However, many theories are very well established and are as close to truth as we get in science. Established theories are backed up with years of experimental evidence, and they are the pinnacle of scientific understanding.

13. The atomic theory states that all matter is composed of small, indestructible particles called atoms. John Dalton formulated this theory.

PROBLEMS

15. Carbon dioxide contains one carbon atom and two oxygen atoms. Water contains one oxygen atom and two hydrogen atoms.

17. **a.** observation   **b.** theory
    c. law   **d.** observation

19. Mass (g) Volume (L) Ratio (g/L)

22.5	1.6	14
35.8	2.55	14.0
70.2	5.00	14.0
98.5	7.01	14.1

The ratio of mass to volume is constant.

21. **a.** All atoms contain a degree of chemical reactivity. The larger the size of an atom, the higher the chemical reactivity of that atom.

   b. There are many correct answers. One example is: Conceivably, when the size of an atom is increased, the surface area of the atom is also increased; an atom with a greater surface area is more likely to react chemically.

CHAPTER 2
QUESTIONS

1. Without units, the results are unclear and it is hard to keep track of what each separate measurement entails.

3. Often scientists work with very large or very small numbers that contain a lot of zeros. Scientific notation allows these numbers to be written more compactly, and the information is more organized.

5. Zeros count as significant digits when they are interior zeros (zeros between two numbers) and when they are trailing zeros (zeros after a decimal point). Zeros are **not** significant digits when they are leading zeros, which are zeros to the left of the first nonzero number.

7. For calculations involving only multiplication and division, the result carries the same number of significant figures as the factor with the fewest significant figures.

9. In calculations involving both multiplication/division and addition/subtraction, do the steps in parentheses first; next determine the correct number of significant figures in the intermediate answer; then do the remaining steps.

11. The basic SI unit of length is the meter. The kilogram is the SI unit of mass. Lastly, the second is the SI unit of time.

13. For measuring a Frisbee, the unit would be the meter and the prefix multiplier would be *centi-*. The final measurement would be in centimeters.

15. **a.** 2.42 cm
    b. 1.79 cm
    c. 21.58 cm
    d. 21.85 cm

17. Units act as a guide in the calculation and are able to show if the calculation is off track. The units must be followed in the calculation, so that the answer is correctly written and understood.

19. A conversion factor is a quantity used to relate two separate units. They are constructed from any two quantities known to be equivalent.

21. The conversion factor is $\dfrac{1 \text{ ft}}{12 \text{ in.}}$. For a feet-to-inches conversion, the conversion factor must be inverted $\left(\dfrac{12 \text{ in.}}{1 \text{ ft}}\right)$.

23. **a.** Sort the information into the **given** information (the starting point for the problem) and the **find** information (the end point).

   b. Create a solution map to get from the given information to the information you are trying to find. This will likely include conversion factors or equations.

   c. Follow the solution map to solve the problem. Carry out mathematical operations and cancel units as needed.

   d. Ask, does this answer make physical sense? Are the units correct? Is the number of significant figures correct?

25. The solution map for converting grams to pounds is:

$$\frac{1 \text{ lb}}{453.59 \text{ g}}$$

27. The solution map for converting meters to feet is:

$$\frac{100 \text{ cm}}{1 \text{ m}} \qquad \frac{1 \text{ ft}}{30.48 \text{ cm}}$$

29. The density of a substance is the ratio of its mass to its volume. Density is a fundamental property of materials and differs from one substance to another. Density can be used to relate two separate units, thus working as a conversion factor. Density is a conversion factor between mass and volume.

PROBLEMS

31. **a.** 3.7692×10^6 **b.** 1.360×10^6
   c. 1.9306×10^7 **d.** 5.68×10^5

33. **a.** 7.461×10^{-11} m   **b.** 1.58×10^{-5} mi
   c. 6.32×10^{-7} m   **d.** 1.5×10^{-5} m

35. **a.** 602,200,000,000,000,000,000,000
   b. 0.00000000000000000000016 C
   c. 299,000,000 m/s
   d. 344 m/s

37. **a.** 32,200,000   **b.** 0.0072
   c. 118,000,000,000   **d.** 0.00000943

39. 2,000,000,000 2×10^9
   1,211,000,000 1.211×10^9
   0.000874 8.74×10^{-4}
   320,000,000,000 3.2×10^{11}

41. **a.** 54.9 mL   **b.** 48.7 °C
   c. 46.83 °C   **d.** 64 mL

43. **a.** 0.005050   **b.** 0.0000000000000060
   c. 220,103   **d.** 0.00108

45. **a.** 4   **b.** 4
   c. 6   **d.** 5

47. **a.** correct   **b.** 3
   c. 7   **d.** correct

49. **a.** 256.0   **b.** 0.0004893
   c. 2.901×10^{-4} **d.** 2.231×10^6

51. **a.** 2.3   **b.** 2.4
   c. 2.3   **d.** 2.4

53. **a.** 42.3   **b.** correct
   c. correct   **d.** 0.0456

55.
8.32466	8.325	8.3	8
84.57225	84.57	85	8×10^1
132.5512	132.6	1.3×10^2	1×10^2

57. **a.** 0.054   **b.** 0.619
   c. 1.2×10^8 **d.** 6.6

59. **a.** 4.22×10^3 **b.** correct
   c. 3.9969   **d.** correct

61. **a.** 110.6   **b.** 41.4
   c. 183.3   **d.** 1.22

63. **a.** correct   **b.** 1.0982
   c. correct   **d.** 3.53

65. **a.** 3.9×10^3 **b.** 632
   c. 8.93×10^4 **d.** 6.34

67. **a.** 3.15×10^3 **b.** correct
   c. correct   **d.** correct

69. **a.** 3.55×10^3 g   **b.** 8.944 m
   c. 4.598×10^{-3} kg   **d.** 18.7 mL

71. **a.** 0.588 L   **b.** 34.1 μg
   c. 10.1 ns   **d.** 2.19×10^{-12} m

73. **a.** 57.2 cm   **b.** 38.4 m
   c. 0.754 km   **d.** 61 mm

75. **a.** 15.7 in   **b.** 91.2 ft
   c. 6.21 mi   **d.** 8478 lb

77.
5.08×10^8 m	5.08×10^5 km	508 Mm
5.08×10^{-1} Gm	5.08×10^{-4} Tm	
2.7976×10^{10} m	2.7976×10^7 km	27,976 Mm
27976×10^1 Gm	2.7976×10^{-2} Tm	
1.77×10^{12} m	1.77×10^9 km	1.77×10^6 Mm
1.77×10^3 Gm	1.77 Tm	
1.5×10^8 m	1.5×10^5 m	1.5×10^2 Mm
0.15 Gm	1.5×10^{-4} Tm	
4.23×10^{11} m	4.23×10^8 km	4.23×10^5 Mm
423 Gm	0.423 Tm	

79. **a.** 2.255×10^7 kg   **b.** 2.255×10^4 Mg
   c. 2.255×10^{13} mg   **d.** 2.255×10^4 metric tons

81. 1.5×10^3 g

83. 5.0×10^1 min

85. 4.7×10^3 cm³

87. **a.** 1.0×10^6 m²   **b.** 1.0×10^{-6} m³
   c. 1.0×10^{-9} m³

89. **a.** 6.2×10^5 pm³   **b.** 6.2×10^{-4} nm³
   c. 6.2×10^{-1} Å³

91. **a.** 2.15×10^{-4} km²   **b.** 2.15×10^4 dm²
   c. 2.15×10^6 cm²

93. 1.49×10^6 mi²

95. 11.4 g/cm³, lead

97. 1.26 g/cm³

99. Yes, the density of the crown is 19.3 g/cm³.

101. **a.** 4.30×10^2 g   **b.** 3.12 L

103. **a.** 3.38×10^4 g (gold); 5.25×10^3 g (sand)

   b. Yes, the mass of the bag of sand is different from the mass of the gold vase; thus, the weight-sensitive pedestal will sound the alarm.

105. 10.6 g/cm^3

107. $2.7 \times 10^3 \dfrac{\text{kg}}{\text{m}^3}$

109. $2.5 \times 10^5 \text{ lbs}$

111. $1.19 \times 10^5 \text{ kg}$

113. 18 km/L

115. 768 mi

117. Metal A is denser than metal B.

119. 2.26 g/cm^3

121. 1.32 cm

123. $108 \text{ km}; 47.2 \text{ km}$

125. $9.1 \times 10^{10} \text{ g/cm}^3$

CHAPTER 3

QUESTIONS

1. Matter is defined as anything that occupies space and possesses mass. It can be thought of as the physical material that makes up the universe.

3. The three states of matter are solid, liquid, and gas.

5. In a crystalline solid, the atoms/molecules are arranged in geometric patterns with repeating order. In amorphous solids, the atoms/molecules do not have long-range order.

7. The atoms/molecules in gases are not in contact with each other and are free to move relative to one another. The spacing between separate atoms/molecules is very far apart. A gas has no fixed volume or shape; rather, it assumes both the shape and the volume of the container it occupies.

9. A mixture is two or more pure substances combined in variable proportions.

11. Pure substances are those composed of only one type of atom or molecule.

13. A mixture is formed when two or more pure substances are mixed together; however, a new substance is not formed. A compound is formed when two or more elements are bonded together and form a new substance.

15. In a physical change, the composition of the substance does not change, even though its appearance might change. However, in a chemical change, the substance undergoes a change in its composition.

17. Energy is defined as the capacity to do work.

19. Kinetic energy is the energy associated with the motion of an object. Potential energy is the energy associated with the position or composition of an object.

21. Three common units for energy are joules, calories, and kilowatt-hours.

23. An endothermic reaction is one that absorbs energy from the surroundings. The products have more energy than the reactants in an endothermic reaction.

25. Heat is the transfer of thermal energy caused by a temperature difference, whereas temperature is a measure of the thermal energy of matter.

27. Heat capacity is the quantity of heat energy required to change the temperature of a given amount of the substance by 1 °C.

29. $°F = \dfrac{9}{5}(°C) + 32$

PROBLEMS

31. **a.** element   **b.** element
   c. compound   **d.** compound

33. **a.** homogeneous   **b.** heterogeneous
   c. homogeneous   **d.** homogeneous

35. **a.** pure substance-element
   b. mixture-homogeneous
   c. mixture-heterogeneous
   d. mixture-heterogeneous

37. **a.** chemical   **b.** physical
   c. physical   **d.** chemical

39. physical–colorless; odorless; gas at room temperature; one liter has a mass of 1.260 g under standard conditions; mixes with acetone; chemical–flammable; polymerizes to form polyethylene

41. **a.** chemical   **b.** physical
   c. chemical   **d.** chemical

43. **a.** physical   **b.** chemical

45. $2.10 \times 10^2 \text{ kg}$

47. **a.** Yes   **b.** No

49. 15.1 g of water

51. **a.** $2.46 \times 10^3 \text{ J}$ **b.** $4.16 \times 10^{-3} \text{ Cal}$
   c. 32.0 Cal   **d.** $2.35 \times 10^5 \text{ J}$

53. **a.** $9.0 \times 10^7 \text{ J}$ **b.** 0.249 Cal
   c. $1.31 \times 10^{-4} \text{ kWh}$ **d.** $1.1 \times 10^4 \text{ cal}$

55.

J	cal	Cal	kWh
225	53.8	5.38×10^{-2}	6.25×10^{-5}
3.44×10^6	8.21×10^5	8.21×10^2	9.54×10^{-1}
1.06×10^9	2.54×10^8	2.54×10^5	295
6.49×10^5	1.55×10^5	155	1.80×10^{-1}

57. $3.697 \times 10^9 \text{ J}$

59. $8 \times 10^2 \text{ kJ}$; 17 days

61. Exothermic.

63. **a.** exothermic, $-\Delta H$
   b. endothermic, $+\Delta H$
   c. exothermic, $-\Delta H$

65. **a.** $1.00 \times 10^2 \text{ °C}$ **b.** $-3.2 \times 10^2 \text{ °F}$
   c. 298 K   **d.** $3.10 \times 10^2 \text{ K}$

67. $-62 \text{ °C}, 211 \text{ K}$

69. $159 \text{ K}, -173 \text{ °F}$

71. -75.5 °F

73.

0.0 K	-459.4 °F	-273.0 °C
30.1 K	82.5 °F	28.1 °C
282 K	47 °F	8.5 °C

75. $9.0 \times 10^3 \text{ J}$

77. 8.7×10^5 J

79. 58 °C

81. 31 °C

83. 1.0×10^1 °C

85. 0.24 J/g°C; silver

87. 2.2 J/g°C

89. When warm drinks are placed into the ice, they release heat, which then melts the ice. The prechilled drinks, on the other hand, are already cold, so they do not release much heat.

91. 612 J

93. 49 °C

95. 70.2 J

97. 1.7×10^4 kJ

99. 67 °C

101. 6.0 kWh

103. 22 g of fuel

105. 78 g

107. 27.2 °C

109. 5.96×10^5 kJ; $25

111. −40°

113. **a.** pure substance   **b.** pure substance
     c. pure substance   **d.** mixture

115. physical change

117. Small temperature changes in the ocean have a great impact on global weather because of the high heat capacity of water.

119. **a.** Sacramento is farther inland than San Francisco, so Sacramento is not as close to the ocean. The ocean water has a high heat capacity and will be able to keep San Francisco cooler in the hot days of summer. However, Sacramento is away from the ocean in a valley, so it will experience high temperatures in the summer.

     b. San Francisco is located right next to the ocean, so the high heat capacity of the seawater keeps the temperature in the city from dropping. In the winter, the ocean actually helps to keep the city warmer, compared to an inland city like Sacramento.

CHAPTER 4
QUESTIONS

1. Democritus theorized that matter was ultimately composed of small, indivisible particles called atoms. Upon dividing matter, one would find tiny, indestructible atoms.

3. Rutherford's gold foil experiment involved sending positively charged alpha particles through a thin sheet of gold foil and detecting if there was any deflection of the particles. He found that most passed straight through, yet some particles showed some deflection. This result contradicts the plum-pudding model of the atom because the plum-pudding model does not explain the deflection of the alpha particles.

5.

Particle	Mass (kg)	Mass (amu)	Charge
Proton	1.67262×10^{-27}	1	+1
Neutron	1.67493×10^{-27}	1	0
Electron	0.00091×10^{-27}	0.00055	−1

7. Matter is usually charge-neutral due to protons and electrons having opposite charges. If matter were not charge-neutral, many unnatural things would occur, such as objects repelling or attracting each other.

9. A chemical symbol is a unique one- or two-letter abbreviation for an element. It is listed below the atomic number for that element on the periodic table.

11. Mendeleev noticed that many patterns were evident when elements were organized by increasing mass; from this observation he formulated the periodic law. He also organized the elements based on this law and created the basis for the periodic table being used today.

13. The periodic table is organized by listing the elements in order of increasing atomic number.

15. Nonmetals have varied properties (solid, liquid, or gas at room temperature); however, as a whole they tend to be poor conductors of heat and electricity, and they all tend to gain electrons when they undergo chemical changes. They are located toward the upper right side of the periodic table.

17. Each column within the main group elements in the periodic table is labeled as a family or group of elements. The elements within a group usually have similar chemical properties.

19. An ion is an atom or group of atoms that has lost or gained electrons and has become charged.

21. **a.** ion charge = 1+   **b.** ion charge = 2+
     c. ion charge = 3+   **d.** ion charge = 2−
     e. ion charge = 1−

23. The percent natural abundance of isotopes is the relative amount of each different isotope in a naturally occurring sample of a given element.

25. Isotopes are noted in this manner: $^A_Z X$. X represents the chemical symbol, A represents the mass number, and Z represents the atomic number.

PROBLEMS

27. **a.** Correct.
     b. False; different elements contain different types of atoms according to Dalton.
     c. False; one cannot have 1.5 hydrogen atoms; combinations must be in simple, whole-number ratios.
     d. Correct.

29. **a.** Correct.
     b. False; most of the volume of the atom is empty space occupied by tiny, negatively charged electrons.
     c. False, the number of negatively charged particles outside the nucleus equals the number of positively charged particles inside the nucleus.
     d. False, the majority of the mass of an atom is found in the nucleus.

31. Solid matter seems to have no empty space within it because electromagnetic forces hold the atoms in a tight arrangement and the variation in density is too small to perceive with our eyes.

33. **a, b, d**

35. **b, d**

37. approximately 1.8×10^3 electrons

39. 5.4×10^{-4} g

41. **a.** 87   **b.** 36   **c.** 91   **d.** 32   **e.** 13

43. a. 18   **b.** 50   **c.** 54   **d.** 8   **e.** 81

45. a. C, 6   **b.** N, 7
c. Na, 11   **d.** K, 19
e. Cu, 29

47. a. manganese, 25   **b.** silver, 47
c. gold, 79   **d.** lead, 82
e. sulfur, 16

49.

Element Name	Element Symbol	Atomic Number
Gold	Au	79
Tin	Sn	50
Arsenic	As	33
Copper	Cu	29
Iron	Fe	26
Mercury	Hg	80

51. a. metal   **b.** metal
c. nonmetal   **d.** nonmetal
e. metalloid

53. a, d, e

55. a, b

57. c, d

59. b, e

61. a. halogen   **b.** noble gas
c. halogen   **d.** neither
e. noble gas

63. a. 6A   **b.** 3A
c. 4A   **d.** 4A
e. 5A

65. b, oxygen; it is in the same group or family.

67. b, chlorine and fluorine; they are in the same family or group.

69. d

71.

Chemical Symbol	Group Number	Group Name	Metal or Nonmetal
K	1A	Alkali Metals	Metals
Br	7A	Halogens	Nonmetal
Sr	2A	Alkaline Earth	Metal
He	8A	Noble Gas	Nonmetal
Ar	8A	Noble Gas	Nonmetal

73. a. e^- **b.** O^{2-} **c.** $2e^-$ **d.** Cl^-

75. a. 2−   **b.** 3+   **c.** 4+   **d.** 1−

77. a. 11 protons, 10 electrons
b. 56 protons, 54 electrons
c. 8 protons, 10 electrons
d. 27 protons, 24 electrons

79. a. False; Ti^{2+} has 22 protons and 20 electrons.
b. True
c. False; Mg^{2+} has 12 protons and 10 electrons.
d. True

81. a. Rb^+ **b.** K^+ **c.** Al^{3+} **d.** O^{2-}

83. a. 3 electrons lost   **b.** 1 electron lost
c. 1 electron gained   **d.** 2 electrons gained

85.

Symbol	Ion Commonly Formed	Number of Electrons in Ion	Number of Protons in Ion
Te	Te^{2-}	54	52
In	In^{3+}	46	49
Sr	Sr^{2+}	36	38
Mg	Mg^{2+}	10	12
Cl	Cl^-	18	17

87. a. $Z = 1, A = 3$ **b.** $Z = 24, A = 52$
c. $Z = 20, A = 42$ **d.** $Z = 73, A = 182$

89. a. $^{16}_{8}O$ **b.** $^{19}_{9}F$
c. $^{23}_{11}Na$ **d.** $^{27}_{13}Al$

91. a. $^{60}_{27}Co$ **b.** $^{22}_{10}Ne$
c. $^{131}_{53}I$ **d.** $^{244}_{94}Pu$

93. a. 11 protons, 12 neutrons
b. 88 protons, 178 neutrons
c. 82 protons, 126 neutrons
d. 7 protons, 7 neutrons

95. 6 protons, 8 neutrons, $^{14}_{6}C$

97. 85.47 amu

99. a. 49.31%
b. 78.91 amu

101. 121.8 amu, Sb

103. 7.8×10^{17} electrons

105. 4.2×10^{-45} m³; 6.2×10^{-31} m³; 6.7×10^{-13}%

107.

Symbol	Number of Protons	Number of Neutrons	A (Mass Number)	Natural Abundance
Sr-84 or $^{84}_{38}Sr$	38	46	84	0.56%
Sr-86 or $^{86}_{38}Sr$	38	48	86	9.86%
Sr-87 or $^{87}_{38}Sr$	38	49	87	7.00%
Sr-88 or $^{88}_{38}Sr$	38	50	88	82.58%

Atomic mass of Sr = 87.62 amu

109.

Symbol	Z	A	Number of Protons	Number of Electrons	Number of Neutrons	Charge
Zn^{2+}	30	64	30	28	34	2+
Mn^{3+}	25	55	25	22	30	3+
P	15	31	15	15	16	0
O^{2-}	8	16	8	10	8	2−
S^{2-}	16	34	16	18	18	2−

111. 153 amu, 52.2%

113. The atomic theory and nuclear model of the atom are both theories because they attempt to provide a broader understanding and model behavior of chemical systems.

115. Atomic mass is measured as the mean value of masses of all isotopes in a sample. In the case of fluorine, only the 19.00 amu isotope is naturally occurring. In the case of chlorine, about 76% of naturally occurring atoms are 35 amu, and 24% are 37 amu.

117. 69.3% Cu-63, 30.7% Cu-65

119. a. Nt-304 = 72%; Nt-305 = 4%; Nt-306 = 24%

b.

120
Nt
304.5

CHAPTER 5

QUESTIONS

1. Yes; when elements combine with other elements, a compound is created. Each compound is unique and contains properties different from those of the elements that compose it.

3. The law of constant composition states that all samples of a given compound have the same proportions of their constituent elements. Joseph Proust formulated this law.

5. The more metallic element is generally listed first in a chemical formula.

7. The empirical formula gives the relative number of atoms of each element in a compound. The molecular formula gives the actual number of atoms of each element in a molecule of the compound.

9. An atomic element is one that exists in nature with a single atom as the basic unit. A molecular element is one that exists as a diatomic molecule as the basic unit. Molecular elements include H_2, N_2, O_2, F_2, Cl_2, Br_2, and I_2.

11. The systematic name can be directly derived by looking at the compound's formula. The common name for a compound acts like a nickname and can only be learned through familiarity.

13. The block that contains the elements for Type II compounds is known as the transition metals.

15. The basic form for the names of Type II ionic compounds is to have the name of the metal cation first, followed by the charge of the metal cation (in parentheses, using Roman numerals), and finally the base name of the nonmetal anion with *-ide* attached to the end.

17. For compounds containing a polyatomic anion, the name of the cation is first, followed by the name for the polyatomic anion. Also, if the compound contains both a polyatomic cation and a polyatomic anion, one would just use the names of both polyatomic ions.

19. The form for naming molecular compounds is to have the first element preceded by a prefix to indicate the number of atoms present. This is then followed by the second element with its corresponding prefix and *-ide* placed on the end of the second element.

21. To correctly name a binary acid, one must begin the first word with *hydro-*, which is followed by the base name of the nonmetal plus *-ic* added on the end. Finally, the word *acid* follows the first word.

23. To name an acid with oxyanions ending with *-ite*, one must take the base name of the oxyanion and attach *-ous* to it; the word *acid* follows this.

PROBLEMS

25. Yes; the ratios of sodium to chlorine in both samples were equal.

27. 2.06×10^3 g

29.

	Mass N_2O	Mass N	Mass O
Sample A	2.85	1.82	1.03
Sample B	4.55	2.91	1.64
Sample C	3.74	2.39	1.35
Sample D	1.74	1.11	0.63

31. NI_3

33. a. Fe_3O_4 **b.** PCl_3
   c. PCl_5 **d.** Ag_2O

35. a. 4   **b.** 4
   c. 6   **d.** 4

37. a. magnesium, 1; chlorine, 2
   b. sodium, 1; nitrogen, 1; oxygen, 3
   c. calcium, 1; nitrogen, 2; oxygen, 4
   d. strontium, 1; oxygen, 2; hydrogen, 2

39.

Formula	Number of $C_2H_3O_2$	Number of C Atoms	Number of H Atoms	Number of O Atoms	Number of Metal Atoms
$Mg(C_2H_3O_2)_2$	2	4	6	4	1
$NaC_2H_3O_2$	1	2	3	2	1
$Cr_2(C_2H_3O_2)_4$	4	8	12	8	2

41. a. CH_3 **b.** NO_2
   c. C_2H_3O **d.** NH_3

43. a. molecular   **b.** atomic
   c. atomic   **d.** molecular

45. a. molecular   **b.** ionic
   c. ionic   **d.** molecular

47. helium $\longrightarrow$ single atoms
   CCl_4 $\longrightarrow$ molecules
   K_2SO_4 $\longrightarrow$ formula units
   bromine $\longrightarrow$ diatomic molecules

49. a. formula units   **b.** single atoms
   c. molecules   **d.** molecules

51. a. ionic; forms only one type of ion
   b. molecular
   c. molecular
   d. ionic; forms more than one type of ion

53. a. Na_2S **b.** SrO
   c. Al_2S_3 **d.** $MgCl_2$

55. a. $KC_2H_3O_2$ **b.** K_2CrO_4
   c. K_3PO_4 **d.** KCN

57. a. Li_3N, Li_2O, LiF   **b.** Ba_3N_2, BaO, BaF_2
   c. AlN, Al_2O_3, AlF_3

59. a. cesium chloride   **b.** strontium bromide
   c. potassium oxide   **d.** lithium fluoride

61. a. chromium(II) chloride   **b.** chromium(III) chloride
   c. tin(IV) oxide   **d.** lead(II) iodide

63. a. forms more than one type of ion, chromium(III) oxide
   b. forms only one type of ion, sodium iodide
   c. forms only one type of ion, calcium bromide
   d. forms more than one type of ion, tin(II) oxide

65. a. barium nitrate   b. lead(II) acetate
    c. ammonium iodide   d. potassium chlorate
    e. cobalt(II) sulfate   f. sodium perchlorate

67. a. hypobromite ion   b. bromite ion
    c. bromate ion   d. perbromate ion

69. a. $CuBr_2$ b. $AgNO_3$
    c. KOH   d. Na_2SO_4
    e. $KHSO_4$ f. $NaHCO_3$

71. a. sulfur dioxide   b. nitrogen triiodide
    c. bromine pentafluoride   d. nitrogen monoxide
    e. tetranitrogen tetraselenide

73. a. CO   b. S_2F_4
    c. Cl_2O d. PF_5
    e. BBr_3 f. P_2S_5

75. a. PBr_5 phosphorus pentabromide
    b. P_2O_3 diphosphorus trioxide
    c. SF_4 sulfur tetraflouride
    d. correct

77. a. oxyacid, nitrous acid, nitrite
    b. binary acid, hydroiodic acid
    c. oxyacid, sulfuric acid, sulfate
    d. oxyacid, nitric acid, nitrate

79. a. hypochlorous acid   b. chlorous acid
    c. chloric acid   d. perchloric acid

81. a. H_3PO_4 b. HBr   c. H_2SO_3

83. a. 63.02 amu   b. 199.88 amu
    c. 153.81 amu   d. 211.64 amu

85. PBr_3, Ag_2O, PtO_2, $Al(NO_3)_3$

87. a. CH_4 b. SO_3 c. NO_2

89. a. 12   b. 4
    c. 12   d. 7

91. a. 8   b. 12   c. 12

93.

Formula	Type	Name
N_2H_4	molecular	dinitrogen tetrahydride
KCl	ionic	potassium chloride
H_2CrO_4	acid	chromic acid
$Co(CN)_3$	ionic	cobalt(III) cyanide

95. a. calcium nitrite
    b. potassium oxide
    c. phosphorus trichloride
    d. correct
    e. potassium iodite

97. a. $Sn(SO_4)_2$ 310.9 amu   b. HNO_2 47.02 amu
    c. $NaHCO_3$ 84.01 amu   d. PF_5 125.97 amu

99. a. platinum(IV) oxide 227.08 amu
    b. dinitrogen pentoxide 108.02 amu
    c. aluminum chlorate 277.33 amu
    d. phosphorus pentabromide 430.47 amu

101. C_2H_4

103. 10 different isotopes can exist. 151.88 amu, 152.88 amu, 153.88 amu, 154.88 amu, 155.88 amu, 156.88 amu, 157.88 amu, 158.88 amu, 159.88 amu, and 160.88 amu.

105. a. molecular element   b. atomic element
     c. ionic compound   d. molecular compound

107. a. NaOCl; NaOH
     b. $Al(OH)_3$; $Mg(OH)_2$
     c. $CaCO_3$
     d. $NaHCO_3$, $Ca_3(PO_4)_2$, $NaAl(SO_4)_2$

CHAPTER 6

QUESTIONS

1. Chemical composition lets us determine how much of a particular element is contained within a particular compound.

3. There are 6.022×10^{23} atoms in 1 mole of atoms.

5. One mole of any element has a mass equal to its atomic mass in grams.

7. a. 30.97 g   b. 195.08 g
   c. 12.01 g   d. 52.00 g

9. Each element has a different atomic mass number. So, the subscripts that represent mole ratios cannot be used to represent the ratios of grams of a compound. The grams per mole of one element always differ from the grams per mole of a different element.

11. a. 11.19 g H≡100 g H_2O
    b. 53.29 g O≡100 g fructose
    c. 84.12 g C≡100 g octane
    d. 52.14 g C≡100 g ethanol

13. The empirical formula gives the smallest whole-number ratio of each type of atom. The molecular formula gives the specific number of each type of atom in the molecule. The molecular formula is always a multiple of the empirical formula.

15. The empirical formula mass of a compound is the sum of the masses of all the atoms in the empirical formula.

PROBLEMS

17. 3.5×10^{24} atoms

19. a. 2.0×10^{24} atoms   b. 5.8×10^{21} atoms
    c. 1.38×10^{25} atoms   d. 1.29×10^{23} atoms

21.

Element	Moles	Number of Atoms
Ne	0.552	3.32×10^{23}
Ar	5.40	3.25×10^{24}
Xe	1.78	1.07×10^{24}
He	1.79×10^{-4}	1.08×10^{20}

23. a. 72.7 dozen
    b. 6.06 gross
    c. 1.74 reams
    d. 1.45×10^{-21} moles

25. 0.321 mol

27. 28.6 g

29. a. 2.05×10^{-2} mol
    b. 0.623 mol
    c. 0.401 mol
    d. 3.21×10^{-3} mol

31.

Element	Moles	Mass
Ne	1.11	22.5
Ar	0.117	4.67 g
Xe	7.62	1.00
He	1.44×10^{-4}	5.76×10^{-4} g

33. 8.07×10^{18} atoms

35. 8.44×10^{22} atoms

37. a. 1.16×10^{23} atoms **b.** 2.81×10^{23} atoms
c. 2.46×10^{22} atoms **d.** 7.43×10^{23} atoms

39. 1.9×10^{21} atoms

41. 1.61×10^{25} atoms

43.

Element	Mass	Moles	Number of Atoms
Na	38.5 mg	1.67×10^{-3}	1.01×10^{21}
C	13.5 g	1.12	6.74×10^{23}
V	1.81×10^{-20} g	3.55×10^{-22}	214
Hg	1.44 kg	7.18	4.32×10^{24}

45. b

47. a. 0.654 mol **b.** 1.22 mol
c. 96.6 mol **d.** 1.76×10^{-5} mol

49.

Compound	Mass	Moles	Molecules
H_2O	112 kg	6.22×10^3	3.74×10^{27}
N_2O	6.33 g	0.144	8.66×10^{22}
SO_2	156	2.44	1.47×10^{24}
CH_2Cl_2	5.46	0.0643	3.87×10^{22}

51. 6.20×10^{21} molecules

53. a. 1.2×10^{23} molecules **b.** 1.21×10^{24} molecules
c. 3.5×10^{23} molecules **d.** 6.4×10^{22} molecules

55. 0.10 mg

57. $\$6.022 \times 10^{21}$ total. $\$8.5 \times 10^{11}$ Each person would be a billionaire.

59. 5.4 mol Cl

61. d, 3 mol O

63. a. 2.5 mol C **b.** 0.230 mol C
c. 22.7 mol C **d.** 201 mol C

65. a. 2 moles H per mole of molecules; 8 H atoms present
b. 4 moles H per mole of molecules; 20 H atoms present
c. 3 moles H per mole of molecules; 9 H atoms present

67. a. 22.3 g **b.** 29.4 g
c. 21.6 g **d.** 12.9 g

69. a. 1.4×10^3 kg **b.** 1.4×10^3 kg
c. 2.1×10^3 kg

71. 84.8% Sr

73. 36.1% Ca; 63.9% Cl

75. 10.7 g

77. 6.6 mg

79. a. 63.65% **b.** 46.68%
c. 30.45% **d.** 25.94%

81. a. 39.99% C; 6.73% H; 53.28% O
b. 26.09% C; 4.39% H; 69.52% O
c. 60.93% C; 15.37% H; 23.69% N
d. 54.48% C; 13.74% H; 31.78% N

83. a. 58.50% O **b.** 42.13% O **c.** 72.71% O

85. Fe_3O_4, 72.36% Fe; Fe_2O_3, 69.94% Fe; $FeCO_3$, 48.20% Fe; magnetite

87. NO_2

89. a. NiI_2 **b.** $SeBr_4$ **c.** $BeSO_4$

91. C_2H_6N

93. a. C_3H_6O **b.** $C_5H_{10}O_2$ **c.** $C_9H_{10}O_2$

95. P_2O_3

97. NCl_3

99. C_4H_8

101. a. C_6Cl_6 **b.** C_2HCl_3 **c.** $C_6H_3Cl_3$

103. 2.43×10^{23} atoms

105. 2×10^{21} molecules

107.

Substance	Mass	Moles	Number of Particles
Ar	0.018 g	4.5×10^{-4}	2.7×10^{20}
NO_2	8.33×10^{-3} g	1.81×10^{-4}	1.09×10^{20}
K	22.4 mg	5.73×10^{-4}	3.45×10^{20}
C_8H_{18}	3.76 kg	32.9	1.98×10^{25}

109. a. CuI_2: 20.03% Cu; 79.97% I
b. $NaNO_3$: 27.05% Na; 16.48% N; 56.47% O
c. $PbSO_4$: 68.32% Pb; 10.57% S; 21.10% O
d. CaF_2: 51.33% Ca; 48.67% F

111. 1.8×10^3 kg rock

113. 59 kg Cl

115. 1.1×10^2 g H

117.

Formula	Molar Mass	%C (by mass)	%H (by mass)
C_2H_4	28.06	85.60%	14.40%
C_4H_{10}	58.12	82.66%	17.34%
C_4H_8	56.12	85.60%	14.40%
C_3H_8	44.09	81.71%	18.29%

119. $C_4H_6O_2$

121. $C_{10}H_{14}N_2$

123. 70.4% KBr, 29.6% KI

125. 29.6 g SO_2

127. 2.66 kg Fe

129. a. 1×10^{57} atoms per star
b. 1×10^{68} atoms per galaxy
c. 1×10^{79} atoms in the universe

131. $C_{16}H_{10}$

CHAPTER 7

QUESTIONS

1. A chemical reaction is the change of one or more substances into different substances, for example, burning wood, rusting iron, and protein synthesis.

3. The main evidence of a chemical reaction includes a color change, the formation of a solid, the formation of a gas, the emission of light, and the emission or absorption of heat.

5. **a.** gas   **b.** liquid
    c. solid   **d.** aqueous

7. **a.** reactants: 4 Ag, 2 O, 1 C products: 4 Ag, 2 O, 1 C balanced: yes
    b. reactants: 1 Pb, 2 N, 6 O, 2 Na, 2 Cl products: 1 Pb, 2 N, 6 O, 2 Na, 2 Cl balanced: yes
    c. reactants: 3 C, 8 H, 2 O products: 3 C, 8 H, 10 O balanced: no

9. If a compound dissolves in water, then it is soluble. If it does not dissolve in water, it is insoluble.

11. When ionic compounds containing polyatomic ions dissolve in water, the polyatomic ions usually dissolve as intact units.

13. The solubility rules are a set of empirical rules for ionic compounds that were deduced from observations on many compounds. The rules help us determine whether particular compounds will be soluble or insoluble.

15. The precipitate will always be insoluble; it is the solid that forms upon mixing two aqueous solutions.

17. Acid–base reactions involve an acid and a base reacting to form water and an ionic compound. An example is the reaction between hydrobromic acid and sodium hydroxide: $HBr + NaOH \longrightarrow H_2O + NaBr$

19. Gas evolution reactions are reactions that evolve a gas. An example is the reaction between hydrochloric acid and sodium bicarbonate: $HCl + NaHCO_3 \longrightarrow H_2O + CO_2 + NaCl$

21. Combustion reactions are a type of redox reaction and are characterized by the exothermic reaction of a substance with O_2. An example is the reaction between methane and oxygen: $CH_4 + 2\,O_2 \longrightarrow CO_2 + 2\,H_2O$

23. A synthesis reaction combines simpler substances to form more complex substances. An example is the reaction between elemental potassium and chloride: $2\,K + Cl_2 \longrightarrow 2\,KCl$. A decomposition decomposes a more complex substance into simpler substances. An example is the decomposition of water: $2\,H_2O \longrightarrow 2\,H_2 + O_2$

PROBLEMS

25. **a.** Yes; there is a color change showing a chemical reaction.
    b. No; the state of the compound changes, but no chemical reaction takes place.
    c. Yes; there is a formation of a solid in a previously clear solution.
    d. Yes; there is a formation of a gas when the yeast is added to the solution.

27. Yes; a chemical reaction has occurred, for the presence of the bubbles is evidence for the formation of a gas.

29. Yes; a chemical reaction has occurred. We know this due to the color change of the hair.

31. **a.** Reactants: 1 Pb, 6 O, 2 Na, 2 Cl Products: 1 Pb; 6 O; 2 Na; 2 Cl; Balanced

b. Reactants: 3 C, 8 H, 2 O; Products: 3 C, 8 H, 10 O ; Not balanced

33. Placing a subscript 2 after H_2O would change the compound from water to hydrogen peroxide (H_2O_2). To balance chemical reactions, one must add coefficients, not subscripts.
$2\,H_2O(l) \longrightarrow 2\,H_2(g) + O_2(g)$

35. **a.** $PbS + 2\,HCl \longrightarrow PbCl_2 + H_2S$
    b. $CO + 3\,H_2 \longrightarrow CH_4 + H_2O$
    c. $Fe_2O_3 + 3\,H_2 \longrightarrow 2\,Fe + 3\,H_2O$
    d. $4\,NH_3 + 5\,O_2 \longrightarrow 4\,NO + 6\,H_2O$

37. **a.** $Mg(s) + 2\,CuNO_3(aq) \longrightarrow 2\,Cu(s) + Mg(NO_3)_2(aq)$
    b. $2\,N_2O_5(g) \longrightarrow 4\,NO_2(g) + O_2(g)$
    c. $Ca(s) + 2\,HNO_3(aq) \longrightarrow H_2(g) + Ca(NO_3)_2(aq)$
    d. $2\,CH_3OH(l) + 3\,O_2(g) \longrightarrow 2\,CO_2(g) + 4\,H_2O(g)$

39. $2\,H_2(g) + O_2(g) \longrightarrow 2\,H_2O(l)$;
$Cl(g) + O_3(g) \longrightarrow ClO(g) + O_2(g)$

41. $2\,Na(s) + 2\,H_2O(l) \longrightarrow H_2(g) + 2\,NaOH(aq)$

43. $2\,SO_2(g) + O_2(g) + 2\,H_2O(l) \longrightarrow 2\,H_2SO_4(aq)$

45. $V_2O_5(s) + 2\,H_2(g) \longrightarrow V_2O_3(s) + 2\,H_2O(l)$

47. $C_{12}H_{22}O_{11}(aq) + H_2O(l) \longrightarrow$
$$4\,CO_2(g) + 4\,C_2H_5OH(aq)$$

49. **a.** $Na_2S(aq) + Cu(NO_3)_2(aq) \longrightarrow$
$$2\,NaNO_3(aq) + CuS(s)$$
    b. $4\,HCl(aq) + O_2(g) \longrightarrow 2\,H_2O(l) + 2\,Cl_2(g)$
    c. $2\,H_2(g) + O_2(g) \longrightarrow 2\,H_2O(l)$
    d. $FeS(s) + 2\,HCl(aq) \longrightarrow FeCl_2(aq) + H_2S(g)$

51. **a.** $BaO_2(s) + H_2SO_4(aq) \longrightarrow BaSO_4(s) + H_2O_2(aq)$
    b. $2\,Co(NO_3)_3(aq) + 3\,(NH_4)_2S(aq) \longrightarrow$
$$Co_2S_3(s) + 6\,NH_4NO_3(aq)$$
    c. $Li_2O(s) + H_2O(l) \longrightarrow 2\,LiOH(aq)$
    d. $Hg_2(C_2H_3O_2)_2(aq) + 2\,KCl(aq) \longrightarrow$
$$Hg_2Cl_2(s) + 2\,KC_2H_3O_2(aq)$$

53. **a.** $2\,Rb(s) + 2\,H_2O(l) \longrightarrow 2\,RbOH(aq) + H_2(g)$
    b. Equation is balanced
    c. $2\,NiS(s) + 3\,O_2(g) \longrightarrow 2\,NiO(s) + 2\,SO_2(g)$
    d. $3\,PbO(s) + 2\,NH_3(g) \longrightarrow 3\,Pb(s)$
$$+ N_2(g) + 3\,H_2O(l)$$

55. $C_6H_{12}O_6(aq) + 6\,O_2(g) \longrightarrow 6\,CO_2(g) + 6\,H_2O(l)$

57. $2\,NO(g) + 2\,CO(g) \longrightarrow N_2(g) + 2\,CO_2(g)$

59. **a.** soluble; Na^+, $C_2H_3O_2^-$
    b. soluble; Sn^{2-}, NO_3^-
    c. insoluble
    d. soluble; Na^+, PO_4^{3-}

61. $AgCl$; $BaSO_4$; $CuCO_3$; Fe_2S_3

63.

Soluble	Insoluble
K_2S	Hg_2I_2
BaS	$Cu_3(PO_4)_2$
NH_4Cl	MgS
Na_2CO_3	$CaSO_4$
K_2SO_4	$PbSO_4$
SrS	$PbCl_2$
Li_2S	Hg_2Cl_2

65. a. NO REACTION

b. $K_2SO_4(aq) + BaBr_2(aq) \longrightarrow BaSO_4(s) + 2 KBr(aq)$

c. $2 NaCl(aq) + Hg_2(C_2H_3O_2)_2(aq) \longrightarrow$
$$Hg_2Cl_2(s) + 2 NaC_2H_3O_2(aq)$$

d. NO REACTION

67. a. $Na_2CO_3(aq) + Pb(NO_3)_2(aq) \longrightarrow$
$$PbCO_3(s) + 2 NaNO_3(aq)$$

b. $K_2SO_4(aq) + Pb(C_2H_3O_2)_2(aq) \longrightarrow$
$$PbSO_4(s) + 2 KC_2H_3O_2$$

c. $Cu(NO_3)_2(aq) + BaS(aq) \longrightarrow$
$$CuS(s) + Ba(NO_3)_2(aq)$$

d. NO REACTION

69. a. correct

b. NO REACTION

c. correct

d. $Pb(NO_3)_2(aq) + 2 LiCl(aq) \longrightarrow$
$$PbCl_2(s) + 2 LiNO_3(aq)$$

71. K^+, NO_3^-

73. a. $Ag^+(aq) + NO_3^-(aq) + K^+(aq) + Cl^-(aq) \longrightarrow$
$$AgCl(s) + K^+(aq) + NO_3^-(aq)$$
$Ag^+(aq) + Cl^-(aq) \longrightarrow AgCl(s)$

b. $Ca^{2+}(aq) + S^{2-}(aq) + Cu^{2+}(aq) + 2 Cl^-(aq) \longrightarrow$
$$CuS(s) + Ca^{2+}(aq) + 2 Cl^-(aq)$$
$Cu^{2+}(aq) + S^{2-}(aq) \longrightarrow CuS(s)$

c. $Na^+(aq) + OH^-(aq) + H^+(aq) + NO_3^-(aq) \longrightarrow$
$$H_2O(l) + Na^+(aq) + NO_3^-(aq)$$
$H^+(aq) + OH^-(aq) \longrightarrow H_2O(l)$

d. $6 K^+(aq) + 2 PO_4^{3-}(aq) + 3 Ni^{2+}(aq) + 6 Cl^-(aq)$
$$\longrightarrow Ni_3(PO_4)_2(s) + 6 K^+(aq) + 6 Cl^-(aq)$$
$3 Ni^{2+}(aq) + 2 PO_4^{3-}(aq) \longrightarrow Ni_3(PO_4)_2(s)$

75. $Hg_2^{2+}(aq) + 2 NO_3^-(aq) + 2 Na^+(aq) + 2 Cl^-(aq) \longrightarrow$
$$Hg_2Cl_2(s) + 2 Na^+(aq) + 2 NO_3^-(aq)$$
$Hg_2^{2+}(aq) + 2 Cl^-(aq) \longrightarrow Hg_2Cl_2(s)$

77. a. $2 Na^+(aq) + CO_3^{2-}(aq) + Pb^{2+}(aq) + 2 NO_3^-(aq)$
$$\longrightarrow PbCO_3(s) + 2 Na^+(aq) + 2 NO_3^-(aq)$$
$Pb^{2+}(aq) + CO_3^{2-}(aq) \longrightarrow PbCO_3(s)$

b. $2 K^+(aq) + SO_4^{2-}(aq) + Pb^{2+}(aq) + 2 CH_3CO_2^-(aq)$
$$\longrightarrow PbSO_4(s) + 2 K^+(aq) + 2 CH_3CO_2^-(aq)$$
$Pb^{2+}(aq) + SO_4^{2-}(aq) \longrightarrow PbSO_4(s)$

c. $Cu^{2+}(aq) + 2 NO_3^-(aq) + Ba^{2+}(aq) + S^{2-}(aq) \longrightarrow$
$$CuS(s) + Ba^{2+}(aq) + 2 NO_3^-(aq)$$
$Cu^{2+}(aq) + S^{2-}(aq) \longrightarrow CuS(s)$

d. NO REACTION

79. $HCl(aq) + KOH(aq) \longrightarrow H_2O(l) + KCl(aq)$
$H^+(aq) + OH^-(aq) \longrightarrow H_2O(l)$

81. a. $2 HCl(aq) + Ba(OH)_2(aq) \longrightarrow 2 H_2O(l) + BaCl_2(aq)$

b. $H_2SO_4(aq) + 2 KOH(aq) \longrightarrow$
$$2 H_2O(l) + K_2SO_4(aq)$$

c. $HClO_4(aq) + NaOH(aq) \longrightarrow$
$$H_2O(l) + NaClO_4(aq)$$

83. a. $HBr(aq) + NaHCO_3(aq) \longrightarrow$
$$H_2O(l) + CO_2(g) + NaBr(aq)$$

b. $NH_4I(aq) + KOH(aq) \longrightarrow$
$$H_2O(l) + NH_3(g) + KI(aq)$$

c. $2 HNO_3(aq) + K_2SO_3(aq) \longrightarrow$
$$H_2O(l) + SO_2(g) + 2 KNO_3(aq)$$

d. $2 HI(aq) + Li_2S(aq) \longrightarrow H_2S(g) + 2 LiI(aq)$

85. b and d are redox reactions; a and c are not.

87. a. $2 C_2H_6(g) + 7 O_2(g) \longrightarrow 4 CO_2(g) + 6 H_2O(g)$

b. $2 Ca(s) + O_2(g) \longrightarrow 2 CaO(s)$

c. $2 C_3H_8O(l) + 9 O_2(g) \longrightarrow 6 CO_2(g) + 8 H_2O(g)$

d. $2 C_4H_{10}S(l) + 15 O_2(g) \longrightarrow$
$$8 CO_2(g) + 10 H_2O(g) + 2 SO_2(g)$$

89. a. $2 Ag(s) + Br_2(g) \longrightarrow 2 AgBr(s)$

b. $2 K(s) + Br_2(g) \longrightarrow 2 KBr(s)$

c. $2 Al(s) + 3 Br_2(g) \longrightarrow 2 AlBr_3(s)$

d. $Ca(s) + Br_2(g) \longrightarrow CaBr_2(s)$

91. a. double displacement

b. synthesis or combination

c. single displacement

d. decomposition

93. a. synthesis   **b.** decomposition

c. synthesis

95. a. $2 Na^+(aq) + 2 I^-(aq) + Hg_2^+(aq) + 2 NO_3^-(aq)$
$$\longrightarrow Hg_2I_2(s) + 2 Na^+(aq) + 2 NO_3^-(aq)$$

b. $2 H^+(aq) + 2 ClO_4^-(aq) + Ba^{2+}(aq) + 2 OH^-(aq)$
$$\longrightarrow 2 H_2O(l) + Ba^{2+}(aq) + 2 ClO_4^-(aq)$$
$H^+(aq) + OH^-(aq) \longrightarrow H_2O(s)$

c. NO REACTION

d. $2 H^+(aq) + 2 Cl^-(aq) + 2 Li^+(aq) + CO_3^{2-}(aq) \longrightarrow$
$$H_2O(l) + CO_2(g) + 2 Li^+(aq) + 2 Cl^-(aq)$$
$2 H^+(aq) + CO_3^{2-}(aq) \longrightarrow H_2O(l) + CO_2(g)$

97. a. NO REACTION

b. NO REACTION

c. $K^+(aq) + HSO_3^-(aq) + H^+(aq) + NO_3^-(aq) \longrightarrow$
$$H_2O(l) + SO_2(g) + K^+(aq) + NO_3^-(aq)$$
$H^+(aq) + HSO_3^-(aq) \longrightarrow H_2O(l) + SO_2(g)$

d. $Mn^{3+}(aq) + 3 Cl^-(aq) + 3 K^+(aq) + PO_4^{3-}(aq) \longrightarrow$
$$MnPO_4(s) + 3 K^+(aq) + 3 Cl^-(aq)$$
$Mn^{3+}(aq) + PO_4^{3-}(aq) \longrightarrow MnPO_4(s)$

99. a. acid–base; $KOH(aq) + HC_2H_3O_2(aq) \longrightarrow$
$$H_2O(l) + KC_2H_3O_2(aq)$$

b. gas evolution; $2 HBr(aq) + K_2CO_3(aq) \longrightarrow$
$$H_2O(l) + CO_2(g) + 2 KBr(aq)$$

c. synthesis; $2 H_2(g) + O_2(g) \longrightarrow 2 H_2O(l)$

d. precipitation; $2 NH_4Cl(aq) + Pb(NO_3)_2(aq) \longrightarrow$
$$PbCl_2(s) + 2 NH_4NO_3(aq)$$

101. a. oxidation–reduction; single displacement

b. gas evolution; acid–base

c. gas evolution; double displacement

d. precipitation; double displacement

103. $3 CaCl_2(aq) + 2 Na_3PO_4(aq) \longrightarrow$
$$Ca_3(PO_4)_2(s) + 6 NaCl(aq)$$
$3 Ca^{2+}(aq) + 6 Cl^-(aq) + 6 Na^+(aq) + 2 PO_4^{3-}(aq)$
$$\longrightarrow Ca_3(PO_4)_2(s) + 6 Na^+(aq) + 6 Cl^-(aq)$$
$3 Ca^{2+}(aq) + 2 PO_4^{3-}(aq) \longrightarrow Ca_3(PO_4)_2(s)$
$3 Mg(NO_3)_2(aq) + 2 Na_3PO_4(aq) \longrightarrow$
$$Mg_3(PO_4)_2(s) + 6 NaNO_3(aq)$$

$3 Mg^{2+}(aq) + 6 NO_3^-(aq) + 6 Na^+(aq) + 2 PO_4^{3-}(aq)$
$\longrightarrow Mg_3(PO_4)_2(s) + 6 Na^+(aq) + 6 NO_3^-(aq)$
$3 Mg^{2+}(aq) + 2 PO_4^{3-}(aq) \longrightarrow Mg_3(PO_4)_2(s)$

105. *Correct answers may vary; representative correct answers are:

   a. addition of a solution containing SO_4^{2-};
$Pb^{2+}(aq) + SO_4^{2-}(aq) \longrightarrow PbSO_4(s)$

   b. addition of a solution containing SO_4^{2-};
$Ca^{2+}(aq) + SO_4^{2-}(aq) \longrightarrow CaSO_4(s)$

   c. addition of a solution containing SO_4^{2-};
$Ba^{2+}(aq) + SO_4^{2-}(aq) \longrightarrow BaSO_4(s)$

   d. addition of a solution containing Cl^-;
$Hg_2^{2+}(aq) + 2 Cl^-(aq) \longrightarrow Hg_2Cl_2(s)$

107. Ca^{2+} and Cu^{2+} were present in the original solution.
1st: $Ca^{2+}(aq) + SO_4^{2-}(aq) \longrightarrow CaSO_4(s)$
2nd: $Cu^{2+}(aq) + CO_3^{2-}(aq) \longrightarrow CuCO_3(s)$

109. 0.168 mol Ca; 6.73 g Ca

111. 0.00128 mol NaCl, 0.0750 g NaCl

113. **a.** chemical   **b.** physical

CHAPTER 8
QUESTIONS

1. Reaction stoichiometry is very important to chemistry. It gives us a numerical relationship between the reactants and products that allows chemists to plan and carry out chemical reactions to obtain products in the desired quantities.

   For example, how much CO_2 is produced when a given amount of C_8H_{10} is burned?

   How much $H_2(g)$ is produced when a given amount of water decomposes?

3. $1 mol\ Cl_2 \equiv 2\ mol\ NaCl$

5. mass A $\longrightarrow$ moles A $\longrightarrow$ moles B $\longrightarrow$ mass B
(A = reactant, B = product)

7. The limiting reactant is the reactant that limits the amount of product in a chemical reaction.

9. The actual yield is the amount of product actually produced by a chemical reaction. The percent yield is the percentage of the theoretical yield that was actually attained.

11. **d**

13. The enthalpy of reaction is the total amount of heat generated or absorbed by a particular chemical reaction. The quantity is important because it quantifies the change in heat for the chemical reaction. It is useful for determining the necessary starting conditions and predicting the outcome of various reactions.

PROBLEMS

15. **a.** 2 mol C   **b.** 1 mol C
   c. 3 mol C   **d.** 1.5 mol C

17. **a.** 2.6 mol NO_2 **b.** 11.6 mol NO_2
   c. 8.90×10^3 mol NO_2 **d.** 2.012×10^{-3} mol NO_2

19. **c**

21. **a.** 3.50 mol HCl   **b.** 3.50 mol H_2O
   c. 0.875 mol Na_2O_2 **d.** 1.17 mol SO_3

23. **a.** 2.4 mol PbO(s), 2.4 mol $SO_2(g)$
   b. 1.6 mol PbO(s), 1.6 mol $SO_2(g)$
   c. 5.3 mol PbO(s), 5.3 mol $SO_2(g)$
   d. 3.5 mol PbO(s), 3.5 mol $SO_2(g)$

25.

mol N_2H_4	mol N_2O_4	mol N_2	mol H_2O
4	2	6	8
6	3	9	12
4	2	6	8
11	5.5	16.5	22
3	1.5	4.5	6
8.26	4.13	12.4	16.5

27. $2 C_4H_{10}(g) + 13 O_2(g) \longrightarrow$
$8 CO_2(g) + 10 H_2O(g)$; 32 mol O_2

29. **a.** $Pb(s) + 2 AgNO_3(aq) \longrightarrow Pb(NO_3)_2(aq) + 2 Ag(s)$
   b. 19 mol $AgNO_3$ **c.** 56.8 mol Ag

31. **a.** 0.157 g O_2 **b.** 0.500 g O_2
   c. 114 g O_2 **d.** 2.86×10^{-4} g O_2

33. **a.** 4.0 g NaCl   **b.** 4.3 g $CaCO_3$
   c. 4.0 g MgO   **d.** 3.1 g NaOH

35. **a.** 8.9 g Al_2O_3, 9.7 g Fe   **b.** 3.0 g Al_2O_3, 3.3 g Fe

37.

Mass CH_4	Mass O_2	Mass CO_2	Mass H_2O
0.645 g	2.57 g	1.77 g	1.45 g
22.32 g	89.00 g	61.20 g	50.12 g
5.044 g	20.11 g	13.83 g	11.32 g
1.07 g	4.28 g	2.94 g	2.41 g
3.18 kg	12.7 kg	8.72 kg	7.14 kg
8.57×10^2 kg	3.42×10^3 kg	2.35×10^3 kg	1.92×10^3 kg

39. **a.** 2.3 g HCl   **b.** 4.3 g HNO_3
   c. 2.2 g H_2SO_4

41. 123 g H_2SO_4, 2.53 g H_2

43. **a.** 2 mol A   **b.** 1.8 mol A
   c. 4 mol B   **d.** 40 mol B

45. **a.** 1.5 mol C   **b.** 3 mol C
   c. 3 mol C   **d.** 96 mol C

47. **a.** 1 mol K   **b.** 1.8 mol K
   c. 1 mol Cl_2 **d.** 14.6 mol K

49. **a.** 1.3 mol MnO_3 **b.** 4.8 mol MnO_3
   c. 0.107 mol MnO_3 **d.** 27.5 mol MnO_3

51. 3 mol A, 0 mol B, 4 mol C

53. **a.** 2 Cl_2 **b.** 3 Cl_2
   c. 2 Cl_2

55. **a.** 1.0 g F_2 **b.** 10.5 g Li
   c. 6.79×10^3 g F_2

57. **a.** 1.3 g $AlCl_3$ **b.** 24.8 g $AlCl_3$
   c. 2.17 g $AlCl_3$

59. 74.6%

61. CaO; 25.7 g $CaCO_3$; 75.5%

63. O_2; 5.07 g NiO; 95.9%

65. Pb^{2+}; 262.7 g $PbCl_2$; 96.09%
67. TiO_2: 0 g, C: 7.0 g, Ti: 5.99 g, CO: 7.00 g
69. **a.** exothermic, $-\Delta H$ **b.** endothermic, $+\Delta H$
    c. exothermic, $-\Delta H$
71. **a.** 55 kJ   **b.** 110 kJ
    c. 28 kJ   **d.** 55 kJ
73. 4.78×10^3 kJ
75. 34.9 g C_8H_{18}
77. N_2
79. 0.152 g Ba^{2+}
81. 1.5 g HCl
83. 3.1 kg CO_2
85. 4.7 g Na_3PO_4
87. 469 g Zn
89. $2\ NH_4NO_3(s) \longrightarrow$
    $2\ N_2(g) + O_2(g) + 4\ H_2O(l)$; 2.00×10^2 g O_2
91. salicylic acid ($C_7H_6O_3$); 2.71 g $C_9H_8O_4$; 74.1%
93. NH_3; 120 kg (CH_4N_2O); 72.9%
95. 2.4 mg $C_4H_6O_4S_2$
97. 1.0×10^3 g CO_2
99. b; the loudest explosion will occur when the ratio is 2 hydrogen to 1 oxygen, for that is the ratio that occurs in water.
101. 2.8×10^{13} kg CO_2 per year; 1.1×10^2 years

CHAPTER 9
QUESTIONS

1. Both the Bohr model and the quantum-mechanical model for the atom were developed in the early 1900s. These models serve to explain how electrons are arranged within the atomic structure and how the electrons affect the chemical and physical properties of each element.

3. White light contains a spectrum of wavelengths and therefore a spectrum of color. Colored light is produced by a single wavelength and is therefore a single color.

5. Energy carried per photon is greater for shorter wavelengths than for longer wavelengths. Wavelength and frequency are inversely related—the shorter the wavelength, the higher the frequency.

7. X-rays pass through many substances that block visible light and are therefore used to image bones and organs.

9. Ultraviolet light contains enough energy to damage biological molecules, and excessive exposure increases the risk of skin cancer and cataracts.

11. Microwaves can only heat things containing water, and therefore the food, which contains water, becomes hot, but the plate does not.

13. The Bohr model is a representation for the atom in which electrons travel around the nucleus in circular orbits with a fixed energy at specific, fixed distances from the nucleus.

15. The Bohr orbit describes the path of an electron as an orbit or trajectory (a specified path). A quantum-mechanical orbital describes the path of an electron using a probability map.

17. The e^- has wave particle duality, which means the path of an electron is not predictable. The motion of a baseball is

predictable. A probability map shows a statistical, reproducible pattern of where the electron is located.

19. The subshells are s (1 orbital, which contains a maximum of 2 electrons); p (3 orbitals, which contain a maximum of 6 electrons); d (5 orbitals, which contain a maximum of 10 electrons); and f (7 orbitals, which contain a maximum of 14 electrons).

21. The Pauli exclusion principle states that separate orbitals may hold no more than 2 electrons, and when 2 electrons are present in a single orbital, they must have opposite spins. When writing electron configurations, the principle means that no box can have more than 2 arrows, and the arrows will point in opposite directions.

23. [Ne] represents $1s^2 2s^2 2p^6$.
    [Kr] represents $1s^2 2s^2 2p^6 3s^2 3p^6 4s^2 3d^{10} 4p^6$.

25.

27. Group 1 elements form 1+ ions because they lose one valence electron in the outer s shell to obtain a noble gas configuration. Group 7 elements form 1− ions because they gain an electron to fill their outer p orbital to obtain a noble gas configuration.

PROBLEMS

29. **a.** 1.0 ns   **b.** 13.21 ms
    c. 4 h 10 min
31. infrared
33. radiowaves < microwaves < infrared < ultraviolet
35. gamma, ultraviolet, or X-rays
37. **a.** radio waves < infrared < X-rays
    b. radio waves < infrared < X-rays
    c. X-rays < infrared < radio waves
39. energies, distances
41. $n = 6 \longrightarrow n = 2$:   410 nm
    $n = 5 \longrightarrow n = 2$:   434 nm

43.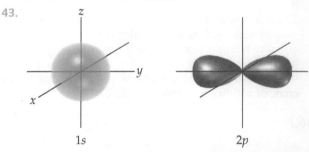

    The 2s and 3p orbitals are bigger than the 1s and 2p orbitals.

45. Electron in the 2s orbital
47. $2p \longrightarrow 1s$
49. **a.** $1s^2 2p^2 2p^6 3s^2 3p^6 4s^2 3d^{10} 4p^6 5s^2$
    b. $1s^2 2s^2 2p^6 3s^2 3p^6 4s^2 3d^{10} 4p^2$
    c. $1s^2 2s^1$
    d. $1s^2 2s^2 2p^6 3s^2 3p^6 4s^2 3d^{10} 4p^6$

51.

a. He

⇅	☐
$1s$	$2s$

b. B

⇅	⇅	↑	☐	☐
$1s$	$2s$		$2p$	

c. Li

⇅	↑	☐	☐	☐
$1s$	$2s$		$2p$	

d. N

⇅	↑	⇅	↓	↓
$1s$	$2s$		$2p$	

53.
a. $[Ar]4s^23d^{10}4p^1$ **b.** $[Ar]4s^23d^{10}4p^3$
c. $[Kr]5s^1$ **d.** $[Kr]5s^24d^{10}5p^2$

55.
a. $[Ar]4s^23d^{10}$ **b.** $[Ar]4s^13d^{10}$
c. $[Kr]5s^24d^2$ **d.** $[Ar]4s^23d^6$

57. Valence electrons are underlined.
a. $1s^22s^22p^63s^23p^6\underline{4s^2}3d^{10}\underline{4p^6}$
b. $1s^22s^22p^63s^23p^6\underline{4s^2}3d^{10}\underline{4p^2}$
c. $1s^22s^22p^6\underline{3s^23p^5}$
d. $1s^22s^22p^63s^23p^64s^23d^{10}4p^6\underline{5s^2}$

59.
a. Br

⇅		⇅	⇅	↑
$4s$			$4p$	

, 1 unpaired electron

b. Kr

⇅		⇅	⇅	⇅
$4s$			$4p$	

, 0 unpaired electron

c. Na

↑
$3s$

, 1 unpaired electron

d. In

⇅		↑	☐	☐
$5s$			$5p$	

, 1 unpaired electron

61. **a.** 6   **b.** 6
c. 7   **d.** 1

63. **a.** ns^1 **b.** ns^2
c. ns^2np^3 **d.** ns^2np^5

65. **a.** $[Ne]3s^23p^1$ **b.** $[He]2s^2$
c. $[Kr]5s^24d^{10}5p^1$ **d.** $[Kr]5s^24d^2$

67. **a.** $[Kr]5s^2$ **b.** $[Kr]5s^24d^1$
c. $[Ar]4s^23d^2$ **d.** $[Kr]5s^24d^{10}5p^4$

69. **a.** 2   **b.** 3
c. 5   **d.** 6

71. Period 1 has two elements. Period 2 has eight elements. The number of subshells is equal to the principal quantum number. For Period 1, $n = 1$ and the s subshell contains only two elements. For Period 2, $n = 2$ and contains s and p subshells that have a total of 8 elements.

73. **a.** Al   **b.** S
c. Ar   **d.** Mg

75. **a.** Cl   **b.** Ga
c. Fe   **d.** Rb

77. **a.** As   **b.** Br
c. cannot tell   **d.** S

79. Pb < Sn < Te < S < Cl

81. **a.** In   **b.** Si
c. Pb   **d.** C

83. F < S < Si < Ge < Ca < Rb

85. **a.** Sr   **b.** Bi
c. cannot tell   **d.** As

87. S < Se < Sb < In < Ba < Fr

89. $18 \, e^-$

91. Alkaline earth metals have the general electron configuration of ns^2. If they lose their two s electrons, they will obtain the stable electron configuration of a noble gas. This loss of electrons will give the metal a 2+ charge.

93. **a.** $1s^22s^22p^63s^23p^6$ **b.** $1s^22s^22p^63s^23p^6$
c. $1s^22s^22p^63s^23p^6$ **d.** $1s^22s^22p^63s^23p^64s^23d^{10}4p^6$
They all have noble gas electron configurations.

95. Metals tend to form positive ions because they tend to lose electrons. Elements on the left side of the periodic table have only a few extra electrons, which they will lose to gain a noble gas configuration. Metalloids tend to be elements with 3 to 5 valence electrons; they could lose or gain electrons to obtain a noble gas configuration. Nonmetals tend to gain electrons to fill their almost full valence shell, so they tend to form negative ions and are on the right side of the table.

97. **a.** Can only have 2 in the s shell and 6 in the p shell: $1s^22s^22p^63s^23p^3$.
b. There is no $2d$ subshell: $1s^22s^22p^63s^23p^2$.
c. There is no $1p$ subshell: $1s^22s^22p^3$.
d. Can only have 6 in the p shell: $1s^22s^22p^63s^23p^3$.

99. Bromine is highly reactive because it reacts quickly to gain an electron and obtain a stable valence shell. Krypton is a noble gas because it already has a stable valence shell.

101. K

103. 660 nm

105. 8 min, 19 sec

107. The quantum-mechanical model provided the ability to understand and predict chemical bonding, which is the basic level of understanding of matter and how it interacts. This model was critical in the areas of lasers, computers, semiconductors, and drug design. The quantum-mechanical model for the atom is considered the foundation of modern chemistry.

109. **a.** 1.5×10^{-34} m   **b.** 1.88×10^{-10} m
Electrons have wave-particle duality, whereas golf balls do not.

111. The ionization energy dips at column 3A because removing an electron from one of those atoms leaves the atom with a fairly stable, filled s-orbital as its valence shell. For the group 6A elements, special stability occurs when those elements lose an electron and achieve a half-filled p-orbital as their valence shell.

113. Ultraviolet light is the only one of these three types of light that contains enough energy to break chemical bonds in biological molecules.

CHAPTER 10
QUESTIONS

1. Bonding theories predict how atoms bond together to form molecules, and they also predict what combinations of atoms form molecules and what combinations do not. Likewise, bonding theories explain the shapes of molecules, which in turn determine many of their physical and chemical properties.

3. Atoms with 8 valence electrons are particularly stable and are said to have an octet. Atoms such as hydrogen, helium, lithium, and beryllium are exceptions to the octet rule as they achieve stability when their outermost shell contains two electrons—a duet. A chemical bond is the sharing or transfer of electrons to attain stable electron configurations among the bonding atoms.

5. The Lewis structure for potassium has 1 valence electron, whereas the Lewis structure for monatomic chlorine has 7 valence electrons. From these structures we can determine that if potassium gives up its one valence electron to chlorine, K^+ and Cl^- are formed; therefore the formula must be KCl.

7. Double and triple bonds are shorter and stronger than single bonds.

9. You determine the number of electrons that go into the Lewis structure of a molecule by summing the valence electrons of each atom in the molecule.

11. The octet rule is not sophisticated enough to be correct every time. For example, some molecules that exist in nature have an odd number of valence electrons and thus will not have octets on all their constituent atoms. Some elements tend to form compounds in nature in which they have more (sulfur) or less (boron) than 8 valence electrons.

13. VSEPR theory predicts the shape of molecules using the idea that electron groups repel each other.

15. **a.** 180°   **b.** 120°
    c. 109.5°

17. Electronegativity is the ability of an element to attract electrons within a covalent bond.

19. A polar covalent bond is a covalent bond that has a dipole moment.

21. If a polar liquid and a nonpolar liquid are mixed, they will separate into distinct regions because the polar molecules will be attracted to one another and will exclude the nonpolar molecules.

PROBLEMS

23. **a.** $1s^22s^22p^3$, ·N̈:
    b. $1s^22s^22p^2$, ·C̈·
    c. $1s^22s^22p^63s^23p^5$, :C̈l·
    d. $1s^22s^22p^63s^23p^6$, :Är:

25. **a.** :Ï: **b.** ·S̈:
    c. ·G̈e·   **d.** ·Ca·

27. :Ẍ: Halogens tend to gain one electron in a chemical reaction.

29. M: Alkaline earth metals tend to lose two electrons in a chemical reaction.

31. **a.** Al^{3+} **b.** Mg^{2+}
    c. $[:S̈e:]^{2-}$ **d.** $[:N̈:]^{3-}$

33. **a.** Kr   **b.** Ne
    c. Kr   **d.** Xe

35. **a.** covalent   **b.** ionic
    c. covalent   **d.** ionic

37. **a.** $Na^+[:F̈:]^-$ **b.** $Ca^{2+}[:Ö:]^{2-}$
    c. $[:B̈r:]^- Sr^{2+}[:B̈r:]^-$ **d.** $K^+[:Ö:]^{2-}K^+$

39. **a.** CaS   **b.** $MgBr_2$
    c. CsI   **d.** Ca_3N_2

41. **a.** $[:F̈:]^- Mg^{2+}[:F̈:]^-$ **b.** $Mg^{2+}[:Ö:]^{2-}$
    c. $Mg^{2+}[:N̈:]^{3-}Mg^{2+}[:N̈:]^{3-}Mg^{2+}$

43. **a.** $Cs^+[:C̈l:]^-$ **b.** $Ba^{2+}[:Ö:]^{2-}$
    c. $[:Ï:]^- Ca^{2+}[:Ï:]^-$

45. **a.** Hydrogen exists as a diatomic molecule because two hydrogen molecules achieve a stable duet when they share their electrons and form a single covalent bond.
    b. Iodine achieves a stable octet when two atoms share electrons and form a single bond.
    c. Nitrogen achieves a stable octet when two atoms share electrons and form a triple bond.
    d. Oxygen achieves a stable octet when two atoms share electrons and form a double bond.

47. **a.** H—P̈—H (with H below)   **b.** :C̈l—S̈—C̈l:
    c. :F̈—F̈:   **d.** H—Ï:

49. **a.** Ö=Ö   **b.** :C≡O:
    c. H—Ö—N̈—Ö   **d.** :Ö=S̈—Ö:

51. **a.** H—C≡C—H   **b.** H—C=C—H (with H H below)
    c. H—N̈=N̈—H   **d.** H—N̈—N̈—H (with H H below)

53. **a.** :N≡N: **b.** S̈=Si=S̈
    c. H—Ö—H   **d.** :Ï—N̈—Ï: (with :Ï: below)

55. **a.** Ö=S̈e—Ö: ⟷ :Ö—S̈e=Ö
    b.
    $[Ö=C—Ö:]^{2-}$ ⟷ $[:Ö—C=Ö:]^{2-}$ ⟷ $[:Ö—C—Ö:]^{2-}$ (each with :O: below)
    c. $[:C̈l—Ö:]^-$ **d.** $[:Ö—C̈l—Ö:]^-$

57. **a.** $\left[\ddot{\underset{\ddot{O}:}{\overset{:\ddot{O}:}{\overset{|}{O}-P-\ddot{O}:}}}\right]^{3-}$ **b.** $[:C\equiv N:]^-$

c. $[:\ddot{O}=\ddot{N}-\ddot{O}:]^- \longleftrightarrow [:\ddot{O}-\ddot{N}=\ddot{O}:]^-$

d. $\left[:\ddot{\underset{:\ddot{O}:}{\overset{|}{O}}}-\overset{|}{\underset{|}{S}}-\ddot{O}:\right]^{2-}$

59. **a.** $:\ddot{C}l-\underset{\overset{|}{:}\ddot{C}l:}{B}-\ddot{C}l:$

b. $\ddot{O}=\dot{N}-\ddot{O}: \longleftrightarrow :\ddot{O}-\dot{N}=\ddot{O}$

c. $H-\underset{\overset{|}{H}}{B}-H$

61. **a.** 4 **b.** 4
    c. 2 **d.** 4
63. **a.** 2 bonding groups, 2 lone pairs
    b. 3 bonding groups, 1 lone pair
    c. 2 bonding groups, 0 lone pair
    d. 4 bonding groups, 0 lone pair
65. **a.** tetrahedral **b.** trigonal planar
    c. linear **d.** trigonal planar
67. **a.** 109.5° **b.** 120°
    c. 180° **d.** 120°
69. **a.** linear, linear
    b. trigonal planar, bent
    c. tetrahedral, bent
    d. tetrahedral, trigonal pyramidal
71. **a.** 180° **b.** 120°
    c. 109.5° **d.** 109.5°
73. **a.** linear, linear
    b. trigonal planar, bent (about both nitrogen atoms)
    c. tetrahedral, trigonal pyramidal (about both nitrogen atoms)
75. **a.** trigonal planar **b.** bent
    c. trigonal planar **d.** tetrahedral
77. **a.** 1.2 **b.** 1.8
    c. 2.8
79. Cl > Si > Ga > Ca > Rb
81. **a.** polar covalent **b.** ionic
    c. pure covalent **d.** polar covalent
83. H_2 < ICl < HBr < CO
85. **a.** polar **b.** nonpolar
    c. nonpolar **d.** polar
87. **a.** $(+):C\equiv O:(-)$ **b.** nonpolar
    c. nonpolar **d.** $(+)H-\ddot{B}r:(-)$
89. **a.** nonpolar **b.** polar
    c. nonpolar **d.** polar

91. **a.** nonpolar **b.** polar
    c. nonpolar **d.** polar
93. **a.** $1s^22s^22p^63s^23p^64s^2$, Ca: (underlined electrons are the ones included)
    b. $1s^22s^22p^33s^23p^64s^23d^{10}4p^1$, Ga:
    c. $[Ar]4s^23d^{10}4p^3$, $\cdot\dot{A}s:$
    d. $[Kr]5s^24d^{10}5p^5$, $:\dot{I}:$
95. **a.** ionic, $K^+[:\ddot{S}:]^{2-}K^+$
    b. covalent, $H-\underset{}{\overset{\ddot{O}:}{\overset{\|}{C}}}-\ddot{F}:$
    c. ionic, $Mg^{2+}[:\ddot{S}\dot{e}:]^{2-}$
    d. covalent, $:\ddot{B}r-\underset{}{\overset{:\ddot{B}r:}{\overset{|}{P}}}-\ddot{B}r:$
97. $:\ddot{C}l-\overset{\overset{\ddot{O}}{\|}}{C}-\ddot{C}l:$ polar, $\underset{Cl \quad Cl}{\overset{\overset{O}{\|}}{C}}$
99. $H-\underset{\overset{|}{H}}{\overset{\overset{H}{|}}{C}}-\overset{\overset{\ddot{O}:}{\|}}{C}-\ddot{O}H$ $H^{\text{IIII}}\underset{\overset{|}{H}}{\overset{\overset{H}{|}}{C}}-\underset{OH}{\overset{\overset{O}{\|}}{C}}$
101. $H:\ddot{C}l: + Na^+[:\ddot{O}:H]^- \longrightarrow H:\ddot{O}:H + Na^+[:\ddot{C}l:]^-$
103. $K\cdot$, $:\ddot{C}l-\ddot{C}l:$, $K^+[:\ddot{C}l:]^-$, Cl reduced, K oxidized
105. **a.** $K^+[:\ddot{O}:H]^-$
    b.
    $K^+[:\ddot{O}=\overset{:\ddot{O}:}{N}:\ddot{O}:]^- \longleftrightarrow K^+[:\ddot{O}:\overset{:\ddot{O}:}{N}:\ddot{O}:]^- \longleftrightarrow K^+[:\ddot{O}:\overset{:\ddot{O}:}{N}=\ddot{O}:]^-$
    c. $Li^+[:\ddot{I}:\ddot{O}:]^-$
    d.
    $Ba^{2+}\left[\overset{:\ddot{O}}{\underset{:\ddot{O}:\quad:\ddot{O}:}{\overset{\|}{C}}}\right]^{2-} \longleftrightarrow Ba^{2+}\left[\overset{:\ddot{O}:}{\underset{:\ddot{O}:\quad\ddot{O}:}{\overset{\ddot{C}}{}}}\right]^{2-} \longleftrightarrow Ba^{2+}\left[\overset{:\ddot{O}:}{\underset{:\ddot{O}:\quad:\ddot{O}:}{\overset{\ddot{C}}{}}}\right]^{2-}$
107. **a.** $\underset{:\ddot{F}:\quad:\ddot{F}:}{\overset{:\ddot{F}:\quad:\ddot{F}:\quad:\ddot{F}}{P}}$ **b.** $\underset{:\ddot{F}\quad:\ddot{F}:}{\overset{:\ddot{F}:\quad:\ddot{F}:}{S}}$
    c. $\underset{:\ddot{F}:\quad:\ddot{F}:}{\overset{:\ddot{F}:\quad:\ddot{F}:}{Se}}$
109. CH_2O_2 or $H-\overset{\overset{:\ddot{O}}{\|}}{C}-\ddot{O}-H$

111. H—Ö—Ö· HOO is not stable because one oxygen atom does not have an octet. The geometry for HOO is *bent*.

113. a. $[\text{:Ö—Ö:}]^{-}$ **b.** $[\text{:Ö:}]^{-}$

c. ·Ö—H   **d.** H—C—Ö—Ö· (with H above and H below the C)

115. a. The structure has 2 bonding electron pairs and 2 lone pairs. The Lewis structure is analogous to that of water, and the molecular geometry is bent.

b. Correct

c. The structure has 3 bonding electron pairs and 1 lone pair. The Lewis structure is analogous to that of NH_3, and the geometry is trigonal pyramidal.

d. Correct

CHAPTER 11

QUESTIONS

1. Pressure is the push (or force) exerted per unit area by gaseous molecules as they collide with the surfaces around them.

3. The kinetic molecular theory makes four main assumptions. The first is that the gas is a collection of molecules in constant motion. Second, there is no attraction or repulsion between the particles, and collisions are perfectly elastic. Third, there is a lot of space in between the particles relative to the particle size. Lastly, the speed of the particles increases with temperature.

5. The pain we experience in our ears during a change in altitude is due to a pressure difference between the cavities inside of our ears and the surrounding air.

7. Boyle's law states that the volume of a gas and its pressure are inversely proportional. This relationship can be explained by the kinetic molecular theory. If the volume of a sample is decreased, the same number of particles are crowded into a smaller space, causing more collisions with the walls of the container. This causes the pressure to increase.

9. When an individual is more than a couple of meters underwater, the air pressure in the lungs is greater than the air pressure at the water's surface. If a snorkel were used, it would move the air from the lungs to the surface, making it very difficult to breathe.

11. Increasing the temperature of the air in the balloon causes it to expand. As the volume of the air increases, the density decreases allowing it to float in the cooler, more dense air surrounding it.

13. Avogadro's law states that the volume of a gas is directly proportional to the amount of gas in moles. Kinetic molecular theory predicts that if the number of gas particles increases at a constant pressure and temperature, the volume increases.

15. The ideal gas law is most accurate when the volume of gas particles is small compared to the space between them. It is also accurate when the forces between particles are not important. The ideal gas law breaks down at high pressures and low temperatures. This breakdown occurs

because the gases are no longer acting according to the kinetic molecular theory.

17. Dalton's law states that the sum of the partial pressures in a gas mixture must equal the total pressure. $P_{tot} = P_A + P_B + P_C + \ldots$

19. Deep-sea divers breathe helium with oxygen because helium, unlike nitrogen, does not have physiological effects under high-pressure conditions. The oxygen concentration in the mixture is low to avoid oxygen toxicity.

21. Vapor pressure is the partial pressure of a gas above its liquid. Partial pressure increases with increasing temperature.

PROBLEMS

23. a. 1.680 atm   **b.** 2.35 atm
     c. 8.64 atm   **d.** 0.599 atm

25. a. 1.7×10^3 torr   **b.** 36 mmHg
     c. 1.28×10^3 mmHg   **d.** 834.2 torr

27.

Pascals	Atmospheres	mmHg	Torr	PSI
882	0.00871	6.62	6.62	0.128
5.65×10^4	0.558	424	424	8.20
1.71×10^5	1.69	1.28×10^3	1.28×10^3	24.8
1.02×10^5	1.01	764	764	14.8
3.32×10^4	0.328	249	249	4.82

29. a. 0.832 atm   **b.** 632 mmHg
     c. 12.2 psi   **d.** 8.43×10^4 Pa

31. a. 809.0 mmHg   **b.** 1.065 atm
     c. 809.0 torr   **d.** 107.9 kPa

33. 518 mmHg

35. 1.8 L

37.

P_1	V_1	P_2	V_2
755 mmHg	2.85 L	885 mmHg	2.43 L
9.35 atm	1.33 L	4.32 atm	2.88 L
192 mmHg	382 mL	152 mmHg	482 mL
211 atm	226 mL	3.82 atm	125 mL

39. 4.0 L

41. 58.9 mL

43.

V_1	T_1	V_2	T_2
1.08 L	25.4 °C	1.33 L	94.5 °C
58.9 mL	77 K	228 mL	298 K
115 cm³	12.5 °C	119 cm³	22.4 °C
232 L	18.5 °C	294 L	96.2 °C

45. 6.8 L

47. 4.33 L

49.

V_1	n_1	V_2	n_2
38.5 mL	1.55×10^{-3}	49.4 mL	1.99×10^{-3}
8.03 L	1.37	26.8 L	4.57
11.2 L	0.628	15.7 L	0.881
422 mL	0.0109	671 mL	0.0174

51. 1.71×10^3 mmHg

53. 0.76 L

55. 877 mmHg

57.

P_1	V_1	T_1	P_2	V_2	T_2
121 atm	1.58 L	12.2 °C	1.54 torr	1.33 L	32.3 °C
721 torr	141 mL	135 K	801 torr	152 mL	162 K
5.51 atm	0.879 L	22.1 °C	4.87 atm	1.05 L	38.3 °C

59. 5.11 L

61. 2.1 mol

63. 1.42 mol

65.

P	V	n	T
1.05 atm	1.19 L	0.112 mol	136 K
112 torr	40.8 L	0.241 mol	304 K
1.50 atm	28.5 mL	1.74×10^{-3} mol	25.4 °C
0.559 atm	0.439 L	0.0117 mol	255 K

67. 0.23 mol

69. 44.0 g/mol

71. 4.00 g/mol

73. 571 torr

75. 10.7 atm

77. 7.00×10^2 mmHg

79. 0.87 atm N_2; 0.25 atm O_2

81. 0.34 atm

83. **a.** 504 L   **b.** 81 L
    c. 49 L   **d.** 6.0×10^2 L

85. **a.** 59.1 L   **b.** 30.0 L
    c. 72.1 L   **d.** 0.125 L

87. **a.** 0.350 g   **b.** 0.221 g
    c. 8.15 g

89. 28 L

91. 33 L H_2; 16 L CO

93. 8.82 L

95. 12.6 g

97. 0.5611 g

99. $V = \dfrac{nRT}{P}$

$$= \frac{1.00 \text{ mol} \left(0.0821 \dfrac{\text{L} \cdot \text{atm}}{\text{mol} \cdot \text{K}} \right) (273 \text{ K})}{1.00 \text{ atm}} = 22.4 \text{ L}$$

101. 27.8 g/mol

103. C_4H_{10}

105. 0.828 g

107. 0.128 g

109. 0.935 L

111. $HCl + NaHCO_3 \longrightarrow CO_2 + H_2O + NaCl$;
    1.11×10^{-3} mol

113. **a.** SO_2, 0.0127 mol   **b.** 65.6%

115. **a.** NO_2, 24.0 g   **b.** 61.6%

117. 11.7 L

119. 356 torr

121. 0.15 atm

123. **c.** From the ideal gas law, we see that pressure is directly proportional to the number of moles of gas per unit volume (n/V). The gas in (c) contains the greatest concentration of particles and thus has the highest pressure.

125. 22.8 g

127. $V_2 = 0.76$ L, actual volume is 0.61 L. Difference is because air contains about 20% oxygen, which condenses into a liquid at −183 °C.

CHAPTER 12
QUESTIONS

1. Intermolecular forces are attractive forces that occur between molecules. Intermolecular forces are what living organisms depend on for many physiological processes. Intermolecular forces are also responsible for the existence of liquids and solids.

3. The magnitude of intermolecular forces relative to the amount of thermal energy in the sample determines the state of the matter.

5. Properties of solids:
   a. Solids have high densities in comparison to gases.
   b. Solids have a definite shape.
   c. Solids have a definite volume.
   d. Solids may be crystalline or amorphous.

7. Surface tension is the tendency of liquids to minimize their surface area. Molecules at the surface have few neighbors to interact with via intermolecular forces.

9. Evaporation is a physical change in which a substance is converted from its liquid form to its gaseous form. Condensation is a physical change in which a substance is converted from its gaseous form to its liquid form.

11. Evaporation below the boiling point occurs because molecules on the surface of the liquid experience fewer attractions to the neighboring molecules and can therefore break away. At the boiling point, evaporation occurs faster because more of the molecules have sufficient thermal energy to break away (including internal molecules).

13. Acetone has weaker intermolecular forces than water. Acetone is more volatile than water.

15. Vapor pressure is the partial pressure of a gas in dynamic equilibrium with its liquid. It increases with increasing temperature, and it also increases with decreasing strength of intermolecular forces.

17. A steam burn is worse than a water burn at the same temperature (100 °C), because when the steam condenses on the skin, it releases large amounts of additional heat.

19. As the first molecules freeze, they release heat, making it harder for other molecules to freeze without the aid of a refrigeration mechanism, which would draw heat out.

21. The melting of ice is endothermic. ΔH for melting is positive (+), whereas ΔH for freezing is negative (−).

23. Dispersion forces are the default intermolecular force present in all molecules and atoms. Dispersion forces are caused by fluctuations in the electron distribution within molecules or atoms. Dispersion forces are the weakest type of intermolecular force and increase with increasing molar mass.

25. Hydrogen bonding is an intermolecular force and is sort of a super dipole–dipole force. Hydrogen bonding occurs

in compounds containing hydrogen atoms bonded directly to fluorine, oxygen, or nitrogen.

27. Dispersion force, dipole–dipole force, hydrogen bond, ion–dipole

29. Molecular solids as a whole tend to have low to moderately low melting points relative to other types of solids; however, strong molecular forces can increase their melting points relative to each other.

31. Ionic solids tend to have much higher melting points relative to the melting points of other types of solids.

33. Water is unique for a couple of reasons. Water has a low molar mass, yet it is still liquid at room temperature and has a relatively high boiling point. Unlike other substances, which contract upon freezing, water expands upon freezing.

PROBLEMS

35. The 55 mL of water in a dish with a diameter of 12 cm will evaporate more quickly because it has a larger surface area.

37. Acetone feels cooler while evaporating from one's hand, for it is more volatile than water and evaporates much faster.

39. The ice's temperature will increase from $-5\,°C$ to $0\,°C$, where it will then stay constant while the ice completely melts. After the melting process is complete, the water will continue to rise steadily in temperature until it reaches room temperature ($25\,°C$).

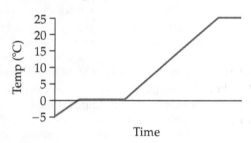

41. Allowing 0.50 g of 100 °C steam to condense on your hand would cause a more severe burn than spilling 0.50 g of 100 °C water on your hand. When the steam condenses on the skin, it releases large amounts of additional heat.

43. The $-8\,°C$ ice chest will cause the water in the watery bag of ice to freeze, which is an exothermic process. The freezing process of the water will release heat, and the temperature of the ice chest will increase.

45. The ice chest filled with ice at 0 °C will be colder after a couple of hours than the ice chest filled with water at 0 °C. This is because the ice can absorb additional heat as it melts.

47. Denver is a mile above sea level and thus has a lower air pressure. Due to this low pressure, the point at which the vapor pressure of water equals the external pressure will occur at a lower temperature.

49. 76.3 kJ

51. 6.8 kJ

53. 10.4 kJ

55. 3.70×10^2 g

57. 12.5 kJ

59. 11.4 kJ

61. 6.53 kJ

63. **a.** dispersion
    b. dispersion
    c. dispersion, dipole–dipole
    d. dispersion, dipole–dipole, hydrogen bonding

65. **a.** dispersion, dipole–dipole
    b. dispersion, dipole–dipole, hydrogen bonding
    c. dispersion
    d. dispersion

67. Ion–dipole forces (between the ions and the water molecules); and hydrogen bonding (between the water molecules themselves)

69. d, because it has the highest molecular weight

71. CH_3OH, due to strong hydrogen bonding

73. NH_3, because it has the ability to form hydrogen bonds

75. These two substances are not miscible, for H_2O is polar and $CH_3CH_2CH_2CH_2CH_3$ is nonpolar.

77. **a.** no   **b.** yes
    c. yes

79. **a.** atomic   **b.** molecular
    c. ionic   **d.** atomic

81. **a.** molecular **b.** ionic
    c. molecular **d.** molecular

83. **c.** LiCl(s); it is an ionic solid and possesses ionic bonds, resulting in a higher melting point.

85. **a.** Ti(s); Ti is a covalent atomic solid, and Ne is a nonbonding atomic solid.
    b. $H_2O(s)$; while both are molecular solids, water has strong hydrogen bonding.
    c. Xe(s); both are nonbonding atomic solids, but Xe has a higher molar mass.
    d. NaCl(s); NaCl(s) is an ionic solid, and $CH_4(s)$ is a molecular solid.

87. $Ne < SO_2 < NH_3 < H_2O < NaF$

89. **a.** 2.6×10^4 J   **b.** 26 kJ
    c. 6.2×10^3 cal   **d.** 6.2 Cal

91. 2.7 °C

93. 1.1×10^2 g

95. 57.5 kJ

97. **a.** H—S̈e—H Bent: Dispersion and dipole–dipole
    b. Ö=S̈—Ö: Bent: Dispersion and dipole–dipole

    c. H—C̈—C̈l: Tetrahedral: Dispersion and dipole–dipole

    d. :Ö=C=Ö: Linear: Dispersion

99. $Na^+[:\ddot{F}:]^-$; $Mg^{2+}[:\ddot{O}:]^{2-}$; MgO has a higher melting point, because the magnitude of the charges on the ions is greater.

101. As the molecular weight increases from Cl to I, the greater the London dispersion forces present, which will increase the boiling point as observed. However, HF is the only compound listed that has the ability to form hydrogen bonds, which explains the anomaly in the trend.

103. 23.6 °C

105. The molecule in the interior has the most neighbors. The molecule on the surface is more likely to evaporate. In three dimensions, the molecules that make up the surface area have the fewest neighbors and are more likely to evaporate than the molecules in the interior.

107. **a.** Yes, if the focus is on the melting of icebergs. No, the melting of an ice cube in a cup of water will *not* raise the level of the liquid in the cup; when the ice cube melts, the volume of the water created will be less than the volume of the initial ice cube.

  b. Yes, for the ice sheets that sit on the continent of Antarctica are above sea level, and if some melted, the water created would be added to the ocean without decreasing the amount of ice below the ocean's surface.

CHAPTER 13
QUESTIONS

1. A solution is a homogeneous mixture of two or more substances. Some examples are air, seawater, soda water, and brass.

3. In a solution, the solvent is the majority component of the mixture, and the solute is the minority component. For example, in a seawater solution, the water is the solvent, and the salt content is the solute.

5. Solubility is the amount of the compound, usually in grams, that will dissolve in a specified amount of solvent.

7. In solutions with solids, soluble ionic solids form strong electrolyte solutions, while soluble molecular solids form nonelectrolyte solutions. Strong electrolyte solutions are solutions containing solutes that dissociate into ions, for example, $BaCl_2$ and $NaOH$.

9. Recrystallization is a common way to purify a solid. In recrystallization, enough solid is put into high-temperature water until a saturated solution is created. Then the solution cools slowly, and crystals result from the solution. The crystalline structure tends to reject impurities, resulting in a purer solid.

11. The bubbles formed on the bottom of a pot of heated water (before boiling) are dissolved air coming out of the solution. These gases come out of solution because the solubility of the dissolved nitrogen and oxygen decreases as the temperature of the water rises.

13. The solubility of gases increases with increasing pressure. When a soda can is opened, the pressure is lowered, decreasing the solubility of carbon dioxide. This causes bubbles of carbon dioxide to come out of the solution.

15. Mass percent is the number of grams of solute per 100 grams of solution. Molarity is defined as the number of moles of solute per liter of solution.

17. The boiling point of a solution containing a nonvolatile solute is higher than the boiling point of the pure solvent. The melting point of the solution, however, is lower.

19. Molality is a common unit of concentration of a solution expressed as number of moles of solute per kilogram of solvent.

21. Water tends to move from lower concentrations to higher concentrations, and when the salt water is being passed through the human body, the salt content draws the water out of the body, causing dehydration.

PROBLEMS

23. **c** and **d** are solutions

25. **a.** solute: salt, solvent: water
  b. solute: sugar, solvent: water
  c. solute: CO_2, solvent: water

27. **a.** hexane   **b.** water
  c. ethyl ether   **d.** water

29. ions, strong electrolyte solution

31. unsaturated

33. recrystallization

35. **a.** no   **b.** yes
  c. yes

37. At room temperature water contains some dissolved oxygen gas; however, the boiling of the water will remove dissolved gases.

39. Under higher pressure, the gas (nitrogen) will be more easily dissolved in the blood. To reverse this process, the diver should ascend to relieve the pressure.

41. **a.** 7.64%   **b.** 3.50%
  c. 4.64%

43. 12%

45.

Mass Solute (g)	Mass Solvent (g)	Mass Solution (g)	Mass%
15.5	238.1	253.6	6.11%
22.8	167.2	190.0	12.0%
28.8	183.3	212.1	13.6%
56.9	315.2	372.1	15.3%

47. 8.9 g NaCl

49. **a.** 1.8 g   **b.** 10.5 mg
  c. 0.46 kg

51. **a.** 2.6 kg   **b.** 1.0×10^2 g
  c. 18 g

53. 1.6×10^2 g

55. 1.3×10^3 g

57. 11 L

59. **a.** 0.194 M   **b.** 0.234 M
  c. 0.41 M

61. **a.** 0.149 M   **b.** 0.461 M
  c. 3.00×10^{-2} M

63. 0.57 M

65. **a.** 1.8 mol   **b.** 0.38 mol
  c. 0.238 mol

67. **a.** 0.59 L   **b.** 0.083 L
  c. 0.15 L

69.

Solute	Mass Solute	Mol Solute	Volume Solution	Molarity
KNO_3	22.5 g	0.223	125 mL	1.78 M
$NaHCO_3$	2.10 g	0.0250	250.0 mL	0.100 M
$C_{12}H_{22}O_{11}$	55.38 g	0.162	1.08 L	0.150 M

71. 2.7 g

73. 19 g

75. 8.8 L

77. a. 0.15 M   **b.** 0.30 M
   c. 0.45 M

79. a. 0.24 M Na^+, 0.12 M SO_4^{2-}
   b. 0.50 M K^+, 0.25 M CO_3^{2-}
   c. 0.11 M Rb^+, 0.11 M Br^-

81. 0.29 M

83. Dilute 0.045 L of the stock solution to 2.5 L.

85. 6.0×10^2 mL

87. 17.7 mL

89. a. 0.025 L   **b.** 0.020 L
   c. 1.03 L

91. 4.45 mL

93. 0.373 M

95. 1.2 L

97. a. 1.0 m   **b.** 3.92 m
   c. 0.52 m

99. 1.49 m

101. a. $-1.6\,°C$ **b.** $-2.70\,°C$
   c. $-8.9\,°C$ **d.** $-4.37\,°C$

103. a. $100.060\,°C$ **b.** $100.993\,°C$
   c. $101.99\,°C$ **d.** $101.11\,°C$

105. $-1.27\,°C$, $100.348\,°C$

107. 2.28 M, 12.3%

109. 0.43 L

111. 319 mL

113. 1.03 M

115. 0.17 L

117. 9.0 mL

119. 8.0×10^1 mL

121. $-3.60\,°C$, $100.992\,°C$

123. $-1.86\,°C$, $100.508\,°C$

125. 1.8×10^2 g/mol

127. $101.8\,°C$

129. 39.8 g glucose, 85.2 g sucrose

131. a. Water will flow from left to right.
   b. Water will flow from right to left.
   c. Water won't flow between the two.

133. 3×10^4 L

CHAPTER 14

QUESTIONS

1. Sour gummy candies are coated with a white powder that is a mixture of citric acid and tartaric acid. The combination of these two acids creates the sour taste.

3. The main component of stomach acid is hydrochloric acid. Its purpose is to help break down food and kill harmful bacteria.

5. The properties of bases are bitter taste, slippery feel, and the ability to turn red litmus paper blue. Some common substances that contain bases are ammonia, Drano, baking soda, and antacids.

7. The Arrhenius definition of an acid is a substance that produces H^+ ions in aqueous solution. An example:
$HCl(aq) \longrightarrow H^+(aq) + Cl^-(aq)$

9. The Brønsted–Lowry definition states that an acid is a proton donor and a base is a proton acceptor. The following is an example of a chemical equation demonstrating this definition:
$$HCl(aq) + H_2O(l) \longrightarrow H_3O^+(aq) + Cl^-(aq)$$
       acid   base

11. An acid–base neutralization reaction occurs when an acid and a base are mixed and the $H^+(aq)$ from the acid combines with the $OH^-(aq)$ from the base to form $H_2O(l)$. An example follows.
$$HCl(aq) + KOH(aq) \longrightarrow H_2O(l) + KCl(aq)$$

13. $2\,HCl(aq) + K_2O(s) \longrightarrow H_2O(l) + 2\,KCl(aq)$

15. A titration is a laboratory procedure in which a reactant in a solution of known concentration is reacted with another reactant in a solution of unknown concentration until the reaction has reached the equivalence point. The equivalence point is the point at which the reactants are in exact stoichiometric proportions.

17. A strong acid is one that will completely dissociate in solution, while a weak acid does not completely dissociate in solution.

19. Monoprotic acids (such as HCl) contain only one hydrogen ion that will dissociate in solution, while diprotic acids (such as H_2SO_4) contain two hydrogen ions that will dissociate in solution.

21. Yes, pure water contains H_3O^+ ions. Through self-ionization, water acts as an acid and a base with itself; water is amphoteric.

23. **a.** $[H_3O^+] > 1.0 \times 10^{-7}\,M$; $[OH^-] < 1.0 \times 10^{-7}\,M$
   b. $[H_3O^+] < 1.0 \times 10^{-7}\,M$; $[OH^-] > 1.0 \times 10^{-7}\,M$
   c. $[H_3O^+] = 1.0 \times 10^{-7}\,M$; $[OH^-] = 1.0 \times 10^{-7}\,M$

25. The pOH of a solution is the negative base-10 logarithm of the concentration of OH^- ions ($-\log[OH^-]$). A change of 2.0 pOH units corresponds to a 100-fold change in $[OH^-]$.

27. A buffer is a solution that resists pH change by neutralizing added acid or added base.

PROBLEMS

29. **a.** acid; $H_2SO_4(aq) \longrightarrow H^+(aq) + HSO_4^-(aq)$
   b. base; $Sr(OH)_2(aq) \longrightarrow Sr^{2+}(aq) + 2\,OH^-(aq)$
   c. acid; $HBr(aq) \longrightarrow H^+(aq) + Br^-(aq)$
   d. base; $NaOH(aq) \longrightarrow Na^+(aq) + OH^-(aq)$

31.

	B-L Acid	B-L Base	Conjugate Acid	Conjugate Base
a.	HBr	H_2O	H_3O^+	Br^-
b.	H_2O	NH_3	NH_4^+	OH^-
c.	HNO_3	H_2O	H_3O^+	NO_3^-
d.	H_2O	C_5H_5N	$C_5H_5NH^+$	OH^-

33. **a, c**

35. **a.** Cl^- **b.** HSO_3^-
   c. CHO_2^- **d.** F^-

37. **a.** NH_4^+ **b.** $HClO_4$
   c. H_2SO_4 **d.** HCO_3^-

39. **a.** $HI(aq) + NaOH(aq) \longrightarrow H_2O(l) + NaI(aq)$
   b. $HBr(aq) + KOH(aq) \longrightarrow H_2O(l) + KBr(aq)$

c. $2\,HNO_3(aq) + Ba(OH)_2(aq) \longrightarrow$
$2\,H_2O(l) + Ba(NO_3)_2(aq)$

d. $2\,HClO_4(aq) + Sr(OH)_2(aq) \longrightarrow$
$2\,H_2O(l) + Sr(ClO_4)_2(aq)$

41. a. $2\,HBr(aq) + 2\,Rb(s) \longrightarrow 2\,RbBr(aq) + H_2(g)$
b. $2\,HBr(aq) + Mg(s) \longrightarrow MgBr_2(aq) + H_2(g)$
c. $2\,HBr(aq) + 2\,Ba(s) \longrightarrow 2\,BaBr(aq) + H_2(g)$
d. $6\,HBr(aq) + 2\,Al(s) \longrightarrow 2\,AlBr_3(aq) + 3\,H_2(g)$

43. a. $MgO(aq) + 2\,HI(aq) \longrightarrow H_2O(l) + MgI_2(aq)$
b. $K_2O(aq) + 2\,HI(aq) \longrightarrow H_2O(l) + 2\,KI(aq)$
c. $Rb_2O(aq) + 2\,HI(aq) \longrightarrow H_2O(l) + 2\,RbI(aq)$
d. $CaO(aq) + 2\,HI(aq) \longrightarrow H_2O(l) + CaI_2(aq)$

45. a. $6\,HClO_4(aq) + Fe_2O_3(s) \longrightarrow$
$2\,Fe(ClO_4)_3(aq) + 3\,H_2O(l)$
b. $H_2SO_4(aq) + Sr(s) \longrightarrow SrSO_4(s) + H_2(g)$
c. $H_3PO_4(aq) + 3\,KOH(aq) \longrightarrow 3\,H_2O(l) + K_3PO_4(aq)$

47. a. 0.1400 M b. 0.138 M
c. 0.08764 M d. 0.182 M

49. 0.1090 M H_2SO_4

51. 16.9 mL

53. a. strong b. weak
c. strong d. weak

55. a. $[H_3O^+] = 1.7$ M b. $[H_3O^+] = 1.5$ M
c. $[H_3O^+] < 0.38$ M d. $[H_3O^+] < 1.75$ M

57. a. strong b. weak
c. strong d. weak

59. a. $[OH^-] = 0.25$ M b. $[OH^-] < 0.25$ M
c. $[OH^-] = 0.50$ M d. $[OH^-] = 1.25$ M

61. a. acidic b. acidic
c. neutral d. basic

63. a. 6.7×10^{-6} M, basic b. 1.1×10^{-6} M, basic
c. 4.5×10^{-9} M, acidic d. 1.4×10^{-11} M, acidic

65. a. 3.7×10^{-3} M, acidic b. 4.0×10^{-13} M, basic
c. 9.1×10^{-5} M, acidic d. 3.0×10^{-11} M, basic

67. a. basic b. neutral
c. acidic d. acidic

69. a. 7.77 b. 7.00
c. 5.66 d. 3.13

71. a. 2.8×10^{-9} M b. 5.9×10^{-12} M
c. 1.3×10^{-3} M d. 6.0×10^{-2} M

73. a. 7.28 b. 6.42
c. 3.86 d. 12.98

75. a. 1.8×10^{-10} M b. 3.4×10^{-2} M
c. 3.2×10^{-13} M d. 1.8×10^{-6} M

77. a. 1.810 b. 11.107
c. 2.724 d. 10.489

79. a. pOH = 8.82, acidic b. pOH = 4.15, basic
c. pOH = 7.00, neutral d. pOH = 2.06, basic

81. a. pOH = 6.08, basic b. pOH = 12.74, acidic
c. pOH = 5.59, basic d. pOH = 1.274, basic

83. a. pH = 5.5, acidic b. pH = 9.8, basic
c. pH = 12.3, basic d. pH = 7.0, neutral

85. c and d are buffers

87. $HCl(aq) + NaF(aq) \longrightarrow HF(aq) + NaCl(aq)$
$HCl(aq) + KC_2H_3O_2(aq) \longrightarrow HC_2H_3O_2(aq) + KCl(aq)$

89. a. $HC_2H_3O_2$ b. NaH_2PO_4
c. $NaCHOO$

91. 50.0 mL

93. 0.16 L

95. 65.2 g

97. 60.0 g/mol

99. 0.17 L

101. a. 2.60, acidic b. 11.75, basic
c. 8.02, basic d. 1.710, acidic

103.

$[H_3O^+]$	$[OH^-]$	pH	pOH	Acidic or Basic
1.0×10^{-4}	1.0×10^{-10}	4.00	10.00	acidic
5.5×10^{-3}	1.8×10^{-12}	2.26	11.74	acidic
3.1×10^{-9}	3.2×10^{-6}	8.50	5.50	basic
4.3×10^{-9}	2.1×10^{-6}	8.32	5.68	basic
2.3×10^{-8}	3.5×10^{-7}	7.55	6.45	basic

105. a. $[H_3O^+] = 0.0088$ M
$[OH^-] = 1.1 \times 10^{-12}$ M
pH = 2.06
b. $[H_3O^+] = 1.5 \times 10^{-3}$ M
$[OH^-] = 6.7 \times 10^{-12}$ M
pH = 2.82
c. $[H_3O^+] = 9.77 \times 10^{-4}$ M
$[OH^-] = 1.02 \times 10^{-11}$ M
pH = 3.010
d. $[H_3O^+] = 0.0878$ M
$[OH^-] = 1.14 \times 10^{-13}$ M
pH = 1.057

107. a. $[OH^-] = 0.15$ M
$[H_3O^+] = 6.7 \times 10^{-14}$ M
pH = 13.18
b. $[OH^-] = 3.0 \times 10^{-3}$ M
$[H_3O^+] = 3.3 \times 10^{-12}$ M
pH = 11.48
c. $[OH^-] = 9.6 \times 10^{-4}$ M
$[H_3O^+] = 1.0 \times 10^{-11}$ M
pH = 10.98
d. $[OH^-] = 8.7 \times 10^{-5}$ M
$[H_3O^+] = 1.1 \times 10^{-10}$ M
pH = 9.94

109. 1.49 L

111. 11.495

113. 3.0×10^{12} H^+ ions

115. 0.024 mol $Sr(OH)_2$, 0.076 mol NaOH

117. a. weak b. strong
c. weak d. strong

119. approximately 8 times more concentrated

Glossary

absolute zero The coldest temperature possible. Absolute zero (0 K or −273 °C or −459 °F) is the temperature at which molecular motion stops. Lower temperatures do not exist.

acid A molecular compound that dissolves in solution to form H^+ ions. Acids have the ability to dissolve some metals and will turn litmus paper red.

acid rain Acidic precipitation in the form of rain; created when fossil fuels are burned, which releases SO_2 and NO_2, which then react with water in the atmosphere to form sulfuric acid and nitric acid.

acid–base reaction A reaction that forms water and typically a salt.

acidic solution A solution containing a concentration of H_3O^+ ions greater than 1.0×10^{-7} M (pH < 7).

activation energy The amount of energy that must be absorbed by reactants before a reaction can occur; an energy hump that normally exists between the reactants and products.

activity series of metals A listing of metals (and hydrogen) in order of decreasing activity, decreasing ability to oxidize, and decreasing tendency to lose electrons.

actual yield The amount of product actually produced by a chemical reaction.

addition polymer A polymer formed by addition of monomers to one another without elimination of any atoms.

alcohol An organic compound containing an —OH functional group bonded to a carbon atom and having the general formula ROH.

aldehyde An organic compound with the general formula RCHO.

alkali metals The Group 1A elements, which are highly reactive metals.

alkaline battery A dry cell employing half-reactions that use a base.

alkaline earth metals The Group 2A elements, which are fairly reactive metals.

alkaloids Organic compounds that are typically found in plants and act as bases.

alkanes Hydrocarbons in which all carbon atoms are connected by single bonds. Noncyclic alkanes have the general formula C_nH_{2n+2}.

alkene A hydrocarbon that contains at least one double bond between carbon atoms. Noncyclic alkenes have the general formula C_nH_{2n}.

alkyl group In an organic molecule, any group containing only singly bonded carbon atoms and hydrogen atoms.

alkyne A hydrocarbon that contains at least one triple bond between carbon atoms. Noncyclic alkynes have the general formula C_nH_{2n-2}.

alpha particle A particle consisting of two protons and two neutrons (a helium nucleus), represented by the symbol ${}^4_2He$.

alpha (α) radiation Radiation emitted by an unstable nucleus, consisting of alpha particles.

alpha (α)-helix The most common secondary protein structure. The amino acid chain is wrapped into a tight coil from which the side chains extend outward. The structure is maintained by hydrogen bonding interactions between NH and CO groups along the peptide backbone of the protein.

amine An organic compound that contains nitrogen and has the general formula NR_3, where R may be an alkyl group or a hydrogen atom.

amino acid A molecule containing an amine group, a carboxylic acid group, and an R group (also called a side chain). Amino acids are the building blocks of proteins.

amorphous A type of solid matter in which atoms or molecules do not have long-range order (e.g., glass and plastic).

amphoteric In Brønsted–Lowry terminology, able to act as either an acid or a base.

anion A negatively charged ion.

anode The electrode where oxidation occurs in an electrochemical cell.

aqueous solution A homogeneous mixture of a substance with water.

aromatic ring A ring of carbon atoms containing alternating single and double bonds.

Arrhenius acid A substance that produces H^+ ions in aqueous solution.

Arrhenius base A substance that produces OH^- ions in aqueous solution.

atmosphere (atm) The average pressure at sea level, 101,325 Pa (760 mmHg).

atom The smallest identifiable unit of an element.

atomic element An element that exists in nature with single atoms as the basic unit.

atomic mass A weighted average of the masses of each naturally occurring isotope of an element; atomic mass is the average mass of the atoms of an element.

atomic mass unit (amu) The unit commonly used to express the masses of protons, neutrons, and nuclei. 1 amu = 1.66×10^{-24} g.

atomic number (Z) The number of protons in the nucleus of an atom.

atomic size The size of an atom, which is determined by how far the outermost electrons are from the nucleus.

atomic solid A solid whose component units are individual atoms (e.g., diamond, C; iron, Fe).

atomic theory A theory stating that all matter is composed of tiny particles called atoms.

Avogadro's law A law stating that the volume (V) of a gas and the amount of the gas in moles (n) are directly proportional.

Avogadro's number The number of entities in a mole, 6.022×10^{23}.

balanced equation A chemical equation in which the numbers of each type of atom on both sides of the equation are equal.

base A molecular compound that dissolves in solution to form OH^- ions. Bases have a slippery feel and turn litmus paper blue.

base chain The longest continuous chain of carbon atoms in an organic compound.

basic solution A solution containing a concentration of OH^- ions greater than 1.0×10^{-7} M (pH > 7).

bent The molecular geometry in which 3 atoms are not in a straight line. This geometry occurs when the central atoms contain 4 electron groups (2 bonding and 2 nonbonding) or 3 electron groups (2 bonding and 1 nonbonding).

benzene (C_6H_6) A particularly stable organic compound consisting of six carbon atoms joined by alternating single and double bonds in a ring structure.

beta particle A form of radiation consisting of an energetic electron and represented by the symbol $_{-1}^{0}e$.

beta (β) radiation Energetic electrons emitted by an unstable nucleus.

beta (β)-pleated sheet A common pattern in the secondary structure of proteins. The protein chain is extended in a zigzag pattern, and the peptide backbones of adjacent strands interact with one another through hydrogen bonding to form sheets.

binary acid An acid containing only hydrogen and a nonmetal.

binary compound A compound containing only two different kinds of elements.

biochemistry The study of the chemical substances and processes that occur in living organisms.

Bohr model A model for the atom in which electrons travel around the nucleus in circular orbits at specific, fixed distances from the nucleus.

boiling point The temperature at which the vapor pressure of a liquid is equal to the pressure above it.

boiling point elevation The increase in the boiling point of a solution caused by the presence of the solute.

bonding pair Electrons that are shared between two atoms in a chemical bond.

bonding theory A model that predicts how atoms bond together to form molecules.

Boyle's law A law maintaining that the volume (V) of a gas and its pressure (P) are inversely proportional.

branched alkane An alkane composed of carbon atoms bonded in chains containing branches.

Brønsted–Lowry acid A proton (H^+ ion) donor.

Brønsted–Lowry base A proton (H^+ ion) acceptor.

buffer A solution that resists pH change by neutralizing added acid or added base.

Calorie (Cal) An energy unit equivalent to 1000 little-c calories.

calorie (cal) The amount of energy required to raise the temperature of 1 g of water by 1 °C.

carbohydrates Polyhydroxyl aldehydes or ketones or their derivatives, containing multiple —OH groups and often having the general formula $(CH_2O)_n$.

carbonyl group A carbon atom double bonded to an oxygen atom.

carboxylic acid An organic compound with the general formula $RCOOH$.

catalyst A substance that increases the rate of a chemical reaction but is not consumed by the reaction.

cathode The electrode where reduction occurs in an electrochemical cell.

cation A positively charged ion.

cell The smallest structural unit of living organisms that has the properties associated with life.

cell membrane The structure that bounds the cell and holds the contents of the cell together.

cellulose A common polysaccharide composed of repeating glucose units linked together.

Celsius (°C) scale A temperature scale often used by scientists. On this scale, water freezes at 0 °C and boils at 100 °C at 1 atm pressure. Room temperature is approximately 22 °C.

chain reaction A self-sustaining chemical or nuclear reaction yielding energy or products that cause further reactions of the same kind.

charge A fundamental property of protons and electrons. Charged particles experience forces such that like charges repel and unlike charges attract.

Charles's law A law stating that the volume (V) of a gas and its temperature (T) expressed in kelvins are directly proportional.

chemical bond The sharing or transfer of electrons to attain stable electron configurations among the bonding atoms.

chemical change A change in which matter changes its composition.

chemical energy The energy associated with chemical changes.

chemical equation An equation that represents a chemical reaction; the reactants are on the left side of the equation, and the products are on the right side.

chemical formula A way to represent a compound. At a minimum, the chemical formula indicates the elements present in the compound and the relative number of atoms of each element.

chemical properties Properties that a substance can display only through changing its composition.

chemical reaction The process by which one or more substances transform into different substances via a chemical change. Chemical reactions often emit or absorb energy.

chemical symbol A one- or two-letter abbreviation for an element. Chemical symbols are listed directly below the atomic number in the periodic table.

chemistry The science that seeks to understand the behavior of matter by studying what atoms and molecules do.

chromosome A biological structure containing genes, located within the nucleus of a cell.

codon A sequence of three bases in a nucleic acid that codes for one amino acid.

colligative properties Physical properties of solutions that depend on the number of solute particles present but not the type of solute particles.

collision theory A theory of reaction rates stating that effective collisions between reactant molecules must take place in order for the reaction to occur.

color change One type of evidence of a chemical reaction, involving the change in color of a substance after a reaction.

combined gas law A law that combines Boyle's law and Charles's law; it is used to calculate how a property of a gas (P, V, or T) changes when two other properties are changed at the same time.

combustion reaction A reaction in which a substance reacts with oxygen, emitting heat and forming one or more oxygen-containing compounds.

complementary base In DNA, a base capable of precise pairing with a specific other DNA base.

complete ionic equation A chemical equation showing all the species as they are actually present in solution.

complex carbohydrate A carbohydrate composed of many repeating saccharide units.

compound A substance composed of two or more elements in fixed, definite proportions.

compressible Able to occupy a smaller volume when subjected to increased pressure. Gases are compressible because, in the gas phase, atoms or molecules are widely separated.

concentrated solution A solution containing large amounts of solute.

condensation A physical change in which a substance is converted from its gaseous form to its liquid form.

condensation polymer A class of polymers that expel atoms, usually water, during their formation or polymerization.

condensed structural formula A shorthand way of writing a structural formula.

conjugate acid–base pair In Brønsted–Lowry terminology, two substances related to each other by the transfer of a proton.

conservation of energy, law of A law stating that energy can be neither created nor destroyed. The total amount of energy is constant and cannot change; it can only be transferred from one object to another or converted from one form to another.

conservation of mass, law of A law stating that in a chemical reaction, matter is neither created nor destroyed.

constant composition, law of A law stating that all samples of a given compound have the same proportions of their constituent elements.

conversion factor A factor used to convert between two separate units; a conversion factor is constructed from any two quantities known to be equivalent.

copolymers Polymers that are composed of two different kinds of monomers and result in chains composed of alternating units rather than a single repeating unit.

core electrons The electrons that are not in the outermost principal shell of an atom.

corrosion The oxidation of metals (e.g., rusting of iron).

covalent atomic solid An atomic solid, such as diamond, that is held together by covalent bonds.

covalent bond The bond that results when two nonmetals combine in a chemical reaction. In a covalent bond, the atoms share their electrons.

critical mass The mass of uranium or plutonium required for a nuclear reaction to be self-sustaining.

crystalline A type of solid matter with atoms or molecules arranged in a well-ordered, three-dimensional array with long-range, repeating order (e.g., salt and diamond).

cytoplasm In a cell, the region between the nucleus and the cell membrane.

Dalton's law of partial pressure A law stating that the sum of the partial pressures of each component in a gas mixture equals the total pressure.

daughter nuclide The nuclide product of a nuclear decay.

decimal part One part of a number expressed in scientific notation.

decomposition A reaction in which a complex substance decomposes to form simpler substances; AB $\longrightarrow$ A + B.

density (*d*) A fundamental property of materials that relates mass and volume and differs from one substance to another. The units of density are those of mass divided by volume, most commonly expressed in g/cm^3, g/mL, or g/L.

derived unit A unit formed from the combination of other units.

dilute solution A solution containing small amounts of solute.

dimer A molecule formed by the joining together of two smaller molecules.

dipeptide Two amino acids linked together via a peptide bond.

dipole moment A measure of the separation of charge in a bond or in a molecule.

diprotic acid An acid containing two ionizable protons.

disaccharide A carbohydrate that can be decomposed into two simpler carbohydrates.

dispersion force The intermolecular force present in all molecules and atoms. Dispersion forces are caused by fluctuations in the electron distribution within molecules or atoms.

displacement A reaction in which one element displaces another in a compound; A + BC $\longrightarrow$ AC + B.

dissociation In aqueous solution, the process by which a solid ionic compound separates into its ions.

disubstituted benzene A benzene in which two hydrogen atoms have been replaced by an atom or group of atoms.

DNA (deoxyribonucleic acid) Long chainlike molecules that occur in the nucleus of cells and act as blueprints for the construction of proteins.

dot structure A drawing that represents the valence electrons in atoms as dots; it shows a chemical bond as the sharing or transfer of electron dots.

double bond The bond that exists when two electron pairs are shared between two atoms. In general, double bonds are shorter and stronger than single bonds.

double displacement A reaction in which two elements or groups of elements in two different compounds exchange places to form two new compounds; AB + CD $\longrightarrow$ AD + CB.

dry cell An ordinary battery (voltaic cell); it does not contain large amounts of liquid water.

duet The name for the two electrons corresponding to a stable Lewis structure in hydrogen and helium.

dynamic equilibrium In a chemical reaction, the condition in which the rate of the forward reaction equals the rate of the reverse reaction.

electrical current The flow of electric charge—for example, electrons flowing through a wire or ions through a solution.

electrical energy Energy associated with the flow of electric charge.

electrochemical cell A device that creates electrical current from a redox reaction.

electrolysis A process in which electrical current is used to drive an otherwise nonspontaneous redox reaction.

electrolytic cell An electrochemical cell used for electrolysis.

electromagnetic radiation A type of energy that travels through space at a constant speed of 3.0×10^8 m/s (186,000 miles/s) and exhibits both wavelike and particlelike behavior. Light is a form of electromagnetic radiation.

electromagnetic spectrum A spectrum that includes all wavelengths of electromagnetic radiation.

electron A negatively charged particle that occupies most of the atom's volume but contributes almost none of its mass.

electron configuration A representation that shows the occupation of orbitals by electrons for a particular element.

electron geometry The geometrical arrangement of the electron groups in a molecule.

electron group A general term for a lone pair, single bond, or multiple bond in a molecule.

electron spin A fundamental property of all electrons that causes them to have magnetic fields associated with them. The spin of an electron can either be oriented up $\left(+\frac{1}{2}\right)$ or down $\left(-\frac{1}{2}\right)$.

electronegativity The ability of an element to attract electrons within a covalent bond.

element A substance that cannot be broken down into simpler substances.

emission spectrum A spectrum associated with the emission of electromagnetic radiation by elements or compounds.

empirical formula A formula for a compound that gives the smallest whole-number ratio of each type of atom.

empirical formula molar mass The sum of the molar masses of all the atoms in an empirical formula.

endothermic Describes a process that absorbs heat energy.

endothermic reaction A chemical reaction that absorbs energy from the surroundings.

energy The capacity to do work.

English system A unit system commonly used in the United States.

enzymes Biological catalysts that increase the rates of biochemical reactions; enzymes are abundant in living organisms.

equilibrium constant (K_{eq}) The ratio, at equilibrium, of the concentrations of the products raised to their stoichiometric coefficients divided by the concentrations of the reactants raised to their stoichiometric coefficients.

equivalence point The point in a reaction at which the reactants are in exact stoichiometric proportions.

equivalent The stoichiometric proportions of elements and compounds in a chemical equation.

ester An organic compound with the general formula RCOOR.

ester linkage A type of bond with the general structure —COO—. Ester linkages join glycerol to fatty acids.

ether An organic compound with the general formula ROR.

evaporation A process in which molecules of a liquid, undergoing constant random motion, acquire enough energy to overcome attractions to neighbors and enter the gas phase.

excited state An unstable state for an atom or a molecule in which energy has been absorbed but not reemitted, raising an electron from the ground state into a higher energy orbital.

exothermic Describes a process that releases heat energy.

exothermic reaction A chemical reaction that releases energy to the surroundings.

experiment A procedure that attempts to measure observable predictions to test a theory or law.

exponent A number that represents the number of times a term is multiplied by itself. For example, in 2^4 the exponent is 4 and represents $2 \times 2 \times 2 \times 2$.

exponential part One part of a number expressed in scientific notation; it represents the number of places the decimal point has moved.

Fahrenheit (°F) scale The temperature scale that is most familiar in the United States; water freezes at 32 °F and boils at 212 °F at 1 atm prssure.

family (of elements) A group of elements that have similar outer electron configurations and therefore similar properties. Families occur in vertical columns in the periodic table.

family (of organic compounds) A group of organic compounds with the same functional group.

fatty acid A type of lipid consisting of a carboxylic acid with a long hydrocarbon tail.

film badge dosimeter Badges used to measure radiation exposure, consisting of photographic film held in a small case that is pinned to clothing.

fission, nuclear The process by which a heavy nucleus is split into nuclei of smaller masses and energy is emitted.

formula mass The average mass of the molecules (or formula units) that compose a compound.

formula unit The basic unit of ionic compounds; the smallest electrically neutral collection of cations and anions that compose the compound.

freezing point depression The decrease in the freezing point of a solvent caused by the presence of a solute.

frequency The number of wave cycles or crests that pass through a stationary point in one second.

fuel cell A voltaic cell in which the reactants are constantly replenished.

functional group A set of atoms that characterizes a family of organic compounds.

fusion, nuclear The combination of light atomic nuclei to form heavier ones with emission of large amounts of energy.

galvanic (voltaic) cell An electrochemical cell that spontaneously produces electrical current.

gamma radiation High-energy, short-wavelength electromagnetic radiation emitted by an atomic nucleus.

gamma rays The shortest-wavelength, most energetic form of electromagnetic radiation. Gamma ray photons are represented by the symbol ${}^{0}_{0}\gamma$.

gas A state of matter in which atoms or molecules are widely separated and free to move relative to one another.

gas-evolution reaction A reaction that occurs in solution and forms a gas as one of the products.

gas formation One type of evidence of a chemical reaction, a gas forms when two substances are mixed together.

Geiger-Müller counter A radioactivity detector consisting of a chamber filled with argon gas that discharges electrical signals when high-energy particles pass through it.

gene A sequence of codons within a DNA molecule that codes for a single protein. Genes vary in length from hundreds to thousands of codons.

genetic material The inheritable blueprint for making organisms.

glycogen A type of polysaccharide; it has a structure similar to that of starch, but the chain is highly branched.

glycolipid A biological molecule composed of a nonpolar fatty acid and hydrocarbon chain and a polar section composed of a sugar molecule such as glucose.

glycoside linkage The link between monosaccharides in a polysaccharide.

ground state The state of an atom or molecule in which the electrons occupy the lowest possible energy orbitals available.

group (of elements) Elements that have similar outer electron configurations and therefore similar properties. Groups occur in vertical columns in the periodic table.

half-cell A compartment in which the oxidation or reduction half-reaction occurs in a galvanic or voltaic cell.

half-life The time it takes for one-half of the parent nuclides in a radioactive sample to decay to the daughter nuclides.

half-reaction Either the oxidation part or the reduction part of a redox reaction.

halogens The Group 7A elements, which are very reactive nonmetals.

heat absorption One type of evidence of a chemical reaction, involving the intake of energy.

heat capacity The quantity of heat energy required to change the temperature of a given amount of a substance by 1 °C.

heat emission One type of evidence of a chemical reaction, involving the evolution of thermal energy.

heat of fusion The amount of heat required to melt one mole of a solid at its melting point with no change in temperature.

heat of vaporization The amount of heat required to vaporize one mole of a liquid at its boiling point with no change in temperature.

heterogeneous mixture A mixture, such as oil and water, that has two or more regions with different compositions.

homogeneous mixture A mixture, such as salt water, that has the same composition throughout.

human genome All of the genetic material of a human being; the total DNA of a human cell.

Hund's rule A rule stating that when filling orbitals of equal energy, electrons will occupy empty orbitals singly before pairing with other electrons.

hydrocarbon A compound that contains only carbon and hydrogen atoms.

hydrogen bond A strong dipole–dipole interaction between molecules containing hydrogen directly bonded to a small, highly electronegative atom, such as N, O, or F.

hydrogenation The chemical addition of hydrogen to a compound.

hydronium ion The H_3O^+ ion. Chemists often use $H^+(aq)$ and $H_3O^+(aq)$ interchangeably to mean the same thing—a hydronium ion.

hypothesis A theory or law before it has become well established; a tentative explanation for an observation or a scientific problem that can be tested by further investigation.

hypoxia A shortage of oxygen in the tissues of the body.

ideal gas law A law that combines the four properties of a gas—pressure (P), volume (V), temperature (T), and number of moles (n) in a single equation showing their interrelatedness: $PV = nRT$ (R = ideal gas constant).

indicator A substance that changes color with acidity level, often used to detect the end point of a titration.

infrared (IR) light The fraction of the electromagnetic spectrum between visible light and microwaves. Infrared light is invisible to the human eye.

insoluble Not soluble in water.

instantaneous dipole A type of intermolecular force resulting from transient shifts in electron density within an atom or molecule.

intermolecular forces Attractive forces that exist between molecules.

International System (SI) The standard set of units for science measurements, based on the metric system.

ion An atom (or group of atoms) that has gained or lost one or more electrons, so that it has an electric charge.

ion product constant (K_W) The product of the H_3O^+ ion concentration and the OH^- ion concentration in an aqueous solution. At room temperature, $K_w = 1.0 \times 10^{-4}$.

ionic bond The bond that results when a metal and a nonmetal combine in a chemical reaction. In an ionic bond, the metal transfers one or more electrons to the nonmetal.

ionic compound A compound formed between a metal and one or more nonmetals.

ionic solid A solid compound composed of metals and nonmetals joined by ionic bonds.

ionization The forming of ions.

ionization energy The energy required to remove an electron from an atom in the gaseous state.

ionizing power The ability of radiation to ionize other molecules and atoms.

isomers Molecules with the same molecular formula but different structures.

isoosmotic Describes solutions having equal osmotic pressure.

isotope scanning The use of radioactive isotopes to identify disease in the body.

isotopes Atoms with the same number of protons but different numbers of neutrons.

Kelvin (K) scale The temperature scale that assigns 0 K to the coldest temperature possible, absolute zero (−273 °C or −459 °F), the temperature at which molecular motion stops. The size of the kelvin is identical to that of the Celsius degree.

ketone An organic compound with the general formula $RCOR$.

kilogram (kg) The SI standard unit of mass.

kilowatt-hour (kWh) A unit of energy equal to 3.6 million joules.

kinetic energy Energy associated with the motion of an object.

kinetic molecular theory A simple model for gases that predicts the behavior of most gases under many conditions.

Le Châtelier's principle A principle stating that when a chemical system at equilibrium is disturbed, the system shifts in a direction that minimizes the disturbance.

lead-acid storage battery An automobile battery consisting of six electrochemical cells wired in series. Each cell produces 2 volts for a total of 12 volts.

Lewis structure A drawing that represents chemical bonds between atoms as shared or transferred electrons; the valence electrons of atoms are represented as dots.

Lewis theory A simple theory for chemical bonding involving diagrams showing bonds between atoms as lines or dots. In this theory, atoms bond together to obtain stable octets (8 valence electrons).

light emission One type of evidence of a chemical reaction, involving the giving off of electromagnetic radiation.

limiting reactant The reactant that determines the amount of product formed in a chemical reaction.

linear Describes the molecular geometry of a molecule containing two electron groups (two bonding groups and no lone pairs).

linearly related A relationship between two variables such that, when they are plotted one against the other, the graph produced is a straight line.

lipid A cellular component that is insoluble in water but soluble in nonpolar solvents.

lipid bilayer A structure formed by lipids in the cell membrane.

liquid A state of matter in which atoms or molecules are packed close to each other (about as closely as in a solid) but are free to move around and by each other.

logarithmic scale A scale involving logarithms. A logarithm entails an exponent that indicates the power to which a number is raised to produce a given number (e.g., the logarithm of 100 to the base 10 is 2).

lone pair Electrons that are only on one atom in a Lewis structure.

main-group elements Groups 1A–8A on the periodic table. These groups have properties that tend to be predictable based on their position in the periodic table.

mass A measure of the quantity of matter within an object.

mass number (A) The sum of the number of neutrons and protons in an atom.

mass percent composition (or mass percent) The percentage, by mass, of each element in a compound.

matter Anything that occupies space and has mass. Matter exists in three different states: solid, liquid, and gas.

melting point The temperature at which a solid turns into a liquid.

messenger RNA (mRNA) Long chainlike molecules that act as blueprints for the construction of proteins.

metallic atomic solid An atomic solid, such as iron, which is held together by metallic bonds that, in the simplest model, consist of positively charged ions in a sea of electrons.

metallic character The properties typical of a metal, especially the tendency to lose electrons in chemical reactions. Elements become more metallic as you move from right to left across the periodic table.

metalloids Those elements that fall along the boundary between the metals and the nonmetals in the periodic table; their properties are intermediate between those of metals and those of nonmetals.

metals Elements that tend to lose electrons in chemical reactions. They are found at the left side and in the center of the periodic table.

meter (m) The SI standard unit of length.

metric system The unit system commonly used throughout most of the world.

microwaves The part of the electromagnetic spectrum between the infrared region and the radio wave region. Microwaves are efficiently absorbed by water molecules and can therefore be used to heat water-containing substances.

millimeter of mercury (mmHg) A unit of pressure that originates from the method used to measure pressure with a barometer. Also called a *torr*.

miscibility The ability of two liquids to mix without separating into two phases, or the ability of one liquid to mix with (dissolve in) another liquid.

mixture A substance composed of two or more different types of atoms or molecules combined in variable proportions.

molality (m) A common unit of solution concentration, defined as the number of moles of solute per kilogram of solvent.

molar mass The mass of one mole of atoms of an element or one mole of molecules (or formula units) for a compound. An element's molar mass in grams per mole is numerically equivalent to the element's atomic mass in amu.

molar solubility The solubility of a substance in units of moles per liter (mol/L).

molar volume The volume occupied by one mole of gas. Under standard temperature and pressure conditions the molar volume of ideal gas is 22.5 L.

molarity (M) A common unit of solution concentration, defined as the number of moles of solute per liter of solution.

mole Avogadro's number (6.022×10^{23}) of particles—especially, of atoms, ions, or molecules. A mole of any element has a mass in grams that is numerically equivalent to its atomic mass in amu.

molecular compound A compound formed from two or more nonmetals. Molecular compounds have distinct molecules as their simplest identifiable units.

molecular element An element that does not normally exist in nature with single atoms as the basic unit. These elements usually exist as diatomic molecules—2 atoms of that element bonded together—as their basic units.

molecular equation A chemical equation showing the complete, neutral formulas for every compound in a reaction.

molecular formula A formula for a compound that gives the specific number of each type of atom in a molecule.

molecular geometry The geometrical arrangement of the atoms in a molecule.

molecular solid A solid whose composite units are molecules.

molecule Two or more atoms joined in a specific arrangement by chemical bonds. A molecule is the smallest identifiable unit of a molecular compound.

monomer An individual repeating unit that makes up a polymer.

monoprotic acid An acid containing only one ionizable proton.

monosaccharide A carbohydrate that cannot be decomposed into simpler carbohydrates.

monosubstituted benzene A benzene in which one of the hydrogen atoms has been replaced by another atom or group of atoms.

net ionic equation An equation that shows only the species that actually participate in a reaction.

neutral solution A solution in which the concentrations of H_3O^+ and OH^- are equal (pH = 7).

neutralization A reaction that takes place when an acid and a base are mixed; the $H^+(aq)$ from the acid combines with the $OH^-(aq)$ from the base to form $H_2O(l)$.

neutron A nuclear particle with no electrical charge and nearly the same mass as a proton.

nitrogen narcosis An increase in nitrogen concentration in bodily tissues and fluids that results in feelings of drunkenness.

noble gases The Group 8A elements, which are chemically unreactive.

nonbonding atomic solid An atomic solid that is held together by relatively weak dispersion forces.

nonelectrolyte solution A solution containing a solute that dissolves as molecules; therefore, the solution does not conduct electricity.

nonmetals Elements that tend to gain electrons in chemical reactions. They are found at the upper right side of the periodic table.

nonpolar molecule A molecule that does not have a net dipole moment.

nonvolatile Describes a compound that does not vaporize easily.

normal alkane (or *n*-alkane) An alkane composed of carbon atoms bonded in a straight chain with no branches.

normal boiling point The boiling point of a liquid at a pressure of 1 atmosphere.

nuclear equation An equation that represents the changes that occur during radioactivity and other nuclear processes.

nuclear radiation The energetic particles emitted from the nucleus of an atom when it is undergoing a nuclear process.

nuclear theory of the atom A theory stating that most of the atom's mass and all of its positive charge are contained in a small, dense nucleus. Most of the volume of the atom is empty space occupied by negatively charged electrons.

nucleic acids Biological molecules, such as deoxyribonucleic acid (DNA) and ribonucleic acid (RNA), that store and transmit genetic information.

nucleotide An individual unit of a nucleic acid. Nucleic acids are polymers of nucleotides.

nucleus (of a cell) The part of the cell that contains the genetic material.

nucleus (of an atom) The small core containing most of the atom's mass and all of its positive charge. The nucleus is made up of protons and neutrons.

observation Often the first step in the scientific method. An observation must measure or describe something about the physical world.

octet The number of electrons, 8, around atoms with stable Lewis structures.

octet rule A rule that states that an atom will give up, accept, or share electrons in order to achieve a filled outer electron shell, which usually consists of 8 electrons.

orbital The region around the nucleus of an atom where an electron is most likely to be found.

orbital diagram An electron configuration in which electrons are represented as arrows in boxes corresponding to orbitals of a particular atom.

organic chemistry The study of carbon-containing compounds and their reactions.

organic molecule A molecule whose main structural component is carbon.

osmosis The flow of solvent from a lower-concentration solution through a semipermeable membrane to a higher-concentration solution.

osmotic pressure The pressure produced on the surface of a semipermeable membrane by osmosis or the pressure required to stop osmotic flow.

oxidation The gain of oxygen, the loss of hydrogen, or the loss of electrons (the most fundamental definition).

oxidation state (or oxidation number) A number that can be used as an aid in writing formulas and balancing equations. It is computed for each element based on the number of electrons assigned to it in a scheme where the most electronegative element is assigned all of the bonding electrons.

oxidation–reduction (redox) reaction A reaction in which electrons are transferred from one substance to another.

oxidizing agent In a redox reaction, the substance being reduced. Oxidizing agents tend to gain electrons easily.

oxyacid An acid containing hydrogen, a nonmetal, and oxygen.

oxyanion An anion containing oxygen. Most polyatomic ions are oxyanions.

oxygen toxicity The result of increased oxygen concentration in bodily tissues.

parent nuclide The original nuclide in a nuclear decay.

partial pressure The pressure due to any individual component in a gas mixture.

pascal (Pa) The SI unit of pressure, defined as 1 newton per square meter.

Pauli exclusion principle A principle stating that no more than 2 electrons can occupy an orbital and that the 2 electrons must have opposite spins.

penetrating power The ability of a radioactive particle to penetrate matter.

peptide bond The bond between the amine end of one amino acid and the carboxylic acid end of another. Amino acids link together via peptide bonds to form proteins.

percent natural abundance The percentage amount of each isotope of an element in a naturally occurring sample of the element.

percent yield In a chemical reaction, the percentage of the theoretical yield that was actually attained.

period A horizontal row of the periodic table.

periodic law A law that states that when the elements are arranged in order of increasing relative mass, certain sets of properties recur periodically.

periodic table An arrangement of the elements in which atomic number increases from left to right and elements with similar properties fall in columns called families or groups.

permanent dipole A separation of charge resulting from the unequal sharing of electrons between atoms.

pH scale A scale used to quantify acidity or basicity. A pH of 7 is neutral; a pH lower than 7 is acidic, and a pH greater than 7 is basic. The pH is defined as follows: $pH = -\log[H_3O^+]$.

phenyl group The term for a benzene ring when other substituents are attached to it.

phospholipid A lipid with the same basic structure as a triglyceride, except that one of the fatty acid groups is replaced with a phosphate group.

phosphorescence The slow, long-lived emission of light that sometimes follows the absorption of light by some atoms and molecules.

photon A particle of light or a packet of light energy.

physical change A change in which matter does not change its composition, even though its appearance might change.

physical properties Those properties that a substance displays without changing its composition.

polar covalent bond A covalent bond between atoms of different electronegativities. Polar covalent bonds have a dipole moment.

polar molecule A molecule with polar bonds that add together to create a net dipole moment.

polyatomic ion An ion composed of a group of atoms with an overall charge.

polymer A molecule with many similar units, called monomers, bonded together in a long chain.

polypeptide A short chain of amino acids joined by peptide bonds.

polysaccharide A long, chainlike molecule composed of many linked monosaccharide units. Polysaccharides are polymers of monosaccharides.

positron A nuclear particle that has the mass of an electron but carries a 1+ charge.

positron emission Expulsion of a positron from an unstable atomic nucleus. In positron emission, a proton is transformed into a neutron.

potential energy The energy of a body that is associated with its position or the arrangement of its parts.

precipitate An insoluble product formed through the reaction of two solutions containing soluble compounds.

precipitation reaction A reaction that forms a solid or precipitate when two aqueous solutions are mixed.

prefix multipliers Prefixes used by the SI system with the standard units. These multipliers change the value of the unit by powers of 10.

pressure The force exerted per unit area by gaseous molecules as they collide with the surfaces around them.

primary protein structure The sequence of amino acids in a protein's chain. Primary protein structure is maintained by the covalent peptide bonds between individual amino acids.

principal quantum number A number that indicates the shell that an electron occupies.

principal shell The shell indicated by the principal quantum number.

products The final substances produced in a chemical reaction; represented on the right side of a chemical equation.

properties The characteristics we use to distinguish one substance from another.

protein A biological molecule composed of a long chain of amino acids joined by peptide bonds. In living organisms, proteins serve many varied and important functions.

proton A positively charged nuclear particle. A proton's mass is approximately 1 amu.

pure substance A substance composed of only one type of atom or molecule.

quantification The assigning of a number to an observation so as to specify a quantity or property precisely.

quantum (pl. quanta) The precise amount of energy possessed by a photon; the difference in energy between two atomic orbitals.

quantum number (n) An integer that specifies the energy of an orbital. The higher the quantum number n, the greater the distance between the electron and the nucleus and the higher its energy.

quantum-mechanical model The foundation of modern chemistry; explains how electrons exist in atoms and how they affect the chemical and physical properties of elements.

quaternary structure In a protein, the way that individual chains fit together to compose the protein. Quaternary structure is maintained by interactions between the R groups of amino acids on the different chains.

R group (side chain) An organic group attached to the central carbon atom of an amino acid.

radio waves The longest wavelength and least energetic form of electromagnetic radiation.

radioactive Describes a substance that emits tiny, invisible, energetic particles from the nuclei of its component atoms.

radioactivity The emission of tiny, invisible, energetic particles from the unstable nuclei of atoms. Many of these particles can penetrate matter.

radiocarbon dating A technique used to estimate the age of fossils and artifacts through the measurement of natural radioactivity of carbon atoms in the environment.

radiotherapy Treatment of disease with radiation, such as the use of gamma rays to kill rapidly dividing cancer cells.

random coil The name given to an irregular pattern of a secondary protein structure.

rate of a chemical reaction (reaction rate) The amount of reactant that changes to product in a given period of time. Also defined as the amount of a product that forms in a given period of time.

reactants The initial substances in a chemical reaction, represented on the left side of a chemical equation.

recrystallization A technique used to purify a solid; involves dissolving the solid in a solvent at high temperature, creating a saturated solution, then cooling the solution to cause the crystallization of the solid.

reducing agent In a redox reaction, the substance being oxidized. Reducing agents tend to lose electrons easily.

reduction The loss of oxygen, the gain of hydrogen, or the gain of electrons (the most fundamental definition).

rem Stands for *roentgen equivalent man*; a weighted measure of radiation exposure that accounts for the ionizing power of the different types of radiation.

resonance structures Two or more Lewis structures that are necessary to describe the bonding in a molecule or ion.

reversible reaction A reaction that is able to proceed in both the forward and reverse directions.

RNA (ribonucleic acid) Long chainlike molecules that occur throughout cells and take part in the construction of proteins.

salt An ionic compound that usually remains dissolved in a solution after an acid–base reaction has occurred.

salt bridge An inverted, U-shaped tube containing a strong electrolyte; completes the circuit in an electrochemical cell by allowing the flow of ions between the two half-cells.

saturated fat A triglyceride composed of saturated fatty acids. Saturated fat tends to be solid at room temperature.

saturated hydrocarbon A hydrocarbon that contains no double or triple bonds between the carbon atoms.

saturated solution A solution that holds the maximum amount of solute under the solution conditions. If additional solute is added to a saturated solution, it will not dissolve.

scientific law A statement that summarizes past observations and predicts future ones. Scientific laws are usually formulated from a series of related observations.

scientific method The way that scientists learn about the natural world. The scientific method involves observations, laws, hypotheses, theories, and experimentation.

scientific notation A system used to write very big or very small numbers, often containing many zeros, more compactly and precisely. A number written in scientific notation consists of a decimal part and an exponential part (10 raised to a particular exponent).

scintillation counter A device used to detect radioactivity in which energetic particles traverse a material that emits ultraviolet or visible light when excited by their passage. The light is detected and turned into an electrical signal.

second (s) The SI standard unit of time.

secondary protein structure Short-range periodic or repeating patterns often found in proteins. Secondary protein structure is maintained by interactions between amino acids that are fairly close together in the linear sequence of the protein chain or adjacent to each other on neighboring chains.

semiconductor A compound or element exhibiting intermediate electrical conductivity that can be changed and controlled.

semipermeable membrane A membrane that selectively allows some substances to pass through but not others.

SI units The most convenient system of units for science measurements, based on the metric system. The set of standard units agreed on by scientists throughout the world.

significant digits (figures) The non–place-holding digits in a reported measurement; they represent the precision of a measured quantity.

simple carbohydrate (simple sugar) A monosaccharide or disaccharide.

single bond A chemical bond in which one electron pair is shared between two atoms.

solid A state of matter in which atoms or molecules are packed close to each other in fixed locations.

solid formation One type of evidence of a chemical reaction involving the formation of a solid.

solubility The amount of a compound, usually in grams, that will dissolve in a certain amount of solvent.

solubility rules A set of empirical rules used to determine whether an ionic compound is soluble.

solubility-product constant (K_{sp}) The equilibrium expression for a chemical equation that represents the dissolving of an ionic compound in solution.

soluble Dissolves in solution.

solute The minority component of a solution.

solution A homogeneous mixture of two or more substances.

solvent The majority component of a solution.

specific heat capacity (or specific heat) The heat capacity of a substance in joules per gram degree Celsius (J/g °C).

spectator ions Ions that do not participate in a reaction; they appear unchanged on both sides of a chemical equation.

standard temperature and pressure (STP) Conditions often assumed in calculations involving gases: $T = 0$ °C (273 K) and $P = 1$ atm.

starch A common polysaccharide composed of repeating glucose units.

states of matter The three forms in which matter can exist: solid, liquid, and gas.

steroid A biological compound containing a 17-carbon 4-ring system.

stock solution A concentrated form in which solutions are often stored.

stoichiometry The numerical relationships among chemical quantities in a balanced chemical equation. Stoichiometry allows us to predict the amounts of products that form in a chemical reaction based on the amounts of reactants.

strong acid An acid that completely ionizes in solution.

strong base A base that completely dissociates in solution.

strong electrolyte A substance whose aqueous solutions are good conductors of electricity.

strong electrolyte solution A solution containing a solute that dissociates into ions; therefore, a solution that conducts electricity well.

structural formula A two-dimensional representation of molecules that not only shows the number and type of atoms, but also how the atoms are bonded together.

sublimation A physical change in which a substance is converted from its solid form directly into its gaseous form.

subshell In quantum mechanics, specifies the shape of the orbital and is represented by different letters (s, p, d, f).

substituent An atom or a group of atoms that has been substituted for a hydrogen atom in an organic compound.

substitution reaction A reaction in which one or more atoms are replaced by one or more different atoms.

supersaturated solution A solution holding more than the normal maximum amount of solute.

surface tension The tendency of liquids to minimize their surface area, resulting in a "skin" on the surface of the liquid.

synthesis A reaction in which simpler substances combine to form more complex substances; A + B $\longrightarrow$ AB.

temporary dipole A type of intermolecular force resulting from transient shifts in electron density within an atom or molecule.

terminal atom An atom that is located at the end of a molecule or chain.

tertiary structure A protein's structure that consists of the large-scale bends and folds due to interactions between the R groups of amino acids that are separated by large distances in the linear sequence of the protein chain.

tetrahedral The molecular geometry of a molecule containing four electron groups (four bonding groups and no lone pairs).

theoretical yield The maximum amount of product that can be made in a chemical reaction based on the amount of limiting reactant.

theory A proposed explanation for observations and laws. A theory presents a model of the way nature works and predicts behavior that extends well beyond the observations and laws from which it was formed.

titration A laboratory procedure used to determine the amount of a substance in solution. In a titration, a reactant in a solution of known concentration is reacted with another reactant in a solution of unknown concentration until the reaction reaches the end point.

torr A unit of pressure named after the Italian physicist Evangelista Torricelli; also called a millimeter of mercury.

transition metals The elements in the middle of the periodic table whose properties tend to be less predictable based simply on their position in the periodic table. Transition metals lose electrons in their chemical reactions, but do not necessarily acquire noble gas configurations.

triglyceride A fat or oil; a tryglyceride is a triester composed of glycerol with three fatty acids attached.

trigonal planar The molecular geometry of a molecule containing three electron groups, three bonding groups, and no lone pairs.

trigonal pyramidal The molecular geometry of a molecule containing four electron groups, three bonding groups, and one lone pair.

triple bond A chemical bond consisting of three electron pairs shared between two atoms. In general, triple bonds are shorter and stronger than double bonds.

Type I compounds Compounds containing metals that always form cations with the same charge.

Type II compounds Compounds containing metals that can form cations with different charges.

ultraviolet (UV) light The fraction of the electromagnetic spectrum between the visible region and the X-ray region. UV light is invisible to the human eye.

units Previously agreed-on quantities used to report experimental measurements. Units are vital in chemistry.

unsaturated fat (or oil) A triglyceride composed of unsaturated fatty acids. Unsaturated fats tend to be liquids at room temperature.

unsaturated hydrocarbon A hydrocarbon that contains one or more double or triple bonds between its carbon atoms.

unsaturated solution A solution holding less than the maximum possible amount of solute under the solution conditions.

valence electrons The electrons in the outermost principal shell of an atom; they are involved in chemical bonding.

valence shell electron pair repulsion (VSEPR) A theory that allows prediction of the shapes of molecules based on the idea that electrons—either as lone pairs or as bonding pairs—repel one another.

vapor pressure The partial pressure of a vapor in dynamic equilibrium with its liquid.

vaporization The phase transition between a liquid and a gas.

viscosity The resistance of a liquid to flow; manifestation of intermolecular forces.

visible light The fraction of the electromagnetic spectrum that is visible to the human eye, bounded by wavelengths of 400 nm (violet) and 780 nm (red).

vital force A mystical or supernatural power that, it was once believed, was possessed only by living organisms and allowed them to produce organic compounds.

vitalism The belief that living things contain a nonphysical "force" that allows them to synthesize organic compounds.

volatile Tending to vaporize easily.

voltage The potential difference between two electrodes; the driving force that causes electrons to flow.

volume A measure of space. Any unit of length, when cubed, becomes a unit of volume.

wavelength The distance between adjacent wave crests in a wave.

weak acid An acid that does not completely ionize in solution.

weak base A base that does not completely dissociate in solution.

weak electrolyte A substance whose aqueous solutions are poor conductors of electricity.

X-rays The portion of the electromagnetic spectrum between the ultraviolet (UV) region and the gamma-ray region.

Photo Credits

Maxwell Art And Photo/Pearson. Page 250 (bottom left): Maxwell Art And Photo/Pearson. Page 250 (bottom right): Maxwell Art And Photo/Pearson. Page 250 (bottom right): Maxwell Art And Photo/Pearson. Page 251 (top left): Maxwell Art And Photo/Pearson. Page 251 (bottom left): Maxwell Art And Photo/Pearson. Page 251 (bottom right): Maxwell Art And Photo/Pearson. Page 254: Maxwell Art And Photo/Pearson. Page 258 (top left): Maxwell Art And Photo/Pearson. Page 258 (top center): Maxwell Art And Photo/Pearson. Page 265 (left): Fundamental Photographs. Page 265 (center left): Fundamental Photographs. Page 265 (center right): Fundamental Photographs. Page 265 (right): Fundamental Photographs. Page 281 (top left): Nancy R. Cohen/Photodisc/Getty Images. Page 281 (top center): Nancy R. Cohen/Photodisc/Getty Images. Page 281 (bottom left): Nancy R. Cohen/Photodisc/Getty Images. Page 281 (bottom): Nancy R. Cohen/Photodisc/Getty Images. Page 281 (top right): Katrina Leigh/Shutterstock. Page 281 (center): Katrina Leigh/Shutterstock. Page 281 (center right): Katrina Leigh/Shutterstock. Page 281 (bottom center): Katrina Leigh/Shutterstock. Page 281 (bottom right): Katrina Leigh/Shutterstock. **Chapter 9** Page 285: AP Photo/Murray Becker. Page 286 (bottom left): Photo Researchers/Alamy. Page 286 (bottom right): INTERFOTO/Alamy. Page 287 (top left): Martin Barraud/OJO Images/Getty Images. Page 287 (bottom left): zooropa/Shutterstock. Page 289 (bottom left): Image courtesy of SPI Corp/www.x20.org. Page 289 (bottom right): Image courtesy of SPI Corp/www.x20.org. Page 290: Larry Mulvehill/Science Source. Page 291 (center left): TEA/Fotolia. Page 291 (bottom center): Richard Megna/Fundamental Photographs. Page 291 (bottom right): Richard Megna/Fundamental Photographs. Page 295 (center left): REUTERS/XXSTRING-ERXX xxxxx/Reuters/Corbis. Page 295 (top right): Science Source. Page 322 (center left): Hisham Ibrahim/Photodisc/Getty Images. Page 322 (bottom right): Library of Congress Prints and Photographs Division, [LC-USZ62-60242]. **Chapter 10** Page 340: Editorial Image, LLC/Alamy. Page 341: Kip Peticolas/Fundamental Photographs. Page 345 (bottom left): Richard Megna/Fundamental Photographs. Page 345 (bottom center): Richard Megna/Fundamental Photographs. Page 355: Tom Grundy/Shutterstock. **Chapter 11** Page 366: Jerry Driendl/Photodisc/Getty Images. Page 371: Larry Brownstein/Photodisc/Getty Images. Page 372: Richard Megna/Fundamental Photographs. Page 377: matka_Wariatka/Shutterstock. Page 387: AP Photo/Pasang Geljen Sherpa. Page 394: LatitudeStock/Alamy. Page 407 (top left): Caspar Benson/Getty Images. Page 407 (bottom left): Pearson. **Chapter 12** Page 413: Tom Brakefield/Photodisc/Getty Images. Page 414 (top left): Anthony West/Corbis. Page 414 (center left): Fundamental Photographs. Page 414 (bottom left): Vetta Collection/iStockphoto/Getty

Images. Page 415 (top right): lostbear/iStockphoto/Getty Images. Page 415 (bottom left): NASA. Page 415 (center right): Fundamental Photographs. Page 417 (top left): Richard Megna/Fundamental Photographs. Page 417 (top center): Richard Megna/Fundamental Photographs. Page 417 (top right): Richard Megna/Fundamental Photographs. Page 417 (bottom): Magnascan/iStockphoto/Getty Images. Page 421: Richard Megna/Fundamental Photographs. Page 424 (bottom center): Photo Researchers/Getty Images. Page 424 (top left): Charles D. Winters/Science Source. Page 427 (top left): Richard Megna/Fundamental Photographs. Page 427 (top center): Richard Haynes/Prentice Hall School Division/Pearson. Page 427 (top right): RGB Ventures LLC dba SuperStock/Alamy. Page 432 (bottom left): KieselUndStein/iStockphoto/Getty Images. Page 432 (bottom center): Matejay/iStockphoto/Getty Images. Page 432 (bottom right): Sashkin/Shutterstock. Page 433 (bottom left): GeoStock/Photodisc/Getty Images. Page 433 (bottom right): Sashkin/Shutterstock. Page 434: Maciej Toporowicz, NYC/Flickr/Getty Images. Page 435 (bottom right): Shutterstock. Page 435 (center left): Kristen Brochmann/Fundamental Photographs. **Chapter 13** Page 448: Louise Gubb/Corbis. Page 451 (top left): Fundamental Photographs. Page 451 (top center): Fundamental Photographs. Page 451 (top right): Fundamental Photographs. Page 452: kevinhillillustration/iStockphoto/Getty Images. Page 453: Maxwell Art And Photo/Pearson. Page 458: Don B. Stevenson/Alamy. Page 466: Chris Howes/Wild Places Photography/Alamy. Page 467: jane/iStockphoto/Getty Images. Page 468: Masonjar/Shutterstock. Page 471 (bottom left): David Kamm/Alamy. Page 471 (bottom right): Derek Trask Inv. Ltd./Alamy. Page 472 (top left): Pearson. Page 472 (top center): Pearson. Page 472 (top right): Pearson. Page 484: Science Source. **Chapter 14** Page 488 (top left): VaLiza/Shutterstock. Page 488 (top right): Richard Megna/Fundamental Photographs. Page 488 (bottom left): Richard Megna/Fundamental Photographs. Page 489: Ivaylo Ivanov/Shutterstock. Page 490 (top left): Maxwell Art And Photo/Pearson. Page 490 (center left): Richard Megna/Fundamental Photographs. Page 494 (top left): Paul Silverman/Fundamental Photographs. Page 494 (bottom left): Richard Megna/Fundamental Photographs. Page 496 (center left): Maxwell Art And Photo/Pearson. Page 496 (top right): Maxwell Art And Photo/Pearson. Page 498 (top left): Richard Megna/Fundamental Photographs. Page 498 (top center): Richard Megna/Fundamental Photographs. Page 498 (top right): Richard Megna/Fundamental Photographs. Page 500 (bottom left): Richard Megna/Fundamental Photographs. Page 500 (bottom right): Richard Megna/Fundamental Photographs. Page 501 (center): Richard Megna/Fundamental Photographs. Page 501 (bottom right): Richard Megna/Fundamental Photographs. Page 512: KonstantinChristian/Shutterstock.

Index

$$x + x - 3 = 4$$
$$x3 =$$